Fifth Edition

IFRS Standards Edition

# BUSINESS ANALYSIS AND VALUATION

Krishna G. Palepu

Paul M. Healy

Erik Peek

***Business Analysis and Valuation:***
***IFRS Standards edition,*** **5th Edition**
**Krishna G. Palepu, Paul M. Healy**
**& Erik Peek**

Publisher: Annabel Ainscow

List Manager: Jenny Grene

Marketing Manager: Sophie Clarke

Senior Content Project Manager:
Sue Povey

Manufacturing Buyer: Elaine Bevan

Typesetter: SPi Global

Text Design: Design Deluxe Ltd

Cover design: Simon Levy Associates

Cover Image(s): nats77/Getty Images

For product information and technology assistance,
contact **emea.info@cengage.com**

For permission to use material from this text or
product, and for permission queries,
email **emea.permissions@cengage.com**

*British Library Cataloguing-in-Publication Data*
A catalogue record for this book is available from the British Library.

ISBN: 978-1-4737-5842-1

**Cengage Learning EMEA**
Cheriton House, North Way, Andover, Hampshire, SP10 5BE
United Kingdom

Cengage Learning products are represented in Canada by Nelson Education Ltd.

For your lifelong learning solutions, visit **www.cengage.co.uk**

Purchase your next print book or e-book at
**www.cengagebrain.com**

Printed in China by RR Donnelley
Print Number: 01          Print Year: 2019

# Brief contents

# Contents

# Preface

Financial statements are the basis for a wide range of business analyses. Managers use them to monitor and judge their firms' performance relative to competitors, to communicate with external investors, to help judge what financial policies they should pursue, and to evaluate potential new businesses to acquire as part of their investment strategy. Securities analysts use financial statements to rate and value companies they recommend to clients. Bankers use them in deciding whether to extend a loan to a client and to determine the loan's terms. Investment bankers use them as a basis for valuing and analyzing prospective buyouts, mergers, and acquisitions. And consultants use them as a basis for competitive analysis for their clients. Not surprisingly, therefore, there is a strong demand among business students for a course that provides a framework for using financial statement data in a variety of business analysis and valuation contexts. The purpose of this book is to provide such a framework for business students and practitioners. This IFRS Standards edition is the European adaptation of the authoritative US edition – authored by Krishna G. Palepu and Paul M. Healy – that has been used in Accounting and Finance departments in universities around the world. In 2007 we decided to write the first IFRS Standards edition because of the European business environment's unique character and the introduction of mandatory IFRS Standards reporting for public corporations in the European Union. This fifth IFRS Standards edition is a thorough update of the successful fourth edition, incorporating new examples, cases, problems and exercises, and regulatory updates.

## This IFRS Standards edition

Particular features of the IFRS Standards edition are the following:

- A large number of examples support the discussion of business analysis and valuation throughout the chapters. The examples are from (mostly European) companies that students will generally be familiar with, such as Audi, BMW, British American Tobacco, BP, Carlsberg, Deutsche Telekom, easyGroup, Hennes and Mauritz, Lufthansa, Renault, Sanofi, Société Générale, and Tesco.
- The chapters dealing with accounting analysis (Chapters 3 and 4) prepare students for the task of analyzing IFRS Standards-based financial statements. All numerical examples of accounting adjustments in Chapter 4 describe adjustments to IFRS Standards-based financial statements. Further, throughout the book we discuss various topics that are particularly relevant to understanding IFRS Standards-based (European) financial reports, such as: the classification of expenses by nature and by function; a principles-based approach versus a rules-based approach to standard setting; the first-time adoption of IFRS Standards; cross-country differences and similarities in external auditing and public enforcement, and cross-country differences in financing structures.
- The terminology that we use throughout the chapters is consistent with the terminology that is used in the IFRS Standards.
- Throughout the chapters, we describe the average performance and growth ratios, the average time-series behavior of these ratios, and average financing policies of a sample of close to 7,800 firms that have been listed on European public exchanges between 1998 and 2017.
- The financial analysis and valuation chapters (Chapters 5-8) focus on firms in the apparel retail sector, primarily Hennes & Mauritz and Inditex. Throughout these chapters, we explicitly differentiate between analyzing and valuing operations and analyzing and valuing non-operating investments. Further, Chapter 8 explicitly discusses implementation differences between equity-based and asset-based valuation approaches.

- Chapter 10 on credit analysis includes a discussion of how credit ratings and default probability estimates can be used in debt valuation. Chapter 11 on M&A analysis includes a discussion on how to perform a purchase price allocation using the tools and techniques from Chapters 5 through 8.
- Data, analyses, problems, and examples have been thoroughly updated in the fifth edition.
- We have updated some of the fourth IFRS Standards edition's cases ('Carrefour SA', 'Forecasting Earnings and Earnings Growth in the European Oil and Gas Industry', 'Two European Hotel Groups') and have included eight new cases: 'Akris: Competition in the High-End Fashion Industry', 'Toshiba: Accounting Fraud', 'Accounting for the iPhone Upgrade Program', 'Valuation Multiples in Fast Fashion', 'Ferrari: The 2015 Initial Public Offering', 'Tesco: From Troubles to Turnaround', 'Spotify's Direct Listing IPO', and 'Valuing Europe's fastest growing company: HelloFresh in 2017'.

## Key features

This book differs from other texts in business and financial analysis in a number of important ways. We introduce and develop a framework for business analysis and valuation using financial statement data. We then show how this framework can be applied to a variety of decision contexts.

### FRAMEWORK FOR ANALYSIS

We begin the book with a discussion of the role of accounting information and intermediaries in the economy, and how financial analysis can create value in well-functioning markets (Chapter 1). We identify four key components, or steps, of effective financial statement analysis:

- Business strategy analysis
- Accounting analysis
- Financial analysis
- Prospective analysis

The first step, business strategy analysis (Chapter 2), involves developing an understanding of the business and competitive strategy of the firm being analyzed. Incorporating business strategy into financial statement analysis is one of the distinctive features of this book. Traditionally, this step has been ignored by other financial statement analysis books. However, we believe that it is critical to begin financial statement analysis with a company's strategy because it provides an important foundation for the subsequent analysis. The strategy analysis section discusses contemporary tools for analyzing a company's industry, its competitive position and sustainability within an industry, and the company's corporate strategy.

Accounting analysis (Chapters 3 and 4) involves examining how accounting rules and conventions represent a firm's business economics and strategy in its financial statements, and, if necessary, developing adjusted accounting measures of performance. In the accounting analysis section, we do not emphasize accounting rules. Instead we develop general approaches to analyzing assets, liabilities, entities, revenues, and expenses. We believe that such an approach enables students to effectively evaluate a company's accounting choices and accrual estimates, even if students have only a basic knowledge of accounting rules and standards. The material is also designed to allow students to make accounting adjustments rather than merely identify questionable accounting practices.

Financial analysis (Chapter 5) involves analyzing financial ratio and cash flow measures of the operating, financing, and investing performance of a company relative to either key competitors or historical performance. Our distinctive approach focuses on using financial analysis to evaluate the effectiveness of a company's strategy and to make sound financial forecasts.

Finally, under prospective analysis (Chapters 6–8) we show how to develop forecasted financial statements and how to use these to make estimates of a firm's value. Our discussion of valuation includes traditional discounted cash flow models as well as techniques that link value directly to accounting numbers. In discussing accounting-based valuation models, we integrate the latest academic research with traditional approaches such as earnings and book value multiples that are widely used in practice.

While we cover all four steps of business analysis and valuation in the book, we recognize that the extent of their use depends on the user's decision context. For example, bankers are likely to use business strategy analysis, accounting analysis, financial analysis, and the forecasting portion of prospective analysis. They are less likely to be interested in formally valuing a prospective client.

### APPLICATION OF THE FRAMEWORK TO DECISION CONTEXTS

The next section of the book shows how our business analysis and valuation framework can be applied to a variety of decision contexts:

- Securities analysis (Chapter 9)
- Credit analysis and distress prediction (Chapter 10)
- Merger and acquisition analysis (Chapter 11)

For each of these topics we present an overview to provide a foundation for the class discussions. Where possible we discuss relevant institutional details and the results of academic research that are useful in applying the analysis concepts developed earlier in the book. For example, the chapter on credit analysis shows how banks and rating agencies use financial statement data to develop analysis for lending decisions and to rate public debt issues. This chapter also presents academic research on how to determine whether a company is financially distressed.

## Using the book

We designed the book so that it is flexible for courses in financial statement analysis for a variety of student audiences – MBA students, Masters in Accounting or Finance students, Executive Program participants, and undergraduates in accounting or finance. Depending upon the audience, the instructor can vary the manner in which the conceptual materials in the chapters, end-of-chapter questions, and case examples are used. To get the most out of the book, students should have completed basic courses in financial accounting, finance, and either business strategy or business economics. The text provides a concise overview of some of these topics, primarily as background for preparing the cases. But it would probably be difficult for students with no prior knowledge in these fields to use the chapters as stand-alone coverage of them.

If the book is used for students with prior working experience or for executives, the instructor can use almost a pure case approach, adding relevant lecture sections as needed. When teaching students with little work experience, a lecture class can be presented first, followed by an appropriate case or other assignment material. It is also possible to use the book primarily for a lecture course and include some of the short or long cases as in-class illustrations of the concepts discussed in the book. Alternatively, lectures can be used as a follow-up to cases to more clearly lay out the conceptual issues raised in the case discussions. This may be appropriate when the book is used in undergraduate capstone courses. In such a context, cases can be used in course projects that can be assigned to student teams.

## Companion website

A companion website accompanies this book. This website contains the following valuable material for instructors and students:

- Instructions for how to easily produce standardized financial statements in Excel.
- Spreadsheets containing: (1) the reported and standardized financial statements of Hennes & Mauritz (H&M) and Inditex; (2) calculations of H&M's and Inditex's ratios (presented in Chapter 5); (3) H&M's forecasted

financial statements (presented in Chapter 6); and (4) valuations of H&M's shares (presented in Chapter 8). Using these spreadsheets students can easily replicate the analyses presented in Chapters 5 through 8 and perform "what-if" analyses – i.e., to find out how the reported numbers change as a result of changes to the standardized statements or forecasting assumptions.

- Spreadsheets containing case material.
- Answers to the discussion questions and case instructions (for instructors only).
- A complete set of lecture slides (for instructors only).

Accompanying teaching notes to some of the case studies can be found at www.harvardbusiness.org or www.thecasecentre.org. Lecturers are able to register to access the teaching notes and other relevant information.

# Acknowledgements

We thank the following colleagues who gave us feedback as we wrote this and the previous IFRS Standards edition:

- Constantinos Adamides, Lecturer, University of Nicosia
- Tony Appleyard, Professor of Accounting and Finance, Newcastle University
- Professor Chelley-Steeley, Professor of Finance, Aston Business School
- Rick Cuijpers, Assistant Professor, Maastricht University School of Business and Economics
- Christina Dargenidou, Professor, University of Exeter
- Dominic Detzen, Assistant Professor, Vrije University
- Karl-Hermann Fischer, Lecturer and Associate Researcher, Goethe University Frankfurt
- Zhan Gao, Lecturer in Accounting, Lancaster University
- Stefano Gatti, Associate Professor of Finance, Bocconi University Milan
- Frøystein Gjesdal, Professor, Norwegian School of Economics
- Igor Goncharov, Professor, WHU Business School
- Aditi Gupta, Lecturer, King's College London
- Shahed Imam, Associate Professor, Warwick Business School
- Otto Janschek, Assistant Professor, WU Vienna
- Marcus Kliaras, Banking and Finance Lecturer, University of Applied Sciences, BFI, Vienna
- Gianluca Meloni, Clinical Professor – Accounting Department, Bocconi University
- Sascha Moells, Professsor in Financial Accounting and Corporate Valuation, Philipps-University of Marburg, Germany
- Jon Mugabi, Lecturer in Finance and Accounting, The Hague University
- Cornelia Neff, Professor of Finance and Management Accounting, University of Applied Sciences Ravens-burg-Weingarten, Germany
- Bartlomiej Nita, Associate Professor, Wroclaw University of Economics
- Nikola Petrovic, Lecturer in Accounting, University of Bristol
- Roswitha Prassl, Teaching and Research Associate, Vienna University for Economics and Business Administration
- Bill Rees, Professor of Financial Analysis, Edinburgh University
- Matthias Schmidt, Professor for Business Administration, Leipzig University
- Harri Seppänen, Assistant Professor, Aalto University School of Economics
- Yun Shen, Lecturer in Accounting, University of Bath
- Radha Shiwakoti, Lecturer, University of Kent
- Ana Simpson, Lecturer, London School of Economics
- Nicos Sykianakis, Assistant Professor, TEI of Piraeus
- Isaac Tabner, Lecturer in Finance, University of Stirling
- Jon Tucker, Professor and Centre Director, Centre for Global Finance, University of the West of England
- Birgit Wolf, Professor of Managerial Economics, Touro College Berlin
- Jessica Yang, Senior Lecturer in Accounting, University of East London

We are *also* very grateful to the publishing team at Cengage Learning for their help and assistance throughout the production of this edition.

The Publisher would like to thank all parties who gave permission for the reproduction of case studies. All cases have been individually credited.

# Authors

**KRISHNA G. PALEPU** is the Ross Graham Walker Professor of Business Administration and Senior Advisor to the President of Harvard University. During the past 25 years, Professor Palepu's research has focused on corporate strategy, governance, and disclosure. Professor Palepu is the winner of the American Accounting Association's Notable Contributions to Accounting Literature Award (in 1999) and the Wildman Award (in 1997).

**PAUL M. HEALY** is the James R. Williston Professor of Business Administration and Senior Associate Dean for Faculty Development at the Harvard Business School. Professor Healy's research has focused on corporate governance and disclosure, mergers and acquisitions, earnings management, and management compensation. He has previously worked at the MIT Sloan School of Management, ICI Ltd, and Arthur Young in New Zealand. Professor Healy has won the Notable Contributions to Accounting Literature Award (in 1990 and 1999) and the Wild-man Award (in 1997) for contributions to practice.

**ERIK PEEK** is Professor of Business Analysis and Valuation at Rotterdam School of Management, Erasmus University, the Netherlands. Prior to joining RSM Erasmus University he has been an Associate Professor at Maastricht University and a Visiting Associate Professor at the Wharton School of the University of Pennsylvania. Professor Peek is a CFA charterholder and holds a PhD from the VU University Amsterdam. His research has focused on international accounting, financial analysis and valuation, and earnings management.

# Framework

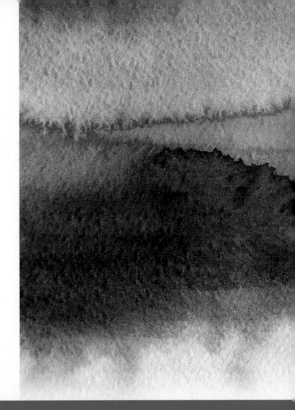

## PART I

1   A framework for business analysis and valuation using financial statements

# 1 A framework for business analysis and valuation using financial statements

This chapter outlines a comprehensive framework for financial statement analysis. Because financial statements provide the most widely available data on public corporations' economic activities, investors and other stakeholders rely on financial reports to assess the plans and performance of firms and corporate managers.

A variety of questions can be addressed by business analysis using financial statements, as shown in the following examples:

- A security analyst may be interested in asking: "How well is the firm I am following performing? Did the firm meet my performance expectations? If not, why not? What is the value of the firm's stock given my assessment of the firm's current and future performance?"
- A loan officer may need to ask: "What is the credit risk involved in lending a certain amount of money to this firm? How well is the firm managing its liquidity and solvency? What is the firm's business risk? What is the additional risk created by the firm's financing and dividend policies?"
- A management consultant might ask: "What is the structure of the industry in which the firm is operating? What are the strategies pursued by various players in the industry? What is the relative performance of different firms in the industry?"
- A corporate manager may ask: "Is my firm properly valued by investors? Is our investor communication program adequate to facilitate this process?"
- A corporate manager could ask: "Is this firm a potential takeover target? How much value can be added if we acquire this firm? How can we finance the acquisition?"
- An independent auditor would want to ask: "Are the accounting policies and accrual estimates in this company's financial statements consistent with my understanding of this business and its recent performance? Do these financial reports communicate the current status and significant risks of the business?"

In almost all countries in the world today, **capital markets** play an important role in channeling financial resources from savers to business enterprises that need capital. Financial statement analysis is a valuable activity when managers have complete information on a firm's strategies, and a variety of institutional factors make it unlikely that they fully disclose this information to suppliers of capital. In this setting, outside analysts attempt to create "inside information" from analyzing financial statement data, thereby gaining valuable insights about the firm's current performance and future prospects.

To understand the contribution that financial statement analysis can make, it is important to understand the role of financial reporting in the functioning of capital markets and the institutional forces that shape financial statements. Therefore we present first a brief description of these forces; then we discuss the steps that an analyst must perform to extract information from financial statements and provide valuable forecasts.

## The role of financial reporting in capital markets

A critical challenge for any economy is the allocation of savings to investment opportunities. Economies that do this well can exploit new business ideas to spur innovation and create jobs and wealth at a rapid pace. In contrast, economies that manage this process poorly dissipate their wealth and fail to support business opportunities.

**FIGURE 1.1** Capital markets

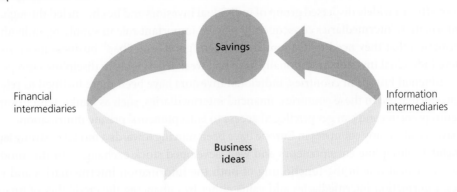

Figure 1.1 provides a schematic representation of how capital markets typically work. Savings in any economy are widely distributed among households. There are usually many new entrepreneurs and existing companies that would like to attract these savings to fund their business ideas. While both savers and entrepreneurs would like to do business with each other, matching savings to business investment opportunities through the use of capital markets – funding business ideas with the highest prospects first – is complicated for at least three reasons:

- Information asymmetry between savers and entrepreneurs. Entrepreneurs typically have better information than savers on the value of business investment opportunities.
- Potentially conflicting interests – credibility problems. Communication by entrepreneurs to savers is not completely credible because savers know that entrepreneurs have an incentive to inflate the value of their ideas.
- Expertise asymmetry. Savers generally lack the financial sophistication needed to analyze and differentiate between the various business opportunities.

The information and incentive issues lead to what economists call the **lemons problem**, which can potentially break down the functioning of the capital market.[1] It works like this. Consider a situation where half the business ideas are "good" and the other half are "bad." If investors cannot distinguish between the two types of business ideas, entrepreneurs with "bad" ideas will try to claim that their ideas are as valuable as the "good" ideas. Realizing this possibility, investors value both good and bad ideas at an average level. Unfortunately, this penalizes good ideas, and entrepreneurs with good ideas find the terms on which they can get financing to be unattractive. As these entrepreneurs leave the capital market, the proportion of bad ideas in the market increases. Over time, bad ideas "crowd out" good ideas, and investors lose confidence in this market.

The emergence of intermediaries can prevent such a market breakdown. Intermediaries are like a car mechanic who provides an independent certification of a used car's quality to help a buyer and seller agree on a price. There are two types of intermediaries in the capital markets. **Financial intermediaries**, such as venture capital firms, banks, collective investment funds, pension funds, and insurance companies, focus on aggregating funds from individual investors and analyzing different investment alternatives to make investment decisions. **Information intermediaries**, such as auditors, financial analysts, credit-rating agencies, and the financial press, focus on providing or assuring information to investors (and to financial intermediaries who represent them) on the quality of various business investment opportunities. Both these types of intermediaries add value by helping investors distinguish "good" investment opportunities from the "bad" ones.

The relative importance of financial intermediaries and information intermediaries varies from country to country for historical reasons. In countries where individual investors traditionally have had strong legal rights to discipline entrepreneurs who invest in "bad" business ideas, such as in the UK, individual investors have been more inclined to make their own investment decisions. In these countries, the funds that entrepreneurs attract may come from a widely dispersed group of individual investors and be channeled through public stock exchanges. Information intermediaries consequently play an important role in supplying individual investors with the information that they need to distinguish between "good" and "bad" business ideas. In contrast, in countries where individual investors traditionally have had weak legal rights to discipline entrepreneurs, such as in many Continental European countries, individual investors have been more inclined to rely on the help of financial intermediaries. In these countries, financial intermediaries, such as banks, tend to supply most of the funds to entrepreneurs and can get privileged access to entrepreneurs' private information.

Over the past decade, many countries in Europe have been moving towards a model of strong **legal protection of investors' rights** to discipline entrepreneurs and well-developed stock exchanges. In this model, financial reporting plays a critical role in the functioning of both the information intermediaries and the financial intermediaries. Information intermediaries add value either by enhancing the credibility of financial reports (as auditors do) or by analyzing the information in the financial statements (as analysts and rating agencies do). Financial intermediaries rely on the information in the financial statements to analyze investment opportunities and supplement this information with other sources of information.

Ideally, the various intermediaries serve as a system of checks and balances to ensure the efficient functioning of the capital markets system. However, this is not always the case as on occasion the intermediaries tend to mutually reinforce rather than counterbalance each other. A number of problems can arise as a result of incentive issues, governance issues within the intermediary organizations themselves, and conflicts of interest, as evidenced by accounting scandals at companies such as Carillion, Olympus, Steinhoff, and Tesco. However, in general this market mechanism functions efficiently, and prices reflect all available information on a particular investment. Despite this overall market efficiency, individual securities may still be temporarily mispriced, thereby justifying the need for financial statement analysis.

In the following section, we discuss key aspects of the financial reporting system design that enable it to play effectively this vital role in the functioning of the capital markets.

## From business activities to financial statements

Corporate managers are responsible for acquiring physical and financial resources from the firm's environment and using them to create value for the firm's investors. Value is created when the firm earns a return on its investment in excess of the return required by its capital suppliers. Managers formulate business strategies to achieve this goal, and they implement them through business activities. A firm's business activities are influenced by its economic environment and its business strategy. The economic environment includes the firm's industry, its input and output markets, and the regulations under which the firm operates. The firm's business strategy determines how the firm positions itself in its environment to achieve a competitive advantage.

As shown in Figure 1.2, a firm's **financial statements** summarize the economic consequences of its business activities. The firm's business activities in any time period are too numerous to be reported individually to outsiders. Further, some of the activities undertaken by the firm are proprietary in nature, and disclosing these activities in detail could be a detriment to the firm's competitive position. The firm's accounting system provides a mechanism through which business activities are selected, measured, and aggregated into financial statement data.

On a periodic basis, firms typically produce five financial reports:

1  An income statement that describes the operating performance during a time period.
2  A balance sheet that states the firm's assets and how they are financed.[2]
3  A cash flow statement that summarizes the cash flows of the firm.

4  A statement of other comprehensive income that outlines the sources of changes in equity that are (a) not the result of transactions with the owners of the firm and (b) not included in the income statement.[3]

5  A statement of changes in equity that summarizes all sources of changes in equity during the period between two consecutive balance sheets, consisting of (a) total comprehensive income – being the sum of profit or loss [item 1] and other comprehensive income [item 4] – and (b) the financial effects of transactions with the owners of the firm.

These statements are accompanied by notes that provide additional details on the financial statement line items, as well as by management's narrative discussion of the firm's activities, performance, and risks in the Management Commentary section.[4]

**FIGURE 1.2**  From business activities to financial statements

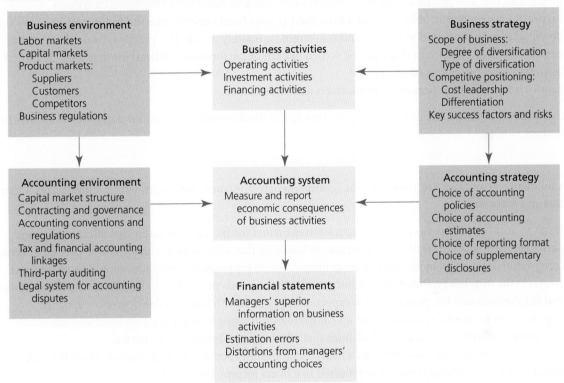

## Influences of the accounting system on information quality

Intermediaries using financial statement data to do business analysis have to be aware that financial reports are influenced both by the firm's business activities and by its accounting system. A key aspect of financial statement analysis therefore involves understanding the influence of the accounting system on the quality of the financial statement data being used in the analysis. The institutional features of accounting systems discussed next determine the extent of that influence.

### FEATURE 1: ACCRUAL ACCOUNTING

One of the fundamental features of corporate financial reports is that they are prepared using accrual rather than cash accounting. Unlike cash accounting, **accrual accounting** distinguishes between the recording of costs or benefits associated with economic activities and the actual payment or receipt of cash. Profit or loss is the primary periodic performance index under accrual accounting. To compute profit or loss, the effects of economic transactions are recorded on the basis of *expected*, not necessarily *actual*, cash receipts and payments. Expected cash receipts from the delivery of products or services are recognized as revenues, and expected cash outflows associated with these revenues are recognized as expenses. Timing differences between the moment of recording costs or benefits and the moment of experiencing cash inflows or outflows result in the recognition of assets and liabilities on the balance sheet.

While many rules and conventions govern a firm's preparation of financial statements, only a few conceptual building blocks form the foundation of accrual accounting. Starting from the balance sheet, the principles that define a firm's **assets, liabilities**, and **equity** are as follows:

- Assets are economic resources controlled by a firm that (a) have the potential to produce future economic benefits and (b) are measurable with a reasonable degree of certainty. An example of an asset is a firm's inventories that will produce economic benefits once sold and delivered to the firm's customers.
- Liabilities are economic obligations of a firm that (a) arise from benefits received in the past, (b) have the potential of being required to be met, and (c) cannot be feasibly avoided by the firm. Examples of liabilities are bonds or bank loans that must be settled in cash or performance obligations that must be settled by providing services to a customer.
- Equity is the difference between a firm's assets and its liabilities.

The definitions of assets, liabilities, and equity lead to the fundamental relationship that governs a firm's balance sheet:

$$Assets = Liabilities + Equity$$

The following definitions are critical to the (comprehensive) income statement, which summarizes a firm's **income** and **expenses**:[5]

- Income or revenue consists of economic resources earned (or increases in assets that affect equity) and performance obligations settled (or decreases in liabilities that affect equity) during a time period. Revenue recognition is governed by the realization principle, which proposes that revenues should be recognized when (a) the firm has provided all, or substantially all, the goods or services to be delivered to the customer and (b) the customer has paid cash or is expected to pay cash with a reasonable degree of certainty.
- Expenses are economic resources used up (or decreases in assets that affect equity) and economic obligations created (or increases in liabilities that affect equity) during a time period.
- Profit or loss is the difference between a firm's income and expenses in a time period. The following fundamental relationship is therefore reflected in a firm's income statement:

$$Profit\ or\ loss = Income - Expenses$$

Note from the preceding definitions that the recognition of income and expenses depends on a firm's measurement of its assets and liabilities. A consistent application of the principles that define assets and liabilities implies that associated elements of income and expenses are recognized in the income statement in the same time period – a process that is also referred to as matching of income and expenses. For example, after a firm has sold and delivered goods to a customer, an increase in the asset "trade receivables" combined with a simultaneous decrease in the asset "inventories" lead to the recognition of associated income and expense in the same time period.

Remeasurements of assets or liabilities may also result in the recognition of income or expense items that are not related to the firm's current economic activities. For instance, when a firm holds inventories that have suddenly become obsolete, writing down the value of such assets will cause the recognition of an expense item that is unrelated to the firm's current economic transactions. In sum, expenses are (a) costs directly associated with revenues recognized in the same period (such as the cost of inventory sold), or (b) costs associated with benefits that are consumed in this time period (such as depreciation on non-current assets used in the period), or (c) resources whose future benefits are not reasonably certain (such as research expenditures or inventory write-downs).

The need for accrual accounting arises from investors' demand for financial reports on a periodic basis. Because firms undertake economic transactions on a continual basis, the arbitrary closing of accounting books at the end of a reporting period leads to a fundamental measurement problem. Because cash accounting does not report the full economic consequence of the transactions undertaken in a given period, accrual accounting is designed to provide more complete information on a firm's periodic performance.

## FEATURE 2: ACCOUNTING CONVENTIONS AND STANDARDS

The use of accrual accounting lies at the center of many important complexities in corporate financial reporting. For example, how should revenues be recognized when a firm sells land to customers and also provides customer financing? If revenue is recognized before cash is collected, how should potential defaults be estimated? Are the outlays associated with research and development activities, whose payoffs are uncertain, assets or expenses when incurred? Are contractual commitments under lease arrangements or post-employment plans liabilities? If so, how should they be valued? Because accrual accounting deals with expectations of future cash consequences of current events, it is subjective and relies on a variety of assumptions. Who should be charged with the primary responsibility of making these assumptions? In the current system, a firm's managers are entrusted with the task of making the appropriate estimates and assumptions to prepare the financial statements because they have intimate knowledge of their firm's business.

The accounting discretion granted to managers is potentially valuable because it allows them to reflect inside information in reported financial statements. However, because investors view profits as a measure of managers' performance, managers have incentives to use their accounting discretion to distort reported profits by making biased assumptions. Further, the use of accounting numbers in contracts between the firm and outsiders provides another motivation for manipulation of accounting numbers. Income management distorts financial accounting data, potentially making them less valuable to external users of financial statements. Therefore the delegation of financial reporting decisions to corporate managers has both costs and benefits.

A number of accounting conventions have been implemented to ensure that managers use their accounting flexibility to summarize their knowledge of the firm's business activities, and not to disguise reality for self-serving purposes. For example, in most countries financial statements are prepared using the concept of prudence, where caution is taken to ensure that assets are not recorded at values above their fair values and liabilities are not recorded at values below their fair values. This reduces managers' ability to overstate the value of the net assets that they have acquired or developed.

**Accounting standards** and rules also limit management's ability to misuse accounting judgment by regulating how particular types of transactions are recorded. For example, accounting standards for leases stipulate how firms are to record contractual arrangements to lease resources. Similarly, post-employment benefit standards describe how firms are to record commitments to provide pensions and other post-employment benefits for employees. These accounting standards, which are designed to convey quantitative information on a firm's performance, are complemented by a set of disclosure principles. The disclosure principles guide the amount and kinds of information that are disclosed and require a firm to provide qualitative information related to assumptions, policies, and uncertainties that underlie the quantitative data presented.

More than 100 countries have delegated the task of setting accounting standards to the International Accounting Standards Board (IASB). For example:

- Since 2005 European Union (EU) companies that have their shares traded on a public exchange must prepare their consolidated financial statements in accordance with International Financial Reporting Standards (IFRS Standards) as promulgated by the IASB and endorsed by the EU. Most EU countries, however, also have their own national accounting standard-setting bodies. These bodies may, for example, set accounting standards for private companies and for single entity financial statements of public companies or comment on the IASB's drafts of new or modified standards.[6]

- UK-based public companies must continue to prepare IFRS Standards-based consolidated financial statements, even after the United Kingdom's exit from the EU.
- Since 2005 and 2007, respectively, Australian and New Zealand public companies must comply with locally adopted IFRS Standards, labelled A-IFRS Standards and NZ-IFRS Standards. These sets of standards include all IFRS Standards requirements as well as some additional disclosure requirements.
- South African public companies have prepared financial statements that comply with IFRS Standards, as published by the IASB, since 2005.
- Some other large economies with stock exchanges that require (most) publicly listed companies to prepare IFRS Standards-compliant financial statements are Brazil (since 2010), Canada (2011), Korea (2011), Mexico (2012), and Russia (2012).

In the United States, the Securities and Exchange Commission (SEC) has the legal authority to set accounting standards. Since 1973 the SEC has relied on the Financial Accounting Standards Board (FASB), a private sector accounting body, to undertake this task.

Uniform accounting standards attempt to reduce managers' ability to record similar economic transactions in dissimilar ways either over time or across firms. Thus the standards create a uniform accounting language, improve the comparability of financial statements, and increase the credibility of financial statements by limiting a firm's ability to distort them. Increased uniformity from accounting standards, however, comes at the expense of reduced flexibility for managers to reflect genuine business differences in a firm's accounting decisions. Rigid accounting standards work best for economic transactions whose accounting treatment is not predicated on managers' proprietary information. However, when there is significant business judgment involved in assessing a transaction's economic consequences (such as in determining the economic benefits of product development), rigid standards (such as requiring the immediate expensing of product development outlays) are likely to be dysfunctional for some companies because the standards prevent managers from using their superior business knowledge to determine how best to report the economics of key business events. Further, if accounting standards are too rigid, they may induce managers to expend economic resources to restructure business transactions to achieve a desired accounting result or forego transactions that may be difficult to report on.

## FEATURE 3: MANAGERS' REPORTING STRATEGY

Because the mechanisms that limit managers' ability to distort accounting data add noise, it is not optimal to use accounting regulation to eliminate managerial flexibility completely. Therefore real-world accounting systems leave considerable room for managers to influence financial statement data. A firm's **reporting strategy** – that is, the manner in which managers use their accounting discretion – has an important influence on the firm's financial statements.

Corporate managers can choose accounting and disclosure policies that make it more or less difficult for external users of financial reports to understand the true economic picture of their businesses. Accounting rules often provide a broad set of alternatives from which managers can choose. Further, managers are entrusted with making a range of estimates in implementing these accounting policies. Accounting regulations usually prescribe minimum disclosure requirements, but they do not restrict managers from *voluntarily* providing additional disclosures.

A superior disclosure strategy will enable managers to communicate the underlying business reality to outside investors. One important constraint on a firm's disclosure strategy is the competitive dynamics in product markets. Disclosure of proprietary information about business strategies and their expected economic consequences may hurt the firm's competitive position. Subject to this constraint, managers can use financial statements to provide information useful to investors in assessing their firm's true economic performance.

Managers can also use financial reporting strategies to manipulate investors' perceptions. Using the discretion granted to them, managers can make it difficult for investors to identify poor performance on a timely basis. For example, managers can choose accounting policies and estimates to provide an optimistic assessment of the firm's true performance. They can also make it costly for investors to understand the true performance by controlling the extent of information that is disclosed voluntarily.

The extent to which financial statements are informative about the underlying business reality varies across firms and across time for a given firm. This variation in accounting quality provides both an important opportunity and a challenge in doing business analysis. The process through which analysts can separate noise from information in financial statements, and gain valuable business insights from financial statement analysis, is discussed in the following section.

## FEATURE 4: AUDITING, LEGAL LIABILITY, AND PUBLIC ENFORCEMENT
### Auditing
Broadly defined as a verification of the integrity of the reported financial statements by someone other than the preparer, **auditing** ensures that managers use accounting rules and conventions consistently over time and that their accounting estimates are reasonable. Therefore auditing improves the quality of accounting data. In Europe, the United States, and most other countries, all listed companies are required to have their financial statements audited by an independent public accountant. The standards and procedures to be followed by independent auditors are set by various institutions. By means of the Revised Statutory Audit Directive and Regulation, the EU has set minimum standards for public audits that are performed on companies from its member countries. These standards prescribe, for example, that the external auditor does not provide any nonaudit services to the audited company that may compromise his independence and place a cap on nonaudit service fees. To maintain independence, the auditor also must not audit the same company for more than ten consecutive years. Further, in most European countries, audits must be carried out in accordance with the International Standards on Auditing (ISA), as promulgated by the International Auditing and Assurance Standards Board (IAASB).

In the United States, independent auditors must follow Generally Accepted Auditing Standards (GAAS), a set of standards comparable to the ISA. All US public accounting firms are also required to register with the Public Company Accounting Oversight Board (PCAOB), a regulatory body that has the power to inspect and investigate audit work, and if needed discipline auditors. Like the Statutory Audit Directive and Regulation in the EU, the US Sarbanes–Oxley Act specifies the relationship between a company and its external auditor, for example, requiring auditors to report to, and be overseen by, a company's audit committee rather than its management.

While auditors issue an opinion on published financial statements, it is important to remember that the primary responsibility for the statements still rests with corporate managers. Auditing improves the quality and credibility of accounting data by limiting a firm's ability to distort financial statements to suit its own purposes. However, as audit failures at companies such as Carillion, Olympus, Steinhoff, and Tesco show, auditing is imperfect. Audits cannot review all of a firm's transactions. They can also fail because of lapses in quality or because of lapses in judgment by auditors who fail to challenge management for fear of losing future business.

Third-party auditing may also reduce the quality of financial reporting because it constrains the kind of accounting rules and conventions that evolve over time. For example, the IASB considers the views of auditors – in addition to other interest groups – in the process of setting IFRS Standards. To illustrate, about one-quarter of the IASB board members have a background as practicing auditor. Further, the IASB is advised by the IFRS Standards Advisory Council, which contains several practicing auditors. Finally, the IASB invites auditors to comment on its policies and proposed standards. Auditors are likely to argue against accounting standards that produce numbers that are difficult to audit, sometimes also if the proposed rules produce relevant information for investors.

### Legal liability
The legal environment in which accounting disputes between managers, auditors, and investors are adjudicated can also have a significant effect on the quality of reported numbers. The threat of lawsuits and resulting penalties have the beneficial effect of improving the accuracy of disclosure. In the EU, the Transparency Directive requires that every member state has established a statutory civil liability regime for misstatements

that managers make in their periodic disclosures to investors. However, legal liability regimes vary in strictness across countries, both within and outside Europe. Under strict regimes, such as that found in the United States, investors can hold managers liable for their investment losses if the investors prove that the firm's disclosures were misleading, that they relied on the misleading disclosures, and that their losses were caused by the misleading disclosures. Under less strict regimes, such as those found in France, Germany, and several other Continental European countries, investors must additionally prove that managers were (grossly) negligent in their reporting or even had the intent to harm investors (i.e., committed fraud).[7] Further, in some countries only misstatements in annual and interim financial reports are subject to liability, whereas in other countries investors can hold managers liable also for misleading ad hoc disclosures.

The potential for significant legal liability might also discourage managers and auditors from supporting accounting proposals requiring risky forecasts – for example, forward-looking disclosures. This type of concern has motivated several European countries to adopt a less strict liability regime.[8]

### Public enforcement

Several countries adhere to the idea that strong accounting standards, external auditing, and the threat of legal liability do not suffice to ensure that financial statements provide a truthful picture of economic reality. As a final guarantee on reporting quality, these countries have public enforcement bodies that either proactively or on a complaint basis initiate reviews of companies' compliance with accounting standards and take actions to correct noncompliance. In the United States, the Securities and Exchange Commission (SEC) performs such reviews and frequently disciplines companies for violations of US GAAP (Generally Accepted Accounting Principles). In recent years, several European countries have also set up proactive enforcement agencies that should enforce listed companies' compliance with IFRS Standards. Examples of such agencies are the French AMF (Autorité des Marchés Financiers), the German DPR (Deutsche Prüfstelle für Rechnungslegung), the Italian CONSOB (Commissione Nazionale per le Società e la Borsa), and the UK Financial Reporting Council. Because each European country maintains control of domestic enforcement, there is a risk that the enforcement of IFRS Standards exhibits differences in strictness and focus across Europe. To coordinate enforcement activities, however, most European enforcement agencies cooperate under the stimulus of the European Securities and Markets Authority (ESMA). One of the ESMA's tasks is to develop mechanisms that lead to consistent enforcement across Europe. For example, the ESMA organizes peer reviews of national enforcement agencies and promotes best practices through the publication of peer review reports and guidelines. The coming years will show whether a decentralized system of enforcement can consistently assure that European companies comply with IFRS Standards.

Public enforcement bodies cannot ensure full compliance of all listed companies. In fact, most proactive enforcement bodies conduct their investigations on a sampling basis. For example, the enforcement bodies may periodically select industry sectors on which they focus their enforcement activities and select individual companies either at random or on the basis of company characteristics such as poor governance. The set of variables that European enforcers most commonly use to select companies includes market capitalization or trading volume (both measuring the company's economic relevance), share price volatility, the likelihood of new equity issues, and the inclusion of the company in an index.[9]

Strict public enforcement can also reduce the quality of financial reporting because, in their attempt to avoid an accounting credibility crisis on public capital markets, enforcement bodies may pressure companies to exercise excessive prudence in their accounting choices.

# Alternative forms of communication with investors

Given the limitations of accounting standards, auditing, and enforcement, as well as the reporting credibility problems faced by management, firms that wish to communicate effectively with external investors are often forced to use alternative media. Next we discuss two alternative ways that managers can communicate with external investors and analysts: meetings with analysts to publicize the firm and expanded voluntary disclosure. These forms of communication are typically not mutually exclusive.

## Public Enforcement Practices

The fact that most countries have a public enforcement agency does not, of course, imply that all countries have equally developed effective enforcement systems. One measure of the development of public enforcement is how much a country spends on enforcement. A study has shown that there still is significant variation worldwide in enforcement agencies' staff and budget size. For example, in the late 2000s, agencies in Italy, the Netherlands, the United Kingdom, and the United States spent more than twice as much as their peers in France, Germany, Spain, and Sweden.[10] Although public enforcement has important preventive effects – it deters violations of accounting rules just through its presence – another measure of its development is an enforcement agency's activity, potentially measured by the number of investigations held and the number of actions taken against public companies. Most agencies disclose annual reports summarizing their activities. In addition, the ESMA periodically publishes extracts from its confidential database of enforcement decisions taken by the national agencies. These reports illustrate that many actions taken by enforcement agencies (a) target poor disclosure quality (45 percent of all actions in 2017) and (b) are recommendations to firms on how to improve their reporting and better comply with IFRS Standards in the future (75 percent of all actions in 2017). In several cases the agencies took corrective actions. Following are two examples of such actions:

- In the year ending in March 2017, the UK Financial Reporting Council reviewed 203 annual reports, 183 on its own initiative and 20 in response to complaints or referrals. In only a few cases a firm had to either restate its current financial statements or adjust the prior period figures in its next financial statements. For example, in 2015 Learning Technologies Group (LTG) acquired Eukleia, a provider of e-learning services, for £8.3 million plus a contingent consideration estimated at £2.2 million, based on future revenue growth. Because part of the contingent consideration was payable to Eukleia's employees, LTG was asked to charge an amount of £335 thousand as remuneration to the comparative income statement for 2016. In its 2015 financial statements, LTG had incorrectly capitalized this amount.
- In May 2016 the German supervisory authority (DPR) publicly "named and shamed" solar power specialist Phoenix Solar AG. The DPR disclosed that Phoenix Solar had reduced transparency by disclosing two different income statements in its 2014 financial statements, one of which did not comply with IFRS Standards 5 on discontinued operations.

### ANALYST MEETINGS

One popular way for managers to help mitigate information problems is to meet regularly with financial analysts that follow the firm. At these meetings management will field questions about the firm's current financial performance and discuss its future business plans. In addition to holding analyst meetings, many firms appoint a director of public relations, who provides further regular contact with analysts seeking more information on the firm.

Conference calls have become a popular forum for management to communicate with financial analysts. Research finds that firms are more likely to host calls if they are in industries where financial statement data fail to capture key business fundamentals on a timely basis.[11] In addition, conference calls themselves appear to provide new information to analysts about a firm's performance and future prospects.[12] Smaller and less heavily traded firms in particular benefit from initiating investor conference calls.[13]

While firms continue to meet with analysts, rules such as the EU Market Abuse Directive affect the nature of these interactions. Under these rules, all EU countries must have regulations and institutions in place that prevent unfair disclosure. Specifically, countries must ensure that exchange-listed companies disclose non-public private information promptly and simultaneously to all investors. This can reduce the information that managers are willing to disclose in conference calls and private meetings, making these less effective forums for resolving information problems.

## VOLUNTARY DISCLOSURE

Another way for managers to improve the credibility of their financial reporting is through voluntary disclosure. Accounting rules usually prescribe minimum disclosure requirements, but they do not restrict managers from voluntarily providing additional information. These could include an articulation of the company's long-term strategy, specification of non-financial leading indicators that are useful in judging the effectiveness of the strategy implementation, explanation of the relationship between the leading indicators and future profits, and forecasts of future performance. Voluntary disclosures can be reported in the firm's annual report, in brochures created to describe the firm to investors, in management meetings with analysts, or in investor relations responses to information requests.[14]

One constraint on expanded disclosure is the competitive dynamics in product markets. Disclosure of proprietary information on strategies and their expected economic consequences may hurt the firm's competitive position. Managers then face a trade-off between providing information that is useful to investors in assessing the firm's economic performance, and withholding information to maximize the firm's product market advantage.

A second constraint in providing voluntary disclosure is management's legal liability. Forecasts and voluntary disclosures can potentially be used by dissatisfied shareholders to bring civil actions against management for providing misleading information. This seems ironic, since voluntary disclosures should provide investors with additional information. Unfortunately, it can be difficult for courts to decide whether managers' disclosures were good-faith estimates of uncertain future events which later did not materialize, or whether management manipulated the market. Consequently, many corporate legal departments recommend against management providing much in the way of voluntary disclosure. One aspect of corporate governance, earnings guidance, has been particularly controversial. There is substantial evidence that the guidance provided by management plays an important role in leading analysts' expectations towards achievable profit targets, and that management guidance is more likely when analysts' initial forecasts are overly optimistic.[15]

Finally, management credibility can limit a firm's incentives to provide voluntary disclosures. If management faces a credibility problem in financial reporting, any voluntary disclosures it provides are also likely to be viewed skeptically. In particular, investors may be concerned about what management is not telling them, particularly since such disclosures are not audited.

# From financial statements to business analysis

Because managers' insider knowledge is a source of both value and distortion in accounting data, it is difficult for outside users of financial statements to separate accurate information from distortion and noise. Not being able to undo accounting distortions completely, investors "discount" a firm's reported accounting performance. In doing so, they make a probabilistic assessment of the extent to which a firm's reported numbers reflect economic reality. As a result, investors can have only an imprecise assessment of an individual firm's performance. **Financial and information intermediaries** can add value by improving investors' understanding of a firm's current performance and its future prospects.

Effective financial statement analysis is valuable because it attempts to get at managers' inside information from public financial statement data. Because intermediaries do not have direct or complete access to this information, they rely on their knowledge of the firm's industry and its competitive strategies to interpret financial statements. Successful intermediaries have at least as good an understanding of the industry economics as do the firm's managers, as well as a reasonably good understanding of the firm's competitive strategy. Although outside analysts have an information disadvantage relative to the firm's managers, these analysts are more objective in evaluating the economic consequences of the firm's investment and operating decisions.

## The Impact of EU Directives on Financial Reporting and Auditing in Europe

During the past 15 years, the European Commission has issued or revised a few Directives and Regulations that significantly affect financial reporting and auditing practices in the EU. The Revised Statutory Audit Directive and Regulation (SAD; effective since 2014) regulates the audit of financial statements. In addition, the Amended Transparency Directive (TD; 2013) and the Revised Market Abuse Directive and Regulation (MAD; 2014) regulate firms' periodic and ad hoc disclosures, with the objective to improve the quality and timeliness of information provided to investors. Some of the highlights of these Directives and Regulations include:

- Prescribing that firms issuing public debt or equity securities (public firms) publish their annual report no more than four months after the financial year-end. The annual report must contain the audited financial statements, a management report, and management's responsibility statement certifying that the financial statements give a true and fair view of the firm's performance and financial position (TD).
- Requiring that public firms publish semiannual financial reports, including condensed financial statements, an interim management report, and a responsibility statement, within two months of the end of the first half of the fiscal year. The firms must also indicate whether the interim financial statements have been audited or reviewed by an auditor (TD).
- Ensuring that each EU member state has a central filing and storage system for public financial reports (TD).
- Requiring that public firms prepare annual financial reports in a single electronic format as of 2020 (TD).
- Requiring that public firms immediately disclose any information that may have a material impact on their security price and prohibiting that insiders to the firm trade on such information before its disclosure (TD, MAD).
- Requiring that the member states impose common criminal sanctions for insider trading offences (MAD).
- Prohibiting that the external auditor provides any nonaudit services to the audited firm that may compromise his independence, such as tax advice and valuation services (SAD).
- Enhancing auditor independence by prescribing that the external auditor does not audit the same firm for more than ten consecutive years, unless a second ten-year period follows a public tender (SAD).
- Requiring that all audits are carried out in accordance with International Standards on Auditing (SAD).
- Requiring that all audit firms are subject to a system of external quality assurance and public oversight (SAD).
- Mandating that each public firm has an audit committee, which monitors the firm's financial reporting process, internal control system and statutory audit (SAD).
- Ensuring that each EU member state designates a competent authority responsible for supervising firms' compliance with the provisions of the Directives (SAD, TD, MAD).

Each EU member state must implement the Directives by introducing new or changing existing national legislation. This has at least two important consequences. First, because the member states have some freedom in deciding how to comply with the Directives, some differences in financial reporting, disclosure, and auditing regulation continue to exist. Second, in spite of the United Kingdom's exit from the EU, national UK legislation reflects many elements of the preceding Directives.

Figure 1.3 provides a schematic overview of how business intermediaries use financial statements to accomplish four key steps:

1 Business strategy analysis.
2 Accounting analysis.
3 Financial analysis.
4 Prospective analysis.

**FIGURE 1.3** Analysis using financial statements

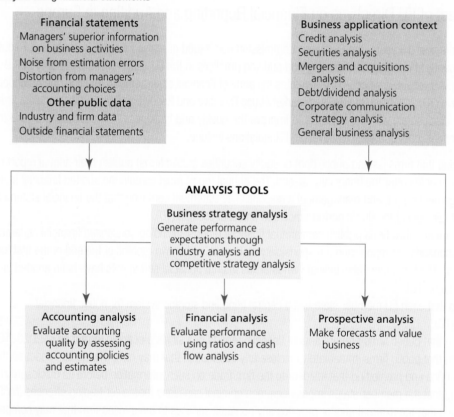

## ANALYSIS STEP 1: BUSINESS STRATEGY ANALYSIS

The purpose of **business strategy analysis** is to identify key profit drivers and business risks and to assess the company's profit potential at a qualitative level. Business strategy analysis involves analyzing a firm's industry and its strategy to create a sustainable competitive advantage. This qualitative analysis is an essential first step because it enables the analyst to frame the subsequent accounting and financial analysis better. For example, identifying the key success factors and key business risks allows the identification of key accounting policies. Assessment of a firm's competitive strategy facilitates evaluating whether current profitability is sustainable. Finally, business analysis enables the analyst to make sound assumptions in forecasting a firm's future performance. We discuss business strategy analysis in further detail in Chapter 2.

## ANALYSIS STEP 2: ACCOUNTING ANALYSIS

The purpose of **accounting analysis** is to evaluate the degree to which a firm's accounting captures the underlying business reality. By identifying places where there is accounting flexibility, and by evaluating the appropriateness of the firm's accounting policies and estimates, analysts can assess the degree of distortion in a firm's accounting numbers. Another important step in accounting analysis is to "undo" any accounting distortions by recasting a firm's accounting numbers to create unbiased accounting data. Sound accounting analysis improves the reliability of conclusions from financial analysis, the next step in financial statement analysis. Accounting analysis is the topic in Chapters 3 and 4.

### ANALYSIS STEP 3: FINANCIAL ANALYSIS

The goal of **financial analysis** is to use financial data to evaluate the current and past performance of a firm and to assess its sustainability. There are two important skills related to financial analysis. First, the analysis should be systematic and efficient. Second, the analysis should allow the analyst to use financial data to explore business issues. Ratio analysis and cash flow analysis are the two most commonly used financial tools. Ratio analysis focuses on evaluating a firm's product market performance and financial policies; cash flow analysis focuses on a firm's liquidity and financial flexibility. Financial analysis is discussed in Chapter 5.

### ANALYSIS STEP 4: PROSPECTIVE ANALYSIS

**Prospective analysis**, which focuses on forecasting a firm's future, is the final step in business analysis. (This step is explained in Chapters 6, 7, and 8.) Two commonly used techniques in prospective analysis are financial statement forecasting and valuation. Both these tools allow the synthesis of the insights from business analysis, accounting analysis, and financial analysis in order to make predictions about a firm's future.

While the intrinsic value of a firm is a function of its future cash flow performance, it is also possible to assess a firm's value based on the firm's current book value of equity and its future return on equity (ROE) and growth. Strategy analysis, accounting analysis, and financial analysis, the first three steps in the framework discussed here, provide an excellent foundation for estimating a firm's intrinsic value. Strategy analysis, in addition to enabling sound accounting and financial analysis, also helps in assessing potential changes in a firm's competitive advantage and their implications for the firm's future ROE and growth. Accounting analysis provides an unbiased estimate of a firm's current book value and ROE. Financial analysis facilitates an in-depth understanding of what drives the firm's current ROE.

The predictions from a sound business analysis are useful to a variety of parties and can be applied in various contexts. The exact nature of the analysis will depend on the context. The contexts that we will examine include securities analysis, credit evaluation, mergers and acquisitions, evaluation of debt and dividend policies, and assessing corporate communication strategies. The four analytical steps previously described are useful in each of these contexts. Appropriate use of these tools, however, requires a familiarity with the economic theories and institutional factors relevant to the context.

There are several ways in which financial statement analysis can add value, even when capital markets are reasonably efficient. First, there are many applications of financial statement analysis whose focus is outside the capital market context – credit analysis, competitive benchmarking, analysis of mergers and acquisitions, to name a few. Second, markets become efficient precisely because some market participants rely on analytical tools such as the ones we discuss in this book to analyze information and make investment decisions.

## Public versus private corporations

This book focuses primarily on publicly traded corporations. In some countries, financial statements of (unlisted) private corporations are also widely available. For example, the United Kingdom as well as member states of the EU require that privately held corporations prepare their financial statements under a common, largely country-specific set of rules and make their financial statements publicly available. All corporations must prepare at least single company financial statements, while parent corporations of large groups must also prepare consolidated financial statements.[16] Consolidated financial statements are typically more appropriate for use in business analysis and valuation because these statements report the combined assets, liabilities, revenues, and expenses of the parent company and its subsidiaries. Single company financial statements report the assets, liabilities, revenues, and expenses of the parent company only and therefore provide little insight into the activities of subsidiaries.

UK and EU laws also require that private corporations' financial statements be audited by an external auditor, although member states may exempt small corporations from this requirement.[17] The way in which private corporations make their financial statements available to the public is typically by filing the statements with a local public register that is maintained by agencies such as the companies' registration office (e.g., Ireland, UK), the chamber of commerce (e.g., Netherlands, Italy), or the national bank (e.g., Belgium).[18]

Private corporations' financial statements can be, and are being, used for business analysis and valuation. For example, venture capitalists, which provide equity funds to mostly private start-up companies, can use financial statements to evaluate potential investments. Nevertheless, although private corporations' financial statements are also subject to accounting standards, their usefulness in business analysis and valuation is less than that of public corporations' financial statements for the following reasons.[19] First, information and incentive problems are smaller in private corporations than in public corporations. Capital suppliers and managers of private corporations maintain close relationships and communicate their information through means other than public financial reports, such as personal communication or ad hoc reports. Because public reporting plays only a small role in communication, managers of private corporations have little incentive to make their public financial statements informative about the underlying business reality. Second, private corporations often produce one set of financial statements that meets the requirements of both tax rules and accounting rules. Tax rules grant managers less discretion in their assumptions than, for example, IFRS Standards. Under tax rules, the recording of costs and benefits is also typically more associated with the payment and receipt of cash than with the underlying economic activities. Consequently, when private corporations' financial statements also comply with tax rules, they are less useful in assessing the corporations' true economic performance.[20]

## Summary

Financial statements provide the most widely available data on public corporations' economic activities; investors and other stakeholders rely on these statements to assess the plans and performance of firms and corporate managers. Accrual accounting data in financial statements are noisy, and unsophisticated investors can assess firms' performance only imprecisely. Financial analysts who understand managers' disclosure and reporting strategies have an opportunity to create inside information from public data, and they play a valuable role in enabling outside parties to evaluate a firm's current and prospective performance.

This chapter has outlined the framework for business analysis with financial statements, using the four key steps: business strategy analysis, accounting analysis, financial analysis, and prospective analysis. The remaining chapters in this book describe these steps in greater detail and discuss how they can be used in a variety of business contexts.

## Core concepts

**Accounting analysis**    Second step of financial statement analysis, aimed at scrutinizing a firm's accounting policies and estimates and undoing the firm's financial statements from any accounting distortions.

**Accounting standards**    Set of rules governing the determination of a company's revenues, profit and (change in) financial position under a system of accrual accounting.

**Accrual accounting**    A system of accounting under which current profit or loss is derived from past and current as well as expected future cash flows arising from business transactions completed in the current period.

**Assets**    Economic resources controlled by a firm that (a) have the potential to produce future economic benefits and (b) are measurable with a reasonable degree of certainty. Examples of economic resources are inventories and property, plant, and equipment.

**Auditing**    Certification of financial statements by an independent public accounting firm, aimed at improving the statements' credibility.

**Business strategy analysis**    First step of financial statement analysis, aimed at identifying a firm's key profit drivers and business risks and qualitatively assessing the firm's profit potential.

**Capital markets**    Markets where entrepreneurs raise funds to finance their business ideas in exchange for equity or debt securities.

**Equity**    The difference between a firm's assets and its liabilities.

**Expenses**    Economic resources (e.g., finished goods inventories) used up and economic obligations (e.g., pension obligations) created in a time period.

**Financial analysis**    Third step of financial statement analysis, which goal is to evaluate (the sustainability of) a firm's current and past financial performance using ratio and cash flow analysis.

**Financial and information intermediaries**    Capital market participants who help to resolve problems of information asymmetry between managers and investors and, consequently, prevent markets from breaking down. Information intermediaries such as auditors or financial analysts improve the (credibility of) information provided by the manager. Financial intermediaries such as banks and collective investment funds specialize in collecting, aggregating, and investing funds from dispersed investors.

**Financial statements**    Periodically disclosed set of statements showing a company's financial performance and change in financial position during a prespecified period. The statements typically include a balance sheet (showing the financial position), a comprehensive income statement and a cash flow statement (describing financial performance), and a statement of changes in equity (outlining the equity effects of comprehensive income and transactions with the owners of the firm). One of the primary purposes of the financial statements is to inform current or potential investors about management's use of their funds, such that they can evaluate management's actions and value their current or potential claim on the firm.

**Income**    Economic resources (e.g., cash and receivables) earned and performance obligations settled during a time period.

**Institutional framework for financial reporting**    Institutions that govern public corporations' financial reporting. These institutions include:

a    Accounting standards set by public or private sector accounting standard-setting bodies, which limit management's accounting flexibility. In the EU, public corporations report under International Financial Reporting Standards, set by the International Accounting Standards Board.

b    Mandatory external auditing of the financial statements by public accountants. In the EU, the Statutory Audit Directive and Regulation have set minimum standards for external audits.

c    Legal liability of management for misleading disclosures. The Transparency Directive requires that each EU Member State has a statutory civil liability regime.

d    Public enforcement of accounting standards. Enforcement activities of individual European public enforcement bodies are coordinated by the European Securities and Markets Authority (ESMA).

**Legal protection of investors' rights**    Laws and regulations aiming at providing investors the rights and mechanisms to discipline managers who control their funds. Examples of such rights and mechanisms are transparent disclosure requirements, the right to vote (by proxy) on important decisions or the right to appoint supervisory directors. In countries where small, minority investors lack such rights or mechanisms, financial intermediaries play an important role in channeling investments to entrepreneurs.

**Lemons problem**    The problem that arises if entrepreneurs have better information about the quality of their business ideas than investors but are not able to credibly communicate this information. If this problem becomes severe enough, investors may no longer be willing to provide funds and capital markets could break down.

**Liabilities**    Economic obligations of a firm arising from benefits received in the past that (a) have the potential of being required to be met and (b) cannot be feasibly avoided by the firm. Examples of economic obligations are bank loans and product warranties.

**Prospective analysis**    Fourth and final step of financial statement analysis, which focuses on forecasting a firm's future financial performance and position. The forecasts can be used for various purposes, such as estimating firm value or assessing creditworthiness.

**Reporting strategy**    Set of choices made by managers in using their reporting discretion, shaping the quality of their financial reports.

## Questions, exercises, and problems

1    Matti, who has just completed his first finance course, is unsure whether he should take a course in business analysis and valuation using financial statements since he believes that financial analysis adds little value, given the efficiency of capital markets. Explain to Matti when financial analysis can add value, even if capital markets are efficient.

2    Accounting statements rarely report financial performance without error. List three types of errors that can arise in financial reporting.

3    A finance student states, "I don't understand why anyone pays any attention to accounting profits, given that a 'clean' number like cash from operations is readily available." Do you agree? Why or why not?

4    Fred argues, "The standards that I like most are the ones that eliminate all management discretion in reporting – that way I get uniform numbers across all companies and don't have to worry about doing accounting analysis." Do you agree? Why or why not?

5    Bill Simon says, "We should get rid of the IASB, IFRS Standards, and EU Accounting and Audit Directives, since free market forces will make sure that companies report reliable information." Do you agree? Why or why not?

6    Juan Perez argues that "Learning how to do business analysis and valuation using financial statements is not very useful, unless you are interested in becoming a financial analyst." Comment.

7    Four steps for business analysis are discussed in the chapter (strategy analysis, accounting analysis, financial analysis, and prospective analysis). As a financial analyst, explain why each of these steps is a critical part of your job and how they relate to one another.

### Problem 1 The Neuer Markt

Many economists believe that innovation is one of the main building blocks of economic growth and job creation. Not all economic infrastructures, however, are equally supportive of innovation. In 1995 venture capital investments in Europe amounted up to 4 percent of total Gross Domestic Product (GDP), compared to 6 percent of GDP in the United States. During the second half of the 1990s, European and US venture capital investments experienced an explosive but distinctively different level of growth. In fact, in 2000 venture capitalists invested an amount equal to 17 percent of European GDP in European companies, while investing 78 percent of US GDP in US companies.[21] The availability of venture capital can be crucial in the development of innovation. Venture capitalists serve an important role as intermediaries in capital markets because they separate good business ideas from bad ones and bestow their reputation on the start-ups that they finance. In addition to providing capital, venture capitalists offer their expertise in management and finance and let start-up companies benefit from their network of contacts. Their close involvement with start-ups' day-to-day operations and their ability to give finance in installments, conditional on start-ups' success, allows venture capitalists to invest in risky business ideas that public capital markets typically ignore.

To improve young, innovative, and fast-growing companies' access to external finance, several European stock exchanges founded separate trading segments for this group of companies at the end of the 1990s. Examples of such trading segments were the Nuovo Mercato in Italy, the Nouveau Marché in France, the NMAX in the Netherlands, and the Neuer Markt in Germany. These new markets coordinated some of their activities under the Euro.NM umbrella. For example, starting in 1999 the markets facilitated cross-border electronic trading to create a pan-European exchange. Another important way of cooperation was to harmonize the admission requirements for new listings.[22] These requirements were not easier to comply with than the admission requirements of the traditional, established trading segments of the European stock exchanges. On the contrary, the common idea was that a separate trading segment for innovative fast-growing companies needed stricter regulation than the established segments that targeted matured companies with proven track records. If this was true, having (some) common listing requirements across European new markets helped to prevent a race to the bottom in which companies would flee to markets with lenient listing requirements and markets would start to compete with each other on the basis of their leniency.

The European new markets had also harmonized some of their disclosure requirements. All new markets required that companies produced quarterly reports of, at least, sales figures. Further, most of the new markets required that companies prepared their financial reports in accordance with either US GAAP or International Accounting Standards. Given the opportunities for electronic cross-border trading, strict disclosure requirements could help in broadening companies' investor base as well as improve investors' opportunities for diversifying their risky investments. However, because the new markets experienced difficulties in further

harmonizing their admission and listing requirements and eventually came to realize that the small cap companies appealed primarily to local investors, their cooperative venture was dissolved in December 2000.

One of the European new markets was the Neuer Markt, a trading segment of the "Deutsche Börse," the German stock exchange. The Neuer Markt's target companies were innovative companies that opened up new markets; used new processes in development, production, or marketing and sales; offered new products or services; and were likely to achieve above-average growth in revenue and profit. On March 10, 1997, the initial public offering of Mobilcom AG started the existence of the exchange. The offering of Mobilcom's 640 thousand shares for an issue price of €31.95 was heavily oversubscribed, as €20 million additional shares could have been sold. Mobilcom's closing price at the end of the first trading day equaled €50.10, yielding an initial return of 56.8 percent. Other success stories followed. For example, on October 30, 1997, Entertainment München, better known as EM.TV, went public on the German Neuer Markt. The Munich-based producer and distributor of children's programs was able to place 600,000 of its common shares at a price set at the upper end of the book-building range, collecting approximately €5.3 million in total. There was a strong demand for the company's shares. At the end of the first trading day, the share price closed at €9.72, up by 9.4 percent. At its peak, in February 2000, EM.TV's share price had increased from € 0.35 (split-adjusted) to slightly more than €120.

At the end of February 2000, being close to its three-year anniversary, the Neuer Markt comprised 229 companies with a total market capitalization of approximately €234 billion. However, in March 2000 the downfall began, in line with the plunge of the NASDAQ exchange. In September 2000 Gigabell AG was the first company to file for insolvency. The total market capitalization of the growth segment of the Deutsche Börse declined further from €121 billion (339 firms) at the end of 2000 to €50 billion (327 firms) at the end of 2001. Because both the "going public" and the "being public" requirements were very strict compared to other segments and markets, several companies left the Neuer Markt, changing to the less regulated Geregelter Markt. During the first years of the 2000s, several Neuer Markt firms were found to have manipulated their financial statements. For example, in September 2000 EM.TV announced that it had overstated the revenue and profit figures of its most recently acquired subsidiaries, the Jim Henson Company and Speed Investments, in the company's semiannual financial statements. Following this announcement, EM.TV's market capitalization declined by more than 30 percent. Other examples include computer games developer Phenomedia and Comroad, a provider of traffic information systems that was found to have falsified more than 90 percent of its 1998–2001 revenues.

On September 26, 2002, the Deutsche Börse announced that it would close its Neuer Markt trading segment in 2003. The remaining Neuer Markt companies could join the exchange's Prime Standard segment, which would adopt the Neuer Markt's strict listing requirements (i.e., quarterly reporting; IAS or US GAAP; at least one analyst conference per year; ad hoc and ongoing disclosures in English), or its General Standard segment, with legal minimum transparency requirements. Approximately two-thirds of the remaining Neuer Markt firms decided to join the Prime Standard segment.

1   Do you think that exchange market segments such as the Euro.NM markets can be a good alternative to venture capital? If not, what should be their function?

2   This chapter described four institutional features of accounting systems that affect the quality of financial statements. Which of these features may have been particularly important in reducing the quality of Neuer Markt companies' financial statements?

3   The decline of the Neuer Markt could be viewed as the result of a lemons problem. Can you think of some mechanisms that might have prevented the market's collapse?

4   What could have been the Deutsche Börse's objective of introducing two new segments and letting Neuer Markt firms choose and apply for admission to one of these segments? When is this strategy most likely to be effective?

## Problem 2 Fair value accounting for financial instruments

One of the key accounting policies of banks and other financial institutions is how they recognize (changes in) the fair value of the securities that they hold in the balance sheet and income statement. Until the implementation of IFRS Standards 9 (effective since 2018), the international rules on the recognition and measurement of financial instruments required a firm to recognize financial securities (other than loans and receivables) at their fair values if the firm did not intend (or was not able) to hold these assets to their maturities (labelled held-for-trading instruments). Changes in the securities' fair values had to be recognized as gains or losses in the income statement. Financial securities that a firm initially intended to hold to their maturities but that were available for sale also had to be recognized at their fair values. However, changes in the fair value of these available-for-sale securities were temporarily recorded in equity and recognized in the income statement once the securities had been sold. If the firm intended to hold the financial instruments to their maturities (held-to-maturity instruments), they had to be recognized at (amortized) historical cost.

How should the fair values of financial instruments be determined? The rules required (and still require) that the values be derived from quoted market prices if an active market for the assets exists (typically referred to as marking to market). If quoted market prices were not available, firms could use their own valuation technique to determine the assets' fair values (referred to as marking to model); however, their valuation had to be based on assumptions that outside market participants would reasonably make, not management's own assumptions.

Complications arose if quoted market prices were available but, at least in the eyes of some, unreliable. For example, the credit crisis of 2008 led to a substantial increase in the uncertainty about the quality and value of asset-backed securities, such as mortgage-backed loans. As a result of the heightened uncertainty, investors fled asset-backed securities, and the market for such securities became highly illiquid. Observable prices from infrequent transactions remained available; however, managers of financial institutions owning asset-backed securities claimed that these prices did not properly reflect the values of the securities if one had the option to hold on to the securities until the crisis was over or the securities matured. In response to these claims, the IASB provided additional guidance and reemphasized that in declining, illiquid markets, managers had the option to use their own valuations to determine fair values. Consequently, many financial institutions chose to move away from marking to market towards adjusting market prices or marking to model.

Prior to the credit market crisis of 2008, an important detail of the international accounting rules for financial instruments was that instruments could not be reclassified between categories (with the exception, of course, of reclassifications from held-to-maturity to available-for-sale). The crisis, however, led some bank managers to change their minds about which securities were actually held for trading purposes and which securities were better held to their maturities. Under great political pressure from the EU, the IASB amended this rule in October 2008.[23] The amendment allowed firms to reclassify securities out of the held-for-trading category in rare circumstances, such as those created by the crisis, if management decided not to sell the securities in the foreseeable future. A survey carried out by the Committee of European Securities Regulators (CESR) revealed that 48 out of 100 European financial institutions reclassified one or more financial instruments in their financial statements for the third quarter of 2008.

1  Discuss how the changes in the reclassification rules affect the balance between noise introduced in accounting data by rigidity in accounting rules and bias introduced in accounting data by managers' systematic accounting choices.

2  The move from marking to market to marking to model during the credit crisis increased managers' accounting flexibility. Managers of financial institutions may have had incentives to bias their valuations of financial instruments. Summarize the main incentives that may have affected these managers' accounting choices.

3  Some politicians argued that fair value accounting needed to be suspended and replaced by historical cost accounting. What is the risk of allowing financial institutions to report their financial securities such as asset-backed securities at historical cost?

## Notes

1  G. Akerlof, "The Market for 'Lemons': Quality Uncertainty and the Market Mechanism," *Quarterly Journal of Economics* (August 1970): 488–500. Akerlof recognized that the seller of a used car knew more about the car's value than the buyer. This meant that the buyer was likely to end up overpaying, since the seller would accept any offer that exceeded the car's true value and reject any lower offer. Car buyers recognized this problem and would respond by making only average-quality offers for used cars, leading sellers with high quality cars to exit the market. As a result, only the lowest quality cars (the "lemons") would remain in the market. Akerlof pointed out that qualified independent mechanics could correct this market breakdown by providing buyers with reliable information on a used car's true value.

2  The IFRS Standards refer to the balance sheet as a "statement of financial position." However, firms are free to choose other titles. Throughout this book, we will refer to the five statements as the income statement, the balance sheet, the cash flow statement, the statement of other comprehensive income, and the statement of changes in equity, which is how they traditionally have been – and still are – called by users of financial statements.

3  Firms are allowed to combine the income statement, which describes the composition of profit or loss, and the statement of other comprehensive income, which describes all other non-owner changes in equity, into one statement.

4  There is no globally accepted name for management's narrative discussion of the firm's performance. In 2010 the IASB issued a (non-binding) Practice Statement Management Commentary, advising on what firms should report in this section. Throughout this book, we will refer to this section as the Management Commentary section, consistent with the IASB's labelling, and assume that it typically contains at least a Letter to the Shareholders and a review of the firm's financial performance during the fiscal year and its financial position at the end of the year.

5  These definitions paraphrase those of the IASB, "The Conceptual Framework for Financial Reporting" (also referred to as the "Conceptual Framework"). Our intent

is to present the definitions at a conceptual, not technical, level. For more complete discussion of these and
related concepts, see the IASB's Conceptual Framework.

6  The EU has given its individual member states the
option to permit or require private companies to use
IFRS Standards for the preparation of their single entity
and/or consolidated financial statements. Similarly,
member states may permit or require public companies
to prepare their single entity financial statements in
accordance with IFRS Standards.

7  For a comprehensive overview of European legal liability
regimes, see C. Gerner-Beuerle, P. Paech, and E.P. Schuster, "Study on Directors' Duties and Liability" (April
2013) or the European Securities and Markets Authority's "Comparison of Liability Regimes in Member States
in Relation to the Prospectus Directive" (May 2013). For
a description of international differences in managers'
legal liability for the information that they provide in
prospectuses, see R. La Porta, F. Lopez-de-Silanes, and
A. Shleifer, "What Works in Securities Laws?" The Journal of Finance 61 (2006): 1–32.

8  See, for example, the UK HM Treasury's report (July
2008) on the "Extension of the Statutory Regime for
Issuer Liability," describing motivations for making
managers subject to civil liability for fraudulent misstatements only.

9  The ESMA has issued guidelines on how enforcers
should select the companies they review, advocating a
combination of risk-based selection with random sampling or rotation. See "ESMA Guidelines on Enforcement of Financial Information" (July 2014).

10  See H.E. Jackson and M.J. Roe, "Public and Private
Enforcement of Securities Laws: Resource-Based Evidence," Journal of Financial Economics 93(2) (2009):
207–238.

11  See Sarah Tasker, "Bridging the Information Gap:
Quarterly Conference Calls as a Medium for Voluntary
Disclosure," Review of Accounting Studies 3(1–2) (1998):
137–167.

12  See Richard Frankel, Marilyn Johnson, and Douglas
Skinner, "An Empirical Examination of Conference Calls
as a Voluntary Disclosure Medium," Journal of Accounting Research 37(1) (Spring 1999): 133–150.

13  See M. Kimbrough, "The Effect of Conference Calls
on Analyst and Market Underreaction to Earnings
Announcements," The Accounting Review 80(1) (January
2005): 189–219.

14  Research on voluntary disclosure includes Mark Lang
and Russell Lundholm, "Cross-Sectional Determinants
of Analysts' Ratings of Corporate Disclosures," Journal
of Accounting Research 31 (Autumn 1993): 246–271;
Lang and Lundholm, "Corporate Disclosure Policy and
Analysts," The Accounting Review 71 (October 1996):
467–492; M. Welker, "Disclosure Policy, Information
Asymmetry and Liquidity in Equity Markets," Contemporary Accounting Research (Spring 1995): 801–827;

Christine Botosan, "The Impact of Annual Report
Disclosure Level on Investor Base and the Cost of Capital," The Accounting Review (July 1997): 323–350; and
Paul Healy, Amy Hutton, and Krishna Palepu, "Stock
Performance and Intermediation Changes Surrounding Sustained Increases in Disclosure," Contemporary
Accounting Research 16(3) (Fall 1999): 485–521. This
research finds that firms are more likely to provide high
levels of disclosure if they have strong earnings performance, issue securities, have more analyst following,
and have less dispersion in analyst forecasts. In addition,
firms with high levels of disclosure policies tend to have
a lower cost of capital and bid-ask spread. Finally, firms
that increase disclosure have accompanying increases in
stock returns, institutional ownership, analyst following,
and share liquidity. In "The Role of Supplementary Statements with Management Earnings Forecasts," Journal of
Accounting Research 41 (2003): 867–890, A. Hutton, G.
Miller, and D. Skinner examine the market response to
management earnings forecasts and find that bad news
forecasts are always informative but that good news forecasts are informative only when they are supported by
verifiable forward-looking statements.

15  See J. Cotter, I. Tuna, and P. Wysocki, "Expectations
Management and Beatable Targets: How Do Analysts
React to Explicit Earnings Guidance," Contemporary
Accounting Research 23(3) (Autumn 2006): 593–628.

16  The EU Accounting Directive (Directive 2013/34/
EU), which governs the preparation of single and consolidated financial statements in the EU, defines large
groups as those meeting at least two of the following
three criteria in two consecutive years:
1  Total assets above €20.0 million.
2  Annual turnover above €40.0 million.
3  More than 250 employees.

17  The EU Accounting Directive (Directive 2013/34/EU)
defines small corporations as those failing to meet two of
the following three criteria in two consecutive years:
1  Total assets above €6.0 million.
2  Annual turnover above €12.0 million.
3  More than 50 employees.

18  It should be noted that although the EU regulations have
partly harmonized private corporations' accounting, the
accessibility of public registers varies greatly and private
corporations' financial statements are therefore in practice not equally available across the EU.

19  See R. Ball and L. Shivakumar, "Earnings Quality in
UK Private Firms: Comparative Loss Recognition
Timeliness," Journal of Accounting and Economics 39
(2005): 83–128; D. Burgstahler, L. Hail, and C. Leuz,
"The Importance of Reporting Incentives: Earnings
Management in European Private and Public Firms,"
The Accounting Review 81 (2006): 983–1016; E. Peek, R.
Cuijpers, and W. Buijink, "Creditors' and Shareholders'
Reporting Demands in Public versus Private Firms: Evi-
dence from Europe," Contemporary Accounting Research

27 (2010): 49–91; and M. Clatworthy and M. Peel, "The Impact of Voluntary Audit and Governance Character-istics on Accounting Errors in Private Companies," *Journal of Accounting and Public Policy* 32 (2013): 1–25.

20  The influence of tax rules is particularly strong on single company financial statements, which in many countries are the basis for tax computations. Although the influ-ence of tax rules on consolidated financial statements is less direct, tax considerations may still affect the preparation of these statements. For example, companies may support their aggressive tax choices by having the consolidated statements conform to the single company statements.

21  See L. Bottazzi and M. Da Rin, "Venture Capital in Europe and the Financing of Innovative Companies," *Economic Policy*, April (2002): 231–269.

22  See L. Bottazzi and M. Da Rin, "Europe's 'New' Stock Markets," Working Paper, July 2002; and M. Goergen, A. Khurshed, J.A. McCahery, and L. Renneboog, "The Rise and Fall of European New Markets: On the Short and Long-run Performance of High-tech Initial Public Offer-ings," Working Paper, European Corporate Governance Institute, September 2003. To be eligible for a listing on one of the two largest new markets, the Nouveau Marché and the Neuer Markt, companies had to meet all of the following admission requirements. First, companies' equity prior to the initial public offering (IPO) had to exceed €1.5 million. Second, companies had to issue more than 100,000 shares, which had to represent more than 20 percent of the companies' nominal capital, at an amount exceeding €5 million. Third, not more than 50 percent of the shares issued were allowed to come from existing shareholders; more than 50 percent of the issued shares had to come from a capital increase. Fourth, man-agers were not allowed to trade their shares during a six-month period following the IPO on the Neuer Markt. Managers of companies listed on the Nouveau Marché could not trade 80 percent of their shares for a period of 12 months. The other new markets had very similar admission requirements.

23  For an illustration of the circumstances surrounding the IASB's decision to amend the reclassification rules, see P. André, A. Cazavan-Jeny, W. Dick, C. Richard, and P. Walton, "Fair Value Accounting and the Banking Crisis in 2008: Shooting the Messenger," *Accounting in Europe,* 6 (2009): 3–24.

## Appendix: Defining Europe

At various places in this book, we refer to "Europe" and "European companies" without intending to imply that all European countries and companies are exactly alike. Because Europe's richness in diver-sity makes it impossible to describe the institutional details of each European country in detail, this book discusses primarily the commonalities between the countries that have chosen to harmonize the dif-ferences among their accounting systems. These countries are the 27 member states of the EU; the three members of the European Economic Area (Iceland, Norway, and Liechtenstein), which are also committed to following EU Accounting Directives; and the United Kingdom, where accounting regula-tion still very much reflects the influence of the EU Accounting Directives. Of particular importance to the topic of this book is that, since 2005 compa-nies from these 31 countries that have their shares publicly traded on a stock exchange are required to prepare their financial statements in accordance with IFRS Standards. A special position is occupied by Switzerland, which is a member of neither the EU nor the European Economic Area. Many of the issues that we address in this book also apply to a large group of Swiss-listed companies, because Switzerland requires its listed companies with international operations to prepare IFRS Standards-based financial statements.

In some of the chapters in this book, we summa-rize the financial ratios, stock returns, and opera-tional characteristics of a representative sample of listed European companies for illustrative purposes. This sample is composed of all domestic compa-nies that were listed on one of the primary stock exchanges (or their predecessors) in the 30 EU/EEA countries, Switzerland, and the United Kingdom between January 1998 (labelled the start of fiscal year 1998) and December 2017 (labelled the end of fiscal year 2017). Table 1.1 shows the ten largest European stock exchanges, or exchange groups, at the end of December 2017 and their countries of operation.

**TABLE 1.1**  European stock exchanges

| Stock exchange | Countries | Total market capitalization of domestic (non-financial) companies at December 2017 (in €billions) |
|---|---|---|
| NYSE Euronext Brussels – Dublin – Paris – Amsterdam – Lisbon | *Belgium, France, Ireland, the Netherlands, Portugal* | 2,696.4 |
| London Stock Exchange Group (Borsa Italiana, LSE) | *United Kingdom, Italy* | 2,413.1 |
| Deutsche Börse | *Germany* | 1,564.2 |
| SIX Swiss Exchange | *Switzerland* | 1,066.5 |
| OMX Exchanges Copenhagen –Tallinn – Helsinki – Reykjavik –Riga – Vilnius – Stockholm | *Denmark, Estonia, Finland, Iceland, Latvia, Lithuania, Sweden* | 884.7 |
| BME Exchanges (Bolsa y Mercados Españoles) | *Spain* | 455.2 |
| Oslo Børs | *Norway* | 184.9 |
| Other | *Various* | 272.4 |

Notes: Total market capitalization is calculated as the sum of the market capitalizations of all domestic non-financial companies that are included in our sample of listed European companies.

Source: Standard & Poor's Compustat Global. Euronext is a Pan-European exchange that was formed from the merger of the exchanges of Amsterdam, Brussels, Dublin, Lisbon, and Paris. OMX Exchanges includes the exchanges of Copenhagen, Helsinki, Stockholm, Tallinn, Riga, and Vilnius. The reported market capitalizations of the Euronext exchange, the OMX Exchanges, and the London Stock Exchange Group represent the total sum of the sizes of the individual segments. Other exchanges include the exchanges of Athens, Bratislava, Bucharest, Budapest, Ljubljana, Luxembourg, Malta, Prague, Sofia, Vienna, Warsaw, and Zagreb.

# CASE

# The role of capital market intermediaries in the dot-com crash of 2000

## The rise and fall of the internet consultants

In the summer of 1999 a host of internet consulting firms made their debut on the Nasdaq. Scient Corporation, which had been founded less than two years earlier in March 1997, went public in May 1999 at an IPO price of $20 per share ($10 on a pre-split basis). Its close on the first day of trading was $32.63. Other internet consulting companies that went public that year included Viant Corporation, IXL Enterprises, and US Interactive (see **Exhibit 1**).

The main value proposition of these companies was that they would be able to usher in the new internet era by lending their information technology and web expertise to traditional "old economy" companies that wanted to gain Web-based technology, as well as to the emerging dot-com sector. Other companies like Sapient Corporation and Cambridge Technology Partners had been doing IT consulting for years, but this new breed of companies was able to capitalize on the burgeoning demand for internet expertise.

Over the following months, the stock prices of the internet consultants rose dramatically. Scient traded at a high of $133.75 in March 2000. However, this was after a 2–1 split, so each share was actually worth twice this amount on a pre-split basis. This stock level represented a 1,238 percent increase from its IPO price and a valuation of 62 times the company's revenues for the fiscal year 2000. Similar performances were put in by the other companies in this group. However, these valuation levels proved to be unsustainable. The stock prices of web consulting firms dropped sharply in April 2000 along with many others in the internet sector, following what was afterwards seen as a general "correction" in the Nasdaq. The prices of the web consultants seemed to stabilize for a while, and many analysts continued to write favorably about their prospects and maintained buy ratings on their stocks. But starting early in September 2000, after some bad news from Viant Corporation and many subsequent analyst downgrades, the stocks went into a free-fall. All were trading in single digits by February of 2001, representing a greater than 95 percent drop from their peak valuations (see **Exhibit 2**).

The dramatic rise and fall of the stock prices of the Web consultants, along with many others in the internet sector, caused industry observers to wonder how this could have happened in a relatively sophisticated capital market like that of the United States. Several well-respected venture capitalists, investment banks, accounting firms, financial analysts, and money management companies were involved in bringing these companies to market and rating and trading their shares (see **Exhibit 3**). Who, if anyone, caused the internet stock price bubble? What, if anything, could be done to avoid the recurrence of such stock market bubbles?

Gillian Elcock, MBA 2001, prepared this case from published sources under the supervision of Professor Krishna Palepu. HBS cases are developed solely as the basis for class discussion. Cases are not intended to serve as endorsements, sources of primary data, or illustrations of effective or ineffective management.

## CONTEXT: THE TECHNOLOGY BULL MARKET

The 1980s and 1990s marked the beginning of a global technology revolution that started with the personal computer (PC) and led to the internet era. Companies like Apple, Microsoft, Intel, and Dell Computer were at the forefront of this new wave of technology that promised to enhance productivity and efficiency through the computerization and automation of many processes.

The capital markets recognized the value that was being created by these companies. Microsoft, which was founded in 1975, had a market capitalization of over $600 billion by the beginning of 2000, making it the world's most valuable company, and its founder, Bill Gates, one of the richest men in the world. High values were also given to many of the other blue-chip technology firms such as Intel and Dell (see **Exhibit 4**).

The 1990s ushered in a new group of companies that were based on information networks. These included AOL, Netscape, and Cisco. Netscape was a visible symbol of the emerging importance of the internet: its browser gave regular users access to the World Wide Web, whereas previously the internet had been mostly the domain of academics and experts. In March 2000, Cisco Systems, which made the devices that routed information across the internet, overtook Microsoft as the world's most valuable company (based on market capitalization). This seemed further evidence of the value shift that was taking place from PC-focused technologies and companies to those that were based on the global information network.

It appeared obvious that the internet was going to profoundly change the world through greater computing power, ease of communication, and the host of technologies that could be built upon it. Opportunities to build new services and technologies were boundless, and they were global in scale. The benefits of the internet were expected to translate into greater economic productivity through the lowering of communication and transaction costs. It also seemed obvious that someone would be able to capitalize upon these market opportunities and that "the next Microsoft" would soon appear. No one who missed out on the original Microsoft wanted to do so the second time around.

A phrase that became popularized during this time was the "new economy." New economy companies, as opposed to old economy ones (exemplified by companies in traditional manufacturing, retail, and commodities), based their business models around exploiting the internet. They were usually small compared to their old economy counter parts, with little need for their real-world "bricks and mortar" structures, preferring to outsource much of the capital intensive parts of the business and concentrate on the higher value-added, information-intensive elements. Traditional companies, finding their market shares and business models attacked by a host of nimble, specialized dot-com start-ups, lived in danger of "being Amazoned." To many, the new economy was the future, and old economy companies would become less and less relevant.

The capital markets seemed to think similarly. From July 1999 to February 2000, as the Nasdaq Composite Index (which was heavily weighted with technology and internet stocks) rose by 74.4 percent, the Dow Jones Industrial Average (which was composed mainly of old economy stocks) fell by 7.7 percent. Investors no longer seemed interested in anything that was not new economy.

Internet gurus and economists predicted the far-reaching effects of the internet. The following excerpts represent the mood of the time:

> *Follow the personal computer and you can reach the pot of gold. Follow anything else and you will end up in a backwater. What the Model T was to the industrial era . . . the PC is to the information age. Just as people who rode the wave of automobile technology – from tire makers to fast food franchisers – prevailed in the industrial era, so the firms that prey on the passion and feed on the force of the computer community will predominate in the information era.*[1]

— George Gilder, 1992

\*\*\*\*\*

---

[1]Mary Meeker, Chris DePuy, "US Investment Research, Technology/New Media, The Internet Report (Excerpt) from *Life After Television* by George Gilder, 1992," *Morgan Stanley* (February 1996).

*Due to technological advances in PC-based communications, a new medium – with the internet, the World Wide Web, and TCP/IP at its core – is emerging rapidly. The market for internet-related products and services appears to be growing more rapidly than the early emerging markets for print publishing, telephony, film, radio, recorded music, television, and personal computers. . . . Based on our market growth estimates, we are still at the very early stages of a powerful secular growth cycle.*[2]

— Mary Meeker, Morgan Stanley Dean Witter, February 1996

*****

*The easy availability of smart capital – the ability of entrepreneurs to launch potentially world-beating companies on a shoestring, and of investors to intelligently spread risk – may be the new economy's most devastating innovation. At the same time, onrushing technological change requires lumbering dinosaurs to turn themselves into clever mammals overnight. Some will. But for many others, the only thing left to talk about is the terms of surrender.*[3]

— *Wall Street Journal*, April 17, 2000

In the new economy gaining market share was considered key because of the benefits of network effects. In addition, a large customer base was needed to cover the high fixed costs often associated with doing business. Profitability was of a secondary concern, and Netscape was one of the first of many internet companies to go public without positive earnings. Some companies deliberately operated at losses because it was essential to spend a lot early to gain market share, which would presumably translate at a later point into profitability. This meant that revenue growth was the true measure of success for many internet companies. Of course there were some dissenting voices, warning that this was just a period of irrational exuberance and the making of a classic stock market bubble. But for the most part, investors seemed to buy into the concept, as evidenced by the values given to several loss-making dotcoms (see **Exhibit 5**).

## SCIENT CORPORATION

The history of Scient, considered a leader in the internet consulting space, is representative of what happened to the entire industry. The firm was founded in November 1997. Its venture capital backers included several leading firms such as Sequioa Capital and Benchmark Capital (see **Exhibit 3**).

Scient described itself as "a leading provider of a new category of professional services called eBusiness systems innovation" that would "rapidly improve a client's competitive position through the development of innovative business strategies enabled by the integration of emerging and existing technologies."[4] Its aim was to provide services in information technology and systems design as well as high-level strategy consulting, previously the domain of companies such as McKinsey and The Boston Consulting Group.

The company grew quickly to almost 2,000 people within three years, primarily organically. Its client list included AT&T, Chase Manhattan, Johnson & Johnson, and Home-store.com.[5] As with any consulting firm, its ability to attract and retain talented employees was crucial, since they were its main assets.

By the fiscal year ending in March 2000, Scient had a net loss of $16 million on revenues of $156 million (see financial statements in **Exhibit 6**). These revenues represented an increase of 653 percent over the previous year. Analysts wrote glowingly about the firm's prospects. In February 2000 when the stock was trading at around $87.25, a Deutsche Banc Alex Brown report stated:

---

[2]Mary Meeker, Chris DePuy, "US Investment Research, Technology/New Media, The Internet Report," *Morgan Stanley* (February 1996).

[3]John Browning, Spencer Reiss, "For the New Economy, the End of the Beginning," *Wall Street Journal* (Copyright 2000 Dow Jones & Company, Inc).

[4]Scient Corporation Prospectus, May 1999. Available from Edgar Online.

[5]Scient Corporation website, www.scient.com/non/content/clients/client_list/index.asp.

*We have initiated research coverage of Scient with a BUY investment rating on the shares. In our view Scient possesses several key comparative advantages: (1) an outstanding management team; (2) a highly scalable and leverageable operating model; (3) a strong culture, which attracts the best and the brightest; (4) a private equity portfolio, which enhances long-term relationships and improves retention; and (5) an exclusive focus on the high-end systems innovation market with eBusiness and industry expertise, rapid time-to-market and an integrated approach. . . . Scient shares are currently trading at roughly 27x projected CY00 revenues, modestly ahead of pure play leaders like Viant (24x) and Proxicom (25x), and ahead of our interactive integrator peer group average of just over 16x. Our 12-month price target is $120. It is a stock we would want to own.[6]*

And in March 2000, when the stock was at $77.75, Morgan Stanley, which had an "outperform" rating, wrote:

*All said we believe Scient continue [sic] to effectively execute on what is a very aggressive business plan. . . . While shares of SCNT trade at a premium valuation to its peer group, we continue to believe that such level is warranted given the company's high-end market focus, short but impressive record of execution, and deep/experienced management team. As well, in our view there is a high probability of meaningful upward revisions to Scient's model.[7]*

Scient's stock reached a high of $133.75 in March 2000 but fell to $44 by June as part of the overall drop in valuation of most of the technology sector. In September the company announced it had authorized a stock repurchase of $25 million. But in December 2000 it lowered its revenue and earnings expectations for the fourth quarter due to the slowdown in demand for internet consulting services. The company also announced plans to lay off 460 positions worldwide (over 20 percent of its workforce) as well as close two of its offices, and an associated $40–$45 million restructuring charge. By February 2001 the stock was trading at $2.94.

Most of the analysts that covered Scient had buy or strong buy ratings on the company as its stock rose to its peak and even after the Nasdaq correction in April 2000. Then, in September, a warning by Viant Corporation of results that would come in below expectations due to a slowdown in e-business spending from large corporate clients, prompted many analysts to downgrade most of the companies in the sector, including Scient (see **Exhibit 7**). Several large mutual fund companies were holders of Scient as its stock rose, peaked, and fell (see **Exhibit 8**).

As the major technology indices continued their slump during late 2000 and early 2001, and the stock prices of the internet consulting firms floundered in the single digits, they received increasing attention from the press:

*Examining the downfall of the eConsultants provides an excellent case study of failed business models. Rose-colored glasses, a lack of a sustainable competitive advantage, and a "me too" mentality are just some of the mistakes these companies made . . . The eConsultants failed to do the one thing that they were supposed to be helping their clients do – build a sustainable business model . . . many eConsultants popped up and expected to be able to take on the McKinseys and Booz-Allens of the world. Now they are discovering that the relationships firmly established by these old economy consultants are integral to building a sustainable competitive advantage.[8]*

*Seems like everything dot-com is being shunned by investors these days. But perhaps no other group has experienced quite the brutality that Web consultancies have. Once the sweethearts of Wall Street, their stocks are now high-tech whipping boys. Even financial analysts, who usually strive to be positive about companies they cover, seem to have given up on the sector. . . . Many of these firms were built on the back of the dot-com boom. Now these clients are gone. At the same time, pressure on bricks-and-mortar companies to build online businesses has lifted, leading to the cancellation or delay of Web projects.[9]*

---

[6]F. Mark D'Annolfo, William S. Zinsmeister, Jeffrey A. Buchbinder, "Scient Corporation Premier Builder of eBusinesses," *Deutsche Banc Alex Brown* (February 14, 2000).

[7]Michael A. Sherrick, Mary Meeker, "Scient Corporation Quarter Update," *Morgan Stanley Dean Witter* (March 2, 2000).

[8]Todd N. Lebor, "The Downfall of internet Consultants," *Fool's Den,* Fool.com (December 11, 2000).

[9]Amey Stone, "Streetwise – Who'll Help the Web Consultants?" *BusinessWeek Online* (New York, February 15, 2001). From http://www.businessweek.com.

The analysts who were formerly excited about Scient's prospects and had recommended the stock when it was trading at almost $80 per share now seemed much less enthusiastic. In January 2001, with the stock around $3.44, Morgan Stanley wrote:

> We maintain our Neutral rating due to greater than anticipated market weakness, accelerating pricing pressure, the potential for increased turnover and management credibility issues. While shares of SCNT trade at a depressed valuation, we continute [sic] to believe that turnover and pricing pressure could prove greater than management's assumptions. While management indicated it would be "aggressive" to maintain its people, we still believe it will be difficult to maintain top-tier talent in the current market and company specific environment.[10]

### PERFORMANCE OF THE NASDAQ

The performance of the stock prices of Scient and its peers mirrored that of many companies in the internet sector. So dramatic was the drop in valuation of these companies, that this period was subsequently often referred to as the "Dot-com crash."

In the months following the crash, the equity markets essentially closed their doors to the internet firms. Several once high-flying dot-coms, operating at losses and starved for cash, filed for bankruptcy, or closed down their operations (see **Exhibit 9**).

The Nasdaq, which had reached a high of 5,132.52 in March of 2000 closed at 2,470.52 in December 2000, a drop of 52 percent from its high. As of February 2001 it had not recovered, closing at 2,151.83.

## The role of intermediaries in a well-functioning market

In a capitalist economy, individuals and institutions have savings that they want to invest, and companies need capital to finance and grow their businesses. The capital markets provide a way for this to occur efficiently. Companies issue debt or equity to investors who are willing to part with their cash now because they expect to earn an adequate return in the future for the risk they are taking.

However, there is an information gap between investors and companies. Investors usually do not have enough information or expertise to determine the good investments from the bad ones. And companies do not usually have the infrastructure and know-how to directly receive capital from investors. Therefore, both parties rely on intermediaries to help them make these decisions. These intermediaries include accountants, lawyers, regulatory bodies (such as the SEC in the US), investment banks, venture capitalists, money management firms, and even the media (see **Exhibit 10**). The focus of this case is on the equity markets in the US.

In a well-functioning system, with the incentives of intermediaries fully aligned in accordance with their fiduciary responsibility, public markets will correctly value companies such that investors earn a normal "required" rate of return. In particular, companies that go public will do so at a value which will give investors this fair rate of investment.

The public market valuation will have a trickle down effect on all intermediaries in the investment chain. Venture capitalists, who typically demand a very high return on investment, and usually exit their portfolio companies through an IPO, will do their best to ensure these companies have good management teams and a sustainable business model that will stand the test of time. Otherwise, the capital markets will put too low a value on the companies when they try to go public. Investment bankers will provide their expertise in helping companies to go public or to make subsequent offerings, and introducing them to investors.

---

[10]Michael A. Sherrick, Mary Meeker, Douglas Levine, "Scient Corporation. Outlook Remains Cloudy, Adjusting Forecasts," *Morgan Stanley Dean Witter* (January 18, 2001).

On the other side of the process, portfolio managers acting on behalf of investors, will only buy companies that are fairly priced, and will sell companies if they become overvalued, since buying or holding an overvalued stock will inevitably result in a loss. Sell-side analysts, whose clients include portfolio managers and therefore investors, will objectively monitor the performance of public companies and determine whether or not their stocks are good or bad investment at any point in time. Accountants audit the financial statements of companies, ensuring that they comply with established standards and represent the true states of the firms. This gives investors and analysts the confidence to make decisions based on these financial documents.

The integrity of this process is critical in an economy because it gives investors the confidence they need to invest their money into the system. Without this confidence, they would not plough their money back into the economy, but instead keep it under the proverbial mattress.

### WHAT HAPPENED DURING THE DOT-COM BUBBLE?

Many observers believed that something went wrong with the system during the dotcom bubble. In April 2001, *BusinessWeek* wrote about "The Great Internet Money Game. How America's top financial firms reaped billions from the Net boom, while investors got burned."[11] The following month, *Fortune* magazine's cover asked, "Can we ever trust Wall Street again?"[12] referring to the way in which, in some people's opinions, Wall Street firms had led investors and companies astray before and after the dot-com debacle.

The implications of the internet crash were far reaching. Many companies that needed to raise capital for investment found the capital markets suddenly shut to them. Millions of investors saw a large portion of their savings evaporate. This phenomenon was a likely contributor to the sharp drop in consumer confidence that took place in late 2000 and early 2001. In addition, the actual decrease in wealth threatened to dampen consumer spending. These factors, along with an overall slowing of the US economy, threatened to put the US into recession for the first time in over ten years.

On a more macro level, the dot-coms used up valuable resources that could have been more efficiently allocated within the economy. The people who worked at failed internet firms could have spent their time and energy creating lasting value in other endeavors, and the capital that funded the dot-coms could have been ploughed into viable, lasting companies that would have benefited the overall economy. However, it could be argued that there were benefits as well, and that the large investment in the technology sector positioned the US to be a world leader in the future.

Nevertheless, the question remained: how could the dot-com bubble occur in a sophisticated capital market system like that of the US? Why did the market allow the valuations of many internet companies to go so high? What was the role of the intermediaries in the process that gave rise to the stock market bubble?

# The intermediaries

One way to try to answer some of these questions is to look more closely at some of the key players in the investing chain. Much of the material in the following section is derived from interviews with representatives from each sector.

### VENTURE CAPITALISTS

Venture capitalists (VCs) provided capital for companies in their early stages of development. They sought to provide a very high rate of return to their investors for the associated risk. This was typically accomplished by

---

[11]Peter Elstrom, "The Great Internet Money Game. How America's top financial firms reaped billions from the Net boom while investors got burned," *BusinessWeek e.biz* (April 16, 2001).
[12]*Fortune,* May 14, 2001.

selling their stake in their portfolio companies either to the public through an IPO, or to another company in a trade sale.

The partners in a VC firm typically had a substantial percentage of their net worth tied up in their funds, which aligned their interests with their investors. Their main form of compensation was a large share of profits (typically 20 percent) in addition to a relatively low fee based on the assets under management.

A large part of a VC's job was to screen good business ideas and entrepreneurial teams from bad ones. Partners at a VC firm were typically very experienced, savvy business people who worked closely with their portfolio companies to both monitor and guide them to a point where they have turned a business idea into a well-managed, fully functional company that could stand on its own. In a sense, their role was to nurture the companies until they reached a point where they were ready to face the scrutiny of the public capital markets after an IPO. Typically, companies would not go public until they had shown profits for at least three quarters.[13]

After the dot-com crash, some investors and the media started pointing fingers at the venture capitalists that had invested in many of the failed dot-coms. They blamed them for being unduly influenced by the euphoria of the market, and knowingly investing in and bringing public companies with questionable business models, or that had not yet proven themselves operationally. Indeed, many of the dot-coms went public within record time of receiving VC funding – a study of venture-backed initial public offerings showed that companies averaged 5.4 years in age when they went public in 1999, compared with eight years in 1995.[14]

Did the venture capital investing process change in a way that contributed to the internet bubble of 2000? According to a partner at a venture capital firm that invested in one of the internet consulting companies, the public markets had a tremendous impact on the way VCs invested during the late 1990s.[15] He felt that, because of expectations of high stock market valuations, VC firms invested in companies during the late 1990s that they would not have invested in under ordinary circumstances. He also believed that the ready availability of money affected the business strategies and attitudes of the internet companies: "If the [management] team knows $50 million is available, it acts differently, e.g., 'go for market share.'"

The VC partner acknowledged that VCs took many internet companies public very early, but he felt that the responsibility of scrutinizing these companies lay largely with the investors that subscribed to the IPOs: "If a mutual fund wants to invest in the IPO of a company that has no track record, profitability, etc. but sees it as a liquidity event, it has made a decision to become a VC. Lots of mutual funds thought 'VC is easy, I want a piece of it.'"

### INVESTMENT BANK UNDERWRITERS

Entrepreneurs relied on investment banks (such as Goldman Sachs, Morgan Stanley Dean Witter, and Credit Suisse First Boston) in the actual process of doing an initial public offering, or "going public." Investment banks provided advisory financial services, helped the companies price their offerings, underwrite the shares, and introduce them to investors, often in the form of a road show.

Investment banks were paid a commission based on the amount of money that the company managed to raise in its offering, typically on the order of 7 percent.[16] Several blue-chip firms were involved in the capital-raising process of the internet consultants (see **Exhibit 3**), and they also received a share of the blame for the dot-com crash in the months that followed it. In an article entitled Just Who Brought Those Duds to Market? the *New York Times* wrote:

> . . . many Wall Street investment banks, from top-tier firms like Goldman Sachs . . . to newer entrants like Thomas Weisel Partners . . . have reason to blush. In one blindingly fast riches-to-rags story, Pets.com filed for bankruptcy just nine months after Merrill Lynch took it public.

[13]Peter Elstrom, "The Great Internet Money Game. How America's top financial firms reaped billions from the net boom while investors got burned," *BusinessWeek e.biz* (April 16, 2001).

[14]Shawn Neidorf, "Venture-Backed IPOs Make a Comeback," *Venture Capital Journal* (Wellesley Hills, August 1, 1999).

[15]Limited partners are the investors in a venture capital fund; the venture capital firm itself usually serves as the general partner.

[16]Source: casewriter interview.

*Of course, investment banks that took these underperforming companies public may not care. They bagged enormous fees, a total of more than $600 million directly related to initial public offerings involving just the companies whose stocks are now under $1.*

*. . . How did investment banks, paid for their expert advice, pick such lemons?*[17]

## SELL-SIDE ANALYSTS

Sell-side analysts worked at investment banks and brokerage houses. One of their main functions was to publish research on public companies. Each analyst typically followed 15 to 30 companies in a particular industry, and his or her job involved forming relationships with and talking to the managements of the companies, following trends in the industry, and ultimately making buy or sell recommendations on the stocks. The recommendations analysts made could be very influential with investors. If a well-respected analyst downgraded a stock, the reaction from the market could be severe and swift, resulting in a same-day drop in the stock price. Sell-side analysts typically interacted with buy-side analysts and portfolio managers at money management companies (the buy-side) to market or "sell" their ideas. In addition, they usually provided support during a company's IPO process, providing research to the buy-side before the company actually went public. Sell-side analysts were usually partly compensated based on the amount of trading fees and investment banking revenue they helped the firm to generate through their research.

In the months following the dot-com crash, sell-side technology and internet analysts found themselves the target of criticism for having buy ratings on companies that had subsequently fallen drastically in price. Financial cable TV channel CNBC ran a report called "Analyzing the Analysts," addressing the issue of whether or not they were to blame for their recommendations of tech stocks. A March 2001 article in the *Wall Street Journal* raised similar issues after it was reported that J.P. Morgan Chase's head of European research sent out a memo requiring all the company's analysts to show their stock recommendation changes to the company involved and to the investment banking division.[18] The previously mentioned issue of *Forbes* featured an article criticizing Mary Meeker, a prominent internet analyst.[19] And a *Financial Times* article entitled "Shoot all the analysts" made a sweeping criticism of their role in the market bubble:

*. . . instead of forecasting earnings per share, they were now in the business of forecasting share prices themselves. And those prices were almost always very optimistic. Now, at last, they have had their comeuppance. Much of what many of them have done in the past several years has turned out to be worthless. High-flying stocks that a year ago were going to be cheap at twice the price have halved or worse – and some analysts have been putting out buy recommendations all the way down. They should learn a little humility and get back to analysis.*[20]

Responding to the media criticism of financial analysts, Karl Keirstead, a Lehman Brothers analyst who followed internet consulting firms, stated:

*It is too easy as they do on CNBC to slam the analysts for recommending stocks when they were very expensive. In the case of the internet consulting firms, looking back before the correction in April 2000, the fundamentals were "nothing short of pristine." The companies were growing at astronomical rates, and it looked as though they would continue to do so for quite a while. Under these assumptions, if you modeled out the financials for these companies and discounted them back at a reasonable rate, they did not seem all that highly valued.*[21]

Keirstead also pointed out that there were times when it was legitimate to have a buy rating on a stock that was "overvalued" based on fundamentals:

[17]Andrew Ross Sorkin, "Just Who Brought Those Duds to Market?" *NYTimes.com* (Copyright 2001 The New York Times Company).

[18]Wade Lambert, Jathon Sapsford, "J.P. Morgan Memo to Analysts Raises Eyebrows," *Wall Street Journal* (Thursday, March 22, 2001).

[19]Peter Elkind, "Where Mary Meeker Went Wrong," *Fortune* (May 14, 2001).

[20]"Shoot all the analysts," *Financial Times* (Tuesday, March 20, 2001).

[21]Source: casewriter interview.

*The future price of a stock is not always tied to the discounted value of cash flow or earnings, it is equal to what someone is willing to pay. This is especially true in periods of tremendous market liquidity and huge interest in young companies with illiquid stocks and steep growth curves that are difficult to project. The valuation may seem too high, but if the fundamentals are improving and Street psychology and hype are building, the stock is likely to rally. Stock pickers must pay as much attention to these factors as the company and industry fundamentals.*

When asked his view on why the buy-side institutions went along with the high valuations that these companies were trading for, Keirstead commented that, "A lot of buy-side analysts and portfolio managers became momentum investors in disguise. They claimed in their mutual fund prospectus that they made decisions based on fundamental analysis. Truth is, they played the momentum game as well."

Keirstead also commented on the criticism analysts had received for being too heavily influenced by the possibility of banking deals when making stock recommendations. He stated that this claim was "completely over-rated." Though there was some legitimacy to the argument and some of analysts' compensation did come from investment banking fees, it was a limited component. Analysts also got significant fees from the trading revenue they generated and the published rankings.[22] He pointed out that critics' arguments were ludicrous because if analysts only made decisions based on banking fees, it would jeopardize their rankings and credibility with their buy-side clients. However, he did note that the potential deal flow could have distorted the view of some technology analysts during the boom.

Finally, Keirstead described the bias that was present on the sell-side to be bullish:

*To be negative when you are a sell-side analyst is to be a contrarian, to stick your neck out. You take a lot of heat, it's tough. And it would have been the wrong call for the last four years. Had I turned short in 1999 when these stocks seemed overvalued, I would have missed a 200 percent increase in the stocks. My view was: I can't be too valuation-sensitive. The stocks are likely to rise as long as the fundamentals hold and that's the position a lot of analysts took.*

Consistent with this optimistic bias, there were very few sell recommendations from analysts during the peak of the internet stock bubble. According to financial information company First Call, more than 70 percent of the 27,000 plus recommendations outstanding on some 6,000 stocks in November 2000 were strong buys or buys, while fewer than 1 percent were sells or strong sells.[23]

## BUY-SIDE ANALYSTS AND PORTFOLIO MANAGERS

The "buy-side" refers to institutions that do the actual buying and selling of public securities, such as mutual fund companies, insurance companies, hedge funds, and other asset managers.

There were two main roles on the buy side: analysts and portfolio managers. Buy-side analysts had some of the same duties as their sell-side counterparts. They were usually assigned to a group of companies within a certain industry and were responsible for doing industry research, talking to the companies' management teams, coming up with earning estimates, doing valuation analysis, and ultimately rating the stock prices of the companies as either "buys" or "sells." The analyst's job was not yet complete, however. Though they did not publish their research, buy-side analysts needed to convince the portfolio managers within their company to follow their recommendations.

Portfolio managers were the ones who actually managed money, whether it was a retail mutual fund or an institutional account. Though they listened to the recommendations of the analysts, they were the ones who were ultimately responsible for buying or selling securities.

The compensation of the buy-side analysts was often linked to how well their stock recommendations do, and in the case of portfolio managers, compensation was determined by the performance of their funds

---

[22]Several financial journals published analyst rankings. The most prominent ranking was by *Institutional Investor* magazine which published annual rankings of sell-side analysts by industry. These rankings were very influential in the analyst and investment community.
[23]Walter Updegrave, "The ratings game," *Money* (New York, January 2001).

relative to an appropriate benchmark return. These compensation schemes were designed to align the incentives of buy-side analysts and portfolio managers with the interests of investors.

Why then, did so many buy-side firms buy and hold on to the internet consulting firms during the market bubble? Did they really believe the companies were worth what they were trading for? Or did they know they were overvalued, but invest in them anyway for other reasons?

According to a former associate at a large mutual fund company, many people within his company knew that most of the internet companies were overvalued before the market correction, but they felt pressure to invest anyway:

> My previous employer is known as a value investor, growth at a reasonable price. At first the general impression in the firm was that a lot of the internet firms would blow up, that they didn't deserve these valuations. But articles were written about my company . . . that it was being left behind because it was not willing to invest in the internet companies. Some of the analysts at the firm began to recommend companies simply because they knew that the stock prices would go up, even though they were clearly overvalued. And portfolio managers felt that if they didn't buy the stocks, they would lag their benchmarks and their competitors – they are rewarded on a one-year term horizon and three-year horizon. It is very important to meet their benchmark, it makes up a material part of their compensation. In addition, they compare against the performance of their peers for marketing purposes.[24]

## The role of information

### THE ACCOUNTING PROFESSION

Independent accountants audited the financial statements of public companies to verify their accuracy and freedom from fraud. If they were reasonably satisfied, they provided an unqualified opinion statement which was attached to the company's public filings. If auditors were not fully satisfied, this is noted as well. Investors usually took heed of the auditor's opinion as it provided an additional level of assurance of the quality of the information they were receiving from companies.

In the year 2000, the accounting profession in the US was dominated by five major accounting firms, collectively referred to as "The Big Five" (Price Waterhouse Coopers, Deloitte & Touche, KPMG, Ernst & Young, and Arthur Andersen). The top 100 accounting firms had roughly a 50 percent share of the market and the Big Five account for about 84 percent of the revenues of the top 100.[25] However, the Big Five made up an even larger percentage of the auditing activity of internet IPOs. Of the 410 internet services and software IPOs between January 1998 and December 2000, 373 of them, or 91 percent, were audited by one of the Big Five accountants.[26]

During the aftermath of the dot-com crash, these firms came under some criticism for not adequately warning investors about the precarious financial position of some of the companies. The *Wall Street Journal* wrote an article addressing the fact that many dotcoms that went bankrupt were not given "going concern" clauses by their auditors. A going concern clause was included by an auditor if it had a substantial doubt that the company would be able to remain in operation for another 12 months:

> In retrospect, critics say, there were early signs that the businesses weren't sustainable, including their reliance on external financing, rather than money generated by their own operations, to stay afloat. You wonder where some of the skepticism was . . . critics say many auditors appear to have presumed the capital markets would remain buoyant. For anybody to have assumed a continuation of those aberrant, irrational conditions was in itself irrational and unjustifiable whether it was an auditor, a board member or an investor . . .[27]

---

[24]Source: casewriter interview.
[25]"Accounting Today Top 100 Survey Shows All is Well," *CPA Journal* (May 1999).
[26]Information extracted from IPO.com website http://www.ipo.com.
[27]Johnathan Weil, "'Going Concerns': Did Accountants Fail to Flag Problems at Dot-Com Casualties?" *Wall Street Journal* (February 9, 2001).

However, in the same article, accountants defended their actions by noting that going concern judgments were subjective, and that they were not able to predict the future any better than the capital markets.

Dr Howard Schilit, founder and CEO of CFRA, an independent financial research organization,[28] believed that accountants certainly had to take a part of the blame for what happened. In his opinion, they "looked the other way when they could have been more rigorous in doing their work."[29] However, he noted that the outcome may not have been materially different even if they did.

One particular criticism he had was that many accountants didn't look closely enough at the substance of transactions and didn't do enough questioning of the circumstances surrounding sales contracts. His hope was that accountants "go back and learn what the basic rules are of when revenues should be booked. The rules haven't changed whether this is the new economy or old economy."

## FASB – A REGULATOR

The Financial Accounting Standards Boards (FASB) was an independent regulatory body in the United States whose mission was to "establish and improve standards of financial accounting and reporting for the guidance and education of the public, including issuers, auditors, and users of financial information."[30] FASB standards were recognized by the Securities and Exchange Commission (SEC), which regulates the financial reporting of public companies in the United States.

The accounting practices of some new economy firms posed challenges for auditors and investors, and though some observers felt that the accountants were not doing a good enough job, others thought that the accounting rules themselves were too ambiguous, and this fact lent itself to exploitation by the companies.

Specific examples included the treatment of barter revenues in the case of companies that exchanged online advertising space, the practice of booking gross rather than net revenues in commission-based businesses (e.g., Priceline.com), and the issue of when to recognize revenues from long-term contracts (e.g., MicroStrategy Inc.). Given that the valuations of many internet firms were driven by how quickly they grew revenues, there was a lot of incentive to inflate this number. In fact, the accounting practices of dot-coms became so aggressive that the SEC had to step in:

> *The Securities & Exchange Commission's crackdown on the aggressive accounting practices that have taken off among many dot-com firms really began . . . when it quietly issued new guidelines to refocus corporate management and investors. . . . To rein in what it saw as an alarming trend in inflated revenue reports, the SEC required companies using lax accounting practices to restate financial results by the end of their next fiscal year's quarter. . . .*
>
> *The SEC has also directed the Financial Accounting Standards Board to review a range of internet company accounting practices that could boost revenues or reduce costs unfairly. Under the scrutiny, more companies are likely to issue restatements of financial results. . . .*[31]

In another spin on the issue, some questioned whether the accounting rules set out by the regulatory bodies had in fact become obsolete for the new economy. In July 2000, leaders in the accounting community told a Senate Banking subcommittee that the United States needed "a new accounting model for the New Economy." A major concern of theirs was that the current rules did not allow companies to report the value of intangible assets on their balance sheets, such as customers, employees, suppliers, and organizations.[32] Others argued that the accounting rules caused internet firms to appear unprofitable when they were actually making money. This was because old economy firms were allowed to capitalize their major investments such as factories, plants,

---

[28]CFRA's mission is to warn investors and creditors about companies experiencing operational problems and particularly those that employ unusual or aggressive accounting practices to camouflage such problems.

[29]Source: casewriter interview.

[30]FASB website: http://accounting.rutgers.edu/raw/fasb/.

[31]Catherine Yang, "Earth to Dot-Com Accountants," *BusinessWeek* (New York, April 3, 2000).

[32]Stephen Barlas, "New accounting model demanded," *Strategic Finance* (Montvale, September 2000).

and equipment, whereas the rules did not allow capitalization of expenditures on R&D and marketing, which created value for many dot-com companies:

> While internet stocks may not be worth what they are selling for, the movement in their prices may not be as crazy as it seems. Many of these companies reporting losses actually make money – lots of it. It all has to do with accounting. Old-economy companies get to capitalize their most important investments, while new economy ones do not. While Amazon.com announces a loss almost every quarter, when it capitalizes its investments in intangibles that loss turns into a $400-million profit.[33]

## Retail investors

The role of the general public in the dot-com craze cannot be ignored. In addition to the people who poured money into mutual funds, many retail investors began trading on their own, often electronically. A group of avid day traders grew up, some of whom quit their regular jobs to devote all their time and energy to trading stocks. Analysts estimated that they made up almost 18 percent of the trading volume of the NYSE and Nasdaq in 2000.[34] Sites such as Yahoo Finance grew in popularity, while chat rooms devoted to stocks and trading proliferated.

The number of accounts of internet stock brokers like Etrade and Ameritrade grew rapidly (Etrade grew from 544 thousand brokerage accounts in 1998 to 3 million in 2000 and Ameritrade grew from 98 thousand accounts in 1997 to 1.2 million in 2000) as they slashed their commissions, some to as low as $8/trade compared to the $50–$300[35] charged by traditional brokerage firms. These companies were dot-coms themselves, and they were able to slash prices partly because they were operating at losses that they were not penalized for by the capital markets. This gave rise to an interesting positive feedback loop: the Etrades of the world, funded by the dot-com frenzied capital markets slashed their prices and therefore encouraged more trading, which continued to fuel the enthusiasm of investors for the markets.

The financial press also became increasingly visible during this period. Several publications like *Barrons* and the *Wall Street Journal* had always been very influential in the financial community. However, a host of other information sources, often on the web, sprang up to support the new demand for information. CNBC and CNNfn, major network channels devoted to the markets, often featured analysts and portfolio managers making stock recommendations or giving their views on the market.

Many of the retail investors did not know much about finance or valuation, and often didn't understand much about the companies whose shares they were buying. They were therefore likely to be heavily influenced by some of the intermediaries previously described, especially the financial press, and the sell-side analysts that publicly upgraded and downgraded companies.

These investors were pointed to by some as having had a large role in driving internet valuations to the levels they went to. The reasoning was that other more sophisticated buyers such as the institutional money managers, may have bought overvalued companies because they thought they could easily sell them later at even higher valuations to "dumb retail investors."

## The companies themselves

The entrepreneurs who founded the internet consulting companies, and the management teams who ran them, could almost be described as bystanders to the process that took the stock prices of their companies to

---

[33]Geoffrey Colvin, "The Net's hidden profits," *Fortune* (New York, April 17, 2000).
[34]Amy S. Butte, "Day Trading and Beyond. A New Niche Is Emerging," *Bear Stearns Equity Research,* April 2000.
[35]Lee Patterson, "If you can't beat 'em . . .," *Forbes* (New York, August 23, 1999).

such lofty highs and then punishing lows. However, they were profoundly affected by these changes in almost every aspect of their businesses.

Obviously there were many benefits to having a high stock price. According to a managing director (MD) at one of the internet consultants, the company was facing a very competitive labor market while trying to grow organically, and having a stock that was doing well helped with recruiting people since the option part of the compensation package was attractive.[36] He also explained that people were proud to be a part of the firm, partly because the stock was doing so well.

As the stock price of the company continued to rise higher and higher, the MD admitted that he did become afraid that the market was overvaluing the company, and that this doubt probably went all the way up to the CEO. As he put it "we were trading at just absurd levels."

When asked about his thoughts on his firm's current stock price, the MD thought that the market had over-reacted and gone to the other extreme. He remarked that investors were worried that the internet consulting firms were facing renewed competition from companies like IBM, the Big Five accounting firms, and the strategy consulting firms. Overall, though the rise and fall of the company's stock price was in many ways a painful experience, this MD thought that the market bubble presented a good opportunity that the company was able to capitalize upon. It was able to do a secondary offering at a high price and now had lots of cash on its balance sheet. His view was that "If you look at competitive sustainability [in this business], it could boil down to the company with the best balance sheet wins."

## The blame game

In the aftermath of the dot-com crash, many tried to pinpoint whose fault it was that the whole bubble occurred in the first place. As mentioned previously, sell-side analysts, often the most visible group in the investment community, came under frequent attack in the media, as did, to some extent, venture capitalists, investment bankers, and even the accounting industry. Company insiders (including the founder of Scient) were also scrutinized for selling large blocks of shares when the stock prices of their companies were near their peaks.[37]

A *Wall Street Journal* article entitled, "Investors, Entrepreneurs All Play the Blame Game," described how these various players were trying to blame each other for what happened:

> With the tech-heavy Nasdaq Composite Index dancing close to the 2,000 mark – down from over 5,000 – internet entrepreneurs and venture capitalists have stepped up their finger-pointing about just who's at fault for the technology meltdown, which continues to topple businesses and once-cushy lifestyles. . . . Fingers pointed right and left – from entrepreneurs to venture capitalists, from analysts to day traders to shareholders – and back around again.[38]

The internet stock market bubble was certainly not the first one to occur. Other notables include the Tulip Craze of the seventeenth century and the Nifty Fifty boom of the 1970s. In all cases market valuations went to unsustainably high levels and ended with a sharp decrease in valuation that left many investors empty-handed.

But the question of what happened in this latest bubble remained: who, if anyone, could be blamed for the dot-com rise and crash? How did the various intermediaries described here affect or cause what happened? Was there really a misalignment of incentives in the system? If so, could it be fixed so that this sort of thing did not happen in the future? Or were market bubbles an inevitable part of the way the economy functioned?

---

[36]Source: casewriter interview.

[37]Mark Maremont, John Hechinger, "If Only You'd Sold Some Stock Earlier – Say $100 Million Worth," *Wall Street Journal* (March 22, 2001).

[38]Rebecca Buckman, "Investors, Entrepreneurs All Play the Blame Game," *Wall Street Journal* (March 5, 2001).

## QUESTIONS

1   What is the intended role of each of the institutions and intermediaries discussed in the case for the effective functioning of capital markets?
2   Are their incentives aligned properly with their intended role? Whose incentives are most misaligned?
3   Who, if anyone, was primarily responsible for the internet stock bubble?
4   What are the costs of such a stock market bubble? As a future business professional, what lessons do you draw from the bubble?

**EXHIBIT 1**  Timeline of the internet consultants – founding and IPO

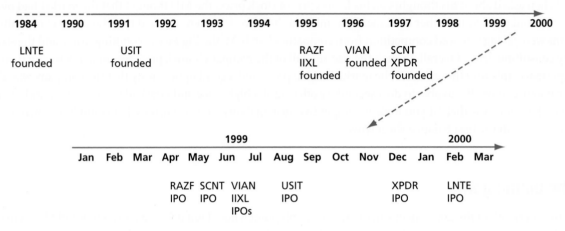

**EXHIBIT 2**  Internet consultants – stock price highs and lows

| Company | IPO Price | Peak Price | % Change IPO to Peak | Date of Peak | Price at End of Feb 2001 | % Change from Peak |
|---|---|---|---|---|---|---|
| Scient | 10 | 133.75 | 1,238% | 10-Mar-00 | 2.94 | −97.8% |
| Viant | 8 | 63.56 | 695% | 14-Dec-99 | 3.06 | −95.2% |
| IXL Enterprises | 12 | 58.75 | 390% | 20-Jan-00 | 1.25 | −97.9% |
| Lante | 20 | 87.50 | 338% | 29-Feb-00 | 1.81 | −97.9% |
| Razorfish | 8 | 56.94 | 612% | 14-Feb-00 | 1.16 | −98.0% |
| US Interactive | 10 | 83.75 | 738% | 4-Jan-00 | 0.56b | −99.3% |
| Xpedior | 19 | 34.75 | 83% | 10-Jan-00 | 0.69 | −98.0% |

aSplit adjusted.

bLast trade on January 11, 2001. Filed for bankruptcy under Chapter 11 in January 2001.

Source: Bloomberg LP, The Center for Research in Security Prices (accessed via Wharton Research Database Services), Marketguide.com.

**EXHIBIT 3** Intermediaries in the capital-raising process of the internet consultants

| Company | Venture Capital Stage Investors | Investment Bank Underwriters | Auditors[a] | Analyst Coverage | Selected Institutional Holders | Venture Funding ($M) | IPO Amount Raised ($M)[b] | IPO Underwriting Fee ($M) | % Institutional Ownership |
|---|---|---|---|---|---|---|---|---|---|
| **Scient** | Sequoia Capital, Benchmark Capital, Stanford Univ., Capital Research, Morgan Stanley Venture Partners, Amerindo Investment Advisors, Palantir Capital | Morgan Stanley Dean Witter, Hambrecht & Quist, Thomas Weisel Partners | PWC | Merrill Lynch, Morgan Stanley Dean Witter, CSFB, Lehman Brothers, UBS Warburg, SG Cowen, others | Capital Research, Putnam, Janus Vanguard, Wellingon, State Street | 31.2 | 60 | 4.2 | 34% (66% of float) |
| **Viant** | Kleiner Perkins Caufield & Byers, Mohr Davidow Ventures, Information Associates, Trident Capital, BancBoston Capital, General Motors, Technology Cross-over Ventures | Goldman Sachs, Credit Suisse First Boston, WIT Capital Corporation | PWC | Goldman Sachs, Merrill Lynch, Lehman Brothers, CSFB, Wasserstein Perella, Bear Stearns, others | Fidelity, T Rowe Price, Putnam, Franklin, State Street, Vanguard, American Century, Goldman Sachs Asset Management | 32.2 | 48 | 3.4 | 34% (67% of float) |
| **IXL** | Greylock Mgmt., Chase Capital Partners, Flatiron Partners, GE Capital, Kelso & Co., TTC Ventures, CB Capital, Portage Venture Partners, Transamerica Technology Finance | Merrill Lynch, BancBoston Robertson Stephens, DLJ, SG Cowen | PWC | Merrill Lynch, Robinson Humphrey, First Union Capital, others | Capital Research, State Street, Vanguard, Goldman Sachs Asset Management, GE Asset Management | 91.0 | 72 | 5.0 | 29% (108% of float) |
| **Lante** | Frontenac Co., Dell Ventures, MSD Capital | Credit Suisse First Boston, Deutsche Bank Alex Brown, Thomas Weisel Partners | PWC | CSFB, Deutsche Bank, Thomas Weisel Partners, others | Fidelity, State Street, Vanguard, Goldman Sachs Asset Management | 26.8 | 80 | 5.6 | 3% (21% of float) |
| **Razorfish** | N/A | Credit Suisse First Boston, BancBoston Robertson Stephens, BTAlex. Brown, Lehman Brothers | AA, PWC | CSFB, Lehman Brothers, SG Cowen, others | Janus, Capital Research, Fidelity, Vanguard, Goldman Sachs Asset Management | N/A | 48 | 3.4 | 8% (14% of float) |
| **US Interactive** | Safeguard Scientific, Technology Leaders | Lehman Brothers, Hambrecht & Quist, Adams Harkness & Hill | KPMG | Lehman Brothers, Hambrecht & Quist, Deutsche Bank Alex Brown, others | T Rowe Price, Prudential, JP Morgan Investment Management, Credit Suisse Asset Mgmt. | N/A | 46 | 2.0 | 4% (6% of float) |
| **Xpedior** | N/A | DLJ, First Union Securities, JP Morgan, The Robinson-Humphrey Group | E&Y | DLJ, First Union Securities, Robinson-Humphrey, others | Capital Research, T Rowe Price, Franklin, Vanguard, John Hancock | N/A | 162 | 11.4 | 2% (10% of float) |

[a]PWC stands for Price Waterhouse Coopers; AA for Arthur Anderson; E&Y for Ernst & Young.

[b]Includes underwriting fee.

[c]As of April 2001.

Source: Compiled by casewriter.

**EXHIBIT 4**  Market capitalization of major technology companies, January 2000

| Company | Market Capitalization ($ billions)[a] | Stock Price (January 3, 2000) |
|---|---|---|
| Microsoft | 603 | 116.56 |
| Intel | 290 | 87.00 |
| IBM | 218 | 116.00 |
| Dell Computer | 131 | 50.88 |
| Hewlett Packard | 117 | 117.44 |
| Compaq Computer | 53 | 31.00 |
| Apple Computer | 18 | 111.94 |

[a]Based on share price close on January 3, 2000 and reported shares outstanding.

Sources: Bloomberg LP, The Center for Research in Security Prices (accessed via Wharton Research Database Services), Edgar Online.

**EXHIBIT 5**  Market valuations given to loss-making dot-coms

| Company | Net Income ('99/'00)[a] ($ millions) | Market Capitalization ($ billions)[b] | Stock Price (January 3, 2000) |
|---|---|---|---|
| Amazon.com | −720 | 30.8 | 89.38 |
| DoubleClick | −56 | 30.1 | 268.00 |
| Akamai Technologies | −58 | 29.7 | 321.25 |
| VerticalNet | −53 | 12.4 | 172.63 |
| Priceline.com | −1,055 | 8.4 | 51.25 |
| E*Trade | −57 | 7.1 | 28.06 |
| EarthLink | −174 | 5.2 | 44.75 |
| Drugstore.com | −116 | 1.6 | 37.13 |

[a]As of end of 1999 or early 2000, depending on fiscal year end.

[b]Based on share price close on January 3, 2000 and reported shares outstanding.

Sources: Bloomberg LP, The Center for Research in Security Prices (accessed via Wharton Research Database Services), Edgar Online.

**EXHIBIT 6**  Scient – consolidated financial statements

**INCOME STATEMENT (in thousands except per-share amounts)**

| | November 7, 1997 (inception) through March 31, 1998 | Year Ended March 31 | |
|---|---|---|---|
| | | 1999 | 2000 |
| Revenues | $179 | $20,675 | $155,729 |
| Operating expenses: | | | |
| Professional services | 102 | 10,028 | 70,207 |
| Selling, general, and administrative | 1,228 | 15,315 | 90,854 |
| Stock compensation | 64 | 7,679 | 15,636 |
| Total operating expenses | 1,394 | 33,022 | 176,697 |
| Loss from operations | (1,215) | (12,347) | (20,968) |
| Interest income and other, net | 56 | 646 | 4,953 |
| Net loss | $(1,159) | $(11,701) | $(16,015) |
| Net loss per share: | | | |
| Basic and diluted | $(0.10) | $(0.89) | $(0.29) |
| Weighted average shares | 11,894 | 13,198 | 54,590 |

**EXHIBIT 6** Scient – consolidated financial statements (Continued)

## BALANCE SHEET (in thousands except per-share amounts)

| | March 31 | |
|---|---|---|
| | 1999 | 2000 |
| **ASSETS** | | |
| Current Assets: | | |
| Cash and cash equivalents | $11,261 | $108,102 |
| Short-term investments | 16,868 | 121,046 |
| Accounts receivable, net | 5,876 | 56,021 |
| Prepaid expenses | 811 | 4,929 |
| Other | 318 | 4,228 |
| Total Current Assets | 35,134 | 294,326 |
| Long-term investments | — | 3,146 |
| Property and equipment, net | 3,410 | 16,063 |
| Other | 268 | 219 |
| | $38,812 | $313,754 |
| **LIABILITIES AND STOCKHOLDERS' EQUITY** | | |
| Current Liabilities: | | |
| Bank borrowings, current | $413 | $1,334 |
| Accounts payable | 832 | 5,023 |
| Accrued compensation and benefits | 2,554 | 33,976 |
| Accrued expenses | 2,078 | 9,265 |
| Deferred revenue | 524 | 6,579 |
| Capital lease obligations, current | 625 | 2,624 |
| Total Current Liabilities | 7,026 | 58,801 |
| Capital lease obligations, long-term | 680 | 2,052 |
| | 8,835 | 61,718 |
| Commitments and contingencies (Note 5) | | |
| Stockholders' equity: | | |
| Convertible preferred stock; issuable in series, $.0001 par value; 10,000 shares authorized; 9,012 and no shares issued and outstanding, respectively | 1 | — |
| Common stock: $.0001 par value; 125,000 shares authorized; 33,134 and 72,491 shares issues and outstanding, respectively | 3 | 7 |
| Additional paid-in capital | 70,055 | 297,735 |
| Accumulated other comprehensive loss | — | (47) |
| Unearned compensation | (27,222) | (16,784) |
| Accumulated deficit | (12,860) | (28,875) |
| Total Stockholders' Equity | 29,977 | 252,036 |
| | $38,812 | $313,754 |

Sources: Scient Corporation 10-K; Edgar Online www.freedgar.com (May 11, 2001).

**EXHIBIT 7** Analyst downgrades of the internet consultants

| Company | Number of Analysts that Downgraded during August 30–September 8, 2000 |
|---|---|
| Viant | 13 |
| Scient | 7 |
| IXL Enterprises | 7 |
| US Interactive | 5 |
| Xpedior | 3 |
| Lante | 1 |
| Razorfish | 0 |

### ANALYST DOWNGRADES OF SCIENT CORPORATION, AUGUST 30–SEPTEMBER 8, 2000

| Institution | Previous Recommendation | New Recommendation | Date of Downgrade |
|---|---|---|---|
| Merrill Lynch | LTBuy | LT Accumulate | 1-Sep-2000 |
| Lehman Brothers | Buy | Outperform | 1-Sep-2000 |
| ING Barings | Buy | Hold | 1-Sep-2000 |
| SG Cowen | Buy | Neutral | 1-Sep-2000 |
| Legg Mason | Buy | Market Perform | 1-Sep-2000 |
| BB&T Capital Markets | Hold | Source of Funds | 1-Sep-2000 |
| First Union Securities | Strong Buy | Buy | 31-Aug-2000 |

Source: I/B/E/S (accessed via Wharton Research Database Services).

**EXHIBIT 8** Selected institutional holders of Scient Corporation, 1999–2000

| Institution | Quarter Ended: June 1999 | September 1999 | December 1999 | March 2000 | June 2000 | September 2000 | December 2000 |
|---|---|---|---|---|---|---|---|
| Capital Research | — | — | — | 265 | 1,079,911 | 586,442 | 586,706 |
| Putnam Investments | 5,000 | — | 625,900 | 2,209,200 | 4,800,800 | 5,749,200 | — |
| Wellington Management | — | — | — | — | — | — | 803,000 |
| State Street | — | 12,450 | 38,167 | 52,867 | 89,667 | 180,668 | 672,352 |
| Janus | 267,300 | 273,915 | 483,730 | 775,085 | 1,359,700 | 4,382,250 | — |

Source: Edgar (SEC).

**EXHIBIT 9** Dot-coms that filed for bankruptcy or closed operations

*(Selected List)*

**August 2000**
Auctions.com
Hardware.com
Living.com
SaviShopper.com
GreatCoffee

**September 2000**
Clickmango.com
Pop.com
FreeScholarships.com
RedLadder.com
DomainAuction.com
Gazoontite.com
Surfing2Cash.com
Affinia.com

**October 2000**
FreeInternet.com
Chipshot.com
Stockpower.com
The Dental Store
More.com
WebHouse
UrbanFetch.com
Boxman.com
RedGorilla.com
Eve.com
MyLackey.com
BigWords.com

Mortgage.com
MotherNature.com
Ivendor
TeliSmart.com

**November 2000**
Pets.com
Caredata.com
Streamline.com
Garden.com
Furniture.com
TheMan.com
Ibelieve.com
eSociety
UrbanDesign.com
HalfthePlanet.com
Productopia.com
BeautyJungle.com
ICanBuy.com
Bike.com
Mambo.com
Babystripes.com
Thirsty.com
Checkout.com

**December 2000**
Quepasa.com
Finance.com
BizBuyer.com
Desktop.com
E-pods.com
Clickabid.com

HeavenlyDoor.com
ShoppingList.com
Babygear.com
HotOffice.com
Goldsauction.com
AntEye.com
EZBid
Admart
I-US.com
Riffage.com

**January 2000**
MusicMaker.com
Mercata
Send.com
CompanyLeader.com
Zap.com
Savvio.com
News Digital Media
TravelNow.com
Foodline.com
LetsBuyIt.com
e7th.cm
CountryCool.com
Ibetcha.com
Fibermarket.com
Dotcomix
NewDigital Media
GreatEntertaining.com
AndysGarage.com
Lucy.com
US Interactive

Sources: Johnathan Weil, "'Going Concerns': Did Accountants Fail to Flag Problems at Dot-Com Casualties?" *Wall Street Journal,* February 2001; Jim Battey, "Dot-com details: The numbers behind the year's e-commerce shake-out," *Infoworld,* March 2001.

**EXHIBIT 10**  Capital flows from investors to companies

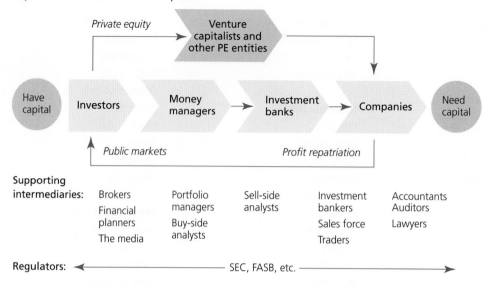

Supporting
intermediaries:

| Brokers | Portfolio | Sell-side | Investment | Accountants |
|---|---|---|---|---|
| Financial | managers | analysts | bankers | Auditors |
| planners | Buy-side | | Sales force | Lawyers |
| The media | analysts | | Traders | |

Regulators:  ←———————————— SEC, FASB, etc. ————————————→

Source: Created by casewriter.

# Business analysis and valuation tools

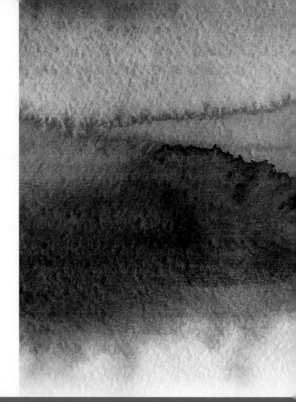

# PART II

# 2 Strategy analysis

Strategy analysis is an important starting point for the analysis of financial statements. Strategy analysis allows the analyst to probe the economics of a firm at a qualitative level so that the subsequent accounting and financial analysis is grounded in business reality. Strategy analysis also allows the identification of the firm's profit drivers and key risks. This in turn enables the analyst to assess the sustainability of the firm's current performance and make realistic forecasts of future performance.

A firm's value is determined by its ability to earn a return on its capital in excess of the cost of capital. What determines whether or not a firm is able to accomplish this goal? While a firm's cost of capital is determined by the capital markets, its profit potential is determined by its own strategic choices:

1 The choice of an industry or a set of industries in which the firm operates (industry choice).
2 The manner in which the firm intends to compete with other firms in its chosen industry or industries (competitive strategy).
3 The way in which the firm expects to create and exploit synergies across the range of businesses in which it operates (corporate strategy).

Strategy analysis therefore involves **industry analysis**, **competitive strategy analysis**, and **corporate strategy analysis**.[1] In this chapter, we will briefly discuss these three steps and use the European airline industry, IKEA, and the easyGroup, respectively, to illustrate the application of the steps.

## Industry analysis

In analyzing a firm's profit potential, an analyst has to first assess the profit potential of each of the industries in which the firm is competing because the profitability of various industries differs systematically and predictably over time. For example, the median ratio of operating profit after taxes to the book value of operating assets for European listed companies between 1998 and 2017 was close to 7 percent. However, the average returns varied widely across specific industries: for the personnel supply services industry, the profitability ratio was four percentage points greater than the population average, and for the gold and silver ore mining industry, it was eight percentage points less than the population average.[2] What causes these profitability differences?

There is a vast body of research in industrial organization on the influence of industry structure on profitability.[3] Relying on this research, strategy literature suggests that the average profitability of an industry is influenced by the "five forces" shown in Figure 2.1.[4] According to this framework, the intensity of competition determines the potential for creating abnormal profits by the firms in an industry. Whether or not the potential profits are kept by the industry is determined by the relative **bargaining power** of the firms in the industry and their customers and suppliers. We will discuss each of these industry profit drivers in more detail below.

### DEGREE OF ACTUAL AND POTENTIAL COMPETITION

At the most basic level, the profits in an industry are a function of the maximum price that customers are willing to pay for the industry's product or service. One of the key determinants of the price is the degree to which there is competition among suppliers of the same or similar products (**industry competition**). At one extreme, if there is a state of perfect competition in the industry, micro-economic theory predicts that prices will be equal to marginal cost, and there will be few opportunities to earn supernormal profits. At the other extreme, if the industry is dominated by a single firm, there will be potential to earn monopoly profits. In reality, the degree of competition in most industries is somewhere in between perfect competition and monopoly.

**FIGURE 2.1** Industry structure and profitability

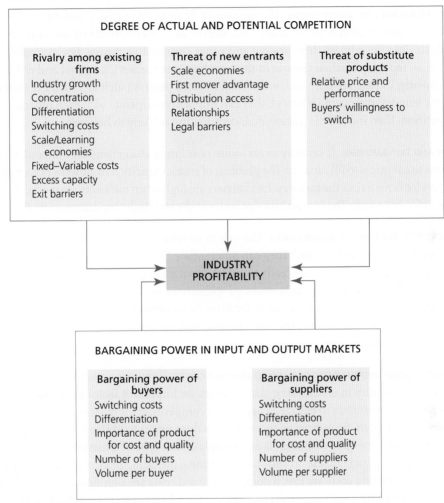

There are three potential sources of competition in an industry:

1  Rivalry between existing firms.
2  Threat of entry of new firms.
3  Threat of substitute products or services.

We will discuss each of these **competitive forces** in the following paragraphs.

### Competitive force 1: Rivalry among existing firms

In most industries the average level of profitability is primarily influenced by the nature of rivalry among existing firms in the industry. In some industries firms compete aggressively, pushing prices close to (and sometimes below) the marginal cost. In other industries firms do not compete aggressively on price. Instead, they find ways to coordinate their pricing, or compete on nonprice dimensions such as innovation, service, or brand image. Several factors determine the intensity of competition between existing players in an industry:

**INDUSTRY GROWTH RATE** If an industry is growing very rapidly, incumbent firms need not grab market share from each other to grow. In contrast, in stagnant industries the only way existing firms can grow is by taking share away from the other players. In this situation one can expect intense rivalry among firms in the industry.

**CONCENTRATION AND BALANCE OF COMPETITORS** The number of firms in an industry and their relative sizes determine the degree of concentration in an industry.[5] The degree of concentration influences the extent to which firms in an industry can coordinate their pricing and other competitive moves. For example, if there is one dominant firm in an industry (such as Google in the search engine market), it can set and enforce the rules of competition. Similarly, if there are only two or three equal-sized players (such as Procter & Gamble, Unilever, and Henkel in the laundry-detergent industry), they can implicitly cooperate with each other to avoid destructive price competition. If an industry is fragmented, competition is likely to be severe.

**EXCESS CAPACITY AND EXIT BARRIERS** If capacity in an industry is larger than customer demand, there is a strong incentive for firms to cut prices to fill capacity. The problem of excess capacity is likely to be exacerbated if there are significant barriers for firms to exit the industry. Exit barriers are high when the assets are specialized or if there are regulations that make exit costly. The competitive dynamics of the steel industry demonstrate these forces at play.

**DEGREE OF DIFFERENTIATION AND SWITCHING COSTS** The extent to which firms in an industry can avoid head-on competition depends on the extent to which they can differentiate their products and services. If the products in an industry are very similar, customers are ready to switch from one competitor to another purely on the basis of price. Switching costs also determine customers' propensity to move from one product to another. When switching costs are low, there is a greater incentive for firms in an industry to engage in price competition. The PC industry, where the standardization of the software and microprocessor has led to relatively low switching costs, is extremely price-competitive.

**SCALE/LEARNING ECONOMIES AND THE RATIO OF FIXED TO VARIABLE COSTS** If there is a steep learning curve or there are other types of scale economies in an industry, size becomes an important factor for firms in the industry. In such situations, there are incentives to engage in aggressive competition for market share. Similarly, if the ratio of fixed to variable costs is high, firms have an incentive to reduce prices to utilize installed capacity. The airline industry, where price wars are quite common, is an example of this type of situation.

As indicated, companies can compete on various dimensions, including price and quality. Price competition is likely if customers' switching costs are low, if companies' fixed costs are significant or if products are subject to decay. Industry profitability comes under pressure especially when companies compete on the same dimension, and even more so when they compete on price. Through competing on different dimensions and targeting different customer groups, companies may succeed to segment the market and preserve industry profitability.

The relationship between rivalry factors and industry profitability is not perfect for various reasons. One reason is that some of the rivalry factors counterbalance each other. For example, in the European laundry-detergent industry, the concentration of competitors is relatively high, as Procter & Gamble, Unilever, and Henkel share most of the European market. There is, however, intense rivalry among these companies because the market exhibits little to no growth. Another reason is the influence of the other competitive forces, such as the threat of new entrants or substitute products, which we will discuss next.

## Competitive force 2: Threat of new entrants

The potential for earning abnormal profits will attract new entrants to an industry. The very threat of new firms entering an industry potentially forces incumbent firms to make additional investments in, for example, advertising or to keep prices low. Therefore the ease with which new firms can enter an industry is a key determinant of its profitability. Several factors determine the height of barriers to entry in an industry:

**SCALE** When there are large economies of scale, new entrants face the choice of having either to invest in a large capacity which might not be utilized right away or to enter with less than the optimum capacity. Either way, new entrants will at least initially suffer from a cost disadvantage in competing with existing firms. Economies of scale might arise from large investments in research and development (the pharmaceutical or jet engine industries), in brand advertising (sportswear industry), or in physical plant and equipment (telecommunications industry). The scale of a firm may not only affect the cost per unit sold, it may also affect customers' demand for a product or service. Scale affects demand, for example, if the usefulness of a product or service increases with the number of users (as with internet communication software such as Skype or social media applications such as Facebook and LinkedIn) or if the perceived reliability or reputation of a company increases with size and is valued by customers (insurance industry).

**FIRST MOVER ADVANTAGE** Early entrants in an industry may deter future entrants if there are first mover advantages. For example, first movers might be able to set industry standards, or enter into exclusive arrangements with suppliers of cheap raw materials. They may also acquire scarce government licences to operate in regulated industries. Finally, if there are learning economies, early firms will have an absolute cost advantage over new entrants. First mover advantages are also likely to be large when there are significant switching costs for customers once they start using existing products. For example, switching costs faced by the users of Microsoft's Windows operating system make it difficult for software companies to market a new operating system.

**ACCESS TO CHANNELS OF DISTRIBUTION AND RELATIONSHIPS** Limited capacity in the existing distribution channels and high costs of developing new channels can act as powerful barriers to entry. For example, a new entrant into the auto industry is likely to face formidable barriers because of the difficulty of developing a dealer network. Similarly, new consumer goods manufacturers find it difficult to obtain supermarket shelf space for their products. Existing relationships between firms and customers in an industry also make it difficult for new firms to enter an industry. Industry examples of this include auditing, investment banking, and advertising.

**LEGAL BARRIERS** There are many industries in which legal barriers such as patents and copyrights in research-intensive industries limit entry. Similarly, licensing regulations limit entry into taxi services, medical services, broadcasting, and telecommunications industries. Tariffs (additional taxes on imports), import quota, or government subsidies can further help to limit the entry of foreign competitors to an industry.

### Competitive force 3: Threat of substitute products

The third dimension of competition in an industry is the threat of substitute products or services. Relevant substitutes are not necessarily those that have the same form as the existing products but those that perform the same function. For example, airlines and high-speed rail systems might be substitutes for each other when it comes to travel over short distances. Similarly, plastic bottles and metal cans substitute for each other as packaging in the beverage industry. In some cases, threat of substitution comes not from customers' switching to another product but from utilizing technologies that allow them to do without, or use less of, the existing products. For example, energy-conserving technologies allow customers to reduce their consumption of electricity and fossil fuels. Similarly, email allows customers to make less use of postal mail.

The threat of substitutes depends on the relative price and performance of the competing products or services and on customers' willingness to substitute. Customers' perception of whether two products are substitutes depends to some extent on whether they perform the same function for a similar price. If two products perform an identical function, then it would be difficult for them to differ from each other in price. However, customers' willingness to switch is often the critical factor in making this competitive dynamic work. For example, even when tap water and bottled water serve the same function, many customers may be unwilling to substitute the former for the latter, enabling bottlers to charge a price premium. Similarly, designer label clothing commands a price premium even if it is not superior in terms of basic functionality because customers place a value on the image offered by designer labels.

## BARGAINING POWER IN INPUT AND OUTPUT MARKETS

While the degree of competition in an industry determines whether there is potential to earn abnormal profits, the *actual profits* are influenced by the industry's bargaining power with its suppliers and customers. On the input side, firms enter into transactions with suppliers of labor, raw materials and components, and finances. On the output side, firms either sell directly to the final customers or enter into contracts with intermediaries in the distribution chain. In all these transactions, the relative economic power of the two sides is important to the overall profitability of the industry firms.

### Competitive force 4: Bargaining power of buyers

Two factors determine the power of buyers: price sensitivity and relative bargaining power. Price sensitivity determines the extent to which buyers care to bargain on price; relative bargaining power determines the extent to which they will succeed in forcing the price down.[6]

**PRICE SENSITIVITY**  Buyers are more price-sensitive when the product is undifferentiated and there are few switching costs. The sensitivity of buyers to price also depends on the importance of the product to their own cost structure. When the product represents a large fraction of the buyers' cost (e.g., the packaging material for soft-drink producers), the buyer is likely to expend the resources necessary to shop for a lower-cost alternative. In contrast, if the product is a small fraction of the buyers' cost (e.g., windshield wipers for automobile manufacturers), it may not pay to expend resources to search for lower-cost alternatives. Further, the importance of the product to the buyers' own product quality also determines whether or not price becomes the most important determinant of the buying decision.

**RELATIVE BARGAINING POWER**  Even if buyers are price-sensitive, they may not be able to achieve low prices unless they have a strong bargaining position. Relative bargaining power in a transaction depends, ultimately, on the cost to each party of not doing business with the other party. The buyers' bargaining power is determined by the number of buyers relative to the number of suppliers, volume of purchases by a single buyer, number of alternative products available to the buyer, buyers' costs of switching from one product to another, and the threat of backward integration by the buyers. For example, in the automobile industry, car manufacturers have considerable power over component manufacturers because auto companies are large buyers with several alternative suppliers to choose from, and switching costs are relatively low. In contrast, in the personal computer industry, computer makers have low bargaining power relative to the operating system software producers because of high switching costs.

### Competitive force 5: Bargaining power of suppliers

The analysis of the relative power of suppliers is a mirror image of the analysis of the buyers' power in an industry. Suppliers are powerful when there are only a few companies and few substitutes are available to their customers. For example, in the soft-drink industry, Coca-Cola and Pepsi are very powerful relative to the bottlers. In contrast, metal can suppliers to the soft-drink industry are not very powerful because of intense competition among can producers and the threat of substitution of cans by plastic bottles. Suppliers also have a lot of power over buyers when the suppliers' product or service is critical to buyers' business. For example, airline pilots have a strong bargaining power in the airline industry. Suppliers also tend to be powerful when they pose a credible threat of forward integration. For example, insurance companies are powerful relative to insurance intermediaries because of their own presence in the insurance-selling business.

# Applying industry analysis: the european airline industry

Let us consider the preceding concepts of industry analysis in the context of the European airline industry. In the early 1980s the European airline industry was highly regulated, and several airlines were partly owned by governments and operated as "flag carriers." Bilateral agreements between European governments severely restricted competition by determining which airlines could operate which routes at what fares. During the ten years from 1987 to 1997, the European Union (EU) gradually liberalized the industry, and reduced government intervention. The industry exhibited steady growth. While the four largest European airlines carried 54 million passengers in 1980, the same airlines carried 147 million passengers in 2000.[7] Despite the steady growth in passenger traffic, however, many of the large European airlines, such as British Airways, KLM, Lufthansa, and SAS, reported volatile performance during the 2000s and on occasion were forced to undergo internal restructuring. Other national carriers, such as Sabena, Swissair, and Alitalia, went through bankruptcy. What accounted for this low profitability? What was the effect of liberalization on competition? What was the European airline industry's future profit potential?

## COMPETITION IN THE EUROPEAN AIRLINE INDUSTRY
Following the liberalization of the industry, the competition has been very intense for a number of reasons:

- Rivalry – industry growth. Between 2001 and 2016, the average annual industry growth was a moderate 4 percent. The industry growth was negative in the years immediately following the September 11, 2001, terrorist attacks and the start of the credit crisis, compared with an average of 5 percent in the other years.[8]
- Rivalry – concentration. The industry was fragmented. While several new airlines had entered the industry after the liberalization period, very few of the inefficient and loss-making national carriers left the industry. Several of these airlines were kept from bankruptcy or being taken over through government intervention or support. Further, regulatory hurdles in restructuring situations made mergers economically less attractive by complicating renegotiations of lease or labor contracts.
- Rivalry – differentiation and switching costs. Services delivered by different airlines on short-haul flights, within Europe, were virtually identical, and, with the possible exception of frequent flyer programs, there were few opportunities to differentiate the products. Switching costs across different airlines were also low because in some areas airports were geographically close and code-sharing agreements increased the number of alternatives that passengers could consider.
- Rivalry – excess capacity. The European airlines had a structural excess capacity problem. Between 2001 and 2016, the five largest European airlines had an average annual passenger load factor, which measures the percentage of passenger seats filled, of 79 percent. Because airlines lacked the opportunity to differentiate, they engaged in price competition in an attempt to fill the empty seats.
- Threat of new entrants – access to distribution channels/legal barriers. The system that most of the large European airports used to allocate their time slots among the airlines could have created barriers to entry. Slots are the rights to land at, or take off from, an airport at a particular date and time. In the twice-yearly allocation of time slots, priority was given to airlines that had slots in the previous season. However, new airlines also successfully managed to enter the European market by using alternative, smaller airports in the vicinity of those used by the established airlines. Most of these new entrants focused on offering low-fare, no-frills flights. Early new entrants were low-cost carriers easyJet and Ryanair, which experienced explosive growth and forced the incumbent airlines to start competing on price. In fact, the total number of passengers that easyJet and Ryanair carried increased from about 18 million passengers in 2001 to 190 million passengers in 2016.
- Threat of new entrants. New entrants had easy access to capital. Purchased aircraft served to securitize loans, or aircraft could be leased. Further, secondhand aircraft became cheap during industry downturns, when troubled airlines disposed of excess capacity.

- Threat of new entrants – legal barriers. After 1997 European airlines faced no legal barriers to enter European markets outside their domestic market. Measures taken by the EU to deregulate the industry made it possible for the airlines to freely operate on any route within the EU, instead of having to conform to bilateral agreements between countries.
- Threat of substitute products. High-speed rail networks were being expanded and provided a potential, not yet fully exploited, substitute for air travel over shorter distances.

## THE POWER OF SUPPLIERS AND BUYERS

Suppliers and buyers had significant power over firms in the industry for these reasons:

- Suppliers' bargaining power. Airlines' primary costs for operating passenger flights were airport fees and handling charges, aircraft depreciation and maintenance, fuel, and labor. Although competition among jet fuel suppliers helped to ensure that the fuel prices that suppliers charged to the airlines did not deviate much from market prices, the fluctuations in fuel market prices were beyond airlines' control. Further, during the 1990s ground handling agents at several European airports were monopolists and charged higher handling fees than agents at airports with competition. Liberalization measures taken by the EU promoted competition among ground handling agents, but during the 2000s few airports still had more than two competing agents. In 2011 the EU proposed to improve competition among agents by increasing the minimum number of competing ground handling agents per airport from two to three. Finally, European airline employees had significant power over their employers since their job security tended to be well protected and the threat of a strike was an efficient bargaining tool in labor negotiations.

   Ninety percent of the aircraft that European airlines had acquired or leased came from two commercial aircraft manufacturers, Airbus and Boeing. The strong dependence of European airlines on only two aircraft suppliers potentially impaired airlines' bargaining power. However, because the overall demand for new aircraft was low, airlines remained relatively powerful in their negotiations with aircraft manufacturers.
- Buyers' bargaining power. Buyers gained more power because of the development of web booking systems, which made market prices transparent. Buyers were price-sensitive since they increasingly viewed air travel as a commodity. Being able to easily compare prices across different airlines substantially increased the buyers' bargaining power.

As a result of the intense rivalry and low barriers to entry in the European airline industry, there was severe price competition among different airlines. Further, also during the 2000s government interference kept the national carriers from entering into mergers. Instead, they created alliances that did not sufficiently reduce or reallocate capacity. These factors led to a low profit potential in the industry. The power of suppliers and buyers reduced the profit potential further.

There were indications of change in the basic structure of the European airline industry. First, most of the established airlines cut capacity in 2002, which led to a three percentage point improvement in the passenger load factor. The average load factor continued to increase from 74 percent in 2002 to close to 84 percent in 2017. Second, in 2003 the merger between two established airlines, Air France and KLM, was one of the first signs of consolidation in the industry. Consolidation progressed slowly when Lufthansa acquired Austrian Airlines, BMI (in 2009) and Brussels Airlines (in 2011) and when British Airways and Iberia merged in 2010. Third, in 2007 the EU negotiated an "open skies" agreement with the United States, which substituted for all the bilateral agreements between European governments and the United States and opened up a new market for European airlines. As Figure 2.2 illustrates, these structural changes have led to a gradual lessening of competition and improvement in profitability. In fact, although during the early 2010s Europe's national carriers reported below normal profitability, earning significantly lower returns on equity than required by investors, the national carriers' profitability has steadily increased in recent years, mirroring the positive trends in the low-fare, no-frills segment of the industry.

**FIGURE 2.2** Profitability in the European airline industry

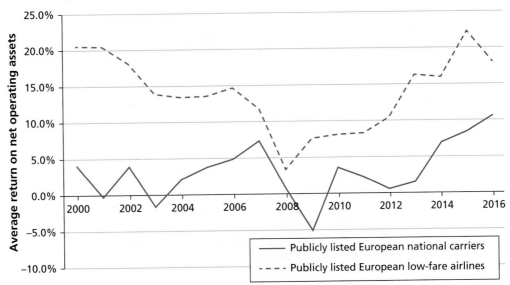

## LIMITATIONS OF INDUSTRY ANALYSIS

A potential limitation of the industry analysis framework discussed in this chapter is the assumption that industries have clear boundaries. In reality, it is often not easy to clearly demarcate industry boundaries. For example, in analyzing the European airline industry, should one focus on the short-haul flight segment or the airline industry as a whole? Should one include charter flights and cargo transport in the industry definition? Should one consider only the airlines domiciled in Europe or also the airlines from other continents that operate flights to Europe? Inappropriate industry definition will result in incomplete analysis and inaccurate forecasts.

# Competitive strategy analysis

The profitability of a firm is influenced not only by its industry structure but also by the strategic choices it makes to cope with or change the industry's competitive forces. A firm may take strategic actions that aim at changing the industry's structure and profit potential. Examples of such actions are the mergers and acquisitions taking place in the European airline industry, which could ultimately reduce the industry's fragmentation and increase average profitability. Alternatively, a firm may take the industry structure as given and choose a set of activities that help it to carve out a profitable position within the industry. While there are many ways to characterize a firm's business strategy, as Figure 2.3 shows, there are two generic competitive strategies: (1) **cost leadership** and (2) **differentiation**.[9] Both these strategies can potentially allow a firm to build a sustainable competitive advantage. Strategy researchers have traditionally viewed cost leadership and differentiation as mutually exclusive strategies. Firms that straddle the two strategies are considered to be "stuck in the middle" and are expected to earn low profitability.[10] These firms run the risk of not being able to attract price-conscious customers because the firms' costs are too high; they are also unable to provide adequate differentiation to attract premium price customers.

## SOURCES OF COMPETITIVE ADVANTAGE

Cost leadership enables a firm to supply the same product or service offered by its competitors at a lower cost. Differentiation strategy involves providing a product or service that is distinct in some important respect valued by the customer. As an example in food retailing, UK-based Sainsbury's competes on the basis of differentiation by emphasizing the high quality of its food and service and by operating an online grocery store. In contrast, Germany-based Aldi and Lidl are discount retailers competing purely on a low-cost basis.

**FIGURE 2.3** Strategies for creating competitive advantage

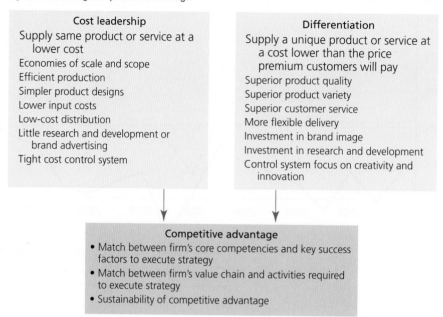

## Competitive strategy 1: Cost leadership

Cost leadership is often the clearest way to achieve competitive advantage. In industries or industry segments where the basic product or service is a commodity, cost leadership might be the only way to achieve superior performance. There are many ways to achieve cost leadership, including economies of scale and scope, economies of learning, efficient production, simpler product design, lower input costs, and efficient organizational processes. If a firm can achieve cost leadership, then it will be able to earn above-average profitability by merely charging the same price as its rivals. Conversely, a cost leader can force its competitors to cut prices and accept lower returns, or to exit the industry. For example, the entry of low-cost carriers to the European airline industry at the end of the 1990s forced the incumbent airlines to change their strategy and focus more on competing through price.

Firms that achieve cost leadership focus on tight cost controls. They make investments in efficient scale plants, focus on product designs that reduce manufacturing costs, minimize overhead costs, make little investment in risky research and development, and avoid serving marginal customers. They have organizational structures and control systems that focus on cost control.

## Competitive strategy 2: Differentiation

A firm following the differentiation strategy seeks to be unique in its industry along some dimension that is highly valued by customers. For differentiation to be successful, the firm has to accomplish three things. First, it needs to identify one or more attributes of a product or service that customers value. Second, it has to position itself to meet the chosen customer need in a unique manner. Finally, the firm has to achieve differentiation at a cost that is lower than the price the customer is willing to pay for the differentiated product or service.

Drivers of differentiation include providing superior intrinsic value via product quality, product variety, bundled services, or delivery timing. Differentiation can also be achieved by investing in signals of value such as brand image, product appearance, or reputation. Differentiated strategies require investments in research and development, engineering skills, and marketing capabilities. The organizational structures and control systems in firms with differentiation strategies need to foster creativity and innovation.

While successful firms choose between cost leadership and differentiation, they cannot completely ignore the dimension on which they are not primarily competing. Firms that target differentiation still need to focus on costs so that the differentiation can be achieved at an acceptable cost. Similarly, cost leaders cannot compete unless they achieve at least a minimum level on key dimensions on which competitors might differentiate, such as quality and service.

## ACHIEVING AND SUSTAINING COMPETITIVE ADVANTAGE

The choice of competitive strategy does not automatically lead to the achievement of competitive advantage. To achieve competitive advantage, the firm has to have the capabilities needed to implement and sustain the chosen strategy. Both cost leadership and differentiation strategy require that the firm makes the necessary commitments to acquire the core competencies needed, and structures its value chain in an appropriate way. Core competencies are the economic assets that the firm possesses, whereas the value chain is the set of activities that the firm performs to convert inputs into outputs. The uniqueness of a firm's core competencies and its value chain determine the sustainability of a firm's competitive advantage.[11] What makes a competitive strategy unique and thus successful in achieving a sustainable competitive advantage?[12]

- Unique core competencies. It is important that the resources supporting the core competencies cannot be acquired easily by competitors or substituted for by other resources. This tends to be the case if resources are, for example, physically unique (such as location or pharmaceutical patents), path-dependent, and the result of a long history of development (such as Microsoft's Windows operating system), or difficult to identify or comprehend for outsiders (what exactly determines Apple's success?).
- System of activities. Another important characteristic of a sustainable competitive strategy is that it comprises a *system* of activities that fit with the strategy and potentially reinforce each other. A coherent system of activities is difficult for competitors to imitate, especially when such activities require a trade-off. For example, when low-cost carriers like Ryanair and easyJet entered the European airline industry, traditional carriers initially responded by lowering service levels (and prices) on short-haul routes. The incumbent airlines would, however, not be able to effectively compete on price without trading off on, for example, the scope of flight networks, the diversity of ticket sales channels, and the quality of service levels in business class, thereby potentially alienating their traditional customer base. This focus on systems of activities distinguishes the concept of competitive strategy from operational effectiveness. Single tools that companies use to achieve operational effectiveness, such as incentive or inventory management systems, can be easily adopted by competitors and thus rarely help to create a sustainable competitive advantage.
- Positioning. To achieve a sustainable competitive advantage – or escape competition – firms often identify or carve out a profitable subsegment of an industry. The identification of such subsegments could be based on (1) particular product or service varieties (e.g., Tesla's focus on selling electric cars), (2) the needs of a particular customer group (e.g., Ferrari's focus on the luxury segment of the car manufacturing industry), or (3) particular access and distribution channels (e.g., online sales versus physical stores).

To evaluate whether a firm is likely to achieve its intended competitive advantage, the analyst should ask the following questions:

- What are the key success factors and risks associated with the firm's chosen competitive strategy?
- Does the firm currently have the resources and capabilities (core competencies) to deal with the key success factors and risks?
- Has the firm made irreversible commitments to bridge the gap between its current capabilities and the requirements to achieve its competitive advantage?
- Has the firm structured its activities (such as research and development, design, manufacturing, marketing and distribution, and support activities) in a way that is consistent with its competitive strategy? Do these activities reinforce each other in some way?
- Has the company been able to identify or carve out a profitable subsegment of the industry?
- Is the company's competitive advantage sustainable? Are there any barriers that make imitation of the firm's strategy difficult?

- Are there any potential changes in the firm's industry structure (such as new technologies, foreign competition, changes in regulation, changes in customer requirements) that might dissipate the firm's competitive advantage? Is the company flexible enough to address these changes? Is the firm or its competitors taking any strategic actions that aim at changing the industry structure?

## APPLYING COMPETITIVE STRATEGY ANALYSIS

Let us consider the concepts of competitive strategy analysis in the context of IKEA. In 2017 Sweden-based IKEA was the world's largest furniture retailer. The company, founded by Ingvar Kamprad as a mail-order company, bought its first furniture factory and showroom in 1953. During the 1960s IKEA started to develop the operating concept that the company is still renowned for: selling flat-packed furniture through large warehouse stores. In those years IKEA also started to expand internationally.

While continuously expanding its worldwide store base, IKEA firmly established itself in the furniture retailing industry by following a low-cost strategy. IKEA's average annual revenue growth rate during the 16 years between 2001 and 2017 was approximately 8 percent. During fiscal year 2017 IKEA generated a gross profit margin of 35 percent on €36.3 billion in revenues. This margin was well above those of some of IKEA's larger peers, such as US-based Target and Sears (both less than 30 percent). IKEA was one of the most successful and, presumably, one of the most profitable furniture retailers in the industry. How did IKEA achieve such performance?

IKEA's superior performance was based on a low-cost competitive strategy that consisted of the following key elements:[13]

- Global strategy. IKEA followed a purely global strategy. In each of the 49 countries where the retailer operated its stores, it targeted the same customer group – young families and young couples – and offered virtually the same selection of furniture. This strategy of strong economic integration and low responsiveness to national cultures helped the company to achieve economies of scale.
- Sourcing of production. IKEA did not own any production facilities other than Swedwood, which supplied 10 percent of its furniture. Instead, the company outsourced its production to manufacturers located throughout the world. Because IKEA had developed a network of more than one thousand suppliers in over 50 countries, the company could choose among a large number of manufacturers. Often, the company was a manufacturer's sole customer. Consequently, IKEA had substantial bargaining power in its dealings with its suppliers, which kept input costs to a minimum.
- Economic designs. Although IKEA outsourced its production, the company kept tight control of the design of its furniture. Its designers worked two to three years ahead of production to have sufficient time to find the most economic design solutions and review potential suppliers.
- Logistics. IKEA incorporated logistics into its strategy. The company operated large warehouse stores on relatively cheap locations outside the city centers. These warehouse stores sold furniture in flat-pack format that customers assembled at home. The integration of stores and warehouses and the use of flat-packs helped IKEA to economize on costs for storage and transportation.
- Sales. IKEA stores were able to employ fewer sales staff than other stores because customers needed little assistance. All warehouse stores were designed such that customers, after having made their choice, picked the flat-packs from the shelves and paid for their purchases at a central location in the store. IKEA also provided its customers with limited after-sales service. Through this strategy, the company was able to keep personnel expenses to a minimum.

As a result of the preceding strategy, IKEA achieved a significant cost advantage over its competitors in the furniture retailing industry. Consequently, IKEA was able to continuously cut prices and maintain the price difference with its competitors. Because over the years the company had made large investments in knowledge of low-cost furniture design, store design, and logistics, the business model was difficult to replicate, making its competitive advantage sustainable. Although IKEA's brand image varied greatly across countries, in some countries it had become a cult brand. In 2017 Interbrand. estimated the value of the IKEA brand at €15.4 billion. This value was similar to the value of brands such as Gillette, Zara, H&M, and Pepsi. The strength of the retailer's brand name, the diversity in its assortment, and the distinctiveness of its designs illustrate that IKEA's strategy also exhibited some characteristics of a differentiation strategy.[14] However, the company's continuous focus on cost control was most likely the main driver of success. IKEA's success inspired some local competitors to attempt to replicate parts of its strategy. However, no competitor to date has been able to replicate the business model on a similar scale.

## Corporate strategy analysis

So far in this chapter we have focused on the strategies at the individual business level. While some companies focus on only one business, many companies operate in multiple businesses. For example, of all companies that were listed on one of the primary European exchanges at the end of 2016, 39 percent operated in more than two business segments.[15] In the 1990s and 2000s, there has been an attempt by US and Western European companies to reduce the diversity of their operations and focus on a relatively few "core" businesses. However, multi-business organizations continue to dominate the economic activity in many countries in the world.

When analyzing a multi-business organization, an analyst has to not only evaluate the industries and strategies of the individual business units but also the economic consequences – either positive or negative – of managing all the different businesses under one corporate umbrella. For example, General Electric has been very successful in creating significant value by managing a highly diversified set of businesses ranging from aircraft engines to light bulbs. In contrast, shareholders of several European conglomerates, such as Siemens and thyssenkrupp, pressured their companies to improve profitability by spinning off their "noncore" divisions.

### SOURCES OF VALUE CREATION AT THE CORPORATE LEVEL

Economists and strategy researchers have identified several factors that influence an organization's ability to create value through a broad corporate scope. Economic theory suggests that the optimal activity scope of a firm depends on the relative transaction cost of performing a set of activities inside the firm versus using the market mechanism.[16] Transaction cost economics implies that the multiproduct firm is an efficient choice of organizational form when coordination among independent, focused firms is costly due to market transaction costs.

Transaction costs can arise out of several sources. They may arise if the production process involves specialized assets such as human capital skills, proprietary technology, or other organizational know-how that is not easily available in the marketplace. Transaction costs also may arise from market imperfections such as information and incentive problems. If buyers and sellers cannot solve these problems through standard mechanisms such as enforceable contracts, it will be costly to conduct transactions through market mechanisms.

For example, as discussed in Chapter 1, public capital markets may not work well when there are significant information and incentive problems, making it difficult for entrepreneurs to raise capital from investors. Similarly, if buyers cannot ascertain the quality of products being sold because of lack of information or cannot enforce warranties because of poor legal infrastructure, entrepreneurs will find it difficult to break into new markets. Finally, if employers cannot assess the quality of applicants for new positions, they will have to rely more on internal promotions rather than external recruiting to fill higher positions in an organization. Emerging economies often suffer from these types of transaction costs because of poorly developed intermediation infrastructure.[17] Even in many advanced economies, examples of high transaction costs can be found. For example, in many countries other than the United States and Western European nations, the venture capital industry is not highly developed, making it costly for new businesses in high technology industries to attract financing. Even in Europe and the United States, transaction costs may vary across economic sectors. For example, until recently electronic commerce was hampered by consumer concerns regarding the security of credit card information sent over the internet.

Transactions inside an organization may be less costly than market-based transactions for several reasons:

- Information. Communication costs inside an organization are reduced because confidentiality can be protected and credibility can be assured through internal mechanisms.
- Enforcement. The headquarters office can play a critical role in reducing costs of enforcing agreements between organizational subunits.
- Asset sharing. Organizational subunits can share valuable non-tradable assets (such as organizational skills, systems, and processes) or non-divisible assets (such as brand names, distribution channels, and reputation).

There are also forces that increase transaction costs inside organizations. Top management of an organization may lack the specialized information and skills necessary to manage businesses across several different industries. This lack of expertise reduces the possibility of actually realizing economies of scope, even when there is potential for such economies. This problem can be remedied by creating a decentralized organization, hiring specialist managers to run each business unit, and providing these managers with proper incentives. However, decentralization will also potentially decrease goal congruence among subunit managers, making it difficult to realize economies of scope.

Whether or not a multi-business organization creates more value than a comparable collection of focused firms is therefore context-dependent.[18] Analysts should ask the following questions to assess whether an organization's corporate strategy has the potential to create value:

- Are there significant imperfections in the product, labor, or financial markets in the industries (or countries) in which a company is operating? Is it likely that transaction costs in these markets are higher than the costs of similar activities inside a well-managed organization?
- Does the organization have special resources such as brand names, proprietary know-how, access to scarce distribution channels, and special organizational processes that have the potential to create economies of scope?
- Is there a good fit between the company's specialized resources and the portfolio of businesses in which the company is operating?
- Does the company allocate decision rights between the headquarters office and the business units optimally to realize all the potential economies of scope?
- Does the company have internal measurement, information, and incentive systems to align interests within the organization and increase coordination across business units?

Empirical evidence suggests that creating value through a multi-business corporate strategy is hard in practice. Several researchers have documented that diversified companies trade at a discount in the stock market relative to a comparable portfolio of focused companies.[19] Studies also show that acquisitions of one company by another, especially when the two are in unrelated businesses, often fail to create value for the acquiring companies.[20] Finally, there is considerable evidence that value is created when multi-business companies increase corporate focus through divisional spin-offs and asset sales.[21]

There are several potential explanations for the preceding diversification discount:

- Empire building. Managers' decisions to diversify and expand are frequently driven by a desire to maximize the size of their organization rather than to maximize shareholder value.
- Incentive misalignment. Diversified companies often suffer from incentive misalignment problems. That is, business unit managers typically have incentives to make investment decisions that benefit their own units but may be suboptimal for the firm as a whole, thereby leading to poor operating performance.
- Monitoring problems. Capital markets find it difficult to monitor and value multi-business organizations because of inadequate disclosure about the performance of individual business segments.

In summary, while companies can theoretically create value through innovative corporate strategies, there are many ways in which this potential fails to get realized in practice. Therefore it pays to be skeptical when evaluating companies' corporate strategies.

## APPLYING CORPORATE STRATEGY ANALYSIS

Let us apply the concepts of corporate strategy analysis to easyGroup, a privately owned company that licences the "easy" brand name to, and holds shares in, various no-frills, low-cost businesses. The company's first and primary holding, easyJet, started operations as a low-fare, short-haul airline company in 1995 and five years later placed 28 percent of its shares on the London Stock Exchange (LSE) at an amount of £224 million. The company grew rapidly and began to pose a serious threat in the short-haul segment to the dominance of leading European airlines like Air France, British Airways, and Lufthansa. The easyJet revenues increased from £46 million in 1997 to £5,047 million in 2017.

Flush with his success in selling cheap short-haul flights, Stelios Haji-Ioannou, the founder of easyJet and private owner of easyGroup, stretched the "easy" brand name to other industries. The new ventures that easyGroup started had a few common characteristics. They primarily sold services with high fixed costs and exploited the fact that the demand for a service could be highly elastic to its price. In fact, when demand was low, the ventures sold their services at often drastically reduced prices. Because the easyGroup ventures consistently offered their services through the internet and rewarded customers for booking in advance, they were able to flexibly adjust prices to demand. Further, because of the no-frills character of services and the bypassing of intermediaries in industries such as the travel industry, the ventures were able to keep tight control over their costs. Following this strategy, easyGroup expanded into car rental, pizza delivery, bus transport, cruise travel, office space rental, cinemas, and hotels. In 2014 easyGroup brought its second company to the stock market, placing a proportion of the shares of easyHotel on the LSE's Alternative Investment Market at an amount of £30 million. In an interview, Haji-Ioannou emphasized his unique position: "Brand extension is very tricky. It's like starting another company, all the time. This is the privilege of entrepreneurs spending their own money."[22]

The diversification of easyGroup into unrelated businesses was not without risks. Haji-Ioannou claimed that easy-Group could create value through its broad corporate focus for the following reasons:[23]

- Through easyJet's rapid growth, its marketing strategy, and the innovations that the airline company had brought to the European airline industry, Haji-Ioannou had gained much exposure for his "easy" brand throughout Europe. Making use of easyJet's valuable brand name and its established reputation in offering no-frills services at low prices, Haji-Ioannou could economize on transaction costs in his new ventures. Customers are likely to have greater trust in new businesses that operate under a familiar brand name. Further, brand-stretching can help to economize on advertising. In fact, Haji-Ioannou admitted on occasions that, without the airline, the other businesses were not likely to survive.
- The easyGroup company had been able to acquire critical expertise in flexible pricing and online selling. This is a general competency that can be exploited in many industries.
- The easyGroup revenues came from licensing the "easy" brand and holding financial stakes in easyJet and the new ventures. Haji-Ioannou planned to take a venture public when it had proven to be successful, as he had done with easyJet. Because easyGroup did not produce the services itself, the company shared the risks of production with the ventures' other stakeholders.

There were also signs that easyGroup was expanding too rapidly and that its diversification beyond air travel was likely to be unsuccessful. Very few of the easyGroup's new business ventures were profitable during their first years of operation. For example, at the end of 2003, the losses incurred by easyGroup's internet café chain added up to an estimated £100 million; easyBus, started in 2003, did not report its first pre-tax profit until 2010; the cruise travel company easyCruise was sold in 2009, shortly thereafter ceasing operations. Further, in many of the industries that easyGroup entered, incumbent companies also had valuable brand names, execution capabilities, and customer loyalty. Therefore these companies were likely to offer formidable competition to easyGroup's individual business lines. The critics of easyGroup also pointed out that expanding rapidly into so many different areas was likely to confuse customers, dilute easyGroup's brand value, and increase the chance of poor execution.

An interesting question to examine is whether there are systematic reasons to believe that a company such as easyGroup can succeed in pursuing a wide focus because its business model – online selling of no-frills services at demand-based prices under one common brand – somehow allows it to manage this diversity in a fundamentally different manner than a traditional company would be able to. The poor financial performance of some of easyGroup's ventures during the 2000s and the continued absence of a successor to star venture easyJet casts some doubt on whether the group can succeed as a diversified company.

## Summary

Strategy analysis is an important starting point for the analysis of financial statements because it allows the analyst to probe the economics of the firm at a qualitative level. Strategy analysis also allows the identification of the firm's profit drivers and key risks, enabling the analyst to assess the sustainability of the firm's performance and make realistic forecasts of future performance.

Whether a firm is able to earn a return on its capital in excess of its cost of capital is determined by its own strategic choices:

1  The choice of an industry or a set of industries in which the firm operates (industry choice).

2  The manner in which the firm intends to compete with other firms in its chosen industry or industries (competitive strategy).

3  The way in which the firm expects to create and exploit synergies across the range of businesses in which it operates (corporate strategy). Strategy analysis involves analyzing all three choices.

Industry analysis consists of identifying the economic factors that drive the industry profitability. In general, an industry's average profit potential is influenced by the degree of rivalry among existing competitors, the ease with which new firms can enter the industry, the availability of substitute products, the power of buyers, and the power of suppliers. To perform industry analysis, the analyst has to assess the current strength of each of these forces in an industry and make forecasts of any likely future changes.

Competitive strategy analysis involves identifying the basis on which the firm intends to compete in its industry. In general, two potential strategies could provide a firm with a competitive advantage: cost leadership and differentiation. Cost leadership involves offering at a lower cost the same product or service that other firms offer. Differentiation involves satisfying a chosen dimension of customer need better than the competition, at an incremental cost that is less than the price premium that customers are willing to pay. To perform strategy analysis, the analyst has to identify the firm's intended strategy, assess whether the firm possesses the competencies required to execute the strategy, and recognize the key risks that the firm has to guard against. The analyst also has to evaluate the sustainability of the firm's strategy.

Corporate strategy analysis involves examining whether a company is able to create value by being in multiple businesses at the same time. A well-crafted corporate strategy reduces costs or increases revenues from running several businesses in one firm relative to the same businesses operating independently and transacting with each other in the marketplace. These cost savings or revenue increases come from specialized resources that the firm has that help it to exploit synergies across these businesses. For these resources to be valuable, they must be non-tradable, not easily imitated by competition, and non-divisible. Even when a firm has such resources, it can create value through a multi-business organization only when it is managed so that the information and agency costs inside the organization are less than the market transaction costs.

The insights gained from strategy analysis can be useful in performing the remainder of the financial statement analysis. In accounting analysis the analyst can examine whether a firm's accounting policies and estimates are consistent with its stated strategy. For example, a firm's choice of functional currency in accounting for its international operations should be consistent with the level of integration between domestic and international operations that the business strategy calls for. Similarly, a firm that mainly sells housing to low-income customers should have higher than average bad debt expenses.

Strategy analysis is also useful in guiding financial analysis. For example, in a cross-sectional analysis, the analyst should expect firms with cost leadership strategy to have lower gross margins and higher asset turnover than firms that follow differentiated strategies. In a time series analysis, the analyst should closely monitor any increases in expense ratios and asset turnover ratios for low-cost firms, and any decreases in investments critical to differentiation for firms that follow differentiation strategy.

Business strategy analysis also helps in prospective analysis and valuation. First, it allows the analyst to assess whether, and for how long, differences between the firm's performance and its industry (or industries) performance are likely to persist. Second, strategy analysis facilitates forecasting investment outlays the firm has to make to maintain its competitive advantage.

## Core concepts

**Bargaining power in input and output markets**     One of the two main drivers of an industry's profit potential. The greater the bargaining power of buyers and suppliers, the lower the industry's profit potential.

**Competitive forces**     Five forces that together determine an industry's profit potential through their influence on the degree of actual and potential competition with the industry or the bargaining power in input and output markets.

**Competitive strategy analysis**     Analysis of the strategic choices that a firm has made to position itself in the industry. Firms typically choose between two mutually exclusive strategies: (1) cost leadership or (2) differentiation. The competitive strategy that a firm has chosen and the industry's profit potential together affect the firm's profitability.

**Corporate strategy analysis**     Analysis of a firm's business structure and processes to establish whether and how the firm has minimized, or can potentially minimize, its transaction costs.

**Cost leadership**     Strategy in which a firm achieves a competitive advantage by producing and delivering its products or services at a lower cost than its competitors.

**Differentiation**     Strategy in which a firm achieves a competitive advantage by producing and delivering products or services with unique features at premium prices.

**Industry analysis**     Analysis of an industry's profit potential.

**Industry competition**     One of the two main drivers of an industry's profit potential. The degree of actual and potential competition is determined by three competitive forces: (1) the rivalry among existing firms in the industry; (2) the threat of new entrants to the industry; and (3) the threat of substitute products.

## Questions, exercises, and problems

1 Judith, an accounting student, states, "Strategy analysis seems to be an unnecessary detour in doing financial statement analysis. Why can't we just get straight to the accounting issues?" Explain to Judith why she might be wrong.

2 What are the critical drivers of industry profitability?

3 One of the fastest growing industries in the past 25 years is the memory chip industry, which supplies memory chips for personal computers and other electronic devices. Yet the average profitability for this industry has been very low. Using the industry analysis framework, list all the potential factors that might explain this apparent contradiction.

4 Joe argues, "Your analysis of the five forces that affect industry profitability is incomplete. For example, in the banking industry, I can

think of at least three other factors that are also important, namely, government regulation, demographic trends, and cultural factors." His classmate Jane disagrees and says, "These three factors are important only to the extent that they influence one of the five forces." Explain how, if at all, the three factors discussed by Joe affect the five forces in the banking industry.

5 Examples of European firms that operate in the pharmaceutical industry are GlaxoSmithKline and Bayer. Examples of European firms that operate in the tour operating industry are Thomas Cook and TUI. Rate the pharmaceutical and tour operating industries as high, medium, or low on the following dimensions of industry structure:

1 Rivalry.

2 Threat of new entrants.

3   Threat of substitute products.

4   Bargaining power of suppliers.

5   Bargaining power of buyers.

Given your ratings, which industry would you expect to earn the highest returns?

6   In 2017 Adidas was a profitable sportswear company. Traditionally, Adidas did not produce most of the shoes, apparel, and accessories that it sold. Instead, the company entered into contracts with independent manufacturers. Adidas also licensed independent companies throughout the world to design, develop, produce, and distribute a selected range of products under its brand name. Gradually, Adidas started to open its own production facilities closer to its consumers in order to become more responsive to changes in consumer trends and demands. Use the five-forces framework and your knowledge of the sportswear industry to explain Adidas's high profitability in 2017.

7   In response to the deregulation of the European airline industry during the 1980s and 1990s, European airlines followed their US peers in starting frequent flyer programs as a way to differentiate themselves from others. Industry analysts, however, believe that frequent flyer programs had only mixed success. Use the competitive advantage concepts to explain why.

8   What are the ways that a firm can create barriers to entry to deter competition in its business? What factors determine whether these barriers are likely to be enduring?

9   Explain why you agree or disagree with each of the following statements:

a   It's better to be a differentiator than a cost leader, since you can then charge premium prices.

b   It's more profitable to be in a high technology than a low technology industry.

c   The reason why industries with large investments have high barriers to entry is because it is costly to raise capital.

10  Very few companies are able to be both cost leaders and differentiators. Why? Can you think of a company that has been successful at both?

11  Many consultants are advising diversified companies in emerging markets such as India, Korea, Mexico, and Turkey to adopt corporate strategies proven to be of value in advanced economies like the United States and Western Europe. What are the pros and cons of this advice?

## Problem 1 The European airline industry

Up until the mid-2010s, the Association of European Airlines (AEA) represented 24 established European airlines, mostly national flag carriers such as Air France–KLM, Lufthansa, Finnair, and SAS, but also some cargo specialists such as TNT and Cargolux. The AEA continuously surveyed its members and published reports and statistics about its members' passenger and cargo traffic and capacity and operating performance. Although the members of the AEA did not represent the whole European airline industry, the AEA statistics were a useful source of information about the state of the industry. In this chapter we described developments in the European airline industry during the period 1995–2016. Table 2.1 is a selection of statistics illustrating the developments in the industry during a sub-period, the years 2004–2014.

Revenue passenger kilometres (RPK) is the number of passengers transported times the average number of kilometres flown. Load factors are defined as the ratio of realized RPKs and available seat kilometres (ASK). Use the preceding information to answer the following questions about whether and how competition in the European airline industry changed between 2004 and 2014:

1   Evaluate how the rivalry among existing firms developed during the period.

2   Consider the consolidated statistics of two large European airlines. Evaluate the influence of fuel prices on the profitability of the airlines' passenger business between 2004 and 2014. If fuel prices had not increased after 2004, what would have been the pre-interest breakeven load factor during the following years (assuming all other factors constant)? What does this imply about the European airline industry?

3   During the period examined, some airlines started to charge fuel surcharges to their customers. For example, in late 2007 KLM started to charge its customers €25 on European flights and €70 on intercontinental flights. Other airlines introduced similar surcharges. How do such practices affect your answer to question 2?

TABLE 2.1 European airline industry statistics

| | 2004 | 2005 | 2006 | 2007 | 2008 | 2009 | 2010 | 2011 | 2012 | 2013 | 2014 |
|---|---|---|---|---|---|---|---|---|---|---|---|
| **Statistics of AEA airlines** | | | | | | | | | | | |
| Market share (RPK) of the 4 largest AEA airlines (%) | 64.8 | 65.4 | 64.3 | 64.9 | 66.4 | 67.0 | 75.8 | 77.7 | 77.1 | 79.5 | 80.8 |
| Revenue passenger kilometres [RPK] (in billions) | 656.7 | 699.5 | 741.6 | 793.1 | 801.1 | 769.0 | 787.5 | 852.1 | 881.0 | 900.4 | 931.9 |
| RPK growth (%) | 9.7 | 6.5 | 6.0 | 6.9 | 1.0 | -4.0 | 2.4 | 8.2 | 3.4 | 2.2 | 3.5 |
| Available seat kilometres [ASK] (billions) | 880.1 | 922.1 | 970.7 | 1,014.4 | 1,040.8 | 1,001.2 | 1,000.2 | 1,089.2 | 1,105.6 | 1,119.9 | 1,155.8 |
| ASK growth (%) | 7.9 | 4.8 | 5.3 | 4.5 | 2.6 | -3.8 | -0.1 | 8.9 | 1.5 | 1.3 | 3.2 |
| Passenger load factor (%) | 74.6 | 75.9 | 76.4 | 78.2 | 77.0 | 76.8 | 78.7 | 78.2 | 79.7 | 80.4 | 80.6 |
| **RPKs of selected low-cost carriers (billions)** | | | | | | | | | | | |
| Air Berlin | – | 22.9 | 24.5 | 46.1 | 44.3 | 43.9 | 47.0 | 52.1 | 50.4 | 48.6 | 49.3 |
| easyJet | – | 27.4 | 31.6 | 37.0 | 47.7 | 50.6 | 56.1 | 61.3 | 65.2 | 67.6 | 72.9 |
| Ryanair | – | 32.7 | 43.4 | 55.4 | 63.1 | 72.2 | 85.7 | 94.3 | 96.3 | 103.8 | 112.5 |
| **Consolidated statistics of two large European airlines** | | | | | | | | | | | |
| Average revenue per RPK (in EUR cents) | 9.09 | 9.23 | 9.77 | 9.81 | 9.82 | 8.73 | 9.58 | 9.40 | 9.82 | 9.60 | 9.31 |
| Average cost per ASK (in EUR cents) | 7.15 | 7.32 | 7.64 | 7.70 | 8.01 | 7.50 | 7.96 | 7.86 | 8.26 | 8.06 | 7.87 |
| Breakeven load factor (%) | 78.7 | 79.3 | 78.2 | 78.5 | 81.6 | 85.8 | 83.2 | 83.7 | 84.1 | 83.9 | 84.5 |
| Fuel cost as a % of total average cost | 14.9 | 19.0 | 21.8 | 22.4 | 26.6 | 21.8 | 24.9 | 26.4 | 30.3 | 29.3 | 28.6 |

Sources: Association of European Airlines; annual reports of selected European airlines.

## Notes

1 The discussion presented here is intended to provide a basic background in strategy analysis. For a more complete discussion of the strategy concepts, see, for example, *Contemporary Strategy Analysis* by Robert M. Grant (Oxford: Blackwell Publishers, 2005); *Economics of Strategy* by David Besanko, David Dranove, and Mark Shanley (New York: John Wiley & Sons, 2004); *Strategy and the Business Landscape* by Pankaj Ghemawat (London: Pearson Education, 2005); and *Corporate Strategy: Resources and the Scope of the Firm* by David J. Collis and Cynthia Montgomery (Burr Ridge, IL: Irwin/McGraw-Hill, 1997).

2 The data to calculate these statistics come from S&P's Compustat Global database. The statistics apply to all companies that were listed between January 1998 and December 2017 on one of the primary European stock exchanges (see the appendix to Chapter 1 for more details about the sample of European companies).

3 For a summary of this research, see *Industrial Market Structure and Economic Performance*, 2nd ed., by F.M. Scherer (Chicago: Rand McNally College Publishing Co., 1980).

4 See *Competitive Strategy* by Michael E. Porter (New York: The Free Press, 1980) and Michael E. Porter, "The Five Competitive Forces That Shape Strategy," *Harvard Business Review* (January 2008).

5 The four-firm concentration ratio is a commonly used measure of industry concentration; it refers to the market share of the four largest firms in an industry.

6 While the discussion here uses the buyer to connote industrial buyers, the same concepts also apply to buyers of consumer products. Throughout this chapter we use the terms buyers and customers interchangeably.

7 The industry statistics in this section are drawn from the Association of European Airlines (AEA) yearbooks and STAR database.

8 The growth rates represent the (weighted) average annual growth rates in the number of passengers on flights from or to the airports of 31 European countries, as reported by Eurostat.

9 For a more detailed discussion of these two sources of competitive advantage, see Michael E. Porter, *Competitive Advantage: Creating and Sustaining Superior Performance* (New York: The Free Press, 1985).

10 Ibid.

11 See *Competing for the Future* by Gary Hammel and C.K. Prahalad (Boston: Harvard Business School Press, 1994) for a more detailed discussion of the concept of core competencies and their critical role in corporate strategy.

12 See Michael E. Porter, "What Is Strategy?" *Harvard Business Review* (November–December, 1996).

13 See Kenny Capell, "IKEA, How the Swedish Retailer Became a Global Cult Brand," *Business Week,* November 14, 2005; K. Kling and I. Goteman, "IKEA CEO Anders Dahlvig on International Growth and IKEA's Unique Corporate Culture and Brand Identity," *Academy of Management Executive* (2003): 31–37; R. Normann and R. Ramirez, "From Value Chain to Value Constellation: Designing Interactive Strategy," *Harvard Business Review* 71 (1993): 65–77; *Yearly Summary FY13*, IKEA Group; Capell, op. cit.

14 One of the strategic challenges faced by corporations is having to deal with competitors who achieve differentiation with low cost. For example, Japanese auto manufacturers have successfully demonstrated that there is no necessary trade-off between quality and cost. The example of IKEA also suggests that combining low cost and differentiation strategies is possible when a firm introduces a significant technical or business innovation. However, such cost advantage and differentiation will be sustainable only if there are significant barriers to imitation by competitors.

15 Business segment data come from Thomson Financial's Worldscope database.

16 The following works are seminal to transaction cost economics: Ronald Coase, "The Nature of the Firm," *Economica* 4 (1937): 386–405; Oliver Williamson, *Markets and Hierarchies: Analysis and Antitrust Implications* (New York: The Free Press, 1975); David Teece, "Toward an Economic Theory of the Multi-Product Firm," *Journal of Economic Behavior and Organization* 3 (1982): 39–63.

17 For a more complete discussion of these issues, see Krishna Palepu and Tarun Khanna, "Building Institutional Infrastructure in Emerging Markets," *Brown Journal of World Affairs* (Winter/Spring 1998); and Tarun Khanna and Krishna Palepu, "Why Focused Strategies May Be Wrong for Emerging Markets," *Harvard Business Review* (July/August 1997).

18 For an empirical study that illustrates this point, see Tarun Khanna and Krishna Palepu, "Is Group Affiliation Profitable in Emerging Markets? An Analysis of Diversified Indian Business Groups," *Journal of Finance* (April 2000): 867–891.

19 See Larry Lang and Rene Stulz, "Tobin's q, Diversification, and Firm Performance," *Journal of Political Economy* 102 (1994): 1248–1280; and Phillip Berger and Eli Ofek, "Diversification's Effect on Firm Value," *Journal of Financial Economics* 37 (1994): 39–65.

20 See Paul Healy, Krishna Palepu, and Richard Ruback, "Which Takeovers Are Profitable: Strategic or Financial?" *Sloan Management Review* 38 (Summer 1997): 45–57.

21 See Katherine Schipper and Abbie Smith, "Effects of Recontracting on Shareholder Wealth: The Case of Voluntary Spinoffs," *Journal of Financial Economics* 12 (December 1983): 437–467; L. Lang, A. Poulsen, and R. Stulz, "Asset Sales, Firm Performance, and the Agency Costs of Managerial Discretion," *Journal of Financial Economics* 37 (January 1995): 3–37.

22 "Stelios on Painting the World Orange," *Brand Strategy* (February 2005): 18–19.

23 Ibid.

# Akris: Competition in the high-end fashion industry

In 1979, Albert Kriemler, a 19-year-old fresh high school graduate, traveled to New York for the first time. Exploring the streets of the Big Apple, he stopped to peer through the shop windows of Bergdorf Goodman, the city's most famous high-end luxury department store. Captivated by the display, he dreamed of one day showcasing his own fashion collection in this "fashion window of the world," which, nine years later, is what he did.

Today, Albert Kriemler is the only Swiss fashion designer whose collections successfully compete with the top segment of the international fashion industry. Akris is also the only Swiss fashion brand that has been elected as a member of the prestigious "Fédération Française de la Couture du Prêt-à-porter des Couturiers et des Créateurs de Mode." Akris is worn by many of the most famous celebrities, among them the US First Lady Michelle Obama, Former US Secretary of State Condoleezza Rice, Princess Charlene of Monaco, and Oscar-winning actress Nicole Kidman.

Together with his brother Peter, Albert Kriemler manages the fashion firm Akris, which was founded and is still based in St. Gallen, Switzerland. Today, the firm's vision reads, "*Akris is the fashion and accessories house for a modern female elite.*"[1] It took only a few years to develop the rather small firm in a remote location in the Eastern part of Switzerland into a globally acclaimed prêt-à-porter brand. Like the "haute couture" fashion segment, the prêt-à-porter segment relies on superior craftsmanship, but is also suitable for everyday wear, thus targeting a broader group of women than haute couture. Expanding its positioning, the company also started a less expensive designer sportswear line called Akris punto.

But what is the secret to such success in the highly competitive fashion industry? How was Akris able to claw its way to the top of the fashion industry? What competitive advantages did Akris gain over the past years? What are Akris's options for future development? What opportunities and threats does the company face? These and other related topics will be illustrated in this case study.

## From a pinafore producer to a globally acclaimed prêt-à-porter brand

Today, Akris is a luxury consumer goods firm. The family-owned business, which is based in St. Gallen, produces and markets prêt-à-porter women's clothing and accessories. But this was not always the case; Akris has changed its game plan a few times since it was founded by Alice Kriemler-Schoch more than 90 years ago.

This case was prepared by Prof. Dr. Günter Müller-Stewens, University of St. Gallen, and Prof. Dr. Markus Menz, University of Geneva, Switzerland. Its objective is to illustrate how a firm gains and sustains a competitive advantage. It is intended to be used as the basis for class discussion rather than to illustrate either effective or ineffective handling of a management situation. Our information sources included interviews with Akris management, as well as publicly available corporate information (press releases, website of Akris AG) and press articles. We would like to thank Albert and Peter Kriemler of Akris for their support.

**Case study reference no** ECCH 312-166-1. This case - German or English version - can be downloaded at The Case Centre: http://www.thecasecentre.org.

[1]Source: Akris.

## MILESTONES

Up to the early 1980s, Akris was a local family business in the former textile center of St. Gallen, a city in the Eastern part of Switzerland with a population of 73,500. The Kriemler family who founded and still owns Akris has been living there for many generations. The third generation of owners systematically developed the firm, which was deeply rooted in its rich tradition, into one of the few globally visible prêt-à-porter brands. Retrospectively, not only the persistence and speed of this development is remarkable, but also the discretion with which it took place: the company did not market its products using celebrity customers, stage image campaigns, or deliberately provoke media attention.

- 1921/22/23: In 1921, Alice Schoch (1896–1972) married Albert Kriemler with whom she has two sons: Max (1922) and Ernst (1923). During the poor times following World War I, Alice Kriemler-Schoch founded the firm in St. Gallen with the seed capital of one sewing machine. She named the firm Akris, an acronym for A(lice)Kri(emler)S(choch). The business mainly manufactured pinafores. Albert traveled, selling the pinafores, but faced stagnating demand in the aftermath of the 1920s' "knitting crisis."
- 1945: After the sudden death of his father, Max Kriemler took over the firm's leadership. He developed the firm from a pinafore producer to a fashion firm. The brand Akris was subsequently expanded with various dress collections.
- 1960s/70s: Max Kriemler established contacts in Paris, primarily because he wanted to produce fashion for couturiers, such as Hubert de Givenchy, St Clair, and Ted Lapidus. The textile connection between St. Gallen and Paris was already well established, as demonstrated by the daily direct train connections between these two cities during that time. From a small pinafore producer with 15 seamstresses, Max Kriemler and his wife Ute Kriemler-Winkhaus develop an internationally oriented business with about 300 employees and CHF 30 m in revenue by the early 1980s. There are production facilities in St. Gallen, Zurich, and Mendrisio (Ticino).
- 1980/82: At the age of 20, Albert Kriemler (born 1960), the son of Max and Ute Kriemler, entered the family business. He was planning on starting an internship at Givenchy in Paris, but when an important employee of his father suddenly died, Albert was asked to help out. In 1982, Albert Kriemler took over responsibility for the Akris collections, although he was not formally educated as a fashion designer.
- 1984: Akris launched an own sales organization in the US, which eventually becomes one of the firm's most important markets.
- 1986: Right after graduating in business administration and law from the University of St. Gallen, Albert's brother Peter Kriemler (born 1962) joined the family business. The brothers officially took over the management of the firm from Max Kriemler. Since then Peter has been the company's managing director with responsibility for management and technical functions, such as logistics and production, while Albert has been responsible for design, creation, and marketing.
- 1980s: Akris had more than 200 employees and had built up revenues of about 50 million Swiss Francs. The fashion was produced at locations in St. Gallen, Zurich, Mendrisio/Ticino and – via a joint venture – in Romania. Owing to the economic downturn at the beginning of the decade, Akris focused on avoiding lay-offs and temporary employment rather than realizing ambitious fashion visions. Being aware of their firm's strategic positioning and focus on German-speaking Europe, the Kriemler brothers realized that Akris was too small and cost-intensive to survive. In addition, the Akris brand seemed to lack a clear image and expressiveness. Keeping their tradition in mind, they started systematically developing Akris into a new fashion brand with global reach. This development was facilitated by a then-recent fashion trend towards more understated clothes without too much obvious luxury.[2]
- 1988: After years of unsuccessful efforts to get in touch with Dawn Mello, the then-fashion director of the luxury department store Bergdorf Goodman in New York, the Kriemler brothers were at last able to present the Akris fashion to her during a meeting, after which she ordered five pieces of clothing.

[2]Cf. Stäubli, R. (2006): Erfolg des Einfachen, in: Doswald, C. (Eds., 2006): JRP Ringier: Zürich, 90–92.

- 1989: Akris opened a showroom in Paris in order to communicate effectively with the most important stakeholders in the fashion industry.
- 1994: A bleak year for Akris as it was severely hit by the recession following the stock market rally. The revenues dropped and the production facilities needed to be downsized to between 240 and 250 employees. The Kriemler brothers were close to giving up.[3]
- 1995: The first global advertising campaign of the Akris brand was launched with the New York-based photographer Steven Klein – a cooperation that lasted for many years.
- 1995: The first Akris store opened in the Rue du Faubourg Saint Honoré in Paris. Akris continuously expanded its points of sale in the US and Canada at its partners Neiman Marcus, Bergdorf Goodman[4], Saks Fifth Avenue, and Holt Renfrew.
- 1995: Akris launched the designer sportswear collection Akris punto, which was then produced in Italy and Slovenia.
- 1997: Akris opened its first store in the US in Boston and first "store-in-store" with Bergdorf Goodman.
- 1999: Akris was the first Swiss fashion brand to be elected as a member of the prestigious "Fédération Française de la Couture du Prêt-à-porter des Couturiers et des Créateurs de Mode" by the federation's 130 industry members. The members are not annually reelected, which allowed Akris to plan for the long run. As a member of the federation, Akris was also afforded the opportunity to present its collections to an international audience twice a year in spring and fall, which it did for the first time in 2004.
- 2000: Akris established its international subsidiary in Tokyo, Japan, in order to its develop business in the Japanese market.
- 2004: Akris presented its fashion at the press défilé at the Carrousel du Louvre in Paris on one the four most important days of the ten-day fashion event for primarily French designers. The most relevant opinion leaders of the international fashion press were present at this event.
- 2005: Foundation of a production joint venture in Rumania.
- 2007: The textile museum of St. Gallen held an exhibition entitled "Akris – Internationally acclaimed fashion from St. Gallen."
- 2008: In the midst of the financial crisis, Akris acquired the German handbag producer Comtesse, an 80-year-old family business with 35 employees after the former owners, Egana-Goldpfeil, filed for bankruptcy. Comtesse has extensive knowhow in processing horsehair as an exclusive material. The acquisition may also help Akris enter Asian markets; handbags are often used as a first step to enter these markets.[5]
- 2009: Akris presented its first handbag and accessory collection.
- 2010: Albert Kriemler awarded the "Star Award" by the Fashion Group International (FIG) in New York. Akris celebrated the 20 years of collaboration with Steven Klein at Bergdorf Goodman.
- 2011: Owing to the Swiss Franc's strength against the Euro, Akris's situation did not look very rosy from Swiss exporters' perspective. Despite the tremendous success of the Akris brand, 2011 was one of the firm's most difficult years in economic terms. Unlike the Swiss watch industry in which most competitors produce in Switzerland, Akris's competitors are primarily located in other currency regions. Akris was forced to lay-off employees and had to relocate the production of certain goods from Ticino, Switzerland, to Artifex in Romania.
- 2012: Akris celebrated its 90-year jubilee in Paris.[6] Doris Leuthard, a Swiss Federal Counselor and an Akris customer, praised Albert Kriemler's collections as "global ambassadors for Switzerland," reflecting "creativity and innovation."
- 2012: Akris launchesde-commerce on the redesigned webpage www.akris.ch.

[3]Cf. Ammann, R. (2004): Der Wert der Schönheit, in: brand eins, No. 8, 26–32.
[4]Since 1987, Bergdorf Goodman is part of the Neiman Marcus Group, which is owned by private equity firms TPG Capital and Warburg Pincus.
[5]For example, Hermès offers its customers relatively less expensive scarfs and ties to experience the brand.
[6]Cf. V. (2012): Akris. Assouline Publishing:New York. Cf. The video: http://www.youtube.com/user/AkrisOfficialChannel

- 2014: Akris celebrated "10 years at Paris Fashion Week" by presenting a collection in collaboration with the artist Thomas Ruff.[7]
- 2015: Akris entered the Chinese market with the opening of three stores in Shanghai.
- 2016: The UK magazine *Wallpaper* awarded Albert Kriemler the "Design Award 2016 Best Alliance" for the best collaboration of the year in the area of design for his co-operation with the Japanese architect Sou Fujimoto. Fujimoto's "House N" was rebuilt in the Grand Palais in Paris for the Akris Défilé spring/summer 2016.
- 2016: The Fashion Institute of Technology awarded Albert Kriemler the Couture Council Award.

## AKRIS TODAY

The still privately owned firm does not disclose any financial or other detailed firm information. However, based on industry data and information from the media, the following can be estimated as of 2016.

- Employees: Overall, the number of employees probably exceeds 1,200 people, of whom 500 work outside the production in the St. Gallen headquarters and in the five regional offices in New York (USA), Seoul (Korea), Shanghai (China), Paris (France), and Tokyo (Japan). In addition, Akris employs 700 people at the various production facilities.
- Revenues: Estimates of Akris' revenue are very speculative, as confirmed by the range of estimates reported in the media. A comparison with other fashion brands shows that, in 2015, Burberry generated revenues of EUR 303,000 per employee and Gucci revenues of EUR 369,000 per employee. It is important to note, however, that these comparisons are only a rough indication of Akris' revenues, as Akris is a mid-sized company.
- Operating margin: The top tier in the fashion industry in terms of operating margin is represented by Hermès, with an EBIT margin of 24–32% over the past decade (in 2015 it was even 31.8%), as well as by Louis Vuitton, which has shown similar results. A comparison with brands like Burberry and Gucci seems more realistic. In 2015, Burberry had an EBIT margin of 13% with 75% of its sales generated by its own stores. Usually, the operating margin achieved in own stores is twice as high as the revenues generated by department stores.

## AKRIS'S LOCATION: ST. GALLEN

Akris is still primarily manufactured at the same location where the firm was founded. The unspectacular headquarter is in the Felsenstrasse 40, close to the old town of St. Gallen; the same building the Kriemler brothers' grandmother bought in 1944.

*"That we are located in St. Gallen is simply luck," comments Albert Kriemler, "because our grandmother said she wanted to produce a pinafore collection and not just raise two sons. But from a historical perspective, Akris does not directly do that for which St. Gallen was actually famous – to produce laces and fabrics. We are in the next stage and produce fashion from fabrics."[8]*

Oftentimes, the Kriemler brothers are asked if and why St. Gallen is the right location for a brand that produces fashion for customers of Bergdorf Goodman in New York. But for Albert Kriemler, the firm's St. Gallen location is highly attractive and useful because of the contrasts it offers:

*"To create fashion means switching between contrasts: between stimulation and relaxation, silence and stress. [. . .] Decisive for me are the opportunity to concentrate, the knowhow of skilled employees, the aura of friendliness and loyalty, a peaceful landscape, and the proximity to the people. [. . .] From a distance, many things become more explicit."[9]*

---

[7]Cf. German Vogue, Januar 2015.
[8]Skupin, B. (2012): Interview Albert Kriemler, http://www.vogue.de/people-parties/designer/interview-albert-kriemler (accessed on 02/07/2012).
[9]Kriemler, A. (2006): Sensibilität. Der Stoff ist das Medium, in: Doswald (Eds., 2006), JRP Ringier: Zürich, 11–15: 12.

In addition, Albert highlights the textile competence, which has been abundant in St. Gallen for more than a century: *"I am engaged in developing fabrics for twelve months a year. For this, St. Gallen is one of best places in the world because it has been an artisanal cluster for many centuries."*[10] At the end of the 19th century, the St. Gallen textile industry boomed and people dreamed of St. Gallen becoming a major city. But the dream was shattered when the British pound devaluated during the First World War and the global economic crisis occurred. Only few local firms were able to survive these developments and renew themselves, some of which are now among the best global embroideries and fabric producers, for example, Forster Rohner, Jakob Schlaepfer, Bischoff Textil, and Union. Forster Rohner's clients include Yves Saint Laurent, Galliano, Prada, and Armani while Jakob Schlaepfer collaborates with international brands, such as Chanel, Dany Attrache, Emanuel Ungaro, and Louis Vuitton. Evidently, St. Gallen also hosts a community of skilled and creative people in the textile industry. But the location also means that firms operating from there are faced with relatively high costs of labor and a strong Swiss Franc. This has been particularly true since the beginning of 2015 when the Swiss National Bank stopped fixing the Euro-Swiss Franc exchange rate.

## The fashion industry and akris

Globally, the year 2015 was a positive year for the luxury goods sector, although sales in China appeared to slow down at the end of the year: The sector's global sales increased by about 13% to USD 253 bn. at the end of 2015. Women's fashion accounted for about 12% of the sector's global sales volume.

2011 was a very good year for the luxury goods industry. Globally, the revenues increased by 10 percent to almost 200 billion US-$. The fashion industry accounted for about a quarter of these sales. Thanks to China's economic growth, the business recovered surprisingly fast after the 2009 financial crisis, during which the revenues dropped to 150 billion US-$.

Interestingly, the larger luxury goods firms were hit less hard by the financial crisis than their smaller rivals.[11]

The luxury goods industry is characterized by three types of firms: (1) small manufactories, (2) medium-sized industrial firms, and (3) large luxury goods conglomerates. Especially the latter have been on the rise over the past few of years. These firms offer multiple brands that either focus on one category of luxury products (e.g., the watch-maker Swatch) or that span multiple categories, such as watches, jewelry, and fashion (e.g., LVMH, Kering, and Richemont). While most of the small and medium-sized firms are privately owned, the large luxury goods conglomerates are typically listed, but even they are often controlled by a strong major shareholder. Recently, private equity firms have also become a more important investor group with regard to luxury goods firms.

### FASHION AS A BUSINESS: CHARACTERISTICS AND TRENDS

Fashion is considered the most difficult business in the luxury goods industry mostly because of its seasonal nature: Firms have to sell each of their two annual collections within about four months, which distinguishes this segment from watches and leather goods. This implies a strong need to further develop and renew the firm's products. Also, unlike the automotive industry's premium segment with its potential to industrialize a mass product, the prêt-à-porter segment's scaling limits are much lower as it requires a substantial amount of craftsmanship and creative competences.

Fashion firms are typically located in one of the fashion centers of the world, particularly in one of the four "fashion capitals" New York, London, Milan, and Paris. To gain credibility regarding the quality of fashion's design, the collections are presented at fashion shows. Of these, the Paris fashion show is the most important, because a jury of fashion professionals elects the designers that are allowed to present their collections. At other relevant fashion shows, for example, in Milan and London, however, fashion firms can buy themselves a slot to present their fashion.

[10]Kriemler, A. (2006): Sensibilität. Der Stoff ist das Medium, in: Doswald (Eds., 2006), JRP Ringier: Zürich, 11–15: 1.
[11]Cf. Bain & Company (2011), Luxury Goods Worldwide Market Study, 10th Edition.

To ensure sufficient brand awareness, large amounts are spent on marketing and advertising. The high margins for which the industry is known are primarily due to offshore production in Eastern Europe and Asia. Once a fashion firm has developed a strong brand, it often attempts to capitalize on it by selling accessories. Many large brands profit from licensing their brands to accessory producers, often enabling these firms to attract additional and broader target groups.

While most high-end fashion firms want to grow, they don't necessarily want to do so at the same pace. Growth is achieved by selling more products to more customers. But the more firms accomplish this, the less attractive these products become to their focal target group because the products become less rare and unique – especially when this development takes place in the firm's existing markets. Over the past few years, there has been a rapid increase in clients from the Middle and Far East, including customers from growing markets such as China, Brazil, Saudi Arabia, and Mongolia. The high-end fashion industry is faced with several specific challenges, some of which are outlined below:

- Controlling of the costs: Even in the high-end fashion industry there are certain limits to transferring increasing costs via the pricing of products to the customers. Exchange rate fluctuations may have a severe impact on the availability of strategic options and the margins.
- Generational change and change in customer preferences: Today, potential customers are significantly younger than in the past. This necessitates different marketing tools and advertising campaigns. Furthermore, the "new" customers are less loyal to a particular brand and are generally more demanding.
- Making luxury accessible in new markets: The internationalization of many high-end fashion brands has several implications that need to be carefully considered. The internationalization should not occur at the expense of existing customers' perception of exclusiveness. It also requires the development of a truly global organization that enables the firm to enter new markets (e.g., supply chain processes, support services in the areas of human resources, sales, etc.). In addition, the internationalization inevitably leads to the questions of if and how the products need to be adapted to local customer preferences.
- Digitalization of the business models: It is becoming increasingly important for firms to develop an integrated online and offline customer experience of its products and services. High-end fashion firms need to be aware that online platforms are an increasingly important means to attract and inform potential customers. The English fashion brand Burberry, for example, shows a live stream of its fashion shows on Facebook. Firms in the high-end fashion industry need to follow this example and develop a convincing digital value proposition.
- Sustainability: Today, luxury goods customers are much more aware of topics such as sustainability. Customers increasingly require an "end-to-end responsibility" that spans the entire value chain of luxury goods producers. *"For the new generation, luxury brands that will not take environmental issues into consideration will lose most of their appeal. Modern brands must address these questions. Ignoring them would be old-fashioned and would equal a return to the previous century,"* says Graydon Carter, Editor of Vanity Fair. Many customers expect commitment to sustainability from *"their"* brand. *"Green luxury"* is cool and shows that responsibility for the environment creates status.

Overall, there is a trend towards consolidation in the high-end fashion industry. Large luxury goods conglomerates that aim at achieving a global competitive advantage by realizing synergies more often acquire traditional smaller brands.

## THE POSITIONING OF AKRIS

Akris is an independent couture house, of which only about a dozen still exist. Since the end of the 1980s, the firm has followed almost the same strategic direction, which is based on the belief that sustainable success in a business requires as much experience with the same activities as possible. The firm is still focused on female customers and predominantly produces women's clothing and accessories. Akris targets women who want to dress elegantly, but who do not want to radically change their look every season. These include "*[. . .] women who want to look attractive but not dramatic, [. . .]*" rather than the "*ladies who lunch.*"[12] The focus is on the successful woman:

> "*The Akris woman is a fashion-minded member of a global elite in business, the art and society. She inspires her peers in balancing femininity, sleek sophistication and purpose. She thinks of fashion as an investment in her personal and professional well-being and poise. She is uncompromising in searching for the best. She covets Akris because she feels strong yet at ease, feminine and always right.*"[13]

The target group is not defined by age. "*The Akris-woman is not defined by her age or nationality, but by her attitude towards her attire,*" says Albert Kriemler, "*[s]he is a woman who knows what she wants: perfectly manufactured and versatile clothes, to express her personality in a discreet way.*"[14] The Akris design defined a "*new, modern and independent form of femininity. [. . .] The Akris philosophy includes: cultivated beauty, understatement, quality, simplicity, contemporary, discretion, and luxury that you feel but do not see at first glance.*"[15]

Akris does not design fashion for a special occasion but for daily life: "*Akris's business model is based on globalized urbaneness.*" The brand achieves an "*alchemy of local roots and internationalization.*"[16] Akris's famous customers are, for example, Queen Rania of Jordan, US First Lady Michelle Obama, Former US Secretary of State Condoleezza Rice, Princess Charlene of Monaco, Oscar-winning actress Nicole Kidman, Cecilia Bartoli, Sandra Bullock, Susan Sarandon, Margaret Thatcher, and several of the Kennedys. Allegedly, unlike many of its competitors, Akris does not pay celebrities to wear its clothes.

Almost 40 percent of the firm's revenues are generated in the US, which is the most difficult market for European designer brands to enter. Despite this difficulty, it is of crucial importance for all major fashion brands with international reach to compete in this market. The remainder of Akris's sales is distributed almost equally between Europe and Asia, and is likely to shift towards Asia in the near future. To be able to meet the very high quality requirements of the value creation process, Akris pursues a strategy of strong vertical integration. Even today, the production is located at its own facilities in Switzerland and Rumania. Akris is financed in a very conservative way and has a relatively low amount of debt, which means the firm is largely independent from financial institutions.

## THE DESIGNER AND HIS PHILOSOPHY

Akris's success is attributable to several different aspects of which Albert Kriemler's design talent is among the most important. Peter Kriemler speaks highly of his brother's talent: "*Albert has the natural talent to create elegant dresses from precious fabrics, characterized by luxury that you feel but that isn't in your face.*"[17] But Albert Kriemler compares his work to that of an architect rather than an artist, because his creations have to fulfill a predefined purpose. Architects need a lot of creativity to create an extraordinary building, but at the same time it must have a certain level of functionality. Both architecture and fashion should respect the context in which they are embedded. Albert "builds" the clothes in which his customers can "live." Not surprisingly, one of his role models is the Viennese Bauhaus-architect Adolf Loos, whose works are a classic example of Modernism in the 1930s. "*He is someone I feel very connected to. He knew the value of texture, materials. He had this sensitivity to fabric and feeling,*" says Albert.[18] Like Adolf Loos, whose work was inspired by materials, often the beauty of wood, Albert's creations are kindled by specific textiles.

---

[12]Griese, I. (2006): Eleganz aus dem Bauch heraus, in: Doswald, C. (Eds., 2006): JRP Ringier: Zürich, 86–87: 86
[13]Source: Akris.
[14]Cf. Ammann, R. (2004): Der Wert der Schönheit, in: brand eins, No. 8, 26–32.
[15]Doswald, C. (Eds., 2006): Akris, JRP Ringier: 7.
[16]Binswanger, D. (2008): Am Anfang war der Stoff, in: Das Magazin, No. 46, 18–29: 26.
[17]Stäubli, R. (2006): Erfolg des Einfachen, in: Doswald, C. (Eds., 2006): JRP Ringier: Zürich, 90–92: 90.
[18]Cf. Martin, J.J. (2015): Albert Kriemler expands Akris's global footprint, in: Wall Street Journal USA, 19/11/2015.

Today, while they are in great demand,[19] top fashion designers are notorious for having "difficult" personalities. John Galliano from Dior, for example, was fired after making anti-Semitic statements. And, as the creatives, many of the top designers show little interest in their firm's business model and economic performance. Albert Kriemler has proven to be just the opposite. He is distinguished, humble, and uses differentiated, elegant language. He is passionate about high-quality fabrics, is technically accurate, and develops visionary designs. And even though he spends 180 days of the year travelling for work, he stays informed about the development of the business. Considering it part of his role as an entrepreneur, he analyzes sales figures, visits stores, and explains the collections to his sales staff.

At the age of 16, Albert would accompany his father when examining and purchasing fabrics. By the time he was in his early 20s, Albert assumed responsibility for 200 employees. His greatest challenge was to identify and develop his own style: *"In the 1980s, I did too many of the things that one was allegedly supposed to do in fashion during that time. We became really good and successful only when we started to do what we really feel and when we decided to continuously learn."*[20]

Today, Albert's fashion is elegant and simple: *"I think that contemporary dresses need to be simple because our life is so complex."*[21] Indeed, Akris's fashion is not chichi, but esthetic, humble, and particularly practical. He feels that the dress is supposed to support the woman and to emphasize her personality, not the other way around.[22] Albert's dresses unfold their effect only when they are worn.[23]

For Albert, it is of the utmost importance to be sensitive towards the fabrics, the customers, and the context: *"One is only able to absorb something if you are sensitive towards it. And only once you have absorbed it are you able to make a difference."*[24] Albert Kriemler's fashion stems from his ability to find a balance between trends and design principles, and between experimentation and innovation and traditions. If he is to continue creating timeless fashion, Albert needs to continuously renew himself:[25] *"The creation of a new collection is successful, if the dresses are worn by different cultures and if the dresses are aligned with the rhythm of life of the contemporary woman – irrespective of her age and nationality."*[26]

Wherever he goes, Albert Kriemler is always seeking inspiration. His inspirations are sometimes more modern and sometimes more traditional. The challenge is to find a balance between the two, transferring past knowledge and ideas to the present.

- Role models and vintages: Albert's role models are the Spanish fashion designer Cristobal Balenciaga, who had a fashion store in Paris from 1937 to 1968, Yves Saint Laurent, who made fashion that was comfortable and supported women's personality, Giorgio Armani, Jil Sander, and American designer Bill Blass. Albert regularly purchases interesting or vintage dresses at auctions.
- Historical textile archive: Akris has a very extensive and well-maintained archive of textile materials and fabrics that covers decades of the firm's history. The archive includes countless fabric samples, which often serve as inspiration for new collections.
- City walks: Albert travels about four months a year. He often walks around New York's and other major cities' up-market, trendy neighborhoods to observe potential customers and get a sense of the latest trends. Albert stays in contact with the people who sell Akris fashion to the end-customers, because he wants to maintain a good understanding of his customers' wants and needs. James J. Gold, then CEO of Bergdorf Goodman, says: "A successful collection is less about advertising than about the special

[19]There were rumors that the designer Marc Jacobs (Louis Vuitton) negotiated with Dior in 2011 for an annual salary of 8–10 million US-$.
[20]Kriemler, A. (2006): Sensibilität. Der Stoff ist das Medium, in: Doswald (Eds., 2006), JRP Ringier: Zürich, 11–15: 15.
[21]Kalt, G. (2008): Swiss house on a roll, in: Financial Times, Beilage "How to spend it", 09/20/2008, 6–10: 8.
[22]Staubli, R. (2006): Erfolg des Einfachen, in: Doswald, C. (Eds., 2006): JRP Ringier: Zürich, 90–92: 90.
[23]Griese, I. (2006): Eleganz aus dem Bauch heraus, in: Doswald, C. (Eds., 2006): JRP Ringier: Zürich, 86–87: 87.
[24]Kriemler, A. (2006): Sensibilität. Der Stoff ist das Medium, in: Doswald (Eds., 2006), JRP Ringier: Zürich, 11–15: 15.
[25]Binswanger, D. (2008): Am Anfang war der Stoff, in: Das Magazin, No. 46, 18–29: 28.
[26]Kriemler, A. (2006): Sensibilität. Der Stoff ist das Medium, in: Doswald (Eds., 2006), JRP Ringier: Zürich, 11–15: 15.

relationship between our sales associates and our clients – that's what gets the product sold. The people at Akris have their ear to the sales floor."[27]

- Architects: Among Albert's friends are the Swiss architects Jacques Herzog and Pierre de Meuron. He dedicated his fall collection of 2007 to them, which was inspired by their surface designs. Other architects like Josef Maria Olbrich, Sou Fujimoto, Tatiana Bilbao, Roberto Burle Marx, and Luis Barrágan also inspired him.
- Artists: Seeking inspiration, Albert regularly meets with contemporary artists. He used to meet with Scottish artist Ian Hamilton Finlay before he passed away and he is in contact with US American expressionist Frank Kleine, who inspired the Akris's fall/winter collection 2012 – a collection that plays around with "verticals." Albert also collaborated with the choreographer John Neumeier several times to create costumes for his ballet performances.

Despite these multiple sources of inspiration, Albert Kriemler's uniqueness and courage to have a distinctive style as a fashion designer contributes to Akris's success. Inspiration and trends are primarily used to renew and improve the existing style. Besides securing a loyal clientele, Albert Kriemler has received many international awards for his fashion, for example, the Museum of Fine Arts' design award and his fashion typically receives very positive critiques by the most influential fashion magazines, such as *Women's Wear Daily*, as well as by the fashion supplements of the *Financial Times* and the *New York Times*.

## The value creation process

To be able to attract and please customers, every single aspect of the value creation process needs to be optimized. Every element needs to fit with the others and must be a consistent part of the entire process. Continuously improving the business and value creation processes ensures that these are difficult to imitate by competitors and that the firm stays agile and is able to address changing conditions in a timely manner. Peter Kriemler motivates this as follows:

> *"Twenty years ago we decided that control would be one of the most important parts of our strategy: controlling our shipments, our production, our research, our deliveries. It was an emotional decision as much as anything, and many people were not so happy originally because it took a long time to put in place, and was expensive. But it allows Albert to create whatever he wants."[28]*

Hence, Akris aligned itself towards the needs of the firm's designer.

In the fashion business, every single aspect is critical – from the fabrics, design and creation of the clothing to the presentation of the final products. It is advantageous for Akris to have these processes performed internally for several reasons. For one, it enables the firm to offer the highest product quality possible. Moreover, Akris designs and produces the dresses at the same location. This close proximity ensures a high level of internal control. Similar to other luxury goods firms for which the quality of the fabrics and processing are decisive, for example Hermès and Louis Vuitton, Akris is characterized by a very high degree of vertical integration. Where necessary, Akris builds long-term external partnerships that are rooted in mutual respect, understanding, and trust. Operating in a cyclical industry, Akris believes that these partnerships are especially important in difficult times. Despite the firm's business philosophy of strong vertical integration, Akris is frequently faced with "make-or-buy" decisions: Which value creation activities should be under the firm's direct control? Which processes could be offshored to less cost-intensive countries?

At the heart of Akris's success is its capability to manage the entire process of producing and selling its fashion collections. The firm's value creation process follows a similar rhythm that is defined by the two main

[27]Rohwedder, C. (2006): A Swiss Brand Excels by Breaking Fashion's Rules, in: Doswald, C. (Eds., 2006): JRP Ringier: Zürich, 89.

[28]Kalt, G. (2008): Swiss house on a roll, in: Financial Times, Beilage "How to spend it", 09/20/2008, 6–10: 10.

annual collections: three months of traveling and three months of creating the new collection. Twice a year, a new collection is shown at the défilé in Paris, which has a significant impact on the respective collection's success. The value creation process consists of the following activities: the selection and development of fabrics, designing and producing clothes, showcasing the collection at the défilé, as well as branding/marketing, logistics, and sales.

## (1) SELECTION AND DEVELOPMENT OF THE FABRICS

Many fashion designers' work is based on cultural or geographic inspiration. Albert Kriemler considers the fabric his point of departure when designing his creations. He begins the process by asking himself how the fabric would feel when worn as a dress: *"I do not search for a suitable fabric after I have designed a dress. The starting point is the fabric. The fabric is the medium of understated luxury that the woman who wears Akris feels."*[29] He uses the fabric to feel the concept and design of a new dress. The materials enable him to unfold his creativity:

> *"Absolute quality of the materials and production is necessary, but not sufficient, to create a relevant collection. The collection needs to prove that it is aesthetic and functional in the woman's daily life in different cultures. The collection must fit with her rhythm of life, working life, and requirements for mobility – and it must make a difference."*[30]

Albert Kriemler is always searching for new interesting materials. He experiments with innovative fabrics that are either developed internally or with external partners, and are often produced by textile firms in St. Gallen.

## (2) DESIGN

After the suitable materials have been selected, designing the dress seems rather simple at a first glance. Albert Kriemler works like a sculptor with a model. Designs are not only developed with professional models, but also with women of different ages and sizes. It requires a lot of passion and patience to develop and finalize a design. A sketch or Polaroid documents every step of the design process, as this may be the best design draft.

In the design phase, Akris relies on a team of extraordinary designers and couturiers who have a pronounced sense of Akris's quality and style. This requires many years of investment in educating the firm's employees and in developing their capabilities. Because Akris has been growing rapidly the past couple of years and needs to deliver ten collections per year (including pre-collections, side collections, and the main défilé collections), it must be able to recruit and educate talented fashion professionals.

## (3) PRODUCTION

The actual production of the dresses is considered the most important part of Akris's value creation process. Albert Kriemler says: *"The product comes to the fore. Certainly, marketing, PR, and advertising can be powerful. But if the product does not match the customer's expectations, these tools do not have a strong effect."*[31] Put differently: *"Ultimately, our dresses communicate what our brand actually stands for."*[32] The first step is cutting the fabrics. This step offers a certain degree of automation potential, but this is technologically demanding because the fabrics have become lighter and, thus, more difficult to process. The next step involves high-quality craftsmanship:

> *"My brother Peter Kriemler and his employees have developed a sophisticated technical program for cutting the fabrics. But afterwards, we need manual work. We use technology but we should not forget what really matters: you need to be incomparable to succeed in a comparison. The difference lies in the manual work, which is nowadays only applied in the haute couture segment."*[33]

[29]Kriemler, A. (2006): Sensibilität. Der Stoff ist das Medium, in: Doswald (Eds., 2006), JRP Ringier: Zürich, 11–15: 12/13.
[30]Kriemler, A. (2006): Sensibilität. Der Stoff ist das Medium, in: Doswald (Eds., 2006), JRP Ringier: Zürich, 11–15: 11.
[31]Kriemler, A. (2006): Sensibilität. Der Stoff ist das Medium, in: Doswald (Eds., 2006), JRP Ringier: Zürich, 11–15: 12.
[32]Binswanger, D. (2008): Am Anfang war der Stoff, in: Das Magazin, No. 46, 18–29: 18.
[33]Kriemler, A. (2006): Sensibilität. Der Stoff ist das Medium, in: Doswald (Eds., 2006), JRP Ringier: Zürich, 11–15: 13.

Albert Kriemler also emphasizes the importance of the "double-face" technique:

*"The most interesting material for modern, luxurious fashion is double-face, a fabric quality with two right hand sides. [. . .] This requires high-end craftsmanship. [. . .] Together with our innovative fabric suppliers, we developed this demanding wool fabric so that it has a new, feathery, and timely quality."*[34]

This type of craftsmanship is consistent with Akris's identity and quality standards. Over the past years, the firm has continuously expanded its portfolio of such fabrics. Among the other aspects that have become characteristic of Akris is its photo prints, which were shown in the summer collection 2008 with pictures of the Scottish artist Ian Hamilton Finlay. To ensure that the demanding customers like the Akris collections, Albert Kriemler continuously communicates with Akris's tailors during the production process. One of the greatest challenges was and still is to cope with the firm's growth. How can the extremely high quality requirements be matched while increasing the production output? Because of the company's growth, Akris expanded its production facilities to Italy and Romania.

## (4) DÉFILÉ

Twice a year, Akris presents its spring and fall collections at the Carrousel du Louvre in Paris. This event is extremely important for the perception of the Akris brand, as the industry's most influential people are in attendance, for example, Anna Wintour, editor-in-chief of the US edition of *Vogue*, Suzy Menkes, formerly with *International Herald Tribune* now with *Vogue Online*, Sabine Nedelchev, editor-in-chief of *Elle*, or Vanessa Freedman of the *New York Times*, as well as VIP customers and the purchasing directors of the world's large luxury department stores. The business press, for example, *The Wall Street Journal* and *Financial Times*, are also important to Akris as many of its potential customers are businesswomen. The online magazine *Vogue.com* has become very influential in the industry, primarily because of its reach and publication speed but also because articles remain online for at least six months.

The outcome of six months' of hard work is presented in just 13 minutes. Everything needs to be perfect in order to communicate the brand image and style to the audience. The success of the entire collection depends on this short presentation and, thus, has a significant impact on the future development of the brand.[35] Here, again, Akris tries to be authentic. As the designer, Albert prefers to remain in the background, only making a brief appearance during the show. The cocktail reception following the Akris fashion show also reflects the firm's values and style and can be described as an *"unconventional mixture of sausages from St. Gallen and champagne."*[36]

## (5) BRANDING/MARKETING

Having a strong brand is critical to success in the luxury goods industry. The brand, however, needs to be based on a fit between the firm's and the collection's history and the current products. The brand is the intangible und emotional part of the products and services. Because of the increasingly large number of brands in the luxury markets, it is critical for the target group to perceive the difference between the respective brand and other brands. To achieve this, some brands intensify their local marketing activities, for example, by hosting exclusive events.

The firm Akris states that

*"Akris is a collection of refined, sleek and versatile pieces, designed in clear architectural lines with exceptional fabrics, body conscious tailoring and sophisticated colors. Collector prints, double-face and horsehair are iconic design elements woven through each collection. Uniting effortless fashion and master craftsmanship. Akris is quintessentially today, yet timeless."* . . . *"Akris punto is a collection of everyday easy to wear items with a sporty and flirtatious twist. Akris punto celebrates the signature dot in unexpected and playful ways.*[37]

---

[34]Kriemler, A. (2006): Sensibilität. Der Stoff ist das Medium, in: Doswald (Eds., 2006), JRP Ringier: Zürich, 11–15: 14.
[35]Cf. Doswald, C. (Eds., 2006): Akris, JRP Ringier: 31.
[36]Binswanger, D. (2008): Am Anfang war der Stoff, in: Das Magazin, No. 46, 18–29: 27.
[37]Source: Akris.

Akris positions its brand as a "clean" brand. In the past, it was not necessary to maintain a large PR department, because Akris has always benefited from favorable attention by the fashion media and other opinion leaders in the industry. Compared to its competitors, Akris has a relatively small marketing budget. The firm invests in carefully selected, long-term partnerships. For example, it has been working in close collaboration with the New York-based photographer Steven Klein for more than ten years. His pictures are used in Akris's advertising campaigns and emphasize the brand's distinctive image.

## (6) LOGISTICS

The global logistics of Akris is one of the firm's main cost drivers and, therefore, requires regular efficiency and quality assessments. The company also needs to assess whether or not it would be more efficient to deliver goods directly from its various production facilities to the target countries. For this reason, Akris established a central, 5,000 square meter logistics center, including a warehouse and a sales and distribution department for international shipping.

## (7) SALES

Akris pays special attention to the locations at which its products are sold:

> "The collection itself is not sufficient. The location where the customer buys the dress is decisive for the perception of the sensitivity. [. . .] Here customers change clothes and undress their shoes. A certain feeling of "protection" and privacy is important. [. . .] While some may consider these aspects as tiny, ignoring them could lead to unconscious irritations. [. . .] Also the interior of the Akris stores is supposed to reflect what Akris stands for: cultivated beauty."[38]

Akris is currently available at about 350 points of sale. About 50 percent of the revenue is derived from department stores ("wholesale," including store-in-stores), while 25 percent is from licensed stores, and 25 percent from own Akris stores ("directly operated stores").

- Department stores (wholesale): The rise of the Akris brand began in luxury department stores in New York. These stores continue to be a very important distribution channel for the brand. Akris is one of Bergdorf Goodman's best-selling designer brands. Here, and in about 50 other locations, Akris presents its fashion in store-in-stores. The firm has been working in close collaboration with other US department store chains, such as Neiman Marcus and Saks Fifth Avenue, for many years. Akris receives valuable feedback from these partners. Bergdorf Goodman, for example, suggested the creation of a pre-collection to bridge the long period between the two large main collections. This led to additional sales in November and had a signaling effect for the next season.
- Flagship stores (retail): Akris started relatively late, in 1997, to sell its products in its own stores. Today, Akris operates its own stores at many attractive locations. In 2016, there were about 20 own Akris stores, which are extremely important because they present the entire Akris collection, which department stores do not typically do due to space restrictions. Furthermore, flagship stores offer the opportunity to optimize interaction with customers via the architecture, interior design, and sales processes – without having competing brands directly next to the Akris display. The Kriemlers have developed these stores in close collaboration with the architects Ferruccio Robbiani and Christopher Sattler.
- E-commerce: The online store has become one of the most important sales channels for many fashion firms. Akris would like to build upon its strong brand and use this channel for remote regions without an Akris point of sale. For example, Akris has been operating online in the US since 2012, which includes a delivery service by an Akris tailor who, if necessary, customizes the purchased dress.

---

[38]Kriemler, A. (2006): Sensibilität. Der Stoff ist das Medium, in: Doswald (Eds., 2006), JRP Ringier: Zürich, 11–15: 14.

# Preparing for the future

Over the past decades, Akris has been characterized by its focus on the long-term, which is particularly notable in the fast-paced high-end fashion industry. Entrepreneurial decisions are long-term oriented and the management aims at optimizing the value creation processes incrementally, while ensuring that the entire process is under Akris' control. The Kriemler brothers are aware that top designers' creativity is not eternal. Albert Kriemler remarks: *"A couture-designer has 20, at most 25 years, to be really good in his profession. My brother and I plan to stay on our own for the next ten years."*[39] Akris had its breakthrough in the 1990s. Therefore, the firm needs to be prepared for a future in which Albert Kriemler's designs may no longer be desirable.

Another important issue that needs to be addressed is Akris's growth. Should the firm diversify or stay focused on women's clothing?

*"Aside from eschewing skimpy styles and other high-fashion mainstays, Akris is unusual in that it sells no profit-boosting accessories, no namesake fragrances. By relying on a few key U.S. retail accounts, subtle marketing and just one brand, Akris tests the industry notion that multi-brand conglomerates are the best route to growth."*[40]

Akris took a first careful step towards diversifying its product offerings by acquiring the handbag brand Comtesse in 2009, which led to the creation of an own handbag collection. Expanding the products may be required if Akris wants to grow further in Asia, where potential customers typically spend more money on brand accessories than on the fashion itself.

Finally, questions regarding the future ownership of Akris are likely to arise over the next few years. To date, Akris has received many acquisition requests. The Kriemler brothers could, for example, sell their business to a strategic investor, such as the fast growing luxury conglomerate LVMH, Richemont, or Kering, or (partly) to a financial investor to finance the future growth. When making the respective decisions it will also be critical to consider the entrepreneurial ethics and attitude of their family business. While the Kriemler brothers envision Akris to become more diversified in the distant future, they prefer not to comment on when and how this development could take place: *"You cannot push things. They have to happen naturally."*[41] *"We're building a group of women who love the brand. And that's what is important. We are in fashion, but we're not trendy."*[42]

## ASSIGNMENT QUESTIONS

1  In which industry does Akris currently operate? What are Akris's core products?

2  What were the most important milestones in Akris's development up to now?

3  What factors are critical to the success of a firm in the high-end fashion industry ("prêt-à-porter-segment") in general? Put differently, how can firms in this industry differentiate themselves from their competitors?

4  How does Akris differentiate itself from its competitors? What are Akris's competitive advantages? How did Akris gain these competitive advantages?

5  What opportunities and risks do you see for the future development of Akris? How would you deal with these opportunities and risks?

6  Please develop three potential growth strategies for Akris. One of the strategies should be based on Akris's status quo as an independent family-owned firm that produces women's fashion. Explain, justify, and evaluate each of your strategies. Which option would you favor? Why?

7  What is special about "sustainability" in the high-end fashion industry? How should Akris address topics related to sustainability in its value creation processes? How would you deal with sustainability in Akris' public relations activities?

[39]Staubli, R. (2006): Erfolg des Einfachen, in: Doswald, C. (Eds., 2006): JRP Ringier: Zürich, 90–92: 92.
[40]Rohwedder (2006), 89.
[41]Albert Kriemler in Kalt, G. (2008): Swiss house on a roll, in: Financial Times, Beilage "How to spend it", 09/20/2008, 6–10: 10.
[42]Cf. Martin, J.J. (2015): Albert Kriemler expands Akris's global footprint, in: Wall Street Journal USA, 19/11/2015

# 3 Accounting analysis: The basics

The purpose of accounting analysis is to evaluate the degree to which a firm's accounting captures its underlying business reality.[1] By identifying places where there is accounting flexibility and by evaluating the appropriateness of the firm's accounting policies and estimates, analysts can assess the degree of distortion in a firm's accounting numbers. Another important skill is adjusting a firm's accounting numbers using cash flow information and information from the notes to the financial statements to "undo" accounting distortions, where possible. Sound accounting analysis improves the reliability of conclusions from financial analysis, the next step in financial statement analysis.

## Factors influencing accounting quality

Because the mechanisms that limit managers' ability to distort accounting data themselves add noise, it is not optimal to use accounting regulation to eliminate managerial flexibility completely. Therefore real-world accounting systems leave considerable room for managers to influence financial statement data. The net result is that information in corporate financial reports is noisy and biased, even in the presence of accounting regulation and external auditing.[2] The objective of **accounting analysis** is to evaluate the degree to which a firm's accounting captures its underlying business reality and to "undo" any accounting distortions. When potential distortions are large, accounting analysis can add considerable value.[3]

There are three potential **sources of noise and bias in accounting data:**

1  That introduced by rigidity in accounting rules.
2  Random forecast errors.
3  Systematic reporting choices made by corporate managers to achieve specific objectives.

Each of these factors is discussed next.

### NOISE FROM ACCOUNTING RULES

Accounting rules introduce noise and bias because it is often difficult to restrict management discretion without reducing the information content of accounting data. For example, revised International Accounting Standard (IAS) 19 issued by the IASB requires firms to recognize pension expense net of a close to risk free return – more specifically, the expected return on high-quality corporate bonds – on the pension plan's investments. Clearly, if the firm's pension plan is making wise investments, in the long run we expect it to earn significantly more than the risk-free rate. However, because IAS 19 does not allow firms to recognize the true expected return on the plan's assets in their income statement, the application of the rule leads to a systematic distortion of reported accounting numbers. Broadly speaking, the degree of distortion introduced by accounting standards depends on how well uniform accounting standards capture the nature of a firm's transactions.

As a solution to the adverse effects of rigid accounting rules, the IASB often defines standards that are based more on broadly stated principles than on detailed rules. For example, most accountants agree that when a firm spends cash on research and development, it essentially makes an investment that should be recorded as such on the balance sheet. In its standard for intangible assets, the IASB leaves much responsibility to the managers and auditors to decide what proportion of development outlays will likely generate future revenues and should thus be considered an asset. In contrast, the US accounting standard for intangible assets issued by the FASB prescribes that all research and development outlays are recognized as expense in the period that they are made. The US standard thus leaves managers much less discretion in the reporting of research and development than the international standard.

The research and development example illustrates what many see as an important difference in the approaches that the IASB and the FASB have been taking to standard-setting. Proponents of the principles-based approach claim that reporting in accordance with principles, instead of technical rules, ensures that the financial statements reflect the economic substance of firms' transactions, instead of their legal form. However, because principles-based standards provide less technical guidance than rules-based standards, they demand more professionalism from auditors in exercising their duties and are more difficult to enforce. Proponents of the rules-based approach therefore claim that using rules-based standards increases the verifiability of the information included in the financial statements, reduces managers' misuse of their reporting discretion, and increases the comparability of financial statements across firms. Because during recent years the FASB and IASB have intensively cooperated to eliminate differences between US GAAP (Generally Accepted Accounting Principles) and IFRS Standards (International Financial Reporting Standards) and to develop new common standards, the distinction between the two approaches to standard-setting has gradually diminished, leaving some international standards to be more principles-based than others.

## FORECAST ERRORS

Another source of noise in accounting data arises from pure forecast error, because managers cannot predict future consequences of current transactions perfectly. For example, when a firm sells products on credit, accrual accounting requires managers to make a judgment about the probability of collecting payments from customers. If payments are deemed "reasonably certain," the firm treats the transactions as sales, creating trade receivables on its balance sheet. Managers then make an estimate of the proportion of receivables that will not be collected. Because managers do not have perfect foresight, actual defaults are likely to be different from estimated customer defaults, leading to a forecast error. The extent of errors in managers' accounting forecasts depends on a variety of factors, including the complexity of the business transactions, the predictability of the firm's environment, and unforeseen economy-wide changes.

## MANAGERS' ACCOUNTING CHOICES

Corporate managers also introduce noise and bias into accounting data through their own accounting decisions. Managers have a variety of incentives to exercise their accounting discretion to achieve certain objectives:[4]

- Accounting-based debt covenants. Managers may make accounting decisions to meet certain contractual obligations in their debt covenants. For example, firms' lending agreements with banks and other debt holders require the firms to meet covenants related to interest coverage, working capital ratios, and net worth, all defined in terms of accounting numbers. Violation of these agreements may be costly because lenders can trigger penalties including demanding immediate payment of their loans. Managers of firms close to violating debt covenants have an incentive to select accounting policies and estimates to reduce the probability of covenant violation. The debt covenant motivation for managers' accounting decisions has been analyzed by a number of accounting researchers.[5]
- Management compensation. Another motivation for managers' accounting choice comes from the fact that their compensation and job security are often tied to reported profits. For example, many top managers receive bonus compensation if they exceed certain prespecified profit targets. This provides motivation for managers to choose accounting policies and estimates to maximize their expected compensation.[6] Stock option awards can also potentially induce managers to manage earnings. Options provide managers with incentives to understate earnings prior to option grants to lower the firm's current share price and hence the option exercise price, and to inflate earnings and share prices at the time of the option exercise.[7]

- Corporate control contests. In corporate control contests, such as hostile takeovers, competing management groups attempt to win over the firm's shareholders. Accounting numbers are used extensively in debating managers' performance in these contests. Therefore managers may make accounting decisions to influence investor perceptions in corporate control contests. Also, when takeovers are not necessarily hostile but structured as a share-for-share merger, the acquiring firm may overstate its performance to boost its share price and by this reduce the share exchange ratio.[8]

- Tax considerations. Managers may also make reporting choices to trade-off between financial reporting and tax considerations. For example, US firms are required to use LIFO inventory accounting for shareholder reporting in order to use it for tax reporting. Under LIFO, when prices are rising, firms report lower profits, thereby reducing tax payments. Some firms may forgo the tax reduction in order to report higher profits in their financial statements. In countries where such a direct link between financial reporting and tax reporting does not exist, tax considerations may still indirectly affect managers' reporting decisions. For example, firms that recognize losses aggressively in their tax statements may support their aggressive tax choices by having the financial reporting treatment of these losses conform to their tax treatment. Having no divergence between the tax treatment and the financial reporting treatment could increase the probability that tax authorities allow the tax treatment.[9]

- Regulatory considerations. Since accounting numbers are used by regulators in a variety of contexts, managers of some firms may make accounting decisions to influence regulatory outcomes. Examples of regulatory situations where accounting numbers are used include actions to end or prevent infringements of competition laws, import tariffs to protect domestic industries, and tax policies.[10]

- Capital market considerations. Managers may make accounting decisions to influence the perceptions of capital markets. When there are information asymmetries between managers and outsiders, this strategy may succeed in influencing investor perceptions, at least temporarily.[11]

- Stakeholder considerations. Managers may also make accounting decisions to influence the perception of important stakeholders in the firm. For example, since labor unions can use healthy profits as a basis for demanding wage increases, managers may make accounting decisions to decrease profit when they are facing union contract negotiations. In countries like Germany, where labor unions are strong, these considerations appear to play an important role in firms' accounting policy. Other important stakeholders that firms may wish to influence through their financial reports include suppliers and customers.[12]

- Competitive considerations. The dynamics of competition in an industry might also influence a firm's reporting choices. For example, a firm's segment disclosure decisions may be influenced by its concern that disaggregated disclosure may help competitors in their business decisions. Similarly, firms may not disclose data on their margins by product line for fear of giving away proprietary information. Finally, firms may discourage new entrants by making profit-decreasing accounting choices.

In addition to accounting policy choices and estimates, the level of disclosure is also an important determinant of a firm's accounting quality. Corporate managers can choose disclosure policies that make it more or less costly for external users of financial reports to understand the true economic picture of their businesses. Accounting regulations usually prescribe minimum disclosure requirements, but they do not restrict managers from voluntarily providing additional disclosures. Managers can use various parts of the financial reports, including the Management Report and notes, to describe the company's strategy, its accounting policies, and its current performance. There is wide variation across firms in how managers use their disclosure flexibility.[13]

## Steps in accounting analysis

In this section we discuss a series of steps that an analyst can follow to evaluate a firm's accounting quality.

## STEP 1: IDENTIFY KEY ACCOUNTING POLICIES

As discussed in Chapter 1, a firm's industry characteristics and its own competitive strategy determine its key success factors and risks. One of the goals of financial statement analysis is to evaluate how well these success factors and risks are being managed by the firm. In accounting analysis therefore the analyst should identify and evaluate the policies and the estimates the firm uses to measure its critical factors and risks.

Key success factors in the banking industry include interest and credit risk management; in the retail industry, inventory management is a key success factor; and for a manufacturer competing on product quality and innovation, research and development and product defects after the sale are key areas of concern. A significant success factor in the leasing business is to make accurate forecasts of residual values of the leased equipment at the end of the lease terms. In each of these cases, the analyst has to identify the accounting measures the firm uses to capture these business constructs, the policies that determine how the measures are implemented, and the key estimates embedded in these policies. For example, the accounting measure a bank uses to capture credit risk is its loan loss reserves, and the accounting measure that captures product quality for a manufacturer is its warranty expenses and reserves. For a firm in the equipment leasing industry, one of the most important accounting policies is the way residual values are recorded. Residual values influence the company's reported profits and its asset base. If residual values are overestimated, the firm runs the risk of having to take large write-offs in the future.

## Critical Accounting Estimates

When identifying a firm's key accounting policies, it is helpful that the IFRS Standards mandate firms to explicitly identify the accounting methods and estimates that require most judgment and are of critical importance to the usefulness of their accounting information. For example, in its 2017 financial statements, cruise company Carnival Corporation & plc reported that ". . . our most significant assets are our ships, ship improvements and ships under construction, which represent 80% of our total assets at November 30, 2017. We make several critical accounting estimates dealing with our ship accounting. First, in order to compute our ships' depreciation expense, which represented 11% of our cruise costs and expenses in 2017, we have to estimate the useful life of each of our ships as well as their residual values. Secondly, we account for ship improvement costs by capitalizing those costs we believe will add value to our ships and have a useful life greater than one year, and depreciate those improvements over their estimated remaining useful life. The costs of repairs and maintenance, including minor improvement costs and dry-dock expenses, are charged to expense as incurred. When we record the retirement of a ship component included within the ship's cost basis, we may have to estimate the net book value of the asset being retired in order to remove it from the ship's cost basis." Other areas of significant judgment identified by Carnival were: (1) the determination of fair values of ships and trademarks for which no active market exists (in impairment tests) and (2) the valuation of potential liabilities related to lawsuits, environmental claims, guest and crew claims, and tax matters.

## STEP 2: ASSESS ACCOUNTING FLEXIBILITY

Not all firms have equal flexibility in choosing their key accounting policies and estimates. Some firms' accounting choice is severely constrained by accounting standards and conventions. For example, even though research and development is a key success factor for biotechnology companies, managers have no accounting discretion in reporting on research activities and, in practice, often make no distinction between development and research because the future benefits of development outlays are too difficult to assess. Similarly, even though marketing and brand building are key to the success of consumer goods firms, they are required to expense all their marketing outlays. In contrast, managing credit risk is one of the critical success factors for banks, and bank managers have the freedom to estimate expected defaults on their loans. Similarly, shipbuilding companies can adequately show the profitability status of their long-term projects because they have the flexibility to recognize proportions of the project revenues during the life of the project.

If managers have little flexibility in choosing accounting policies and estimates related to their key success factors (as in the case of biotechnology firms), accounting data are likely to be less informative for understanding the firm's economics. In contrast, if managers have considerable flexibility in choosing the policies and estimates (as in the case of banks), accounting numbers have the potential to be informative, depending upon how managers exercise this flexibility.

Regardless of the degree of accounting flexibility a firm's managers have in measuring their key success factors and risks, they will have some flexibility with respect to several other accounting policies. For example, all firms have to make choices with respect to depreciation policy (straight-line or accelerated methods), inventory accounting policy (FIFO or average cost), policy for amortizing intangible assets other than goodwill (useful life assumptions), and policies regarding the estimation of pension and other post-employment benefits (discount rate for liabilities, rates of increase in wages, and healthcare costs). Since all these policy choices can have a significant impact on the reported performance of a firm, they offer an opportunity for the firm to manage its reported numbers.

## Accounting Flexibility

Carnival calculates the average useful life and residual value of its ships as the weighted average of the useful lives and residual values of the ships' major components, such as cabins and engines. Management's estimate of the average useful life of its ships is 30 years; the residual value is set at 15 percent of the ships' initial cost. In the notes to the financial statements, management illustrates its accounting flexibility as follows: "... if we change our assumptions in making our determinations as to whether improvements to a ship add value, the amounts we expend each year as repair and maintenance costs could increase, which would be partially offset by a decrease in depreciation expense, resulting from a reduction in capitalized costs. Our fiscal 2017 depreciation expense would have increased by approximately $41 million assuming we had reduced our estimated 30-year ship useful life estimate by one year at the time we took delivery or acquired each of our ships. In addition, our 2017 ship depreciation expense would have increased by approximately $215 million assuming we had estimated our ships to have no residual value at the time of their delivery or acquisition." In 2017 $41 million was equivalent to roughly 1.5 percent of the company's operating income.

### STEP 3: EVALUATE ACCOUNTING STRATEGY

When managers have accounting flexibility, they can use it either to communicate their firm's economic situation or to hide true performance. Some of the strategy questions one could ask in examining how managers exercise their accounting flexibility include the following:

- Reporting incentives. Do managers face strong incentives to use accounting discretion to manage earnings? For example, is the firm close to violating bond covenants? Or are the managers having difficulty meeting accounting-based bonus targets? Does management own a significant amount of shares? Is the firm in the middle of a takeover battle or union negotiations? Managers may also make accounting decisions to reduce tax payments or to influence the perceptions of the firm's competitors.
- Deviations from the norm. How do the firm's accounting policies compare to the norms in the industry? If they are dissimilar, is it because the firm's competitive strategy is unique? For example, consider a firm that reports a lower provision for warranty costs than the industry average. One explanation is that the firm competes on the basis of high quality and has invested considerable resources to reduce

the rate of product failure. An alternative explanation is that the firm is merely understating its warranty provision.

- Accounting changes. Has the firm changed any of its policies or estimates? What is the justification? What is the impact of these changes? For example, if warranty expenses decreased, is it because the firm made significant investments to improve quality?
- Past accounting errors. Have the company's policies and estimates been realistic in the past? For example, firms may overstate their revenues and understate their expenses during the year by manipulating quarterly or semiannual reports, which are not subject to a full-blown external audit. However, the auditing process at the end of the fiscal year forces such companies to make large year-end adjustments, providing an opportunity for the analyst to assess the quality of the firm's interim reporting. Similarly, firms that depreciate fixed assets too slowly will be forced to take a large write-off later. A history of write-offs may be therefore a sign of prior earnings management.
- Structuring of transactions. Does the firm structure any significant business transactions so that it can achieve certain accounting objectives? Enron structured acquisitions of joint venture interests and hedging transactions with special purpose entities to avoid having to show joint venture liabilities, and to avoid reporting investment losses in its financial statements.[14] Although structuring of transactions has been made substantially more difficult under currently prevailing accounting rules, if present, such behavior may suggest that the firm's managers are willing to expend economic resources merely to achieve an accounting objective.

## STEP 4: EVALUATE THE QUALITY OF DISCLOSURE

Managers can make it more or less easy for an analyst to assess the firm's accounting quality and to use its financial statements to understand business reality. While accounting rules require a certain amount of minimum disclosure, managers have considerable choice in the matter. Disclosure quality therefore is an important dimension of a firm's accounting quality.

In assessing a firm's disclosure quality, an analyst could ask the following questions:

- Strategic choices. Does the company provide adequate disclosures to assess the firm's business strategy and its economic consequences? For example, some firms use management's narrative report in their financial statements to clearly lay out the firm's industry conditions, its competitive position, and management's plans for the future. Others use the report to puff up the firm's financial performance and gloss over any competitive difficulties the firm might be facing.
- Accounting choices. Do the notes to the financial statements adequately explain the key accounting policies and assumptions and their logic? For example, if a firm's revenue and expense recognition policies differ from industry norms, the firm can explain its choices in a note. Similarly, when there are significant changes in a firm's policies, notes can be used to disclose the reasons.
- Discussion of financial performance. Does the firm adequately explain its current performance? The Management Report section of the annual report provides an opportunity to help analysts understand the reasons behind a firm's performance changes. Some firms use this section to link financial performance to business conditions. For example, if profit margins went down in a period, was it because of price competition or because of increases in manufacturing costs? If the selling and general administrative expenses went up, was it because the firm was investing in a differentiation strategy, or because unproductive overhead expenses were creeping up?
- Non-financial performance information. If accounting rules and conventions restrict the firm from measuring its key success factors appropriately, does the firm provide adequate additional disclosure to help outsiders understand how these factors are being managed? For example, if a firm invests in product quality and customer service, accounting rules do not allow the management to capitalize these outlays, even when the future benefits are certain. The firm's review of its operations can be used to highlight how

these outlays are being managed and their performance consequences. For example, the firm can disclose physical indexes of defect rates and customer satisfaction so that outsiders can assess the progress being made in these areas and the future cash flow consequences of these actions.

- Segment information. If a firm is in multiple business segments, what is the quality of segment disclosure? Some firms provide excellent discussion of their performance by product segments and geographic segments. Others lump many different businesses into one broad segment. The level of competition in an industry and management's willingness to share desegregated performance data influence a firm's quality of segment disclosure.
- Bad news. How forthcoming is the management with respect to bad news? A firm's disclosure quality is most clearly revealed by the way management deals with bad news. Does it adequately explain the reasons for poor performance? Does the company clearly articulate its strategy, if any, to address the company's performance problems?
- Investor relations. How good is the firm's investor relations program? Does the firm provide fact books with detailed data on the firm's business and performance? Is the management accessible to analysts?

## STEP 5: IDENTIFY POTENTIAL RED FLAGS

In addition to the preceding steps, a common approach to accounting quality analysis is to look for "red flags" pointing to questionable accounting quality. These indicators suggest that the analyst should examine certain items more closely or gather more information on them. Some common red flags are the following:

- Unexplained changes in accounting, especially when performance is poor. This may suggest that managers are using their accounting discretion to "dress up" their financial statements.[15]
- Unexplained transactions that boost profits. For example, firms might undertake balance sheet transactions, such as asset sales or debt-for-equity swaps, to realize gains in periods when operating performance is poor.[16]
- Unusual increases in trade receivables in relation to sales increases. This may suggest that the company is relaxing its credit policies or artificially loading up its distribution channels to record revenues during the current period. If credit policies are relaxed unduly, the firm may face receivable write-offs in subsequent periods as a result of customer defaults. If the firm accelerates shipments to its distributors, it may face either product returns or reduced shipments in subsequent periods.
- Unusual increases in inventories in relation to sales increases. If the inventory build-up is due to an increase in finished goods inventory, it could be a sign that demand for the firm's products is slowing down, suggesting that the firm may be forced to cut prices (and hence earn lower margins) or write down its inventory. A buildup in work-in-progress inventory tends to be good news on average, probably signaling that managers expect an increase in sales. If the buildup is in raw materials, it could suggest manufacturing or procurement inefficiencies, leading to an increase in cost of sales (and hence lower margins).[17]
- An increasing gap between a firm's reported profit and its cash flow from operating activities. While it is legitimate for accrual accounting numbers to differ from cash flows, there is usually a steady relationship between the two if the company's accounting policies remain the same. Therefore any *change* in the relationship between reported profits and operating cash flows might indicate subtle changes in the firm's accrual estimates. For example, a firm undertaking large construction contracts might use the percentage-of-completion method to record revenues. While operating profits and operating cash flows are likely to differ for such a firm, they should bear a steady relationship to each other. Now suppose the firm increases revenues in a period through an aggressive application of the percentage-of-completion method. Then its profits will go up, but its cash flow remains unaffected. This change in the firm's accounting quality will be manifested by a *change* in the relationship between the firm's profits and cash flows.
- An increasing gap between a firm's reported profit and its tax profit. Once again, it is quite legitimate for a firm to follow different accounting policies for financial reporting and tax accounting as long as the

tax law allows it. However, the relationship between a firm's book and tax accounting is likely to remain constant over time, unless there are significant changes in tax rules or accounting standards. Thus an *increasing* gap between a firm's reported profit and its tax profit may indicate that financial reporting to shareholders has become more aggressive. For example, warranty expenses are estimated on an accrual basis for financial reporting, but they are recorded on a cash basis for tax reporting in many countries. Unless there is a big change in the firm's product quality, these two numbers bear a consistent relationship to each other. Therefore a change in this relationship can be an indication either that product quality is changing significantly or that financial reporting estimates are changing.

- A tendency to use financing mechanisms like research and development partnerships, special purpose entities, and the sale of receivables with recourse. While these arrangements may have a sound business logic, they can also provide management with an opportunity to understate the firm's liabilities and/or overstate its assets.[18]

- Unexpected large asset write-offs. This may suggest that management is slow to incorporate changing business circumstances into its accounting estimates. Asset write-offs may also be a result of unexpected changes in business circumstances.[19]

- Large year-end adjustments. A firm's annual reports are audited by the external auditors, but its interim financial statements are usually only reviewed. If a firm's management is reluctant to make appropriate accounting estimates (such as provisions for uncollectible receivables) in its interim statements, it could be forced to make adjustments at the end of the year as a result of pressure from its external auditors. A consistent pattern of year-end adjustments therefore may indicate aggressive management of interim reporting.[20]

- Qualified audit opinions or changes in independent auditors that are not well justified. These may indicate a firm's aggressive attitude or a tendency to "opinion shop" – a tendency to search for an auditor who is willing to provide an unqualified opinion.

- Poor internal governance mechanisms. Internal governance agents, such as independent directors or supervisors, audit committees, and internal auditors, are responsible for assuring the flow of credible information to external parties. When a firm's supervising directors or audit committee lack independence from management or its internal control system has deficiencies, accounting may be of questionable quality.[21] A lack of independence can be the result of, for example, family bonds, economic relationships, or prior working relationships.

- Related-party transactions or transactions between related entities. These transactions may lack the objectivity of the marketplace, and managers' accounting estimates related to these transactions are likely to be more subjective and potentially self-serving.[22]

While the preceding list provides a number of red flags for potentially poor accounting quality, it is important to do further analysis before reaching final conclusions. Each of the red flags has multiple interpretations; some interpretations are based on sound business reasons, and others indicate questionable accounting. It is therefore best to use the red flag analysis as a starting point for further probing, not as an end point in itself.[23]

### STEP 6: RECAST FINANCIAL STATEMENTS AND UNDO ACCOUNTING DISTORTIONS

If the accounting analysis suggests that the firm's reported numbers are misleading, analysts should attempt to restate the reported numbers to reduce the distortion to the extent possible. It is, of course, virtually impossible to perfectly undo the distortion using outside information alone. However, some progress can be made in this direction by using the cash flow statement and the notes to the financial statements.

A firm's cash flow statement provides a reconciliation of its performance based on accrual accounting and cash accounting. If the analyst is unsure of the quality of the firm's accrual accounting, the cash flow statement provides an alternative benchmark of its performance. The cash flow statement also provides information on how individual line items in the income statement diverge from the underlying cash flows. For example, if an analyst is concerned that the firm is aggressively capitalizing certain costs that should be expensed, the information in the cash flow statement provides a basis to make the necessary adjustment.

The notes to the financial statements also provide information that is potentially useful in restating reported accounting numbers. For example, when a firm changes its accounting policies, it provides a note indicating the effect of that change if it is material. Similarly, some firms provide information on the details of accrual estimates such as the provision for doubtful receivables. The IAS 12 tax disclosures in the notes to the financial statements usually provide information on the differences between a firm's accounting policies for shareholder reporting and tax reporting. Since tax reporting is often more conservative than shareholder reporting, the information in the tax note can be used to estimate what the profit or loss reported to shareholders would be under more conservative policies.

Undoing accounting distortions also entails recasting a firm's financial statements using standard reporting nomenclature and formats. Firms frequently use somewhat different formats and terminology for presenting their financial results. **Recasting the financial statements** using a standard template therefore helps ensure that performance metrics used for financial analysis are calculated using comparable definitions across companies and over time.

The following section shows how to recast the firm's financial statements into a template that uses standard terminology and classifications. In Chapter 4 we show how to make accounting adjustments for some of the most common types of accounting distortions.

## Recasting financial statements

Firms sometimes use different nomenclature and formats to present their financial results. For example, the asset minority equity investments can be reported separately using titles such as "investments in associates" and "investments accounted for using the equity method," or they can be included in the line item Financial Assets. Interest Income can be reported as a subcategory of Revenue, shown lower down the income statement as part of Other Income and Expenses, or it is sometimes reported as Interest Expense, Net of Interest Income.

These differences in financial statement terminology, classifications, and formats can make it difficult to compare performance across firms, and sometimes to compare performance for the same firm over time. The first task for the analyst in accounting analysis is therefore to recast the financial statements into a common format. This involves designing a template for the balance sheet, income statement, cash flow statement, and statement of comprehensive income that can be used to standardize financial statements for any company.

### SOME COMPLICATIONS

One particular obstacle that the analyst must overcome in recasting IFRS Standards-based income statements is that the international standards allow firms to classify their operating expenses in two ways: by nature or by function. The classification by nature defines categories with reference to the cause of operating expenses. Firms using this classification typically distinguish between the cost of materials, the cost of personnel, and the cost of non-current assets (depreciation and amortization). In contrast, the classification by function defines categories with reference to the purpose of operating expenses. Under this classification, firms typically differentiate between costs that are incurred for the purpose of producing the products or services sold – labelled Cost of Sales – and costs for overhead activities such as administrative work and marketing – which hereafter we label Selling, General, and Administrative Expenses (SG&A). Only income statements that are prepared using the latter classification include the line item **Gross Profit**, which is defined as the difference between Revenue and Cost of Sales and measures the efficiency of a firm's production activities.

Although the **classification of operating expenses by function** potentially provides better information about the efficiency and profitability of a firm's operating activities, some analysts prefer the **classification of expenses by nature** because this classification is less arbitrary and requires less judgment from management. The coexistence of two classifications generally will not cause problems as long as the choice for a particular classification is industry-related. For example, firms that operate in the airline industry are more likely to classify their expenses by nature, whereas manufacturing firms are more likely to classify their expenses by function. Firms that operate in similar industries may, however, prefer different classifications, possibly because they were used to different local disclosure traditions or rules prior to the adoption of IFRS Standards.

A further complication may be that firms use similar terminology under different approaches. For example, in 2017 Hennes & Mauritz (H&M) reported that its Gross Profit was 54.0 percent of Revenue, while Inditex, owner of brands such as Zara and Massimo Dutti and one of H&M's main competitors, reported that its Gross Profit was 56.3 percent of Revenue. Because the two firms classified their expenses differently, however, these amounts were not comparable. Inditex's (mislabelled) Gross Profit was calculated by subtracting the nature-based cost of merchandise from Revenue, whereas H&M's Gross Profit reflected the difference between Revenue and the function-based Cost of Sales, which included depreciation and the cost of procurement personnel. Fortunately, the IFRS Standards require that when firms classify their expenses by function, they should also report a classification of expenses by nature in the notes to the financial statements. Hence the analyst can always recast H&M's income statement into the format that Inditex used.

## CATEGORIES OF FINANCIAL STATEMENT ITEMS

Bearing in mind that the accounting analysis is one step in a larger process of analyzing a business, the design of standardized statements primarily depends on how such statements will be used in the following steps of the process. Although the use of standardized statements may vary according to the end objective of the business analysis – that is, whether a user is, for example, valuing investors' equity claim or assessing the firm's credit-worthiness – two general rules apply to most common types of business analysis:

1 Business activities versus financing activities. Analysts typically analyze and value a firm's business activities separately from the firm's sources of financing because both have different value implications: whereas business activities affect the firm's creation of value, financing activities affect the allocation of value among the firm's capital providers more than the value itself. As we will see in a later chapter, for example, a common approach to equity valuation is to estimate equity value as the value of a residual claim on a firm's business assets or, alternatively stated, as the value of a firm's business assets after subtracting the value of its fixed financing obligations. To follow such an approach, the standardized financial statements must clearly separate business from financial assets or liabilities.

2 Aggregation versus disaggregation. In many business analysis and valuation applications, a central task is to predict the amount, timing, and uncertainty of a firm's future cash flows or profits. Although aggregation of line items in the standardized financial statements generally helps to remove unnecessary details, the statements must be sufficiently disaggregated to enable users to separately analyze items that have materially different future performance consequences. This is why we distinguish, for example, operating from investment items, current from non-current items, and continued from discontinued operations.

In sum, following the preceding general rules, we classify balance sheet items along the following dimensions:

- Business (operating and investment) versus financial assets or liabilities.
- Current versus non-current assets or liabilities.
- Assets or liabilities from continued versus discontinued operations.

This classification is useful not only because managers' business and financing decisions have different valuation implications and thus must be separately analyzed, but also because the three categories of assets and liabilities receive different accounting treatments. For example, in contrast to most operating assets, several financial and discontinued assets are recognized at their fair values rather than at their historical cost. Consistent with the approach used for the balance sheet, in the income statement, we distinguish business items, such as revenue, cost of sales, and investment income, from financial items, such as interest expense and income from discontinued operations.

Tables 3.1, 3.2, 3.3, 3.4, and 3.5 present the format used throughout the book to standardize the income statement, balance sheet, and cash flow statement, respectively.

To create standardized financials for a company, the analyst classifies each line item in that firm's financial statements using the appropriate account name from the templates set out in the tables. This may require using information from the notes to the financial statements to ensure that accounts are classified appropriately. For example, applying the templates to standardize the 2017 financial statements for apparel retailer Hennes & Mauritz AB is shown in appendix B at the end of this chapter.

**TABLE 3.1**  Standardized income statement format (classification of operating expenses by function)

| Standard income statement accounts | Description | Sample line items classified in account |
|---|---|---|
| **Business – Operating items** | | |
| *Revenue* | Revenues generated through the use of operating assets. | Sales<br>Turnover<br>Membership fees<br>Commissions<br>Licences |
| *Cost of Sales (by function)* | Expenses recognized to account for the use of operating assets in production or procurement activities. | Cost of merchandise sold<br>Cost of products sold<br>Cost of revenues<br>Cost of services<br>Depreciation on manufacturing facilities |
| *SG&A (by function)* | Expenses recognized to account for the use of operating assets in selling, distribution, or overhead activities. | General and administrative<br>Marketing and sales<br>Distribution expenses<br>Servicing and maintenance<br>Depreciation on selling and administrative facilities<br>Amortization of intangibles |
| *Other Operating Income, Net of Other Operating Expense (by function)* | Recurring income from noncore operating activities *minus* recurring expenses that are not directly related to current-period revenues but primarily incurred to generate other operating income or future revenues. | Research and development<br>Start-up costs |

**TABLE 3.1** Standardized income statement format (classification of operating expenses by function) (Continued)

| Standard income statement accounts | Description | Sample line items classified in account |
|---|---|---|
| **Business – Investment items** | | |
| *Investment Income* | Non-interest income generated from (non-operating) investment assets. | Result from associate companies<br>Share of the profit or loss from associates accounted for using the equity method<br>Dividend income<br>Rental income |
| *Interest Income* | Interest accrued on investment assets during the period (net of the amortization of costs of acquiring the assets). | Interest income<br>Interest earned |
| **Financial items** | | |
| *Interest Expense* | Interest accrued on financial liabilities during the period (including the amortization of costs of issuing financial liabilities). | Interest expense<br>Finance cost<br>Interest charge on non-current provisions<br>Post-employment/pension benefits interest cost<br>Amortization of issue costs on loans<br>Dividend on preference shares |
| *Profit/Loss to Non-Controlling Interest* | Portion of net group income that is attributable to minority interests. | Minority interest |
| **Other items** | | |
| *Net Non-Recurring Income or Expense* | Gains *minus* losses from non-recurring transactions or events. | Foreign exchange gains/losses<br>Special charges<br>Gains/losses on sale of investments/non-current assets<br>Asset impairments<br>Restructuring charges |
| *Tax Expense* | Current and deferred tax expense or credit (arising from business or financing activities). | Provision for taxes |
| *Profit/Loss of Discontinued Operations* | Net after-tax profit or loss generated by operations that have been discontinued or will be sold. | |
| *Profit/Loss to Ordinary Shareholders* | Profit or loss attributable to ordinary shareholders, i.e., excluding profit/loss of discontinued operations and profit/loss attributable to non-controlling interests. | Net income |

**TABLE 3.2** Standardized income statement format (classification of operating expenses by nature)

| Standard income statement accounts | Description | Sample line items classified in account |
|---|---|---|
| **Business – Operating items** | | |
| *Revenue* | Revenues generated through the use of operating assets. | Sales<br>Turnover<br>Membership fees<br>Commissions<br>Licences |
| *Cost of Materials (by nature)* | Expenses recognized to account for the cost of inventories sold or used during the period. | Cost of outsourced work and services received<br>Raw materials and work subcontracted<br>Cost of components<br>Changes in inventories and own work capitalized (correction) |
| *Personnel Expense (by nature)* | Expenses recognized to account for the cost of personnel during the period. | Salaries and wages<br>Social security<br>Post-employment/Pension benefit service cost<br>Share-based payments |
| *Depreciation and Amortization (by nature)* | Expenses recognized to account for the cost of non-current operating assets used during the period. | Depreciation on property, plant and equipment<br>Amortization of intangibles |
| *Other Operating Income, Net of Other Operating Expense (by nature)* | Recurring income from noncore operating activities *minus* expenses that are:<br><br>• recognized to account for operating expenditures or the use of operating assets;<br>• recurring in nature; and<br>• not classified as cost of materials, personnel expense or depreciation and amortization. | Transport and distribution costs<br>Operating lease installments<br>Insurance premiums |
| **Investment, financial and other items** | See Table 3.1 | |

**TABLE 3.3** Standardized balance sheet format – assets

| Standard balance sheet accounts | Description | Sample line items classified in account |
|---|---|---|
| **Business – Operating items** | Business assets related to the company's core business activities. | |
| *Cash and Cash Equivalents* | Fair value of cash and cash equivalents used in the financing of short-term business activities. | Cash and cash equivalents<br>Short-term investments<br>Time deposits |
| *Trade Receivables* | Claims against customers (to be settled within one year). | Accounts receivable<br>Trade debtors |

**TABLE 3.3** Standardized balance sheet format – assets (Continued)

| Standard balance sheet accounts | Description | Sample line items classified in account |
|---|---|---|
| *Inventories* | Net cost of inventories produced or acquired. | Inventory<br>Finished goods<br>Raw materials<br>Work-in-progress<br>Stocks |
| *Other Current Assets* | Claims against others than customers (to be settled within one year) or expenditures incurred for next year's operations (other than the cost of inventories). | Prepaid expenses<br>Claims for tax refunds<br>Amounts due from affiliates<br>Amounts due from employees |
| *Derivatives – Asset* | Fair value of investments in derivative financial instruments. | (Non-) current derivative financial Instruments |
| *Non-Current Tangible Assets* | Depreciated cost of tangible resources to be used in the long-term operations of the firm. | Property, plant, and equipment<br>Land and buildings |
| *Non-Current Intangible Assets* | Amortized cost of intangible resources to be used in the long-term operations of the firm. | Goodwill<br>Software/product development costs<br>Deferred financing costs<br>Deferred subscriber acquisition costs<br>Deferred catalogue costs<br>Deferred charges<br>Trademarks and licences |
| **Business – Investment items** | Business assets unrelated to the company's core business activities. | |
| *Minority Equity Investments* | Cost of minority investments in subsidiaries plus the accumulated share in subsidiaries' retained earnings. | Investments accounted for using the equity method<br>Investments in associates |
| *Other Non-Operating Investments* | Cost or fair value of investments in (non-equity) assets that are not used in the company's core business activities. | Finance lease receivables<br>Derivative financial Instruments<br>Biological assets<br>Investment property |
| **Other items** | | |
| *Deferred Tax Asset* | Non-current tax claims arising from the company's business and financing activities. | |
| *Assets Held for Sale* | Assets that were used in operations that have been discontinued or will be sold. | Current assets classified as held for sale<br>Non-current assets classified as held for sale |

**TABLE 3.4**  Standardized balance sheet format – liabilities and equity

| Standard balance sheet accounts | Description | Sample line items classified in account |
|---|---|---|
| **Business – Operating items** | (Non-interest-bearing) liabilities arising from the company's business activities. | |
| *Trade Payables* | Suppliers' claims against the company (to be settled within one year). | Accounts payable<br>Trade creditors |
| *Other Current Liabilities* | Claims against the company held by others than suppliers (to be settled within one year) or revenues to be earned in next year's operations. | Accrued expenses<br>Amounts due to related parties<br>Income tax liabilities<br>Social Security and payroll taxes<br>Dividends payable<br>Current deferred (unearned) revenue<br>Current provisions |
| *Derivatives – Liability* | Fair value of investments in derivative financial instruments. | |
| *Other Non-Current Liabilities (non-interest-bearing)* | Non-interest-bearing, non-current liabilities arising from the company's business activities. | Non-current deferred (unearned) revenues<br>Other non-current liabilities |
| **Financial items** | Liabilities incurred to finance the company's business activities | |
| *Current Debt* | Current interest-bearing liabilities or current portion of non-current interest-bearing liabilities. | Current borrowings<br>Notes payable<br>Bank overdrafts<br>Current portion of non-current borrowings<br>Current portion of finance lease obligation |
| *Non-Current Debt* | Non-current interest-bearing liabilities. | Long-term borrowings/financial liabilities<br>Subordinated debentures<br>Finance lease obligations<br>Convertible debentures<br>Provision for post-employment benefits<br>Provision for decommissioning costs<br>Other non-current provisions |
| *Preference Shares* | Preferred shareholders' investment in the company. | Preference shares<br>Convertible preference shares |
| *Non-Controlling Interest in Equity* | Consolidated subsidiaries' minority shareholders' share in the company's net assets. | |

**TABLE 3.4**  Standardized balance sheet format – liabilities and equity (Continued)

| Standard balance sheet accounts | Description | Sample line items classified in account |
|---|---|---|
| *Ordinary Shareholders' Equity* | Ordinary shareholders' investment in the company. | Share capital<br>Share premium<br>Retained earnings<br>Treasury share/Own share purchased but not canceled<br>Other reserves |
| **Other items** | | |
| *Deferred Tax Liability* | Non-current tax claims against the company arising from the company's business and financing activities. | |
| *Liabilities Held for Sale* | Liabilities related to operations that have been discontinued or will be sold. | |

**TABLE 3.5**  Standardized cash flow sheet format

| Standard balance sheet accounts | Description | Sample line items classified in account |
|---|---|---|
| **Business – Operating/Investment items** | | |
| *Profit Before Interest and Tax* | Profit/loss plus net interest expense and tax expense. | |
| *Taxes Paid* | Tax payments made during the current fiscal period. | |
| *Non-Operating Gains (Losses)* | Adjustment to profit for non-cash gains (and losses) resulting from non-operating activities. | Gain (loss) on disposal of investments/non-current assets<br>Cumulative effect of accounting changes<br>Gain (loss) on foreign exchange |
| *Non-Current Operating Accruals* | Adjustment to profit for accruals related to changes in the book value of non-current assets or liabilities that result from the company's operating activities. | Depreciation and amortization<br>Deferred revenues/costs<br>Deferred taxes<br>Impairment of non-current assets<br>Other non-cash charges to operations<br>Equity earnings of affiliates/unconsolidated subs, net of cash received<br>Minority interest<br>Stock bonus awards |
| *Interest Received* | Interest payments received on other non-operating investments. | |
| *Dividends Received* | Dividend payments received from subsidiaries. | |

**TABLE 3.5** Standardized cash flow sheet format (Continued)

| Standard balance sheet accounts | Description | Sample line items classified in account |
|---|---|---|
| *Net (Investments in) or Liquidation of Operating Working Capital* | Net changes in working capital components arising from the company's operating activities. | Changes in:<br>Trade receivables<br>Other receivables<br>Prepaid expenses<br>Trade payables<br>Accrued expenses (liabilities)<br>Due from affiliates<br>Accounts payable and accrued expenses<br>Refundable/payable income taxes<br>Inventories<br>Provision for doubtful accounts<br>Other current liabilities (excluding current debt) |
| *Net (Investment in) or Liquidation of Non-Current Operating or Investment Assets* | Net changes in the book value of non-current assets arising from the company's business activities. | Purchase/disposal of non-current assets<br>Acquisition of research and development<br>Acquisition/sale of business<br>Capital expenditures<br>Acquisition of subsidiaries and equity investments<br>Capitalization of development costs<br>Cost in excess of the fair value of net assets acquired<br>Investment in financing leases |
| **Financial items** | | |
| *Interest Paid* | Interest payments made on financial liabilities. | Interest paid<br>Dividends paid on preference shares |
| *Net Debt (Repayment) or Issuance* | Net change in current and non-current debt arising from issuances and/or repayments. | Principal payments on debt<br>Borrowings (repayments) under credit facility<br>Issuance (repayment) of long-term debt<br>Net increase (decrease) in short-term borrowings<br>Notes payable<br>Issue (redemption) of preferred securities |
| *Dividend (Payments)* | Dividend payments made during the current fiscal year. | Cash dividends paid on ordinary shares<br>Distributions |
| *Net Share (Repurchase) or Issuance* | Net change in shareholders' equity arising from issuances and/or repurchases. | Proceeds from issuance of ordinary shares<br>Issue of ordinary share for services<br>Issue of subsidiary equity<br>Purchase (issue) of treasury shares<br>Capital contributions |

## Extensible Business Reporting Language

An increasing number of firms worldwide prepare and report their financial statements using the Extensible Business Reporting Language (XBRL). These XBRL statements typically complement the traditional financial statements, but in future years XBRL reporting may start to replace the traditional way of financial reporting. XBRL is a language that supports the internet-based communication of financial information. The basic idea underlying this language is that it provides a "tag" for every individual item in a company's financial statements, including the notes, which describes the main characteristics of the item. Tags contain information about, for example, the accounting standards that the company uses to prepare the item as well as the fiscal year and the broader category of items to which the item belongs. The data items including their tags are reported in an XBRL instance document, which the company makes publicly available through the internet. By using the appropriate software that recognizes the tags, an analyst can then extract only the needed information from the instance document and ignore irrelevant items. One advantage of XBRL reporting is therefore that it substantially reduces the time that the analyst needs to collect and summarize financial statement information.

The process of tagging data items is somewhat similar to the process of recasting financial statements. Because companies use accepted taxonomies to categorize their financial statement items, they take over some of the analyst's work of standardizing the financial statements. The IASB XBRL team has developed the IFRS Standards taxonomy, which classifies all possible data items that may appear in an IFRS Standards-based financial statement and defines the relationships among them. The use of the IFRS Standards taxonomy for XBRL reporting by listed companies may therefore eventually reduce the importance of recasting IFRS Standards-based financial statements.

## Accounting analysis pitfalls

There are several potential pitfalls and common misconceptions in accounting analysis that an analyst should avoid.

### CONSERVATIVE ACCOUNTING IS NOT "GOOD" ACCOUNTING

Some firms take the approach that it pays to be conservative in financial reporting and to set aside as much as possible for contingencies. This logic is commonly used to justify the expensing of research and advertising, and the rapid write-down of intangible assets other than goodwill. It is also used to support large loss reserves for insurance companies, for merger expenses, and for restructuring charges.

From the standpoint of a financial statement user, it is important to recognize that conservative accounting is not the same as "good" accounting. Financial statement users want to evaluate how well a firm's accounting captures business reality in an unbiased manner, and conservative accounting can be as misleading as aggressive accounting in this respect.

It is certainly true that it can be difficult to estimate the economic benefits from many intangibles. However, the intangible nature of some assets does not mean that they do not have value. Indeed, for many firms these types of assets are their most valued ones. For example, Swiss-based pharmaceutical Novartis's two most valued assets are its research capabilities that permit it to generate new drugs and its sales force that enables it to sell those drugs to doctors. Yet neither is recorded on Novartis's balance sheet. From the investors' point of view, accountants' reluctance to value intangible assets does not diminish their importance. If they are not included in financial statements, investors have to look to alternative sources of information on these assets.

Further, conservative accounting often provides managers with opportunities for reducing the volatility of reported earnings, typically referred to as "earnings smoothing," which may prevent analysts from recognizing poor performance in a timely fashion. Finally, over time investors are likely to figure out which firms are conservative and may discount their management's disclosures and communications.

## NOT ALL UNUSUAL ACCOUNTING IS QUESTIONABLE

It is easy to confuse unusual accounting with questionable accounting. While unusual accounting choices might make a firm's performance difficult to compare with other firms' performance, such an accounting choice might be justified if the company's business is unusual. For example, firms that follow differentiated strategies or firms that structure their business in an innovative manner to take advantage of particular market situations may make unusual accounting choices to properly reflect their business. Therefore it is important to evaluate a company's accounting choices in the context of its business strategy.

Similarly, it is important not to necessarily attribute all *changes* in a firm's accounting policies and accruals to earnings management motives.[24] Accounting changes might be merely reflecting changed business circumstances. For example, as already discussed, a firm that shows unusual increases in its inventory might be preparing for a new product introduction. Similarly, unusual increases in receivables might merely be due to changes in a firm's sales strategy. Unusual decreases in the allowance for uncollectible receivables might be reflecting a firm's changed customer focus. It is therefore important for an analyst to consider all possible explanations for accounting changes and investigate them using the qualitative information available in a firm's financial statements.

## COMMON ACCOUNTING STANDARDS ARE NOT THE SAME AS COMMON ACCOUNTING PRACTICES

Listed firms in the EU and elsewhere prepare their consolidated financial statements under a common set of accounting standards, IFRS Standards. The adoption of IFRS Standards makes financial statements more comparable across countries and lowers the barriers to cross-border investment analysis. It is important, however, not to confuse the adoption of common accounting *standards* such as IFRS Standards with the introduction of common accounting *practices*.[25]

In Chapter 1 we discussed some international differences that remained in place after the adoption of IFRS Standards. For example, although the EU sets minimum standards for external auditing, it remains up to the member countries to implement and enforce such rules. Further, IFRS Standards may not be similarly enforced throughout Europe because all European countries have their own public enforcement bodies. Finally, the role of financial reports in communication between managers and investors differs across firms and countries. In Chapter 1 we also discussed the reporting differences between private corporations and public corporations. Similar, potentially smaller differences exist between widely held and closely held listed firms. The analyst should therefore carefully consider these aspects of a firm's reporting environment.

# Value of accounting data and accounting analysis

What is the value of accounting information and accounting analysis? Given the incentives and opportunities for managers to affect their firms' reported accounting numbers, some have argued that accounting data and accounting analysis are not likely to be useful for investors.

Researchers have examined the value of earnings and return on equity (ROE) by comparing stock returns that could be earned by an investor who has perfect foresight of firms' earnings, ROE, and cash flows for the following year.[26] To assess the importance of earnings, the hypothetical investor is assumed to buy shares of firms with subsequent earnings increases and sell shares with subsequent earnings decreases. If this strategy had been followed each year during the period 1964 to 1996, the hypothetical investor would have earned an average return of 37.5 percent. If a similar investment strategy were followed using ROE, buying shares with subsequent increases in ROE and selling shares with ROE decreases, an even higher annual return, 43 percent, would be earned. In contrast, cash flow data appear to be considerably less valuable than earnings or ROE information. Annual returns generated from buying shares with increased subsequent cash flow from operations and selling shares with cash flow decreases would be only 9 percent. This suggests that next period's earnings and ROE performance are more relevant information for investors than cash flow performance.

Overall, this research suggests that the institutional arrangements and conventions created to mitigate potential misuse of accounting by managers are effective in providing assurance to investors. The research indicates that investors do not view earnings management so pervasive as to make earnings data unreliable.

A number of research studies have examined whether superior accounting analysis is a valuable activity. By and large, this evidence indicates that there are opportunities for superior analysts to earn positive stock returns. Studies show that companies criticized in the financial press for misleading financial reporting subsequently suffered an average share price drop of 8 percent.[27] Firms where managers appeared to inflate reported earnings prior to an equity issue and subsequently reported poor earnings performance had more negative share price performance after the offer than firms with no apparent earnings management.[28] Finally, US firms subject to SEC investigation for earnings management showed an average share price decline of 9 percent when the earnings management was first announced and continued to have poor share price performance for up to two years.[29]

These findings imply that analysts who are able to identify firms with misleading accounting are able to create value for investors. The findings also indicate that the stock market ultimately sees through earnings management. For all of these cases, earnings management is eventually uncovered and the share price responds negatively to evidence that firms have inflated prior earnings through misleading accounting.

## Summary

In summary, accounting analysis is an important step in the process of analyzing corporate financial reports. The purpose of accounting analysis is to evaluate the degree to which a firm's accounting captures the underlying business reality. Sound accounting analysis improves the reliability of conclusions from financial analysis, the next step in financial statement analysis.

There are six key steps in accounting analysis. The analyst begins by identifying the key accounting policies and estimates, given the firm's industry and its business strategy. The second step is to evaluate the degree of flexibility available to managers, given the accounting rules and conventions. Next, the analyst has to evaluate how managers exercise their accounting flexibility and the likely motivations behind managers' accounting strategy. The fourth step involves assessing the depth and quality of a firm's disclosures. The analyst should next identify any red flags needing further investigation. The final accounting analysis step is to restate accounting numbers to remove any noise and bias introduced by the accounting rules and management decisions.

Chapter 4 discusses how to implement these concepts and shows how to make some of the most common types of adjustments.

## Core concepts

**Accounting analysis**    Evaluation of the potential accounting flexibility that management has and the actual accounting choices that it makes, focusing on the firm's key accounting policies. The accounting analysis consists of the following six steps:

1   Identification of the firm's key accounting policies.

2   Assessment of management's accounting flexibility.

3   Evaluation of management's reporting strategy.

4   Evaluation of the quality of management's disclosures.

5   Identification of potential red flags or indicators of questionable accounting quality.

6   Correction of accounting distortions.

**Classification of operating expenses by function**    Classification in which firms distinguish categories of operating expense with reference to the *purpose* of the expense. This classification typically distinguishes (at least) the following categories of expenses: (a) Cost of Sales and (b) Selling, General, and Administrative Expenses.

**Classification of operating expenses by nature**    Classification in which firms distinguish categories of operating expense with reference to the *cause* of the expense. This classification typically distinguishes the following categories of expenses: (a) Cost of Materials, (b) Personnel Expense, and (c) Depreciation and Amortization.

**Gross profit**    Difference between Revenue and Cost of Sales.

**Recasting of financial statements**    Process of standardizing the formats and nomenclature of firms' financial statements (income statement, balance sheet, cash flow statement).

**Sources of noise and bias in accounting data**    Three potential sources of noise and bias in accounting data are:

a   Rigid accounting standards.

b   Management's forecast errors.

c   Management's reporting strategy (accounting choices).

## Questions, exercises, and problems

1   Many firms recognize revenues at the point of shipment. This provides an incentive to accelerate revenues by shipping goods at the end of the quarter. Consider two companies: one ships its product evenly throughout the quarter, and the other ships all its products in the last two weeks of the quarter. Each company's customers pay 30 days after receiving shipment. Using accounting ratios, how can you distinguish these companies?

2   a   If management reports truthfully, what economic events are likely to prompt the following accounting changes?

   ●   Increase in the estimated life of depreciable assets.

   ●   Decrease in the allowance for doubtful accounts as a percentage of gross trade receivables.

   ●   Recognition of revenues at the point of delivery rather than at the point cash is received.

   ●   Capitalization of a higher proportion of development expenditures.

b   What features of accounting, if any, would make it costly for dishonest managers to make the same changes without any corresponding economic changes?

3   The conservatism (or prudence) principle arises because of concerns about management's incentives to overstate the firm's performance. Joe Banks argues, "We could get rid of conservatism and make accounting numbers more useful if we delegated financial reporting to independent auditors rather than to corporate managers." Do you agree? Why or why not?

4   A fund manager states, "I refuse to buy any company that makes a voluntary accounting change, since it's certainly a case of management trying to hide bad news." Can you think of any alternative interpretation?

5   On this book's companion website, there is a spreadsheet containing the financial statements of the following:

a   Vodafone plc for the fiscal year ended March 31, 2018.

b   The Unilever Group for the fiscal year ended December 31, 2017.

c   Audi AG for the fiscal year ended December 31, 2017.

d   Use the templates shown in Tables 3.1–3.5 to recast these companies' financial statements.

## Problem 1 Key accounting policies

Consider the following companies.

*Juventus F.C. S.p.A.* is an Italian publicly listed football club. The club's primary sources of revenue are:

a   Season and single ticket sales.

b   Television, radio, and media rights.

c   Sponsorship and advertising contracts.

d   The disposal of players' registration rights.

Players' registration rights are recognized on the balance sheet at cost and amortized over the players' contract terms. The club owns its stadium ("Juventus Stadium"), which opened in 2011, but leases the land adjacent to its stadium from the City of Turin under an operating lease arrangement. The operating lease has a term of 99 years and involves a lease payment, made in advance, of close to €13 million. To help finance the €105 million construction cost of the stadium, Juventus entered into an agreement with a large sports marketing agency, selling the exclusive naming rights for the new stadium for a period of 12 years. In exchange for the naming rights, Juventus received an advance payment of €38.5 million.

*Spyker Cars N.V.* is a small Netherlands-based designer and manufacturer of exclusive sports cars, which had its initial public offering in 2004 but delisted from the Amsterdam Stock Exchange in 2013. During the first five years as a publicly listed company, Spyker's annual revenues went down from a maximum of €19.7 million (in 2006) to €6.6 million (in 2009). In these years, Spyker produced 242 new cars (including demonstration cars) and sold 194 cars. At the end of 2009, it held 28 cars in stock. Further, in 2009 the company spent close to €9.8 million on development, which it added to its development asset of €27.3 million, and €14,000 on research. Because Spyker had been loss-making since its IPO, the car manufacturer had €97 million in tax-deductible carry forward losses at the end of 2009.

*J Sainsbury plc* is a UK-based publicly listed retailer that operates more than 2,200 supermarkets and convenience stores and has an estimated 16 percent market share in the United Kingdom. During the period 2010–2014 the company's operating profit margin averaged around 3.6 percent; during the period 2015–2017 the operating profit margin averaged around 1.5 percent, reaching a level of 1.6 percent in the year ending on March 10, 2018 (fiscal 2017). In March 2018 the net book value of Sainsbury's land and buildings was £7.9 billion. A significant part of the company's supermarket properties was pledged as security for long-term borrowings. In 2018 Sainsbury had 187 thousand employees (121 thousand full-time equivalents); many of them participated in one of the retailer's defined-benefit pension plans. At the presentation of the fiscal 2017 results, Sainsbury announced that it had agreed to acquire supermarket chain Asda for an amount of £7.3 billion in cash and shares.

1   Identify the key accounting policies for each of these companies.

2   What are these companies' primary areas of accounting flexibility? (Focus on the key accounting policies.)

## Problem 2 Fashion retailers' key accounting policies

In their 2017 financial statements, five international fashion retailers – that is, Burberry, Esprit, French Connection, Inditex, and Next – explicitly discussed their "key accounting policies." The following table summarizes the accounting policies that were denoted as "key" by at least one of the five retailers (x = mentioned as key accounting policy; o = not mentioned):

| | Burberry | Esprit | French Connection | Inditex | Next |
|---|---|---|---|---|---|
| Depreciation and/or impairment of property, plant, and equipment | X | X | 0 | X | 0 |
| Employee/post-retirement benefits | 0 | 0 | 0 | X | X |
| Fair value of financial instruments | 0 | 0 | 0 | X | X |
| Impairment of goodwill | 0 | X | 0 | 0 | 0 |
| Impairment of trade receivables | 0 | 0 | 0 | 0 | X |
| Impairment of trademarks | 0 | X | 0 | 0 | 0 |
| Inventory valuation/provision for obsolete inventory | X | X | X | X | X |
| Lease terms and commitments | 0 | 0 | 0 | X | 0 |
| Provision for product returns | 0 | 0 | 0 | 0 | X |
| Provision for store closures/onerous leases | X | X | 0 | 0 | X |
| Provisions for litigation | 0 | 0 | 0 | X | 0 |
| Recoverability of deferred tax assets | 0 | X | 0 | X | 0 |
| Valuation of investments in subsidiaries | 0 | 0 | X | 0 | 0 |

1. Based on your knowledge of the fashion retail industry, for each of the above accounting policies, discuss why the accounting policy is considered as "key" by one or more of the five fashion retailers.

2. Discuss which economic, industry, or firm-specific factors may explain the observed variation in key accounting policies across the five retailers.

## Problem 3 Euro Disney and the first five steps of accounting analysis

*Euro Disney S.C.A.* is a holding company, holding 82 percent of the shares of Euro Disney Associés S.C.A., which operates, amongst others, the Disneyland Park, Walt Disney Studios Park, Disneyland Hotel, and Davy Crockett Ranch in Paris and holds 99.99 percent of the shares of EDL Hotels S.C.A. EDL Hotels operates all of the Disney Hotels in Paris (except for the Disneyland Hotel and Davy Crockett Ranch).

Until 2012 Euro Disney Associés leased the Disneyland Park (including land) under a finance lease from Euro Disneyland S.N.C., which was owned by (1) a syndicate of banks and financial institutions (83 percent participation) and (2) a wholly-owned

subsidiary of the US-based Walt Disney Company (17 percent participation). EDL Hotels S.C.A. rented land to a group of six special-purpose financing companies that, in turn, owned the hotels on the land and leased these hotels back to EDL Hotels. All special-purpose financing companies were fully consolidated in Euro Disney's financial statements, despite the absence of ownership in some cases. In 2012 Euro Disney Associés and EDL Hotels exercised their options to acquire the Disneyland Park and hotels from the special-purpose financing companies.

Euro Disney's primary sources of revenue are its two theme parks (entrance fees, merchandise, food and beverage, special events) and its seven hotels and Disney Village (room rental, merchandise, food and beverage, dinner shows, convention revenues). Disney Village offers themed dining, entertainment, and shopping facilities. The company has, on average, around 15 thousand employees. The company and its subsidiaries are considered as one French economic and labor unit and have negotiated around 30 collective bargaining agreements with the various trade unions represented in the unit. The majority of the company's employees (about 90 percent) have a permanent contract. To cope with the seasonal nature of the business, Euro Disney is able to move employees from its theme parks to its hotels and vice versa. Approximately 5.5 percent of total personnel expenses consist of training costs.

In 2012, after a long period of poor performance, Euro Disney restructured its financial obligations. As part of the restructuring, the company obtained two new loans (with an interest rate of 4 percent and a face value of €615.9 million) and a €100 million revolving credit facility from the Walt Disney Company that helped Euro Disney settle all outstanding loans from other creditors, thus effectively turning the Walt Disney Company into Euro Disney's only creditor. Prior to the restructuring, Euro Disney's debt agreements included debt covenants requiring the company to maintain minimum ratios of adjusted operating income (before depreciation and amortization) to total debt service obligations. The loan agreements with the Walt Disney Company include only negative debt covenants, limiting Euro Disney's ability to make new investments or attract new debt capital. At the end of 2016 Euro Disney's debt to total assets ratio was 77 percent (down from 82 percent in 2014).

Euro Disney S.C.A. is publicly listed on the Euronext Paris stock exchange. By the end of fiscal 2016, 76.7 percent of its shares were owned by the Walt Disney Company (up from 39.8 percent in 2014), and 23.3 percent were in the hands of dispersed shareholders. The company has a supervisory board with 12 members, three of which are representatives of the Walt Disney Company, an audit committee, and a nominations committee. Euro Disney S.C.A. as well as both operating companies of Euro Disney S.C.A., that is, Euro Disney Associés and Euro Disney Hotels, are managed by the management company Euro Disney S.A.S. (referred to as the *Gérant),* an indirect wholly-owned subsidiary of the Walt Disney Company. At the end of fiscal year 2016, the CEO of the *Gérant* (Euro Disney S.A.S.) was Catherine Powell, who replaced Tom Wolber in July 2016. For the management services provided to the holding and operating companies, the *Gérant* receives management fees consisting of a fixed percentage of revenues plus a performance-related portion. The aggregate compensation for the nine independent supervisory board members was €298,908 in 2016. The three representatives of the Walt Disney Company received

an annual fixed salary, a bonus, restricted stocks, and stock options from the Walt Disney Company. In 2016 the CEO of the *Gérant* (Euro Disney S.A.S.) received an annual salary of € 502,991. The CEO's employment contract further promised her:

1 A discretionary annual bonus based on individual performance relative to the objectives of the company and the Walt Disney Company Parks & Resorts operating segment.

2 Discretionary grants of the company's stock options, the Walt Disney Company's stock options, and the Walt Disney Company's restricted stock.

3 The use of a company car.

In addition to the CEO (*président*), the executive committee of the *Gérant* consisted of three senior vice presidents and six vice presidents.

Euro Disney reported net losses in 2014, 2015, and 2016. Whereas the company's total revenues decreased by 6.9 percent to €1,278 million in 2016, direct operating costs and marketing, sales, and general expenses increased by 4.0 and 7.0 percent, respectively. Euro Disney's operating cash flows amounted to €78, €69, and -€68 million (negative) in 2014, 2015, and 2016, respectively. In all three years, the cash flows used in investing activities were more than the operating cash flows, resulting in negative free cash flows. In 2016 Euro Disney's free cash flow decreased from -€65 million (negative) to -€261 million (negative) as a consequence of decreased operating performance and increased investments in attractions and hotel renovation.

The company's trade receivables to sales ratio decreased from 5.9 percent in 2014 to 4.1 percent in 2016. Liabilities for deferred revenues as a percentage of sales increased from 10.8 percent in 2014 to 11.7 percent in 2016. The allowance for uncollectible receivables increased from 1.4 percent (of gross trade receivables) in 2014 to 1.9 percent in 2016 (after having been 3.2 percent in 2009); the allowance for inventories obsolescence decreased from 8.9 percent (of gross inventories) in 2014 to 8.3 percent in 2016. During fiscal year 2016, Euro Disney did not make any voluntary change in its accounting methods; profit or loss included an impairment charge of €565 million related to tangible and intangible assets. Related party transactions consisted primarily of the payment of royalties and management fees to the *Gérant*, payments to the *Gérant* to reimburse the direct and indirect costs of the technical and administrative services provided, and interest payments to the Walt Disney Company. Such payments amounted to 12.9 percent of revenues in 2016 (or 9.8 percent excluding interest charges). Euro Disney's tax expense was zero in 2014, 2015, and 2016. At the end of fiscal year 2016, the company's unused tax loss carryforwards amounted to €2.7 billion and could be carried forward indefinitely. The company's 2016 financial statements received an unqualified audit opinion.

At the end of fiscal 2016, Euro Disney's share price was €1.18. The company's average share return since the end of fiscal 2008 had been −55 percent (or −9

percent annually). During fiscal 2014 the company's share return had been -6 percent.

1  Identify the key accounting policies (step 1) and primary areas of accounting flexibility (step 2) for Euro Disney.

2  What incentives may influence management's reporting strategy (step 3)? Did the changes made in 2012 affect management's incentives?

3  What disclosures would you consider an essential part of the company's annual report, given its key success factors and key accounting policies (step 4)?

4  What potential red flags can you identify (step 5)?

## Notes

1  Accounting analysis is sometimes also called quality of earnings analysis. We prefer to use the term accounting analysis because we are discussing a broader concept than merely a firm's earnings quality.

2  Thus, although accrual accounting is theoretically superior to cash accounting in measuring a firm's periodic performance, the distortions it introduces can make accounting data less valuable to users. If these distortions are large enough, current cash flows may measure a firm's periodic performance better than accounting profits. The relative usefulness of cash flows and accounting profits in measuring performance therefore varies from firm to firm. For empirical evidence on this issue, see P. Dechow, "Accounting Earnings and Cash Flows as Measures of Firm Performance: The Role of Accounting Accruals," *Journal of Accounting and Economics* 18 (July 1994): 3–42; and A. Charitou, C. Clubb, and A. Andreou, "The Effect of Earnings Permanence, Growth and Firm Size on the Usefulness of Cash Flows and Earnings in Explaining Security Returns: Empirical Evidence for the UK," *Journal of Business Finance and Accounting* 28 (June/July 2001): 563–594.

3  For example, a recent study shows that accounting adjustments made by Moody's (credit) analysts help to explain stock prices and analysts' target prices and recommendations (G. De Franco, F. Wong, and Y. Zhou, "Accounting Adjustments and the Valuation of Financial Statement Note Information in 10-K Filings," *Accounting Review* 86 (2011): 1577–1604). Further, Abraham Briloff wrote a series of accounting analyses of public companies in *Barron's* over several years. On average, the share prices of the analyzed companies changed by about 8 percent on the day these articles were published, indicating the potential value of performing such analysis. For a more complete discussion of this evidence, see G. Foster,

"Briloff and the Capital Market," *Journal of Accounting Research* 17 (Spring 1979): 262–274.

4  For a complete discussion of these motivations, see *Positive Accounting Theory*, by R. Watts and J. Zimmerman (Englewood Cliffs, NJ: Prentice-Hall, 1986). A summary of this research is provided by P. Healy and J. Wahlen, "A Review of the Earnings Management Literature and Its Implications for Standard Setting," *Accounting Horizons* 13 (December 1999): 365–383; and T. Fields, T. Lys, and L. Vincent in "Empirical Research on Accounting Choice," *Journal of Accounting and Economics* 31 (September 2001): 255–307.

5  The most convincing evidence supporting the covenant hypothesis is reported in a study of the accounting decisions by firms in financial distress: A. Sweeney, "Debt-Covenant Violations and Managers' Accounting Responses," *Journal of Accounting and Economics* 17 (May 1994): 281–308.

6  Studies that examine the bonus hypothesis generally report evidence supporting the view that managers' accounting decisions are influenced by compensation considerations. See, for example, P. Healy, "The Effect of Bonus Schemes on Accounting Decisions," *Journal of Accounting and Economics* 7 (April 1985): 85–107; R. Holthausen, D. Larcker, and R. Sloan, "Annual Bonus Schemes and the Manipulation of Earnings," *Journal of Accounting and Economics* 19 (February 1995): 29–74; and F. Guidry, A. Leone, and S. Rock, "Earnings-Based Bonus Plans and Earnings Management by Business Unit Managers," *Journal of Accounting and Economics* 26 (January 1999): 113–142.

7  For empirical evidence that CEOs of firms with scheduled awards make opportunistic voluntary disclosures to maximize stock award compensation, see D. Aboody and R. Kasznik, "CEO Stock Option Awards and the

Timing of Corporate Voluntary Disclosures," *Journal of Accounting and Economics* 29 (February 2000): 73–100.

8  L. DeAngelo, "Managerial Competition, Information Costs, and Corporate Governance: The Use of Accounting Performance Measures in Proxy Contests," *Journal of Accounting and Economics* 10 (January 1988): 3–36; and M. Erickson and S. Wang, "Earnings Management by Acquiring Firms in Stock for Stock Mergers," *Journal of Accounting and Economics* 27 (1999): 149–176.

9  The trade-off between taxes and financial reporting in the context of managers' accounting decisions is discussed in detail in *Taxes and Business Strategy* by M. Scholes and M. Wolfson (Englewood Cliffs, NJ: Prentice-Hall, 1992). Many empirical studies have examined firms' LIFO/FIFO choices.

10  Several researchers have documented that firms affected by such situations have a motivation to influence regulators' perceptions through accounting decisions. For example, J. Jones documents that firms seeking import protections make profit-decreasing accounting decisions in "Earnings Management during Import Relief Investigations," *Journal of Accounting Research* 29(2) (Autumn 1991): 193–228. Similarly, W. Beekes finds that UK water and electricity companies make profit-decreasing accounting choices in years of regulatory price reviews in "Earnings Management in Response to Regulatory Price Review. A Case Study of the Political Cost Hypothesis in the Water and Electricity Sectors in England and Wales," Working paper, Lancaster University, 2003. A number of studies find that banks that are close to minimum capital requirements overstate loan loss provisions, understate loan write-offs, and recognize abnormal realized gains on securities portfolios (see S. Moyer, "Capital Adequacy Ratio Regulations and Accounting Choices in Commercial Banks," *Journal of Accounting and Economics* 12 (1990): 123–154; M. Scholes, G.P. Wilson, and M. Wolfson, "Tax Planning, Regulatory Capital Planning, and Financial Reporting Strategy for Commercial Banks," *Review of Financial Studies* 3 (1990): 625–650; A. Beatty, S. Chamberlain, and J. Magliolo, "Managing Financial Reports of Commercial Banks: The Influence of Taxes, Regulatory Capital and Earnings," *Journal of Accounting Research* 33(2) (1995): 231–261; and J. Collins, D. Shackelford, and J. Wahlen, "Bank Differences in the Coordination of Regulatory Capital, Earnings and Taxes," *Journal of Accounting Research* 33(2) (Autumn 1995): 263–291. Finally, Petroni finds that financially weak property-casualty insurers that risk regulatory attention understate claim loss reserves: K. Petroni, "Optimistic Reporting in the Property Casualty Insurance Industry," *Journal of Accounting and Economics* 15 (December 1992): 485–508.

11  P. Healy and K. Palepu, "The Effect of Firms' Financial Disclosure Strategies on Stock Prices," *Accounting Horizons* 7 (March 1993): 1–11. For a summary of the empirical evidence, see P. Healy and J. Wahlen,

"A Review of the Earnings Management Literature and Its Implications for Standard Setting," *Accounting Horizons* 13 (December 1999): 365–384.

12  In "Stakeholders' Implicit Claims and Accounting Method Choice," *Journal of Accounting and Economics* 20 (December 1995): 255–295, R. Bowen, L. DuCharme, and D. Shores argue that, based on theory and anecdotal evidence, managers choose long-run income-increasing accounting methods as a result of ongoing implicit claims between a firm and its customers, suppliers, employees, and short-term creditors.

13  Financial analysts pay close attention to managers' disclosure strategies; Standard and Poor's publishes scores that rate the disclosure of companies from around the world. For a discussion of these ratings, see, for example, T. Khanna, K. Palepu, and S. Srinivasan, "Disclosure Practices of Foreign Companies Interacting with US Markets," *Journal of Accounting Research* 42 (May 2004): 475–508.

14  See P. Healy and K. Palepu, "The Fall of Enron," *Journal of Economic Perspectives* 17(2) (Spring 2003): 3–26.

15  For detailed analyses of companies that made such changes, see R. Schattke and R. Vergoossen, "Barriers to Interpretation: A Case Study of Philips Electronics NV," *Accounting and Business Research* 27 (1996): 72–84, and K. Palepu, "Anatomy of an Accounting Change," in *Accounting and Management: Field Study Perspectives*, edited by W. Bruns, Jr. and R. Kaplan (Boston: Harvard Business School Press, 1987).

16  Examples of this type of behavior are documented by J. Hand in his study, "Did Firms Undertake Debt-Equity Swaps for an Accounting Paper Profit or True Financial Gain?" *The Accounting Review* 64 (October 1989): 587–623, and by E. Black, K. Sellers, and T. Manley in "Earnings Management Using Asset Sales: An International Study of Countries Allowing Noncurrent Asset Revaluation," *Journal of Business Finance and Accounting* 25 (November/December 1998): 1287–1317.

17  For an empirical analysis of inventory buildups, see V. Bernard and J. Noel, "Do Inventory Disclosures Predict Sales and Earnings?" *Journal of Accounting, Auditing, and Finance* (Fall 1991).

18  For research on accounting and economic incentives in the formation of R&D partnerships, see A. Beatty, P. Berger, and J. Magliolo, "Motives for Forming Research and Development Financing Organizations," *Journal of Accounting and Economics* 19 (April 1995): 411–442. An overview of Enron's use of special purpose entities to manage earnings and window-dress its balance is provided by P. Healy and K. Palepu, "The Fall of Enron," *Journal of Economic Perspectives* 17(2) (Spring 2003): 3–26.

19  For an empirical examination of asset write-offs, see J. Elliott and W. Shaw, "Write-offs as Accounting Procedures to Manage Perceptions," *Journal of Accounting Research* 26 (1988): 91–119.

20  R. Mendenhall and W. Nichols report evidence consistent with managers taking advantage of their discretion

to postpone reporting bad news until the year-end. See R. Mendenhall and W. Nichols, "Bad News and Differential Market Reactions to Announcements of Earlier-Quarter versus Fourth-Quarter Earnings," *Journal of Accounting Research,* Supplement (1988): 63–86.

21　K. Peasnell, P. Pope, and S. Young report evidence that independent outside directors prevent earnings management. See K. Peasnell, P. Pope, and S. Young, "Board Monitoring and Earnings Management: Do Outside Directors Influence Abnormal Accruals?," *Journal of Business Finance and Accounting* 32 (September 2005): 1311–1346.

22　The role of insider transactions in the collapse of Enron are discussed by P. Healy and K. Palepu, "The Fall of Enron," *Journal of Economic Perspectives* 17(2) (Spring 2003): 3–26.

23　This type of analysis is presented in the context of provisions for bad debts by M. McNichols and P. Wilson in their study, "Evidence of Earnings Management from the Provisions for Bad Debts," *Journal of Accounting Research,* Supplement (1988): 1–31.

24　This point has been made by several accounting researchers. For a summary of research on earnings management, see K. Schipper, "Earnings Management," *Accounting Horizons* (December 1989): 91–102.

25　See H. Daske, L. Hail, C. Leuz, and R. Verdi, "Mandatory IFRS Standards Reporting around the World: Early Evidence on the Economic Consequences," *Journal of Accounting Research* 46 (2008): 1085–1142.

26　See J. Chang, "The Decline in Value Relevance of Earnings and Book Values," unpublished dissertation, Harvard University, 1998. Evidence is also reported by J. Francis and K. Schipper, "Have Financial Statements Lost Their Relevance?," *Journal of Accounting Research* 37(2) (Autumn 1999): 319–352; and W.E. Collins, E. Maydew, and I. Weiss, "Changes in the Value-Relevance of Earnings and Book Value over the Past Forty Years," *Journal of Accounting and Economics* 24 (1997): 39–67.

27　See G. Foster, "Briloff and the Capital Market," *Journal of Accounting Research* 17(1) (Spring 1979): 262–274.

28　See S. H. Teoh, I. Welch, and T. J. Wong, "Earnings Management and the Long-Run Market Performance of Initial Public Offerings," *Journal of Finance* 53 (December 1998a): 1935–1974; S.H. Teoh, I. Welch and T.J. Wong, "Earnings Management and the Post-Issue Underperformance of Seasoned Equity Offerings," *Journal of Financial Economics* 50 (October 1998): 63–99; and S. Teoh, T. Wong, and G. Rao, "Are Accruals During Initial Public Offerings Opportunistic?," *Review of Accounting Studies* 3(1–2) (1998): 175–208.

29　See P. Dechow, R. Sloan, and A. Sweeney, "Causes and Consequences of Earnings Manipulation: An Analysis of Firms Subject to Enforcement Actions by the SEC," *Contemporary Accounting Research* 13(1) (1996): 1–36; and M.D. Beneish, "Detecting GAAP Violation: Implications for Assessing Earnings Management among Firms with Extreme Financial Performance," *Journal of Accounting and Public Policy* 16 (1997): 271–309.

# Appendix A: First-time adoption of IFRS Standards

The widespread use of IFRS Standards to prepare financial statements is a relatively recent phenomenon. By the end of 2004, around 1,000 firms worldwide prepared their financial statements in conformity with IFRS Standards. Since the mandated introduction of IFRS Standards-based reporting in, amongst other countries, the EU, the United Kingdom, Australia (2005), New Zealand (2007), Brazil (2010), Canada, and Korea (2011), however, the number of IFRS Standards users has grown explosively to over 27,000 firms. Although the worldwide move to using one common set of accounting rules yields many advantages for the analyst, the switch from local to international accounting rules also complicates the accounting analysis a little.

In the first year that a firm applies IFRS Standards, it is required to provide the current year's IFRS Standards-based financial figures as well as restate the prior year's balance sheet and income statement for comparative purposes. This means that the firm traces back every historical event and assumption that is relevant to a particular line item on the opening balance sheet of the prior year, recalculates the impact of these events and assumptions on the items, and essentially produces its first IFRS Standards-based opening balance sheet as though it had applied the IFRS Standards all along (though applying current IFRS Standards). The firm then records all the events during the prior year and the current year in accordance with IFRS Standards. To avoid the misuse of hindsight, when preparing its opening IFRS Standards-based balance sheet, the first-time IFRS Standards adopter cannot use information that it received after the balance sheet date.

In their first IFRS Standards-based financial statements, firms have to disclose at least the following information to illustrate the effects of IFRS Standards adoption on their financial figures:

• A description of the sources of differences between equity reported under previous accounting standards and under IFRS Standards as well as the effects of these differences in quantitative terms. The firm must provide such reconciliations for equity in both its opening and its closing comparative balance sheets.

- A reconciliation of profit or loss reported under previous accounting standards and under IFRS Standards for the prior year.

Some firms also voluntarily disclose the opening IFRS Standards-based balance sheet of the prior year, improving the analyst's dataset, but they are not required to do so.

Unfortunately, in practice it is difficult for a first-time IFRS Standards adopter to trace back every relevant historical event because it may not have collected or stored all the necessary data in the past. Further, the informational benefits of recalculating and restating certain line items may not outweigh the associated costs. For example, firms that consolidate the translated values of subsidiaries' foreign currency-denominated assets on their balance sheets recognize the cumulative translation difference, which arises because exchange rates fluctuate over the years, as a separate component in equity. When these firms adopt IFRS Standards, they would face the tedious task of recalculating all cumulative translation differences on their subsidiaries. Because separately reporting restated cumulative translation differences generates little additional information, however, first-time IFRS Standards adopters can choose to add the cumulative translation differences to equity and reset the line item to zero upon adoption. To facilitate the first-time preparation of an IFRS Standards-based opening balance sheet, the rules on the first-time IFRS Standards application allow more of these exemptions and even prohibit some restatements.

## Appendix B: Recasting financial statements into standardized templates

The following tables show the financial statements for Hennes and Mauritz AB for the year ended November 30, 2017. The first column in each statement presents the recast financial statement classifications that are used for each line item. Note that the classifications are not applied to subtotal lines such as Total current assets. The recast financial statements for Hennes and Mauritz are prepared by simply totalling the balances of line items with the same standard classifications. For example, on the recast balance sheet are four line items classified as Non-Current Intangible Assets: Brands, Customer relations, Capitalized expenditure (mostly IT-related) and Goodwill.

Hennes & Mauritz reported balance sheet (SEK millions)

| Classifications | Fiscal year November 30 | 2017 |
|---|---|---|
| | **ASSETS** | |
| Non-Current Intangible Assets | Brands | 18 |
| Non-Current Intangible Assets | Customer relations | 8 |
| Non-Current Tangible Assets | Leasehold and similar rights | 592 |
| Non-Current Intangible Assets | Goodwill | 64 |
| Non-Current Intangible Assets | Capitalized development expenditure | 6,361 |
| Non-Current Tangible Assets | Buildings and land | 824 |
| Non-Current Tangible Assets | Equipment, tools, fixtures and fittings | 38,994 |
| Other Non-Operating Investments | Long-term receivables | 1,039 |
| Deferred Tax Asset | Deferred tax receivables | 2,916 |
| | **Total fixed assets** | **50,816** |

| Classifications | Fiscal year November 30 | 2017 |
|---|---|---|
| Inventories | Stock-in-trade | 33,712 |
| Trade Receivables | Accounts receivable | 5,297 |
| Other Current Assets | Tax receivables | 2,375 |
| Other Current Assets | Other receivables | 1,377 |
| Derivatives – Asset | Forward contracts | 497 |
| Other Current Assets | Prepaid expenses | 2,770 |
| Cash and Cash Equivalents | Short-term investments | 601 |
| Cash and Cash Equivalents | Cash and cash equivalents | 9,117 |
| | **Total current assets** | **55,746** |
| Total Assets | **Total assets** | **106,562** |
| | **LIABILITIES AND SHAREHOLDERS' EQUITY** | |
| Ordinary Shareholders' Equity | Share capital | 207.0 |
| Ordinary Shareholders' Equity | Reserves | 1,015.0 |
| Ordinary Shareholders' Equity | Retained earnings | 42,307.0 |
| Ordinary Shareholders' Equity | Profit for the year | 16,184.0 |
| | **Equity** | **59,713.0** |
| Non-Current Debt | Provisions for pensions | 445 |
| Deferred Tax Liability | Other interest-bearing liabilities | 350 |
| Deferred Tax Liability | Deferred tax liabilities | 5,331 |
| | **Total noncurrent liabilities** | **6,126** |
| Trade Payables | Accounts payable | 7,215 |
| Other Current Liabilities | Tax liabilities | 918 |
| Current Debt | Liabilities to credit institutions | 9,745 |
| Current Debt | Other interest-bearing liabilities | 125 |
| Derivatives – Liability | Forward contracts | 903 |
| Other Current Liabilities | Other liabilities | 2,769 |
| Other Current Liabilities | Accrued expenses and prepaid income | 19,048 |
| | **Total current liabilities** | **40,723** |
| Total Liabilities and Shareholders' Equity | **Total liabilities and shareholders' equity** | **106,562** |

## Hennes & Mauritz reported income statement (SEK millions)

| Classifications | Fiscal year ended November 30 | 2017 |
|---|---|---|
| Revenue | Sales, excluding VAT | 200,004 |
| Cost of Sales (function) | Cost of goods sold | (91,914) |
| | **Gross profit** | **108,090** |
| SG&A (function) | Selling expenses | (80,427) |
| SG&A (function) | Administrative expenses | (7,081) |
| Interest Expense | Interest expense – provision for pensions (taken from note 18) | (13) |
| | **Operating profit** | **20,569** |
| Interest Income | Interest income and similar items | 281 |
| Interest Expense | Interest expense and similar items | (41) |
| | **Profit after financial items** | **20,809** |
| Tax Expense | Tax | (4,625) |
| Profit/Loss to Ordinary Shareholders | **Profit for the year** | **16,184** |
| | **INCOME STATEMENT ITEMS BY NATURE** | |
| Personnel Expenses (nature) | Salaries, other remuneration and payroll overheads | (35,634) |
| Depreciation and Amortization (nature) | Depreciation – within cost of goods sold | (736) |
| Depreciation and Amortization (nature) | Depreciation – within selling expenses | (7,175) |
| Depreciation and Amortization (nature) | Depreciation – within administrative expenses | (577) |

## Hennes & Mauritz reported cash flow statement (SEK millions)

| Classifications | Fiscal year ended November 30 | 2017 |
|---|---|---|
| Profit Before Interest and Tax | Profit after financial items | 20,809 |
| Profit Before Interest and Tax | Net interest expense | (227) |
| Interest Paid | Interest paid | (41) |
| Interest Received | Interest received | 281 |
| Interest Paid | Interest paid – provision for pensions (note 18) | (13) |
| | Adjustment for: | |
| Non-Current Operating Accruals | Provisions for pensions | 9 |
| Non-Current Operating Accruals | Depreciation | 8,488 |
| Taxes Paid | Tax paid | (6,051) |
| Non-Current Operating Accruals | Other | (20) |
| Net (Investments in) or Liquidation of Operating Working Capital | Changes in current receivables | (1,115) |
| Net (Investments in) or Liquidation of Operating Working Capital | Changes in stock-in-trade | (2,414) |
| Net (Investments in) or Liquidation of Operating Working Capital | Changes in current liabilities | 1,881 |
| | **Cash flow from current operations** | **21,587** |

| Classifications | Fiscal year ended November 30 | 2017 |
|---|---|---|
| Net (Investments in) or Liquidation of Non-Current Operating or Investment Assets | Investment in leasehold and similar rights | (102) |
| Net (Investments in) or Liquidation of Non-Current Operating or Investment Assets | Investment in other intangible assets | (2,058) |
| Net (Investments in) or Liquidation of Non-Current Operating or Investment Assets | Investment in buildings and land | (27) |
| Net (Investments in) or Liquidation of Non-Current Operating or Investment Assets | Investment in equipment | (10,284) |
| Net (Investments in) or Liquidation of Non-Current Operating or Investment Assets | Other investments | (25) |
| | **Cash flow from investing activities** | **(12,496)** |
| Net Debt (Repayment) or Issuance | Short-term loans | 7,677 |
| Net Debt (Repayment) or Issuance | Amortization finance lease | (57) |
| Dividend (Payments) | Dividend | (16,137) |
| | **Cash flows from financing activities** | **(8,517)** |
| | Exchange rate effect | (302) |
| | Cash flow for the year | 272 |
| | Cash and cash equivalents at beginning of year | 9,446 |
| | **Cash and cash equivalents at end of year** | **9,718** |

The standardized financial statements for Hennes and Mauritz AB are as follows:

Hennes & Mauritz standardized balance sheet (SEK millions)

| | 2017 |
|---|---|
| **ASSETS** | |
| Non-Current Tangible Assets | 40,410 |
| Non-Current Intangible Assets | 6,451 |
| Minority Equity Investments | 0 |
| Other Non-Operating Investments | 1,039 |
| Deferred Tax Asset | 2,916 |
| Derivatives – Asset | 497 |
| **Total Non-Current Assets** | **51,313** |
| Inventories | 33,712 |
| Trade Receivables | 5,297 |
| Other Current Assets | 6,522 |
| Cash and Cash Equivalents | 9,718 |
| **Total Current Assets** | **55,249** |
| **Assets Held for Sale** | **0** |
| **Total Assets** | **106,562** |

|  | 2017 |
|---|---|
| **LIABILITIES AND SHAREHOLDERS' EQUITY** | |
| **Ordinary Shareholders' Equity** | **59,713** |
| **Non-Controlling Interest in Equity** | **0** |
| **Preference Shares** | **0** |
| Non-Current Debt | 795 |
| Deferred Tax Liability | 5,331 |
| Derivatives – Liability | 903 |
| Other Non-Current Liabilities (non-interest-bearing) | 0 |
| **Non-Current Liabilities** | **7,029** |
| Trade Payables | 7,215 |
| Other Current Liabilities | 22,735 |
| Current Debt | 9,870 |
| **Current Liabilities** | **39,820** |
| **Liabilities Held for Sale** | **0** |
| **Total Liabilities and Shareholders' Equity** | **106,562** |

Hennes & Mauritz standardized income statement (SEK millions)

|  | 2017 |
|---|---|
| **Revenue** | 200,004 |
| Operating expenses | (179,422) |
| **Operating profit** | **20,582** |
| Investment income | 0 |
| Net non-recurring income or expense | 0 |
| Net interest expense (income) | |
| Interest income | 281 |
| Interest expense | (54) |
| **Profit before taxes** | **20,809** |
| Tax expense | (4,625) |
| **Profit after taxes** | **16,184** |
| Profit/loss to non-controlling interest | 0 |
| **Profit to ordinary shareholders** | **16,184** |

|                                                                 | 2017     |
|-----------------------------------------------------------------|----------|
| **Operating expenses**                                          |          |
| Classification by function:                                     |          |
| Cost of Sales (function)                                        | (91,914) |
| SG&A (function)                                                 | (87,508) |
| Other Operating Income, Net of Other Operating Expenses (function) | 0     |
| Classification by nature:                                       |          |
| Cost of Materials (nature)                                      | (91,178) |
| Personnel Expenses (nature)                                     | (35,634) |
| Depreciation and Amortization (nature)                          | (8,488)  |
| Other Operating Income, Net of Other Operating Expenses (nature) | (44,122) |

Hennes & Mauritz standardized cash flow statement (SEK millions)

|                                                                 | 2017     |
|-----------------------------------------------------------------|----------|
| Profit Before Interest and Tax                                  | 20,582   |
| Taxes Paid                                                      | (6,051)  |
| Non-Operating Losses (Gains)                                    | 0        |
| Non-Current Operating Accruals                                  | 8,477    |
| **Operating Cash Flow before Working Capital Investments**      | **23,008** |
| Net (Investments in) or Liquidation of Operating Working Capital | (1,648) |
| **Operating Cash Flow before Investment in Non-Current Assets** | **21,360** |
| Interest Received                                               | 281      |
| Dividends Received                                              | 0        |
| Net (Investments in) or Liquidation of Non-Current Operating or Investment Assets | (12,496) |
| **Free Cash Flow Available to Debt and Equity**                 | **9,145** |
| Interest Paid                                                   | (54)     |
| Net Debt (Repayment) or Issuance                                | 7,620    |
| **Free Cash Flow Available to Equity**                          | **16,711** |
| Dividend (Payments)                                             | (16,137) |
| Net share (Repurchase) or Issuance                              | 0        |
| **Net Increase (Decrease) in Cash Balance**                     | **574**  |

# Toshiba: Accounting fraud

**IVEY** | Publishing

On July 22, 2015, Masashi Muromachi was appointed president of Toshiba Corporation (Toshiba) after the resignation of the former chief executive officer (CEO), Hisao Tanaka. Tanaka had resigned over the revelation of a JP¥151.8 billion (US$1.2 billion)[1] accounting scandal that shocked the world. At a press conference, Muromachi commented on his new role: "I am strongly feeling the social responsibility of alarming and causing trouble to our 400,000 shareholders, including domestic and international investors, as well as our clients and the authorities concerned. We will devote ourselves wholeheartedly to regain your trust, and revive Toshiba under the new management."[2] Toshiba, a Japanese multinational conglomerate with net sales of ¥6.5 trillion and total assets of ¥6.2 trillion, had been widely criticized in the news for the multibillion-dollar accounting fraud. The company's stock prices had declined by 38 percent since it announced the accounting probe,[3] and the company had withdrawn the dividend that had been declared earlier.[4]

The impact of the decreased share prices and the withdrawal of the declared dividend due to the accounting scandal had been challenging for investors in the company, who had always regarded Toshiba as a reputable company. On September 30, 2015, shareholders protested at an investor meeting, questioning the company officials as to what went wrong. As the *Hürriyet Daily News* noted, "Nearly 2000 shareholders turned up to an investor meeting outside Tokyo, peppering a new management team with questions about the affair which led to the resignation of Toshiba's president and seven other top executives in July."[5]

The investors were wondering the same as everyone else watching the scandal unfold: how could a company with a 140-year history do this, and why? "There was no explanation of what we [wanted] to know most: why it happened and who is to blame," said one investor.[6] Understanding investors' concerns and the damage done by the accounting fraud to Toshiba's investors worldwide, Muromachi, the newly appointed CEO, apologized

*Anupam Mehta wrote this case solely to provide material for class discussion. The author does not intend to illustrate either effective or ineffective handling of a managerial situation. The author may have disguised certain names and other identifying information to protect confidentiality.*

---

[1]All currency amounts are in Japanese yen (¥) unless otherwise specified; JP¥1 = US$0.0082 on October 5, 2015.
[2]Michal Addady, "Toshiba's Accounting Scandal Is Much Worse than We Thought," *Fortune*, September 8, 2015, accessed September 12, 2015, http://fortune.com/2015/09/08/toshiba-accounting-scandal.
[3]Pavel Alpeyev and Takashi Amano, "Toshiba Executives Resign over $1.2 Billion Accounting Scandal," Bloomberg, July 21, 2015, accessed September 17, 2015, www.bloomberg.com/news/articles/2015-07-21/toshiba-executives-resign-over-1-2-billion-accounting-scandal.
[4]"Toshiba Cancels Dividend over Accounting Probe," RTÉ News, May 11, 2015, accessed September 16, 2015, www.rte.ie/news/business/2015/0511/700223-toshiba-accounting-dividend.
[5]"Toshiba Management Faces Investor Wrath over Accounting Scandal," *Hürriyet Daily News*, September 3, 2015, accessed September 16, 2015, www.hurriyetdailynews.com/toshiba-management-faces-investor-wrath-over-accounting-scandal-.aspx?pageID=238&nID=89184&NewsCatID=345.
[6]"Toshiba Investors Still Puzzled about Bad Books," *Nikkei Asian Review*, July 2, 2015, accessed October 14, 2015, http://asia.nikkei.com/magazine/20150702-ASIA-S-STARTUPS-SWITCHED-ON/Business/Toshiba-investors-still-puzzledabout-bad-books.

to investors: "Toshiba Corporation expresses [its] sincere apologies to our shareholders, customers, business partners, and all other stakeholders for any concern or inconvenience caused by issues relating to the appropriateness of its accounting."[7]

However, investors were still haunted by the unsolved puzzle of the accounting scandal. What would the company do in response to this crisis?

## About the company

Toshiba was founded in 1938 with the merger of two firms, Shibaura Seisaku-sho (established in 1875) and Tokyo Denki (established in 1890). The Toshiba Group expanded and was driven by a combination of acquisitions and organic growth in the 1940s and 1950s. The company name was officially changed to Toshiba Corporation in 1978.

Since then, Toshiba, headquartered in Tokyo, Japan, had dealt in various products and services, including information technology equipment and systems, industrial and social infrastructure systems, electronic components and materials, consumer electronics, office equipment, household appliances, lighting, and logistics.[8] As of March 31, 2015, the company's financial and stock data included common stock valued at ¥439 billion and net sales of ¥6.7 trillion (US$55 billion), with 4 billion shares issued.[9] The company employed approximately 200,000 people.[10] Toshiba marketed itself as committed to improving the quality of life for all people and ensuring progress in the world community.[11]

Domestically, Toshiba was listed on the Tokyo Stock Exchange (TSE), Nagoya Stock Exchange, and Osaka Securities Exchange. As of March 2015 Toshiba had diversified into energy and infrastructure, community solutions, health care systems and services, electronic devices and components, lifestyle products and services, and others.

## Financial performance

### FINANCIAL PERFORMANCE BEFORE 2008

Toshiba had enjoyed good overall sales and performance until 2008, with the net sales of the company growing from ¥5.2 trillion to ¥7.2 trillion by the end of March 2008. At the beginning of 2008, Toshiba was in fourth position in the global portable personal computer market.

### FINANCIAL PERFORMANCE, 2009–2014

During 2009, Toshiba recorded disappointing results. The company implemented action programs to improve its profitability by bringing in a ¥319.2 billion public offering to increase its capital expenditure (mainly for strategic investments). From 2009 to 2013, Toshiba's total sales decreased from ¥6.5 trillion to ¥5.8 trillion, a fall of approximately 11 percent. In June 2013 Hisao Tanaka was named the president and CEO of Toshiba Group, while Asotosh Nishida held the position of chairman of the board of directors. The economic growth the firm had experienced was better than the previous year, but in terms of global economic growth, issues with the external business environment persisted.

[7]Masashi Muromachi, Toshiba, "Toshiba's New Management Team Is Determined to Regain Your Trust," message from the president, accessed October 14, 2015, www.toshiba.co.jp/worldwide/about/message.html.

[8]"Companies," Toshiba, accessed December 2, 2015, www.toshiba.co.jp/worldwide/about/company/index.html.

[9]"Corporate Data," Toshiba, accessed December 8, 2015, https://www.toshiba.co.jp/worldwide/about/corp_data.html.

[10]"Company Overview," Toshiba, accessed June 17, 2016, https://toshiba.semicon-storage.com/us/corporate/taec/company-overview.html.

[11]"Corporate Philosophy," Toshiba, accessed December 10, 2015, www.toshiba.co.jp/csr/en/policy/aim.htm.

For the fiscal year ending in March 2014, all business segments showed better sales and growth; as a result, the overall net sales of the company increased to ¥6.5 trillion, up from ¥5.8 trillion in the year ending March 2013. The operating income rose to ¥290 million, an increase of 47 percent, for the same period (see **Exhibits 1**, **2**, and **3**).

### FINANCIAL PERFORMANCE, Q1 2015

For the first quarter of the financial year ending March 31, 2015, the net sales of the company stood at ¥1,349 billion. In terms of operating income, the company incurred an operating loss of ¥11 billion, leading to a net income (loss) attributable to shareholders amounting to ¥12.3 billion.[12]

## The facts of the accounting fraud

On February 12, 2015, Toshiba received an order from the Securities and Exchange Surveillance Commission (SESC) to allow a disclosure inspection with respect to some projects in which a percentage of completion method of accounting, among other methods, was used (see **Exhibit 4**). The Japanese market regulator investigated Toshiba's accounting methods under the authority granted by Article 177 of the *Financial Instruments and Exchange Act*.[13]

The SESC's investigation was launched in response to a whistleblowing tip, the details of which were never disclosed. It was then unclear whether the irregularities were due to errors or were deliberate. Technology experts helped to recover deleted and old email messages that connected Toshiba with accounting fraud. The recovered emails contained messages suggesting the use of misleading practices, confirming that the irregularities were not simply errors: they were intentional manipulations.

An internal investigation committee was set up by Toshiba to investigate the company's book of accounts from financial year (FY) 2009 through the third quarter of FY2014. FY2008 was also included, but as a comparison year for the FY2009 securities report.[14] When the committee revealed the various fraudulent distortions across various Toshiba companies, Toshiba had no other choice but to establish an independent investigation committee, which first met on May 8, 2015. The independent investigation committee consisted of members from outside the company, as opposed to the company-appointed members of the internal committee.

The problem was identified as accounting fraud when investigators found evidence of overstated profits in various Toshiba business units, including the visual products unit, the personal computer unit, and the semiconductor unit. It was found that the total amount of contract costs was underestimated, and contract losses were not recorded in a timely manner.

The fraud had began under CEO Atsutoshi Nishida in 2008, in the middle of the global financial crisis, which had drastically reduced Toshiba's profitability.[15] The fraud had evidently continued with the same intensity under the next CEO, Norio Sasaki.

In June 2013 Hisao Tanaka, a long-time manager of procurement and manufacturing in Toshiba's consumer electronics division, was promoted to the position of president and CEO. As part of his management strategy,

---

[12]Toshiba, *Annual Report: Financial Review*, 2015, accessed September 25, 2015, www.toshiba.co.jp/about/ir/en/finance/ar.

[13]*Kin'yū shōhin torihiki-hō [Financial Instruments and Exchange Act]*, Act No. 25 of 1948, Japan, accessed June 16, 2016, www.fsa.go.jp/common/law/fie01.pdf.

[14]Toshiba, "Notice on Media Coverage of Investigation on Appropriateness of Toshiba's Accounting," press release, July 4, 2015, accessed October 5, 2015, www.toshiba.co.jp/about/ir/en/news/20150704_1.pdf.

[15]Tyler Durden, "Japan Inc. Rocked by Massive Accounting Fraud: Toshiba CEO Quits After Admitting 7 Years of Cooked Books," ZeroHedge, July 21, 2015, accessed October 5, 2015, https://www.zerohedge.com/news/2015-07-21/japan-inc-rocked-massive-accounting-scandal-toshiba-ceo-quits-after-admitting-7-year.

Tanaka pushed his employees to meet their budget targets.[16] The fraud continued under Tanaka in this budget-conscious environment and eventually ended in scandal.

Toshiba had a policy of personnel rotation after every few years, which had complicated (and perhaps facilitated) the fraud issue. Due to this policy, by the time a project was finished, the person who initiated it was gone, and his or her successor was held responsible for the losses of the project, if any. This system led to making immediate goals a priority, even if it meant taking orders at a loss.

In one of Toshiba's manufacturing contracts, the cost of the ordered work was expected to exceed the negotiated price; however, the company did not record a provision on the balance sheet for any loss-making contracts. In another project, Toshiba exaggerated its cost reductions. A review of the contract work concluded that ¥1.7 billion could be shed in costs; however, in reality, the costs were only reduced by ¥100 million.[17]

To meet its profit targets, Toshiba implemented a plan to carry over and overstate profits by adjusting profits and losses—a practice that had been going on since 2008. It was determined that Toshiba used a cash-based method for its accounting instead of using the accrual method. The company had also requested that its vendors issue postdate invoices in order to show those expenses in the next quarter, even though the expenses had already been incurred. The company had also failed to record some items, such as valuation losses, loan loss allowances, and so on.[18] Eight of the 16 members of the board resigned after the fraud became known.[19]

## Toshiba's corporate culture

According to a summary of the investigator's report, "Toshiba had a corporate culture in which management decisions could not be challenged." The investigation report further stated that "[e]mployees were pressured into inappropriate accounting by postponing loss reports or moving certain costs into later years." Toshiba's accounting fraud occurred less than four years after the Olympus Corporation scandal with accounting fraud.[20] In light of these instances of fraud in Japan, Japan's finance minister, Taro Aso, called the accounting fraud at Toshiba "very regrettable" and "a blow to the country's efforts to regain the confidence of global investors." He also added, "If [Japan] fails to implement appropriate corporate governance, it could lose the market's trust."[21]

## The situation by September 2015

The fraud was detected on July 21, 2015, and showed overstated earnings of ¥152 billion. On August 3, 2015, Toshiba was removed from the Dow Jones Sustainability World Index.[22] Toshiba planned to decide in late September how to punish its non-executives who were caught in the fraud. To prevent the reoccurrence of such a situation, Toshiba said that it would scrap its monthly president's meetings, where employees were told by top management to achieve unrealistic targets.[23] The company also decided to sell some of its assets to

[16]Richard Trenholm, "Toshiba CEO Quits as Accounting Scandal Adds Up to $1.22 Billion," CNET, July 21, 2015, accessed December 11, 2015, www.cnet.com/news/toshiba-ceo-quits-over-1-22bn-accounting-scandal.

[17]Independent Investigation Committee for Toshiba Corporation, *Investigation Report: Summary Version* (Tokyo: Toshiba Corporation, July 20, 2015), accessed June 17, 2016, www.toshiba.co.jp/about/ir/en/news/20150725_1.pdf.

[18]"Toshiba Accounting Scandal Snowballs to 24 Cases, ¥54.8 Billion," *Japan Times*, June 13, 2015, accessed October 5, 2015, www.japantimes.co.jp/news/2015/06/13/business/corporate-business/toshiba-accounting-scandal-snowballs-to-24-cases-%C2%A554-8-billion/#.VjAsVbcrLIV.

[19]Durden, op. cit.

[20]Three executives from Olympus Corporation pleaded guilty to accounting fraud, covering up losses of US$1.7 billion over 13 years; Terje Langeland, "Olympus Sued for $273 Million After 13-Year Fraud," Bloomberg, April 9, 2014, https://www.bloomberg.com/news/articles/2014-04-09/olympus-sued-for-273-million-after-13-year-fraud.

[21]Sean Farrell, "Toshiba Boss Quits over £780m Accounting Scandal," *Guardian*, July 21, 2015, accessed December 2, 2015, https://www.theguardian.com/world/2015/jul/21/toshiba-boss-quits-hisao-tanaka-accounting-scandal.

[22]S & P Dow Jones Indices, McGraw Hill Financial, "Toshiba Corporation to be Removed from Dow Jones Sustainability Index," press release, July 27, 2015, accessed December 12, 2015, https://www.sustainability-indices.com/media/4/b/8/4b8046f37fa1c5b60da5527a6794d3ba_150727-statement-toshiba-exclusion-vdef_tcm10-13258.pdf.

[23]"Toshiba Unveils More Exec Pay Cuts over Accounting Scam," *Japan Times*, July 30, 2015, accessed December 11, 2015, https://www.japantimes.co.jp/news/2015/07/30/business/corporate-business/toshiba-unveils-pay-cuts-affecting-16-execs-accounting-scam/.

recover part of the funds lost to the fraud. By September 29, 2015, Toshiba's shares were at ¥292.8,[24] a signficiant decrease from the peak stock price of ¥539.9, attained in December 2014.[25]

Mark Newman, an analyst at Sanford Bernstein, said that the financial impact was likely to be manageable because of Toshiba's flash-memory business. That business supplied smartphone makers such as Apple Inc., and was expected to provide a majority of the company's operating profit in the current year.[26] Yoshihiro Nakatani, a senior fund manager at Asahi Life Asset Management, had recommendations for Toshiba:

> *They need to change into a more transparent organization, which could mean the executives stepping down and bringing more outside directors. . . . There is an increasing chance of a downgrade. . . . Concerns are mounting that this will begin to affect the company's relationship with financial institutions.[27]*

On September 14, 2015, the TSE, under its Securities Listing Regulations, designated the shares of the company as "Securities on Alert," effective September 15, 2015. The TSE required payment from the company in the amount of ¥91.2 million as a listing agreement violation penalty.[28] The fears of Toshiba's shareholders intensified. What were the reasons behind this accounting fraud? What would its implications be?

[24]The highest value for Toshiba shares was ¥539.9 on December 5, 2014. The lowest value as of the time of writing was ¥158.0 on February 12, 2016. (Toshiba Corporation, "Tokyo Stock Quote—Toshiba Corp.," Bloomberg, accessed June 16, 2016.

[25]"Toshiba Corp. 6502.JP," *Wall Street Journal,* accessed December 10, 2015, http://quotes.wsj.com/JP/6502. The highest value for Toshiba shares was ¥539.9 on December 5, 2014. The lowest value as of the time of writing was ¥158.0 on February 12, 2016.

[26]Eric Pfanner, "Toshiba Still Struggles with Fukushima Impact," *Wall Street Journal,* June 22, 2015, accessed June 17, 2016, https://www.wsj.com/articles/toshiba-still-struggles-with-fukushima-impact-1434998874.

[27]"Toshiba Chiefs to Quit as Panel Finds 'Organized' Accounting Fraud: Sources," *Japan Times,* July 16, 2015, accessed December 10, 2015, www.japantimes.co.jp/news/2015/07/16/business/corporate-business/toshiba-chiefs-quit-panel-findsorganized-accounting-fraud-sources.

[28]Toshiba, "Notice on Designation of Toshiba Shares as 'Securities on Alert' and Imposition of Listing Agreement Violation Penalty," press release, September 14, 2015, accessed December 12, 2015, www.toshiba.co.jp/about/ir/en/news/20150914_1.pdf

**EXHIBIT 1**  Consolidated statements of income, toshiba group (¥ billions)

| Net sales, operating income (loss), net income (loss) | 2009 | 2010 | 2011 | 2012 | 2013 | 2014 |
|---|---|---|---|---|---|---|
| Net sales | 6,364,800 | 6,129,900 | 6,270,700 | 5,994,300 | 5,727,000 | 6,502,500 |
| Cost of sales | 5,103,905 | 4,710,778 | 4,781,880 | 4,538,563 | 4,313,956 | 4,854,349 |
| Selling, general, and administrative expenses | 1,493,754 | 1,301,472 | 1,250,128 | 1,253,156 | 1,215,289 | 1,357,430 |
| Operating income (loss) | −232,859 | 117,600 | 238,700 | 202,600 | 197,700 | 290,800 |
| Income (loss) from continuing operations | −259,677 | 27,200 | 194,700 | 145,400 | 159,600 | 180,900 |
| Income taxes | 61,562 | 33,534 | 407,200 | 64,200 | 59,315 | 96,299 |
| Net income (loss) attributable | −343,559 | −19,700 | 137,800 | 70,100 | 77,400 | 50,800 |

Note: Financial data reported for financial year ended March 31st.

Source: Toshiba, *Annual Report: Financial Review*, 2008–2014, accessed September 25, 2015, www.toshiba.co.jp/about/ir/en/finance/ar.

**EXHIBIT 2**  Consolidated statements of income, toshiba group (¥ millions)

| Assets | 2009 | 2010 | 2011 | 2012 | 2013 | 2014 |
|---|---|---|---|---|---|---|
| Current assets | 2,720,631 | 2,761,606 | 2,799,668 | 3,009,513 | 3,160,440 | 3,209,224 |
| Long-term receivables and investments | 534,853 | 622,854 | 660,380 | 701,225 | 706,188 | 664,646 |
| Property, plant, and equipment | 1,089,579 | 978,726 | 900,205 | 851,365 | 884,680 | 960,035 |
| Other assets | 1,108,162 | 1,087,987 | 1,019,066 | 1,190,634 | 1,348,694 | 1,407,718 |
| **Total assets** | **5,453,225** | **5,451,173** | **5,379,319** | **5,752,737** | **6,100,002** | **6,241,623** |

| Liabilities and equity | 2009 | 2010 | 2011 | 2012 | 2013 | 2014 |
|---|---|---|---|---|---|---|
| Short-term debt | 1,033,884 | 257,364 | 311,762 | 326,141 | 433,128 | 203,523 |
| Other current liabilities | 2,033,889 | 2,231,081 | 2,186,547 | 2,343,421 | 2,304,311 | 2,388,523 |
| Total current liabilities | 3,067,773 | 2,488,445 | 2,498,309 | 2,669,562 | 2,737,439 | 2,592,046 |
| Long-term debt | 776,768 | 960,938 | 769,544 | 909,620 | 1,038,448 | 1,184,864 |
| Other long-term liabilities | 849,403 | 874,168 | 931,850 | 943,344 | 908,038 | 812,386 |
| Total long-term liabilities | 1,626,171 | 1,835,106 | 1,701,394 | 1,852,964 | 1,946,486 | 1,997,250 |
| Equity attributable to shareholders of Toshiba Corporation | 447,346 | 797,455 | 868,119 | 863,481 | 1,034,268 | 1,229,066 |
| Equity attributable to noncontrolling interests | 311,935 | 330,167 | 311,497 | 366,730 | 381,809 | 423,261 |
| **Total liabilities and equity** | **5,453,225** | **5,451,173** | **5,379,319** | **5,752,737** | **6,100,002** | **6,241,623** |

Note: Financial data reported for financial year ended March 31st.

Source: Toshiba, *Annual Report: Financial Review*, 2008–2014, accessed September 25, 2015, www.toshiba.co.jp/about/ir/en/finance/ar.

**EXHIBIT 3**  Consolidated statement of cash flows, toshiba group (¥ millions)

| Cash flows | 2009 | 2010 | 2011 | 2012 | 2013 | 2014 |
|---|---|---|---|---|---|---|
| Net cash provided by (used in) operating activities | −16,011 | 451,445 | 374,084 | 334,997 | 132,316 | 286,586 |
| Net cash used in investing activities | −335,308 | −252,922 | −214,700 | −377,227 | −196,347 | −246,555 |
| **Free cash flows**[†] | **−351,319** | **198,523** | **159,384** | **−42,230** | **−64,031** | **40,031** |
| Net cash provided by (used in) financing activities | 478,452 | −277,861 | −154,716 | −240 | 41,772 | −89,309 |
| Effect of exchange rate changes on cash and cash equivalents | −31,989 | 2,994 | −13,277 | −2,065 | 17,123 | 11,449 |
| Net increase (decrease) in cash and cash equivalents | 95,144 | −76,344 | −8,609 | −44,535 | −5,136 | −37,829 |
| Cash and cash equivalents at beginning of year | 248,649 | 343,793 | 267,449 | 258,840 | 214,305 | 209,169 |
| **Cash and cash equivalents at end of year** | **343,793** | **267,449** | **258,840** | **214,305** | **209,169** | **171,340** |

[†] Free cash flow = Net cash provided by operating activities + Net cash used in investing activities

Note: Financial data reported for financial year ended March 31st.

Source: Toshiba, *Annual Report: Financial Review*, 2008–2014, accessed September 25, 2015, www.toshiba.co.jp/about/ir/en/finance/ar.

**EXHIBIT 4**  Percentage of completion method of accounting

This method of accounting recognizes a portion of revenue associated with a long-term contract in each accounting period of construction or production under the contract. The percentage of completion is typically estimated by dividing the total construction costs incurred to date by the total estimated costs of the contract or job.

$$\% \ complete = \frac{Total \ Construction \ or \ Production \ Costs \ to \ Date}{Total \ Estimated \ Costs \ of \ Contract}$$

Total estimated revenue, or gross profit, is then multiplied by this percentage of completion to derive the total revenue or gross profit that has been earned to date.

$$Gross \ Profit \ to \ Date = \% \ Complete \times Total \ Estimated \ Gross \ Profit$$

Percentage of completion follows the accrual principle of accounting and matches expenses with related revenue.

Source: Roman L. Weil, Katherine Schipper, and Jennifer Francis, *Student Solutions Manual to Financial Accounting: An Introduction to Concepts, Methods, and Uses*, 14th. ed. (Mason, OH: Cengage Learning, 2014).

# 4 Accounting analysis: Accounting adjustments

We learned in Chapter 3 that accounting analysis requires the analyst to adjust a firm's accounting numbers using cash flow information and information from the notes to the financial statements to "undo" accounting distortions (where possible).

Once the financial statements have been standardized, the analyst is ready to identify any distortions in financial statements. The analyst's primary focus should be on those accounting estimates and methods that the firm uses to measure its key success factors and risks. If there are differences in these estimates and/or methods between firms or for the same firm over time, the analyst's job is to assess whether they reflect legitimate business differences and therefore require no adjustment, or whether they reflect differences in managerial judgment or bias and require adjustment. In addition, even if accounting rules are adhered to consistently, accounting distortions can arise because accounting rules themselves do a poor job of capturing firm economics, creating opportunities for the analyst to adjust a firm's financials in a way that presents a more realistic picture of its performance.

This chapter discusses the most common types of accounting distortions that can arise and shows how to make adjustments to the standardized financial statements to undo these distortions.

A balance sheet approach is used to identify whether there have been any distortions to assets, liabilities, or shareholders' equity. Once any asset and liability misstatements have been identified, the analyst can make adjustments to the balance sheet at the beginning and/or end of the current year, as well as any needed adjustments to revenues and expenses in the latest income statement. This approach ensures that the most recent financial ratios used to evaluate a firm's performance and forecast its future results are based on financial data that appropriately reflect its business economics.

In some instances, information taken from a firm's notes to the balance sheet, cash flow statement, and statement of comprehensive income enables the analyst to make a precise adjustment for an accounting distortion. However, for many types of accounting adjustments the company does not disclose all of the information needed to perfectly undo the distortion, requiring the analyst to make an approximate adjustment to the financial statements.

## Recognition of assets

Accountants define assets as resources that a firm owns or controls as a result of past business transactions and which can produce future economic benefits that are measurable with a reasonable degree of certainty. Assets can take a variety of forms, including cash, marketable securities, receivables from customers, inventories, tangible assets, non-current investments in other companies, and intangibles.

**Distortions in asset** values generally arise because there is ambiguity about whether:

- The firm owns or controls the economic resources in question.
- The economic resources can provide future economic benefits that can be measured with reasonable certainty.
- The fair values of assets fall below their book values.
- Fair value estimates are accurate.

## WHO OWNS OR CONTROLS RESOURCES?

For most resources used by a firm, ownership or control is relatively straightforward: the firm using the resource owns the asset. However, some types of transactions make it difficult to assess who owns a resource. For example, who owns or controls a resource that has been leased? Is it the lessor or the lessee? Or consider a firm that factors a customer receivable with a bank. If the bank has recourse against the firm should the customer default, is the real owner of the receivable the bank or the company? Or consider a firm owning 49 percent of another firm's ordinary shares. Does the firm control all of the investment's assets or only the net investment it legally owns?

Accounting rules often leave some discretion to managers and auditors in deciding whether their company owns or controls an asset. Leaving discretion to managers and auditors can be preferred over imposing detailed and mechanical rules if the latter solution causes managers to structure their transactions such that they avoid recognizing an asset. Following this idea, the IASB frequently takes a principles-based approach to setting accounting standards, thereby granting managers greater reporting discretion than under a rules-based approach. For example, the international standard for preparing consolidated financial statements (IFRS Standards 10) requires that firm A reports all the assets of firm B on its balance sheet when firm A has the power to govern activities of firm B that affect firm A's variable return on its investment in firm B. This broadly defined principle anticipates situations where firm A owns less than half of firm B's voting shares but has other ways to influence firm B's decisions, such as through board memberships or contractual agreements. The standard leaves much responsibility to managers and auditors to decide which subsidiaries are economically owned by the company.

While reporting discretion is necessary to benefit from managers' insider knowledge about the economic substance of their company's transactions, it also permits managers to misrepresent transactions and satisfy their own financial reporting objectives. Accounting analysis therefore involves assessing whether a firm's reported assets adequately reflect the key resources that are under its control, and whether adjustments are required to compare its performance with that of competitors. In situations where standard setters or auditors impose rigid and mechanical accounting rules on managers to reduce reporting discretion, accounting analysis is also important because these detailed rules permit managers to structure contracts and transactions in such a way that they satisfy their own reporting objectives.

Although firms are generally inclined to understate the assets that they control, thereby inflating the return on capital invested, they may sometimes pretend to control subsidiaries for the sake of inflating asset and revenue growth. For example, in the period from 1999 to 2001, Dutch food retailer Royal Ahold fraudulently reported the assets, liabilities, revenues, and operating profits of jointly controlled joint ventures in its financial statements as if the company fully controlled the joint ventures. The correct accounting treatment would have been to report only half of the joint ventures' assets and liabilities on Ahold's balance sheet and only half of the joint ventures' revenues, expenses, and operating profits in Ahold's income statement. By fully consolidating the joint ventures, Royal Ahold overstated its revenues by a total amount of €27.6 billion and its annual revenue growth by an average of 24 percent. Analyzing the accounting of a firm that follows a strategy of growing through acquisitions, such as Ahold, thus would include identifying subsidiaries that are fully consolidated but not fully owned and assessing their impact on the firm's net assets, revenues, and growth figures.

Asset ownership issues also arise indirectly from the application of rules for revenue recognition. Firms are permitted to recognize revenues only when their product has been shipped or their service has been provided to the customer. Revenues are then considered "earned," and the customer has a legal commitment to pay for the product or service. As a result, for the seller, recognition of revenue frequently coincides with "ownership" of a receivable that is shown as an asset on its balance sheet. Accounting analysis that raises questions about whether or not revenues have been earned therefore often affects the valuation of assets.

Ambiguity over whether a company owns an asset creates a number of opportunities for accounting analysis:

- Despite management's best intentions, financial statements sometimes do a poor job of reflecting the firm's economic assets because it is difficult for accounting rules to capture all of the subtleties associated with ownership and control.
- Accounting rules on ownership and control are the result of a trade-off between granting reporting discretion, which opens opportunities for earnings management, and imposing mechanical, rigid reporting criteria, which opens opportunities for the structuring of transactions. Because finding the perfect balance between discretion and rigidity is a virtually impossible task for standard setters, accounting rules cannot always prevent important assets being omitted from the balance sheet even though the firm bears many of the economic risks of ownership.
- There may be legitimate differences in opinion between managers and analysts over residual ownership risks borne by the company, leading to differences in opinion over reporting for these assets.
- Aggressive revenue recognition, which boosts reported earnings, is also likely to affect asset values.

## CAN ECONOMIC BENEFITS BE MEASURED WITH REASONABLE CERTAINTY?

It is almost always difficult to accurately forecast the future benefits associated with capital outlays because the world is uncertain. A company does not know whether a competitor will offer a new product or service that makes its own obsolete. It does not know whether the products manufactured at a new plant will be the type that customers want to buy. A company does not know whether changes in oil prices will make the oil drilling equipment that it manufactures less valuable.

Accounting rules deal with these challenges by stipulating which types of resources can be recorded as assets and which cannot. For example, the economic benefits from research and development are generally considered highly uncertain: research projects may never deliver promised new products, the products they generate may not be economically viable, or products may be made obsolete by competitors' research. International rules (IAS 38) therefore require that research outlays be expensed and development outlays only be capitalized if they meet stringent criteria of technical and economic feasibility (which they rarely do in industries such as the pharmaceutical industry). In contrast, the economic benefits from plant acquisitions are considered less uncertain and are required to be capitalized.

Rules that require the immediate expensing of outlays for some key resources may be good accounting, but they create a challenge for the analyst – namely, they lead to less timely financial statements. For example, if all firms expense R&D, financial statements will reflect differences in R&D success only when new products are commercialized rather than during the development process. The analyst may attempt to correct for this distortion by capitalizing key R&D outlays and adjusting the value of the intangible asset based on R&D updates.[1]

## HAVE FAIR VALUES OF ASSETS DECLINED BELOW BOOK VALUE?

An asset is impaired when its fair value falls below its book value. In most countries accounting rules require that a loss be recorded for permanent asset impairments. International rules (IAS 36) specify that an impairment loss be recognized on a non-current asset when its book value exceeds the recoverable amount, which the rules define as the greater of the asset's fair value less costs of disposal and the discounted cash flows expected to be generated from future use. If this condition is satisfied, the firm is required to report a loss for the difference between the asset's recoverable amount and its book value.

Of course markets for many non-current operating assets are illiquid and incomplete, making it highly subjective to infer their fair values. Further, if the cash flows of an individual asset cannot be identified, IAS 36 requires that the impairment test be carried out for the smallest possible *group* of assets that has identifiable cash flows, called the cash generating unit. Consequently, considerable management judgment is involved in defining the boundaries of cash generating units, deciding whether an asset is impaired and determining the value of any impairment loss. For the analyst, this raises the possibility that asset values are misstated. In fact, the more assets are combined in one cash generating unit, the more likely it is that the impairment of one asset (or a set of assets) is offset by the surplus value created by the other assets in the cash generating unit. This can create situations where no financial statement loss is reported for an individual asset that is economically impaired but whose impairment is concealed in the group.

## ARE FAIR VALUE ESTIMATES ACCURATE?

Managers estimate fair values of assets not only for asset impairment testing. One other use of fair value estimates is to adjust the book value of assets when firms use the revaluation method instead of the historical cost method. The international accounting rules for non-current assets (IAS 16) allow firms to record their non-current assets at fair value instead of their historical cost prices. When doing so, firms must regularly assess whether the reported book values deviate from the assets' fair values and, if necessary, make adjustments. Although revaluation adjustments are recorded in the statement of other comprehensive income (not in the income statement), revaluations do affect earnings through the depreciation expense because, under this method depreciation is determined by reference to the assets' fair value.

Fair value estimates are also needed to calculate goodwill in business combinations. Specifically, the amount by which the acquisition cost exceeds the fair value of the acquired net assets is recorded on the balance sheet as goodwill. The international standard for business combinations (IFRS Standards 3) requires that the amount of goodwill is not amortized, but regularly tested for impairment. This may create the incentive for managers to understate the fair value of acquired net assets and, consequently, overstate goodwill, thereby reducing future depreciation charges at a cost of increasing the risk of impairment.

Finally, international rules on the recognition and measurement of financial instruments (IFRS Standards 9) require a firm to recognize equity investments and debt investments held for trading (rather than for the purpose of collecting contractual cash flows till maturity) at their fair values. With a few exceptions, changes in the fair value of such assets are immediately recognized in profit or loss.

The task of determining fair values is delegated to management, with oversight by the firm's auditors, potentially leaving opportunities for management bias in valuing assets and for legitimate differences in opinion between managers and analysts over asset valuations. In most cases, management bias will lead to overstated assets since managers will prefer not to recognize an impairment or prefer to overstate nonamortized goodwill in business combinations. However, managers can also bias asset values downward by "taking a bath," reducing future expenses, and increasing future earnings.

To reduce management's discretion in determining the fair value of financial assets, their values must be derived from quoted market prices, if an active market for the assets exists (typically referred to as marking to market). If quoted market prices are not available, firms can use their own valuation technique to determine the assets' fair values (referred to as marking to model); however, their valuation should be based on assumptions that outside market participants would reasonably make, not management's own assumptions. During the credit market crisis of 2008, trading in asset-backed securities came to a halt because of the high uncertainty surrounding the value of these securities. As fewer transactions in asset-backed securities took place at increasingly volatile prices, financial institutions owning such securities argued that market prices could no longer be reliably used to determine the securities' fair values. Following the guidance of the IASB, many financial institutions started to adjust market prices or use their own valuations to assess fair value. Of course, this move away from using observable market prices increases managers' accounting flexibility and increases the importance as well as the difficulty of establishing whether financial institutions' fair value estimates are reliable.

In summary, distortions in assets are likely to arise when there is ambiguity about whether the firm owns or controls a resource, when there is a high degree of uncertainty about the value of the economic benefits to be derived from the resource, and when there are differences in opinion about the value of asset impairments. Opportunities for accounting adjustments can arise in these situations if:

- Accounting rules do not do a good job of capturing the firm's economics.
- Managers use their discretion to distort the firm's performance.
- There are legitimate differences in opinion between managers and analysts about economic uncertainties facing the firm that are reflected in asset values.

## Asset distortions

Asset overstatements are likely to arise when managers have incentives to increase reported earnings, such as discussed in Chapter 3. Thus adjustments to assets also typically require adjustments to the income statement in the form of either increased expenses or reduced revenues. Asset understatements typically arise when managers have incentives to deflate reported earnings. This may occur when the firm is performing exceptionally well and managers decide to store away some of the current strong earnings for a rainy day. Income smoothing, as it has come to be known, can be implemented by overstating current period expenses (and understating the value of assets) during good times. Asset (and expense) understatements can also arise in a particularly bad year, when managers decide to "take a bath" by understating current period earnings to create the appearance of a turnaround in following years.

Accounting rules themselves can also lead to the understatement of assets. For example, IAS 38 requires firms to expense outlays for research and advertising because, even though they may create future value for owners, their outcomes are highly uncertain. In these cases the analyst may want to make adjustments to the balance sheet and income statement to ensure that they reflect the economic reality of the transactions.

Asset understatements can also arise when managers have incentives to understate liabilities. For example, if a firm records lease transactions as operating leases or if it factors receivables with recourse, neither the assets nor the accompanying obligations are shown on its balance sheet. Yet in some instances this accounting treatment does not reflect the underlying economics of the transactions – the lessee may effectively own the leased assets, and the firm that sells receivables may still bear all of the risks associated with ownership. The analyst may then want to adjust the balance sheet (and also the income statement) for these effects.

Accounting analysis involves judging whether managers have understated or overstated assets (and also earnings) and, if necessary, adjusting the balance sheet and income statement accordingly. The most common items that can lead to overstatement or understatement of assets (and earnings) are the following:

- Depreciation and amortization on non-current assets.
- Impairment of non-current assets.
- Leased assets (in financial statements with fiscal year-ends before 2019).
- Intangible assets.
- The timing of revenue (and receivables) recognition.
- Allowances (e.g., allowances for doubtful accounts or loan losses).
- Write-downs of current assets.

We illustrate below some of the types of distortions that understate or overstate assets and show corrections that the analyst can make to ensure that assets are reflected appropriately.

Note that some of the accounting methods that we describe can be used by managers to both understate and overstate assets. The corrections that we describe for asset understatement can of course be easily modified to undo the effects of asset overstatement (and vice versa).

## Deferred Taxes on Adjustments

**M**ost firms use different accounting rules for business reporting and tax reporting. As a consequence, the assets and liabilities that firms report in their financial statements may differ in value from the assets and liabilities that they report in their tax statements. Consider a firm whose property, plant, and equipment have a book value of €300 in its financial statements but a tax base of €100 in its tax statements. Ignoring future investments, the firm will record a total amount of €300 in depreciation in its future financial statements, whereas it can only record an amount of €100 in tax-deductible depreciation in its future tax statements. Because the firm's tax statements are not publicly available, the analyst must estimate the firm's future tax deductions based on the book value of property, plant, and equipment as reported in the financial statements. This book value, however, overstates the firm's future tax deductions by an amount of €200 (€300 − €100). The IFRS Standards therefore require that the firm discloses the amount of overstatement of future tax deductions in its current financial statements. To do this, the firm recognizes a deferred tax liability on its balance sheet. Given a tax rate of 35 percent, the deferred tax liability equals €70 ([€300 − €100] × €0.35). This liability essentially represents the tax amount that the firm must pay in future years, in excess of the tax expense that the firm will report in its future financial statements. It also represents the tax amount that the firm would have to pay immediately were the firm to sell the asset for its current carrying amount. All additions to (reductions in) the deferred tax liability are accompanied by the recognition of a deferred tax expense (income) in the firm's income statement. Assets whose book values in the financial statements are below the tax bases recorded in the tax statements create a deferred tax asset.

When the analyst makes adjustments to the firm's assets or liabilities to undo any distortions, the deferred tax liability (or asset) is also affected. This is because the adjustments do not affect the tax statements and, consequently, change the difference between book values and tax bases. For example, when the analyst reduces the book value of property, plant, and equipment by €50, the deferred tax liability is reduced by an amount of €17.50 (€50 × €0.35) to €52.50 ([€250 − €100] × € 0.35).

The international accounting standard for income taxes requires that deferred taxes be recognized on any difference between book values and tax bases with the exception of a few differences, such as those related to:

- Nondeductible assets and nontaxable liabilities.
- Nondeductible goodwill and nontaxable negative goodwill.

### Overstated depreciation for non-current assets

Because non-current assets such as manufacturing equipment decrease in value over time, accounting rules require that firms systematically depreciate the book values of these assets. The reduction in the book value of the assets must be recognized as depreciation or amortization expense in the income statement. Managers make estimates of asset lives, salvage values, and amortization schedules for depreciable non-current assets. If these estimates are optimistic, non-current assets and earnings will be overstated. This issue is likely to be most pertinent for firms in heavy asset businesses (e.g., airlines, utilities), whose earnings contain large depreciation components. Firms that use tax depreciation estimates of asset lives, salvage values, or amortization rates are likely to amortize assets more rapidly than justifiable given the assets' economic usefulness, leading to non-current asset understatements.

In 2012 Lufthansa, the German national airline, reported that it depreciated its aircraft over 12 years on a straight-line basis, with an estimated residual value of 15 percent of initial cost. These assumptions imply that Lufthansa's annual depreciation expense was, on average, 7.1 percent ([1 − 0.15]/12) of the initial cost of its aircraft. In contrast, industry peers such as Air France-KLM and British Airways were using straight-line depreciation rates between 4 and 5 percent (of initial cost).

For the analyst these differences raise several questions. Do Lufthansa, Air France-KLM, and British Airways fly different types of routes, potentially explaining the differences in their depreciation policies? Alternatively, do they have different asset management strategies? For example, does Lufthansa use newer planes to attract more business travelers, to lower maintenance costs, or to lower fuel costs? If there do not appear to be operating differences that explain the differences in the two firms' depreciation rates, the analyst may well decide that it is necessary to adjust the depreciation rates for one or both firms to ensure that their performance is comparable.

To adjust for the effect of different depreciation policies, the analyst could decrease Lufthansa's depreciation rates to match those of its industry peers. The following financial statement adjustments would then be required in Lufthansa's financial statements:

1  Increase the book value of the fleet at the beginning of the year to adjust for the relatively high deprecia-tion rates that had been used in the past. The necessary adjustment is equal to the following amount: original minus adjusted depreciation rate × average asset age × initial asset cost. At the beginning of 2012, Lufthansa reported in the notes to its financial statements that its fleet of aircraft had originally cost €22,486 million and that accumulated depreciation was €12,238 million. This implies that the average age of Lufthansa's fleet was 7.6 years, calculated as follows:

| (€ millions unless otherwise noted) | | |
|---|---|---|
| Aircraft cost, 1/1/2012 | €22,486 | Reported |
| Depreciable cost | €19,113.1 | Cost × (1 − 0.15) |
| Accumulated depreciation, 1/1/2012 | €12,238 | Reported |
| Accumulated depreciation/Depreciable cost | 64.03% | |
| Depreciable life | 12 years | Reported |
| Average age of aircraft | 7.684 years | 12 × 0.6403 years |

If Lufthansa used similar life and salvage estimates as its peers and set its annual depreciation rate at 4.5 percent, given the average age of its fleet, accumulated depreciation would have been €7,775 (7.684 × 0.045 × 22,486) versus the reported €12,238. Consequently, the company's Non-Current Tangible Assets would have been higher by €4,463 (12,238 − 7,775).

2  Calculate the offsetting increase in equity (retained earnings) and in the deferred tax liability. Given the 25 percent marginal tax rate, the adjustment to Non-Current Tangible Assets would have required off-setting adjustments of €1,116 (0.25 × 4,463) to the Deferred Tax Liability and €3,347 (0.75 × 4,463) to Shareholders' Equity.

3  Reduce the depreciation expense (and increase the book value of the fleet) to reflect the lower deprecia-tion for the current year. Assuming that €1,902 million net new aircraft purchased in 2012 were acquired throughout the year, and therefore require only half a year of depreciation, the depreciation expense for 2012 (included in Cost of Sales) would have been €1,055 million {0.045 × [22,486 + (1,902/2)]} versus the €1,660 {(0.85/12) × [22,486 + (1,902/2)]} million reported by the company. Thus Cost of Sales would decline by €605 million.

4  Increase the tax expense, profit or loss, and the balance sheet values of equity and the deferred tax liability. Given the 25 percent tax rate for 2012, the Tax Expense for the year would increase by €151 million (0.25 × 605). On the balance sheet, these changes would increase Non-Current Tangible Assets by €605 mil-lion, increase Deferred Tax Liability by €151 million, and increase Shareholders' Equity by €454 million.

Note that these changes are designed to show Lufthansa's results as if it had always used the same deprecia-tion assumptions as its industry peers, rather than to reflect a change in the assumptions for the current year going forward. This enables the analyst to be able to compare ratios that use assets (e.g., return on assets) for the two companies. By making the adjustments, the analyst substantially improves the comparability of Lufthansa's and its peers' financial statements.

In summary, if Lufthansa were using the same depreciation method as its peers, its financial statements for the years ended December 31, 2011 and 2012 would have to be modified as follows (references to the preceding described steps are reported in brackets):

| (€ millions) | Adjustments December 31, 2011 | | Adjustments December 31, 2012 | |
|---|---|---|---|---|
| | Assets | Liabilities | Assets | Liabilities |
| **Balance sheet** | | | | |
| Non-Current Tangible Assets | +4,463 (1) | | +4,463 (1) | |
| | | | +605 (3) | |
| Deferred Tax Liability | | +1,116 (2) | | +1,116 (2) |
| | | | | +151 (4) |
| Shareholders' Equity | | +3,347 (2) | | +3,347 (2) |
| | | | | +454 (4) |
| **Income statement** | | | | |
| Cost of Sales | | | | −605 (3) |
| Tax Expense | | | | +151 (4) |
| Profit or Loss | | | | +454 (4) |

In fiscal year 2013 Lufthansa decided to change its assumption about the economic useful life of its aircraft and lower its annual depreciation rate to slightly less than 5 percent, thereby underlining the practical relevance of the preceding adjustments. The change helped Lufthansa to increase operating profit and bring its accounting for aircraft more into line with the industry norm. However, following the international accounting rules, Lufthansa adopted the new depreciation policy "prospectively," without adjusting past depreciation and reducing accumulated depreciation accordingly. Making Lufthansa's operating performance fully comparable with that of its peers in the years prior to and the earliest years after the change in policy would thus continue to require making some of the adjustments discussed above.

### Leased assets off balance sheet

One of the objectives of the balance sheet is to report the assets for which a firm receives the rewards and bears the risks. These can also be assets the firm does not legally own but leases from another firm. The international standard on leases, IFRS Standards 16, therefore requires that a company leasing an asset recognizes a lease asset and a lease liability on its balance sheet, reflecting the company's right of using the asset and its obligation to make the rental payments.

Prior to the adoption of IFRS Standards 16, which became effective for fiscal years starting on or after January 1, 2019, firms had two ways in which they could record their leased assets. Under the finance lease method, the firm recorded the asset and an offsetting lease liability on its balance sheet. During the lease period, the firm then recognized depreciation on the asset as well as interest on the lease liability, comparable to what firms currently do under IFRS Standards 16. In contrast, under the operating lease method, the firm recognized the lease payment as an expense in the period in which it occurred, keeping the leased asset off its balance sheet. Assessing whether a lease arrangement should be considered an operating lease or a finance lease required judgment, helped by a set of criteria laid down in the old lease standard. The distinction depended on whether the lessee had effectively accepted most of the risks of ownership, such as obsolescence and physical deterioration.

The changes in lease accounting practices that result from the adoption of IFRS Standards 16 may have a substantial effect on the comparability of financial statements over time. This is likely to be an important issue for the analysis of heavy asset industries where there are options for leasing (e.g., airlines).[2] To increase the comparability of financial statements that have been prepared under different lease rules, an analyst could capitalize operating lease commitments in pre-2019 financial statements using the approach described in the following example.[3]

In 2017 Air Canada, the Canadian airline company, accounted for part of its rented flight equipment using the operating lease method. These rented resources were excluded from Air Canada's balance sheet, making it difficult for an analyst to compare Air Canada's 2017 financial position with that in the years after the adoption of IFRS Standards 16. To correct this accounting, the analyst can use the information on noncancelable lease commitments presented in Air Canada's lease note to estimate the value of the assets and liabilities that are omitted from the balance sheet. The leased equipment is then depreciated over the life of the lease, and the lease payments are treated as interest and debt repayment.

On December 31, 2016 and 2017, Air Canada reports the following minimum future rental payments for aircraft:

| ($ millions) | December 31, 2016 | December 31, 2017 |
| --- | --- | --- |
| After 1 year | 482 | 509 |
| After 2 years | 434 | 443 |
| After 3 years | 362 | 329 |
| After 4 years | 255 | 242 |
| After 5 years | 166 | 182 |
| After more than 5 years | 308 | 643 |
| Total | 2,007 | 2,348 |

Because Air Canada does not show the present value of its operating lease commitments, the analyst must decide how to allocate the lump sum values of $308 and $643 over year 6 and beyond, and estimate a suitable interest rate on the lease debt. It is then possible to compute the present value of the lease payments.

Air Canada indicates that its (weighted average) effective annual interest rate on finance lease obligations is 9.5 percent and the actual lease expense reported in 2017 is $503 million. For 2017 one assumption that the analyst can make is that the annual rental payments in the sixth, seventh, and eighth year are equal to the rental payment in the fifth year and that the remainder of the lump sum value, $97 ($643 - 3 \times 182$), is due in the ninth year. Likewise, for 2016 the rental payment in the sixth year is equal to the rental payment in the fifth year, and the remainder of the lump sum value, $142 ($308 - 1 \times 166$), is due in the seventh year. Under this assumption, with a discount rate of 9.5 percent, the present values of the minimum rental payments for the years ended December 31, 2016, and December 31, 2017, are as follows:

| ($ millions) | December 31, 2016 | December 31, 2017 |
| --- | --- | --- |
| Within one year | 440.2 | 464.8 |
| Over one year | 1,092.0 | 1,236.9 |
| Total | 1,532.2 | 1,701.7 |

Unfortunately, the average lease term and the initial cost of the aircraft – being the present values of the minimum lease payments at the inception of the leases – are not perfectly known to the outside analyst. Therefore a necessary assumption to make is that the net book value (initial cost minus accumulated past depreciation) of Air Canada's leased aircraft is equal to the present value of the lease obligation. Under this assumption the analyst can determine that the average remaining lease term at the end of fiscal year 2016 is close to 5.1 years in the following manner:

| Future rental payments | | Rental payment will be made during . . . | Annuity of future rental payments (@ 9.5%) | Proportion | Column 2 × Column 4 |
|---|---|---|---|---|---|
| $48m | [482 – 434] | 1 year | 43.8 | 0.0286 | 0.0286 |
| $72m | [434 – 362] | 2 years | 125.8 | 0.0821 | 0.1642 |
| $107m | [362 – 255] | 3 years | 268.5 | 0.1752 | 0.5256 |
| $89m | [255 – 166] | 4 years | 285.2 | 0.1861 | 0.7445 |
| $0m | [166 – 166] | 5 years | 0.0 | 0.0000 | 0.0000 |
| $24m | [166 – 142] | 6 years | 106.1 | 0.0692 | 0.4154 |
| $142m | [142 – 0] | 7 years | 702.8 | 0.4587 | 3.2110 |
| | | | 1,532.2 | 1.0000 | 5.0893 |

In the preceding calculation, the analyst essentially splits up all scheduled lease payments into seven different contracts, each contract with a different remaining lease term ranging from one to seven. Contract 1 consists of one payment of $48 million (reflecting the decrease in Air Canada's minimum rental payments from year 1 to year 2, i.e., 482 – 436) in year 1; contract 2 consists of two payments of $72 million (reflecting the decrease in Air Canada's minimum rental payments from year 2 to year 3, i.e., 434 – 362) in years 1 and 2; contract 3 consists of three payments of $107 million (362 – 255) in years 1 through 3; and so on. Consequently, the value of contract 1 is the present value of a single payment of $48 million one year from now; the value of contract 2 is the present value of a two-year annuity of $72 million per year; the value of contract 3 is the present value of a three-year annuity of $107 million per year; and so on. The weights that are used to calculate the weighted average remaining lease term, in the fourth and fifth columns, are derived from the relative values of each of the seven contracts.

Given this information, the analyst can make the following adjustments to Air Canada's beginning and ending balance sheets, and to its income statement for the year ended December 31, 2017:

1  Capitalize the present value of the lease commitments for December 31, 2016, increasing Non-Current Tangible Assets and Non-Current Debt by $1,532.2.

2  Calculate the value of any change in lease assets and lease liabilities during the year from new lease transactions. On December 31, 2016, Air Canada's liability for lease commitments in 2018 and beyond was $1,092.0. If there had been no changes in these commitments, one year later (on December 31, 2017), they would have been valued at $1,195.7 (1,092.0 × 1.095). Yet Air Canada's actual lease commitment on December 31, 2017, was $1,701.7. Further, Air Canada's actual lease expense in 2017 of $503 exceeded the "anticipated" amount of $482 (see the table above showing the minimum future rental payments, second column). The difference between the actual and anticipated lease expense reflects another change in Air Canada's lease commitments. In total, these differences indicate that the company increased its leased aircraft capacity by $527.0 ([1,701.7 − 1,195.7] + [503.0 − 482.0]). Air Canada's Non-Current Tangible Assets and Non-Current Debt therefore increased by $527.0 during 2017.

3  Add back the operating lease expense in the income statement, included in Cost of Sales. As previously mentioned, the operating lease expense, which is equal to the cash payment that Air Canada made to its lessors, is $503. When lease liabilities are recorded on the balance sheet, as under the finance lease method, the lease payment must be treated as the sum of interest and debt repayment (see next item), instead of being recorded as an expense.

4  Apportion the lease payment between Interest Expense and repayment of Non-Current Debt. The portion of this that is shown as Interest Expense is the interest rate (9.5 percent) multiplied by the beginning lease liability ($1,532.2) plus interest on the increase in the leased liability for 2017 ($527.0), prorated throughout the year. The interest expense for 2017 is therefore $170.6 (0.095 × 1,532.2 + 0.5 × 0.095 × 527.0). The Non-Current Debt repayment portion is then the remainder of the total lease payment, $332.4 (503.0 − 170.6).

5  Reflect the change in lease asset value and the expense from depreciation during the year. The depreciation expense for 2017 (included in Cost of Sales) is the beginning cost of leased equipment at the end of 2016 ($1,532.2) divided by the average lease term (5.1 years), plus depreciation on the increase in leased equipment for 2017 ($527.0), prorated throughout the year. Consequently, the depreciation expense for 2017 is $352.1 ([1,532.2/5.1] + [0.5 × 527.0 × 1/5.1]).

6  Make any needed changes to the Deferred Tax Liability to reflect differences in earnings under the finance and operating lease methods. Air Canada's expenses under the finance lease method are $522.7 ($352.1 depreciation expense plus $170.6 interest expense) versus $503.0 under the operating lease method. Air Canada will not change its tax books, but for financial reporting purposes, it will show lower earnings before tax and thus a lower Tax Expense through deferred taxes. Given its 26.6 percent tax rate, the Tax Expense will decrease by $5.2 (0.266 × [503.0 − 522.7]) and the Deferred Tax Liability will decrease by the same amount.

In summary, the adjustments to Air Canada's financial statements on December 31, 2016, and December, 2017, are as follows:

| ($ millions) | Adjustments December 31, 2016 | | Adjustments December 31, 2017 | |
| --- | --- | --- | --- | --- |
| | Assets | Liabilities | Assets | Liabilities |
| **Balance sheet** | | | | |
| Non-Current Tangible Assets: | | | | |
| Beginning capitalization | +1,532.2 (1) | | +1,532.2 (1) | |
| New leases | | | +527.0 (2) | |
| Annual depreciation | | | −352.1 (5) | |
| Non-Current Debt: | | | | |
| Beginning debt | | +1,532.2 (1) | | +1,532.2 (1) |
| New leases | | | | +527 (2) |
| Debt repayment | | | | −332.4 (4) |
| Deferred Tax Liability | | | | −5.2 (6) |
| Shareholders' Equity | | | | −14.5 (6) |
| **Income statement** | | | | |
| Cost of Sales: | | | | |
| Lease expense | | | | −503.0 (3) |
| Depreciation expense | | | | +352.1 (5) |
| Interest Expense | | | | +170.6 (4) |
| Tax Expense | | | | −5.2 (6) |
| Profit or Loss | | | | −14.5 (6) |

These adjustments increase Air Canada's fixed assets by 18 percent in 2016 and 2017, reducing the company's fixed asset turnover (revenue/fixed assets) from the reported value of 172 percent to 146 percent in 2016, and from 176 percent to 148 percent in 2017. Note that an alternative method for calculating depreciation (under item 5) is to assume that the scheduled debt repayments for the first to the seventh year following fiscal 2016 accurately reflect the consumption pattern of the future economic benefits arising from the leased assets. Under this method, which is sometimes referred to as the interest-based or present value method, the depreciation expense for 2017 is $332.4, as calculated under item 4, and the adjustment's effect on Profit or Loss is zero.

### Key intangible assets off balance sheet

Some firms' most important assets are excluded from the balance sheet. Examples include investments in R&D, software development outlays, and brands and membership bases that are created through advertising and promotions. International accounting rules (IAS 38) specifically prohibit the capitalization of research outlays, primarily because it is believed that the benefits associated with such outlays are too uncertain. New products or software may never reach the market due to technological infeasibility or to the introduction of superior products by competitors. Expensing the cost of intangibles has two implications for analysts. First, the omission of intangible assets from the balance sheet inflates measured rates of return on capital (either return on assets or return on equity).[4] For firms with key omitted intangible assets, this has important implications for forecasting long-term performance; unlike firms with no intangibles, competitive forces will not cause their rates of return to fully revert to the cost of capital over time. For example, pharmaceutical firms have shown very high rates of return over many decades, in part because of the impact of R&D accounting. A second effect of expensing outlays for intangibles is that it makes it more difficult for the analyst to assess whether the firm's business model works. Under the matching concept, operating profit is a meaningful indicator of the success of a firm's business model, since it compares revenues and the expenses required to generate them. Immediately expensing outlays for intangible assets runs counter to matching and, therefore, makes it more difficult to judge a firm's operating performance. Consistent with this, research shows that investors view R&D and advertising outlays as assets rather than expenses.[5] Understated intangible assets are likely to be important for firms in pharmaceutical, software, branded consumer products, and subscription businesses.

How should the analyst approach the omission of intangibles? One way is to leave the accounting as is, but to recognize that forecasts of long-term rates of return will have to reflect the inherent biases that arise from this accounting method. A second approach is to capitalize intangibles and amortize them over their expected lives.

For example, consider the case of Sanofi, one of the largest pharmaceutical companies in the world. Sanofi does not capitalize most of its R&D costs because regulatory uncertainties surrounding the development and marketing of new products mean that the recognition criteria for research expenditures are rarely met. What adjustment would be required if the analyst decided to capitalize all of Sanofi's R&D and to amortize the intangible asset using the straight-line method over the expected life of R&D investments? Assume for simplicity that R&D spending occurs evenly throughout the year, that only half a year's amortization is taken on the latest year's spending, and that the average expected life of R&D investments is approximately five years. Given R&D outlays for the years 2012 to 2017, the R&D asset at the end of 2017 is €12,947 million (rounded), calculated as follows:

| Year | R&D Outlay | Proportion Capitalized 31/12/16 | Asset 31/12/16 | Proportion Capitalized 31/12/17 | Asset 31/12/17 |
|---|---|---|---|---|---|
| 2017 | €5,472m | | | $(1 - [1/5 \times 0.5])$ | €4,925m |
| 2016 | 5,172 | $(1 - [1/5 \times 0.5])$ | €4,655m | $(1 - [1/5 \times 1.5])$ | 3,620 |
| 2015 | 5,082 | $(1 - [1/5 \times 1.5])$ | 3,557 | $(1 - [1/5 \times 2.5])$ | 2,541 |
| 2014 | 4,667 | $(1 - [1/5 \times 2.5])$ | 2,334 | $(1 - [1/5 \times 3.5])$ | 1,400 |
| 2013 | 4,605 | $(1 - [1/5 \times 3.5])$ | 1,382 | $(1 - [1/5 \times 4.5])$ | 461 |
| 2012 | 4,741 | $(1 - [1/5 \times 4.5])$ | 474 | | |
| Total | | | €12,401 | | €12,947m |

In this table the proportion capitalized is calculated as 1 *minus* the amortization rate *times* the number of amortization years passed since the R&D outlay was incurred.

The R&D amortization expenses (included in Other Operating Expenses) for 2016 and 2017 are €4,803 million and €4,927 million (rounded), respectively, and are calculated as follows:

| Year | R&D Outlay | Proportion Amortized in 2016 | Expense in 2016 | Proportion Amortized in 2017 | Expense in 2017 |
|------|-----------|------------------------------|-----------------|------------------------------|-----------------|
| 2017 | €5,472m | | | 1/5 × 0.5 | €547m |
| 2016 | 5,172 | 1/5 × 0.5 | €517m | 1/5 | 1,034 |
| 2015 | 5,082 | 1/5 | 1,016 | 1/5 | 1,016 |
| 2014 | 4,667 | 1/5 | 933 | 1/5 | 933 |
| 2013 | 4,605 | 1/5 | 921 | 1/5 | 921 |
| 2012 | 4,741 | 1/5 | 948 | 1/5 × 0.5 | 474 |
| 2011 | 4,665 | 1/5 × 0.5 | 467 | | |
| Total | | | €4,803m | | €4,927m |

The calculations in this table are based on the idea that, for example, of the €4,741 million R&D outlay incurred in 2012, one half of one-fifth is amortized in 2012 (i.e., half a year's amortization in the first year), one-fifth is amortized in each of the four years between 2013 and 2016, and the remaining one half of one-fifth is amortized in 2017.

Since Sanofi will continue to expense R&D immediately for tax purposes, the change in reporting method will give rise to a Deferred Tax Liability. Given a marginal tax rate of 34 percent, this liability will equal 25 percent of the value of the Intangible Asset reported (0.34 × 12,401 in 2016; 0.34 × 12,947 in 2017), with the balance increasing Shareholders' Equity.

In summary, the adjustments required to capitalize R&D for Sanofi for the years 2016 and 2017 are as follows:

| (€ millions) | Adjustments December 31, 2016 Assets | Liabilities | Adjustments December 31, 2017 Assets | Liabilities |
|--------------|------|-------------|------|-------------|
| **Balance sheet** | | | | |
| Non-Current Intangible Assets | +12,401 | | +12,947 | |
| Deferred Tax Liability | | +4,266 | | +4,454 |
| Shareholders' Equity | | +8,135 | | +8,493 |
| **Income statement** | | | | |
| Other Operating Expenses | | −5,172 | | −5,472 |
| Other Operating Expenses | | +4,803 | | +4,927 |
| Tax Expense | | +127 | | +187 |
| Profit or Loss | | +242 | | +358 |

## Accelerated recognition of revenues

Managers typically have the best information on the uncertainties governing revenue recognition – whether a product or service has been provided to customers and whether cash collection is reasonably likely. However, managers may also have incentives to accelerate the recognition of revenues, boosting reported earnings for the period. Earnings and trade receivables (or accrued income in case invoicing has not yet occurred, or contracts in progress in case of long-term contracts) will then be overstated.

Consider UK-based Healthcare Locums plc, a company that recruits medical specialists for temporary or permanent placement at health and social care providers. In 2008 the recruitment company recognized revenue from permanent placements at the date that the candidate accepted the job offer. This acceptance date could be significantly earlier than the start date of the candidate, especially in the company's growing segment of international placements. In fact, in the United States, lengthy visa applications could delay permanent placements by up to four years, leading some analysts to argue that Healthcare Locums' permanent placement revenue recognition policy was too aggressive.

During the years 2005 to 2008, Healthcare Locums recognized the following revenue and cost of sales in its permanent placement segment:

| (£ millions) | 2008 | 2007 | 2006 | 2005 |
|---|---|---|---|---|
| Revenue | 5.3 | 4.0 | 3.2 | 1.0 |
| Cost of Sales | 0.8 | 0.4 | 0.4 | 0.1 |

Assume that an analyst estimates that candidates accepting a permanent position in 2005 start their new jobs in 2005, 2006, 2007, or 2008 with equal probabilities (25 percent in each of the four years). This assumption would imply, for example, that 50 percent $(1 - [2 \times 25\%])$ of the revenues on job offers accepted in 2007 were still unearned at the end of 2008. In fact, at the end of 2008 a total amount of £6.8 million in revenues would be considered unearned, as calculated in the following manner:

| Year | Contract amount | Proportion unearned end-2008 | Amount unearned end-2008 |
|---|---|---|---|
| 2008 | £5.3m | $1 - [1 \times 25\%]$ | 4.0 |
| 2007 | £4.0m | $1 - [2 \times 25\%]$ | 2.0 |
| 2006 | £3.2m | $1 - [3 \times 25\%]$ | 0.8 |
| Total | | | 6.8 |

In a similar manner we can calculate that the total cost associated with the revenues considered unearned at the end of 2008 would amount to £0.9 million:

| Year | Contract cost | Proportion unearned end-2008 | Cost associated with unearned revenues end-2008 |
|---|---|---|---|
| 2008 | £0.8m | $1 - [1 \times 25\%]$ | 0.6 |
| 2007 | £0.4m | $1 - [2 \times 25\%]$ | 0.2 |
| 2006 | £0.4m | $1 - [3 \times 25\%]$ | 0.1 |
| Total | | | 0.9 |

If the analyst decided to adjust for the distortions created by Healthcare Locums' aggressive revenue recognition policy, the following changes would have to be made to the company's 2008 financial reports:

1  To account for the revenues that were still unearned at the end of 2008, Trade Receivables would decrease by £6.8 million. In addition, Other Current/Non-Current Assets (in particular, prepaid expenses) would increase by £0.9 million to account for the costs associated with the unearned revenues.
2  Given that Healthcare Locums' marginal tax rate was 28.5 percent, the preceding adjustments would result in offsetting decreases in the Deferred Tax Liability of £1.7 million ($0.285 \times [0.9 - 6.8]$) and Shareholders' Equity of £4.2 million ($[1 - 0.285] \times [0.9 - 6.8]$).
3  The analyst's estimate of Healthcare Locums' 2008 revenues under a policy of recognizing revenues when candidates start (rather than when they accept) equals £3.4 million ($0.25 \times 1.0 + 0.25 \times 3.2 + 0.25 \times 4.0 + 0.25 \times 5.3$). Revenue would therefore decline by £1.9 million ($5.3 - 3.4$).
4  Cost of Sales would decline to reflect the reduction in revenues. For Healthcare Locums, the cost of permanent placement revenues is £0.8 million under the current revenue recognition policy and would be £0.4 million ($[0.25 \times 0.1 + 0.25 \times 0.4 + 0.25 \times 0.4 + 0.25 \times 0.8]$) under the adjusted policy. Hence Cost of Sales would decline by £0.4 million ($0.8 - 0.4$).
5  The decline in pre-tax profit would result in a lower Tax Expense. Given the marginal tax rate of 28.5 percent, the decline in the Tax Expense is £0.4 million $[(1.9 - 0.4) \times 0.285]$.

The full effect of the adjustment on the financial statements would therefore be as follows:[6]

| (£ millions) | Adjustments | |
| --- | --- | --- |
| | Assets | Liabilities and Equity |
| **Balance sheet** | | |
| Trade Receivables | −6.8 (1) | |
| Other Current/Non-Current Assets | +0.9 (1) | |
| Deferred Tax Liability | | −1.7 (2) |
| Shareholders' Equity | | −4.2 (2) |
| **Income statement** | | |
| Revenue | | −1.9 (3) |
| Cost of Sales | | −0.4 (4) |
| Tax Expense | | −0.4 (5) |
| Profit or Loss | | −1.1 (5) |

In 2009 Healthcare Locums voluntarily changed its revenue recognition policy for permanent placement revenues. Because of this accounting change, the company restated its permanent placement revenues for prior years. The outcome was that revenues for 2008 were reduced by £1.9 million. Profit was reduced by £1.4 million (or 12 percent of unrestated profit), leading to a significant drop in the company's stock price.

Accelerated revenue recognition is also a relevant concern when analyzing the financial statements of a company that engages in long-term contracts with its customers, agreeing to provide services or construct a product over a longer period of time. The international accounting rules on revenue recognition allow such a company to recognize revenues in increments during the contract period, as the company satisfies each of its contractual obligations. Under these rules, managers have an incentive to overstate the proportion of long-term contractual obligations satisfied at the end of a fiscal period.

Consider Denmark-based Vestas Wind Systems, a company specializing in developing, manufacturing, and installing wind turbines. In 2017 (and prior years) Vestas had several contracts requiring the company to supply and install wind turbines during periods that extended into the next fiscal year. At the end of the fiscal year, the company recognized revenues on such contracts in proportion to the contracts' rate of completion, despite the fact that the risks (and rewards) of owning the wind turbines would not be transferred to the customer before the contracts' completion. The effect of this accounting treatment on the company's financial statements was to:

- Accelerate the recognition of revenues.
- Create a non-current asset labeled "construction contracts in progress," reflecting the difference between (1) revenues recognized and (2) billings made on contracts in progress.

In the notes to its financial statements, Vestas disclosed the following information about revenues recognized on its projects in progress during the fiscal years 2016 and 2017:

| (€ millions) | 2017 | 2016 |
|---|---|---|
| Sales value of construction contracts in progress | 825 | 605 |
| Progress billings | (902) | (659) |
| Net "construction contracts in progress" asset (liability) | (77) | (54) |

If there is significant uncertainty about the remaining risks of Vestas's projects in progress, the analyst may decide to recalculate revenues and earnings under the assumption that revenues on supply-and-installation projects are not recognized before completion. This would require making the following adjustments to the 2017 financial statements:

1 Reduce Revenue by the sales value of contracts in progress at the end of 2017, being €825 million. This adjustment would also require an offsetting adjustment to Other Current Assets (in particular, contracts in progress) of €825 million. To estimate the effect of the revenue adjustment on Vestas's Cost of Sales, assume that the gross margin on the contracts in progress is equal to the company's average gross margin in 2017 of 19.7 percent. Hence decrease Cost of Sales and increase Inventories by €662 million ([1 − 0.197] × 825).

2 Under the new accounting treatment, prepayments on contracts in progress that Vestas received in 2017 give rise to a current liability. Therefore increase Other Current Assets (in particular, contracts in progress) and increase Other Current Liabilities (in particular, prepayments from customers) by €902 million, being the amount of progress billings in 2017.

3 Assume that contracts in progress at the end of 2016 – with a sales value of €605 – were completed during 2017, increasing Revenue in 2017 by €605 million. The value of the Cost of Sales adjustment can again be estimated based on the average gross margin in 2016, which was 20.8 percent. Hence increase Cost of Sales by €479 million ([1 − 0.208] × 1,800).

4 The net effect on pre-tax profit of the adjustments to Revenue and Cost of Sales is −€37 million ([605 − 479] − [825 − 662]). The decline in pre-tax profit would result in a lower Tax Expense. Thus, given Vestas's marginal tax rate of 22 percent, reduce the Tax Expense by €8 million (0.22 × 37). As a result of these adjustments, Profit or Loss decreases by €19 million.

5 The effect of the preceding adjustments on the Deferred Tax Liability and Shareholders' Equity is not equal to that on the Tax Expense and Profit or Loss (see item 4). This is because the amounts of Revenue (605) and Cost of Sales (479) recognized under item 3 were originally incorporated in Vestas's 2016 balance sheet and therefore require no additional balance sheet adjustments. Instead, given the adjustments made under item 1 and the marginal tax rate of 22 percent, reduce the Deferred Tax Liability by €36 million (0.22 × [825 − 662]) and Shareholders' Equity by €127 million (0.78 × [825 − 662]).

The full effect of the adjustment on the quarterly financial statements would therefore be as follows:

| (€ millions) | Adjustments | |
| --- | --- | --- |
| | Assets | Liabilities and Equity |
| **Balance sheet** | | |
| Other Current Assets | −825 (1) | |
| | +902 (2) | |
| Inventories | +662 (1) | |
| Other Current Liabilities | | +902 (2) |
| Deferred Tax Liability | | −36 (5) |
| Shareholders' Equity | | −127 (5) |
| **Income statement** | | |
| Revenue | | −825 (1) |
| | | +605 (3) |
| Cost of Sales | | −662 (1) |
| | | +479 (3) |
| Tax Expense | | −8 (4) |
| Profit or Loss | | −19 (4) |

### Delayed write-downs of non-current assets

Deteriorating industry or firm economic conditions can affect the value of non-current assets as well as current assets. When the fair value of an asset falls below its book value, the asset is "impaired." Firms are required to recognize impairments in the values of non-current assets when they arise. However, since secondhand markets for non-current assets are typically illiquid and incomplete, estimates of asset valuations and impairment are inherently subjective. This is particularly true for intangible assets such as goodwill, which is the amount by which the cost of business acquisitions exceeds the fair value of the acquired assets. As a result, managers can use their reporting judgment to delay write-downs on the balance sheet and avoid showing impairment charges in the income statement.[6] This issue is likely to be particularly critical for heavily asset-intensive firms in volatile markets (e.g., airlines) or for firms that follow a strategy of aggressive growth through acquisitions and report substantial amounts of goodwill.[7] Warning signs of impairments in non-current assets include declining non-current asset turnover, declines in return on assets to levels lower than the weighted average cost of capital, write-downs by other firms in the same industry that have also suffered deteriorating asset use, and overpayment for or unsuccessful integration of key acquisitions. Managers may sometimes also have incentives to overstate asset impairment. Overly pessimistic management estimates of non-current asset impairments reduce current period earnings and boost earnings in future periods.

Consider car manufacturer Renault's minority investment in Nissan. In its financial statements for the fiscal year ending on December 31, 2017, Renault's management described that the company's 43.7 percent stake in Nissan and its agreements with Nissan's management did not give it sufficient influence to control Nissan's major financial and operating decisions. Renault therefore used the equity method to account for its investment in Nissan, thus recognizing the investment on the balance sheet at its initial cost and periodically adjusting the investment's book value for Renault's share in Nissan's profit or loss as well as dividends received. On December 31, 2017, the book value of the investment in Nissan amounted to €19,135 million (corresponding to around 18 percent of Renault's balance sheet total), including goodwill of €686 million. In the notes to its financial statements, Renault disclosed that based on Nissan's end-of-year share price, the market value of the company's investment in Nissan was close to €15,244 million, almost €4 billion less than the investment's book value (compared with €0.9 billion in 2016). Nonetheless, Renault's management concluded that its own valuation of Nissan, in which it assumed a cost of capital of 8 percent and a long-term (infinite) growth rate of 4 percent, did not give reason to recognize an impairment on the investment.

An analyst might argue that the valuation assumptions used by Renault's management are too optimistic and decide that the observed market value of the investment is a more reliable estimate of the investment's fair value. To record an additional write-down of €3,891 million (19,135 − 15,244) in the December 2017 financials, it would be necessary to make the following balance sheet adjustments:

1  Reduce Non-Current Intangible Assets and increase Non-Recurring Expense by €3,891 million.
2  Reduce the Deferred Tax Liability and the Tax Expense for the tax effect of the write-down. Assuming a 34.4 percent tax rate, this amounts to €1,338 million.
3  Reduce Shareholders' Equity and Profit or Loss for the after-tax effect of the write-down (€2,553 million).

| (£ millions) | Adjustment | |
| --- | --- | --- |
| | **Assets** | **Liabilities and Equity** |
| **Balance sheet** | | |
| Non-Current Intangible Assets | −3,891 (1) | |
| Deferred Tax Liability | | −1,338 (2) |
| Shareholders' Equity | | −2,553 (3) |
| **Income statement** | | |
| Non-Recurring Expense | | +3,891 (1) |
| Tax Expense | | −1,338 (2) |
| Profit or Loss | | −2,553 (3) |

### Delayed write-downs of current assets

If current assets become impaired – that is, their book values fall below their realizable values – accounting rules generally require that they be written down to their fair values. Current asset impairments also affect earnings since write-offs are charged directly to earnings. Deferring current asset write-downs is therefore one way for managers to boost reported profits.[8] Analysts who cover firms where management of inventories and receivables is a key success factor (e.g., the retail and manufacturing industries) need to be particularly cognizant of this form of earnings management. If managers over-buy or over-produce in the current period, they are likely to have to offer customers discounts to get rid of surplus inventories. In addition, providing customers with credit carries risks of default. Warning signs for delays in current asset write-downs include growing days' inventory and days' receivable, write-downs by competitors, and business downturns for a firm's major customers.

Consider the example of Imtech, a Dutch industrial services company. In November 2012 an ABN AMRO analyst issued a research report pointing to the potential deterioration of the quality of Imtech's trade receivables. Using the company's segment information, the analyst estimated that the average number of days that Imtech needed to collect its German and Eastern European receivables had increased from 147 days in the first half of 2010 to 232 days in the first half of 2012, whereas receivables' collection period in other geographic segments had remained stable. The analysts showed that the increase in receivables had helped Imtech to recognize substantial amounts of non-cash revenues and, consequently, boost its profit margins.

Imtech's semiannual financial statements showed that at the end of June 2012, Imtech's current receivables (of all geographic segments combined) had a carrying value of €2,197 million; Imtech's total revenues during the 12-month period ending in June 2012 amounted to €5,436 million. The average collection period of Imtech's current receivables – also referred to as days receivables outstanding – thus equaled 148 days (2,197 / [5,436/365]). In contrast, at the end of June 2010, days receivables outstanding amounted to 123 days (1,460 / [4,327/365]). Assuming that the normal collection period is close to 123 days – which was the average collection period at the beginning of 2010 – Imtech's disclosures suggest that an approximate amount of €365 million (2,197 – [123/365] × 5,436) in receivables outstanding was impaired in June 2012. To account for the potential impairment of receivables, the analyst would need to make the following adjustments:

1  Reduce Receivables and increase Non-Recurring Expense by €365 million.
2  Reduce the Deferred Tax Liability and the Tax Expense for the tax effect of the write-down. Given a 28.1 percent tax rate, this amounts to €103 million.
3  Reduce Shareholders' Equity and Profit or Loss for the after-tax effect of the write-down (€262 million).

| (€ millions) | Adjustment | |
| --- | --- | --- |
|  | Assets | Liabilities and Equity |
| **Balance sheet** | | |
| Receivables | −365 (1) | |
| Deferred Tax Liability | | −103 (2) |
| Shareholders' Equity | | −262 (3) |
| **Income statement** | | |
| Non-Recurring Expense | | +365 (1) |
| Tax Expense | | −103 (2) |
| Profit or Loss | | −262 (3) |

Whereas Imtech's management initially hastened to deny the analyst's claims that the quality of its receivables had eroded, early 2013 management announced a €100 million write-off on a theme park construction project, because of the uncollectibility of the project's receivables. The company postponed the publication of its 2012 financial statements to further investigate irregularities at its German division and later announced another €270 million write-off on German and Polish projects. During 2013 Imtech's stock price decreased by close to 70 percent.

Managers potentially have an incentive to overstate current asset write-downs during years of exceptionally strong performance, or when the firm is financially distressed. By overstating current asset impairments and overstating expenses in the current period, managers can show lower future expenses, boosting earnings in years of sub-par performance or when a turnaround is needed. Overstated current asset write-downs can also arise when managers are less optimistic about the firm's future prospects than the analyst is.

### Allowances

Managers make estimates of expected customer defaults on trade receivables and loans. If managers underestimate the value of these allowances, assets and earnings will be overstated. Warning signs of inadequate allowances include growing days receivable, business downturns for a firm's major clients, and growing loan delinquencies. If managers overestimate allowances for doubtful accounts or loan losses, trade receivables and loans will be understated.

Consider the allowances for loan losses reported by the French banking and insurance company Société Générale (SG) in the years 2014–2017. At the end of 2017, 4.7 percent of SG's loans were past due, down from 6.7 percent in 2014. From 2014 to 2017, SG reported the following values for its gross outstanding loans and allowances:

| Year | Gross loans | Allowances for loan losses | Allowances / Gross loans (%) |
|------|-------------|----------------------------|------------------------------|
| 2014 | 385,789 | 14,758 | 3.83% |
| 2015 | 420,036 | 13,978 | 3.33% |
| 2016 | 440,874 | 13,281 | 3.01% |
| 2017 | 437,403 | 11,214 | 2.56% |

These numbers show that the relative size of SG's allowance for loan losses gradually decreased across the four years, arguably in sync with the decrease in SG's loans past due.

On December 31, 2017, SG reported the following values for its allowances and write-offs:

| Allowances for loan losses (€ millions) | December 31, 2017 | December 31, 2016 | December 31, 2015 |
|------------------------------------------|-------------------|-------------------|-------------------|
| Balance at beginning of year | 13,281 | 13,978 | 14,758 |
| Provision for/(recovery of) loan losses | 1,162 | 1,393 | 2,019 |
| Write-offs | (3,077) | (2,208) | (3,252) |
| Other changes (e.g., changes in consolidation, exchanges rates) | −152 | 118 | 453 |
| Balance at end of year | 11,214 | 13,281 | 13,978 |

If the analyst decided that the observed decrease in SG's loan loss allowances during the years 2014 to 2017 was too large and that the allowance in 2016 and 2017 should have been 3.3 percent rather than 3.01 and 2.56 percent, the following adjustments would have to be made:

1  Given a provisioning percentage of 3.3 percent, the new beginning and ending balances of the loan loss allowance for 2016 and 2017 are €14,549 million ($0.033 \times 440,874$) and €14,434 million ($0.033 \times 437,403$), respectively. Decrease Net Loans on December 31, 2016, by €1,268 million ($13,281 - 14,549$) and decrease Net Loans on December 31, 2017, by €3,220 million ($11,214 - 14,434$), respectively, to reflect the adjustment to the allowance.

2  Given the company's marginal tax rate of 34.4 percent, decrease the Deferred Tax Liability for 2016 by €436 million ($0.344 \times 1,268$), and decrease Shareholders' Equity for 2016 by €832 million ($[1 - 0.344] \times 1,268$). Likewise, decrease the Deferred Tax Liability for 2017 by €1,108 million ($0.344 \times 3,220$), and decrease Shareholders' Equity for 2017 by €2,112 million ($[1 - 0.344] \times 3,220$).

3  Adjust the other (consolidation- and exchange rate-related) changes in the loan loss allowance to reflect the use of a lower provisioning percentage. Assuming that these other changes remain proportional to the beginning balance of the allowance, decrease other changes in 2017 by €15 million to a new value of −€167 million ($[-152/13,281] \times 14,549$).

**4**  Because the actual loan write-offs for 2017 remain unchanged (€3,077) and the adjusted other changes in the loan loss allowance amount to −€167 million (as calculated under item 3), the adjusted provision for bad debts is €3,129 million (14,434 − [14,549 − 3,077 − 167]). Given the unadjusted loan loss provision for 2017 of €1,162 million, increase Operating Expenses for 2017 by €1,967 million (3,129 − 1,162).

**5**  Given the tax rate of 34.4 percent, decrease the Tax Expense for 2017 by €677 million (0.344 × 1,967) and decrease Profit or Loss by €678 million ([1 − 0.344] × 1,034).

The adjustment to the December 31, 2016, and December 31, 2017, financial statements would therefore be as follows:

| (€ millions) | Adjustments December 31, 2016 | | Adjustments December 31, 2017 | |
|---|---|---|---|---|
|  | Assets | Liabilities | Assets | Liabilities |
| **Balance sheet** | | | | |
| Net Loans | −1,268 (1) | | −3,220 (1) | |
| Deferred Tax Liability | | −436 (2) | | −1,108 (2) |
| Shareholders' Equity | | −832 (2) | | −2,112 (2) |
| | | | | |
| **Income statement** | | | | |
| Operating Expenses | | | | +1,967 (4) |
| Tax Expense | | | | −677 (5) |
| Profit or Loss | | | | −1,290 (5) |

Note that the balance sheet effects of the adjustments described under items 3 through 5 have been implicitly incorporated into the balance sheet by the adjustments described under item 1. For example, the adjustment to Net Loans (of −€3,220 million) on December 31, 2017, is equal to the adjustment to Net Loans (−1,268) on December 31, 2016, minus the adjustment to Operating Expenses (1,967) minus the adjustment to the other changes in the loan loss allowance (−15). Similarly, the adjustment to Shareholders' Equity (of −€2,112 million) on December 31, 2017, is equal to the adjustment to Shareholders' Equity (−832) on December 31, 2016, plus the adjustment to Profit or Loss (−1,290) plus the Other Comprehensive Income effect of the adjustment to the other changes in the loan loss allowance ([1 − 0.344] × 15). Therefore, under items 3 through 5, no further adjustments to the balance sheet are needed.

This adjustment would decrease SG's return on equity for 2017 by 1.9 percentage points (from 5.4 to 3.5 percent). This example illustrates that a seemingly small adjustment to a bank's loan loss allowance can have a significant effect on profitability.

Understated allowances are also a point of attention when analyzing the financial statements of loss-making firms. When a firm reports a loss in its tax statements, it does not receive an immediate tax refund, but becomes the holder of a claim against the tax authorities, called a tax loss carryforward, which can be offset against future taxable profits. The period over which the firm can exercise this claim differs across tax jurisdictions. The international accounting standard for income taxes requires that firms record a deferred tax asset for a tax loss carryforward that is probable of being realized (through the availability of future taxable profit). Because changes in this deferred tax asset affect earnings through the tax expense, managers can manage earnings upwards by overstating the probability of realization.

During its first five years of operations, from 2001 to 2005, the Dutch manufacturer of exclusive cars Spyker Cars N.V. had been loss-making. In December 2005 and December 2004, when Spyker reported net losses of €1.9 million and €5.0 million, respectively, the company reported the following losses carried forward and deferred tax assets:

| (€ thousands) | December 31, 2005 | December 31, 2004 |
|---|---|---|
| Total loss carried forward | 19,822 | 15,687 |
| × Tax rate | 29.6% | 34.5% |
| = Calculated deferred tax | 5,867 | 5,412 |
| – Allowance | (1,467) | (3,058) |
| = Recognized deferred tax asset | 4,400 | 2,354 |

Spyker deducted an allowance from its calculated deferred tax assets because management deemed it not probable that the tax loss carryforwards could be fully realized in future years. The allowance, however, was substantially lower in 2005 than in 2004 because management expected an increase in Spyker's future profitability, justifying a decrease in the allowance from 56.5 percent of the deferred tax asset to 25 percent.

Any increase (decrease) in the deferred tax asset is offset by a decrease (increase) in the tax expense. If the analyst believed that management's optimism in 2005 was unwarranted and decided to increase the allowance to 56.5 percent, it would be necessary to reduce the Deferred Tax Asset, Shareholders' Equity, and Profit or Loss by €1,848 thousand ($[0.565 - 0.250] \times 5.867$) and increase the Tax Expense by the same amount.

| | Adjustments | |
|---|---|---|
| (€ millions) | Assets | Liabilities and Equity |
| **Balance sheet** | | |
| Deferred Tax Asset | −1,848 | |
| Shareholders' Equity | | −1,848 |
| **Income statement** | | |
| Tax Expense | | +1,848 |
| Profit or Loss | | −1,848 |

In the years 2006–2008, Spyker kept reporting pre-tax losses. At the end of 2007, Spyker's management decided to deduct an allowance of 100 percent from its deferred tax asset, thereby removing the asset from its balance sheet in full, after being pressured by the Dutch enforcement body.

## Key Analysis Questions

The following are some of the questions an analyst can probe when analyzing whether a firm's assets exhibit distortions:

- *Depreciation and amortization.* Are the firm's depreciation and amortization rates in line with industry practices? If not, is the firm aggressive or conservative in its estimates of the assets' useful lives? What does the deferred tax liability for depreciation and amortization suggest about the relationship between reported depreciation and tax depreciation?

- *Asset impairment.* Have industry or firm economic conditions deteriorated such that non-current assets' fair values could have fallen below their book values? Have industry peers recently recognized asset impairments? Does the firm have a history of regular write-downs, suggesting a tendency to delay?
- *Leased assets.* Did the firm have a material amount of off-balance sheet lease commitments prior to its adoption of IFRS Standards 16 in 2019? Did this lead to a large change in capitalized leases at the time of adoption, thereby distorting comparative financial figures?
- *Intangible assets.* Does the firm make material investments in non-current intangible assets, such as research and development, that are omitted from the balance sheet? If so, are these investments likely to yield future economic benefits? Does the immediate expensing of these investments lead to artificially permanent abnormal earnings?
- *Revenue recognition.* Are trade receivables abnormally high (relative to revenue), suggesting aggressive revenue recognition?
- *Allowances.* Did the firm make unexplained changes in its allowance for doubtful accounts (or loan losses)? Is the size of the allowance in line with industry practices? Did the characteristics of the firm's receivables (e.g., concentration of credit risk) change such that the firm should adjust its allowance? Are the allowances that the firm recognizes systematically smaller or greater than its write-offs? Is it likely that the firm's deferred tax assets for losses carried forward can be realized?

## Recognition of liabilities

Liabilities are defined as economic (cash or performance) obligations that arise from benefits received in the past, have the potential of being required to be met, and cannot be feasibly avoided. Liabilities include obligations to customers that have paid in advance for products or services; commitments to public and private providers of debt financing; obligations to federal and local governments for taxes; commitments to employees for unpaid wages and post-employment benefits; and obligations from court or government fines or environmental clean-up orders.

**Distortions in liabilities** generally arise because there is ambiguity about whether (1) an obligation has really been incurred and/or (2) the obligation can be measured.

### HAS AN OBLIGATION BEEN INCURRED?

For most liabilities there is little ambiguity about whether an obligation has been incurred. For example, when a firm buys supplies on credit, it has incurred an obligation to the supplier. However, for some transactions it is more difficult to decide whether there is any such obligation. For example, if a firm announces a plan to restructure its business by laying off employees, has it made a commitment that would justify recording a liability? Or, if a software firm receives cash from its customers for a five-year software licence, should the firm report the full cash inflow as revenues, or should some of it represent the ongoing commitment to the customer for servicing and supporting the licence agreement?

### CAN THE OBLIGATION BE MEASURED?

Many liabilities specify the amount and timing of obligations precisely. For example, a 20-year €100 million bond issue with an 8 percent coupon payable semiannually specifies that the issuer will pay the holders €100 million in 20 years, and it will pay out interest of €4 million every six months for the duration of the loan. However, for some liabilities it is difficult to estimate the amount of the obligation. For example, a firm that is responsible for an environmental clean-up clearly has incurred an obligation, but the amount is highly uncertain.[9] Similarly, firms that provide post-employment benefits for employees have incurred commitments that depend on uncertain future events, such as employee mortality rates, and on future inflation rates, making valuation of the obligation subjective. Future warranty and insurance claim obligations fall into the same category – the commitment is clear but the amount depends on uncertain future events.

Accounting rules frequently specify when a commitment has been incurred and how to measure the amount of the commitment. However, as discussed earlier, accounting rules are imperfect – they cannot cover all contractual possibilities and reflect all of the complexities of a firm's business relationships. They also require managers to make estimates of future events to value the firm's commitments. Thus the analyst may decide that some important obligations are omitted from the financial statements or, if included, are understated, either because of management bias or because there are legitimate differences in opinion between managers and analysts over future risks and commitments. As a result, analysis of liabilities is usually with an eye to assessing whether the firm's financial commitments and risks are understated and/or its earnings overstated.

## Liability distortions

Liabilities are likely to be understated when the firm has key commitments that are difficult to value and therefore not considered liabilities for financial reporting purposes. Understatements are also likely to occur when managers have strong incentives to overstate the soundness of the firm's financial position or to boost reported earnings. By understating leverage, managers present investors with a rosy picture of the firm's financial risks. Earnings management also understates liabilities (namely deferred or unearned revenues) when revenues are recognized upon receipt of cash, even though not all services have been provided.

Accounting analysis involves judging whether managers have understated liabilities and, if necessary, adjusting the balance sheet and income statement accordingly. The most common forms of liability understatement arise when the following conditions exist:

- Deferred revenues are understated through aggressive revenue recognition.
- Provisions are understated.
- Post-employment obligations, such as pension obligations, are not fully recorded.

In addition, prior to the adoption of the new international standard on leases (IFRS Standards 16) in 2019, key lease assets and liabilities could be excluded from the balance sheet if a firm structured lease transactions to fit the accounting definition of an operating lease. To ensure that a firm's true financial commitments and risks are reflected on its balance sheet also before 2019, and hence improve comparability of the firm's financial position over time, the analyst can restate pre-2019 operating leases as finance leases, as discussed in the "Asset distortions" section.

### Deferred revenues understated

If cash has already been received but the product or service has yet to be provided, a liability (called unearned or deferred revenues) is created. This liability reflects the company's commitment to provide the service or product to the customer and is extinguished once that is accomplished. Firms that recognize revenues prematurely, after the receipt of cash but prior to fulfilling their product or service commitments to customers, understate deferred revenue liabilities and overstate earnings. Firms that bundle service contracts with the sale of a product are particularly prone to deferred revenue liability understatement since separating the price of the product from the price of the service is subjective.

Consider the case of MicroStrategy, a software company that bundles customer support and software updates with its initial licensing agreements. This raises questions about how much of the contract price should be allocated to the initial licence versus the company's future commitments. In March 2000 MicroStrategy conceded that it had incorrectly overstated revenues on contracts that involved significant future customization and consulting by $54.5 million. As a result, it would have to restate its financial statements for 1999 as well as for several earlier years. To undo the distortion to 1999 financials, the following adjustments would have to be made:

1   In the quarter that the contracts were booked by the company, Revenue would decline and deferred revenues (included in Other Current Liabilities) would increase by $54.5 million.
2   Cost of Sales would decline and prepaid expenses (inventory for product companies) would increase to reflect the lower revenues. As noted earlier, MicroStrategy's cost of licence revenues is only 3 percent of licence revenues, implying that the adjustment to prepaid expenses (included in Other Current Assets) and Cost of Sales is modest ($1.6 million).
3   The decline in pre-tax profit would result in a lower Tax Expense in the company's financial reporting books (but presumably not in its tax books). Given MicroStrategy's marginal tax rate of 35 percent, the decline in the Tax Expense as well as in the Deferred Tax Liability is $18.5 million [($54.5 − 1.6) × 0.35].

The full effect of the adjustment on the quarterly financial statements would therefore be as follows:

| | Adjustments | |
|---|---|---|
| (€ millions) | Assets | Liabilities and Equity |
| **Balance sheet** | | |
| Other Current Assets | +1.6 (2) | |
| Other Current Liabilities | | +54.5 (1) |
| Deferred Tax Liability | | −18.5 (3) |
| Shareholders' Equity | | −34.4 |
| **Income statement** | | |
| Revenue | | −54.5 (1) |
| Cost of Sales | | −1.6 (2) |
| Tax Expense | | −18.5 (3) |
| Profit or Loss | | −34.4 |

MicroStrategy's March 10 announcement that it had overstated revenues prompted the SEC to investigate the company. In the period when it announced its overstatements, MicroStrategy's stock price plummeted 94 percent, compared to the 37 percent drop by the NASDAQ in the same period.

### Provisions understated

Many firms have obligations that are likely to result in a future outflow of cash or other resources but for which the exact amount is hard to establish. Examples of such uncertain liabilities are liabilities that arise from obligations to clean up polluted production sites or to provide warranty coverage for products sold. International accounting rules prescribe that a firm recognizes a provision—or non-financial liability—on its balance sheet for such uncertain liabilities when:

1   It is probable that the obligation will lead to a future outflow of cash.
2   The firm has no or little discretion to avoid the obligation.
3   The firm can make a reliable estimate of amount of the obligation.

When an uncertain liability does not meet these requirements for recognition, the firm discloses the liability only in the notes to the financial statements, as a "contingent liability." The international rules for the recognition of provisions may result in the understatement of a firm's liabilities. Because of the uncertainty surrounding the obligations, managers have much discretion in deciding whether obligations are probable as well as in estimating the amount of the obligation. Further, the use of a probability threshold below which uncertain liabilities are not recognized may lead to situations in which obligations with a relatively low probability but with a high expected value remain off-balance. An analyst may therefore decide that some of a firm's contingent liabilities are less uncertain than management asserts and undo the distortion by recognizing the liability on-balance as a provision. Additionally, the analyst may be of the opinion that low-probability obligations that nevertheless expose the firm to substantial risks because of their high expected value must also be recognized on the balance sheet.

At the end of the fiscal year 2017, British American Tobacco plc (BAT) was defendant in thousands of product liability cases – either directly or through some of its subsidiaries. The notes to the company's financial statements indicated that "in a number of these cases, the amounts of compensatory and punitive damages sought are significant" and could potentially add up to billions of British pounds. The company also reported that in several cases that went to trial before the balance sheet date, judges had awarded substantial damages against BAT (or its subsidiaries). Nevertheless, the company chose not to recognize a provision for potential damages because it considered it improbable that individual cases would result in an outflow of resources, even though in the aggregate the cases could have a material effect on the company's cash flow.

Assume that an analyst estimates the present value of future damages and settlements, discounted at BAT's average borrowing rate of 4 percent, to be £1 billion. In this particular situation, the analyst could base such an estimate on the historical probability that a tobacco company would lose a product liability case times the average damages awarded. Sometimes a firm's notes on contingent liabilities provide an indication of the size of the liability. For BAT, the following adjustments would have to be made to recognize the liability of £1 billion:

1 At the end of fiscal year 2017, the liability of £1 billion would be recognized as Non-Current Debt. Given BAT's marginal tax rate of 19 percent, Shareholders' Equity would decline by £0.81 billion (1.0 billion $\times$ [1 − 0.19]) and the Deferred Tax Liability would decline by £0.19 billion (1.0 billion $\times$ 0.19).

2 Because the non-current provision is a discounted liability, the provision increases as interest accrues. In 2018 BAT's income statement would include additional Interest Expense for an amount of £40 million (1.0 billion $\times$ 0.04). Tax Expense and the Deferred Tax Liability would decline by £7.6 million (40 million $\times$ 0.19) and Profit or Loss and Shareholders' Equity would decline by £32.4 million (40 million $\times$ [1 − 0.19]). The additional Interest Expense would result in an increase in Non-Current Debt.

The full effect of the adjustments would be as follows:

| (£ millions) | Adjustments December 31, 2017 | | Adjustments December 31, 2018 | |
|---|---|---|---|---|
| | Assets | Liabilities | Assets | Liabilities |
| **Balance sheet** | | | | |
| Non-Current Debt | | +1,000.0 (1) | | +1,000.0 (1) |
| | | | | +40.0 (2) |
| Deferred Tax Liability | | −190.0 (1) | | −190.0 (1) |
| | | | | −7.6 (2) |
| Shareholders' Equity | | −810.0 (1) | | −810.0 (1) |
| | | | | −32.4 (2) |
| **Income statement** | | | | |
| Interest Expense | | | | +40.0 (2) |
| Tax Expense | | | | −7.6 (2) |
| Profit or Loss | | | | −32.4 (2) |

### Post-employment benefit obligations understated

Many firms make commitments to provide pension benefits and other post-employment benefits, such as healthcare, to their employees. International accounting rules require managers to estimate and report the present value of the commitments that have been earned by employees over their years of working for a firm. This obligation is offset by any assets that the firm has committed to post-employment plans to fund future plan benefits. If the funds set aside in the post-employment plan are greater (less) than the plan commitments, the plan is overfunded (underfunded).

Estimating the post-employment benefit obligations requires judgment – managers, with the help of actuaries, have to make forecasts of future wage and benefit rates, worker attrition rates, and the expected lives of retirees.[10] If these forecasts are too low, the firm's benefit obligations (as well as the annual post-employment benefit expense reported in the income statement) will be understated.[11] As a result, for labor-intensive firms that offer attractive post-employment benefits to employees, it is important that the analyst assesses whether reported post-employment plan liabilities reflect the firms' true commitments.

International accounting rules require that firms estimate the value of post-employment commitments, called the post-employment benefit obligation, as the present value of future expected payouts under the plans. The obligation under pension plans is the present value of plan commitments factoring in the impact of future increases in wage rates and salary scales on projected payouts. For other post-employment plans, such as post-employment healthcare or life insurance, the firm's obligation is calculated as the present value of expected future benefits for employees and their beneficiaries.

Each year the firm's post-employment obligations are adjusted to reflect the following factors:

- Current service cost. Defined benefit plans typically provide higher benefits for each additional year of service with the company. For example, a company may promise its employees pension benefits in the amount of 2 percent of their career-average pay for every year worked. The value of incremental benefits earned from another year of service is called the current service cost, and increases the firm's obligation each year.
- Interest cost. The passage of time increases the present value of the firm's obligation. The interest cost recognizes this effect, and it is calculated by multiplying the obligation at the beginning of the year by the discount rate. The discount rate is set equal to the expected return on high-quality corporate bonds.
- Actuarial gains and losses. Each year the actuarial assumptions used to estimate the firm's commitments are reviewed and, if appropriate, changes are made. The effect of these changes is shown as Actuarial Gains and Losses.
- Past service cost. Occasionally companies may decide to amend their post-employment plans. For example, during recent years some companies have switched from linking pension benefits to employees' career-end pay to linking pension benefits to employees' career-average pay. Because these amendments affect the future payouts under the plans, they also affect the current post-employment benefit obligation. The effect of these amendments is shown as Past Service Cost (or Benefit).
- Benefits paid. The plan commitments are reduced as the plan makes payments to retirees each year.
- Other. The post-employment obligations can change because of changes in foreign exchange rates, changes in consolidation, plan curtailments, and plan settlements.

For example, in the notes to its financial statements, brewing company Carlsberg provided the following information on its post-employment benefit obligation for the years ended December 31, 2017 and 2016:

| (DKK millions) | December 31, 2017 | December 31, 2016 |
| --- | --- | --- |
| Benefit obligation at beginning of year | 14,772 | 14,229 |
| Current service cost | 215 | 310 |
| Interest cost | 251 | 296 |
| Actuarial (gains)/losses | (704) | 1,477 |
| Benefits paid | (689) | (643) |
| Other (e.g., foreign exchange adjustments, settlements) | (810) | (897) |
| Benefit obligation at end of year | 13,035 | 14,772 |

Carlsberg's obligation at the end of 2017 was DKK13.0 billion, an 11.8 percent decrease over the prior year.

To meet their commitments under post-employment plans, firms make contributions to the plans. These contributions are then invested in equities, debt, and other assets. Plan assets therefore are increased each year by new company (and employee) contributions. They are also increased or decreased by the returns generated each year from plan investments. Finally, plan assets decline when the plan pays out benefits to retirees. For the years ended December 31, 2017 and 2016, Carlsberg's post-employment assets were as follows:

| (DKK millions) | December 31, 2017 | December 31, 2016 |
| --- | --- | --- |
| Fair value of plan assets at beginning of year | 9,935 | 9,034 |
| Actual return on plan assets | 711 | 696 |
| Contributions to plans | 209 | 1,232 |
| Benefits paid | (570) | (491) |
| Other (e.g., foreign exchange adjustments) | (567) | (536) |
| Fair value of plan assets at end of year | 9,718 | 9,935 |

The difference between Carlsberg's post-employment plan obligations and the plan assets, DKK3.32 billion (13,035 − 9.718), represents the company's unfunded obligation to employees under the plan. The company reports a liability on its balance sheet for a similar amount.

Of course, estimating post-employment obligations requires significant judgment. It requires actuaries to forecast the future payouts under the plans, which in turn involves making projections of employees' service with the firm, retirement ages, and life expectancies, as well as future wage rates. It also requires actuaries to select an interest rate to estimate the present value of the future benefits. For example, Carlsberg projected that future salaries would grow at 2.1 percent per year, on average. It also assumed that the appropriate discount rate, measured as the expected return on high-quality bonds, was 1.8 percent, up from 1.5 percent in 2016. Given the management judgment involved in making these forecasts and assumptions, analysts should question whether reported obligations adequately reflect the firm's true commitments. Luckily, many companies provide additional disclosures in their notes that help analysts to assess the influence of management's assumptions on their post-employment obligation estimates. For example, Carlsberg discloses that a 0.5 percent increase in the discount rate would decrease the post-employment benefit obligation by close to DKK1.0 billion.

What does accounting for post-employment benefits imply for financial analysis? It is reasonable for the analyst to raise several questions about a firm's post-employment obligations, particularly for firms in labor-intensive industries.

1   Are the assumptions made by the firm to estimate its post-employment obligations realistic? These include assumptions about the discount rate, which is supposed to represent the current market interest rate for high-quality corporate bonds, as well as assumptions about increases in wage and benefit costs. If these assumptions are optimistic (pessimistic), the obligations recorded on the books understate (overstate) the firm's real economic commitment. In the preceding example, the analyst may find that the 1.8 percent discount rate, which reflects the contemporaneous rate for corporate bonds, understates the "true" expected risk-free return and thus conclude that the current discount rate is too low. If the analyst decided that Carlsberg's discount rate must increase by 0.5 percent, the post-employment obligation would have to be decreased by DKK1.0 billion, with offsetting increases in equity (for the after-tax effect) and the deferred tax liability. The adjustment to Carlsberg's 2017 balance sheet, assuming a 22 percent tax rate, would be as follows:

| (DKK billions) | Adjustment | |
| --- | --- | --- |
| | Assets | Liabilities and Equity |
| **Balance sheet** | | |
| Long-Term Debt | | −1.00 |
| Deferred Tax Liability | | +0.22 |
| Shareholders' Equity | | +0.78 |

2   What effect do post-employment benefit assumptions play in the income statement? The post-employment benefit expense each year comprises:

a   Current and past service cost, plus
b   Interest cost on the net post-employment benefit liability (or asset).

For Carlsberg, in 2017 the post-employment benefit expense equaled DKK314 million. Note that this cost is not equal to the change (decrease) in Carlsberg's net unfunded obligation in 2017 of −DKK1,520 million ([13,035 − 14,772] − [9,718 − 9,935]). This is because international accounting rules require companies to include several components of this change in other comprehensive income, a component of equity, rather than in the income statement. In particular, to mitigate the effect of fluctuations in the value of pension plans and commitments on companies' profits, the following components – labelled "remeasurements" – are recognized outside the income statement:

a   Actuarial gains and losses, plus
b   Excess return on plan assets, calculated as the actual return minus the discount rate times the fair value of plan assets.

Although it makes sense to recognize such volatile remeasurements separate from the more persistent post-employment cost components, the differential treatment of the components strengthens managers' incentive to (temporarily) understate post-employment obligations. In fact, corrections on the obligation that follow a period of unwarranted optimism (e.g., low forecasts of future wage and benefit rates) will be classified as actuarial gains and losses and immediately recognized in equity, thus by-passing the income statement. To assess the risk that management is overly optimistic in its post-employment assumptions, the analyst could evaluate the company's history of amounts recognized in other comprehensive income.

Finally, past service cost relates to employees' prior service years rather than to the company's current performance. From an analyst's perspective, such costs should therefore not be considered as permanent and ideally excluded from profit (or classified as Net Non-Recurring Income or Expense) using the information from the notes to the financial statements.

## Key Analysis Questions

The following are some of the questions an analyst can probe when analyzing whether a firm's liabilities exhibit distortions:

- *Unearned revenues.* Has the firm recognized revenues for services or products that have yet to be provided?
- *Provisions.* Did the firm disclose contingent liabilities that expose the firm to material risks? If so, can the expected value of such liabilities be estimated and recognized on the balance sheet? Did the firm make unexplained changes in its provisions? Is the size of the provisions in line with industry practices?
- *Post-employment benefits.* Are the assumptions made by the firm to estimate its post-employment obligations realistic? Does the firm have a history of actuarial losses? Has the firm recognized past service cost?

# Equity distortions

Accounting treats stockholders' equity as a residual claim on the firm's assets, after paying off the other claimholders. Consequently, equity distortions arise primarily from distortions in assets and liabilities. For example, distortions in assets or liabilities that affect earnings also lead to **distortions in equity**. However, there are forms of equity distortions that would not typically arise in asset and liability analyses. One particular issue is how firms account for contingent claims on their net assets that they sometimes provide to outside stakeholders. Two examples of such contingent claims are employee stock options and conversion options on convertible bonds.

### CONTINGENT CLAIMS

A stock option gives the holder the right to purchase a certain number of shares at a predetermined price, called the exercise or strike price, for a specified period of time, termed the exercise period. In the 1990s stock options became the most significant component of compensation for many corporate executives. Proponents of options argue that they provide managers with incentives to maximize shareholder value and make it easier to attract talented managers. Convertible bonds also contain a stock option component. Holders of these bonds have the right to purchase a certain number of shares in exchange for their fixed claim. When deciding on how to account for these contingent claims in a firm's financial statements, the following two factors are important to consider:

- Although providing a contingent claim does not involve a cash outflow for the firm, the claim is by no means costless to the firm's shareholders. The potential exercise of the option dilutes current shareholders' equity and as such imposes an economic cost on the firm's shareholders. To improve current profit or loss as a measure of the firm's current economic performance, the economic cost of contingent claims should therefore be included in the income statement in the same period in which the firm receives the benefits from these claims.
- The contingent claims are valuable to those who receive them. Employees are willing to provide services to the firm in exchange for employee stock options. Convertible bond holders are willing to charge a lower interest rate to the firm in exchange for the conversion option. If in future years the firm wishes to receive similar services or similar low interest rates without providing contingent claims on its net assets, it must be willing to give up other resources. To improve current profit or loss as a predictor of the firm's future profit or loss the income statement should therefore include an expense that reflects the value of the contingent claims to the recipients.

These two factors underline the importance of accurately recording the cost of options in a firm's income statement. International rules require firms to report stock options using the fair value method (discussed in IFRS Standards 2). The fair value method requires firms to record an expense for stock option compensation when the options are granted. The value of the options on the grant date is estimated using a recognized valuation model, such as the Black-Scholes model, and is then expensed over the vesting period.[12] Prior to the European adoption of IFRS Standards, the local accounting rules in most European countries permitted firms to report stock options using the intrinsic value method. Under the intrinsic value method, no compensation expense is reported at the grant date for the vast majority of stock options awarded, where the exercise price is equal to the firm's current stock price. If the options are subsequently exercised, there is also no expense recorded, and the new stock that is issued is valued at the exercise price rather than its higher market value.

Although there is no question that Black-Scholes valuations present a more accurate reflection of the economic cost of stock option awards to the firm's shareholders than the zero cost reported under the intrinsic value method, these valuations can be highly sensitive to management's assumptions about its share price characteristics. For example, when using the Black-Scholes model to value options, managers can understate the stock option expense by understating the expected future share price volatility or overstating the expected future dividend yield. One task of the analyst is therefore to assess the adequacy of management's valuation assumptions. Additionally, research suggests that employees attach much lower values than the Black-Scholes values to the nonmarketable options that they receive. This implies that when a firm plans to replace its stock option awards with cash-based forms of compensation, the analyst should assess whether a decrease in the compensation expense can be expected.

International accounting rules also require a firm to separate the debt from the equity component of convertible bonds. To do so, the firm first estimates what the fair value of the bonds would have been if the conversion option had not been attached to the bonds. This fair value is equal to the present value of the future fixed payments on the bonds, discounted at the firm's effective interest rate on nonconvertible bonds. The value of the equity component is then set equal to the proceeds of the bond issue minus the fair value of the debt component. The economic cost of the conversion option is included in the income statement by calculating the interest expense on the bonds on the basis of the (higher) effective interest rate on nonconvertible bonds. Under these rules, firms may have the incentive to understate the effective interest rate on nonconvertible bonds, thereby understating the convertible bonds' equity component and effective interest expense.

## Summary

Once the financial statements are standardized, the analyst can determine what accounting distortions exist in the firm's assets, liabilities, and equity. Common distortions that overstate assets include delays in recognizing asset impairments, underestimated allowances, aggressive revenue recognition leading to overstated receivables, and optimistic assumptions on long-term asset depreciation. Asset understatements can arise if managers overstate asset write-offs or make conservative assumptions for asset depreciation. They can also arise because accounting rules require outlays for key assets (e.g., research outlays and brands) to be immediately expensed.

For liabilities, the primary concern for the analyst is whether the firm understates its real commitments. This can arise from off-balance liabilities, from understated provisions, from questionable management judgment and limitations in accounting rules for estimating post-employment liabilities, and from aggressive revenue recognition that understates unearned revenue obligations. Equity distortions frequently arise when there are distortions in assets and liabilities.

Adjustments for distortions can therefore arise because accounting standards, although applied appropriately, do not reflect a firm's economic reality. They can also arise if the analyst has a different point of view than management about the estimates and assumptions made in preparing the financial statements. Once distortions have been identified, the analyst can use cash flow statement information and information from the notes to the financial statements to make adjustments to the balance sheet at the beginning and/or end of the current year, as well as any needed adjustments to revenues and expenses in the latest income statement. This ensures that the most recent financial ratios used to evaluate a firm's performance and to forecast its future results are based on financial data that appropriately reflect its business economics.

Several points are worth remembering when undertaking accounting analysis. First, the bulk of the analyst's time and energy should be focused on evaluating and adjusting accounting policies and estimates that describe the firm's key strategic value drivers. Of course this does not mean that management bias is not reflected in other accounting estimates and policies, and the analyst should certainly examine them. But given the importance of evaluating how the firm is managing its key success factors and risks, the bulk of the accounting analysis should be spent examining those policies that describe these factors and risks. Similarly, the analyst should focus on adjustments that have a material effect on the firm's liabilities, equity, or earnings. Immaterial adjustments cost time and energy but are unlikely to affect the analyst's financial and prospective analysis.

It is also important to recognize that many accounting adjustments can only be approximations rather than precise calculations, because much of the information necessary for making precise adjustments is not disclosed. The analyst should therefore try to avoid worrying about being overly precise in making accounting adjustments. By making even crude adjustments, it is usually possible to mitigate some of the limitations of accounting standards and problems of management bias in financial reporting.

## Core concepts

**Examples of asset value distortions**     Examples of asset value distortions are:

a   Non-current asset understatement resulting from overstated depreciation or amortization.
b   Non-current asset understatement resulting from off-balance sheet operating leases (prior to the adoption of IFRS Standards 16 in 2019).
c   Non-current asset understatement resulting from the immediate expensing of investments in intangible assets (such as research).
d   Current asset (receivables) understatement resulting from the sales of receivables.
e   Current asset (receivables) overstatement resulting from accelerated revenue recognition.
f   Non-current or current asset overstatement resulting from delayed write-downs.
g   Current asset overstatement resulting from underestimated allowances (e.g., for doubtful receivables or inventories obsolescence).

**Examples of liability distortions**     Examples of liability distortions are:

a   Liability understatement resulting from understated unearned revenues (e.g., revenues from long-term service contracts).
b   Liability understatement resulting from understated provisions.
c   Liability understatement resulting from the sales of receivables (with recourse).
d   Non-current liability understatement resulting from off-balance sheet operating leases (prior to the adoption of IFRS Standards 16 in 2019).
e   Liability understatement resulting from post-employment obligations that are (partly) kept off-balance.

**Sources of asset value distortions**     Managers may strategically bias or accounting rules may force them to bias the book values of assets if there is uncertainty about:

a   Who owns or controls the economic resources that potentially give rise to the assets.
b   Whether the economic resources will provide future economic benefits that can be reliably measured.
c   What the fair value of the assets is.
d   Whether the fair value of the asset is less than its book value.

**Sources of liability distortions**    Managers may strategically bias or accounting rules may force them to bias the book values of liabilities if there is uncertainty about:

a   Whether an obligation has occurred.
b   Whether the obligation can be reliably measured.

**Sources and examples of equity distortions**    Distortions in assets and liabilities can lead to equity distortions. However, contingent claims such as employee stock options or convertible bonds can directly cause distortions in equity.

## Questions, exercises, and problems

1   Refer to the Lufthansa example on asset depreciation estimates in this chapter. What adjustments would be required if Lufthansa's aircraft depreciation was computed using an average life of 25 years and salvage value of 5 percent (instead of the reported values of 12 years and 15 percent)? Show the adjustments to the 2011 and 2012 balance sheets, and to the 2012 income statement.

2   At the end of 2017, the Rolls-Royce Group reported in its footnotes that its plant and equipment had an original cost of £5,035 million and that accumulated depreciation was £2,984. Rolls-Royce depreciates its plant and equipment on a straight-line basis under the assumption that the assets have an average useful life of 12 years (assume a 10 percent salvage value). Rolls-Royce's tax rate equals 19.25 percent. What adjustments should be made to Rolls-Royce's (1) balance sheet at the end of 2017 and (2) income statement for the year 2018, if you assume that the plant and equipment have an average useful life of ten years (and a 10 percent salvage value)?

3   Car manufacturers Renault and Fiat Chrysler disclosed the following information in their 2017 financial statements:

| | Renault | Fiat Chrysler |
|---|---|---|
| Property, plant, and equipment (PP&E) at cost | €41,343m | €66,247m |
| Accumulated depreciation on PP&E | €27,761m | €37,233m |
| Deferred tax liability for depreciation of PP&E | €1,745m | €1,891m |
| Statutory tax rate | 34.4% | 19.25% |

Purely based on the companies' deferred tax liabilities, which of the two companies appears to be most conservative in its depreciation policy?

4   On December 31, 2017, Belgian-Dutch food retailer Ahold-Delhaize disclosed the following information about its operating lease commitments:

| (€ millions) | 2017 | 2016 |
|---|---|---|
| Within one year | €1,141 | €1,218 |
| Between one and five years | 3,522 | 3,754 |
| After five years | 2,927 | 3,478 |
| Total | 7,590 | 8,450 |

Ahold-Delhaize's operating lease expense in 2017 amounted to €979 million and its statutory tax rate was 25 percent. Assume that Ahold-Delhaize records its finance lease liabilities at an interest rate of 7.5 percent. Use this rate to capitalize Ahold-Delhaize's operating leases at December 2016 and 2017.

a   Record the adjustment to Ahold-Delhaize's balance sheet at the end of 2016 to reflect the capitalization of operating leases.

b   How would this reporting change affect Ahold-Delhaize's income statement in 2017?

c   When bringing operating lease commitments to the balance sheet, some analysts assume that in each year of the lease term, depreciation on the operating lease assets is exactly equal to the difference between (a) the operating lease payment and (b) the estimated interest expense on the operating lease obligation. Explain how this simplifies the adjustments. Do you consider this a valid assumption?

5   Refer to the Sanofi example on intangibles in this chapter. What would be the value of Sanofi's R&D asset at the end of fiscal years 2016 and 2017 if the average expected life of its R&D investments is only three years?

6   Under IFRS Standards, firms can capitalize development outlays, whereas under US GAAP such outlays must be expensed as incurred. In its 2016 IFRS Standards-based financial statements, Philips Electronics recognized a development asset of €1,079 million (€992 million in 2015). The company's development expenditures and total R&D expenditures during the period 2007–2016 were as follows (all amounts in millions):

| | Development expenditures | Total R&D expenditures |
|---|---|---|
| 2007 | €233 | €1,629 |
| 2008 | €154 | €1,622 |
| 2009 | €233 | €1,542 |
| 2010 | €219 | €1,493 |
| 2011 | €241 | €1,610 |
| 2012 | €347 | €1,831 |
| 2013 | €357 | €1,733 |
| 2014 | €323 | €1,766 |
| 2015 | €315 | €1,971 |
| 2016 | €318 | €2,021 |

Philips's statutory tax rate is 25.0 percent.

a   Estimate the average expected life of Philips's investments in development at the end of 2016.

b   Using the estimate derived under a, what adjustments should an analyst make to the 2016 beginning balance sheet and 2016 income statement to immediately expense all development outlays and derecognize the development asset?

c   What adjustments should be made to the 2016 beginning balance sheet and 2016 income statement to recognize an asset for both research and development investments? Assume that the average expected life of Philips's investments in research at the end of 2015 and 2016 is equal to that of Philips's development investments at the end of 2016.

7   What approaches would you use to estimate the value of brands? What assumptions underlie these approaches? As a financial analyst, what would you use to assess whether the brand value of £8.3 billion reported by consumer goods company Reckitt Benckiser plc in 2017 for its health and hygiene brands such as Strepsils, Nurofen, and Clearasil was a reasonable reflection of the future benefits from these brands? What questions would you raise with the firm's CFO about the firm's brand assets?

8   In early 2003 Bristol-Myers Squibb announced that it would have to restate its financial statements as a result of stuffing as much as $3.35 billion worth of products into wholesalers' warehouses from 1999 through 2001. The company's revenue and cost of sales during this period were as follows:

| (millions) | 2001 | 2000 | 1999 |
|---|---|---|---|
| Revenue | $18,139 | $17,695 | $16,502 |
| Cost of sales | $5,454 | $4,729 | $4,458 |

The company's marginal tax rate during the three years was 35 percent. What adjustments are required to correct Bristol-Myers Squibb's balance sheet for December 31, 2001? What assumptions underlie your adjustments? How would you expect the adjustments to affect

Bristol-Myers Squibb's performance in the coming few years?

9   As the CFO of a company, what indicators would you look at to assess whether your firm's non-current assets were impaired? What approaches could be used, either by management or an independent valuation firm, to assess the value of any asset impairment? As a financial analyst, what indicators would you look at to assess whether a firm's non-current assets were impaired? What questions would you raise with the firm's CFO about any charges taken for asset impairment?

10  On September 30, 2017, Germany-based Ceconomy (which owns consumer electronics retailer MediaMarktSaturn) reported in its annual financial statements that it held inventories for 52 days' sales. The inventories had a book value of €2,553 million. Ceconomy's statutory tax rate was 30.5 percent.

   a   How much excess inventory do you estimate Ceconomy is holding in September 2017 if the firm's optimal Days' Inventories is 45 days?

   b   Calculate the inventory impairment charge for Ceconomy if 50 percent of this excess inventory is deemed worthless. Record the changes to Ceconomy's financial statements from adjusting for this impairment.

11  On December 31, 2016 and 2017, Deutsche Telekom AG had net trade receivables in the amount of €9,179 million and €9,553 million, respectively. The following proportion of the receivables was past due on the reporting date:

| | 2016 | 2017 |
|---|---|---|
| Not past due on the reporting date | 3,074 (33.5%) | 4,107 (43.0%) |
| Past due on the reporting date | 6,105 (66.5%) | 5,446 (57.0%) |
| Total | 9,179 (100.0%) | 9,553 (100.0%) |

The changes in Deutsche Telekom's allowance for doubtful receivables were as follows:

| Item | 2016 | 2017 |
|---|---|---|
| Allowance on January 1 | 1,502 | 1,567 |
| Currency translation adjustments | 10 | (19) |
| Additions (allowance recognized as expense) | 757 | 698 |
| Use | (596) | (490) |
| Reversal | (106) | (99) |
| Allowance on December 31 | 1,567 | 1,657 |

Assume that Deutsche Telekom's statutory tax rate was 31.4 percent in 2016 and 2017. Further assume that an analyst wishes to recognize an additional allowance for 20 percent of the receivables that are past due on the reporting date.

   a   What adjustments should the analyst make to Deutsche Telekom's balance sheet at the end of 2016?

   b   What adjustments should the analyst make to Deutsche Telekom's 2017 income statement?

12  Refer to the British American Tobacco example on provisions in this chapter. The cigarette industry is subject to litigation for health hazards posed by its products. In the United States, the industry has been negotiating a settlement of these claims with state and federal governments. As the CFO for UK-based British American Tobacco (BAT), which is affected through its US subsidiaries, what information would you report to investors in the annual report on the firm's litigation risks? How would you assess whether the firm should record a provision for this risk, and if so, how would you assess the value of this provision? As a financial analyst following BAT, what questions would you raise with the CFO over the firm's litigation provision?

13  Refer to the Carlsberg example on post-employment benefits in this chapter. Discuss the components of the pension expense. In your opinion, is it reasonable to exclude some components of the change in the unfunded obligation from earnings? Is the calculation of the pension charge in the income statement appropriate (from an analyst's perspective)?

14  Some argue that (1) because estimating the value of contingent claims (such as executive stock options) is surrounded with uncertainty and (2) the claims do not represent a cash outlay, the value of these claims should not be included in the income statement as an expense. Do you agree with these arguments?

## Problem 1 Impairment of non-current assets

Consider the acquisitions by Germany-based media company EM.TV & Merchandising AG of the Jim Henson Company, creator of *The Muppet Show*, and Speed Investments Ltd., co-owner of the commercial rights to Formula One motor racing. At the end of the 1990s, EM.TV pursued a strategy of aggressive growth through the acquisitions of TV and marketing rights for well-known cartoon characters, such as *The Flintstones*, and popular sporting events. After its initial public offering on the Neuer Markt segment of the German Stock Exchange in October 1997, EM.TV's share price soared from €0.35 (split-adjusted) to a high of just above €120 in February 2000. Its high share price helped EM.TV to finance several acquisitions through a secondary stock offering and the issuance of convertible debt. In March and May 2000, respectively, the company made its two largest acquisitions with the intention of expanding its international reputation. The company acquired the Jim Henson Company for €699 million and Speed Investment for €1.55 billion. At the time of the acquisition, Speed Investment's book value of equity was negative and the amount of goodwill that EM.TV recognized on the investment was €2.07 billion. The rationale of capitalizing this amount of goodwill on EM.TV's balance sheet is that it could truly represent the future economic benefits that EM.TV expects to receive from its investment but that are not directly attributable to the investment's recorded assets and liabilities. However, the analyst should consider the possibility that EM.TV has overpaid for its new investments, especially in times where its managers are flush with free cash flow.

At the end of the fiscal year, when EM.TV's share price had already declined to €5.49, the company was forced to admit that it had overpaid for its latest acquisitions. Goodwill impairment charges for the year ending in December 2000 amounted to €340 million for the Jim Henson Company and €600 million for Speed Investment. In its annual report, EM.TV commented that "the salient factor for the write-offs was that, at the time of the acquisitions, the expert valuation was determined by the positive expectations of the capital markets. This was particularly expressed through the use of corresponding multiples." Despite the large write-offs, a considerable amount of goodwill, related to the acquisition of Speed Investment, remained part of EM.TV's assets. This amount of €1.41 billion was equal to 170 percent of EM.TV's book value of equity.

Given the questionable financial health of Speed Investment, did the initial €2.07 billion of goodwill ever represent a true economic asset? Was it reasonable to expect to receive €2.07 billion in future economic benefits from a firm that had not been able to earn profits in the past? If not, was the €600 million write-down adequate?

1   What balance sheet adjustments should an analyst make if she decided to record an additional write-down of €1.41 billion in the December 2000 financials?

2   What effect would this additional write-down have on EM.TV's depreciation expense in 2001? (Assume that the adjustments to EM.TV's balance sheet are in conformity with current IFRS Standards.)

## Problem 2 Audi, BMW, and Skoda's research and development

Car manufacturers Audi, BMW Group, and Skoda Auto spend considerable amounts on research and development and capitalize a proportion of these amounts each year. Each manufacturer systematically amortizes development cost assets, presumably using the straight-line method, following the start of the production of a developed car model or component. In the notes to their financial statements, the firms report the following (average) estimated product lives:

- Audi: Four to nine years.
- BMW: Usually five to twelve years.
- Skoda: One to nine years, according to the product life cycle.

In 2017, the proportion of capitalized development expenditures that concerned costs for products under development (i.e., models or components that are not yet in production) was 36 percent for Audi and 34 percent for Skoda (BMW did not disclose this proportion).

Audi and BMW both focus their activities on the premium sector of the automobile market. Skoda operates primarily in the lower segments of the market. Both Audi and Skoda are majority owned by Volkswagen Group and share car platforms and production facilities with their major shareholder. BMW is publicly listed and independent (from other car manufacturers).

The following table displays the firms' research and development expenditures and the amount capitalized and amortized during the years 2007–2017.

| | 2017 | 2016 | 2015 | 2014 | 2013 | 2012 | 2011 | 2010 | 2009 | 2008 | 2007 |
|---|---|---|---|---|---|---|---|---|---|---|---|
| **BMW Group (€ millions)** | | | | | | | | | | | |
| Research and development expense | 4,920 | 4,294 | 4,271 | 4,135 | 4,118 | 3,993 | 3,610 | 3,082 | 2,587 | 2,825 | 2,920 |
| Amortization and impairment | −1,236 | −1,222 | −1,166 | −1,068 | −1,069 | −1,130 | −1,209 | −1,260 | −1,226 | −1,185 | −1,109 |
| Development costs capitalized in the current year | 2,424 | 2,092 | 2,064 | 1,499 | 1,744 | 1,089 | 972 | 951 | 1,087 | 1,224 | 1,333 |
| Total R&D expenditure | 6,108 | 5,164 | 5,169 | 4,566 | 4,793 | 3,952 | 3,373 | 2,773 | 2,448 | 2,864 | 3,144 |
| Capitalized development costs (asset) at the end of the year | 8,409 | 7,221 | 6,351 | 5,453 | 5,022 | 4,347 | 4,388 | 4,625 | 4,934 | 5,073 | 5,034 |
| End-of-year total assets | 193,483 | 188,535 | 172,174 | 154,803 | 138,377 | 131,850 | 123,429 | 110,164 | 101,953 | 101,086 | 88,997 |
| Revenue | 98,678 | 94,163 | 92,175 | 80,401 | 76,059 | 76,848 | 68,821 | 60,477 | 50,681 | 53,197 | 56,018 |
| Operating profit | 9,880 | 9,386 | 9,593 | 9,118 | 7,978 | 8,300 | 8,018 | 5,111 | 289 | 921 | 4,212 |
| **Audi (€ millions)** | | | | | | | | | | | |
| Research and development expense | 3,590 | 3,640 | 3,718 | 3,685 | 3,287 | 2,942 | 2,641 | 2,469 | 2,050 | 2,161 | 2,226 |
| Amortization and impairment | −1025 | −871 | −739 | −681 | −528 | −429 | −397 | −567 | −480 | −530 | −656 |
| Development costs capitalized in the current year | 1,244 | 1,677 | 1,261 | 1,311 | 1,207 | 923 | 595 | 629 | 528 | 547 | 497 |
| Total R&D expenditure | 3,809 | 4,446 | 4,240 | 4,315 | 3,966 | 3,436 | 2,839 | 2,531 | 2,098 | 2,178 | 2,067 |
| Capitalized development costs (asset) at the end of the year | 5,666 | 5,447 | 4,642 | 4,120 | 3,489 | 2,810 | 2,249 | 2,051 | 1,989 | 1,940 | 1,923 |
| End-of-year total assets | 63,680 | 61,090 | 56,763 | 50,769 | 45,156 | 40,425 | 37,019 | 30,772 | 26,550 | 26,056 | 22,578 |
| Revenue | 60,128 | 59,317 | 58,420 | 53,787 | 49,880 | 48,771 | 44,096 | 35,441 | 29,840 | 34,196 | 33,617 |
| Operating profit | 4,671 | 3,052 | 4,836 | 5,150 | 5,030 | 5,380 | 5,348 | 3,340 | 1,604 | 2,772 | 2,705 |

| | 2017 | 2016 | 2015 | 2014 | 2013 | 2012 | 2011 | 2010 | 2009 | 2008 | 2007 |
|---|---|---|---|---|---|---|---|---|---|---|---|
| **Skoda Auto (CZK millions)** | | | | | | | | | | | |
| Research and development expense | 13,293 | 12,452 | 10,355 | 10,214 | 6,709 | 7,345 | 9,133 | 8,222 | 7,139 | 5,721 | 4,812 |
| Amortization and impairment | −5,006 | −5,917 | −4,148 | −2,672 | −2,461 | −2,497 | −3,072 | −3,658 | −2,899 | −2,326 | −2,450 |
| Development costs capitalized in the current year | 7,111 | 3,475 | 4,110 | 5,428 | 4,326 | 6,104 | 3,306 | 3,093 | 1,493 | 2,066 | 3,097 |
| Total R&D expenditure | 15,398 | 10,010 | 10,317 | 12,970 | 8,574 | 10,952 | 9,367 | 7,657 | 5,733 | 5,461 | 5,459 |
| Capitalized development costs (asset) at the end of the year | 18,621 | 16,516 | 18,958 | 18,995 | 16,239 | 14,333 | 10,726 | 10,492 | 11,057 | 12,463 | 12,725 |
| End-of-year total assets | 250,859 | 228,180 | 202,615 | 176,869 | 152,001 | 159,986 | 153,557 | 135,736 | 118,376 | 122,456 | 115,781 |
| Revenue | 407,400 | 347,987 | 314,997 | 299,318 | 243,624 | 262,649 | 252,562 | 219,454 | 187,858 | 200,182 | 221,967 |
| Operating profit | 40,531 | 30,892 | 35,154 | 21,598 | 12,537 | 17,917 | 18,257 | 11,316 | 5,924 | 13,620 | 19,784 |

1 Estimate the average economic lives of the car manufacturers' development assets. What assumptions make your estimates of the average economic lives consistent with those reported by the manufacturers?

2 The percentages of R&D expenditures capitalized fluctuate over time and differ between car manufacturers. Which factors may explain these fluctuations and differences? As an analyst, what questions would you raise with the CFO about the levels of and fluctuations in these capitalization percentages?

3 In accordance with IAS 38, the three car manufacturers do not capitalize research expenditures. From an analyst's perspective, which arguments would support capitalization (rather than immediate expensing) of research expenditures?

4 What adjustments to the car manufacturers' 2017 financial statements are required if you decide to capitalize (and gradually amortize) the firms' entire R&D? Which of the three manufacturers is most affected by these adjustments?

## Problem 3 H&M and Inditex's non-current assets

Hennes & Mauritz (H&M) and Inditex are publicly listed apparel retailers. The following information is taken from their financial statements for the fiscal years ending on November 30, 2017, and January 31, 2018, respectively (hereafter referred to as fiscal 2017):

| | H&M fiscal 2017 | Inditex fiscal 2017 |
|---|---|---|
| Book value of land, buildings, and leasehold improvements at the beginning of the year | SEK 850m | €1,816m |
| Equipment at cost at the beginning of the year | SEK 63,727m | €10,391m |
| Book value of equipment at the beginning of the year | SEK 35,994m | €5,146m |
| Cost of equipment acquired during the year | SEK 11,035m | €1,499m |
| Buildings and leasehold improvements depreciation expense | SEK 32m | €36m |
| Equipment depreciation expense | SEK 7,711m | €930m |
| Revenue | SEK 200,004m | €25,336m |

Both retailers had non-cancelable operating leases related to land, buildings, and equipment. Under the operating lease agreements, the companies were committed to paying the following amounts:

| Due in ... | H&M | | Inditex | |
| --- | --- | --- | --- | --- |
| | fiscal 2017 | fiscal 2016 | fiscal 2017 | fiscal 2016 |
| Year 1 | SEK 16,219m | SEK 16,068m | €1,453m | €1,385m |
| Years 2–5 | SEK 41,788m | SEK 41,605m | €2,386m | €2,358m |
| After year 5 | SEK 20,330m | SEK 23,820m | €1,092m | €1,239m |
| Actual lease payment made during the year | SEK 19,126m | SEK 20,554m | €1,913m | €1,820m |

The statutory tax rates of H&M and Inditex were 22 and 25 percent, respectively. Assume that in 2017 the incremental borrowing rate of H&M and Inditex was 3 percent and that all land, buildings, and equipment had zero residual values. Further assume that both retailers recognized half a year of depreciation on assets acquired during the year.

1   Two measures of the efficiency of a firm's investment policy are (a) the ratio of land, buildings, leasehold improvements, and equipment to revenue and (b) the ratio of depreciation to revenue. Calculate both ratios for H&M and Inditex based on the reported information. Which of the two companies appears to be relatively more efficient in its investment policy?

2   Calculate the depreciation rates that H&M and Inditex use for their equipment.

3   What adjustments to (a) the beginning book value of H&M's equipment and (b) the equipment depreciation expense would be required if you assume that H&M uses Inditex's depreciation rate?

4   What adjustments to (a) the beginning book value of H&M's and Inditex's land, buildings, and equipment and (b) H&M's and Inditex's depreciation expense would be required if you capitalize the retailers' operating leases?

5   Recalculate the investment efficiency measures using the adjusted data. Do the adjustments affect your assessment of the retailers' investment efficiency?

## Notes

1   See P. Healy, S. Myers, and C. Howe, "R&D Accounting and the Tradeoff Between Relevance and Objectivity," *Journal of Accounting Research* 40 (June 2002): 677–711, for analysis of the value of capitalizing R&D and then annually assessing impairment.
2   V. Beattie, K. Edwards, and A. Goodacre show that adjustments to capitalize operating leases have a significant impact on leverage and other key financial ratios of UK firms. See "The Impact of Constructive Operating Lease Capitalisation on Key Accounting Ratios," *Accounting and Business Research* 28 (Autumn 1998): 233–254.
3   Some research suggests that the distinction between finance and operating lease obligation is not arbitrary. In their study "Recognition Versus Disclosure:

An Investigation of the Impact on Equity Risk Using UK Operating Lease Disclosures," *Journal of Business Finance and Accounting* 27 (November/December 2000): 1185–1224, V. Beattie, A. Goodacre, and S. Thomson find that UK investors interpret the operating lease obligation as an obligation that increases a firm's equity risk but less so than ordinary debt.
4   P. Healy, S. Myers, and C. Howe, "R&D Accounting and the Tradeoff Between Relevance and Objectivity," *Journal of Accounting Research* 40 (June 2002): 677–711, show that the magnitude of this bias is sizable.
5   See, e.g., B. Bublitz and M. Ettredge, "The Information in Discretionary Outlays: Advertising, Research and Development," *The Accounting Review* 64 (1989): 108–124; M. Hirschey and J. Weygandt, "Amortization Policy for Advertising and Research and Development Expenditures," *Journal of Accounting Research* 23 (1985): 326–335;

B. Lev and T. Sougiannis, "The Capitalization, Amortization, and Value-Relevance of R&D," *Journal of Accounting and Economics* 21 (1996): 107–138; P. Green, A. Stark, and H. Thomas, "UK Evidence on the Market Valuation of Research and Development Expenditures," *Journal of Business Finance and Accounting* 23 (March 1996): 191–216; D. Aboody and B. Lev, "The Value-Relevance of Intangibles: The Case of Software Capitalization," *Journal of Accounting Research* 36 (1998): 161–191; and M. Ballester, M. Garcia-Ayuso, and J. Livnat, "The Economic Value of the R&D Intangible Asset," *European Accounting Review* 12 (2003): 605–633.

6  J. Francis, D. Hanna, and L. Vincent find that management is more likely to exercise judgment in its self-interest for goodwill write-offs and restructuring charges than for inventory or PP&E write-offs. See "Causes and Effects of Discretionary Asset Write-Offs," *Journal of Accounting Research* 34 (Supplement, 1996): 117–134.

7  P. Healy, K. Palepu, and R. Ruback find that acquisitions add value for only one-third of the 50 largest acquisitions during the early 1980s, suggesting that acquirers frequently do not recover goodwill. See "Which Takeovers Are Profitable – Strategic or Financial?" *Sloan Management Review*, Summer 1997. Studying a sample of 519 UK acquirers between 1983 and 1995, S. Sudarsanam and A. Mahate find in their study "Glamour Acquirers, Method of Payment and Post-acquisition Performance: The UK Evidence," *Journal of Business Finance and Accounting* 30 (January 2003): 299–341 that the risk of not recovering goodwill is especially large for glamour acquirers, who have experienced a large share price run-up prior to the acquisition.

8  J. Elliott and D. Hanna find that the market anticipates large write-downs by about one quarter, consistent with managers being reluctant to take write-downs on a timely basis. See "Repeated Accounting Write-Offs and the Information Content of Earnings," *Journal of Accounting Research* 34 (Supplement, 1996): 135–155.

9  Mary E. Barth and Maureen McNichols discuss ways for investors to estimate the value of environmental liabilities. See "Estimation and Market Valuation of Environmental Liabilities Relating to Superfund Sites," *Journal of Accounting Research* 32 (Supplement, 1994): 177–209.

10  Defined contribution plans, where companies agree to contribute fixed amounts today to cover future benefits, require very little forecasting to estimate their annual cost since the firm's obligation is limited to its annual obligation to contribute to the employees' pension funds.

11  E. Amir and E. Gordon show that firms with larger post-retirement benefit obligations and more leverage tend to make more aggressive estimates of post-retirement obligation parameters. See "A Firm's Choice of Estimation Parameters: Empirical Evidence from SFAS No. 106," *Journal of Accounting, Auditing and Finance* 11(3) (Summer 1996).

12  The Black-Scholes option pricing model estimates the value of an option as a nonlinear function of the exercise price, the remaining time to expiration, the estimated variance of the underlying stock, and the risk-free interest rate. Studies of the valuation of executive stock options include T. Hemmer, S. Matsunaga, and T. Shevlin, "Optimal Exercise and the Cost of Granting Employee Stock Options with a Reload Provision," *Journal of Accounting Research* 36 (No. 2, 1998): 231–255; C. Cuny and P. Jorion, "Valuing Executive Stock Options with Endogenous Departure," *Journal of Accounting and Economics* 20 (September 1995): 193–206; and S. Huddart, "Employee Stock Options," *Journal of Accounting and Economics* 18 (September 1994): 207–232.

# CASE

## Accounting for the iPhone Upgrade Program (A)

*The iPhone has become one of the most important, world-changing and successful products in history. Last week [July 27, 2016] we passed another major milestone when we sold the billionth iPhone. We never set out to make the most, but we've always set out to make the best products that make a difference.*

— Tim Cook, Apple CEO[1]

## Introduction

On September 9, 2015, Apple Inc. (Apple) launched its new iPhone 6s and iPhone 6s Plus models and, at the same time, announced the "iPhone Upgrade Program," a new way to purchase those iPhone models in Apple's retail stores throughout the U.S.[2] Under the program, eligible consumers could buy an iPhone 6s and 6s Plus and, as a form of payment, agree to a 24-month loan in partnership with Citizens Bank (Citizens).[3] An iPhone purchased under the program was unlocked, meaning customers were able to switch their wireless carrier according to their contract terms. The offer included Apple's AppleCare+ service, which provided extended warranty and software support compared to the regular one-year limited warranty. After one year the iPhone customer could turn in her old iPhone, get a new iPhone model, and enter into a new installment loan agreement, with a new two-year payment obligation.[4] In the event the iPhone upgrade program was terminated by the customer, the customer was responsible for any outstanding balances due under the terms of the loan with Citizens.[5]

Following the announcement, several financial analysts reacted positively to the new upgrade program; some of them described it as a "smart move" forward.[6] According to one UBS analyst, the "Upgrade Program

HBS Professors Jonas Heese and Krishna G. Palepu, Professor H. David Sherman (Northeastern University), and Case Researcher Monica Baraldi (Case Research & Writing Group) prepared this case. This case was developed from published sources. Funding for the development of this case was provided by Harvard Business School and not by the company. HBS cases are developed solely as the basis for class discussion. Cases are not intended to serve as endorsements, sources of primary data, or illustrations of effective or ineffective management.

[1]Jasper Hamill, "Apple Has Flogged One Billion iPhones in Less than a Decade," *The Sun*, July 28, 2016, https://www.thesun.co.uk/news/1516139/apple-has-flogged-one-billion-iphones-in-less-than-a-decade/, accessed July 2016.

[2]Thomas Gryta and Ryan Knutson, "Apple Wants to Sell You an iPhone for $32 a Month," *The Wall Street Journal*, http://blogs.wsj.com/digits/2015/09/09/apple-wants-to-sell-you-an-iphone-for-32-a-month/, accessed July 2016.

[3]Deirdre Fernandes, "Citizens Is the Bank behind Apple's New iPhone Upgrade Plan," *The Boston Globe*, September 10, 2015, http://www.betaboston.com/news/2015/09/10/citizens-bank-to-offer-loans-for-iphone-subscriptions/, accessed August 2016.

[4]Apple, "iPhone Upgrade Program Terms & Conditions," Apple Web site, http://www.apple.com/legal/sales-support/iphoneupgrade_us/, accessed July 2016.

[5]Apple, "iPhone Upgrade Program Terms & Conditions."

[6]Steven Milunovich, "Apple Inc. Upgrade Program a Net EPS Positive and Could Boost Multiple on Recognition of Annuity Revenue," UBS Securities LLC., September 15, 2015, via Thomson ONE, accessed August 2016.

increases stickiness and makes the iPhone look more like an annuity business."[7] Another J.P. Morgan analyst estimated that Apple's margin for an iPhone sold under the new program could be four times higher than that for iPhones sold through the carrier channel, as Apple was charging $50 more per device under this program.[8] A UBS analyst wrote that the iPhone Upgrade Program "could be a big deal," as it allowed Apple to take control of the customer relationship.[9] One observer predicted that 75% of Apple's iPhone customers would eventually switch to an annual upgrade, increasing Apple's U.S. iPhone unit sales by 10% over three years.[10]

Other business analysts were more skeptical about the program, as it came with risks related to competition from wireless carriers. Because carriers made money when phone users paid them for service, and because phone users tended to stick with a single carrier long-term, carriers had an incentive to try to lock in customers by selling them phones that came with a two-year contract. They could do this by offering other brands of phones at lower prices than Apple.[11] "Apple's move is perhaps a bit threatening, in that it incrementally erodes the carrier's relationship with the customer," said one senior analyst.[12]

Next to the strategic implications of the Upgrade Program, analysts tried to understand the accounting implications, especially for recognition of revenue, which the Upgrade Program could have on Apple's financials. Some assumed "no dramatic change" in revenue recognition, while others were waiting for more guidance from Apple.

In an effort to increase iPhone sales, Apple was pushing the Upgrade Program hard for the 2015 holidays in its retail stores, on its website, and in unsolicited e-mails.[13]

## Company background

The iPhone went on sale for the first time at the end of June 2007 and, at a starting price of $500, was immediately criticized by bloggers and news commentators for being too expensive compared to an average smartphone priced roughly around $200.[14] The doubts were soon dispelled. By the end of 2007, Apple sold two million iPhones, and almost seven million in the last quarter of fiscal year 2008.[15] From a strategic perspective, between 2007 and 2014 Apple had been "remarkably consistent"[16] in maintaining a smartphone price somewhere near $700 and annually launching anticipated handsets which featured incremental or radical innovations.[17] Apple typically released new iPhone models in the fall, increasing Apple's smartphone units sold and boosting revenue during the first quarter of the fiscal year, which typically started on October 1.[18]

In 2015, Apple faced a challenging and changing competitive environment. The major wireless service providers such as AT&T, Sprint, T-Mobile, and Verizon were competing for subscribers in a mature U.S.

[7]Steven Milunovich, "Apple Inc. Upgrade Program a Net EPS Positive and Could Boost Multiple on Recognition of Annuity Revenue."

[8]Rod Hill, "Apple Inc., iPhone Upgrade Program Deep Dive," J.P. Morgan, September 15, 2015, via Thomson ONE, accessed July 2016.

[9]Steven Milunovich, "Apple Inc. Upgrade Program a Net EPS Positive and Could Boost Multiple on Recognition of Annuity Revenue."

[10]Philip Elmer-DeWitt, "Apple's Secret Plan to Boost iPhone Sales Is Working," *Fortune*, December 15, 2015, http://fortune.com/2015/12/15/apple-iphone-upgrade-program/, accessed August 2016.

[11]Rod Hill, "Apple Inc., iPhone Upgrade Program Deep Dive;" Munster, Gene, "Apple Inc., Early Take On iPhone Upgrade Program Metrics," PiperJaffray, January 22, 2016, via Thomson ONE, accessed July 2016.

[12]Thomas Gryta and Ryan Knutson, "Apple Takes Aim at Wireless Phone Companies," *The Wall Street Journal*, September 9, 2015, http://www.wsj.com/articles/apple-takes-aim-at-wireless-phone-companies-1441845365, accessed July 2016.

[13]Philip Elmer-DeWitt, "Apple's Secret Plan to Boost iPhone Sales Is Working."

[14]Statista, "Average Price of PDAs/Smartphones, after Discount, in the United States between 4th Quarter 2006 and 4th Quarter 2009 (in U.S. Dollars)," Statista, http://www.statista.com/statistics/185718/average-price-for-pdas-and-smartphones-in-the-united-states-since-2006/, accessed August 2016.

[15]Statista, "Global Apple iPhone Sales from 3rd Quarter 2007 to 2nd Quarter 2016 (in Million Units)," Statista, http://www.statista.com/statistics/263401/global-apple-iphone-sales-since-3rd-quarter-2007/, accessed August 2016.

[16]Vlad Savov, "The Entire History of iPhone vs. Android Summed Up in Two Charts," The Verge, June 1, 2016, http://www.theverge.com/2016/6/1/11836816/iphone-vs-android-history-charts, accessed August 2016.

[17]Wayne Williams, "Just How Innovative Was Each iPhone Release?," *Betanews*, September 5, 2014, http://betanews.com/2014/09/05/just-how-innovative-was-each-iphone-release/, accessed August 2016.

[18]Jack Linshi, "This 1 Chart Shows How Intense the Apple-Samsung Rivalry Really Is," *Time*, April 29, 2015, http://time.com/3840414/samsung-apple-market-share/, accessed August 2016.

market.[19] Most consumers already had a cell phone and switched carriers infrequently. The average phone upgrade frequency in the U.S. had risen from 18 months in 2010 to an estimated 26 months in 2015.[20] The average contract between the consumer and the wireless carrier stretched across two years in which the customer had to sign an agreement with the carrier and pay early-termination fees "in exchange for a discounted price on a phone."[21] However, new trends were emerging.

In the summer of 2015, two-year contracts were disappearing,[22] unlocked phones were becoming more popular, and consumers were accepting the idea of paying the full cost of a phone upfront in exchange for the freedom to select their preferred carrier at any time.[23] By 2013, T-Mobile was the first carrier that no longer sold two-year contracts. "Once T-Mobile did it, all the others followed,"[24] said an industry insider. Furthermore, new players were entering the mobile market. Google was testing a wireless service, Google Fi, which would allow consumers to switch from T-Mobile to Sprint and back multiple times.[25]

Apple's management decided that it was time to innovate the iPhone business model. In September 2015 the company announced the new iPhone Upgrade Program. For the first time, Apple financed iPhone sales directly to customers without locking them to any particular carrier.[26]

## iPhone upgrade program

Under the new iPhone Upgrade Program, available only through Apple's retail stores in the U.S., the company began offering a 24-month payment plan for the unlocked iPhones 6s and 6s Plus and the AppleCare+ service for $32.41 and $44.92 a month, respectively. Customers could upgrade to a new device after making 12 payments and could switch to new service carriers according to the contractual terms. (See **Exhibit 1** for the iPhone Upgrade Program terms and conditions.)

From a consumer perspective, the new program did not provide any savings on the device. The final payment would end up being about $778 for the iPhone 6s, which reflected the combined stand-alone prices of the iPhone 6s ($649) and the AppleCare+ coverage ($129). However, as Apple typically did not increase the price of its new iPhone models, the upgrade program made it attractive for customers to upgrade. One expert reported that "[t]he leasing program[a] may seem like Apple is doing consumers a favor, but it's really an effort to ensure people buy new phones or continue paying more for the old one if they decide to hold on to it."[27] One consumer columnist wrote: "It [the iPhone Upgrade Program] is a decent deal if you're one who simply must upgrade to the latest, greatest gadget as soon as it comes out. But if you're like me and you keep your phones for years, then you're probably better off buying instead of [essentially] leasing."[28]

[19]Joanna Stern, "Kill the Wireless Contract! Buy Your Own Phone," *The Wall Street Journal*, February 25, 2015, http://www.wsj.com/articles/kill-the-wireless-contract-buy-your-own-phone-1424807865, accessed July 2016.

[20]Thomas Gryta and Ryan Knutson, "Apple's iPhone: The Biggest Change Is How You'll Pay for It," *The Wall Street Journal*, September 8, 2015, http://www.wsj.com/articles/apples-iphone-the-biggest-change-is-how-youll-pay-for-it-1441754856, accessed July 2016.

[21]Ryan Knutson, "Sprint to Abandon Two-Year Contracts," *The Wall Street Journal*, August 18, 2015, http://www.wsj.com/articles/sprint-to-abandon-two-year-contracts-1439837235, accessed July 2016.

[22]Ryan Knutson, "Sprint to Abandon Two-Year Contracts."

[23]Joanna Stern, "Kill the Wireless Contract! Buy Your Own Phone."

[24]Cade Metz, "New iPhone Means We'll Soon Escape the Captivity of Carriers," *Wired*, September 14, 2015, http://www.wired.com/2015/09/new-iphone-means-well-soon-escape-captivity-carriers/, accessed July 2016.

[25]Cade Metz, "New iPhone Means We'll Soon Escape the Captivity of Carriers."

[26]Thomas Gryta and Ryan Knutson, "Apple Takes Aim at Wireless Phone Companies."

[a]Under the Upgrade Program, consumers purchased and owned the phone. However, due to the payment plan structure of the accompanying loan and the ability for a consumer to turn in their phone early, some analysts referred to the program as a leasing program.

[27]ABC News, "What You Should Know about New Lease Program for Apple iPhone 6s and 6sPlus," ABC News website, September 11, 2015, http://wtnh.com/2015/09/11/what-you-should-know-about-new-lease-program-for-apple-aapl-iphone-6s-and-6s-plus/, accessed August 2016.

[28]Susanna Kim, "What you should know about new lease program for apple iPhone 6s and 6sPlus," ABCNews, September 24, 2015, http://abcnews.go.com/Technology/lease-program-apple-aapl-iphone-6s-6s/story?id=33657547, accessed November 2016.

Product innovation at Apple had anticipated the company's new strategy in the mobile business segment. A multi-carrier SIM[b] enabled the new iPhones 6s and 6s Plus to run on any wireless network in the world. This innovation would allow consumers to move between cellular carriers according to their preference.[29] One respected Silicon Valley inventor said of Tim Cook and Apple: "They've opened up the floodgates. The strongest tie that an operator has to a user is a financial one, where there's either a pre-paid plan or an installment plan. With this new Apple [multi-carrier SIM], that goes away."[30]

From a strategic perspective, the new iPhone Upgrade Program opened several possibilities for Apple's iPhone business. First, customers were allowed to access high-end handsets with a limited upfront payment. The program encouraged a higher turnover of the phone, at a time when the average iPhone replacement cycle was longer than two years.[31] Second, sales of iPhone units had slowed in 2014 and 2015, and observers noticed that sales of services, such as Internet services, AppleCare, and Apple Pay, were becoming more and more relevant.[32] With reference to the "Services" business segment, Cook said: "The growth was broad-based, with App Store revenue up 37% to a new all-time high, in addition to a strong increase in Apple Music, iCloud, and AppleCare."[33] (See **Exhibit 2** for Apple's revenue and units sold by product.)

The program also allowed Apple to enter the market for used iPhones, especially in developing countries where new iPhone models had significantly lower customer penetration. One AT&T senior executive said, "If they [Apple] are successful there will be a lot of slightly used pre-owned iPhones or handsets out there. We'll be really interested in talking to them about partnering with them to utilize those [used iPhones]."[34] Financial analysts were forecasting profitable market opportunities. Gartner estimated that the high-end second-hand smartphone market would reach $14 billion by 2017,[35] but for analysts it was difficult to find "meaningful data to support an estimate," as one observer wrote.[36] A UBS analyst reported, "Our best guess for iPhone users who are using a second-hand iPhone is somewhere around 35 million to 45 million or roughly 10% of the user base, growing by 5 to 7 million each quarter prior to the launch of the iPhone 6s and 6s Plus. With an increasing supply of iPhones traded-in within 1-2 years, we believe the available stock of used iPhones will rise."[37]

In India, where Apple had a 2% market share, 70% of smartphones sold for less than $150. In 2016, in an effort to increase its sales, Apple was seeking permission from government officials to sell pre-owned iPhones in India. Above all, Apple saw growth potential in China's rising middle class. Chinese customers still viewed the iPhone as a luxury product. However, Apple faced strong competition in China, especially from Xiaomi and Huawei. In 2015, Xiaomi, a Chinese company headquartered in Beijing, grew at a 23% annual rate. Its management had projected 100 million smartphone shipments for that year.[38] Xiaomi controlled 15.8% of

[b]Most mobile devices contained SIM cards, or subscriber identity module cards. These were removable smart cards that stored a mobile device's identifying features, technological elements enabling voice encryption, and the user's contacts and message data. They enabled the device to connect to a specified carrier's cellular network.

[29]Sam Oliver, "Apple Unveils New Multi-Carrier Apple SIM Bundled with new iPads," AppleInsider, October 16, 2014, http://appleinsider.com/articles/14/10/16/apple-unveils-new-multi-carrier-apple-sim-bundled-with-new-ipads, accessed August 2016.

[30]Cade Metz, "New iPhone Means We'll Soon Escape the Captivity of Carriers."

[31]Puneet Sikka, "Has Apple's iPhone Upgrade Program Led to Faster Upgrades?," Market Realist, April 19, 2016, http://marketrealist.com/2016/04/apples-iphone-upgrade-program-helped-faster-upgrades/, accessed August 2016.

[32]Hannes Sverrisson, "Services. The New iPhone!," Seeking Alpha, July 27, 2016, http://seekingalpha.com/article/3992035-services-new-iphone, accessed July 2016.

[33]Hannes Sverrisson, "Services. The New iPhone."

[34]Reinhardt Krause, "Apple Used-iPhone Market Could Boom From Upgrades," *Investor's Business Daily*, September 16, 2015, http://www.investors.com/apple-iphone-upgrade-program-fuels-used-iphone-market/, accessed August 2016.

[35]Steven Milunovich, "Apple Inc. Upgrade Program a Net EPS Positive and Could Boost Multiple on Recognition of Annuity Revenue," UBS Securities LLC., September 15, 2015, via Thomson ONE, accessed August 2016.

[36]Steven Milunovich, "Apple Inc. Upgrade Program a Net EPS Positive and Could Boost Multiple on Recognition of Annuity Revenue."

[37]Reinhardt Krause, "Apple Used-iPhone Market Could Boom From Upgrades."

[38]Sam Mattera, "This New Smartphone Could Be the iPhone's Biggest Competition in China," The Motley Fool, March 14, 2016, http://www.fool.com/investing/general/2016/03/14/this-new-smartphone-could-be-the-iphones-biggest-c.aspx, accessed August 2016.

the smartphone market, followed by Huawei (15.4%) and Apple (12.2%).[39] The Chinese market was especially resistant to the introduction of iPhone 6 models since, according to a 2014 market analysis, smartphones from national brands had a competitive price and were perceived as having good quality.[40]

Finally, the iPhone Upgrade Program created new alliances. It redefined commercial and competitive terms with phone carriers such as AT&T, T-Mobile, and Verizon. A former Verizon senior executive said: "Apple's move is a sign it wants to wrest control of customers from wireless carriers. Companies that control the customer relationship have more leverage in pricing and sales."[41] A top manager at Sprint stated, "Apple is trying to do nothing more than shorten the cycle so they can sell more iPhones."[42] A T-Mobile senior executive was supportive of Apple's new strategy, saying "it would allow customers to try out other carriers."[43]

The Upgrade Program relied on a partnership with Citizens Bank. Citizens was a subsidiary of Citizens Financial Group, one of the oldest financial institutions in the U.S., headquartered in Providence, Rhode Island.[44] Citizens provided the two-year installment loan for consumers who paid a monthly amount tied to a credit card for the purchased iPhone. When the plan was launched, Citizens was Apple's only financial partner.[45] One observer noticed that, for several years, Citizens had offered loans for college students and teachers to purchase Apple products. Some saw Citizens' collaboration with Apple as a low risk partnership for the bank, which controlled the credit risk related to the contract, decided on eligibility for each Apple customer applying to the Upgrade Program, and likely received interest payments from Apple to grant Apple's customers 0% loans.[c] At the end of 2015, Citizens added $220 million in loans to its balance sheet, which, according to one analyst, accounted for 250,000 iPhone 6s sales in Apple Stores.[46]

## iPhone revenue recognition

The revenue recognition for Apple's iPhone had undergone several changes over the years. Before fiscal year 2010, Apple reported revenues from its iPhone sales using the subscription method of accounting.[47] iPhone products fell under the software revenue recognition rules pursuant to American Institute of Certified Public Accountants (AICPA) Statement of Position (SOP) No. 97-2.[48] Apple used subscription accounting as it periodically provided new software updates to iPhone customers free of charge, making the iPhone a product "in which the hardware and the operating system software were tightly bundled."[49] SOP 97-2 required companies to use subscription accounting for such software-enabled hardware devices. Under subscription accounting, Apple recognized the revenue and cost of goods sold for the iPhone on a straight-line basis over the product's estimated 24-month economic life. Thus, Apple's quarterly revenues reflected only one-eighth of the total

---

[39]Adam Rogers, "Apple Sees Growth Potential in China's Rising Middle Class," Market Realist, January 6, 2016, http://marketrealist. com/2016/01/apple-sees-growth-potential-chinas-rising-middle-class/, accessed August 2016.

[40]Statista, "Main Reasons Not to Purchase an Apple iPhone 6/6 Plus among Smartphone Users in China as of September 2014," Statista Web site, http://www.statista.com.ezp-prod1.hul.harvard.edu/statistics/369701/china-main-reasons-against-iphone-6-purchase/, accessed August 2016.

[41]Thomas Gryta and Ryan Knutson, "Apple Takes Aim at Wireless Phone Companies."

[42]Thomas Gryta and Ryan Knutson, "Apple Takes Aim at Wireless Phone Companies."

[43]Thomas Gryta and Ryan Knutson, "Apple Takes Aim at Wireless Phone Companies."

[44]Citizens Bank, "About Us," Citizens Bank Web site, http://investor.citizensbank.com/about-us.aspx, accessed August 2016.

[45]Deirdre Fernandes, "Citizens Is the Bank behind Apple's New iPhone Upgrade Plan."

[c]One analyst believed that "Apple is effectively paying an interest rate in the realm of 6–12% annualized." Gene Munster, "Thoughts on iPhone Upgrade Plan Economics and iPhone User Survey," Piper Jaffray, November 23, 2015, via Thomson ONE, accessed November 2016.

[46]Ian Kar, "Apple's iPhone Upgrade Program Is Off to a Slow Start, but the Real Test Is in September," Quartz, January 29, 2016, http://qz.com/600547/the-iphone-upgrade-program-could-be-apples-major-key/, accessed August 2016; Gene Muster, "Early Take On iPhone Program Metrics," Piper Jaffray Analyst Report, January 22, 2016, Thomson ONE, accessed July 2016.

[47]Philip Elmer-DeWitt, "Spotlight on Apple's Hidden Revenue Stream," Fortune, January 20, 2009, http://fortune.com/2009/01/20/spotlight-on-apples-hidden-revenue-stream/, accessed August, 2016.

[48]FASB, "Statement of Position 97-2 Software Revenue Recognition," FASB Web site, October 27, 1997, http://www.fasb.org/jsp/FASB/Document_C/DocumentPage?cid=1176156442593&acceptedDisclaimer=true, accessed August 2016; Apple, 2008 Form 10-K, p. 55, http://investor.apple.com/secfiling.cfm?filingid=1193125-08-224958&cik=, accessed August 2016.

[49]Walter Isaacson, The Innovators. (New York: Simon & Schuster, 2014) p. 381.

revenue from iPhone sales during that quarter. This resulted in a deferral of the remaining revenue and cost of goods sold, although the company received and reported the related cash flow in the fiscal quarter when the sale happened. As long as iPhone sales increased each quarter, the deferral balance followed the same trend. (See **Exhibit 3** for an illustration of the iPhone subscription accounting.) By the fourth quarter of 2008, Apple's deferred revenues reached $7.8 billion, at which point Apple decided to provide additional information to analysts and investors that gave Apple's watchers a look at Apple's revenue numbers without the use of subscription accounting.[50] (See **Exhibit 4** on Apple's deferred revenue.)

In 2009, the Financial Accounting Standards Board (FASB) ratified Emerging Issues Task Force (EITF) Issue No. 09-3[51] ("2009 rule"),[d] which Apple immediately supported and adopted in the first quarter of fiscal year 2010.[52] The "2009 rule" allowed Apple to split multi-element arrangements, such as the iPhone, into separate deliverables. In the case of the iPhone the first deliverable was the hardware and software "essential to the functionality of the hardware device at the time of sale;"[53] the second deliverable was related to the right to receive "future unspecified software upgrades and features relating to the product's essential software."[54] Following the "2009 rule," Apple was able to recognize the iPhone hardware revenue as soon as the iPhone was sold, while the revenue recognition for the frequently updated software was based on an estimated value to be recognized over the life of the iPhone, similar to using subscription accounting. (See **Exhibit 5** for an illustration of the iPhone accounting under the "2009 rule.")

In May 2014, the FASB issued the Accounting Standards Update (ASU) No. 14-09, Revenue from Contracts with Customers, which amended the existing accounting standards for revenue recognition.[55] ASU 14-09 aimed to provide a comprehensive and uniform framework for revenue recognition across entities and industries, thus replacing special rules such as EITF 09-3. Similar to the "2009 rule," the core principle of ASU 14-09 was to identify separate deliverables (referred to as performance obligations under the new standard) and their respective transaction prices. Revenue was recognized when a performance obligation was satisfied. Apple was considering adopting the standard in either its first quarter of 2018 or 2019.[56]

Beginning in September 2015, Apple estimated the revenue allocated to the software deliverable to be about $10 to reflect the increase in competitive offers for similar products at little to no cost for users. This reduced the amount Apple could reasonably charge for these deliverables on a standalone basis. Thus, when selling an iPhone, Apple only deferred up to $10 for the software component.[57]

### iPhone revenue recognition under the upgrade program

The iPhone Upgrade Program introduced additional accounting complexities. Next to the handset and the software, the Upgrade Program also required the customer to subscribe for AppleCare+ and gave the customer the right to trade in her used phone.[58] Upon exercise of the trade-in right and purchase of a new iPhone, the customer enrolled in a new two-year 0% loan with Citizens, Apple satisfied the customer's outstanding balance due to Citizens on the original device, and Apple paid interest to Citizens for granting the new loan.

---

[50]Daniel Eran Dilger, "Inside Apple's iPhone Subscription Accounting Changes," AppleInsider, October 21, 2009, http://appleinsider.com/articles/09/10/21/inside_apples_iphone_subscription_accounting_changes/page/2, accessed July 2016.

[51]FASB, "FASB Emerging Issues Task Force," FASB Web site, June 4, 2009, http://www.fasb.org/cs/BlobServer?blobcol=urldata&blobtable=MungoBlobs&blobkey=id&blobwhere=1175818951112&blobheader=application%2Fpdf, accessed August 2016.

[d]The title "2009 rule" is not an official term. The case authors use the expression "2009 rule" only to improve clarity and comprehension of the case narrative.

[52]Philip Elmer-DeWitt. "Accounting Rule Change in Apple's Favor," *Fortune*, September 14, 2009, http://fortune.com/2009/09/14/accounting-rule-change-in-apples-favor/, accessed August 2016; Joe Wilcox, "Accounting Change Lifts Apple Fiscal Q1 2010 Results to over $15.6 billion," *Betanews*, January 25, 2010, http://betanews.com/2010/01/25/accounting-change-lifts-apple-fiscal-q1-2010-results-to-over-15-6-billion/, accessed August 2016.

[53]Apple, 2010 Form 10-K, p. 50.

[54]Apple, 2010 Form 10-K, p. 50.

[55]FASB, "Update No. 2014-09—Revenue from Contracts with Customers (Topic 606)," FASB Web site, 2016, http://www.fasb.org/cs/ContentServer?c=Page&pagename=FASB%2FPage%2FSectionPage&cid=1176156316498, accessed August 2016.

[56]Apple, 2015 Form 10-K, p. 30, http://investor.apple.com/secfiling.cfm?filingid=1193125-15-356351&cik=320193, accessed August 2016.

[57]Apple, 2015 Form 10-K, p. 45.

[58]Apple, "iPhone Upgrade Program Terms & Conditions."

The revenue from AppleCare+ was deferred and recognized ratably over the service coverage period of two year. In presenting the Q4 2015 financials, Apple CFO Luca Maestri explained that Apple would be "deferring the portion of revenue related to AppleCare+."[59]

Apple accounted for the trade-in right as a guarantee liability and recognized revenue for the iPhone net of the value of such right. According to an accounting experts, trade-in rights were typically treated like a right to return the purchased item. To determine the value of this right (and consequently the guarantee liability), Apple had to estimate the number of customers exercising the right and the point in time customers exercised the right. The difference between the sales price and the expected value of the trade-in right is the revenue that should be recognized at the time of sale, whereas the expected value of the trade-in right is recorded as a guarantee liability on Apple's books. Recognizing such liability resulted in a deferral of the remaining revenue and cost of goods sold, although Apple received and reported the full cash from the sale of the phone from Citizens in the fiscal quarter when the sale happened. The more iPhones sold under the program and the earlier customers exercised the trade-in right, the larger the guarantee liability, and consequently the less revenue could be recognized at the time of sale. The deferred part of cost of goods sold represents the expected value of the returned phone and is recorded as a Right of Return Asset on the firm's balance sheet. (See **Exhibit 6** for an illustration of the iPhone accounting under the new Upgrade Program and **Exhibit 7** for Apple's revenue recognition policies.)

At the end of each financial reporting period, the estimate of the firm's return expectations were updated. Changes in this estimate were accounted for as adjustments to the amount of revenue and cost of goods sold recognized. In 2015, Apple described in its 10-K that it recognized subsequent changes to the guarantee liability within revenue.[60]

The Upgrade Program carried three additional issues that were not directly related to revenue recognition but nonetheless impacted Apple's financials: the value of a right of return asset, refurbishment costs, and inventory impairments of refurbished phones.

- Value of Right of Return Asset Apple promised its customers to take back the used iPhones and pay the outstanding balance due to Citizens if certain conditions were met. If, at the time of sale, the company expected that the outstanding balance was larger than the value of the returned phone, the company would adjust the right of return asset as well as costs of goods sold accordingly. (See **Exhibit 8** for market prices of used and refurbished iPhones). In addition, Apple had to periodically check if the carrying amount of the right of return asset was still recoverable. If Apple determined that the fair value of the used iPhones decreased, it recorded an impairment loss equal to the amount by which the book value of its iPhones exceeded the fair value (net realizable value) of these iPhones.
- Refurbishment Costs When receiving used iPhones, Apple was likely to incur some costs to refurbish these phones. Such costs would be capitalized and recorded in an inventory asset account.
- Value of refurbished iPhones In much the same manner as for the right of return asset, Apple also had to periodically check if the carrying amount of the refurbished iPhones was still recoverable. If Apple determined that the fair value of the refurbished iPhones decreased, it recorded an impairment loss equal to the amount by which the book value of its iPhones exceeded the fair value (net realizable value) of these iPhones.

The Upgrade Program required Apple's management to exercise judgment on several dimensions. The guarantee liability, for instance, required Apple's management to forecast customers' decision to upgrade their iPhone during the two-year program. The upgrade could take place any time after six months, with the expectation of completing the necessary 12 monthly payments, until the end of the two-year program.

---

[59]Luca Maestri, "Apple's (AAPL) CEO Tim Cook on Q4 2015 Results - Earnings Call Transcript," Seeking Alpha, October 27, 2015, http://seekingalpha.com/article/3611256-apples-aapl-ceo-tim-cook-q4-2015-results-earnings-call-transcript?part=single, accessed August 2016.
[60]Ernst&Young, "Revenue Recognition – Multiple Elements Arrangements," Ernst&Young Web site, revised May 2015, www.ey.org, accessed July 2016.

The expected loss from buying back the used iPhones from its customers also had to be estimated. Such loss was likely to be affected by the level of innovation of the new iPhones as well as the supply and demand of refurbished iPhones.

## Conclusion

Apple's second fiscal quarter, ending in March 2016, was seen as a turning point for the company. For the first time in thirteen years, Apple's revenue declined 13% (to $50.6 billion) compared to the net sales of the previous year. (See **Exhibits 9** and **10** for Apple's annual reports.) The company sold 16% fewer iPhones than in the same quarter in 2015. Apple stock dropped 14% following the earnings call in April 2016. (See **Exhibit 11** for Apple's share price.) There were different reactions to the news. Cook described the revenue decline as a "pause" and not the reflection of a fundamental shift in Apple's business.[61] Analysts were trying to understand the reason for the decline. "There's no question that Apple's best days are behind it. The company grew at astronomical rates, and it's now so big that its ability to grow at those rates doesn't exist anymore," said one analyst.[62] According to other analysts, the revenue decline could be related to a period of slowing replacement sales, a strong dollar depressing international sales, and slow growth for services such as Apple Music and iCloud.[63]

Most of all, analysts focused on iPhone sales. Some observers noticed that the iPhone 7, expected to be released in the fall of 2016, would show only subtle changes, like the removal of the headphone plug to make a thinner phone, and might not be a stellar driver of sales.[64] Most relevant changes, like the edge-to-edge organic light emitting diode (OLED) screen and a longer battery life, were expected to be introduced on the market at the time of the 10th anniversary of the product in 2017.[65] The same observers noticed that minor innovations to the iPhone 5 in the past led to a 13% sales increase, while the introduction of the larger display in 2014 generated a 37% increase at the end of 2015 fiscal year.[66] The slower growth trend had also been confirmed by the iPhone 6s and 6s Plus, which resembled the previous year's models and had not generated great enthusiasm.[67] Consequently, analysts forecasted a drop in unit sales as high as 20%.[68] According to another analyst, the incentive for Android customers to switch to the iPhone was lower than in the past due to the high degree of innovation and improvement that Android devices introduced, such as the curved screen of Samsung's S7 Edge and Motorola's modular Moto Z.[69]

Cook was very optimistic about the Upgrade Program and its impact on iPhone sales: "We are going to give you things that you can't live without, that you just don't even know you need today. You will look back and wonder 'how did I live without this?'"[70] According to Cook, in January 2016 only 40% of iPhone users had an

[61]Ben Popper, "Apple Sees Its Revenue Decline for the First Time in 13 Years," The Verge, April 26, 2016, http://www.theverge.com/2016/4/26/11510312/apple-q2-second-quarter-2016-earnings, accessed July 2016.

[62]Katie Kuehner-Hebert, "Apple's Q2 Results Miss on iPhone Sales Drop," CFO Magazine, April 27 2016, http://ww2.cfo.com/financial-performance/2016/04/apples-q2-results-miss-iphone-sales-drop/, accessed July 2016.

[63]Vindu Goel, "iPhone Sales Drop, and Apple's 13-Year Surge Ebbs," The New York Times, April 26, 2016, http://www.nytimes.com/2016/04/27/technology/apple-q2-earnings-iphone.html?_r=0, accessed July 2016.

[64]Daisuke Wakabayashi and Eva Dou, "Apple Unlikely to Make Big Changes for Next iPhone," The Wall Street Journal, June 21, 2016, http://www.wsj.com/articles/apple-unlikely-to-make-big-changes-for-next-iphone-1466526489, accessed July 2016.

[65]Daisuke Wakabayashi and Eva Dou, "Apple Unlikely to Make Big Changes for Next iPhone;" Gordon Kelly, "Apple Leak Reveals Massive iPhone 7 Upgrade," Forbes, July 14, 2016, http://www.forbes.com/sites/gordonkelly/2016/07/14/apple-leak-big-iphone-7-battery-upgrade/#c308652608ec, accessed July 2016.

[66]Daisuke Wakabayashi and Eva Dou, "Apple Unlikely to Make Big Changes for Next iPhone."

[67]Daisuke Wakabayashi and Eva Dou, "Apple Unlikely to Make Big Changes for Next iPhone."

[68]Tim Bradshaw, "Apple Earnings: What to Expect," Financial Times, July 26, 2016, https://next.ft.com/content/bf644bd0-52ee-11e6-9664-e0b-dc13c3bef, accessed July 2016.

[69]Trefis, "iPhone Unlikely to See Meaningful Update This Year, How Will This Impact Apple?"Trefis web site, June 22, 2016, http://www.trefis.com/stock/aapl/articles/361949/iphone-unlikely-to-see-meaningful-update-this-year-how-will-this-impact-apple/2016-06-22, accessed July 2016.

[70]Todd Haselton, "Apple's Tim Cook: "We're Going to Give You Things You Can't Live Without," TechnoBuffalo, May 3, 2016, http://www.technobuffalo.com/2016/05/03/apple-tim-cook-cnbc-jim-cramer-mad-money/, accessed July 2016.

iPhone 6s or 6s Plus. Many users with an old device were likely tied to a standard two-year contract, most likely stipulated in 2014. By 2016, these customers represented an opportunity to increase sales.[71]

Apple's observation on iPhones sales trends was confirmed by field experts. At the beginning of 2016, RBC Capital Markets expected 20% of the 6,400 customers it surveyed to sign up for Apple's iPhone Upgrade Program.[72] Credit Suisse noted, "[A]ssuming about 30% of iPhone users join, the Upgrade Program would add about 50 million iPhone sales by 2017."[73]

Could the iPhone Upgrade Program bring new life to the product? How could Apple forecast its revenues under the new Upgrade Program? Should the company push the Upgrade Program or were there other priorities related to the impact such a program could have on Apple's financials?

---

[71]Seeking Alpha, "Apple's (AAPL) CEO Tim Cook on Q1 2016 Results - Earnings Call Transcript," Seeking Alpha Web site, January 26, 2016, http://seekingalpha.com/article/3836826-apples-aapl-ceo-tim-cook-q1-2016-results-earnings-call-transcript, accessed August 2016.

[72]Adam Rogers, "iPhone Upgrade Program: An Important Apple Initiative," Market Realist, January 6, 2016, http://marketrealist.com/2016/01/iphone-upgrade-program-important-apple-initiative/, accessed July 2016.

[73]Ian Kar, "Apple's iPhone Upgrade Program Is Off to a Slow Start, but the Real Test is in September."

**Exhibit 1**   iPhone upgrade program terms and conditions

Apple offers the iPhone Upgrade Program described below under the following terms and conditions ("Terms & Conditions"). When you enroll in an iPhone Upgrade Program, you are agreeing to these Terms & Conditions.

- **iPhone Upgrade Program.** The iPhone Upgrade Program is available to qualified customers and consists of the purchase and activation of an eligible iPhone, AppleCare+ for iPhone, and includes an option to upgrade to a new eligible iPhone pursuant to the conditions set forth below.
- **Conditions for Upgrade Option.** You may exercise your Upgrade Option to purchase a new eligible iPhone, subject to availability, under all of the following conditions:
  - *Payments.* You have paid the equivalent of at least twelve (12) installment payments under your Installment Loan plus any taxes and fees paid at the time of enrollment;
  - *Installment Loan.* Your account with Bank is in good standing under the terms of your Installment Loan at the time of purchase at an Apple Retail Store or at time of purchase and shipment from apple.com; and
  - *AppleCare+.* You have continuously maintained AppleCare+ with your Financed iPhone.
- **Exercising your Upgrade Option.** To exercise your Upgrade Option you must:
  - Trade in your Financed iPhone in good physical and operational condition, as directed by Apple; and
  - Enroll in a new iPhone Upgrade Program which includes applying for and entering into a new 24-month 0% APR installment loan ("New Installment Loan") with Bank.
- **Timing.** You must exercise your Upgrade Option prior to the expiration date of your Installment Loan.
- **Early Upgrade Option.** At any time six (6) months after the date of enrollment, you can become upgrade eligible by making advance payments so that you have paid the equivalent of at least twelve (12) installment payments under your Installment Loan plus any taxes and fees paid at the time of enrollment.
- **Termination of Original Installment Loan After Exercising Upgrade Option.** Upon successfully exercising your Upgrade Option, entering into a New Installment Loan, and completing your First Installment Payment on your New Installment Loan with Bank as outlined above, Apple will pay any remaining balance due under your original Installment Loan on your behalf to the Bank, and Bank will consider your original Installment Loan to be paid in full. Subsequent monthly payments will be made under the terms of your New Installment Loan, subject to the conditions of "Return of New, Upgraded iPhone After Exercising Upgrade Option," as set forth below.
- **Prompt Return of Financed iPhone.** If you exercise your Upgrade Option and do not return your original Financed iPhone as directed by Apple within 14 days, your original Installment Loan will be reinstated and you will be responsible for any missed and/or remaining installment payments, as well as any installment payments under your New Installment Loan.
- **Condition of Financed iPhone when Exercising your Upgrade Option.** As noted above, your Financed iPhone must be in good physical and operational condition when exercising your Upgrade Option as determined solely by Apple or Apple's trade-in service provider ("Trade-In Service Provider"). For a Financed iPhone to be considered in good physical and operational condition, the Financed iPhone must:
  - Power on and hold a charge;
  - Have an intact and functioning display;
  - Have no breaks or cracks; and
  - Have Activation Lock disabled (you may be asked to disable at the time of upgrade).
  - If exercising your Upgrade Option via apple.com, you must also remove the SIM card prior to returning the original Financed iPhone.
- **Repairs under AppleCare+.** If your Financed iPhone is not in good physical and operational condition, you will need to exercise your service rights set forth in the AppleCare+ Terms and Conditions, including paying any applicable service fee(s) required under the AppleCare+ plan. In the event you have already exhausted your service rights set forth in the AppleCare+ Terms and Conditions, or the necessary repair is not covered by AppleCare+, you must have your Financed iPhone repaired at an Apple Store or through an Apple Authorized Service Provider at the prevailing service rates, or, depending on the extent of repairs needed, pay the prevailing out of warranty replacement cost of the Financed iPhone. If you are upgrading via apple.com and repairs are not available under AppleCare+ as outlined above, we will return your original iPhone to you, the Installment Loan associated with the original Financed iPhone will be reinstated, and you will be responsible for any missed and/or remaining installment payments as well as any installment payments under your New Installment Loan.

Source: Adapted from Apple Web site, http://www.apple.com/legal/sales-support/iphoneupgrade_us/, accessed July 2016.

**EXHIBIT 2** Apple's revenue and units sold by products, FY2007–FY2016

| | FY2016 | | FY2015 | | FY2014 | | FY2013 | | FY2012 | |
|---|---|---|---|---|---|---|---|---|---|---|
| | Units (K) | Revenue ($M) | Units (K) | Revenue ($M) | Units (K) | Revenue ($M) | Units (K) | Revenue ($M) | Units (K) | Revenue ($M) |
| **Product Summary:** | | | | | | | | | | |
| Desktop | | | | | | | | | 4,656 | $6,040 |
| Portables | | | | | | | | | 13,502 | 17,181 |
| **Subtotal CPUs** | **13,598** | **$22,831** | **20,587** | **$25,471** | **18,906** | **$24,079** | **16,341** | **$21,483** | **18,158** | **$23,221** |
| iTunes, Software and Services | | 24,348 | | 19,909 | | 18,063 | | 16,051 | | 12,890 |
| iPhone and related products and services | 211,884 | 136,700 | 231,218 | 155,041 | 169,219 | 101,991 | 150,257 | 91,279 | 125,046 | 78,692 |
| iPad and related products and services | 45,590 | 20,628 | 54,856 | 23,227 | 67,977 | 30,283 | 71,033 | 31,980 | 58,310 | 30,945 |
| iPod | | 11,132 | | 10,067 | 14,377 | 2,286 | 26,379 | 4,411 | 35,165 | 5,615 |
| Accessories | | | | | | 6,093 | | 5,706 | | 5,145 |
| **Total Apple** | | **$215,639** | | **$233,715** | | **$182,795** | | **$170,910** | | **$156,508** |

| | FY2011 | | FY2010 | | FY2009 | | FY2008 | | FY2007 | |
|---|---|---|---|---|---|---|---|---|---|---|
| | Units (K) | Revenue ($M) | Units (K) | Revenue ($M) | Units (K) | Revenue ($M) | Units (K) | Revenue ($M) | Units (K) | Revenue ($M) |
| **Product Summary:** | | | | | | | | | | |
| Desktop | 4,669 | $6,439 | 4,627 | $6,201 | 3,182 | $4,324 | 3,712 | $5,603 | 2,714 | $4,020 |
| Portables | 12,066 | 15,344 | 9,035 | 11,278 | 7,214 | 9,535 | 6,003 | 8,673 | 4,337 | 6,294 |
| **Subtotal CPUs** | **16,735** | **21,783** | **13,662** | **17,479** | **10,396** | **13,859** | **9,715** | **14,276** | **7,051** | **10,314** |
| iTunes, Software and Services | | 9,268 | | 7,521 | | 6,447 | | 5,547 | | 4,004 |
| iPhone and related products and services | 72,293 | 47,057 | 39,989 | 25,179 | 20,731 | 13,033 | 11,627 | 1,844 | 1,389 | 123 |
| iPad and related products and services | 32,394 | 20,358 | 7,458 | 4,958 | 0 | 0 | | | | |
| iPod | 42,620 | 7,453 | 50,312 | 8,274 | 54,132 | 8,091 | 54,828 | 9,153 | 51,630 | 8,305 |
| Accessories | | 2,330 | | 1,814 | | 1,475 | | 1,659 | | 1,260 |
| **Total Apple** | | **$108,249** | | **$65,225** | | **$42,905** | | **$32,479** | | **$24,006** |

Source: Compiled from Apple Inc. Form 10-K, various years.

Note: Apple stopped reporting separate data on Desktop and Portables product segment sales after fiscal year 2012.

**Exhibit 3**  Illustration of the iPhone subscription accounting

Assume that Apple sold the iPhone 6s for $649 (without AppleCare+) and that Apple allocated $10 of revenue to the software deliverable. The software deliverable is excluded from the illustration below, reducing the revenue for the iPhone 6s to $639. After excluding the software deliverable, assume that the gross profit was $192 (30%). The subscription accounting for the iPhone sale would be as follows:

Q1 (iPhone was sold to consumer):

| | | |
|---|---|---|
| Dr. Cash | 639 | |
| Cr. Revenue (1/8) | | 80 |
| Cr. Deferred Revenue (7/8) | | 559 |
| Dr. Cost of Goods Sold (1/8) | 56 | |
| Dr. Deferred Cost of Goods Sold (7/8) | 391 | |
| Cr. Inventory | | 447 |

Q2 to Q8 (remaining quarters of iPhone's economic life):

| | | |
|---|---|---|
| Dr. Deferred Revenue | 80 | |
| Cr. Revenue | | 80 |
| Dr. Cost of Goods Sold | 56 | |
| Cr. Deferred Cost of Goods Sold | | 56 |

Source: Casewriter.

Note: "Dr." means "debit" and "Cr." means "credit."

**Exhibit 4**  Unaudited condensed schedule of deferred revenue (in $ millions), 2008–2015

| Deferred Revenue | 09/26/15 | 09/27/14 | 09/28/13 | 09/29/12 | 09/24/11 | 09/25/10 | 09/26/09 | 09/27/08 |
|---|---|---|---|---|---|---|---|---|
| Current | 8,940 | 8,491 | 7,435 | 5,953 | 4,091 | 2,984 | 10,305 | 4,853 |
| Non-current | 3,624 | 3,031 | 2,625 | 2,648 | 1,686 | 1,139 | 4,485 | 3,029 |
| Total | 12,564 | 11,522 | 10,060 | 8,601 | 5,777 | 4,123 | 14,790 | 7,882 |

Source: Capital IQ, accessed July 2016.

**Exhibit 5**  Illustration of the iPhone accounting under the "2009 rule" ($)

Assume that Apple sold the iPhone 6s for $649 (without AppleCare+) and that Apple allocated $10 of revenue to the software deliverable. The software deliverable is excluded from the illustration below, reducing the revenue for the iPhone 6s to $639. After excluding the software deliverable, assume that the gross profit was $192 (30%). The accounting for the iPhone sale under the "2009 rule" would be as follows:

Q1 (iPhone was sold to consumer):

| | | |
|---|---|---|
| Dr. Cash | 639 | |
| Cr. Revenue | | 639 |
| Dr. Cost of Goods Sold | 447 | |
| Cr. Inventory | | 447 |

Source: Casewriter.

Note: "Dr." means "debit" and "Cr." means "credit."

**Exhibit 6**  Illustration of the iPhone accounting under the new upgrade program ($)

Assume that Apple sold the iPhone 6s for $649 (without AppleCare+) and that Apple allocated $10 of revenue to the software deliverable. The software deliverable is excluded from the illustration below, reducing the revenue for the iPhone 6s to $639. After excluding the software deliverable, assume that the gross profit was $192 (30%). Apple assumed that the consumer exercised the trade-in option after one year and that the market value of the returned phone was not lower than the book value of the returned phone at the point in time Apple purchased it back from the customer. The accounting for the iPhone sale under the upgrade program would be as follows:

Q1 (iPhone was sold to consumer):

| | | | |
|---|---|---|---|
| Dr. Cash | | 639 | |
| | Cr. Revenue | | 319.5 |
| | Cr. Guarantee liability for trade-in option | | 319.5 |
| Dr. Cost of Goods Sold | | 223.5 | |
| Dr. Right of Return Asset | | 223.5 | |
| | Cr. Inventory | | 447 |

After one year (exercise of trade-in option):

| | | | |
|---|---|---|---|
| Dr. Guarantee liability for trade-in option | | 319.5 | |
| | Cr. Cash | | 319.5 |
| Dr. Inventory | | 223.5 | |
| | Cr. Right of Return Asset | | 223.5 |

Source: Casewriter.

Note: "Dr" means "debit" and "Cr" means "credit."

**Exhibit 7**  Apple Inc. FY 2015 revenue recognition policy—notes to consolidated financial statements

The Company records deferred revenue when it receives payments in advance of the delivery of products or the performance of services. This includes amounts that have been deferred for unspecified and specified software upgrade rights and non-software services that are attached to hardware and software products. The Company sells gift cards redeemable at its retail and online stores, and also sells gift cards redeemable on iTunes Store, App Store, Mac App Store and iBooks Store for the purchase of digital content and software. The Company records deferred revenue upon the sale of the card, which is relieved upon redemption of the card by the customer. Revenue from AppleCare service and support contracts is deferred and recognized over the service coverage periods. AppleCare service and support contracts typically include extended phone support, repair services, web-based support resources and diagnostic tools offered under the Company's standard limited warranty. The Company records reductions to revenue for estimated commitments related to price protection and other customer incentive programs. For transactions involving price protection, the Company recognizes revenue net of the estimated amount to be refunded. For the Company's other customer incentive programs, the estimated cost of these programs is recognized at the later of the date at which the Company has sold the product or the date at which the program is offered. The Company also records reductions to revenue for expected future product returns based on the Company's historical experience. Revenue is recorded net of taxes collected from customers that are remitted to governmental authorities, with the collected taxes recorded as current liabilities until remitted to the relevant government authority.

In September 2015, the Company introduced the iPhone Upgrade Program, which is available to customers who purchase an iPhone 6s and 6s Plus in one of its U.S. physical retail stores and activate the purchased iPhone with one of the four national carriers. The iPhone Upgrade Program provides customers the right to trade in that iPhone for a new iPhone, provided certain conditions are met. One of the conditions of this program requires the customer to finance the initial purchase price of the iPhone with a third-party lender. Upon exercise of the trade-in right and purchase of a new iPhone, the Company satisfies the customer's outstanding balance due to the third-party lender on the original device. The Company accounts for the trade-in right as a guarantee liability and recognizes arrangement revenue net of the fair value of such right with subsequent changes to the guarantee liability recognized within revenue.

Source: Excerpted from Apple Web site, http://files.shareholder.com/downloads/AAPL/2531064259x0x861262/2601797E-6590-4CAA-86C9-962348440FFC/2015_Form_10-K_As-filed_.pdf, p. 45 and p. 64, accessed July 2016.

**Exhibit 8** Price of used and refurbished iPhone 6s

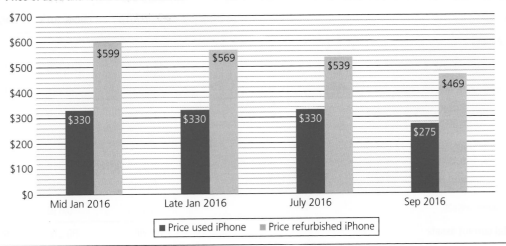

Source: Compiled from Appleinsider.com and Gazelle.com; historical data from these sites accessed via http://archive.org/web/. Trade-in prices from Appleinsider.com refer to prices on Gazelle.com.

**Exhibit 9** Apple Inc. consolidated statements of operations (in $ millions)*, 2014–2016

|  | 09/24/2016 | 09/26/2015 | 09/27/2014 |
|---|---|---|---|
| **Net sales** | $215,639 | $233,715 | $182,795 |
| Cost of sales | 131,376 | 140,089 | 112,258 |
| **Gross Margin** | 84,263 | 93,626 | 70,537 |
| Operating expenses: |  |  |  |
| Research and Development | 10,045 | 8,607 | 6,041 |
| Selling, general and administrative | 14,194 | 14,329 | 11,993 |
| Total operating expenses | 24,239 | 22,396 | 18,034 |
| Operating income | 60,024 | 71,230 | 52,503 |
| Other income/(expenses), net | 1,348 | 1,285 | 980 |
| Income before provision for income taxes | 61,372 | 72,515 | 53,483 |
| Provision for income taxes | 15,685 | 19,121 | 13,973 |
| **Net income** | 45,687 | 53,394 | 39,510 |
| Earnings per share |  |  |  |
| Basic | $8.35 | $9.28 | $6.49 |
| Diluted | $8.31 | $9.22 | $6.45 |
| Shares used in computing earnings per share |  |  |  |
| Basic | 5,470,820 | 5,753,421 | 6,085,572 |
| Diluted | 5,500,281 | 5,793,069 | 6,122,663 |
| Cash dividends declared per share | $2.18 | $1.98 | $1.82 |

Source: Excerpted from company Web site, FY2016 10-K, http://investor.apple.com/financials.cfm, accessed November 2016.

Note: * Except number of shares which are reflected in thousands and per share amounts.

**Exhibit 10**  Unaudited condensed consolidated balance sheets (in $ millions)*, 2014–2016

| ASSETS | 09/24/2016 | 09/26/2015 | 09/27/2014 |
|---|---|---|---|
| **Current Assets**: | | | |
| Cash and cash equivalent | $20,484 | $21,120 | $13,844 |
| Short-term marketable securities | 46,671 | 20,481 | 11,233 |
| Accounts Receivable | 15,754 | 16,849 | 17,460 |
| Inventories | 2,132 | 2,349 | 2,111 |
| Deferred tax assets | – | 5,546 | 4,318 |
| Vendor non-trade receivables | 13,545 | 13,494 | 9,759 |
| Other current assets | 8,283 | 9,539 | 9,806 |
| **Total current assets** | 106,869 | 89,378 | 68,531 |
| Long-term marketable securities | 170,430 | 164,065 | 130,162 |
| Property, plant and equipment, net | 27,010 | 22,471 | 20,624 |
| Goodwill | 5,414 | 5,116 | 4,616 |
| Acquired intangible assets, net | 3,206 | 3,893 | 4,142 |
| Other non-current assets | 8,757 | 5,556 | 3,764 |
| **Total assets** | 321,686 | 290,479 | 231,839 |
| **liabilities and shareholders' equity** | | | |
| **Current liabilities**: | | | |
| Accounts payable | 37,294 | 35,490 | 30,196 |
| Accrued expenses | 22,027 | 25,181 | 18,453 |
| **Deferred revenue** | 8,080 | 8,940 | 8,491 |
| Commercial paper | 8,105 | 8,499 | 6,308 |
| Current portion of long-term debt | 3,500 | 2,500 | |
| **Total current liabilities** | 79,006 | 80,610 | 63,448 |
| **Deferred revenue, non-current** | 2,930 | 3,624 | 3,031 |
| Long-term debt | 75,427 | 53,463 | 28,987 |
| Other non-current liabilities | 36,074 | 33,427 | 24,826 |
| **Total liabilities** | 193,437 | 171,124 | 120,292 |

(*continued*)

**EXHIBIT 10** Unaudited condensed consolidated balance sheets (in $ millions)*, 2014–2016 (Continued)

| ASSETS | 09/24/2016 | 09/26/2015 | 09/27/2014 |
|---|---|---|---|
| **Commitment and contingencies**(Note 10) **Shareholders' equity** | | | |
| Common stock and additional paid-in capital, $0.00001 per value: 12,600,000 shares authorized; 5,336,166 and 5,578,753 shared issued and outstanding, respectively | 31,251 | 27,416 | 23,313 |
| Retained earnings | 96,364 | 92,284 | 87,152 |
| Accumulated other comprehensive income/(loss) | 634 | (345) | 1,082 |
| **Total shareholders' equity** | 128,249 | 119,355 | 111,547 |
| **Total liabilities and shareholders' equity** | 321,686 | 290,479 | 231,839 |

**Note 10 – Commitments and Contingencies**

[. . .] The Company offers an iPhone Upgrade Program, which is available to customers who purchase an iPhone 6s and 6s Plus in its U.S. retail and online stores and activate the purchased iPhone with one of the four U.S. national carriers. The iPhone Upgrade Program provides customers the right to trade in that iPhone for a new iPhone, provided certain conditions are met. One of the conditions of this program requires the customer to finance the initial purchase price of the iPhone with a third-party lender. Upon exercise of the trade-in right and purchase of a new iPhone, the Company satisfies the customer's outstanding balance due to the third-party lender on the original device. The Company accounts for the trade-in right as a guarantee liability and recognizes arrangement revenue net of the fair value of such right with subsequent changes to the guarantee liability recognized within revenue. [. . .]

Source: Excerpted from company website, FY2016 10-K, http://investor.apple.com/financials.cfm, accessed November 2016.

Note: * Except number of shares which were reflected in thousands and par value.

**Exhibit 11** Apple Inc. Share Pricing ($), April 15–May 16, 2016

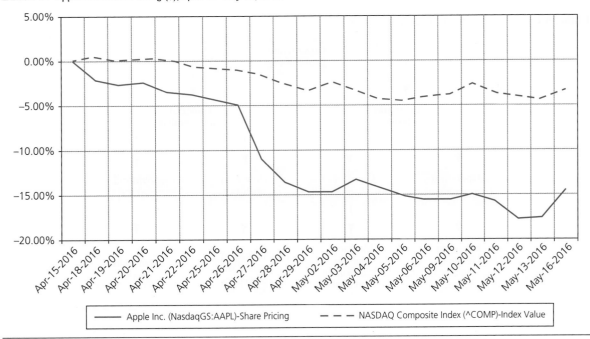

Source: Compiled from Capital IQ, accessed August 2016.

# 5 Financial analysis

The goal of financial analysis is to assess the performance of a firm in the context of its stated goals and strategy. There are two principal tools of financial analysis: ratio analysis and cash flow analysis. **Ratio analysis** involves assessing how various line items in a firm's financial statements relate to one another. Cash flow analysis allows the analyst to examine the firm's liquidity and how the firm is managing its operating, investment, and financing cash flows.

Financial analysis is used in a variety of contexts. Ratio analysis of a company's present and past performance provides the foundation for making forecasts of future performance. As we will discuss in later chapters, financial forecasting is useful in company valuation, credit evaluation, financial distress prediction, security analysis, and mergers and acquisitions analysis.

## Ratio analysis

The value of a firm is determined by its profitability and growth. As shown in Figure 5.1, the firm's growth and profitability are influenced by its product market and financial market strategies. The product market strategy is implemented through the firm's competitive strategy, operating policies, and investment decisions. Financial market strategies are implemented through financing and dividend policies.

**FIGURE 5.1** Drivers of a firm's profitability and growth

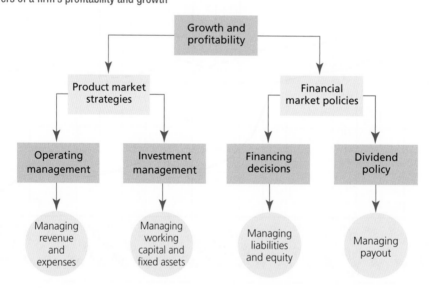

Thus the four levers that managers can use to achieve their growth and profit targets are:

1 Operating management.
2 Investment management.
3 Financing strategy.
4 Dividend policies.

The objective of ratio analysis is to evaluate the effectiveness of the firm's policies in each of these areas. Effective ratio analysis involves relating the financial numbers to the underlying business factors in as much detail as possible. While ratio analysis may not give all the answers to an analyst regarding the firm's performance, it will help the analyst frame questions for further probing.

In ratio analysis, the analyst can:

1 Compare ratios for a firm over several years (a time-series comparison).
2 Compare ratios for the firm and other firms in the industry (cross-sectional comparison).
3 Compare ratios to some absolute benchmark.

In a **time-series comparison**, the analyst can hold firm-specific factors constant and examine the effectiveness of a firm's strategy over time. **Cross-sectional comparison** facilitates examining the relative performance of a firm within its industry, holding industry-level factors constant. For most ratios there are no absolute benchmarks. The exceptions are measures of rates of return, which can be compared to the cost of the capital associated with the investment. For example, subject to distortions caused by accounting, the rate of return on equity (ROE) can be compared to the cost of equity capital.

In the following discussion, we will illustrate these approaches using the example of apparel retailers Hennes & Mauritz AB (H&M) and Inditex SA. We will compare these retailers' ratios for the fiscal year 2017 with their own ratios for the fiscal year 2016, and with the ratios of a group of competitors for the same fiscal years.[1] During the years 2014 through 2017, H&M saw its return on equity steadily decline. In contrast, Inditex showed constant profitability during these years. Analyzing the companies' performance over time allows us to assess which factors contributed to the retailers' financial performance. Comparison of Hennes & Mauritz with Inditex and other industry peers allows us to see the impact of different strategic choices on financial ratios. While making some different competitive choices, H&M also follows different investment and financing strategies than its industry peers. For example, the retailer holds, on average, less cash and securities to finance future expansions and uses more debt financing and shorter-term leases than Inditex. We will illustrate how these differences among the companies affect their ratios. We will also try to see which strategy is delivering better performance for shareholders.

In order to facilitate replication of the ratio calculations presented below, we present in the appendix to this chapter two versions of the financial statements of H&M. The first set of financial statements is presented in the standardized format described in Chapter 3. These "standardized and adjusted financial statements" not only put industry peers' financials in one standard format to facilitate direct comparison but also have been adjusted for one form of asset/liability understatement: the omission from the balance sheet of operating lease assets and liabilities. We also present H&M's financial statements in a second format in the appendix. These statements, labelled "Condensed Financial Statements," are essentially a recasting of the standardized and adjusted financial statements to facilitate the calculation of several ratios discussed in the chapter. We will discuss later in the chapter how this recasting process works.[2]

## Background information on Hennes & Mauritz, Inditex, and their industry
## Hennes & Mauritz

Sweden-based Hennes & Mauritz AB (normally referred to as H&M) is an internationally operating apparel retailer that is publicly listed on the Stockholm Stock Exchange. During the fiscal year ended November 30, 2017 (labelled fiscal 2017), the company employed close to 171 thousand employees, operated 4,739 stores in 56 countries around the world under eight brands (such as H&M, & Other Stories, and Weekday), and generated close to €20.2 billion (SEK200.0 billion) of revenue. In 2017 H&M derived about 68 percent of its total revenues from selling apparel within Europe. Sales in North and South America and Asia and Oceania accounted for 17 and 15 percent of total revenue, respectively. In 44 countries, including France, Germany, the United Kingdom, the United States, and China, the apparel retailer also sold its products through the internet. At the end of 2017, H&M had plans to open a net total of 220 new stores worldwide and start internet sales in a few new markets, including India.

## Inditex

Spain-based Inditex SA is H&M's largest international peer. The company is publicly listed on the Spanish Stock Exchanges but is closely held by its founder Amancio Ortega Gaona, who controls close to 60 percent of the company's share capital. During the fiscal year ending on January 31, 2018 (labelled fiscal 2017), Inditex employed close to 172 thousand employees and operated 7,475 stores in 96 countries around the world under eight different brands, such as Zara, Pull & Bear, and Massimo Dutti. The company generated slightly more than €25.3 billion of revenue, of which it earned about 18 percent in Spain, 47 percent in Europe (excluding Spain), 15 percent in the Americas, and 20 percent in the rest of the world. In 2017 Inditex also sold its apparel online in 49 countries. At the end of 2017, Inditex planned to open a net total of 150 to 200 new stores worldwide and start internet sales in a few new markets, including Australia and New Zealand.

## The industry

H&M and Inditex operate in the branded apparel segment of the retail industry. The apparel retail industry is a cyclical industry, implying that the demand for apparel typically depends on consumers' discretionary spending and varies with economic cycles. Accordingly, industry growth rates were negatively affected by the economic slowdown that followed the credit crisis of 2008 and continued through the European sovereign debt crisis. Industry growth slowly picked up around 2015.

The apparel retail industry is competitive. Around 2017, the following factors contributed to the industry's profit potential:

- Moderate growth. In the decade following the start of the credit crisis, industry growth had been moderate to low. Future growth rates of the global apparel retail industry were expected to remain moderate but increase to around 4 to 5 percent, with most of the growth coming from emerging markets and online sales.
- Importance of pricing and supply chain management. With moderate growth, price-sensitive customers and increasing competition from low-cost retailers, pricing decisions and inventory and supply chain management were instrumental to preserving margins.
- Perishable nature of fashion. Consumers' fast-changing tastes and expectations required apparel retailers to (a) excel in monitoring customer trends and preferences, using state-of-the-art digital analytics and artificial intelligence technologies, and (b) keep design and production cycles efficient and short. Only by doing so, could the retailers avoid inventory markdowns or write-offs.

- Omnichannel shopping. The current generation of consumers increasingly used online shopping platforms and, in the process, came to expect more convenience, support, and speedy delivery. The possibility of comparing online information, reviews, and prices also made customers more willing to switch brands and more conscious of quality and brand values.
- Sourcing of production. Motivated by the need to be price-competitive, some apparel retailers outsourced production to low-cost labor markets. Production outsourcing introduced some risks. For example, it made quality control more challenging, complicated supply chain management, and made companies potentially subject to reputational damage from poor labor practices and conditions.
- Private labels and specialty retailing. One of the primary ways to differentiate was through branding. Related to this, selling private labels and specialty retailing had become increasingly popular. Private labels help apparel retailers to capture a bigger portion of the margin, become more flexible in responding to fashion trends, and build brand equity.

## The strategy

Hennes & Mauritz and Inditex pursue a differentiation strategy, focusing on "fast fashion" retailing. The fast fashion retailing strategy is characterized by the following two features: the retailer (1) sells trendy, affordable products and (2) is able to respond quickly to changing trends by using digital analytics and maintaining short production and lead times. Core competencies that help H&M and Inditex to achieve this strategy are the following:

- In-house design. H&M and Inditex employ large teams of in-house designers. The retailers' designer teams work on several collections simultaneously and continuously monitor customer preferences to spot and anticipate new fashion trends.
- Competitive pricing. H&M and Inditex aim to keep their prices affordable by being cost-efficient. H&M does so, for example, by outsourcing production to a large number of independent manufacturers coordinated by self-operated production offices around the world. To optimize logistics and minimize inventory costs, Inditex makes use of local suppliers, logistics centres located in one country (Spain) from where it ships its products across the world, and a sophisticated inventory management system.
- Brand. The H&M and Zara (Inditex) brands have high customer awareness. H&M has achieved this through high-profile advertising campaigns and collaborations with star designers and celebrities. One of the brand values that H&M increasingly communicates to customers is that of a sustainable brand, being committed to supporting social development in production countries and reducing the environmental impact of its activities. Inditex does not advertise; the company builds brand awareness primarily through the presence and appeal of its stores.
- Size and growth. Both H&M and Zara are pursuing a growth strategy, implying that they expand their store network by 8 to 12 percent every year. This growth strategy helps the retailers to achieve economies of scale in, for example, design, production (sourcing), and advertising. The expansion of H&M and Inditex into emerging markets also helps the companies to become less dependent on saturated mature markets. The retailers' comparatively low dependence on debt financing and high profitability provides them with the financial flexibility they need to realize their growth plans.

Some of the activities that H&M and Inditex undertake as part of their strategy potentially reinforce each other, thus contributing to the strategy's sustainability. In particular, the retailers' carefully developed brand identity helps them to build customer loyalty, especially among their target group of fashion conscious customers. In addition, because of their superior design competencies and, especially in the case of Inditex, superior inventory management, the retailers are able to frequently renew their assortments during a season and entice their target customers to make return visits to their stores, which further supports customer loyalty creation. Finally, the retailers' size and growth strategy help create the economies of scale that make them price-competitive.

H&M and Inditex's strong brand names, high customer loyalty, superior fast fashion design teams, and price competitiveness thus jointly contribute to achieving high inventory turnover, little to no inventory markdowns, and superior margins. Their strategy is, of course, not without risks. The retailers' international expansion and production make their profitability sensitive to foreign exchange rate fluctuations. H&M is also strongly dependent on its suppliers. Unexpected interruptions in deliveries could seriously increase production and lead times and impair the company's fast fashion strategy. Further, because H&M and Inditex use a great deal of cotton in their garments, inflation in cotton prices adversely affect the retailers' profit margin. Finally, H&M's focus on the low-priced segment of the market makes the retailer vulnerable to competition from general merchandise retailers or discount apparel retailers such as Primark. To counter this risk, in recent years the company has introduced new brands and store concepts (such as "& Other Stories"), typically focused on the higher priced segments of the market. By doing so H&M followed the example of Inditex, which has traditionally sold its apparel under eight different brands in varying price segments.

## MEASURING OVERALL PROFITABILITY

The starting point for a systematic analysis of a firm's performance is its return on equity (ROE), defined as

$$ROE = \frac{\text{Profit or loss}}{\text{Shareholders' equity}}$$

ROE is a comprehensive indicator of a firm's performance because it provides an indication of how well managers are employing the funds invested by the firm's shareholders to generate returns. On average, over long periods, large publicly traded firms in Europe generate ROEs in the range of 8 to 10 percent.

In the long run, the value of the firm's equity is determined by the relationship between its ROE and its cost of equity capital – the return that the firm's equity holders require on their equity investment in the firm. That is, those firms that are expected over the long run to generate ROEs in excess of the cost of equity capital should have market values in excess of book value, and vice versa. (We will return to this point in more detail in Chapter 7 on valuation.)

A comparison of ROE with the cost of capital is useful not only for contemplating the value of the firm but also in considering the path of future profitability. The generation of consistent supernormal profitability will, absent significant barriers to entry, attract competition. For that reason, ROEs tend over time to be driven by competitive forces towards a "normal" level – the cost of equity capital. Thus one can think of the cost of equity capital as establishing a benchmark for the ROE that would be observed in a long-run competitive equilibrium. Deviations from this level arise for two general reasons. One is the industry conditions and competitive strategy that cause a firm to generate supernormal (or subnormal) economic profits, at least over the short run. The second is distortions due to accounting.

In computing ROE, one can use either the beginning equity or the ending equity or an average of the two. Conceptually, the average equity is appropriate, particularly for rapidly growing companies that see their balance sheet change significantly throughout the year. However, for most companies, this computational choice makes little difference as long as the analyst is consistent. Therefore in practice most analysts use ending balances for simplicity. This comment applies to all ratios discussed in this chapter where one of the items in the ratio is a flow variable (items in the income statement or cash flow statement) and the other item is a stock variable (items in the balance sheet). Because of its conceptual superiority, throughout this chapter we use the average balances of the stock variables.

Table 5.1 shows the ROE based on reported earnings for Hennes & Mauritz, Inditex, and their industry peers. Hennes & Mauritz's ROE decreased from 31.2 to 26.8 percent between 2016 and 2017 despite a moderate increase in revenue (of 4 percent), suggesting that unfavourable market conditions affected the company's performance disproportionally compared to its sales. Compared to historical trends of ROE in the European economy, Hennes & Mauritz's earnings performance in 2017 can be viewed as being significantly above average. Further, its ROE in 2017 was more than adequate to cover reasonable estimates of its cost of equity capital.[3]

**TABLE 5.1** Return on equity for Hennes & Mauritz and its industry peers

| Ratio | H&M 2017 | H&M 2016 | Inditex 2017 | Inditex 2016 | Other peers 2017 |
|---|---|---|---|---|---|
| *Return on equity* (%) | 26.8 | 31.2 | 25.7 | 26.1 | 21.1 |

In 2017 Hennes & Mauritz's performance was also ahead of its peers' ROE. In particular, Inditex's ROE was 25.7 percent, a decrease from 26.1 percent in 2016. The average ROE of H&M's other peers showed an increase from 16.9 to 21.1 percent. At that performance the industry peers were also earning excess returns relative to the historical trends of ROE in the economy, as well as to their own cost of equity. The superior performance of H&M and Inditex relative to their peers is reflected in the difference in the companies' ratio of market value of equity to book value. As we will discuss in Chapter 7, ROE is a key determinant of a company's market value-to-book value ratio. As of the end of fiscal 2017, the market value-to-book value ratios of H&M and Inditex were 5.5 and 6.7, respectively, while the same ratio was 4.2 for the other apparel retailers.

## DECOMPOSING PROFITABILITY: TRADITIONAL APPROACH

A company's ROE is affected by two factors: how profitably it employs its assets and how big the firm's asset base is relative to shareholders' investment. To understand the effect of these two factors, ROE can be decomposed into return on assets (ROA) and a measure of financial leverage, the equity multiplier, as follows:

$$\text{ROE} = \text{ROA} \times \text{Equity multiplier}$$
$$= \frac{\text{Profit or loss}}{\text{Total assets}} \times \frac{\text{Total assets}}{\text{Equity}}$$

ROA tells us how much profit a company is able to generate for each euro of assets invested. The equity multiplier indicates how many euros of assets the firm is able to deploy for each euro invested by its shareholders.

The ROA itself can be decomposed as a product of two factors:

$$\text{ROA} = \frac{\text{Profit or loss}}{\text{Revenue}} \times \frac{\text{Revenue}}{\text{Total assets}}$$

The ratio of profit or loss to revenue is called net profit margin or return on revenue (ROR); the ratio of revenue to total assets is known as asset turnover. The profit margin ratio indicates how much the company is able to keep as profits for each euro of revenue it makes. Asset turnover indicates how many euros of revenue the firm is able to generate for each euro of its assets.

Table 5.2 displays the three drivers of ROE for our apparel retailers: net profit margins, asset turnover, and equity multipliers. In 2017 the decrease in ROE experienced by Hennes & Mauritz and Inditex is largely driven by a decrease in their net profit margins. The increase in the retailers' financial leverage ratios helps to partly offset the ROE effect of the net profit margin decrease.

The traditional decomposition of ROE suggests that H&M has superior operating performance relative to the other industry peers, as indicated by its higher ROA, but inferior operating performance relative to Inditex. Although H&M currently generates ten cents of revenue more than Inditex for each euro invested in assets, the retailer's ROA is lower than Inditex's ROA because of its lower and gradually declining net profit margin.

**TABLE 5.2** Traditional decomposition of ROE

| Ratio | H&M 2017 | H&M 2016 | Inditex 2017 | Inditex 2016 | Other peers 2017 |
|---|---|---|---|---|---|
| Net profit margin (ROR) (%) | 8.1 | 9.7 | 13.3 | 13.6 | 6.5 |
| × Asset turnover | 1.13 | 1.14 | 1.03 | 1.01 | 1.05 |
| = Return on assets (ROA) (%) | 9.2 | 11.0 | 13.7 | 13.7 | 6.8 |
| × Equity multiplier | 2.92 | 2.83 | 1.87 | 1.91 | 3.10 |
| = Return on equity (ROE) (%) | 26.8 | 31.2 | 25.7 | 26.1 | 21.2 |

H&M's operating performance is leveraged by its more aggressive financial management relative to Inditex, which causes its ROE to exceed that of Inditex by one percentage point in 2017.

## DECOMPOSING PROFITABILITY: ALTERNATIVE APPROACH

Even though the preceding approach is popularly used to decompose a firm's ROE, it has several limitations. In the computation of ROA, the denominator includes the assets claimed by all providers of capital to the firm, but the numerator includes only the earnings available to equity holders (after interest payments have been deducted). The assets themselves include both operating assets and non-operating investments such as minority equity investments and excess cash. Further, profit or loss includes profit from operating and investment activities, as well as interest income and expense, which are consequences of financing decisions. Often it is useful to distinguish between these sources of performance for at least three reasons:

1   As we will see in Chapters 6 through 8, valuing operating assets requires different tools from valuing non-operating investments. Specifically, financial statements include much detailed information about the financial and risk consequences of operating activities, which enables the analyst to take an informed approach to the analysis and valuation of such activities. In contrast, what comprises the non-operating investments and drives their profitability is often not easily identified from the financial statements, thus forcing the analyst to use shortcut methods or rely on a firm's own fair value disclosures to assess the value of such assets.

2   Operating, investment, and financing activities contribute differently to a firm's performance and value, and their relative importance may vary significantly across time and firms. For example, as we will show in this chapter, whereas close to 33 percent of Inditex's invested capital has been allocated to non-operating investments that earn an average return of less than 1 percent, Hennes & Mauritz and the retailers' other industry peers have only 1 and 17 percent of their capital invested in such low-performing non-operating assets. Mixing operating with non-operating assets would obfuscate the effect that these investments have on retailers' performance. Further, an increase in financial leverage may not only have a direct positive effect on return on equity but also an indirect negative effect through increasing a firm's financial risk and borrowing costs. The traditional decomposition of ROE does not make this explicit: whereas the equity multiplier reflects the direct effect of leverage, the net profit margin reflects the indirect effect.

3   Finally, the preceding financial leverage ratio does not recognize the fact that some of a firm's liabilities are in essence non-interest-bearing operating liabilities.

These issues are addressed by an alternative approach to decomposing ROE discussed below. Before discussing this alternative ROE decomposition approach, we need to define some terminology (see Table 5.3) used in this section as well as in the rest of this chapter.

**TABLE 5.3**  Definitions of accounting items used in ratio analysis

| Item | Definition |
|---|---|
| **Income statement items** | |
| *Interest expense after tax* | Interest expense × (1 − Tax rate)[a] |
| *Net investment profit after tax (NIPAT)* | (Investment income + Interest income) × (1 − Tax rate) |
| *Net operating profit after tax (NOPAT)* | Profit or loss − Net investment profit after tax + Interest expense after tax |
| **Balance sheet items** | |
| *Operating working capital* | (Current assets − Excess cash and cash equivalents) − (Current liabilities − Current debt and current portion of non-current debt)[b] |
| *Net non-current operating assets* | Non-current tangible and intangible assets + (Net) derivatives − (Net) deferred tax liability − Non-interest-bearing non-current liabilities |
| *Non-operating investments* | Minority equity investments + Other non-operating investments + Excess cash and cash equivalents |
| *Net operating assets* | Operating working capital + Net non-current operating assets |
| *Business assets* | Net operating assets + Non-operating investments |
| *Debt* | Total interest-bearing non-current liabilities + Current debt and current portion of non-current debt |
| *Invested capital* | Debt + Group equity |

a. This calculation treats interest expense as absolute value, independent of how this figure is reported in the income statement.

b. Excess cash and cash equivalents is defined as total cash and cash equivalents minus the cash balance needed for operations. In the analysis of Hennes & Mauritz and its peers, we set the cash balance needed for operations equal to 5 percent of revenue, the long-term average cash balance in the European apparel retail industry.

We use the terms defined in Table 5.3 to recast the financial statements of Hennes & Mauritz, Inditex, and their industry peers. The retailers' recast financial statements, of which H&M's are shown in the appendix to this chapter, are used to decompose ROE in the following manner:

$$\text{ROE} = \frac{\text{NOPAT} + \text{NIPAT}}{\text{Equity}} - \frac{\text{Interest expense after tax}}{\text{Equity}}$$

$$= \frac{\text{NOPAT} + \text{NIPAT}}{\text{Invested Capital}} \times \frac{\text{Invested Capital}}{\text{Equity}} - \frac{\text{Interest expense after tax}}{\text{Debt}} \times \frac{\text{Debt}}{\text{Equity}}$$

$$= \frac{\text{NOPAT} + \text{NIPAT}}{\text{Invested Capital}} \times \left(1 + \frac{\text{Debt}}{\text{Equity}}\right) - \frac{\text{Interest expense after tax}}{\text{Debt}} \times \frac{\text{Debt}}{\text{Equity}}$$

$$= \frac{\text{NOPAT} + \text{NIPAT}}{\text{Invested Capital}} + \left(\frac{\text{NOPAT} + \text{NIPAT}}{\text{Invested Capital}} - \frac{\text{Interest expense after tax}}{\text{Debt}}\right) \times \frac{\text{Debt}}{\text{Equity}}$$

= Return on invested capital + (Return on invested capital − Effective interest rate) × Financial leverage

= Return on invested capital + Spread × Financial leverage

Return on invested capital is a measure of how profitably a company is able to deploy its operating and non-operating assets to generate profits. This would be a company's ROE if it were financed with all equity. Spread is the incremental economic effect from introducing debt into the capital structure. This economic effect of borrowing is positive as long as the return on invested capital is greater than the cost of borrowing.

Firms that do not earn adequate returns to pay for interest cost, reduce their ROE by borrowing. Both the positive and negative effect is magnified by the extent to which a firm borrows relative to its equity base. The ratio of debt to equity provides a measure of this financial leverage. A firm's spread times its financial leverage therefore provides a measure of the financial leverage gain to the shareholders.

To separate the effect on profitability of a firm's non-operating investments from its operating activities, the return on invested capital (ROIC) can be split up into an operating and an investment component:

$$\text{ROE} = \frac{\text{NOPAT}}{\text{Invested capital}} + \frac{\text{NIPAT}}{\text{Invested capital}}$$

$$= \frac{\text{NOPAT}}{\text{Net operating assets}} \times \frac{\text{Net operating assets}}{\text{Invested capital}} + \frac{\text{NIPAT}}{\text{Non-operating investments}} \times \frac{\text{Non-operating investments}}{\text{Invested capital}}$$

$$= \text{Return on net operating assets} \times \frac{\text{Net operating assets}}{\text{Invested capital}} + \text{Return on non-operating investments} \times \frac{\text{Non-operating investments}}{\text{Invested capital}}$$

In other words, the return that a firm earns on its invested capital is a weighted average of its return on net operating assets (RNOA) and its return on non-operating investments (RNOI). For the average firm the return on non-operating investments is lower than the return on net operating assets. Therefore non-operating investments typically decrease the return on invested capital relative to the return on net operating assets.

Finally, return on net operating assets can be further decomposed into NOPAT margin and operating asset turnover as follows:

$$\text{RNOA} = \frac{\text{NOPAT}}{\text{Revenue}} \times \frac{\text{Revenue}}{\text{Net operating assets}}$$

NOPAT margin – the first term in the preceding equation – is a measure of how profitable a company's sales are from an operating perspective. Operating asset turnover – the second term in the preceding equation – measures the extent to which a company is able to use its net operating assets to generate revenue.

Table 5.4 presents the decomposition of ROE for Hennes & Mauritz, Inditex, and their peers. The ratios in this table show that there can be a significant difference between ROA and return on invested capital (ROIC). In 2017, for example, Inditex's ROA was 13.7 percent, while its ROIC was 19.1 percent. This difference between the retailer's ROIC and ROA can be largely attributed to the company's current operating liabilities, such as trade payables, and (non-interest-bearing) deferred tax liabilities, which reduce the amount of net operating assets relative to the amount of total assets. That is, Inditex has large current operating liabilities such as trade payables, which help finance a large proportion of the company's current operating assets. The difference between Inditex's ROA and its return on net operating assets is even more remarkable: its return on net operating assets in 2014 was 28.0 percent, or around 14 percentage points above the ROA. One of the reasons that Inditex's return on net operating assets is dramatically larger than its ROA is that the firm holds a significant amount of excess cash and cash equivalents (of estimably 14 percent of revenue), possibly to finance its future expansion investments. As indicated, we classify excess cash as a non-operating investment. At 28.0 percent, Inditex's return on net operating assets is significantly larger than Hennes & Mauritz's return on net operating assets of 12.3 percent. This superior operating performance of Inditex would have been obscured by using the simple ROA measure. This shows that, for at least some firms, it is important to adjust the simple ROA to take into account non-operating investments and financial structure.

The decomposition of returns on invested capital into investment and operating returns shows that the returns on net operating assets of Inditex and the other industry peers were substantially larger than their returns on invested capital in 2017. This is because Inditex and its peers invested 33 and 26 percent, respectively, in low-earning non-operating investments such as marketable securities (cash equivalents). Although these typically liquid and low-risk investments were likely needed to finance the firms' growth plans, their immediate effect was to reduce overall business performance.

**TABLE 5.4** Distinguishing operating, investment, and financing components in ROE decomposition

| Ratio | H&M 2017 | H&M 2016 | Inditex 2017 | Inditex 2016 | Other peers 2017 |
|---|---|---|---|---|---|
| Net operating profit margin (%) | 8.6 | 10.3 | 13.4 | 13.7 | 7.2 |
| × Net operating asset turnover | 1.43 | 1.42 | 2.09 | 2.02 | 1.73 |
| = Return on net operating assets (%) | 12.3 | 14.6 | 28.0 | 27.6 | 12.5 |
| Return on net operating assets (%) | 12.3 | 14.6 | 28.0 | 27.6 | 12.5 |
| × (Net operating assets/invested capital) | 0.99 | 0.98 | 0.67 | 0.68 | 0.74 |
| + Return on non-operating investments (%) | 21.4 | 6.0 | 0.9 | 0.9 | 0.7 |
| × (Non-operating investments/invested capital) | 0.01 | 0.02 | 0.33 | 0.32 | 0.26 |
| = Return on invested capital (%) | 12.3 | 14.5 | 19.1 | 19.1 | 9.4 |
| Spread (%) | 10.8 | 12.8 | 17.5 | 17.4 | 7.6 |
| × Financial leverage | 1.34 | 1.31 | 0.37 | 0.40 | 1.55 |
| = Financial leverage gain (%) | 14.4 | 16.8 | 6.5 | 7.1 | 11.8 |
| ROE = Return on invested capital + financial leverage gain (%) | 26.8 | 31.2 | 25.7 | 26.1 | 21.2 |

The appropriate benchmark for evaluating return on invested capital is the weighted average cost of debt and equity capital, or WACC. [4] In the long run, the value of the firm's assets is determined by where return on invested capital stands relative to this norm. Moreover, over the long run and absent some barrier to competitive forces, return on invested capital will tend to be pushed towards the weighted average cost of capital. Since the WACC is lower than the cost of equity capital, return on invested capital tends to be pushed to a level lower than that to which ROE tends. The average return on invested capital for large firms in Europe, over long periods of time, is in the range of 6 to 8 percent. Hennes & Mauritz and Inditex's returns on invested capital in 2017 exceed this range, indicating that their operating and investment performance is above average.

In 2017 Hennes & Mauritz saw its NOPAT margin decrease and its operating asset turnover remain flat, at levels below those of Inditex. H&M's marginally lower margin is consistent with the observation that H&M has a stronger focus on the lower-priced segment of the apparel industry and, on average, is asking lower premium prices than Inditex. Inditex's higher operating asset turnover shows that the company is able to utilize its net operating assets more efficiently than H&M, which allows Inditex to leverage its higher margin and, consequently, earn a notably higher return on its net operating assets.

Hennes & Mauritz and Inditex are also able to create shareholder value through their financing strategy. In 2016 the spread between H&M's return on invested capital and its after-tax interest cost was 12.8 percent; its debt as a percent of its equity was 131 percent. Both these factors contributed to a net increment of 16.8 percent to its ROE. Thus, while H&M's return on invested capital in 2016 was 14.5 percent, its ROE was 31.2 percent (rounded). In 2017 H&M's spread decreased to 10.8 percent and its financial leverage increased to 134 percent, leading to a 14.4 percent net increment to ROE due to its debt policy. With a return on invested capital of 12.3 percent in that year, its ROE went down to 26.8 percent (rounded). Overall, these trends indicate that whereas leverage can help to improve ROE, it also increases equity risk; that is, leverage amplifies the negative ROE effect of reductions in the retailer's operating and investment efficiency.

Inditex had low leverage in 2017, to the tune of 37 percent. As a result, even though Inditex had a positive spread of 17.5 percent, the retailer had a relatively modest financial leverage gain of 6.5 percent. This financial leverage gain helped to produce a ROE of 25.7 percent, which was less than H&M's ROE in spite of Inditex's superior operating performance. With a higher level of leverage, Inditex could have exploited its spread to produce an even higher ROE. Note, again, that an increase in Inditex's financial leverage would also raise its equity risk and, consequently, increase its cost of equity, thus reducing the benefits of leverage. Given the large spread, however, the higher cost of equity would not likely offset the higher financial leverage gain. We will discuss the relationship between leverage and the cost of equity in more detail in Chapter 8.

## ASSESSING OPERATING MANAGEMENT: DECOMPOSING NET PROFIT MARGINS

A firm's net profit margin or ROS shows the profitability of the company's operating activities. Further decomposition of a firm's ROS allows an analyst to assess the efficiency of the firm's operating management. A popular tool used in this analysis is the common-sized income statement in which all the line items are expressed as a ratio of revenue. This type of analysis is also referred to as vertical analysis.

Common-sized income statements make it possible to compare trends in income statement relationships over time for the firm, and trends across different firms in the industry. Income statement analysis allows the analyst to ask the following types of questions:

1  Are the company's margins consistent with its stated competitive strategy? For example, a differentiation strategy should usually lead to higher gross margins than a low-cost strategy.
2  Are the company's margins changing? Why? What are the underlying business causes? Changes in competition, changes in input costs, or poor overhead cost management?
3  Is the company managing its overhead and administrative costs well? What are the business activities driving these costs? Are these activities necessary?

To illustrate how the income statement analysis can be used, common-sized income statements for Hennes & Mauritz, Inditex, and the other industry peers are shown in Table 5.5. The table also shows some commonly used profitability ratios. We will use the information in Table 5.5 to investigate why Hennes & Mauritz had a net profit margin (or return on revenue) of 8.1 percent in 2017 and 9.7 percent in 2016, while Inditex and the other industry peers had net margins of 13.3 and 6.5 percent, respectively, in 2017. Hennes & Mauritz classifies its expenses by function in the income statement and discloses a classification of its expenses by nature in the notes to the financial statements. In contrast, Inditex classifies its expenses by nature only. Consequently, we can decompose H&M's net profit margins both by function and by nature, but can only compare expenses by nature. Because not all other industry peers follow International Financial Reporting Standards (IFRS Standards), and thus use inconsistent classifications, we can split up their operating expenses neither by nature nor by function.

### Decomposition by function

Although not required to do so by the international accounting rules, some firms classify their operating expensing according to function. The decomposition of operating expenses by function is potentially more informative than the decomposition by nature. This is because the functional decomposition requires the firm to use judgment in dividing total operating expenses into expenses that are directly associated with products sold or services delivered (cost of sales) and expenses that are incurred to manage operations (selling, general, and administrative expense).

The difference between a firm's revenue and cost of sales is gross profit. Gross profit margin is an indication of the extent to which revenues exceed direct costs associated with sales, and it is computed as

$$\text{Gross profit margin} = \frac{\text{Revenue} - \text{Cost of sales}}{\text{Revenue}}$$

Gross margin is influenced by two factors: (1) the price premium that a firm's products or services command in the marketplace and (2) the efficiency of the firm's procurement and production process. The price premium a firm's products or services can command is influenced by the degree of competition and the extent to which its products are unique. The firm's cost of sales can be low when it can purchase its inputs at a lower cost than competitors and/or run its production processes more efficiently. This is generally the case when a firm has a low-cost strategy.

**TABLE 5.5** Common-sized income statement and profitability ratios

| Ratio | H&M 2017 | H&M 2016 | Inditex 2017 | Inditex 2016 | Other peers 2017 |
|---|---|---|---|---|---|
| **Line items as a percentage of revenue (%)** | | | | | |
| Revenue | 100.0 | 100.0 | 100.0 | 100.0 | 100.0 |
| Net operating expense | (88.9) | (86.7) | (82.1) | (82.2) | (89.4) |
| Net non-recurring income or expense | 0.0 | 0.0 | (0.5) | (0.2) | 0.1 |
| Net operating profit before tax | 11.1 | 13.3 | 17.3 | 17.7 | 10.6 |
| Investment and interest income | 0.1 | 0.1 | 0.3 | 0.3 | 0.2 |
| Interest expense | (0.8) | (0.9) | (0.4) | (0.5) | (1.2) |
| Tax expense | (2.3) | (2.8) | (3.9) | (3.9) | (3.1) |
| Profit or loss | 8.1 | 9.7 | 13.3 | 13.6 | 6.5 |
| | | | | | |
| **Net operating expense line items as a percent of revenue (by nature) (%)** | | | | | |
| Personnel expense | (17.8) | (16.9) | (15.6) | (15.6) | N.A. |
| Cost of materials | (45.6) | (44.3) | (43.7) | (43.0) | N.A. |
| Depreciation and amortization | (13.0) | (13.8) | (10.5) | (11.8) | N.A. |
| Other operating income/expense | (12.5) | (11.7) | (12.3) | (11.7) | N.A. |
| | | | | | |
| **Operating expense line items as a percent of revenue (by function) (%)** | | | | | |
| Cost of sales | (46.0) | (44.8) | N.A. | N.A. | N.A. |
| Selling, general, and administrative expense | (43.0) | (42.0) | N.A. | N.A. | N.A. |
| | | | | | |
| **Key profitability ratios (%)** | | | | | |
| Gross profit margin | 54.0 | 55.2 | N.A. | N.A. | N.A. |
| EBITDA margin | 24.2 | 27.2 | 28.1 | 29.7 | N.A. |
| NOPAT margin | 8.6 | 10.3 | 13.4 | 13.7 | 7.2 |
| Net profit margin | 8.1 | 9.7 | 13.3 | 13.6 | 6.5 |

Table 5.5 indicates that Hennes & Mauritz's gross margin in 2017 decreased to 54.0 percent. The primary cause of this decline is that competitive pressures from online retailers, discount retailers such as Primark or ASOS, and mid-market retailers such as Inditex, in combination with growing stale inventory, forced H&M to further mark down its products. In addition, because H&M sources its products from countries other than those where it sells most of its products, its gross margin is sensitive to fluctuations in currency exchange rates. Adverse movements in currency exchange rates, together with small increases in the cost of materials and transportation, caused a further reduction in H&M's gross margin.

A company's selling, general, and administrative (SG&A) expenses are influenced by the operating activities it has to undertake to implement its competitive strategy. As discussed in Chapter 2, firms with differentiation strategies have to undertake activities to achieve differentiation. A company competing on the basis of quality and rapid introduction of new products is likely to have higher R&D costs relative to a company competing purely on a cost basis. Similarly, a company that attempts to build a brand image, distribute its products through full-service retailers, and provide significant customer service is likely to have higher selling and administration costs relative to a company that sells through warehouse retailers or direct mail and does not provide much customer support.

A company's SG&A expenses are also influenced by the efficiency with which it manages its overhead activities. The control of operating expenses is likely to be especially important for firms competing on the basis of low cost. However, even for differentiators, it is important to assess whether the cost of differentiation is commensurate with the price premium earned in the marketplace.

The ratio of SG&A expense to revenue in Table 5.5 allows us to evaluate the effectiveness with which Hennes & Mauritz managed its SG&A expenses. This ratio shows how much a company is spending to generate each euro of revenue. In 2017 H&M's SG&A-to-revenue ratio increased from 42.0 to 43.0 percent. The increased markdowns that we discussed earlier also affected H&M's SG&A-to-revenue ratio by reducing the denominator in the ratio. Another important factor to consider when interpreting the SG&A-to-revenue ratio is the stickiness of SG&A expenses. In particular, in periods during which consumer demand and, in turn, revenue per store decline, changes in selling expenditures typically lag behind revenue changes, thus increasing the ratio of these costs to revenue. Conversely, in times when sales pick up, excess sales capacity may get reutilized, helping to decrease the ratio of SG&A costs to revenue.

Stickiness of SG&A expenses occurs because it is costly for firms to temporarily cut capacity in down periods and bring back capacity when sales recover. For example, in many countries labor regulations make it difficult to lay off personnel. Also, temporarily cutting back on personnel could be difficult in stores that require a minimum amount of staffing to function efficiently, or raise concerns about finding adequate replacements in the future. To illustrate the effect of cost stickiness, consider H&M's revenue and SG&A expense on a per-store basis. In 2017 revenue per store decreased by 5.3 percent, from SEK46.5 million to SEK44.0 million, or by 4.0 percent when excluding the effect of markdowns; however, the ratio of SG&A to the average number of stores operated decreased less, by only 3.0 percent, from SEK19.5 million to SEK18.9 million. This observation signals that H&M's management was not able to cut back sufficiently on its sales capacity following the drop in consumer demand. Consequently, the SG&A-to-revenue ratio went up in 2017.

Note that a retailer's expenditures on procurement can be just as sticky as selling expenditures. However, procurement costs that are related to unsold products end up on the firm's balance sheet as part of inventories. The temporary capitalization of these costs dampens the positive effect of revenue declines on the cost of sales to revenue ratio, though it leads to an increase in the inventories to revenue ratio. We will return to this issue in the section on asset turnover.

### Decomposition by nature

The international accounting rules require that all firms reporting under IFRS Standards classify and disclose their operating expenses by nature, either in the income statement or in the notes to the financial statements. Like most European firms, Hennes & Mauritz and Inditex distinguish four expense categories:

1  Cost of materials.
2  Personnel expense.
3  Depreciation and amortization.
4  Other operating expenses.

Table 5.5 indicates that Hennes & Mauritz experienced a significant increase in personnel expense in 2017. As argued earlier, this is partly because personnel expenses tend to exhibit stickiness in the presence of a revenue-per-store decline, such as in 2017, given that it is costly to lay off personnel and often difficult to cut salaries. An advantage of classifying operating expenses by nature is that these expenses can be more easily related to their main drivers, such as the number of employees or the number of stores operated. This helps us to further analyze the development in Hennes & Mauritz's personnel expenses. In 2017 Hennes & Mauritz's average workforce grew by 7.5 percent to 123,178 employees, which given the company's lower revenue growth of 4.0 percent, led to a worsening of employee productivity. In particular, revenue per employee decreased by 3.0 percent to SEK1.62 million (or €164 thousand). H&M's personnel cost per employee increased by 1.8 percent to SEK289 thousand per employee (which is equal to €29 thousand per employee), which in combination with the decrease in employee productivity led to a net increase in the personnel expense-to-revenue ratio.

In 2017 Inditex spent on average €23.1 thousand per employee, up 2.8 percent from €22.4 thousand per employee in 2016, which illustrates that the company had a less expensive workforce than H&M. The difference in average cost per employee between H&M and Inditex can be partly attributed to the fact that Inditex operates its own manufacturing facilities and thus employs more low-cost production employees than H&M. Because of these manufacturing activities, Inditex also needs a larger workforce than H&M, making Inditex's average employee productivity lower at €147 thousand in revenue per employee.

Hennes & Mauritz experienced a decrease in its depreciation and amortization expense of roughly 0.8 percent. However, with a value of 13.0 percent H&M's depreciation and amortization-to-revenue ratio remains notably higher than that of Inditex. The depreciation difference between the two retailers is consistent with the observation that Inditex is able to generate a higher amount of revenue than H&M from a smaller investment base, as we will discuss in more detail in the next section.

Hennes & Mauritz saw its cost of materials to revenue ratio increase in 2017 from 44.3 to 45.6 percent. When we compare Hennes & Mauritz's with Inditex's cost of materials (of 43.7 percent), we see that H&M's cost of materials as a percent of revenue is higher. This difference between the two retailers is not surprising given that Inditex's greater presence in the higher-priced segments of the apparel industry allows the company to have a greater average price markup on its products than H&M. The difference in cost of materials as a percent of revenue is small only because H&M has comparatively cheap suppliers, often in lower-wage countries, making its outsourcing strategy relatively cost-efficient compared with Inditex's strategy to self-manufacture part of its assortment and concentrate production in Europe.

### NOPAT margin and EBITDA margin

Given that Hennes & Mauritz, Inditex, and their peers are pursuing different pricing, distribution, marketing, and production strategies, it is not surprising that they have different cost structures. The question is, when these costs are netted out, which company is performing better? Two ratios provide useful signals here: net operating profit margin (NOPAT margin) and EBITDA margin:

$$\text{NOPAT margin} = \frac{\text{Net operating profit after tax}}{\text{Revenue}}$$

$$\text{EBITDA margin} = \frac{\text{Earnings before interest, tax, depreciation and amortization}}{\text{Revenue}}$$

NOPAT margin provides a comprehensive indication of the operating performance of a company because it reflects all operating policies and eliminates the effects of debt policy. EBITDA margin provides similar information, except that it excludes depreciation and amortization expense, a significant non-cash operating expense. Some analysts prefer to use EBITDA margin because they believe that it focuses on "cash" operating items. While this is to some extent true, it can be potentially misleading for two reasons. EBITDA is not strictly a cash concept because revenue, cost of sales, and SG&A expenses often include non-cash items. Also, depreciation and amortization is a real operating expense, and it reflects to some extent the consumption of resources. Therefore ignoring it can be misleading.

From Table 5.5 we see that H&M's NOPAT margin and EBITDA margin worsened between 2016 and 2017. Inditex also saw both its NOPAT margin and its EBITDA margin worsen. In 2017 Inditex was able to retain close to 13 cents in net operating profits for each euro of revenue, which is more than the 9 and 7 cents that H&M and the other industry peers were able to retain. Inditex also had a higher EBITDA margin than H&M.

Recall that in Table 5.3 we define NOPAT as profit or loss plus interest expense and minus investment profit after tax. Therefore NOPAT is influenced by any non-recurring income (expense) items included in profit or loss. We can calculate a "recurring" NOPAT margin by eliminating these items, which we labelled "Net Non-Recurring Income or Expense" in the standardized income statement. For Inditex, the average recurring NOPAT margin was 13.8 percent in 2017. The 2017 margin is higher than the NOPAT margin number we discussed above, suggesting that a portion of the retailer's expenses are related to sources other than its core, recurring operations and investments. These sources include impairment and foreign exchange rate losses that Inditex reported in its financial statements. Recurring NOPAT may be a better benchmark to use when one is extrapolating current performance into the future because it reflects margins from the core business activities of a firm.

### Tax expense

Taxes are an important element of firms' total expenses. Through a wide variety of tax planning techniques, firms can attempt to reduce their tax expenses. [5] Two measures can be used to evaluate a firm's tax expense. One is the ratio of tax expense to revenue, and the other is the ratio of tax expense to earnings before tax (also known as the average tax rate). The firm's tax note provides a detailed account of why its average tax rate differs from the statutory tax rate.

When evaluating a firm's tax planning, the analyst should ask two questions: (1) Are the company's tax policies sustainable, or is the current tax rate influenced by one-time tax credits? (2) Do the firm's tax planning strategies lead to other business costs? For example, if the operations are located in tax havens, how does this affect the company's profit margins and asset utilization? Are the benefits of tax planning strategies (reduced taxes) greater than the increased business costs?

Table 5.5 shows that Hennes & Mauritz's tax rate decreased between 2016 and 2017. Hennes & Mauritz's taxes as a percentage of revenue were lower than those of Inditex. The primary reason for this is that H&M's pre-tax profits as a percent of revenue were lower. Despite the fact that the statutory tax rate of 30 percent in Inditex's country of domicile is substantially higher than the statutory rate of 22 percent in H&M's country of domicile, Inditex is able to effectively pay the same average rate as H&M by earning a greater proportion of its profits in low-tax countries. Specifically, in 2014 Inditex's effective tax rate was 22.5 percent (calculated as tax/[profit or loss + tax], i.e., 3.86%/[13.31% + 3.86%]), whereas H&M's and the other industry peers' effective tax rates were 22.9 percent (2.31%/[8.09% + 2.31%]) and 32.3 percent (3.11%/[6.51% + 3.11%]).

In summary, we conclude that Hennes & Mauritz's return on revenue came under pressure because of increased competition and markdowns, adverse currency exchange rate movements, and increases in input costs – reflected by an increase in both the cost of sales-to-revenue ratio and the SG&A-to-revenue ratio. In comparison with Inditex, Hennes & Mauritz has a lower net profit margin and a lower NOPAT margin, which is likely explained by the companies' different competitive positions, their different pricing strategies and Inditex's lower depreciation on non-current assets. Inditex and H&M have higher net profit margins and higher NOPAT margins than the other industry peers, resulting from the retailers' high operating efficiency.

### EVALUATING INVESTMENT MANAGEMENT: DECOMPOSING ASSET TURNOVER

Asset turnover is the second driver of a company's return on equity. Since firms invest considerable resources in their assets, using them productively is critical to overall profitability. A detailed analysis of asset turnover allows the analyst to evaluate the effectiveness of a firm's investment management.

There are two primary areas of asset management: (1) working capital management and (2) management of non-current operating assets. Working capital is defined as the difference between a firm's current assets and current liabilities. However, this definition does not distinguish between operating components (such as trade receivables, inventories, and trade payables) and the financing and investment components (such as excess cash, marketable securities, and notes payable). An alternative measure that makes this distinction is operating working capital, as defined in Table 5.3:

Operating working capital  =  (Current assets − Excess cash and cash equivalents)

− (Current liabilities − Current debt and current portion of non-current debt)

### Working capital management

The components of operating working capital that analysts primarily focus on are trade receivables, inventories, and trade payables. A certain amount of investment in working capital is necessary for the firm to run its normal operations. For example, a firm's credit policies and distribution policies determine its optimal level of trade receivables. The nature of the production process and the need for buffer stocks determine the optimal level of inventories. Finally, trade payables are a routine source of financing for the firm's working capital, and payment practices in an industry determine the normal level of trade payables.

The following ratios are useful in analyzing a firm's working capital management: operating working capital as a percentage of revenue, operating working capital turnover, trade receivables turnover, inventories turnover, and trade payables turnover. The turnover ratios can also be expressed in number of days of activity that the operating working capital (and its components) can support. The definitions of these ratios are as follows:

$$\text{Operating working capital-to-sales ratio} = \frac{\text{Operating working capital}}{\text{Revenue}}$$

$$\text{Operating working capital turnover} = \frac{\text{Revenue}}{\text{Operating working capital}}$$

$$\text{Trade receivables turnover} = \frac{\text{Revenue}}{\text{Trade receivables}}$$

$$\text{Inventories turnover} = \frac{\text{Cost of sales}}{\text{Inventories}} \text{ or } \frac{\text{Cost of materials}}{\text{Inventories}}$$

$$\text{Trade payables turnover} = \frac{\text{Purchases}}{\text{Trade payables}} \text{ or } \frac{\text{Cost of sales}}{\text{Trade payables}} \text{ or } \frac{\text{Cost of materials}}{\text{Trade payables}}$$

$$\text{Days' receivables} = \frac{\text{Trade receivables}}{\text{Average revenue per day}} = \frac{\text{Trade receivables}}{\text{Revenue}/360}$$

$$\text{Days' inventories} = \frac{\text{Inventories}}{\text{Average cost of sales per day}} \text{ or } \frac{\text{Inventories}}{\text{Average cost of materials per day}}$$

$$\text{Days' payables} = \frac{\text{Trade payables}}{\text{Average purchases per day}} \text{ or } \frac{\text{Trade payables}}{\text{Average cost of sales per day}} \text{ or } \frac{\text{Trade payables}}{\text{Average cost of materials per day}}$$

Operating working capital turnover indicates how many euros of revenue a firm is able to generate for each euro invested in its operating working capital. Trade receivables turnover, inventories turnover, and trade payables turnover allow the analyst to examine how productively the three principal components of working capital are being used. Days' receivables, days' inventories, and days' payables are another way to evaluate the efficiency of a firm's working capital management.[6]

### Non-current assets management

Another area of investment management concerns the utilization of a firm's non-current operating assets. It is useful to define a firm's investment in non-current operating assets as follows:

$$\text{Net non-current operating assets} = \text{Total non-current operating assets}$$
$$- \text{Non-interest bearing non-current liabilities}$$

Non-current operating assets generally consist of net property, plant, and equipment (PP&E), intangible assets such as goodwill, and derivatives used to hedge operating risks. Non-interest-bearing non-current liabilities include items such as (net) deferred taxes.

The efficiency with which a firm uses its net non-current operating assets is measured by the following two ratios: net non-current operating assets as a percentage of revenue and net non-current operating asset turnover. Net non-current operating asset turnover is defined as:

$$\text{Net non-current operating asset turnover} = \frac{\text{Revenue}}{\text{Net non-current operating assets}}$$

PP&E is the most important non-current asset in a firm's balance sheet. The efficiency with which a firm's PP&E is used is measured by the ratio of PP&E to revenue, or by the PP&E turnover ratio:

$$\text{PP\&E turnover} = \frac{\text{Revenue}}{\text{Net property, plant and equipment}}$$

The preceding ratios allow the analyst to explore a number of business questions in four general areas:

1  How well does the company manage its inventories? Does the company use modern manufacturing techniques? Does it have good vendor and logistics management systems? If inventories ratios are changing, what is the underlying business reason? Are new products being planned? Is there a mismatch between the demand forecasts and actual sales?
2  How well does the company manage its credit policies? Are these policies consistent with its marketing strategy? Is the company artificially increasing revenue by loading the distribution channels?
3  Is the company taking advantage of trade credit? Is it relying too much on trade credit? If so, what are the implicit costs?
4  Are the company's investments in plant and equipment consistent with its competitive strategy? Does the company have a sound policy of acquisitions and divestitures?

Table 5.6 shows the asset turnover ratios for Hennes & Mauritz, Inditex, and their peers. Between 2016 and 2017 Hennes & Mauritz became less efficient in its working capital management, as can be seen from the increase in operating working capital as a percentage of revenue and the decrease in operating working capital turnover. Working capital management worsened primarily because of a decrease in inventories turnover. The decrease in inventories turnover is consistent with the information disclosed by H&M that, because of increased competition and lower consumer demand, it experienced more difficulty in selling its products and needed to mark down its inventory more frequently in 2017. Hennes & Mauritz's non-current operating asset utilization slightly improved in 2017: both its net non-current operating asset turnover and its PP&E turnover increased, albeit marginally. These small increases in turnover signal that H&M's price decisions, increasingly marking down products, did not really help to stimulate sales.

Inditex managed its inventories more efficiently than H&M in 2017. Although the two retailers followed a similar fast fashion strategy, having its own manufacturing facilities, sourcing from local suppliers, and having one centralized logistics centre helped Inditex to more promptly respond to changes in customers' tastes and demands. As a consequence, Inditex was more successful in the execution of the fast fashion strategy than H&M, as evidenced by its lower days' inventories. Consistent with this difference in success, Inditex also achieved better non-current operating asset utilization ratios in 2017 relative to Hennes & Mauritz. Illustrating that Inditex is a clear leader and pioneer in fast fashion, the other industry peers also have lower inventory turnover and net non-current operating asset turnover (on average) than Inditex.

A second factor that, next to its high inventory turnover, allows Inditex to make much smaller investments in working capital than its industry peers is the company's extensive use of supplier financing. Inditex's 2017 days' payables ratio indicates that the company paid its suppliers after 115 days, on average. In contrast, H&M and the other industry peers paid their suppliers much quicker, after 29 and 55 days on average, thereby forcing these companies' to finance part of their inventories in other ways than through supplier credit. The differences in the companies' working capital management become even more visible when considering the average number of days it takes each company to collect cash from its customers since the moment it has paid its suppliers. This measure, which is also referred to as the cash conversion cycle, has the following definition:

$$\text{Cash conversion cycle} = \text{Days' inventories} + \text{Days' receivables} - \text{Days' payables}$$

**TABLE 5.6** Asset management ratios

| Ratio | H&M 2017 | H&M 2016 | Inditex 2017 | Inditex 2016 | Other peers 2017 |
|---|---|---|---|---|---|
| Operating working capital/Revenue (%) | 11.7 | 10.3 | −1.4 | −2.3 | 11.5 |
| Net non-current operating assets/Revenue (%) | 58.4 | 59.9 | 49.3 | 51.8 | 57.8 |
| PP&E/Revenue (%) | 57.0 | 58.9 | 49.5 | 51.9 | 44.8 |
| Operating working capital turnover | 8.56 | 9.69 | −69.73 | −42.89 | 8.71 |
| Net non-current operating asset turnover | 1.71 | 1.67 | 2.03 | 1.93 | 1.73 |
| PP&E turnover | 1.76 | 1.70 | 2.02 | 1.93 | 2.23 |
| Trade receivables turnover | 39.30 | 43.20 | 116.81 | 117.86 | 17.31 |
| Days' receivables | 9.2 | 8.3 | 3.1 | 3.1 | 20.8 |
| Inventories turnover | 2.79 | 3.01 | 4.23 | 4.23 | 3.96 |
| Days' inventories | 129.2 | 119.4 | 85.1 | 85.1 | 91.0 |
| Trade payables turnover | 12.60 | 12.86 | 3.14 | 3.10 | 6.52 |
| Days' payables | 28.6 | 28.0 | 114.5 | 116.0 | 55.2 |
| Cash conversion cycle (in days) | 109.8 | 99.8 | −26.4 | −27.8 | 56.6 |

Whereas in 2017 H&M and the other industry peers had cash conversion cycles of 110 and 57 days, Inditex had a negative cash conversion cycle of −26 days. This shows that Inditex paid its suppliers after the company received cash from its customers and underlines the exceptional efficiency of the company's working capital management.

## EVALUATING FINANCIAL MANAGEMENT: FINANCIAL LEVERAGE

Financial leverage enables a firm to have an asset base larger than its equity. The firm can augment its equity through borrowing and the creation of other liabilities like trade payables, provisions, and deferred taxes. Financial leverage increases a firm's ROE as long as the cost of the liabilities is less than the return from investing these funds. In this respect it is important to distinguish between interest-bearing liabilities such as notes payable, other forms of current debt and non-current debt that carry an explicit interest charge, and other forms of liabilities. Some of these other forms of liability, such as trade payables or deferred taxes, do not carry any interest charge at all. Other liabilities, such as finance lease obligations or pension obligations, carry an implicit interest charge.

While financial leverage can potentially benefit a firm's shareholders, it can also increase their risk. Unlike equity, liabilities have predefined payment terms, and the firm faces risk of financial distress if it fails to meet these commitments. There are a number of ratios to evaluate the degree of risk arising from a firm's financial leverage.

### Current liabilities and short-term liquidity

The following ratios are useful in evaluating the risk related to a firm's current liabilities:

$$\text{Current ratio} = \frac{\text{Current assets}}{\text{Current liabilities}}$$

$$\text{Quick ratio} = \frac{\text{Cash and cash equivalents} + \text{Trade receivables (net)}}{\text{Current liabilities}}$$

$$\text{Cash ratio} = \frac{\text{Cash and cash equivalents}}{\text{Current liabilities}}$$

$$\text{Operating cash flow ratio} = \frac{\text{Cash flow from operations}}{\text{Current liabilities}}$$

All these ratios attempt to measure the firm's ability to repay its current liabilities. The first three compare a firm's current liabilities with its current assets that can be used to repay those liabilities. The fourth ratio focuses on the ability of the firm's operations to generate the resources needed to repay its current liabilities.

Since both current assets and current liabilities have comparable duration, the current ratio is a key index of a firm's short-term liquidity. Analysts view a current ratio of more than one to be an indication that the firm can cover its current liabilities from the cash realized from its current assets. However, the firm can face a short-term liquidity problem even with a current ratio exceeding one when some of its current assets are not easy to liquidate. Further, firms whose current assets have high turnover rates, such as food retailers, can afford to have current ratios below one. Quick ratio and cash ratio capture the firm's ability to cover its current liabilities from liquid assets. Quick ratio assumes that the firm's trade receivables are liquid. This is true in industries where the credit-worthiness of the customers is beyond dispute, or when receivables are collected in a very short period. When these conditions do not prevail, cash ratio, which considers only cash and cash equivalents, is a better indication of a firm's ability to cover its current liabilities in an emergency. Operating cash flow is another measure of the firm's ability to cover its current liabilities from cash generated from operations of the firm.

The liquidity ratios for Hennes & Mauritz, Inditex, and their peers are shown in Table 5.7. Most of the retailers' liquidity situation in 2017 was comfortable, thanks to their large cash balances and sound operating cash flows. H&M's liquidity ratios worsened in 2017 but remained at acceptable levels.

**TABLE 5.7** Liquidity ratios

| Ratio | H&M 2017 | H&M 2016 | Inditex 2017 | Inditex 2016 | Other peers 2017 |
|---|---|---|---|---|---|
| Current ratio | 1.49 | 1.78 | 1.55 | 1.49 | 2.64 |
| Quick ratio | 0.42 | 0.59 | 0.89 | 0.86 | 1.65 |
| Cash ratio | 0.27 | 0.42 | 0.85 | 0.82 | 1.31 |
| Operating cash flow ratio | 1.14 | 1.65 | 1.10 | 1.17 | 0.60 |

## Debt and long-term solvency

A company's financial leverage is also influenced by its debt financing policy. There are several potential benefits from debt financing. First, debt is typically cheaper than equity because the firm promises predefined payment terms to debt holders. Second, in most countries, interest on debt financing is tax deductible whereas dividends to shareholders are not tax deductible. Third, debt financing can impose discipline on the firm's management and motivate it to reduce wasteful expenditures. Fourth, it is often easier for management to communicate their proprietary information on the firm's strategies and prospects to private lenders than to public capital markets. Such communication can potentially reduce a firm's cost of capital. For all these reasons, it is optimal for firms to use at least some debt in their capital structure. Too much reliance on debt financing, however, is potentially costly to the firm's shareholders. The firm will face financial distress if it defaults on the interest and principal payments. Debt holders also impose covenants on the firm, restricting the firm's operating, investment, and financing decisions.

The optimal capital structure for a firm is determined primarily by its business risk. A firm's cash flows are highly predictable when there is little competition or there is little threat of technological changes. Such firms have low business risk and hence they can rely heavily on debt financing. In contrast, if a firm's operating cash flows are highly volatile and its capital expenditure needs are unpredictable, it may have to rely primarily on equity financing. Managers' attitude towards risk and financial flexibility also often determine a firm's debt policies.

There are a number of ratios that help the analyst in this area. To evaluate the mix of debt and equity in a firm's capital structure, the following ratios are useful:

$$\text{Liabilities-to-equity ratio} = \frac{\text{Total liabilities}}{\text{Shareholder' equity}}$$

$$\text{Debt-to-equity ratio} = \frac{\text{Current debt} + \text{Non-current debt}}{\text{Shareholders' equity}}$$

$$\text{Debt-to-capital ratio} = \frac{\text{Current debt} + \text{Non-current debt}}{\text{Current debt} + \text{Non-current debt} + \text{Shareholder' equity}}$$

The first ratio restates the assets-to-equity ratio (one of the three primary ratios underlying ROE) by subtracting one from it. The second ratio provides an indication of how many euros of debt financing the firm is using for each euro invested by its shareholders. The third ratio measures debt as a proportion of total capital. In calculating all the preceding ratios, it is important to include all interest-bearing obligations, whether the interest charge is explicit or implicit. Recall that examples of line items that carry an implicit interest charge include finance lease obligations and pension obligations. Analysts sometimes include any potential off-balance sheet obligations that a firm may have, such as noncancelable operating leases, in the definition of a firm's debt. We discussed the methods to do so in Chapter 4.

The ease with which a firm can meet its interest payments is an indication of the degree of risk associated with its debt policy. The interest coverage ratio provides a measure of this construct:

$$\text{Interest coverage (earnings basis)} = \frac{\text{Profit or loss} + \text{Interest expense} + \text{Tax expense}}{\text{Interest expense}}$$

$$or \; \frac{\text{Profit or loss} + \text{Interest expense after tax}}{\text{Interest expense after tax}}$$

$$\text{Interest coverage (cash flow basis)} = \frac{\text{Cash flow from operations} + \text{Interest paid} + \text{Taxes paid}}{\text{Interest paid}}$$

The earnings-based coverage ratio indicates the euros of earnings available for each euro of required interest payment; the cash flow-based coverage ratio indicates the euros of cash generated by operations for each euro of required interest payment. In both these ratios, the denominator is the interest expense. In the numerator we add taxes back because taxes are computed only after interest expense is deducted. A coverage ratio of one implies that the firm is barely covering its interest expense through its operating activities, which is a very risky situation. The larger the coverage ratio, the greater the cushion the firm has to meet interest obligations.

One can also calculate debt coverage ratios that measure a firm's ability to measure all fixed financial obligations, such as interest payments, lease payments, and debt repayments, by appropriately redefining the numerator and denominator in the above ratios. In doing so it is important to remember that while some fixed charge payments, such as interest and lease rentals, are paid with pre-tax euros, others, such as debt repayments, are made with after-tax euros. For example, a debt coverage ratio that takes into account the tax deductibility of interest and lease payments is the following:

$$\text{Debt coverage (earnings basis)} = \frac{\text{Profit or loss} + \text{Interest and lease expenses} \times (1 - \text{tax rate})}{\text{Interest and lease expense} \times (1 - \text{tax rate}) + \text{Debt repayments}}$$

We show debt and coverage ratios for Hennes & Mauritz, Inditex, and their peers in Table 5.8. Hennes & Mauritz's liabilities-to-equity and debt-to-equity ratios increased marginally in 2017. The company's interest coverage decreased but remained at a comfortable level. Inditex's debt ratios indicate that it has been following a less aggressive debt policy than Hennes & Mauritz and the other industry peers. Its interest coverage ratios in 2017 are far above the other retailer's ratios. Overall, the interest coverage ratios illustrate that the apparel retailers' current earnings and cash flows are, on average, more than sufficient to cover their interest expenses.

**TABLE 5.8** Debt and coverage ratios

| Ratio | H&M 2017 | H&M 2016 | Inditex 2017 | Inditex 2016 | Other peers 2017 |
|---|---|---|---|---|---|
| Liabilities-to-equity | 1.92 | 1.83 | 0.87 | 0.91 | 2.12 |
| Debt-to-equity | 1.34 | 1.31 | 0.37 | 0.40 | 1.55 |
| Debt-to-capital | 0.57 | 0.57 | 0.27 | 0.29 | 0.61 |
| Interest coverage (earnings-based) | 14.02 | 15.10 | 41.57 | 39.39 | 8.85 |
| Interest coverage (cash flow-based) | 38.66 | 39.10 | 97.08 | 93.77 | 8.29 |

## Key Analysis Questions

S ome of the business questions to ask when the analyst is examining a firm's debt policies are:

- Does the company have enough debt? That is, is it exploiting the potential benefits of debt – interest tax shields, management discipline, and easier communication?
- Does the company have too much debt given its business risk? What type of debt covenant restrictions does the firm face? Is it bearing the costs of too much debt, risking potential financial distress and reduced business flexibility?
- What is the company doing with the borrowed funds? Investing in working capital? Investing in fixed assets? Are these investments profitable?
- Is the company borrowing money to pay dividends? If so, what is the justification?

### Ratios of disaggregated data

So far we have discussed how to compute ratios using information in the financial statements. Analysts often probe these ratios further by using disaggregated financial and physical data, taken from the Management Commentary or segment disclosures in the financial statements. For example, for a multi-business company, one could analyze the information by individual business segments. Such an analysis can reveal potential differences in the performance of each business unit, allowing the analyst to pinpoint areas where a company's strategy is working and where it is not. It is also possible to probe financial ratios further by computing ratios of physical data pertaining to a company's operations. The appropriate physical data to look at varies from industry to industry. As an example in retailing, one could compute productivity statistics such as revenue per store, revenue per square meter, customer transactions per store, and amount of revenue per customer transaction; in the hotel industry, room occupancy rates provide important information; in the cellular telephone industry, acquisition cost per new subscriber and subscriber retention rate are important. These disaggregated ratios are particularly useful for young firms and young industries, where accounting data may not fully capture the business economics due to conservative accounting rules.

### PUTTING IT ALL TOGETHER: ASSESSING SUSTAINABLE GROWTH RATE

Analysts often use the concept of sustainable growth as a way to evaluate a firm's ratios in a comprehensive manner. A firm's **sustainable growth rate** is defined as:

$$\text{Sustainable growth rate} = \text{ROE} \times (1 - \text{Dividend payout ratio})$$

We have already discussed the analysis of ROE in the previous four sections. The dividend payout ratio is defined as:

$$\text{Dividend payout ratio} = \frac{\text{Cash dividends paid}}{\text{Profit or loss}}$$

A firm's dividend payout ratio is a measure of its dividend policy. Firms pay dividends for several reasons. They provide a way for the firm to return to its shareholders any cash generated in excess of its operating and investment needs. When there are information asymmetries between a firm's managers and its shareholders, dividend payments can serve as a signal to shareholders about managers' expectations of the firm's future prospects. Firms may also pay dividends to attract a certain type of shareholder base.

Sustainable growth rate is the rate at which a firm can grow while keeping its profitability and financial policies unchanged. A firm's return on equity and its dividend payout policy determine the pool of funds available for growth. Of course the firm can grow at a rate different from its sustainable growth rate if its profitability, payout policy, or financial leverage changes. Therefore the sustainable growth rate provides a benchmark against which a firm's growth plans can be evaluated. Figure 5.2 shows how a firm's sustainable growth rate can be linked to all the ratios discussed in this chapter. These linkages allow an analyst to examine the drivers of a firm's current sustainable growth rate. If the firm intends to grow at a higher rate than its sustainable growth rate, one could assess which of the ratios are likely to change in the process. This analysis can lead to asking business questions such as these: Where is the change going to take place? Is management expecting profitability to increase? Or asset productivity to improve? Are these expectations realistic? Is the firm planning for these changes? If the profitability is not likely to go up, will the firm increase its financial leverage or cut dividends? What is the likely impact of these financial policy changes?

**FIGURE 5.2** Sustainable growth rate framework for financial ratio analysis

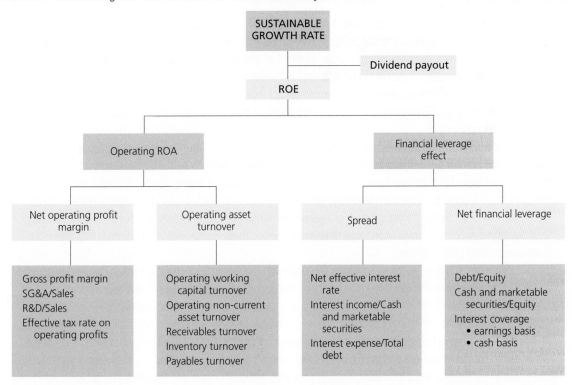

Conflicts of interest between managers and shareholders can also have implications for dividend policy decisions. Shareholders of a firm with high profits and free cash flows and few profitable investment opportunities want managers to adopt a dividend policy with high payouts, thus reducing the sustainable growth rate. This will deter managers from growing the firm by investing in new projects that are not valued by shareholders or from spending the free cash flows on management perks. If a firm's sustainable growth rate is much higher than warranted by the firm's growth opportunities, one could evaluate the possible reasons for why management has not changed its dividend policy: Is management expecting profitability to decrease? If profitability is not expected to decline, has the firm reduced or will it reduce leverage? Are there contractual or legal constraints preventing the firm from paying higher dividends?

Table 5.9 shows the sustainable growth rate and its components for Hennes & Mauritz and its peers. In 2016 and 2017 Hennes & Mauritz had a higher ROE but also a higher dividend payout ratio than Inditex, leading to a lower sustainable growth rate.

**TABLE 5.9**  Sustainable growth rate

| Ratio (%) | H&M 2017 | H&M 2016 | Inditex 2017 | Inditex 2016 | Other peers 2017 |
|---|---|---|---|---|---|
| ROE | 26.8 | 31.2 | 25.7 | 26.1 | 21.2 |
| Dividend payout ratio | 99.7 | 86.6 | 63.1 | 59.2 | 49.9 |
| Sustainable growth rate | 0.1 | 4.2 | 9.5 | 10.7 | 10.6 |

## Constraints on Dividend Policies

A firm's dividend policy affects its sustainable growth, financing decisions and conflicts with its shareholders. The following factors impose some constraints on dividend policy:

- *Tax costs of dividends.* Classical models of the tax effects of dividends predict that if the capital gains tax rate is less than the rate on dividend income, investors will prefer that the firm either pays no dividends, so that they subsequently take gains as capital accumulation, or that the firm undertakes a share repurchase, which qualifies as a capital distribution. Today many practitioners and theorists believe that taxes play only a minor role in determining a firm's dividend policy since a firm can attract investors with various tax preferences. Thus a firm that wishes to pay high dividend rates will attract shareholders that are tax-exempt institutions, which do not pay taxes on dividend income.

- *Contractual constraints.* One of the concerns of a firm's creditors is that when the firm is in financial distress, managers will pay a large dividend to shareholders. This problem is likely to be particularly severe for a firm with highly liquid assets, since its managers can pay a large dividend without selling assets. To limit these types of ploys, managers agree to restrict dividend payments to shareholders. Such dividend covenants usually require the firm to maintain certain minimum levels of retained earnings and current asset balances, which effectively limit dividend payments in times of financial difficulty. However, these constraints on dividend policy are unlikely to be severe for a profitable firm.

- *Legal constraints.* In many European countries corporate law mandates restrictions on firms' dividend payouts, primarily with the objective of protecting the rights of creditors. Such legal dividend restrictions replace or complement the restrictions that creditors may impose on borrowers by means of debt covenants.[7] Legal dividend restrictions typically require that companies transfer a fixed percentage of their current profits to a legal reserve, unless the legal reserve exceeds a certain percentage of total capital. Companies then can distribute dividends out of the remainder of current profits plus the current amount of retained earnings. Legal dividend restrictions of this kind can be found in most Western European countries, although mandated transfers to legal reserves do not exist in Finland, Ireland, the Netherlands, and the United Kingdom.

Hennes & Mauritz's sustainable growth rate in 2017 was close to zero and substantially lower than the company's average growth rate during the prior five years of 10.6 percent. This observation may have raised the question of whether the company's 2017 dividend payout was sustainable. However, Hennes & Mauritz's debt and interest coverage ratios showed earlier that the retailer's leverage position is still comfortable and stronger than that of the other industry peers. If H&M anticipates that the decrease in profitability is only temporary, it can decide to maintain its dividends and finance near-term investments with debt, thereby letting leverage increase a bit further.

Inditex's sustainable growth rates of 2016 and 2017 are close to the company's long-term average growth rate of around 10 percent. Given Inditex's below-normal leverage, this raises the question of whether the company would be better off by increasing its dividend payout ratio, consequently reducing excess cash or making more use of debt to finance its growth than it has done previously. One possible reason for Inditex's management not to increase dividends, and thus reduce excess cash or take on higher leverage, is that the company's majority shareholder derives private benefits from having control over the operating assets and excess cash balance. Another possible reason is that management expects that the current profitability level will not persist and wants to avoid cutting dividends in the future.

## HISTORICAL PATTERNS OF RATIOS FOR EUROPEAN FIRMS

To provide a benchmark for analysis, Table 5.10 reports historical values of the key ratios discussed in this chapter. These ratios are calculated using financial statement data for our sample of 7,771 publicly listed European companies. The table shows the median values of ROE, its key components, and the sustainable growth rate for each of the years 1998 to 2017, and the average for this 20-year period. The data in the table show that the average ROE during this period has been 8.4 percent, average return on invested capital has been 6.4 percent, and the average spread between the return on invested capital and net borrowing costs after tax has been 2.7 percent. The average sustainable growth rate for European companies during this period has been 5.4 percent. Of course an individual company's ratios might depart from these economy-wide averages for a number of reasons, including industry effects, company strategies, and management effectiveness. Nonetheless, the average values in the table serve as useful benchmarks in financial analysis.

# Cash flow analysis

The ratio analysis discussion focused on analyzing a firm's income statement (net profit margin analysis) or its balance sheet (asset turnover and financial leverage). The analyst can get further insights into the firm's operating, investing, and financing policies by examining its cash flows. Cash flow analysis also provides an indication of the quality of the information in the firm's income statement and balance sheet. As before, we will illustrate the concepts discussed in this section using Hennes & Mauritz's and Inditex's cash flows.

## CASH FLOW AND FUNDS FLOW STATEMENTS

All companies reporting in conformity with IFRS Standards are required to include a statement of cash flows in their financial statements under IAS 7. In the reported cash flow statement, firms classify their cash flows into three categories: cash flow from operations, cash flow related to (non-current, operating, and non-operating) investments, and cash flow related to financing activities. Cash flow from operations is the cash generated by the firm from the sale of goods and services after paying for the cost of inputs and operations. Cash flow related to investment activities shows the cash paid for capital expenditures, intercorporate investments, acquisitions, and cash received from the sales of non-current assets. Cash flow related to financing activities shows the cash raised from (or paid to) the firm's shareholders and debt holders.

**TABLE 5.10** Historical values of key financial ratios

| Year | ROE (%) | NOPAT margin (%) | Operating asset turnover | Return on net operating assets (%) | Return on invested capital (%) | Spread (%) | Financial leverage | Sustainable growth rate (%) |
|---|---|---|---|---|---|---|---|---|
| 1998 | 12.1 | 4.5 | 2.04 | 9.1 | 8.6 | 3.9 | 0.65 | 7.8 |
| 1999 | 10.5 | 4.4 | 1.85 | 7.8 | 7.7 | 3.5 | 0.67 | 6.5 |
| 2000 | 9.6 | 4.2 | 1.78 | 7.3 | 7.0 | 2.7 | 0.67 | 6.1 |
| 2001 | 4.1 | 3.1 | 1.48 | 4.0 | 4.0 | 0.2 | 0.62 | 2.2 |
| 2002 | 5.2 | 2.7 | 1.65 | 4.6 | 4.5 | 0.5 | 0.65 | 2.5 |
| 2003 | 6.9 | 3.0 | 1.78 | 5.7 | 5.4 | 1.5 | 0.63 | 3.7 |
| 2004 | 9.4 | 3.8 | 1.85 | 7.0 | 6.8 | 3.0 | 0.60 | 5.9 |
| 2005 | 10.7 | 4.5 | 1.82 | 7.9 | 7.6 | 4.1 | 0.56 | 6.9 |
| 2006 | 11.5 | 4.7 | 1.77 | 8.6 | 8.1 | 4.4 | 0.56 | 7.7 |
| 2007 | 11.6 | 5.1 | 1.72 | 8.6 | 8.3 | 4.2 | 0.55 | 7.6 |
| 2008 | 8.3 | 4.2 | 1.65 | 7.2 | 6.7 | 2.1 | 0.57 | 5.8 |
| 2009 | 5.3 | 3.3 | 1.46 | 5.0 | 4.7 | 1.1 | 0.59 | 3.4 |
| 2010 | 7.8 | 4.1 | 1.54 | 6.7 | 6.0 | 2.6 | 0.54 | 5.5 |
| 2011 | 7.8 | 4.2 | 1.58 | 6.7 | 6.3 | 2.6 | 0.53 | 5.6 |
| 2012 | 7.1 | 3.9 | 1.56 | 6.2 | 5.7 | 2.1 | 0.53 | 5.0 |
| 2013 | 6.9 | 3.7 | 1.52 | 6.0 | 5.5 | 2.2 | 0.53 | 4.6 |
| 2014 | 7.9 | 4.2 | 1.52 | 6.6 | 6.0 | 2.8 | 0.52 | 5.1 |
| 2015 | 8.3 | 4.2 | 1.49 | 6.6 | 6.0 | 3.1 | 0.52 | 5.4 |
| 2016 | 8.7 | 4.6 | 1.48 | 6.9 | 6.2 | 3.5 | 0.53 | 5.7 |
| 2017 | 9.2 | 4.6 | 1.50 | 7.1 | 6.5 | 3.9 | 0.53 | 5.9 |
| Average | 8.4 | 4.0 | 1.65 | 6.8 | 6.4 | 2.7 | 0.58 | 5.4 |

Source: Financial statement data for all nonfinancial companies publicly listed on one of the primary European exchanges (Compustat Global database).

Firms use two cash flow statement formats: the direct format and the indirect format. The key difference between the two formats is the way they report cash flow from operating activities. In the direct cash flow format, which is used by only a small number of firms in practice, operating cash receipts and disbursements are reported directly. In the indirect format, firms derive their operating cash flows by making accrual adjustments to profit or loss (such as done in Hennes & Mauritz's cash flow statement shown in the appendix to this chapter). Because the indirect format links the cash flow statement with the firm's income statement and balance sheet, many analysts and managers find this format more useful.

You may recall from Chapter 3 that profit or loss differs from operating cash flows because revenues and expenses are measured on an accrual basis. There are two types of accruals embedded in profit or loss. First, there are current accruals like credit sales and unpaid expenses. Current accruals result in changes in a firm's current assets (such as trade receivables, inventories, and prepaid expenses) and current liabilities (such as trade payables and current provisions). The second type of accruals included in the income statement is non-current accruals such as depreciation, deferred taxes, and equity income from unconsolidated subsidiaries. To derive cash flow from operations from profit or loss, adjustments have to be made for both these types of accruals. In addition, adjustments have to be made for non-operating gains included in profit or loss such as profits from asset sales.

The indirect cash flow format explicitly details the accrual adjustments that need to be made to profit or loss in order to arrive at operating cash flows. If a firm uses the direct cash flow format, it is useful for analysts to know how to prepare an approximate indirect cash flow statement. The first step to doing so is to calculate a firm's working capital from operations, defined as profit or loss adjusted for non-current accruals, and gains from the sale of non-current assets. Information about non-current accruals such as depreciation and deferred taxes or non-operating gains can typically be taken from the income statement or the notes to the financial statements. The second step is to convert working capital from operations to cash flow from operations by making the relevant adjustments for current accruals related to operations.

Information on current accruals can be obtained by examining changes in a firm's current assets and current liabilities. For example, the change in inventories can be seen as representing an investment in current assets that is not yet recognized as an expense; this change is thus included in cash flow from operations but not (yet) in profit or loss. Typically, operating accruals represent changes in all the current asset accounts other than cash and cash equivalents and changes in all the current liabilities other than notes payable and the current portion of non-current debt.[8] Cash from operations can be calculated as follows:

Working capital from operations

− Increase (or + decrease) in trade receivables

− Increase (or + decrease) in inventories

− Increase (or + decrease) in other current assets excluding cash and cash equivalents

+ Increase (or − decrease) in trade payables

+ Increase (or − decrease) in other current liabilities excluding debt

In most cases working capital from operations adjusted for changes in the balance sheet values of current assets and liabilities will not be exactly equal to the operating cash flow disclosed in the direct cash flow statement. Therefore the analyst needs to add a category of other, unexplained accruals to the self-constructed indirect cash flow statement to make the operating cash flows in the two cash flow statements match. This complication arises because year-to-year changes in the balance sheet values of current assets and liabilities are affected by events such as changes in consolidation or foreign currency exchange rate changes, whereas the current accruals in the indirect cash flow statement are not.

## ANALYZING CASH FLOW INFORMATION

Cash flow analysis can be used to address a variety of questions regarding a firm's cash flow dynamics:

- How strong is the firm's internal cash flow generation? Is the cash flow from operations positive or negative? If it is negative, why? Is it because the company is growing? Is it because its operations are unprofitable? Or is it having difficulty managing its working capital properly?
- Does the company have the ability to meet its short-term financial obligations, such as interest payments, from its operating cash flow? Can it continue to meet these obligations without reducing its operating flexibility?
- How much cash did the company invest in growth? Are these investments consistent with its business strategy? Did the company use internal cash flow to finance growth, or did it rely on external financing?
- Did the company pay dividends from internal free cash flow, or did it have to rely on external financing? If the company had to fund its dividends from external sources, is the company's dividend policy sustainable?
- What type of external financing does the company rely on? Equity, current debt, or non-current debt? Is the financing consistent with the company's overall business risk?

- Does the company have excess cash flow after making capital investments? Is it a long-term trend? What plans does management have to deploy the free cash flow?

While the information in reported cash flow statements can be used to answer the preceding questions directly in the case of some firms, it may not be easy to do so always for a number of reasons. First, even though IAS 7 provides broad guidelines on the format of a cash flow statement, there is still significant variation across firms in how cash flow data are disclosed. Therefore, to facilitate a systematic analysis and comparison across firms, analysts often recast the information in the cash flow statement using their own cash flow model. Second, firms may choose to include interest expense in computing their cash flow from operating activities. However, this item is not strictly related to a firm's operations but a function of financial leverage. Therefore it is useful to restate the cash flow statement to take this into account.

Analysts use a number of different approaches to restate the cash flow data. One such model is shown in Table 5.11. This presents cash flow from operations in two stages. The first step computes cash flow from operations before operating working capital investments. In computing this cash flow, the model excludes interest expense. To compute this number starting with a firm's profit before interest and taxes, an analyst subtracts or adds back three types of items:

1  Subtract taxes paid adjusted for the tax shield on interest payments, i.e., taxes paid plus (1 − tax rate) × interest paid. The tax shield adjustment is made to ensure that the restated cash flow from operations does not depend on the financing structure of the firm.
2  Add back non-operating gains or losses typically arising out of asset disposals or asset write-offs because these items are investment-related and will be considered later.
3  Add back non-current operating accruals such as depreciation and deferred taxes because these are non-cash operating charges.

**TABLE 5.11**  Cash flow analysis

| Line item (SEK or € millions) | H&M 2017 | H&M 2016 | Inditex 2017 | Inditex 2016 |
|---|---|---|---|---|
| Profit before Interest and Tax | 22,125.8 | 25,519.5 | 4,432.2 | 4,163.1 |
| Taxes Paid plus Tax Shield on Interest Paid | (6,402.5) | (4,845.0) | (1,060.7) | (829.1) |
| Non-Operating Losses (Gains) | 0.0 | 0.0 | 34.0 | 10.5 |
| Non-Current Operating Accruals | 26,059.2 | 26,471.5 | 2,869.8 | 2,835.8 |
| Operating Cash Flow before Working Capital Investments | 41,782.5 | 47,146.0 | 6,275.3 | 6,180.3 |
| Net (Investments in) or Liquidation of Operating Working Capital | (1,648.0) | (3,390.0) | (449.0) | (274.7) |
| Operating Cash Flow before Investment in Non-Current Assets | 40,134.5 | 43,756.0 | 5,826.3 | 5,905.6 |
| Interest Received | 281.0 | 224.0 | 26.0 | 21.5 |
| Dividends Received | 0.0 | 0.0 | 0.0 | 0.0 |
| Net (Investments in) or Liquidation of Non-Current Operating or Investment Assets | (27,553.1) | (29,608.3) | (2,600.7) | (4,052.1) |
| Free Cash Flow Available to Debt and Equity | 12,862.4 | 14,371.7 | 3,251.7 | 1,875.1 |
| Interest Paid after Tax | (1,246.3) | (1,329.5) | (75.6) | (74.8) |
| Net Debt (Repayment) or Issuance | 5,094.9 | (697.2) | (107.1) | (46.8) |
| Free Cash Flow Available to Equity | 16,711.0 | 12,345.0 | 3,069.0 | 1,753.5 |
| Dividend (Payments) | (16,137.0) | (16,137.0) | (2,127.0) | (1,871.5) |
| Net Share (Repurchase) or Issuance | 0.0 | 0.0 | 0.0 | 0.0 |
| Net Increase (Decrease) in Cash Balance | 574.0 | (3,792.0) | 942.0 | (118.0) |

Several factors affect a firm's ability to generate positive cash flow from operations. Healthy firms that are in a steady state should generate more cash from their customers than they spend on operating expenses. In contrast, growing firms – especially those investing cash in research and development, advertising and marketing, or building an organization to sustain future growth – may experience negative operating cash flow. Firms' working capital management also affects whether they generate positive cash flow from operations. Firms in the growing stage typically invest some cash flow in operating working capital items like accounts receivable, inventories, and accounts payable. Net investments in working capital are a function of firms' credit policies (trade receivables), payment policies (trade payables, prepaid expenses, and provisions), and expected growth in sales (inventories). Thus, in interpreting firms' cash flow from operations after working capital, it is important to keep in mind their growth strategy, industry characteristics, and credit policies.

The cash flow analysis model next focuses on cash flows related to long-term investments. These investments take the form of capital expenditures, intercorporate investments, and mergers and acquisitions. Any positive operating cash flow after making operating working capital investments allows the firm to pursue long-term growth opportunities. If the firm's operating cash flows after working capital investments are not sufficient to finance its long-term investments, it has to rely on external financing to fund its growth. Such firms have less flexibility to pursue long-term investments than those that can fund their growth internally. There are both costs and benefits from being able to fund growth internally. The cost is that managers can use the internally generated free cash flow to fund unprofitable investments. Such wasteful capital expenditures are less likely if managers are forced to rely on external capital suppliers. Reliance on external capital markets may make it difficult for managers to undertake long-term risky investments if it is not easy to communicate to the capital markets the benefits from such investments.

Any excess cash flow after these long-term investments is free cash flow that is available for both debt holders and equity holders. Payments to debt holders include interest payments and principal payments. Firms with negative free cash flow have to borrow additional funds to meet their interest and debt repayment obligations, or cut some of their investments in working capital or long-term investments, or issue additional equity. This situation is clearly financially risky for the firm.

Cash flow after payments to debt holders is free cash flow available to equity holders. Payments to equity holders consist of dividend payments and share repurchases. If firms pay dividends despite negative free cash flow to equity holders, they are borrowing money to pay dividends. While this may be feasible in the short-term, it is not prudent for a firm to pay dividends to equity holders unless it has a positive free cash flow on a sustained basis. On the other hand, firms that have a large free cash flow after debt payments run the risk of wasting that money on unproductive investments to pursue growth for its own sake. An analyst therefore should carefully examine the investment plans of such firms.

The model in Table 5.11 suggests that the analyst should focus on a number of cash flow measures:

1 Cash flow from operations before investment in working capital and interest payments, to examine whether the firm is able to generate a cash surplus from its operations.
2 Cash flow from operations after investment in working capital, to assess how the firm's working capital is being managed and whether it has the flexibility to invest in non-current assets for future growth.
3 Free cash flow available to debt and equity holders, to assess a firm's ability to meet its interest and principal payments.
4 Free cash flow available to equity holders, to assess the firm's financial ability to sustain its dividend policy and to identify potential agency problems from excess free cash flow.

These measures have to be evaluated in the context of the company's business, its growth strategy, and its financial policies. Further, changes in these measures from year to year provide valuable information on the stability of the cash flow dynamics of the firm.

Finally, as we will discuss in Chapter 7, free cash flow available to debt and equity and free cash flow available to equity are critical inputs into the cash flow-based valuation of firms' assets and equity, respectively.

## Key Analysis Questions

The cash flow model in Table 5.11 can also be used to assess a firm's earnings quality, as discussed in Chapter 3. The reconciliation of a firm's net profit with its cash flow from operations facilitates this exercise. The following are some of the questions an analyst can probe in this respect:

- Are there significant differences between a firm's profit or loss and its operating cash flow? Is it possible to clearly identify the sources of this difference? Which accounting policies contribute to this difference? Are there any one-time events contributing to this difference?
- Is the relationship between cash flow and profit or loss changing over time? Why? Is it because of changes in business conditions or because of changes in the firm's accounting policies and estimates?
- What is the time lag between the recognition of revenues and expenses and the receipt and disbursement of cash flows? What type of uncertainties need to be resolved in between?
- Are the changes in receivables, inventories, and payables normal? If not, is there adequate explanation for the changes?

### ANALYSIS OF HENNES & MAURITZ'S AND INDITEX'S CASH FLOW

Hennes & Mauritz and Inditex reported their cash flows using the indirect cash flow statement. Table 5.11 recasts these statements using the approach discussed above so that we can analyze the two companies' cash flow dynamics.

Cash flow analysis presented in Table 5.11 shows Hennes & Mauritz had an operating cash flow before working capital investments of SEK41.8 billion in 2017, a decrease from SEK47.1 billion in 2016. The difference between earnings and these cash flows is primarily attributable to the depreciation and amortization charge included in the company's income statement. Hennes & Mauritz's decrease in operating cash flow is smaller than its decrease in profitability because a substantially larger portion of the company's tax expense was current and thus paid in cash in 2017. H&M's taxes paid increased by more than 30 percent. In contrast to H&M, Inditex experienced an increase in operating cash flow, primarily caused by an increase in the company's operating profit.

Both Hennes & Mauritz and Inditex generated more than adequate cash flow from operations to meet their total investments in non-current assets. Consequently, in 2017 Hennes & Mauritz had SEK12.9 billion of free cash flow available to debt and equity holders; Inditex's free cash flow to debt and equity holders was €3.2 billion.

In 2017 Hennes & Mauritz was a net borrower, increasing the free cash flow available to equity holders. The company utilized this free cash flow to pay dividends. In 2016 distributions to equity holders exceeded the free cash flow to equity in, and Hennes & Mauritz drew down its cash balance, just like it had done in the prior three years. Doing so helped the company to gradually decrease its emphasis on non-operating investments and, consequently, slow down the decline in its return on invested capital.

Inditex paid €75.6 million in interest (net of taxes) and was a net repayer of debt, leaving it with €3,069.0 million in free cash flow available to equity holders. The company distributed a smaller amount of cash to its shareholders – €2,127 million in dividends – causing an increase in the company's cash balance of about €942 million. During the years 2013 through 2017, Inditex's cash balance change averaged €240 million, equivalent to around 5 percent of its cash balance. Inditex's dividend payout thus seems to be consistent with its growth rate; that is, also after making all necessary investments in non-current assets and working capital to support the company's growth plans, the excess cash flow left is sufficient to sustain its dividend policy.

# SUMMARY

This chapter presents two key tools of financial analysis: ratio analysis and cash flow analysis. Both these tools allow the analyst to examine a firm's performance and its financial condition, given its strategy and goals. Ratio analysis involves assessing the firm's income statement and balance sheet data. Cash flow analysis relies on the firm's cash flow statement.

The starting point for ratio analysis is the company's ROE. The next step is to evaluate the three drivers of ROE, which are net profit margin, asset turnover, and financial leverage. Net profit margin reflects a firm's operating management, asset turnover reflects its investment management, and financial leverage reflects its liability management. Each of these areas can be further probed by examining a number of ratios. For example, common-sized income statement analysis allows a detailed examination of a firm's net margins. Similarly, turnover of key working capital accounts, like accounts receivable, inventories, and accounts payable, and turnover of the firm's fixed assets allow further examination of a firm's asset turnover. Finally, short-term liquidity ratios, debt policy ratios, and coverage ratios provide a means of examining a firm's financial leverage.

A firm's sustainable growth rate – the rate at which it can grow without altering its operating, investment, and financing policies – is determined by its ROE and its dividend policy. The concept of sustainable growth provides a way to integrate the ratio analysis and to evaluate whether a firm's growth strategy is sustainable. If a firm's plans call for growing at a rate above its current sustainable rate, then the analyst can examine which of the firm's ratios is likely to change in the future.

Cash flow analysis supplements ratio analysis in examining a firm's operating activities, investment management, and financial risks. Firms reporting in conformity with IFRS Standards are currently required to report a cash flow statement summarizing their operating, investment, and financing cash flows. Since there are wide variations across firms in the way cash flow data are reported, analysts often use a standard format to recast cash flow data. We discussed in this chapter one such cash flow model. This model allows the analyst to assess whether a firm's operations generate cash flow before investments in operating working capital, and how much cash is being invested in the firm's working capital. It also enables the analyst to calculate the firm's free cash flow after making long-term investments, which is an indication of the firm's ability to meet its debt and dividend payments. Finally, the cash flow analysis shows how the firm is financing itself, and whether its financing patterns are too risky.

The insights gained from analyzing a firm's financial ratios and its cash flows are valuable in forecasts of the firm's future prospects.

## Core concepts

**Alternative approach to ROE decomposition**    Decomposition of return on equity into NOPAT margin, asset turnover, return on non-operating investments, financial spread, and financial leverage. Return on net operating assets is the product of NOPAT margin and asset turnover. Return on invested capital is the weighted average of the returns on operating assets and non-operating investments. The financial leverage gain is the product of financial spread and financial leverage.

$$\text{ROE} = \left[ \frac{\text{NOPAT}}{\text{Revenue}} \times \frac{\text{Revenue}}{\text{Net operating assets}} \right] \times \frac{\text{Net operating assets}}{\text{Business assets}}$$

$$+ \left[ \frac{\text{NIPAT}}{\text{Non-operating investments}} \right] \times \frac{\text{Non-operating investments}}{\text{Business assets}}$$

$$+ \text{Spread} \times \frac{\text{Debt}}{\text{Equity}}$$

$$\begin{aligned}
&&&\text{Return on net operating assets }\times \frac{\text{Net operating assets}}{\text{Business assets}}\\
&=&&+\text{Return on non-operating investments}\times \frac{\text{Non-operating investments}}{\text{Business assets}}\\
&&&+\text{Spread}\times \frac{\text{Debt}}{\text{Equity}}\\
&=&&\text{Return on invested capital}+\text{Spread}\times \frac{\text{Debt}}{\text{Equity}}\\
&=&&\text{Return on invested capital}+\text{Financial leverage gain}
\end{aligned}$$

where

$$\text{Spread}=\text{Return on invested capital}-\frac{\text{Interest expense after tax}}{\text{Debt}}$$

**Asset turnover analysis**    Decomposition of asset turnover into its components, with the objective of identifying the drivers of (changes in) a firm's asset turnover and assessing the efficiency of a firm's investment management. The asset turnover analysis typically distinguishes between working capital turnover (receivables, inventories, and payables) and non-current operating assets turnover (PP&E and intangible assets).

**Cross-sectional comparison**    Comparison of the ratios of one firm to those of one or more other firms from the same industry.

**Financial leverage analysis**    Analysis of the risk related to a firm's current liabilities and mix of non-current debt and equity. The primary considerations in the analysis of financial leverage are whether the financing strategy (1) matches the firm's business risk and (2) optimally balances the risks (e.g., financial distress risk) and benefits (e.g., tax shields, management discipline).

**Profit margin analysis**    Decomposition of the profit margin into its components, typically using common-sized income statements. The objective of profit margin analysis is to identify the drivers of (changes in) a firm's margins and assess the efficiency of a firm's operating management. The operating expenses that impact the profit margin can be decomposed by function (e.g., cost of sales, SG&A) or by nature (e.g., cost of materials, personnel expense, depreciation, and amortization).

**Ratio analysis**    Analysis of financial statement ratios to evaluate the four drivers of firm performance:

1  Operating policies.

2  Investment policies.

3  Financing policies.

4  Dividend policies.

**Sustainable growth rate**    The rate at which a firm can grow while keeping its profitability and financial policies unchanged.

$$\text{Sustainable growth rate}=\text{ROE}\times \left(1-\frac{\text{Cash dividends paid}}{\text{Profit or loss}}\right)$$

**Time-series comparison**    Comparison of the ratios of one firm over time.

**Traditional approach to ROE decomposition**    Decomposition of return on equity into profit margin, asset turnover, and financial leverage:

$$\text{ROE}=\frac{\text{Profit or loss}}{\text{Revenue}}\times \frac{\text{Revenue}}{\text{Assets}}\times \frac{\text{Assets}}{\text{Shareholders' equity}}$$

## Questions, exercises, and problems

1  Which of the following types of firms do you expect to have particularly high or low asset turnover? Explain why.

   - A supermarket.
   - A pharmaceutical company.
   - A jewellery retailer.
   - A steel company.

2  Which of the following types of firms do you expect to have high or low sales margins? Why?

   - A supermarket.
   - A pharmaceutical company.
   - A jewellery retailer.
   - A software company.

3  Sven Broker, an analyst with an established brokerage firm, comments: "The critical number I look at for any company is operating cash flow. If cash flows are less than earnings, I consider a company to be a poor performer and a poor investment prospect." Do you agree with this assessment? Why or why not?

4  In 2018 Dutch-Belgian food retailer Ahold-Delhaize had a return on equity of 12 percent, whereas France-based Groupe Casino's return was only 2 percent. Use the decomposed ROE framework to provide possible reasons for this difference.

5  Joe Investor asserts, "A company cannot grow faster than its sustainable growth rate." True or false? Explain why.

6  What are the reasons for a firm having lower cash from operations than working capital from operations? What are the possible interpretations of these reasons?

7  ABC Company recognizes revenue at the point of shipment. Management decides to increase revenue for the current quarter by filling all customer orders. Explain what impact this decision will have on:

   - Days' receivable for the current quarter.
   - Days' receivable for the next quarter.
   - Revenue growth for the current quarter.
   - Revenue growth for the next quarter.
   - Return on revenue for the current quarter.
   - Return on revenue for the next quarter.

8  What ratios would you use to evaluate operating leverage for a firm?

9  What are the potential benchmarks that you could use to compare a company's financial ratios? What are the pros and cons of these alternatives?

10  The International Financial Reporting Standards do not allow companies to use LIFO for inventory valuation, whereas US GAAP does allow a choice between LIFO and FIFO. In a period of rising prices, how would the following ratios be affected by the accounting decision to select LIFO, rather than FIFO, for inventory valuation?

   - Gross margin.
   - Current ratio.
   - Asset turnover.
   - Debt-to-equity ratio.
   - Average tax rate.

## Problem 1 ROE decomposition

Tesco plc is one of the world's largest food retailers. Fiscal year 2014 (the year ended February 28, 2015) was a rocky year for the retailer. The company's sales and margins had come under pressure as a result of strong competition in the industry. Further, in September 2014 company management announced that it had overstated earnings in previous fiscal years through the accelerated recognition of supplier rebates. The events led to a management change in which Dave Lewis took over as chief executive and John Allen took over as chairman. In April 2015 Dave Lewis announced a record (pre-tax) loss of £6.4 billion – one of the largest losses in UK history. This loss was attributable, at least in part, to a £4.7 billion impairment of property, plant, and equipment, a £0.7 billion impairment of (non-operating) investment assets, and a restructuring charge of £0.6 billion.

The following tables show the standardized and adjusted income statements and balance sheets of Tesco, for the years ended February 28, 2014, 2015, 2016, and 2017. Operating lease obligations have been capitalized, and the operating lease expense has been replaced with depreciation and interest expense, following the procedure described in Chapter 4. Further, to help you better analyze the retail activities of Tesco, the net assets of Tesco Bank have been included as one separate balance sheet item, labelled "Net investment in Tesco Bank"; Tesco Bank's pre-tax profit is separately reported in the income statement.

Tesco's statutory tax rate was 23.1 percent in 2013, 21.2 percent in 2014, 20.1 percent in 2015, and 20.0 percent in 2016.

| Standardized and adjusted income statement (£ millions) | 2016 | 2015 | 2014 | 2013 |
|---|---|---|---|---|
| Revenue | 54,905 | 52,978 | 61,260 | 62,554 |
| Cost of sales | (51,417) | (49,227) | (58,639) | (57,239) |
| SG&A | (1,734) | (1,836) | (1,827) | (1,657) |
| Operating profit | 1,754 | 1,915 | 1,488 | 3,658 |
| Net non-recurring income or expense | (450) | (564) | (6,112) | (456) |
| Pre-tax profit/loss of Tesco Bank | 77 | 161 | 194 | 194 |
| Investment and interest income | (59) | 8 | 67 | 192 |
| Interest expense | (1,177) | (1,318) | (1,329) | (1,329) |
| Profit before taxes | 145 | 202 | (6,376) | 2,259 |
| Tax expense | 87 | 54 | 657 | (347) |
| Profit after taxes | 58 | 256 | (5,719) | 1,912 |
| Profit/Loss to Non-Controlling Interest | 14 | 9 | 25 | 4 |
| Profit or loss | 72 | 265 | (5,694) | 1,916 |

| Items included in non-recurring income/expense (£ millions) | 2016 | 2015 | 2014 | 2013 |
|---|---|---|---|---|
| Impairment of net non-current operating assets | (31) | (440) | (4,677) | (734) |
| Impairment of non-operating investments | 0 | 0 | (712) | 0 |
| Restructuring costs | (199) | (126) | (566) | 0 |
| Reversal of commercial income recognized in previous years | 0 | 0 | (208) | 0 |
| Other | (220) | 2 | 51 | 278 |

*(continued)*

| Standardized and adjusted balance sheet (£ millions) | 2016 | 2015 | 2014 | 2013 |
|---|---|---|---|---|
| Non-current tangible assets | 25,475 | 25,636 | 30,051 | 34,308 |
| Non-current intangible assets | 1,615 | 1,700 | 2,548 | 2,542 |
| Minority equity investments | 668 | 709 | 860 | 209 |
| Other non-operating investments | 385 | 430 | 312 | 392 |
| Net investment in Tesco Bank | 2,478 | 2,374 | 2,241 | 2,168 |
| Deferred tax asset | 707 | 49 | 514 | 73 |
| Derivatives | 1,589 | 1,708 | 1,699 | 1,576 |
| **Total non-current assets** | **32,917** | **32,606** | **38,225** | **41,268** |
| Trade receivables | 1,963 | 2,116 | 2,722 | 3,402 |
| Inventories | 1,475 | 1,406 | 2,121 | 2,190 |
| Other current assets | 21 | 13 | 11 | 12 |
| Cash and cash equivalents | 6,548 | 6,545 | 2,758 | 3,494 |
| **Total current assets** | **10,007** | **10,080** | **7,612** | **9,098** |
| **Assets held for sale** | **344** | **236** | **139** | **2,487** |
| **TOTAL ASSETS** | **43,268** | **42,922** | **45,976** | **52,853** |
| | | | | |
| **Shareholders' equity** | **6,438** | **8,626** | **7,071** | **14,715** |
| **Non-Controlling Interest in Equity** | **(24)** | **(10)** | **0** | **7** |
| Non-current debt | 23,373 | 21,331 | 25,256 | 22,486 |
| Deferred tax liability | 74 | 103 | 158 | 570 |
| Derivatives | 668 | 951 | 1,035 | 869 |
| Other non-current liabilities | 324 | 275 | 0 | 0 |
| **Total non-current liabilities** | **24,439** | **22,660** | **26,449** | **23,925** |
| Current debt | 4,672 | 4,293 | 4,831 | 5,595 |
| Trade payables | 5,012 | 4,527 | 5,612 | 5,508 |
| Other current liabilities | 2,560 | 2,826 | 2,008 | 1,910 |
| **Total current liabilities** | **12,244** | **11,646** | **12,451** | **13,013** |
| **Liabilities held for sale** | **171** | **0** | **5** | **1,193** |
| **TOTAL LIABILITIES AND SHAREHOLDERS' EQUITY** | **43,268** | **42,922** | **45,976** | **52,85** |

| Segment information | 2016 | 2015 | 2014 | 2013 |
|---|---|---|---|---|
| **UK and Ireland** | | | | |
| Store space (sq. ft. millions) | 43.40 | 45.07 | 45.84 | 45.29 |
| Revenue (£ billion) | 43.52 | 43.08 | 42.93 | 43.06 |
| Operating profit (£ millions) | 519 | 597 | 467 | 2,191 |
| Net operating assets (£ billion) | 9.71 | 9.88 | 8.67 | 10.80 |
| | | | | |
| **International** | | | | |
| Store space (sq. ft. millions) | 45.34 | 45.85 | 66.75 | 67.26 |
| Revenue (£ billion) | 11.38 | 9.90 | 18.33 | 19.50 |
| Operating profit (£ billion) | 421 | 314 | 729 | 930 |
| Net operating assets (£ billion) | 4.72 | 4.75 | 9.75 | 10.70 |

1  Calculate Tesco's net operating profit after tax, net investment profit after tax, interest after tax, operating working capital, net non-current operating assets, non-operating investments, business assets, debt, and capital for the years 2013–2016.

2  Decompose Tesco's return on equity for the years 2013–2016 using the traditional approach.

3  Decompose Tesco's return on equity for the years 2013–2016 using the alternative approach. What explains the difference between Tesco's return on assets and its return on net operating assets?

4  Analyze the underlying drivers of the change in Tesco's return on equity, also making use of the non-financial statistics and segment information. Which factors explain the decrease in return on equity in 2014? To what extent can you conclude that Tesco's transformation plan is effective in 2015 and 2016?

## Problem 2 Ratios of three fashion retailers

Exhibit P2 displays a selected set of financial ratios for the years 2015–2017 of three fashion retailers: US-based Gap, UK-based Next, and Japan-based Uniqlo (Fast Retailing). Using this set of ratios, analyze the retailers' financial performance.

1  The return on equity (ROE) decomposition shows that the underlying drivers of ROE performance vary across retailers. Which economic or strategic factors may explain these differences in the components of ROE?

2  How did performance trends (during the period 2015 to 2017) differ among the three retailers? Which factors contributed most to these differences?

EXHIBIT P2 Ratio analysis of Gap, Next, and Uniqlo

| ROE decomposition | Gap | | | Next | | | Uniqlo | | |
|---|---|---|---|---|---|---|---|---|---|
| | 2017 (%) | 2016 (%) | 2015 (%) | 2017 (%) | 2016 (%) | 2015 (%) | 2017 (%) | 2016 (%) | 2015 (%) |
| Net operating profit margin (including other expense/income) | 6.3 | 5.4 | 6.6 | 16.3 | 17.2 | 17.4 | 6.9 | 3.2 | 7.1 |
| Net operating profit margin (excluding other expense/income) | 6.4 | 6.1 | 6.9 | 16.4 | 17.3 | 17.6 | 6.7 | 5.9 | 6.9 |
| × Operating asset turnover | 1.63 | 1.55 | 1.55 | 1.31 | 1.35 | 1.47 | 2.94 | 2.82 | 2.77 |
| = Return on Net Operating Assets | 10.5 | 9.5 | 10.7 | 21.4 | 23.2 | 25.9 | 19.8 | 16.6 | 19.3 |
| Return on Net Operating Assets | 10.5 | 9.5 | 10.7 | 21.4 | 23.2 | 25.9 | 19.8 | 16.6 | 19.3 |
| x (Net Operating Assets/Invested Capital) | 0.89 | 0.91 | 0.92 | 0.97 | 0.98 | 0.97 | 0.50 | 0.57 | 0.64 |
| + Return on Non-Operating Investments | 1.1 | 0.5 | 0.5 | 2.1 | 1.7 | 1.5 | 0.7 | 0.4 | 0.3 |
| x (Non-Operating Investments/ Invested Capital) | 0.11 | 0.09 | 0.08 | 0.03 | 0.02 | 0.03 | 0.50 | 0.43 | 0.36 |
| = Return on Invested Capital | 9.5 | 8.7 | 9.9 | 20.9 | 22.8 | 25.2 | 10.2 | 9.7 | 12.3 |
| Spread | 7.4 | 6.7 | 8.3 | 18.3 | 20.2 | 22.9 | 9.4 | 8.6 | 11.2 |
| × Financial leverage | 2.60 | 3.04 | 2.98 | 5.43 | 6.55 | 8.22 | 0.87 | 0.61 | 0.35 |
| = Financial leverage gain | 19.2 | 20.4 | 24.7 | 99.2 | 132.0 | 187.9 | 8.2 | 5.2 | 4.0 |
| ROE = Return on Invested Capital + Financial leverage gain | 28.7 | 29.1 | 34.6 | 120.0 | 154.9 | 213.1 | 18.4 | 14.9 | 16.3 |

| Line items as a percent of revenue | Gap | | | Next | | | Uniqlo | | |
|---|---|---|---|---|---|---|---|---|---|
| | 2017 (%) | 2016 (%) | 2015 (%) | 2017 (%) | 2016 (%) | 2015 (%) | 2017 (%) | 2016 (%) | 2015 (%) |
| Revenue | 100.0 | 100.0 | 100.0 | 100.0 | 100.0 | 100.0 | 100.0 | 100.0 | 100.0 |
| Net operating expense | (89.4) | (90.0) | (89.1) | (79.9) | (78.5) | (78.0) | (89.9) | (90.7) | (89.3) |
| Non-recurring income/expense | (0.2) | (1.1) | (0.3) | (0.1) | 0.0 | (0.2) | 0.3 | (4.0) | 0.2 |
| Net operating profit before tax | 10.4 | 8.8 | 10.6 | 20.0 | 21.4 | 21.8 | 10.4 | 5.3 | 10.9 |
| Investment income | 0.0 | 0.0 | 0.0 | 0.0 | 0.0 | 0.0 | 0.0 | 0.0 | 0.0 |
| Interest income | 0.1 | 0.1 | 0.0 | 0.0 | 0.0 | 0.0 | 0.3 | 0.1 | 0.1 |
| Interest expense | (1.6) | (1.7) | (1.3) | (2.2) | (2.2) | (1.8) | (0.4) | (0.4) | (0.3) |
| Tax expense | (3.6) | (2.9) | (3.5) | (3.3) | (3.8) | (4.1) | (3.5) | (2.0) | (3.8) |
| Net profit | 5.3 | 4.4 | 5.8 | 14.6 | 15.5 | 16.0 | 6.9 | 3.0 | 7.0 |

| Operating expense line items as a percent of revenue | Gap | | | Next | | | Uniqlo | | |
|---|---|---|---|---|---|---|---|---|---|
| | 2017 (%) | 2016 (%) | 2015 (%) | 2017 (%) | 2016 (%) | 2015 (%) | 2017 (%) | 2016 (%) | 2015 (%) |
| Cost of sales | (61.7) | (63.7) | (63.8) | (66.6) | (66.2) | (65.2) | (51.2) | (51.6) | (49.5) |
| SG&A | (27.7) | (26.4) | (25.3) | (13.3) | (12.4) | (12.7) | (38.7) | (39.1) | (39.8) |

| Asset management ratios | Gap | | | Next | | | Uniqlo | | |
|---|---|---|---|---|---|---|---|---|---|
| | 2017 | 2016 | 2015 | 2017 | 2016 | 2015 | 2017 | 2016 | 2015 |
| Operating working capital/Revenu (%) | 6.2 | 6.7 | 7.9 | 25.4 | 20.9 | 16.3 | 10.7 | 10.7 | 8.6 |
| Net non-current operating assets/Revenue (%) | 55.0 | 57.9 | 56.5 | 51.3 | 53.4 | 51.7 | 23.3 | 24.8 | 27.4 |
| PP&E/Revenue (%) | 53.6 | 55.9 | 54.9 | 55.2 | 55.9 | 53.2 | 21.7 | 19.7 | 18.2 |
| Operating working capital turnover | 16.00 | 14.89 | 12.73 | 3.94 | 4.77 | 6.13 | 9.37 | 9.35 | 11.61 |
| Net non-current asset turnover | 1.82 | 1.73 | 1.77 | 1.95 | 1.87 | 1.94 | 4.30 | 4.03 | 3.65 |
| PP&E turnover | 1.86 | 1.79 | 1.82 | 1.81 | 1.79 | 1.88 | 4.61 | 5.08 | 5.50 |
| Trade receivables turnover | 51.39 | 50.29 | 56.72 | 3.83 | 4.24 | 5.00 | 39.71 | 39.72 | 36.48 |
| Days' receivables | 7.0 | 7.2 | 6.3 | 94.0 | 84.9 | 71.9 | 9.1 | 9.1 | 9.9 |
| Inventories turnover | 5.12 | 5.33 | 5.36 | 3.05 | 3.07 | 3.26 | 3.40 | 3.48 | 3.45 |
| Days' inventories | 70.4 | 67.5 | 67.2 | 118.2 | 117.1 | 110.3 | 105.7 | 103.5 | 104.4 |
| Trade payables turnover | 8.08 | 8.39 | 8.82 | 8.09 | 7.11 | 6.64 | 4.84 | 4.97 | 4.54 |
| Days' payables | 44.6 | 42.9 | 40.8 | 44.5 | 50.6 | 54.2 | 74.4 | 72.5 | 79.2 |
| Cash conversion cycle | 32.8 | 31.7 | 32.7 | 167.7 | 151.5 | 128.0 | 40.5 | 40.1 | 35.0 |

## Problem 3 The Fiat Group in 2008

In 2009, following the worldwide credit crisis, several US-based car manufacturers, such as Chrysler and General Motors, approached bankruptcy and needed to be bailed out by the US government and private investors. Italy-based Fiat Group SpA. decided to help rescue Chrysler by acquiring 20 to 35 percent of the car manufacturer's shares. In exchange, Fiat would get access to Chrysler's vehicle platforms and manufacturing facilities, which could eventually help the Italian manufacturer re-enter the US market. Following the initial rumors about private negotiations between Fiat and Chrysler and Fiat's (coinciding) announcement that it would not pay a dividend for 2008, Fiat's share price dropped by more than 25 percent in one week. The question arose whether Fiat's performance was really stronger than Chrysler's.

The following tables show the financial statements of the Fiat Group SpA. for the fiscal years 2006–2008. In all three years, Fiat earned a return on equity in excess of 12 percent. Decompose Fiat's return on equity and evaluate the drivers of the company's performance during the period 2006–2008. What trends can you identify in the company's performance? What has been the likely effect of the credit crisis on Fiat? (To simplify the analysis, classify Fiat's customer financing assets as non-operating investments; revenues of these financing activities are included in interest income.)

| Income statement (€ millions) | 2008 | 2007 | 2006 |
|---|---|---|---|
| Revenue | 58,421 | 57,550 | 50,755 |
| Cost of sales | −48,646 | −48,168 | −42,991 |
| Selling, general, and administrative costs | −5,075 | −4,924 | −4,697 |
| Research and development costs | −1,497 | −1,536 | −1,401 |
| Other income (expenses) | −23 | 88 | 105 |
| **Trading profit** | **3,180** | **3,010** | **1,771** |
| Gains (losses) on the disposal of investments | 20 | 190 | 607 |
| Restructuring costs | −165 | −105 | −450 |
| Other unusual income (expenses) | −245 | −166 | −47 |
| **Operating profit/(loss)** | **2,790** | **2,929** | **1,881** |
| Interest income | 1,188 | 1,301 | 1,372 |
| Interest expense | −1,526 | −1,651 | −1,782 |
| Other financial income (expenses) | -427 | 9 | 14 |
| Result from investments | 162 | 185 | 156 |
| **Profit before taxes** | **2,187** | **2,773** | **1,641** |
| Income taxes | −466 | −719 | −490 |
| **Profit from continuing operations** | **1,721** | **2,054** | **1,151** |
| Profit from discontinued operations | 0 | 0 | 0 |
| **Profit or loss** | **1,721** | **2,054** | **1,151** |

| Balance sheet (€ millions) | 2008 | 2007 | 2006 |
|---|---|---|---|
| Intangible assets | 7,048 | 6,523 | 6,421 |
| Property, plant, and equipment | 12,607 | 11,246 | 10,540 |
| Investment property | 0 | 10 | 19 |
| Investments and other financial assets | 2,177 | 2,214 | 2,280 |
| Leased assets | 505 | 396 | 247 |
| Defined benefit plan assets | 120 | 31 | 11 |
| Deferred tax assets | 2,386 | 1,892 | 1,860 |
| **Total non-current assets** | **24,843** | **22,312** | **21,378** |
| Inventories | 11,346 | 9,990 | 8,548 |
| Trade receivables | 4,390 | 4,384 | 4,944 |
| Receivables from financing activities | 13,136 | 12,268 | 11,743 |
| Current tax receivables | 770 | 1,153 | 808 |
| Other current assets | 2,600 | 2,291 | 2,278 |
| Current financial assets | 967 | 1,016 | 637 |
| Cash and cash equivalents | 3,683 | 6,639 | 7,736 |
| **Total current assets** | **36,892** | **37,741** | **36,694** |
| Assets held for sale | 37 | 83 | 332 |
| **TOTAL ASSETS** | **61,772** | **60,136** | **58,404** |
| **Shareholders' equity** | **10,354** | **10,606** | **9,362** |
| **Non-controlling interest in equity** | **747** | **673** | **674** |
| Employee benefits | 3,366 | 3,597 | 3,761 |
| Other provisions | 4,778 | 4,965 | 4,850 |
| Asset-backed financing | 6,663 | 6,820 | 8,344 |
| Other debt | 14,716 | 11,131 | 11,844 |
| Other financial liabilities | 1,202 | 188 | 105 |
| Trade payables | 13,258 | 14,725 | 12,603 |
| Current tax payables | 331 | 631 | 311 |
| Deferred tax liabilities | 170 | 193 | 263 |
| Other current liabilities | 6,185 | 6,572 | 5,978 |
| Liabilities held for sale | 2 | 35 | 309 |
| **TOTAL SHAREHOLDERS' EQUITY AND LIABILITIES** | **61,772** | **60,136** | **58,404** |

*(continued)*

| Cash flow statement (€ millions) | 2008 | 2007 | 2006 |
|---|---|---|---|
| Profit or loss | 1,721 | 2,054 | 1,151 |
| Amortization and depreciation (net of vehicles sold under buy-back commitments) | 2,901 | 2,738 | 2,969 |
| (Gains) losses on disposal | −50 | −297 | −575 |
| Other non-cash items | 253 | −138 | 7 |
| Dividends received | 84 | 81 | 69 |
| Change in provisions | −161 | 6 | 229 |
| Change in deferred taxes | −490 | −157 | −26 |
| Change in items due to buy-back commitments | -88 | 34 | −18 |
| Change in working capital | −3,786 | 1,588 | 812 |
| **Cash flows from (used in) operating activities** | **384** | **5,909** | **4,618** |
| **Cash flows from (used in) investment activities** | **−6,310** | **−4,601** | **−1,390** |
| **Cash flows from (used in) financing activities** | **3,127** | **-2,375** | **−1,731** |
| Translation exchange differences | −159 | −33 | −173 |
| **Total change in cash and cash equivalents** | **−2,958** | **−1,100** | **1,324** |

## Problem 4 Ahold versus Delhaize

On June 24, 2015, two grocery retailers, Netherlands-based Ahold and Belgium-based Delhaize, announced their intention to engage in a merger of equals. By merging their activities, the two companies hoped to achieve €500 million of annual cost savings as well as increase their market power in the United States, where they earned about 60 percent of their revenues. The merger of the two companies would create the fourth largest grocery retailer in Europe and the fifth largest grocery retailer in the United States. The terms of the deal implied that Delhaize shareholders would receive 4.75 Ahold shares in exchange for each of their shares. Further, Ahold would return €1 billion to its shareholders before completion of the merger with Delhaize, as a consequence of which Ahold shareholders would own close to 61 percent of all shares after the merger. For comparison, at the end of fiscal year 2014, Ahold's total assets comprised only about 54 percent of the two companies' assets combined; similarly, Ahold's book equity comprised about 47 percent of combined book equity.

Using Ahold's and Delhaize's financial statements, an analyst prepared the following set of standardized statements. To better understand the differences between and similarities of the two merging companies as well as understand why Ahold shareholders would receive a larger stake in the combined company than Delhaize shareholders, the analyst wanted to compare the pre-merger performance of both companies. She had jotted down a few notes that could help her to interpret the numbers:

- In 2014 and 2013 Ahold's (Delhaize's) investment property had a book value of €560 and €543 million (€84 and €100 million), respectively.
- At the end of fiscal 2013 Ahold held an amount of €1,467 million in short-term deposits after having sold its 60 percent equity stake in the Swedish supermarket chain ICA. In 2014 Ahold used the proceeds of the ICA sale to increase its share buy-back program from €500 million to €2 billion.
- For both companies intangible assets have arisen from acquisitions in Europe and the United States.
- The total number of stores operated by Ahold amounted to 3,206 in 2014 and 3,131 in 2013; Delhaize operated 3,468 stores in 2014 and 3,534 stores in 2013. Ahold had a workforce of

126 thousand full time equivalent (fte) in 2014 (123 thousand fte in 2013); Delhaize had a workforce of 114 thousand in 2014 (121 thousand fte in 2013).

1  Decompose Ahold's and Delhaize's returns on equity (ROE) in 2014 and 2013. Which economic or strategic factors may explain the observed differences in the components of ROE? Which factors may explain why Ahold shareholders received a majority stake in the new company?

2  On the day prior to the announcement, Ahold's share price was €18.96. Based on this share price, the acquisition price for Delhaize amounted to €9,260 million. Prepare pro-forma financial statements and a pro-forma ROE decomposition for the combined company for fiscal 2014. When doing so, assume for simplicity that Delhaize's assets and liabilities have been reported at their fair values and take into account the anticipated annual (pre-tax) cost savings of €500 million. What will be the effect of the merger on the companies' ratios?

| | Ahold | | Delhaize | |
|---|---|---|---|---|
| Standardized balance sheet (€ millions) | 2014 | 2013 | 2014 | 2013 |
| Non-current intangible assets | 1,763 | 1,563 | 3,910 | 3,691 |
| Non-current tangible assets | 6,150 | 5,712 | 4,015 | 3,973 |
| Derivatives – asset | — | — | 9 | 1 |
| Minority equity investments | 206 | 197 | 30 | 24 |
| Other non-operating investments | 1,077 | 991 | 162 | 170 |
| Deferred tax asset | 494 | 411 | 46 | 71 |
| **Total non-current assets** | **9,690** | **8,874** | **8,172** | **7,930** |
| Cash and cash equivalents | 1,947 | 4,016 | 1,600 | 1,149 |
| Trade receivables | 728 | 665 | 623 | 618 |
| Inventories | 1,589 | 1,450 | 1,399 | 1,353 |
| Other current assets | 177 | 109 | 273 | 294 |
| **Total current assets** | **4,441** | **6,240** | **3,895** | **3,414** |
| **Assets held for sale** | **7** | **28** | **60** | **250** |
| **Total assets** | **14,138** | **15,142** | **12,127** | **11,594** |
| Trade payables | 2,655 | 2,387 | 2,112 | 1,993 |
| Current debt | 520 | 453 | 258 | 381 |
| Other current liabilities | 1,291 | 1,254 | 770 | 712 |
| **Total current liabilities** | **4,466** | **4,094** | **3,140** | **3,086** |
| Non-current debt | 4,402 | 4,122 | 3,108 | 2,862 |
| Derivatives - liability | — | — | 26 | 8 |
| Deferred tax liability | 150 | 123 | 302 | 443 |
| Other non-current liabilities (non-interest-bearing) | 276 | 235 | 58 | 64 |
| **Total non-current liabilities** | **4,828** | **4,480** | **3,494** | **3,377** |
| **Ordinary shareholders' equity** | **4,844** | **6,520** | **5,447** | **5,068** |
| **Non-controlling interests** | **—** | **—** | **6** | **5** |
| **Liabilities held for sale** | **—** | **48** | **40** | **58** |
| **Total equity and liabilities** | **14,138** | **15,142** | **12,127** | **11,594** |

*(continued)*

| Standardized income statement (€ millions) | Ahold | | Delhaize | |
|---|---|---|---|---|
| | 2014 | 2013 | 2014 | 2013 |
| Revenue | 32,774 | 32,615 | 21,361 | 20,593 |
| Cost of sales | (24,088) | (23,933) | (16,222) | (15,579) |
| SG&A | (7,425) | (7,380) | (4,338) | (4,221) |
| Other operating income, net of other operating expense | — | — | 72 | 69 |
| Other income, net of other expense | (11) | (63) | (436) | (317) |
| Investment and interest income | 30 | 17 | 20 | 13 |
| Interest expense | (241) | (298) | (202) | (201) |
| Tax expense | (248) | (153) | (66) | (85) |
| Profit after taxes | 791 | 805 | 189 | 272 |
| Profit/loss to non-controlling interest | - | - | (1) | (3) |
| Net gain/loss from discontinued operations | (197) | 1,732 | (99) | (90) |
| Profit or loss | 594 | 2,537 | 89 | 179 |
| Present value of operating lease commitments (@11%) | 2,715 | 2,413 | 835 | 821 |
| Operating lease expense | 690 | 705 | 296 | 278 |
| . . . of which implicit interest (estimate) | 282 | 270 | 91 | 99 |
| . . . of which implicit depreciation (estimate) | 408 | 435 | 205 | 179 |
| Statutory tax rate | 25% | 25% | 34% | 34% |
| Dividends | 414 | 457 | 158 | 142 |
| Share repurchases | 1,232 | 768 | 0 | 0 |

## NOTES

1 For Hennes & Mauritz, we will call the fiscal year ending November 2016 as the year 2016, and the fiscal year ending November 2017 as the year 2017. For Inditex, we will call the fiscal year ending January 2017 as the year 2016, and the fiscal year ending January 2018 as the year 2017.

2 A spreadsheet containing the three versions of the financial statements of Hennes & Mauritz and Inditex as well as all ratios described throughout this chapter is available on the companion website of this book. This spreadsheet also shows how we capitalized omitted operating lease assets on Hennes & Mauritz's and Inditex's balance sheet before calculating all ratios.

3 We discuss in greater detail in Chapter 8 how to estimate a company's cost of equity capital. Analysts following Hennes & Mauritz and Inditex estimated their equity betas at around 0.7 to 0.9 in 2017. The historical return on long-term treasury bonds was approximately 4 percent. If one assumes a risk premium of 5 percent, the two firms' cost of equity is between 7.5 and 8.5 percent. Lower assumed risk premiums will, of course, lead to lower estimates of equity capital.

4 Both Hennes & Mauritz and Inditex have a solid financial position and a relatively low cost of debt. Given the level of leverage, the weighted average cost of capital will be lower than the cost of equity. We will discuss in Chapter 8 how to estimate a company's weighted average cost of capital.

5 See *Taxes and Business Strategy* by Myron Scholes and Mark Wolfson (Englewood Cliffs, NJ: Prentice-Hall, 1992).

6 Average revenue (or average cost of sales) is calculated as annual revenue (or annual cost of sales) divided by the

number of days in the year. There are a number of issues related to the calculation of turnover ratios in practice. First, in calculating all the turnover ratios, the assets used in the calculations can either be beginning of the year values, year-end values or an average of the beginning and ending balances in a year. We use the average values in our calculations. Second, strictly speaking, one should use credit sales to calculate trade receivables turnover and days' receivables. But since it is usually difficult to obtain data on credit sales, total sales are used instead. Similarly, in calculating trade payables turnover or days' payables, cost of sales (or cost of materials) is substituted for purchases for data availability reasons. Third, the ratios for income statements classified by function differ from those for income statements classified by nature. Turnover ratios for the two types of statements are therefore not perfectly comparable.

7  See Christian Leuz, Dominic Deller, and Michael Stubenrath, "An international comparison of accounting-based payout restrictions in the United States, United Kingdom, and Germany," *Accounting and Business Research* 28 (1998): 111–129.

8  Changes in cash and cash equivalents are excluded because this is the amount being explained by the cash flow statement. Changes in current debt and the current portion of non-current debt are excluded because these accounts represent financing flows, not operating flows.

## Appendix: Hennes & Mauritz AB financial statements

**Standardized and Adjusted Statements of Earnings (SEK millions)**

| Fiscal year ended November 30 | 2017 | 2016 | 2015 |
|---|---|---|---|
| **Revenue** | **200,004** | **192,267** | **180,861** |
| Operating expenses | (177,878) | (166,747) | (152,516) |
| **Operating profit** | **22,125.8** | **25,520** | **28,345** |
| Investment income | 0 | 0 | 0 |
| Net non-recurring income or expense | 0 | 0 | 0 |
| Interest income | 281 | 224 | 310 |
| Interest expense | (1,598) | (1,705) | (1,413) |
| **Profit before taxes** | **20,809** | **24,039** | **27,242** |
| Tax expense | (4,625) | (5,403) | (6,344) |
| **Profit after taxes** | **16,184** | **18,636** | **20,898** |
| Profit/Loss to non-controlling Interest | 0 | 0 | 0 |
| **Profit/loss to ordinary shareholders** | **16,184** | **18,636** | **20,898** |
| **OPERATING EXPENSES** | | | |
| Classification by function: | | | |
| Cost of sales (function) | (91,914) | (86,090) | (77,694) |
| SG&A (function) | (85,964) | (80,657) | (74,822) |
| Other operating income, net of other operating expenses (function) | 0 | 0 | 0 |
| Classification by nature: | | | |
| Personnel expenses (nature) | (35,634) | (32,561) | (29,952) |
| Depreciation and amortization (nature) | (26,070) | (26,480) | (25,571) |
| Other operating income, net of other operating expenses (nature) | (24,996) | (22,463) | (20,024) |

Source: 2017–2015 annual reports of Hennes & Mauritz AB and authors' calculations.

**Standardized and Adjusted Balance Sheets (SEK millions)**

| Fiscal year ended November 30 | 2017 | 2016 | 2015 |
|---|---|---|---|
| **ASSETS** | | | |
| Non-current tangible assets | 113,191 | 114,629 | 111,693 |
| Non-current intangible assets | 6,451 | 4,717 | 3,455 |
| Minority equity investments | 0 | 0 | 0 |
| Other non-operating investments | 1,039 | 1,014 | 862 |
| Deferred tax asset | 2,916 | 2,862 | 2,338 |
| Derivatives – asset | 497 | 848 | 707 |
| **Total non-current assets** | **124,094** | **124,070** | **119,055** |
| Inventories | 33,712 | 31,732 | 24,833 |
| Trade receivables | 5,297 | 4,881 | 4,021 |
| Other current assets | 6,522 | 3,756 | 3,025 |
| Cash and cash equivalents | 9,718 | 9,446 | 12,950 |
| **Total current assets** | **55,249** | **49,815** | **44,829** |
| **Assets held for sale** | **0** | **0** | **0** |
| **Total assets** | **179,343** | **173,885** | **163,884** |
| **LIABILITIES AND SHAREHOLDERS'EQUITY** | | | |
| **Ordinary shareholders' equity** | **59,713** | **61,236** | **58,049** |
| **Non-Controlling Interest in Equity** | **0** | **0** | **0** |
| **Preference shares** | **0** | **0** | **0** |
| Non-current debt | 73,576 | 76,046 | 78,520 |
| Deferred tax liability | 5,331 | 4,898 | 4,378 |
| Derivatives – liability | 903 | 1,176 | 302 |
| Other non-current liabilities (non-interest bearing) | 0 | 0 | 0 |
| **Non-current liabilities** | **79,810** | **82,120** | **83,200** |
| Trade payables | 7,215 | 7,262 | 6,000 |
| Other current liabilities | 22,735 | 21,140 | 16,635 |
| Current debt | 9,870 | 2,127 | 0 |
| **Current liabilities** | **39,820** | **30,529** | **22,635** |
| **Liabilities held for sale** | **0** | **0** | **0** |
| **Total liabilities and shareholders' equity** | **179,343** | **173,885** | **163,884** |

Source: 2017–2015 annual reports of Hennes & Mauritz AB and authors' calculations.

**Standardized and Adjusted Statements of Cash Flows (SEK millions)**

| Fiscal year ended November 30 | 2017 | 2016 | 2015 |
|---|---|---|---|
| Profit before interest and tax | 22,126 | 25,520 | 28,345 |
| Taxes paid plus tax shield on interest paid | (6,403) | (4,845) | (7,392) |
| Non-operating losses (gains) | 0 | 0 | 0 |
| Non-current operating accruals | 26,059 | 26,471 | 25,599 |
| **Operating cash flow before working capital investments** | **41,782** | **47,146** | **46,552** |
| Net (investments in) or liquidation of operating working capital | (1,648) | (3,390) | (2,580) |
| **Operating cash flow before investment in non-current assets** | **40,134** | **43,756** | **43,972** |
| Interest received | 281 | 224 | 310 |
| Dividends received | 0 | 0 | 0 |
| Net (investments in) or liquidation of operating or investment non-current assets | (27,553) | (29,608) | (34,111) |
| **Free cash flow available to debt and equity** | **12,862** | **14,372** | **10,171** |
| Interest paid after tax | (1,246) | (1,330) | (1,043) |
| Net debt (repayment) or issuance | 5,095 | (697) | 5,329 |
| **Free cash flow available to equity** | **16,711** | **12,345** | **14,457** |
| Dividend (payments) | (16,137) | (16,137) | (16,137) |
| Net share (repurchase) or issuance | 0 | 0 | 0 |
| **Net increase (decrease) in cash balance** | **574** | **(3,792)** | **(1,680)** |

Source: 2017–2015 annual reports of Hennes & Mauritz AB and authors' calculations.

**Condensed Statements of Earnings (SEK millions)**

| Fiscal year ended November 30 | 2017 | 2016 | 2015 |
|---|---|---|---|
| **Revenue** | **200,004.0** | **192,267.0** | **180,861.0** |
| **Net operating profit after tax** | 17,211.1 | 19,790.8 | 21,758.4 |
| Profit or loss | 16,184.0 | 18,636.0 | 20,898.0 |
| − Investment profit after tax | (219.2) | (174.7) | (241.8) |
| + Interest expense after tax | 1,246.3 | 1,329.5 | 1,102.2 |
| = **Net operating profit after tax** | **17,211.1** | **19,790.8** | **21,758.4** |
| of which: **Net other expense after tax** | 0 | 0 | 0 |
| = Net other expense (income) | 0 | 0 | 0 |
| × (1 − Tax rate) | 78% | 78% | 73.7% |
| = **Net other expense after tax** | 0 | 0 | 0 |
| + **Net investment profit after tax** | **219.2** | **174.7** | **241.8** |
| = Investment and interest income | 281.0 | 224.0 | 310.0 |
| × (1 − Tax rate) | 78.0% | 78.0% | 78.0% |
| = **Net investment profit after tax** | **219.2** | **174.7** | **241.8** |

| | | | |
|---|---|---|---|
| **– Interest expense after tax** | **1,246.3** | **1,329.5** | **1,102.2** |
| = Interest expense | 1,597.8 | 1,704.5 | 1,413.1 |
| × (1 – Tax rate) | 78.0% | 78.0% | 78.0% |
| = **Interest expense after tax** | **1,246.3** | **1,329.5** | **1,102.2** |
| = **Profit or loss** | **16,184.0** | **18,636.0** | **20,898.0** |

Source: Authors' calculations.

**Condensed Balance Sheets (SEK millions)**

| Fiscal year ended November 30 | 2017 | 2016 | 2015 |
|---|---|---|---|
| **Ending operating working capital** | | | |
| Operating cash | 9,718.0 | 9,446.0 | 9,043.1 |
| + Trade receivables | 5,297.0 | 4,881.0 | 4,021.0 |
| + Inventories | 33,712.0 | 31,732.0 | 24,833.0 |
| + Other current assets | 6,522.0 | 3,756.0 | 3,025.0 |
| – Trade payables | 7,215.0 | 7,262.0 | 6,000.0 |
| – Other current liabilities | 22,735.0 | 21,140.0 | 16,635.0 |
| = **Ending operating working capital** | **25,299.0** | **21,413.0** | **18,287.1** |
| **+ Ending net non-current operating assets** | | | |
| Non-current tangible assets | 113,190.7 | 114,628.8 | 111,693.0 |
| + Non-current intangible assets | 6,451.0 | 4,717.0 | 3,455.0 |
| + Derivatives (assets net of liabilities) | (406.0) | (328.0) | 405.0 |
| – Deferred tax liabilities (net of assets) | 2,415.0 | 2,036.0 | 2,040.0 |
| – Other non-current liabilities (non-interest – bearing) | 0.0 | 0.0 | 0.0 |
| = **Ending net non-current operating assets** | **116,820.7** | **116,981.8** | **113,513.0** |
| **+ Ending non-operating investments** | | | |
| Excess cash | 0.0 | 0.0 | 3,907.0 |
| Minority equity investments | 0.0 | 0.0 | 0.0 |
| + Other non-operating investments | 1,039.0 | 1,014.0 | 862.0 |
| = **Ending non-operating investments** | **1,039.0** | **1,014.0** | **4,769.0** |
| = **Total business assets** | **143,158.7** | **139,408.8** | **136,569.0** |
| **Ending Debt** | | | |
| Current debt | 9,870.0 | 2,127.0 | 0.0 |
| + Non-current debt | 73,575.7 | 76,045.8 | 78,520.0 |
| + Preference shares | 0.0 | 0.0 | 0.0 |
| = **Ending debt** | **83,445.7** | **78,172.8** | **78,520.0** |

**+ Ending group equity**

| | | | |
|---|---:|---:|---:|
| Ordinary shareholders' equity | 59,713.0 | 61,236.0 | 58,049.0 |
| + Non-controlling interest in equity | 0.0 | 0.0 | 0.0 |
| − Net assets held for sale | 0.0 | 0.0 | 0.0 |
| **= Group equity** | **59,713.0** | **61,236.0** | **58,049.0** |
| **= Invested capital** | **143,158.7** | **139,408.8** | **136,569.0** |

Source: Authors' calculations.

# CASE

# Carrefour S.A.

Analyst Chrystelle Moreau of Leblanc Investissements, a small Paris-based investment firm, glanced through the annual report of Groupe Carrefour for the fiscal year 2017 that she had just downloaded. She had just seen the retailer's stock price drop by 8 percent, shortly after the company's announcement of its most recent annual results. The announcement had truly surprised the analyst, as Carrefour had seemed to be on a road towards recovery. The past decade had been a worrisome period for Carrefour's shareholders; during the period the company's share price had decreased by almost 60 percent. However, after Georges Plassat took over as Carrefour's Chairman and Chief Executive Officer (CEO) in 2012 and announced his new strategy, getting Carrefour "back to basics," several signs – such as a solid return on equity of 9 to 12 percent – had pointed in the direction of a turnaround.

During the 1990s Carrefour had been one of Moreau's favourite shares. The company had created a great reputation for its broad assortment and low prices, and had shown an outstanding share price performance. During the first half of the 2000s, however, Carrefour's share price fell from about €80 to €40, despite the fact that the company consistently earned returns on equity in excess of 17 percent. Carrefour's core strengths had long been its low prices, its wide product offering, and the convenience of finding all of its products in one place, that is, in its hypermarkets.[1] However, the company's business model gradually became outdated, particularly as internet shopping became increasing popular. Carrefour also lost market share in the food segment of the retail market, presumably because, as some analysts argued, the company's relatively expensive hypermarkets prevented it from being sufficiently price competitive.

In 2005 Jose Luis Duran took over from Daniel Bernard as the CEO of Carrefour, determined to put an end to Carrefour's over-aggressive expansion abroad and its incoherent pricing strategy in France.[2] However, in 2008, soon after the privately held investment firm Colony Capital and French billionaire Bernard Arnault had acquired a 14 percent stake in Carrefour (and 20 percent of the voting rights), they forced out Duran and welcomed Lars Olofsson as the new CEO in an effort to speed up the company's change process. Two pillars of Olofsson's turnaround plan were the offering and marketing of competitive low prices and the realization of cost savings. Olofsson also developed plans to streamline the company, resulting in, for example, the spin-off the retailer's hard discount division (Dia) in 2011. Olofsson's actions did not, however, help to improve Carrefour's financial performance. During the fiscal years 2009 through 2011, the retailer's share price decreased by 26 percent (adjusted for the Dia spin-off). Having seen the value of their investment more than halve since acquisition, in early 2012 Arnault and Colony Capital intervened and replaced Olofsson with George Plassat, the former Chairman and CEO of France-based apparel company Vivarte.

Plassat faced several challenges when he started. Not only had Carrefour's hypermarket concept proven to be difficult to revive, consumers' perception that the retailer lacked price competitiveness also appeared to be very persistent. Furthermore, shareholders Colony Capital and Arnault were seen by outsiders as stimulants of managerial myopia.[3] Finally, Carrefour's management seemed to have insufficient oversight of its international

---

Professor Erik Peek prepared this case. The case is intended solely as the basis for class discussion and is not intended to serve as an endorsement, source of primary data, or illustration of effective or ineffective management.

[1] See "Bread, Cheese, New Boss?" *The Economist,* January 14, 2012.
[2] See "Carrefour at Crossroads," *The Economist,* October 20, 2005.
[3] See "New Carrefour Chief Faces Unenviable Task," *Financial Times,* January 26, 2012.

operations, in 32 countries, as illustrated, for example, by the occurrence of accounting irregularities at the company's Brazilian business. Plassat's plan to remediate the situation was to cut costs, withdraw from several international markets, and give more authority to regional store managers to help them respond to local demands.[4] Between 2011 and 2015, Carrefour's return on equity (after excluding non-recurring items) increased from 3.3 percent to 11.8 percent, supporting a gradual increase in dividends from 52 cents to 70 cents per share.

Following the 2017 earnings announcement, the analyst was reconsidering Carrefour's inclusion in her firm's high-dividend yield fund. Carrefour's dividend yield had been close to a respectable level of 3 percent in 2015 and 2016. However, Carrefour's management now proposed to cut the company's dividends by a third, a drastic decision that the Carrefour's management had taken earlier in 2011. Moreau wondered which factors explained this decision. In particular, she wanted to get a better understanding of what had caused Carrefour's performance improvement during the past years as well as the company's current financial position. Furthermore, she wondered whether Carrefour would remain an attractive stock to her firm's high-dividend yield fund or, if not, whether it could become attractive again in the near term.

## Company background

France-based food and nonfood retailer Carrefour was established in 1959 by the Fournier and Defforey families and opened its first hypermarket in Sainte-Genévieve-de-Bois in 1963. The hypermarket concept was the store concept that Carrefour would eventually become most famous for. The typical characteristic of such hypermarkets is that they offer a wide assortment of food as well as nonfood products at economic prices and are of a much greater size than the traditional supermarkets. Specifically, the size of hypermarkets can range from 2,400 to 23,000 square metres. In comparison, Carrefour's regular supermarkets, operating under the name Carrefour Market, and convenience stores, such as the Carrefour City and Carrefour Express stores, have sales areas ranging from 90 to 4,000 square metres.

In 1979 Carrefour opened its first hard discount stores under the "Ed" banner in France and under the "Dia" banner in Spain. The hard discount stores sold a much smaller variety of products than the hypermarkets (on average 800 products versus 20,000 to 80,000) in a much smaller store space (between 200 and 800 square metres) at discount prices. Some of the discount products were sold under its own brand names, such as the Dia brand name. After having transformed its Ed stores into Dia stores at the end of the 2000s, Carrefour spun off its hard discount division in 2011. To achieve this, the company paid out a special dividend of one Dia share for each ordinary Carrefour share on July 5, 2011, leading to a decrease in the company's market capitalization by close to €2.3 billion (or 12 percent).

During the 1970s and 1980s, Carrefour expanded across the oceans and established hypermarkets in, for example, Brazil (1975), Argentina (1982), and Taiwan (1989). The international and intercontinental expansion of Carrefour took off especially in the 1990s when Carrefour opened a large number of hypermarkets in Southern Europe (Greece, Italy, and Turkey), Eastern Europe (Poland), Asia (China, Hong Kong, Korea, Malaysia, Singapore, and Thailand), and Latin America (Mexico, Chile, and Colombia). The company's intercontinental expansion primarily occurred through the opening of hypermarkets. Most of Carrefour's smaller supermarkets were located throughout Europe.

In addition to its traditional food and nonfood retailing activities, the company soon offered travelling, financial, and insurance services to its customers in Brazil, France, and Spain. For example, Carrefour has its own payment card, the "Pass" card, which it introduced in the early 1980s. In the beginning, the Pass card offered customers priority at store check-outs and allowed them to pay their bills in installments. Later the card became linked to a credit card and customers could borrow money for out-of-store purchases. By the end of 2017 Carrefour's financial services unit had €6.3 billion in credit outstanding throughout the world.

---

[4] See "Carrefour Unveils Turnround Plan," *Financial Times,* August 30, 2012.

One of the key events in Carrefour's history took place in 1999, when it merged with Promodès, a large French food retailer that owned the Champion supermarket chain. At the time of the merger, Carrefour and Promodès were, respectively, the sixth and ninth largest retailers in the world and held market shares of around 18 and 12 percent in France. After the merger the combined company, which continued under the name Carrefour, became Europe's largest retailer, the world's second largest retailer, and the world's most international supermarket chain. An important trigger for the merger was that in the late 1990s, US-based Walmart, the world's largest retailer, was expanding its operations to Europe and posed a potential threat to the French retailer's strong position in its home market.

The integration of the operations of Promodès and Carrefour went slowly, and the merger of the two retailers was the start of a difficult period. Immediately following the merger, Carrefour acquired a few other supermarket chains, such as Norte in Argentina, GS in Italy, and GB in Belgium, emphasizing its desire to aggressively expand its operations and become the leading international retailer. However, over the years competition in the food retailing industry substantially increased, and all retailers came under pressure to cut prices. Carrefour's revenue growth in its home market suffered from the competition of France-based Leclerc and Auchan, which focused their strategy on cutting prices and gaining market share. Although Carrefour did join its French rivals in cutting prices, the company aimed much more at improving its margins than increasing sales volumes. Only in 2003, when Carrefour's revenue growth in France approached zero, did the company start to put more emphasis on competing on price, gaining market share, and stimulating customer loyalty.

Between 2005 and 2008 Carrefour's then-CEO Jose Luis Duran managed to restore the retailer's (organic) revenue and profit growth. During this period Carrefour redesigned its store layout, further widened its product offering, and expanded its assortment of Carrefour-branded products. Carrefour also abandoned its multi-banner strategy and gradually brought all store concepts under the Carrefour banner, with the exception of the retailer's hard discount division, to improve branding. Further, the retailer withdrew operations from some of its less profitable geographic segments. However, being unsatisfied with the speed of change and Carrefour's profitability, the company's primary shareholders, Arnault and Colony Capital, forced out Duran at the end 2008.

In 2009 Lars Olofsson took over as the CEO of Carrefour and introduced a new three-year transformation plan. The transformation plan involved increasing customers' awareness of Carrefour's price competitiveness. Furthermore, the plan aimed at achieving significant cost savings, gradually reducing days inventories (by seven days), and revitalizing the hypermarket concept. To achieve the latter Carrefour launched the Carrefour Planet concept in 2010. Carrefour Planet stores were redesigned, more spacious hypermarkets organized in distinct product areas: market, organic, frozen, beauty, fashion, baby, home, and leisure-multimedia. The primary goals of this redesign were to provide a more focused offering of nonfood products, improve the hypermarkets' attractiveness, win back customers, and improve store traffic. After a successful pilot with the conversion of two hypermarkets in 2010, Carrefour decided to convert around 250 additional hypermarkets into Carrefour Planet stores between 2011 and 2013. At the end of 2011 Carrefour had opened 81 Carrefour Planet stores, of which 29 and 39 were located in France and Spain, respectively.

In March 2011 Carrefour's management announced its intention to spin off its hard discount unit Dia. Management argued that Dia's business model was significantly different from Carrefour's, which reduced the synergies from combining the two companies. In addition, management revealed its plans to spin off its property into a separate publicly listed entity. However, while Carrefour did complete the spin-off of Dia, the retailer decided to postpone its property spin-off plans under pressure from activist investors who feared that the spin-off would be too costly and value-destroying. It would take until 2014 for Carrefour to realize its property spin-off plans through the establishment of Carmila, a publicly listed entity that owned and managed shopping centres adjacent to Carrefour's hypermarkets and in which Carrefour held a 42 percent stake.

Carrefour had been listed on the Paris Stock Exchange (Euronext) since 1970. The company's stock price performance during the years 2005 through 2017 is summarized in **Exhibit 1**.

## CARREFOUR FROM 2012 TO 2017

In its 2011 financial statements Carrefour's management disclosed the following outlook for 2012:

> In 2012, the Group intends to maintain strict financial discipline in response to a still challenging business environment. It will pursue initiatives [. . .] with the goal of reducing costs by approximately 400 million euros. [. . .] Expenditure for the deployment of the new Carrefour Planet hypermarket concept will be sharply reduced in 2012, with priority going to expanding the store network in key growth markets. Investments for the year will total between 1,600 million euros and 1,700 million euros.

For comparison, in 2011 investments in tangible and intangible fixed assets had amounted to €2,330 million, of which €369 million had resulted from remodelling expenditures incurred for the development of Carrefour Planet hypermarkets in Europe. Because the performance of the Carrefour Planet stores had been lower than expected in 2011, management decided to convert only 11 hypermarkets into Carrefour Planet stores (compared with 81 in 2011) and put a further roll out of the conversion plan on hold. Some of the other strategic actions that management planned to take in 2012 were to further improve Carrefour's price positioning; revamp a large selection of Carrefour-branded products; accelerate cost savings and investments in e-commerce, including the expansion of the number of Drives where customers could pick up their online orders; and increase the number of (smaller) convenience stores.

In the years 2011 to 2013 Carrefour withdrew operations from several countries, including Greece, Portugal, Turkey, Colombia, Indonesia, and Malaysia, the years thereafter focusing on ten countries. **Exhibit 2** provides information about Carrefour's operations, performance, and store formats by geographic segment during the period 2012 to 2017. The retailer used the proceeds from its asset sales to pay off debt, gradually reducing its total debt from a total of €24.2 billion at the end of fiscal year 2012 to €19.3 billion at the end of fiscal 2017. Capital expenditures rose from €1.6 billion in 2012 to €2.4 billion in 2017, with a focus on investments in store refurbishment, IT, and internet services.[5] In the second half of 2013 and the first half of 2014, the first signs arose that the store improvements and greater autonomy for regional store managers helped to attract more customers, improve store turnover, and grow market share in several markets, including its domestic market.[6] Some markets, such as Italy and China, remained a concern.[7] In China, Carrefour struggled to compete with local incumbent hypermarkets with well-developed local supply and distribution networks.

By the beginning of 2017 Carrefour announced its fifth consecutive year of like-for-like sales growth. During 2016 the retailer had opened more convenience stores in countries such as Brazil and Spain, further developing its multi-store format strategy. As part of this strategy, Carrefour had also reacquired discount chain Dia France in June 2014. Price competition remained fierce, especially in the retailer's home market, cost reductions were difficult to achieve, and the financial performance of Carrefour's Chinese operations remained worrisome.[8] One of Carrefour's other key challenges was to further develop its omnichannel approach, combining its in-store sales with online sales. Amazon's takeover of Wholefoods highlighted the changes that took place in the food retail industry; online competition not only affected Carrefour's sales of nonfood products but also became increasingly in the retailer's food segment. Some analysts argued that Plassat had insufficiently prepared Carrefour for this development; in 2016 Carrefour's online sales amounted to €1.2 billion.

In July 2017 Alexandre Bompard replaced George Plassat as CEO of Carrefour, becoming the retailer's fourth CEO in 12 years. Half a year later, in January 2018, Bompard announced a new cost-cutting programme, targeting a cost savings of €2 billion, and a new digital strategy, promising to boost investments in digitization.

---

[5] See "Carrefour Profits Surge on Asset Sales," *Financial Times,* March 7, 2013.
[6] See "Carrefour Rights the Boat Everybody Thought Was Going to Sink," *Financial Times,* November 3, 2013.
[7] See "Carrefour Says Recovery Plans Are Starting to Bear Fruit," *Financial Times,* January 16, 2014.
[8] See "Carrefour Posts Fifth Consecutive Year of Sales Growth," *Financial Times,* January 19, 2017.

## CASINO

One of Carrefour's French competitors was Groupe Casino. Though being smaller than Carrefour in terms of revenues (€37.8 billion revenue in 2017), the retailer was fairly comparable in terms of strategy. In particular, like Carrefour, Casino had adopted a multi-format strategy, operating hypermarkets (Géant), supermarkets (Casino and Monoprix), convenience stores (Petite Casino and Franprix), and discount stores (Leader Price). Close to 75 percent of Casino's stores were located in France, where Casino was one of the largest food retailers; however, in 2017 the retailer earned half of its revenues outside France or online (5.3 percent). The retailer's key international markets were Brazil and Colombia.

Casino held a 40 percent stake in Mercialys, a real estate investment company that owned the Casino group's shopping centres, and a 50 percent stake in three banking joint ventures, which helped the company to offer financial services through its stores. In 2017 Casino's return on equity was 7.3 percent. **Exhibit 4** shows a summary of Casino's financial performance in fiscal years 2016 and 2017.

## TESCO

One of Carrefour's European industry peers was UK-based Tesco, one of the world's largest retailers, together with Carrefour and Walmart. Historically, the strategies of Carrefour and Tesco exhibited some similarities. Particularly, both retailers engaged in international expansion and reserved a substantial amount of store space for nonfood products. Like Carrefour, Tesco offered financial services, such as banking and insurance services, to its customers. Tesco also operated a successful online grocery store. Following a period of fierce competition, declining performance, and an accounting scandal, Tesco went through a significant restructuring in 2015. Part of the restructuring was that Tesco focused more strongly on its domestic market and sold or closed several stores in its international segments. Whereas 60 percent of Tesco's store space was located outside of the United Kingdom in 2013, the size of international store space had decreased to close to 50 percent in 2016.

The company had different store formats, which all operated under the Tesco banner. Tesco Express and Metro stores were the smallest type of stores (with up to 5,000 square metres) and focused on selling food products. Tesco's Superstores occupied between 7,000 and 16,000 square metres and offered both food and nonfood products. Since 1997 Tesco also operated Extra stores, which offered a wide range of food and nonfood lines, including electrical equipment, clothing, and health and pharmaceutical products. These stores had store spaces of approximately 20,000 square metres. Tesco's Superstores and Extra stores were thus comparable, at least in size and assortment, to Carrefour's Hypermarkets.

In the fiscal year ending on February 24, 2018, Tesco's return on equity was 8.6 percent. **Exhibit 7** shows a summary of Tesco's financial performance in fiscal years 2016 and 2017.

**EXHIBIT 1**  Carrefour's stock price and the MSCI Europe price index from December 2011 to March 2018 (price on December 31, 2011 = 100)

**EXHIBIT 2**  Carrefour's operations, performance, and store formats by geographic segment

| (in € mn) | Fiscal year | France | Rest of Europe | Latin America | Asia | Global functions |
|---|---|---|---|---|---|---|
| *Revenue* | 2017 | 35,835 | 21,112 | 16,042 | 5,907 | 0 |
| | 2016 | 35,877 | 20,085 | 14,507 | 6,176 | 0 |
| | 2015 | 36,272 | 19,724 | 14,290 | 6,659 | 0 |
| | 2014 | 35,336 | 19,191 | 13,891 | 6,288 | 0 |
| | 2013 | 35,438 | 19,220 | 13,786 | 6,443 | 0 |
| | 2012 | 35,341 | 20,873 | 14,174 | 6,400 | 0 |
| *Recurring operating* | 2017 | 692 | 677 | 715 | 4 | (83) |
| *income* | 2016 | 1,031 | 712 | 711 | (58) | (45) |
| | 2015 | 1,191 | 567 | 705 | 13 | (31) |
| | 2014 | 1,271 | 425 | 685 | 97 | (92) |
| | 2013 | 1,198 | 388 | 627 | 131 | (106) |
| | 2012 | 929 | 509 | 608 | 168 | (74) |
| *Tangible and intangible* | 2017 | 10,759 | 6,865 | 3,268 | 1,079 | 465 |
| *fixed assets* | 2016 | 10,789 | 7,301 | 3,600 | 1,216 | 405 |
| | 2015 | 10,146 | 7,082 | 2,731 | 1,291 | 331 |
| | 2014 | 10,080 | 7,005 | 3,263 | 1,338 | 129 |
| | 2013 | 9,058 | 6,855 | 2,877 | 1,255 | 108 |
| | 2012 | 8,854 | 7,365 | 3,304 | 1,249 | 145 |

| (in € mn) | Fiscal year | France | Rest of Europe | Latin America | Asia | Global functions |
|---|---|---|---|---|---|---|
| Capital expenditures | 2017 | 903 | 636 | 526 | 164 | 150 |
| | 2016 | 1,287 | 625 | 519 | 174 | 144 |
| | 2015 | 957 | 579 | 517 | 204 | 122 |
| | 2014 | 988 | 536 | 622 | 214 | 51 |
| | 2013 | 997 | 409 | 457 | 261 | 35 |
| | 2012 | 602 | 345 | 308 | 257 | 35 |
| Depreciation and amortization expense | 2017 | (692) | (459) | (221) | (178) | (81) |
| | 2016 | (616) | (414) | (183) | (199) | (74) |
| | 2015 | (602) | (389) | (180) | (213) | (87) |
| | 2014 | (610) | (380) | (174) | (189) | (28) |
| | 2013 | (622) | (393) | (187) | (184) | (39) |
| | 2012 | (620) | (456) | (219) | (186) | (43) |
| Total sales area (square metres, thousands) | 2017 | 5,764 | 5,599 | 2,408 | 2,736 | 1,111 |
| | 2016 | 5,719 | 5,449 | 2,335 | 2,758 | 0 |
| | 2015 | 5,668 | 6,039 | 2,258 | 2,734 | 828 |
| | 2014 | 5,189 | 5,753 | 2,173 | 2,757 | 761 |
| | 2013 | 5,071 | 5,539 | 2,088 | 2,765 | 712 |
| | 2012 | 5,075 | NA | 2,045 | 2,592 | 608 |
| Number of hypermarkets | 2017 | 247 | 460 | 193 | 365 | 111 |
| | 2016 | 243 | 439 | 316 | 374 | 0 |
| | 2015 | 242 | 489 | 304 | 369 | 77 |
| | 2014 | 237 | 489 | 291 | 375 | 67 |
| | 2013 | 234 | 475 | 277 | 371 | 64 |
| | 2012 | 232 | 524 | 272 | 350 | NA |
| Number of supermarkets | 2017 | 1,060 | 1,756 | 147 | 58 | 222 |
| | 2016 | 1,062 | 1,777 | 168 | 38 | 0 |
| | 2015 | 1,003 | 2,096 | 168 | 29 | 166 |
| | 2014 | 960 | 1,819 | 169 | 19 | 148 |
| | 2013 | 949 | 1,656 | 169 | 17 | 126 |
| | 2012 | 964 | 2,336 | 168 | 16 | NA |
| Number of convenience stores | 2017 | 4,267 | 2,446 | 521 | 41 | 52 |
| | 2016 | 4,222 | 2,312 | 468 | 27 | 0 |
| | 2015 | 4,263 | 2,464 | 404 | 8 | 42 |
| | 2014 | 3,673 | 2,035 | 370 | 0 | 33 |
| | 2013 | 3,458 | 1,795 | 316 | 0 | 24 |
| | 2012 | 3,405 | 1,433 | 235 | 0 | NA |
| Number of cash & carry stores | 2017 | 144 | 42 | 153 | 2 | 13 |
| | 2016 | 143 | 13 | 0 | 2 | 0 |
| | 2015 | 142 | 18 | 0 | 0 | 12 |
| | 2014 | 143 | 19 | 0 | 0 | 13 |
| | 2013 | 138 | 19 | 0 | 5 | 12 |
| | 2012 | 140 | 21 | 0 | 4 | NA |

**EXHIBIT 3** Carrefour's consolidated and adjusted income statements, balance sheets, and cash flow statements, 2012 to 2017 (in € millions)

The following financial statements are based on information taken from Carrefour's 2012 – 2017 annual reports and the author's own calculations. The financials have been adjusted for off-balance operating lease and (partly) standardized.

| INCOME STATEMENT - € mn | 2017 | 2016 | 2015 | 2014 | 2013 | 2012 |
|---|---|---|---|---|---|---|
| Revenue – retail | 78,897 | 76,645 | 76,945 | 74,706 | 74,888 | 76,789 |
| Revenue – Carrefour banque | 379 | 417 | 461 | 527 | 538 | 490 |
| Financing fees and commissions | 1,005 | 956 | 869 | 719 | 846 | 841 |
| **Total revenue** | **80,281** | **78,018** | **78,275** | **75,952** | **76,272** | **78,120** |
| Cost of sales | (62,692) | (60,714) | (60,838) | (59,270) | (59,828) | (61,523) |
| SG&A expenses | (16,431) | (15,771) | (15,675) | (14,823) | (14,741) | (14,977) |
| Operating expenses – Carrefour banque | (305) | (325) | (336) | (333) | (321) | (282) |
| Net other operating income or expense | 1,021 | 1,021 | 924 | 757 | 744 | 733 |
| Non-operating investment income | 249 | 208 | 248 | 253 | 265 | 336 |
| **Operating profit** | **2,123** | **2,437** | **2,598** | **2,536** | **2,391** | **2,407** |
| Impairment losses | (1,039) | (130) | (115) | (77) | (128) | (236) |
| Restructuring costs | (279) | (154) | (237) | (111) | (52) | (285) |
| Other net non-recurring income or expense | (100) | (148) | 48 | 243 | 169 | (435) |
| Interest income | 25 | 27 | 32 | 35 | 49 | 53 |
| Interest expense | (476) | (604) | (609) | (616) | (739) | (880) |
| **Profit before taxes** | **254** | **1,428** | **1,717** | **2,010** | **1,690** | **624** |
| Tax expense | (620) | (482) | (577) | (688) | (600) | (347) |
| Tax expense – Carrefour banque | 2 | (12) | (20) | (21) | (31) | (41) |
| Profit/loss to non-controlling interest | (169) | (148) | (143) | (118) | (101) | (83) |
| **Profit/loss to ordinary shareholders** | **(533)** | **786** | **977** | **1,183** | **958** | **153** |

| OPERATING EXPENSES BY NATURE - € mn | 2017 | 2016 | 2015 | 2014 | 2013 | 2012 |
|---|---|---|---|---|---|---|
| Personnel Expenses | (8,599) | (8,240) | (8,209) | (7,762) | (7,679) | (7,566) |
| Depreciation and Amortization | (2,680) | (2,482) | (2,414) | (2,209) | (2,221) | (2,272) |

| TAX EXPENSE ITEMS - € mn | 2017 | 2016 | 2015 | 2014 | 2013 | 2012 |
|---|---|---|---|---|---|---|
| Theoretical income tax expense | (88) | (492) | (652) | (764) | (631) | (199) |
| Differences between the French and overseas corporate income tax rates | (40) | 19 | 67 | 59 | 236 | 110 |
| Tax effect of permanent differences | (213) | (80) | (36) | 56 | (222) | (277) |
| Other, including deferred tax expense | (100) | (69) | (41) | (126) | (161) | (226) |
| **Recurring tax expense** | **(441)** | **(622)** | **(662)** | **(775)** | **(778)** | **(592)** |
| Non-recurring tax items | (179) | 140 | 85 | 87 | 178 | 245 |
| **Total tax expense** | **(620)** | **(482)** | **(577)** | **(688)** | **(600)** | **(347)** |

| OTHER INFORMATION - € mn | 2017 | 2016 | 2015 | 2014 | 2013 | 2012 |
|---|---|---|---|---|---|---|
| Effect of exchange rate changes on revenue | 0.4% | −3.1% | −1.1% | −3.1% | −3.1% | −0.7% |
| Profit/loss of discontinued operations | 1 | (40) | 4 | 67 | 306 | 1,081 |

| BALANCE SHEET - € mn | 2017 | 2016 | 2015 | 2014 | 2013 | 2012 |
|---|---|---|---|---|---|---|
| Non-current tangible assets | 16,463 | 16,668 | 15,156 | 15,381 | 13,935 | 15,143 |
| Non-current intangible assets | 9,341 | 9,906 | 9,509 | 9,543 | 9,044 | 9,409 |
| Consumer credit granted by financial services companies | 2,455 | 2,371 | 2,351 | 2,560 | 2,381 | 2,360 |
| Minority equity investments | 1,355 | 1,361 | 1,433 | 1,471 | 496 | 384 |
| Other non-operating investments | 2,275 | 2,063 | 2,032 | 2,140 | 1,887 | 2,042 |
| Deferred tax asset | 636 | 829 | 744 | 759 | 931 | 752 |
| **Total non-current assets** | **32,525** | **33,198** | **31,225** | **31,854** | **28,674** | **30,090** |
| Inventories | 6,690 | 7,039 | 6,362 | 6,213 | 5,738 | 5,658 |
| Trade receivables | 2,750 | 2,682 | 2,269 | 2,260 | 2,213 | 2,144 |
| Consumer credit granted by financial services companies | 3,866 | 3,902 | 3,658 | 3,420 | 3,221 | 3,286 |
| Other current assets | 1,741 | 1,951 | 1,873 | 1,989 | 1,487 | 1,263 |
| Cash and cash equivalents | 3,593 | 3,305 | 2,724 | 3,113 | 4,757 | 6,573 |
| **Total Current Assets** | **18,640** | **18,879** | **16,886** | **16,995** | **17,416** | **18,924** |
| **Assets Held for Sale** | **16** | **31** | **66** | **49** | **301** | **465** |
| **Total Assets** | **51,181** | **52,108** | **48,177** | **48,898** | **46,391** | **49,479** |

| BALANCE SHEET - € mn | 2017 | 2016 | 2015 | 2014 | 2013 | 2012 |
|---|---|---|---|---|---|---|
| Ordinary shareholders' equity | 10,061 | 10,427 | 9,631 | 9,190 | 7,843 | 7,303 |
| Non-controlling interest in equity | 2,099 | 1,582 | 1,039 | 1,037 | 754 | 874 |
| Non-current debt | 12,797 | 12,526 | 12,761 | 13,505 | 13,994 | 16,905 |
| Consumer credit financing | 2,661 | 1,935 | 1,921 | 1,589 | 1,765 | 1,966 |
| Deferred tax liability | 489 | 543 | 508 | 523 | 521 | 476 |
| Non-current liabilities | 15,947 | 15,004 | 15,190 | 15,617 | 16,280 | 19,347 |
| Trade payables | 15,082 | 15,396 | 13,648 | 13,384 | 12,854 | 12,925 |
| Consumer credit financing | 2,817 | 3,395 | 3,328 | 3,718 | 3,145 | 3,032 |
| Other current liabilities | 4,095 | 4,413 | 4,341 | 4,194 | 3,808 | 3,462 |
| Current debt | 1,069 | 1,875 | 966 | 1,757 | 1,683 | 2,263 |
| Current liabilities | 23,063 | 25,079 | 22,283 | 23,053 | 21,490 | 21,682 |
| Liabilities held for sale | 11 | 16 | 34 | 1 | 24 | 273 |
| Total liabilities and shareholders' equity | 51,181 | 52,108 | 48,177 | 48,898 | 46,391 | 49,479 |

| CASH FLOW STATEMENT - € mn | 2017 | 2016 | 2015 | 2014 | 2013 | 2012 |
|---|---|---|---|---|---|---|
| Profit before interest and tax | 676 | 1,922 | 2,167 | 2,512 | 2,206 | 1,264 |
| Taxes paid | (738) | (444) | (837) | (1,011) | (1,265) | (797) |
| Non-operating losses (gains) | 960 | (208) | (247) | (467) | (550) | 362 |
| Non-current operating accruals | 2,745 | 2,543 | 2,518 | 2,279 | 2,278 | 2,357 |
| Net (investments in) or liquidation of operating working capital | 157 | 454 | 276 | 18 | (284) | (42) |
| Operating cash flow | 3,800 | 4,267 | 3,877 | 3,331 | 2,385 | 3,144 |
| Dividends received | 76 | 79 | 8 | (4) | 30 | 30 |
| Net (Investments in) or liquidation of non-current assets | (3,819) | (4,132) | (3,251) | (4,507) | (893) | (317) |
| Free cash flow available to debt and equity | 58 | 214 | 635 | (1,180) | 1,522 | 2,857 |
| Interest paid | (275) | (321) | (289) | (355) | (379) | (458) |
| Net debt (repayment) or issuance | (329) | 518 | (603) | (206) | (2,595) | 723 |
| Free cash flow available to equity | (546) | 411 | (257) | (1,741) | (1,452) | 3,122 |
| Dividend (payments) | (292) | (207) | (488) | (219) | (209) | (258) |
| Net share (repurchase) or issuance | 1,408 | 245 | 606 | 298 | (8) | (3) |
| Net increase (decrease) in cash balance | 570 | 449 | (139) | (1,662) | (1,669) | 2,861 |

**EXHIBIT 4**  Summary of industry peers' accounting performance in the fiscal years 2016 and 2017

| | Casino | | Tesco | |
|---|---|---|---|---|
| | **2017** | **2016** | **2017** | **2016** |
| **Panel A: ROE decomposition** | | | | |
| NOPAT Margin (%) | 3.3 | 3.0 | 2.3 | 2.1 |
| × Net Operating Asset Turnover | 1.94 | 1.82 | 2.33 | 2.21 |
| = Return on Net Operating Assets (%) | 6.5 | 5.5 | 5.4 | 4.6 |
| Return on Net Operating Assets (%) | 6.5 | 5.5 | 5.4 | 4.6 |
| x (Net Operating Assets/Invested Capital) | 0.83 | 0.75 | 0.81 | 0.77 |
| + Return on Non-Operating Investments (%) | 1.8 | 4.0 | 2.9 | 0.2 |
| x (Non-Operating Investments/Invested Capital) | 0.17 | 0.25 | 0.19 | 0.23 |
| = Return on Invested Capital (%) | 5.7 | 5.1 | 4.9 | 3.6 |
| Spread (%) | 1.4 | 1.3 | 2.0 | 0.6 |
| × Financial Leverage | 1.10 | 1.07 | 1.91 | 4.16 |
| = Financial Leverage Gain (%) | 1.6 | 1.4 | 3.8 | 2.7 |
| ROE = Return on Invested Capital + Financial Leverage Gain (%) | 7.3 | 6.5 | 8.6 | 6.3 |
| **Panel B: Other ratios** | | | | |
| Personnel expense-to-revenue (%) | −12.1 | −12.2 | −12.8 | −13.4 |
| Operating working capital/Revenue (%) | −3.9 | −6.2 | −6.0 | −5.6 |
| Net non-current assets/Revenue (%) | 55.4 | 61.1 | 49.0 | 51.1 |
| PP&E/Revenue (%) | 25.8 | 28.8 | 45.9 | 46.5 |
| Operating working capital turnover | −25.50 | −16.04 | −16.56 | −17.95 |
| Net non-current asset turnover | 1.80 | 1.64 | 2.04 | 1.96 |
| PP&E turnover | 3.88 | 3.47 | 2.18 | 2.15 |
| Trade receivables turnover | 39.98 | 40.94 | 38.08 | 38.12 |
| Days' receivables | 9.0 | 8.8 | 9.5 | 9.4 |
| Inventories turnover | 7.41 | 6.86 | 27.15 | 25.33 |
| Days' inventories | 48.6 | 52.5 | 13.3 | 14.2 |
| Trade payables turnover | 4.32 | 3.94 | 10.23 | 11.53 |
| Days' payables | 83.4 | 91.3 | 35.2 | 31.2 |
| Cash conversion cycle | −25.8 | −30.0 | −12.5 | −7.6 |
| Debt-to-invested capital | 0.52 | 0.52 | 0.66 | 0.81 |
| Interest coverage (earnings based) | 1.63 | 1.13 | 2.56 | 1.16 |

Source: Casino's and Tesco's 2016 – 2017 annual reports and author's own calculations. The ratios in this table have been calculated (a) using the end-of-year balances of balance sheet items, (b) after adjusting the financial statements for off-balance operating lease, and (c) after excluding other income and expense from NOPAT and net income.

# 6 Prospective analysis: Forecasting

Most financial statement analysis tasks are undertaken with a forward-looking decision in mind – and, much of the time, it is useful to summarize the view developed in the analysis with an explicit forecast of a firm's future performance and financial position. Managers need forecasts to formulate business plans and provide performance targets; analysts need forecasts to help communicate their views of the firm's prospects to investors; and bankers and debt market participants need forecasts to assess the likelihood of loan repayment. Moreover, there are a variety of contexts (including but not limited to security analysis) where the forecast is usefully summarized in the form of an estimate of the firm's value. This estimate can be viewed as an attempt to best reflect in a single summary statistic the manager's or analyst's view of the firm's prospects.

**Prospective analysis** includes two tasks – forecasting and valuation – that together represent approaches to explicitly summarizing the analyst's forward-looking views. In this chapter we focus on forecasting; valuation is the topic of the next two chapters. Forecasting is not so much a separate analysis as it is a way of summarizing what has been learned through business strategy analysis, accounting analysis, and financial analysis. However, certain techniques and knowledge can help a manager or analyst structure the best possible forecast, conditional on what has been learned in the previous steps. Below we summarize an approach to structuring the forecast, offer information useful in getting started, explore the relationship between the other analytical steps and forecasting, and give detailed steps to forecast earnings, balance sheet data, and cash flows. The key concepts discussed in this chapter are illustrated using a forecast for Hennes & Mauritz, the apparel retailer examined in Chapter 5.

## The overall structure of the forecast

The best way to forecast future performance is to do it comprehensively – producing not only an earnings forecast but also a forecast of cash flows and the balance sheet. A **comprehensive forecasting approach** is useful, even in cases where one might be interested primarily in a single facet of performance, because it guards against unrealistic implicit assumptions. For example, if an analyst forecasts growth in revenue and earnings for several years without explicitly considering the required increases in working capital and plant assets and the associated financing, the forecast might possibly imbed unreasonable assumptions about asset turnover, leverage, or equity capital infusions.

A comprehensive approach involves many forecasts, but in most cases they are all linked to the behaviour of a few key "drivers." The drivers vary according to the type of business involved, but for businesses outside the financial services sector, the revenue forecast is nearly always one of the key drivers; profit margin is another. When operating asset turnover is expected to remain stable – often a realistic assumption – working capital accounts and investment in plant should track the growth in revenue closely. Most major expenses also track revenues, subject to expected shifts in profit margins. By linking forecasts of such amounts to the revenue forecast, one can avoid internal inconsistencies and unrealistic implicit assumptions.

In some contexts the manager or analyst is interested ultimately in a forecast of cash flows, not earnings per se. Nevertheless, even forecasts of cash flows tend to be grounded in practice on forecasts of accounting numbers, including revenue, earnings, assets, and liabilities. Of course, it would be possible in principle to move *directly* to forecasts of cash flows – inflows from customers, outflows to suppliers and laborers, and so forth – and in some businesses this is a convenient way to proceed. In most cases, however, the growth prospects, profitability, and investment and financing needs of the firm are more readily framed in terms of accrual-based revenues, operating earnings, assets, and liabilities. These amounts can then be converted to cash flow measures by adjusting for the effects of non-cash expenses and expenditures for working capital and plant.

## A PRACTICAL FRAMEWORK FOR FORECASTING

The most practical approach to forecasting a company's financial statements is to focus on projecting **"condensed" financial statements**, as used in the ratio analysis in Chapter 5, rather than attempting to project detailed financial statements that the company reports. There are several reasons for this recommendation. First, this approach involves making a relatively small set of assumptions about the future of the firm so that the analyst will have more ability to think about each of the assumptions carefully. A detailed line item forecast is likely to be very tedious, and an analyst may not have a good basis to make all the assumptions necessary for such forecasts. Further, for most purposes condensed financial statements are all that are needed for analysis and decision making. We therefore approach the task of financial forecasting with this framework.

Recall that the condensed income statement that we used in Chapter 5 consists of the following elements: revenue, net operating profit after tax (NOPAT), net investment profit after tax (NIPAT), interest expense after tax, and profit or loss. The condensed balance sheet consists of net operating working capital, net non-current operating assets, non-operating investments, debt, and equity. Also recall that we start with a balance sheet at the beginning of the forecasting period. Assumptions about investment in working capital and non-current assets, and how we finance these assets, results in a balance sheet at the end of the forecasting period; assumptions about how we use the average assets available during the period and run the firm's operations will lead to the income statement for the forecasting period.

In Chapter 5 we learned how to decompose return on equity in order to separately analyze the consequences on profitability of management's (1) operating decisions, (2) non-operating investments, and (3) financing decisions. To make full use of the information generated through the return on equity decomposition, the forecasting task should follow the same process, forecasting operating items first, then non-operating investment items, and finally financing items.

### Operating items

To forecast the operating section of the condensed income statement, one needs to begin with an assumption about next-period revenue. Beyond that an assumption about NOPAT margin is all that is needed to prepare the operating income statement items for the period. To forecast the operating section of the condensed balance sheet for the end of the period (or the equivalent, the beginning of the next period), we need to make the following additional assumptions:

1 The ratio of operating working capital to revenue to estimate the level of working capital needed to support revenue-generating activities.
2 The ratio of net non-current operating assets to revenue to calculate the expected level of net non-current operating assets.

### Non-operating investment items

Forecasting the investment sections of the condensed income statement and balance sheet requires that one makes assumptions about the following two items:

1 The ratio of non-operating investments to revenue to calculate the expected level of non-operating investments.
2 The return on non-operating investments.

NIPAT margin then follows as the product of the ratio of non-operating investments to revenue and the return on non-operating investments (after tax).

## Financing items

To forecast the financing sections of the condensed income statement and balance sheet, one needs to make assumptions about:

1  The ratio of debt to capital to estimate the levels of debt and equity needed to finance the estimated amount of assets in the balance sheet.
2  The average interest rate (after tax) that the firm will pay on its debt.

Using these forecasts, net interest expense after tax can be calculated as the product of the average interest rate after tax and the debt-to-capital ratio. Note that a ninth forecast, that of the firm's tax rate, is implicit in three of the preceding forecasts (NOPAT margin, NIPAT margin, and interest rate after tax).

Once we have the condensed income statement and balance sheet, it is relatively straightforward to compute the condensed cash flow statement, including cash flow from operations before working capital investments, cash flow from operations after working capital investments, free cash flow available to debt and equity, and free cash flow available to equity. We will discuss a practical example of how to go through all the forecasting process's preceding steps later in this chapter.

## INFORMATION FOR FORECASTING

The three levels of analysis that precede prospective analysis – strategy, accounting, and financial analysis – can lead to informed decisions by an analyst about expected performance, especially in the short and medium term. Specifically, the primary goal of financial analysis is to understand the historical relationship between a firm's financial performance and economic factors identified in the strategy and accounting analysis, such as the firm's macroeconomic environment, industry and strategy, and accounting decisions. Forecasting can be seen as performing a reverse financial analysis, primarily addressing the question of what the effect will be of anticipated changes in relevant economic factors on the firm's future performance and financial position, conditional on the historical relationships identified in the financial analysis. Thus much of the information generated in the strategic, accounting, and financial analysis is of use when going through the following steps of the forecasting process.

### Step 1: Predict changes in environmental and firm-specific factors

The first step in forecasting is to assess how the firm's economic environment, such as macroeconomic conditions and industry competitiveness, will change in future years and how the firm has indicated to respond to such changes. Throughout this chapter we will use the example of Hennes & Mauritz, one of the apparel retailers discussed in Chapter 5, to illustrate the mechanics of forecasting. A thorough step 1 analysis of H&M for the year 2018 must be grounded in an understanding of questions such as these:

- From a macroeconomic analysis. How will the economic situation in H&M's geographic segments develop?
- From industry and business strategy analysis. Will the growth in online retailing increase price competition in the industry? Is it expected that new discount retailers or general merchandise retailers will enter the lower-priced segment of the apparel retail industry, thereby increasing competition in H&M's primary segment? Can H&M's multi-branding strategy help the company to become stronger in the mid-market segment of the apparel retail industry? Will H&M's brand recognition, strong advertising campaigns, and investments in multichannel retailing (online and physical stores) help the firm to restore customer loyalty, avoid price competition, and reduce the occurrence of inventory markdowns? Will H&M's bargaining power over its suppliers decrease if its need for production flexibility, which is inherent to the fast fashion strategy, requires the retailer to develop longer term and more integrated relationships with its suppliers? How will the average labor costs in production countries develop in the near future? What will be the effect of consumers' increased demand for ethical and sustainable clothing on the costs of outsourced production? How long will H&M maintain its policy of outsourcing all production to independent suppliers? Will H&M be able to successfully replicate its strategy in emerging markets? What will be the performance consequences of H&M's foreign currency risk exposure?

- From accounting analysis. Are there any aspects of H&M's accounting that suggest past earnings and assets are misstated, or expenses or liabilities are misstated? If so, what are the implications for future accounting statements?

### Step 2: Assess the relationship between step 1 factors and financial performance

After having obtained a thorough understanding of what economic factors are relevant and how these factors are expected to change in future years, the next step of the forecasting process is to assess how such future changes will translate into financial performance trends. This second step strongly builds on the financial analysis. In particular, observations on how sensitive Hennes & Mauritz's past ratios have been to variations in, for example, economic growth, price competition, and input prices can help the analyst learn what will happen to the firm's ratios if the anticipated changes crystallize. The financial analysis of H&M helps to understand questions that include the following: What were the sources of H&M's above-average performance in 2016? Which economic factors caused the firm's profitability to decrease in 2017 (and by how much)? Are these factors and their performance effects permanent or transitory? Is there any discernible longer term pattern in H&M's past performance? If so, are there any reasons why this trend is likely to continue or change?

### Step 3: Forecast condensed financial statements

Based on the outcomes of steps 1 and 2, one can produce forecasts of the line items in the firm's condensed financial statements, most particularly of the operating statement items. For Hennes & Mauritz, the key challenge in building forecasts is to predict whether the firm will be able to maintain – or possibly improve – its above-average margins and turnover and grow its revenue at the same rate at which it expands its store network or whether increasing online competition, adverse economic conditions in some of its markets, increasing input prices, or the continuing investments in multichannel retailing will lead to a decline in operating performance. Forecasts of non-operating investment performance and financing structure typically rely less on business strategy information and build strongly on firm-specific information about investment and financing plans as well as historical trends in these measures, which we will discuss in the next section.

## Performance behavior: A starting point

The preceding forecasting framework implicitly assumes that sufficient information is available, or is generated in prior steps of the business analysis process, to produce detailed, informed forecasts. Quite often such information is not sufficiently obtainable, especially when preparing longer term forecasts. Therefore every forecast has, at least implicitly, an initial "benchmark" or point of departure – some notion of how a particular ratio, such as revenue growth or profit margins, would be expected to behave in the absence of detailed information. By the time one has completed a business strategy analysis, an accounting analysis, and a detailed financial analysis, the resulting forecast might differ significantly from the original point of departure. Nevertheless, simply for purposes of having a starting point that can help anchor the detailed analysis, it is useful to know how certain key financial statistics behave "on average" for all firms. As a general rule, the lower the quality and richness of the available information, the more emphasis one ultimately places on the initial benchmark.

In the case of some key statistics, such as earnings, a point of departure based only on prior behaviour of the number is more powerful than one might expect. Research demonstrates that some such benchmarks for earnings are almost as accurate as the forecasts of professional security analysts, who have access to a rich information set (we return to this point in more detail shortly). Thus the benchmark often is not only a good starting point but also close to the amount forecast after detailed analysis. Larger departures from the benchmark could be justified only in cases where the firm's situation is demonstrably different from the average situation and after having performed a careful and thorough analysis.

Reasonable points of departure for forecasts of key accounting numbers can be based on the evidence summarized next. Such evidence may also be useful for checking the reasonableness of a completed forecast.

## REVENUE GROWTH BEHAVIOUR

Revenue growth rates tend to be "mean-reverting": firms with above-average or below-average rates of revenue growth tend to revert over time to a "normal" level (historically in the range of 5 to 7 percent for European firms) within three to ten years. Figure 6.1 documents this effect for 1998 through 2017 for all the publicly traded European (nonfinancial) firms covered by the Compustat Global database. All firms are ranked in terms of their revenue growth in 1998 (year 1) and formed into five portfolios based on the relative ranking of their revenue growth in that year. Firms in portfolio 1 are in the top 20 percent of rankings in terms of their revenue growth in 1998, those in portfolio 2 fall into the next 20 percent, while those in portfolio 5 are in the bottom 20 percent when ranked by revenue growth. The revenue growth rates of firms in each of these five portfolios are traced from 1995 through the subsequent nine years (years 2 to 10). The same experiment is repeated with every year between 1999 and 2008 as the base year (year 1). The results are averaged over the 11 experiments, and the resulting revenue growth rates of each of the five portfolios for years 1 through 10 are plotted in the figure.

**FIGURE 6.1** Behaviour of revenue growth for European firms over time, 1998–2017

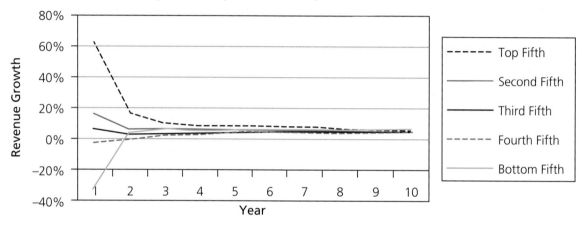

The figure shows that the group of firms with the highest growth initially – revenue growth rates of just over 60 percent – experience a decline to about 10 percent growth rate within two years and are never above 10 percent in the next seven years. Those with the lowest initial revenue growth rates, minus 32 percent, experience an increase to about a 7 percent growth rate by year 3, and average about 5 percent annual growth in years 4 through 10. One explanation for the pattern of revenue growth seen in Figure 6.1 is that as industries and companies mature, their growth rate slows down due to demand saturation and intra-industry competition. Therefore, even when a firm is growing rapidly at present, it is generally unrealistic to extrapolate the current high growth indefinitely. Of course, how quickly a firm's growth rate reverts to the average depends on the characteristics of its industry and its own competitive position within an industry.

## EARNINGS BEHAVIOUR

Earnings have been shown on average to follow a process that can be approximated by a "random walk" or "random walk with drift." Thus the prior year's earnings figure is a good starting point in considering future earnings potential. As will be explained, it is reasonable to adjust this simple benchmark for the earnings changes of the most recent quarter (that is, changes relative to the comparable quarter of the prior year after controlling for the long-run trend in the series). Even a simple random walk forecast – one that predicts next year's earnings will be equal to last year's earnings – is surprisingly useful. One study documents that professional analysts' year-ahead forecasts are only 22 percent more accurate, on average, than a simple random walk forecast.[1] Thus a final earnings forecast usually will not differ dramatically from a random walk benchmark.

The implication of the evidence is that, in beginning to contemplate future earnings possibilities, a useful number to start with is last year's earnings; the average level of earnings over several prior years is not useful.

Long-term trends in earnings tend to be sustained on average, and so they are also worthy of consideration. If quarterly or semiannual data are also included, then some consideration should usually be given to any departures from the long-run trend that occurred in the most recent quarter or half year. For most firms, these most recent changes tend to be partially repeated in subsequent quarters or half years.[2]

## RETURNS ON EQUITY BEHAVIOUR

Given that prior earnings serves as a useful benchmark for future earnings, one might expect the same to be true of rates of return on investment, like ROE. That, however, is not the case for two reasons. First, even though the *average* firm tends to sustain the current earnings level, this is not true of firms with unusual levels of ROE. Firms with abnormally high (low) ROE tend to experience earnings declines (increases).[3]

Second, firms with higher ROEs tend to expand their investment bases more quickly than others, which causes the denominator of the ROE to increase. Of course, if firms could earn returns on the new investments that match the returns on the old ones, then the level of ROE would be maintained. However, firms have difficulty pulling that off. Firms with higher ROEs tend to find that, as time goes by, their earnings growth does not keep pace with growth in their investment base, and ROE ultimately falls.

The resulting behaviour of ROE and other measures of return on investment is characterized as "mean-reverting": firms with above-average or below-average rates of return tend to revert over time to a "normal" level (for ROE, historically in the range of 8 to 10 percent for European firms) within no more than ten years.[4] Figure 6.2 documents this effect for European firms from 1998 through 2017. All firms are ranked in terms of their ROE in 1998 (year 1) and formed into five portfolios. Firms in portfolio 1 have the top 20 percent ROE rankings in 1998, those in portfolio 2 fall into the next 20 percent, and those in portfolio 5 have the bottom 20 percent. The average ROE of firms in each of these five portfolios is then traced through nine subsequent years (years 2 to 10). The same experiment is repeated with every year between 1999 and 2008 as the base year (year 1), and the subsequent years as years 2 to 10. Figure 6.2 plots the average ROE of each of the five portfolios in years 1 to 10 averaged across these eleven experiments.

**FIGURE 6.2** Behaviour of ROE for European firms over time, 1998–2017

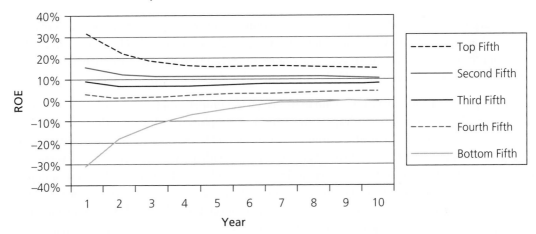

Though the five portfolios start out in year 1 with a wide range of ROEs (−31 percent to +31 percent), by year 10 the pattern of **mean-reversion** is clear. The most profitable group of firms initially – with average ROEs of 31 percent – experience a decline to 17 percent within three years. By year 10 this group of firms has an ROE of 15 percent. Those with the lowest initial ROEs (−31 percent) experience a dramatic increase in ROE and then level off at 0 percent in year 10.

The pattern in Figure 6.2 is not a coincidence; it is exactly what the economics of competition would predict. The tendency of high ROEs to fall is a reflection of high profitability attracting competition; the tendency of low ROEs to rise reflects the mobility of capital away from unproductive ventures towards more profitable ones. Despite the general tendencies documented in Figure 6.2, there are some firms whose ROEs may remain above or below normal levels for long periods of time. In some cases the phenomenon reflects the strength of a sustainable competitive advantage (e.g., Apple), but in other cases it is purely an artifact of conservative accounting methods.

A good example of the latter phenomenon is pharmaceutical firms, whose major economic asset, the intangible value of research and development, is not recorded on the balance sheet and is therefore excluded from the denominator of ROE. For those firms, one could reasonably expect high ROEs – in excess of 20 percent – over the long run, even in the face of strong competitive forces.

## THE BEHAVIOUR OF COMPONENTS OF ROE

The behaviour of rates of return on equity can be analyzed further by looking at the behaviour of its key components. Recall from Chapter 5 that ROEs and profit margins are linked as follows:

$$\text{ROE} = (\text{NOPAT margin} \times \text{Operating asset turnover}) \times \frac{\text{Net operating assets}}{\text{Invested capital}}$$

$$+ \text{Return on non-operating investments} \times \frac{\text{Investment assets}}{\text{Invested capital}} + \text{Spread} \times \text{Financial leverage}$$

Thus the primary components of ROE are NOPAT margin, operating asset turnover, return on non-operating investments, the proportion of capital invested in operating assets and non-operating investments, spread, and financial leverage. The time-series behaviour of the components of ROE for European companies for 1998 through 2017 are shown in a series of figures in the appendix to this chapter. Some major conclusions can be drawn from these figures:

1 Operating asset turnover tends to be rather stable, in part because it is so much a function of the technology of the industry. The only exception to this is the set of firms with very high asset turnover, which tends to decline somewhat over time before stabilizing.
2 Financial leverage also tends to be stable, simply because management policies on capital structure aren't often changed.
3 NOPAT margin and spread stand out as the most variable components of ROE; if the forces of competition drive abnormal ROEs towards more normal levels, the change is most likely to arrive in the form of changes in profit margins and the spread. The change in spread is itself driven by changes in NOPAT margin, because the cost of borrowing is likely to remain stable if leverage remains stable

To summarize, profit margins, like ROEs, tend to be driven by competition to "normal" levels over time. What constitutes normal varies widely according to the technology employed within an industry and the corporate strategy pursued by the firm, both of which influence turnover and leverage.[5] In a fully competitive equilibrium, profit margins should remain high for firms that must operate with a low turnover, and vice versa.

The preceding discussion of rates of return and margins implies that a reasonable point of departure for forecasting such a statistic should consider more than just the most recent observation. One should also consider whether that rate or margin is above or below a normal level. If so, then without detailed information to the contrary, one would expect some movement over time to that norm. Of course, this central tendency might be overcome in some cases – for example, where the firm has erected barriers to competition that can protect margins, even for extended periods. The lesson from the evidence, however, is that such cases are unusual.

In contrast to rates of return and margins, it is reasonable to assume that asset turnover, financial leverage, and net interest rate remain relatively constant over time. Unless there is an explicit change in technology or financial policy being contemplated for future periods, a reasonable point of departure for assumptions for these variables is the current period level. The only exceptions to this appear to be firms with either very high asset turnover that experience some decline in this ratio before stabilizing or firms with a very low debt-to-capital ratio that appears to increase leverage before stabilizing.

As we proceed with the steps involved in producing a detailed forecast, note that we draw on the preceding knowledge of the behaviour of accounting numbers to some extent. However, it is important to keep in mind that the described *average* behaviour will not fit all firms well. The art of financial statements analysis requires not only knowing what the "normal" patterns are but also having expertise in identifying those firms that will *not* follow the norm.

# Forecasting assumptions

In this section we apply the previously described forecasting framework to the example of Hennes & Mauritz. After providing some background information about macroeconomic and industry factors, we will forecast the line items of H&M's condensed financial statements following the order outlined in the previous section. For each line item, we will go through the three steps of the forecasting process, thereby relying on the outcomes of H&M's business strategy and financial analyses. In cases where we lack information, we will discuss whether it is more appropriate to rely on forecasts implied by the historical time-series patterns of European financial ratios. Although our forecasts are grounded in realistic assumptions, we emphasize that rather than providing a full-fledged forecasting analysis, the main purpose of the example is to illustrate the basics of the forecasting process and provide a sound basis for the next step of the prospective analysis, the valuation of H&M. Therefore, at some points in the analysis, we take the liberty of making some necessary simplifying assumptions.

## BACKGROUND: MACROECONOMIC AND INDUSTRY GROWTH

In the first quarter of 2018, the European economy had just experienced the strongest growth in a year since the start of the worldwide credit crisis in 2008. Following the crisis and the associated economic slowdown, several European governments took drastic budget cuts, thereby reducing consumers' discretionary income. During the first half of the 2010s, significant uncertainty about the consequences of one of the European countries defaulting or restructuring its debt impaired consumer confidence and stalled economic recovery. Around the beginning of 2015, low oil prices, economic reforms, economic stimulus programs, and a significant depreciation of the euro helped to create the necessary conditions for an economic upswing. During the spring of 2018, the Directorate-General for Economic and Financial Affairs of the European Commission identified a temporary cooling of economic activity but expected near-term economic growth in the EU to remain strong. Economic factors that could moderate growth were expected changes to the European Central Bank's monetary stimulus program and labor supply and production capacity constraints. The Directorate-General forecast that annual Private Consumption growth in the EU – an aggregate measure of the growth in households' purchases – would be 1.8 percent for both 2018 and 2019. Table 6.1 shows the realized and predicted Private Consumption growth rates for (1) the EU, (2) H&M's European markets, and (3) all countries where H&M operates. These growth rates illustrate that economy-wide growth was expected to remain strong in 2018 and 2019, albeit slightly lower than in the prior two years. Realized growth rates and growth prospects in H&M's non-European markets exceeded those in the European markets, suggesting that H&M worldwide expansion helped the retailer to improve growth opportunities.

**TABLE 6.1** Realized and expected economic growth rates

|  | 2016 (%) | 2017 (%) | 2018e (%) | 2019e (%) |
|---|---|---|---|---|
| European Union | 2.4 | 1.9 | 1.8 | 1.8 |
| Weighted average of H&M's European markets | 2.2 | 2.1 | 2.1 | 2.0 |
| Weighted average of H&M's World markets | 2.5 | 2.5 | 2.5 | 2.4 |

Source: European Economic Forecast Spring 2018 – Directorate-General for Economic and Financial Affairs and OECD Economic Outlook.

The apparel retail industry is a cyclical industry. Because consumers tend to delay their purchases of apparel during periods of economic uncertainty, apparel retailers' sales typically vary with economic cycles. Table 6.2 shows the realized and predicted near-term industry growth rates for the apparel industry. The industry growth rates are moderate, though higher than the economy-wide growth rates. Because H&M generates a comparatively large proportion of its revenues in developed (European) markets, where expected industry growth is substantially lower than in emerging markets, the average industry growth rate in H&M's markets is noticeably lower than the worldwide average industry growth rate.

**TABLE 6.2**  Realized and expected industry growth rates

|  | 2016 (%) | 2017e (%) | 2018e (%) | 2019e (%) |
|---|---|---|---|---|
| Worldwide industry growth rate | 4.3 | 4.5 | 4.9 | 5.2 |
| Weighted average industry growth rate in H&M's World markets | 2.6 | 2.7 | 3.0 | 3.2 |

Source: Marketline.

## REVENUE GROWTH

A good starting point for developing a forecast of short-term revenue growth is management's outlook. Management typically provides guidance about future revenue and margins in the Management Report section of the annual report but sometimes also in interim reports, press releases, and analyst conferences. The analyst's task is to critically challenge the assumptions underlying management's expectations, using information about macro-economic, industry, and firm-specific factors.

At the presentation of the 2017 annual report, H&M's management expressed the expectation that the firm would grow its store network by approximately 220 stores in 2018 and by around 4 percent per annum in the immediate years thereafter. H&M plans to shift its focus from physical stores to online, growing its online sales (of SEK25 billion in 2017) by 20 percent per annum. Based on this information, it is relatively straightforward to predict the number of stores that H&M will operate during the next two to three years. We can also easily project revenue from online sales. Table 6.3 displays our estimates of the worldwide number of H&M stores and revenue from online sales during the years 2018–2020, calculated under the assumption that in 2019 and 2020 the store growth rate will be 4 percent, close to its 2018 value, and the online sales growth rate will be 20 percent.

**TABLE 6.3**  Expected growth in H&M's store network and online sales

|  | 2016 | 2017 | 2018e | 2019e | 2020e |
|---|---|---|---|---|---|
| Store growth rate (%) | 9.8 | 8.2 | 4.4 | 4.0 | 4.0 |
| Number of stores added during the year | 427 | 388 | 220 | 198 | 206 |
| Number of stores at the end of the year | 4,351 | 4,739 | 4,959 | 5,157 | 5,363 |
| Average number of stores | 4,137.5 | 4,545.0 | 4,849.0 | 5,058.0 | 5,260.0 |
| Online sales growth rate (%) |  | 20.0 | 20.0 | 20.0 | 20.0 |
| Revenue from online sales (SEK millions) | 20,833 | 25,000 | 30,000 | 36,000 | 43,200 |

The number of stores is, however, not H&M's only revenue driver; the other driver, which certainly is more challenging to predict, is the amount of revenue per store. Table 6.4 shows the calculation of H&M's revenue per store during the years 2015–2017. To exclude revenue from online sales from these calculations, we must assume that online sales grew by 20 percent per annum throughout the period, given that H&M started to disclose its revenue from online sales only at the end of 2017. H&M's revenue per store – calculated as the ratio between total revenue and the average number of stores operated during the year – decreased from SEK44.0 million per store in 2015 to SEK38.5 million per store in 2017. Key questions at this point in the analysis therefore are: What economic factors explain the significant decline in H&M's store productivity? How will these factors develop during the next three years?

**TABLE 6.4** Decomposition of changes in H&M's store productivity

|  | 2015 | 2016 | 2017 |
|---|---|---|---|
| Revenue (in SEK millions) | 180,861 | 192,267 | 200,004 |
| Revenue excluding online sales (in SEK millions) | 163,500 | 171,434 | 175,004 |
| Average number of stores | 3,717.5 | 4,137.5 | 4,545.0 |
| Revenue per store (in SEK millions) | 44.0 | 41.4 | 38.5 |
| Percentage point change in revenue per store (%p), |  | −5.8 | −7.1 |
| consisting of: |  |  |  |
| • the effect of currency exchange rate changes (%p) |  | −0.6 | +1.0 |
| • the cannibalization effect of online sales (%p) |  | −1.0 | −1.2 |
| • the effect of changes in H&M's store portfolio mix (%p) |  | −1.0 | −0.6 |
| • the effect of inventory markdowns (%p) |  | −1.0 | −1.3 |
| • the effect of changes in consumer demand (%p) |  | −2.2 | −5.0 |

The following factors contributed to the decline of H&M's revenue per store:

- Foreign currency exchange rate changes. Hennes & Mauritz operates stores in 56 different countries and, consequently, is exposed to exchange rate risk. H&M disclosed that in 2016 revenue growth in Swedish Krona (SEK) was 0.6 percentage point lower than revenue growth in local currencies. In 2017 the effect of changes in currency exchange rates was positive, increasing H&M revenue growth in Swedish Krona by 1.0 percentage point.
- Cannibalization effect of online sales. A potential side effect of the fact that H&M shifts its focus to online sales is that the retailer's online activities start to compete with and, consequently, cannibalize in-store sales. Let us assume that one half of H&M's new online sales, which amounted to SEK1,736 million in 2016 and SEK2,084 million in 2017, was taken away from the retailer's in-store sales. This would imply that the increase in online sales led to a reduction of revenue per store of 1.0 percentage point in 2016 (1,736/[1,736 + 171,434]) and 1.2 percentage point in 2017 (2,084/[2,084 + 175,004]).
- Changes in H&M's store portfolio mix. Because store productivity varies across markets and H&M is continuously optimizing and expanding its store network, changes in the composition of H&M's store portfolio unavoidably lead to changes in the retailer's average store productivity. If Hennes & Mauritz shifts its focus away from geographic segments with high store productivity, such as its European market, overall store productivity will decrease. The retailer did so in 2016 and 2017, causing its average revenue per store to go down by, respectively, 0.8 and 0.4 percentage points. Furthermore, in 2016 and 2017 H&M invested especially in stores operated under the retailer's new banners, which have a lower average

productivity than the retailer's H&M-branded stores. Consequently, average revenue per store decreased by an additional 0.2 percentage point in both years.

- Inventory markdowns. In 2016 and 2017 intense competition continued to negatively affect consumers' demand for H&M products. In both years, the retailer needed to mark down its inventories more frequently than in prior years, causing declines in revenue per store of 1.0 and 1.3 percentage points.
- Changes in consumer demand. Under the assumption that changes in H&M's revenue per store that cannot be explained by the preceding four economic factors can be attributed to consumer demand effects, we conclude that declining demand reduced the retailer's revenue per store by 2.2 percentage points in 2016 and 5.0 percentage points in 2017.

Table 6.4 summarizes the quantitative impact of these three factors on H&M's average store productivity. The next step in forecasting revenue growth is to assess the persistence of each of the effects in future years. When doing so, the following considerations are particularly important:

- Foreign currency exchange rate changes. Much research suggests that exchange rates between currencies can be reasonably modelled as a random walk, implying that the current exchange rate is the best possible estimate of next year's exchange rate. If the exchange rates between the Swedish Krona and other major currencies indeed follow a random walk, the change in H&M's store productivity that is due to changes in exchange rates in 2017 should be considered as permanent.
- Changes in H&M's store portfolio mix. Without detailed information, it is reasonable to assume that the 2017 change in revenue per store that is due to the change in H&M's store portfolio is a permanent change. Furthermore, because H&M plans to grow its comparatively less productive stores under new banners at a higher pace than its H&M-branded stores, we expect that future changes in the store portfolio mix will lead to an additional annual 0.2 percentage point decrease in revenue per store during the years 2018 to 2020.
- Cannibalization effect of online sales. H&M disclosed that it plans to grow its online sales at a growth rate of 20 percent per annum. If one half of all future increases in online sales cannibalizes H&M's in-store sales, revenue per store will decrease by an additional 0.1 percentage point in 2018 and by an additional 0.2 percentage point in both 2019 and 2020.
- Changes in consumer demand and inventory markdowns. At the end of fiscal year 2017, H&M's management announced that it would take several actions to improve store productivity, such as integrating physical and online stores and making more use of digital analytics and artificial intelligence to better align the company's assortment with customers' needs. Trusting that these actions will have the desired effect, it is reasonable to expect that consumer demand will improve and markdowns will decrease in the years 2018 and beyond.

Given these considerations, we assume that after the observed decline, revenue per store will gradually rebound during the years 2018 to 2020. Table 6.5 summarizes the consequences of the preceding assumptions for H&M's revenue growth forecasts between 2018 and 2020.

The preceding growth forecasts assume that in the near term Hennes & Mauritz will maintain moderate growth, backed by its brand equity and ability to further develop its new brands and online business. While long-term trends in the apparel retail market are uncertain, it is reasonable to assume that Hennes & Mauritz will not be immune to the long-run forces of competition and mean reversion. Two factors that may lead to increased future competition are the consistently moderate growth in the apparel retail industry and the market entrance of new discount retailers and online retailers. Consequently, without detailed information we assume that revenue growth forecasts after 2020 will gradually revert to the average growth rate of the world economy, from 8 percent in 2020 to 3 percent in 2027.

**TABLE 6.5** Expected revenue growth for H&M

|  | 2017 | 2018e | 2019e | 2020e |
|---|---|---|---|---|
| (Expected) effect on revenue per store of: |  |  |  |  |
| • currency exchange rate changes (%p) | 1.0 | 1.0 | 1.0 | 1.0 |
| • changes in cannibalization by online sales (%p) | −1.2 | −1.3 | −1.5 | −1.7 |
| • changes in H&M's store portfolio mix(%p) | −0.6 | −0.8 | −1.0 | −1.2 |
| • changes in inventory markdowns (%p) | −1.3 | −1.0 | −0.5 | 0.0 |
| • changes in consumer demand (%p) | −5.0 | −4.0 | −2.0 | 0.0 |
| (a) Total (expected) effect on revenue per store (%) | −7.1 | −6.1 | −4.0 | −1.9 |
| (b) Revenue per store in 2016 (in SEK millions) | 41.4 | 41.4 | 41.4 | 41.4 |
| + (Expected) change in revenue per store (a × b) | −2.9 | −2.5 | −1.7 | −0.8 |
| = (Expected) revenue per store | 38.5 | 38.9 | 39.7 | 40.6 |
| × (Expected) average number of stores (from Table 6.3) | 4,545.0 | 4,849.0 | 5,058.0 | 5,260.0 |
| = (Expected) revenue from in-store sales | 175,004 | 188,792 | 200,976 | 213,736 |
| + (Expected) revenue from online sales (from Table 6.3) | 25,000 | 30,000 | 36,000 | 43,200 |
| = (Expected) revenue | 200,004 | 218,792 | 236,976 | 256,936 |
| Implied revenue growth rate (%) |  | 9.4 | 8.3 | 8.4 |

## NOPAT MARGINS

In 2017 Hennes & Mauritz's NOPAT margin decreased to 8.6 percent, after a decrease from 12.0 percent to 10.3 percent in 2016. The following economic factors, some of which we discussed in Chapter 5, contributed to the changes in H&M's margins:

- Foreign currency exchange rate changes. Hennes & Mauritz outsources its production to independent suppliers, which are paid in euros or US dollars, but generates revenues across the world in various currencies. The retailer's exposure to foreign currencies therefore differs between its input and output markets, making its margin between revenues and costs susceptible to foreign currency fluctuations. For example, given that H&M generates slightly more than 13 percent of its revenue in the United States but purchases a much larger proportion of its goods in US dollars, the company's NOPAT margin worsens if the US dollar appreciates relative to the Swedish Krona (H&M's reporting currency). Hennes & Mauritz disclosed that currency exchange rate changes led to an increase in revenue and SG&A expenses of, respectively, 1.0 and 1.5 percent in 2017. These changes, in turn, increased the SG&A-to-revenue ratio by 0.5 percentage point (1.015/1.010 − 1) and, given an SG&A-to-revenue ratio of 33.5 percent and a tax rate of 22 percent, decreased the NOPAT margin by close to 0.1 percentage point (0.5 × [1 − 0.22] × 0.335). Further, we estimate that exchange rate changes led to an increase in cost of sales of 1.7 percent in 2017, which given H&M's cost of sales-to-revenue ratio of 35.8 percent, led to a 0.2 percentage point decrease in the NOPAT margin ([1.017/1.010 − 1] × [1 − 0.22] × 0.358).[6] In sum, we estimate that the currency exchange rate changes contributed to a 0.3 percentage point decrease in H&M's NOPAT margin in 2017. Using similar calculations, we can derive that exchange rate changes decreased H&M's NOPAT margin by 0.4 percentage point in 2016.

- Inventory markdowns. In a January 2018 conference call, H&M's management disclosed that markdowns led to a 1.3 percent reduction in revenue in 2017, compared with a 1.0 percent reduction in 2016. Because markdowns reduce revenue but leave operating expense unchanged, they contribute to a net decrease in the NOPAT margin. Given a NOPAT margin of 8.6 percent, the 1.3 percent reduction in revenue led to a 1.2 percentage point decrease in H&M's NOPAT margin for 2017 ($-1 \times \{1/[1 - 0.013] - 1\} \times \{1 - 0.086\}$). In 2016 the 1.0 percent markdown effect on revenue led to a 0.9 percentage point decrease in the NOPAT margin ($-1 \times \{1/[1 - 0.010] - 1\} \times \{1 - 0.103\}$).
- Effective tax rate. In 2016 H&M's effective tax rate decreased from 23.3 percent to 22.5 percent. Given H&M's pretax margin of 13.3 percent ($1/[1 - 22.5\%]$ times the NOPAT margin of 10.3 percent), the change in the effective tax rate increased the company's NOPAT margin by close to 0.1 percentage point ($13.3 \times [0.233 - 0.225]$). The effect of change in the effective tax rate was not material in 2017.
- SG&A cost stickiness. We discussed in Chapter 5 that in periods of store productivity declines, stickiness of SG&A expenses can lead to a change in the SG&A-to-revenue ratio. As we previously discussed, changes in consumer demand resulted in 2.2 percent and 5.0 percent decreases in revenue per store in 2016 and 2017. If we assume that H&M needs around half a year to adjust its SG&A expense to decreases in store productivity, the 2.2 percent and 5.0 percent productivity decreases changed the retailer's NOPAT margin by $-0.3$ percentage point ($-0.5 \times \{1/[1 - 0.022] - 1\} \times \{1 - 0.22\} \times 0.327$) in 2016 and $-0.7$ percentage point ($-0.5 \times \{1/[1 - 0.050] - 1\} \times \{1 - 0.22\} \times 0.335$) in 2017.
- Net effect of other factors. In 2016 and 2017 Hennes & Mauritz gradually expanded its online activities to new geographic segments. In addition, the retailer broadened its product range and increased the number of stores that it operated under alternative brand names, such as COS and & Other Stories, in the higher-priced segments of the apparel market. Although these expansions should help H&M earn higher margins, especially in the long run, they may also require additional initial investments of which a portion is immediately expensed in the income statement. We assume that the portions of the NOPAT decrease that cannot be explained by the preceding four economic factors can be attributed to the net effect of new online activities and changes in H&M's store mix.

Table 6.6 summarizes the effects of the previously described factors on H&M's NOPAT margins in 2016 and 2017. In assessing the persistence of each of the NOPAT effects in future years, we take the following considerations into account:

TABLE 6.6  Decomposition of changes in H&M's NOPAT margin

|  | 2015 | 2016 | 2017 |
|---|---|---|---|
| Revenue (in SEK millions) | 180,861 | 192,267 | 200,004 |
| NOPAT (in SEK millions) | 21,758 | 19,791 | 17,211 |
| NOPAT margin (%) | 12.0 | 10.3 | 8.6 |
| Annual percentage point change (%p) in NOPAT margin, consisting of: |  | −1.7 | −1.7 |
| • the effect of foreign currency exchange rate changes (%p) |  | −0.4 | −0.3 |
| • the effect of inventory markdowns (%p) |  | −0.9 | −1.2 |
| • the effect of effective tax rate changes (%p) |  | +0.1 | +0.0 |
| • the effect of SG&A cost stickiness (%p) |  | −0.3 | −0.7 |
| • the net effect of other factors (e.g., changes in store mix and product range, online activities) (%p) |  | −0.2 | +0.5 |

- Foreign currency exchange rate changes. Assuming that the current exchange rate is the best possible estimate of the next year's exchange rate, we consider the change in H&M's NOPAT margin that is due to changes in exchange rates in 2017 as permanent.
- Inventory markdowns. Although inventory markdowns remain a common phenomenon in H&M's industry, especially in the near term, we expect that the actions taken by H&M's to restore store productivity will help to reduce future inventory markdowns. In particular, we assume that the negative NOPAT margin effect of inventory markdowns will gradually approach zero during the coming three years.
- Effective tax rate. We anticipate no further changes in H&M's effective tax rate.
- SG&A cost stickiness. Because Hennes & Mauritz can gradually adjust its SG&A expenditures to the 2017 change in store productivity but also because store productivity will gradually revert to a higher level, we expect that the negative cost stickiness effect that we observed in 2017 will fully revert during 2018.
- Net effect of other factors. H&M's management anticipates increased additional investments in online activities and new stores in the higher-priced segment of the market. We assume that these additional investments will lead to a gradual improvement of H&M's NOPAT margin, by an additional 0.20 percentage point in each of the next three years.

Table 6.7 shows what these assumptions imply for H&M's NOPAT margin between 2018 and 2020. Based on our assumptions, NOPAT margin would gradually increase to 11.1 percent in 2020.

**TABLE 6.7** Expected NOPAT margins for H&M

|  | 2017 (%) | 2018e (%) | 2019e (%) | 2020e (%) |
|---|---|---|---|---|
| NOPAT margin in 2016 (%) (Expected) effect on NOPAT margin of: | 10.3 | 10.3 | 10.3 | 10.3 |
| • foreign currency exchange rate changes (%p) | −0.3 | −0.3 | −0.3 | −0.3 |
| • inventory markdowns (%p) | −1.2 | −0.8 | −0.4 | +0.0 |
| • effective tax rate (%p) | +0.0 | +0.0 | +0.0 | +0.0 |
| • SG&A cost stickiness (%p) | −0.7 | +0.0 | +0.0 | +0.0 |
| • other factors (%p) | +0.5 | +0.7 | +0.9 | +1.1 |
| = (Expected) NOPAT margin (%) | 8.6 | 9.9 | 10.5 | 11.1 |

Recall that the NOPAT margin of H&M's competitor Inditex was 13.4 percent in 2017; the average NOPAT margin of the other industry peers was 7.2 percent. Based on the historical trends in the European economy, we expect that in the long run H&M's NOPAT margin will gradually move closer to that of its industry peers. One factor that may contribute to the mean reversion of H&M's margin is, for example, that consumers' increasing demand for sustainable products, rising labor costs in production countries, and H&M's need for developing long-term relationships with its suppliers will make it gradually more expensive for H&M to outsource its production. Hence we expect that the firm's NOPAT margin will gradually decrease from 11.1 percent in 2020 to 7 percent in 2027.

## WORKING CAPITAL TO REVENUE

Hennes & Mauritz's working capital consists of the following components: (1) operating cash, (2) trade receivables, (3) inventories, (4) trade payables, and (5) other current assets and liabilities. In 2017 days' receivables and day's payables were 9.2 and 28.6 days, respectively. The ratios varied marginally during the prior four years, and their 2017 values were close to the five-year averages. Therefore without detailed information, we consider it reasonable to assume that during the forecasting period days' receivables and days' payables will remain constant at 9.2 and 28.6 days, respectively.

In 2017 H&M's days' inventories decreased from its 2016 level of 119.4 days to 129.2 days. The firm's average days' inventories was 106.3 days between 2011 and 2015. The decrease in inventories turnover reflects that consumer demand declined in 2016 and 2017. Because we anticipate improvements in consumer demand during fiscal 2018 and beyond, we predict that during the next three years days' inventories will gradually revert to a level of 105 days.

Finally, without information to the contrary, we assume that average operating cash and net other current assets/liabilities as a percentage of revenue remain at a level of 5.0 and −8.4 percent, respectively. Table 6.8 details the calculation of our working capital-to-revenue forecasts. Note that, technically speaking, the inventories-to-revenue and payables-to-revenue ratios also depend on the gross margin forecasts, as both days' inventories and days' payables are a function of cost of sales instead of revenue. However, to simplify calculations and because the effect is non-material, we calculate the inventories-to-revenue and payables-to-revenue forecasts using a constant cost of sales-to-revenue ratio (of 45 percent).

**TABLE 6.8**  Working capital-to-revenue forecasts for H&M

|  | 2017 | 2018e | 2019e | 2020e |
|---|---|---|---|---|
| (a) Days' receivables | 9.2 | 9.2 | 9.2 | 9.2 |
| (b) Days' inventories | 129.2 | 121.1 | 113.1 | 105.0 |
| (c) Days' payables | 28.6 | 28.6 | 28.6 | 28.6 |
| Receivables to revenue [(a)/365] (%) |  | 2.5 | 2.5 | 2.5 |
| Inventories to revenue [0.4 × (b)/365] (%) |  | 15.1 | 14.1 | 13.1 |
| Payables to revenue [−0.4 × (c)/365] (%) |  | −3.6 | −3.6 | −3.6 |
| Operating cash to revenue (%) |  | 5 | 5 | 5 |
| Net other current assets/liabilities to revenue (%) |  | −8.4 | −8.4 | −8.4 |
| Working capital to revenue (%) |  | 10.6 | 9.6 | 8.6 |

## NON-CURRENT ASSETS TO REVENUE

The forecasts of net non-current operating assets to revenue are closely linked with the previously described forecasts of H&M's store productivity. Specifically, under an assumption that the investment in net non-current operating assets per store will remain constant in the next few years, store productivity (revenue per store) and net non-current operating assets to revenue will follow the same trend. In 2017 net non-current operating assets per store amounted to SEK25.7 million per store, down from SEK27.9 million per store in 2016. Net non-current operating assets per store may further decrease if H&M continues to shift its focus from larger H&M-branded stores to less asset-intensive stores operated under one of the new banners. However, it is reasonable to expect that such a positive effect will be more than offset by the investments that Hennes & Mauritz needs to make in new technology to further develop its online activities. In 2017 the cost of these investments was SEK2,058 million, or SEK0.5 million per store. We therefore expect that net non-current assets per store will gradually increase, by SEK0.5 million per year, during the years 2018–2020. Table 6.9 shows what this assumption, in combination with our earlier forecasts of revenue and store growth, implies for our net non-current assets-to-revenue forecasts. Because we assumed that store productivity will slightly increase and revenue from online sales will grow at a high rate between 2018 and 2020, net non-current operating assets as a percentage of revenue will decrease from 58.4 percent in 2017 to 55.7 percent in 2020. Without detailed information to the contrary, we assume that in the years beyond 2020, store productivity and investments per store will remain constant (or both increase at the inflation rate), which implies that net non-current operating assets-to-revenue ratio remains constant at 55.7 percent.

**TABLE 6.9** Net non-current operating assets-to-revenue forecasts for H&M

|  | 2017 | 2018e | 2019e | 2020e |
|---|---|---|---|---|
| Net non-current operating assets per store (SEK millions) | 25.7 | 26.2 | 26.7 | 27.2 |
| × Average number of stores (see Table 6.3) | 4,545 | 4,849 | 5,058 | 5,260 |
| = Net non-current operating assets (SEK millions) | 116,901 | 127,145 | 135,154 | 143,182 |
| / Revenue (see Table 6.5) (SEK millions) | 200,004 | 218,792 | 236,976 | 256,936 |
| = Net non-current operating assets to revenue (%) | 58.4 | 58.1 | 57.0 | 55.7 |

## NON-OPERATING INVESTMENTS

At the end of fiscal year 2017, Hennes & Mauritz had almost no non-operating investments. During the period 2012 through 2016, H&M gradually reduced its excess cash balance, which we classified as non-operating investments, from 11.6 percent of invested capital to 0 percent. The retailer did so by paying out high dividends in spite of its substantial investments in growth. Given the retailer's current cash flow performance, it is likely that in the near term H&M will maintain its zero excess cash balance, giving priority to dividends. Consequently, we assume that the non-operating investments-to-revenue ratio will remain steady at 0.5 percent during the years 2018 and beyond. We further assume that the (after-tax) return on non-operating investments will remain constant at a normalized level of 3.0 percent, close to the long-term European average return.

## CAPITAL STRUCTURE

Between 2014 and 2017, H&M's debt-to-capital ratio fluctuated only slightly from year to year, with an average of around 0.57. Given the low historical variance in leverage and without any concrete information that management plans to change the firm's capital structure, we assume that the debt-to-capital ratio will remain 57.2 percent throughout the forecasting period. In 2017 Hennes & Mauritz's after-tax interest rate was low, at 1.5 percent, also as a consequence of low market rates. Because at the end of 2017 investors expected that market interest rates would increase in the medium term, we let H&M's after-tax interest rate gradually increase from 1.5 percent in 2018 to 2.5 percent in 2023.

# From assumptions to forecasts

The analysis of Hennes & Mauritz's performance in Chapter 5 and the preceding discussions about general market behaviour and H&M's strategic positioning lead to the conclusion that in the near and medium term it is likely that the company can, at least temporarily, earn substantial abnormal profits.

Table 6.10 shows the forecasting assumptions for years 2018 to 2027. Table 6.11 shows the forecasted income statements and beginning of the year balance sheets for these same fiscal years. Recall that the balance sheet at the beginning of fiscal 2018 is the same as the balance sheet reported by the company for the year ending November 30, 2017. Further note that, technically speaking, our forecasts of assets-to-revenue ratios express average (rather than ending or beginning) assets as a percentage of revenue. To simplify calculations when translating these ratios into monetary values, we treat all ratios as forecasts of ending assets to revenue. In other words, we implicitly assume that all required investments are made immediately after the start of the fiscal year.

We have chosen a ten-year forecasting period because we believe that the firm should reach such a steady state of performance by the end of the period, such that a few simplifying assumptions about its subsequent performance are sufficient to estimate firm value (discussed in further detail in Chapter 8). For example, as we will discuss in Chapter 8, a reasonable assumption for the period following the forecasting period is that a portion of the firm's abnormal profits will be competed away and the performance of the firm will revert towards the mean, as has been the general trend that we have seen earlier in the chapter.

**TABLE 6.10** Forecasting assumptions for Hennes & Mauritz

| Forecast year | 2018 (%) | 2019 (%) | 2020 (%) | 2021 (%) | 2022 (%) | 2023 (%) | 2024 (%) | 2025 (%) | 2026 (%) | 2027 (%) |
|---|---|---|---|---|---|---|---|---|---|---|
| Revenue growth rate | 9.4 | 8.3 | 8.4 | 7.6 | 6.8 | 6.0 | 5.3 | 4.5 | 3.8 | 3.0 |
| NOPAT margin | 9.9 | 10.5 | 11.1 | 10.5 | 9.9 | 9.3 | 8.7 | 8.1 | 7.6 | 7.0 |
| Operating working capital/ revenue | 10.6 | 9.6 | 8.6 | 8.6 | 8.6 | 8.6 | 8.6 | 8.6 | 8.6 | 8.6 |
| Net non-current operating assets/revenue | 58.1 | 57.0 | 55.7 | 55.7 | 55.7 | 55.7 | 55.7 | 55.7 | 55.7 | 55.7 |
| Non-operating investments/ revenue | 0.5 | 0.5 | 0.5 | 0.5 | 0.5 | 0.5 | 0.5 | 0.5 | 0.5 | 0.5 |
| After tax return on non-operating investments | 3.0 | 3.0 | 3.0 | 3.0 | 3.0 | 3.0 | 3.0 | 3.0 | 3.0 | 3.0 |
| After-tax cost of debt | 1.5 | 1.7 | 1.9 | 2.1 | 2.3 | 2.5 | 2.5 | 2.5 | 2.5 | 2.5 |
| Debt-to-capital | 57.2 | 57.2 | 57.2 | 57.2 | 57.2 | 57.2 | 57.2 | 57.2 | 57.2 | 57.2 |

In addition to these assumptions, we also assume that revenue will continue to grow at 3.0 percent in 2028 and all the balance sheet ratios remain constant, to compute the beginning balance sheet for 2028 and cash flows for 2027.

Our strategic analysis led to an expectation of significant revenue growth, because of H&M's store network expansion, an increase in store productivity, and an increase in online sales. As shown in Table 6.10, we assume that revenue will increase at 9.4 percent, which is higher than the 4.0 percent revenue growth that the company achieved in 2017. This growth rate leads to an expected revenue level in 2018 of SEK218,792 million, up from SEK200,004 million in 2017 as Table 6.11 shows. The assumptions together lead to a projected SEK20,426 million profit in fiscal year 2018 compared with a reported profit of SEK16,184 million in 2017.

In making longer-term forecasts, in this instance for years 2 to 10, we have relied on our analysis of the firm and its prospects as well as the time-series behaviour of various performance ratios discussed earlier. Given our assumption of gradually declining store growth, we assume that H&M will see a decrease in its revenue growth rate to 8.3 and 8.4 percent in years 2 and 3. Thereafter, revenue growth will continue to gradually decline as the effect of competition gets stronger.

We assume a pattern of moderately increasing and then declining NOPAT margins over time. The assumption that the NOPAT margin increases in the medium term is consistent with our assessment of the effects of decreasing inventory markdowns, SG&A cost stickiness reversal, and changes in the store portfolio mix. The assumed time-series trend for the second half of the forecasting period is consistent with that documented earlier in the chapter for firms with initially high NOPAT. While Hennes & Mauritz clearly has a significant competitive advantage, it is prudent to assume, given the history of European firms, that this advantage will decline over time. Overall, we assume that the company's NOPAT margin reaches its peak of 11.1 percent in year 3 and then declines to reach a value of 7 percent by year 9.

H&M currently has a 11.7 percent ratio of working capital to revenue. Based on the inventories turnover assumption for years 1–3, this ratio is projected to decline to 8.6 percent. The forecast assumes that a ratio of 8.6 percent is maintained throughout the forecast horizon. Based on the assumed shift towards more online sales, the ratio of net non-current assets to revenue is expected to decrease to 55.7 percent in year 3 and remain steady thereafter. As H&M will likely give priority to maintaining dividends over growing excess cash to finance new stores, the investment assets-to-revenue ratio is held constant at 0.5 percent.

**TABLE 6.11** Forecasted financial statements for Hennes & Mauritz

| Fiscal year | 2018 | 2019 | 2020 | 2021 | 2022 | 2023 | 2024 | 2025 | 2026 | 2027 |
|---|---|---|---|---|---|---|---|---|---|---|
| **Beginning balance sheet (SEK millions)** | | | | | | | | | | |
| Beginning operating working capital | 25,299.0 | 23,192.0 | 22,749.7 | 22,096.5 | 23,775.8 | 25,392.6 | 26,916.1 | 28,342.7 | 29,618.1 | 30,743.6 |
| + Beginning net non-current operating assets | 116,820.7 | 127,118.2 | 135,076.3 | 143,113.4 | 153,989.9 | 164,461.3 | 174,329.0 | 183,568.4 | 191,829.0 | 199,118.5 |
| + Beginning non-operating investments | 1,039.0 | 1,094.0 | 1,184.9 | 1,284.7 | 1,382.3 | 1,476.3 | 1,564.9 | 1,647.8 | 1,722.0 | 1,787.4 |
| **= Business assets** | **143,158.7** | **151,404.2** | **159,010.9** | **166,494.6** | **179,148.0** | **191,330.2** | **202,810.0** | **213,558.9** | **223,169.1** | **231,649.5** |
| Debt | 83,445.7 | 86,603.2 | 90,954.2 | 95,234.9 | 102,472.7 | 109,440.9 | 116,007.3 | 122,155.7 | 127,652.7 | 132,503.5 |
| + Group equity | 59,713.0 | 64,801.0 | 68,056.7 | 71,259.7 | 76,675.3 | 81,889.3 | 86,802.7 | 91,403.2 | 95,516.4 | 99,146.0 |
| **= Invested capital** | **143,158.7** | **151,404.2** | **159,010.9** | **166,494.6** | **179,148.0** | **191,330.2** | **202,810.0** | **213,558.9** | **223,169.1** | **231,649.5** |
| **Income statement (SEK millions)** | | | | | | | | | | |
| Revenue | 218,792.0 | 236,976.0 | 256,936.0 | 276,463.1 | 295,262.6 | 312,978.4 | 329,566.3 | 344,396.3 | 357,483.9 | 368,208.4 |
| Net operating profit after tax | 21,646.0 | 24,866.8 | 28,502.9 | 29,028.6 | 29,231.0 | 29,107.0 | 28,672.3 | 27,896.1 | 27,168.8 | 25,774.6 |
| + Net investment profit after tax | 31.2 | 32.8 | 35.5 | 38.5 | 41.5 | 44.3 | 46.9 | 49.4 | 51.7 | 53.6 |
| **= Net business profit after tax** | **21,677.2** | **24,899.6** | **28,538.4** | **29,067.1** | **29,272.5** | **29,151.3** | **28,719.2** | **27,945.5** | **27,220.5** | **25,828.2** |
| − Net interest expense after tax | −1,251.7 | −1,472.3 | −1,728.1 | −1,999.9 | −2,356.9 | −2,736.0 | −2,900.2 | −3,053.9 | −3,191.3 | −3,312.6 |
| **= Profit or loss** | **20,425.5** | **23,427.3** | **26,810.3** | **27,067.2** | **26,915.6** | **26,415.3** | **25,819.0** | **24,891.6** | **24,029.2** | **22,515.6** |
| Return on net operating assets (%) | 15.2 | 16.5 | 18.1 | 17.6 | 16.4 | 15.3 | 14.2 | 13.2 | 12.3 | 11.2 |
| ROE (%) | 34.2 | 36.2 | 39.4 | 38.0 | 35.1 | 32.3 | 29.7 | 27.2 | 25.2 | 22.7 |
| BV of equity growth rate (%) | 8.5 | 5.0 | 4.7 | 7.6 | 6.8 | 6.0 | 5.3 | 4.5 | 3.8 | 3.8 |
| Profit or loss | 20,425.5 | 23,427.3 | 26,810.3 | 27,067.2 | 26,915.6 | 26,415.3 | 25,819.0 | 24,891.6 | 24,029.2 | 22,515.6 |
| − Change in operating working capital | 2,107.0 | 442.3 | 653.2 | −1,679.3 | −1,616.8 | −1,523.5 | −1,426.6 | −1,275.4 | −1,125.5 | −922.3 |
| − Change in net non-current operating assets | −10,297.5 | −7,958.1 | −8,037.1 | −10,876.5 | −10,471.4 | −9,867.7 | −9,239.4 | −8,260.6 | −7,289.5 | −5,973.6 |
| + Change in non-operating investments | −55.0 | −90.9 | −99.8 | −97.6 | −94.0 | −88.6 | −82.9 | −74.2 | −65.4 | −53.6 |
| + Change in debt | 3157.5 | 4351 | 4280.7 | 7237.8 | 6968.2 | 6566.4 | 6148.4 | 5497 | 4850.8 | 3975.1 |
| **= Free cash flow to equity** | **15,337.5** | **20,171.6** | **23,607.3** | **21,651.6** | **21,701.6** | **21,501.9** | **21,218.5** | **20,778.4** | **20,399.6** | **19,541.2** |
| Net operating profit after tax | 21,646.0 | 24,866.8 | 28,502.9 | 29,028.6 | 29,231.0 | 29,107.0 | 28,672.3 | 27,896.1 | 27,168.8 | 25,774.6 |
| − Change in operating working capital | 2,107.0 | 442.3 | 653.2 | −1,679.3 | −1,616.8 | −1,523.5 | −1,426.6 | −1,275.4 | −1,125.5 | −922.3 |
| − Change in net non-current operating assets | −10,297.5 | −7,958.1 | −8,037.1 | −10,876.5 | −10,471.4 | −9,867.7 | −9,239.4 | −8,260.6 | −7,289.5 | −5,973.6 |
| **= Free cash flow from operations** | **13,455.5** | **17,351.0** | **21,119.0** | **16,472.8** | **17,142.8** | **17,715.8** | **18,006.3** | **18,360.1** | **18,753.8** | **18,878.7** |

We do not show the beginning balance sheet forecasted for 2028 here, but it is implicit in the calculation of cash flows for 2027. As stated in Table 6.10, we assume that revenue continues to grow in 2028 and that all the balance sheet ratios continue to be the same, to derive the beginning balance sheet for 2028.

Hennes & Mauritz's capital structure remains relatively unchanged. As a result, the ratio of debt to book value of capital of 57.2 percent is maintained for the duration of the forecast horizon. This assumption of a constant capital structure policy is consistent with the general pattern observed in the historical data discussed earlier in the chapter. The forecast assumes that H&M's cost of debt increases from 1.9 percent, or an after-tax cost of 1.5 percent, to 3.2 percent, or an after-tax cost of 2.5 percent.

Having made this set of key assumptions, it is a straightforward task to derive the forecasted income statements and beginning balance sheets for years 2018 through 2027 as shown in Table 6.11. Under these forecasts, H&M's revenue will grow to SEK368,208 million, 84 percent above the level in 2017. By 2027 the firm will have net operating assets of SEK229,862 million and shareholders' equity of SEK99,146 million. Consistent with market-wide patterns of mean-reversion in returns, H&M's return on beginning equity will decline from 26.8 percent in 2017 to 22.7 percent by 2027, and return on beginning net operating assets will show a similar pattern.

## CASH FLOW FORECASTS

Once we have forecasted income statements and balance sheets, we can derive cash flows for the years 2018 through 2027. Note that we need to forecast the beginning balance sheet for 2028 to compute the cash flows for 2025. This balance sheet is not shown in Table 6.11. For the purpose of illustration, we assume that all the revenue growth and the balance sheet ratios remain the same in 2028 as in 2027. Based on this, we project a beginning balance sheet for 2028 and compute the cash flows for 2027. Free cash flow from operations is equal to net operating profit after tax (NOPAT) minus increases in operating working capital and net non-current operating assets. Cash flow to equity is cash flow to capital minus interest after tax plus increase in debt. These two sets of forecasted cash flows are presented in Table 6.11. As the table shows, the free cash flow from operating assets increases from SEK13,456 million to SEK18,879 million by 2027. In addition, the firm is expected to increase the free cash flow it generates to its equity holders from SEK15,338 million in 2018 to SEK19,541 million by 2027.

# Sensitivity analysis

The projections discussed thus far represent nothing more than an estimation of a most likely scenario for Hennes & Mauritz. Managers and analysts are typically interested in a broader range of possibilities. For example, an analyst estimating the value of Hennes & Mauritz might consider the sensitivity of the projections to the key assumptions about revenue growth, profit margins, and asset utilization. What if rising labor costs in H&M's production countries lead to a substantial increase in cost of sales? Alternatively, what if H&M's investments in online activities pay off significantly and asset turnover grows at a faster rate than assumed in the preceding forecasts? It is wise to also generate projections based on a variety of assumptions to determine the sensitivity of the forecasts to these assumptions.

There is no limit to the number of possible scenarios that can be considered. One systematic approach to **sensitivity analysis** is to start with the key assumptions underlying a set of forecasts and then examine the sensitivity to the assumptions with greatest uncertainty in a given situation. For example, if a company has experienced a variable pattern of gross margins in the past, it is important to make projections using a range of margins. Alternatively, if a company has announced a significant change in its expansion strategy, asset utilization assumptions might be more uncertain. In determining where to invest one's time in performing sensitivity analysis, it is therefore important to consider historical patterns of performance, changes in industry conditions, and changes in a company's competitive strategy.

In the case of Hennes & Mauritz, two likely alternatives to the forecast can be readily envisioned. The forecast presented expects that H&M's revenue per store will improve during the years 2018 to 2020. A downside case for H&M would have the firm improve store productivity at a lower rate. On the upside, the projected decrease in H&M's NOPAT margin between 2021 and 2027 because of the effects of competition could turn out to be too pessimistic, flattening the decline in the company's NOPAT margin.

## SEASONALITY AND INTERIM FORECASTS

Thus far we have concerned ourselves with annual forecasts. However, traditionally for security analysts in the United States and increasingly for security analysts in Europe, forecasting is very much a quarterly exercise. Forecasting quarter by quarter raises a new set of questions. How important is seasonality? What is a useful point of departure for **interim forecasts** – the most recent quarter's performance? The comparable quarter of the prior year? Some combination of the two? How should quarterly data be used in producing an annual forecast? Does the item-by-item approach to forecasting used for annual data apply equally well to quarterly data? Full consideration of these questions lies outside the scope of this chapter, but we can begin to answer some of them.

Seasonality is a more important phenomenon in revenue and earnings behaviour than one might guess. It is present for more than just the retail sector firms that benefit from holiday sales. Seasonality also results from weather-related phenomena (e.g., for electric and gas utilities, construction firms, and motorcycle manufacturers), new product introduction patterns (e.g., for the automobile industry), and other factors. Analysis of the time-series behaviour of earnings for US firms suggests that at least some seasonality is present in nearly every major industry.

The implication for forecasting is that one cannot focus only on performance of the most recent quarter as a point of departure. In fact, the evidence suggests that, in forecasting earnings, if one had to choose only one quarter's performance as a point of departure, it would be the comparable quarter of the prior year, not the most recent quarter. Note how this finding is consistent with the reports of analysts or the financial press; when they discuss a quarterly earnings announcement, it is nearly always evaluated relative to the performance of the comparable quarter of the prior year, not the most recent quarter.

Research has produced models that forecast revenue, earnings, or EPS based solely on prior quarters' observations. Such models are not used by many analysts, because analysts have access to much more information than such simple models contain. However, the models are useful for helping those unfamiliar with the behaviour of earnings data to understand how it tends to evolve through time. Such an understanding can provide a useful general background, a point of departure in forecasting that can be adjusted to reflect details not revealed in the history of earnings, or a "reasonableness" check on a detailed forecast.

One model of the earnings process that fits well across a variety of industries is the so-called Foster model.[7] Using $Q_t$ to denote earnings (or EPS) for quarter $t$, and $E(Q_t)$ as its expected value, the Foster model predicts that:

$$E(Q_t) = Q_{t-4} + \delta + \varphi(Q_{t-1} - Q_{t-5})$$

Foster shows that a model of the same form also works well with quarterly revenue data.

The form of the Foster model confirms the importance of seasonality because it shows that the starting point for a forecast for quarter $t$ is the earnings four quarters ago, $Q_{t-4}$. It states that, when constrained to using only prior earnings data, a reasonable forecast of earnings for quarter $t$ includes the following elements:

- The earnings of the comparable quarter of the prior year ($Q_{t-4}$).
- A long-run trend in year-to-year quarterly earnings increases ($\delta$).
- A fraction ($\phi$) of the year-to-year increase in quarterly earnings experienced most recently ($Q_{t-1} - Q_{t-5}$).

The parameters $\delta$ and $\phi$ can easily be estimated for a given firm with a simple linear regression model available in most spreadsheet software.[8] For most firms the parameter $\phi$ tends to be in the range of 0.25 to 0.50, indicating that 25 to 50 percent of an increase in quarterly earnings tends to persist in the form of another increase in the subsequent quarter. The parameter $\delta$ reflects in part the average year-to-year change in quarterly earnings over past years, and it varies considerably from firm to firm.

Research indicates that the Foster model produces one-quarter-ahead forecasts that are off by $.30 to $.35 per share, on average.[9] Such a degree of accuracy stacks up surprisingly well with that of security analysts, who obviously have access to much information ignored in the model. As one would expect, most of the evidence supports analysts being more accurate, but the models are good enough to be "in the ball park" in most circumstances. While it would certainly be unwise to rely completely on such a naïve model, an understanding of the typical earnings behaviour reflected by the model is useful.

# Summary

Forecasting represents the first step of prospective analysis and serves to summarize the forward-looking view that emanates from business strategy analysis, accounting analysis, and financial analysis. Although not every financial statement analysis is accompanied by such an explicit summarization of a view of the future, forecasting is still a key tool for managers, consultants, security analysts, investment bankers, commercial bankers, and other credit analysts, among others.

The best approach to forecasting future performance is to do it comprehensively – producing not only an earnings forecast but a forecast of cash flows and the balance sheet as well. Such a comprehensive approach provides a guard against internal inconsistencies and unrealistic implicit assumptions. The approach described here involves line-by-line analysis, so as to recognize that different items on the income statement and balance sheet are influenced by different drivers. Nevertheless, it remains the case that a few key projections – such as revenue growth and profit margin – usually drive most of the projected numbers.

The forecasting process should be embedded in an understanding of how various financial statistics tend to behave on average, and what might cause a firm to deviate from that average. Without detailed information to the contrary, one would expect revenue and earnings numbers to persist at their current levels, adjusted for overall trends of recent years. However, rates of return on investment (ROEs) tend, over several years, to move from abnormal to normal levels – close to the cost of equity capital – as the forces of competition come into play. Profit margins also tend to shift to normal levels, but for this statistic "normal" varies widely across firms and industries, depending on the levels of asset turnover and leverage. Some firms are capable of creating barriers to entry that enable them to fight these tendencies towards normal returns, even for many years, but such firms are the unusual cases.

Forecasting should be preceded by a comprehensive business strategy, accounting, and financial analysis. It is important to understand the dynamics of the industry in which the firm operates and its competitive positioning within that industry. Therefore, while general market trends provide a useful benchmark, it is critical that the analyst incorporates the views developed about the firm's prospects to guide the forecasting process.

For some purposes, including short-term planning and security analysis, forecasts for quarterly periods are desirable. One important feature of quarterly data is seasonality; at least some seasonality exists in the revenue and earnings data of nearly every industry. An understanding of a firm's intra-year peaks and valleys is a necessary ingredient of a good forecast of performance on a quarterly basis.

Forecasts provide the input for estimating a firm's value, which can be viewed as the best attempt to reflect the manager's or analyst's view of the firm's prospects in a set of summary statistics. The process of converting forecasts into a value estimate is labeled valuation and is discussed next.

# Core concepts

**Comprehensive forecasting approach**   Forecasting of the (condensed) income statement, balance sheet, and cash flow statement to make sure that the performance forecast does not imbed unreasonable assumptions about future asset turnover, leverage, or equity changes.

**Condensed financial statements**   Recommended focus of the forecasting task. The condensed financial statements consist of the following elements:

1   Income statement: Revenue, net operating profit after tax, net interest expense after tax, profit or loss.
2   Balance sheet: Operating working capital, net non-current operating assets, non-operating investments, debt, shareholders' equity, invested capital.
3   Cash flow statement: Profit or loss (net operating profit after taxes), change in operating working capital, change in net non-current assets, change in debt.

**Interim forecasts**    of quarterly performance. A key issue in interim forecasting is the seasonality of performance, that is, the tendency of quarterly performance to exhibit within-year time–series patterns that repeat themselves across years.

**Mean-reversion**    Tendency of financial ratios to revert to the industry or economy average over time. Financial ratios or indicators that tend to revert to the mean are: revenue growth, return on equity, return on assets, and financial spread. Financial ratios that have a low tendency to revert to the mean are: operating asset turnover and financial leverage.

**Prospective analysis**    Fourth and final step of financial statement analysis, which focuses on forecasting a firm's future financial performance and position. The forecasts can be used for various purposes, such as estimating firm value or assessing creditworthiness.

**Sensitivity analysis**    Analysis of how sensitive performance forecasts are to (realistic) changes in the key assumptions made to produce the forecast. In a sensitivity analysis, the analyst typically produces forecasts under various scenarios.

## Questions, exercises, and problems

1   GlaxoSmithKline is one of the largest pharmaceutical firms in the world, and over an extended period of time in the recent past, it consistently earned higher ROEs than the pharmaceutical industry as a whole. As a pharmaceutical analyst, what factors would you consider to be important in making projections of future ROEs for GlaxoSmithKline? In particular, what factors would lead you to expect GlaxoSmithKline to continue to be a superior performer in its industry, and what factors would lead you to expect GlaxoSmithKline's future performance to revert to that of the industry as a whole?

2   An analyst claims, "It is not worth my time to develop detailed forecasts of revenue growth, profit margins, etcetera, to make earnings projections. I can be almost as accurate, at virtually no cost, using the random walk model to forecast earnings." What is the random walk model? Do you agree or disagree with the analyst's forecast strategy? Why or why not?

3   Which of the following types of businesses do you expect to show a high degree of seasonality in quarterly earnings? Explain why.

- A supermarket.
- A pharmaceutical company.
- A software company.
- An auto manufacturer.
- A clothing retailer.

4   What factors are likely to drive a firm's outlays for new capital (such as plant, property, and equipment) and for working capital (such as receivables and inventory)? What ratios would you use to help generate forecasts of these outlays?

5   How would the following events (reported this year) affect your forecasts of a firm's future profit or loss?

- An asset write-down.
- A merger or acquisition.
- The sale of a major division.
- The initiation of dividend payments.

6   Consider the following two earnings forecasting models:

$$\text{Model 1: } E_t(EPS_{t+1}) = EPS_t$$

$$\text{Model 2: } E_t(EPS_{t+1}) = \frac{1}{5}\sum_{i=0}^{4} EPS_{t-i}$$

$E_t(EPS_{t+1})$ is the expected forecast of earnings per share for year $t + 1$, given information available at $t$. Model 1 is usually called a random walk model for earnings, whereas Model 2 is called a mean-reverting model. The earnings per share for Telefónica for the period 2012 to 2016 are as follows:

| Year | 1 | 2 | 3 | 4 | 5 |
|------|------|------|------|------|------|
| EPS | €0.80 | €0.93 | €0.62 | €0.07 | €0.42 |

a   What would be the year 6 forecast for earnings per share for each model?

**b** Actual earnings per share for Telefónica in year 6 were €0.56. Given this information, what would be the year 7 forecast for earnings per share for each model? Why do the two models generate quite different forecasts? Which do you think would better describe earnings per share patterns? Why?

**7** An investment banker states, "It is not worth my while to worry about detailed long-term forecasts. Instead, I use the following approach when forecasting cash flows beyond three years. I assume that revenues grow at the rate of inflation, capital expenditures are equal to depreciation, and that net profit margins and working-capital-to-revenue ratios stay constant."

What pattern of return on equity is implied by these assumptions? Is this reasonable?

## Problem 1 Predicting Tesco's 2017/2018 earnings

On April 12, 2017, UK-based retailer Tesco plc presented its financial statements for the fiscal year ending on February 28, 2017, announcing its first annual increase in like-for-like sales in seven years. The following tables show a selection of Tesco's (standardized and adjusted) financial figures for the fiscal years 2014/2015, 2015/2016, and 2016/2017 (i.e., the fiscal years ending on February 28, 2015, 2016, and 2017, respectively):

| Income statement (£ millions) | 2016/17 | 2015/16 | 2014/15 |
|---|---|---|---|
| **Revenue** | 54,905 | 52,978 | 61,260 |
| Operating expenses | (53,151) | (51,063) | (60,466) |
| **Operating profit** | 1,754 | 1,915 | 1,488 |
| Net non-recurring income or expense | (450) | (564) | (6,112) |
| Investment and interest income | 18 | 169 | 261 |
| Interest expense | (1,177) | (1,318) | (1,329) |
| Tax expense | 87 | 54 | 657 |
| Profit/Loss to Non-Controlling Interest | 14 | 9 | 25 |
| **Profit or loss** | 72 | 265 | (5,694) |

| Balance sheet (£ millions) | 2016/17 | 2015/16 | 2014/15 |
|---|---|---|---|
| Net non-current tangible assets | 25,475 | 25,636 | 30,051 |
| Net non-current intangible assets | 1,615 | 1,700 | 2,548 |
| Net other non-current operating assets | 1,230 | 428 | 1,020 |
| Excess cash | 4,901 | 4,956 | 920 |
| Minority equity investments | 668 | 709 | 860 |
| Other non-operating investments | 2,863 | 2,804 | 2,553 |
| Trade receivables | 1,963 | 2,116 | 2,722 |
| Inventories | 1,475 | 1,406 | 2,121 |
| Operating cash | 1,647 | 1,589 | 1,838 |
| Trade payables | (5,012) | (4,527) | (5,612) |
| Other current liabilities (net) | (2,539) | (2,813) | (1,997) |
| **BUSINESS ASSETS** | 34,286 | 34,004 | 37,024 |

| Income statement (£ millions) | 2016/17 | 2015/16 | 2014/15 |
|---|---|---|---|
| Equity | 6,241 | 8,380 | 6,937 |
| Debt | 28,045 | 25,624 | 30,087 |
| **INVESTED CAPITAL** | **34,286** | **34,004** | **37,024** |

| Other information (£ millions) | 2016/17 | 2015/16 | 2014/15 |
|---|---|---|---|
| Depreciation of non-current tangible assets | 1,554 | 1,540 | 2,085 |
| Amortization of non-current intangible assets | 245 | 255 | 257 |
| Non-current tangible assets at cost | 40,811 | 40,839 | 46,488 |
| Dividends paid | 0 | 0 | 914 |

In 2014/2015 non-recurring expense included (a) a £4.7 billion impairment of property, plant, and equipment, (b) a restructuring charge of £0.6 billion, (c) a £0.7 billion impairment of non-operating investments, and (d) a £0.2 billion reversal of commercial income overstated in prior years. Adjustments have been made to the financial statements such that "other non-operating investments" include the net assets of Tesco Bank (£2.2, £2.4, and £2.5 billion in 2014/2015, 2015/2016, and 2016/2017, respectively) and "investment income" includes Tesco Bank's pre-tax profit (£194, £161, and £77 million in 2014/2015, 2015/2016, and 2016/2017). Consequently, all other assets are those used in Tesco's retailing activities; further, revenue and operating expenses are those arising from Tesco's retailing activities.

In addition to disclosing the financial statements, Tesco's management also provided guidance about future investment plans, financing strategies, and performance expectations. In particular, the following information became available to investors and analysts on the publication date:

- In 2016/2017, Tesco opened 729 thousand square feet of new store space but closed or repurposed a substantially larger amount of store space, that is, 2.9 million square feet. The retailer plans to open 724 thousand square feet of new store space in 2017/2018 and, again, close or repurpose a larger amount of store space of 1.65 million square feet, thereby aiming to replace underperforming stores.

- Group capital expenditure during 2016/2017 was £1.13 billion (of which £0.73 billion had been spent in the United Kingdom and Ireland), slightly up from £0.93 billion in 2015/2016. Tesco's management provided no information on expected capital expenditure in 2017/2018. Assuming that new store space were equally expensive as in 2016/2017, 2017/2018 capital expenditures would probably be close to £1.3 billion.

- Tesco's effective tax rate was 32.4 percent (adjusted for one-time items); this effective tax rate may have been somewhat distorted by the fact that Tesco's pre-tax profit was relatively low (close to zero). The statutory tax rate was 20 percent.

- In 2016/2017 Tesco made substantial repayments on its borrowings. Net cash flows from borrowings amounted to −£1.85 billion (versus -£0.74 billion in 2015/2016). However, the retailer's debt-to-capital ratio increased because of a £3.4 billion increase in its net pension obligation, following a significant drop in the company's pension discount rate from 3.8 to 2.5 percent. Management decided to adjust its approach for setting the pension discount rate in 2017/2018, which would lead to a 0.3 percentage point increase in the pension discount rate. In the notes to the 2016/2017 financial statements, Tesco's management disclosed that a 0.1 percent increase in the discount rate corresponds with a £0.5 billion decrease in the net pension obligation.

- Management targets to have a net operating profit margin (before tax) of 3.5 to 4.0 percent by 2018/2019.

Management also disclosed information about revenue, like-for-like growth rates, and realized and planned store openings (see table).

| (£ millions) | UK & Ireland | International |
|---|---|---|
| **2015/2016 (Realized):** | | |
| Revenues | 43,080 | 9,898 |
| Trading profit (before exceptional items) | 503 | 320 |
| Exchange rate effect on revenue | (0.4%) | (6.0%) |
| Like-for-like revenue growth rate (at constant rates) | (0.7%) | 2.0% |
| **2016/2017 (Realized):** | | |
| Revenue | 43,524 | 11,381 |
| Trading profit (before exceptional items) | 803 | 320 |
| Exchange rate effect on revenue | 0.6% | 12.9% |
| Like-for-like revenue growth rate (at constant rates) | 0.9% | 1.3% |
| Square feet store space (× 1,000): | | |
| Beginning-of-year | 45,068 | 45,846 |
| Openings | 180 | 549 |
| Closures, disposals, repurposing | (1,850) | (1,056) |
| End-of-year | 43,398 | 45,339 |
| **2017/2018 (Expected):** | | |
| Square feet store space (× 1,000): | | |
| Beginning-of-year | 43,398 | 45,339 |
| Openings | 223 | 501 |
| Closures, disposals, repurposing | (22) | (1,627) |
| End-of-year | 43,599 | 44,213 |

1  Predict Tesco's 2017/2018 revenue using the information about the company's store space, revenues, and like-for-like growth (per geographical segment).

2  Predict the 2017/2018 book values of Tesco's net non-current operating assets, operating working capital, and investment assets using the information about the company's investment plans. Make simplifying assumptions where necessary.

3  Estimate Tesco's 2017/2018 net operating profit after tax, net investment profit after tax, interest expense after tax, and debt-to-equity ratio using the preceding information.

4  Early in 2015 Tesco's management indicated that "future dividends will be considered within the context of the performance of the group, free cash flow generation and the level of indebtedness." What do the preceding estimates (and your estimate of Tesco's 2017/2018 tax expense) imply for the company's free cash flow to equity holders in 2017/2018? If Tesco targets a cash percentage of 3 percent of revenue, how likely is it that Tesco will be able to pay dividends and/or reduce its debt in 2017/2018?

## Notes

1  See Patricia O'Brien, "Analysts' Forecasts as Earnings Expectations," *Journal of Accounting and Economics* (January 1988): 53–83.

2  See George Foster, "Quarterly Accounting Data: Time Series Properties and Predictive Ability Results," *The Accounting Review* (January 1977): 1–21.

3  See Robert Freeman, James Ohlson, and Stephen Penman, "Book Rate-of-Return and Prediction of Earnings Changes: An Empirical Investigation," *Journal of Accounting Research* (Autumn 1982): 639–653.

4  See Stephen H. Penman, "An Evaluation of Accounting Rate-of-Return," *Journal of Accounting, Auditing, and Finance* (Spring 1991): 233–256; Eugene Fama and Kenneth French, "Size and Book-to-Market Factors in Earnings and Returns," *Journal of Finance* (March 1995): 131–156; and Victor Bernard, "Accounting-Based Valuation Methods: Evidence on the Market-to-Book Anomaly and Implications for Financial Statements Analysis," University of Michigan, working paper (1994). Ignoring the effects of accounting artifacts, ROEs should be driven in a competitive equilibrium to a level approximating the cost of equity capital.

5  A "normal" profit margin is that which, when multiplied by the turnover achievable within an industry and with a viable corporate strategy, yields a return on investment that just covers the cost of capital. However, as mentioned above, accounting artifacts can cause returns on investment to deviate from the cost of capital for long periods, even in a competitive equilibrium.

6  During fiscal year 2017, the average percentage change in the euro-to-SEK exchange rate amounted to 2.1 percent; the US dollar-to-SEK exchange rate increased by 1.4 percent, on average. Assuming, for simplicity, that half of H&M's cost of sales is paid in US dollars and the other half is paid in euros, we can estimate that exchange rate changes led to an increase in cost of sales of 1.7 percent (0.5 × 2.1 + 0.5 × 1.4).

7  See Foster, op. cit. A somewhat more accurate model is furnished by Brown and Rozeff, but it requires interactive statistical techniques for estimation. See Lawrence D. Brown and Michael Rozeff, "Univariate Time Series Models of Quarterly Accounting Earnings per Share," *Journal of Accounting Research* (Spring 1979): 179–189.

8  To estimate the model, we write in terms of realized earnings (as opposed to expected earnings) and move $Q_{t-4}$ to the left-hand side:

$$Q_t - Q_{t-4} = \delta + \phi(Q_{t-1} - Q_{t-5}) + e_t$$

We now have a regression where $(Q_t - Q_{t-4})$ is the dependent variable, and its lagged value – $(Q_{t-1} - Q_{t-5})$ – is the independent variable. Thus, to estimate the equation, prior earnings data must first be expressed in terms of year-to-year changes; the change for one quarter is then regressed against the change for the most recent quarter. The intercept provides an estimate of $\delta$, and the slope is an estimate of $\phi$. The equation is typically estimated using 24 to 40 quarters of prior earnings data.

9  See O'Brien, op. cit.

## Appendix: The behavior of components of roe

In Figure 6A we show that ROEs tend to be mean-reverting. In this appendix we show the behaviour of the key components of ROE – return on net operating assets, operating margin, operating asset turnover, return on non-operating investments, spread, and financial leverage. These ratios are computed using the same portfolio approach described in the chapter, based on the data for all European firms for the time period 1998 through 2017.

**FIGURE 6A.1** Behaviour of return on net operating assets for European firms over time, 1998–2017

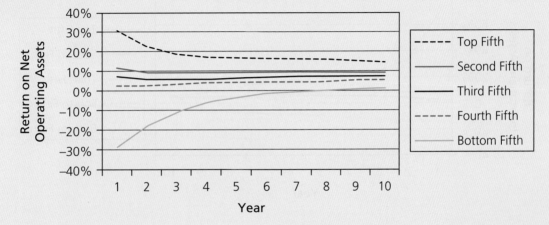

**FIGURE 6A.2** Behaviour of NOPAT margin for European firms over time, 1998–2017

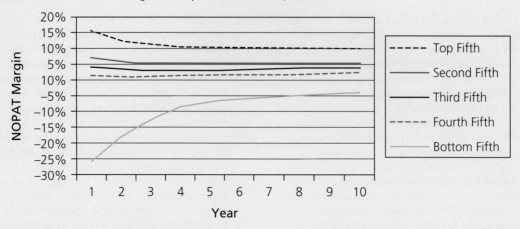

**FIGURE 6A.3** Behaviour of operating asset turnover for European firms over time, 1998–2017

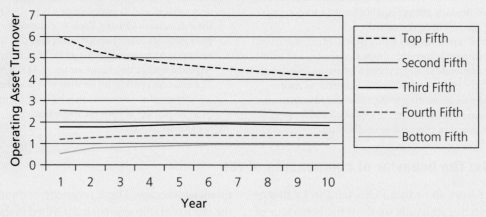

**FIGURE 6A.4** Behaviour of return on non-operating investments for European firms over time, 1998–2017

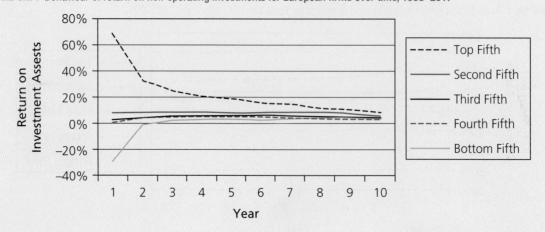

**FIGURE 6A.5** Behaviour of spread for European firms over time, 1998–2017

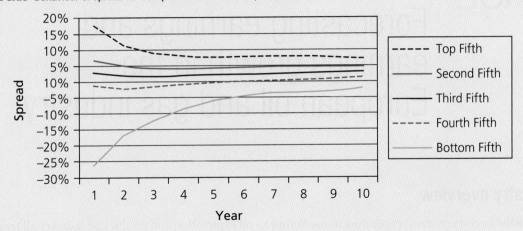

**FIGURE 6A.6** Behaviour of financial leverage for European firms over time, 1998–2017

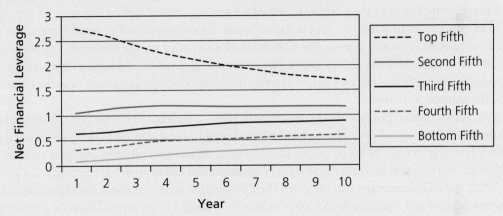

# CASE

## Forecasting earnings and earnings growth in the European oil and gas industry

## Industry overview

In 2018 the largest companies operating in the European oil exploration and production industry all tended to operate on a global scale. They were typically categorized as "price takers" because they had little control over the prices that they could ask from their customers. One reason for this small influence on prices was that the 14 oil-producing developing countries that coordinated their production activities through the OPEC organization had a strong influence on the worldwide oil supply and crude oil prices. Although the OPEC countries possessed roughly 80 percent of the worldwide proved oil reserves, they supplied less than 45 percent of the worldwide oil production to stabilize prices at higher levels. Other supply and demand factors that affected oil prices were (global) economic growth, the availability of alternative energy resources, and oil production in developed markets such as the United States. National taxes also influenced local prices and demand for oil. For example, in Europe fuel prices were, on average, three times as high as fuel prices in the United States, tempering the demand in Europe.

During the 2000s crude oil prices soared to record levels. While at the end of 1999 the price for a barrel of crude oil was close to $25, the crude oil price approached $110 per barrel by the end of 2011. There were several possible reasons for this strong increase in the oil price.[1] The increasing demand for oil from emerging economies such as China had led to a situation in which the amount of oil demanded had approached the maximum production capacity. While the OPEC countries had increased their production to record levels, they had invested insufficiently in new capacity and were unable to further increase oil supply. Oil supply had also come under pressure because of the low interest rates, which made it less expensive for oil producers to carry inventories and strategically limit production. Further, oil prices were strongly affected by speculative trading in the commodity markets in response to the political instability in the Middle East and oil-producing African countries.

In 2014 oil prices plunged, from a level of $110 per barrel at the beginning of the year to $56 per barrel by the end of the year. Important drivers of this oil price decline were (a) an economic slowdown in China, (b) high production in the United States, and (c) unwillingness of the OPEC countries to cut their production. The price decline had a strong effect on the profitability of oil and gas companies and forced these companies to find ways to cut costs, improve efficiency, and reduce investments. **Exhibit 1** shows the (Brent) crude oil price between January 2005 and March 2018 as well as the prices of oil futures during the first half of 2018.

Because oil and gas companies were price takers, their success critically depended on (1) their ability to grow and (2) the efficiency of their exploration and production activities. Although the growth of the energy

Professor Erik Peek prepared this case. The case is intended solely as the basis for class discussion and is not intended to serve as an endorsement, source of primary data, or illustration of effective or ineffective management.

[1] See "The Structure of the Oil Market and Causes of High Prices" by Pelin Berkmen, Sam Ouliaris, and Hossein Samiei, *International Monetary Fund*, 2005; "The Effect of Monetary Policy on Real Commodity Prices" by Jeffrey A. Frankel, in: *Asset Prices and Monetary Policy*, University of Chicago Press, 2008.

markets typically followed the growth in gross domestic product, oil and gas companies could grow at a faster or slower rate than the economy average for the following reasons. First, some companies were able to open up new markets, primarily in the emerging countries. The most important emerging market since the 2000s had been China, which had contributed almost one-third to the total worldwide increase in oil consumption. Second, although the demand for energy tended to follow the growth of the economy, the supply of oil and gas was limited by the natural availability of the energy sources. By the end of the 2000s many industry analysts feared that oil and gas companies' proved developed oil and gas reserves would be reduced in the near future. However, by 2017 several of the major oil companies started to prepare for a scenario in which the demand for oil would gradually decline, ultimately leaving a proportion of their existing reserves unused. Third, companies could diversify into other segments of the energy market. For example, oil and natural gas companies produced or started to produce coal, nuclear energy, or hydroelectric energy.

Whereas oil prices were one of the primary drivers of oil and gas companies' profitability, various other developments also affected companies' profit margins. First, because oil was traded in US dollars, a weak (strong) dollar implied that it was expensive (inexpensive) for oil companies to buy resources in other currencies. Second, steel prices were rising, making oil and gas companies' capital investments more and more expensive. Third, and most importantly, exploration costs varied over time. For example, during the first half of the 2000s exploration costs per barrel of oil equivalent (BOE) had risen sharply.[2]

Oil and gas companies that had operations in developing countries were also subject to a substantial degree of country risk. Many companies were extending their operations to developing countries, for example, in West Africa or around the Caspian Sea, because they were running out of reserves in the developed countries. Operations in such developing countries could, however, be disrupted by political crises, acts of war, and expropriation or nationalization of reserves and production facilities by governments. For example, in 2006 Bolivia announced plans to nationalize its oil and gas fields, which were then owned by several international oil and gas producers. Similarly, in early 2012 Argentina decided to take back control of YPF, the Argentinian operating branch of Spain-based oil producer Repsol.

## OIL AND GAS COMPANIES' ACCOUNTING AND DISCLOSURE

As argued, because oil and gas companies are price takers, their future profitability depends primarily on (1) the quantity and quality of their current oil and gas reserves, (2) their ability to efficiently extract and produce oil and gas, and (3) their ability to replace extracted reserves. Some inherent characteristics of oil and gas companies' exploration and development activities, however, make accounting for these activities a difficult exercise. Particularly, because the future economic benefits of current exploration and development expenditures are hard to establish, deciding on which expenditures must be capitalized as assets and which expenditures must be categorized as "unsuccessful" and immediately written off can be problematic.

Most oil and gas companies use the "successful efforts method" of accounting for exploration and development activities. Under this method, the key financial reporting estimate is for proved oil and gas reserves. Accounting standards consider oil and gas reserves to be proved when the company has government and regulatory approval for the extraction of reserves and is able to bring the reserves quickly to the market in a commercially viable manner. Companies make these estimates using geological information about each reservoir, reservoir production histories, and reservoir pressure histories. The distinction between proved and unproved reserves is important because only exploration expenditures that are associated with proved reserves are capitalized as assets. Specifically, under the successful efforts method, companies capitalize their exploration expenditures for a short period, after which they choose between continued capitalization and immediate amortization based on whether the exploration has successfully led to the booking of proved reserves. In addition, oil companies' depreciation, depletion, and amortization of production plants are typically calculated

---

[2]See "Oil Companies' Profits: Not Exactly What They Seem to Be," *The Economist*, October 28, 2004.

using the unit-of-production method, where the expected production capacity is derived from the proved reserves. The following paragraphs from BP plc's 2017 Annual Report describe how BP accounts for exploration and development expenditures and illustrate the basic idea underlying the successful efforts method:

*Exploration licence and leasehold property acquisition costs are capitalized within intangible assets and are reviewed at each reporting date to confirm that there is no indication that the carrying amount exceeds the recoverable amount. This review includes confirming that exploration drilling is still under way or planned or that it has been determined, or work is under way to determine, that the discovery is economically viable based on a range of technical and commercial considerations, and sufficient progress is being made on establishing development plans and timing. If no future activity is planned, the remaining balance of the licence and property acquisition costs is written off. [. . .]*

*Geological and geophysical exploration costs are recognized as an expense as incurred. Costs directly associated with an exploration well are initially capitalized as an intangible asset until the drilling of the well is complete and the results have been evaluated. These costs include employee remuneration, materials and fuel used, rig costs and payments made to contractors. If potentially commercial quantities of hydrocarbons are not found, the exploration well costs are written off. If hydrocarbons are found and, subject to further appraisal activity, are likely to be capable of commercial development, the costs continue to be carried as an asset. [. . .]*

*When proved reserves of oil and natural gas are determined and development is approved by management, the relevant expenditure is transferred to property, plant, and equipment. [. . .]*

*Expenditure on the construction, installation, and completion of infrastructure facilities such as platforms, pipelines, and the drilling of development wells, including service and unsuccessful development or delineation wells, is capitalized within property, plant, and equipment and is depreciated from the commencement of production as described below in the accounting policy for property, plant, and equipment. [. . .]*

*Oil and natural gas properties, including related pipelines, are depreciated using a unit-of-production method. The cost of producing wells is amortized over proved developed reserves. Licence acquisition, common facilities, and future decommissioning costs are amortized over total proved reserves.*

The method that BP uses to account for its exploration and development expenditures is similar to the method used by many other oil and gas companies, including Royal Dutch Shell and Statoil. Most oil and gas companies also provide supplemental disclosures about their oil and gas reserves. These disclosures typically show (1) the exploration and development costs that the company incurred during the year, (2) the exploration and development costs that the company capitalized over the years, (3) the results of the company's oil and gas exploration and development activities, and (4) the movements in the company's proved and unproved oil and gas reserves during the year. **Exhibit 2** summarizes the supplemental information that BP, Royal Dutch Shell, and Statoil provided in annual reports for the fiscal year ended on December 31, 2017.

## A description of three European oil and gas companies

Following are the descriptions of three European companies that operated in the oil and gas industry in 2017: BP, Royal Dutch Shell, and Statoil.

### BP

In 2017 BP was one the world's ten largest publicly listed oil and gas companies in terms of revenues. The company had upstream (oil exploration and production) and downstream (sales and distribution) operations in more than 70 countries, in which it employed approximately 74,000 people. Between December 31, 2012, and December 31, 2017, BP's share price increased by 20.1 percent, which in combination with the company's dividends yielded an average annual return of 8.7 percent. By the end of 2017 BP's market value was close to £104 billion.

BP's shares were widely held. In 2017 the company's largest shareholder owned less than 7 percent of BP's ordinary shares outstanding. Like many other oil and gas companies, BP had excess cash that it returned to its shareholders through share repurchases and dividends. In 2017 the company started a new share repurchase programme under which it repurchased ordinary shares for an amount of $343 million in the first year. BP was a financially healthy company, evidenced by the fact that Standard and Poor's had rated BP's public debt at A.

In the first half of 2010 an oil spill caused by an explosion at one of BP's operations had caused significant environmental damage in the Gulf of Mexico. Following the oil spill, BP had committed to an extensive clean up, to supporting the economic restoration of the area affected by the oil spill, and to creating a $20 billion Deepwater Horizon Oil Spill Trust from which individual claims and settlements could be funded. During the six years following the Deepwater Horizon incident, BP restructured its asset portfolio, making substantial asset sales, to generate sufficient funds for the $63 billion charge arising from the incident but also to deal with effects of record low oil and gas prices. The low oil and gas prices also forced BP to cut cost and improve production efficiency. By the end of 2016, when oil prices were stabilizing, BP started to gradually shift its focus towards growth again and cautiously increased its capital expenditures. Throughout 2017 BP made several acquisitions in the effort to rebuild its oil and gas reserves. However, in the expectation that the global demand for oil would gradually decline, creating an oversupply and in turn putting oil prices under pressure, BP also invested more and more in unconventional energy resources, such as shale gas and renewables. Nonetheless, in 2017 only around 1 percent of the company's revenues came from its alternative energy business.

BP's capital expenditures in the exploration and production segment totalled $14.5 billion in 2017.[3] The company's proved developed and undeveloped reserves increased by 568 million barrels of oil equivalent (BOE) because of discoveries and improvements in recovery techniques. BP's daily production in 2017 was approximately 2.2 million BOEs. BP's primary geographical segment were the United States and the United Kingdom, where it generated, respectively, 35 percent and 20 percent of its revenues.

## ROYAL DUTCH SHELL

By the beginning of 2018, Royal Dutch Shell plc was, like BP, one of the world's ten largest publicly listed energy and petrochemical group and larger than BP in terms of revenues and market capitalization. The company employed around 84,000 people in more than 70 countries. The shares of Royal Dutch Shell were widely held. The company's largest shareholder held around 6 percent of the company's ordinary share capital.

Royal Dutch Shell's core activities were the production, development, and retailing of oil and natural gas. One third of Royal Dutch Shell's revenues in 2017 came from its European operations, 22 percent of its revenues came from its US operations, and 38 percent of its revenues were made in non-European countries from the Eastern Hemisphere. During the period from 2013 to 2017, Royal Dutch Shell realized an average total share return of 6.5 percent, reaching a market capitalization of €234 billion on December 31, 2017. Shell repurchased shares for a total amount of $409 million in 2015, but stopped its repurchase programme in 2016.

Royal Dutch Shell was one of the few large oil and gas companies that made a large investment during the industry's downturn at the beginning of 2015, acquiring UK-based BG Group for a price of £35 billion. However, the Anglo Dutch company also felt the consequences of the 2014 oil price decline, reporting a 44 percent drop in profitability for fiscal year 2016. To avoid cutting dividends Shell focused on cutting costs, abandoning high-cost projects, and improving production efficiency, like BP and many of the other oil majors. During 2016 and 2017, the company aggressively cut jobs, decreasing its number of employees from 90 to 84 thousand, and announced plans for selling noncore assets, targeting a total of $30 billion in proceeds. Royal Dutch Shell saw its debt rise, motivating rating agency Standard and Poor's to downgrade the company's debt from AA to A. In 2016 profitability and cash flows came from the company's refining and marketing

[3]Note that BP's reporting currency was US dollars, whereas the company's shares were traded in British pounds.

activities (downstream) rather than exploration and production (upstream). Upstream profits rebounded at the beginning of 2017, when oil prices started to improve. Like BP, Royal Dutch Shell cautiously increased its investments in alternative energy resources during 2017. The company, for example, announced plans to start supplying electricity to business consumers, initially on a smaller scale in the United Kingdom.

Royal Dutch Shell's capital expenditures in the exploration and production segments were $13.6 billion in 2017, when its daily oil and gas production level amounted to 3.3 million BOEs.

## STATOIL

Of the three described European oil and gas companies – BP, Royal Dutch Shell, and Statoil – Statoil was the smallest. In 2017 the company operated in more than 30 countries, employing approximately 20.2 thousand people. During the period 2013 to 2017, the company's share price had increased by an annual average of 9 percent (including dividends), to reach a market value of NOK572.5 billion (€58.2 billion) on December 31, 2017. Statoil had one large shareholder, the government of Norway, which held close to 67 percent of the company's ordinary share capital.

In fiscal 2015 Statoil saw its profits decline as a result of the low oil and gas prices. Like BP and Shell, Statoil consequently reduced its investments and took actions to cut costs. In 2016 the oil and gas producer recognized an impairment charge of $2.3 billion after adjusting the valuation of its oil reserves to its new oil price expectations. However, Statoil saw its profits recover during the first quarter of 2017, when oil prices started to rebound to higher levels. At the end of 2017 Standard and Poor's rated Statoil's public debt at A.

Statoil's operating activities were focused on exploring for, producing, and retailing oil and natural gas. The company had most of its operations located in Norway and North America and was less geographically diversified than BP and Royal Dutch Shell. Specifically, the company generated 66 of its upstream revenues in Norway, 12 percent in the United States and Canada, and 19 percent in Algeria, Angola, Azerbaijan, and Brazil. Statoil had 49 percent of its non-current assets located in Norway. In early 2018 Statoil's management decided to change the company's name to Equinor, as a first step in repositioning the company as a "broad energy company" rather than an oil and gas company.

In 2017 the company made capital expenditures of $9.4 billion, down by 7 percent compared to 2016, but anticipated an increase in capital spending by 17 percent in the next year. In its 2017 Annual Report the company identified as one of its primary ambitions to remain in the top quartile of its peer group for unit of production cost, underlining management's focus on production efficiency.

## Questions

1   What are the European oil and gas companies' drivers of profitability? What are their key risks?

2   Using the supplemental information summarized in **Exhibit 2**, analysts can produce several ratios that provide insight into the efficiency of the companies' exploration, development, and production activities as well as their growth opportunities. Develop a set of ratios that provide such insights. How efficient are the three oil and gas companies in exploration and production?

3   **Exhibit 3** summarizes analysts' one-year-horizon (2018), two-year-horizon (2019), and three-year-horizon (2020) forecasts of revenue growth and profit margins. For each of the three oil and gas companies, provide arguments justifying the most pessimistic scenarios as well as arguments justifying the most optimistic scenarios.

4   Given your answers to the previous questions, what are your forecasts of the oil and gas companies' profit or loss for fiscal year 2018? What are your expectations about each of the companies' long-term earnings growth (i.e., growth in 2019 and 2020)?

**EXHIBIT 1**  Crude Brent oil prices

Source: Thomson Datastream.

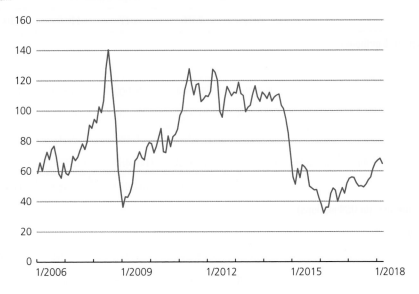

| Crude Brent oil futures for delivery in | Crude Brent oil futures prices during the first half of 2018 | | |
| --- | --- | --- | --- |
| | Price in US$ per barrel on December 31, 2017 | Price in US$ per barrel on March 31, 2018 | Price in US$ per barrel on June 30, 2018 |
| December 2018 | 63.64 | 65.06 | 76.35 |
| December 2019 | 60.17 | 61.26 | 71.43 |
| December 2020 | 58.33 | 58.51 | 67.46 |
| December 2021 | 57.55 | 56.91 | 64.74 |
| December 2022 | 57.43 | 56.29 | 62.86 |

Source: Thomson Datastream.

**EXHIBIT 2** Supplementary information about BP's, Royal Dutch Shell's, and Statoil's oil and natural gas reserves

| | BP | | Royal Dutch Shell | | Statoil | |
|---|---|---|---|---|---|---|
| | **2017** | **2016** | **2017** | **2016** | **2017** | **2016** |
| **Capitalized costs (in US$ millions)** | | | | | | |
| Gross capitalized costs: | | | | | | |
| Proved properties | 226,054 | 215,564 | 276,002 | 286,509 | 173,954 | 159,284 |
| Unproved properties | 17,886 | 18,524 | 23,707 | 25,582 | 12,627 | 13,563 |
| Auxiliary equipment and facilities | NA | NA | 6,112 | 6,418 | NA | NA |
| Accumulated depreciation and impairment losses | (134,186) | (123,993) | (141,452) | (139,057) | (120,170) | (109,160) |
| Net capitalized costs | 109,754 | 110,095 | 164,369 | 179,452 | 66,411 | 63,687 |
| **Costs incurred for the year (in US$ millions)** | | | | | | |
| Acquisition of properties: | | | | | | |
| Proved | 1,773 | 1,439 | 2,275 | 104 | 365 | 9 |
| Unproved | 958 | 1,967 | 548 | 501 | 862 | 2,477 |
| Exploration and appraisal costs | 1,655 | 1,402 | 2,829 | 3,384 | 1,235 | 1,437 |
| Development costs | 10,695 | 11,145 | 10,996 | 58,071 | 8,102 | 8,804 |
| Total costs | 15,081 | 15,953 | 16,648 | 62,060 | 10,564 | 12,727 |
| **Results of oil and natural gas exploration and production activities (in US$ millions)** | | | | | | |
| Sales and other operating revenues: | | | | | | |
| To third parties | 6,687 | 4,085 | 9,295 | 7,234 | 2,037 | 1,187 |
| To group companies | 22,094 | 15,725 | 35,101 | 28,405 | 24,759 | 18,725 |
| Total revenue | 28,781 | 19,810 | 44,396 | 35,639 | 26,796 | 19,912 |
| Exploration expenditure | (2,080) | (1,721) | (1,945) | (2,108) | (1,059) | (2,952) |
| Production costs | (5,614) | (6,006) | (12,800) | (13,493) | NA | NA |
| Production taxes | (1,775) | (683) | (2,841) | (1,624) | NA | NA |
| Production costs (including taxes) | (7,389) | (6,689) | (15,641) | (15,117) | (3,610) | (3,569) |
| Other operating costs | (2,469) | (2,548) | (2,312) | (3,734) | (2,156) | (1,908) |
| Depreciation, depletion, and amortization | (12,385) | (11,213) | (19,762) | (18,928) | (8,297) | (11,208) |
| Impairment and gains (losses) on sale of business and fixed assets | (179) | 2,747 | NA | NA | NA | NA |
| Profit before taxation | 4,279 | 386 | 4,736 | (4,248) | 11,674 | 275 |
| Taxes | (632) | 335 | (2,678) | 163 | (8,056) | (2,636) |
| Results of operations | 3,647 | 721 | 2,058 | (4,085) | 3,619 | (2,361) |

| | BP | | Royal Dutch Shell | | Statoil | |
|---|---|---|---|---|---|---|
| | 2017 | 2016 | 2017 | 2016 | 2017 | 2016 |
| **Proved developed and undeveloped reserves of crude oil and natural gas liquids (in million barrels)** | | | | | | |
| Reserves at the beginning of the year: | | | | | | |
| Developed reserves | 2,753 | 2,453 | 4,321 | 3,592 | 1,382 | 1,394 |
| Undeveloped reserves | 1,398 | 1,529 | 1,674 | 1,398 | 1,023 | 1,061 |
| Total reserves | 4,151 | 3,982 | 5,995 | 4,990 | 2,405 | 2,455 |
| Revision of previous estimates | 637 | 533 | 530 | 297 | 362 | 183 |
| Increase due to improvements in recovery techniques | 29 | 78 | 73 | 24 | NA | NA |
| Extensions and discoveries | 6 | 6 | 374 | 126 | 289 | 96 |
| Purchases of reserves-in-place | 53 | 38 | 666 | 1,207 | 34 | 62 |
| Sales of reserves-in-place | (10) | (112) | (2,058) | (12) | (38) | (14) |
| Production | (419) | (375) | (631) | (637) | (371) | (378) |
| Reserves at the end of the year | | | | | | |
| Developed reserves | 2,808 | 2,753 | 3,923 | 4,321 | 1,390 | 1,382 |
| Undeveloped reserves | 1,639 | 1,398 | 1,026 | 1,674 | 1,292 | 1,023 |
| Total reserves | 4,447 | 4,151 | 4,949 | 5,995 | 2,682 | 2,405 |
| **Proved developed and undeveloped reserves of natural gas (in billion cubic feet)** | | | | | | |
| Reserves at the beginning of the year: | | | | | | |
| Developed reserves | 13,398 | 15,009 | 21,783 | 17,256 | 10,584 | 11,901 |
| Undeveloped reserves | 15,490 | 15,553 | 7,476 | 6,683 | 4,053 | 2,723 |
| Total reserves | 28,888 | 30,563 | 29,259 | 23,939 | 14,637 | 14,624 |
| Revision of previous estimates | (983) | (211) | 2,304 | 532 | 1363 | 1265 |
| Increase due to improvements in recovery techniques | 1,009 | 534 | 140 | 10 | NA | NA |
| Extensions and discoveries | 2,082 | 399 | 1,925 | 551 | 857 | 462 |
| Purchases of reserves-in-place | 552 | 438 | 277 | 7,537 | 90 | 16 |
| Sales of reserves-in-place | (4) | (750) | (248) | (77) | 0 | (70) |
| Production | (2,281) | (2,085) | (3,333) | (3,233) | (1,873) | (1,661) |
| Reserves at the end of the year | | | | | | |
| Developed reserves | 15,266 | 13,398 | 24,693 | 21,783 | 10,958 | 10,584 |
| Undeveloped reserves | 13,997 | 15,490 | 5,631 | 7,476 | 4,115 | 4,053 |
| Total reserves | 29,263 | 28,888 | 30,324 | 29,259 | 15,073 | 14,637 |
| Conversion rate: × billion cubic feet of gas = 1 million barrel of oil equivalents | 5.80 | 5.80 | 5.80 | 5.80 | 5.80 | 5.80 |

Source: Annual Reports for the fiscal year ended on December 31, 2017, of BP, Royal Dutch Shell, and Statoil. Average exchange rates in 2017 (2016): $1 = £0.77 ($1 = £0.75); $1 = €0.89 ($1 = €0.91).

**EXHIBIT 3**  Analysts' forecasts for fiscal years 2018, 2019, and 2020 at mid-2018

### Forecasts of revenue growth

| Fiscal year 2018 relative to fiscal year 2017 | Most pessimistic forecast | Consensus forecast | Most optimistic forecast |
|---|---|---|---|
| BP | 4.8% | 13.4% | 27.3% |
| Royal Dutch Shell | −0.9% | 9.6% | 24.1% |
| Statoil | −2.2% | 13.6% | 32.9% |

| Fiscal year 2019 relative to fiscal year 2017 | Most pessimistic forecast | Consensus forecast | Most optimistic forecast |
|---|---|---|---|
| BP | 1.5% | 16.0% | 42.2% |
| Royal Dutch Shell | −1.3% | 12.6% | 33.3% |
| Statoil | −6.4% | 14.6% | 28.5% |

| Fiscal year 2020 relative to fiscal year 2017 | Most pessimistic forecast | Consensus forecast | Most optimistic forecast |
|---|---|---|---|
| BP | −13.0% | 4.5% | 29.3% |
| Royal Dutch Shell | −3.5% | 19.9% | 45.4% |
| Statoil | 7.7% | 23.0% | 38.2% |

### Forecasts of net profit margins

| Fiscal year 2018 | Most pessimistic forecast | Consensus forecast | Most optimistic forecast |
|---|---|---|---|
| BP | 2.9% | 3.6% | 5.9% |
| Royal Dutch Shell | 5.0% | 6.3% | 7.9% |
| Statoil | 5.1% | 7.8% | 13.8% |

| Fiscal year 2019 | Most pessimistic forecast | Consensus forecast | Most optimistic forecast |
|---|---|---|---|
| BP | 3.1% | 3.9% | 5.9% |
| Royal Dutch Shell | 4.9% | 6.7% | 8.0% |
| Statoil | 5.4% | 8.1% | 13.4% |

| Fiscal year 2020 | Most pessimistic forecast | Consensus forecast | Most optimistic forecast |
|---|---|---|---|
| BP | 3.3% | 4.4% | 6.2% |
| Royal Dutch Shell | 4.3% | 6.5% | 7.7% |
| Statoil | 5.3% | 7.9% | 10.4% |

Source: Thomson I/B/E/S.

**EXHIBIT 4** Standardized financial statements and financial ratios of BP, Royal Dutch Shell, and Statoil for the fiscal year ended December 31, 2017

### CONSOLIDATED INCOME STATEMENTS – BP ($ millions)

| Fiscal year ended December 31 | 2017 | 2016 | 2015 |
|---|---|---|---|
| Revenue | 240,208 | 183,008 | 222,894 |
| Operating expenses | (231,753) | (186,753) | (230,376) |
| **Operating profit** | **8,455** | **(3,745)** | **(7,482)** |
| Investment and interest income | 2,507 | 1,960 | 1,810 |
| Net non-recurring income or expense | (1,216) | 1,664 | (1,909) |
| Interest expense | (2,566) | (2,174) | (1,991) |
| **Profit before taxes** | **7,180** | **(2,295)** | **(9,572)** |
| Tax expense | (3,712) | 2,467 | 3,171 |
| **Profit after taxes** | **3,468** | **172** | **(6,401)** |
| Profit or loss to non-controlling interest | (79) | (57) | (82) |
| **Profit or loss to ordinary shareholders** | **3,389** | **115** | **(6,483)** |

### CONSOLIDATED BALANCE SHEETS – BP ($ millions)

| Fiscal year ended December 31 | 2017 | 2016 | 2015 | 2014 |
|---|---|---|---|---|
| ASSETS | | | | |
| Non-current tangible assets | 142,363 | 142,928 | 144,082 | 148,350 |
| Non-current intangible assets | 29,906 | 29,377 | 30,287 | 32,775 |
| Minority equity investments | 24,985 | 22,701 | 17,834 | 19,156 |
| Other non-operating investments | 8,792 | 4,827 | 7,597 | 7,836 |
| Deferred tax asset | 4,469 | 4,741 | 1,545 | 2,309 |
| Derivatives – asset | 7,142 | 7,375 | 8,651 | 9,607 |
| **Total non-current assets** | **217,657** | **211,949** | **209,996** | **220,033** |
| Inventories | 19,011 | 17,655 | 14,142 | 18,373 |
| Trade receivables | 18,916 | 13,393 | 13,754 | 19,837 |
| Other current assets | 8,112 | 9,962 | 11,078 | 13,628 |
| Cash and cash equivalents | 25,711 | 23,528 | 26,608 | 30,092 |
| **Total current assets** | **71,750** | **64,538** | **65,582** | **81,930** |
| **Assets held for sale** | **0** | **0** | **578** | **0** |
| **Total assets** | **289,407** | **276,487** | **276,156** | **301,963** |
| LIABILITIES AND SHAREHOLDERS' EQUITY | | | | |
| **Ordinary shareholders' equity** | **98,491** | **95,286** | **97,216** | **111,441** |
| **Non-controlling interest in equity** | **1,913** | **1,557** | **1,171** | **1,201** |
| Non-current debt | 98,140 | 94,124 | 105,363 | 104,166 |
| Deferred tax liability | 7,982 | 7,238 | 9,599 | 13,893 |
| Derivatives – liability | 6,569 | 8,504 | 7,522 | 6,888 |
| Other non-current liabilities | 14,394 | 14,415 | 3,800 | 4,448 |
| **Non-current liabilities** | **127,085** | **124,281** | **126,284** | **129,395** |
| Trade payables | 26,983 | 21,575 | 16,838 | 23,074 |
| Other current liabilities | 23,872 | 23,142 | 22,452 | 26,157 |
| Current debt | 11,063 | 10,646 | 12,098 | 10,695 |
| **Current liabilities** | **61,918** | **55,363** | **51,388** | **59,926** |
| **Liabilities held for sale** | **0** | **0** | **97** | **0** |
| **Total liabilities and shareholders' equity** | **289,407** | **276,487** | **276,156** | **301,963** |

Source: Annual financial statements of BP (standardized and adjusted for operating leases). Average exchange rate in 2017 (2016): $1 = £0.77 ($1 = £0.75).

(continued)

**EXHIBIT 4** Standardized financial statements and financial ratios of BP, Royal Dutch Shell, and Statoil for the fiscal year ended December 31, 2017 (Continued)

## ROE DECOMPOSITION – BP

| Ratio | 2017 | 2016 | 2015 |
|---|---|---|---|
| Net operating profit margin | 1.9% | −0.5% | −2.1% |
| × Operating asset turnover | 1.44 | 1.06 | 1.17 |
| = Return on net operating assets | 2.7% | −0.6% | −2.5% |
| Return on net operating assets | 2.7% | −0.6% | −2.5% |
| × (Net operating assets/Invested capital) | 0.81 | 0.83 | 0.86 |
| + Return on non-operating investments | 5.2% | 4.4% | 4.6% |
| × (Non-operating investments/Invested capital) | 0.19 | 0.17 | 0.14 |
| = Return on invested capital | 3.2% | 0.3% | −1.5% |
| Spread | 1.2% | −1.3% | -2.9% |
| × Financial leverage | 1.08 | 1.14 | 1.10 |
| = Financial leverage gain | 1.3% | −1.5% | −3.1% |
| ROE = Return on invested capital + Financial leverage gain | 4.5% | −1.2% | −4.6% |

Source: Author's own calculations. Ratios have been calculated after excluding net non-recurring income or expense.

## CONSOLIDATED INCOME STATEMENTS – ROYAL DUTCH SHELL ($ millions)

| Fiscal year ended December 31 | 2017 | 2016 | 2015 |
|---|---|---|---|
| **Revenue** | **305,179** | **233,591** | **264,960** |
| Operating expenses | (281,623) | (224,890) | (253,633) |
| **Operating profit** | **23,556** | **8,701** | **11,327** |
| Investment and interest income | 4,225 | 3,545 | 3,527 |
| Net non-recurring income or expense | (4,190) | (1,902) | (9,326) |
| Interest expense | (4,539) | (3,724) | (2,388) |
| **Profit before taxes** | **19,052** | **6,620** | **3,140** |
| Tax expense | (4,695) | (829) | 153 |
| **Profit after taxes** | **14,357** | **5,791** | **3,293** |
| Profit or loss to non-controlling interest | (458) | (202) | (261) |
| **Profit or loss to ordinary shareholders** | **13,899** | **5,589** | **3,032** |

## CONSOLIDATED BALANCE SHEETS – ROYAL DUTCH SHELL ($ millions)

| Fiscal year ended December 31 | 2017 | 2016 | 2015 | 2014 |
|---|---|---|---|---|
| ASSETS | | | | |
| Non-current tangible assets | 248,204 | 260,133 | 206,967 | 218,588 |
| Non-current intangible assets | 24,180 | 23,967 | 6,283 | 7,076 |
| Minority equity investments | 27,927 | 33,255 | 30,150 | 31,558 |
| Other non-operating investments | 19,415 | 16,961 | 16,495 | 14,101 |
| Deferred tax asset | 13,791 | 14,425 | 11,033 | 8,131 |
| **Total non-current assets** | **333,517** | **348,741** | **270,928** | **279,454** |

**EXHIBIT 4** Standardized financial statements and financial ratios of BP, Royal Dutch Shell, and Statoil for the fiscal year ended December 31, 2017 (Continued)

**CONSOLIDATED BALANCE SHEETS – ROYAL DUTCH SHELL ($ millions)**

| Fiscal year ended December 31 | 2017 | 2016 | 2015 | 2014 |
|---|---|---|---|---|
| Inventories | 25,223 | 21,775 | 15,822 | 19,701 |
| Trade receivables | 30,721 | 25,766 | 20,607 | 28,393 |
| Other current assets | 19,148 | 19,898 | 25,177 | 30,077 |
| Cash and cash equivalents | 20,312 | 19,130 | 31,752 | 21,607 |
| **Total current assets** | **95,404** | **86,569** | **93,358** | **99,778** |
| **Total assets** | **428,921** | **435,310** | **364,286** | **379,232** |
| LIABILITIES AND SHAREHOLDERS' EQUITY | | | | |
| **Ordinary shareholders' equity** | **194,356** | **186,646** | **162,876** | **171,966** |
| **Non-controlling interest in equity** | **3,456** | **1,865** | **1,245** | **820** |
| Non-current debt | 133,907 | 150,775 | 115,713 | 104,600 |
| Deferred tax liability | 13,007 | 15,274 | 8,976 | 12,052 |
| Other non-current liabilities | 4,428 | 6,925 | 4,528 | 3,582 |
| **Non-current liabilities** | **151,342** | **172,974** | **129,217** | **120,234** |
| Trade payables | 33,196 | 28,069 | 23,795 | 32,131 |
| Other current liabilities | 31,311 | 32,488 | 37,558 | 42,907 |
| Current debt | 15,260 | 13,268 | 9,595 | 11,174 |
| **Current liabilities** | **79,767** | **73,825** | **70,948** | **86,212** |
| **Total liabilities and shareholders' equity** | **428,921** | **435,310** | **364,286** | **379,232** |

Source: Annual financial statements of Royal Dutch Shell (standardized and adjusted for operating leases). Average exchange rate in 2017 (2016): $1 = €0.89 ($1 = €0.91).

**ROE DECOMPOSITION – ROYAL DUTCH SHELL**

| Ratio | 2017 | 2016 | 2015 |
|---|---|---|---|
| Net operating profit margin | 5.8% | 3.1% | 3.6% |
| × Operating asset turnover | 1.01 | 0.87 | 1.12 |
| = Return on net operating assets | 5.9% | 2.8% | 4.0% |
| Return on net operating assets | 5.9% | 2.8% | 4.0% |
| × (Net operating assets/Invested capital) | 0.86 | 0.83 | 0.82 |
| + Return on non-operating investments | 6.5% | 4.9% | 5.1% |
| × (Non-operating investments/Invested capital) | 0.14 | 0.17 | 0.18 |
| = Return on invested capital | 6.0% | 3.1% | 4.2% |
| Spread | 3.8% | 1.2% | 2.7% |
| × Financial leverage | 0.81 | 0.82 | 0.72 |
| = Financial leverage gain | 3.1% | 1.0% | 1.9% |
| ROE = Return on invested capital + Financial leverage gain | 9.1% | 4.1% | 6.1% |

Source: Author's own calculations. Ratios have been calculated after excluding net non-recurring income or expense.

(continued)

**EXHIBIT 4** Standardized financial statements and financial ratios of BP, Royal Dutch Shell, and Statoil for the fiscal year ended December 31, 2017 (Continued)

## CONSOLIDATED INCOME STATEMENTS – STATOIL ($ millions)

| Fiscal year ended December 31 | 2017 | 2016 | 2015 |
|---|---|---|---|
| Revenue | 60,971 | 45,688 | 57,900 |
| Operating expenses | (48,289) | (43,980) | (50,718) |
| Operating profit | 12,682 | 1,708 | 7,182 |
| Investment and interest income | 188 | (119) | (29) |
| Net non-recurring income or expense | 1,055 | (1,301) | (5,527) |
| Interest expense | (506) | (467) | (1,569) |
| Profit before taxes | 13,419 | (179) | 57 |
| Tax expense | (8,822) | (2,724) | (5,225) |
| Profit after taxes | 4,597 | (2,903) | (5,168) |
| Profit or loss to non-controlling interest | (8) | (20) | (22) |
| Profit or loss to ordinary shareholders | 4,589 | (2,923) | (5,190) |

## CONSOLIDATED BALANCE SHEETS – STATOIL ($ millions)

| Fiscal year ended December 31 | 2017 | 2016 | 2015 | 2014 |
|---|---|---|---|---|
| ASSETS | | | | |
| Non-current tangible assets | 70,725 | 67,035 | 71,664 | 89,105 |
| Non-current intangible assets | 8,621 | 9,243 | 9,452 | 11,458 |
| Minority equity investments | 2,551 | 2,245 | 824 | 1,127 |
| Other non-operating investments | 13,507 | 12,287 | 14,404 | 12,440 |
| Deferred tax asset | 2,441 | 2,195 | 2,022 | 1,732 |
| Derivatives – asset | 1,762 | 2,311 | 3,239 | 4,740 |
| Total non-current assets | 99,607 | 95,316 | 101,605 | 120,602 |
| Inventories | 3,398 | 3,227 | 2,502 | 3,193 |
| Trade receivables | 7,649 | 5,504 | 4,464 | 2,687 |
| Other current assets | 1,776 | 2,335 | 2,207 | 8,525 |
| Cash and cash equivalents | 4,390 | 5,090 | 8,623 | 11,182 |
| Total current assets | 17,213 | 16,156 | 17,796 | 25,587 |
| Assets held for sale | 1,369 | 537 | 0 | 0 |
| Total assets | 118,189 | 112,009 | 119,401 | 146,189 |
| LIABILITIES AND SHAREHOLDERS' EQUITY | | | | |
| Ordinary shareholders' equity | 39,862 | 35,073 | 40,272 | 51,227 |
| Non-controlling interest in equity | 24 | 27 | 36 | 57 |
| Non-current debt | 50,732 | 52,264 | 55,024 | 60,597 |
| Deferred tax liability | 7,654 | 6,427 | 7,421 | 9,613 |
| Derivatives – liability | 1,303 | 1,928 | 1,549 | 1,498 |
| Non-current liabilities | 59,689 | 60,619 | 63,994 | 71,708 |
| Trade payables | 3,181 | 2,358 | 2,052 | 2,928 |
| Other current liabilities | 10,454 | 7,771 | 8,975 | 14,226 |
| Current debt | 4,979 | 6,107 | 4,072 | 6,043 |
| Current liabilities | 18,614 | 16,236 | 15,099 | 23,197 |
| Liabilities held for sale | 0 | 54 | 0 | 0 |
| Total liabilities and shareholders' equity | 118,189 | 112,009 | 119,401 | 146,189 |

Source: Annual financial statements of Statoil (standardized and adjusted for operating leases).

**EXHIBIT 4**  Standardized financial statements and financial ratios of BP, Royal Dutch Shell, and Statoil for the fiscal year ended December 31, 2017 (Continued)

## ROE DECOMPOSITION – STATOIL

| Ratio | 2017 | 2016 | 2015 |
|---|---|---|---|
| Net operating profit margin | 6.6% | −3.3% | 0.1% |
| × Operating asset turnover | 0.79 | 0.58 | 0.64 |
| = Return on net operating assets | 5.2% | −1.9% | 0.0% |
| Return on net operating assets | 5.2% | −1.9% | 0.0% |
| × (Net operating assets/Invested capital) | 0.83 | 0.82 | 0.83 |
| + Return on non-operating investments | 0.9% | −0.5% | −0.1% |
| × (Non-operating investments/Invested capital) | 0.17 | 0.18 | 0.17 |
| = Return on invested capital | 4.5% | −1.6% | 0.0% |
| Spread | 3.8% | −2.2% | −1.8% |
| × Financial leverage | 1.56 | 1.57 | 1.37 |
| = Financial leverage gain | 5.9% | −3.5% | −2.5% |
| ROE = Return on invested capital + Financial leverage gain | 10.4% | −5.1% | −2.5% |

Source: Author's own calculations. Ratios have been calculated after excluding net non-recurring income or expense.

# 7 Prospective analysis: Valuation theory and concepts

The previous chapter introduced forecasting, the first stage of prospective analysis. In this and the following chapter, we describe valuation, the second and final stage of prospective analysis. This chapter focuses on valuation theory and concepts, and the following chapter discusses implementation issues.

Valuation is the process of converting a forecast into an estimate of the value of the firm's assets or equity. At some level, nearly every business decision involves valuation, at least implicitly. Within the firm, capital budgeting involves consideration of how a particular project will affect firm value. Strategic planning focuses on how value is influenced by larger sets of actions. Outside the firm, security analysts conduct valuation to support their buy/sell decisions, and potential acquirers (often with the assistance of investment bankers) estimate the value of target firms and the synergies they might offer. Even credit analysts, who typically do not explicitly estimate firm value, must at least implicitly consider the value of the firm's equity "cushion" if they are to maintain a complete view of the risk associated with lending activity.

In practice, a wide variety of valuation approaches are employed. For example, in evaluating the fairness of a takeover bid, investment bankers commonly use five to ten different methods of valuation. Among the available methods are the following:

- Discounted dividends. This approach expresses the value of the firm's equity as the present value of forecasted future dividends.
- Discounted cash flow (DCF) analysis. This approach involves the production of detailed, multiple-year forecasts of cash flows. The forecasts are then discounted at the firm's estimated cost of capital to arrive at an estimated present value.
- Discounted abnormal profit. Under this approach the value of the firm's equity is expressed as the sum of its book value and the present value of forecasted **abnormal profits (or losses)**.
- Discounted abnormal profit growth. This approach defines the value of the firm's equity as the sum of its capitalized next-period profit or loss forecast and the present value of forecasted **abnormal profit growth** beyond the next period.
- Valuation based on price multiples. Under this approach a current measure of performance or single forecast of performance is converted into a value by applying an appropriate price multiple derived from the value of comparable firms. For example, firm value can be estimated by applying a price-to-earnings ratio to a forecast of the firm's profit (earnings) for the coming year. Other commonly used multiples include price-to-book ratios and price-to-revenue ratios.

These methods are developed throughout the chapter, and their pros and cons discussed. All of the preceding approaches can be structured in two ways. The first is to directly value the equity of the firm, since this is usually the variable the analyst is directly interested in estimating. The second is to value the net operating assets and non-operating investments of the firm and then to deduct the value of debt claims to arrive at the final equity value estimate. Theoretically, both approaches should generate the same values. However, as we will see in the next chapter, there are implementation issues in reconciling the approaches. In this chapter we illustrate valuation using an all-equity firm to simplify the discussion. A brief discussion of the theoretical issues in valuing a firm's assets is included in Appendix A.

# Defining value for shareholders

How should shareholders think about the value of their equity claims on a firm? Finance theory holds that the value of any financial claim is simply the present value of the cash payoffs that its claimholders receive. Since shareholders receive cash payoffs from a company in the form of dividends, the value of their equity is the present value of future dividends (including any liquidating dividend).[1]

$$\text{Equity value} = \text{PV of expected future dividends}$$

If we denote $r_e$ as the cost of equity capital (the relevant discount rate), the **equity value** is as follows:

$$\text{Equity value}_0 = \frac{\text{Dividend}_1}{\left(1+r_e\right)} + \frac{\text{Dividend}_2}{\left(1+r_e\right)^2} + \frac{\text{Dividend}_3}{\left(1+r_e\right)^3} + \ldots$$

Notice that the valuation formula views a firm as having an indefinite life. But in reality firms can go bankrupt or get taken over. In these situations shareholders effectively receive a terminating dividend on their shares.

In practice, analysts tend to produce detailed forecasts for a finite near-term period, referred to as the forecast horizon, and make simplifying assumptions about firm performance after the forecast horizon. Using a forecast horizon of three years, equity value can be written as follows:

$$\text{Equity value}_0 = \frac{\text{Dividend}_1}{\left(1+r_e\right)} + \frac{\text{Dividend}_2}{\left(1+r_e\right)^2} + \frac{\text{Dividend}_3}{\left(1+r_e\right)^3}$$
$$+ \text{PV of dividends beyond year 3}$$

In this equation, the last term represents the terminal value – in this particular model the expected value of equity at the end of the forecast horizon.

If a firm had a constant dividend growth rate ($g^{\text{div}}$) indefinitely, its value would simplify to the following formula:

$$\text{Equity value}_0 = \frac{\text{Dividend}_1}{r_e - g^{\text{div}}}$$

To better understand how the discounted dividend approach works, consider the following example. At the beginning of year 1, Down Under Company raises €60 million of equity and uses the proceeds to buy a fixed asset. Operating profits before depreciation (all received in cash) and dividends for the company are expected to be €40 million in year 1, €50 million in year 2, and €60 million in year 3, at which point the company terminates (having a terminal value of zero). The firm pays no taxes. Assuming straight-line depreciation to zero (of €20 million per year), the firm's profits thus equal €20 million in year 1, €30 million in year 2, and €40 million in year 3. If the cost of equity capital for this firm is 10 percent, the value of the firm's equity is computed as follows:

| Year | Dividend | PV factor | PV of dividend |
|------|----------|-----------|----------------|
|      | (a) | (b) | (a) × (b) |
| 1 | €40m | 0.9091 | €36.4m |
| 2 | 50 | 0.8264 | 41.3 |
| 3 | 60 | 0.7513 | 45.1 |
| Equity value | | | €122.8m |

The preceding valuation formula is called the dividend discount model. It forms the basis for most of the popular theoretical approaches for equity valuation. Despite its theoretical importance, the dividend discount model is not a very useful valuation model in practice. This is because equity value is created primarily through the investment and operating activities of a firm. Dividend payments tend to be a by-product of such activities, and their timing and amount depends strongly on the firm's investment opportunities. Within a period of five to ten years, which tends to be the focus of most prospective analyses, dividends may therefore reveal very little about the firm's equity value. For example, high-growth start-up firms tend not to pay out dividends until later into their life cycle, but they nonetheless have value when they start their operations. Predicting long-run dividends for these firms is a tedious, virtually impossible task. Because the first stage of the prospective analysis, as discussed in Chapter 6, typically produces comprehensive, detailed forecasts for the near term but unavoidably makes simplifying assumptions for the longer term, useful valuation models value near-term profitability and growth directly rather than indirectly through long-run dividends. The remainder of this chapter discusses how the dividend discount model can be recast to generate such useful models. The models that we discuss are the discounted cash flow, discounted abnormal profit, discounted abnormal profit growth, and price multiple models of value.

## The discounted cash flow model

As we described in the previous section, the value of an asset or investment is the present value of the net cash payoffs that the asset generates. The **discounted cash flow** valuation model clearly reflects this basic principle of finance. The model defines the value of a firm's business assets as the present value of cash flows generated by these assets (OCF) minus the investments made in new business assets (Investment) or, alternatively stated, as the sum of the **free cash flows to debt and equity** holders discounted at the cost of capital $(r_c)$.

$$\text{Business value}_0 = \text{PV of free cash flows to debt and equity}$$

$$= \frac{OCF_1 - Investment_1}{(1+r_c)} + \frac{OCF_2 - Investment_2}{(1+r_c)^2} + \frac{OCF_3 - Investment_3}{(1+r_c)^3}$$

$$+ \text{PV of free cash flows to debt and equity beyond year 3}$$

Note that in this equation OCF excludes interest payments (unlike the operating cash flows reported in IFRS Standards-based cash flow statements), as these are distributions to debt holders.

The cash flows that are available to equity holders are the cash flows generated by the firm's business assets minus investment outlays, adjusted for cash flows from and to debt holders, such as interest payments, debt repayments, and debts issues. As discussed in Chapter 5, operating cash flows to equity holders are simply profit or loss plus depreciation and amortization less changes in working capital. Investment outlays are expenditures for non-current operating assets and non-operating investments less asset sales. Finally, net cash flows from debt owners are issues of new debt less retirements. By rearranging these terms, the free cash flows to equity can be written as follows:

$$\text{Free cash flows to equity} = \text{Profit or loss} - \Delta BVA + \Delta BVD$$

where $\Delta BVA$ is the change in book value of business assets (changes in working capital plus investment expenditures less depreciation and amortization expense), and $\Delta BVD$ is the change in book value of (interest-bearing) debt. Using the discounted cash flow model, equity value is thus estimated as follows:

$$\text{Equity value}_0 = \text{PV of free cash flow to equity}$$

$$= \frac{\text{Profit or loss}_1 - \Delta BVA_1 + \Delta BVD_1}{(1+r_e)} + \frac{\text{Profit or loss}_2 - \Delta BVA_2 + \Delta BVD_2}{(1+r_e)^2}$$

$$+ \frac{\text{Profit or loss}_3 - \Delta BVA_3 + \Delta BVD_3}{(1+r_e)^3} + \text{PV of free cash flow to equity beyond year 3}$$

If we assume a forecast horizon of three years, the last term in this equation again represents the terminal value. Valuation under this method therefore involves the following three steps:

**Step 1:** Forecast free cash flows available to equity holders over a finite forecast horizon (usually five to ten years; three years in the preceding example) using detailed information obtained during the first three steps of the business analysis process.

**Step 2:** Forecast free cash flows beyond the terminal year based on some simplifying assumption (to estimate the terminal value).

**Step 3:** Discount free cash flows to equity holders at the cost of equity. The discounted amount represents the estimated value of free cash flows available to equity.

Returning to the Down Under Company example, there is no debt, so the free cash flows to owners are simply the operating profits before depreciation. Since the company's cost of equity is assumed to be 10 percent, the present value of the free cash flows is as follows:

| Year | Profit or loss | Change in book value of business assets | Change in book value of debt | Free cash flows to equity | PV factor | PV of free cash flows |
|------|----------------|------------------------------------------|------------------------------|---------------------------|-----------|------------------------|
|      | (a)            | (b)                                      | (c)                          | (d) = (a) − (b) + (c)     | (e)       | (d) × (e)              |
| 1    | €20m           | −€20m                                    | €0m                          | €40m                      | 0.9091    | €36.4m                 |
| 2    | 30             | −20                                      | 0                            | 50                        | 0.8264    | 41.3                   |
| 3    | 40             | −20                                      | 0                            | 60                        | 0.7513    | 45.1                   |
| Equity value | | | | | | €122.8m |

Earlier we indicated that the discounted cash flow model can be obtained by recasting the dividend discount model. To see how this works, recall our formulation of the free cash flows to equity holders in terms of profit or loss, the change in the book value of business assets ($\Delta$BVA), and the change in the book value of debt ($\Delta$BVD). In the recast financial statements, which we described in Chapter 5 and use throughout this book, the change in the book value of business assets minus the change in the book value of debt is equal to the change in the book value of equity ($\Delta$BVE). The free cash flows to equity can therefore be written as:

$$\text{Free cash flow to equity} = \text{Profit or loss} - \Delta\text{BVA} + \Delta\text{BVD}$$
$$= \text{Profit or loss} - \Delta\text{BVE}$$
$$= \text{Dividends}$$

which illustrates the relationship between free cash flows to equity and dividends.[2]

As discussed in Chapter 6, the key ingredient to an accurate prediction of future free cash flows is a full set of predicted future (condensed) income statements and balance sheets. Given the prominence of profit or loss forecasts in most prospective analyses, models have been developed that express equity value directly in terms of expected profits (or losses), book values of equity, and cost of equity, thus further sharpening the focus of the valuation exercise. The following sections describe two of these accounting-based valuation models: the **discounted abnormal profit model** and the **discounted abnormal profit growth model**. In a later section, we also show that these accounting-based valuation models can help in better understanding the rationale underlying valuation based on price multiples.

# The discounted abnormal profit model

As discussed in Chapter 3, there is a link between dividends, profits, and equity. At the end of each accounting period, profit (or loss) for the period is added to (subtracted from) retained earnings, a component of equity. Dividends are taken out of retained earnings. Stated differently, if all equity effects (other than capital transactions) flow through the income statement,[3] the expected book value of equity for existing shareholders at the end of year 1 ($BVE_1$) is simply the book value at the beginning of the year ($BVE_0$) plus expected profit or loss (Profit or loss$_1$) less expected dividends (Dividend$_1$).[4] This relation can be written as follows:

$$\text{Dividend}_1 = \text{Profit or loss}_1 + BVE_0 - BVE_1$$

By substituting this identity for dividends into the dividend discount formula and rearranging the terms, equity value can be rewritten as follows:[5]

$$\text{Equity value} = \text{Book value of equity} + \text{PV of future abnormal profits}$$

Abnormal profits (or losses) are profit or loss adjusted for a capital charge, which is computed as the discount rate multiplied by the beginning book value of equity. Abnormal profits incorporate an adjustment to reflect the fact that accountants do not recognize any opportunity cost for equity funds used. Thus, using a forecast horizon of three years, the discounted abnormal profit valuation formula is:

$$\text{Equity value}_0 = BVE_0 + \frac{\text{Profit or loss}_1 - r_e \cdot BVE_0}{(1+r_e)} + \frac{\text{Profit or loss}_2 - r_e \cdot BVE_1}{(1+r_e)^2}$$

$$+ \frac{\text{Profit or loss}_3 - r_e \cdot BVE_2}{(1+r_e)^3} + \text{PV of abnormal profits beyond year 3}$$

where the last term in the equation denotes the terminal value.

The profit-based formulation, which is also referred to in practice as the residual income model, has intuitive appeal. If a firm can earn only a normal rate of return on its book value, then investors should be willing to pay no more than book value for its shares. Investors should pay more or less than book value if profits are above or below this normal level. Thus the deviation of a firm's market value from book value depends on its ability to generate "abnormal profit." The formulation also implies that a firm's equity value reflects the cost of its existing net assets (i.e., its book equity) plus the net present value of future growth options (represented by cumulative abnormal profits and losses).

To illustrate the profit-based valuation approach, let's return to the Down Under Company example. Assuming the company depreciates its fixed assets using the straight-line method, its accounting-based profits will be €20 million lower than dividends in each of the three years. Further, the book value of equity at the beginning of years 2 and 3 equals prior year's beginning book value plus prior year's profit or loss minus prior year's dividends. The firm's beginning book equity, profit or loss, abnormal profits, and valuation will be as follows:

| Year | Beginning book equity | Profit or loss | Capital charge | Abnormal profits | PV factor | PV of abnormal profits |
|---|---|---|---|---|---|---|
| | (a) | (b) | (c) = $r_e$ × (a) | (d) = (b) − (c) | (e) | (d) × (e) |
| 1 | €60m | €20m | €6m | €14m | 0.9091 | €12.7m |
| 2 | 40 | 30 | 4 | 26 | 0.8264 | 21.5 |
| 3 | 20 | 40 | 2 | 38 | 0.7513 | 28.6 |
| Cumulative PV of abnormal profits in years 1–3 | | | | | | 62.8 |
| PV of abnormal profits beyond year 3 | | | | | | 0.0 |
| + Beginning book value of equity | | | | | | 60.0 |
| = Equity value | | | | | | €122.8m |

Notice that the value of Down Under's equity is exactly the same as that estimated using the discounted cash flow method. This should not be surprising. Both methods are derived from the dividend discount model. And in estimating value under the two approaches, we have used the same underlying assumptions to forecast profits and cash flows.

## Key Analysis Questions

**V**aluation of equity under the discounted abnormal profit method requires the analyst to answer the following questions:

- What are expected future profits or losses and book values of equity (and therefore abnormal profits) over a finite forecast horizon (usually five to ten years) given the firm's industry competitiveness and the firm's positioning?
- What is expected future abnormal profit or loss beyond the final year of the forecast horizon (called the "terminal year") based on some simplifying assumption? If abnormal returns are expected to persist, what are the barriers to entry that deter competition?
- What is the firm's cost of equity used to compute the present value of abnormal profits and losses? (We will discuss cost of equity estimation in more detail in Chapter 8.)

### ACCOUNTING METHODS AND DISCOUNTED ABNORMAL PROFIT

One question that arises when valuation is based directly on profits (or losses) and book values is how the estimate is affected by managers' choice of accounting methods and accrual estimates. Would estimates of value differ for two otherwise identical firms if one used more conservative accounting methods than the other? We will see that, provided analysts recognize the impact of differences in accounting methods on future profits (and hence their profit or loss forecasts), the accounting effects per se should have no influence on their value estimates. There are two reasons for this. First, accounting choices that affect a firm's current profit or loss also affect its book value, and therefore they affect the capital charges used to estimate future abnormal profits. For example, conservative accounting not only lowers a firm's current profit or loss and book equity but also reduces future capital charges and inflates its future abnormal profits. Second, double-entry bookkeeping is by nature self-correcting. Inflated profits for one period have to be ultimately reversed in subsequent periods.

To understand how these two effects undo the effect of differences in accounting methods or accrual estimates, let's return to Down Under Company and see what happens if its managers choose to be conservative and expense some unusual costs that could have been capitalized as inventory in year 1. This accounting decision causes profits and ending book value to be lower by €10 million. The inventory is then sold in year 2. For the time being, let's say the accounting choice has no influence on the analyst's view of the firm's real performance.

Managers' choice reduces abnormal profit in year 1 and book value at the beginning of year 2 by €10 million. However, future profits will be higher, for two reasons. First, future profits will be higher (by €10 million) when the inventory is sold in year 2 at a lower cost of sales. Second, the benchmark for normal profits (based on book value of equity) will be lower by €10 million. The €10 million decline in abnormal profit in year 1 is perfectly offset (on a present value basis) by the €11 million higher abnormal profit in year 2. As a result, the value of Down Under Company under conservative reporting is identical to the value under the earlier accounting method (€122.8 million).

| Year | Beginning book equity | Profit or loss | Capital charge | Abnormal profits | PV factor | PV of abnormal profits |
|---|---|---|---|---|---|---|
| | (a) | (b) | (c) = $r_e \times$ (a) | (d) = (b) − (c) | (e) | (d) × (e) |
| 1 | €60m | €10m | €6m | €4m | 0.9091 | €3.6m |
| 2 | 30 | 40 | 3 | 37 | 0.8264 | 30.6 |
| 3 | 20 | 40 | 2 | 38 | 0.7513 | 28.6 |
| Cumulative PV of abnormal profits in years 1–3 | | | | | | 62.8 |
| PV of abnormal profits beyond year 3 | | | | | | 0.0 |
| + Beginning book value of equity | | | | | | 60.0 |
| = Equity value | | | | | | €122.8m |

Provided the analyst is aware of biases in accounting data that arise from managers' using aggressive or conservative accounting choices, abnormal profit-based valuations are unaffected by the variation in accounting decisions. This shows that strategic and accounting analyses are critical precursors to abnormal profit valuation. The strategic and accounting analysis tools help the analyst to identify whether abnormal profits arise from sustainable competitive advantage or from unsustainable accounting manipulations. For example, consider the implications of failing to understand the reasons for a decline in profit from a change in inventory policy for Down Under Company. If the analyst mistakenly interpreted the decline as indicating that the firm was having difficulty moving its inventory, rather than that it had used conservative accounting, she might reduce expectations of future profits. The estimated value of the firm would then be lower than that reported in our example. To avoid such mistakes, the analyst would be wise to go through all steps of the accounting analysis, including step 6 (undo accounting distortions), and then perform the financial and prospective analyses using the restated financial statements.

## The discounted abnormal profit growth model

As previously discussed, abnormal profit is the amount of profit that a firm generates in excess of the opportunity cost for equity funds used. The annual change in abnormal profit is generally referred to as abnormal profit growth and can be rewritten as follows:

$$
\begin{aligned}
&\text{Abnormal profit growth}\\
&= \text{change in abnormal profit}\\
&= \left(\text{Profit or loss}_2 - r_e \cdot \text{BVE}_1\right) - \left(\text{Profit or loss}_1 - r_e \cdot \text{BVE}_0\right)\\
&= \left(\text{Profit or loss}_2 - r_e \cdot \left[\text{BVE}_0 + \text{Profit or loss}_1 - \text{Dividends}_1\right]\right) - \left(\text{Profit or loss}_1 - r_e \cdot \text{BVE}_0\right)\\
&= \text{Profit or loss}_2 + r_e \cdot \text{Dividends}_1 - \left(1 + r_e\right) \cdot \text{Profit or loss}_1\\
&= \Delta \text{Profit or loss}_2 - r_e \cdot \left(\text{Profit or loss}_1 - \text{Dividends}_1\right)\\
&\left(= \text{abnormal change in profit}\right)
\end{aligned}
$$

This formula shows that abnormal profit growth is actual profit growth benchmarked against normal profit growth. Normal profit growth is calculated as the portion of prior period profit or loss that is retained in the firm times a normal rate of return. When abnormal profit growth is zero, the firm functions like a savings account. In this particular case, the firm earns an abnormal return on its existing investment but is able to earn only a normal rate of return on the additional investments that it finances from its retained profit. Consequently, an investor would be indifferent between reinvesting profits in the firm or receiving all profits in dividends.

The discounted dividend model can also be recast to generate a valuation model that defines equity value as the capitalized sum of (1) next-period profit or loss and (2) the discounted value of abnormal profit growth beyond the next period. Using a forecast horizon of three years, the **discounted abnormal profit growth** valuation formula is:[6]

$$Equity\ value_0 = \frac{Profit\ or\ loss_1}{r_e}$$

$$+\frac{1}{r_e}\left[\frac{\Delta Profit\ or\ loss_2 - r_e \cdot (Profit\ or\ loss_1 - Dividend_1)}{(1+r_e)}\right.$$

$$+\frac{\Delta Profit\ or\ loss_3 - r_e \cdot (Profit\ or\ loss_2 - Dividend_2)}{(1+r_e)^2}$$

$$\left. + PV\ of\ abnormal\ profit\ growth\ beyond\ year\ 3 \right]$$

This approach, under which valuation starts with capitalizing next-period profit or loss, has practical appeal because investment analysts spend much time and effort on estimating near-term profit as the starting point of their analysis. The valuation formula shows that differences between equity value and capitalized next-period profit or loss are explained by abnormal changes in profit – or changes in abnormal profit – beyond the next period. Notice that this formula also views the firm as having an indefinite life. However, the formula can be easily used for the valuation of a finite-life investment by extending the investment's life by one year and setting profits and dividends equal to zero in the last year. For example, consider the profits and dividends of the Down Under Company during its three years of existence. Capitalized year 1 profit is equal to €200.0 million (20.0/0.1). Abnormal profit growth equals €12.0 million in year 2 (30.0 + 40.0 × 0.1 − 20.0 × 1.1) and €12.0 million in year 3 (40.0 + 50.0 × 0.1 − 30.0 × 1.1). In year 4, when profit and dividends are zero, abnormal profit growth is −€38.0 million (0.0 + 60.0 × 0.1 − 40.0 × 1.1). The total value of the firm's equity is computed as follows:

| Year | Profit or loss | Retained profits | Normal profit growth | Abnormal profit growth | PV factor | PV of abnormal profit growth |
|---|---|---|---|---|---|---|
| | (a) | (b) = (a) − Dividends | (c) = $r_e$ × (b)$_{t-1}$ | (d) = Δ(a) − (c) | (e) | (d) × (e) |
| 1 | €20m | −€20m | | | | |
| 2 | 30 | −20 | −€2m | €12 | 0.9091 | €10.91m |
| 3 | 40 | −20 | −2 | 12 | 0.8264 | 9.92 |
| 4 | 0 | 0 | −2 | −38 | 0.7513 | −28.55 |
| Cumulative PV of abnormal profit growth | | | | | | −7.72 |
| + Profit or loss in year 1 | | | | | | 20.00 |
| = | | | | | | €12.28m |
| × 1/$r_e$ | | | | | | 10.00 |
| = Equity value | | | | | | €122.8m |

Note that the Down Under Company gradually reduces its investment because the annual dividend payments exceed annual profits. Consequently, normal profit growth is negative, and the firm's abnormal profit growth is greater than its actual profit growth in years 2 and 3.

Like the abnormal profit method, the value estimate from the abnormal profit growth model is not affected by the firm's accounting choices. For example, recall the situation where the Down Under Company reports conservatively and expenses unusual costs that could have been capitalized in year 1, thereby reducing profit by €10.0 million. Under conservative accounting, the value of capitalized year 1 profit decreases from €200.0 million to €100.0 million. This reduction, however, is exactly offset by an increase in the discounted value of abnormal profit growth, as shown in the following table:

| Year | Profit or loss | Retained profits | Normal profit growth | Abnormal profit growth | PV factor | PV of abnormal profit growth |
|------|---------------|------------------|---------------------|-----------------------|-----------|------------------------------|
| | (a) | (b) = (a) − Dividends | (c) = $r_e \times (b)_{t-1}$ | (d) = Δ(a) − (c) | (e) | (d) × (e) |
| 1 | €10m | −€30m | | | | |
| 2 | 40 | −10 | −€3m | €33 | 0.9091 | €30.00m |
| 3 | 40 | −20 | −1 | 1 | 0.8264 | 0.83 |
| 4 | 0 | 0 | −2 | −38 | 0.7513 | −28.55 |
| Cumulative PV of abnormal profit growth | | | | | | 2.28 |
| + Profit or loss in year 1 | | | | | | 10.00 |
| = | | | | | | €12.28m |
| × $1/r_e$ | | | | | | 10.00 |
| = Equity value | | | | | | €122.8m |

This value is again identical to the value estimated under the discounted dividends and abnormal profit approaches.

## Demonstration Case: Hennes & Mauritz AB

During the first week following the publication of the financial statements for the fiscal year ending on November 30, 2017, several analysts updated their forecasts of H&M's 2018 and 2019 revenue and profit or loss. Analysts' average expectations were as follows:

| SEK bn | 2017 realized | 2018 expected | 2019 expected |
|--------|---------------|---------------|---------------|
| Revenue | 200.0 | 215.8 | 232.0 |
| Profit or loss | 16.2 | 19.2 | 20.7 |

## Required:

1. These forecasts are not sufficient to estimate the value of H&M's equity. Forecast H&M's ending operating working capital, net non-current assets, debt and group equity under the simplifying assumption that the future growth in these items follows revenue growth.

2. Assume that H&M's cost of equity is 8 percent. Calculate:

   a. Dividends in 2018 and 2019.

   b. Abnormal profits in 2018 and 2019.

   c. Abnormal profit growth in 2019.

   d. Free cash flows to equity in 2018 and 2019.

3. To estimate H&M's equity value, we need to make an assumption about what will happen to H&M's profits, dividends, equity, debt, and assets after 2019. In the next chapter, we will discuss several assumptions that the analyst can make. For now, we make the somewhat unrealistic but convenient assumption that in 2020 H&M liquidates all its assets at their book values, uses the proceeds to pay off debt, and pays out the remainder to its equity holders. What does this assumption imply about:

   a. The book value of H&M's assets and liabilities at the end of 2020?

   b. H&M's profit or loss in 2020?

   c. H&M's final dividend payment in 2020?

   d. H&M's free cash flow to equity holders in 2020?

   e. H&M's abnormal profit growth in 2020 and 2021 (!)?

4. Estimate H&M's equity value at the end of fiscal 2017 using:

   a. The discounted dividends model and the discounted cash flow model.

   b. The discounted abnormal profit model.

   c. The discounted abnormal profit growth model.

# Answers:

1. Expected revenue growth in 2018 and 2019 is 7.9 percent (15.8/200.0) and 7.5 percent (16.2/215.8), respectively. The values of the four balance sheet items at the end of 2017 are known. Based on the expected revenue growth rates, the expected values at the end of 2018 and 2019 are:

| SEK bn | 2017 realized | 2018 expected | 2019 expected |
|---|---|---|---|
| Operating working capital | 25.3 | 27.3 | 29.3 |
| Net non-current assets | 117.9 | 127.2 | 136.8 |
| Debt | 83.4 | 90.0 | 96.7 |
| Group equity | 59.8 | 64.5 | 69.4 |
| Assets/Invested capital | 143.2 | 154.5 | 166.1 |

2. **Calculations:**

   a. $\text{Dividends}_{2018} = \text{Equity}_{2017} + \text{Profit}_{2018} - \text{Equity}_{2018} = 59.8 + 19.2 - 64.5 = 14.5$

   $\text{Dividends}_{2019} = \text{Equity}_{2018} + \text{Profit}_{2019} - \text{Equity}_{2019} = 64.5 + 20.7 - 69.4 = 15.8$

   b. $\text{Abnormal Profit}_{2018} = \text{Profit}_{2018} - r_e \times \text{Equity}_{2017} = 19.2 - 8\% \times 59.8 = 14.4$

   $\text{Abnormal Profit}_{2019} = \text{Profit}_{2019} - r_e \times \text{Equity}_{2018} = 20.7 - 8\% \times 64.5 = 15.5$

   c. $\text{Abnormal Profit growth}_{2019} = \Delta\text{Profit}_{2019} - r_e \times (\text{Profit}_{2018} - \text{Dividends}_{2018}) =$
   $1.5 - 8\% \times (19.2 - 14.5) = 1.1$

   (Check that Abnormal Profit growth = $\Delta$Abnormal profit [see b].)

   d. $\text{FCF to Equity}_{2018} = \text{Profit}_{2018} - \Delta\text{Assets}_{2018} + \Delta\text{Debt}_{2018} = 19.2 - 11.3 + 6.6 = 14.5$

   $\text{FCF to Equity}_{2019} = \text{Profit}_{2019} - \Delta\text{Assets}_{2019} + \Delta\text{Debt}_{2019} = 20.7 - 11.6 + 6.7 = 15.8$

   (Note that the free cash flows to equity holders is equal to the dividends paid out to equity holders.)

3. **Calculations:**

   a. H&M's assets and liabilities will have book values of zero at the end of 2020.

   b. H&M's profit or loss will be zero in 2020 because all assets have been sold at their book values (i.e., profit on the sale = 0).

   c. The final dividend payment in 2020 will be equal to the ending book value in 2019: $\text{Dividends}_{2020}$
   $= \text{Equity}_{2019} + \text{Profit}_{2020} - \text{Equity}_{2020} = 69.4 + 0 - 0 = 69.4$

   d. $\text{FCF to Equity}_{2020} = \text{Profit}_{2020} - \Delta\text{Assets}_{2020} + \Delta\text{Debt}_{2020} = 0 - (-166.1) + (-96.7) = 69.4$
   (Note that the final free cash flow to equity holders is equal to the final dividend.)

   e. $\text{Abnormal Profit}_{2020} = \text{Profit}_{2020} - r_e \times \text{Equity}_{2019} = 0 - 8\% \times 69.4 = -5.6$

   f. $\text{Abnormal Profit growth}_{2020} = \Delta\text{Profit}_{2020} - r_e \times (\text{Profit}_{2019} - \text{Dividends}_{2019}) = -20.7 - 8\% \times (20.7 - 15.8)$
   $= -21.1$

   $\text{Abnormal Profit growth}_{2021} = \Delta\text{Profit}_{2021} - r_e \times (\text{Profit}_{2020} - \text{Dividends}_{2020}) = 0 - 8\% \times (0 - 69.4) = 5.6$

   (Check that Abnormal profit growth = $\Delta$Abnormal profit [see e and 2b].)

4. **Calculations:**

   a. Note that H&M's expected dividends are exactly equal to its free cash flows to equity holders. Using the discounted dividends (DIV) model (or discounted cash flow model), H&M's equity value is calculated as follows:

   $$\text{Equity value}_{\text{end 2017}} = \frac{\text{DIV}_{2018}}{(1+r_e)} + \frac{\text{DIV}_{2019}}{(1+r_e)^2} + \frac{\text{DIV}_{2020}}{(1+r_e)^3}$$

   $$= \frac{14.5}{(1.08)} + \frac{15.8}{(1.08)^2} + \frac{69.4}{(1.08)^3} = 82.1$$

   b. Using the discounted abnormal profit (AP) model, H&M's equity value is calculated as follows:

   $$\text{Equity value}_{\text{end 2017}} = \text{BVE}_{2017} + \frac{\text{AP}_{2018}}{(1+r_e)} + \frac{\text{AP}_{2019}}{(1+r_e)^2} + \frac{\text{AP}_{2020}}{(1+r_e)^3}$$

   $$= 59.8 + \frac{14.4}{(1.08)} + \frac{15.5}{(1.08)^2} + \frac{-5.6}{(1.08)^3} = 82.1$$

   c. Using the discounted abnormal profit growth (APG) model, H&M's equity value is calculated as follows:

   $$\text{Equity value}_{\text{end 2017}} = \frac{\text{Profit or loss}_{2018}}{r_e} + \frac{1}{r_e}\left[\frac{\text{APG}_{2019}}{(1+r_e)} + \frac{\text{APG}_{2020}}{(1+r_e)^2} + \frac{\text{APG}_{2021}}{(1+r_e)^3}\right]$$

   $$= \frac{19.2}{0.08} + \frac{1}{0.08}\left[\frac{1.1}{(0.08)} + \frac{-21.1}{(0.08)^2} + \frac{5.6}{(0.08)^3}\right] = 82.1$$

At the end of 2017, H&M had 1,655,072 thousand shares outstanding. The equity value estimate of SEK82.1 billion thus corresponds with an estimate of SEK49.58 per share. On February 1, 2018, one day after H&M's annual earnings announcement, the company's closing share price was SEK139.52. Our estimate of equity value per share is substantially lower than the actual share price because we made very conservative assumptions about H&M's performance after 2019. In the next chapter we will discuss methods to arrive at more realistic (less conservative) equity value estimates.

# Valuation using price multiples

Valuations based on price multiples are widely used by analysts. The primary reason for the popularity of this method is its simplicity. Unlike the discounted dividend, discounted abnormal profit (growth), and discounted cash flow methods, **multiple-based valuations** do not require detailed multiyear forecasts of a number of parameters such as growth, profitability, and cost of capital.

Valuation using multiples involves the following three steps:

**Step 1:** Select a measure of performance or value (e.g., profit, revenue, cash flows, book equity, book assets) as the basis for multiple calculations. The two most commonly used metrics are based on profit and book equity.

**Step 2:** Calculate price multiples for comparable firms, that is, the ratio of the market value to the selected measure of performance or value.

**Step 3:** Apply the comparable firm multiple to the performance or value measure of the firm being analyzed.

Under this approach, the analyst relies on the market to undertake the difficult task of considering the short- and long-term prospects for growth and profitability and their implications for the values of the comparable firms. Then the analyst assumes that the pricing of those other firms is applicable to the firm at hand.

## MAIN ISSUES WITH MULTIPLE-BASED VALUATION

On the surface, using multiples seems straightforward. Unfortunately, in practice it is not as simple as it would appear. Identification of "comparable" firms is often quite difficult. There are also some choices to be made concerning how multiples will be calculated. Finally, understanding why multiples vary across firms, and how applicable another firm's multiple is to the one at hand, requires a sound knowledge of the determinants of each multiple.

### *Selecting comparable firms*

Ideally, price multiples used in a comparable firm analysis are those for firms with similar operating and financial characteristics. Firms within the same industry are the most obvious candidates. But even within narrowly defined industries, it is often difficult to identify comparable firms. Many firms are in multiple industries, making it difficult to identify representative benchmarks. In addition, firms within the same industry frequently have different strategies, growth opportunities, and profitability, creating selection problems.

One way of dealing with these issues is to average across *all* firms in the industry. The analyst implicitly hopes that the various sources of noncomparability cancel each other out so that the firm being valued is comparable to a "typical" industry member. Another approach is to focus only on those firms within the industry that are most similar.

For example, consider using multiples to value Hennes & Mauritz (H&M) or Inditex. Business and financial databases classify both companies in the apparel retail industry. Their competitors include Abercrombie & Fitch, Esprit, Gap, Fast Retailing (Uniqlo), and Next. The average price-earnings (PE) ratio for a profitable subset of these direct competitors was 19.2 and the average price-to-book (PB) ratio was 4.7. However, it is unclear whether these multiples are useful benchmarks for valuing H&M and Inditex. Not all of these competitors follow a similar strategy or financing policy, and some of them operate on a smaller scale, in terms of both revenue and geographic reach. In addition, not all competitors exhibit similar growth rates as H&M and Inditex.

A potential problem of choosing comparable firms from different countries is that a variety of factors that influence multiples may differ across countries. For example, the cost of equity, which is inversely related to the price-earnings multiple, is affected by the risk-free interest rate and the equity risk premium. Further, the expected profit growth rate, which positively affects the price-earnings multiple, partly depends on a country's future economic growth. Consequently, international differences in risk-free interest rates, equity risk premiums, and growth expectations lead to international differences in price-earnings multiples. In addition, international differences in accounting practices may lead to systematic international differences in profits or losses, which is the denominator in price-earnings multiples. The most obvious way to get around this problem is to choose comparable firms from one country. This is, however, often not feasible in smaller equity markets.

The alternative solution is to explicitly take into account the country factors that affect multiples. For example, when using the multiples of the preceding group of competitors, it is important to realize that at the time that the multiples were calculated, risk-free interest rates in Japan (domicile of Fast Retailing) were much lower than the risk-free interest rate in, for example, the United States (domicile of Abercrombie & Fitch and Gap). This may have reduced the average price-earnings multiple of Abercrombie & Fitch and Gap in comparison with the price-earnings multiple of Fast Retailing.

### Multiples for firms with poor performance

Price multiples can be affected when the denominator variable is performing poorly. This is especially common when the denominator is a flow measure, such as profits or cash flows. For example, one of H&M's competitors, Esprit, reported losses in 2017, making the price-earnings ratios negative. Because negative price-earnings ratios have no sensible meaning, these are ignored in the calculation of the average price-earnings ratio.

What are analysts' options for handling the problems for multiples created by transitory shocks to the denominator? One option is to simply exclude firms with large transitory effects from the set of comparable firms, as we did above. If poor performance is due to a one-time write-down or special item, analysts can simply exclude that effect from their computation of the comparable multiple. For example, in 2011 Esprit recorded a small profit of HK $0.06 per share, including close to HK $1.91 per share (after tax) in impairment and restructuring charges. If these charges were excluded, Esprit's profit would be HK $1.97 per share, and its price-earnings ratio would change from an unrealistically high value of 395.2 to a more informative value of 12.3. This change shows the sensitivity of price-earnings multiples to transitory shocks. Finally, analysts can reduce the effect on multiples of temporary problems in past performance by using a denominator that is a forecast of future performance rather than the past measure itself. Multiples based on forecasts are termed *leading* multiples, whereas those based on historical data are called *trailing* multiples. Leading multiples are less likely to include one-time gains and losses in the denominator, simply because such items are difficult to anticipate.

### Adjusting multiples for leverage

Price multiples should be calculated in a way that preserves consistency between the numerator and denominator. Consistency is an issue for those ratios where the denominator reflects performance *before* servicing debt. Examples include the price-to-revenue multiple and any multiple of operating profits or operating cash flows. When calculating these multiples, the numerator should include not just the market value of equity but the value of debt as well.

## DETERMINANTS OF VALUE-TO-BOOK AND VALUE-EARNINGS MULTIPLES

Even across relatively closely related firms, price multiples can vary considerably. The abnormal profit valuation method provides insight into factors that lead to differences in value-to-book multiples across firms. Similarly, the abnormal profit growth valuation method helps to explain why value-to-earnings multiples vary across firms.

If the abnormal profit formula is scaled by book value, the left-hand side becomes the equity value-to-book ratio as opposed to the equity value itself. The right-hand side variables now reflect three multiple drivers: (1) profit or loss deflated by book value, or our old friend return on equity (ROE), discussed in Chapter 5, (2) the growth in equity book value over time, and (3) the firm's cost of equity. The actual valuation formula is as follows:

$$\text{Equity value-to-book ratio}_0 = 1 + \frac{\text{ROE}_1 - r_e}{(1 + r_e)} + \frac{(\text{ROE}_2 - r_e)(1 + g_1^{\text{equity}})}{(1 + r_e)^2}$$
$$+ \frac{(\text{ROE}_3 - r_e)(1 + g_1^{\text{equity}})(1 + g_2^{\text{equity}})}{(1 + r_e)^3} + \dots$$

where $g_t^{equity}$ = growth in book value of equity (BVE) from year t-1 to year t or:

$$\frac{BVE_t - BVE_{t-1}}{BVE_{t-1}}$$

A firm's value-to-book ratio is largely driven by the magnitude of its future abnormal ROEs, defined as ROE less the cost of equity capital (ROE – $r_e$). Firms with positive abnormal ROE are able to invest their net assets to create value for shareholders and will have price-to-book ratios greater than one. In contrast, firms with negative abnormal ROEs are unable to invest shareholder funds at a rate greater than their cost of capital and have ratios below one.

The magnitude of a firm's value-to-book multiple also depends on the amount of growth in book value. Firms can grow their equity base by issuing new equity or by reinvesting profits. If this new equity is invested in positive valued projects for shareholders – that is, projects with ROEs that exceed the cost of capital – the firm will boost its equity value-to-book multiple. Conversely, for firms with ROEs that are less than the cost of capital, equity growth further lowers the multiple.

The valuation task can now be framed in terms of two key questions about the firm's "value drivers":

- Will the firm be able to generate ROEs that exceed its cost of equity capital? If so, for how long?
- How quickly will the firm's investment base (book value) grow?

If desired, the equation can be rewritten so that future ROEs are expressed as the product of their components: profit margins, asset turnover, and leverage. Thus the approach permits us to build directly on projections of the same accounting numbers utilized in financial analysis (see Chapter 5) without the need to convert projections of those numbers into cash flows. Yet in the end, the estimate of value should be the same as that from the dividend discount model.[7]

Returning to the Down Under Company example, the implied equity value-to-book multiple can be estimated as follows:

|  | Year 1 | Year 2 | Year 3 |
|---|---|---|---|
| Beginning book value of equity | €60m | €40m | €20m |
| Profit or loss | €20m | €30m | €40m |
| ROE | 0.33 | 0.75 | 2.00 |
| – Cost of equity | 0.10 | 0.10 | 0.10 |
| = Abnormal ROE | 0.23 | 0.65 | 1.90 |
| × (1 + cumulative book equity growth) | 1.00 | 0.67 | 0.33 |
| = Abnormal ROE scaled by book value growth | 0.23 | 0.43 | 0.63 |
| × PV factor | 0.909 | 0.826 | 0.751 |
| = PV of abnormal ROE scaled by book equity growth | 0.212 | 0.358 | 0.476 |
| Cumulative PV of abnormal ROE scaled by book equity growth | 1.046 | | |
| + 1.00 | 1.000 | | |
| = Equity value-to-book multiple | 2.046 | | |

The equity value-to-book multiple for Down Under is therefore 2.046, and the implied equity value is €122.8 (€60 times 2.046), once again identical to the dividend discount model value.

The equity value-to-book formulation can also be used to construct the equity value-earnings multiple as follows:

$$\text{Equity value-to-earnings multiple} = \text{Equity value-to-book multiple} \times \frac{\text{Book value of equity}}{\text{Profit or loss}}$$

$$= \frac{\text{Equity value-to-book multiple}}{\text{ROE}}$$

In other words, the same factors that drive a firm's equity value-to-book multiple also explain its equity value-earnings multiple. The key difference between the two multiples is that the value-earnings multiple is affected by the firm's current level of ROE performance, whereas the value-to-book multiple is not. Firms with low current ROEs therefore have very high value-earnings multiples and vice versa. If a firm has a zero or negative ROE, its PE multiple is not defined. Value-earnings multiples are therefore more volatile than value-to-book multiples.

The following data for a subset of firms in the apparel retail industry illustrate the relation between ROE, the price-to-book ratio, and the price-earnings ratio:

| Company | ROE | Price-to-book ratio | Price-earnings ratio |
|---|---|---|---|
| Abercrombie & Fitch | 1.6% | 1.2 | 86.4 |
| Fast Retailing | 16.4% | 4.4 | 28.0 |
| Gap | 27.5% | 4.2 | 15.2 |

Both the price-to-book and price-earnings ratios are high for Fast Retailing. Investors therefore expect that in the future Fast Retailing will generate higher ROEs than its current level (16.4 percent). In contrast, Gap has a high price-to-book ratio but a moderate price-earnings ratio (15.2). This indicates that investors expect that Gap will continue to generate positive abnormal ROEs but that the current level of ROE (27.5 percent) will be sustained. Finally, Abercrombie & Fitch has a relatively low price-to-book ratio (1.2) and a high price-earnings multiple. Investors apparently expect Abercrombie & Fitch to substantially improve its currently low performance (1.6 percent) but not to earn large abnormal ROEs in the future.

The effect of future growth in profit on the price-earnings multiple can also be seen from the model that arises when we scale the abnormal profit growth valuation formula by next-period profit. The valuation formula then becomes:

$$\text{Leading equity value-to-earnings ratio} =$$

$$\frac{1}{r_e} + \frac{1}{r_e}\left[\frac{g_2^{\text{profit}} + (d_1 - 1)r_e}{(1 + r_e)} + \frac{(1 + g_2^{\text{profit}})\left[g_3^{\text{profit}} + (d_2 - 1)r_e\right]}{(1 + r_e)^2} + \dots\right]$$

where

$$d_t = \text{dividend payout ratio in year t}$$

$$g_t^{\text{profit}} = \text{growth in profit (P) from year t} - 1 \text{ to year t or } \frac{P_t - P_{t-1}}{P_{t-1}}$$

In this formula, future profit growth rates and dividend payouts are the basis for estimating price-earnings multiples.[8] Consider the profit growth rates and dividend payout ratios of the Down Under Company. The profit growth rates ($g_t^{\text{profit}}$) are 50, 33, and −100 percent in years 2, 3, and 4, respectively. Dividend payouts are

200 percent, 167 percent, and 150 percent in years 1, 2, and 3, respectively. Substituting these percentages in the leading price-earnings formula yields:

Leading equity value-to-earnings ratio =

$$\frac{1}{r_e} + \frac{1}{r_e}\left[\frac{g_2^{\text{profit}} + (d_1 - 1)r_e}{(1 + r_e)} + \frac{(1 + g_2^{\text{profit}})[g_3^{\text{profit}} + (d_2 - 1)r_e]}{(1 + r_e)^2}\right.$$

$$\left. + \frac{(1 + g_2^{\text{profit}})(1 + g_3^{\text{profit}})[g_4^{\text{profit}} + (d_3 - 1)r_e]}{(1 + r_e)^3} + \ldots\right]$$

$$= \frac{1}{0.1} + \frac{1}{0.1}\left[\frac{0.5 + 0.1}{(1.1)} + \frac{1.5 \times [0.33 + 0.067]}{(1.1)^2} + \frac{1.5 \times 1.33 \times [-1 + 0.05]}{(1.1)^3}\right] = 6.14$$

The price-earnings multiple of 6.14 is consistent with a value of equity of €122.8 (6.14 × €20).

## Key Analysis Questions

To value a firm using multiples, an analyst must assess the quality of the variable used as the multiple basis and determine the appropriate peer firms to include in the benchmark multiple. Analysts are therefore likely to be interested in answering the following questions:

- How well does the denominator used in the multiple reflect the firm's performance? For example, if profits or book equity are used as the denominator, has the firm made conservative or aggressive accounting choices that are likely to unwind in the coming years? Is the firm likely to show strong growth in profits or book equity? If profits are the denominator, does the firm have temporarily poor or strong performance?
- What is the sustainability of the firm's growth and ROE based on the competitive dynamics of the firm's industry and product market and its own competitive position?
- Which are the most suitable peer companies to include in the benchmark multiple computation? Have these firms had growth (profit or book values), profitability, and quality of earnings comparable to the firm being analyzed? Do they have the same risk characteristics?

## Shortcut forms of profit-based valuation

The discounted abnormal profit valuation formula can be simplified by making assumptions about the relation between a firm's current and future abnormal profits or losses. Similarly, the equity value-to-book formula can be simplified by making assumptions about long-term ROEs and growth.

### ABNORMAL PROFIT (GROWTH) SIMPLIFICATION

Several assumptions about the relation between current and future abnormal profits or losses are popular for simplifying the abnormal profit model and the abnormal profit growth model. First, abnormal profits are assumed to follow a random walk. The random walk model for abnormal profits implies that an analyst's best guess about future expected abnormal profits are current abnormal profit. The model assumes that past shocks to abnormal profits persist forever but that future shocks are random or unpredictable. The random walk model can be written as follows:

$$\text{Forecasted AP}_1 = \text{AP}_0$$

Forecasted $AP_1$ is the forecast of next year's abnormal profit, and $AP_0$ is current period abnormal profit. Under the model, forecasted abnormal profit for two years ahead are simply abnormal profit in year 1, or once again current abnormal profit. In other words, the best guess of abnormal profit in any future year is just current abnormal profit. It is also possible to include a drift term in the model, allowing profits to grow by a constant amount, or at a constant rate in each period.

How does the preceding assumption about future abnormal profits simplify the discounted abnormal profit valuation model? If abnormal profits follow a random walk, all future forecasts of abnormal profits are simply current abnormal profits. Consequently, the present value of future abnormal profits can be calculated by valuing the current level of abnormal profits as a perpetuity. It is then possible to rewrite value as follows:

$$\text{Equity value} = BVE_0 + \frac{AP_0}{r_e}$$

Equity value is the book value of equity at the end of the year plus current abnormal profit divided by the cost of capital. The perpetuity formula can be adjusted to incorporate expectations of constant growth in future abnormal profit.

A logical consequence of the previous assumption is also that future abnormal profit growth equals zero. When abnormal profit growth in any future year is zero, the abnormal profit growth valuation model can be rewritten as follows:

$$\text{Equity value} = \frac{\text{Profit}_1}{r_e}$$

Equity value is then set equal to the capitalized value of next-period profit.

In reality, shocks to abnormal profits are unlikely to persist forever. Firms that have positive shocks are likely to attract competitors that will reduce opportunities for future abnormal performance. Firms with negative abnormal profit shocks are likely to fail or to be acquired by other firms that can manage their resources more effectively. The persistence of abnormal performance will therefore depend on strategic factors such as barriers to entry and switching costs, discussed in Chapter 2. To reflect this, analysts frequently assume that current shocks to abnormal profit decay over time. Under this assumption, abnormal profits are said to follow an autoregressive model. Forecasted abnormal profits are then:

$$\text{Forecasted } AP_1 = \beta AP_0$$

$\beta$ is a parameter that captures the speed with which abnormal profits decay over time. If there is no decay, $\beta$ is one and abnormal profits follow a random walk. If $\beta$ is zero, abnormal profits decay completely within one year. Estimates of $\beta$ using actual company data indicate that for a typical firm, $\beta$ is approximately 0.6. However, it varies by industry, and is smaller for firms with large accruals and onetime accounting charges.[9]

Note that if the rate of decay in abnormal profits, $\beta$, is constant, the perpetual growth rate in abnormal profits equals $\beta - 1$. The autoregressive model therefore implies that equity values can again be written as a function of current abnormal profit or loss and book values:[10]

$$\text{Equity value} = BVE_0 + \frac{\beta AP_0}{r_e - (\beta - 1)}$$

This formulation implies that equity values are simply the sum of current book value plus current abnormal profit or loss weighted by the cost of equity capital and persistence in abnormal profits.

Under the assumption that abnormal profits follow an autoregressive model, abnormal profit growth in year 1, or the change in abnormal profit , can be rewritten as $(\beta - 1)AP_0$ and the abnormal profit growth model simplifies to:

$$\text{Equity value} = \frac{\text{Profit or loss}_1}{r_e} + \frac{(1 + r_e)}{r_e}\left[\frac{(\beta - 1)AP_1}{r_e - (\beta - 1)}\right]$$

This formula illustrates that equity values can be expressed as the sum of capitalized next-period profit or loss plus next-period abnormal profit weighted by the cost of equity capital and persistence in abnormal profits.

An advantage of the abnormal profit growth model over the abnormal profit model is that the former model can be simplified by making assumptions about the change in abnormal profit. This can be useful in situations where the analyst believes, for example, that a firm has a sustainable competitive advantage but expects that the growth in abnormal profit will gradually decay over time. Under the assumption that:

$$\text{Forecasted } (AP_2 - AP_1) = \beta(AP_1 - AP_0)$$

the abnormal profit growth model simplifies to:

$$\text{Equity value} = \frac{\text{Profit or loss}_1}{r_e} + \frac{(1+r_e)}{r_e}\left[\frac{\beta(AP_1 - AP_0)}{r_e - (\beta - 1)}\right]$$

## ROE AND GROWTH SIMPLIFICATIONS

It is also possible to make simplifications about long-term ROEs and equity growth to reduce forecast horizons for estimating the equity value-to-book multiple. Firms' long-term ROEs are affected by factors such as barriers to entry in their industries, change in production or delivery technologies, and quality of management. As discussed in Chapter 6, these factors tend to force abnormal ROEs to decay over time. One way to model this decay is to assume that ROEs revert to the mean. Forecasted ROE after one period then takes the following form:

$$\text{Forecasted ROE}_1 = ROE_0 + \beta(ROE_0 - \overline{ROE})$$

$\overline{ROE}$ is the steady state ROE (either the firm's cost of capital or the long-term industry ROE) and $\beta$ is a "speed of adjustment factor" that reflects how quickly it takes the ROE to revert to its steady state.[11]

Growth rates in the book value of equity are driven by several factors. First, the size of the firm is important. Small firms can sustain very high growth rates for an extended period, whereas large firms find it more difficult to do so. Second, firms with high rates of growth are likely to attract competitors, which reduces their growth rates. As a result, steady-state rates of growth in book equity are likely to be similar to rates of growth in the overall economy, which have averaged 2–4 percent per year.

The long-term patterns in ROE and book equity growth rates imply that for most companies there is limited value in making forecasts for valuation beyond a relatively short horizon, generally five to ten years. Powerful economic forces tend to lead firms with superior or inferior performance early in the forecast horizon to revert to a level that is comparable to that of other firms in the industry or the economy. For a firm in steady state, that is, expected to have a stable ROE and book equity growth rate ($g^{equity}$), the value-to-book multiple formula simplifies to the following:

$$\text{Equity value-to-book multiple} = 1 + \frac{ROE_0 - r_e}{r_e - g^{equity}}$$

Of course, analysts can make a variety of simplifying assumptions about a firm's ROE and growth. For example, they can assume that they decay slowly or rapidly to the cost of capital and the growth rate for the economy. They can assume that the rates decay to the industry or economy average ROEs and book value growth rates. The valuation formula can easily be modified to accommodate these assumptions.

## Comparing valuation methods

We have discussed four methods of valuation derived from the dividend discount model: discounted dividends, discounted abnormal profit (or abnormal ROEs), discounted abnormal profit growth, and discounted cash flows. Since the methods are all derived from the same underlying model, no one version can be considered superior to the others. As long as analysts make the same assumptions about firm fundamentals, value estimates under all four methods will be identical. However, we next discuss important differences between the models.

## FOCUS ON DIFFERENT ISSUES

The methods frame the valuation task differently and can in practice focus the analyst's attention on different issues. The profit-based approaches frame the issues in terms of accounting data such as profit or loss and book values. Analysts spend considerable time analyzing historical income statements and balance sheets, and their primary forecasts are typically for these variables.

Defining values in terms of ROEs has the added advantage that it focuses analysts' attention on ROE, the same key measure of performance that is decomposed in a standard financial analysis. Furthermore, because ROEs control for firm scale, it is likely to be easier for analysts to evaluate the reasonableness of their forecasts by benchmarking them with ROEs of other firms in the industry and the economy. This type of benchmarking is more challenging for free cash flows and abnormal profits.

## DIFFERENCES IN REQUIRED STRUCTURE

The methods differ in the amount of analysis and structure required for valuation. The discounted abnormal profit and ROE methods require analysts to construct both pro forma income statements and balance sheets to forecast future profits and book values. In contrast, the discounted abnormal profit growth model requires analysts to forecast future profits and dividends. The discounted cash flow method requires analysts to forecast income statements and changes in working capital and long-term assets to generate free cash flows. Finally, the discounted dividend method requires analysts to forecast dividends.

The discounted abnormal profit (growth), ROE, and free cash flow models all require more structure for analysis than the discounted dividend approach. They therefore help analysts to avoid structural inconsistencies in their forecasts of future dividends by specifically allowing for firms' future performance and investment opportunities. Similarly, the discounted abnormal profit/ROE method requires more structure and work than the discounted cash flow method and the discounted abnormal profit growth method to build full pro forma balance sheets. This permits analysts to avoid inconsistencies in the firm's financial structure.

## DIFFERENCES IN TERMINAL VALUE IMPLICATIONS

A third difference between the methods is in the effort required for estimating terminal values. Terminal value estimates for the abnormal profit, abnormal profit growth, and ROE methods tend to represent a much smaller fraction of total value than under the discounted cash flow or dividend methods. On the surface, this would appear to mitigate concerns about the aspect of valuation that leaves the analyst most uncomfortable. Is this apparent advantage real? As explained below, the answer turns on how well value is already reflected in the accountant's book value.

The abnormal profit and abnormal profit growth valuations do not eliminate the discounted cash flow terminal value problem, but they do reframe it. Discounted cash flow terminal values include the present value of *all* expected cash flows beyond the forecast horizon. Under abnormal profit valuation, that value is broken into two parts: the present values of *normal* profits and *abnormal* profits beyond the terminal year. The terminal value in the abnormal profit technique includes only the *abnormal* profits. The present value of normal profits is already reflected in the original book value. Similarly, under the abnormal profit growth approach, the present value of near-term abnormal profits is already reflected in next-period profit or the growth in profits over the forecast horizon. The terminal value includes only the *changes in abnormal* profits that are expected to occur in the years beyond the terminal year.

The abnormal profit and abnormal profit growth approaches therefore recognize that current book value and profits over the forecast horizon already reflect many of the cash flows expected to arrive after the forecast horizon. The approaches build directly on accrual accounting. For example, under accrual accounting, book equity can be thought of as the minimum recoverable future benefits attributable to the firm's net assets. In addition, revenues are typically realized when earned, not when cash is received. The discounted cash flow approach, on the other hand, "unravels" all of the accruals, spreads the resulting cash flows over longer horizons, and then reconstructs its own "accruals" in the form of discounted expectations of future cash flows. The essential difference between the two approaches is that abnormal profit (growth) valuation recognizes that the accrual process may already have performed a portion of the valuation task, whereas the discounted cash flow approach ultimately moves back to the primitive cash flows underlying the accruals.

The usefulness of the accounting-based perspective thus hinges on how well the accrual process reflects future cash flows. The approach is most convenient when the accrual process is "unbiased," so that profits or losses can be abnormal only as the result of economic rents and not as a product of accounting itself.[12] The forecast horizon then extends to the point where the firm is expected to approach a competitive equilibrium and earn only normal profits on its projects. Subsequent abnormal profits would be zero, and the terminal value at that point would be zero. In this extreme case, *all* of the firm's value is reflected in the book value and profits projected over the forecast horizon.

Of course, accounting rarely works so well. For example, many firms expense research and development costs, and book values fail to reflect any research and development assets. As a result, firms that spend heavily on research and development – such as pharmaceuticals – tend on average to generate abnormally high profits even in the face of stiff competition. Purely as an artifact of research and development accounting, abnormal profits would be expected to remain positive indefinitely for such firms, and under the abnormal profit approach, the terminal value could represent a substantial fraction of total value.

If desired, the analyst can alter the accounting approach used by the firm in his or her own projections. "Better" accounting would be viewed as that which reflects a larger fraction of the firm's value in book values and profits over the forecast horizon.[13] This same view underlies analysts' attempts to "normalize" profits; the adjusted numbers are intended to provide better indications of value, even though they reflect performance only over a short horizon.

Research has focused on the performance of abnormal profit-based valuation relative to discounted cash flow and discounted dividend methods. The findings indicate that over relatively short forecast horizons (ten years or less), valuation estimates using the abnormal profit approach generate more precise estimates of value than either the discounted dividend or discounted cash flow models. This advantage for the abnormal profit-based approach persists for firms with conservative or aggressive accounting, indicating that accrual accounting does a reasonably good job of reflecting future cash flows.[14] The performance of the abnormal profit growth valuation model has not yet been extensively studied. However, the model's close relationship to the abnormal profit model makes it subject to many of the same practical advantages.

Research also indicates that abnormal profit estimates of value outperform traditional multiples, such as price-earnings ratios, price-to-book ratios, and dividend yields, for predicting future share price movements.[15] Firms that have high abnormal profit model estimates of value relative to current price show positive abnormal future stock returns, whereas firms with low estimated value-to-price ratios have negative abnormal share price performance.

## Key Analysis Questions

The previous discussion on the trade-offs between different methods of valuing a company raises several questions for analysts about how to compare methods and to consider which is likely to be most reliable for their analysis:

- What are the key performance parameters that the analyst forecasts? Is more attention given to forecasting accounting variables, such as profits or losses and book values, or to forecasting cash flow variables?

- Has the analyst linked forecasted income statements and balance sheets? If not, is there any inconsistency between the two statements or in the implications of the assumptions for future performance? If so, what is the source of this inconsistency and does it affect discounted profit-based and discounted cash flow methods similarly?
- How well does the firm's accounting capture its underlying assets and obligations? Does it do a good enough job that we can rely on book values as the basis for long-term forecasts? Alternatively, does the firm rely heavily on off-balance sheet assets, such as R&D, which makes book values poorly reflect the lower bound on long-term performance?
- Has the analyst made very different assumptions about long-term performance in the terminal value computations under the different valuation methods? If so, which set of assumptions is more plausible given the firm's industry and its competitive positioning?

## Summary

Valuation is the process by which forecasts of performance are converted into estimates of price. A variety of valuation techniques are employed in practice, and no single method clearly dominates others. In fact, since each technique involves different advantages and disadvantages, there are gains to considering several approaches simultaneously.

For shareholders, a firm's equity value is the present value of future dividends. This chapter described four valuation techniques directly based on this dividend discount definition of value: discounted dividends, discounted abnormal profits/ROEs, discounted abnormal profit growth, and discounted free cash flows. The discounted dividend method attempts to forecast dividends directly. The abnormal profit approach expresses the value of a firm's equity as book value plus discounted expectations of future abnormal profits. The abnormal profit growth approach defines equity value as capitalized next-period profit or loss plus the present value of future changes in abnormal profits. Finally, the discounted cash flow method represents a firm's equity value by expected future free cash flows discounted at the cost of equity.

Although these four methods were derived from the same dividend discount model, they frame the valuation task differently. In practice they focus the analyst's attention on different issues and require different levels of structure in developing forecasts of the underlying primitive, future dividends.

Price multiple valuation methods were also discussed. Under these approaches, analysts estimate ratios of current price to historical or forecasted measures of performance for comparable firms. The benchmarks are then used to value the performance of the firm being analyzed. Multiples have traditionally been popular, primarily because they do not require analysts to make multiyear forecasts of performance. However, it can be difficult to identify comparable firms to use as benchmarks. Even across highly related firms, there are differences in performance that are likely to affect their multiples.

The chapter discussed the relation between two popular multiples, value-to-book and value-earnings ratios, and the discounted abnormal profit valuation. The resulting formulations indicate that value-to-book multiples are a function of future abnormal ROEs, book value growth, and the firm's cost of equity. The value-earnings multiple is a function of the same factors and also the current ROE.

## Core Concepts

**Abnormal profit**    Difference between profit or loss and a capital charge. The capital charge is calculated as the cost of equity times the beginning of the period book value of equity.

**Abnormal profit growth**    Change in abnormal profit. The change in abnormal profit can be rewritten as the abnormal change in profit, which is calculated as the difference between the actual period change in profit or loss and the expected change in profit or loss. The expected change in profit or loss is calculated as the cost of equity times prior period's retained profit or loss:

$$\text{Abnormal profit growth } (APG) = \Delta\text{Profit or loss}_2 - r_e \cdot \left(\text{Profit or loss}_1 - \text{Dividend}_1\right)$$

**Discounted abnormal profit growth model**    Model expressing equity value as a function of next-period profit or loss and the present value of abnormal profit growth (APG) beyond the next period:

$$\text{Equity value} = \frac{\text{Profit or loss}_1}{r_e} + \frac{1}{r_e}\left[\frac{APG_2}{(1+r_e)} + \frac{APG_3}{(1+r_e)^2} + \ldots\right]$$

**Discounted abnormal profit model**    Model expressing equity value as the sum of the beginning book value of equity and the present value of future abnormal profits (AP):

$$\text{Equity value} = BVE_0 + \frac{AP_1}{(1+r_e)} + \frac{AP_2}{(1+r_e)^2} + \ldots$$

**Discounted cash flow model**    Model expressing equity value as the present value of future free cash flows to equity (FCFE):

$$\text{Equity value} = \frac{FCFE_1}{(1+r_e)} + \frac{FCFE_2}{(1+r_e)^2} + \ldots$$

**Equity value**    Present value of expected future dividends (DIV):

$$\text{Equity value} = \frac{DIV_1}{(1+r_e)} + \frac{DIV_2}{(1+r_e)^2} + \frac{DIV_3}{(1+r_e)^3} + \ldots$$

This dividend-discount model can be recast to generate the discounted abnormal profit model, the discounted abnormal profit growth model, and the discounted free cash flow model.

**Free cash flow to debt and equity**    Cash flow available for distribution to creditors and shareholders. The free cash flow to debt and equity is equal to: profit or loss + after tax net interest expense – change in operating working capital – change in net non-current assets.

**Free cash flow to equity**    Cash flow available for distribution to shareholders. The free cash flow to equity is equal to: profit or loss – change in operating working capital – change in net non-current assets + change in debt.

**Multiple-based valuation**    Use of price multiples – ratios of market value to a measure of firm performance (e.g., profit) or value (e.g., book value of equity) – of comparable firms to value equity.

## Summary of notations used in this chapter

| | |
|---|---|
| AP | Abnormal profit |
| APG | Abnormal profit growth |
| BVA | Book value of business assets |
| BVE | Book value of equity |

| BVD | Book value of debt |
|---|---|
| DIV | Dividends |
| $g^{div}$ | Dividend growth rate |
| $g^{equity}$ | Growth rate in the book value of equity |
| $g^{profit}$ | Growth rate in profit |
| OCF | Operating cash flow |
| P | Profit |
| PB | Price-to-book ratio |
| PE | Price-to-earnings ratio |
| PV | Present value |
| $r_e$ | Cost of equity |
| $r_c$ | Cost of capital |

## Questions, exercises, and problems

1  Jonas Borg, an analyst at EMH Securities, states: "I don't know why anyone would ever try to value profits. Obviously, the market knows that profits can be manipulated and only values cash flows." Discuss.

2  Explain why terminal values in accounting-based valuation are significantly smaller than those in DCF valuation.

3  Manufactured Earnings is a "darling" of European analysts. Its current market price is €15 per share, and its book value is €5 per share. Analysts forecast that the firm's book value will grow by 10 percent per year indefinitely, and the cost of equity is 15 percent. Given these facts, what is the market's expectation of the firm's long-term average ROE?

4  Given the information in question 3, what will be Manufactured Earnings' share price if the market revises its expectations of long-term average ROE to 20 percent?

5  Analysts reassess Manufactured Earnings' future performance as follows: growth in book value increases to 12 percent per year, but the ROE of the incremental book value is only 15 percent. What is the impact on the market-to-book ratio?

6  How can a company with a high ROE have a low PE ratio?

7  What types of companies have:
   a. A high PE and a low market-to-book ratio?
   b. A high PE ratio and a high market-to-book ratio?
   c. A low PE and a high market-to-book ratio?
   d. A low PE and a low market-to-book ratio?

8  Free cash flows (FCF) used in DCF valuations discussed in the chapter are defined as follows:

FCF to debt and equity
= Profit before interest and taxes × (1 − tax rate) + Depreciation − Capital expenditures −/+ Increase/decrease in working capital

FCF to equity = Profit or loss + Depreciation − Capital expenditures −/+Increase/decrease in working capital +/− Increase/decrease in debt

Which of the following items affect free cash flows to debt and equity holders? Which affect free cash flows to equity alone? Explain why and how.

- An increase in trade receivables.
- A decrease in gross margins.
- An increase in property, plant, and equipment.
- An increase in inventories.

- Interest expense.
- An increase in prepaid expenses.
- An increase in notes payable to the bank.

9  Sta - Rite Company is valued at $20 per share. Analysts expect that it will generate free cash flows to equity of $4 per share for the foreseeable future. What is the firm's implied cost of equity capital?

10  Janet Stringer argues that "the DCF valuation method has increased managers' focus on short-term rather than long-term performance, since the discounting process places much heavier weight on short-term cash flows than long-term ones." Comment.

## Problem 1 Estimating Hugo Boss's equity value

Hugo Boss AG is a German designer, manufacturer, and distributer of men's and women's clothing, operating in the higher end of the clothing retail industry. During the period 2004–2017, the company consistently earned returns on equity in excess of 20 percent, with peaks around 50 to 60 percent, grew its book value of equity (before special dividends) by 5 percent per year, on average, and paid out 65–80 percent of its profit as dividends.

On March 29, 2018, before the publication of the first-quarter results, when Hugo Boss's 69.0 million common shares trade at about €71 per share, an analyst produces the following forecasts for Hugo Boss.

| Income statement (€ millions) | 2018E | 2019E | 2020E |
|---|---|---|---|
| Revenue | 2,798 | 2,925 | 3,101 |
| Profit before interest and tax | 345 | 381 | 419 |
| Interest expense | (8) | (7) | (6) |
| Profit before tax | 337 | 374 | 413 |
| Tax expense | (88) | (97) | (107) |
| Profit/loss | 249 | 277 | 306 |

| Balance sheet (€ millions) | 2017R | 2018E | 2019E | 2020E |
|---|---|---|---|---|
| Net operating assets | 1,167 | 1,195 | 1,249 | 1,324 |
| Investment assets | 57 | 58 | 60 | 65 |
| Business assets | 1,224 | 1,253 | 1,309 | 1,389 |
| Shareholders' equity | 915 | 972 | 1,039 | 1,130 |
| Current and non-current debt | 309 | 281 | 270 | 259 |
| Invested capital | 1,224 | 1,253 | 1,309 | 1,389 |

Assume that Hugo Boss's cost of equity equals 10 percent.

1  Calculate free cash flows to equity, abnormal profits, and abnormal profit growth for the years 2018–2020.

2  Assume that in 2021 Hugo Boss AG liquidates all its assets at their book values, uses the proceeds to pay off debt, and pays out the remainder to its equity holders. What does this assumption imply about the company's:

a. Free cash flow to equity holders in 2021 and beyond?

b. Abnormal profits in 2021 and beyond?

c. Abnormal profit growth in 2021 and beyond?

3  Estimate the value of Hugo Boss's equity on March 29, 2018, using the preceding forecasts and

assumptions. Check that the discounted cash flow model, the abnormal profit model, and the abnormal profit growth model yield the same outcome.

4   The analyst estimates a target price of €77 per share. What is the expected value of Hugo Boss's equity at the end of 2020 that is implicit in the analysts' forecasts and target price?

5   Under the assumption that the historical trends in the company's ROE (i.e., approximately 25 percent), payout ratio (80 percent), and book equity growth (5 percent) continue in the future, what would be your estimate of Hugo Boss's equity value-to-book ratio?

## Problem 2 Estimating Adidas's equity value

Germany-based Adidas is one of the world's largest producers of sportswear. On March 15, 2018, one day after the publication of Adidas's 2017 financial statements, an analyst produces a set of near-term forecasts of Adidas's 2018–2020 performance and financial position.

| Income statement (€ mn) | 2017R | 2018E | 2019E | 2020E |
|---|---|---|---|---|
| Revenue | 21,218 | 22,785 | 24,731 | 26,762 |
| Net operating profit after tax | 1,366 | 1,644 | 1,916 | 2,211 |
| Net investment profit after tax | 32 | 21 | 14 | 15 |
| Interest expense after tax | (43) | (45) | (50) | (51) |
| Profit or loss | 1,355 | 1,620 | 1,880 | 2,175 |

| Balance sheet (€ millions) | 2017R | 2018E | 2019E | 2020E |
|---|---|---|---|---|
| Net operating working capital | 2,380 | 2,620 | 2,918 | 2,997 |
| Net non-current operating assets | 4,591 | 5,013 | 5,564 | 5,941 |
| Non-operating investments | 1,597 | 974 | 627 | 722 |
| Business assets | 8,568 | 8,607 | 9,109 | 9,660 |
| Debt | 2,551 | 2,630 | 2,827 | 2,905 |
| Group equity | 6,017 | 5,977 | 6,282 | 6,755 |
| Invested capital | 8,568 | 8,607 | 9,109 | 9,660 |

On the day that the analyst issues her forecasts, Adidas's closing share price equals €193. The analyst assumes that Adidas's long-term tax rate equals 30 percent, the company's diluted number of shares outstanding is 204 million, and the company's required return on operating assets and cost of equity are both 9 percent. The analyst estimates that the fair value of Adidas's net operating assets equals €31,554 million.

1   Check whether all changes in the book value of equity that the analyst predicts can be fully explained through profits and dividends. Why is this an important property of the analyst's equity estimates?

2   Based on a market value of €39,372 million on March 15, 2018, and the analyst's estimates, Adidas's leading market value-to-earnings ratio is 24.3. What does this ratio suggest about the analyst's expectations about future abnormal profit growth?

3   Calculate abnormal NOPAT and free cash flow from operations for the years 2018–2020. Note that free cash flow from operations is defined as: NOPAT – Change in net operating assets.

4   Assume that abnormal NOPAT in 2021 and beyond is zero. Estimate the value of Adidas's net operating assets (NOA) at the end of 2017.

What might explain the difference between your NOA value estimate and the analyst's estimate (of €31,554 million)?

5  Calculate the present value of the free cash flow from operations for the years 2018–2020 and compare this present value to your NOA estimate calculated under item 4. What explains the difference between these two amounts? Why is this difference equal to the present value of Adidas's net operating assets at the end of 2020?

## Notes

1  From a theoretical perspective, it is preferred to express equity *per share* as a function of dividends *per share*. This is because only the discounted dividends *per share* model accurately accounts for the wealth transfer from new shareholders to the current shareholders that occurs when a firm offers shares to new shareholders in future years at a price that is not equal to the prevailing market price. To simplify the discussion of the other valuation models, however, we describe all models on a "total equity value basis," thereby implicitly assuming that future capital transactions do not affect the firm's current equity value per share – that is, are value neutral.

2  In practice, firms do not have to pay out all of their free cash flows as dividends; they can retain surplus cash in the business. The conditions under which a firm's dividend decision affects its value are discussed by M.H. Miller and F. Modigliani in "Dividend Policy, Growth, and the Valuation of Shares," *Journal of Business* 34 (October 1961): 411–433.

3  The incorporation of all non-owner changes in equity into profit is called clean surplus accounting. It is analogous to "comprehensive income," the concept defined in Chapter 1.

4  Changes in book value also include new capital contributions. However the dividend discount model assumes that new capital is issued at fair value. As a result, any incremental book value from capital issues is exactly offset by the discounted value of future dividends to new shareholders. Capital transactions therefore do not affect firm valuation.

5  Appendix B to this chapter provides a simple proof of the profit-based valuation formula.

6  The abnormal profit growth model and its properties are extensively discussed in the following articles: J.A. Ohlson and B.E. Juettner-Nauroth, "Expected EPS and EPS Growth as Determinants of Value," *Review of Accounting Studies* (2005): 349–365; J.A. Ohlson, "On Accounting-Based Valuation Formulae," *Review of Accounting Studies* (2005): 323–347; S.H. Penman, "Discussion of 'On Accounting-Based Valuation Formulae' and 'Expected EPS and EPS Growth as Determinants of Value,'" *Review of Accounting Studies* (2005): 367–378.

7  It may seem surprising that one can estimate value with no explicit attention to two of the cash flow streams considered in DCF analysis – investments in working capital and capital expenditures. The accounting-based technique recognizes that these investments cannot possibly contribute to value without impacting abnormal profits, and that therefore only their profit impacts need be considered. For example, the benefit of an increase in inventory turnover surfaces in terms of its impact on ROE (and thus, abnormal profit), without the need to consider explicitly the cash flow impacts involved.

8  This model must not be confused with the PEG ratio. The PEG ratio, which is defined as the price-earnings ratio divided by the short-term profit growth rate, is a rule-of-thumb used by some analysts to determine whether a share is overpriced. The rule suggests that shares whose PEG ratio is above one are overpriced. Valuation using the PEG ratio has, however, no clear theoretical basis.

9  See P.M. Dechow, A.P. Hutton, and R.G. Sloan, "An Empirical Assessment of the Residual Income Valuation Model," *Journal of Accounting and Economics* 23 (January 1999): 1–34.

10  This formulation is a variant of a model proposed by James Ohlson, "Earnings, Book Values, and Dividends in Equity Valuation," *Contemporary Accounting Research* 11 (Spring 1995): 661–687. Ohlson includes in his forecasts of future abnormal profits a variable that reflects relevant information other than current abnormal profit. This variable then also appears in the equity valuation formula. Empirical research by Dechow, Hutton, and Sloan, "An Empirical Assessment of the Residual Income Valuation Model," *Journal of Accounting and Economics* 23 (January 1999), indicates that financial analysts' forecasts of abnormal profits do reflect considerable information other than current abnormal profit, and that this information is useful for valuation.

11  This specification is similar to the model for dividends developed by J. Lintner, "Distribution of Incomes of Corporations among Dividends, Retained Earnings, and Taxes," *American Economic Review* 46 (May 1956): 97–113.

12  Unbiased accounting is that which, in a competitive equilibrium, produces an expected ROE equal to the cost of capital. The actual ROE thus reveals the presence of economic rents. Market value accounting is a special case of unbiased accounting that produces an expected ROE equal to the cost of capital, even when the firm is *not* in a competitive equilibrium. That is, market value accounting reflects the present value of future economic rents in book value, driving the expected ROEs to a

normal level. For a discussion of unbiased and biased accounting, see G. Feltham and J. Ohlson, "Valuation and Clean Surplus Accounting for Operating and Financial Activities," *Contemporary Accounting Research* 11(2) (Spring 1995): 689–731.

13 In Bennett Stewart's book on EVA valuation, *The Quest for Value* (New York: HarperBusiness, 1999), he recommends a number of accounting adjustments, including the capitalization of research and development.

14 S. Penman and T. Sougiannis, "A Comparison of Dividend, Cash Flow, and Earnings Approaches to Equity Valuation," *Contemporary Accounting Research* (Fall 1998): 343–383, compares the valuation methods using actual realizations of profits, cash flows, and dividends to estimate prices. J. Francis, P. Olsson, and D. Oswald, "Comparing Accuracy and Explainability of Dividend, Free Cash Flow, and Abnormal Earnings Equity Valuation Models," *Journal of Accounting Research* 38 (Spring 2000): 45–70, estimates values using *Value Line forecasts*.

15 See C. Lee and J. Myers, "What Is the Intrinsic Value of the Dow?" *The Journal of Finance* 54 (October 1999): 1693–1741.

## Appendix A: asset valuation methodologies

All of the valuation approaches discussed in this chapter can also be structured to estimate the value of a firm's business assets (including the tax shield on debt) rather than its equity. Switching from equity valuation to asset (enterprise/firm) valuation is often as simple as substituting financial measures related to equity for financial measures related to the firm's business assets. For example, in the profit-based valuation model, profit or loss (the earnings flow to equity) is replaced by NOPAT plus NIPAT (the earnings generated through operations and non-operating investments), and book value of the business assets replaces the book value of equity. Value multiples are based on ROEs for the equity formulation and on returns on invested capital for valuing business assets (or invested capital). And the discount rate for equity models is the cost of equity compared to the (weighted average) cost of capital ($r_c$ or WACC) for asset valuation models.

The formulae used for asset valuation under the various approaches are presented next.

### Abnormal profit valuation

Under the profit-based approach, the value of invested capital (business assets plus the tax shield on debt) is:

$$\text{Business value}_0 = BVA_0 + \frac{NOPAT_1 + NIPAT_1 - r_c \cdot BVA_0}{(1+r_c)} + \frac{NOPAT_2 + NIPAT_2 - r_c \cdot BVA_1}{(1+r_c)^2} + \ldots$$

BVA is the book value of the firm's business assets, NOPAT is net operating profit (before interest) after tax, NIPAT is net investment profit after tax, and $r_c$ is the firm's cost of capital (weighted average cost of debt and equity). From this firm value the analyst can deduct the market value of debt to generate an estimate of the value of equity.

Similarly, the value of the net operating assets is:

$$\text{Net operating asset value}_0$$
$$= BVNOA_0 + \frac{NOPAT_1 - r_{NOA} \cdot BVNOA_0}{(1+r_{NOA})} + \frac{NOPAT_2 - r_{NOA} \cdot BVNOA_1}{(1+r_{NOA})^2} + \ldots$$

where BVNOA is the book value of the firm's net operating assets, NOPAT is net operating profit after tax, and $r_{NOA}$ is the firm's required return on net operating assets.

## Valuation using price multiples

The multiple valuation can be structured as the debt plus equity value-to-book assets ratio by scaling the preceding business asset valuation formula by the book value of business assets. The valuation formula then becomes:

$$\text{Business value-to-book ratio}_0 = 1 + \frac{\text{ROIC}_1 - r_c}{(1+r_c)} + \frac{(\text{ROIC}_2 - r_c)(1+g_1^{assets})}{(1+r_c)^2}$$

$$+ \frac{(\text{ROIC}_3 - r_c)(1+g_1^{assets})(1+g_2^{assets})}{(1+r_c)^3} + \ldots$$

where

ROIC = return on invested capital, as defined in Chapter 5.

$r_c$ = cost of capital (weighted average cost of debt and equity)

$g_1^{assets}$ = growth in book value of invested capital/business assets (BVA) from year $t$-1 to year $t$ or

$$\frac{\text{BVA}_t - \text{BVA}_{t-1}}{\text{BVA}_{t-1}}$$

The value of the firm's business assets to the book value of the assets therefore depends on its ability to generate asset returns that exceed its cost of capital, and on its ability to grow its asset base. The value of equity under this approach is then the estimated multiple times the current book value of business assets less the market value of debt.

## Discounted cash flow model

The free cash flow formulation can be structured by estimating the value of claims to debt and equity and then deducting the market value of debt. The value of invested capital (business value) is computed as follows:

$$\text{Business value}_0 = \frac{\text{NOPAT}_1 + \text{NIPAT}_1 - \Delta\text{BVA}_1}{(1+r_c)} + \frac{\text{NOPAT}_2 + \text{NIPAT}_2 - \Delta\text{BVA}_2}{(1+r_c)^2} + \ldots$$

The firm's asset valuation therefore depends on the expected free cash flows from business assets during the forecast horizon, the forecasted terminal value of the free cash flows, and the (weighted average) cost of capital.

# Appendix B: reconciling the discounted dividends, discounted abnormal profit, and discounted abnormal profit growth models

To derive the abnormal profit model from the dividend discount model, consider the following two-period valuation:

$$\text{Equity value}_0 = \frac{\text{Dividend}_1}{(1+r_e)} + \frac{\text{Dividend}_2}{(1+r_e)^2}$$

With clean surplus accounting, dividends can be expressed as a function of profit or loss and the book value of equity (BVE):

$$\text{Dividend}_t = \text{Profit or loss}_t + \text{BVE}_{t-1} - \text{BVE}_t$$

Substituting this expression into the dividend discount model yields the following:

$$\text{Equity value}_0$$
$$= \frac{\text{Profit or loss}_1 + \text{BVE}_0 - \text{BVE}_1}{(1+r_e)}$$
$$+ \frac{\text{Profit or loss}_2 + \text{BVE}_1 - \text{BVE}_2}{(1+r_e)^2}$$

This can be rewritten as follows:

$$\text{Equity value}_0 = \frac{\text{Profit or loss}_1 - r_e \text{BVE}_0 + (1+r_e)\text{BVE}_0 - \text{BVE}_1}{(1+r_e)}$$

$$+ \frac{\text{Profit or loss}_2 - r_e \text{BVE}_1 + (1+r_e)\text{BVE}_1 - \text{BVE}_2}{(1+r_e)^2}$$

$$= \text{BVE}_0 + \frac{\text{Profit or loss}_1 - r_e \text{BVE}_0}{(1+r_e)} + \frac{\text{Profit or loss}_2 - r_e \text{BVE}_1}{(1+r_e)^2}$$

$$- \frac{\text{BVE}_2}{(1+r_e)^2}$$

The value of equity is therefore the current book value plus the present value of future abnormal profits. As the forecast horizon expands, the final term (the present value of liquidating book value) becomes inconsequential under the assumption that the long-term growth in the book value of equity is less than the cost of equity. A simple and appealing condition under which this assumption holds is when the firm has a constant dividend payout ratio.

To derive the abnormal profit growth model from the dividend discount model consider the same two-period dividend model and express dividends in the second (and final) period as a function of profit or loss and first-period dividends:

$$\text{Dividend}_2 = \text{Profit or loss}_2 + \text{Profit or loss}_1 - \text{Dividend}_1$$

Substituting this expression into the dividend discount model yields the following:

$$\text{Equity value}_0 = \frac{\text{Profit or loss}_1 + \text{Dividends}_1 - \text{Profit or loss}_1}{(1+r_e)}$$

$$+ \frac{\text{Profit or loss}_1 + \text{Profit or loss}_2 - \text{Dividends}_1}{(1+r_e)^2}$$

This can be rewritten as follows:

$$\text{Equity value}_0 = \frac{\text{Profit or loss}_1}{(1+r_e)} + \frac{\text{Profit or loss}_1}{(1+r_e)^2}$$

$$- \frac{(\text{Profit loss}_1 - \text{Dividends}_1)(1+r_e)}{(1+r_e)^2}$$

$$+ \frac{(\text{Profit or loss}_2 - \text{Dividends}_1)}{(1+r_e)^2}$$

$$= \frac{\text{Profit or loss}_1}{(1+r_e)} + \frac{\text{Profit or loss}_1}{(1+r_e)^2}$$

$$+ \frac{\text{Profit or loss}_2 + r_e \text{Dividends}_1 - (1+r_e)\text{Profit or loss}_1}{(1+r_e)^2}$$

The value of equity is therefore the capitalized value of first-period profit or loss plus the present value of second-period abnormal profit growth. Note that in contrast to the abnormal profit model, the abnormal profit growth model does not assume clean surplus accounting.

CASE

# Valuation Multiples in Fast Fashion

Sweden-based Hennes & Mauritz AB (H&M) and Spain-based Industria de Diseno Textil S.A. (Inditex) are two of the world's largest fast fashion retailers. During the 2000s both companies were considered pioneers of "fast fashion," a strategy aimed at achieving high inventory turnover with trendy fashion designed and produced at a high pace. In the early 2010s H&M lost its leading position in the fast fashion industry to Inditex, which seemingly managed to have created the better model for success in fast fashion. These developments were reflected in the retailers' valuations. Whereas Inditex traded at a discount to H&M at the end of 2007, with a price-to-book ratio of 5.2 versus 9.0 for H&M, Inditex had gained the edge by the end of 2017, trading at a price-to-book ratio of 6.0 versus 3.8 for H&M.

## The industry

The fashion retail industry is a strongly cyclical industry in which consumer demand may strongly vary with economic cycles. During the period 2007 to 2017, growth rates in the fashion retail industry ranged from 3 to 5 percent, with most growth coming from emerging economies, especially at the end of the period. Consumers' high price sensitivity forced fashion retailers to search for differentiation opportunities, for example, by building strong brand recognition or, alternatively, find ways to keep production costs and selling prices low. One commonly used way to reduce costs was to source products from low-cost labor markets, often in Asia; Hennes & Mauritz did so extensively. Another approach was to develop private labels, which helped retailers to get greater operating flexibility and capture a larger portion of the margin.

To cope with price competition and improve profitability, some fashion retailers, including Hennes & Mauritz and Inditex, pursued a so-called "fast fashion strategy." This strategy aimed at building a loyal and frequently returning customer base, primarily by (a) monitoring and quickly responding to changes in fashion trends, (b) minimizing production and lead times, and (c) frequently renewing store assortments. Fast fashion strategies helped to improve profitability via at least three channels. First, frequently returning customers – attracted by the frequent assortment renewals – helped the retailers to increase impulse sales, store productivity, and asset turnover. Second, fast fashion retailers operated on a large scale, which helped them to keep input prices low through scale economies and their strong bargaining power over suppliers. Third and finally, fast fashion retailers had a strong brand equity, which sometimes allowed them to charge premium prices and earn higher margins, especially in the earlier years of the fast fashion era.

In addition to the above strategic choices, several other factors had a significant influence on retailers' profitability and growth. First, as growth opportunities were limited in mature markets such as Western Europe, one of the few ways to achieve above-average growth rates was to expand into emerging economies. Such a strategy was not without risks. Next to the fact that emerging economies tended to be more volatile, the

Professor Erik Peek prepared this case. The case is intended solely as the basis for class discussion and is not intended to serve as an endorsement, source of primary data, or illustration of effective or ineffective management.

303

profit margins of internationally operating retailers such as H&M and Inditex also became increasingly sensitive to foreign currency exchange rate fluctuations. For example, whereas H&M initially focused its growth investments on Europe and the United States, Inditex entered the emerging markets much earlier. This caused Inditex to grow faster than H&M; however, after the beginning of the 2010s the growing weakness in emerging markets' currencies also started to put Inditex's strong margins and growth under pressure.

Second, some fashion retailers used multi-brand strategies to diversify across market segments and, consequently, avoid being too much affected by strong competition in one – typically lower-end – segment of the market. For example, at the end of the 2000s Inditex operated fashion stores under several different banners, such as Zara, Pull & Bear, and Massimo Dutti. In contrast, H&M operated its stores under only one brand name and, consequently, primarily targeted one customer group, that of the trend-sensitive younger customer. During the economic downturn starting at the end of the 2000s, this strong focus harmed H&M's profitability because the retailer's younger customers were also most affected by the downturn and thus the most price-sensitive customers. This effect of the economic downturn was further amplified by the entrance of discount fashion retailers such as Primark.

Third, during the period 2007 to 2017 online sales and omni-channel strategies – combining online sales with physical stores – grew strongly in importance. This development forced fashion retailers to make significant and timely investments in new technology that supported online sales and optimized customer convenience. Later in the period, increased digitization of logistic processes and the monitoring of customer preferences and trends forced fast fashion retailers to invest in artificial intelligence to stay at par with competition. These investments could have a negative effect on short-term performance. The increasing importance of online sales also made consumers less brand-loyal and more price-sensitive, thus further intensifying competition.

## Hennes & Mauritz between 2007 and 2017

The fiscal year ending on November 30, 2007, was a year of strong performance for Hennes & Mauritz AB (H&M). In that year the fashion retailer's return on equity and return on net operating assets were close to 30 percent. Soon after the end of fiscal 2007, investors became increasingly concerned about the potential of a US recession and a global economic slowdown – a slowdown that could be expected to have especially adverse consequences for the strongly cyclical global fashion industry. Although at the beginning of 2008 H&M was still the darling of fashion investors and traded at a premium to, for example, one of its main competitors Inditex, some clouds were appearing on the horizon. While input costs, such as prices of cotton and costs of logistics, were steadily rising, the developing economic downturn withheld retailers from passing on cost increases to consumers, thereby putting margins under pressure. A potential upside to this development was that the largest global fashion retailers, such as H&M and Inditex, had more bargaining power over their suppliers, which gave them a competitive edge over their smaller peers. Another factor that protected H&M's margins during this period was the weakness of the US dollar, H&M's primary sourcing currency. Consequently, at the end of fiscal 2008, H&M reported to investors that it had managed to keep margins stable and that it planned to continue its strategy of growing the company's store portfolio by 10 to 15 percent per year, despite the recent start of a worldwide economic crisis, weakened like-for-like revenue growth expectations, and the increasing pressure on margins.

Like-for-like sales fell during the first part of 2009 but picked up again by the end of the fiscal year, which temporarily raised investor optimism. However, after a strong first half in 2010, H&M's fortune turned. A significant weakening of the euro, H&M's primary selling currency, against the US dollar, H&M's primary sourcing currency, contributed to a gradual erosion of the retailer's margins. On top of this, H&M's margin suffered from cotton prices reaching record high levels and markdowns increasing as a result of intensifying price competition. Further, economic turmoil in some of Europe's former growth markets, such as Greece, Portugal, and Spain, slowed down the company's growth. In fiscal 2011 H&M's NOPAT margin declined from 18.0 to 14.9 percent, while the company's revenue growth rate declined from 7.0 to 1.4 percent. Some analysts argued that H&M's declining performance signaled that the retailer's superior margins and turnover had been the result of high operational efficiency rather than a sustainable competitive advantage. Other analysts criticized H&M for being late with its investments in emerging markets, late with developing online activities, and inconsistent in its strategy – having become "not the best of fashion and not the best of price."

During the following years H&M maintained its aggressive growth strategy but made some changes: the retailer added more stores in Asia and gradually moved towards a multi-brand strategy, introducing new store concepts such as COS and &Other Stories. Nonetheless, the company's sourcing strategy as well as its focus on price-sensitive younger consumers kept its influence on performance. In particular, H&M's dependence on external suppliers, mostly located in Asia or Eastern Europe, made the company much slower in getting its products to the market than its largest rival Inditex. Further, increases in input costs could not be passed on to consumers because of the continued economic downturn and increases in competition from online and discount retailers; on the contrary, H&M was forced to frequently mark down its products to get rid of inventory pile-ups. While decreasing cotton prices and positive foreign currency developments softened the decline, H&M's NOPAT margin decreased from 14.9 percent in 2012 to 13.7 percent in 2014; net operating asset turnover decreased from 1.44 in 2012 to 1.32 in 2014.

The NOPAT margin continued to decrease between 2015 and 2017, primarily because of weaknesses in H&M's strategy execution, investments in online technology, increased markdowns, and the adverse effects of a strong US dollar. By the end of fiscal 2017 Hennes & Mauritz had shifted its focus from growing its portfolio of physical stores towards growing online. Rather than targeting a store growth rate of 10 to 15 percent, from 2017 onwards the retailer targeted an annual revenue growth rate from 10 to 15 percent. Investors and analysts appeared skeptical about H&M's ability to change the tide; during the months following the retailer's 2017 earnings announcement, H&M's share price decreased from SEK155 to a low of SEK120.

## Inditex between 2007 and 2017

Between 2007 and 2017 Inditex's performance was substantially less volatile than that of its industry peer Hennes & Mauritz. At the end of the 2000s Inditex lagged behind H&M in terms of profitability and market valuation. However, a few factors helped Inditex to take over as the world's largest fashion retailer and to steadily outperform its main industry peer after H&M ran into troubles in 2011. In particular, Inditex had been earlier with expanding its operations to emerging markets, which not only allowed the company to grow at a steady rate but also softened the effects of the European economic downturn at the beginning of the 2010s. Further, Inditex's strategic choice to produce most of its fashion close to home and ship its products across the world from one central warehouse located in Spain helped the company to become a leader in the execution of the fast fashion strategy, achieve high and stable store productivity, and avoid significant markdowns. To illustrate the difference in execution, between 2007 and 2017 Inditex's days' inventories averaged at 82 days, compared with 104 days for H&M.

In 2008 and 2009, Inditex's performance suffered from the global downturn, a recession in its home market, Spain, and weak currencies in emerging economies. In particular, the company's like-for-like revenue growth turned moderately negative, its NOPAT margin reached a low of 12.5 percent, and management decided to temporarily reduce store openings. However, the company managed to compensate its weaknesses in recessionary markets with cost cutting, rapid expansions into growth markets such as China, Japan, and South Korea, and expanding online. Between 2010 and 2012, when Inditex grew its store space by around 10 to 11 percent per year, especially outside Europe, the company returned to double-digit revenue growth and improved its NOPAT margin to levels above 14 percent, making investors increasingly convinced about the company's strategy execution, operating efficiency, and growth chances.

In the first half of 2013 investors learned that Inditex was also not immune to setbacks. Although the retailer continued to increase store space and improve its online presence, also in its primary international markets, revenue growth slowed, partly as a consequence of devaluations of the yen and emerging market currencies. Inditex sought to boost growth by shifting away from smaller stores to larger, more productive flagship stores and by more aggressively expanding its online activities. The company's environment turned for the better at the end of 2014, when the euro weakened and sales grew sharply again.

During the years 2015 to 2017 Inditex continued to show solid like-for-like revenue growth, averaging at almost 8 percent per year. NOPAT margins remained fairly stable, around 13.5 percent, despite the negative impact of declines in the value of the Brazilian real, the Mexican peso, and the Russian ruble. Inditex also continued to enter new markets, such as New Zealand, Vietnam, and Paraguay, highlighting that the company had not yet reached the limits of its growth potential. Nonetheless, being concerned about the potential impact of emerging market currencies on Inditex's margins, investors became gradually more cautious in their views on the company's profit potential. Between April 2017 and April 2018 Inditex's share price decreased by almost 27 percent, from €35.21 to €25.78.

## Multiple-based valuation

**Exhibits 1 and 2** show a summary of the financial performance and financial position of Hennes & Mauritz and Inditex during the years 2007 to 2017. The exhibits also report the two retailers' share prices during these years, measured at the end of each fiscal year as well as three and six months after the fiscal year end dates. During 2007–2017 H&M's price-to-book ratio ranged from 3.8 to 11.7; Inditex's price-to-book ratio ranged from 4.3 to 8.6. The retailers' price-to-earnings ratios were even more volatile, ranging from 14.1 to 30.1 for H&M and from 16.0 to 35.5 for Inditex. Analysts estimated that during 2007–2017, the retailers' cost of equity varied between 7 and 9 percent, whereas their required returns on net operating assets varied between 6.5 and 8.5 percent.

## Questions

1  Which multiples are potentially useful in valuing Hennes & Mauritz and Inditex? What are their advantages and disadvantages?
2  What explains these multiples' variation over time? What explains the differences in the multiples of H&M and Inditex between 2007 and 2017? Do you consider these multiples justified?
3  Using your knowledge about the drivers of H&M's and Inditex's multiples, can you value the four industry peers of H&M and Inditex, described in **Exhibit 3**?

**EXHIBIT 1** Financial and share price information of Hennes & Mauritz for the years 2007–2017

| SEK mln | 2017 | 2016 | 2015 | 2014 | 2013 | 2012 | 2011 | 2010 | 2009 | 2008 | 2007 |
|---|---|---|---|---|---|---|---|---|---|---|---|
| Revenue | 200,004 | 192,267 | 180,861 | 151,419 | 128,562 | 120,799 | 109,999 | 108,483 | 101,393 | 88,532 | 78,346 |
| Net operating profit after tax | 17,211 | 19,791 | 21,758 | 20,710 | 17,631 | 17,662 | 16,435 | 19,511 | 17,688 | 15,651 | 13,970 |
| of which: Net non-recurring expense after tax | 0 | 0 | 0 | 0 | 0 | 0 | 0 | 0 | 0 | 0 | 0 |
| Net investment profit after tax | 219 | 175 | 242 | 256 | 286 | 395 | 419 | 262 | 336 | 763 | 571 |
| Interest expense after tax | 1,246 | 1,330 | 1,102 | 990 | 765 | 1,190 | 1,033 | 1,092 | 1,640 | 1,121 | 953 |
| Profit or loss | 16,184 | 18,636 | 20,898 | 19,976 | 17,152 | 16,867 | 15,821 | 18,681 | 16,384 | 15,294 | 13,588 |
| | | | | | | | | | | | |
| Tax rate | 22.0% | 22.0% | 22.0% | 22.0% | 22.0% | 26.3% | 26.3% | 26.3% | 28.0% | 28.0% | 28.0% |
| Cost of sales-to-revenue | −46.0% | −44.8% | −43.0% | −41.2% | −40.9% | −40.5% | −39.9% | −37.1% | −38.4% | −38.5% | −38.9% |
| SG&A expense-to-revenue | −43.0% | −42.0% | −41.4% | −41.1% | −41.1% | −40.2% | −40.3% | −38.8% | −38.0% | −37.0% | −35.9% |
| Revenue growth in local currencies | 3.0% | 7.0% | 11.0% | 14.0% | 9.0% | 11.0% | 8.0% | 15.0% | 4.0% | 11.0% | 17.0% |
| Like-for-like revenue growth | - | - | - | - | 0.0% | 1.0% | −1.0% | 5.0% | −5.0% | −1.0% | 5.0% |
| | | | | | | | | | | | |
| Net operating assets | 142,120 | 138,395 | 131,800 | 114,918 | 92,542 | 83,852 | 77,631 | 73,316 | 71,690 | 62,630 | 47,339 |
| Non-operating investments | 1,039 | 1,014 | 4,769 | 9,831 | 11,455 | 11,731 | 16,385 | 19,952 | 17,506 | 18,775 | 17,300 |
| of which: excess cash | 0 | 0 | 3,907 | 9,122 | 10,796 | 11,103 | 15,777 | 19,434 | 16,955 | 18,299 | 17,047 |
| Debt | 83,446 | 78,173 | 78,520 | 73,193 | 58,749 | 51,748 | 49,912 | 49,096 | 48,216 | 44,455 | 32,546 |
| Ordinary shareholders' equity | 59,713 | 61,236 | 58,049 | 51,556 | 45,248 | 43,835 | 44,104 | 44,172 | 40,613 | 36,950 | 32,093 |
| Non-controlling interest in equity | 0 | 0 | 0 | 0 | 0 | 0 | 0 | 0 | 0 | 0 | 0 |
| Invested capital | 143,159 | 139,409 | 136,569 | 124,749 | 103,997 | 95,583 | 94,016 | 93,268 | 88,829 | 81,405 | 64,639 |

*(continued)*

**EXHIBIT 1**  Financial and share price information of Hennes & Mauritz for the years 2007–2017    (Continued)

| SEK mln | 2017 | 2016 | 2015 | 2014 | 2013 | 2012 | 2011 | 2010 | 2009 | 2008 | 2007 |
|---|---|---|---|---|---|---|---|---|---|---|---|
| Average number of stores | 4,545 | 4,138 | 3,718 | 3,322 | 2,954 | 2,624 | 2,339 | 2,097 | 1,863 | 1,630 | 1,434 |
| PP&E-to-revenue | 56.6% | 58.9% | 58.6% | 59.9% | 59.2% | 57.3% | 60.2% | 59.2% | 59.4% | 55.9% | 50.7% |
| Days' inventories | 129.2 | 119.4 | 103.5 | 105.1 | 110.3 | 107.7 | 104.7 | 98.1 | 87.4 | 87.7 | 90.2 |
| Operating cash flow | 40,134 | 43,756 | 43,972 | 40,714 | 38,291 | 31,998 | 29,487 | 33,977 | 29,136 | 25,156 | 21,754 |
| Investment cash flow (plus interest received) | (27,272) | (29,384) | (33,801) | (38,632) | (29,164) | (16,672) | (15,809) | (22,079) | (22,381) | (19,737) | (8,834) |
| Change in debt (minus interest paid) | 3,849 | (2,027) | 4,286 | 13,366 | 6,344 | 673 | (314) | (190) | 2,463 | 11,456 | 2,605 |
| Free cash flow to equity | 16,711 | 12,345 | 14,457 | 15,448 | 15,471 | 15,999 | 13,364 | 11,709 | 9,218 | 16,876 | 15,525 |
| Number of shares outstanding (mln) | 1,655.1 | 1,655.1 | 1,655.1 | 1,655.1 | 1,655.1 | 1,655.1 | 1,655.1 | 1,655.1 | 1,655.1 | 1,655.1 | 1,655.1 |
| Share price at fiscal year-end | 197.10 | 267.90 | 323.50 | 319.40 | 278.00 | 215.90 | 214.00 | 237.40 | 206.15 | 149.00 | 199.50 |
| Share price 3 months after the fiscal year-end | 137.42 | 238.60 | 279.10 | 363.80 | 289.20 | 232.10 | 237.80 | 207.00 | 216.25 | 168.75 | 174.50 |
| Share price 6 months after the fiscal year-end | 132.88 | 216.50 | 256.00 | 336.20 | 282.80 | 228.00 | 215.80 | 229.30 | 222.35 | 180.25 | 165.75 |
| Exchange rate SEK 1 = € X | 0.101 | 0.102 | 0.108 | 0.108 | 0.112 | 0.116 | 0.108 | 0.108 | 0.096 | 0.097 | 0.107 |

**EXHIBIT 2** Financial and share price information of Inditex for the years 2007–2017

| € mln | 2017 | 2016 | 2015 | 2014 | 2013 | 2012 | 2011 | 2010 | 2009 | 2008 | 2007 |
|---|---|---|---|---|---|---|---|---|---|---|---|
| Revenue | 25,336.0 | 23,310.5 | 20,900.4 | 18,116.5 | 16,724.4 | 15,946.1 | 13,792.6 | 12,524.8 | 11,080.8 | 10,404.2 | 9,433.0 |
| Net operating profit after tax | 3,401.4 | 3,189.0 | 2,885.5 | 2,522.2 | 2,416.2 | 2,407.1 | 1,985.9 | 1,784.9 | 1,381.8 | 1,312.2 | 1,308.3 |
| of which: Net non-recurring expense after tax | 101.3 | 30.1 | 47.1 | 51.9 | 64.6 | 43.8 | 14.5 | 33.4 | 34.0 | 26.9 | 10.6 |
| Net investment profit after tax | 51.0 | 51.8 | 56.8 | 40.7 | 15.7 | 16.6 | 14.1 | 16.1 | 8.0 | 20.3 | 10.4 |
| Interest expense after tax | 80.4 | 79.7 | 60.0 | 52.7 | 50.3 | 49.0 | 54.5 | 59.8 | 67.6 | 70.9 | 61.0 |
| Profit or loss | 3,372.0 | 3,161.1 | 2,882.2 | 2,510.2 | 2,381.6 | 2,374.7 | 1,945.5 | 1,741.3 | 1,322.1 | 1,261.6 | 1,257.8 |
| Tax rate | 25.0% | 25.0% | 28.0% | 30.0% | 30.0% | 30.0% | 30.0% | 30.0% | 30.0% | 30.0% | 30.0% |
| Personnel expense-to-revenue | −15.6% | −15.6% | −16.0% | −16.2% | −16.1% | −16.0% | −16.2% | −16.0% | −16.2% | −16.4% | −15.6% |
| Cost of materials-to-revenue | −43.7% | −43.0% | −42.2% | −41.7% | −40.7% | −40.2% | −40.7% | −40.8% | −42.9% | −43.2% | −43.3% |
| Revenue growth in local currencies | 10.0% | 13.0% | 15.0% | 11.0% | 8.0% | 14.0% | 11.0% | 10.0% | 9.0% | 12.0% | 17.0% |
| Like-for-like revenue growth | 5.0% | 10.0% | 8.5% | 5.0% | 3.0% | 6.0% | 4.0% | 3.0% | 0.0% | 0.0% | 5.0% |
| Net operating assets | 12,454.2 | 11,805.5 | 11,262.1 | 10,885.9 | 9,052.2 | 8,219.8 | 7,143.0 | 5,972.7 | 6,200.0 | 5,880.7 | 5,561.5 |
| Non-operating investments | 5,925.2 | 5,880.3 | 5,040.7 | 3,988.2 | 3,488.8 | 3,378.9 | 3,047.4 | 3,046.9 | 2,065.0 | 1,133.6 | 1,159.5 |
| of which: excess cash | 3,664.2 | 2,950.4 | 3,180.5 | 2,892.1 | 3,010.5 | 3,045.6 | 2,777.1 | 2,807.2 | 1,866.1 | 946.1 | 994.2 |
| Debt | 4,857.4 | 4,934.3 | 4,852.0 | 4,405.4 | 3,262.7 | 3,116.8 | 2,734.8 | 2,596.4 | 2,894.5 | 2,265.7 | 2,503.7 |
| Ordinary shareholders' equity | 13,497.0 | 12,713.4 | 11,410.2 | 10,430.7 | 9,246.2 | 8,445.9 | 7,414.8 | 6,386.2 | 5,329.2 | 4,721.7 | 4,193.1 |
| Non-controlling interest in equity | 25.0 | 38.2 | 40.6 | 38.0 | 32.1 | 35.9 | 40.8 | 37.0 | 41.4 | 26.9 | 23.9 |
| Invested capital | 18,379.4 | 17,685.8 | 16,302.8 | 14,874.1 | 12,541.1 | 11,598.7 | 10,190.3 | 9,019.6 | 8,265.0 | 7,014.3 | 6,720.8 |

(continued)

**EXHIBIT 2** Financial and share price information of Inditex for the years 2007–2017  (Continued)

| € mln | 2017 | 2016 | 2015 | 2014 | 2013 | 2012 | 2011 | 2010 | 2009 | 2008 | 2007 |
|---|---|---|---|---|---|---|---|---|---|---|---|
| Average number of stores | 7,383.5 | 7,152.5 | 6,848.0 | 6,511.5 | 6,174.5 | 5,768.0 | 5,285.5 | 4,825.5 | 4,435.5 | 3,977.5 | 3,411.0 |
| PP&E-to-revenue | 49.5% | 51.9% | 54.0% | 53.9% | 50.4% | 47.9% | 49.0% | 51.5% | 56.1% | 55.8% | 57.0% |
| Days' inventories | 85.1 | 85.1 | 82.8 | 84.3 | 86.2 | 80.2 | 79.9 | 77.8 | 77.5 | 82.6 | 80.7 |
| Operating cash flow | 5,826 | 5,906 | 6,193 | 4,737 | 4,219 | 4,410 | 3,539 | 3,657 | 3,308 | 2,558 | 2,419 |
| Investment cash flow (plus interest received) | (2,575) | (4,031) | (4,551) | (4,368) | (2,837) | (3,222) | (2,576) | (1,500) | (2,240) | (1,588) | (1,808) |
| Change in debt (minus interest paid) | (183) | (122) | 444 | 1,013 | 47 | 336 | 61 | (422) | 547 | (289) | 479 |
| Free cash flow to equity | 3,069 | 1,754 | 2,086 | 1,382 | 1,429 | 1,524 | 1,023 | 1,735 | 1,615 | 681 | 1,090 |
| Number of shares outstanding (mln) | 3,113.2 | 3,113.6 | 3,113.2 | 3,113.8 | 3,115.6 | 3,116.7 | 3,116.7 | 3,116.7 | 3,116.7 | 3,116.7 | 3,116.7 |
| Share price at fiscal year-end | 28.87 | 30.54 | 30.19 | 26.14 | 22.14 | 20.64 | 13.34 | 11.04 | 9.13 | 5.98 | 6.70 |
| Share price 3 months after the fiscal year-end | 25.78 | 35.21 | 28.04 | 28.68 | 21.63 | 20.41 | 13.59 | 12.11 | 9.33 | 6.48 | 7.00 |
| Share price 6 months after the fiscal year-end | 28.05 | 33.59 | 30.94 | 31.18 | 21.86 | 20.04 | 16.77 | 12.63 | 10.15 | 7.55 | 6.21 |

**EXHIBIT 3** Financial information of other fashion retailers for the years 2016 and 2017

| Millions of local currency | Abercrombie & Fitch (US; $) | | Fast Retailing (Japan; ¥) | | Gap (US; $) | | Next (UK; £) | |
|---|---|---|---|---|---|---|---|---|
| | 2017 | 2016 | 2017 | 2016 | 2017 | 2016 | 2017 | 2016 |
| Revenue | 3,493 | 3,327 | 1,861,917 | 1,786,473 | 15,855 | 15,516 | 4,056 | 4,097 |
| Net operating profit after tax (recurring) | 59 | 55 | 125,173 | 105,061 | 1,019 | 953 | 665 | 707 |
| Profit or loss (recurring) | 20 | 13 | 125,074 | 102,249 | 867 | 792 | 596 | 637 |
| Net operating assets | 2,301 | 2,480 | 670,708 | 593,755 | 9,784 | 9,648 | 3,064 | 3,149 |
| Non-operating investments | 713 | 572 | 712,213 | 571,031 | 1,169 | 1,200 | 108 | 65 |
| Debt | 1,761 | 1,800 | 620,880 | 567,128 | 7,809 | 7,944 | 2,690 | 2,704 |
| Ordinary shareholders' equity | 1,242 | 1,243 | 731,769 | 574,500 | 3,144 | 2,904 | 483 | 511 |
| Non-controlling interest in equity | 10 | 9 | 30,272 | 23,159 | 0 | 0 | 0 | 0 |
| Invested capital | 3,014 | 3,052 | 1,382,921 | 1,164,787 | 10,953 | 10,848 | 3,172 | 3,214 |
| NOPAT margin | 1.7% | 1.7% | 6.7% | 5.9% | 6.4% | 6.1% | 16.4% | 17.3% |
| Operating asset turnover | 1.41 | 1.25 | 3.14 | 2.65 | 1.64 | 1.49 | 1.29 | 1.39 |
| Return on (beginning) net operating assets | 2.4% | 2.1% | 21.1% | 15.6% | 10.6% | 9.2% | 21.1% | 24.0% |
| Return on (beginning) equity | 1.6% | 1.0% | 21.8% | 13.6% | 29.8% | 31.1% | 116.7% | 204.2% |
| Revenue growth | 5.0% | -5.5% | 4.2% | 6.2% | 2.2% | -1.8% | -1.0% | -1.9% |
| PP&E-to-revenue | 62.5% | 70.9% | 21.7% | 19.7% | 53.6% | 55.9% | 55.2% | 55.9% |
| Days' inventories | 105.3 | 116.0 | 105.7 | 103.5 | 70.4 | 67.5 | 118.2 | 117.1 |
| Exchange rate (€) at year end | 0.8068 | 0.9347 | 0.0076 | 0.0087 | 0.8068 | 0.9347 | 1.1370 | 1.1719 |

# 8 Prospective analysis: Valuation implementation

To move from the valuation theory discussed in the previous chapter to the actual task of valuing a company, we have to deal with three key issues. First, we have to estimate the cost of capital to discount our forecasts. Second, we have to make forecasts of financial performance stated in terms of abnormal profits and book values, or free cash flows, over the life of the firm. Third, we need to choose between an equity valuation or an asset valuation approach and understand the consequences of this choice. Figure 8.1 shows a condensed "fair-value" balance sheet, including the (primary) performance forecasts and discount rates used to value assets and claims. This figure shows that there are various approaches that an analyst can follow to value a firm's equity. Possible valuation approaches are:

- To value the firm's equity directly as, for example, the sum of its book value of equity and the present value of forecasted profits or losses, discounted at the cost of equity.
- To value the firm's business assets as the sum of these assets' book values and the present value of forecasted NOPAT plus NIPAT – discounted at the (weighted average) cost of capital – first and then calculate equity value as the difference between the value of business assets and the (pre-tax) value of debt claims. As we will discuss in this chapter, this (business) asset valuation approach is a useful alternative to the equity valuation approach, especially if the analyst anticipates significant changes in leverage over the forecast horizon.
- To separately value net operating assets as the sum of these assets' book values and the present value of forecasted NOPAT – discounted at the **required return on net operating assets** – first and then calculate equity value as the sum of the value of net operating assets and the value of non-operating investments minus the after-tax value of debt claims. Or equivalently, calculate equity value as the sum of the values of net operating assets, non-operating investments, and the tax shield on debt minus the pre-tax value of debt claims. This (operating) asset valuation approach is especially useful if the value of non-operating investments can be easily obtained from the financial statements and/or if the analyst anticipates significant changes in the relative size of non-operating investments over the forecast horizon.

The first part of this chapter provides guidance on calculating the discount rates used under each of these three approaches: the cost of equity (equity valuation), the cost of capital (business asset valuation), and the required return on net operating assets (operating asset valuation). The second part of this chapter explains that the forecasting task itself is divided into two subcomponents: (1) detailed forecasts over a finite number of years and (2) a forecast of **terminal value**, which represents a summary forecast of performance beyond the period of detailed forecasts. This part builds on the forecast developed in Chapter 6 and provides guidance on computing a terminal value and synthesizing the different pieces of the analytical process to estimate firm or equity value.

## Computing a discount rate

To value a company's equity (directly), the analyst discounts cash flows available to equity holders, abnormal profit (growth), or abnormal ROE. The proper discount rate to use is the cost of equity.

**FIGURE 8.1**  Condensed fair-value balance sheet

| Assets | | | Claims | | |
|---|---|---|---|---|---|
| **Asset** | **Primary performance forecast** | **Discount rate** | **Claim** | **Primary performance forecast** | **Discount rate** |
| Value of net operating assets | NOPAT | Required return on net operating assets $(r_{NOA})$ | After-tax value of debt claims | Interest expense after tax | Cost of debt $(r_d)$ |
| + Value of non-operating investments | + NIPAT | Required return on non-operating investments $(r_{NOI})$ | + Value of equity claim | + Profit or loss | Cost of equity $(r_e)$ |
| + Value of the tax shield on debt | | | + Value of the tax shield on debt | | |
| = Business value | = NOPAT + NIPAT | Weighted average cost of capital (WACC, $r_c$) | Value of invested capital | = Profit or loss + Interest expense after tax | Weighted average cost of capital (WACC, $r_c$) |

## ESTIMATING THE COST OF EQUITY

Estimating the **cost of equity** $(r_e)$ can be difficult, and a full discussion of the topic lies beyond the scope of this chapter. In any case, even an extended discussion would not supply answers to all the questions that might be raised in this area because the field of finance is in a state of flux over what constitutes an appropriate measure of the cost of equity.

### The capital asset pricing model

One common approach to estimating the cost of equity is to use the **capital asset pricing model** (CAPM). The main idea of the CAPM is that investors holding a portfolio of investments (only) care about – and thus want to be compensated for – the risk that an asset contributes to the portfolio. This type of risk, labelled beta or systematic risk, is the risk created by the correlation between the asset's return and the returns of the other investments in the portfolio. The CAPM therefore expresses the cost of equity as the sum of a required return on riskless assets plus a premium for beta or systematic risk:

$$r_e = r_f + \beta \left[ E(r_m) - r_f \right]$$

where $r_f$ is the riskless rate; $[E(r_m) - r_f]$ is the risk premium expected for the market as a whole, expressed as the excess of the expected return on the market index over the riskless rate; and $\beta$ is the systematic risk of the equity.

To compute $r_e$ one must estimate three parameters: the riskless rate, $r_f$, the market risk premium $[E(r_m) - r_f]$, and systematic risk, $\beta$. To estimate the required return on riskless assets, analysts often use the expected rate of return on intermediate-term government bonds, based on the observation that it is cash flows beyond the short-term that are being discounted.[1] Theory calls for the use of a short-term rate, but if that rate is used here, a difficult practical question arises: how does one reflect the premium required for expected inflation over long horizons? While the premium could, in principle, be treated as a portion of the term $[E(r_m) - r_f]$, it is probably easier to use an intermediate – or long-term – riskless rate that presumably reflects expected inflation.

The systematic, non-diversifiable or beta risk ($\beta$) of a share reflects the sensitivity of its cash flows and profits (and hence stock price) to economy-wide market movements.[2] A firm whose performance increases or decreases at the same rate as changes in the economy as a whole will have a beta of one. Firms whose performance is highly sensitive to economy-wide changes, such as luxury goods producers, capital goods manufacturers, and construction firms, will have beta risks that exceed one. And firms whose profits and cash flows are less sensitive to economic changes, such as regulated utilities or supermarkets, will have betas that are lower than one. Financial services firms, such as Bloomberg and Thomson Financial, provide estimates of beta for publicly listed companies that are based on the historical relation between the firm's stock returns and the returns on the market index. These estimates provide a useful way to assess publicly traded firms' beta risks. For firms that are not publicly traded, analysts can use betas for publicly traded firms in the same industries, adjusting for any differences in financial leverage, as an indicator of the likely beta risk.

## Apparel Retailers' Betas

One way to estimate systematic risk is to regress the firm's stock returns over some recent time period against the returns on the market index. In this regression the slope coefficient on the market index represents an estimate of a company's (historical) $\beta$. Using monthly returns on the MSCI World Index as the measure for market returns, the estimated relationship between Hennes & Mauritz's monthly stock returns and the market index between January 2013 and December 2017 is as follows:

$$\text{Monthly return H\&M} = -0.01 + 0.93 \times \text{Monthly market return (R}^2 = 25.4\%)$$

This equation indicates that H&M's historical beta estimate is 0.93. When changing the starting year of the estimation period from 2013 to years between 2006 and 2012, the beta estimate ranges from 0.3 in the earlier years to 0.9 in later years.

Similar regressions estimated using the monthly stock returns of Inditex indicate that Inditex's equity beta is close to 0.7, illustrating the greater cyclicality of H&M.

Finally, the market risk premium is the amount that investors demand as additional return for bearing beta risk. It is the excess of the expected return on the market index over the riskless rate $r_f$. When $r_f$ is measured as the rate on intermediate-term government bonds, then average worldwide common stock returns (based on the returns to a 21-country, common-currency equity index) have exceeded that rate by slightly less than 5 percent over the 1900–2017 period.[3] This excess return constitutes an estimate of the market risk premium $[E(r_m) - r_f]$. Based on the risk premium's historical means and variances between 1900 and 2017, plausible estimates of future market risk premiums for the "world market" are somewhere between 4.5 and 5.5 percent. However, it is important to realize that the market risk premium has varied substantially across countries and will likely continue to do so, albeit to a lesser degree when worldwide stock markets will further integrate and worldwide disclosure and securities regulation will be further harmonized.[4] In addition, while the historical risk premium has been calculated over a long time period, the premium is likely to change over time because of, for example, the changing risk preferences of investors.

### The firm size effect

Although the preceding CAPM is often used to estimate the cost of capital, the evidence indicates that the model is incomplete. Assuming stocks are priced competitively, stock returns should be expected to compensate investors only for the cost of their capital. Thus long-run average returns should be close to the cost of capital and should (according to the CAPM) vary across stocks according to their systematic risk. However, factors beyond just systematic risk seem to play some role in explaining variation in long-run average returns. The most important such factor is labelled the "size effect": smaller firms (as measured by market capitalization) tend to generate higher returns in subsequent periods.[5] Why this is so is unclear. It could mean either that smaller firms are riskier than indicated by the CAPM or that they are underpriced at the point their market capitalization is measured, or some combination of both.

## Hennes & Mauritz's Risk Premium

At the end of 2017 the average nominal yield on ten-year government bonds in the euro area was close to 1.0 percent (Source: Eurostat). Yields had been driven down to abnormally low levels during the economic crisis, partly because of investors fleeing to higher quality bond investments and bond market interventions by the European Central Bank. Consequently, the average yield had even dropped below the expected long-term inflation rate, thereby making the yield a poor measure of investors' expectation of the long-term risk-free rate of return.

The long-term historical average real return on (worldwide) governments bonds between 1900 and 2017 had been close to 2.1 percent. Using the long-term average bond return to measure the expected *real* risk-free rate and assuming that at the end of 2017 the expected long-term inflation rate in the euro area amounted to 1.9 percent (Source: ECB), we estimate the expected *nominal* risk-free rate at 4 percent (2.1 percent + 1.9 percent). Assuming that the market risk premium equals 5 percent, the CAPM-based estimate of H&M's cost of equity equals:

$$\text{Cost of equity} = 4\% \ (r_f) + 0.93 \ (\beta) \times 5\% \ (E(r_m) - r_f) = 8.7 \text{ percent}$$

Average stock returns for European firms (from 17 European countries) varied across size deciles from 1990 to 2017 as shown in Table 8.1. The table shows that historically investors in firms in the two smallest size deciles of the size distribution have realized returns that are, on average, 5.5 to 12.3 percent higher than the returns earned in the top size decile. Note, however, that if we use firm size as an indicator of the cost of capital, we are implicitly assuming that large size is indicative of lower risk. Yet finance theorists have not developed a well-accepted explanation for why that should be the case.

One method for combining the cost of capital estimates is based on the CAPM and the "size effect." The approach calls for adjustment of the CAPM-based cost of capital, based on the difference between the average return on the market index used in the CAPM and the average return on firms of size comparable to the firm being evaluated. The resulting cost of capital is:

$$r_e = r_f + \beta \left[ E(r_m) - r_f \right] + r_{SIZE}$$

**TABLE 8.1** European firms' stock returns and firm size

| Size deciles | Market value of largest company in decile, in 2017 (€ millions) | Average premium 1990–2017 (% return differential with decile 10) |
|---|---|---|
| *1-small* | 11.4 | 12.3% |
| *2* | 29.5 | 5.5% |
| *3* | 58.0 | 4.4% |
| *4* | 119.8 | 5.1% |
| *5* | 225.8 | 3.5% |
| *6* | 464.9 | 2.6% |
| *7* | 950.7 | 2.3% |
| *8* | 2,208.2 | 1.3% |
| *9* | 6,502.9 | 1.8% |
| *10-large* | 221,671.8 | 0.0% |

Source: Duff & Phelps' 2018 International Valuation Handbook.

## Hennes & Mauritz's Size Premium

At the end of fiscal year 2017, the market value of H&M's shares was approximately €32,928 million, down from €45,386 million one year earlier. Although the equity value that we estimate for Hennes & Mauritz may deviate from its market price, this value is likely to fall within the top size decile of the European market. Consequently, it is unnecessary to adjust H&M's cost of equity estimate for a size effect.

In light of the continuing debate on how to measure the cost of capital, it is not surprising that managers and analysts often consider a range of estimates. In addition to the question about whether the historical risk premium of about 5 percent is valid today,[6] there is debate over whether beta is a relevant measure of risk and whether other metrics such as size should be reflected in cost of capital estimates. Since these debates are still unresolved, it is prudent for analysts to use a range of risk premium estimates in computing a firm's cost of capital.

### Adjusting the cost of equity for changes in leverage

The beta risk of a firm's equity changes as a function of its leverage. As the leverage increases, the sensitivity of the firm's equity performance to economy-wide changes also increases. To see this, recall from Chapter 5 that return on equity (ROE) can be decomposed in the following manner:

$$ROE = \text{Return on invested capital}$$
$$+ \left(\text{Return on invested capital} - \text{Effective interest rate}\right) \times \frac{\text{Debt}}{\text{Equity}}$$

This equation shows that if debt equals equity, a 2 percent increase in return on invested capital (ROIC) after an economy-wide recovery will increase ROE by 4 percent, all else equal. In contrast, if debt is two times equity, the same increase in ROIC will increase ROE by 6 percent. Hence the equity beta of a firm does not only reflect the sensitivity of its assets' performance to economy-wide movements (labelled **asset beta**) but also the financial leverage effect on its equity performance. If an analyst is contemplating changing capital structure during the forecasting period relative to the historical capital structure of the firm, or changing the capital structure over time during the forecasting period, it is important to re-estimate the equity beta and to take these changes into account. We describe here a simple approach to this task.

We begin with the observation that the beta of a portfolio of assets is the weighted average of the assets' individual betas. Similarly, the beta of a firm's business assets is equal to the weighted average of its debt and equity betas, weighted by the proportion of debt and equity in its capital structure, taking into account the tax shield on debt:

$$\beta_{\text{BUSINESS}} = \frac{(1 - \text{Tax rate}) \times \text{Debt}}{(1 - \text{Tax rate}) \times \text{Debt} + \text{Equity}} \beta_{\text{DEBT}} + \frac{\text{Equity}}{(1 - \text{Tax rate}) \times \text{Debt} + \text{Equity}} \beta_{\text{EQUITY}}$$

A firm's equity beta can be estimated directly using its stock returns and the capital asset pricing model. Its debt beta can be inferred from the capital asset pricing model if we have information on its current interest rate and the risk-free rate, using the CAPM formula. From these estimated equity and debt betas at the current capital structure, we can infer the firm's asset beta.

When the firm's capital structure changes, its equity and debt betas will change, but its asset beta remains the same. We can take advantage of this fact to estimate the expected equity beta for the new capital structure. We first have to get an estimate of the interest rate on debt at the new capital structure level. Once we have this information, we can estimate the implied debt beta using the capital asset pricing model and the risk-free rate. Now we can estimate the equity beta for the new capital structure using the identity that the new equity beta and the new debt beta, weighted by the new capital structure weights, have to add up to the asset beta estimated earlier.

For many firms that have a low probability of bankruptcy, the current interest rate will be close to the risk-free rate and the debt beta will be close to zero. To simplify the calculation of leverage-adjusted betas, many analysts thus assume that the debt beta equals zero. Under this assumption, the equity and asset betas have the following relationship:

$$\beta_{\text{EQUITY}} = \left[ 1 + (1 - \text{Tax rate}) \times \frac{\text{Debt}}{\text{Equity}} \right] \beta_{\text{BUSINESS}}$$

Note that in this equation, debt and equity are measured in terms of economic values rather than book values. We will next discuss some of the complications involved in obtaining these economic values.

### Adjusting the cost of equity for changes in non-operating investments

In the previous discussion we conveniently ignored the fact that the business assets of some firms consist in significant part of non-operating investments and, just as importantly, that the relevance of such investments may change during the forecasting period. For example, in Chapter 5 we described that at the end of 2017 Hennes & Mauritz had no excess cash – a non-operating investment asset. The retailer had gradually reduced its excess cash holdings from 15 percent of revenue in 2010 to 0 percent in 2015. Because the beta of excess cash and cash equivalents (fixed income securities) is close to zero and therefore significantly different from the average beta of the other business assets, changes in the holdings of excess cash and similar non-operating investments, either during the beta estimation period or during the forecast horizon, will also lead to changes in the firm's equity beta. We describe next how the equity beta can be re-estimated to take such changes into account.

Because the beta of a portfolio of assets is the weighted average of the assets' individual betas, the following equation – which sets the weighted average of the two types of asset betas equal to the weighted average of the debt and equity beta – should hold:

$$\beta_{\text{BUSINESS}} = \frac{\text{Net operating assets}}{\text{Business assets}} \beta_{\text{NOA}} + \frac{\text{Non-operating investments}}{\text{Business assets}} \beta_{\text{NOI}}$$

$$= \frac{(1 - \text{Tax rate}) \times \text{Debt}}{(1 - \text{Tax rate}) \times \text{Debt} + \text{Equity}} \beta_{\text{DEBT}} + \frac{\text{Equity}}{(1 - \text{Tax rate}) \times \text{Debt} + \text{Equity}} \beta_{\text{EQUITY}}$$

Rearranging the equation leads to the following relationship between the equity beta and the betas of net operating assets ($\beta_{\text{NOA}}$), non-operating investments ($\beta_{\text{NOI}}$), and debt:

$$\beta_{\text{EQUITY}} = \left[ 1 + \frac{(1 - \text{Tax rate}) \times \text{Debt} - \text{Non-operating investments}}{\text{Equity}} \right] \beta_{\text{NOA}}$$

$$+ \left[ \frac{\text{Non-operating investments}}{\text{Equity}} \right] \beta_{\text{NOI}} - \left[ \frac{(1 - \text{Tax rate}) \times \text{Debt}}{\text{Equity}} \right] \beta_{\text{DEBT}}$$

In this equation debt, equity, and non-operating investments are all measured in terms of economic values, not book values. When analyzing a financially healthy industrial (non-financial) firm whose investment assets consist mostly of cash and marketable fixed income securities, such as Hennes & Mauritz, it is reasonable to assume that the betas of the non-operating investments and debt equal zero, such that the equity beta depends only on the beta of the net operating assets.

### Weights of debt, non-operating investments, and equity

The weights assigned to debt, non-operating investments, and equity in the preceding equations represent their respective fractions of total capital provided, measured in terms of economic values. Computing an economic value for debt should not be difficult. International accounting standards (IFRS Standards 7) require that firms disclose the economic value of their liabilities in the notes to the financial statements. Further, if interest rates have not changed significantly since the time the debt was issued, it is reasonable to use book values rather than economic values in the beta leverage-adjustment. If interest rates have changed and economic value information is not available from the financial statements, the value of the debt can be estimated by discounting the future payouts at current market rates of interest applicable to the firm.

The tricky problem we face is assigning an economic value to equity. That is the very amount we are trying to estimate in the first place! How can the analyst possibly assign a market value to equity at this intermediate stage, given that the estimate will not be known until all steps in the valuation analysis are completed? The most feasible approach to the problem is to use averages of the historical ratios of debt and non-operating investments to market capitalization (market value of equity) that we observed during the period in which the equity beta has been estimated. This approach is appropriate because the equity beta estimate reflects a firm's operating and financial risk during the estimation period rather than a firm's expected or targeted operating and financial risk.

If historical market values are not available, another way around the problem is to start with book value of equity as a weight for purposes of calculating an initial estimate of the leverage-adjusted equity beta, which in turn can be used in the discounting process to generate an initial estimate of the value of equity. That initial estimate can then be used in place of the guess to arrive at a new equity beta, and a second estimate of the value of equity can be produced. This process can be repeated until the value used to calculate the leverage-adjusted equity beta and the final estimated value converge.

## ESTIMATING THE REQUIRED RETURN ON NET OPERATING ASSETS

To value a company's net operating assets, the analyst discounts abnormal net operating profit after tax (NOPAT), abnormal return on net operating assets (RNOA), or free cash flows from operating assets. The proper discount rate to use therefore depends on the beta of the firm's net operating assets. Based on the theoretical relationship between the equity beta and the betas of the operating assets and non-operating investments, which we described earlier, this beta can be calculated as:

$$
\begin{aligned}
\beta_{NOA} =& \left[\frac{\text{Equity}}{(1-\text{Tax rate})\times\text{Debt}+\text{Equity}-\text{Non-operating investments}}\right]\beta_{EQUITY} \\
&+\left[\frac{(1-\text{Tax rate})\times\text{Debt}}{(1-\text{Tax rate})\times\text{Debt}+\text{Equity}-\text{Non-operating investments}}\right]\beta_{DEBT} \\
&-\left[\frac{\text{Non-operating investments}}{(1-\text{Tax rate})\times\text{Debt}+\text{Equity}-\text{Non-operating investments}}\right]\beta_{NOI}
\end{aligned}
$$

For financially healthy firms whose non-operating investments consist of low risk instruments such as excess cash or fixed income securities, like Hennes & Mauritz, the calculation can again be simplified by setting the beta of the non-operating investments equal to zero. After having derived the beta of the net operating assets, one can plug the beta into the CAPM formula to calculate the required return on net operating assets. Similarly, one can plug the non-operating investments beta into the CAPM formula to derive the required return on non-operating investments.

## ESTIMATING THE WEIGHTED AVERAGE COST OF CAPITAL

To value the sum of a company's business assets and the tax shield on debt directly, analysts may discount abnormal NOPAT plus NIPAT, or cash flows available to both debt and equity holders, at the **weighted average cost of capital** (WACC). The WACC is calculated by weighting the costs of debt and equity capital according to their respective market values:

$$
\text{WACC} = \frac{\text{Debt}}{\text{Debt}+\text{Equity}}(1-\text{Tax rate})\times\text{Cost of debt}+\frac{\text{Equity}}{\text{Debt}+\text{Equity}}\times\text{Cost of equity}
$$

# Hennes & Mauritz's Required Return on Net Operating Assets

**D**uring the years 2013–2017, the ratio of H&M's after-tax book value of debt to market value of equity ranged from 0.10 to 0.20 and averaged at 0.13.

|  | 2017 | 2016 | 2015 | 2014 | 2013 |
|---|---|---|---|---|---|
| Book/market value of debt (SEK bn) | 83.4 | 78.2 | 78.5 | 73.2 | 58.7 |
| × (1 − Tax rate) (%) | 78.0 | 78.0 | 78.0 | 78.0 | 78.0 |
| After-tax value of debt (SEK bn) | 65.1 | 61.0 | 61.2 | 57.1 | 45.8 |
| Market value of equity (SEK bn) | 326.2 | 443.4 | 535.4 | 528.6 | 460.1 |
| Leverage ratio (%) | 20.0 | 13.8 | 11.4 | 10.8 | 10.0 |

Given H&M's low leverage and high creditworthiness, it is safe to assume that the market value of the company's debt is close to its book value. Footnote disclosures in the company's financial statements, made in accordance with international accounting standard IFRS Standards 7, also confirm this. Using the average after-tax leverage ratio of 0.13 and our previous equity beta estimate of 0.93 (and assuming that the H&M's debt beta equals zero), H&M's asset beta can be easily derived as follows:

$$\beta_{BUSINESS} = \frac{1}{[0.13+1]} \times \beta_{EQUITY} = \frac{1}{1.13} \times 0.93 = 0.82$$

Between 2013 and 2017, the ratio between the market/book value of H&M's non-operating investments to the market value of its equity ranged from 0 to 0.02 and averaged at 0.01.

|  | 2017 | 2016 | 2015 | 2014 | 2013 |
|---|---|---|---|---|---|
| Book/market value of non-operating investments | 1.0 | 1.0 | 0.9 | 5.3 | 7.6 |
| Market value of equity | 326.2 | 443.4 | 535.4 | 528.6 | 460.1 |
| Investment ratio | 0.3 | 0.2 | 0.2 | 1.0 | 1.7 |

Using this information (and assuming that the H&M's non-operating investments beta and debt beta equal zero), the net operating asset beta of H&M can be calculated as follows:

$$\beta_{NOA} = \left[\frac{Equity}{(1-Tax\ rate)\times Debt + Equity - Non\text{-}operating\ investments}\right]\beta_{EQUITY}$$

$$= \left[\frac{1}{0.13+1-0.01}\right] \times 0.93 = 0.83$$

Using the beta of the net operating assets and the CAPM formula, one can calculate the required return on net operating assets ($r_{NOA}$) under the assumption that in future years H&M's operating risk will remain close to its historical level:

$$r_{NOA} = 4\ \%\ (r_f) + 0.83\ (\beta_{NOA}) \times 5\ \%\ (E(r_m)-r_f) = 8.2\ percent$$

# Using Industry Betas

T he previous estimates of H&M's cost of equity and required return on net operating assets were based on our firm-specific estimate of H&M's equity beta. H&M's equity beta appears to be high relative to the equity betas of its industry peers. An obvious explanation for this difference in equity betas is that H&M's currently weak competitive position has increased the retailer's exposure to economy-wide fluctuations, thus increasing its systematic risk relative to the other peers. In our forecasting analysis we assumed, however, that over time H&M's competitive position and performance would improve. Given this assumption, it makes sense to also assume that in the long run the systematic risk of H&M's net operating assets will approach the industry average. Consequently, the industry asset beta should be used as an input in calculating H&M's cost of equity and required return on net operating assets. To do so, we take the following approach.

First, we calculate the industry equity beta as the equity value-weighted average of the retailers' individual betas. Using the equity beta estimation procedure described earlier, the weighted average equity beta of the six industry peers that we examined in Chapter 5 is 0.78.

Second, we estimate the industry beta of net operating assets by adjusting the equity beta for the average degree of leverage and the proportion of non-operating investments in the industry. During the years 2013–2017, the ratio of six retailers' after-tax book value of debt to market value of equity ranged from 0.09 to 0.11 and averaged at 0.10.

|  | 2017 | 2016 | 2015 | 2014 | 2013 |
|---|---|---|---|---|---|
| After tax book/market value of debt (€bn) | 15.1 | 16.2 | 14.8 | 13.5 | 11.2 |
| Market value of equity (€bn) | 135.8 | 143.9 | 158.5 | 140.4 | 123.5 |
| Industry leverage ratio (%) | 11.1 | 11.3 | 9.3 | 9.6 | 9.1 |

Given the industry's comparatively low leverage and high creditworthiness, it is safe to assume that the market value of the industry's debt is close to its book value. Between 2013 and 2017, the ratio between the market/book value of the industry's non-operating investments to the market value of its equity ranged from 0.06 to 0.10 and averaged at 0.08.

|  | 2017 | 2016 | 2015 | 2014 | 2013 |
|---|---|---|---|---|---|
| Book/market value of non-operating investments (€bn) | 13.5 | 13.1 | 9.6 | 8.3 | 8.2 |
| Market value of equity (€bn) | 135.8 | 143.9 | 158.5 | 140.4 | 123.5 |
| Investment ratio (%) | 9.9 | 9.1 | 6.1 | 5.9 | 6.6 |

Using this information (and assuming that the industry's non-operating investments beta and debt beta equal zero), the average net operating asset beta of the five industry peers can be calculated as follows:

$$\beta_{NOA} = \left[ \frac{Equity}{(1 - Tax\ rate) \times Debt + Equity - Investment\ assets} \right] \beta_{EQUITY}$$

$$= \left[ \frac{1}{0.10 + 1 - 0.08} \right] \times 0.78 = 0.76$$

Third, given our assumption that H&M's competitive position gradually improves, it is reasonable to expect that H&M's net operating asset beta will move from its current level of 0.83 towards the peers' net operating beta, potentially settling around 0.76. This would imply that H&M's required return on net operating assets is equal to:

$$r_{NOA} = 4\% \ (r_f) + 0.76 \ (\beta_{NOA}) \times 5\% \ (E(r_m) - r_f) = 7.8 \text{ percent}$$

Fourth and finally, assuming that H&M's future debt and investment ratios will remain close to their 2017 levels of, respectively, 0.20 and 0, the retailer's future equity beta can be derived as follows:

$$\beta_{EQUITY} = \left[1 + \frac{(1 - \text{Tax rate}) \times \text{Debt} - \text{Investment assets}}{\text{Equity}}\right] \beta_{NOA}$$

$$= \left[1 + \frac{0.20 - 0}{1}\right] \times 0.76 = 0.91$$

Consequently, our estimate of H&M's cost of equity is:

$$\text{Cost of equity} = 4\% \ (r_f) + 0.91 \ (\beta) \times 5\% \ (E(r_m) - r_f) = 8.6 \text{ percent}$$

Throughout this chapter we will use a required return on net operating assets of 7.8 percent and a cost of equity of 8.6 percent to value H&M's net operating assets and equity. To put our cost of equity estimate into context, early 2018 analysts following H&M were using costs of equity between 8.0 and 9.2 percent in their valuations.

Note that for most firms the WACC is not equal to the required return on business assets, which is the return that we obtain when plugging the beta of business assets into the CAPM formula. Whereas discounting abnormal NOPAT and NIPAT at the WACC gives us an estimate of the value of business assets *plus* the value of the tax shield on debt, discounting NOPAT and NIPAT at the required return on business assets gives us an estimate of the value of business assets only. In other words, when using the required return on business assets rather than the WACC, the analyst must separately value the tax shield on debt, as we will illustrate later in this chapter.

### Estimating the cost of debt

The cost of debt is the interest rate on the debt. It can be used to calculate the WACC, the value debt capital, or the present value of the tax shield on debt in asset valuation. If the assumed capital structure in future periods is the same as the historical structure, then the current interest rate on debt will be a good proxy for this. However, if the analyst assumes a change in capital structure, then it is important to estimate the expected interest rate given the new level of debt ratio. One approach to this would be to estimate the expected credit rating of the company at the new level of debt and use the appropriate interest rates for that credit category. We discuss the estimation of credit ratings in further detail in Chapter 10.

It is also worth noting that the cost of debt will change over time if market interest rates are expected to change. This can arise if investors expect inflation to increase or decrease over the forecast horizon. Since we typically discount nominal profits or cash flows, the cost of debt is a nominal rate and will change over time to reflect changes in inflation. This can be handled by scaling the cost of debt up or down over time to reflect expected changes in interest rates each year. If interest rates are projected to rise by 3 percent as a result of expected inflation, the cost of debt for the firm we are analyzing should also increase by 3 percent. The yield curve, which shows how investors expect interest rates to change over time can be used to assess whether time-varying interest rates are likely to be important in the analysis.

Finally, in the WACC calculation, the cost of debt should be expressed on a net-of-tax basis. In most settings the market rate of interest can be converted to a net-of-tax basis by multiplying it by one minus the marginal corporate tax rate.

## DETAILED FORECASTS OF PERFORMANCE

The horizon over which detailed forecasts are to be made is itself a choice variable. We will discuss later in this chapter how the analyst might make this choice. Once it is made, the next step is to consider the set of assumptions regarding a firm's performance that are needed to arrive at the forecasts. We described in Chapter 6 the general framework of financial forecasting and illustrated the approach using Hennes & Mauritz.

The key to sound forecasts is that the underlying assumptions are grounded in a company's business reality. Strategy analysis provides a critical understanding of a company's value proposition and whether current performance is likely to be sustainable in future. Accounting analysis and ratio analysis provide a deep understanding of a company's current performance and whether the ratios themselves are reliable indicators of performance. It is therefore important to see the valuation forecasts as a continuation of the earlier steps in business analysis rather than as a discreet exercise not connected from the rest of the analysis.

Since valuation involves forecasting over a long time horizon, it is not practical to forecast all the line items in a company's financial statements. Instead, the analyst has to focus on the key elements of a firm's performance. Specifically, we forecasted H&M's condensed income statement, beginning balance sheet, and free cash flows for a period of ten years starting in fiscal year 2018 (the year beginning in December 2017). We will use these same forecasting assumptions and financial forecasts, which are repeated here in Tables 8.2 and 8.3, as a starting point to value Hennes & Mauritz as of December 1, 2017. A spreadsheet containing H&M's actual and forecasted financial statements as well as the valuation described in this chapter is available on the companion website of this book.

## MAKING PERFORMANCE FORECASTS FOR VALUING H&M

As discussed in Chapter 7, the forecasts required to convert the preceding financial forecasts into estimates of value differ depending on whether we wish to value a firm's equity or its assets. To value equity, the essential inputs are:

- Abnormal profits: profit or loss less shareholders' equity at the beginning of the year times cost of equity.
- Abnormal profit growth: the change in profit less the cost of equity times prior period's change in equity (or the change in abnormal profit).
- Free cash flow to equity: net income less the increase in operating working capital less the increase in net non-current assets plus the increase in debt.

TABLE 8.2  Forecasting assumptions for Hennes & Mauritz

| Forecast year | 2018 (%) | 2019 (%) | 2020 (%) | 2021 (%) | 2022 (%) | 2023 (%) | 2024 (%) | 2025 (%) | 2026 (%) | 2027 (%) |
|---|---|---|---|---|---|---|---|---|---|---|
| Revenue growth rate | 9.4 | 8.3 | 8.4 | 7.6 | 6.8 | 6.0 | 5.3 | 4.5 | 3.8 | 3.0 |
| NOPAT margin | 9.9 | 10.5 | 11.1 | 10.5 | 9.9 | 9.3 | 8.7 | 8.1 | 7.6 | 7.0 |
| Operating working capital/ revenue | 10.6 | 9.6 | 8.6 | 8.6 | 8.6 | 8.6 | 8.6 | 8.6 | 8.6 | 8.6 |
| Net non-current operating assets/revenue | 58.1 | 57.0 | 55.7 | 55.7 | 55.7 | 55.7 | 55.7 | 55.7 | 55.7 | 55.7 |
| Non-operating investments/ revenue | 0.5 | 0.5 | 0.5 | 0.5 | 0.5 | 0.5 | 0.5 | 0.5 | 0.5 | 0.5 |
| After-tax return on non-operating investments | 3.0 | 3.0 | 3.0 | 3.0 | 3.0 | 3.0 | 3.0 | 3.0 | 3.0 | 3.0 |
| After-tax cost of debt | 1.5 | 1.7 | 1.9 | 2.1 | 2.3 | 2.5 | 2.5 | 2.5 | 2.5 | 2.5 |
| Debt to capital | 57.2 | 57.2 | 57.2 | 57.2 | 57.2 | 57.2 | 57.2 | 57.2 | 57.2 | 57.2 |

**TABLE 8.3** Forecasted financial statements for Hennes & Mauritz

| Fiscal year | 2018 | 2019 | 2020 | 2021 | 2022 | 2023 | 2024 | 2025 | 2026 | 2027 |
|---|---|---|---|---|---|---|---|---|---|---|
| **Beginning balance sheet (SEK millions)** | | | | | | | | | | |
| Beginning operating working capital | 25,299.0 | 23,192.0 | 22,749.7 | 22,096.5 | 23,775.8 | 25,392.6 | 26,916.1 | 28,342.7 | 29,618.1 | 30,743.6 |
| + Beginning net non-current operating assets | 116,820.7 | 127,118.2 | 135,076.3 | 143,113.4 | 153,989.9 | 164,461.3 | 174,329.0 | 183,568.4 | 191,829.0 | 199,118.5 |
| + Beginning non-operating investments | 1,039.0 | 1,094.0 | 1,184.9 | 1,284.7 | 1,382.3 | 1,476.3 | 1,564.9 | 1,647.8 | 1,722.0 | 1,787.4 |
| **= Business assets** | **143,158.7** | **151,404.2** | **159,010.9** | **166,494.6** | **179,148.0** | **191,330.2** | **202,810.0** | **213,558.9** | **223,169.1** | **231,649.5** |
| Debt | 83,445.7 | 86,603.2 | 90,954.2 | 95,234.9 | 102,472.7 | 109,440.9 | 116,007.3 | 122,155.7 | 127,652.7 | 132,503.5 |
| + Group equity | 59,713.0 | 64,801.0 | 68,056.7 | 71,259.7 | 76,675.3 | 81,889.3 | 86,802.7 | 91,403.2 | 95,516.4 | 99,146.0 |
| **= Invested capital** | **143,158.7** | **151,404.2** | **159,010.9** | **166,494.6** | **179,148.0** | **191,330.2** | **202,810.0** | **213,558.9** | **223,169.1** | **231,649.5** |
| **Income statement (SEK millions)** | | | | | | | | | | |
| Revenue | 218,792.0 | 236,976.0 | 256,936.0 | 276,463.1 | 295,262.6 | 312,978.4 | 329,566.3 | 344,396.8 | 357,483.9 | 368,208.4 |
| Net operating profit after tax | 21,646.0 | 24,866.8 | 28,502.9 | 29,028.6 | 29,231.0 | 29,107.0 | 28,672.3 | 27,896.1 | 27,168.8 | 25,774.6 |
| + Net investment profit after tax | 31.2 | 32.8 | 35.5 | 38.5 | 41.5 | 44.3 | 46.9 | 49.4 | 51.7 | 53.6 |
| **= Net business profit after tax** | **21,677.2** | **24,899.6** | **28,538.4** | **29,067.1** | **29,272.5** | **29,151.3** | **28,719.2** | **27,945.5** | **27,220.5** | **25,828.2** |
| − Net interest expense after tax | −1,251.7 | −1,472.3 | −1,728.1 | −1,999.9 | −2,356.9 | −2,736.0 | −2,900.2 | −3,053.9 | −3,191.3 | −3,312.6 |
| **= Profit or loss** | **20,425.5** | **23,427.3** | **26,810.3** | **27,067.2** | **26,915.6** | **26,415.3** | **25,819.0** | **24,891.6** | **24,029.2** | **22,515.6** |
| Return on net operating assets (%) | 15.2 | 16.5 | 18.1 | 17.6 | 16.4 | 15.3 | 14.2 | 13.2 | 12.3 | 11.2 |
| ROE (%) | 34.2 | 36.2 | 39.4 | 38.0 | 35.1 | 32.3 | 29.7 | 27.2 | 25.2 | 22.7 |
| BV of net operating assets growth rate (%) | 5.8 | 5.0 | 4.7 | 7.6 | 6.8 | 6.0 | 5.3 | 4.5 | 3.8 | 3.0 |
| BV of equity growth rate (%) | 8.5 | 5.0 | 4.7 | 7.6 | 6.8 | 6.0 | 5.3 | 4.5 | 3.8 | 3.8 |
| Profit or loss | 20,425.5 | 23,427.3 | 26,810.3 | 27,067.2 | 26,915.6 | 26,415.3 | 25,819.0 | 24,891.6 | 24,029.2 | 22,515.6 |
| − Change in operating working capital | 2,107.0 | 442.3 | 653.2 | −1,679.3 | −1,616.8 | −1,523.5 | −1,426.6 | −1,275.4 | −1,125.5 | −922.3 |
| − Change in net non-current operating assets | −10,297.5 | −7,958.1 | −8,037.1 | −10,876.5 | −10,471.4 | −9,867.7 | −9,239.4 | −8,260.6 | −7,289.5 | −5,973.6 |
| − Change in non-operating investments | −55.0 | −90.9 | −99.8 | −97.6 | −94.0 | −88.6 | −82.9 | −74.2 | −65.4 | −53.6 |
| + Change in debt | 3,157.5 | 4,351 | 4,280.7 | 7,237.8 | 6,968.2 | 6,566.4 | 6,148.4 | 5,497 | 4,850.8 | 3,975.1 |
| **= Free cash flow to equity** | **15,337.5** | **20,171.6** | **23,607.3** | **21,651.6** | **21,701.6** | **21,501.9** | **21,218.5** | **20,778.4** | **20,399.6** | **19,541.2** |
| Net operating profit after tax | 21,646.0 | 24,866.8 | 28,502.9 | 29,028.6 | 29,231.0 | 29,107.0 | 28,672.3 | 27,896.1 | 27,168.8 | 25,774.6 |
| − Change in operating working capital | 2,107.0 | 442.3 | 653.2 | −1,679.3 | −1,616.8 | −1,523.5 | −1,426.6 | −1,275.4 | −1,125.5 | −922.3 |
| − Change in net non-current operating assets | −10,297.5 | −7,958.1 | −8,037.1 | −10,876.5 | −10,471.4 | −9,867.7 | −9,239.4 | −8,260.6 | −7,289.5 | −5,973.6 |
| **= Free cash flow from operations** | **13,455.5** | **17,351.0** | **21,119.0** | **16,472.8** | **17,142.8** | **17,715.8** | **18,006.3** | **18,360.1** | **18,753.8** | **18,878.7** |

Alternatively, to value a company's net operating assets, the significant performance forecasts would be:

- Abnormal NOPAT: Net operating profit after tax (NOPAT) less total net operating assets at the beginning of the year times the required return on net operating assets.
- Abnormal NOPAT growth: the change in NOPAT less the required return on net operating assets times prior period's change in net operating assets (or the change in abnormal NOPAT).
- Free cash flow from operating assets: NOPAT less the increase in operating working capital less the increase in net non-current operating assets.

Table 8.4 shows H&M's performance forecasts for all six of these financial statement variables for the ten-year period 2018–2027.

As discussed earlier, to derive cash flows in 2027, we need to make assumptions about the revenue growth rate and balance sheet ratios in 2028. The cash flow forecasts shown in Table 8.4 are based on the simple assumption that the revenue growth and beginning balance sheet ratios in 2028 remain the same as in 2027. We discuss the sensitivity of this assumption and the terminal value assumption later in the chapter.

Hennes & Mauritz's projected abnormal ROE increases from 25.6 percent in 2018 to 30.8 percent in 2020 and then declines again due to the forces of competition. Abnormal return on net operating assets (RNOA), abnormal NOPAT, and abnormal profit show a similar trend. A slightly different pattern is shown for cash flow to equity and cash flow from operations. Projected cash flows are slightly more volatile under the influence of two opposing effects of competition. On the one hand, competition negatively affects the cash flow that H&M generates from its operations; on the other hand, competition reduces H&M's future investments through its moderating effect on the retailer's growth, thereby positively affecting free cash flows.

## TERMINAL VALUES

Explicit forecasts of the various elements of a firm's performance generally extend for a period of five to ten years. The final year of this forecast period is labelled the *terminal year* (selection of an appropriate terminal year is discussed later in this section). **Terminal value** is then the present value of either abnormal profits or free cash flows occurring beyond the terminal year. Since this involves forecasting performance over the remainder of the firm's life, the analyst must adopt some assumption that simplifies the process of forecasting. A key question is whether it is reasonable to assume a continuation of the terminal year performance or whether some other pattern is expected.

Clearly, the continuation of a revenue growth that is significantly greater than the average growth rate of the economy is unrealistic over a very long horizon. That rate would likely outstrip inflation in the euro and the real growth rate of the world economy. Over many years, it would imply that the firm would grow to a size greater than that of all the other firms in the world combined. But what would be a suitable alternative assumption? Should we expect the firm's revenue growth rate to ultimately settle down to the rate of inflation? Or to a higher rate, such as the nominal GDP growth rate? And perhaps equally important, will a firm that earns abnormal profits continue to do so by maintaining its profit margins on a growing, or even existing, base of revenue?

To answer these questions, we must consider how much longer the rate of growth in industry sales can outstrip overall economic growth, and how long a firm's competitive advantages can be sustained. Clearly, looking 11 or more years into the future, any forecast is likely to be subject to considerable error. Next we discuss a variety of alternative approaches to the task of calculating a terminal value.

TABLE 8.4  Performance forecasts for Hennes & Mauritz

| Fiscal year | 2018 | 2019 | 2020 | 2021 | 2022 | 2023 | 2024 | 2025 | 2026 | 2027 |
|---|---|---|---|---|---|---|---|---|---|---|
| **Equity valuation (SEK millions)** | | | | | | | | | | |
| Abnormal profit | 15,290.2 | 17,854.4 | 20,957.4 | 20,938.9 | 20,321.5 | 19,372.8 | 18,354.0 | 17,030.9 | 15,814.8 | 13,989.0 |
| Abnormal ROE (%) | 25.6 | 27.6 | 30.8 | 29.4 | 26.5 | 23.7 | 21.1 | 18.6 | 16.6 | 14.1 |
| Free cash flow to equity | 15,337.5 | 20,171.6 | 23,607.3 | 21,651.6 | 21,701.6 | 21,501.9 | 21,218.5 | 20,778.4 | 20,399.6 | 19,541.2 |
| Abnormal profit growth | | 2,564.2 | 3,103.0 | −18.6 | −617.3 | −948.7 | −1,018.9 | −1,323.0 | −1,216.1 | −1,825.7 |
| **Asset valuation (SEK millions)** | | | | | | | | | | |
| Abnormal NOPAT | 10,560.7 | 13,142.6 | 16,192.5 | 16,142.2 | 15,365.3 | 14,298.4 | 12,975.2 | 11,367.0 | 9,895.9 | 7,845.4 |
| Abnormal RNOA (%) | 9.0 | 10.3 | 11.9 | 11.2 | 9.9 | 8.6 | 7.4 | 6.1 | 5.1 | 3.9 |
| Free cash flow from operations | 13,455.5 | 17,351.0 | 21,119.0 | 16,472.8 | 17,142.8 | 17,715.8 | 18,006.3 | 18,360.1 | 18,753.8 | 18,878.7 |
| Abnormal NOPAT growth | | 2,581.9 | 3,049.9 | −50.2 | −777.0 | −1,066.9 | −1,323.2 | −1,608.1 | −1,471.1 | −2,050.6 |
| **Present value factors:** | | | | | | | | | | |
| Equity | 0.921 | 0.848 | 0.781 | 0.719 | 0.662 | 0.610 | 0.561 | 0.517 | 0.476 | 0.438 |
| Net operating assets | 0.928 | 0.861 | 0.798 | 0.740 | 0.687 | 0.637 | 0.591 | 0.548 | 0.509 | 0.472 |

## TERMINAL VALUES WITH THE COMPETITIVE EQUILIBRIUM ASSUMPTION

Fortunately, in many if not most situations, how we deal with the seemingly imponderable questions about long-range growth in revenue simply *does not matter very much!* In fact, under plausible economic assumptions, there is no practical need to consider revenue growth beyond the terminal year. Such growth may be *irrelevant,* so far as the firm's current value is concerned!

How can long-range growth in revenue *not* matter? The reasoning revolves around the forces of competition. One impact of competition is that it tends to constrain a firm's ability to identify on a consistent basis growth opportunities that generate supernormal profits. The other dimension that competition tends to impact is a firm's margins.

Ultimately, we would expect high profits to attract enough competition to drive down a firm's margins, and therefore its returns, to a normal level. At this point, the firm will earn its cost of capital, with no abnormal returns or terminal value. (Recall the evidence in Chapter 6 concerning the reversion of ROEs to normal levels over horizons of five to ten years.)

Certainly a firm may at a point in time maintain a competitive advantage that permits it to achieve returns in excess of the cost of capital. When that advantage is protected with patents or a strong brand name, the firm may even be able to maintain it for many years, perhaps indefinitely. With hindsight, we know that some such firms – like Coca-Cola – were able not only to maintain their competitive edge but also to expand it across dramatically increasing investment bases. However, with a few exceptions, it is reasonable to assume that the terminal value of the firm will be zero under the **competitive equilibrium assumption**, obviating the need to make assumptions about long-term growth rates.

## COMPETITIVE EQUILIBRIUM ASSUMPTION ONLY ON INCREMENTAL REVENUE

An alternative version of the competitive equilibrium assumption is to assume that a firm will continue to earn abnormal profits forever on the revenues it had in the terminal year, but there will be no abnormal profit on any incremental revenue beyond that level. If we invoke the competitive equilibrium assumption on incremental revenue for years beyond the terminal year, then it does not matter what revenue growth rate we use beyond that year, and we may as well simplify our arithmetic by treating revenues *as if* they will be constant at the terminal year level. Then return on invested capital, ROE, NOPAT, profit or loss, free cash flow to debt and equity, and free cash flow to equity will all remain constant at the terminal year level. For example, by treating Hennes & Mauritz as if its competitive advantage can be maintained only on the nominal revenue level achieved in the year 2027, we will be assuming that in *real* terms its competitive advantage will shrink. Under this scenario, it is easy to estimate the terminal value by dividing the 2027 level of each of the variables by the appropriate discount rate. Under the abnormal profit (NOPAT) growth valuation method, H&M's abnormal profit (NOPAT) growth beyond 2027 and its terminal value will be zero. As one would expect, terminal values in this scenario will be higher than those with no abnormal returns on all revenue in years 2028 and beyond. This is entirely due to the fact that we are now assuming that H&M can retain indefinitely its superior performance on its existing base of revenue.

## TERMINAL VALUE WITH PERSISTENT ABNORMAL PERFORMANCE AND GROWTH

Each of the approaches described above appeals in some way to the "competitive equilibrium assumption." However, there are circumstances where the analyst is willing to assume that the firm may defy competitive forces and earn abnormal rates of return on new projects for many years. If the analyst believes supernormal profitability can be extended to larger markets for many years, it can be accommodated within the context of valuation analysis.

One possibility is to project profits and cash flows over a longer horizon, that is, until the competitive equilibrium assumption can reasonably be invoked. In the case of Hennes & Mauritz, for example, we could assume that the supernormal profitability will continue for five years beyond 2027 (for a total forecasting horizon of 15 years from the beginning of the forecasting period), but after that period, the firm's ROE and return on net operating assets will be equal to its cost of equity and its required return on net operating assets.

Another possibility is to project growth in abnormal profits or cash flows at some constant rate. For instance, one could expect H&M to maintain its advantage on a revenue base that remains constant in *real* terms, implying that revenue grows beyond terminal year 2027 at the expected long-run European inflation rate of between 2 and 4 percent. Beyond our terminal year, 2027, as the revenue growth rate remains constant at the inflation rate, abnormal profit (growth), free cash flows, and book values of assets and equity also grow at the constant inflation rate. This is simply because we held all other performance ratios constant in this period. As a result, abnormal return on net operating assets and abnormal ROE remain constant at the same level as in the terminal year.

This approach is more aggressive than the preceding assumptions about terminal value, but it may be more realistic. After all, there is no obvious reason why the *real* size of the investment base on which H&M earns abnormal returns should depend on inflation rates. The approach, however, still relies to some extent on the competitive equilibrium assumption. The assumption is now invoked to suggest that supernormal profitability can be extended only to an investment base that remains constant in real terms. In rare situations, if the company has established a market dominance that the analyst believes is immune to the threat of competition, the terminal value can be based on both positive real revenue growth and abnormal profits.

When we assume that the abnormal performance persists at the same level as in the terminal year, projecting abnormal profits (growth) and free cash flows is a simple matter of growing them at the assumed revenue growth rate. Since the rate of abnormal profits and cash flows growth is constant starting in the year after the terminal year, it is also straightforward to discount those flows. The present value of the flow stream is the flow at the end of the first year (after the terminal year) divided by the difference between the discount rate and steady-state growth rate, provided that the discount rate exceeds the growth rate. There is nothing about this valuation method that requires reliance on the competitive equilibrium assumption, so it could be used with *any* rate of growth in revenue. The question is not whether the arithmetic is available to handle such an approach but rather how realistic it is.

## TERMINAL VALUE BASED ON A PRICE MULTIPLE

A popular approach to terminal value calculation is to apply a multiple to abnormal profit, cash flows, or book values of the terminal period. The approach is not as ad hoc as it might at first appear. Note that under the assumption of no revenue growth, abnormal profits or cash flows beyond the terminal year remain constant. Capitalizing these flows in perpetuity by dividing by the cost of capital is equivalent to multiplying them by the inverse of the cost of capital. For example, in the case of Hennes & Mauritz, capitalizing free cash flows to equity at its cost of equity of 8.6 percent is equivalent to assuming a terminal cash flow multiple of 11.6 (1/0.086). Thus applying a multiple in this range to H&M is similar to discounting all free cash flows beyond 2027 while invoking the competitive equilibrium assumption on incremental revenue.

The mistake to avoid here is to capitalize the future abnormal profits or cash flows using a multiple that is too high. The profit or cash flow multiples might be high currently because the market anticipates abnormally profitable growth. However, once that growth is realized, the price-earnings multiple should fall to a normal level. It is that normal price-earnings ratio, applicable to a stable firm or one that can grow only through zero net present value projects, that should be used in the terminal value calculation. Thus multiples in the range of 7 to 13 – close to the reciprocal of cost of equity and required return on net operating assets – should be used here. Higher multiples are justifiable only when the terminal year is closer and there are still abnormally profitable growth opportunities beyond that point. A similar logic applies to the estimation of terminal values using book value multiples.

## SELECTING THE TERMINAL YEAR

A critical question posed by the preceding discussion is how long to make the detailed forecast horizon. When the competitive equilibrium assumption is used, the answer is whatever time is required for the firm's returns on incremental investment projects to reach that equilibrium – an issue that turns on the sustainability of the firm's competitive advantage. As indicated in Chapter 6, historical evidence indicates that most firms in Europe should expect ROEs to revert to normal levels within five to ten years. But for the typical firm, we can justify ending the forecast horizon even earlier – note that the return on *incremental* investment can be normal even while the return on *total* investment (and therefore ROE) remains abnormal. Thus a five- to ten-year forecast horizon should be more than sufficient for most firms. Exceptions would include firms so well insulated from competition (perhaps due to the power of a brand name) that they can extend their investment base to new markets for many years and still expect to generate supernormal returns.

## ESTIMATES OF HENNES & MAURITZ'S TERMINAL VALUE

### Choosing terminal year

In the case of Hennes & Mauritz, the terminal year used is ten years beyond the current one. Table 8.3 shows that the ROE (and return on net operating assets) is forecasted to decline at the end of these ten years, from the unusually high 30.8 percent in 2020 to 22.7 percent (rounded) by 2027. At this level the company will earn an abnormal return on equity of 14.1 percent (rounded), since its cost of equity is estimated to be 8.6 percent.

Based on the foregoing strategic assessment of Hennes & Mauritz, we believe that the firm has created a competitive advantage that should be sustainable in the long term. Consequently, we assume that the firm will have reached a steady state of performance in 2027 and extending the forecast horizon will not lead to further insights into how market dynamics will impact H&M's performance. The overall projection, therefore, expects that while H&M's current level of abnormal performance is not sustainable and that growth will slow and margins will get squeezed, the firm has created a market position that will allow it to make some level of abnormal profits in the long-term. Based on this logic, we will fix 2027 as the terminal year for H&M and attempt to estimate its terminal value at that time.

### Terminal value under varying assumptions

Table 8.5 shows H&M's terminal value under the various theoretical approaches we discussed above. Scenario 1 of this table shows the terminal value if we assume that H&M will continue to grow its revenue at 3.0 percent beyond fiscal year 2027, and that it will continue to earn the same level of abnormal returns as in 2027 (that is,

**TABLE 8.5**  Terminal values for Hennes & Mauritz under various assumptions (using abnormal profit methodology)

| Scenario number | Approach | Scenario | Terminal revenue growth (%) | Terminal NOPAT margin (%) | Value beyond the forecast horizon (AP terminal value) (SEK bn) |
|---|---|---|---|---|---|
| 1 | Persistent abnormal performance | Revenue growth and margins based on detailed analysis and forecast | 3.0 | 7.0 | 112.8 |
| 2 | Abnormal returns on constant revenue (real terms) | Revenue grows at the rate of inflation, margins maintained | 2.0 | 7.0 | 94.7 |
| 3 | Abnormal returns on constant revenue (nominal terms) | Essentially zero revenue growth, margins maintained | 0.0 | 7.0 | 71.3 |
| 4 | Competitive equilibrium | Margins reduced so no abnormal profit | 3.0 | 3.2 | 0.0 |

we assume that all the other forecasting assumptions will be the same as in 2027). Under this scenario, terminal values in the abnormal profit model ($\text{TV}_{\text{AP}}$), the abnormal profit growth model ($\text{TV}_{\text{APG}}$), and the free cash flow model ($\text{TV}_{\text{FCF}}$) are as follows:

$$\text{TV}_{\text{AP}} = \frac{(1+g) \times \text{AP}_{2027}}{(r_e - g) \times (1 + r_e)^T} = \frac{1.03 \times \text{AP}_{2027}}{(0.086 - 0.03) \times (1.086)^{10}}$$

$$\text{TV}_{\text{APG}} = \frac{1}{r_e} \times \frac{g \times \text{AP}_{2027}}{(r_e - g) \times (1 + r_e)^{T-1}} = \frac{1}{0.086} \times \frac{0.03 \times \text{AP}_{2027}}{(0.086 - 0.03) \times (1.086)^{9}}$$

$$\text{TV}_{\text{FCF}} = \frac{(1+g) \times \text{FCFE}_{2027}}{(r_e - g) \times (1 + r_e)^T} = \frac{1.03 \times \text{FCFE}_{2027}}{(0.086 - 0.03) \times (1.086)^{10}}$$

where $r_e$ is the cost of equity, g is the terminal growth rate, and $\text{AP}_{2027}$ and $\text{FCFE}_{2027}$ are expected abnormal profit and free cash flow to equity for fiscal 2027, respectively. Using the abnormal profit methodology this scenario leads to a terminal value of SEK112.8 billion.

Scenario 2 calculates the terminal value assuming that H&M will maintain its margins only on revenues that grow at the long-run expected rate of inflation, assumed to be 2 percent, dropping the terminal value in the abnormal profit model to SEK94.7 billion. Scenario 3 shows the terminal value if we assume that the company's competitive advantage can be maintained only on the nominal revenue level achieved in 2027. As a result, revenue growth beyond the terminal year is assumed to be zero, which is equivalent to assuming that incremental revenues do not produce any abnormal returns. The terminal value under this scenario drops to SEK71.3 billion.

The final scenario invokes the competitive equilibrium assumption, i.e., margins will be eroded such that the firm will have no abnormal returns irrespective of the rate of revenue growth, leading to no terminal value in the abnormal profit model. For the sake of illustration, the expected revenue growth of 3.0 percent is maintained. To portray the competitive equilibrium, margins are lowered to eliminate any competitive advantage that H&M will have. In this final scenario, the terminal values are as follows:

$$\text{TV}_{\text{AP}} = 0$$

$$\text{TV}_{\text{APG}} = \frac{1}{r_e} \times \frac{-1 \times \text{AP}_{2027}}{(1 + r_e)^T} = \frac{1}{0.086} \times \frac{-1 \times \text{AP}_{2027}}{(1.086)^{10}}$$

$$\text{TV}_{\text{FCF}} = \frac{\text{BVE}_{2027}}{(1 + r_e)^T} = \frac{\text{BVE}_{2027}}{(1.086)^{10}}$$

where $\text{BVE}_{2027}$ is H&M's end-of-year book value of equity in fiscal 2027.

## Computing Estimated Values

Table 8.6 shows the estimated value of Hennes & Mauritz's net operating assets and equity, each using three different methods discussed in Chapter 7. The value of net operating assets is estimated using abnormal NOPAT, abnormal NOPAT growth, and free cash flows from operations. The value of equity is estimated using abnormal profit, abnormal profit growth, and free cash flow to equity. These values are computed using the financial forecasts in Table 8.4 and the terminal value forecast under the persistent abnormal performance scenario.

In Table 8.6, present values of abnormal NOPAT (growth) and free cash flow from operations are computed using a required return on net operating assets of 7.8 percent; present values of abnormal profit (growth) and free cash flow to equity are computed using a cost of equity of 8.6 percent. Note that under the abnormal profit

(NOPAT) growth valuation approach, abnormal profit (NOPAT) growth values in year $t$ are multiplied by the corresponding discount factors in year $t-1$. Under the assumptions and forecasts we have made, Hennes & Mauritz's estimated equity value per share is SEK175.90 and the total value of the firm's net operating assets is SEK309.8 billion.

**TABLE 8.6** Valuation summary for Hennes & Mauritz using various methodologies

| | Beginning book value | Value from forecast period 2018–2027 | Value beyond forecast horizon (terminal value) | Total value | Value per share (SEK) |
|---|---|---|---|---|---|
| **Equity value (SEK billions)** | | | | | |
| Abnormal profit | 59.7 | 118.7 | 112.8 | 291.1 | 175.90 |
| Abnormal profit growth | N.A. | 249.7 | 41.5 | 291.1 | 175.90 |
| Free cash flows to equity | N.A. | 133.6 | 157.5 | 291.1 | 175.90 |
| **Net operating assets value (SEK billions)** | | | | | |
| Abnormal NOPAT | 142.1 | 88.3 | 79.4 | 309.8 | N.A. |
| Abnormal NOPAT growth | N.A. | 277.9 | 32.0 | 309.8 | N.A. |
| Free cash flows from operations | N.A. | 118.7 | 191.2 | 309.8 | N.A. |

Value estimates presented in each scenario show that the abnormal profit method, abnormal profit growth method, and the free cash flow method result in the same value, as claimed in Chapter 7. A necessary condition to achieve this equality of value estimates is that we assume that H&M is in a steady state at the end of the forecast horizon. Such a steady state requires that the company's growth rate, margin, turnover rates and financing structure remain unchanged during the terminal year and all years beyond the terminal year. If a firm is assumed not to be in a steady state at the end of the forecast horizon – for example, revenue growth in the terminal year is 6 percent, whereas the terminal growth rate is 2 percent – the discounted cash flow model will not produce the same value estimate as the profit-based valuation models.

Note also that H&M's terminal value represents a larger fraction of the total value of assets and equity under the free cash flow method relative to the other methods. As discussed in Chapter 7, this is due to the fact that the abnormal returns and profit methods rely on a company's book value of assets and equity, so the terminal value estimates are estimates of incremental values over book values. Similarly, under the abnormal profit growth method, the terminal value estimates reflect only the changes in abnormal profit that are expected to occur beyond the terminal year. In contrast, the free cash flow approach ignores the book values, so the terminal value forecasts are estimates of total value during this period.

The primary calculations in the above estimates treat all flows as if they arrive at the end of the year. Of course, they are likely to arrive throughout the year. If we assume for the sake of simplicity that cash flows will arrive mid-year, then we should adjust our value estimates upward by the amount $[1 + (r/2)]$, where r is the discount rate. Further, the value estimates displayed in Table 8.6 are values on December 1, 2017 but our forecasts are partly based on information published after fiscal 2017, for example at H&M's FY2017 earnings announcement on January 31, 2018. To calculate H&M's equity value on February 1, 2018 we should multiply the December 1 estimates by $(1 + r)^{N/365}$, where N denotes the number of days between December 1, 2017 and February 1, 2015:

$$\text{Equity value on February 1, 2018} = \text{SEK175.90} \times (1 + 0.086)^{62/365} = \text{SEK178.38}$$

## FROM ASSET VALUES TO EQUITY VALUES

The net operating asset value estimates displayed in Table 8.6 can also be used to derive an estimate of H&M's equity value. To calculate equity value we should make the following adjustments to the net operating assets value:

|  | Value of net operating assets |
|---|---|
| Add: | Value of non-operating investments |
| Add: | Value of net assets held for sale |
| Add: | Present value of the tax shield on debt |
| = | Business or enterprise value |
| Subtract: | Value of debt |
| Subtract: | Value of non-controlling interests |
| = | Equity value |

The asset value estimate that we calculated reflects the value of the firm's net operating assets had the firm been financed with 100 percent equity. The introduction of debt into the firm's capital structure can, however, increase firm value because the associated interest payments create a valuable tax shield. We therefore include the present value of the tax shield on debt in our calculation of firm value, in addition to the value of non-operating investments and net assets held for sale, to calculate the total value of the firm (also referred to as the enterprise value). To derive the value of ordinary shareholders' equity, we subtract the value of all non-equity claims.

### Value of non-operating investments

In accordance with the International Financial Reporting Standards, firms disclose the economic values of many of their non-operating investments either on the balance sheet or in the notes to their financial statements. Determining the economic values of, for example, marketable securities or long-term receivables is therefore relatively straightforward. At least two types of non-operating investments are potentially more complicated to value. These assets are (1) investment property and (2) minority equity investments.

Under IAS 40, firms can choose between recognizing their investment property at fair value or at cost. If recognized at cost, the fair value of the investment property must be disclosed in the notes to the financial statements. To obtain the economic value of investment property, an analyst should therefore check the firm's accounting policy for investment property and use information from the notes, if necessary, to adjust the investment property's book value.

The IFRS Standards require that a firm use the equity method to account for minority equity investments (also referred to as associates) over which it has significant influence (but not control). The equity method requires that the equity investment is recorded at its initial cost and in subsequent periods adjusted for the firm's share in the investment's profit or loss. Consequently, the balance sheet value of the minority equity investment reflects what portion the firm owns of the investment's book value of equity, not its economic value. An analyst therefore has the challenging task of estimating the value of minority equity investment based on very limited information.

Consider the associates of Next plc, one of H&M's industry peers. In its financial statements, Next discloses that at the end of fiscal years 2016 and 2017 its investment in associates had a book value of £2.1 million. Further, in both fiscal years, Next's share in the associates' profits was £1.0 million. Given the low materiality of the investment, relative to Next's market value of £7.6 billion, a simple, acceptable solution would be to assume that the associates' economic value is equal to its book value of £2.1 million. An alternative, conceptually preferred approach is to use one of the shortcut valuation formulae from Chapter 7. For example, note that the associates' average return on equity was 48 percent in 2012 (1.0/2.1). Assuming a future return on equity of 48 percent (as in 2016 and 2017), a long-run growth rate of 2 percent (equal to the long-term inflation rate), and a cost of equity of 9 percent, the theoretical equity value-to-book multiple for Next's associates can be calculated as:

$$\text{Equity-value-to-book multiple} = 1 + \frac{ROE_0 - r_e}{r_e - g^{equity}} = 1 + \frac{0.48 - 0.09}{0.09 - 0.02} = 6.57$$

Based on a multiple of 6.57 the economic value of Next's investment in associates equals £13.8 million. Whether this multiple approach is preferred over using the book value of the investment should be decided based on factors such as the volatility of the associates' performance and the materiality of the investment.

In the notes to its financial statements Hennes & Mauritz discloses that the fair value of its non-operating investments is not significantly different from their book value. We therefore assume that the firm's investment assets have a book value and an economic value of SEK1,039 million.

### Value of net assets held for sale

Because we removed net assets held for sale from the balance sheet before calculating financial ratios and valuing net operating assets, we must add back the assets' economic value to the value of the firm. In the absence of detailed information, we have no other option than to set the economic value estimate of net assets held for sale equal to the assets' book values. IFRS Standards 5 requirements imply that non-current assets held for sale are recorded on the balance sheet at their fair values if such fair values are lower than the assets' original carrying values. It is therefore likely that especially in cases where firms sell unprofitable or loss-making assets the book values of net assets held for sale are a reasonable approximation of the assets' fair values.

In 2017, Hennes & Mauritz did not have any non-current assets that the firm classified as held for sale.

### Present value of the tax shield on debt

The present value of the tax shield on debt can be written as follows:

$$\text{Present value of tax shield} = \frac{\text{Interest expense}_1 \times \text{Tax rate}_1}{(1 + r_{ts})} + \frac{\text{Interest expense}_2 \times \text{Tax rate}_2}{(1 + r_{ts})^2} + \ldots$$

where interest expense is the pre-tax interest expense forecast, tax rate is the expected future tax rate, and $r_{ts}$ is the discount rate of the tax shield. Researchers and practitioners do not fully agree on which discount rate must be used in the valuation of the tax shield. Because we predict that Hennes & Mauritz remains profitable and will continue to have a low financial risk, the tax benefits arising from future interest deductions can be considered close to risk-free. Consequently, using the risk-free rate as the discount rate seems appropriate. However, some might argue that the realization of tax benefits from interest deductions depends on H&M's future profitability and growth and, consequently, is subject to business risk. In the calculations below, we will use the risk-free rate. However, we caution the reader that it is not inconceivable that H&M's future interest deductions are at least weakly subject to business risk. If so, our valuation of the tax shield on debt will be biased upwards.

Table 8.7 displays the calculation of the present value of the tax shield on debt for Hennes & Mauritz. Note that the discount factor in 2027 includes the effect of the terminal value, which is based on a terminal growth rate of 3 percent and a terminal discount rate of 4 percent (equal to the long-term risk-free rate of return). The calculation shows that the present value of the tax shield at the beginning of fiscal 2018 is equal to SEK72,948.3 million.

### Value of debt

As indicated earlier in this chapter, international accounting standards (IFRS Standards 7) require that firms disclose the economic value of their liabilities in the notes to the financial statements. If interest rates have not changed significantly since the time the debt was issued, it is reasonable to assume that the economic value of debt is equal to its book value. If interest rates have changed and economic value information is not available from the financial statements, the value of the debt can be estimated by discounting the future payouts at current market rates of interest applicable to the firm.

**TABLE 8.7** Present value of the tax shield on debt for Hennes & Mauritz

| Fiscal year | 2018 | 2019 | 2020 | 2021 | 2022 | 2023 | 2024 | 2025 | 2026 | 2027 |
|---|---|---|---|---|---|---|---|---|---|---|
| Interest expense | 1,604.7 | 1,887.6 | 2,215.5 | 2,564.0 | 3,021.7 | 3,507.7 | 3,718.2 | 3,915.3 | 4,091.4 | 4,246.9 |
| Tax rate (%) | 22.0 | 22.0 | 22.0 | 22.0 | 22.0 | 22.0 | 22.0 | 22.0 | 22.0 | 22.0 |
| Tax shield | 353.0 | 415.3 | 487.4 | 564.1 | 664.8 | 771.7 | 818.0 | 861.4 | 900.1 | 934.3 |
| Discount factor | 0.962 | 0.925 | 0.889 | 0.855 | 0.822 | 0.790 | 0.760 | 0.731 | 0.703 | 73.069 |
| Present value of tax shield | 339.5 | 383.9 | 433.3 | 482.2 | 546.4 | 609.9 | 621.6 | 629.4 | 632.4 | 68,269.7 |
| Total present value SEK72,948.3m | | | | | | | | | | |

## Value of non-controlling interests

The balance sheet item non-controlling interest in equity reflects the share of the net assets that is attributable to outside shareholders. The economic value of this outside claim on the value of the firm should thus be excluded from the value of ordinary shareholders' equity. In most cases, the economic value of non-controlling interest is not material relative to the value of the firm. If so, it is reasonable to set the economic value equal to the book value of the claim. If the claim is sufficiently large, an alternative approach to valuing the claim is to use a multiple approach, like the one we used to value the investment in associates earlier. When using a multiple approach the share of profit that is attributable to minority shareholders can be taken from the income statement.

For Hennes & Mauritz, the book value of non-controlling interest in equity equals zero.

## Deriving Hennes & Mauritz's equity value

Based on the foregoing discussion, we can derive Hennes & Mauritz's equity value as follows:

| | | |
|---|---|---|
| | Value of net operating assets: | SEK309.845.8m |
| Add: | Value of investment assets | +1,039.0m |
| Add: | Value of net assets held for sale | +0.0m |
| Add: | Present value of the tax shield on debt | +72,948.3m |
| = | Business or enterprise value | SEK383,833.1m |
| Subtract: | Value of debt | −83,445.7m |
| Subtract: | Value of non-controlling interests | −0.0m |
| = | Equity value | SEK300,387.4 |

Based on this approach, our estimate of H&M's equity value equals SEK300.4 billion, or SEK181.50 per share (or SEK184.06 per share on February 1, 2018), which is slightly more than our equity value estimate under the direct approach discussed earlier.

## ASSET VALUATION VERSUS EQUITY VALUATION

The example of Hennes & Mauritz shows that asset-based approach to valuation (i.e., valuing net operating assets first, then deriving equity value) does not always produce the same equity value estimate as the equity-based approach (i.e., directly valuing equity). In fact, the asset-based approach has one advantage over the equity-based approach that tends to make this approach the more accurate of the two: discount factors in the asset-based approach are based on the required return on net operating assets, whereas discount factors in the equity-based approach are based on the cost of equity. As we discussed earlier, the cost of equity varies as a function of a firm's degree of leverage and the proportion of funds invested in investment assets. If leverage or the importance of investment assets changes over the forecast horizon, future cost of equity estimates should be adjusted accordingly. Unfortunately, this is a difficult task, leading most analysts to use a constant cost of equity instead. In contrast, the required return on net operating assets only depends on the systematic risk of a firm's net operating assets, at least in theory, and is presumably insensitive to changes in leverage or investment assets. Consequently, the asset-based approach to valuation makes use of the fact that the economic values of several claims and assets can be easily taken from the financial statements and circumvents some of the complications associated with cost of equity estimation.

## VALUE ESTIMATES VERSUS MARKET VALUES

As the preceding discussion shows, valuation involves a substantial number of assumptions by analysts. Therefore the estimates of value will vary from one analyst to another. The only way to ensure that one's estimates are reliable is to make sure that the assumptions are grounded in the economics of the business being valued. It is also useful to check the assumptions against the time-series trends for performance ratios discussed in Chapter 6. While it is quite legitimate to make assumptions that differ markedly from these trends in any given case, it is important for the analyst to be able to articulate the business and strategy reasons for making such assumptions.

When a company being valued is publicly traded, it is possible to compare one's own estimated value with the market value of a company. When an estimated value differs substantially from a company's market value, it is useful for the analyst to understand why such differences arise. A way to do this is to redo the valuation exercise and figure out what valuation assumptions are needed to arrive at the observed stock price. One can then examine whether the market's assumptions are more or less valid relative to one's own assumptions. As we discuss in the next chapter, such an analysis can be invaluable in using valuation to make buy or sell decisions in the security analysis context.

In the case of Hennes & Mauritz, our estimated value of the firm's equity per share (SEK184.06) is above the observed value, of SEK139.52, at the beginning of February 2018, when the market had assimilated the announced results for the fiscal year ended November 30, 2017. In the months following the valuation date, H&M's share price fluctuated between SEK120 and SEK154. Analysts' target prices ranged from SEK120 to SEK175. Clearly the market was making less optimistic assumptions than our own. The differences in the two sets of assumptions might be related to growth rates, NOPAT margins, or asset turns. One could run different scenarios regarding each of these variables and test the sensitivity of the estimated value to these assumptions.

## SENSITIVITY ANALYSIS

Recall that in Chapter 6, we developed what we believed to be a reasonable assessment of H&M's expected future performance. The resulting valuation seems to be more optimistic than the market's expectations, as the imputed value per share is higher than the traded value per share at the time. However, we acknowledged that the company's future could play out in multiple ways and propose two alternative scenarios. As shown in Table 8.8, if H&M is not able to improve its store productivity between 2018 and 2020 and grows its online sales by only 10 percent per annum (resulting in revenue growth rates of 7.2, 5.0, and 4.0 percent in 2018, 2019, and 2020, respectively), its value per share would be only SEK159. Alternatively, if H&M's NOPAT margin would gradually decrease from 11.1 percent in 2020 to 5.0 percent (rather than 7.0 percent) in 2027, because of increased competition, its shares would be worth SEK131.50 per share, close to what the average analyst expected at in February 2018. The changes in equity value in these scenarios are driven primarily by changes in revenue growth and margins, performance measures that are most strongly affected by the forces of competition.

**TABLE 8.8** Equity valuation under various scenarios using abnormal profit

| Scenario | Beginning book value | Value from forecast period 2018–2027 | Value beyond forecast horizon (terminal value) | Total value | Value per share (SEK) |
|---|---|---|---|---|---|
| No improvement in store productivity and low online sales growth between 2018 and 2020 | 59.7 | 106.7 | 96.8 | 263.2 | 159.00 |
| Stronger decline in NOPAT between 2020 and 2027 | 59.7 | 104.5 | 53.4 | 217.6 | 131.50 |

# Some practical issues in valuation

The preceding discussion provides a blueprint for doing valuation. In practice, the analyst has to deal with a number of other issues that have an important effect on the valuation task. We discuss next three frequently encountered complications – accounting distortions, negative book values, and excess cash.

## DEALING WITH ACCOUNTING DISTORTIONS

We know from the discussion in Chapter 7 that accounting methods per se should have no influence on firm value (except as those choices influence the analyst's view of future real performance). Yet the abnormal returns and profit valuation approaches used here are based on numbers that vary with accounting method choices.

Since accounting choices must affect both profits *and* book value, and because of the self-correcting nature of double-entry bookkeeping (all "distortions" of accounting must ultimately reverse), estimated values will not be affected by accounting choices, *as long as the analyst recognizes the accounting distortions.*[7]

If accounting reliability is a concern, the analyst has to expend resources on accounting adjustments. When a company uses "biased" accounting – either conservative or aggressive – the analyst needs to recognize the bias to ensure that value estimates are not biased. If a thorough analysis is not performed, a firm's accounting choices can influence analysts' perceptions of the real performance of the firm and hence the forecasts of future performance. Accounting choice would affect expectations of future profits and cash flows, and distort the valuation, regardless of whether the valuation is based on DCF or discounted abnormal profit. For example, if a firm overstates current revenue growth through aggressive revenue recognition, failure to appreciate the effect is likely to lead the analyst to overstate future revenues, affecting both profit and cash flow forecasts.

An analyst who encounters biased accounting has two choices – either to adjust current profits and book values to eliminate managers' accounting biases, or to recognize these biases and adjust future forecasts accordingly. Whereas both approaches lead to the same estimated firm value, the choice will have an important impact on what fraction of the firm's value is captured within the forecast horizon, and what remains in the terminal value. Holding forecasting horizon and future growth opportunities constant, higher accounting quality allows a higher fraction of a firm's value to be captured by the current book value and profits and the abnormal profits within the forecasting horizon.

## DEALING WITH NEGATIVE BOOK VALUES

A number of firms have losses and negative book values of equity. Firms in the start-up phase have negative equity, as do those in high technology industries. These firms incur large investments whose payoff is uncertain. Accountants write off these investments as a matter of conservatism, leading to negative book equity. Examples of firms in this situation include biotechnology firms, internet firms, telecommunication firms, and other high technology firms. A second category of firms with negative book equity are those that are performing poorly, resulting in cumulative losses exceeding the original investment by the shareholders.

Negative book equity and losses make it difficult to use the accounting-based approach to value a firm's equity. There are several possible ways to get around this problem. The first approach is to value the firm's assets (using, for example, abnormal return on net operating assets or abnormal NOPAT) rather than equity. Then, based on an estimate of the value of the firm's debt, one can estimate the equity value. Another alternative is to "undo" accountants' conservatism by capitalizing the investment expenditures written off. This is possible if the analyst is able to establish that these expenditures are value creating. A third alternative, feasible for publicly traded firms, is to start from the observed share price and work backwards. Using reasonable estimates of cost of equity and steady-state growth rate, the analyst can calculate the average long-term level of abnormal profit or abnormal profit growth needed to justify the observed share price. Then the analytical task can be framed in terms of examining the feasibility of achieving this abnormal profit (growth) "target."

It is important to note that the value of firms with negative book equity often consists of a significant option value. For example, the value of high-tech firms is not only driven by the expected earnings from their current technologies but also by the payoff from technology options embedded in their research and development efforts. Similarly, the value of troubled companies is driven to some extent by the "abandonment option" – shareholders with limited liability can put the firm to debt holders and creditors. One can use the options theory framework to estimate the value of these "real options."[8]

### DEALING WITH EXCESS CASH FLOW

Firms with large free cash flows also pose a valuation challenge. In our asset valuation approach, we separately valued non-operating investments and thus implicitly assumed that cash beyond the level required to finance a company's operations can be paid out to the firm's shareholders. Excess cash flows are assumed to be paid out to shareholders either in the form of dividends or share repurchases. Notice that these cash flows are already incorporated into the valuation process when they are earned, so there is no need to take them into account when they are paid out.

It is important to recognize that both the accounting-based valuations and the discounted cash flow valuation assume a dividend payout that can potentially vary from period to period. This dividend policy assumption is required as long as one wishes to assume a constant level of financial leverage, a constant cost of equity, and a constant required return on net operating assets used in the valuation calculations. As discussed in a later chapter, firms rarely have such a variable dividend policy in practice. However, this in itself does not make the valuation approaches invalid, as long as a firm's dividend policy does not affect its value. That is, the valuation approaches assume that the well-known Modigliani–Miller theorem regarding the irrelevance of dividends holds.

A firm's dividend policy can affect its value if managers do not invest free cash flows optimally. For example, if a firm's managers are likely to use excess cash to undertake value-destroying acquisitions, then our approach overestimates the firm's value. If the analyst has these types of concerns about a firm, one approach is to first estimate the firm according to the approach described earlier and then adjust the estimated value for whatever agency costs the firm's managers may impose on its investors. One approach to evaluating whether a firm suffers from severe agency costs is to examine how effective its corporate governance processes are.

## Summary

We illustrate in this chapter how to apply the valuation theory discussed in Chapter 7. The chapter explains the set of business and financial assumptions one needs to make to conduct the valuation exercise. It also illustrates the mechanics of making detailed valuation forecasts and terminal values of profits, free cash flows, and accounting rates of return. We also discuss how to compute cost of equity and the required return on net operating assets. Using a detailed example, we show how a firm's equity values and asset values can be computed using profits, cash flows, and rates of return. The sensitivity of equity and firm value to the assumptions, both during the forecast horizon and for the terminal value, are highlighted. Finally, we offer ways to deal with some commonly encountered practical issues, including accounting distortions, negative book values, and excess cash balances.

## Core concepts

**Asset beta**    Sensitivity of a firm's assets' performance to economy-wide movements. The asset beta can be derived from the firm's equity beta, its debt to equity ratio, and its tax rate:

$$\beta_{BUSINESS} = \frac{(1- \text{Tax rate}) \times \text{Debt}}{(1- \text{Tax rate}) \times \text{Debt} + \text{Equity}} \beta_{DEBT}$$
$$+ \frac{\text{Equity}}{(1- \text{Tax rate}) \times \text{Debt} + \text{Equity}} \beta_{EQUITY}$$

The asset beta remains constant if leverage changes and can be used to calculate the effect of a change in leverage on the equity beta.

**Capital asset pricing model**    Model expressing the cost of equity as a function of (1) the risk-free rate ($r_f$) and (2) a risk premium for systematic risk ($[E(r_m) − r_f]$):

$$r_e = r_f + \beta \left[ E(r_m) - r_f \right]$$

The risk-free rate is typically the rate of return on intermediate-term government bonds. Systematic or beta risk (β) is the risk from correlation of the firm's return and the market return.

**Competitive equilibrium assumption**    Assumption that competitive forces will drive down a firm's abnormal profit until it reaches an equilibrium stage in which the firm's return on equity equals it cost of equity. If it is assumed that the firm reaches this equilibrium stage in or before the terminal year, the terminal value is equal to zero in the abnormal profit (growth) model and is equal to the discounted terminal-year book value of equity in the free cash flow model.

**Cost of equity**    Rate of return that equity investors demand on their investment and discount rate in the equity valuation model. One way to estimate the cost of equity is to use the capital asset pricing model. Firm size may also affect the cost of equity: small firms tend to have higher (required) rates of return.

**Required return on net operating assets**    Rate of return that equity and debt investors demand on their operating investments and discount rate in the (operating) asset valuation model. The required return on net operating assets can be calculated using the CAPM model and an estimate of the operating asset beta:

$$\beta_{NOA} = \left[ \frac{\text{Equity}}{(1- \text{Tax rate}) \times \text{Debt} + \text{Equity} - \text{Non-operating investments}} \right] \beta_{EQUITY}$$
$$+ \left[ \frac{(1- \text{Tax rate}) \times \text{Debt}}{(1- \text{Tax rate}) \times \text{Debt} + \text{Equity} - \text{Non-operating investments}} \right] \beta_{DEBT}$$
$$- \left[ \frac{\text{Non-operating investments}}{(1- \text{Tax rate}) \times \text{Debt} + \text{Equity} - \text{Non-operating investments}} \right] \beta_{NOI}$$

The weights must be calculated using the market values of debt, equity, and investment assets.

**Terminal value**    Present value of abnormal profits (growth) or free cash flows occurring beyond the last year of the forecasting period (labelled terminal year).

**Weighted average cost of capital (WACC)**    Rate of return that equity and debt investors demand on their investment and discount rate in the (business) asset valuation model. The WACC is the weighted average of the *after-tax* cost of debt and the cost of equity:

$$WACC = \frac{Debt}{Debt + Equity}(1 - Tax\ rate) \times Cost\ of\ debt + \frac{Equity}{Debt + Equity} \times Cost\ of\ equity$$

The weights must be calculated using the market values of debt and equity.

## Questions, exercises, and problems

1  A spreadsheet containing Hennes & Mauritz's actual and forecasted financial statements as well as the valuation described in this chapter is available on the companion website of this book. How will the forecasts in Table 8.3 and the value estimates in Table 8.6 for H&M change if the company defies the forces of competition and maintains a revenue growth rate of 10 percent from 2018 to 2025 (and all the other assumptions are kept unchanged)?

2  Calculate H&M's cash payouts to its shareholders in the years 2018–2027 that are implicitly assumed in the projections in Table 8.3.

3  How will the abnormal profit calculations in Table 8.4 change if the cost of equity assumption is changed to 10 percent?

4  How will the terminal values in Table 8.6 change if the revenue growth rate in years 2028 and beyond is 4 percent, and the company keeps forever its abnormal returns at the same level as in fiscal 2027 (keeping all the other assumptions in the table unchanged)? If revenue growth is 3 percent in 2027 and 4 percent in 2028, why are the equity value estimates of the free cash flow model and the abnormal profit model no longer the same?

5  Calculate the proportion of terminal values to total estimated values of equity under the abnormal profit method, the abnormal profit growth

method, and the discounted cash flow method. Why are these proportions different?

6  Under the competitive equilibrium assumption, the terminal value in the discounted cash flow model is the present value of the end-of-year book value of equity in the terminal year. Explain.

7  Under the competitive equilibrium assumption, the terminal value in the discounted abnormal profit growth model is the present value of abnormal profit in the terminal year times minus one, capitalized at the cost of equity. Explain.

8  What will be H&M's cost of equity if the equity market risk premium is 6 percent?

9  Assume that H&M changes its capital structure so that its market value weight of debt to capital increases to 45 percent, and its after-tax interest rate on debt at this new leverage level is 4 percent. Assume that the equity market risk premium is 5 percent. What will be the cost of equity at the new debt level? What will be the weighted average cost of capital?

10  Nancy Smith says she is uncomfortable making the assumption that H&M's dividend payout will vary from year to year. If she makes a constant dividend payout assumption, what changes does she have to make in her other valuation assumptions to make them internally consistent with each other?

## Problem 1 Hugo Boss's and Adidas's terminal values

Refer to Problem 1 in Chapter 7.

1   The analyst following Hugo Boss estimates a target price of €77 per share. Under the assumption that the company's profit margins, asset turnover, and capital structure remain constant after 2020, what is the terminal growth rate that is implicit in the analysts' forecasts and target price?

2   Using the analyst's forecasts, estimate Hugo Boss's equity value under the following three scenarios:

   a   Hugo Boss enters into a competitive equilibrium in 2021.
   b   After 2020 Hugo Boss's competitive advantage can be maintained only on the nominal revenue level achieved in 2020.
   c   After 2020 Hugo Boss's competitive advantage can be maintained on a revenue base that remains constant in real terms.

3   Using the analyst's forecasts, estimate Hugo Boss's equity value under the assumption that the company's profitability gradually reverts to its required level (i.e., $AP_t = 0.75 \times AP_{t-1}$) after the terminal year.

Refer to Problem 2 in Chapter 7.

4   Using the analyst's forecasts, estimate the value of Adidas's net operating assets using the discounted cash flow and the abnormal profit models under the assumption that free cash flows and abnormal NOPATs grow at 3 percent annually after 2020.

5   Why is the value estimate obtained from the DCF model different from the value estimate obtained from the abnormal NOPAT model?

## Problem 2 Anheuser-Busch InBev S.A.

In November 2008 the Belgian InBev S.A. completed the acquisition of US-based Anheuser-Busch. The brewer acquired Anheuser-Busch for close to €40 billion, of which it classified approximately €25 billion as goodwill. At the end of the fiscal year ending on December 31, 2008, Anheuser-Busch InBev's (AB InBev) net assets amounted to €61,357 million, consisting of €64,183 million in non-current assets and −€2,826 million in working capital. The company's book value of equity amounted to €16,126 million.

Early May, 2009, when AB Inbev's 1,593 million common shares trade at about €24 per share, an analyst produces the following forecasts for the company and issues an "overweight" (buy) recommendation.

1   The analyst estimates that AB InBev's weighted average cost of capital is 9 percent and assumes that the free cash flow to debt and equity grows

| Forecasts (€ millions) | 2009 | 2010 | 2011 | 2012 | 2013 | 2014 | 2015 | 2016 | 2017 | 2018 |
|---|---|---|---|---|---|---|---|---|---|---|
| Revenue | 28,475 | 26,688 | 27,909 | 29,047 | 30,089 | 31,011 | 31,810 | 32,470 | 32,311 | 32,658 |
| NOPAT | 6,169 | 6,294 | 6,729 | 7,003 | 7,254 | 7,476 | 7,669 | 7,828 | 7,790 | 7,874 |
| Depreciation and amortization | 2,297 | 2,158 | 2,228 | 2,318 | 2,402 | 2,475 | 2,539 | 2,592 | 2,579 | 2,607 |
| Investment in non-current assets | −1,526 | −1,441 | −1,549 | −1,743 | −1,805 | −1,860 | −1,909 | −1,948 | −1,939 | −1,959 |
| Investment in working capital | 485 | 580 | 669 | 435 | 451 | 465 | 477 | 487 | 485 | 490 |
| Free cash flow to debt and equity | 7,425 | 7,590 | 8,077 | 8,014 | 8,301 | 8,556 | 8,777 | 8,958 | 8,915 | 9,011 |

indefinitely at a rate of 1 percent after 2018. Show that under these assumptions the equity value per share estimate exceeds AB InBev's share price.

2   Calculate AB InBev's expected abnormal NOPATs between 2009 and 2018 based on the preceding information. How does the implied trend in abnormal NOPAT compare with the general trends in the economy?

3   Estimate AB InBev's equity value using the abnormal NOPAT model (under the assumption that the WACC is 9 percent and the terminal growth rate is 1 percent). Why do the discounted cash flow model and the abnormal NOPAT model yield different outcomes?

4   What adjustments to the forecasts are needed to make the two valuation models consistent?

## Notes

1   See T. Copeland, M. Goedhart, and D. Wessels, *Valuation: Measuring and Managing the Value of Companies,* 6th ed. (Hoboken, New Jersey: John Wiley & Sons, 2015).

2   One way to estimate systematic risk is to regress the firm's stock returns over some recent time period against the returns on the market index. The slope coefficient represents an estimate of β. More fundamentally, systematic risk depends on how sensitive the firm's operating profits are to shifts in economy-wide activity and the firm's degree of leverage. Financial analysis that assesses these operating and financial risks should be useful in arriving at reasonable estimates of β.

3   The average return reported here is the arithmetic mean as opposed to the geometric mean. Ibbotson and Associates explain why this estimate is appropriate in this context (see *Stocks, Bonds, Bills, and Inflation,* 2002 Chicago Yearbook). This estimate of the worldwide equity risk premium is an arithmetic mean derived from statistics reported in E. Dimson, P. Marsh, and M. Staunton, "Credit Suisse Global Investment Returns Sourcebook," which updates the evidence in "Global Evidence on the Equity Risk Premium," *Journal of Applied Corporate Finance* 15(4) (2003): 8–19.

4   E. Dimson, P. Marsh, and M. Staunton (2003), op. cit., argue that when estimating future equity risk premiums, it is preferred to take a global approach than a country-by-country approach. Reasons for taking a global approach are, for example, that many country-specific events that affected historical risk premiums are non-recurring and that worldwide capital markets have integrated significantly. In their study "International Differences in the Cost of Equity Capital: Do Legal Institutions and Securities Matter," *Journal of Accounting Research* 44(3) (2006): 485–531, L. Hail and C. Leuz provide evidence that international differences in the strictness of disclosure and securities regulation and enforcement also create international differences in firms' cost of equity. Harmonization of such regulations within, for example, the European Union may therefore also reduce the country variations in risk premiums.

5   See Mathijs A. van Dijk, "Is Size Dead? A Review of the Size Effect in Equity Returns," *Journal of Banking and Finance* 35 (2011): 3263–3274.

6   See William R. Gebhardt, Charles M.C. Lee, and Bhaskaran Swaminathan, "Toward an Ex-Ante Cost of Capital," *Journal of Accounting Research* 39 (2001): 135–176; and James Claus and Jacob Thomas, "Equity Premia as Low as Three Percent? Evidence from Analysts' Earnings Forecasts for Domestic and International Stock Markets," *The Journal of Finance* 56 (October 2001): 1629–1666.

7   Valuation based on discounted abnormal profit does require one property of the forecasts: that they be consistent with "clean surplus accounting." Such accounting requires the following relation:

End-of-period book value = Beginning book value + profit or loss − dividends ± capital contributions/ withdrawals

Clean surplus accounting rules out situations where some gain or loss is excluded from profit or loss but is still used to adjust the book value of equity. For example, under IFRS Standards, gains and losses on foreign currency translations are handled this way. In applying the valuation technique described here, the analyst would need to deviate from IFRS Standards in producing forecasts and treat such gains/losses as a part of profit or loss. However, the technique does *not* require that clean surplus accounting has been applied *in the past* – so the existing book value, based on IFRS Standards or any other set of principles, can still serve as the starting point. All the analyst needs to do is apply clean surplus accounting in his/her forecasts. That much is not only easy but is usually the natural thing to do anyway.

8   If losses are likely to be transitory, this may be a reason to extend the forecast horizon. P. Joos and G. Plesko find that the probability of losses being transitory is negatively related to the size of the loss and positively related to the size of the firm, revenue growth, whether the loss is the first loss, and whether the firm pays out dividends. If a loss is likely to be permanent, the value of the firm is driven by the value of the abandonment option. See P. Joos and G. Plesko, "Valuing Loss Firms," *The Accounting Review* 80 (2005): 847–870.

# Ferrari: The 2015 Initial Public Offering

*The Ferrari is a dream—people dream of owning this special vehicle, and for most people it will remain a dream apart from those lucky few.*

— Enzo Ferrari, Founder, Ferrari

It was October 20, 2015, the day before what was anticipated to be the first day of public trading for the stock of legendary Italian sports car company Ferrari NV (Ferrari). Sergio Marchionne, chairman of Ferrari and CEO of its parent company, Fiat Chrysler Automobiles NV (FCA), had announced a year previously that FCA would be spinning off Ferrari into a separately traded company. As an independent company, the shares of Ferrari (under the aptly named ticker symbol RACE) would be listed on the New York Stock Exchange (NYSE), with an eventual listing in Milan. Marchionne's plan was to sell 10% of Ferrari's shares in an initial public offering (IPO), and the money raised in the offering would go to FCA.

The worth of the Ferrari shares had been the subject of fierce debate among analysts and investors, especially after FCA set an initial price range of USD48 to USD52 per share in early October.[1] Following the road-show meetings with potential investors in both Europe and the United States, Marchionne knew there was strong demand for the 17.175 million shares that would be offered for sale in the IPO. If the offer price was set too low, FCA would leave money on the table, which suggested pricing the deal at the top of the initial range or beyond. However, if the offer price was set too high, poor first-day trading returns would sour the investor's initial experience with the company. It was time now for Marchionne—in negotiation with lead bank UBS—to set the price at which the company's IPO shares would be offered to investors that evening.

## Ferrari—A background[2]

The history of Ferrari, the business, was inextricably linked to Ferrari, the man. Enzo Ferrari, born to a lower-middle-class family in Modena, Italy, in 1898, felt a powerful draw to racing from a young age. He moved to Turin to work for Fiat after the First World War only to have his application hurtfully rejected. He eventually landed an assistant job at a new automobile manufacturer nearby, and it was there that he competed in his first race in 1919. Despite his passion for racing, he was not immediately successful; he finished fourth. Enzo Ferrari joined the team of racecar maker Alfa Romeo as a test driver, and his role soon grew to include racing Alfa

[1] USD = U.S. dollars, EUR= euros.
[2] The background on Ferrari is partially drawn from Drew D. Johnson, ed., *International Directory of Company Histories: Volume 146* (Detroit: St James Press, 2013). Thomas Derdak, "Ferrari S.p.A," pp 140–146.

Romeos on behalf of the company and selling cars to wealthy clients around northern Italy. Over the years, he raced his way to multiple victories and built a large dealership from which he sold and serviced Alfa cars. In the late 1920s, Alfa Romeo encountered financial difficulties and shut down its involvement in the racing circuit.

Unable to be around cars and not race them, Enzo Ferrari founded his own racing *scuderia* ("stable" or "team") in 1929—Scuderia Ferrari. Over the ensuing years he continued to run both his dealership and Scuderia Ferrari (which Alfa Romeo frequently used to represent the company at races). Alfa Romeo eventually bought 80% of Scuderia Ferrari and returned the management of the racing program to company headquarters. Following the acquisition, Enzo Ferrari realized that he would never achieve his ambition of running Alfa Romeo's racing program and left the company in 1939 after two decades of service. The parting agreement forbade him from racing or using the name Scuderia Ferrari for the next four years, so he returned to one of his old scuderia buildings in Modena the next year and established his own manufacturing firm while waiting out the racing ban.

However, with Italy's involvement in the Second World War, Mussolini's fascist government forced Enzo Ferrari to focus his manufacturing operation on building aircraft engines for the war rather than cars. When Allied forces bombed the factory, Enzo Ferrari moved his operations from Modena to Maranello. After the war, Enzo Ferrari debuted his first Ferrari racecar, which quickly won a high-profile race in Turin in front of Italy's elite. Before long, members of European society were contacting Ferrari for cars of their own. The following year Ferrari's car designers finished a nonracing road car. During the following decade these hand-made cars, produced in batches of 10, became the prize of every car enthusiast in Europe and North America, with a client list including kings, princes, and members of America's wealthiest families.

Despite his commercial business success, Enzo Ferrari's single focus continued to be racing. Throughout the 1950s and 1960s, he used the profits from his sports car sales to fund competition in Grand Prix and Formula 1 races. Enzo Ferrari was so present on the racing circuit that he became Italy's national symbol of motor racing. His negligence toward road car production (and the ensuing design and production flaws) became evident, and Ferrari sales declined throughout the 1960s.

Refusing to cut costs and miss races, Enzo Ferrari sought external funds to keep the company afloat. He went to Fiat for help, an ironic turn following his longtime disdain for Fiat. In 1969, Fiat purchased 50% of Ferrari shares and took control of all road car production. Ferrari retained ownership in the remaining 50% and continued to manage the racing operation. Fiat's efforts to modernize the factory and update the manufacturing process paid off, and by 1980, annual road car production reached 2,000, more than double what it had been prior to Fiat's involvement. At the time of Enzo Ferrari's death in 1988, Fiat's stake in Ferrari was 90%, with the remaining 10% held by the Ferrari family.

## Ferrari—The car business

After Ferrari's death, his namesake company entered a period of aimlessness and decline—annual sales consisted of only 2,000 cars in the early 1990s. In 1992, Fiat hired Luca Cordero di Montezemolo, a marketing maven who had once worked as both an assistant to Enzo Ferrari and later as the Ferrari team leader, as chairman of Ferrari. Montezemolo wasted no time in making sweeping changes at the automaker. The product line grew from two outdated models to nine new ones and a commitment to engineering excellence was instilled.

A key aspect of Montezemolo's quality and branding strategy over the period from 1992 to 2014 involved holding production volumes below demand in order to instill a perception of exclusivity. In 2014, for example, Ferrari sold just 7,255 cars compared to the nearly 40,000 cars sold by FCA's sister company, Maserati.[3] The restricted production created long waiting lists, but customers who were designated as preferred customers due to their regular purchases were allowed to bypass the waiting list. This policy prompted many buyers to regularly purchase Ferrari cars just to stay on the preferred customer list. Ferrari also produced limited-edition "halo" cars that were exclusively sold to a select group of loyal customers. One notable such offering was the roofless F60

[3] *Ward's Automotive Yearbook* (Southfield, MI: Penton Media, 2016).

America, which was announced in 2014; only 10 of the USD2.5 million roadsters were produced and all were sold in advance of the cars' actual production, with commitments based simply on a full-scale maquette. The limited production policy ensured high resale value. For example, in August 2014 Bonhams auctioned a 1962 Ferrari GTO for a jaw-dropping USD38 million.[4] Montezemolo believed that the waiting list and limited-edition model policies promoted the Ferrari brand without jeopardizing customer satisfaction. Ferrari had recently been named the most powerful brand in the world by Brand Finance, the intangible-asset-valuation consultancy.

By 2014, Montezemolo's restricted-volume strategy was creating increased tension with the leadership at Ferrari's parent company, FCA. In September, Marchionne, who was business-school educated and had long pushed Ferrari management to increase volume, asked Montezemolo to leave the company. On his way out, Montezemolo reportedly said that Ferrari was now American, and that statement wasn't meant as a compliment.[5] After Montezemolo left, Marchionne stepped in as chairman and immediately pushed for higher volume—particularly to China and the Middle East. Marchionne indicated that Ferrari shipment volume would rise to 9,000 units by 2019. He maintained that the volume increase was justified by both "growing demand in emerging markets" and "demographic changes as the size and spending capacity of target clients." By maintaining restricted volumes in Europe and the Americas, Marchionne believed Ferrari could maintain its levels of perceived exclusivity and preserve the value of brand, even with a higher vehicle output. **Exhibit 1** provides Ferrari historical data on shipments by car model.

In 2015, the company had four sports cars and two grand touring cars in production, in addition to a half-dozen limited-edition vehicles (see **Exhibit 2** for descriptions of the current product line). Ferrari's brand power was such that the average car selling price exceeded USD267,000, and Ferrari was one of the most profitable companies in the global auto-manufacturing industry, with operating margins far greater than industry average. **Exhibits 3** and **4** provide financial statement information for Ferrari.

In addition to its revenue from car, engine, and parts sales, Ferrari maintained a steady stream of income, totaling roughly 15% of yearly sales, from its sponsorships and licensing activities, a line of business that was developed under Montezemolo's leadership. Not only did Ferrari lend its name to its Formula 1 racing team and collect on those sponsorship agreements and shared revenues with the Formula 1 World Championship commercial revenue, but, starting in the mid-1990s, the company also licensed its brand power and iconic prancing horse logo to a "select number of producers and retailers of luxury and lifestyle goods" ranging from watches and sportswear to perfume and video games.[6] Ferrari launched its first retail store in 2002, and by 2015, the company sold Ferrari-branded merchandise through 32 franchised or company-owned Ferrari stores and on its website. In 2010, the first Ferrari theme park, Ferrari World, opened in Abu Dhabi and featured the world's fastest roller coaster—Formula Roussa. Ferrari management believed there were ongoing opportunities to expand the company's brand presence further "in attractive and growing lifestyle categories . . . including sportswear, watches, accessories, consumer electronics and theme parks, which . . . [would] enhance the brand experience of…loyal clients and Ferrari enthusiasts."[7]

## FCA

The formation of FCA resulted from the merger of Fiat, the leading Italian car manufacturer, which had been founded in 1899, and Chrysler, the third-largest U.S. auto company, which had been founded in 1925. The two companies partially merged in 2009, as Fiat hoped to expand its exposure beyond a struggling European market and Chrysler hoped to use Fiat's technology to build more fuel-efficient, smaller cars to sell in North America. Over the next few years, Fiat bought additional stakes in Chrysler before assuming full ownership in early 2014, in the midst of a highly competitive year for the global automotive sector.

[4]Mark Ewing, "Ferrari at the Crossroads," *Forbes*, December 15, 2014, 106–108.
[5]Ewing.
[6]Ferrari prospectus.
[7]Ferrari prospectus.

FCA was currently the world's seventh-largest automaker. With operations in approximately 40 countries, FCA designed, manufactured, distributed, and sold vehicles for both the mass market (under the Abarth, Alfa Romeo, Chrysler, Dodge, Fiat, Fiat Professional, Jeep, Lancia, and Ram brands) and the luxury market (under the Maserati and Ferrari brands). Despite its broad portfolio of vehicles, FCA received disproportionate benefits from its luxury automotive sector—FCA's luxury brand division provided 21% of 2014's EBIT despite just 5% of revenue. **Exhibit 5** provides operating details on FCA's car portfolio.

Facing a range of competitive and economic threats in 2014, Marchionne announced a five-year business plan. The plan sought to aggressively reorganize the company over the period from 2014 to 2018 by focusing on strengthening, differentiating, and globalizing FCA's portfolio of brands and standardizing production architecture for multiple brands to increase productivity. Soon after the plan was announced and just weeks after Montezemolo's exit, Marchionne announced the intended separation of Ferrari from FCA. The plan provided that FCA would sell 17.175 million shares in an IPO, with the proceeds going to FCA. Several months after the IPO, FCA would spin off the 80% of Ferrari stock it held. The spin-off entailed simply distributing FCA holdings in Ferrari to the existing FCA shareholders as a stock dividend. Following the spin-off, 90% of Ferrari shares would be publicly traded and the other 10% retained by the Ferrari family. FCA saw the upcoming Ferrari IPO and spin-off as having several purposes.

1  Generate a large cash payment to FCA through the sale of the IPO shares, while simultaneously transferring some of FCA's debt to Ferrari (Ferrari debt was expected to be EUR2.3 billion after the deal).
2  Promote and extend the value of Ferrari's brand among the world's premier luxury lifestyle companies.
3  Allow Ferrari direct access to sources of equity and debt capital on favourable terms.
4  Attract American investors by listing on the NYSE—historically one of Ferrari's most important product markets.
5  Attract and reward technical and management talent by allowing them to have direct ownership in Ferrari.
6  Unlock "hidden value" that shareholders were not currently attributing to FCA share values under the consolidated structure. While the entire FCA group (including Ferrari) was trading for a market capitalization of EUR21 billion, Marchionne believed that both Ferrari and the rest of FCA would trade for much more than that if the companies traded independently.

## The premium car industry

The premium car industry historically included a wide range of entry points. In order to categorize the industry further, some analysts divided the sector into a normal premium segment and a super luxury segment.[8] Normal premium brands included Audi (owned by Volkswagen), Mercedes (owned by Daimler), BMW, and Japanese luxury brands Lexus and Infiniti. The super luxury brands included lower-volume makers such as Ferrari, Rolls-Royce (owned by BMW), Porsche, Bentley, and Bugatti (all three owned by Volkswagen), all of which shared a historic European legacy as a key component of their branding power.

Some argued that Ferrari's business was closer to such luxury-good firms as Hermès or Prada than that of car manufacturers. These firms maintained similarly high-margin, low-volume, and low-volatility business models. While the level of Ferrari's capital investment was much higher than that required of most luxury goods firms, Ferrari spent substantially less on advertising and used Formula 1 as its marketing tool. **Exhibit 6** provides capital market and financial data for car-related companies and luxury brands.

In 2015, the premium car industry exhibited continued strength in its traditional markets in the developed world while also enjoying growing demand from China, the world's single-largest automotive market.[9] WardsAuto

[8]Christian Breitsprecher et al., "Premium Car Makers—the Sweetest Piece of the Pie," *Macquarie*, January 6, 2014, 42.
[9]Breitsprecher et al.:., 31.

claimed that the annual growth of units of the Chinese luxury car sales had exceeded 20% over the past five years and now exceeded 1.5 million units per year.[10] While the global car market expanded by 3.5% in 2014, the premium sector enjoyed considerably more gains. For example, in 2014 BMW Group sold over 1.8 million BMW-brand cars and over 4,000 Rolls-Royce–brand cars, up 9.5% and 11.9%, respectively, from the previous year.

## The IPO process

The process of going public—selling publicly traded equity for the first time—was an arduous undertaking that, at a minimum, required about three months. (**Table 1** provides a timetable for a typical IPO.)

**Table 1.** Timetable for typical U.S. IPO (in days).

| | | | | | | | | |
|---|---|---|---|---|---|---|---|---|
| **Prior to Day 1: Organizational "all-hands" meeting** | 1 | 2 | 3 | 4 | 5 | 6 | 7 | **1–14: Quiet period** |
| | 8 | 9 | 10 | 11 | 12 | 13 | 14 | |
| **15–44: Due diligence** | 15 | 16 | 17 | 18 | 19 | 20 | 21 | |
| Underwriter interviews management, suppliers, and customers; reviews financial statements; drafts preliminary registration statement. Senior management of underwriter gives OK on issue. | 22 | 23 | 24 | 25 | 26 | 27 | 28 | |
| | 29 | 30 | 31 | 32 | 33 | 34 | 35 | |
| | 36 | 37 | 38 | 39 | 40 | 41 | 42 | |
| **45: Registration (announcement)** | | | | | | | | |
| | 43 | 44 | 45 | 46 | 47 | 48 | 49 | **45–75: SEC review period** |
| **50: Prospectus (red herring)** | 50 | 51 | 52 | 53 | 54 | 55 | 56 | SEC audit or reviews for compliance with SEC regulations. |
| | 57 | 58 | 59 | 60 | 61 | 62 | 63 | Underwriter assembles syndicate and initiates road show. |
| | 64 | 65 | 66 | 67 | 68 | 69 | 70 | |
| | 71 | 72 | 73 | 74 | 75 | 76 | 77 | **76–89: Road show** |
| **76–89:** Letters of comment received from SEC; amendments filed with SEC | 78 | 79 | 80 | 81 | 82 | 83 | 84 | Preliminary price range set. Underwriters, issuing firm's management present deal to institutional investors, build book of purchase orders. |
| **90: Effective date; shares offered** | 85 | 86 | 87 | 88 | 89 | 90 | 91 | **91: Trading begins** |
| | 92 | 93 | 94 | 95 | 96 | 97 | 98 | **98: Settlement** |

Source: Created by author based on industry standards.

[10]Mike Dean, Alexander Haissl, and Fei Teng, "European Autos 2015 Outlook," Credit Suisse, January 9, 2015.

Before initiating the equity-issuance process, private firms needed to fulfill a number of prerequisites: generate a credible business plan; gather a qualified management team; create an outside board of directors; prepare audited financial statements, performance measures, and projections; and develop relationships with investment bankers, lawyers, and accountants. Frequently, firms held "bake-off" meetings to discuss the equity-issuance process with various investment banks before selecting a lead underwriter. Important considerations when choosing an underwriter included the proposed compensation package, track record, analyst research support, distribution capabilities, and aftermarket market-making support. After the firm satisfied the prerequisites, the equity-issuance process began with a meeting of all the key participants (management, underwriters, accountants, and legal counsel for both the underwriters and the issuing firm) to plan the process and reach agreement on specific terms. Throughout the process, additional meetings could be called to discuss problems and review progress.

Following the initiation of the equity-issuance process, the company was commonly prohibited from publishing information outside the prospectus. The company could continue established, normal advertising activities, but any increased publicity designed to raise awareness of the company's name, products, or geographical presence in order to create a favorable attitude toward the company's securities could be considered illegal. This requirement was known as the "quiet period."

The underwriter's counsel generally prepared a letter of intent that provided most of the terms of the underwriting agreement but was not legally binding. The underwriting agreement described the securities to be sold, set forth the rights and obligations of the various parties, and established the underwriter's compensation. Because the underwriting agreement was not signed until the offering price was determined (just before distribution began), both the firm and the underwriter were free to pull out of the agreement any time before the offering date. If the firm did withdraw the offer, the letter of intent generally required the firm to reimburse the underwriter for direct expenses.

Selling securities required a registration process with the government's security regulatory agency. In the United States, the Security and Exchange Commission (SEC) called for preparation of the prospectus (part I of the registration statement), answers to specific questions, copies of the underwriting contract, company charter and bylaws, and a specimen of the security (included in part II of the registration statement), all of which required considerable attention from the parties on the offering firm's team. One of the important features of the registration process was the performance of due-diligence procedures by the company and the bankers. Due diligence referred to the process of providing reasonable grounds that there was nothing in the registration statement that was significantly untrue or misleading and was motivated by the liability of all parties to the registration statement for any material misstatements or omissions. Due-diligence procedures involved such things as reviewing company documents, contracts, and tax returns; visiting company offices and facilities; soliciting "comfort letters" from company auditors; and interviewing company and industry personnel.

During this period, the lead underwriter began to form the underwriting syndicate, which comprised a number of investment banks that agreed to buy portions of the offering at the offer price less the underwriting discount. The underwriting discount provided the bulk of compensation for the underwriter as it paid a discounted price for the IPO shares and then turned around and sold them for the full offering price. In addition to the syndicate members, dealers were enlisted to sell a certain number of shares on a "best-effort" basis. The dealers received a fixed reallowance, or concession, for each share sold. The selling agreement provided the contract to members of the syndicate, granted power of attorney to the lead underwriter, and stipulated (a) the management fee that each syndicate member was required to pay the lead underwriter, (b) the share allocations, and (c) the dealer reallowances or concessions. Because the exact terms of the agreement were not specified until approximately 48 hours before selling began, the agreement did not become binding until just before the offering. The original contract specified a range of expected compensation levels; the selling agreement was structured so that the contract became binding when it was orally approved via telephone by the syndicate members after the effective date.

The SEC review process started when the registration statement was filed and the statement was assigned to a branch chief of the Division of Corporate Finance. As part of the SEC review, the statement was given to accountants, attorneys, analysts, and industry specialists. The SEC review process was laid out in the Securities Act of 1933, which according to its preamble aspired to "provide full and fair disclosure of the character of securities sold in interstate commerce." Under the Securities Act, the registration statement became effective 20 days after the filing date. If, however, the SEC found anything in the registration statement that was regarded as materially untrue, incomplete, or misleading, the branch chief sent the registrant a letter of comment detailing the deficiencies. Following a letter of comment, the issuing firm was required to correct and return the amended statement to the SEC. Unless an acceleration was granted by the SEC, the amended statement restarted the 20-day waiting period.

While the SEC was reviewing the registration statement, the underwriter was engaged in book-building activities, which involved surveying potential investors to construct a schedule of investor demand for the new issue. To generate investor interest, the preliminary offering prospectus or "red herring" (so called because the prospectus was required to have the words "preliminary prospectus" on the cover in red ink) was printed and offered to potential investors. During this period, underwriters generally organized a one-to-two-week "road show" tour, which enabled managers to discuss their investment plans, display their management potential, and answer questions from financial analysts, brokers, and institutional investors in locations across the country or abroad. Finally, companies could place "tombstone ads" in various financial periodicals announcing the offering and listing the members of the underwriting syndicate.

By the time the registration statement was ready to become effective, the underwriter and the offering firm's management negotiated the final offering price and the underwriting discount. The negotiated price depended on perceived investor demand and current market conditions (e.g., price multiples of comparable companies, previous offering experience of industry peers). Once the underwriter and the management agreed on the offering price and discount, the underwriting agreement was signed, and the final registration amendment was filed with the SEC. The company and the underwriter generally asked the SEC to accelerate the final pricing amendment, which was usually granted immediately by phone. The offering was then ready for public sale. The final pricing and acceleration of the registration statement typically happened within a few hours.

During the morning of the effective day, the lead underwriter confirmed the selling agreement with the members of the syndicate. Following confirmation of the selling agreement, selling began. Members of the syndicate sold shares of the offering through oral solicitations to potential investors. Because investors were required to receive a final copy of the prospectus with the confirmation of sale, and the law allowed investors to back out of purchase orders upon receipt of the final prospectus, the offering sale was not realized until underwriters actually received payment. Underwriters would generally cancel orders if payment was not received within five days of the confirmation.

SEC Rule 10b-7 permitted underwriters to engage in price-stabilization activities for a limited period during security distribution. Under this rule, underwriters often posted stabilizing bids at or below the offer price, which provided some price stability during the initial trading of an IPO.

The offering settlement, or closing, occurred 7 to 10 days after the effective date, as specified in the underwriting agreement. At this meeting, the firm delivered the security certificates to the underwriters and dealers, and the lead underwriter delivered the prescribed proceeds to the firm. In addition, the firm traditionally delivered an updated comfort letter from its independent accountants. Following the offering, the underwriter generally continued to provide valuable investment-banking services by distributing research literature and acting as a market maker for the company.

# Pricing the Ferrari IPO

As the date of the Ferrari IPO approached, an active debate around the appropriate valuation for Ferrari continued to make waves in the investment community. **Exhibit 7** contains samples of analyst and reporter opinions on the value of the shares. **Exhibit 8** provides a base-case financial forecast for Ferrari based on Marchionne's volume-expansion forecast. The cost of capital had been estimated to be 5.0% in euro based on market data for comparable companies. This figure was consistent with the relatively low risk that analysts associated with Ferrari's expected cash flows. Although Ferrari was incorporated in the Netherlands, because the company headquarters and operations were in Italy, Ferrari profits would be taxed in Italy at a tax rate of 38%.

The number of Ferrari shares outstanding was to increase from 172 million before the offering to 189 million after the offering.[11] To facilitate trading in U.S. dollars on the NYSE, U.S.-dollar Ferrari certificates would be authorized for trading in the United States based on euro-denominated Ferrari shares held in trust. The trust would facilitate transfer of all dividends and voting privileges between the certificate holder and the company as if the certificate were equivalent to the underlying share. This arrangement was common in the United States to allow the shares of non-U.S. companies to trade on U.S. exchanges.

The level of comparable price multiples played an important role in the valuation of IPO firms, but for Ferrari there were no perfect "pure plays" (publicly traded companies that were solely in the exact same business). World IPO volume was down from 2014, but European IPO volume was up. Back in March, Autotrader, the British website for buying and selling used cars, had gone public at an enterprise-to-EBITDA multiple of 26 times. In June, the American producer of wearable activity trackers, Fitbit, had priced its IPO at 21 times EBITDA. Last week, the large British payment-processing company Worldpay had gone public at 19 times EBITDA. Concurrently, it was expected that Poste Italiane, Italy's postal service, would price its IPO at a multiple of 8 times EBITDA. The only related auto manufacturer transaction was the 2012 acquisition of Aston Martin by a private equity firm that had occurred at an EBITDA multiple of 9.9 times. But Aston Martin had been poorly performing and unprofitable at the time of the acquisition and had a much lower brand loyalty than Ferrari. **Exhibit 9** provides prevailing capital market information.

The current interest reports suggested that investor interest in the Ferrari IPO was so high that the deal was expected to be as much as 10 times oversubscribed. Indeed, following the road show in Europe the previous week, UBS claimed that the book was well oversubscribed. These signals left Marchionne wondering if pricing the stock within range might leave money on the table.

The contrasting view, however, held that pricing too high would send a message of imprudence to the investment community and risk losing subsequent upsurges in price. Some analysts had, after all, expressed concern that Ferrari might struggle as an independent entity because of its small scale. Others worried that once Ferrari as a public company, management would be pushed to think more about numbers and sales than preserving brand exclusivity.

---

[11]Since FCA, rather than Ferrari, would receive the cash proceeds of the offering, the appropriate number of shares to consider in pricing the company was the post-money shares of 189 million. Table 1. Timetable for typical U.S. IPO (in days).

**Exhibit 1**  Ferrari car shipments

| | Full Year | | | First Half of Year | |
|---|---|---|---|---|---|
| | **2012** | **2013** | **2014** | **2014** | **2015** |
| **By Model Type** | | | | | |
| Sports Cars | | | | | |
| V8 | 4,274 | 3,944 | 3,651 | 2,077 | 1,581 |
| V12 | 481 | 1,401 | 1,565 | 900 | 645 |
| Total | 4,755 | 5,345 | 5,216 | 2,977 | 2,226 |
| GT Cars | | | | | |
| V8 | 1,589 | 1,219 | 1,645 | 454 | 1,280 |
| V12 | 1,061 | 436 | 394 | 237 | 188 |
| Total | 2,650 | 1,655 | 2,039 | 691 | 1,468 |
| **By Geography** | | | | | |
| Europe, Middle East, and Africa | | | | | |
| United Kingdom | 686 | 686 | 705 | 408 | 456 |
| Germany | 755 | 659 | 616 | 353 | 214 |
| Switzerland | 366 | 350 | 332 | 181 | 155 |
| Italy | 318 | 206 | 243 | 132 | 139 |
| France | 330 | 273 | 253 | 138 | 129 |
| Middle East | 423 | 472 | 521 | 232 | 185 |
| Rest of EMEA | 825 | 663 | 604 | 349 | 320 |
| Total EMEA | 3,703 | 3,309 | 3,274 | 1,793 | 1,598 |
| Americas | | | | | |
| Americas | 2,208 | 2,382 | 2,462 | 1,199 | 1,287 |
| Asia Pacific | | | | | |
| Greater China | 789 | 572 | 675 | 289 | 261 |
| Rest of APAC | 705 | 737 | 844 | 387 | 548 |
| Total APAC | 1,494 | 1,309 | 1,519 | 676 | 809 |
| Total | 7,405 | 7,000 | 7,255 | 3,668 | 3,694 |

Middle East includes the United Arab Emirates, Saudi Arabia, Bahrain, Lebanon, Qatar, Oman, and Kuwait.

Rest of Europe, Middle East, and Africa (EMEA) includes Africa and the other European markets not separately identified.

Americas includes the United States of America, Canada, Mexico, the Caribbean, and Central and South America.

Greater China includes China, Hong Kong, and Taiwan.

Rest of Asia Pacific (APAC) mainly includes Japan, Australia, Singapore, Indonesia, and South Korea.

Source: Ferrari prospectus.

**Exhibit 2**  Ferrari car models in October 2015

## Sports cars

### 458 ITALIA

The 458 Italia is a two-seater sports car with a 570 hp mid-rear mounted V8 engine, launched in 2009. Its longitudinally-mounted engine is influenced by Ferrari's Formula 1 racing technology, and has been engineered to reach 9,000 rpm, a first on an eight cylinder road car. The 458 Italia is designed as a pure sports car, for drivers seeking spirited performance on and off the track. The cabin features a reinterpretation of Ferrari's traditional sports car interior themes, with clean and simple yet innovative components. The redesigned and intuitive ergonomics have resulted in a completely driver-oriented layout. We discontinued production of the 458 Italia, which is being replaced by the 488 GTB, in May 2015.

### 488 GTB

Our latest sports car, the 488 GTB a two seater berlinetta with a 670 hp mid-rear mounted V8 engine, is replacing the 458 Italia. It was launched in March 2015, 40 years after we unveiled our first ever mid-rear-engined V8 model (the 308 GTB). Its large signature air intake scallop evokes the original 308 GTB and is divided into two sections by a splitter. Designed for track-level performance, the 488 GTB can also provide enjoyment to non-professional drivers for everyday use. Accelerating from 0-200 km/h in only 8.3 seconds, its new 3902 cc V8 turbo engine is at top of the class for power output, torque and response times. In the cabin, the seamless integration of the new satellite control clusters, angled air vents and instrument panel heightens the sense that the cockpit is completely tailored around the driver, leading to an extremely sporty yet comfortable ambiance.

### 458 SPIDER

Launched in 2011, the 458 Spider is a two seat coupe with a 570 hp mid-rear mounted V8 engine and is the world's first mid-rear-engine car with a retractable hard top. If offers the full experience of sports car driving, especially on mixed and challenging surfaces, but aims to cater to those who do not need to constantly push their car to the limit on the track. Unlike the 458 Italia, the engine air intakes have been moved to the rear spoiler, close to the gearbox, clutch and oil radiators. Like the 458 Italia and the 458 Speciale (see below), the Spider draws inspiration from Formula 1 single-seaters, and has been made 12 percent more aerodynamic than its convertible predecessors, such as the F430. Among its other awards, it was named 2012's "Best of the Best" convertible by the Robb Report (a prominent luxury periodical).

We currently expect to stop producing the 458 Spider by the end of July 2015.

### F12BERLINETTA

Launched in 2012, the F12berlinetta is equipped with a 740 hp V12 engine. It is the most powerful high performance Ferrari sports car ever built. Built around evolved transaxle architecture with cutting-edge components and control systems, it sets a new standard in aerodynamics and handling. Though conceived as a performance automobile, the F12berlinetta is capable of both high speed and long-distance driving.

## Grand touring (GT) cars

### CALIFORNIA T

The California T, which followed the great success of our 2008 California model, is equipped with a 560 hp V8 turbo engine. Launched in 2014, it is the only GT car in the segment to combine a retractable hard top, rear seats, and a ski passage to the spacious trunk. Its new turbocharged V8 engine comes with a variable boost management system. This makes it the only turbo engine in the world with close to no turbo lag. It also features a revised rear and interior design and a 15 percent reduction in fuel consumption compared to its predecessor.

### FF

Launched in 2011, the FF, our first four-wheel drive model, is equipped with a 660 hp V12 engine. Among its main innovations, the FF features the patented lightweight 4RM system, which transmits torque to all four wheels, thus allowing a 50 percent saving in weight compared to a traditional four-wheel drive system and a lower center of gravity to be maintained. Part of our GT class, the FF features an elegant two door, four seat sporting layout, and the best cabin and luggage space and occupant comfort in its class.

## Special series cars

### 458 SPECIALE

The 458 Speciale was launched in 2013 and features a 605 hp V8 engine. It is aimed at clients willing to trade some on board comfort for a more track focused car. With a Ferrari-patented special active aerodynamics designed by the Ferrari Design Centre and Pininfarina, it is currently our most aerodynamic road car. Building on the integration of Formula 1 technology, on-track handling is enhanced by Ferrari's Side Slip Angle Control (SSC) system, which employs an algorithm to analyze the car's side slip, compare it to the car's projected trajectory and work with the electronic differential to instantly change the torque distribution between the rear wheels. The Speciale is available as a two seat coupe. We currently expect to stop producing the 458 Speciale by October 2015.

## 458 SPECIALE A

The 458 Speciale A (equipped with a 605 hp V8 engine) debuted at the 2014 Paris Auto Show and features the most powerful naturally aspirated V8 engine ever produced for a Ferrari spider. It is the latest variant of the 458 models, and celebrates the remarkable success of this line. It adopts the innovative retractable hard top that has become a signature of Ferrari spiders and features significantly improved combustion, mechanical, and volumetric efficiency. The 499 models produced come as a two seat coupe. We currently expect to stop producing the 458 Speciale A by November 2015.

## Limited edition supercars, fuoriserie, and one-offs

### LAFERRARI

Launched in 2013, LaFerrari is the latest in our line of supercars. Planned for a total production run of just 499 cars, LaFerrari is our first car with hybrid technology. Alongside its powerful rear-wheel drive layout V12 engine (which generates 800 hp), the hybrid system comprises two electric motors and a special battery consisting of cells developed by the Scuderia Ferrari where the F138 KERS technology was pioneered. Because the battery generates an additional 163 hp, LaFerrari has a combined total of 963 hp. LaFerrari's HY-KERS system is designed to achieve seamless integration and rapid communication between the V12 and electric motor, thus blending extreme performance with maximum efficiency. Thanks to the hybrid technology, LaFerrari generates almost 50 percent more horsepower than the Enzo, its predecessor, and 220 hp more than the F12, our most powerful car to date. Acceleration: 0 to 200 km/h in less than 7 seconds. 0 to 300 km/h in 15 seconds.

Source: Ferrari prospectus.

## F60 AMERICA

The F60 America, a V12 open air roadster, celebrates our 60 years in the United States and is available to U.S. clients only. It combines two of our American clients' great passions - the modified V12 engine and open-top driving. The exterior is finished in North American Racing Team livery, with special 60th anniversary prancing horse badges adorning the wheel arches. Inside, the F60America features bespoke cabin trim, with the driver's side finished in red and the passenger side in black - a nod to our historic competition cars. We have pre-sold ten F60s, with scheduled production and delivery between 2015 and 2016.

## SERGIO

The Sergio is a 605 hp V8 2-seater *barchetta* named after Sergio Pininfarina. The car celebrates the spirit and core values of the historic company on the 60th anniversary of its collaboration with Ferrari. The Sergio's performance and dynamics are designed for excellence even when pushed to the limits. Based on the 458 Spider, it retains the latter's technological content as well as all of the functional aspects of its cockpit. It is powered by the latest 605 hp model of Ferrari's naturally aspirated 4,497 cubic centimeter V8 engine, which has won multiple categories of the International Engine of the Year award from Engine Technology International magazine in three of the last four years. This power unit also guarantees a 0 to 100 km/h acceleration in just three seconds. We produced six Sergio cars, all of which have been sold and will be dispatched to our clients by the end of 2015.

## ONE-OFFS

Finally, in order to meet the varying needs of our most loyal and discerning clients, we also from time to time produce one-off models. While based on the chassis and equipped with engines of one of the current range models for registration purposes, these cars reflect the exact exterior and interior design and specifications required by the clients, and are produced as a single, unique car.

**Exhibit 3**  Ferrari income statement (millions of euro)

| | 2012 | 2013 | 2014 | First Half 2015 |
|---|---|---|---|---|
| Sales | | | | |
| Cars and Spare Parts (1) | 1,695 | 1,655 | 1,944 | 1,007 |
| Engines (2) | 77 | 188 | 311 | 121 |
| Sponsorship, Commercial and Brand (3) | 385 | 412 | 417 | 212 |
| Other (4) | 69 | 80 | 91 | 46 |
| Total Sales | 2,225 | 2,335 | 2,762 | 1,387 |
| Cost of Sales excluding Dep and Amort | 961 | 964 | 1,217 | 592 |
| Depreciation & Amortization Expense | 238 | 270 | 289 | 130 |
| Selling, General, and Admin. Expense | 243 | 260 | 300 | 152 |
| Research & Development | 431 | 479 | 541 | 291 |
| Other Operating Expense | 17 | −2 | 26 | 4 |
| Operating Income (EBIT) | 335 | 364 | 389 | 218 |
| Net Financial Income (Expense) | −1 | 3 | 9 | −27 |
| Profit before Tax | 335 | 366 | 398 | 191 |
| Income Tax Expense | 101 | 120 | 133 | 65 |
| Net Profit | 233 | 246 | 265 | 126 |
| Capital Expenditures | 258 | 271 | 330 | 151 |

(1)   Includes the net revenues generated from shipments of our cars, including any personalization revenue generated on these cars and sales of spare parts.
(2)   Includes the net revenues generated from the sale of engines to Maserati for use in their cars, and the revenues generated from the rental of engines to other Formula 1 racing teams
(3)   Includes the net revenues earned by our Formula 1 racing team through sponsorship agreements and our share of the Formula 1 World Championship commercial revenues and net revenues generated through the Ferrari brand, including merchandising, licensing, and royalty income.
(4)   Primarily includes interest income generated by the Ferrari Financial Services group and net revenues from the management of the Mugello racetrack.

Source: Company prospectus.

**Exhibit 4** Ferrari balance sheet (millions of euro)

| | 31-Dec-2013 | 31-Dec-2014 | 30-Jun-2015 |
|---|---|---|---|
| Cash and cash equivalents | 798 | 1,077 | 258 |
| Trade receivables | 206 | 184 | 154 |
| Receivables from financing activities | 863 | 1,224 | 1,181 |
| Inventories | 238 | 296 | 352 |
| Other current assets | 115 | 64 | 100 |
| Total current assets | 2,219 | 2,845 | 2,045 |
| Investments and other financial assets | 37 | 47 | 48 |
| Deferred tax assets | 42 | 112 | 149 |
| Property, plant, and equipment | 568 | 585 | 589 |
| Intangible Assets (1) | 242 | 265 | 283 |
| Goodwill | 787 | 787 | 787 |
| Total assets | 3,895 | 4,641 | 3,900 |
| Trade payables | 486 | 536 | 578 |
| Current tax payables | 104 | 110 | 182 |
| Other current liabilities | 475 | 774 | 836 |
| Total current liabilities | 1,065 | 1,420 | 1,595 |
| Long-term debt | 317 | 510 | 2,267 |
| Other liabilities | 197 | 233 | 239 |
| Total equity | 2,316 | 2,478 | −201 |
| Total liabilities and equity | 3,895 | 4,641 | 3,900 |

(1)   Costs incurred for car project development are recognized as asset following the conditions of IAS38. Capitalized development costs are amortized on a straight-line basis over the estimated life of the model (generally four to eight years).

Source: Company prospectus.

**Exhibit 5** FCA car shipments by brand (thousands of units)

| | 2013 | 2014 |
|---|---|---|
| Mass-Market Vehicle Brands | | |
| NAFTA (U.S., Canada, Mexico) | 2,100 | 2,500 |
| LATAM (Latin America) | 900 | 800 |
| APAC (Asia Pacific) | 200 | 300 |
| EMEA (Europe, Middle East, Africa) | 1,100 | 1,200 |
| Total | 4,300 | 4,800 |
| Maserati | 20 | 40 |
| Ferrari | 7 | 7 |

Mass-market brands: Abarth, Alfa Romeo, Chrysler, Dodge, Fiat, Fiat Professional, Jeep, Lancia, and Ram.

Source: Created by author from data found in the FCA 2014 annual report.

**Exhibit 6** Data for comparable companies (in millions of euros)

| | Total Revenue | Capital Expend | EBITDA | Projected Growth Rate | Market Value of Equity | Total Debt | Cash |
|---|---|---|---|---|---|---|---|
| **Auto Manufacturers** | | | | | | | |
| BMW | 80,401 | 6,099 | 16,426 | 6.1% | 56,562 | 77,506 | 7,688 |
| Daimler | 129,872 | 6,307 | 18,514 | 6.9% | 77,906 | 86,689 | 15,543 |
| Fiat Chrysler | 96,090 | 8,121 | 8,271 | 4.6% | 18,657 | 33,724 | 23,601 |
| Ford Motor | 108,619 | 5,626 | 8,537 | 10.1% | 52,925 | 98,484 | 25,743 |
| General Motors | 117,554 | 8,946 | 6,674 | 4.5% | 46,554 | 38,710 | 24,391 |
| Honda Motor | 96,196 | 6,374 | 12,730 | 6.9% | 51,128 | 52,483 | 11,427 |
| Hyundai Motor | 63,924 | 3,385 | 7,233 | 6.8% | 33,631 | 40,802 | 19,547 |
| Kia Motors | 33,730 | 1,446 | 2,800 | 1.6% | 16,977 | 3,535 | 5,502 |
| Nissan Motor | 82,101 | 11,432 | 10,879 | 6.2% | 40,013 | 51,796 | 6,698 |
| Peugeot | 53,607 | 2,428 | 3,318 | 7.0% | 12,230 | 21,914 | 10,521 |
| Renault | 41,055 | 2,703 | 3,967 | 8.9% | 23,096 | 36,299 | 14,049 |
| Tata Motors | 33,811 | 4,100 | 5,647 | 5.5% | 16,701 | 10,952 | 7,125 |
| Tesla Motors | 2,411 | 731 | 9 | 94.9% | 26,400 | 2,051 | 1,590 |
| Toyota Motor | 196,622 | 24,233 | 30,260 | 3.2% | 186,069 | 147,344 | 40,497 |
| Volkswagen | 202,458 | 16,613 | 23,048 | 3.5% | 52,916 | 139,021 | 34,143 |
| **Luxury Brands** | | | | | | | |
| Burberry Group | 3,221 | 199 | 745 | 2.6% | 7,691 | 90 | 865 |
| Cie Financiere | 10,410 | 708 | 2,902 | 3.1% | 38,986 | 3,093 | 8,553 |
| Hermes International | 4,119 | 279 | 1,478 | 6.8% | 35,297 | 41 | 1,481 |
| LVMH Moet Hennessy | 30,638 | 1,848 | 7,027 | 2.1% | 80,731 | 9,243 | 4,648 |
| Prada | 3,552 | 362 | 954 | 1.9% | 8,772 | 519 | 720 |
| Tiffany & Co. | 3,248 | 189 | 819 | 4.7% | 9,125 | 989 | 648 |

Figures as of end of 2014, except Equity Value, which is as of October 2015. The projected growth rate is equal to the 5-year compound annual growth rate of operating profits from 2014 actuals to 2019 forecast.

Data source: FactSet; the projected growth rate is obtained based on Value Line Investment Survey (August–October 2015) and author estimates.

**Exhibit 7**   Selected quotations from analysts and reporters

*"Indications of interest [in Ferrari] have been high... with some reports stating that the deal could be as much as 10 times oversubscribed...The indications of interest and the valuation cited yesterday's media reports certainly confirm our thesis that Ferrari deserves a luxury goods stock multiple."*

—Richard Hilgert, "Daimler AG," Morningstar Equity Research, October 1, 2015.

*"Fiat wants its crown jewel to fetch a high price... yet this pricey offer, plus the burdens of maintaining Ferrari's specialness, could end up repelling investors...Though Ferrari's operating margin is higher than its peers, thanks to the high price of its products, it has been stuck between 14% and 16% since 2010.... Ferrari shares are [pricey], at 36 times last year's earnings at the midpoint of their IPO range."*

—Abheek Bhattacharya, "Ferrari IPO: Why This Engine Runs Too Rich," Wall Street Journal, October 20, 2015.

*"Ferrari isn't geared to the auto cycle and has exceptionally high pricing power, with strong cash conversion and brand value. As such, we think it could also be valued in line with the top end of luxury goods companies."*

—Alexander Haissl and Fei Teng, "European Auto OEMs," Credit Suisse, July 15, 2015.

*"The Chief Executive of UBS recently...[said] that it was 'almost impossible to think that the Ferrari IPO can't be successful."*

—FT reporters, "Red Faces as Banker Revs up Ferrari IPO," Financial Times, October 9, 2015.

*"The demand for Ferrari shares has significantly surpassed the amount offered in the luxury sports carmaker's US IPO, and the final price might exceed the top end of the initial price range by 20%."*

—"Ferrari IPO Demand Well Above Offer, Final Price Might Jump 20%," SeeNews Italy, October 19, 2015.

*"We believe Ferrari will struggle as an independent entity given a lack of scale."*

—Mike Dean, Alexander Haissl, and Fei Teng, "European Autos 2015 Outlook," Credit Suisse, January 9, 2015.

*"Ferrari has pricing power, however, Ferrari's products sell at a similar price to comparable products. Ferrari is not "hard" luxury. Its products need updating and refreshing."*

—George Galliers, Chris McNally, and Arndt Ellinghorst, "Ferrari," Evercore, November 16, 2015.

*"In our view, the success and desirability of Ferrari's road cars lies precisely in their exclusivity. We do not think that Montezemolo arbitrarily imposed the 7,000 unit cap on Ferrari production back in May 2013, but rather that this represented the apex of the supply/demand price maximization equation...A decision to produce significantly more might drive Ferrari into lower and less rarefied segments where completion is much more acute from extremely well capitalized manufacturers."*

—Stephen Reitman, Erwann Dagorne, and Philippe Barrier, "FCA—Analysing the Ferrari IPO and FCA Thereafter," Societe Generale, July 29, 2015.

**Exhibit 8**  Ferrari forecast (millions of euro, except as noted)

| Assumptions | 2014 | 2015 | 2016 | 2017 | 2018 | 2019 |
|---|---|---|---|---|---|---|
| Growth in Cars Shipped | 3.6% | 7.0% | 5.0% | 4.0% | 4.0% | 3.0% |
| Growth in Revenue/Car | | 5.0% | 5.0% | 5.0% | 5.0% | 5.0% |
| Growth in Engine Revenue | | 3.0% | 3.0% | 3.0% | 3.0% | 3.0% |
| Growth in Other Revenue | | 3.0% | 6.0% | 6.0% | 6.0% | 6.0% |
| Operating Margin—Cars | 12.5% | 13.0% | 13.5% | 14.0% | 14.0% | 14.0% |
| Operating Margin—Engines | 9.1% | 10.0% | 10.0% | 10.0% | 10.0% | 10.0% |
| Operating Margin—All Other Revenue | 24.9% | 25.0% | 27.0% | 28.0% | 30.0% | 30.0% |
| Net Working Capital Turnover | 1.9 | 2.0 | 2.1 | 2.2 | 2.2 | 2.2 |
| Net Fixed Asset Turnover | 3.2 | 3.2 | 3.3 | 3.5 | 3.7 | 3.8 |
| Deprec & Amort/PPE | 34% | 34% | 34% | 34% | 34% | 34% |
| Financial Forecast | | | | | | |
| Car Shipments (000s) | 7.26 | 7.76 | 8.15 | 8.48 | 8.82 | 9.08 |
| Avg Revenue per Car (Euro 000s) | 268 | 281 | 295 | 310 | 326 | 342 |
| Car Revenue | 1,944 | 2,184 | 2,408 | 2,629 | 2,871 | 3,105 |
| Engine Revenue | 311 | 320 | 330 | 340 | 350 | 361 |
| All Other Revenue | 507 | 523 | 554 | 587 | 623 | 660 |
| Total Revenue | 2,762 | 3,027 | 3,292 | 3,556 | 3,844 | 4,126 |
| Operating Profit—Cars | 243 | 284 | 325 | 368 | 402 | 435 |
| Operating Profit—Engines | 28 | 32 | 33 | 34 | 35 | 36 |
| Operating Profit—All Other Revenue | 126 | 131 | 150 | 164 | 187 | 198 |
| Total Operating Profit | 398 | 447 | 508 | 567 | 624 | 669 |
| Net Working Capital | 1,425 | 1,513 | 1,568 | 1,617 | 1,747 | 1,875 |
| Net PP&E and Int. Assets | 851 | 932 | 998 | 1,016 | 1,039 | 1,086 |
| Dep & Amort | 289 | 317 | 339 | 345 | 353 | 369 |

Source: Created by author based on author estimates.

**Exhibit 9**  Capital markets data (October 19, 2015)

Government Bond Yields (Italy)

| | |
|---|---|
| 1 year | 0.23% |
| 10 year | 1.70% |

Corporate Bonds

| | Euro |
|---|---|
| AAA | 1.91% |
| AA | 1.99% |
| A | 2.30% |
| BBB | 3.43% |
| BB | 4.98% |
| B | 6.79% |

Exchange Rate

| | |
|---|---|
| USD/EUR | 1.1375 |

Source: Created by author based on data from ADB Analisi Data Borsi, Merrill Lynch, and author estimates.

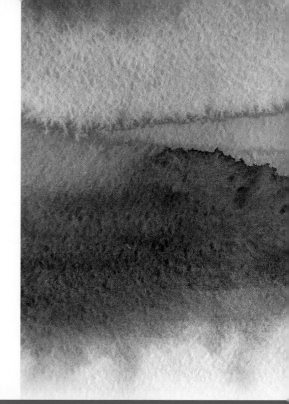

# Business analysis and valuation applications

# PART III

# 9 Equity security analysis

Equity **security analysis** is the evaluation of a firm and its prospects from the perspective of a current or potential investor in the firm's shares. Security analysis is one step in a larger investment process that involves:

1  Establishing the objectives of the investor.
2  Forming expectations about the future returns and risks of individual securities.
3  Combining individual securities into portfolios to maximize progress towards the investment objectives.

Security analysis is the foundation for the second step, projecting future returns and assessing risk. Security analysis is typically conducted with an eye towards identification of mispriced securities in hopes of generating returns that more than compensate the investor for risk. However, that need not be the case. For analysts who do not have a comparative advantage in identifying mispriced securities, the focus should be on gaining an appreciation for how a security would affect the risk of a given portfolio, and whether it fits the profile that the portfolio is designed to maintain.

Security analysis is undertaken by individual investors, by analysts at brokerage houses (sell-side analysts), and by analysts who work at the direction of fund managers for various institutions (buy-side analysts). The institutions employing buy-side analysts include collective investment funds, pension funds, insurance companies, universities, and others.

A variety of questions are dealt with in security analysis:

- A sell-side analyst asks: Is the industry I am covering attractive, and if so why? How do different firms within the industry position themselves? What are the implications for my earnings forecasts? Given my expectations for a firm, do its shares appear to be mispriced? Should I recommend this share as a buy, a sell, or a hold?
- A buy-side analyst for a "value share fund" asks: Does this security possess the characteristics we seek in our fund? That is, does it have a relatively low ratio of price to earnings, low price-to-book value, and other fundamental indicators? Do its prospects for earnings improvement suggest good potential for high future returns on the security?
- An individual investor asks: Does this security offer the risk profile that suits my investment objectives? Does it enhance my ability to diversify the risk of my portfolio? Is the firm's dividend payout rate low enough to help shield me from taxes while I continue to hold the security?

As the preceding questions underscore, there is more to security analysis than estimating the value of equity securities. Nevertheless, for most sell-side and buy-side analysts, the key goal remains the identification of mispriced securities.

## Investor objectives and investment vehicles

The investment objectives of individual savers in the economy are highly idiosyncratic. For any given saver they depend on factors such as income, age, wealth, tolerance for risk, and tax status. For example, savers with many years until retirement are likely to prefer to have a relatively large share of their portfolio invested in equities, which offer a higher expected return than fixed income (or debt) securities and higher short-term variability.

Investors in high tax brackets are likely to prefer to have a large share of their portfolio in shares that generate tax-deferred capital gains rather than shares that pay dividends or interest-bearing securities.

**Collective investment funds** (mutual funds, unit trusts, OEICs, SICAVs, or BEVEKs as they are termed in some countries) have become popular investment vehicles for savers to achieve their investment objectives.[1] Collective investment funds sell shares in professionally managed portfolios that invest in specific types of equity and/or fixed income securities. They therefore provide a low-cost way for savers to invest in a portfolio of securities that reflects their particular appetite for risk.

The major classes of collective investment funds include:

1 Money market funds that invest in commercial paper, certificates of deposit, and treasury bills.
2 Bond funds that invest in debt instruments.
3 Equity funds that invest in equity securities.
4 Balanced funds that hold money market, bond, and equity securities.
5 Real estate funds that invest in commercial real estate.

Within the bond and equities classes of funds, however, there are wide ranges of fund types. For example, bond funds include:

- *Corporate bond funds* that invest in investment-grade rated corporate debt instruments.[2]
- *Government bond funds* that invest in government debt instruments.
- *High yield funds* that invest in non-investment-grade rated corporate debt.
- *Mortgage funds* that invest in mortgage-backed securities.

Equity funds include:

- *Income funds* that invest in equities that are expected to generate dividend income.
- *Growth funds* that invest in equities expected to generate long-term capital gains.
- *Income and growth funds* that invest in equities that provide a balance of dividend income and capital gains.
- *Value funds* that invest in equities that are considered to be undervalued.
- *Short funds* that sell short equity securities that are considered to be overvalued.
- *Index funds* that invest in equities that track a particular market index, such as the MSCI World Index or the DJ Euro Stoxx 50.
- *Sector funds* that invest in equities in a particular industry segment, such as the technology or health sciences sectors.
- *Regional funds* that invest in equities from a particular country or geographic region, such as Japan, the Asia-Pacific region, or the United States.

Since the 1990s hedge funds have gained increased prominence, and the assets controlled by these funds have grown significantly. While generally open only to institutional investors and certain qualified wealthy individuals, hedge funds are becoming an increasingly important force in the market. Hedge funds employ a variety of investment strategies, including:

- *Market neutral funds* that typically invest equal amounts of money in purchasing undervalued securities and shorting overvalued ones to neutralize market risk.
- *Short selling funds,* which short sell the securities of companies that they believe are overvalued.
- *Special situation funds* that invest in undervalued securities in anticipation of an increase in value resulting from a favourable turn of events.

These fund types employ very different strategies. But, for many, fundamental analysis of companies is the critical task. This chapter focuses on applying the tools we developed in Part 2 of the book to analyze equity securities.

# Equity security analysis and market efficiency

How a security analyst should invest his or her time depends on how quickly and efficiently information flows through markets and becomes reflected in security prices. In the extreme, information would be reflected in security prices fully and immediately upon its release. This is essentially the condition posited by the *efficient markets hypothesis*. This hypothesis states that security prices reflect all available information, as if such information could be digested without cost and translated immediately into demands for buys or sells without regard to frictions imposed by transactions costs. Under such conditions it would be impossible to identify mispriced securities on the basis of public information.

In a world of efficient markets, the expected return on any equity security is just enough to compensate investors for the unavoidable risk the security involves. Unavoidable risk is that which cannot be "diversified away" simply by holding a portfolio of many securities. Given efficient markets, the investor's strategy shifts away from the search for mispriced securities and focuses instead on maintaining a well-diversified portfolio. Aside from this, the investor must arrive at the desired balance between risky securities and risk-free short-term government bonds. The desired balance depends on how much risk the investor is willing to bear for a given increase in expected returns.

The preceding discussion implies that investors who accept that share prices already reflect available information have no need for analysis involving a search for mispriced securities. If all investors adopted this attitude, of course no such analysis would be conducted, mispricing would go uncorrected, and markets would no longer be efficient![3] This is why the efficient markets hypothesis cannot represent an equilibrium in a strict sense. In equilibrium there must be just enough mispricing to provide incentives for the investment of resources in security analysis.

The existence of some mispricing, even in equilibrium, does not imply that it is sensible for just anyone to engage in security analysis. Instead, it suggests that securities analysis is subject to the same laws of supply and demand faced in all other competitive industries: it will be rewarding only for those with the strongest comparative advantage. How many analysts are in that category depends on a number of factors, including the liquidity of a firm's shares and investor interest in the company.[4] For example, about 30 sell-side professional analysts follow British Petroleum, a company with highly liquid shares and considerable investor interest. Many other buy-side analysts track the firm on their own account without issuing formal reports to outsiders. For the smallest publicly traded firms in Europe, there is typically no formal following by analysts, and would-be investors and their advisors are left to form their own opinions on a security.

## MARKET EFFICIENCY AND THE ROLE OF FINANCIAL STATEMENT ANALYSIS

The degree of **market efficiency** that arises from competition among analysts and other market agents is an empirical issue addressed by a large body of research spanning the past four decades. Such research has important implications for the role of financial statements in security analysis. Consider, for example, the implications of an extremely efficient market, where information is fully impounded in prices within minutes of its revelation. In such a market, agents could profit from digesting financial statement information in two ways. First, the information would be useful to the select few who receive newly announced financial data, interpret it quickly, and trade on it within minutes. Second, and probably more important, the information would be useful for gaining an understanding of the firm, so as to place the analyst in a better position to interpret other news (from financial statements as well as other sources) as it arrives.

On the other hand, if prices of securities fail to reflect financial statement data fully, even days or months after its public revelation, market agents could profit from such data by creating trading strategies designed to exploit systematic ways in which the publicly available data are ignored or discounted in the price-setting process.

## MARKET EFFICIENCY AND MANAGERS' FINANCIAL REPORTING STRATEGIES

The degree to which markets are efficient also has implications for managers' approaches to communicating with their investment communities. The issue becomes most important when the firm pursues an unusual strategy, or when the usual interpretation of financial statements would be misleading in the firm's context. In such a case the communication avenues managers can successfully pursue depend not only on management's credibility but also on the degree of understanding present in the investment community.

## EVIDENCE OF MARKET EFFICIENCY

There is an abundance of evidence consistent with a high degree of efficiency in securities markets.[5] In fact, during the 1960s and 1970s, the evidence was so one-sided that the efficient markets hypothesis gained widespread acceptance within the academic community and had a major impact on the practicing community as well.

Evidence pointing to very efficient securities markets comes in several forms:

- When information is announced publicly, the markets react very quickly.
- It is difficult to identify specific funds or analysts who have consistently generated abnormally high returns.
- A number of studies suggest that share prices reflect a rather sophisticated level of fundamental analysis.

While a large body of evidence consistent with efficiency exists, recent years have witnessed a re-examination of the once widely accepted thinking. A sampling of the research includes the following:

- On the issue of the speed of share price response to news, a number of studies suggest that, even though prices react quickly, the initial reaction tends to be incomplete.[6]
- A number of studies point to trading strategies that could have been used to outperform market averages.[7]
- Some related evidence – still subject to ongoing debate about its proper interpretation – suggests that, even though market prices reflect some relatively sophisticated analyses, prices still do not fully reflect all the information that could be garnered from publicly available financial statements.[8]

The controversy over the efficiency of securities markets is unlikely to be resolved soon. However, some lessons are accepted by most researchers. First, securities markets not only reflect publicly available information, but they also anticipate much of it before it is released. The open question is, what fraction of the response remains to be impounded in price once the day of the public release comes to a close? Second, even in most studies that suggest inefficiency, the degree of mispricing is relatively small for large firms.

Finally, even if some of the evidence is currently difficult to align with the efficient markets hypothesis, it remains a useful benchmark (at a minimum) for thinking about the behaviour of security prices. The hypothesis will continue to play that role unless it can be replaced by a more complete theory. Some researchers are developing theories that encompass the existence of market agents who are forced to trade for unpredictable "liquidity" reasons, and prices that differ from so-called "fundamental values," even in equilibrium. Also, behavioural finance models recognize that cognitive biases can affect investor behaviour.[9]

# Approaches to fund management and securities analysis

Approaches used in practice to manage funds and analyze securities are quite varied. One dimension of variation is the extent to which the investments are actively or passively managed. Another variation is whether a quantitative or a traditional fundamental approach is used. Security analysts also vary considerably in terms of whether they produce formal or informal valuations of the firm.

## ACTIVE VERSUS PASSIVE MANAGEMENT

**Active portfolio management** relies heavily on security analysis to identify mispriced securities. The passive portfolio manager serves as a price taker, avoiding the costs of security analysis and turnover while typically seeking to hold a portfolio designed to match some overall market index or sector performance. Combined approaches are also possible. For example, one may actively manage 20 percent of a fund balance while passively managing the remainder. The growing popularity of passively managed funds in Europe over the past 20 years serves as testimony to the growing belief that it is difficult to consistently earn returns that are superior to broad market indices.

## QUANTITATIVE VERSUS TRADITIONAL FUNDAMENTAL ANALYSIS

Actively managed funds must depend on some form of security analysis. Some funds employ "technical analysis," which attempts to predict share price movements on the basis of market indicators (prior share price movements, volume, etc.). In contrast, "fundamental analysis," the primary approach to security analysis, attempts to evaluate the current market price relative to projections of the firm's future profits and cash flow generating potential. Fundamental analysis involves all the steps described in the previous chapters of this book: business strategy analysis, accounting analysis, financial analysis, and prospective analysis (forecasting and valuation). In recent years some analysts have supplemented traditional fundamental analysis, which involves a substantial amount of subjective judgment, with more quantitative approaches.

The quantitative approaches themselves are quite varied. Some involve simply "screening" shares on the basis of some set of factors, such as trends in analysts' earnings revisions, price-earnings ratios, price-book ratios, and so on. Whether such approaches are useful depends on the degree of market efficiency relative to the screens. Quantitative approaches can also involve implementation of some formal model to predict future stock returns. Longstanding statistical techniques such as regression analysis and probit analysis can be used, as can more recently developed computer-intensive techniques such as neural network analysis. Again, the success of these approaches depends on the degree of market efficiency and whether the analysis can exploit information in ways not otherwise available to market agents as a group.

Quantitative approaches play a more important role in security analysis today than they did a decade or two ago. However, by and large, analysts still rely primarily on the kind of fundamental analysis involving complex human judgments, as outlined in our earlier chapters.

## FORMAL VERSUS INFORMAL VALUATION

Full-scale, formal valuations based on the methods described in Chapter 7 have become more common, especially in recent years. However, less formal approaches are also possible. For example, an analyst can compare his or her long-term earnings projection with the consensus forecast to generate a buy or sell recommendation. Alternatively, an analyst might recommend a share because his or her earnings forecast appears relatively high in comparison to the current price. Another possible approach, that might be labelled "marginalist," involves no attempt to value the firm. The analyst simply assumes that if he or she has unearthed favourable (or unfavourable) information believed not to be recognized by others, the share should be bought (or sold).

Unlike many security analysts, investment bankers produce formal valuations as a matter of course. Investment bankers, who estimate values for purposes of bringing a private firm to the public market, for evaluating a merger or buyout proposal, for issuing a fairness opinion or for making a periodic managerial review, must document their valuation in a way that can be readily communicated to management and, if necessary, to the courts.

# The process of a comprehensive security analysis

Given the variety of approaches practised in security analysis, it is impossible to summarize all of them here. Instead, we briefly outline **steps to be included in a comprehensive security analysis**. The amount of attention focused on any given step varies among analysts.

## SELECTION OF CANDIDATES FOR ANALYSIS

No analyst can effectively investigate more than a small fraction of the securities on a major exchange, and thus some approach to narrowing the focus must be employed. Sell-side analysts are often organized within an investment house by industry or sector. Thus they tend to be constrained in their choices of firms to follow. However, from the perspective of a fund manager or an investment firm as a whole, there is usually the freedom to focus on any firm or sector.

As noted earlier, funds typically specialize in investing in shares with certain risk profiles or characteristics (e.g., growth shares, "value" shares, technology shares, cyclical shares). Managers of these types of funds seek to focus the energies of their analysts on identifying shares that fit their fund objective. In addition, individual investors who seek to maintain a well-diversified portfolio without holding many shares also need information about the nature of a firm's risks and how they fit with the risk profile of their overall portfolio.

An alternative approach to security selection is to screen firms on the basis of some potential mispricing followed by a detailed analysis of only those shares that meet the specified criteria. For example, one fund managed by a large insurance company screens shares on the basis of recent "earnings momentum," as reflected in revisions in the earnings projections of sell-side and buy-side analysts. Upward revisions trigger investigations for possible purchase. The fund operates on the belief that earnings momentum is a positive signal of future price movements. Another fund complements the earnings momentum screen with one based on recent short-term share price movements, in the hopes of identifying earnings revisions not yet reflected in share prices.

## Key analysis questions

Depending on whether fund managers follow a strategy of targeting equities with specific types of characteristics or of screening shares that appear to be mispriced, the following types of questions are likely to be useful:

- What is the risk profile of a firm? How volatile is its earnings stream and share price? What are the key possible bad outcomes in the future? What is the upside potential? How closely linked are the firm's risks to the health of the overall economy? Are the risks largely diversifiable, or are they systematic?
- Does the firm possess the characteristics of a growth share? What is the expected pattern of revenue and earnings growth for the coming years? Is the firm reinvesting most or all of its earnings?
- Does the firm match the characteristics desired by "income funds"? Is it a mature or maturing company, prepared to "harvest" profits and distribute them in the form of high dividends?
- Is the firm a candidate for a "value fund"? Does it offer measures of earnings, cash flow, and book value that are high relative to the price? What specific screening rules can be implemented to identify misvalued shares?

## INFERRING MARKET EXPECTATIONS

If the security analysis is conducted with an eye towards the identification of mispricing, it must ultimately involve a comparison of the analyst's expectations with those of "the market." One possibility is to view the observed share price as the reflection of market expectations and to compare the analyst's own estimate of value with that price. However, a share price is only a "summary statistic." It is useful to have a more detailed idea of the market's expectations about a firm's future performance, expressed in terms of revenue, earnings, and other measures. For example, assume that an analyst has developed new insights about a firm's near-term revenue. Whether those insights represent new information for the stock market, and whether they indicate that a "buy" recommendation is appropriate, can be easily determined if the analyst knows the market consensus revenue forecast.

Around the world a number of agencies summarize analysts' forecasts of revenue and earnings. Forecasts for the next year or two are commonly available, and for many firms, a "long-run" earnings growth projection is also available – typically for three to five years. Some agencies provide continuous online updates to such data, so if an analyst revises a forecast, that can be made known to fund managers and other analysts within seconds.

As useful as analysts' forecasts of revenue and earnings are, they do not represent a complete description of expectations about future performance, and there is no guarantee that consensus analyst forecasts are the same as those reflected in market prices. Further, financial analysts typically forecast performance for only a few years, so that even if these do reflect market expectations, it is helpful to understand what types of long-term forecasts are reflected in share prices. Armed with the models in Chapters 7 and 8 that express price as a function of future cash flows or earnings, an analyst can draw some educated inferences about the expectations embedded in share prices.

For example, consider the valuation of apparel retailer Burberry plc. On June 30, 2018, Burberry's share price was 2,272 pence. For the year ended March 31 2018, the company reported that earnings per share had increased from 77 pence the prior year to 82 pence, reflecting the company's solid performance in a challenging environment. Burberry's book value of equity per share was 331 pence. By the end of June analysts were forecasting that Burberry would experience a moderate decline in profitability in fiscal 2018, with earnings per share projected to go down by 2 percent to 80 pence. Gradually increasing growth was projected for the following years: 6 percent in 2019 (85 pence), 13 percent in 2020 (96 pence), and 13 percent in 2021 (108 pence).[10] Analysts expected Burberry to pay out approximately 55 percent of its annual earnings in dividends.

How do consensus forecasts by analysts reconcile with the market valuation of Burberry? What are the market's implicit assumptions about the short-term and long-term earnings growth for the company? By altering the amounts for key value drivers and arriving at combinations that generate an estimated value equal to the observed market price, the analyst can infer what the market might have been expecting for Burberry in June 2018. Table 9.1 summarizes the combinations of earnings growth, book value growth, and cost of capital that generate prices comparable to the market price of 2,272 pence.

Burberry has an equity beta of 0.9. Given a risk-free rate of 4 percent and a market risk premium between 4.5 and 5.5 percent (see Chapter 8), Burberry's cost of equity capital probably lies between 8.1 and 9.0 percent. Critical questions for judging the market valuation of Burberry include how quickly the company's abnormal profitability will erode and how quickly earnings growth will revert to the same level as average firms in the economy, historically around 4 percent. The analysis reported in Table 9.1 presents three scenarios for Burberry's earnings growth that are consistent with an observed market price of 2,272 pence. The three scenarios assume that earnings growth reverts to the economy average after 2021 and that Burberry's dividend payout ratio between 2018 and 2021 is 55 percent.

Table 9.1 shows the implications for Burberry's earnings growth in 2020 and 2021 if competition drives down earnings in 2018 and 2019. This analysis indicates that with an 8.1 percent cost of equity and a significant deterioration of earnings performance (i.e., 10 percent decline in 2018 and 2019), earnings need to grow by close to 38 percent per year in 2020 and 2021 to justify the 2,272 pence share price. However, if growth is –2 and 6 percent in 2018 and 2019, respectively, as the consensus predicts, expected earnings growth remains close to its longer-term historical average during the next two years (before approaching the economy average of 4 percent after 2021). The 2,272 pence share price is also consistent with a scenario that predicts constant earnings growth of 11.5 percent between 2018 and 2021. The value of Burberry's equity is computed as in Table 9.2. Because one quarter of the fiscal year passed on June 30, two adjustments must be made in the analysis. First, the present value factor for the first five years equals $(1 - r_e)^{-(t - 0.25)}$. Second, the book value on June 30 is set equal to the book value on April 1 times $(1 + r_e)^{0.25}$.

Unless the analyst has good indications that Burberry's abnormal profitability will rebound after two years, given the company's 2,272 pence share price, it is unlikely that the market anticipates that earnings will be hit by competition or other adverse factors in 2018 and 2019. Burberry's share price more likely reflects the expectation that earnings growth will remain close to its historical average of 10–15 percent in the near term, before reverting to the economy average in the longer term. This type of scenario analysis provides the analyst with insights about investors' expectations for Burberry and is useful for judging whether the share is correctly valued. Security analysis need not involve such a detailed attempt to infer market expectations. However, whether or not the analysis is explicit, a good analyst understands what economic scenarios could plausibly be reflected in the observed price.

**TABLE 9.1** Alternative assumptions about value drivers for Burberry consistent with the observed market price of 2,272 pence

| | 2018 | 2019 | 2020 | 2021 | After 2021 | Implied earnings per share in 2021 |
|---|---|---|---|---|---|---|
| **Assumed equity costs of capital of 8.1%** | | | | | | |
| *Earnings growth:* | | | | | | |
| *Scenario 1* | −2.0% | 6.0% | 22.1% | 22.1% | 4.0% | 127 pence |
| *Scenario 2* | −10.0% | −10.0% | 38.4% | 38.4% | 4.0% | 127 pence |
| *Scenario 3* | 11.5% | 11.5% | 11.5% | 11.5% | 4.0% | 127 pence |
| **Assumed equity cost of capital of 9.0%** | | | | | | |
| *Earnings growth:* | | | | | | |
| *Scenario 1* | −2.0% | 6.0% | 42.8% | 42.8% | 4.0% | 154 pence |
| *Scenario 2* | −10.0% | −10.0% | 52.5% | 52.5% | 4.0% | 154 pence |
| *Scenario 3* | 16.9% | 16.9% | 16.9% | 16.9% | 4.0% | 153 pence |

**TABLE 9.2** Computing the value of Burberry's equity (in pence)

| Year | Beginning book value | Earnings (11.5% annual growth) | Abnormal profit (8.1% cost of equity) | PV factor | PV of abnormal profit |
|---|---|---|---|---|---|
| *2018* | 331.0p | 91.4p | 64.6p | 0.9433 | 60.95 |
| *2019* | 372.1 | 101.9 | 71.8 | 0.8726 | 62.65 |
| *2020* | 418.0 | 113.7 | 79.8 | 0.8072 | 64.42 |
| *2021* | 469.2 | 126.7 | 88.7 | 0.7467 | 66.26 |
| *After 2021* | | | 92.3 | 18.2125 | 1,680.77 |
| *Cumulative PV of abnormal profits* | | | | | 1,935.06 |
| *+ Book value on June 30, 2018* | | | | | 337.51 |
| *= Equity value per share* | | | | | 2,272.57p |

# Key analysis questions

**B**y using the discounted abnormal profit/ROE valuation model, analysts can infer the market's expectations for a firm's future performance. This permits analysts to ask whether the market is overvaluing or undervaluing a company. Typical questions that analysts might ask from this analysis include the following:

- What are the market's assumptions about long-term ROE and growth? For example, is the market forecasting that the company can grow its earnings without a corresponding level of expansion in its asset base (and hence equity)? If so, how long can this persist?
- How do changes in the cost of capital affect the market's assessment of the firm's future performance? If the market's expectations seem to be unexpectedly high or low, has the market reassessed the company's risk? If so, is this change plausible?

## DEVELOPING THE ANALYST'S EXPECTATIONS

Ultimately, a security analyst must compare his or her own view of a share with the view embedded in the market price. The analyst's view is generated using the same tools discussed in Chapters 2 through 8. The final product of this work is, of course, a forecast of the firm's future earnings and cash flows and an estimate of the firm's value. However, that final product is less important than the understanding of the business and its industry that the analysis provides. It is such understanding that enables the analyst to interpret new information as it arrives and to infer its implications.

## Key analysis questions

In developing expectations about the firm's future performance using the financial analysis tools discussed throughout this book, the analyst is likely to ask the following types of questions:

- How profitable is the firm? In light of industry conditions, the firm's corporate strategy, and its barriers to competition, how sustainable is that rate of profitability?
- What are the opportunities for growth for this firm?
- How risky is this firm? How vulnerable are operations to general economic downturns? How highly levered is the firm? What does the riskiness of the firm imply about its cost of capital?
- How do answers to the preceding questions compare to the expectations embedded in the observed share price?

## THE FINAL PRODUCT OF SECURITY ANALYSIS

For financial analysts, the final product of security analysis is a recommendation to buy, sell, or hold the share (or some more refined ranking). The recommendation is supported by a set of forecasts and a report summarizing the foundation for the recommendation. Analysts' reports often delve into significant detail and include an assessment of a firm's business as well as a line-by-line income statement, balance sheet, and cash flow forecasts for one or more years.

In making a recommendation to buy or sell a share, the analyst has to consider the investment time horizon required to capitalize on the recommendation. Are anticipated improvements in performance likely to be confirmed in the near term, allowing investors to capitalize quickly on the recommendation? Or do expected performance improvements reflect long-term fundamentals that will take several years to play out? Longer investment horizons impose greater risk on investors that the company's performance will be affected by changes in economic conditions that cannot be anticipated by the analyst, reducing the value of the recommendation. Consequently, thorough analysis requires not merely being able to recognize whether a share is misvalued, but being able to anticipate when a price correction is likely to take place.

Because there are additional investment risks from following recommendations that require long-term commitments, security analysts tend to focus on making recommendations that are likely to pay off in the short term. This potentially explains why so few analysts recommended selling dotcom and technology shares during the late 1990s when their prices would be difficult to justify on the basis of long-term fundamentals. It also explains why analysts recommended Enron's share at its peak, even though the kind of analysis performed in this chapter would have shown that the future growth and ROE performance implied by this price would be extremely difficult to achieve. It also implies that to take advantage of long-term fundamental analysis can often require access to patient, long-term capital.

# Performance of security analysts and fund managers

Extensive research has been done on the performance of security analysts and fund managers during the past three decades. A few of the key findings are summarized here.

## PERFORMANCE OF SECURITY ANALYSTS

Despite the failure of security analysts to foresee the dramatic price declines for dotcom and telecommunications shares at the beginning of the 2000s and financials in 2008, or to detect the financial shenanigans and overvaluation of companies such as Carillion, Enron, Olympus, Steinhoff, and Tesco, research shows that analysts generally add value in the capital market. Analyst earnings forecasts are more accurate than those produced by time-series models that use past earnings to predict future earnings.[11] Of course, this should not be too surprising since analysts can update their earnings forecasts between quarters to incorporate new firm and economy information, whereas time-series models cannot. In addition, share prices tend to respond positively to upward revisions in analysts' earnings forecasts and recommendations, and negatively to downward revisions.[12] Finally, research finds that analysts play a valuable role in improving market efficiency. For example, share prices for firms with a higher analyst following more rapidly incorporate information on accruals and cash flows than prices of less followed firms.[13]

Several factors seem to be important in explaining analysts' earnings forecast accuracy. Not surprisingly, forecasts of near-term earnings are much more accurate than those of long-term performance.[14] This probably explains why analysts typically make detailed forecasts for only one or two years ahead. Studies of differences in earnings forecast accuracy across analysts find that analysts who are more accurate tend to specialize by industry and by country and work for large, well-funded firms that employ other analysts who follow the same industry.[15]

Although analysts perform a valuable function in the capital market, research shows that their forecasts and recommendations tend to be biased. Early evidence on bias indicated that analyst earnings forecasts tended to be optimistic and that their recommendations were almost exclusively for buys.[16] Several factors potentially explain this finding. First, security analysts at brokerage houses are typically compensated on the basis of the trading volume that their reports generate. Given the costs of short selling and the restrictions on short selling by many institutions, brokerage analysts have incentives to issue optimistic reports that encourage investors to buy shares rather than to issue negative reports that create selling pressure. Second, analysts who work for investment banks are rewarded for promoting public issues by current clients and for attracting new banking clients, creating incentives for optimistic forecasts and recommendations. Studies show that analysts who work for lead underwriters make more optimistic long-term earnings forecasts and recommendations for firms raising equity capital than unaffiliated analysts.[17]

Evidence indicates that during the late 1990s there was a marked decline in analyst optimism for forecasts of near-term earnings.[18] One explanation offered for this change is that during the late 1990s analysts relied heavily on private discussions with top management to make their earnings forecasts. Management allegedly used these personal connections to manage analysts' short-term expectations downwards so that the firm could subsequently report earnings that beat analysts' expectations. In response to concerns about this practice, in October 2000 the US SEC approved Regulation Fair Disclosure, which prohibits management from making selective disclosures of nonpublic information. In Europe the EU Transparency and Market Abuse Directives, adopted in 2004, may counter such practices, albeit less directly.

There also has been a general decline in sell-side analysts' optimistic recommendations during the past few years. Many large investment banks now require analysts to use a forced curve to rate shares, leading to a greater number of lower ratings. Factors that underlie this change include a sharp rise in trading by hedge funds, which actively seek shares to short sell. In contrast, traditional money management firms are typically restricted from short selling and are more interested in analysts' buy recommendations than their sells. Second, regulatory changes require tight separation between investment banking and equity research at investment banks.

## PERFORMANCE OF FUND MANAGERS

Measuring whether collective investment and pension fund managers earn superior returns is a difficult task for several reasons. First, there is no agreement about how to estimate benchmark performance for a fund. Studies have used a number of approaches – some have used the capital asset pricing model (CAPM) as a benchmark while others have used multifactor pricing models. For studies using the CAPM, there are questions about what type of market index to use. For example, should it be an equal or value-weighted index, an exchange-related index, or a broader market index? Second, many of the traditional measures of fund performance abstract from market-wide performance, which understates fund abnormal performance if fund managers can time the market by reducing portfolio risk prior to market declines and increasing risks before a market run-up. Third, given the overall volatility of stock returns, statistical power is an issue for measuring fund performance. Finally, tests of fund performance are likely to be highly sensitive to the time period examined. Value or momentum investing could therefore appear to be profitable depending on when the tests are conducted.

Perhaps because of these challenges, there is no consistent evidence that actively managed collective investment funds generate superior returns for investors. While some studies find evidence of positive abnormal returns for the industry, others conclude that returns are generally negative.[19] Of course, even if collective investment fund managers on average can only generate "normal" returns for investors, it is still possible for the best managers to show consistently strong performance. Some studies do in fact document that funds earning positive abnormal returns in one period continue to outperform in subsequent periods. However, more recent evidence suggests that these findings are caused by general momentum in stock returns and fund expenses rather than superior fund manager ability.[20] Researchers have also examined which, if any, investment strategies are most successful. However, no clear consensus appears – several studies have found that momentum and high turnover strategies generate superior returns, whereas others conclude that value strategies are better.[21]

Finally, recent research has examined whether fund managers tend to buy and sell many of the same shares at the same time. They conclude that there is evidence of "herding" behaviour, particularly by momentum fund managers.[22] This could arise because managers have access to common information, because they are affected by similar cognitive biases, or because they have incentives to follow the crowd.[23] For example, consider the calculus of a fund manager who holds a share but who, through long-term fundamental analysis, estimates that it is misvalued. If the manager changes the fund's holdings accordingly and the share price returns to its intrinsic value in the next quarter, the fund will show superior relative portfolio performance and will attract new capital. However, if the share continues to be misvalued for several quarters, the informed fund manager will underperform the benchmark and capital will flow to other funds. In contrast, a risk-averse manager who simply follows the crowd will not be rewarded for detecting the misvaluation, but neither will this manager be blamed for a poor investment decision when the share price ultimately corrects, since other funds made the same mistake.

There has been considerably less research on the performance of pension fund managers. Overall, the findings show little consistent evidence that pension fund managers either over perform or under perform traditional bench-marks.[24]

## Summary

Equity security analysis is the evaluation of a firm and its prospects from the perspective of a current or potential investor in the firm's shares. Security analysis is one component of a larger investment process that involves:

1  Establishing the objectives of the investor or fund.

2  Forming expectations about the future returns and risks of individual securities.

3  Combining individual securities into portfolios to maximize progress towards the investment objectives.

Some security analysis is devoted primarily to assuring that a share possesses the proper risk profile and other desired characteristics prior to inclusion in an investor's portfolio. However, especially for many professional buy-side and sell-side security analysts, the analysis is also directed towards the identification of mispriced securities. In equilibrium, such activity will be rewarding for those with the strongest comparative advantage. They will be the ones able to identify any mispricing at the lowest cost and exert pressure on the price to correct the mispricing. What kinds of efforts are productive in this domain depends on the degree of market efficiency. A large body of existing evidence is supportive of a high degree of efficiency in stock markets, but recent evidence has reopened the debate on this issue.

In practice, a wide variety of approaches to fund management and security analysis are employed. However, at the core of the analyses are the same steps outlined in Chapters 2 through 8 of this book: business strategy analysis, accounting analysis, financial analysis, and prospective analysis (forecasting and valuation). For the professional analyst, the final product of the work is, of course, a forecast of the firm's future earnings and cash flows, and an estimate of the firm's value. But that final product is less important than the understanding of the business and its industry that the analysis provides. It is such understanding that positions the analyst to interpret new information as it arrives and infer its implications.

Finally, the chapter summarizes some key findings of the research on the performance of both sell-side and buy-side security analysts.

## Core concepts

**Active versus passive portfolio management**    Active portfolio management involves the use of security analysis to identify mispriced securities; passive portfolio management implies holding a portfolio of securities to match the risk and return of a market or sector index.

**Collective investment funds**    Funds selling shares in professionally managed portfolios of securities with similar risk, return, and/or style characteristics.

**Market efficiency**    Degree to which security prices reflect all available information. Market inefficiencies can lead to security mispricing and increase opportunities for earning abnormal investment returns through the use of comprehensive security analysis.

**Security analysis**    Projecting future returns and assessing risks of a security with the objective of identifying mispriced securities or understanding how the security affects the risk, return, and style characteristics of a portfolio.

**Steps of security analysis**    Comprehensive security analysis consists of the following steps:

1.  Selection of candidates for analysis on the basis of risk, return, or style characteristics, industry membership, or mispricing indicators.

2.  Inferring market expectations about the firm's future profitability and growth from the current security price.

3.  Developing expectations about the firm's profitability and growth using the four steps of business analysis.

4.  Making an investment decision after comparing own expectations with those of the market.

## Questions

1   Despite many years of research, the evidence on market efficiency described in this chapter appears to be inconclusive. Some argue that this is because researchers have been unable to precisely link company fundamentals to share prices. Comment.

2   Geoffrey Henley, a professor of finance, states: "The capital market is efficient. I don't know why anyone would bother devoting their time to following individual shares and doing fundamental analysis. The best approach is to buy and hold a well-diversified portfolio of shares." Do you agree? Why or why not?

3   What is the difference between fundamental and technical analysis? Can you think of any trading strategies that use technical analysis? What are the underlying assumptions made by these strategies?

4   Investment funds follow many different types of investment strategies. Income funds focus on shares with high dividend yields, growth funds invest in shares that are expected to have high capital appreciation, value funds follow shares that are considered to be undervalued, and short funds bet against shares they consider to be overvalued. What types of investors are likely to be attracted to each of these types of funds? Why?

5   Intergalactic Software Plc went public three months ago. You are a sophisticated investor who devotes time to fundamental analysis as a way of identifying mispriced shares. Which of the following characteristics would you focus on in deciding whether to follow this share?

  - The market capitalization.
  - The average number of shares traded per day.
  - The bid–ask spread for the share.
  - Whether the underwriter that took the firm public is a Top Five investment banking firm.
  - Whether its audit company is a Big Four firm.
  - Whether there are analysts from major brokerage firms following the company.
  - Whether the share is held mostly by retail or institutional investors.

6   There are two major types of financial analysts: buy-side and sell-side. Buy-side analysts work for investment firms and make recommendations that are available only to the management of funds within that firm. Sell-side analysts work for brokerage firms and make recommendations that are used to sell shares to the brokerage firms' clients, which include individual investors and managers of investment funds. What would be the differences in tasks and motivations of these two types of analysts?

7   Many market participants believe that sell-side analysts are too optimistic in their recommendations to buy shares and too slow to recommend sells. What factors might explain this bias?

8   Joe Klein is an analyst for an investment banking firm that offers both underwriting and brokerage services. Joe sends you a highly favourable report on a share that his firm recently helped go public and for which it currently makes the market. What are the potential advantages and disadvantages in relying on Joe's report in deciding whether to buy the share?

9   Intergalactic Software's shares have a market price of €20 per share and a book value of €12 per share. If its cost of equity capital is 15 percent and its book value is expected to grow at 5 percent per year indefinitely, what is the market's assessment of its steady state return on equity? If the share price increases to €35 and the market does not expect the firm's growth rate to change, what is the revised steady state ROE? If instead the price increase was due to an increase in the market's assessments about long-term book value growth rather than long-term ROE, what would the price revision imply for the steady state growth rate?

10  Joe states, "I can see how ratio analysis and valuation help me do fundamental analysis, but I don't see the value of doing strategy analysis." Can you explain to him how strategy analysis could be potentially useful?

# Notes

1 OEIC stands for "Open-Ended Investment Company" and is a UK collective investment fund. SICAV stands for "Société d'Investissement a Capital Variable" and is an open-ended collective investment fund in France and Luxembourg. BEVEK stands for "Beleggingsvennootschap met Veranderlijk Kapitaal" and is an open-ended collective investment fund in Belgium.

2 Investment-grade rated bonds have received a credit rating by Moody's of Baa or above and/or a credit rating by Standard & Poor's of BBB or above. We discuss these rating categories in more detail in Chapter 10.

3 P. Healy and K. Palepu, "The Fall of Enron," *Journal of Economic Perspectives* 17(2) (Spring 2003): 3–26, discuss how weak money manager incentives and long-term analysis contributed to the share price run-up and subsequent collapse for Enron. A similar discussion on factors affecting the rise and fall of dot-com shares is provided in "The Role of Capital Market Intermediaries in the Dot-Com Crash of 2000," Harvard Business School Case 101–110, 2001.

4 See R. Bhushan, "Firm Characteristics and Analyst Following," *Journal of Accounting and Economics* 11(2/5), July 1989: 255–275, and P. O'Brien and R. Bhushan, "Analyst Following and Institutional Ownership," *Journal of Accounting Research* 28, Suppl. (1990): 55–76.

5 Reviews of evidence on market efficiency are provided by E. Fama, "Efficient Capital Markets: II," *Journal of Finance* 46 (December 1991): 1575–1617; S. Kothari, "Capital Markets Research in Accounting," *Journal of Accounting and Economics* 31 (September 2001): 105–231; and C. Lee, "Market Efficiency in Accounting Research," *Journal of Accounting and Economics* 31 (September 2001): 233–253.

6 For example, see V. Bernard and J. Thomas, "Evidence That Stock Prices Do Not Fully Reflect the Implications of Current Earnings for Future Earnings," *Journal of Accounting and Economics* 13 (December 1990): 305–341.

7 Examples of studies that examine a "value share" strategy include J. Lakonishok, A. Shleifer, and R. Vishny, "Contrarian Investment, Extrapolation, and Risk," *Journal of Finance* 49 (December 1994): 1541–1578; and R. Frankel and C. Lee, "Accounting Valuation, Market Expectation, and Cross-Sectional Stock Returns," *Journal of Accounting and Economics* 25 (June 1998): 283–319.

8 For example, see J. Ou and S. Penman, "Financial Statement Analysis and the Prediction of Stock Returns," *Journal of Accounting and Economics* 11 (November 1989): 295–330; R. Holthausen and D. Larcker, "The Prediction of Stock Returns Using Financial Statement Information," *Journal of Accounting and Economics* 15 (June/September 1992): 373–411; and R. Sloan, "Do Stock Prices Fully Reflect Information in Accruals and Cash Flows about Future Earnings?" *The Accounting Review* 71 (July 1996): 298–325.

9 For an overview of research in behavioural finance, see *Advances in Behavioral Finance* by R. Thaler (New York: Russell Sage Foundation, 1993), and *Inefficient Markets: An Introduction to Behavioral Finance* by A. Shleifer (Oxford: Oxford University Press, 2000).

10 These forecasts were taken from I/B/E/S.

11 Time-series model forecasts of future annual earnings are the most recent annual earnings (with or without some form of annual growth), and forecasts of future quarterly earnings are a function of growth in earnings for the latest quarter relative to both the last quarter and the same quarter one year ago. See L. Brown and M. Rozeff, "The Superiority of Analyst Forecasts as Measures of Expectations: Evidence from Earnings," *Journal of Finance* 33 (1978): 1–16; L. Brown, P. Griffin, R. Hagerman, and M. Zmijewski, "Security Analyst Superiority Relative to Univariate Time-Series Models in Forecasting Quarterly Earnings," *Journal of Accounting and Economics* 9 (1987): 61–87; and D. Givoly, "Financial Analysts' Forecasts of Earnings: A Better Surrogate for Market Expectations," *Journal of Accounting and Economics* 4(2) (1982): 85–108.

12 See D. Givoly and J. Lakonishok, "The Information Content of Financial Analysts' Forecasts of Earnings: Some Evidence on Semi-Strong Efficiency," *Journal of Accounting and Economics* 2 (1979): 165–186; T. Lys and S. Sohn, "The Association between Revisions of Financial Analysts' Earnings Forecasts and Security Price Changes," *Journal of Accounting and Economics* 13 (1990): 341–364; and J. Francis and L. Soffer, "The Relative Informativeness of Analysts' Stock Recommendations and Earnings Forecast Revisions," *Journal of Accounting Research* 35(2) (1997): 193–212.

13 See M. Barth and A. Hutton, "Information Intermediaries and the Pricing of Accruals," working paper, Stanford University, 2000.

14 See P. O'Brien, "Forecasts Accuracy of Individual Analysts in Nine Industries," *Journal of Accounting Research* 28 (1990): 286–304.

15 See G. Bolliger, "The Characteristics of Individual Analysts' Forecasts in Europe," *Journal of Banking and Finance* 28 (2004): 2283–2309; M. Clement, "Analyst Forecast Accuracy: Do Ability, Resources, and Portfolio Complexity Matter?" *Journal of Accounting and Economics* 27 (1999): 285–304; J. Jacob, T. Lys, and M. Neale, "Experience in Forecasting Performance of Security Analysts," *Journal of Accounting and Economics* 28 (1999): 51–82; and S. Gilson, P. Healy, C. Noe, and K. Palepu, "Analyst Specialization and Conglomerate Stock Breakups," *Journal of Accounting Research* 39 (December 2001): 565–573.

16 See L. Brown, G. Foster, and E. Noreen, "Security Analyst Multi-Year Earnings Forecasts and the Capital Market," *Studies in Accounting Research,* No. 21 (Sarasota, FL), American Accounting Association; M. McNichols and P. O'Brien, in "Self-Selection and Analyst Coverage," *Journal of Accounting Research,* Supplement (1997): 167–208, find that analyst bias arises primarily because analysts issue recommendations on firms for which they have favourable information and withhold recommending firms with unfavourable information.

17 See H. Lin and M. McNichols, "Underwriting Relationships, Analysts' Earnings Forecasts and Investment Recommendations," *Journal of Accounting and Economics* 25(1) (1998): 101–128; R. Michaely and K. Womack, "Conflict of Interest and the Credibility of Underwriter Analyst Recommendations," *Review of Financial Studies* 12(4) (1999): 653–686; and P. Dechow, A. Hutton, and R. Sloan, "The Relation between Analysts' Forecasts of Long-Term Earnings Growth and Stock Price Performance Following Equity Offerings," *Contemporary Accounting Research* 17(1) (2000): 1–32.

18 See L. Brown, "Analyst Forecasting Errors: Additional Evidence," *Financial Analysts' Journal* (November/December 1997): 81–88; and D. Matsumoto, "Management's Incentives to Avoid Negative Earnings Surprises," *The Accounting Review* 77 (July 2002): 483–515.

19 For example, evidence of superior fund performance is reported by M. Grinblatt and S. Titman, "Mutual Fund Performance: An Analysis of Quarterly Holdings," *Journal of Business* 62 (1994): 393–416, and by D. Hendricks, J. Patel, and R. Zeckhauser, "Hot Hands in Mutual Funds: Short-Run Persistence of Relative Performance," *The Journal of Finance* 48 (1993): 93–130. In contrast, negative fund performance is shown by M. Jensen, "The Performance of Mutual Funds in the Period 1945–64," *The Journal of Finance* 23 (May 1968): 389–416, and B. Malkiel, "Returns from Investing in Equity Mutual Funds from 1971 to 1991," *Journal of Finance* 50 (June 1995): 549–573.

20 M. Grinblatt and S. Titman, "The Persistence of Mutual Fund Performance," *Journal of Finance* 47 (December 1992): 1977–1986, and D. Hendricks, J. Patel, and R. Zeckhauser, "Hot Hands in Mutual Funds: Short-Run Persistence of Relative Performance," *Journal of Finance* 48 (March 1993): 93–130, find evidence of persistence in mutual fund returns. However, M. Carhart, "On Persistence in Mutual Fund Performance," *The Journal of Finance* 52 (March 1997): 57–83, shows that much of this is attributable to momentum in stock returns and to fund expenses; B. Malkiel, "Returns from Investing in Equity Mutual Funds from 1971 to 1991," *The Journal of Finance* 50 (June 1995): 549–573, shows that survivorship bias is also an important consideration.

21 See M. Grinblatt, S. Titman, and R. Wermers, "Momentum Investment Strategies, Portfolio Performance, and Herding: A Study of Mutual Fund Behavior," *The American Economic Review* 85 (December 1995): 1088–1105.

22 For example, J. Lakonishok, A. Shleifer, and R. Vishny, "Contrarian Investment, Extrapolation, and Risk," *Journal of Finance* 49 (December 1994): 1541–1579, find that value funds show superior performance, whereas M. Grinblatt, S. Titman, and R. Wermers, "Momentum Investment Strategies, Portfolio Performance, and Herding: A Study of Mutual Fund Behavior," *The American Economic Review* 85 (December 1995): 1088–1105, find that momentum investing is profitable.

23 See D. Scharfstein and J. Stein, "Herd Behavior and Investment," *The American Economic Review* 80 (June 1990): 465–480; and P. Healy and K. Palepu, "The Fall of Enron," *Journal of Economic Perspectives* 17(2) (Spring 2003): 3–26.

24 For evidence on performance by pension fund managers, see J. Lakonishok, A. Shleifer, and R. Vishny, "The Structure and Performance of the Money Management Industry," *Brookings Papers on Economic Activity* (Washington, DC: American Accounting Association, 1992), 339–392; T. Coggin, F. Fabozzi, and S. Rahman, "The Investment Performance of US Equity Pension Fund Managers: An Empirical Investigation," *The Journal of Finance* 48 (July 1993): 1039–1056; and W. Ferson and K. Khang, "Conditional Performance Measurement Using Portfolio Weights: Evidence for Pension Funds," *Journal of Financial Economics* 65 (August 2002): 249–282.

# Valuation at Novartis

In early 2007, Novartis announced record annual earnings of $7.2 billion for the year ended December 31, 2006, representing a 17 percent increase over the prior year. The company's return on beginning book equity of 21.7 percent far exceeded the company's estimate of its cost of equity (8.5 percent). Further, since 2003, the company had grown earnings by an average of 17 percent per year, and its return on beginning book equity had increased steadily from 16.8 percent. Despite this superior performance, the company's stock performance had lagged that of the S&P500 and Swiss Market indexes, growing by an average of 10 percent per year (see **Exhibit 1**). In addition, its price-to-earnings multiple had declined steadily from 22.9 2003 to 19.4 in 2006 (see **Exhibit 9**).

Several explanations for the gap between the company's earnings and stock performance were plausible. First, given the sustained strong performance of the pharmaceutical industry and the company's past success, market expectations were likely to be high. Merely meeting those heady expectations would generate only normal stock price appreciation. A second explanation was that the market questioned whether Novartis could sustain such strong performance, perhaps because of heightened regulatory oversight and proposed changes in the US medical system, or as a result of concerns about the viability of the company's unique strategy of investing in both branded pharmaceuticals and generics. Finally, it was possible that investors had under-estimated Novartis and the stock was undervalued. For Novartis's management, understanding which of these best explained the company's situation was a necessary first step before deciding on an appropriate course of action.

## The pharmaceutical industry

The pharmaceutical industry had an impressive track record of generating strong growth and returns for shareholders over an extended period. From 2003 to 2006, the industry reported revenue and earnings growth of 11 percent per year, and had an average return on book equity of 17.5 percent.[1] Two forces had combined to help create this sustained high performance. First, the industry had been remarkably successful in creating new innovative drugs to address patient needs. This was a costly process. Only one in 5,000 to 10,0000 compounds tested in the laboratory reached the market, and of these only 30 percent were a commercial success.[2] As a result

[1] Source: Capital IQ.
[2] See "Pharmaceutical Industry Profile 2007," Pharmaceutical Research and Manufacturers of America website, www.phrma.org/publications.

of extensive testing and regulatory approval to ensure drug efficacy and safety, total drug development time lasted around fourteen years and cost more than $800 million per drug. On average, in 2006 pharmaceutical companies spent $55.2 billion (17.5 percent of sales) on research and development.[3] However, patent protection of new compounds prevented competitors from copying successful new innovations and enabled innovators to recover the heavy costs of drug discovery and development. The average effective patent life for branded drugs was 11.5 years.[4]

A second factor behind the industry's performance was its strong sales and marketing capability. On average, pharmaceutical companies spent around 30 percent of sales on sales and marketing costs. In many markets, drug companies employed an army of sales reps who visited doctors to convince them to prescribe their firms' drugs. However, given the time constraints faced by physicians, sales rep visits were typically short, enabling the reps to drop off promotional materials and free sample drugs. Drug companies therefore frequently organized educational conferences, dinners, and other events to enable sales reps to spend time with doctors. Firms also appealed directly to patients by consumer advertising. By 2005, direct-to-consumer advertising was $4.2 billion.[5]

In early 2007, the pharmaceutical industry faced a number of challenges. Public concern over the cost of medical care and drugs had escalated, particularly in the US, the most expensive (and also most profitable) health care market in the world. For the first time in fifteen years politicians had seriously begun debating whether the health care system in the US needed to be changed. Candidates for the 2008 presidential elections from both political parties were in the process of developing new health care initiatives to solve dual problems of a large uninsured population and the increased cost of health care. While increased access to health care could potentially benefit the pharmaceutical industry, there was also a significant risk that changes would increase the power of health care providers (including federal and state governments) which would use their leverage to obtain price cuts of as much as 40 percent, reducing the industry's profitability and the financial resources available for developing new drugs.

A second challenge had emerged following publication of research showing adverse cardiac risks for patients using Merck's blockbuster Vioxx painkiller. Merck had voluntarily withdrawn Vioxx from the market in September 2004 following the publication. However, research findings from a 2001 study presented to the company also showed cardiac risks, leading critics to allege that the company had over-promoted the drug and underplayed its risks. By early 2007, roughly 22,000 lawsuits in US state and federal courts had been filed against Merck. Analysts estimated that company's legal liabilities could range from $4 billion to more than $25 billion. Merck opted to defend each suit separately on its merits. Of the 17 cases tried as of March 28, 2007, Merck won ten, lost five, and two had ended in mistrials.[6] Merck planned to or had appealed the cases it had lost. However, the problems had increased pressure on the Food and Drug Administration, which regulated drug approvals in the US, to be more cautious in approving new drugs and to respond more promptly to drug safety questions.

In addition, it appeared that the industry was becoming less productive in discovering and commercializing new drugs to replace those going off patent. Drug development costs had increased from $54 million per new drug in 1976 to $231 million in 1987 and to $802 million in 2001.[7] A study by Bain & Co. discovered that by 2003, only one in thirteen drugs that reached animal testing actually reached the market, down from one in eight in the late 1990s. Opinions were divided on the causes of this decline. Some argued that it was becoming more difficult to discover breakthrough drugs. Others pointed to increased regulatory oversight to improve drug safety. Despite questions about research productivity, spending on R&D continued to grow, both in dollar

[3]Ibid.
[4]Ibid.
[5]Julie M. Donohue, Marisa Cevasco, and Meredith B. Rosenthal, "A Decade of Direct-to-Consumer Advertising of Prescription Drugs," *New England Journal of Medicine,* Vol. 357 (August 16, 2007): 673–681.
[6]Standard & Poor's Healthcare, "Pharmaceuticals Industry Survey," May 10, 2007.
[7]"Pharmaceutical Industry Profile 2007, Pharmaceutical Research and Manufacturers of America website, www.phrma.org/publications.

terms and as a percentage of sales. In 2006, industry R&D totaled $55.2 billion, a 7.8 percent increase over the prior year. As a percentage of sales, R&D increased from 12.9 percent in 1985 to 17.5 percent in 2006.[8]

Finally, the industry faced increased pricing pressure from generics companies that produced and marketed drugs for which patent protection had expired. Generics drugs sold at 30 percent to 90 percent discounts relative to prices of brand-name drugs prior to patent expiration. Analysts estimated that in the first year after patent expiration, a brand-name drug could lose more than 80 percent of its volume to generics. The generics share of the US prescription drug market had grown from 19 percent in 1994, to 47 percent in 2000, and 54 percent in 2005.[9] This growth was driven by managed care providers, which substituted generics drugs for the brand names to reduce costs. Generics companies followed a very different business model than traditional pharma companies. They spent much less on research and development, and on marketing and sales. Their focus was on aggressively challenging existing brand name drugs about to lose patent protection since the first to market was granted six-month period of market exclusivity. Once this six-month period ended, however, other generics firms were free to enter the market, leading to intense competition.

## Novartis

Novartis was founded in 1996 through the merger of Ciba-Geigy and Sandoz. Under the leadership of Daniel Vasella, who was appointed CEO in 1999, Novartis grew through a combination of successful new drug discoveries and selected acquisitions. From 1999 to 2006, revenues increased from $20.4 billion to $36 billion, and operating earnings grew from $4.6 to $8.1 billion (see **Exhibit 2** for Novartis's income statement and balance sheet data for the period 1999 to 2006).[10] During this period Novartis was among the industry leaders in introducing new drugs, including Femura (for breast cancer), Excelon (for Alzheimers), Dio-van/Co-Diovan (for hypertension), Visudyne (for age-related macular degeneration), Glee-vac/Gilvec (for chronic myeloid leukemia), and Zometa (for cancer complications).[11] It also successfully refocused by divesting its agribusiness and made several key acquisitions, including contact lens maker Wesley Jessen for $845 million in 2000, generics companies Lek ($959 million in 2002), Eon and Hexal ($8.4 billion in 2005), and Chiron, a biopharmaceutical, vaccine, and diagnostics firm for $6.3 billion in 2006.[12]

By early 2007, Novartis comprised four divisions: Pharmaceuticals, Sandoz (its generics business), Consumer Health, and Vaccines and Diagnostics. The company's strategy was to provide customers with a full complement of the health care products they needed, including branded drugs, generic drugs, vaccines, and over-the-counter medicines.

Pharmaceuticals, the largest division with sales of $26.6 billion, boasted highly successful drugs in the cardiovascular, oncology, and neuroscience areas (see **Exhibit 3** for data on the company's top twenty drug sales and **Exhibit 4** for sales by drug maturity). Sales growth at Pharma exceeded 12 percent for 2006 with profit margins of 28.7 percent. The unit's strong performance was expected to continue in 2007 and 2008 with approvals pending in the US and Europe for a number of new drugs, including Exforge and Tek-turna (hypertension), Galvus (type 2 diabetes), and Lucentis (for blindness). A total of 138 new projects were in progress at the end of 2006, 36 percent classified as new molecular entities, and the remainder as life cycle management projects. Fifteen projects had been submitted to regulatory authorities, thirteen were in phase III (large clinical trials), and another

---

[8]Ibid.
[9]"Insights 2006, Highlights from the Pharmaceutical Industry Profile, Pharmaceutical Research and Manufacturers of America website, www.phrma.org/publications.
[10]Source: Novartis annual reports, 1999 to 2006.
[11]Ibid.
[12]Source: Capital IQ.

76 were in phase II clinical trials.[13] The company's major competitors in this sector included GlaxoSmithKline, Johnson & Johnson, Merck, and Pfizer (see **Exhibit 5** for data on the performance of these firms).

Sandoz, with sales of $5.6 billion in 2006, was the world's second-largest generics business. In 2003, Novartis consolidated its different generics businesses using the Sandoz brand. It subsequently invested in building the generics business with acquisitions of Lek, Hexal, and Eon. Novartis was the only major pharma company with a generics drug business. In commenting on the strategy, CEO Vasella explained that the company viewed "generic medicines as a critical complement to innovative medicines." Large purchasers like Wal-Mart, and private and state-run health care providers want to buy a range of generic and patented products.[14] Also, generic drugs were projected to increase their market share as patents for many large drug companies were scheduled to expire in the US market. However, some analysts expressed doubts about the move, pointing out that "competition is high in the (generics) sector, fueled by the entry of low-cost producers from emerging markets like India which (has) hurt (generic drug) margins and profitability."[15] In 2006, Sandoz sales grew by 27 percent and operating profit margins increased to 12 percent as a result of the completion of the Hexal and Eon acquisitions, and rapid growth in the US and Eastern European markets. Key competitors in this sector included Teva Pharmaceutical Industries, Watson Pharmaceuticals, and a range of smaller companies (see **Exhibit 6** for data on the performance of key competitors in the industry).

The Consumer Health division included several businesses, Over-the Counter (OTC), Animal Health, CIBA Vision, and Gerber. In 2006, the group's Medical Nutrition unit was sold to Nestlé for $2.5 billion. Consumer Health sales from continuing operations grew by 8 percent to $6.5 billion. This was led by strong performance in OTC, which jumped from sixth largest in sales to the fourth largest in the world, and in Animal Health which jumped three positions to number five. The group's other major business units included eye lens firm CIBA Vision and Gerber, the leading baby nutrition company in the US Key competitors in this sector included Johnson & Johnson, Schering-Plough, Reckitt and Benkiser, and Pfizer (see **Exhibit 7** for data on the performance of key competitors).

The Vaccines and Diagnostics unit arose from the acquisition of Chiron. 2006 sales for the post-acquisition eight months were $956 million, up 42 percent over the comparable period for 2005. This increase was driven by a sharp increase in influenza vaccines in the US market. Novartis reported that given novel new products and innovations in manufacturing technologies it anticipated double digit growth in this segment during the following decade. Key competitors in this sector included Johnson & Johnson, Sanofi-Aventis, Merck, and Abbott Laboratories (see **Exhibit 8** for data on the performance of competitors).

## Valuation

The health care industry had experienced declining stock multiples from 2003 to 2006. Price-to-earnings multiples during the period had dropped steadily from 47.8 to 33.0, despite strong earnings growth in 2006. Price-to-book multiples had declined from 6.0 to 4.0 during the same period despite sustained strong returns on book equity (see **Exhibit 9**).

In early 2007, Novartis's price to earnings multiple was higher than that of three of its five leading competitors (GlaxoSmithKline, Pfizer, and Johnson & Johnson). Yet its price to book multiple was lower than that all but Pfizer (see **Exhibit 10**). Despite continued strong earnings performance, its record of new drug introductions,

---

[13]Source: Novartis 2006 annual report.
[14]Tom Wright, "Novartis to become generics leader," *International Herald Tribune,* February 22, 2005.
[15]Ibid.

and its strong pipeline of future new drugs, management was puzzled by the stock's three-year record of merely tracking the S&P index. What assumptions was the market making about Novartis's future performance? How were questions about the future of the industry, and the company's unique strategy affecting its valuation? And what actions if any should the company's management team take to respond to market's assessments?

**EXHIBIT 1** Stock performance for Novartis and indices for the period 2003 to 2006

|         | Novartis | Swiss Market Index | S&P 500 Index | Morgan Stanley World Pharmaceutical Index |
|---------|----------|--------------------|---------------|--------------------------------------------|
| 2003    | 13%      | 21%                | 26%           | 3%                                         |
| 2004    | 4%       | 5%                 | 9%            | −8%                                        |
| 2005    | 22%      | 36%                | 3%            | 19%                                        |
| 2006    | 2%       | 17%                | 14%           | 7%                                         |
| Average | 10%      | 20%                | 13%           | 5%                                         |

Sources: Novartis 2006 annual report for performance of Novartis stock, Swiss market index, and Pharmaceutical Index, and Standard & Poor's for S&P500 Index.

EXHIBIT 2  Novartis's income statement for the years ended December 31, 1999, to 2006 in $US millions

| | 1999 | 2000 | 2001 | 2002 | 2003 | 2004 | 2005 | 2006 |
|---|---|---|---|---|---|---|---|---|
| Total Revenue | 20,380 | 21,846 | 18,762 | 20,877 | 24,930 | 27,277 | 31,319 | 36,749 |
| Cost of Goods Sold | 6,166 | 6,321 | 4,744 | 4,994 | 6,457 | 6,700 | 8,259 | 10,299 |
| **Gross Profit** | **14,214** | **15,525** | **14,018** | **15,883** | **18,473** | **20,577** | **23,060** | **26,450** |
| Selling General & Administrative Expense | 6,939 | 7,785 | 7,153 | 7,883 | 9,235 | 9,989 | 11,078 | 12,411 |
| R&D Expense | 2,665 | 2,874 | 2,528 | 2,843 | 3,729 | 4,152 | 4,493 | 5,349 |
| Other Operating Expense | — | — | — | 65 | 15 | 270 | 350 | 548 |
| **Operating Income** | **4,609** | **4,865** | **4,337** | **5,092** | **5,494** | **6,166** | **7,139** | **8,142** |
| Interest Expense | (340) | (315) | (218) | (194) | (243) | (261) | (294) | (266) |
| Interest and Invest. Income | 725 | 705 | 404 | 484 | 340 | 400 | 408 | 375 |
| **Net Interest Expense** | **385** | **391** | **186** | **290** | **97** | **139** | **114** | **109** |
| Income/(loss) from Affiliates | 240 | 60 | 83 | (7) | (279) | 68 | 193 | 264 |
| Currency Exchange Gains (Loss) | (213) | (124) | (152) | 69 | 64 | 95 | 115 | 38 |
| Other Non-Operating Inc. (Expense) | (68) | (77) | (86) | 333 | 272 | (66) | (107) | (316) |
| EBT Excl. Unusual Items | 4,953 | 5,115 | 4,368 | 5,777 | 5,648 | 6,402 | 7,454 | 8,237 |
| EBT Incl. Unusual Items | 5,347 | 5,599 | 4,692 | 5,698 | 5,734 | 6,410 | 7,162 | 8,301 |
| Income Tax Expense | 1,151 | 1,123 | 844 | 959 | 947 | 1,045 | 1,090 | 1,282 |
| Minority Int. in Earnings | (17) | (26) | (12) | (14) | (44) | (15) | (11) | (27) |
| **Earnings from Continuing Operations** | **4,180** | **4,450** | **3,836** | **4,725** | **4,743** | **5,350** | **6,061** | **6,992** |
| Earnings of Discontinued Operations | — | — | — | — | — | 15 | 69 | 183 |
| **Net Income** | **4,180** | **4,450** | **3,836** | **4,725** | **4,743** | **5,365** | **6,130** | **7,175** |
| **Per Share Items** | | | | | | | | |
| Basic EPS | $1,575 | $1,703 | $1,492 | $1,878 | $1,993 | $2,278 | $2,628 | $3,059 |
| Basic EPS Excluding Extra Items | 1.575 | 1.703 | 1.492 | 1.878 | 1.993 | 2.271 | 2.598 | 2.981 |
| Weighted Average Basic Shares Outstanding | 2,653.8 | 2,613.5 | 2,571.7 | 2,515.3 | 2,380.1 | 2,355.5 | 2,332.8 | 2,345.2 |
| Dividends per Share | $0.5 | $0.52 | $0.54 | $0.68 | $0.8 | $0.86 | $0.94 | $1.11 |
| Payout Ratio % | 29.1% | 28.6% | 33.1% | 28.9% | 35.0% | 35.3% | 34.4% | 28.6% |

EXHIBIT 2  Novartis's income statement for the years ended December 31, 1999, to 2006 in $US millions (Continued)

| | 1999 | 2000 | 2001 | 2002 | 2003 | 2004 | 2005 | 2006 |
|---|---|---|---|---|---|---|---|---|
| **ASSETS** | | | | | | | | |
| Cash and Short-Term Investments | 10,250 | 12,667 | 13,346 | 12,542 | 13,259 | 13,358 | 10,449 | 7,848 |
| Accounts Receivable | 4,420 | 3,261 | 3,223 | 4,982 | 5,480 | 6,334 | 6,663 | 8,041 |
| Inventory | 4,323 | 2,544 | 2,477 | 2,963 | 3,346 | 3,558 | 3,725 | 4,498 |
| Other Current Assets | 2,776 | 1,858 | 1,544 | 328 | 188 | 670 | 606 | 1,017 |
| **Total Current Assets** | **21,770** | **20,330** | **20,590** | **20,815** | **22,273** | **23,920** | **21,443** | **21,404** |
| Net Property, Plant & Equipment | 7,323 | 5,573 | 5,458 | 6,321 | 7,597 | 8,497 | 8,679 | 10,945 |
| Long-term Investments | 4,967 | 1,864 | 5,362 | 7,789 | 8,362 | 9,206 | 8,996 | 8,424 |
| Goodwill | 963 | 1,276 | 1,382 | 1,704 | 1,477 | 1,899 | 7,279 | 10,659 |
| Other Intangibles | 1,044 | 2,313 | 2,563 | 2,691 | 3,231 | 3,430 | 5,177 | 8,205 |
| Deferred Charges, Long Term | 11 | 9 | — | — | — | 300 | 838 | 2,366 |
| Other Long-Term Assets | 2,896 | 2,547 | 2,917 | 3,527 | 3,976 | 3,001 | 2,757 | 4,468 |
| **Total Assets** | **41,134** | **35,919** | **40,222** | **45,025** | **49,317** | **52,488** | **57,732** | **68,008** |
| **LIABILITIES** | | | | | | | | |
| Accounts Payable | 1,237 | 982 | 1,090 | 1,266. | 1,665 | 2,020 | 1,961 | 2,487 |
| Short-term Borrowings | 4,197 | 2,287 | 2,281 | 2,399 | 2,235 | 3,142 | 5,768 | 5,220 |
| Current Portion of Long-Term Debt | 498 | 46 | 776 | 111 | 45 | 680 | 1,122 | 1,340 |
| Other Current Liabilities | 4,999 | 3,870 | 4,407 | 4,496 | 5,375 | 6,007 | 6,477 | 7,187 |
| **Total Current Liabilities** | **10,931** | **7,184** | **8,553** | **8,272** | **9,320** | **11,849** | **15,328** | **16,234** |
| Long-Term Debt | 1,534 | 1,409 | 1,506 | 2,729 | 3,191 | 2,736 | 1,319 | 656 |
| Minority Interest | 139 | 48 | 63 | 66 | 90 | 138 | 174 | 183 |
| Pension & Other Post-Retirement Benefits | 1,543 | 965 | 1,084 | 1,342 | 1,573 | 2,706 | 2,797 | 2,679 |
| Deferred Tax Liability, Non-Current | 2,289 | 2,153 | 2,341 | 2,821 | 3,138 | 2,340 | 3,472 | 5,290 |
| Other Non-Current Liabilities | 1,336 | 1,408 | 1,223 | 1,526 | 1,576 | 1,542 | 1,652 | 1,855 |
| **Total Liabilities** | **17,772** | **13,168** | **14,770** | **16,756** | **18,888** | **21,311** | **24,742** | **26,897** |
| Total Common Equity | 23,362 | 22,751 | 25,452 | 28,269 | 30,429 | 31,177 | 32,990 | 41,111 |
| **Total Liabilities and Equity** | **41,134** | **35,919** | **40,222** | **45,025** | **49,317** | **52,488** | **57,732** | **68,008** |

Source: Standard & Poor's Capital IQ data.

**EXHIBIT 3**  Sales for Novartis pharmaceutical division's top 20 drugs in 2006

| Brands | Therapeutic Area | USA USD millions | % change in local currencies | Rest of world USD millions | % change in local curriencies | Total USD millions | % change in USD | % change in local currencies |
|---|---|---|---|---|---|---|---|---|
| Diovan/Co-Diovan | Hypertension | 1,858 | 20 | 2,365 | 12 | 4,223 | 15 | 15 |
| Gleevec/Glivec | Chronic myeloid leukemia | 630 | 20 | 1,924 | 16 | 2,554 | 18 | 17 |
| Lotrel | Hypertension | 1,352 | 26 | | | 1,352 | 5 | 4 |
| Zometa | Cancer complications | 696 | −1 | 587 | 12 | 1,283 | 5 | 4 |
| Lamisil (group) | Fungal infections | 574 | 7 | 404 | −31 | 978 | −14 | −13 |
| Neural/Sandimmun | Transplantation | 125 | −17 | 793 | −1 | 918 | −4 | −4 |
| Sandostatin (incl. LAR) | Acromegaly | 367 | −2 | 548 | 4 | 915 | 2 | 2 |
| Lescol | Cholesterol reduction | 256 | 0 | 469 | −8 | 725 | −5 | −5 |
| Trileptal | Epilepsy | 549 | 19 | 172 | 11 | 721 | 17 | 17 |
| Femara | Breast cancer | 338 | 40 | 381 | 27 | 719 | 34 | 33 |
| **Top ten products total** | | **6,745** | **15** | **7,643** | **7** | **14,388** | **10** | **10** |
| Voltaren (group) | Inflammation/pain | 8 | 60 | 682 | 0 | 690 | 0 | 1 |
| Zelnorm/Zelmac | Irritable bowel syndrome | 488 | 37 | 73 | 20 | 561 | 34 | 34 |
| Exelon | Alzheimer's disease | 187 | 9 | 338 | 12 | 525 | 12 | 11 |
| Tegretol (incl. CR/XR) | Epilepsy | 120 | 10 | 271 | −5 | 391 | −1 | −1 |
| Visudyne | Macular degeneration | 70 | −62 | 284 | −6 | 354 | −27 | −27 |
| Miacalcic | Osteoporosis | 199 | −13 | 140 | 3 | 339 | −7 | −7 |
| Comtan/Stalevo Group | Parkinson's disease | 157 | 18 | 182 | 24 | 339 | 22 | 21 |
| Foradil | Asthma | 14 | 0 | 317 | −1 | 331 | 0 | −1 |
| Ritalin/Focalin (group) | Attention deficit/ hyperactive disorder | 264 | 47 | 66 | 6 | 330 | 37 | 37 |
| Famvir | Viral infections | 166 | 10 | 102 | −3 | 268 | 6 | 5 |
| **Top twenty products total** | | **8,418** | **14** | **10,098** | **5** | **18,516** | **9** | **9** |
| Rest of portfolio | | 1,054 | 43 | 3,006 | 14 | 4,060 | 21 | 21 |
| **Total Division net sales** | | **9,472** | **17** | **13,104** | **7** | **22,576** | **11** | **11** |

Source: Novartis 2006 annual report.

**EXHIBIT 4**  2006 sales for Novartis pharmaceutical division by drug maturity

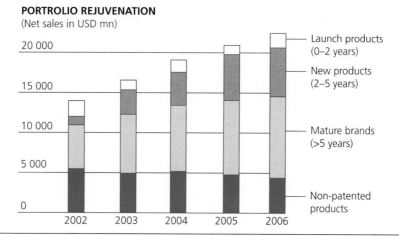

**PORTROLIO REJUVENATION**
(Net sales in USD mn)

Source: Novartis 2006 annual report.

**EXHIBIT 5**  Performance of key competitors in the pharmaceutical industry (in $US mn)

|  | 2000 | 2001 | 2002 | 2003 | 2004 | 2005 | 2006 |
|---|---|---|---|---|---|---|---|
| **Revenues** | | | | | | | |
| AstraZeneca plc | 19,200 | 16,480 | 17,841 | 18,849 | 21,426 | 23,950 | 26,475 |
| GlaxoSmithKline plc | 23,074 | 25,021 | 28,963 | 32,439 | 32,852 | 32,075 | 39,334 |
| Johnson & Johnson | 11,954 | 14,851 | 17,151 | 19,517 | 22,128 | 22,322 | 23,267 |
| Merck & Co. Inc. | 23,320 | 19,732 | 20,130 | 21,038 | 21,494 | 20,679 | 20,375 |
| Novartis | 11,202 | 12,159 | 15,183 | 16,020 | 18,497 | 20,515 | 23,000 |
| Pfizer | 24,027 | 26,949 | 29,843 | 39,631 | 46,133 | 44,284 | 45,083 |
| Weighted average sales growth | | 2.1% | 12.1% | 22.1% | 53.6% | 6.0% | 11.2% |
| **EBIT** | | | | | | | |
| AstraZeneca plc | 4,008 | 3,954 | 4,356 | 4,202 | 4,770 | 6,502 | 8,216 |
| GlaxoSmithKline plc | 6,455 | 6,256 | 8,157 | 10,348 | 10,400 | 10,586 | 13,958 |
| Johnson & Johnson | 4,175 | 4,928 | 5,787 | 5,896 | 7,376 | 6,365 | 6,894 |
| Merck & Co. Inc. | 11,564 | 12,200 | 12,723 | 13,250 | 13,507 | 13,158 | 13,649 |
| Novartis | 3,334 | 3,420 | 4,353 | 4,423 | 5,253 | 6,014 | 6,703 |
| Pfizer | 8,859 | 10,936 | 12,920 | 6,837 | 21,510 | 19,594 | 20,718 |
| Weighted average EBIT margin | 34.0% | 36.2% | 37.4% | 30.5% | 35.0% | 34.2% | 34.8% |
| **Net Operating Assets** | | | | | | | |
| AstraZeneca plc | na | na | 21,576 | 23,573 | 25,616 | 24,840 | 29,932 |
| GlaxoSmithKline plc | 29,017 | 26,278 | 29,950 | 33,927 | 36,165 | 28,242 | 33,179 |
| Johnson & Johnson | 9,209 | 10,591 | 11,112 | 15,351 | 16,058 | 16,091 | 18,799 |
| Merck & Co. Inc. | na | na | na | na | na | na | na |
| Novartis | 10,423 | 11,225 | 12,118 | 13,836 | 14,914 | 14,655 | 20,418 |
| Pfizer | 15,854 | 16,881 | 18,541 | 81,522 | 81,651 | 74,406 | 72,497 |
| Weighted average revenues to net operating assets | 1.09 | 1.22 | 1.17 | 0.75 | 0.81 | 0.90 | 0.90 |

Notes: Data are actual reported segment data reported at each year end. Changes in the performance measures therefore include the effect of any acquisitions or divestitures, such as Pfizer's acquisition of Pharmacia in mid-2003. EBIT are earnings before interest and taxes. Net operating assets are operating assets less non-interest-bearing liabilities.

Source: Standard & Poor's Capital IQ data.

**EXHIBIT 6**  Performance of key competitors in the generics industry (in $US mn)

| | 2000 | 2001 | 2002 | 2003 | 2004 | 2005 | 2006 |
|---|---|---|---|---|---|---|---|
| **Revenues** | | | | | | | |
| Novartis | 1,973 | 2,433 | 2,809 | 2,906 | 3,045 | 4,712 | 5,983 |
| Teva Pharmaceutical Inds. Ltd. | 1,548 | 1,838 | 2,240 | 2,885 | 4,276 | 4,703 | 7,821 |
| Watson Pharmaceuticals Inc. | 423 | 552 | 650 | 749 | 1,239 | 1,247 | 1,517 |
| Weighted average sales growth rate | | 22.3% | 18.2% | 14.8% | 30.9% | 24.6% | 43.7% |
| **EBIT** | | | | | | | |
| Novartis | 242 | 281 | 406 | 473 | 235 | 342 | 736 |
| Teva Pharmaceutical Inds. Ltd. | 223 | 297 | 427 | 692 | 307 | 981 | 372 |
| Watson Pharmaceuticals Inc. | na | na | na | na | na | 356 | 321 |
| Weighted average EBIT margin | 13.2% | 13.5% | 16.5% | 20.1% | 7.4% | 15.8% | 9.3% |
| **Net Operating Assets** | | | | | | | |
| Novartis | 2,575 | 3,362 | 4,673 | 4,321 | 5,379 | 14,057 | 15,009 |
| Teva Pharmaceutical Inds. Ltd. | 1,439 | 1,367 | 2,521 | 3,205 | 5,973 | 6,094 | na |
| Watson Pharmaceuticals Inc. | na | na | na | na | na | na | na |
| Weighted average revenues to net operating assets | 0.88 | 0.90 | 0.70 | 0.77 | 0.64 | 0.47 | 0.40 |

Notes: Data are actual reported segment data reported at each year end. Changes in the performance measures therefore include the effect of any acquisitions or divestitures, such as Novartis's acquisition of Hexal and Eon in mid-2005. EBIT are earnings before interest and taxes. Net operating assets are operating assets less non-interest-bearing liabilities.

Source: Standard & Poor's Capital IQ data.

**EXHIBIT 7**  Performance of key competitors in the consumer health industry (in $US mn)

|  | 2000 | 2001 | 2002 | 2003 | 2004 | 2005 | 2006 |
|---|---|---|---|---|---|---|---|
| **Revenues** | | | | | | | |
| GlaxoSmithKline plc | 3,963 | 4,776 | 5,178 | 5,817 | 6,156 | 5,155 | 6,165 |
| Johnson & Johnson | 6,904 | 6,320 | 6,564 | 7,431 | 8,333 | 9,096 | 9,774 |
| Novartis | 4,880 | 5,098 | 5,532 | 5,938 | 5,595 | 6,092 | 6,579 |
| Pfizer Animal Health | 5,547 | 5,310 | 2,530 | 4,640 | 5,469 | 6,084 | 2,311 |
| Reckit & Benkiser | na | 4,665 | 5,334 | 6,279 | 7,053 | 6,848 | 9,262 |
| Schering Plough (Consumer & Animal Health) | na | 1,341 | 1,412 | 1,662 | 1,855 | 1,944 | 2,033 |
| Average sales growth rate | | 1.0% | −3.5% | 19.6% | 8.5% | 2.2% | 2.6% |
| **EBIT** | | | | | | | |
| GlaxoSmithKline plc | 618 | 628 | 777 | 1,056 | 1,268 | 1,229 | 1,338 |
| Johnson & Johnson | 867 | 1,004 | 1,229 | 1,393 | 1,444 | 1,592 | 1,374 |
| Novartis | 598 | 659 | 886 | 821 | 919 | 952 | 1,068 |
| Pfizer Animal Health | 813 | 787 | 546 | 671 | 1,019 | 1,103 | 419 |
| Reckitt & Benckiser | na | 675 | 861 | 1,140 | 1,358 | 1,363 | 1,979 |
| Schering Plough (Consumer & Animal Health) | | 281 | 267 | 195 | 322 | 355 | 348 |
| Weighted average EBIT margin | 13.6% | 14.7% | 17.2% | 16.6% | 18.4% | 18.7% | 18.1% |
| **Net Operating Assets** | | | | | | | |
| GlaxoSmithKline plc | 3,271 | 5,596 | 5,986 | 8,850 | 7,095 | 4,204 | 5,423 |
| Johnson & Johnson | 4,761 | 4,209 | 5,056 | 5,371 | 6,142 | 6,275 | 25,380 |
| Novartis | 4,688 | 4,576 | 5,136 | 5,417 | 6,155 | 6,863 | 6,480 |
| Pfizer Animal Health | 3,840 | 3,553 | 2,105 | 7,514 | 7,878 | 8,158 | 1,951 |
| Reckitt & Benckiser | na | na | na | na | 5,737 | 5,370 | 10,634 |
| Schering Plough (Consumer & Animal Health) | na | na | na | na | na | na | na |
| Weighted average revenues to net operating assets | 1.29 | 1.20 | 1.08 | 0.88 | 0.99 | 1.08 | 0.68 |

Notes: Data are actual reported segment data reported at each year end. Changes in the performance measures therefore include the effect of any acquisitions or divestitures, such as Proctor & Gamble's acquisition of Gillette in 2005, Pfizer's acquisition of its animal health business in 2003 and the sale of its consumer health business to Johnson & Johnson in 2006. Net operating assets are operating assets less non-interest-bearing liabilities. EBIT are earnings before interest and taxes.

Source: Standard & Poor's Capital IQ data.

**EXHIBIT 8** Performance of key competitors in the vaccines and diagnostics industry (in $US mn)

| | 2000 | 2001 | 2002 | 2003 | 2004 | 2005 | 2006 |
|---|---|---|---|---|---|---|---|
| **Revenues** | | | | | | | |
| Abbot Labs Vaccines | 2,924 | 2,929 | 2,897 | 3,040 | 3,378 | 3,756 | 3,979 |
| J&J Medical Devices & Diagnostics | 10,281 | 11,146 | 12,583 | 14,914 | 16,887 | 19,096 | 20,283 |
| Merck Vaccines | na | na | na | na | 973 | 984 | 1,706 |
| Novartis | na | na | na | na | na | na | 1,187 |
| Sanofi-Aventis Vaccines | na | na | na | na | 925 | 2,512 | 3,436 |
| Weighted average sales growth rate | 33.2% | 6.6% | 10.0% | 16.0% | 12.9% | 18.9% | 11.6% |
| **EBIT** | | | | | | | |
| Abbot Labs Vaccines | 331 | 357 | 220 | 249 | 378 | 495 | 431 |
| J&J Medical Devices & Diagnostics | 1,696 | 2,001 | 2,489 | 3,370 | 3,924 | 5,240 | 6,126 |
| Merck Vaccines | na | na | na | na | 881 | 767 | 893 |
| Novartis | na | na | na | na | na | na | (26) |
| Sanofi-Aventis Vaccines | na | na | na | na | (1,374) | 220 | 673 |
| Weighted average EBIT margin | 15.4% | 16.8% | 17.5% | 20.2% | 17.2% | 25.5% | 26.5% |
| **Net Operating Assets** | | | | | | | |
| Abbot Labs Vaccines | na | na | na | na | 3,691 | 3,742 | 4,073 |
| J&J Medical Devices & Diagnostics | 12,745 | 13,645 | 15,052 | 16,082 | 15,805 | 16,540 | 18,601 |
| Merck Vaccines | na | na | na | na | na | na | na |
| Novartis | na | na | na | na | na | na | 5,609 |
| Sanofi-Aventis Vaccines | na | na | na | na | 7,099 | 8,130 | 8,582 |
| Weighted average sales to net operating assets | 0.81 | 0.82 | 0.84 | 0.93 | 0.80 | 0.89 | 0.78 |

Notes: Data are actual reported segment data reported at each year end. Changes in the performance measures therefore include the effect of any acquisitions or divestitures, such as Novartis's acquisition of Chiron in 2006 and Sanofi's acquisition of Aventis in 2004. Net operating assets are operating assets less non-interest-bearing liabilities. EBIT are earnings before interest and taxes.

Source: Standard & Poor's Capital IQ data.

**EXHIBIT 9** Health care industry and Novartis valuation multiples for the period 2003 to 2006

| | 2003 | 2004 | 2005 | 2006 |
|---|---|---|---|---|
| **Health care Industry** | | | | |
| Price-to-earnings multiple | 47.8 | 40.1 | 34.4 | 33.0 |
| Price-to-book multiple | 6.0 | 4.7 | 4.3 | 4.0 |
| Return on equity % | 13.3% | 12.7% | 12.7% | 13.4% |
| Revenue growth % | 14.4% | 13.6% | 8.8% | 16.0% |
| Earnings growth | 26.5% | 19.1% | 12.6% | 21.7% |
| **Novartis AG** | | | | |
| Price to Earnings Multiple | 22.9 | 21.2 | 21.0 | 19.4 |
| Price to Book Multiple | 3.4 | 3.3 | 3.9 | 3.3 |

Note: Multiples are based on year-end financial information and stock price data from March 31 the following year.

Source: Standard & Poor's Capital IQ data.

**EXHIBIT 10** Valuation and multiples for leading pharmaceutical companies based on financial statement data for fiscal year-end 2006 and stock price data on March 31, 2007

| Company | Stock Price ($US) | Market Equity Capitalization ($US mn) | Enterprise Value ($US mn) | Book Equity | Price-Book Multiple | Diluted EPS ($US) | PE Multiple | ROE | Beta |
|---|---|---|---|---|---|---|---|---|---|
| Johnson & Johnson | 60.26 | 174,451 | 176,960 | 39,318 | 4.4 | 3.734 | 16.1 | 28.3% | 0.33 |
| Pfizer Inc. | 25.26 | 178,761 | 159,169 | 71,217 | 2.5 | 1.515 | 16.7 | 16.1% | 0.69 |
| Roche Holding AG | 177.64 | 153,227 | 146,024 | 32,590 | 4.7 | 7.46 | 23.8 | 21.6% | 0.16 |
| GlaxoSmithKline plc | 27.37 | 153,337 | 158,650 | 18,388 | 8.3 | 1.85 | 14.8 | 64.6% | 0.27 |
| Novartis AG | 57.59 | 135,233 | 134,780 | 41,111 | 3.3 | 2.962 | 19.4 | 17.5% | 0.33 |
| Merck & Co. Inc. | 44.17 | 95,848 | 96,377 | 17,560 | 5.5 | 2.027 | 21.8 | 25.0% | 0.96 |
| Weighted average | | | | | 4.7 | | 18.4 | 24.1% | 0.43 |

Notes: Market capitalization is the stock price multiplied by the number of shares outstanding. Earnings per share are diluted earnings per share excluding extraordinary items. Enterprise value is the market equity capitalization plus the book value of interest-bearing debt and minority interest, less cash and marketable securities and earnings. ROE is net income as a percentage of average book equity. Beta is the systematic risk of the stock, estimated by regressing the firm's stock for the previous 36 months on the S&P 500 index returns. The weighted average price-book and PE multiples are weighted by the market capitalizations of the firms, whereas the weighted ROE is weighted by their relative book equity values. Data for Glaxo-SmithKline plc and Roche Holding AG are translated into $US using exchange rates on March 31, 2007.

Source: Standard & Poor's Capital IQ data.

# 10 Credit analysis and distress prediction

Credit analysis is the evaluation of a firm from the perspective of a holder or potential holder of its debt, including trade payables, loans, and public debt securities. A key element of credit analysis is the prediction of the likelihood a firm will face financial distress. Credit analysis is involved in a wide variety of decision contexts:

- A commercial banker asks: Should we extend a loan to this firm? If so, how should it be structured? How should it be priced?
- If the loan is granted, the banker must later ask: Are we still providing the services, including credit, that this firm needs? Is the firm still in compliance with the loan terms? If not, is there a need to restructure the loan, and if so, how? Is the situation serious enough to call for accelerating the repayment of the loan?
- A potential investor asks: Are these debt securities a sound investment? What is the probability that the firm will face distress and default on the debt? Does the yield provide adequate compensation for the default risk involved?
- An investor contemplating purchase of debt securities in default asks: How likely is it that this firm can be turned around? In light of the high yield on this debt relative to its current price, can I accept the risk that the debt will not be repaid in full?
- A potential supplier asks: Should I sell products or services to this firm? The associated credit will be extended only for a short period, but the amount is large, and I should have some assurance that collection risks are manageable.

Finally, there are third parties – those other than borrowers and lenders – who are interested in the general issue of how likely it is that a firm will avoid financial distress:

- An auditor asks: How likely is it that this firm will survive beyond the short run? In evaluating the firm's financials, should I consider it a going concern?
- An actual or potential employee asks: How confident can I be that this firm will be able to offer employment over the long term?
- A potential customer asks: What assurance is there that this firm will survive to provide warranty services, replacement parts, product updates, and other services?
- A competitor asks: Will this firm survive the current industry shakeout? What are the implications of potential financial distress at this firm for my pricing and market share?

This chapter develops a framework to evaluate a firm's creditworthiness and assess the likelihood of financial distress.

## Why do firms use debt financing?

Before discussing the credit market and credit analysis, it is worth understanding why firms use debt financing. Debt financing is attractive to firms for two key reasons:

- Corporate interest tax shields. In many countries tax laws provide for the corporate tax deductibility of interest paid on debt. No such corporate tax shield is available for dividend payments or retained earnings. Therefore corporate tax benefits should encourage firms with high effective tax rates and few forms of tax shields other than interest to favour debt financing.

- Management incentives for value creation. Firms with relatively high leverage face pressures to generate cash flows to meet payments of interest and principal, reducing resources available to fund unjustifiable expenses and investments that do not maximize shareholder value. Debt financing therefore focuses management on value creation, reducing conflicts of interest between managers and shareholders.

However, in addition to these **benefits of debt**, there are also **costs of debt** financing. As a firm increases its use of debt financing, it increases the likelihood of financial distress, where it is unable to meet interest or principal repayment obligations to creditors. When a firm is in serious financial distress, its owners' claims are likely to be restructured. This can take place under formal bankruptcy proceedings or out of bankruptcy, depending on the jurisdiction in which the firm operates. Financial distress has multiple negative consequences for the firm:

- Legal costs of financial distress. Restructurings are likely to be costly, since the parties involved have to hire lawyers, bankers, and accountants to represent their interests, and to pay court costs if there are formal legal proceedings. These are often called the direct costs of financial distress.
- Costs of foregone investment opportunities. Distressed firms face significant challenges in raising capital, as potential new investors and creditors will be wary of becoming embroiled in the firm's legal disputes. Thus firms in distress are often unable to finance new investments even though they may be profitable for its owners.
- Costs of conflicts between creditors and shareholders. When faced with financial distress, creditors focus on the firm's ability to service its debt while shareholders worry that their equity will revert to the creditors if the firm defaults. Thus managers face increased pressure to make decisions that typically serve the interests of the stockholders, and creditors react by increasing the costs of borrowing for the firm's stockholders.

## Debt Financing and Free Cash Flow

The debt introduced as a result of leveraged buyouts (LBOs) is viewed by many as an example of debt creating pressure for management to refocus on value creation for shareholders. The increased debt taken with the LBO forces management to eliminate unnecessary perks, to limit diversification into unrelated industries, and to cancel unprofitable projects. For example, in 2017 the German pharmaceutical company Stada – a specialist in the production of generic drugs – was being acquired for €4.3 billion by private equity firms Bain and Cinven, in one of the largest European leveraged buyout deals in five years. The funds used to finance this large leveraged buyout included €825 million of high-yield bonds, €400 million of revolving loans, and €1.95 billion of syndicated loans. Stada had the typical characteristics of a leveraged buyout target. The generic drugs producer operated in a mature, competitive industry and had relatively stable cash flows, but was being accused by an activist investor of underperforming and having weak corporate governance.

Financial ratio and prospective analysis can help analysts assess whether there are currently free cash flow inefficiencies at a firm as well as risks of future inefficiencies. Symptoms of excessive management perks and investment in unprofitable projects include the following:

- *High ratios of general and administrative expenses and overhead to revenue.* If a firm's ratios are higher than those for its major competitors, one possibility is that management is wasting money on perks.
- *Significant new investments in unrelated areas.* If it is difficult to rationalize these new investments, there might be free cash flow problems.
- *High levels of expected operating cash flows (net of essential capital expenditures and debt retirements) from pro forma income and cash flow statements.*
- *Poor management incentives to create additional shareholder value,* evidenced by a weak linkage between management compensation and firm performance.

Firms are more likely to fall into financial distress if they have high business risks and their assets are easily destroyed in financial distress. For example, firms with human capital and brand intangibles are particularly sensitive to financial distress since dissatisfied employees and customers can leave or seek alternative suppliers. In contrast, firms with tangible assets can sell their assets if they get into financial distress, providing additional security for lenders and lowering the costs of financial distress. Firms with intangible assets are therefore less likely to be highly leveraged than firms whose assets are mostly tangible.

The preceding discussion implies that a firm's long-term decisions on the use of debt financing reflect a trade-off between the corporate interest tax shield and incentive benefits of debt against the costs of financial distress. As the firm becomes more highly leveraged, the costs of leverage presumably begin to outweigh the tax and monitoring benefits of debt.

Table 10.1 shows median leverage ratios for publicly traded stocks in selected industries for the fiscal years 1998–2017. Median ratios are reported for all listed companies and for large companies (with market capitalizations greater than €300 million) only.

Median debt-to-book equity ratios are highest for the electric services and auto leasing industries, which are typically not highly sensitive to economy risk and whose core assets are primarily physical equipment and property that are readily transferable to debt holders in the event of financial distress. In contrast, the software and pharmaceutical industries' core assets are their research staffs and sales force representatives. These types of assets can easily be lost if the firm gets into financial difficulty as a result of too much leverage. In all likelihood management would be forced to cut back on R&D and marketing, allowing their most talented researchers and sales representatives to be subject to offers from competitors. To reduce these risks, firms in these industries have relatively conservative capital structures.[1] Construction and air transportation firms have leverage in between these extremes, reflecting the need to balance the impact of having extensive physical assets and being subject to more volatile revenue streams.

It is also interesting to note that large firms tend to have higher leverage than small firms in the same industries. This probably reflects the fact that larger firms tend to have more product offerings and to be more diversified geographically, reducing their vulnerability to negative events for a single product or market, and enabling them to take on more debt.

TABLE 10.1  Median interest-bearing debt-to-book equity and interest-bearing debt-to-market equity for selected European industries in 1998–2017

| | Interest-bearing debt-to-book equity | |
|---|---|---|
| Industry | All listed firms | Large listed firms |
| Computer programming and data processing | 19% | 27% |
| Pharmaceutical | 35% | 38% |
| Air transportation | 89% | 103% |
| Heavy construction | 91% | 147% |
| Electric services | 117% | 136% |
| Truck, auto rental, and leasing | 189% | 207% |

# The market for credit

An understanding of **credit analysis** requires an appreciation of the various players in the market for credit. We now briefly describe the major **suppliers of debt financing**.

## COMMERCIAL BANKS

Commercial banks are very important players in the market for credit. Since banks tend to provide a range of services to a client and have intimate knowledge of the client and its operations, they have a comparative advantage in extending credit in settings where (1) knowledge gained through close contact with management reduces the perceived riskiness of the credit and (2) credit risk can be contained through careful monitoring of the firm. This is even more so in countries where commercial banks also provide investment banking services to their clients. Examples of investment banking services are asset management, investment advice, and the underwriting of clients' securities. Banks that engage in investment banking sometimes hold substantial equity stakes in other companies, including their clients' operations. The combination of commercial banking and investment banking services, which is called universal banking, therefore not only helps banks to become better informed about their clients' operations but also makes banks more influential over their clients through the equity stakes that they control. Following the global financial crisis of 2008, the universal banking model came under pressure as a result of stricter capital requirements and regulatory pressure to make banks simpler.[2]

Bank lending operations are constrained by a low tolerance for risk to ensure that the overall loan portfolio will be of acceptably high quality to bank regulators. Because of the importance of maintaining public confidence in the banking sector and the desire to shield government deposit insurance from risk, governments have incentives to constrain banks' exposure to credit risk. Banks also tend to shield themselves from the risk of shifts in interest rates by avoiding fixed-rate loans with long maturities. Because banks' capital mostly comes from short-term deposits, such long-term loans leave them exposed to increases in interest rates, unless the risk can be hedged with derivatives. Thus banks are less likely to play a role when a firm requires a very long-term commitment to financing. However, in some cases banks place the debt with investors looking for longer-term credit exposure.

## NON-BANK FINANCIAL INSTITUTIONS

Banks face competition in the commercial lending market from a variety of sources. Finance companies compete with banks in the market for asset-based lending (i.e., the secured financing of specific assets such as receivables, inventory, or equipment). Insurance companies are also involved in a variety of lending activities. Since life insurance companies face obligations of a long-term nature, they often seek investments of long duration (e.g., long-term bonds or loans to support large, long-term commercial property and development projects). Investment bankers are prepared to place debt securities with private investors or in the public markets (discussed next). Various government agencies are another source of credit.

## PUBLIC DEBT MARKETS

Some firms have the size, strength, and credibility necessary to bypass the banking sector and seek financing directly from investors, either through sales of commercial paper or through the issuance of bonds. Such debt issues are facilitated by the assignment of a **public debt rating**, which measures the underlying credit strength of the firm and determines the yield that must be offered to investors.

Banks often provide financing in tandem with a public debt issue or other source of financing. In highly levered transactions, such as leveraged buyouts, banks commonly provide financing along with public debt that has a lower priority in case of bankruptcy. The bank's "senior financing" would typically be scheduled for earlier retirement than the public debt, and it would carry a lower yield. For smaller or start-up firms, banks often provide credit in conjunction with equity financing from venture capitalists. Note that in the case of both the leveraged buyout and the start-up company, the bank helps provide the cash needed to make the deal happen, but it does so in a way that shields it from risks that would be unacceptably high in the banking sector.

## SELLERS WHO PROVIDE FINANCING

Another sector of the market for credit is manufacturers and other suppliers of goods and services. As a matter of course, such firms tend to finance their customers' purchases on an unsecured basis for periods of 30 to 60 days. Suppliers will on occasion also agree to provide more extended financing, usually with the support of a secured note. A supplier may be willing to grant such a loan in the expectation that the creditor will survive a cash shortage and remain an important customer in the future. However, the customer would typically seek such an arrangement only if bank financing is unavailable because doing so could constrain flexibility in selecting among and/or negotiating with suppliers.

# Country differences in debt financing

## COUNTRY FACTORS AND CREDIT TYPES

The preceding described suppliers of credit are not equally important in every country. One source of differences across countries is the extent to which national bankruptcy laws protect credit providers. A stylized classification of bankruptcy laws involves two groups: laws that provide extensive creditor protection in the case of default versus laws that are oriented towards keeping the company in default a going concern and shielding the company from the influence of creditors. The former types of laws typically offer creditors a first right to repossess collateral and enforce other contractual rights when their borrower is in default. These laws therefore increase the probability that creditors recover their loans but reduce the probability that borrowers survive bankruptcy. The latter types of laws typically impose court-administered bankruptcy procedures on the borrower in default and its creditors as well as an automatic stay on the borrower's assets. An automatic stay on the assets means that creditors cannot repossess their collateral during the period in which the borrower's financial obligations are being restructured. The United Kingdom is an example of a European country that has strong creditor protection laws. Examples of European countries that have weak creditor protection laws, or borrower-friendly bankruptcy laws, are France, Italy, and Portugal. Germany takes a position in between these two extremes. In Germany courts impose bankruptcy procedures on the borrower and its creditors, but there is no automatic stay on the borrower's assets, and creditors have considerable influence on the borrower's reorganization process.[3]

The orientation of a country's bankruptcy laws can affect the characteristics of credit provided in various ways. A few examples of how legal differences matter are the following:

● Multiple-bank borrowing. In countries where the legal rights of banks are weakly protected and banks experience difficulties in repossessing collateral when a borrower defaults, they are likely to be hesitant in extending long-term credit. As an alternative, companies may borrow smaller proportions of debt from multiple banks. Because it is more difficult for a company in default to renegotiate its loans with multiple banks than with one bank, multiple-bank borrowing reduces the company's incentive to strategically default. Research has found that multiple-bank borrowing is most common in Belgium, France, Italy, Spain, and Portugal, where banks are indeed weakly protected in case of bankruptcy.[4]

● Supplier financing. Supplier financing is also an efficient alternative form of debt financing when creditor rights are weakly protected.[5] A reason for this is that suppliers are often well informed about their debtors' operations and they have a straightforward way to discipline their debtors. That is, in case of default of payment, suppliers can repossess the delivered goods and withhold future deliveries. In fiscal year 2017 public companies in Belgium, France, Italy, Spain, and Portugal had an average payables-to-revenue ratio of 18.4 percent. The ratio ranged from 16.3 percent in Belgium to 23.4 percent in Italy. In contrast, public companies in Denmark, Finland, Germany, the Netherlands, Norway, Sweden, Switzerland, and the United Kingdom had an average payables-to-revenue ratio of 10.3 percent.

● Off-balance sheet financing. Research has indicated that in countries where companies' access to bank debt is restricted or relatively expensive, companies may also resort to off-balance sheet financing.[6] One example of off-balance sheet financing is the factoring of receivables, where companies sell their customer receivables to a lender at a discount. In the first half of the 2000s, the use of factoring was fastest growing in Eastern Europe, where bankruptcy laws were weak. Further, companies in Italy made relatively more use of factoring than companies in other parts of Europe.

- Public debt. Public debt markets are also not equally developed in all parts of the world. Table 10.2 shows the average annual total proceeds of public debt issues (made by publicly listed non-financial companies) as a percentage of Gross Domestic Product (GDP) or total equity market capitalization in 12 European countries during the period 2005 to 2014. These percentages show that publicly listed non-financial companies issued comparatively more public debt in Belgium, France, and Italy, suggesting that public debt is sometimes used as an alternative to bank debt in countries with borrower-friendly bankruptcy laws.

**TABLE 10.2** Public debt issues in 12 European countries (2005–2014)

| Country | Average annual total proceeds as a percentage of GDP | Average annual total proceeds as a percentage of total equity market capitalization |
|---|---|---|
| Belgium | 2.89% | 7.56% |
| Denmark | 0.58% | 1.29% |
| Finland | 1.46% | 2.10% |
| France | 2.34% | 4.45% |
| Germany | 0.52% | 1.87% |
| Italy | 1.02% | 5.56% |
| Netherlands | 0.93% | 2.19% |
| Portugal | 0.20% | 0.79% |
| Spain | 0.38% | 0.94% |
| Sweden | 0.59% | 0.90% |
| Switzerland | 0.81% | 0.57% |
| UK | 0.94% | 1.19% |

Source: SDC Global New Issues database and Compustat Global.

## COUNTRY FACTORS AND THE OPTIMAL MIX OF DEBT AND EQUITY

In summary, the preceding discussion shows that in countries with borrower-friendly, creditor-unfriendly bankruptcy laws:

- Creditors extend more short-term debt because this allows them to frequently review the borrower's financial position and adjust the terms of the loan when necessary.
- Companies make greater use of supplier financing.
- Companies make greater use of off-balance sheet financing such as the factoring of customer receivables.
- Public debt markets tend to be more developed.

The net effect of these country differences in loan maturity, off-balance sheet financing, supplier financing, and public debt markets' importance on country differences in leverage is unfortunately anything but straightforward. For example, we showed that Belgian, French, and Italian companies have, on average, greater amounts of trade payables on their balance sheets. In these three countries, however, equity markets are still not as well developed as in some other parts of Europe. Thus supplier financing might just as well serve as a substitute for long-term debt and equity, leaving the debt-to-capital ratio unchanged.

To provide a rough indication of how the mix of debt and equity financing varies across Europe, Table 10.3 shows median debt-to-equity, cash-to-equity, and net debt-to-equity ratios for 13 European countries in 2017. Denmark, Sweden, Switzerland, and the United Kingdom tend to have the lowest net debt-to-equity ratios. Cash and marketable securities holdings of the median company in these countries tend to be close to the book value of its interest-bearing debt. Maybe surprisingly, the net interest-bearing debt-to-equity ratios are highest in countries with borrower-friendly, creditor-unfriendly bankruptcy laws, such as Italy, Portugal, and Spain. Two reasons may explain this.

First, in countries where bankruptcy laws shield management from its creditors in situations of financial distress, the threat of creditors intervening in the company's operations and repossessing collateral is less severe. Consequently, managers in these countries may feel comfortable with taking on more debt. As argued, despite being weakly protected, creditors are willing to extend debt because they can force borrowers to borrow smaller proportions of debt from multiple banks and can choose to extend loans with short maturities.

Second, the net debt-to-equity ratios are lowest in the countries where equity markets are most developed, such as the United Kingdom and Switzerland. Companies from these countries can more easily use equity financing as an alternative to debt financing than companies from countries with weakly developed equity markets, such as Portugal and Italy.

**TABLE 10.3**  Median cash and marketable securities holdings and leverage for 13 European countries in 2017

| Country | Interest-bearing debt-to-book equity (%) | Cash and cash equivalents-to-book equity (%) | Net interest-bearing debt-to-book equity (%) | Net interest-bearing debt-to-market equity (%) |
|---|---|---|---|---|
| Portugal | 124 | 20 | 108 | 121 |
| Spain | 107 | 24 | 74 | 31 |
| Italy | 84 | 29 | 54 | 30 |
| Belgium | 67 | 21 | 53 | 24 |
| France | 64 | 34 | 32 | 13 |
| Netherlands | 64 | 23 | 43 | 14 |
| Finland | 57 | 23 | 31 | 14 |
| Germany | 57 | 27 | 27 | 11 |
| Norway | 56 | 28 | 33 | 16 |
| Switzerland | 44 | 27 | 8 | 1 |
| Sweden | 38 | 20 | 21 | 8 |
| Denmark | 36 | 16 | 22 | 9 |
| UK | 33 | 22 | 18 | 8 |

## The credit analysis process in private debt markets

Credit analysis is more than just establishing the creditworthiness of a firm, that is, its ability to pay its debts at the scheduled times. The decision to extend credit is not a binary one – the firm's exact value, its upside potential, and its distance from the threshold of creditworthiness are all equally important. There are ranges of creditworthiness, and it is important for purposes of pricing and structuring a loan to understand where a firm lies within that range. While downside risk must be the primary consideration in credit analysis, a firm with growth potential offers opportunities for future income-generating financial services from a continuing relationship.

This broader view of credit analysis involves most of the issues already discussed in the prior chapters on business strategy analysis, accounting analysis, financial analysis, and prospective analysis. Perhaps the greatest difference is that credit analysis rarely involves any explicit attempt to estimate the value of the firm's equity. However, the determinants of that value are relevant in credit analysis because a larger equity cushion translates into lower risk for the creditor.

Next we describe a representative but comprehensive series of steps that are used by commercial lenders in credit analysis. However, not all credit providers follow these guidelines. For example, when compared to a banker, manufacturers conduct a less extensive analysis on their customers, since the credit is very short-term and the manufacturer is willing to bear some credit risk in the interest of generating a profit on the sale.

We present the steps in a particular order, but they are in fact all interdependent. Thus analysis at one step may need to be rethought depending on the analysis at some later step.

## STEP 1: CONSIDER THE NATURE AND PURPOSE OF THE LOAN

Understanding the purpose of a loan is important not just for deciding whether it should be granted but also for structuring the loan based on duration, purpose, and size. Loans might be required for only a few months, for several years, or even as a permanent part of a firm's capital structure. Loans might be used for replacement of other financing, to support working capital needs, or to finance the acquisition of long-term assets or another firm.

The required amount of the loan must also be established. When bankruptcy laws provide a bank sufficient protection, it would typically prefer to be the sole financier of small and medium-sized companies. This preference is not only to gain an advantage in providing a menu of financial services to the firm but also to maintain a superior interest in case of bankruptcy. If other creditors are willing to subordinate their positions to the bank, that would of course be acceptable so far as the bank is concerned.

Often the commercial lender deals with firms that may have parent-subsidiary relations, posing the question of the appropriate counterparty. In general, the entity that owns the assets that will serve as collateral (or that could serve as such if needed in the future) acts as the borrower. If this entity is the subsidiary and the parent presents some financial strength independent of the subsidiary, a guarantee of the parent could be considered.

National bankruptcy laws in the country where the potential borrower is located also affect the maturity of the loan. When the bankruptcy laws provide weak protection to the credit provider, it may decide only to extend a loan with a short maturity. Short-term loans carry the advantage that the lender can frequently review the borrower and make adjustments to the terms of the loan when necessary.[7] Commercial lenders are inclined to shorten loan maturities, especially when lending to firms with little collateral, such as in tangible-intensive firms.[8]

## STEP 2: CONSIDER THE TYPE OF LOAN AND AVAILABLE SECURITY

The type of loan is a function of not only its purpose but also the financial strength of the borrower. Thus, to some extent, the loan type will be dictated by the financial analysis described in step 3. Some of the possibilities are as follows:

- Open line of credit. An open line of credit permits the borrower to receive cash up to some specified maximum on an as-needed basis for a specified term, such as one year. To maintain this option, the borrower pays a fee (e.g., 3/8 of 1 percent) on the unused balance, in addition to the interest on any used amount. An open line of credit is useful in cases where the borrower's cash needs are difficult to anticipate.

- Revolving line of credit. When it is clear that a firm will need credit beyond the short run, financing may be provided in the form of a "revolver." The terms of a revolver, which is sometimes used to support working capital needs, require the borrower to make payments as the operating cycle proceeds and inventory and receivables are converted to cash. However, it is also expected that cash will continue to be advanced so long as the borrower remains in good standing. In addition to interest on amounts outstanding, a fee is charged on the unused line.
- Working capital loan. Such a loan is used to finance inventory and receivables, and it is usually secured. The maximum loan balance may be tied to the balance of the working capital accounts. For example, the loan may be allowed to rise to no more than 80 percent of receivables less than 60 days old.
- Term loan. Term loans are used for long-term needs and are often secured with long-term assets such as plant or equipment. Typically, the loan will be amortized, requiring periodic payments to reduce the loan balance.
- Mortgage loan. Mortgages support the financing of real estate, have long terms, and require periodic amortization of the loan balance.
- Lease financing. Lease financing can be used to facilitate the acquisition of any asset, but is most commonly used for equipment, including vehicles and buildings. Leases may be structured over periods of one to 15 years, depending on the life of the underlying asset.

Much bank lending is done on a secured basis, especially with smaller and more highly leveraged companies. Security will be required unless the loan is short-term and the borrower exposes the bank to minimal default risk. When security is required, an important consideration is whether the amount of available security is sufficient to support the loan. The amount that a bank will lend on given security involves business judgment, and it depends on a variety of factors that affect the liquidity of the security in the context of a situation where the firm is distressed. It also depends on the extent to which creditor protection laws permit banks to quickly repossess collateral in the event of default. In countries where bankruptcy laws provide weak creditor protection, such as France, banks typically require more collateral for a given loan amount.[9] The following are some rules of thumb often applied in commercial lending to various categories of security:

- Receivables. Trade receivables are usually considered the most desirable form of security because they are the most liquid. An average bank allows loans of 50 to 80 percent of the balance of nondelinquent accounts. The percentage applied is lower when:

  1  There are many small accounts that would be costly to collect in case the firm is distressed.
  2  There are a few very large accounts, such that problems with a single customer could be serious.
  3  Bankruptcy laws are creditor-unfriendly and preclude the bank claiming and collecting the receivables while the borrower in default is being restructured.
  4  The customer's financial health is closely related to that of the borrower, so that collectibility is endangered just when the borrower is in default.

  On the latter score, banks often refuse to accept receivables from affiliates as effective security.
- Inventory. The desirability of inventory as security varies widely. The best-case scenario is inventory consisting of a common commodity that can easily be sold to other parties if the borrower defaults. More specialized inventory, with appeal to only a limited set of buyers, or inventory that is costly to store or transport is less desirable. An average bank typically lends up to 60 percent on raw materials, 50 percent on finished goods, and 20 percent on work in process.
- Machinery and equipment. Machinery and equipment is less desirable as collateral. It is likely to be used, and it must be stored, insured, and marketed. Keeping the costs of these activities in mind, banks typically will lend only up to 50 percent of the estimated value of such assets in a forced sale such as an auction.

- Real estate. The value of real estate as collateral varies considerably. Banks will often lend up to 80 percent of the appraised value of readily saleable real estate. On the other hand, a factory designed for a unique purpose would be much less desirable.

Even when a loan is not secured initially, a bank can require a "negative pledge" on the firm's assets – a pledge that the firm will not use the assets as security for any other creditor. In that case, if the borrower begins to experience difficulty and defaults on the loan, and if there are no other creditors in the picture, the bank can demand the loan become secured if it is to remain outstanding.

## STEP 3: CONDUCT A FINANCIAL ANALYSIS OF THE POTENTIAL BORROWER

This portion of the analysis involves all the steps discussed in our chapters on business strategy analysis, accounting analysis, and financial analysis. The emphasis, however, is on the firm's ability to service the debt at the scheduled rate. All the factors that could impact that ability, such as the presence of off-balance sheet lease obligations and the sustainability of the firm's operating profit stream, need to be carefully examined. The focus of the analysis depends on the type of financing under consideration. For example, if a short-term loan is considered to support seasonal fluctuations in inventory, the emphasis would be on the ability of the firm to convert the inventory into cash on a timely basis. In contrast, a term loan to support plant and equipment must be made with confidence in the long-run earnings prospects of the firm. This step incorporates both an assessment of the potential borrower's financial status using ratio analysis and a forecast to determine future payment prospects.

### Ratio analysis

Ultimately, since the key issue in the financial analysis is the likelihood that cash flows will be sufficient to repay the loan, lenders focus much attention on solvency ratios: the magnitude of various measures of profits and cash flows relative to debt service and other requirements. Therefore ratio analysis from the perspective of a creditor differs somewhat from that of an owner. There is greater emphasis on cash flows and earnings available to *all* claimants (not just owners) *before* taxes (since interest is tax-deductible and paid out of pre-tax euros). The *funds flow coverage ratio* illustrates the creditor's perspective:

$$\text{Funds flow coverage} = \frac{\text{EBIT} + \text{Depreciation}}{\text{Interest} + \dfrac{\text{Debt repayment}}{(1 - \text{tax rate})} + \dfrac{\text{Preference dividends}}{(1 - \text{tax rate})}}$$

Earnings before both interest and taxes in the numerator are compared directly to the interest expense in the denominator, because interest expense is paid out of pre-tax euros. In contrast, any payment of principal scheduled for a given year is nondeductible and must be made out of after-tax profits. In essence, with a 50 percent tax rate, one euro of principal payment is "twice as expensive" as a one-euro interest payment. Scaling the payment of principal by (1 − tax rate) accounts for this. The same idea applies to preference dividends, which are not tax-deductible.

The funds flow coverage ratio provides an indication of how comfortably the funds flow can cover unavoidable expenditures. The ratio excludes payments such as dividend payments to ordinary shareholders and capital expenditures on the premise that they could be reduced to zero to make debt payments if necessary.[10] Clearly, however, if the firm is to survive in the long run, funds flow must be sufficient to not only service debt but also maintain plant assets. Thus long-run survival requires a funds flow coverage ratio well in excess of 1.[11]

To the extent that the ratio exceeds 1, it indicates the "margin of safety" the lender faces. When such a ratio is combined with an assessment of the variance in its numerator, it provides an indication of the probability of nonpayment. However, it would be overly simplistic to establish any particular threshold above which a ratio indicates a loan is justified. A creditor clearly wants to be in a position to be repaid on schedule, even when the borrower faces a reasonably foreseeable difficulty. That argues for lending only when the funds flow coverage is expected to exceed 1, even in a recession scenario – and higher if some allowance for capital expenditures is prudent.

The financial analysis should produce more than an assessment of the risk of nonpayment. It should also identify the nature of the significant risks. At many commercial banks it is standard operating procedure to summarize the analysis of the firm by listing the key risks that could lead to default and factors that could be used to control those risks if the loan were made. That information can be used in structuring the detailed terms of the loan so as to trigger default when problems arise, at a stage early enough to permit corrective action.

### Forecasting

Implicit in the discussion of ratio analysis is a forward-looking view of the firm's ability to service the loan. Good credit analysis should also be supported by explicit forecasts. The basis for such forecasts is usually management, though lenders perform their own tests as well. An essential element of this step is a sensitivity analysis to examine the ability of the borrower to service the debt under a variety of scenarios such as changes in the economy or in the firm's competitive position. Ideally, the firm should be strong enough to withstand the downside risks such as a drop in revenues or a decrease in profit margins.

At times it is possible to reconsider the structure of a loan so as to permit it to "cash flow." That is, the term of the loan might be extended or the amortization pattern changed. Often a bank will grant a loan with the expectation that it will be continually renewed, thus becoming a permanent part of the firm's financial structure (labelled an "evergreen" loan). In that case the loan will still be written as if it is due within the short term, and the bank must assure itself of a viable "exit strategy." However, the firm would be expected to service the loan by simply covering interest payments.

## STEP 4: ASSEMBLE THE DETAILED LOAN STRUCTURE, INCLUDING LOAN COVENANTS

If the analysis thus far indicates that a loan is in order, the final step is to assemble the detailed structure. Having previously determined the type of loan and repayment schedule, the focus shifts to the loan covenants and pricing.

### Writing loan covenants

Loan covenants specify mutual expectations of the borrower and lender by specifying actions the borrower will and will not take. Covenants generally fall into three categories:

1   Those that require certain actions such as regular provision of financial statements.
2   Those that preclude certain actions such as undertaking an acquisition without the permission of the lender.
3   Those that require maintenance of certain financial ratios.

Loan covenants must strike a balance between protecting the interests of the lender and providing the flexibility management needs to run the business. The covenants represent a mechanism for ensuring that the business will remain as strong as the two parties anticipated at the time the loan was granted.

The principal covenants that govern the management of the firm include restrictions on other borrowing, pledging assets to other lenders, selling substantial assets, engaging in mergers or acquisitions, and paying of dividends. The financial covenants should seek to address the significant risks identified in the financial analysis, or to at least provide early warning that such risks are surfacing. Some commonly used financial covenants include:

- Maintenance of minimum net worth. This covenant assures that the firm will maintain an "equity cushion" to protect the lender. Covenants typically require a level of net worth rather than a particular level of profit. In the final analysis, the lender may not care whether that net worth is maintained by generating profit, cutting dividends, or issuing new equity. Tying the covenant to net worth offers the firm the flexibility to use any of these avenues to avoid default.

- Minimum coverage ratio. Especially in the case of a long-term loan, such as a term loan, the lender may want to supplement a net worth covenant with one based on coverage of interest or total debt service. The preceding funds flow coverage ratio would be an example. Maintenance of some minimum coverage helps assure that the ability of the firm to generate funds internally is strong enough to justify the long-term nature of the loan.
- Maximum ratio of total liabilities to net worth. This ratio constrains the risk of high leverage and prevents growth without either retaining earnings or infusing equity.
- Minimum net working capital balance or current ratio. Constraints on this ratio force a firm to maintain its liquidity by using cash generated from operations to retire current liabilities (as opposed to acquiring long-lived assets).
- Maximum ratio of capital expenditures to earnings before depreciation. Constraints on this ratio help prevent the firm from investing in growth (including the illiquid assets necessary to support growth) unless such growth can be financed internally, with some margin remaining for debt service.

Required financial ratios are typically based on the levels that existed at the time that the agreement was executed, perhaps with some allowance for deterioration but often with some expected improvements over time. Violation of a covenant represents an event of default that could cause immediate acceleration of the debt payment, but in most cases the lender uses the default as an opportunity to re-examine the situation and either waive the violation or renegotiate the loan.

Covenants are included not only in private lending agreements but also in public debt agreements. However, public debt agreements tend to have less restrictive covenants for two reasons. First, since negotiations resulting from a violation of public debt covenants are costly (possibly involving not just the trustee, but bondholders as well), the covenants are written to be triggered only in serious circumstances. Second, public debt is usually issued by stronger, more creditworthy firms, though there is a large market for high-yield debt. For the most financially healthy firms with strong debt ratings, very few covenants will be used, generally only those necessary to limit dramatic changes in the firm's operations, such as a major merger or acquisition.

Dividend payout restrictions are not only included in debt contracts, but may also be mandated by law. For example, in several Continental European countries firms are legally obliged to transfer a proportion of their profits to a legal reserve, out of which they cannot distribute dividends. The law then prescribes the minimum legal reserve that a company must maintain.

### Loan pricing

A detailed discussion of loan pricing falls outside the scope of this text. The essence of pricing is to assure that the yield on the loan is sufficient to cover:

1 The lender's cost of borrowed funds.
2 The lender's costs of administering and servicing the loan.
3 A premium for exposure to default risk.
4 At least a normal return on the equity capital necessary to support the lending operation.

The price is often stated in terms of a deviation from a bank's base rate – the rate charged to stronger borrowers. For example, a loan might be granted at base rate plus 2 percent. An alternative base is LIBOR, or the London Interbank Offered Rate, the rate at which large banks from various nations lend large blocks of funds to each other.

Banks compete actively for commercial lending business, and it is rare that a yield includes more than two percentage points to cover the cost of default risk. If the spread to cover default risk is, say, 1 percent, and the bank recovers only 50 percent of amounts due on loans that turn out bad, then the bank can afford only 2 percent of its loans to fall into that category. This underscores how important it is for banks to conduct a thorough analysis and to contain the riskiness of their loan portfolio.

# Financial statement analysis and public debt

Fundamentally, the issues involved in analysis of public debt are no different from those of bank loans and other private debt issues. Institutionally, however, the contexts are different. Bankers can maintain very close relations with clients so as to form an initial assessment of their credit risk and monitor their activities during the loan period. In the case of public debt, the investors are distanced from the issuer. To a large extent, they must depend on professional debt analysts, including debt raters, to assess the riskiness of the debt and monitor the firm's ongoing activities. Such analysts and debt raters thus serve an important function in closing the information gap between issuers and investors.

## THE MEANING OF DEBT RATINGS

A firm's debt rating influences the yield that must be offered to sell the debt instruments. After the debt issue, the rating agencies continue to monitor the firm's financial condition. Changes in the rating are associated with fluctuation in the price of the securities. The three major debt rating agencies in the world are Moody's, Standard and Poor's, and Fitch Ratings.

Using Moody's labelling system, the highest possible rating is Aaa. Proceeding downwards from Aaa, the ratings are Aa, A, Baa, Ba, B, Caa, Ca, and C, where C indicates debt in default. Similarly, under Standard and Poor's labelling system, the highest possible rating is AAA, followed by AA, A, BBB, BB, B, CCC, CC, C, and D (where D indicates default). Table 10.4 presents examples of firms in rating categories AA (or Aa) through CCC (or Caa), as well as the average interest expense as a percentage of total debt across all firms in each category. As of early 2018, none of the European public non-financial companies rated by Standard and Poor's (S&P) had the financial strength to merit an AAA rating. Among the few that had an AAA rating but received a downgrade in 2007 or 2008 are the European firms Novartis and Nestle – both among the largest, most profitable firms in the world. AA firms are also very strong and include pharmaceuticals Novo Nordisk, Roche, and Sanofi. Firms rated AAA and AA have the lowest costs of debt financing; during the period 1998 to 2017 their average interest expense was roughly 3.5 percent of total debt.

TABLE 10.4  Debt ratings: European example firms and average interest expense by category

| S&P debt rating | Equivalent Moody's debt rating | European example firms early 2018 | Percentage of firms with same rating, 2013–2017 | Average (pre-tax) interest expense to debt, fiscal 1998–2017 |
|---|---|---|---|---|
| AA | Aa | Nestlé, Novartis, Novo Nordisk, Roche, Sanofi | 2.0% | 3.5% |
| A | A | Airbus, Anheuser-Busch InBev, Bayer, BMW, Daimler, Diageo, LVMH II, Royal Dutch Shell, Unilever | 16.3% | 3.6% |
| Baa | BBB | AstraZeneca, British American Tobacco, Continental, Enel, Groupe Danone, Heineken, Vodafone | 40.0% | 3.7% |
| BB | Ba | Fiat Chrysler, Nokia, Smurfit Kappa, Telecom Italia, Tesco, ThyssenKrupp | 25.2% | 4.8% |
| B | B | Hapag-LLoyd, NH Hotel Group, Thomas Cook | 13.7% | 6.3% |
| CCC | Caa | Astaldi, Deoleo, Public Power Corp | 2.9% | 6.7% |

Source: S&P, Moody's, and Compustat Global.

To be considered investment grade, a firm must achieve a rating of BBB (Baa) or higher. Many funds are precluded by their articles from investing in any bonds below that grade. Even to achieve a grade of BBB is difficult. Vodafone, one the largest telecommunications companies in Europe, was rated as "only" BBB, or barely investment grade in 2018. Car manufacturer Fiat Chrysler and paper and packaging companies Smurfit Kappa and Stora Enso were in the BB category. The B category included Hapag-LLoyd, NH Hotel Group, and Thomas Cook, all of which were facing financial difficulty. In Europe only a few of the industrial companies rated by S&P are in a category below the B category. An example of a firm that was rated CCC in 2018 is Spain-based olive oil processing company Deoleo, which had reported a series of losses, suffered from the effect of increasing olive oil prices, and was going through a financial restructuring to avoid bankruptcy.

Table 10.4 shows that the cost of debt financing rises markedly once firms' debt falls below investment grade. For example, between 1998 and 2017 the interest expenses of companies with BBB (Baa)-rated debt were 3.7 percent of debt, on average; interest rates for BB (Ba)-rated companies were 4.8 percent; and interest rates for firms with B-rated debt were 6.3 percent.

Table 10.5 shows median financial ratios for firms by debt rating category. Firms with AAA or AA ratings have very strong earnings and cash flow performance as well as minimal leverage. Firms in the BBB class are only moderately leveraged, with about 54 percent of capital coming in the form of debt. Earnings tend to be relatively strong, as indicated by an interest coverage (NOPAT plus NIPAT/ interest after tax) of 5.0 and a cash flow debt coverage (operating cash flow/ debt) of around 23 percent. Firms with B or CCC ratings (and lower), however, face significant risks: they typically report small profits or losses, have high leverage, and have interest coverage ratios close to 1.

**TABLE 10.5** Debt ratings: Median financial ratios by category

| S&P's debt rating | Median ratios for overall category between 1998 and 2017 (European non-financial companies only) | | | |
|---|---|---|---|---|
| | Return on invested capital (%) | Interest coverage (times) | Operating cash flow to debt (%) | Debt to capital (%) |
| AAA/AA | 9.6 | 10.0 | 40.7 | 43.3 |
| A | 8.8 | 5.9 | 26.0 | 52.6 |
| BBB | 7.6 | 5.0 | 23.4 | 53.5 |
| BB | 6.3 | 3.1 | 19.1 | 51.9 |
| B | 3.6 | 1.3 | 13.0 | 60.7 |
| <B | 0.7 | 0.5 | 9.5 | 65.1 |

Source: S&P and Compustat Global.
Interest coverage is calculated as NOPAT plus NIPAT to interest after tax.

## FACTORS THAT DRIVE DEBT RATINGS

Research demonstrates that some of the variation in debt ratings can be explained as a function of selected financial statement ratios, even as used within a quantitative model that incorporates no subjective human judgment. Some debt rating agencies rely heavily on quantitative models, and such models are commonly used by insurance companies, banks, and others to assist in the evaluation of the riskiness of debt issues for which a public rating is not available.

**TABLE 10.6** Factors used in quantitative models of debt ratings

|  | Firm 1 | Firm 2 | Firm 3 |
|---|---|---|---|
| *Profitability measures* | Return on net capital | Return on net capital | Return on net capital |
| *Leverage measures* | Non-current debt to capitalization | Non-current debt to capitalization Total debt to total capital | Non-current debt to capitalization |
| *Profitability and leverage* | Interest coverage Cash flow to non-current debt | Interest coverage Cash flow to non-current debt | Fixed charge coverage Coverage of current debt and fixed charges |
| *Firm size* | Revenue | Total assets |  |
| *Other* |  | Standard deviation of return Subordination status |  |

Table 10.6 lists the factors used by three different firms in their quantitative debt rating models. The firms include one insurance company and one bank, which use the models in their private placement activities, and an investment research firm, which employs the models in evaluating its own debt purchases and holdings. In each case profitability and leverage play an important role in the rating. Two firms also use firm size as an indicator, with larger size associated with higher ratings.

Several researchers have estimated quantitative models used for debt ratings. Two of these **debt rating prediction models**, developed by Kaplan and Urwitz and shown in Table 10.7, highlight the relative importance of the factors.[12] Model 1 has the greater ability to explain variation in bond ratings. However, it includes some factors based on equity market data, which are not available for all firms. Model 2 is based solely on financial statement data.

The factors in Table 10.7 are listed in the order of their statistical significance in Model 1. An interesting feature is that the most important factor explaining debt ratings is not a financial ratio at all – it is simply firm size! Large firms tend to get better ratings than small firms. Whether the debt is subordinated or unsubordinated is the next most important factor, followed by a leverage indicator. Profitability appears less important, but in part that reflects the presence in the model of multiple factors (ROA and interest coverage) that capture profitability. It is only the explanatory power that is *unique* to a given variable that is indicated by the ranking in Table 10.7. Explanatory power common to the two variables is not considered.

When applied to a sample of bonds that were not used in the estimation process, the Kaplan-Urwitz Model 1 predicted the rating category correctly in 44 of 64 cases, or 63 percent of the time. Where it erred, the model was never off by more than one category, and in about half of those cases its prediction was more consistent with the market yield on the debt than was the actual debt rating. The discrepancies between actual ratings and those estimated using the Kaplan-Urwitz model indicate that rating agencies incorporate factors other than financial ratios in their analysis. These are likely to include the types of strategic, accounting, and prospective analyses discussed throughout this book.

We have also estimated a debt ratings prediction model that is conceptually similar to the Kaplan-Urwitz model but includes the factors from Table 10.5 (plus firm size and performance volatility) as predictors. The sample of debt ratings that we used to estimate the model is a sample of 1,453 ratings of public debt securities of European non-financial companies that were issued by Standard & Poor's or Moody's (or outstanding) during the years 1998 to 2017. Table 10.8 lists the factors and their coefficients in order of their statistical significance. When applied to the sample of 1,453 European debt ratings, the model predicted the rating category correctly for 48 percent of the companies. The model was off by one category for 45 percent of the companies and off by two or three categories for 7 percent of the companies.

**TABLE 10.7** Kaplan-Urwitz models of debt ratings

| Firm or debt characteristic | Variable reflecting characteristic | Coefficients | |
|---|---|---|---|
| | | Model 1 | Model 2 |
| | Model intercept | 5.67 | 4.41 |
| *Firm size* | Total assets[a] | 0.0009 | 0.0010 |
| *Subordination status of debt* | 1 = subordinated; 0 = unsubordinated | −2.36 | −2.56 |
| *Leverage* | Non-current debt to total assets | −2.85 | −2.72 |
| *Systematic risk* | Market model beta, indicating sensitivity of share price to market-wide movements (1 = average)[b] | −0.87 | – |
| *Profitability* | Profit or loss to total assets | 5.13 | |
| *Unsystematic risk* | Standard deviation of residual from market model (average = 0.10) | −2.90 | – |
| *Riskiness of profit stream* | Coefficient of variation in profit or loss over five years (standard deviation/mean) | – | −0.53 |
| *Interest coverage* | Pre-tax funds flow before interest to interest expense | 0.007 | 0.006 |

The score from the model is converted to a bond rating as follows:

If score > 6.76, predict Aaa/AAA; score 6.76 − 5.19, predict Aa/AA; score 5.19 − 3.28, predict A; score 3.28 − 1.57, predict Baa/BBB; score 1.57 − 0.00, predict Ba/BB; score < 0.00, predict B

a. The coefficient in the Kaplan-Urwitz model was estimated at 0.005 (Model 1) and 0.006 (Model 2). Its scale has been adjusted to reflect that the estimates were based on assets measured in US dollars from the early 1970s. Given that $1 from 1972 was approximately equivalent to $5.86 in 2017, the original coefficient has been divided by 5.86. On December 31, 2017, $1 was approximately equal to £0.74, €0.83, DKK6.21, and SEK8.21.

b. Market model is estimated by regressing stock returns on the market index, using monthly data for the prior five years.

**TABLE 10.8** Debt ratings prediction model estimated on a sample of European public debt securities

| Firm or debt characteristic | Variable reflecting characteristic | Coefficients |
|---|---|---|
| | Model intercept | 1.678 |
| *Firm size* | Natural logarithm of invested capital (in € billions) | 0.480 |
| *Profitability* | Return on invested capital | 4.193 |
| *Riskiness of profit stream* | Standard deviation of return on invested capital over five years | −3.632 |
| *Interest coverage* | NOPAT plus NIPAT to interest expense after tax | 0.018 |
| *Cash flow performance* | Operating cash flow to debt | 0.591 |
| *Leverage* | Debt to capital | −0.369 |

Note that all variables in the model are expressed as fractions (instead of percentages). To reduce the influence of extreme observations, interest coverage and cash flow performance are capped above at, respectively, 30 and 1; minimum firm size is capped below at 0. The score from the model is converted to a debt rating as follows:

If score > 4.93, predict AA/Aa (or higher); score 4.93 − 3.55, predict A; score 3.55 − 2.14, predict BBB/Baa; score 2.14 − 1.24, predict BB/Ba; score 1.24 − 0.00, predict B; score < 0.00, predict CCC/Caa (or lower)

In the "European" debt ratings prediction model, factors similar to those in the Kaplan-Urwitz model are most significant. That is, European debt ratings between 1998 and 2017 were driven by firm size, profitability, riskiness of the profit stream, interest coverage, cash flow performance, and leverage (in order of statistical significance). We did not include equity market data in the model to make it usable for privately held firms, which may be one of the reasons why this model predicts debt ratings slightly less accurately than the Kaplan-Urwitz model.

Given that debt ratings can be explained reasonably well in terms of a handful of financial ratios, one might question whether ratings convey any news to investors – anything that could not already have been garnered from publicly available financial data. The answer to the question is yes, at least in the case of debt rating downgrades. That is, downgrades are greeted with drops in both bond and share prices.[13] To be sure, the capital markets anticipate much of the information reflected in rating changes. But that is not surprising, given that the changes often represent reactions to recent known events and that the rating agencies typically indicate in advance that a change is being considered.

# Prediction of distress and turnaround

The key task in credit analysis is assessing the probability that a firm will face financial distress and fail to repay a loan. A related analysis, relevant once a firm begins to face distress, involves considering whether it can be turned around. In this section we consider evidence on the predictability of these states.

The prediction of either distress or turnaround is a complex, difficult, and subjective task that involves all of the steps of analysis discussed throughout this book: business strategy analysis, accounting analysis, financial analysis, and prospective analysis. Purely quantitative models of the process can rarely serve as substitutes for the hard work the analysis involves. However, research on such models does offer some insight into which financial indicators are most useful in the task. Moreover, there are some settings where extensive credit checks are too costly to justify and where quantitative distress prediction models are useful. For example, the commercially available "Zeta" model is used by some manufacturers and other firms to assess the creditworthiness of their customers.[14]

## MODELS FOR DISTRESS PREDICTION

Several **financial distress prediction models** have been developed over the years.[15] They are similar to the debt rating models, but instead of predicting ratings, they predict whether a firm will face some state of distress, typically defined as bankruptcy, with a specified period such as one year. One study suggests that the factors most useful (on a stand-alone basis) in predicting bankruptcy one year in advance are the firm's level of profitability, the volatility of that profitability (as measured by the standard deviation of ROE), and its leverage.[16] Interestingly, liquidity measures turn out to be much less important. Current liquidity won't save an unhealthy firm if it is losing money at a fast pace.

A number of more robust, multifactor models have also been designed to predict financial distress. One such model, the Altman Z-score model, weights five variables to compute a bankruptcy score.[17] For public companies the model is as follows:[18]

$$Z = 1.2(X_1) + 1.4(X_2) + 3.3(X_3) + 0.6(X_4) + 1.0(X_5)$$

where  $X_1$ = net working capital/total assets (measure of liquidity)

$X_2$ = retained earnings/total assets (measure of cumulative profitability)

$X_3$ = EBIT/total assets (measure of return on assets)

$X_4$ = market value of equity/book value of total liabilities (measure of market leverage)

$X_5$ = revenue/total assets (measure of revenue generating potential of assets)

The model predicts bankruptcy when $Z < 1.81$. The range between 1.81 and 2.67 is labelled the "grey area." The following table presents calculations for apparel retailer French Connection, for two consecutive fiscal years:

| | **Model coefficient** | **Fiscal 2017** | | **Fiscal 2016** | |
|---|---|---|---|---|---|
| | | **Ratio** | **Score** | **Ratio** | **Score** |
| Net working capital/Total assets | 1.2 | 0.289 | 0.347 | 0.222 | 0.266 |
| Retained earnings/Total assets | 1.4 | 0.315 | 0.441 | 0.237 | 0.332 |
| EBIT/Total assets | 3.3 | 0.016 | 0.054 | -0.003 | -0.011 |
| Market value of equity/Book value of total liabilities | 0.6 | 0.408 | 0.245 | 0.264 | 0.158 |
| Revenue/Total assets | 1.0 | 1.232 | 1.232 | 0.889 | 0.889 |
| | | | 2.319 | | 1.635 |

French Connection's Z-scores highlight its relatively poor but slowly improving performance. In the past few years, difficult market conditions in the traditional segment of the apparel retail industry drove down the retailer's margins and made it report below-normal returns on equity. In fiscal 2016 French Connection's liabilities were almost four times greater than its market capitalization, an indication of its precarious financial state. French Connection's focus on closing down unprofitable stores helped the retailer to improve profitability and reduce its debt, such that its Z-score moved from the "distress area" to the "grey area" in 2017.

Such models have some ability to predict failing and surviving firms. Altman reports that when the model was applied to a holdout sample containing 33 failed and 33 nonfailed firms (the same proportion used to estimate the model), it correctly predicted the outcome in 63 of 66 cases. However, the performance of the model would degrade substantially if applied to a holdout sample where the proportion of failed and nonfailed firms was not forced to be the same as that used to estimate the model.

The Altman Z-score model was estimated on a sample of US firms. When applying this model to a sample of non-US firms, the following complications must be considered. First, accounting practices may differ from country to country. In particular, under some accounting systems total liabilities may be substantially understated because of firms' use of off-balance sheet financing. When comparing the Altman Z-scores of two firms with different accounting practices, the preferred approach would be to undo these firms' financial statements from accounting distortions and bring all off-balance sheet liabilities on the balance sheet before calculating the scores. Second, although the model may be equally useful across countries in predicting financial distress, the likelihood that financial distress leads to bankruptcy depends on national bankruptcy laws and thus varies from country to country.

One way to overcome the preceding problems is to use distress prediction models that were estimated in a particular firm's home country. An international survey of distress prediction models suggests that more than 40 variants of such models exist worldwide.[19] A common characteristic of these models is that they all include some measures of profitability and leverage. For example, one model that was developed by Taffler and is commonly used in the United Kingdom calculates Z-scores as follows:[20]

$$Z = 3.20 + 12.18(X_1) + 2.50(X_2) - 10.68(X_3) + 0.0289(X_4)$$

where   $X_1$ = profit before tax/current liabilities
       $X_2$ = current assets/total liabilities
       $X_3$ = current liabilities/total assets
       $X_4$ = no-credit interval (in days)

The no-credit interval is defined as immediate assets (current assets excluding inventories and prepaid expenses) minus current liabilities divided by total operating expenses excluding depreciation and multiplied by 365 days. This variable measures how long the firm can finance its current operations when other sources of short-term finance are unavailable. The model predicts bankruptcy when Z < 0.

While simple distress prediction models like the Altman and the Taffler models cannot serve as a replacement for in-depth analysis of the kind discussed throughout this book, they do provide a useful reminder of the power of financial statement data to summarize important dimensions of the firm's performance. In addition, they can be useful for screening large numbers of firms prior to more in-depth analysis of corporate strategy, management expertise, market position, and financial ratio performance.

### INVESTMENT OPPORTUNITIES IN DISTRESSED COMPANIES

The debt securities of firms in financial distress trade at steep discounts to par value. Some hedge fund managers and investment advisors specialize in investing in these securities – even purchasing the debt of firms operating under bankruptcy protection. Investors in these securities can earn attractive returns if the firm recovers from its cash flow difficulties.

Distressed debt investors assess whether the firm is likely to overcome its immediate cash flow problems and whether it has a viable long-run future. Two elements of the framework laid out in Part 2 of this book are particularly relevant to analyzing distressed opportunities. The first is a thorough analysis of the firm's industry and competitive positioning and an assessment of its business risks. This is followed by the construction of well-reasoned forecasts of its future cash flow and earnings performance in light of the business analysis.

## Credit ratings, default probabilities, and debt valuation

Debt rating prediction models and financial distress prediction models can help in estimating the value of debt. To illustrate how, consider the following debt valuation formula, which defines debt value as a function of future contractual coupon and face value payments; the expected return on debt (denoted as $r_d$); and the expected cumulative probabilities that a firm will default on its debt payments within one to T years (denoted as $\pi_1,\ldots, \pi_T$).

$$\text{Debt value} = \frac{(1-\pi_1)\times \text{Coupon}_1}{(1+r_d)} + \frac{(1-\pi_2)\times \text{Coupon}_2}{(1+r_d)^2} + \frac{(1-\pi_T)\times \text{Coupon}_T +(1-\pi_T)\times \text{Face value}}{(1+r_d)^T}$$

Note that, for simplicity, this formula assumes that debt holders will receive nothing if the firm defaults on its loans. In practice, however, recovery rates on defaulting debt are often greater than zero. Some studies estimate recovery rates on, for example, senior unsecured bonds at close to 50 percent. It is possible to adjust the debt valuation formula for such non-zero recovery rates, albeit at the expense of making calculations somewhat more complicated. Including the possibility that in case of default debt holders receive $\rho$ percent of face value, changes the debt valuation formula to:

$$\text{Debt value} = \frac{(1-\pi_1)\times \text{Coupon}_1 + \pi_1 \times \rho \times \text{Face value}}{(1+r_d)} + \frac{(1-\pi_2)\times \text{Coupon}_2 +(\pi_2 -\pi_1)\times \rho \times \text{Face value}}{(1+r_d)^2} +\ldots$$
$$+ \frac{(1-\pi_T)\times \text{Coupon}_T +(1-\pi_T)\times \text{Face value} +(\pi_T -\pi_{T-1})\times \rho \times \text{Face value}}{(1+r_d)^T}$$

Assuming for the moment that the contractual payments and the required return on default risk-free debt are known, there are essentially two practical approaches to estimating debt value. First, an analyst can explicitly estimate expected default probabilities and recovery rates (if relevant), and use the preceding formulae to calculate debt value. Second, and alternatively, as a short-cut approach an analyst can discount the contractual payments at the effective yield on debt with similar default risk characteristics, as in the following debt valuation formula.

$$\text{Debt value} = \frac{\text{Coupon}_1}{(1+y)} + \frac{\text{Coupon}_2}{(1+y)^2} +\ldots+ \frac{\text{Coupon}_T + \text{Face value}}{(1+y)^T}$$

Under this approach the effective yield $(y)$ conveniently summarizes the analyst's expectations about future default $(\pi_1,\ldots, \pi_T)$, recovery rates $(\rho)$ and the required return on debt $(r_d)$ into one rate of return $(y)$. Debt rating and financial distress prediction models can thus contribute to debt valuation by informing the analyst on either expected default probabilities and required returns on debt or effective yields.

Table 10.9 shows Standard and Poor's estimates of the percentage of firms that default within one to eight years in seven debt rating categories ranging from AAA to CCC. The debt rating agency derives these percentages from European companies' historical default rates between 1981 and 2017. The percentages in Table 10.9 indicate that firms with CCC ratings have a 40.1 percent probability to default within three years, compared with an 8.9 percent probability for firms with B ratings. In the lower rating categories, the marginal probability to default (measured as the year-to-year change in the cumulative probability) decreases over time. For example, firms with CCC ratings that do not default during the first year have an average marginal probability of only 8.96 percent (35.56 – 26.60) to default in the second year (compared with a default probability of 26.60 percent in the first year). This is because some of the low-rated firms that survive the first year improve their financial health and move up to higher rating categories.

One complication in estimating debt value using the preceding default probability percentages is that the expected return on debt – $r_d$ in the debt valuation formula – is not simply equal to the riskless rate of return. Instead, the expected return on debt depends on the debt's systematic risk and various other (non-default) risk factors, all of which in turn may be a function of a firm's financial health. In a manner analogous to the calculation of the cost of equity, the expected return on debt can be estimated using an extended version of the CAPM model (see Chapter 8), which expresses the expected return on debt as the sum of a required return on riskless assets plus (1) a premium for beta or systematic risk and (2) a premium for other risk factors:

$$r_d = r_f + \beta\left[E\left(r_m\right) - r_f\right] + r_{OTHER}$$

where $r_f$ is the riskless rate; $[E(r_m)-r_f]$ is the risk premium expected for the market as a whole, expressed as the excess of the expected return on the market index over the riskless rate, $\beta$ is the systematic risk of the debt; and $r_{OTHER}$ is the premium for other risks.

Contrary to equity betas, debt betas cannot be easily obtained for each individual firm. To circumvent the complication of estimating firm-specific betas, some analysts therefore assume that financial health is the main driver of debt betas and set the firm-specific debt beta equal to the average debt beta in the firm's debt rating category. Such debt beta estimates typically range from close to zero for low-risk AAA/Aaa-rated debt to 0.4 or higher for high-risk CCC/Caa-rated debt. Much research has shown, however, that default risk probabilities and systematic risk do fully explain the observed variation in bond prices or expected returns on debt $(r_d)$. Which other risk factors are relevant in debt valuation remains a topic of debate, although many researchers agree that

**TABLE 10.9** European companies' default probabilities by debt rating category

| S&P debt rating | Cumulative probability (in %) that the firm defaults within . . . year(s) | | | | | | |
|---|---|---|---|---|---|---|---|
| | 1 | 2 | 3 | 4 | 5 | 6 | 7 |
| AAA | 0.00 | 0.00 | 0.00 | 0.00 | 0.00 | 0.00 | 0.00 |
| AA | 0.00 | 0.03 | 0.07 | 0.13 | 0.21 | 0.28 | 0.32 |
| A | 0.04 | 0.08 | 0.12 | 0.18 | 0.28 | 0.36 | 0.47 |
| BBB | 0.07 | 0.21 | 0.36 | 0.50 | 0.60 | 0.82 | 1.04 |
| BB | 0.38 | 1.25 | 2.12 | 2.87 | 3.96 | 4.90 | 5.86 |
| B | 2.25 | 5.75 | 8.88 | 11.29 | 13.37 | 14.77 | 15.57 |
| CCC/C | 26.60 | 35.56 | 40.05 | 44.17 | 46.37 | 46.37 | 47.27 |

Source: Standard & Poor's. Reproduced with permission.

the risk of incurring losses from debt instruments' low liquidity (referred to as liquidity risk) is a significant determinant of the expected return on debt.[21]

The uncertainty about the exact effect of systematic risk, liquidity risk, and other risk factors on debt value explains the popularity of using effective yields as an alternative (short-cut) approach to debt valuation. To follow this approach all that an analyst needs to assess is the average effective yield in the firm's debt rating category. If for a particular firm a debt rating is unavailable, the debt rating prediction models, which we described in one of the previous sections, can be used to produce an approximate estimate of the firm's creditworthiness. Table 10.10 shows the average spread (difference) between the effective yields in six debt rating categories ranging from A to B and that in category AAA/AA. During the period 2013 to 2017, the median effective yield on A-rated corporate bonds was 0.4 percent higher than the effective yield on AAA/AA-rated corporate bonds; the median effective yield spread between B-rated corporate bonds and AAA/AA-rated bond was 4.9 percent. Note that the effective yield increases sharply once firms' debt falls below investment grade BBB. This yield increase compensates debt holders for the substantially higher default risk, higher beta risk, and potentially higher liquidity risk. Further, keep in mind that the effective yields in Table 10.10 are those of long-term bonds with average maturities greater than five years. Because the marginal default probabilities of lower-rated bonds tend to decrease over the forecast horizon (as can be seen from Table 10.9), the effective yield spreads for lower-rated short-term bonds likely exceed those reported in Table 10.10.

**TABLE 10.10**  Spreads between the effective yields on AAA/AA-rated long-term corporate bonds and those on lower-rated bonds between 2013 and 2017

| Debt rating (S&P) | Effective yield spreads(%) | | |
| --- | --- | --- | --- |
| | Lower quartile | Median | Upper quartile |
| AAA/AA | 0.0 | 0.0 | 0.0 |
| A | 0.3 | 0.4 | 0.4 |
| BBB | 1.1 | 1.3 | 1.4 |
| BB | 2.5 | 2.9 | 3.2 |
| B | 4.3 | 4.9 | 5.3 |

Source: Bank of America – Merrill Lynch Corporate Bond Indices

Consider the following example to illustrate how debt rating prediction models and effective yield spreads can be used to value debt. The following table presents the calculation of apparel retailer Next plc's debt rating score at the end of the fiscal year ending January 2018 (fiscal year 2017):

| | | Next plc | |
| --- | --- | --- | --- |
| | Model coefficient | Ratio | Score |
| Intercept | 1.678 | 1.000 | 1.678 |
| Firm size | 0.480 | 1.069 | 0.513 |
| Profitability | 4.193 | 0.377 | 1.581 |
| Riskiness of profit stream | −3.632 | 0.069 | −0.251 |
| Interest coverage | 0.018 | 21.709 | 0.391 |
| Cash flow performance | 0.591 | 0.800 | 0.473 |
| Leverage | −0.369 | 0.695 | −0.256 |
| | | | 4.129 |

The debt rating score of 4.129 corresponds with a debt rating of A. At the end of fiscal 2017, Next plc had three bonds outstanding, one of which was a £250 million 4.375 percent coupon bond due on October 2, 2026. This bond had been issued at an effective yield of close to 4.5 percent. At the end of January 2018, the effective yield on AA/Aa-rated UK corporate bonds was close to 2.4 percent. Given an expected yield spread of 0.4 percent for A-rated corporate bonds (relative to AA/Aa-rated bonds), Next's effective yield at the end of January 2018 can therefore be estimated at 2.8 percent, and the value of the retailer's £250 million bond is:

| Payment date | Coupon (4.375% × £250) and face value (a) | Discount factor (b) | (a) × (b) |
|---|---|---|---|
| Oct. 2018 | 10.938 | $1/(1+0.028)^{9/12}$ | 10.713 |
| Oct. 2019 | 10.938 | $1/(1+0.028)^{21/12}$ | 10.421 |
| Oct. 2020 | 10.938 | $1/(1+0.028)^{33/12}$ | 10.138 |
| Oct. 2021 | 10.938 | $1/(1+0.028)^{45/12}$ | 9.862 |
| Oct. 2022 | 10.938 | $1/(1+0.028)^{57/12}$ | 9.593 |
| Oct. 2023 | 10.938 | $1/(1+0.028)^{69/12}$ | 9.332 |
| Oct. 2024 | 10.938 | $1/(1+0.028)^{69/12}$ | 9.077 |
| Oct. 2025 | 10.938 | $1/(1+0.028)^{69/12}$ | 8.830 |
| Oct. 2026 | 260.938 | $1/(1+0.028)^{81/12}$ | 204.926 |
| | | | £282.892 |

This bond value estimate of £282.9 million is close to 13 percent above par value. For comparison, in early 2018 Next's £250 million bond traded at a price of between 109 and 111 percent of par value. The observed market price and our fundamental estimates of debt value need not be equal, given that transaction prices are subject to the influence of investor sentiment. In fact, a possible explanation for any observed differences may be that on the valuation date, credit yield spreads of lower-rated bonds, such as those issued by Next, were temporarily below or above their historical averages.

## Summary

Debt financing is attractive to firms with high marginal tax rates and few non-interest tax shields, making interest tax shields from debt valuable. Debt can also help create value by deterring management of firms with high, stable profits/cash flows and few new investment opportunities from over-investing in unprofitable new ventures.

However, debt financing also creates the risk of financial distress, which is likely to be particularly severe for firms with volatile earnings and cash flows, and intangible assets that are easily destroyed by financial distress.

Prospective providers of debt use credit analysis to evaluate the risks of financial distress for a firm. Credit analysis is important to a wide variety of economic agents – not just bankers and other financial intermediaries but also public debt analysts, industrial companies, service companies, and others.

At the heart of credit analysis lie the same techniques described in Chapters 2 through 8: business strategy analysis, accounting analysis, financial analysis, and portions of prospective analysis. The purpose of the analysis is not just to assess the likelihood that a potential borrower will fail to repay the loan. It is also important to identify the nature of the key risks involved, and how the loan might be structured to mitigate or control those risks. A well-structured loan provides the lender with a viable "exit strategy," even in the case of default. Properly designed accounting-based covenants are essential to this structure.

Fundamentally, the issues involved in analysis of public debt are no different from those involved in evaluating bank loans or other private debt. Institutionally, however, the contexts are different. Investors in public debt are usually not close to the borrower and must rely on other agents, including debt raters and other analysts, to assess creditworthiness. Debt ratings, which depend heavily on firm size and financial measures of performance, have an important influence on the market yields that must be offered to issue debt.

The key task in credit analysis is the assessment of the probability of default. The task is complex, difficult, and to some extent, subjective. A few financial ratios can help predict financial distress with some accuracy. The most important indicators for this purpose are profitability, volatility of profits, and leverage. While a number of models predict distress based on financial indicators, they cannot replace the in-depth forms of analysis discussed in this book.

## Core concepts

**Benefits of debt**    Two benefits of debt financing are:

1   The tax deductibility of interest payments creates a corporate tax shield.
2   Debt reduces the free cash flow that is available to management and, consequently, strengthens managerial incentives for value creation.

**Costs of debt**    Three potential costs of debt financing are:

1   Too much debt can lead to financial distress and costly debt restructurings.
2   Financial distress can make a firm forego valuable investment opportunities.
3   Financial distress creates conflicts between creditors, who wish to maximize the value of the firm's assets, and shareholders, who wish to maximize the value of equity.

**Country differences in debt financing**    The use of debt financing differs across countries because of institutional differences, such as differences in the legal protection of creditors' interests. Institutional differences affect, amongst others, the occurrence of multiple-bank borrowing, the use of supplier financing, the use of off-balance sheet financing (such as factoring of receivables), and the development of public debt markets. The ultimate effect of institutional differences on firms' leverage ratios is complex and uncertain.

**Credit analysis**    Credit analysis includes assessing the creditworthiness of a firm; determining the type of loan, loan structure, and the necessity of security and/or loan covenants; and assessing whether the firm's future growth opportunities can be valuable to the lender. The credit analysis process consists of the following four steps:

1   Understanding why the firm applies for a loan and for what purpose the loan will be used.
2   Determining the type of loan on the basis of the purpose of the loan and the firm's financial strength. This step also includes determining the type of security that will be required to reduce the lender's risk (and thereby the cost of debt).
3   Analyzing the creditworthiness of the firm using ratio analysis and forecasting.
4   Determining the loan structure, including loan covenants and price (interest rate).

**Debt rating prediction models**    Quantitative models explaining firms' public debt ratings on the basis of observable firm and debt characteristics. An example of a debt rating prediction model is the Kaplan-Urwitz model. The primary firm characteristics used to predict debt ratings are: firm size, profitability, leverage, and interest coverage.

**Financial distress prediction models**    Quantitative models predicting the likelihood that a firm will become financially distressed within a period of typically one year (on the basis of observable firm characteristics). An example of a financial distress prediction model is the Altman Z-score model. Some firm characteristics used to predict financial distress are: (cumulative) profitability, leverage, and liquidity.

**Public debt ratings**    Scores assigned to the financial condition of firms issuing public debt by debt rating agencies such as Fitch, Moody's and Standard and Poor's.

**Suppliers of debt financing**    Major suppliers of debt financing are: commercial banks, non-bank financial institutions such as finance and insurance companies, public debt markets, and suppliers of goods and services.

## Questions

1  What are the critical performance dimensions for (a) a retailer and (b) a financial services company that should be considered in credit analysis? What ratios would you suggest looking at for each of these dimensions?

2  Why would a company pay to have its public debt rated by a major rating agency (such as Fitch, Moody's or Standard & Poor's)? Why might a firm decide not to have its debt rated?

3  Some have argued that the market for original-issue junk bonds developed in the United States in the late 1970s as a result of a failure in the rating process. Proponents of this argument suggest that rating agencies rated companies too harshly at the low end of the rating scale, denying investment-grade status to some deserving companies. What are proponents of this argument effectively assuming were the incentives of rating agencies? What economic forces could give rise to this incentive?

4  Many debt agreements require borrowers to obtain the permission of the lender before undertaking a major acquisition or asset sale. Why would the lender want to include this type of restriction?

5  Betty Li, the finance director of a company applying for a new loan, states, "I will never agree to a debt covenant that restricts my ability to pay dividends to my shareholders because it reduces shareholder wealth." Do you agree with this argument?

6  A bank extends three loans to the following companies: an Italy-based biotech firm; a France-based car manufacturer; and a UK-based food retailer. How may these three loans differ from each other in terms of loan maturity, required collateral, and loan amount?

7  Cambridge Construction plc follows the percentage-of-completion method for reporting long-term contract revenues. The percentage of completion is based on the cost of materials shipped to the project site as a percentage of total expected material costs. Cambridge's major debt agreement includes restrictions on net worth, interest cover age, and minimum working capital requirements. A leading analyst claims that "the company is buying its way out of these covenants by spending cash and buying materials, even when they are not needed." Explain how this may be possible.

8  Can Cambridge improve its Z score by behaving as the analyst claims in question 7? Is this change consistent with economic reality?

9  A banker asserts, "I avoid lending to companies with negative cash from operations because they are too risky." Is this a sensible lending policy?

10  A leading retailer finds itself in a financial bind. It doesn't have sufficient cash flow from operations to finance its growth, and it is close to violating the maximum debt-to-assets ratio allowed by its covenants. The marketing director suggests, "We can raise cash for our growth by selling the existing stores and leasing them back. This source of financing is cheap since it avoids violating either the debt-to-assets or interest coverage ratios in our covenants." Do you agree with his analysis? Why or why not? As the firm's banker, how would you view this arrangement?

# Notes

1  Rahim Bah and Pascal Dumontier provide empirical evidence that R&D-intensive firms in Europe, Japan, and the United States have lower debt and pay out lower dividends than non-R&D firms. See Rahim Bah and Pascal Dumontier, "R&D Intensity and Corporate Financial Policy: Some International Evidence," *Journal of Business Finance and Accounting* 28 (June/July 2001): 671–692.

2  Some arguments that have been raised in other countries against universal banking are the following. First, because of their investment banking activities, universal banks may incur greater risks than other commercial banks and, consequently, jeopardize the stability of a country's financial system. Second, universal banks may become too powerful because of their size and hold back competition in the banking industry. Third, universal banks could potentially misuse inside information about clients that they obtained through their lending activities in securities trading. In the United States, these concerns led to ban on universal banking until 1999. For a discussion of the potential advantages and disadvantages of universal banking, see, for example, George J. Benston, "Universal Banking," *Journal of Economic Perspectives* (1994): 121–143.

3  See Sergei A. Davydenko and Julian R. Franks, "Do Bankruptcy Codes Matter? A Study of Defaults in France, Germany and the UK," Working Paper, University of Toronto and London Business School, 2005.

4  See Steven Ongena and David C. Smith, "What Determines the Number of Bank Relationships? Cross-Country Evidence," *Journal of Financial Intermediation* (2000): 26–56.

5  See Asli Demirgüç-Kunt and Vojislav Maksimovic, "Firms as Financial Intermediaries: Evidence from Trade Credit Data," Working Paper, World Bank and University of Maryland, 2001.

6  See Marie H.R. Bakker, Leonora Klapper, and Gregory F. Udell, "Financing Small and Medium-Sized Enterprises with Factoring: Global Growth and Its Potential in Eastern Europe," Working Paper, World Bank and Indiana University, 2004.

7  See Asli Demirgüç-Kunt and Vojislav Maksimovic, "Institutions, Financial Markets, and Firm Debt Maturity," *Journal of Financial Economics* 54 (1999): 295–336.

8  See Mariassunta Giannetti, "Do Better Institutions Mitigate Agency Problems? Evidence from Corporate Finance Choices," *Journal of Financial and Quantitative Analysis* 38 (2003): 185–212.

9  Sergei A. Davydenko and Julian R. Franks, op. cit.

10  The same is true of preference dividends. However, when preference shares are cumulative, any dividends missed must be paid later, when and if the firm returns to profitability.

11  Other relevant coverage ratios are discussed in Chapter 5.

12  Robert Kaplan and G. Urwitz, "Statistical Models of Bond Ratings: A Methodological Inquiry," *Journal of Business* (April 1979): 231–261.

13  See Robert Holthausen and Richard Leftwich, "The Effect of Bond Rating Changes on Common Stock Prices," *Journal of Financial Economics* (September 1986): 57–90; and John Hand, Robert Holthausen, and Richard Leftwich, "The Effect of Bond Rating Announcements on Bond and Stock Prices," *Journal of Finance* (June 1992): 733–752.

14  See *Corporate Financial Distress* by Edward Altman (New York: John Wiley, 1993).

15  See Edward Altman, "Financial Ratios, Discriminant Analysis, and the Prediction of Corporate Bankruptcy," *Journal of Finance* (September 1968): 589–609; Altman, *Corporate Financial Distress*, op. cit.; William Beaver, "Financial Ratios as Predictors of Distress," *Journal of Accounting Research*, Suppl. (1966): 71–111; James Ohlson, "Financial Ratios and the Probabilistic Prediction of Bankruptcy," *Journal of Accounting Research* (Spring 1980): 109–131; and Mark Zmijewski, "Predicting Corporate Bankruptcy: An Empirical Comparison of the Extant Financial Distress Models," Working Paper, SUNY at Buffalo, 1983.

16  Zmijewski, op. cit.

17  Altman, *Corporate Financial Distress*, op. cit.

18  For private firms, Altman, ibid., adjusts the public model by changing the numerator for the variable $X_4$ from the market value of equity to the book value. The revised model follows:

$$Z = 0.717(X_1) + 0.847(X_2) + 3.107(X_3) + 0.420(X_4) + 0.998(X_5)$$

where  $X_1$ = net working capital/total assets

$X_2$ = retained earnings/total assets

$X_3$ = EBIT/total assets

$X_4$ = book value of equity/book value of total liabilities

$X_5$ = revenue/total assets

The model predicts bankruptcy when $Z < 1.20$. The range between 1.20 and 2.90 is labelled the "grey area."

19  See E. Altman and P. Narayanan, "An International Survey of Business Failure Classification Models," *Financial Markets, Institutions and Instruments* (May 1997): 1–57, for an extensive description of various non-US bankruptcy prediction models.

20  The Taffler model and tests of its predictive accuracy are described in R. Taffler, "The Assessment of Company Solvency and Performance Using a Statistical Model," *Accounting and Business Research* (1983): 295–307; and R. Taffler, "Empirical Models for the Monitoring of UK Corporations," *Journal of Banking and Finance* (1984): 199–227.

21  See, for example, E. Elton, M. Gruber, D. Agrawal, and D. Mann, "Explaining the Rate Spread on Corporate Bonds." *Journal of Finance* (2001): 247–277, P. Collin-Dufresne, R. Goldstein, and J. Spencer Martin, "The Determinants of Credit Spread Changes," *Journal of Finance* (2001): 2177–2207, and L. Chen, D. Lesmond, and J. Wei, "Corporate Yield Spreads and Bond Liquidity," *Journal of Finance* (2007): 119–149 for discussions of what factors explain corporate bond spreads.

# Getronics' debt ratings

Getronics NV is a Netherlands-based provider of Information and Communication Technology (ICT) services. The company originates from a leveraged management buyout of Geveke Electronics NV and was taken public by its privately held owner SHV Holdings NV in 1985. Following its initial public offering, the company adopted a strategy of aggressive expansion through internal growth, acquisitions, and strategic investments. Between 1985 and 1999 Getronics managed to double its revenue and earnings every three years, on average. In 1999 the company turned from being a moderate player in the European ICT industry into one of the world's largest ICT service providers through its acquisition of US-based Wang Global. This acquisition more than doubled Getronics' revenues (from €1.5 billion to €3.7 billion) and almost tripled the company's employee base.

To finance the acquisition of Wang Global, Getronics needed to issue new shares and attract a substantial amount of new debt. Therefore the company entered into a €500 million syndicated revolving variable-rate credit facility, which would mature on April 2004, and issued €350 million of subordinated convertible bonds. The subordinated convertible bonds bore an annual interest rate of 0.25 percent but would be redeemed at 113.21 percent of their face value if they remained unconverted until the maturity date (April 2004). Hence the yield to maturity of unconverted bonds was 2.75 percent. The bonds' conversion price was €14.53 per ordinary share, while Getronics' share price on December 31, 1999, had reached €26.40.

At the end of fiscal year 1999, Getronics had 343,724,237 ordinary shares and 21,950,000 cumulative preference shares outstanding. The preference shares earned cumulative dividend, paid annually in arrears, at 5.7 percent and had been issued at €10.75 per share (€236 million in total).

During fiscal year 2000 Getronics issued €500 million of new subordinated convertible bonds (with an annual interest rate of 0.25 percent, a redemption price of 116.01 percent, and a conversion price of €36.98), maturing in March 2005, and reduced its debt under the revolving credit facility by €150 million. Getronics' share price at the end of 2000 was €6.26; by the end of 2001 it had dropped further to €3.64.

During fiscal year 2001 Getronics temporarily lowered the conversion price of its subordinated convertible bonds to persuade its bondholders to convert their bonds into ordinary shares. As a result, convertible debt with a total book value €295 million was converted into equity, increasing the number of outstanding shares with 61,078,827. In 2003 Getronics eventually redeemed its outstanding subordinated convertible bonds by paying the bondholders €325 million in cash and agreeing to repay the remaining €250 million through quarterly installment payments during a five-year period. The interest rate on the new installment bonds equaled 13 percent. To finance the redemption, Getronics issued new unsubordinated convertible bonds, maturing in five years, for an amount of €100 million (with an annual interest rate of 5.5 percent, a redemption price of 100 percent, and a conversion price of €1.58). At the end of 2003 Getronics' share price was €1.66.

In 2004 and 2005 Getronics issued 100 million and 48.5 million new shares. The company used the proceeds of the 2004 issue to redeem its installment bonds early. In addition, the company obtained a new €175 credit facility in 2004 – which was replaced by a €300 credit facility in 2005 – to help finance the redemption as well as replace a €100 credit facility and issued new unsubordinated convertible bonds (with an annual interest rate of 5.5 percent and a redemption price of 100 percent) in 2005. As a consequence of the adoption of IFRS

Professor Erik Peek prepared this case. The case is intended solely as the basis for class discussion and is not intended to serve as an endorsement, source of primary data, or illustration of effective or ineffective management.

Standards in 2005, Getronics reclassified its cumulative preference shares from equity to debt. The par value and premium reserve of these shares (i.e., the book value of the new debt) amounted to €235 million.

Fiscal year 2006 was another challenging year for Getronics. The company incurred unexpected losses in Italy and had to recognize an impairment charge of €65 million on goodwill relating to the Wang Global acquisition and, consequently, reported a significant net loss. During 2006 Getronics did not change much of its borrowings other than replacing maturing bonds with new unsubordinated convertible bonds. The losses continued in 2007, when competitors started to consider the company as a takeover candidate. On July 31, 2007, Royal KPN NV announced its interest in acquiring Getronics. On October 22, 2007, KPN completed its acquisition.

**EXHIBIT 1** Getronics NV – summary of events

| Date | Event/announcement |
| --- | --- |
| May 5, 1999 | Getronics acquires US-based industry peer Wang Global; the company finances the acquisition through a mixture of new equity (€0.7 billion common and €0.3 billion preferred) and debt (€0.5 billion loans and €0.3 billion convertible bonds). The amount of goodwill that Getronics recognized on the transaction is close to €2.4 billion. |
| February 9, 2000 | Getronics sells its ATM business, realizing a profit on the sale. |
| March 3, 2000 | Annual results 1999 announcement. The acquisition of Wang Global boosts the company's results. Getronics announces ambitious growth plans. |
| March 16, 2000 | Getronics issues €450 million in subordinated convertible debt (to replace maturing debt). |
| First half 2000 | End of the dotcom bubble. Technology shares decline. |
| August 17, 2000 | First half-year report. |
| November 22, 2000 | Getronics announces that this year's earnings will be below expectations. Getronics' share price declines by 42 percent. |
| February 5, 2001 | Getronics signs €75 million contract with Shell. |
| February 28, 2001 | Annual results 2000 announcement. |
| June 1, 2001 | Getronics' CEO Cees van Luijk resigns and is succeeded by Peter van Voorst. |
| August 16, 2001 | First half-year report. |
| December 11, 2001 | Getronics exchanges €295.3 million of subordinated convertible bonds for equity. |
| December 18, 2001 | Getronics signs €90 million contract with Barclays. |
| March 5, 2002 | Annual results 2001 announcement. Getronics decides to freeze wages of its employees after incurring a record loss. |
| April 22, 2002 | Getronics announces that it plans to repurchase some of its outstanding convertible bonds. |
| August 13, 2002 | Getronics' share price drops by close to 40 percent after rumours that the company is close to applying for bankruptcy. |
| August 15, 2002 | First half-year report. |
| December 31, 2002 | Getronics repays all its amounts outstanding under the €500 million credit facility. |
| February 12, 2003 | Getronics offers (mostly institutional) subordinated convertible bondholders equity in exchange for their bonds. Convertible bondholders deny the offer, resulting in a conflict between management and bondholders. |

*(Continued)*

**EXHIBIT 1**  Getronics NV – summary of events (Continued)

| Date | Event/announcement |
|------|--------------------|
| February 21, 2003 | CEO Peter van Voorst and CFO Jan Docter step down. The new CEO of Getronics is Klaas Wagenaar. |
| March 4, 2003 | Annual results 2002 announcement. |
| March 21, 2003 | Getronics announces to reduce debt by selling assets rather than offering bondholders equity. |
| April 22, 2003 | Getronics sells Getronics HR Solutions for €315 million in cash (and realizes a profit on the sale of €270 million). |
| June 10, 2003 | Getronics immediately repays bondholders €325 million (in cash) and agrees for the repayment of the remaining €250 million in installments. The agreement resolves the company's conflict with its convertible bondholders. |
| July 1, 2003 | Getronics obtains a loan of €100 million, which will be used to replace a €200 million credit facility. |
| August 13, 2003 | First half-year report. |
| October 13, 2003 | Getronics issues €100 million in convertible debt (to replace maturing debt). |
| February 4, 2004 | Getronics sells 100 million new shares to institutional investors (proceeds: €233 million). The proceeds are used to repay €250 million in subordinated installment bonds on March 30, 2004. |
| March 2, 2004 | Annual results 2003 announcement. |
| April 19, 2004 | Getronics obtains a new credit facility of €175 million from a consortium of banks. |
| August 11, 2004 | First half-year report. |
| November 1, 2004 | Getronics announces the acquisition of industry peer PinkRoccade N.V for the amount of €350 million. The company will obtain a new credit facility of €125 million that, together with the credit facility obtained in April, will be used to finance the acquisition. |
| March 3, 2005 | Annual results 2004 announcement. |
| April 11, 2005 | Getronics issues new shares (proceeds: €388 million). |
| August 3, 2005 | First half-year report. |
| September 29, 2005 | Getronics issues €150 million in unsecured convertible debt (to replace maturing bonds). |
| March 2, 2006 | Annual results 2005 announcement. Getronics also announces that its Italian subsidiary has committed fraud, hiding €15 million in expenses. |
| April 20, 2006 | Getronics receives four bids for its Italian subsidiary. |
| June 23, 2006 | Getronics sells its Italian subsidiary to Eutelia for an estimated amount of €135 million, realizing a loss of €50 million. The sale helps the company to meet its debt covenants again. |
| August 1, 2006 | First half-year report. Disappointing results cause share prices to decline by close to 24 percent. Getronics announces restructuring plans. |
| November 15, 2006 | CFO Theo Janssen resigns unexpectedly. Two other Board Members follow his example. |
| December 14, 2006 | Getronics issues €95 million in convertible bonds (to replace maturing bonds). |
| February 27, 2007 | Annual results 2006 announcement. Getronics announces its annual results early. The company realized an unexpected loss of €145 million. |
| July 30, 2007 | Royal KPN acquires Getronics. |

**EXHIBIT 2** Getronics NV – financial information (in € mn)

| | 2007 H2 | 2007 H1 | 2006 H2 | 2006 H1 | 2005 H2 | 2005 H1 | 2004 H2 | 2004 H1 | 2003 H2 | 2003 H1 | 2002 H2 | 2002 H1 | 2001 H2 | 2001 H1 | 2000 H2 | 2000 H1 |
|---|---|---|---|---|---|---|---|---|---|---|---|---|---|---|---|---|
| Revenue | 1,224 | 1,280 | 1,285 | 1,342 | 1,271 | 1,322 | 918 | 1,188 | 1,263 | 1,363 | 1,757 | 1,838 | 2,048 | 2,101 | 2,214 | 1,913 |
| Cost of sales | −996 | −1,051 | −1,007 | −1,095 | −988 | −1,079 | −740 | −981 | −1,044 | −1,131 | −1,463 | −1,495 | −1,703 | −1,723 | −1,768 | −1,514 |
| **Gross profit** | **228** | **229** | **278** | **247** | **283** | **243** | **178** | **207** | **219** | **232** | **294** | **343** | **345** | **378** | **446** | **399** |
| Selling expenses | −91 | −97 | −96 | −111 | −95 | −98 | −68 | −86 | −85 | −92 | −124 | −132 | −135 | −131 | −131 | −125 |
| General and administrative expenses | −153 | −108 | −107 | −110 | −98 | −106 | −67 | −94 | −106 | −128 | −126 | −151 | −145 | −162 | −180 | −161 |
| Other expenses/income | 0 | −13 | −2 | −11 | −30 | −3 | −3 | 6 | −5 | 176 | −33 | −2 | −15 | −69 | −29 | 37 |
| Amortization/impairment of intangible assets | −13 | −88 | −65 | 0 | 0 | 0 | 0 | 0 | −22 | −21 | −403 | −30 | −983 | −49 | −50 | −48 |
| **Earnings before interest and taxes (EBIT)** | **−29** | **−77** | **8** | **15** | **60** | **36** | **40** | **33** | **1** | **167** | **−392** | **28** | **−933** | **−33** | **56** | **102** |
| Interest income | 14 | 11 | 8 | 5 | 10 | — | 7 | — | 3 | — | 4 | 8 | — | — | — | — |
| Interest expense (including preferred dividends) | −43 | −33 | −48 | −28 | −33 | −40 | −13 | −17 | −35 | −12 | −30 | −21 | −30 | −30 | −37 | −19 |
| **Earnings before taxes (EBT)** | **−58** | **−99** | **−32** | **−8** | **37** | **−4** | **34** | **16** | **−31** | **155** | **−418** | **15** | **−963** | **−63** | **19** | **83** |
| Income taxes | 6 | −9 | −38 | 24 | 24 | 0 | 60 | −4 | 22 | 74 | −9 | −11 | −12 | −14 | −26 | −22 |
| Income from discontinued operations (net of income taxes) | 1 | 0 | −34 | −57 | −53 | 0 | −50 | 0 | 13 | 0 | 0 | 0 | −1 | 1 | 1 | −6 |
| **Group profit or loss** | **−51** | **−108** | **−104** | **−41** | **8** | **−4** | **44** | **12** | **4** | **229** | **−427** | **4** | **−976** | **−76** | **−6** | **55** |
| Intangible fixed assets | 517 | 534 | 681 | 896 | 913 | 925 | 530 | 553 | 606 | — | 654 | 1,213 | 1,238 | 2,196 | 2,201 | 2,258 |
| Tangible fixed assets | 109 | 102 | 95 | 107 | 113 | 143 | 73 | 76 | 100 | — | 144 | 177 | 185 | 240 | 223 | 202 |
| Other non-current assets | 322 | 281 | 281 | 352 | 283 | 241 | 147 | 191 | 140 | — | 91 | 79 | 88 | 100 | 168 | 161 |
| **Total non-current assets** | **948** | **917** | **1,057** | **1,355** | **1,309** | **1,309** | **750** | **820** | **846** | **833** | **889** | **1,469** | **1,511** | **2,536** | **2,592** | **2,621** |

**EXHIBIT 2** Getronics NV – financial information (in € mn) (Continued)

| | 2007 H2 | 2007 H1 | 2006 H2 | 2006 H1 | 2005 H2 | 2005 H1 | 2004 H2 | 2004 H1 | 2003 H2 | 2003 H1 | 2002 H2 | 2002 H1 | 2001 H2 | 2001 H1 | 2000 H2 | 2000 H1 |
|---|---|---|---|---|---|---|---|---|---|---|---|---|---|---|---|---|
| **Total current assets** | 701 | 714 | 793 | 841 | 907 | 963 | 889 | 872 | 1,083 | 1,042 | 1,287 | 1,564 | 1,752 | 1,805 | 1,882 | 1,604 |
| – of which cash and cash equivalents | 134 | 122 | 174 | 144 | 251 | 141 | 236 | 217 | 429 | 214 | 296 | 269 | 387 | 250 | 292 | 150 |
| **Assets held for sale** | 0 | 161 | 90 | 22 | 181 | — | — | — | — | — | — | — | — | — | — | — |
| **Total assets** | 1,649 | 1,792 | 1,940 | 2,218 | 2,397 | 2,272 | 1,639 | 1,692 | 1,929 | 1,875 | 2,176 | 3,033 | 3,263 | 4,341 | 4,474 | 4,225 |
| **Shareholders' equity** | 409 | 321 | 408 | 524 | 597 | 602 | 357 | 386 | 65 | 86 | –112 | 288 | 298 | 975 | 1,023 | 1,083 |
| **Non-controlling interest in equity** | 0 | 0 | 0 | 0 | 0 | 0 | 0 | 2 | 2 | 1 | 2 | 2 | 3 | 3 | 4 | 3 |
| **Preference shares** | — | — | — | — | — | — | — | — | 234 | 234 | 234 | 234 | 234 | 234 | 234 | 234 |
| **Subordinated convertibles** | — | — | — | — | — | — | — | — | — | — | 520 | 522 | 554 | 849 | 849 | 849 |
| Short-term interest bearing debt | 67 | 223 | 137 | 85 | 100 | 10 | 6 | 2 | 105 | 38 | 15 | 12 | 24 | 20 | 15 | 15 |
| Long-term debt | 347 | 340 | 323 | 551 | 337 | 453 | 197 | 199 | 330 | 301 | 80 | 367 | 427 | 542 | 435 | 395 |
| Provisions | — | — | — | — | — | — | — | — | — | 286 | 337 | 391 | 411 | 413 | 458 | 452 |
| Employee benefit plans | 95 | 110 | 119 | 155 | 160 | 185 | 202 | 237 | 126 | — | — | — | — | — | — | — |
| Provisions for liabilities and charges | 27 | 16 | 26 | 51 | 39 | 40 | 22 | 23 | 81 | — | — | — | — | — | — | — |
| Deferred income tax liabilities | 10 | 7 | 6 | 20 | 12 | 72 | 12 | 51 | 50 | — | — | — | — | — | — | — |
| Other non-current liabilities | 13 | 29 | 24 | 6 | 15 | 0 | 4 | 0 | 0 | — | — | — | — | — | — | — |
| **Non-current liabilities and short-term debt** | 559 | 725 | 635 | 868 | 663 | 760 | 443 | 512 | 692 | 625 | 432 | 770 | 862 | 975 | 908 | 862 |

*(continued)*

**EXHIBIT 2**  Getronics NV – financial information (in € mn) (Continued)

| | 2007 H2 | 2007 H1 | 2006 H2 | 2006 H1 | 2005 H2 | 2005 H1 | 2004 H2 | 2004 H1 | 2003 H2 | 2003 H1 | 2002 H2 | 2002 H1 | 2001 H2 | 2001 H1 | 2000 H2 | 2000 H1 |
|---|---|---|---|---|---|---|---|---|---|---|---|---|---|---|---|---|
| **Current liabilities (excl. short-term debt)** | 681 | 684 | 862 | 814 | 888 | 910 | 839 | 792 | 936 | 929 | 1,100 | 1,217 | 1,312 | 1,305 | 1,456 | 1,194 |
| **Liabilities from discontinued activities** | 0 | 62 | 35 | 12 | 249 | — | — | — | — | — | — | — | — | — | — | — |
| **Total equity and liabilities** | 1,649 | 1,792 | 1,940 | 2,218 | 2,397 | 2,272 | 1,639 | 1,692 | 1,929 | 1,875 | 2,176 | 3,033 | 3,263 | 4,341 | 4,474 | 4,225 |
| Cash flow from operations | 12 | −148 | 144 | −142 | 95 | −160 | 34 | −141 | 96 | −103 | 175 | 5 | 229 | −27 | −16 | −13 |
| Cash flow from capital expenditures | 13 | −26 | 65 | −81 | −28 | −344 | −19 | −1 | 32 | 259 | 150 | −17 | 22 | −83 | −29 | −127 |
| Cash flow from financing activities | −20 | 115 | −203 | 127 | 48 | 403 | 9 | −53 | 92 | −231 | −307 | −97 | −114 | 68 | 181 | 130 |
| Market capitalization at year end | 771 | 674 | 753 | 1,031 | 1,392 | 1,196 | 846 | 856 | 679 | 458 | 237 | 790 | 1,489 | 1,667 | 2,116 | 5,458 |
| Statutory tax rate (%) | 25.50 | 25.50 | 29.60 | 29.60 | 31.50 | 31.50 | 34.50 | 34.50 | 34.50 | 34.50 | 34.50 | 34.50 | 34.50 | 34.50 | 34.50 | 34.50 |

Sources: 2000–2007 annual and semiannual reports of Getronics NV. Financial figures for the years 2004 through 2007 have been prepared using International Financial Reporting Standards (IFRS Standards); financial figures for the years 2000–2003 have been prepared using Dutch accounting standards.

# Mergers and acquisitions

11

Mergers and acquisitions have long been a popular form of corporate investment. There is no question that these transactions provide a healthy return to target shareholders. However, their value to acquiring shareholders is less understood. Many skeptics point out that given the hefty premiums paid to target shareholders, acquisitions tend to be negative-valued investments for acquiring shareholders.[1]

A number of questions can be examined using financial analysis for mergers and acquisitions:

- Securities analysts can ask: Does a proposed acquisition create value for the acquiring firm's shareholders?
- Risk arbitrageurs can ask: What is the likelihood that a hostile takeover offer will ultimately succeed, and are there other potential acquirers likely to enter the bidding?
- Acquiring management can ask: Does this target fit our business strategy? If so, what is it worth to us, and how can we make an offer that can be successful?
- Target management can ask: Is the acquirer's offer a reasonable one for our shareholders? Are there other potential acquirers that would value our company more than the current bidder?
- Investment bankers can ask: How can we identify potential targets that are likely to be a good match for our clients? And how should we value target firms when we are asked to issue fairness opinions?

In this chapter we focus primarily on the use of financial statement data and analysis directed at evaluating whether a merger creates value for the acquiring firm's shareholders. However, our discussion can also be applied to these other merger contexts. The topic of whether acquisitions create value for acquirers focuses on evaluating:

1 Motivations for acquisitions.
2 The pricing of offers.
3 Forms of payment.
4 The likelihood that an offer will be successful.

Throughout the chapter we use US-based DuPont's acquisition of Denmark-based Danisco in 2011 to illustrate how financial analysis can be used in a merger context.

## Motivation for merger or acquisition

There are a variety of reasons why firms merge or acquire other firms. Some acquiring managers may want to increase their own power and prestige. Others, however, realize that business combinations provide an opportunity to create new economic value for their shareholders. **Merger or acquisition benefits** include the following:

1 **Taking advantage of economies of scale.** Mergers are often justified as a means of providing the two participating firms with increased economies of scale. Economies of scale arise when one large firm can perform a function more efficiently than two smaller firms. For example, Danisco and DuPont were both R&D-intensive companies, were partners in a biofuel-producing joint venture and had overlap between their industrial enzymes and cultures (Danisco) and health and nutrition (DuPont) segments. The merger may therefore provide operating synergies from eliminating duplicate functions and from reducing

research costs. At the time of the merger, management estimated that it would save $130 million annually by 2013, for example, by sharing research and development and sales facilities.

2 **Improving target management.** Another common motivation for acquisition is to improve target management. A firm is likely to be a target if it has systematically underperformed its industry. Historical poor performance could be due to bad luck, but it could also be due to the firm's managers making poor investment and operating decisions, or deliberately pursuing goals that increase their personal power but cost shareholders. In the years 2006 through 2009 Danisco had reported low growth, negative abnormal profitability, and market-to-book ratios below one. However, during the last fiscal year ending prior to the merger announcement, Danisco had managed to grow revenues by 5.5 percent and increase its market-to-book ratio to 1.5. Further, for the following three fiscal years, analysts reckoned that Danisco's revenues would increase by an average of 8 percent and return on equity would revert to a normal level of 10.5 percent, making it less likely that DuPont's motive to acquire Danisco was to replace its management.

3 **Combining complementary resources.** Firms may decide that a merger will create value by combining complementary resources of the two partners. For example, a firm with a strong research and development unit could benefit from merging with a firm that has a strong distribution unit. In the DuPont-Danisco merger, the two firms appeared to have complementary capabilities and resources. DuPont was strong in biomass processing and microbe engineering, whereas Danisco was the world's second-largest manufacturer of enzymes. Combining these activities would help the companies to obtain a stronger position in biotechnology and, for example, develop cost-effective biofuels. Further, through a strong sales organization and close collaboration with customers Danisco had managed to become the global leader in several (bio-based) segments of the competitive food ingredients industry. Danisco's sales organization could thus help to strengthen DuPont's access to several food application markets.

4 **Capturing tax benefits.** Companies may obtain several tax benefits from mergers and acquisitions. The major benefit is the acquisition of operating tax losses. If a firm does not expect to earn sufficient profits to fully utilize operating loss carryforward benefits, it may decide to buy another firm that is earning profits, provided that these profits are made in the same tax jurisdiction as where the loss carryforwards arose. The operating losses and loss carryforwards of the acquirer can then be offset against the target's taxable profit. A second tax benefit often attributed to mergers is the tax shield that comes from increasing leverage for the target firm. That is, the interest expense on the additional debt is tax-deductible and lowers the target firm's tax payments. This was particularly relevant for leveraged buyouts in the 1980s.[2]

5 **Providing low-cost financing to a financially constrained target.** If capital markets are imperfect, perhaps because of information asymmetries between management and outside investors, firms can face capital constraints. Information problems are likely to be especially severe for newly formed, high-growth firms. These firms can be difficult for outside investors to value since they have short track records, and their financial statements provide little insight into the value of their growth opportunities. Further, since they typically have to rely on external funds to finance their growth, capital market constraints for high-growth firms are likely to affect their ability to undertake profitable new projects. Public capital markets are therefore likely to be costly sources of funds for these types of firms. An acquirer that understands the business and is willing to provide a steady source of finance may therefore be able to add value.[3]

6 **Creating value through restructuring and break-ups.** Acquisitions are often pursued by financial investors such as leveraged buy-out firms that expect to create value by breaking up the firm. The break-up value is expected to be larger than the aggregate worth of the entire firm. Often a consortium of financial investors will acquire a firm with a view of unlocking value from various components of the firm's asset base.

7 **Increasing product-market rents.** Firms also can have incentives to merge to increase product-market rents. By merging and becoming a dominant firm in the industry, two smaller firms can collude to restrict their output and raise prices, thereby increasing their profits. This circumvents problems that arise in cartels of independent firms, where firms have incentives to cheat on the cartel and increase their output. DuPont focused its activities on biotechnology and chemicals. Danisco operated primarily in the food

ingredients and industrial enzymes industries. Because the companies operated in related segments but were not directly competing, the merger was not expected to significantly increase product-market rents other than through a possible increase in the companies' bargaining power over their suppliers.

While product-market rents make sense for firms as a motive for merging, the two partners are unlikely to announce their intentions when they explain the merger to their investors, since most countries have competition (antitrust) laws that regulate mergers between two firms in the same industry. For example, in the EU large mergers must be approved by the European Commission, which examines whether mergers do not impede effective competition by creating a dominant market position. National mergers are generally reviewed by national competition authorities. In the United States there are three major antitrust statutes – the Sherman Act of 1890, the Clayton Act of 1914, and the Hart-Scott-Rodino Act of 1976.

Anticompetitive concerns were less significant for the DuPont-Danisco merger because the merging companies were not directly competing in the same markets. Merger approval was obtained from the US Federal Trade Commission (FTC), China's Ministry of Commerce, and the European Commission.

While many of the motivations for acquisitions are likely to create new economic value for shareholders, some are not. Firms that are flush with cash but have few new profitable investment opportunities are particularly prone to using their surplus cash to make acquisitions. Shareholders of these firms would probably prefer that managers pay out any surplus or "free" cash flows as dividends, or use the funds to repurchase their firm's shares. However, these options reduce the size of the firm and the assets under management's control. Management may therefore prefer to invest the free cash flows to buy new companies, even if they are not valued by shareholders. Of course managers will never announce that they are buying a firm because they are reluctant to pay out funds to shareholders.

They may explain the merger using one of the motivations discussed above, or they may argue that they are buying the target at a bargain price.

Another motivation for mergers that is valued by managers but not shareholders is diversification. Diversification was a popular motivation for acquisitions in the 1960s and early 1970s. Acquirers sought to dampen their earnings volatility by buying firms in unrelated businesses. Diversification as a motive for acquisitions has since been widely discredited. Modern finance theorists point out that in a well-functioning capital market, investors can diversify for themselves and do not need managers to do so for them. In addition, diversification has been criticized for leading firms losing sight of their major competitive strengths and expanding into businesses where they do not have expertise.[4] These firms eventually recognize that diversification-motivated acquisitions do not create value, leading to divestitures of business units.

## Key Analysis Questions

In evaluating a proposed merger, analysts are interested in determining whether the merger creates new wealth for acquiring and target shareholders, or whether it is motivated by managers' desires to increase their own power and prestige. Key questions for financial analysis are likely to include:

- *What is the motivation(s) for an acquisition and any anticipated benefits disclosed by acquirers or targets?*
- *What are the industries of the target and acquirer?* Are the firms related horizontally (the firms are suppliers of similar products) or vertically (one firm is the other firm's supplier)? How close are the business relations between them? If the businesses are unrelated, is the acquirer cash-rich and reluctant to return free cash flows to shareholders?
- *What are the key operational strengths of the target and the acquirer?* Are these strengths complementary? For example, does one firm have a renowned research group and the other a strong distribution network?

- *Is the acquisition a friendly one, supported by target management, or hostile?* A hostile takeover is more likely to occur for targets with poorly performing management who oppose the acquisition to preserve their jobs. However, as discussed below, this typically reduces acquirer management's access to information about the target, increasing the risk of overpayment.
- *What is the pre-merger performance of the two firms?* Performance metrics are likely to include ROE, gross margins, general and administrative expenses to revenue, and working capital management ratios. On the basis of these measures, is the target a poor performer in its industry, implying that there are opportunities for improved management? Is the acquirer in a declining industry and searching for new directions?
- *What is the tax position of both firms?* What are the average and marginal current tax rates for the target and the acquirer? Does the acquirer have operating loss carryforwards and the target taxable profits?

This analysis should help the analyst understand what specific benefits, if any, the merger is likely to generate.

# Acquisition pricing

A well-thought-out economic motivation for a merger or acquisition is a necessary but insufficient condition for creating value for acquiring shareholders. The acquirer must be careful to avoid overpaying for the target. Overpayment makes the transaction highly desirable and profitable for target shareholders, but it diminishes the value of the deal to acquiring shareholders. A financial analyst can use the following methods to assess whether the acquiring firm is overpaying for the target (**target value analysis**).

### ANALYZING PREMIUM OFFERED TO TARGET SHAREHOLDERS

One popular way to assess whether the acquirer is overpaying for a target is to compare the premium offered to target shareholders to premiums offered in similar transactions. If the acquirer offers a relatively high **acquisition premium**, the analyst is typically led to conclude that the transaction is less likely to create value for acquiring shareholders.

Premiums differ significantly for friendly and hostile acquisitions. Premiums tend to be about 30 percent higher for hostile deals than for friendly offers, implying that hostile acquirers are more likely to overpay for a target.[5] There are several reasons for this. First, a friendly acquirer has access to the internal records of the target, making it much less likely that the acquirer will be surprised by hidden liabilities or problems once it has completed the deal. In contrast, a hostile acquirer does not have this advantage in valuing the target and is forced to make assumptions that may later turn out to be false. Second, the delays that typically accompany a hostile acquisition often provide opportunities for competing bidders to make an offer for the target, leading to a bidding war.

Comparing a target's premium to values for similar types of transactions is straightforward to compute, but it has several practical problems. First, it is not obvious how to define a comparable transaction. European takeover premiums differ on various dimensions. As argued, average premiums are greater in hostile takeovers than in friendly takeovers. Further, takeover premiums vary by means of payment. Equity-financed acquisitions (share-for-share mergers) require lower premiums than cash-financed acquisitions because the former type makes the target firms' shareholders also shareholders of the new company. Target shareholders thereby keep benefiting – through capital gains – from the synergies created by the merger. Takeover premiums may also depend on the target firms' country of domicile. When a target firm is located in a country with strict takeover rules, the target firm's shareholders may have more power to negotiate higher premiums. Research has indicated that during the years 1993 to 2001 takeover premiums in the United Kingdom, where hostile takeovers were more common and takeover rules were stricter, were on average higher than in Continental Europe.[6]

A second problem in using premiums offered to target shareholders to assess whether an acquirer overpaid is that measured premiums can be misleading if an offer is anticipated by investors. The share price run-up for the target will then tend to make estimates of the premium appear relatively low. This limitation can be partially offset by using target share prices one month prior to the acquisition offer as the basis for calculating premiums. However, in some cases offers may have been anticipated for even longer than one month.

Finally, using target premiums to assess whether an acquirer overpaid ignores the value of the target to the acquirer after the acquisition. The acquirer expects to benefit from the merger by improving the target firm's operating performance through a combination of economies of scale, improved management, tax benefits, and spillover effects derived from the acquisition. Clearly, acquirers will be willing to pay higher premiums for targets that are expected to generate higher merger benefits. Thus examining the premium alone cannot determine whether the acquisition creates value for the acquiring shareholder.

## ANALYZING VALUE OF THE TARGET TO THE ACQUIRER

A second and more reliable way of assessing whether the acquirer has overpaid for the target is to compare the offer price to the estimated value of the target to the acquirer. This latter value can be computed using the valuation techniques discussed in Chapters 7 and 8. The most popular methods of valuation used for mergers and acquisitions are earnings multiples and discounted cash flows. Since a comprehensive discussion of these techniques is provided earlier in the book, we focus here on implementation issues that arise for valuing targets in mergers and acquisitions.

We recommend first computing the value of the target as an independent firm. This provides a way of checking whether the valuation assumptions are reasonable, because for publicly listed targets we can compare our estimate with pre-merger market prices. It also provides a useful benchmark for thinking about how the target's performance, and hence its value, is likely to change once it is acquired.

### Earnings multiples

To estimate the value of a target to an acquirer using earnings multiples, we have to forecast earnings for the target and decide on an appropriate earnings multiple, as follows:

- Step 1: Forecasting earnings. Earnings forecasts are usually made by first forecasting next year's profit or loss for the target assuming no acquisition. Historical revenue growth rates, gross margins, and average tax rates are useful in building a pro forma earnings model. Once we have forecasted the profit for the target prior to an acquisition, we can incorporate into the pro forma model any improvements in earnings performance that we expect to result from the acquisition. Performance improvements can be modelled as:
  - Higher operating margins through economies of scale in purchasing, or increased market power.
  - Reductions in expenses as a result of consolidating research and development staffs, sales forces, and/or administration.
  - Lower average tax rates from taking advantage of operating tax loss carryforwards.
- Step 2: Determining the price-earnings multiple. How do we determine the earnings multiple to be applied to our earnings forecasts? If the target firm is listed, it may be tempting to use the preacquisition price-earnings multiple to value post-merger earnings. However, there are several limitations to this approach. First, for many targets earnings growth expectations and risk characteristics are likely to change after a merger, implying that there will be a difference between the pre- and post-merger price-earnings multiples. Post-merger earnings should then be valued using a multiple for firms with comparable growth and risk characteristics (see the discussion in Chapter 7). A second problem is that pre-merger price-earnings multiples are unavailable for unlisted targets. Once again it becomes necessary to decide which types of listed firms are likely to be good comparables. In addition, since the earnings being valued are the projected earnings for the next 12 months or the next full fiscal year, the appropriate benchmark ratio should be a forward price-earnings ratio. Finally, if a pre-merger price-earnings multiple is appropriate for valuing post-merger earnings, care is required to ensure that the multiple is calculated prior to any acquisition announcement because the price will increase in anticipation of the premium to be paid to target shareholders.

Table 11.1 summarizes how price-earnings multiples are used to value a target firm before an acquisition (assuming it will remain an independent entity), and to estimate the value of a target to a potential acquirer.

**TABLE 11.1**  Summary of price-earnings valuation for targets

| | |
|---|---|
| *Value of target as an independent firm* | Target earnings forecast for the next year, assuming no change in ownership, multiplied by its *pre-merger* PE multiple |
| *Value of target to potential acquirer* | Target *revised* earnings forecast for the next year, incorporating the effect of any operational changes made by the acquirer, multiplied by its *post-merger* PE multiple |

### Limitations of price-earnings valuation

As explained in Chapter 7, there are serious limitations to using earnings multiples for valuation. In addition to these limitations, the method has two more that are specific to merger valuations:

1 PE multiples assume that merger performance improvements come either from an immediate increase in earnings or from an increase in earnings growth (and hence an increase in the post-merger PE ratio). In reality, improvements and savings can come in many forms – gradual increases in earnings from implementing new operating policies, elimination of over-investment, better management of working capital, or paying out excess cash to shareholders. These types of improvements are not naturally reflected in PE multiples.

2 PE models do not easily incorporate any spillover benefits from an acquisition for the acquirer because they focus on valuing the earnings of the target.

### Discounted abnormal profit, abnormal profit growth, or cash flows

As discussed in Chapters 7 and 8, we can also value a company using the discounted abnormal profit, discounted abnormal profit growth, and discounted free cash flow methods. These require us to first forecast the abnormal profit, abnormal profit growth, or free cash flows for the firm and then discount them at the cost of capital, as follows.

- Step 1: Forecast abnormal profits/abnormal profit growth/free cash flows. A pro forma model of expected future profits and cash flows for the firm provides the basis for forecasting abnormal profits, abnormal profit growth, and free cash flows. As a starting point, the model should be constructed under the assumption that the target remains an independent firm. The model should reflect the best estimates of future revenue growth, cost structures, working capital needs, investment and research and development needs, and cash requirements for known debt retirements, developed from financial analysis of the target. The abnormal profit (growth) method requires that we forecast earnings or net operating profit after tax (NOPAT) for as long as the firm expects new investment projects to earn more than their cost of capital. Under the free cash flow approach, the pro forma model will forecast free cash flows to either the firm or to equity, typically for a period of five to ten years. Once we have a model of the abnormal profits, abnormal profit growth or free cash flows, we can incorporate any improvements in earnings/free cash flows that we expect to result from the acquisition. These will include the cost savings, cash received from asset sales, benefits from eliminating over-investment, improved working capital management, and paying out excess cash to shareholders.

- Step 2: Compute the discount rate. If we are valuing the target's postacquisition NOPAT or cash flows to the firm, the appropriate discount rate is the required return on net operating assets for the target, using its expected *postacquisition* capital structure. Alternatively, if the target equity cash flows are being valued directly or if we are valuing abnormal profits, the appropriate discount rate is the target's *postacquisition cost of equity* rather than its required return on net operating assets. Two common mistakes are to use the acquirer's cost of capital or the target's *preacquisition* cost of capital to value the post-merger earnings/cash flows from the target.

The computation of the target's postacquisition cost of capital can be complicated if the acquirer plans to make a change to the target's capital structure after the acquisition, since the target's costs of debt and equity will change. As discussed in Chapter 8, this involves estimating the asset beta for the target, calculating the new equity and debt betas under the modified capital structure, and finally computing the revised cost of equity capital or weighted cost of capital. As a practical matter, the effect of these changes on the weighted average cost of capital is likely to be quite small unless the revision in leverage has a significant effect on the target's interest tax shields or its likelihood of financial distress.

Table 11.2 summarizes how the discounted abnormal profit/cash flow methods can be used to value a target before an acquisition (assuming it will remain an independent entity) and to estimate the value of a target firm to a potential acquirer.

- Step 3: Analyze sensitivity. Once we have estimated the expected value of a target, we will want to examine the sensitivity of our estimate to changes in the model assumptions. For example, answering the following questions can help the analyst assess the risks associated with an acquisition:
  - What happens to the value of the target if it takes longer than expected for the benefits of the acquisition to materialize?
  - What happens to the value of the target if the acquisition prompts its primary competitors to respond by also making an acquisition? Will such a response affect our plans and estimates?

**TABLE 11.2** Summary of discounted abnormal profit/abnormal profit growth/cash flow valuation for targets

| | |
|---|---|
| *Value of target without an acquisition* | a. Present value of abnormal profits/abnormal profit growth/free cash flows to target equity assuming no acquisition, discounted at *pre-merger* cost of equity; or |
| | b. present value of abnormal NOPAT/abnormal NOPAT growth/free cash flows to target debt and equity assuming no acquisition, discounted at *pre-merger* required return on net operating assets, plus value of investment assets less value of debt. |
| *Value of target to potential acquirer* | a. Present value of abnormal profits/abnormal profit growth/free cash flows to target equity, *including benefits from merger,* discounted at *post-merger* cost of equity; or |
| | b. present value of abnormal NOPAT/abnormal NOPAT growth/free cash flows to target, *including benefits from merger,* discounted at *post-merger* required return on net operating assets, plus value of investment assets less value of debt. |

## Key analysis questions

To analyze the pricing of an acquisition, the analyst is interested in assessing the value of the acquisition benefits to be generated by the acquirer relative to the price paid to target shareholders. Analysts are therefore likely to be interested in answers to the following questions:

- What is the premium that the acquirer paid for the target's shares? What does this premium imply for the acquirer in terms of future performance improvements to justify the premium?
- What are the likely performance improvements that management expects to generate from the acquisition? For example, are there likely to be increases in the revenues for the merged firm from new products, increased prices, or better distribution of existing products? Alternatively, are there cost savings as a result of taking advantage of economies of scale, improved efficiency, or a lower cost of capital for the target?
- What is the value of any performance improvements? Values can be estimated using multiples or discounted abnormal profit/cash flow methods.

## DUPONT'S PRICING OF DANISCO

The DuPont-Danisco acquisition was structured as a cash tender offer. For each share they held, Danisco shareholders would receive DKK665. DuPont's DKK32.3 ($5.8) billion price for Danisco represented a 29 percent premium to target shareholders over the market value on December 17, 2010, one day after Danisco's most recent quarterly earnings announcement and a few weeks prior to the disclosure of the cash tender offer.

With average takeover premiums in cash-financed acquisitions of 26 percent, the premium that DuPont offered to Danisco shareholders is slightly above average. Prior to the acquisition announcement, Danisco's leading PE multiple (based on expected earnings for the next fiscal year) was close to 18. Given management's estimate that the acquisition would create cost savings of about DKK0.5 billion (after tax), analysts' consensus (pre-merger) earnings forecast for 2011 of DKK1.4 billion, and a PE multiple of 18, Danisco's post-merger value could be estimated at DKK34.2 billion (18 × [1.4 + 0.5]). This multiple-based value estimate is more than the offer price of DKK32.3 billion, which suggests that DuPont's management expected that the anticipated cost savings would not persist or were somewhat uncertain.

The market reaction to the acquisition announcement on January 10, 2011, suggests that analysts believed that the deal would not create value for DuPont's shareholders – DuPont's share price decreased by 1.5 percent, during the 11 days prior to the announcement to the actual announcement day. By the tenth trading day after the announcement, DuPont's share was still down 1.5 percent, or $0.7 billion. Given the $1.3 billion premium that DuPont paid for Danisco, investors believed that the merger would create value of $0.6 billion.

# Acquisition financing and form of payment

Even if an acquisition is undertaken to create new economic value and is priced judiciously, it may still destroy shareholder value if it is inappropriately financed. Several financing options are available to acquirers, including issuing shares or warrants to target shareholders, or acquiring target shares using surplus cash or proceeds from new debt. The trade-offs between these options from the standpoint of target shareholders usually hinge on their tax and transaction cost implications, which, for acquirers, can affect the firm's capital structure and provide new information to investors.

As we discuss next, the financing preferences of target and acquiring shareholders can diverge. **Acquisition financing** arrangements can therefore increase or reduce the attractiveness of an acquisition from the standpoint of acquiring shareholders. As a result, a complete analysis of an acquisition will include an examination of the implications of the financing arrangements for the acquirer.

## EFFECT OF FORM OF PAYMENT ON ACQUIRING SHAREHOLDERS

From the perspective of the acquirer, the form of payment is essentially a financing decision. As discussed in Chapter 10, in the long term firms choose whether to use debt or equity financing to balance the tax and incentive benefits of debt against the risks of financial distress. For acquiring shareholders the costs and benefits of different financing options usually depend on how the offer affects their firm's capital structure, any information effects associated with different forms of financing.

### Capital structure effects of the form of financing

In acquisitions where debt financing or surplus cash are the primary form of consideration for target shares, the acquisition increases the financial leverage of the acquirer. This increase in leverage may be part of the acquisition strategy, since one way an acquirer can add value to an inefficient firm is to lower its taxes by increasing interest tax shields. However, in many acquisitions an increase in postacquisition leverage is a side effect of the method of financing and not part of a deliberate tax-minimizing strategy. The increase in leverage can then potentially reduce shareholder value for the acquirer by increasing the risk of financial distress.

To assess whether an acquisition leads an acquirer to have too much leverage, financial analysts can assess the acquirer's financial risk following the proposed acquisition by these methods:

- Analyze the business risks and the volatility of the combined, postacquisition cash flows against the level of debt in the new capital structure, and the implications for possible financial distress.
- Assess the pro forma financial risks for the acquirer under the proposed financing plan. Popular measures of financial risk include debt-to-equity and interest coverage ratios, as well as projections of cash flows available to meet debt repayments. The ratios can be compared to similar performance metrics for the acquiring and target firms' industries to determine whether post-merger ratios indicate that the firm's probability of financial distress has increased significantly.
- Examine whether there are important off-balance sheet liabilities for the target and/or acquirer that are not included in the pro forma ratio and cash flow analysis of postacquisition financial risk.
- Determine whether the pro forma assets for the acquirer are largely intangible and therefore sensitive to financial distress. Measures of intangible assets include ratios such as market-to-book equity and tangible assets to the market value of equity.

### Information problems and the form of financing

In the short term, information asymmetries between managers and external investors can make managers reluctant to raise equity to finance new projects. Managers' reluctance arises from their fear that investors will interpret the decision as an indication that the firm's equity is overvalued. In the short term, this effect can lead managers to deviate from the firm's long-term optimal mix of debt and equity. As a result, acquirers are likely to prefer using internal funds or debt to finance an acquisition, because these forms of consideration are less likely to be interpreted negatively by investors.[7]

The information effects imply that firms forced to use equity financing are likely to face a share price decline when investors learn of the method of financing.[8] From the viewpoint of financial analysts, the financing announcement may therefore provide valuable news about the preacquisition value of the acquirer. On the other hand, it should have no implications for analysis of whether the acquisition creates value for acquiring shareholders, since the news reflected in the financing announcement is about the *preacquisition* value of the acquirer and not about the *postacquisition* value of the target to the acquirer.

A second information problem arises if the acquiring management does not have good information about the target. Equity financing then provides a way for acquiring shareholders to share the information risks with target shareholders. If the acquirer finds out after the acquisition that the value of the target is less than previously anticipated, the accompanying decline in the acquirer's equity price will be partially borne by target shareholders who continue to hold the acquirer's shares. In contrast, if the target's shares were acquired in a cash offer, any postacquisition loss would be fully borne by the acquirer's original shareholders. The risk-sharing benefits from using equity financing appear to be widely recognized for acquisitions of private companies, where public information on the target is largely unavailable.[9] In practice it appears to be considered less important for acquisitions of large public corporations.[10]

### Corporate control and the form of payment

There is a significant difference between the use of cash and shares in terms of its impact on the voting control of the combined firm postacquisition. Financing an acquisition with cash allows the acquirer to retain the structure and composition of its equity ownership. On the other hand, depending on the size of the target firm relative to the acquirer, an acquisition financed with shares could have a significant impact on the ownership and control of the firm postacquisition. This could be particularly relevant to a family-controlled acquirer.

Therefore the effects of control need to be balanced against the other costs and benefits when determining the form of payment.

Research has found that European acquirers whose primary shareholder controls between 40 and 60 percent of the equity votes indeed have a preference for cash as the primary form of consideration.[11] For shareholders who hold an equity stake between 40 and 60 percent, the threat of losing control after a share-for-share exchange is most imminent.

## EFFECT OF FORM OF PAYMENT ON TARGET SHAREHOLDERS

The key payment considerations for target shareholders are the tax and transaction cost implications of the acquirer's offer.

### Tax effects of different forms of consideration

Target shareholders care about the after-tax value of any offer they receive for their shares. In many countries, whenever target shareholders receive cash for their shares, they are required to pay capital gains tax on the difference between the takeover offer price and their original purchase price. Alternatively, if they receive shares in the acquirer as consideration, they can defer any taxes on the capital gain until they sell the new shares. To qualify for the deferral of capital gains taxes, governments may require additional conditions to be met.[12] In the United Kingdom taxes on capital gains from takeovers can be deferred only when the acquirer and the target firm operate in the same industry. In the United States the acquisition must be undertaken as a tax-free reorganization. Within the EU not only capital gains on national but also within-border share-for-share exchanges can be deferred. The EU Merger Directive guarantees that the option to defer capital gains taxes, if allowed for national mergers, applies also to cross-border share-for-share exchanges.

Tax laws that allow the deferral of capital gains taxes appear to cause target shareholders to prefer a share offer to a cash one. This is certainly likely to be the case for a target founder who still has a significant stake in the company. If the company's share price has appreciated over its life, the founder will face substantial capital gains tax on a cash offer and will therefore probably prefer to receive shares in the acquiring firm. However, cash and share offers can be tax-neutral for some groups of shareholders. For example, consider the tax implications for risk arbitrageurs, who take a short-term position in a company that is a takeover candidate in the hope that other bidders will emerge and increase the takeover price. They have no intention of holding shares in the acquirer once the takeover is completed and will pay ordinary income tax on any short-term trading gain. Cash and share offers therefore have identical after-tax values for risk arbitrageurs. Similarly, tax-exempt institutions are likely to be indifferent to whether an offer is in cash or shares.

### Transaction costs and the form of payment

Transaction costs are another factor related to the form of financing that can be relevant to target shareholders. Transaction costs are incurred when target shareholders sell any shares received as consideration for their shares in the target. These costs will not be faced by target shareholders if the bidder offers them cash. Transaction costs are unlikely to be significant for investors who intend to hold the acquirer's shares following a share acquisition. However, they may be relevant for investors who intend to sell, such as risk arbitrageurs.

## DUPONT'S FINANCING OF DANISCO

DuPont offered Danisco shareholders DKK665 in cash for each Danisco share. Given Danisco's 48,574 shares outstanding, this implied a total offer of DKK32.3 billion. By using cash to finance the acquisition, DuPont increased its financial leverage and let its shareholders fully bear any future losses arising from the acquisition. The choice for cash to finance the acquisition suggests that the risk of postacquisition losses was small, presumably because of Danisco's public status and transparency as well as the company's relatively small size.

## Key Analysis Questions

For an analyst focused on the acquiring firm, it is important to assess how the method of financing affects the acquirer's capital structure and its risks of financial distress by asking the following questions:

- What is the leverage for the newly created firm? How does this compare to leverage for comparable firms in the industry?
- What are the projected future cash flows for the merged firm? Are these sufficient to meet the firm's debt commitments? How much of a cushion does the firm have if future cash flows are lower than expected? Is the firm's debt level so high that it is likely to impair its ability to finance profitable future investments if future cash flows are below expectations?

## Acquisition outcome

The final question of interest to the analyst evaluating a potential acquisition is whether it will indeed be completed. If an acquisition has a clear value-based motive, the target is priced appropriately, and its proposed financing does not create unnecessary financial risks for the acquirer, it may still fail because the target receives a higher competing bid, there is opposition from **entrenched target management**, or the transaction fails to receive necessary regulatory approval. Therefore, to evaluate the likelihood that an offer will be accepted, the financial analyst has to understand whether there are potential competing bidders who could pay an even higher premium to target shareholders than is currently offered. They also have to consider whether target managers are entrenched and, to protect their jobs, likely to oppose an offer, as well as the political and regulatory environment in which the target and the acquirer operate.

### OTHER POTENTIAL ACQUIRERS

If there are other potential bidders for a target, especially ones who place a higher value on the target, there is a strong possibility that the bidder in question will be unsuccessful. Target management and shareholders have an incentive to delay accepting the initial offer to give potential competitors time to also submit a bid. From the perspective of the initial bidder, this means that the offer could potentially reduce shareholder value by the cost of making the offer (including substantial investment banking and legal fees). In practice, a losing bidder can usually recoup these losses and sometimes even make healthy profits from selling to the successful acquirer any shares it has accumulated in the target.

## Key Analysis Questions

The financial analyst can determine whether there are other potential acquirers for a target and how they value the target by asking the following questions:

- Are there other firms that could also implement the initial bidder's acquisition strategy? For example, if this strategy relies on developing benefits from complementary assets, look for potential bidders who also have assets complementary to the target. If the goal of the acquisition is to replace inefficient management, what other firms in the target's industry could provide management expertise?
- Who are the acquirer's major competitors? Could any of these firms provide an even better fit for the target?

## TARGET MANAGEMENT ENTRENCHMENT

If target managers are entrenched and fearful for their jobs, it is likely that they will oppose a bidder's offer. Some firms have implemented "golden parachutes" for top managers to counteract their concerns about job security at the time of an offer. Golden parachutes provide top managers of a target firm with attractive compensation rewards should the firm get taken over. However, many firms do not have such schemes, and opposition to an offer from entrenched management is a very real possibility.

In some European countries the entrenchment of management is facilitated by legal provisions that allow a company to install various takeover defenses. For example, in most countries, firms can limit the number of votes that a shareholder can exercise at a shareholders' meeting. A voting cap effectively reduces the voting power that a potential acquirer can obtain. Another example of a takeover defense mechanism, which is commonly used in the Netherlands, is the issuance of depository receipts by an administrative office that is controlled by the firm whose shares the office holds.[13] Holders of depository receipts have the right to receive dividends but no voting rights. Instead, the administrative office retains and exercises the voting rights. This construction makes it difficult for an acquiring firm to obtain any voting power.

While the existence of takeover defenses for a target indicates that its management is likely to fight a bidding firm's offer, defenses do not often prevent an acquisition from taking place. Instead, they tend to cause delays, which increase the likelihood that there will be competing offers made for the target, including offers by friendly parties solicited by the target management, called "white knights." Takeover defenses therefore increase the likelihood that the bidder in question will be outbid for the target, or that it will have to increase its offer significantly to win a bidding contest. These risks may discourage acquirers from embarking on a potentially hostile acquisition. Nonetheless, in recent years hostile takeovers have become more rather than less popular in Europe. For example, in 2006 steel producer Mittal Steel was engaged in a hostile takeover attempt for industry peer Arcelor. Arcelor called in the help of "white knight" Severstal, but eventually was forced by its shareholders to accept Mittal's offer. The takeover battle had caused a delay of five months and had driven up the takeover price by 49 percent, or €8.4 billion.

**Takeover regulations** have the objectives of preventing management entrenchment and protecting minority shareholders during European takeovers. During the 1990s national takeover regulations in Europe began converging towards the UK regime model. In 2004 the European Commission issued a heavily debated Takeover Directive, which applies to companies whose shares are traded on a (regulated) public exchange. The most important rules in this Directive are the following:[14]

- The equal-treatment rule and the mandatory-bid rule aim at protecting minority shareholders in takeovers. The mandatory-bid rule prescribes that the acquiring firm makes an offer for all remaining shares, once its equity stake exceeds a predefined threshold. In Denmark, Italy, and the United Kingdom, this threshold is, for example, 30 percent. The equal-treatment rule requires that the acquiring firm makes equally favourable offers to the controlling and minority shareholders of the target firm.
- Under the squeeze-out rule, the acquiring firm can force the remaining minority shareholders to sell their shares at the tender offer price, once the firm holds a predefined equity stake of, usually, between 80 and 95 percent. Under the sell-out rule, the remaining shareholders can force the acquiring firm to buy their shares at a fair price.
- The board-neutrality rule requires that during takeovers management will not take actions that may frustrate the takeover.

Another proposed rule, the breakthrough rule, did make it into the final Directive but can be opted out of by individual countries. The breakthrough rule mandates that a firm that has acquired a predefined percentage of shares can exercise votes on its shares as if all outstanding shares, including the firm's shares, carry one vote per share. For example, the breakthrough rule guarantees that an acquiring firm that owns 90 percent of the target firm's ordinary shares can exercise exactly 90 percent of the votes during a shareholders' meeting of the target firm, irrespective of the takeover defense mechanisms that are in place.

The rules in the EU Takeover Directive can affect the analysis of a takeover offer. For example, in some jurisdictions the laws prescribe that when the mandatory-bid rule comes into effect, the acquiring firm must offer the remaining shareholders no less than the highest price it has paid to other shareholders. This rule, of course, invites the investor to strategically wait until the last moment before accepting the offer. The board-neutrality rule reduces management entrenchment through postbid takeover defenses and therefore reduces the probability that a target firm will oppose an acquisition. The breakthrough rule, if implemented, can remove firms' prebid takeover defenses, such as voting caps.

## Key Analysis Questions

To assess whether the target firm's management is entrenched and therefore likely to oppose an acquisition, analysts can ask the following questions:

- Does the target firm have takeover defenses designed to protect management? If so, do national takeover rules reduce the effect of such defenses? Further, do national takeover rules regulate that minority shareholders receive a fair price?
- Has the target been a poor performer relative to other firms in its industry? If so, management's job security is likely to be threatened by a takeover, leading it to oppose any offers.
- Is there a golden parachute plan in place for target management? Golden parachutes provide attractive compensation for management in the event of a takeover to deter opposition to a takeover for job security reasons.

### ANTITRUST AND SECURITY ISSUES

Regulators such as the European Commission's DG for Competition and the Federal Trade Commission in the United States assess the effects of an acquisition on the competitive dynamics of the industry in which the firms operate. The objective is to ensure that no one firm, through mergers and acquisitions, creates a dominant position that can impede effective competition in specific geographies or product markets.

### ANALYSIS OF OUTCOME OF DUPONT'S OFFER FOR DANISCO

Analysts covering Danisco had little reason to question whether Danisco would be sold to DuPont. The offer was a friendly one that had received the approval of Danisco's management and board of directors. There probably was some risk of another biotech or chemical firm entering the bidding for Danisco. For example, following the merger announcement there were rumors that Netherlands-based DSM, which owned a 5 percent equity stake in Danisco, would launch a competing bid. However, DSM's management considered DuPont's bid too high and sold its equity stake to DuPont in May 2011. Eventually, none of DuPont's competitors made a bid for Danisco.

In Denmark takeover regulations require the acquirer to hold at least 90 percent of the target's shares before it can squeeze out the remaining shareholders. Following the acquisition announcement US-based hedge fund Elliott International gradually increased its stake in Danisco to 10.02 percent, making the acquisition outcome uncertain and pressuring DuPont to raise its bid from DKK665 per share to DKK700 per share. After calling the DKK700 bid "final," Elliott ended its activism and surrendered its shares to DuPont. Elliott's interference in the DuPont-Danisco merger raised the premium received by Danisco's shareholders and thus illustrates how European takeover regulations can support shareholder activism and, consequently, protect shareholders' interests during a takeover.

# Reporting on mergers and acquisitions: purchase price allocations

The acquisition price that an acquiring firm pays to the target firm's shareholders compensates them for the transfer of a potentially widespread collection of assets and liabilities. For example, in the DuPont-Danisco acquisition DuPont's management paid Danisco's shareholders DKK32.3 billion in cash and assumed Danisco's liabilities in exchange for receiving ownership of not only Danisco's physical equipment and buildings but also its technology, in-process research and development, customer relationships, and sales force. The International Accounting Reporting Standards on business combinations (IFRS Standards 3) require that acquiring firms separately identify and value the assets and liabilities that are transferred in a merger or acquisition to provide a basis for reporting the transaction in the acquirer's post-merger consolidated financial statements. The process of doing so is typically referred to as a **purchase price allocation** and relies strongly on the valuation tools discussed in previous chapters.[15]

The objective of a purchase price allocation is essentially twofold. First, the exercise aims to allocate the acquisition price, being the fair value of the consideration transferred to the target firm's shareholders, to the separately identifiable assets (and liabilities), such as buildings, machinery, or patents. Second, the allocation aims to determine the remaining proportion of the acquisition price that cannot be allocated to individual assets and as such is assumed to be the fair value of the synergies created from using all assets in combination. This remaining proportion is labelled "goodwill" and reported as a separate line item in the acquirer's postacquisition consolidated financial statements. Consequently, a purchase price allocation helps outside investors to assess whether the acquisition price is reasonable given the identifiable assets acquired or whether the amount of goodwill arising from the merger or acquisition is too large to be justified by the expected M&A synergies. Further, the distinction between goodwill and other intangible assets is relevant because it affects future financial statements. Accountants assume that goodwill has an indefinite economic useful life and must therefore be regularly tested for impairment rather than amortized over a predefined period. In contrast, most other intangible assets have finite economic lives and must thus be systematically amortized, thereby creating periodic charges to future income statements. Given the differences in accounting treatments, managers are not likely to be indifferent to the choice between goodwill and other intangibles in a purchase price allocation.

Purchase price allocations consist of the following five steps:

- Step 1: Determine the value of the target firm. The first step in a purchase price allocation is to determine the value of the target firm as the sum of the fair values of (1) the consideration transferred to the target firm's shareholders and (2) the target firm's interest-bearing debt. In the following steps, this target firm value will be allocated among the separately identifiable assets and goodwill.

- Step 2: Estimate the rate of return implicit in the M&A transaction. The second step of a purchase price allocation is to estimate the discount rate that sets the target firm value equal to the sum of (a) the fair value of the target firm's investment assets plus (b) the present value of the target firm's *postacquisition* free cash flows from operations. Benchmarking this internal rate of return estimate against the target firm's normally required return on net operating assets provides an initial assessment of whether the acquirer overpaid for the target. In particular, if the internal rate of return is significantly lower than the normally required return, this may indicate that the acquisition price is too high to be justified by expected M&A synergies and warrants further investigation of whether goodwill on the transaction is impaired.

- Step 3: Identify the contributory assets. The third step identifies the target firm's assets that are separately identifiable and contribute to the target firm's *postacquisition* free cash flows. These assets are commonly referred to as the "contributory assets." Contributory assets can be working capital components (e.g., such as trade receivables, inventories, and trade payables), non-current tangible assets (e.g., property, plant, and equipment), or non-current intangible assets (e.g., trademarks, software, customer relationships, and the assembled workforce).

Part of this step is also to determine the required return on each of the identified contributory assets. These required returns have at least two purposes. First, following the idea that the required return on a portfolio of assets is a weighted average of the required returns on the individual assets in the portfolio, the asset value-weighted average of the required returns on the contributory assets must be equal to the internal rate of return estimated under step 2. This equality helps to derive the implied required return on goodwill, thereby providing an initial indication of the riskiness of the transaction. Second, the required returns help to estimate each asset's contribution to future free cash flows, also referred to as contributory asset charges, which become relevant in the next step.

- Step 4: Value the contributory assets. Different types of contributory assets may require different valuation techniques. For example, whereas the valuation of property, plant, and equipment typically relies on external appraisers' value estimates, the value of brand names must be derived from royalty rates that companies pay to make use of a brand. The following set of valuation approaches can be used in purchase price allocations:
  - Cost approach. The value of an asset can be assumed equal to the cost of replacing it with a similar asset or reproducing the asset, thereby taking into account the age and condition of the asset.
  - Market approach. If there is an active market on which similar assets are frequently traded, transaction prices from this market can be used to determine the current market value of an asset.
  - Income approach. If the net cash flows generated by an individual asset can be reliably measured, the value of the asset can be derived from the present value of its cash flows. The international accounting rules describe various methods to estimate the cash flows of an individual asset, such as:
    - The direct cash flow forecast method, under which the asset's value is the present value of the cash flows directly attributable to the asset. This method is especially appropriate for assets that generate predictable and separable cash flows, such as financial assets.
    - The relief-from-royalty method, under which the asset's value is the present value of future royalties saved by owning the asset. This method tends to be used for valuing brands (trademarks), patent rights, or technologies.
    - The multi-period excess earnings method, under which the asset's value is the present value of future cash flows generated by the asset *in excess of* charges for the unavoidable use of other contributory assets. This method helps to value, for example, customer relationships.

  The international accounting standards on business combinations set a clear order of priority, preferring the market approach over the income approach and preferring the income approach over the cost approach. In addition, the rules prescribe that similar approaches are used for similar types of assets or liabilities.

  Note that the multi-period excess earnings method requires the calculation of contributory asset charges, which are defined as the product of the required return on a contributory asset and the contributory asset's value. For example, when valuing Danisco's customer relationships, the contributory asset charges reflect the economic cost of capital tied up in assets that are needed to serve the existing customers, such as working capital, property, plant and equipment, or the assembled workforce. Consequently, assets that are valued using the multi-period excess earnings method can be valued only after all other contributory assets have been valued.

- Step 5: Calculate and evaluate goodwill. The final step in the purchase price allocation process calculates goodwill as the difference between the value of the target firm, as derived in step 1, and the sum of the values of the contributory assets, as calculated in step 4. The derived goodwill amount can be evaluated for reasonableness in various ways. First, the amount of goodwill is not likely to be (significantly) smaller than the premium paid in the acquisition. This is because all other assets identified in the purchase price allocation process were owned by the target firm and must have been valued by investors – at least theoretically – also prior to the merger or acquisition. Consequently, the acquisition premium imposes a (soft) lower bound on the goodwill calculation. Second, purchase price allocations of prior comparable mergers and acquisitions, usually in the same industry, serve as a useful benchmark against which to compare proportions of the acquisition price allocated to the various intangible assets and goodwill. Third, as indicated, the expected return on goodwill that is implicit in the purchase price allocation can be derived from the overall internal rate of return and the individual required returns of contributory assets. As a rule of thumb, if the difference between this expected return on goodwill and the target firm's normally required return on net operating assets is small, some of the risk and uncertainty surrounding the realization of presented synergies may have been ignored in the purchase price allocation, which makes it more likely that goodwill is impaired.

In the next section we will illustrate each of the preceding steps using the example of the DuPont-Danisco acquisition.

## DANISCO'S PURCHASE PRICE ALLOCATION

### Target firm value

To acquire Danisco, DuPont paid Danisco's shareholders DKK32.30 billion in cash and assumed interest-bearing debt and other non-current liabilities to the amount of DKK4.45 billion. This offer thus valued Danisco's assets at DKK36.75 billion.

On April 29, 2011, DuPont announced that close to 48 percent of Danisco's shareholders had tendered their shares and that it would raise the price of its tender offer. DuPont's offer would become unconditional only if more than 80 percent of Danisco's shareholders would tender their shares before May 13. On May 19, 2011, DuPont announced that it had completed the acquisition of 92.2 percent of Danisco's share capital, thereby obtaining formal control over Danisco's operations. Prior to this date, the relevant regulatory authorities, including China's Ministry of Commerce and the European Commission, had given their approval to the acquisition. Following the international accounting rules on business combinations, we denote the date on which DuPont obtained control (May 19) as the "acquisition date" and consider this date as the date of valuation in the purchase price allocation.

### Internal rate of return

Danisco's equity beta, estimated over a ten-year period immediately prior to the acquisition date, is close to 0.8. The firm's operating asset beta, estimated using the procedures described in Chapter 8, is close to 0.6. Given a long-term risk free rate of 4.8 percent and a market risk premium of 5.3 percent (based on market circumstances in 2011; see also Chapter 8), Danisco's required return on net operating assets can thus be estimated at approximately 8 percent (4.8% + 0.6 × 5.3%).

Table 11.3 displays the estimation of the internal rate of return on the acquisition. In this table forecasts of Danisco's future revenue and free cash flows are based on analyst forecasts issued close to the time DuPont announced its intention to acquire Danisco. The estimation shows that the internal rate of return on the Danisco acquisition is approximately 7.852 percent. This internal rate of return is very close to the estimate of Danisco's required return on net operating assets, which suggests that Danisco is reasonably priced, albeit under the assumption that the anticipated synergy effects are justified.

### Contributory assets

In DuPont's acquisition of Danisco, the following identifiable assets were transferred:

- Tangible assets: working capital and property, plant, and equipment.
- Intangible assets: customer relationships, brand names, technology, and in-process research and development.

The risk of the intangible assets can be considered equal to the average risk of Danisco's operations. It is therefore reasonable to assume that the required return on intangible assets is equal to the average required return on net operating assets, which is 8 percent.16 In contrast, the risk of tangible assets is lower. A typical assumption made in purchase price allocations is that the required return on property, plant, and equipment is equal to the yield on long-term corporate bonds, whereas the required return on working capital is equal to the yield on short-term debt.

**TABLE 11.3** Estimation of the internal rate of return on DuPont's acquisition of Danisco

| Forecast year | 2011/ 2012 | 2012/ 2013 | 2013/ 2014 | 2014/ 2015 | 2015/ 2016 | 2016/ 2017 | 2017/ 2018 | 2018/ 2019 |
|---|---|---|---|---|---|---|---|---|
| Revenue | 16.44 | 17.21 | 18.01 | 18.85 | 19.74 | 20.68 | 21.30 | 21.94 |
| Operating profit | 2.41 | 2.55 | 2.72 | 2.86 | 3.01 | 3.17 | 3.26 | 3.36 |
| − Tax (30 percent) | −0.72 | −0.77 | −0.81 | −0.86 | −0.90 | −0.95 | −0.98 | −1.01 |
| NOPAT | 1.68 | 1.79 | 1.90 | 2.00 | 2.11 | 2.22 | 2.28 | 2.35 |
| − Change in net operating assets | 0.41 | 0.47 | 0.49 | 0.47 | 0.49 | 0.52 | 0.63 | 0.64 |
| Preacquisition free cash flow | 1.28 | 1.32 | 1.42 | 1.53 | 1.61 | 1.70 | 1.66 | 1.71 |
| + M&A synergies | 0.20 | 0.40 | 0.50 | 0.52 | 0.53 | 0.55 | 0.56 | 0.58 |
| Postacquisition free cash flow | 1.48 | 1.72 | 1.92 | 2.04 | 2.14 | 2.25 | 2.22 | 2.29 |
| × Partial year factor | 0.8667 | 1.0000 | 1.0000 | 1.0000 | 1.0000 | 1.0000 | 1.0000 | 1.0000 |
| × Discount factor @ 7.852% | 0.9678 | 0.9019 | 0.8362 | 0.7753 | 0.7189 | 0.6665 | 0.6180 | 0.5730 |
| Present value of postacquisition free cash flows | 1.07 | 1.19 | 1.18 | 1.18 | 1.16 | 1.13 | 1.02 | 0.98 |
| Value between May 19, 2011, and March 31, 2019 | | | | | | | | 8.93 |
| Terminal value | | | | | | | | 27.82 |
| Target firm value (in DKK billions) | | | | | | | | 36.75 |

Assumptions:
- Forecasts of revenue, operating profits, and free cash flows (until 2016/2017) are based on analyst forecasts issued close to the acquisition announcement date.
- The acquisition increases free cash flows by DKK0.2 billion in fiscal 2011/2012, by DKK0.4 billion in fiscal 2012/2013, and by DKK0.5 billion in fiscal 2013/2014. This assumption is based on management's expectation that the acquisition will help to achieve annual cost savings in the amount of DKK0.5 billion (after tax) by 2013.
- After 2013/2014, the cash flow effect of the acquisition grows at an annual rate of 3 percent, being the long-run growth rate of the economy.
- The terminal growth rate equals 3 percent. Forecasts in 2017/2018 and 2018/2019 are based on the assumption that all income statement and balance sheet items grow at an annual rate of 3 percent to impose a steady state prior to the terminal year.
- The valuation date is May 19, 2011. Cash flows in year 1 occur halfway between May 19, 2011, and March 31, 2012. Cash flows in the other years occur halfway through the fiscal year, which runs from April 1 to March 31.
- The partial year factor in 2011/2012 is the number of days between May 19, 2011, and March 31, 2012, divided by 366.

In May 2011, the one-year EURIBOR rate was 2.1 percent; the yield on long-term AAA corporate bonds was 5.0 percent. Given a model-based credit rating for Danisco of BBB (see Chapter 10) and an associated yield spread of about 1 percent, we estimate Danisco's required returns on working capital and property and on plant and equipment at 3 and 6 percent, respectively, before tax and 2.1 and 4.2 percent, respectively, after tax.

### Valuation of tangible assets

External appraisers valued Danisco's working capital at DKK3.98 billion and its property, plant, and equipment at DKK8.60 billion. In its third quarter financial statements, for the quarter ended on January 31, 2011, the book values of working capital and of property, plant, and equipment were DKK3.10 billion and DKK5.60 billion, respectively.

The fair value of working capital can sometimes be assumed equal to its book value; however, inventories are likely subject to revaluation. The difference between the fair value and the book value of Danisco's working capital of DKK0.88 billion (3.98 – 3.10) is close to 33 percent of the May 19 book value of Danisco's inventories. This revaluation percentage seems reasonable but conservative given Danisco's past year's gross profit margin of 47 percent of revenue and selling costs of 17.5 percent of revenue. In particular, these ratios suggest a revaluation percentage of 56 percent, estimated as follows:

| | |
|---|---|
| Gross profit as a percentage of revenue: | 47.0 percent |
| Less: cost to sell | 17.5 percent |
| = markup as a percentage of selling price: | 29.5 percent |
| Divide by: (1 − gross profit margin): | 53.0 percent |
| = markup as a percentage of cost: | 55.7 percent |

The fair value estimates and required returns on working capital and property, plant, and equipment can be used to estimate future contributory asset charges only after making some necessary additional assumptions. Specifically, to calculate the future annual averages of the fair values of working capital and property, plant, and equipment, we must assume the following:

- The annual growth in the fair value of working capital follows revenue growth.
- The annual changes in the book value of property, plant, and equipment are as predicted by analysts (close to the acquisition announcement date).
- The difference between the fair value and the book value of property, plant, and, equipment grows at a constant rate of 3 percent annually to reflect the effect of inflation.

Table 11.4 summarizes the implications of these assumptions for the contributory asset charges between 2011/2012 and 2018/2019. The contributory asset charges (after tax) for working capital are close to 0.52 percent of revenue; the contributory asset charges for property, plant, and equipment range from 2.20 to 2.29 percent.

### Valuation of trade names and technology

The most commonly used method to value intellectual property rights such as trademarks, patents, or copyrights is the relief-from-royalty method. The rationale of this method is that intellectual property rights derive their value from the royalties that a firm would be willing to pay to acquire the right to use the intellectual property or, alternatively, from the royalties that a firm would be relieved from by owning the intellectual property rights. Possible sources of royalty rates are industry peers' financial statements, management estimates, or commercial databases.

DuPont's 2011 financial statement disclosures regarding the Danisco acquisition indicate that the fair value of Danisco's trade names was estimated at DKK2.92 billion. Table 11.5 shows how the relief-from-royalty method can be used to value Danisco's trade names or, alternatively, estimate what royalty rate is implicit in the value that DuPont assigned to these trade names. The calculations show that a value estimate of DKK2.92 billion is consistent with a (pre-tax) royalty rate of 1.13 percent. This royalty rate seems low but reasonable given that trade names are significantly less valuable in Danisco's business-to-business industry than in consumer-to-business industries.

When valuing Danisco's technology, DuPont distinguished and separately valued two categories: indefinite-lived technology (microbial cell factories), with an estimated value of DKK1.54 billion, and definite-lived technology (e.g., patents), with an estimated value of DKK2.96 billion. Table 11.6 shows the calculation of royalty rates that are consistent with these value estimates. We estimate the royalty rate of Danisco's indefinite-lived technology at 0.60 percent. Further, under the assumption that the average useful life of Danisco's definite-lived technology is eight years, we estimate that the royalty rate of this technology gradually decreases from 6.53 percent in fiscal 2011/2012 to 0.82 percent (rounded) in fiscal 2018/2019.

**TABLE 11.4** Estimation of the contributory asset charges for working capital and property, plant, and equipment

| | | 2011/ 2012 | 2012/ 2013 | 2013/ 2014 | 2014/ 2015 | 2015/ 2016 | 2016/ 2017 | 2017/ 2018 | 2018/ 2019 |
|---|---|---|---|---|---|---|---|---|---|
| Revenue growth rate (see Table 11.3) | (a) | 4.26% | 4.63% | 4.66% | 4.69% | 4.72% | 4.75% | 3.00% | 3.00% |
| Beginning fair value of working capital | (b) | 3.98 | 4.15 | 4.34 | 4.54 | 4.76 | 4.98 | 5.22 | 5.37 |
| Annual change in the fair value of working capital | (a) × (b) = (c) | 0.17 | 0.19 | 0.20 | 0.21 | 0.22 | 0.24 | 0.16 | 0.16 |
| Average fair value of working capital | (b) + 0.5 × (c) = (d) | 4.06 | 4.25 | 4.44 | 4.65 | 4.87 | 5.10 | 5.30 | 5.46 |
| Contributory charge @ 2.1 percent | 0.021 × (d) = (e) | 0.09 | 0.09 | 0.09 | 0.10 | 0.10 | 0.11 | 0.11 | 0.11 |
| Contributory charge as a percentage of revenue | (e)/revenue = (f) | 0.52% | 0.52% | 0.52% | 0.52% | 0.52% | 0.52% | 0.52% | 0.52% |
| Beginning book value of PP&E | (g) | 5.60 | 5.87 | 6.19 | 6.52 | 6.83 | 7.14 | 7.47 | 7.98 |
| Change in book value of PP&E | Forecasts = (h) | 0.27 | 0.32 | 0.33 | 0.31 | 0.32 | 0.33 | 0.50 | 0.52 |
| Average book value of PP&E | (g) + 0.5 × (h) = (i) | 5.74 | 6.03 | 6.35 | 6.67 | 6.98 | 7.31 | 7.73 | 8.24 |
| Beginning PP&E fair-book value difference | (j) | 3.00 | 3.09 | 3.18 | 3.28 | 3.38 | 3.48 | 3.58 | 3.69 |
| Change in fair-book value difference | 0.03 × (j) = (k) | 0.09 | 0.09 | 0.10 | 0.10 | 0.10 | 0.10 | 0.11 | 0.11 |
| Average PP&E fair-book value difference | (j) + 0.5 × (k) = (l) | 3.05 | 3.14 | 3.23 | 3.33 | 3.43 | 3.53 | 3.64 | 3.74 |
| Average fair value of PP&E | (i) + (l) = (m) | 8.78 | 9.17 | 9.58 | 10.00 | 10.41 | 10.84 | 1.36 | 1.98 |
| Contributory charge @ 4.2 percent | 0.042 × (m) = (n) | 0.37 | 0.39 | 0.40 | 0.42 | 0.44 | 0.46 | 0.48 | 0.50 |
| Contributory charge as a percentage of revenue | (n)/revenue = (o) | 2.24% | 2.24% | 2.24% | 2.23% | 2.22% | 2.20% | 2.24% | 2.29% |

**TABLE 11.5** Estimation of Danisco's trade names royalty rate

| | | 2011/ 2012 | 2012/ 2013 | 2013/ 2014 | 2014/ 2015 | 2015/ 2016 | 2016/ 2017 | 2017/ 2018 | 2018/ 2019 |
|---|---|---|---|---|---|---|---|---|---|
| Revenue | Given | 16.44 | 17.21 | 18.01 | 18.85 | 19.74 | 20.68 | 21.30 | 21.94 |
| × Royalty rate (%) | Plug-in | 1.134% | 1.134% | 1.134% | 1.134% | 1.134% | 1.134% | 1.134% | 1.134% |
| = Royalties saved (pre-tax) | | 0.19 | 0.20 | 0.20 | 0.21 | 0.22 | 0.23 | 0.24 | 0.25 |
| × (1 − tax rate) | 30% | 0.70 | 0.70 | 0.70 | 0.70 | 0.70 | 0.70 | 0.70 | 0.70 |
| = Royalties saved (after tax) | | 0.13 | 0.14 | 0.14 | 0.15 | 0.16 | 0.16 | 0.17 | 0.17 |
| × Partial year factor | | 0.8667 | 1.0000 | 1.0000 | 1.0000 | 1.0000 | 1.0000 | 1.0000 | 1.0000 |
| × Discount factor | 8% | 0.9672 | 0.9002 | 0.8335 | 0.7717 | 0.7146 | 0.6616 | 0.6126 | 0.5673 |
| = Present value of royalties saved | | 0.11 | 0.12 | 0.12 | 0.12 | 0.11 | 0.11 | 0.10 | 0.10 |
| Present value of royalties saved between May 19, 2011, and March 31, 2019 | | | | | | | | | 0.89 |
| Terminal value | | | | | | | | | 2.03 |
| Value of trade names | | | | | | | | | 2.92 |

**TABLE 11.6** Estimation of Danisco's definite-lived and indefinite-lived technology royalty rates

| | | 2011/ 2012 | 2012/ 2013 | 2013/ 2014 | 2014/ 2015 | 2015/ 2016 | 2016/ 2017 | 2017/ 2018 | 2018/ 2019 |
|---|---|---|---|---|---|---|---|---|---|
| **Indefinite-lived technology** | | | | | | | | | |
| Revenue | Given | 16.44 | 17.21 | 18.01 | 18.85 | 19.74 | 20.68 | 21.30 | 21.94 |
| × Royalty rate (% ) | Plug-in | 0.597% | 0.597% | 0.597% | 0.597% | 0.597% | 0.597% | 0.597% | 0.597% |
| = Royalties saved (pre-tax) | | 0.10 | 0.10 | 0.11 | 0.11 | 0.12 | 0.12 | 0.13 | 0.13 |
| × (1 − tax rate) | 30% | 0.70 | 0.70 | 0.70 | 0.70 | 0.70 | 0.70 | 0.70 | 0.70 |
| = Royalties saved (after tax) | | 0.07 | 0.07 | 0.08 | 0.08 | 0.08 | 0.09 | 0.09 | 0.09 |
| × Partial year factor | | 0.8667 | 1.0000 | 1.0000 | 1.0000 | 1.0000 | 1.0000 | 1.0000 | 1.0000 |
| × Discount factor | 8% | 0.9672 | 0.9002 | 0.8335 | 0.7717 | 0.7146 | 0.6616 | 0.6126 | 0.5673 |
| = Present value of royalties saved | | 0.06 | 0.06 | 0.06 | 0.06 | 0.06 | 0.06 | 0.05 | 0.05 |
| Present value of royalties saved between May 19, 2011, and March 31, 2019 | | | | | | | | | 0.47 |
| Terminal value | | | | | | | | | 1.07 |
| Value of indefinite-lived technology | | | | | | | | | 1.54 |
| **Definite-lived technology** | | | | | | | | | |
| Revenue | Given | 16.44 | 17.21 | 18.01 | 18.85 | 19.74 | 20.68 | 21.30 | 21.94 |
| × Royalty rate (% ) | Plug-in | 6.528% | 5.712% | 4.896% | 4.080% | 3.264% | 2.448% | 1.632% | 0.816% |
| = Royalties saved (pre-tax) | | 1.07 | 0.98 | 0.88 | 0.77 | 0.64 | 0.51 | 0.35 | 0.18 |
| × (1 − tax rate) | 30% | 0.70 | 0.70 | 0.70 | 0.70 | 0.70 | 0.70 | 0.70 | 0.70 |
| = Royalties saved (after tax) | | 0.75 | 0.69 | 0.62 | 0.54 | 0.45 | 0.35 | 0.24 | 0.13 |
| × Partial year factor | | 0.8667 | 1.0000 | 1.0000 | 1.0000 | 1.0000 | 1.0000 | 1.0000 | 1.0000 |
| × Discount factor | 8% | 0.9672 | 0.9002 | 0.8335 | 0.7717 | 0.7146 | 0.6616 | 0.6126 | 0.5673 |
| = Present value of royalties saved | | 0.63 | 0.62 | 0.51 | 0.42 | 0.32 | 0.23 | 0.15 | 0.07 |
| Present value of royalties saved between May 19, 2011, and March 31, 2019 | | | | | | | | | 2.96 |
| Terminal value (assumed average useful life is eight years) | | | | | | | | | 0.00 |
| Value of definite-lived technology | | | | | | | | | 2.96 |

Note that in the preceding calculations we assume that the amortization on acquired intangible assets is not tax-deductible. If, in contrast to our assumption, such amortization would be tax-deductible, the value estimates would need to be upwardly adjusted to account for the tax amortization benefit. For example, if Danisco's definite-lived technology were tax-deductible on a straight-line basis over a five year period, we would need to increase the technology's value by a factor of 1.3219. Table 11.7 shows how this factor can be calculated by considering a hypothetical asset with a pre-tax value of 100, which is amortized over five years.

**TABLE 11.7** Calculation of the tax amortization benefit factor

|  |  | Year 1 | Year 2 | Year 3 | Year 4 | Year 5 |
|---|---|---|---|---|---|---|
| Tax amortization | 1/5 per year | 20.00 | 20.00 | 20.00 | 20.00 | 20.00 |
| Tax amortization benefit (TAB) | 30% | 6.00 | 6.00 | 6.00 | 6.00 | 6.00 |
| × Partial year factor |  | 0.8667 | 1.0000 | 1.0000 | 1.0000 | 1.0000 |
| × Discount factor | @8% | 0.9672 | 0.9002 | 0.8335 | 0.7717 | 0.7146 |
| = Present value of TABs |  | 5.03 | 5.40 | 5.00 | 4.63 | 4.29 |
| Asset tax base | (a) |  |  |  |  | 100 |
| – Total value of TABs | (b) |  |  |  |  | 24.35 |
| = After-tax value | (a) – (b) = (c) |  |  |  |  | 75.65 |
| Tax amortization benefit factor | (a)/(c) |  |  |  |  | 1.3219 |

## Assembled workforce

Danisco's workforce is an intangible asset that is of significant value to DuPont. Although the international accounting rules do not allow DuPont to recognize the value of Danisco's assembled workforce as a separate line item in its postacquisition financial statements, the valuation of the workforce is relevant as an input to the valuation of customer relationships later in the purchase price allocation exercise. Purchase price allocation experts typically assume that the target firm's assembled workforce has value to an acquirer for the following reasons:

- Experienced employees are more efficient than newly hired employees. For example, in fiscal 2009/2010, Danisco had an average of 6,853 employees and spent DKK2.5 billion on salaries. Assuming that 90 percent of Danisco's employees were experienced employees and that inexperienced employees are only 80 percent as efficient as experienced employees during a period of six months, the company's experienced workforce helped it to avoid inefficiencies for an amount of DKK0.225 billion (90% × 20% × 6/12 × 2.5), or 1.6 percent of revenue.
- Companies incur recruitment and training costs when hiring new employees. Assuming that the average recruitment and training costs for Danisco were DKK37 thousand (€5 thousand) per employee, having 90 percent experienced employees helped the company to avoid recruitment and training costs of DKK0.228 billion (90% × 6,853 × 37), or 1.7 percent of revenue, in 2009/2010.

Under the preceding assumptions, the cost to replace Danisco's assembled workforce is 3.3 percent of revenue. That is, using the cost method the value of the company's workforce can be estimated as a fixed percentage of its revenue, as shown in Table 11.8.

Note that the valuation of Danisco's assembled workforce affects the valuation of its customer relationships in two ways. First, the growth in the annual values of the assembled workforce can be considered an investment that needs to be added back to the cash flows from customer relationships. Second, the assembled workforce is a contributory asset that helps to generate cash flows from customer relationships and therefore should give rise to contributory charges. In Table 11.8, we calculate the contributory charges under the assumption that the required return on Danisco's assembled workforce is equal to the average required return on net operating assets of 8 percent.

## Customer relationships

The previous steps of the purchase price allocation exercise have laid the groundwork for the valuation of Danisco's customer relationships. To value customer relationships using the multi-period excess earnings method, we must first determine which proportion of Danisco's revenue, operating expenses, and growth investments can be attributed to the company's existing customers. A common method of doing so is to (a) establish one attrition rate, being the average rate per year at which customers switch between suppliers; and (b) estimate customer relationships' remaining economic life. Because Danisco is the market leader in many of its segments, sells several highly specialized and patented products, and has invested significantly in developing close relationships with customers and creating customer loyalty, we can expect that the company's customer attrition rate is relatively low, to the tune of less than 10 percent. In Table 11.9, which details the valuation of Danisco's customer relationships, we therefore assume that Danisco's customer relationships attrite by 8.25 percent annually over a remaining economic life of 25 years. To estimate free cash flows from existing customers before contributory add backs and charges, we further assume that the company's gross profit margin, selling and administrative costs-to-revenue ratio, and tax rate (for revenue from existing customers) remain constant at 41.5, 17.5, and 30.0 percent, respectively. These percentages are close to the average ratios forecasted by analysts.

**TABLE 11.8**  Estimation of the contributory asset charges for and investments in Danisco's assembled workforce

|  |  | 2011/ 2012 | 2012/ 2013 | 2013/ 2014 | 2014/ 2015 | 2015/ 2016 | 2016/ 2017 | 2017/ 2018 | 2018/ 2019 |
|---|---|---|---|---|---|---|---|---|---|
| Revenue | (a) | 16.44 | 17.21 | 18.01 | 18.85 | 19.74 | 20.68 | 21.30 | 21.94 |
| Assembled workforce [AWF] value as a percentage of revenue | (b) | 3.30% | 3.30% | 3.30% | 3.30% | 3.30% | 3.30% | 3.30% | 3.30% |
| Beginning AWF value | $(a)_{t-1} \times (b)_{t-1} = (c)$ | 0.52 | 0.54 | 0.57 | 0.59 | 0.62 | 0.65 | 0.68 | 0.70 |
| Ending AWF value | $(a) \times (b) = (d)$ | 0.54 | 0.57 | 0.59 | 0.62 | 0.65 | 0.68 | 0.70 | 0.72 |
| Investment in AWF (add back) | $(d) - (c) = (e)$ | 0.02 | 0.03 | 0.03 | 0.03 | 0.03 | 0.03 | 0.02 | 0.02 |
| Average AWF value | $(c) + 0.5 \times (d) = (f)$ | 0.53 | 0.56 | 0.58 | 0.61 | 0.64 | 0.67 | 0.69 | 0.71 |
| Contributory charge @ 8 percent | $0.08 \times (f) = (g)$ | 0.04 | 0.04 | 0.05 | 0.05 | 0.05 | 0.05 | 0.06 | 0.06 |
| Contributory charge as (g)/ revenue = (h) a percentage of revenue | | 0.26% | 0.26% | 0.26% | 0.26% | 0.26% | 0.26% | 0.26% | 0.26% |

As a next step in calculating excess earnings, we must subtract the contributory asset charges that we estimated earlier from the free cash flows from existing customers. We account for the following charges:

- Trade names royalty charges: 0.794 percent of revenue from existing customers. This after-tax percentage is equivalent to a pre-tax percentage of 1.134 percent, as estimated in Table 11.5.
- Indefinite-lived technology royalty charges: 0.418 percent of revenue from existing customers (or 0.597 percent before tax, as estimated in Table 11.6).
- Definite-lived technology royalty charges: 4.570 percent of revenue from existing customers (or 6.528 percent before tax, as estimated in Table 11.6). This after-tax percentage is the percentage estimated for fiscal 2011/2012. We use this percentage throughout the forecasting period under the assumption that in future years Danisco will reinvest to maintain its 2011/2012 technology level.
- Returns on working capital and property, plant, and equipment, calculated as the annual contributory charges (as a percentage of revenue) for working capital and PP&E, taken from Table 11.4, times revenue from existing customers.

**TABLE 11.9** Valuation of Danisco's customer relationships

| | | 2011/ 2012 | 2012/ 2013 | 2013/ 2014 | 2014/ 2015 | 2015/ 2016 | 2016/ 2017 | 2017/ 2018 | 2018/ 2019 |
|---|---|---|---|---|---|---|---|---|---|
| Revenue | Given | 16.44 | 17.21 | 18.01 | 18.85 | 19.74 | 20.68 | 21.30 | 21.94 |
| End-of-year customer retention rate | | 92.00% | 84.64% | 77.87% | 71.64% | 65.91% | 60.64% | 55.78% | 51.32% |
| Average customer retention rate | | 96.00% | 88.32% | 81.25% | 74.75% | 68.77% | 63.27% | 58.21% | 53.55% |
| Revenue from existing customers | | 15.79 | 15.20 | 14.63 | 14.09 | 13.58 | 13.08 | 12.40 | 11.75 |
| Gross profit | 41.50% | 6.55 | 6.31 | 6.07 | 5.85 | 5.63 | 5.43 | 5.15 | 4.88 |
| Selling and administrative costs | 17.50% | −2.76 | −2.66 | −2.56 | −2.47 | −2.38 | −2.29 | −2.17 | −2.06 |
| Operating profit | | 3.79 | 3.65 | 3.51 | 3.38 | 3.26 | 3.14 | 2.98 | 2.82 |
| Tax | 30.00% | −1.14 | −1.09 | −1.05 | −1.01 | −0.98 | −0.94 | −0.89 | −0.85 |
| NOPAT | | 2.65 | 2.55 | 2.46 | 2.37 | 2.28 | 2.20 | 2.08 | 1.97 |
| Change in net operating assets | | −0.39 | −0.41 | −0.39 | −0.35 | −0.34 | −0.33 | −0.36 | −0.35 |
| Free cash flows from existing customers before add backs/CACs | | 2.26 | 2.14 | 2.06 | 2.01 | 1.94 | 1.87 | 1.72 | 1.63 |
| Add backs: | | | | | | | | | |
| Assembled workforce growth investment | | 0.02 | 0.02 | 0.02 | 0.02 | 0.02 | 0.02 | 0.01 | 0.01 |
| Contributory asset charges: | | | | | | | | | |
| Return on working capital | | −0.08 | −0.08 | −0.08 | −0.07 | −0.07 | −0.07 | −0.06 | −0.06 |
| Return on property, plant, and equipment | | −0.35 | −0.34 | −0.33 | −0.31 | −0.30 | −0.29 | −0.28 | −0.27 |
| Trade names royalties saved | 0.794% | −0.13 | −0.12 | −0.12 | −0.11 | −0.11 | −0.10 | −0.10 | −0.09 |
| Technology royalties saved | 5.099% | −0.79 | −0.76 | −0.73 | −0.70 | −0.68 | −0.65 | −0.62 | −0.59 |
| Return on the assembled workforce | | −0.04 | −0.04 | −0.04 | −0.04 | −0.04 | −0.03 | −0.03 | −0.03 |
| Excess earnings | | 0.89 | 0.83 | 0.80 | 0.80 | 0.77 | 0.75 | 0.64 | 0.60 |
| Partial year factor | | 0.8667 | 1.0000 | 1.0000 | 1.0000 | 1.0000 | 1.0000 | 1.0000 | 1.0000 |
| Discount factor | | 0.9672 | 0.9002 | 0.8335 | 0.7717 | 0.7146 | 0.6616 | 0.6126 | 0.5673 |
| Present value of excess earnings | | 0.75 | 0.74 | 0.66 | 0.61 | 0.55 | 0.49 | 0.39 | 0.33 |
| Present value of excess earnings between May 19, 2011 and March 31, 2019 | | | | | | | | | 4.52 |
| Terminal value | | | | | | | | | 2.10 |
| Value of trade names | | | | | | | | | 6.62 |

- Return on the assembled workforce, calculated as the annual contributory charges (as a percentage of revenue) for the assembled workforce, taken from Table 11.8, times revenue from existing customers. In addition to subtracting the return, we add back the annual growth investment in the assembled workforce that is attributable to existing customers, as described earlier.

Table 11.9 shows the excess earnings from customer relationships that result after subtracting the preceding charges. Because the remaining economic life of Danisco's customer relationships is 25 years but we have detailed forecasts for only eight years, we must do some simplifying for the 17-year period after the terminal year 2018/2019. Specifically, we assume that excess earnings decrease at a constant rate between 2018/2019 and 2035/2036 and that excess earnings are equal to zero after 2035/2036. Under these assumptions, the terminal value is defined as:

$$TV_{\text{Customer relationships}} = \frac{(1+g) \times \text{Excess earnings}_{2018/2019}}{(1+r)^T (r-g)} - \frac{(1+g)^{18} \times \text{Excess earnings}_{2018/2019}}{(1+r)^{T+17} (r-g)}$$

where r is the required return on net operating assets and g is the terminal growth rate. Given a revenue growth rate of 3 percent and an attrition rate of 8.25 percent, the terminal growth rate equals −5.24 percent ([1 +0.03] × [1 − 0.0825]).

The calculations shown in Table 11.9 show that our estimate of the value of Danisco's customer relationships is DKK6.62 billion. This value estimate is equal to the value disclosed in DuPont's 2011 financial statements.

### Goodwill

The fair value estimates derived in the previous sections help us to estimate goodwill. Goodwill is defined as the difference between the total value of Danisco and the sum of the fair values of the identifiable assets. Recall that goodwill includes the fair value of Danisco's assembled workforce because the international accounting rules on business combinations do not allow DuPont to separately recognize this asset. Table 11.10 shows that based on the above fair value estimates and Danisco's value of DKK36.75 billion, the value of goodwill can be estimated at DKK9.39 billion. This value is slightly greater than the acquisition premium. The implied expected return on goodwill, which can be derived from the required returns on the identifiable assets and the internal rate of return on the acquisition, equals 13.40 percent.

**TABLE 11.10**  Calculation of goodwill

|  | Fair value | Return |
|---|---|---|
| Total value of Danisco (as implied by the acquisition price) | 36.75 | 7.85% |
| Less: fair values of . . . |  |  |
| Working capital | 3.98 | 2.10% |
| Property, plant, and equipment | 8.60 | 4.20% |
| Other assets (including in-process R&D)[a] | 0.75 | 8.00% |
| Trade names | 2.92 | 8.00% |
| Indefinite-lived technology | 1.54 | 8.00% |
| Definite-lived technology | 2.96 | 8.00% |
| Customer relationships | 6.62 | 8.00% |
| = Goodwill (including assembled workforce), net of deferred tax | 9.39 | 13.40% |
| Add: Deferred taxes | 5.17 |  |
| = Goodwill (as reported) | 14.55 |  |

[a]Taken from DuPont's 2011 annual financial statements.

Note that the goodwill estimate shown in Table 11.10 is the net of deferred taxes. Although the identifiable assets are revalued to their fair values for financial reporting purposes, the assets' tax bases may not change by the same amount, depending on the tax jurisdiction. If the amount of revaluation exceeds the change in the assets' tax base, this will give rise to a deferred tax liability.[17] The international accounting rules prescribe that such increase in the deferred tax liability is accompanied by an increase in goodwill of the same amount. In the example of the Danisco acquisition, DuPont recognized deferred tax liabilities for the amount of DKK5.17 billion. Consequently, the total value of goodwill equaled DKK14.55 billion (9.39 + 5.17).

## Summary

This chapter summarizes how financial statement data and analysis can be used by financial analysts interested in evaluating whether an acquisition creates value for an acquiring firm's shareholders. Obviously, much of this discussion is also likely to be relevant to other merger participants, including target and acquiring management and their investment banks.

For the external analyst, the first task is to identify the acquirer's acquisition strategy. We discuss a number of strategies. Some of these are consistent with maximizing acquirer value, including acquisitions to take advantage of economies of scale, improve target management, combine complementary resources, capture tax benefits, provide low-cost financing to financially constrained targets, and increase product-market rents.

Other strategies appear to benefit managers more than shareholders. For example, some unprofitable acquisitions are made because managers are reluctant to return free cash flows to shareholders or because managers want to lower the firm's earnings volatility by diversifying into unrelated businesses.

The financial analyst's second task is to assess whether the acquirer is offering a reasonable price for the target. Even if the acquirer's strategy is based on increasing shareholder value, it can overpay for the target. Target shareholders will then be well rewarded but at the expense of acquiring shareholders. We show how the ratio, pro forma, and valuation techniques discussed earlier in the book can all be used to assess the worth of the target to the acquirer.

The method of financing an offer is also relevant to a financial analyst's review of an acquisition proposal. If a proposed acquisition is financed with surplus cash or new debt, it increases the acquirer's financial risk. Financial analysts can use ratio analysis of the acquirer's postacquisition balance sheet and pro forma estimates of cash flow volatility and interest coverage to assess whether demands by target shareholders for consideration in cash lead the acquirer to increase its risk of financial distress.

Finally, the financial analyst is interested in assessing whether a merger is likely to be completed once the initial offer is made, and at what price. This requires the analyst to determine whether there are other potential bidders, and whether target management is entrenched and likely to oppose a bidder's offer.

## Core concepts

**Acquisition financing**     Methods of acquisition financing are through equity issues, debt issues, or the use of surplus cash. The latter two methods increase financial leverage and potentially increase distress risk. Information problems make acquirers reluctant to use equity to finance the acquisition. Different forms of payment may have different tax effects across countries.

**Acquisition premium**    Premium offered to target shareholders. Acquisition premiums tend to be:

1   Higher for hostile than friendly takeovers.

2   Higher for cash-financed than equity-financed (share-for-share) acquisitions.

3   Higher when the target country's takeover rules are stricter.

**Entrenched target management**    Target management's use of takeover defense mechanisms to deter the acquisition. The use of takeover defense mechanisms may discourage acquisitions or drive up acquisition premiums.

**Merger and acquisition benefits**    Mergers or acquisitions can create value through:

1   Increasing economies of scale.

2   Improving the target firm's management.

3   Combining complementary resources.

4   Capturing tax benefits such as operating tax losses or interest tax shields.

5   Providing a source of finance to the target.

6   Restructuring.

7   Increasing product market rents.

**Purchase price allocation**    Allocation of the total value of a target firm, as implied by the acquisition price, to individual identifiable assets, with the primary objectives of explaining the acquisition price and calculating goodwill.

**Takeover regulations**    Rules aimed at preventing target management entrenchment, such as the EU Takeover Directive.

**Target value analysis**    Target value analysis includes estimating the value of a target both as an independent firm and to the potential acquirer, using earnings multiples or using discounted abnormal profit of cash flow methods. Earnings multiple-based valuations tend to ignore the long-term effects of the acquisition.

# Questions

1   Since the year 2000 there has been a noticeable increase in mergers and acquisitions between firms in different countries (termed cross-border acquisitions). What factors could explain this increase? What special issues can arise in executing a cross-border acquisition and in ultimately meeting your objectives for a successful combination?

2   Private equity firms have become an important player in the acquisition market. These private investment groups offer to buy a target firm, often with the cooperation of management, and then take the firm private. Private equity buyers tend to finance a significant portion of the acquisition with debt.

   a   What types of firms would make ideal candidates for a private equity buyout? Why?

   b   How might the acquirer add sufficient value to the target to justify a high buyout premium?

3   Kim Silverman, finance director of the First Public Bank, notes: "We are fortunate to have a cost of capital of only 10 percent. We want to leverage this advantage by acquiring other banks that have a higher cost of funds. I believe that we can add significant value to these banks by using our lower cost financing." Do you agree with Silverman's analysis? Why or why not?

4   The Munich Beer Company plans to acquire Liverpool Beer Co. for £60 per share, a 50 percent premium over the current market price. Jan Höppe, the financial director of Munich Beer, argues that this valuation can easily be justified, using a price-earnings analysis. "Munich

Beer has a price-earnings ratio of 15, and we expect that we will be able to generate long-term earnings for Liverpool Beer of £5 per share. This implies that Liverpool Beer is worth £75 to us, well above our £60 offer price." Do you agree with this analysis? What are Höppe's key assumptions?

5  You have been hired by GS Investment Bank to work in the merger department. The analysis required for all potential acquisitions includes an examination of the target for any off-balance sheet assets or liabilities that have to be factored into the valuation. Prepare a checklist for your examination.

6  A target company is currently valued at €50 in the market. A potential acquirer believes that it can add value in two ways: €15 of value can be added through better working capital management, and an additional €10 of value can be generated by making available a unique technology to expand the target's new product offerings. In a competitive bidding contest, how much of this additional value will the acquirer have to pay out to the target's shareholders to emerge as the winner?

7  A leading oil exploration company decides to acquire an internet company at a 50 percent premium. The acquirer argues that this move creates value for its own shareholders because it can use its excess cash flows from the oil business to help finance growth in the new internet segment. Evaluate the economic merits of this claim.

8  Under current International Financial Reporting Standards, acquirers are required to capitalize goodwill and report any subsequent declines in value as an impairment charge. What performance metrics would you use to judge whether goodwill is impaired?

## NOTES

1  In a review of studies of merger returns, Michael Jensen and Richard Ruback, "The Market for Corporate Control: The Scientific Evidence," *Journal of Financial Economics* 11 (April 1983): 5–50, conclude that target shareholders earn positive returns from takeovers, but that acquiring shareholders only break even.

2  See Steven Kaplan, "Management Buyouts: Evidence on Taxes as a Source of Value," *Journal of Finance* 44 (1989): 611–632.

3  Krishna Palepu, "Predicting Takeover Targets: A Methodological and Empirical Analysis," *Journal of Accounting and Economics* 8 (March 1986): 3–36.

4  Chapter 2 discusses the pros and cons of corporate diversification and evidence on its implications for firm performance.

5  See Paul Healy, Krishna Palepu, and Richard Ruback, "Which Mergers Are Profitable – Strategic or Financial?," *Sloan Management Review* 38(4) (Summer 1997): 45–58. For empirical evidence on European target firms' cumulative stock returns around the takeover announcement, see Martina Martynova and Luc Renneboog, "Mergers and Acquisitions in Europe," Working Paper, Tilburg University, 2006. This study reports that 60 days after a hostile takeover announcement, European target firms' share prices have run up by, on average, 45 percent since 60 days prior to the announcement. In contrast, after friendly takeover announcements, share prices have run up by, on average, 10 percent. The average difference in price run-up of 35 percent can be interpreted as the average difference in (expected) takeover premiums.

6  See, for example, Martina Martynova and Luc Renneboog, op. cit.

7  See Stewart Myers and Nicholas Majluf, "Corporate Financing and Investment Decisions When Firms Have Information That Investors Do Not," *Journal of Financial Economics* (June 1984): 187–221.

8  For evidence see Nicholas Travlos, "Corporate Takeover Bids, Methods of Payments, and Bidding Firms' Stock Returns," *Journal of Finance* 42 (1987): 943–963.

9  See S. Datar, R. Frankel, and M. Wolfson, "Earnouts: The Effects of Adverse Selection and Agency Costs on Acquisition Techniques," *Journal of Law, Economics, and Organization* 17 (2001): 201–238.

10  See Mara Faccio and Ronald W. Masulis, "The Choice of Payment Method in European Mergers and Acquisitions," *Journal of Finance* 60 (2005): 1345–1388.

11  See Mara Faccio and Ronald W. Masulis, op. cit.

12  In several European countries, such as in Belgium, Denmark, and Germany, individual shareholders pay no or little taxes on the capital gains that they make from selling or exchanging their shares in a takeover, provided that they have held the shares for a defined period, typically being a period of one or two years. For these shareholders

the after-tax value of a takeover offer does not depend on whether they receive cash or shares as consideration.

13  See Rezaul Kabir, Dolph Cantrijn, and Andreas Jeunink, "Takeover Defenses, Ownership Structures, and Stock Returns in the Netherlands: An Empirical Analysis," *Strategic Management Journal* 18 (1997): 97–109.

14  Marc Goergen, Marina Martynova, and Luc Renneboog give a complete description of the most important rules in the EU Takeover Directive in their study "Corporate Governance Convergence: Evidence from Takeover Regulation Reforms in Europe," *Oxford Review of Economic Policy* 21 (2005): 243–268.

15  The Appraisal Foundation summarizes some of the best practices in purchase price allocations in "The Identification of Contributory Assets and Calculation of Economic Rents" (May 2010).

16  Purchase price allocation experts have debated on whether one should use the required return on net operating assets or the internal rate of return on the acquisition to measure the required return on intangible assets. Some experts prefer using the internal rate of return because of the complexities surrounding the estimation of required returns on net operating assets (see Chapter 8).

17  See Chapter 4 for a discussion of deferred taxes.

# Glencore/Xstrata: Playing Aida's Triumphal March on Top of the Everest

## 1. The deal background

### 1.1 INTRODUCTION

It was early December 2011 when Ivan Glasenberg and Mick Davis met for a low-key dinner at a hotel in the West End of London. The two have known each other since their days at Witwatersrand University in South Africa. At the time, they were the CEO of Switzerland-based commodity trader giant Glencore and the CEO of Switzerland-based miner Xstrata, respectively. On the menu was the prospect of a merger codenamed 'Everest', recalling a joint Himalayan expedition they had done together a few years earlier.

Indeed, on 2 February 2012, Xstrata publicly announced that it received an approach and it was in discussions with Glencore regarding a possible all-share merger of equals. In accordance with U.K. corporate law – Rule 2.6(a) of the City Code on Takeovers and Mergers – Glencore was required to announce whether or not it intended to make an offer by 1 March.

The news did not come in as a shock. In fact, the merger between the two companies had long been expected. Glencore already had a 34% ownership stake in Xstrata, and both companies had long recognized the underlying strategic rationale for bringing together production and marketing capabilities with increased scale and greater diversity of earnings.

Still, on each previous attempt to close a deal between the two parties, an agreement upon the terms of the transaction could not be reached, due to differing views of relative value, as well as to the optimal structure and governance arrangements for the combined entity.

This case was prepared by Professor Stefano Gatti (SDA Bocconi School of Management), Carlo Chiarella (Università Bocconi), and Nicolò Nava (Università Bocconi) as a basis for class discussion rather than to illustrate better or worse valuation methodologies or ineffective handling of an administrative situation. This document may contain "forward-looking statements" as defined in the Private Securities Litigation Reform Act of 1995. These statements involve risks, uncertainties and other factors that could cause actual results to differ materially from those which are anticipated. In addition, this document has been prepared with didactical purposes only: all forward-looking data, figures, and projections and all forward-looking statements included have to be considered as not representative of any actual situation. All evaluation considerations included in this document have been developed with the only purpose to provide students a better understanding of valuation techniques using available public information and are not, to all extents, related to any confidential document produced to advise any of the companies mentioned in this document. Neither the results of the analysis nor any other conclusion that one can reach through this document has to be considered indicative of any actual market situation and therefore the authors decline any responsibility for improper use of the data mentioned in this document. The authors do not undertake any obligation to update the forward-looking statements contained or incorporated in this document to reflect actual results, changes in assumptions, or changes in other factors affecting these forward-looking statements. The authors would like to thank Renzo Cenciarini, Alberto Dell'Acqua, and Leonardo Etro for their comments and suggestions on earlier versions of the case.

Hosting an evening of *Aida* in Covent Garden a couple of years earlier, Mr. Davis joked to his guests that when a deal was once completed he switched his ringtone to "Aida's Triumphal March." If all went to plan this time round, Mr. Davis's phone could well be playing that tune again.

This new attempt to close the deal, however, differed from previous approaches as Glencore's Initial Public Offering in May 2011 provided for a market valuation which substantively improved transparency, alleviating concerns over the appropriate value of its assets.

Interestingly, the merger would in some way bring back together the two companies whose histories were inextricably linked since March 2002, when Xstrata acquired Glencore's coal assets in South Africa and Australia and, at the same time, did an IPO. In addition to this, the two parties already had a long-standing relationship as they had been working together for more than ten years through a number of marketing agreements by which Glencore marketed around one-third of Xstrata's total sales.

## 1.2 INVOLVED COMPANIES OVERVIEW
### Target: Xstrata Plc
At the time of the merger, Xstrata (XTA) was the fifth largest diversified mining group in the world, with leading positions in copper, coal, ferrochrome, zinc and nickel. The company had operations and projects in more than 20 countries and was organized along five main business units: (1) Copper; (2) Coal; (3) Nickel; (4) Zinc; and (5) Alloys.

Xstrata's history started in 1926 when the Swiss company Südelektra was established to invest in infrastructure and power projects in Latin America. Beginning in 1990, it built a portfolio of businesses operating in the natural resources sector, and in March 2002 it went public through an IPO on the London and Swiss Stock Exchanges.

In the following years, the company grew dramatically by means of acquisitions. Key elements were the acquisitions of Enex and Duiker coal assets in 2002, of MIM in 2003 and of Falconbridge in 2006. At the time of the merger with Glencore, Xstrata had a great potential of growth with over 20 approved projects across all five business units to be delivered within 2014.

At the time of the merger, Glencore already owned a significant stake in Xstrata and was, indeed, its major shareholder. In addition to this, the CEO of Glencore Ivan Glasenberg sat on Xstrata's 13-member board as a non-executive director. The top three shareholders in Xstrata, including Glencore, owned roughly 50% of the company's shares (see Table A1 below).

**TABLE A1**  XTA shareholding structure (Source: company data)[1]

| Xstrata Shareholding Structure | |
| --- | --- |
| Glencore International plc | 33.64% |
| BlackRock plc | 5.66% |
| Qatar Holding LLC | 3.58% |
| Standard Life Investments Ltd | ≈ 2% |
| Schroders plc | ≈ 1.5% |

In 2012 the company generated revenues of over $31.6 billion, down 6.7% from the previous year, and a profit of $1.18 billion, which was 79% lower with respect to that of the previous year. A general fall in commodity

[1]For Glencore, BlackRock and Qatar Holding, data as of 8 March 2012: Xstrata, *2011 Annual Report*. For Standard Life and Schroders: Kevin Crowley, Jesse Riseborough and Jacqueline Simmons, "Glencore's $39 billion Xstrata offer hinges on 'super' 16%", *Bloomberg Businessweek*, 23 February 2012.

**FIGURE A1**  XTA revenues split by business unit and geographical area (Source: company data)

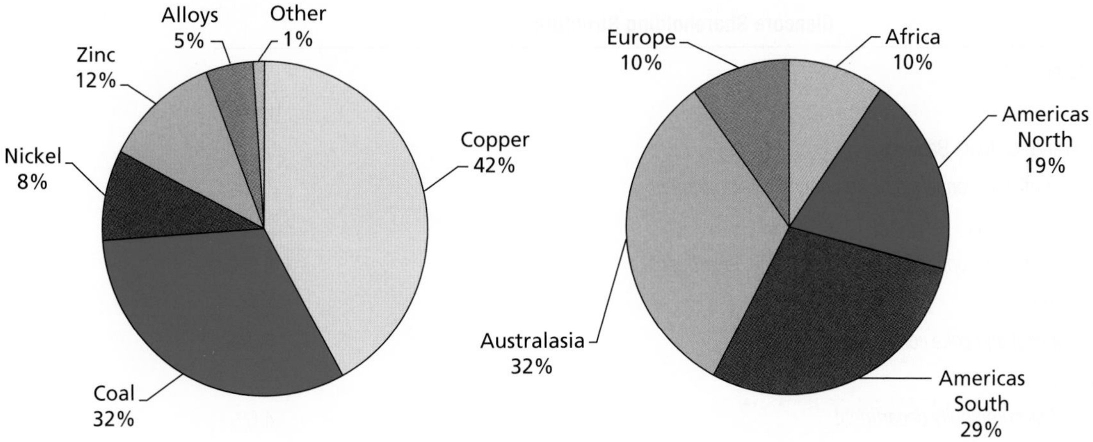

prices was one of the reasons for this fall in the company's operating performance. Figure A1 illustrates Xstrata's revenues by business unit and geographical area.

### Bidder: Glencore International plc

At the time of the merger, Glencore (GLEN) was the leading commodities trader in the world. It operated on a global scale distributing physical commodities sourced from third parties as well as own production to a wide range of industrial consumers, including the automotive, steel, power generation, oil and food processing industries. The company was organized along three business segments: (1) Metals and Minerals; (2) Energy Products; and (3) Agricultural Products. Each division was responsible for all the activities relating to the commodities they covered.

Glencore's roots dated back to 1974 when it was founded as Marc Rich & Co. and initially focused on the marketing of metals, minerals and crude oil. In the subsequent years, the company expanded its reach by acquiring an established Dutch grain trading company in 1981, which created the basis for its Agricultural Products business segment, and added coal to its Energy Products business segment. Starting in 1987, Glencore developed from a purely commodity marketing company into a diversified natural resources group through key acquisitions in mining, smelting, refining and processing.

In 1994 the founder Marc Rich sold its stake through a management buyout (MBO). According to people familiar with the matter, the reason behind this was a failed attempt to control the zinc market. Rich spent more than $1 billion and his bid resulted in a $172 million loss, nearly jeopardizing the future of the firm. The buyback of the founder's 51% stake began in March 1993 and was led by Willy Strothotte, who became newly established Glencore's CEO, and Ivan Glasenberg, who succeeded Strothotte at the helm in 2002.

Finally, in May 2011 Glencore listed in London and Hong Kong raising $10 billion. However, the company was still sort of employee-owned at the time of the merger, given the fact that all major shareholders were directors of Glencore. In particular, the seven top shareholders controlled a stake slightly in excess of 40% of the company (see Table A2 next page).

The company closed the year 2012 with revenues totaling over $214.4 billion, an increase of 15% with respect to the previous year, and profits of roughly $1 billion, a dramatic 75% lower than 2011 because of adverse industry conditions. The charts on next page (see Figure A2) break down Glencore's revenues by business segment and geographical area.

**TABLE A2**  GLEN shareholding structure (Source: company data)[2]

| Glencore Shareholding Structure | |
| --- | --- |
| Ivan Glasenberg | |
| *CEO* | 15.8% |
| Daniel Francisco Maté Badenes | |
| *co-director of zinc, copper and lead commodity department* | 6% |
| Aristotelis Mistakidis | |
| *co-director of zinc, copper and lead commodity department* | 5.9% |
| Tor Peterson | |
| *director of coal and coke commodity department* | 5.3% |
| Alex Beard | |
| *director of oil commodity department* | 4.6% |
| William Macaulay | |
| *non-executive director* | 1.79% |
| Steven Kalmin | |
| *CFO* | 1% |

**FIGURE A2**  GLEN revenues split by business unit and geographical area (Source: company data)

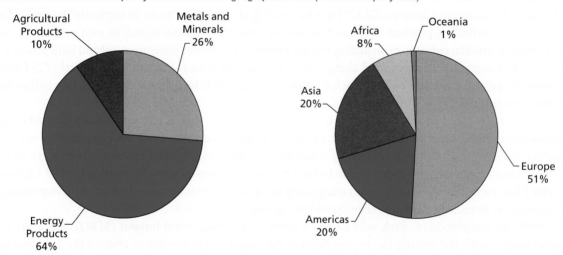

## 1.3 SECTOR OVERVIEW: THE GLOBAL MINING INDUSTRY

2012 was a roller-coaster year for commodity prices (Figure A3). China surpassed the U.S. as the world's biggest trading nation, which could promise well for commodity demand in the years to come, but China's economy slowed to 7.8% GDP growth, after several years of double-digit growth, and markets and observers were cautious as they waited to see how China's economy would transition in the near term.

Regardless of investor uncertainty, copper, zinc, silver, and gold all saw price improvements in 2012 (Table A3). For what concerns copper, some investors were betting global production would begin to wane as

[2]Data as of 26 March 2012. Glencore, *2011 Annual Report*, p.98.

**FIGURE A3** HSBC Global Base Metals Index (Source: HSBC Research)[3]

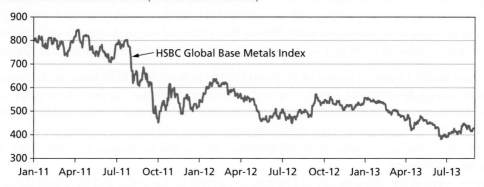

higher costs and shaky markets led to a delay in project development and slow production in the short term. The expectation was that a production slowdown would create supply constraints down the road which could help support strong prices long-term, if copper demand remained steady.

On the side of gold, instead, purchases were sustained by investors' demand of an inflation hedge and a solid long-term investment amid the global economic unease and by an increase in demand from central banks around the world.

**TABLE A3** Annual performance of selected mining commodities in 2012 (Source: PwC)[4]

| Annual performance of selected mining commodities in 2012 | |
| --- | --- |
| Zinc | +11% |
| Silver | +9% |
| Gold | +7% |
| Copper | +3% |
| Met Coal | +0.4% |
| Iron Ore | +0.2% |
| Nickel | −10% |
| Thermal Coal | −15% |

Amid this uncertainty, Rio Tinto, Anglo American, Barrick Gold and Kinross, to name the main headline grabbers, all had to break the news to shareholders in 2012 of multi-billion dollar write-downs. As a consequence, shareholders were then discouraging executives from pursuing expensive acquisitions. Markets and commentators then expected mega-mergers were to be placed on the shelf while executives sought to prove they were being prudent with shareholders' dollars and able to realize positive results on the many acquisitions of the past few years.

With mega-mergers out of the way and the importance of the bottom-line front and centre, industry observers argued that the short-term would be all about asset rationalization and that scan deal activity could be driven mainly by major miners either looking to divest non-core assets or to de-risk projects through joint ventures. Still, commentators also argued that opportunities may arise from junior miners finding value creation in one

[3]HSBC Global Research, https://www.research.hsbc.com/ibcom/out/indices/facility/summary?detail=.JCBM.
[4]PwC, Down, but not out, *Global Mining Deals,* March 2013, p. 4.

another by merging to create a stronger, more resilient company. For example, miner with a stellar asset but weak cash position may consider merging with a company that has a strong cash position, but struggling assets.

In terms of business scale and scope, BHP Billiton, Rio Tinto and Anglo American were the most direct competitors of the combined entity that would emerge from a merger between Glencore and Xstrata.

- BHP Billiton resulted from the merger of BHP and Billiton in June 2001. BHP, based in Australia, was engaged in mining, development, production, and marketing of iron ore, copper, oil and gas, diamonds, silver, lead, zinc, and other natural resources. It was also the market leader in value added flat steel products. Billiton, based in Indonesia, was a top player in the metals and minerals mining industry and also one of the major producers of aluminum and alumina, chrome and manganese ores and alloys, steaming coal, nickel and titanium.
- Rio Tinto was one of the oldest metals and mining companies in the world, and its origins dated as far back as 1873. A leading producer of copper in the world it also dealt with aluminum, copper, diamonds, coal, uranium, gold, industrial minerals and iron. It was headquartered in the U.K., while the company major assets were in Australia and North America.
- Anglo American was originally a gold mining company headquartered in the U.K. and founded in 1917. In 1945, the company expanded its business into coal mining. It went public in 1999 and then it diversified into several commodities such as iron ore, manganese, metallurgical coal, thermal coal, copper and nickel. The company was a top ten company in the metal and mining industry and was the global leader in both platinum and diamonds, as well as the fourth-largest producer of iron ore.

The entity emerging from the merger would differ from other big diversified miners in three main ways:

(i) its marketing division would be the largest marketer of industrial, agricultural and energy products globally.

(ii) while being the most diversified by geography and commodity (see Figure A4 and Figure A5), it would have no iron ore earnings and its industrial business would be primarily focused on copper, coal and zinc with a growing contribution from oil. Its mining assets would be positioned, in aggregate, in the middle of their respective cost curves. BHP Billiton and Rio Tinto had a slightly better cost position and their assets also had a slightly longer life of mine, but these differences mainly reflected their iron ore operations.

(iii) management and employees would own around 37% of the company's equity, while ownership in other peer firms was well below 1% (seven company executives were among the top-10 shareholders, compared with none in industry peers, see Figure A6).

## 1.4 THE MERGER RATIONALE

In the words of Xstrata CEO Mick Davis, at the time of the announcement, the merger between the two companies offered *"a unique opportunity to create a new business model"* in order *to "respond to a changing environment"*, characterized by the shift of the sources of supply to more disparate locations and the shift of demand growth to emerging Asian economies. Moreover, the deal represented *"the logical step for two complementary businesses".*[5]

Integration was expected to provide to the combined firm more flexible control over inputs and improved supply chain coordination and increased market power.

EBITDA synergies were expected to be of at least $500 million in the first year, predominantly related to marketing. The significant majority of these synergies would be due to the possibility to create additional value from marketing Xstrata's output which was not already marketed through Glencore's trading arm. It was estimated that 60% of these synergies would emanate from the Metals and Minerals business segment, one third from the Energy Products business segment and the remainder from cost cutting.

[5]Glencore and Xstrata, *News Release*, 7 February 2012.

**FIGURE A4** Large diversified global miners' 2012 EBIT split by commodity (Source: company data, Morgan Stanley research)

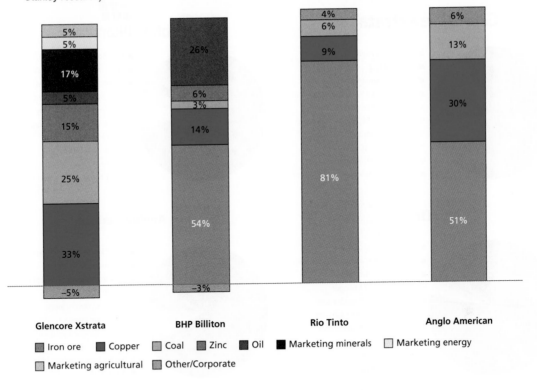

**FIGURE A5** Large diversified global miners' 2012 revenues split by geographical area (Source: Morgan Stanley research)

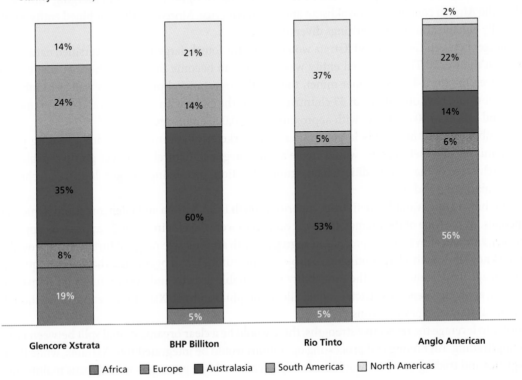

**FIGURE A6** Large diversified global miners' ownership structure (Source: Thomson Reuters)

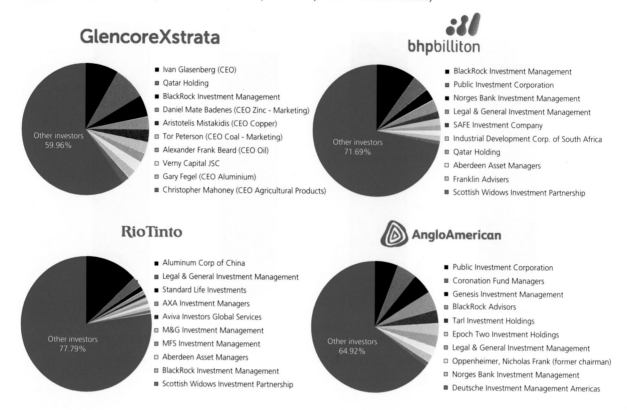

The new company would feature strong presence in key current and future mining regions in all core commodities and would be ideally positioned to take advantage of opportunities in emerging mining regions, including the African copper-belt, Kazakhstan and South America. Moreover, the combined entity would enjoy substantially enhanced scale and earnings diversification.

The merger between Glencore and Xstrata would create the fourth-largest global diversified natural resources company in the world. The combined entity was expected to become the largest thermal coal exporter and zinc producer, the third-largest copper miner, the fourth-largest nickel producer, as well as number seven in FTSE 100. It would have operations in 33 countries around the globe with 101 mines and over 50 metallurgical facilities and offices in 40 countries with approximately 130,000 employees.

The combination of the world's largest trader and marketer of commodities with a leading portfolio of industrial mining and metals assets would create a fully integrated natural resources group capable to capture value at each stage of the commodities chain, from extraction, processing, freight, logistics, technology and storage  to marketing and trading.

The combined group would benefit from superior growth from Xstrata and Glencore's complementary project pipelines. At the time of the merger, the two companies were developing over 25 approved copper, thermal coal, nickel, zinc and alloys growth projects in aggregate, with an extensive range of further unapproved options. Matching know-how with a larger number of project opportunities, and overlaying that with adequate risk and capital management, should raise the probability of profitable growth and good returns on reinvestment. In this respect, applying Glencore's stricter capital allocation philosophy to Xstrata's asset portfolio should reduce the risk of substantial capex overruns.

In order to leverage the respective strengths, there would be a clear organizational split between mining and marketing/trading. All mining and processing operations would be integrated into Xstrata's, while the marketing, logistics and trading activities would be led by Glencore. Mine managers would focus mainly on volume targets, unit costs and capex efficiency, while traders would focus on working capital control and maximizing revenue per ton. This alignment of incentives and skills should increase the probability that mines outperform peers on costs, volumes, and capex efficiency. Diversified miners have set up their own marketing operations too, but none would match the scale of the combined entity resulting from a merger between Glencore and Xstrata (in terms of people, client relationships and logistics capabilities).

## MERGER TERMS AND CHRONOLOGY

On 6 February 2012, Glencore announced its bid of 2.80 shares for each Xstrata share it did not already own. The figure represented a premium of 15.2% on the undisturbed price on 1 February, and 27.9% on the average price over the three-month period ending on 1 February. The offer was structured as a Scheme of Arrangement and all Xstrata shares already beneficially owned by Glencore, about 34% of ordinary issued capital, were therefore excluded from the transaction.

Further terms of the merger provided for Xstrata chairman Sir John Bond, CEO Mick Davis and CFO Trevor Reid to keep their roles in the combined group. Glencore CEO Ivan Glasenberg and CFO Steven Kalmin, on the other hand, would take up deputy roles. Finally, a retention package was designed for some 70 Xstrata executives and directors with the aim to prevent key employees from leaving their job once the transaction was completed.[6]

The terms of the merger, despite Xstrata board's approval, were not deemed satisfactory by shareholders. Indeed, after months of rumors, on 26 June Qatar Holding stated it expected a 3.25x exchange ratio from Glencore. The Qatari Sovereign Wealth Fund had been increasing its stake in Xstrata since before the deal's announcement in February and then owned about 10% of shares. The request for a higher ratio was motivated on the basis of the asserted need to balance the benefits resulting from the merger and to acknowledge the long-term prospects of the mining company.

Criticism also clustered around the retention package (worth about £170 million in total) for lack of performance clauses attached. Xstrata chairman and board were criticized for failing to consult with shareholders.

Qatar Holding's move seriously endangered the smooth proceeding of the deal. In a U.K. Court-sanctioned Scheme of Arrangement scenario, Glencore had to win the support of 75% of voting shareholders[7] but, being prevented from voting its 34% stake in Xstrata, a group representing 16.5% could block the deal. Moreover, assuming standard attendance at the meeting, commentators argued that a group of only 11–12% against could prove decisive.

In addition to Qatar, other naysayers included Knight Vinke, Standard Life, Schroders, the Norwegian Government Pension Fund and Fidelity, who together controlled about 5.5% of Xstrata shares.

---

[6] Retention measures were offered to each of the Xstrata Executive Directors (Mr. Davis, Mr. Reid and Mr. Zaldumbide), other members of Xstrata's Management and the Xstrata Senior Employees (64 people), in addition to entitlements to salary, benefits and any discretionary performance bonuses payable pursuant to the terms of each individual's contract. Payment of all retention awards would be in tranches following completion of the merger and the value of each tranche would be equal to the total of an individual's current annual salary, pension and other benefits, and the bonus awarded in February 2012 (except for Mr. Zaldumbide who did not receive retirement or other benefits and whose tranches would be equal to 150% of his current annual salary and the bonus awarded). The payment of each retention award was conditional upon completion of the merger and the individual not being dismissed for cause in accordance with his or her employment contract before the date of payment of the award. Mr. Davis' retention award was payable in three equal tranches on the first, second and third anniversaries, respectively, of the Effective Date. Each payment would be paid as to two-thirds in cash and one-third in newly-issued Glencore Shares (in the form of the grant of a nil-cost option exercisable for up to ten years). Mr. Davis' award would be accelerated if his employment was terminated at any time for any reason (other than if he was dismissed for cause in accordance with his contract of employment) of if Mr. Davis resigned for a "valid reason" as defined in his contract of employment. The retention awards of the other members of Xstrata's Management and the Xstrata Senior Employees were payable in two equal tranches in cash on the first and second anniversaries, respectively, of the Effective Date. In each case, retention awards were subject to the same conditions for payment as Mr. Davis' award. For these purposes, "valid reason" includes a material change to the terms of employment and benefits or compensation, Glencore ceasing to comply with the governance structure and a change of control of Glencore. The maximum aggregate amount payable to participants to the Management Incentive Plan is as set out in the table below.

[7]"If a majority in number representing 75% in value of the creditors or class of creditors or members or class of members (as the case may be), present and voting either in person or by proxy at the meeting summoned under section 896, agree a compromise or arrangement, the court may, on an application under this section, sanction the compromise or arrangement". *Companies Act 2006*, Part 26, sec. 899, par. 1.

| | 2013 | 2014 | 2015 |
|---|---|---|---|
| Mick Davis | £9,598,475 | £9,598,475 | £9,598,475 |
| Trevor Reid | £5,451,848 | £5,451,848 | – |
| Santiago Zaldumbide | £3,942,785 | £3,942,785 | – |
| Management | £16,088,493 | £16,088,493 | – |
| Senior Employees | £46,447,660 | £46,447,660 | – |

Adapted from Glencore, *Scheme Circular*, 31 May 2012, pp. 30–33.

In response to the dissatisfaction of Xstrata's investors on the terms of the bid and their threat to block the deal, Glasenberg told Reuters: "*This is a merger of equals. Xstrata has got most senior jobs. Most previous mergers of equals were done at a ratio of equals, this has been done at a premium. We believe it is a fair deal. Fair to all shareholders*".

## The Problem

The turning point was on the evening of 6 September, when Glencore CEO Ivan Glasenberg met Qatar's Prime Minister Sheikh Hamad Bin Jasim Bin Al-Thani in a London hotel. The meeting is mediated by former U.K. Prime Minister Tony Blair, who has been serving as a senior adviser to J.P. Morgan, one of Xstrata's financial advisers, since 2008.

Ivan Glasenberg is on his way to the hotel where he is going to meet Sheik Hamad. While stuck in London's traffic, he reflects on how to unlock the situation and get the deal back on track. Mr. Glasenberg believes that by increasing the exchange ratio to 3.05x an agreement can be reached, but Qatar's Prime Minister has proven to be a tough negotiator in the past months.

Now, suppose you are the chief executive of Glencore.

Firstly, you are reconsidering what are the reasons why you opted for a stock-for-stock bid under a scheme of arrangement.

Secondly, you want to estimate what is the minimum exchange ratio that would be acceptable for Xstrata's shareholders and what is the maximum exchange ratio that you could offer. Based on your DCF valuation of the post-merger combined firm, is your original offer of 2.80x acceptable for the target? Is the 3.25x request by Qatar Holding suitable for your company? Where would a revised bid of 3.05x stand in the range of the mutually acceptable terms?

Finally, you want to analyze the acquisition premium implied by a revised proposal of 3.05x on the basis of: the (i) historical market exchange ratio between the two firms, the (ii) relative contribution to the combined firm, and (iii) precedent comparable transactions.

## Appendix 1 – Deal Tear Sheet

### GLENCORE INTERNATIONAL PLC TO ACQUIRE 66% STAKE IN XSTRATA PLC

Glencore bids to acquire the remaining 65.9% interest, or 1,964 mil ordinary shares, which it did not already own in Xstrata in a stock swap transaction, via scheme of arrangement. Glencore originally offers 2.80 new ordinary shares per Xstrata share, and the exchange ratio is then revised to 3.05 under new terms. Upon completion, Xstrata will be delisted from London and Swiss Stock Exchanges. Glencore will be renamed Glencore Xstrata International PLC.

## Deal Purpose

The purpose of the transaction is for the companies to benefit from enhanced scale and diversification in the global resources industry, gain presence at each stage of the commodities chain, establish footprint in emerging regions for natural resources investment and to create synergies.

## Deal Summary

| | | | |
|---|---|---|---|
| Deal Value (USD $m) | 34,739.08 | Deal Attitude | Friendly |
| Shares Held/Sought | 34.08% / 65.92% | Shares Sought | 1,964,290,000 |
| Acquisition Technique | Scheme of Arrangement, Merger of Equals | Consideration | Stock Swap |
| Synergies (EBIT $m) | 500 | | |
| Date First Announced | 02/02/2012 | Initial ER | 2.80x |
| Date Revised | 07/09/2012 | Revised ER | 3.05x |

| Financials | Xstrata | | Glencore | |
|---|---|---|---|---|
| (USD $m) | 2011 | 2012 | 2011 | 2012 |
| Total assets | 74,832 | 83,113 | 86,165 | 105,537 |
| Net assets | 45,701 | 46,791 | 32,335 | 34,300 |
| Net debt | 8,422 | 15,084 | 12,938 | 11,457 |
| Equity (BV) | 43,664 | 44,452 | 29,265 | 31,266 |
| Revenues | 33,877 | 31,618 | 186,152 | 214,436 |
| EBITDA | 11,648 | 8,122 | 6,464 | 5,943 |
| EBIT | 8,460 | 4,791 | 5,398 | 4,470 |
| Net income | 5,713 | 3,652 | 4,048 | 1,004 |
| Dividends | 586 | 797 | 346 | 1,066 |
| Shares outstanding (000) | 2,968,763 | 2,971,497 | 6,087,322 | 6,988,783 |
| Market Cap (01/02/2012) | – | 53,616.33 | – | 48,283.86 |
| Rating (S&P / Moody's) | – | BBB+/Baa2 | – | BBB/Baa2 |

| Key Ratios | Xstrata | | Glencore | |
|---|---|---|---|---|
| | 2011 | 2012 | 2011 | 2012 |
| EV/Sales | 1.70 | 1.92 | 0.37 | 0.43 |
| EV/EBITDA | 4.98 | 5.61 | 16.17 | 11.61 |
| EV/EBIT | 6.89 | 7.77 | 21.53 | 14.80 |
| P/E | 8.07 | 9.24 | 8.76 | 10.53 |
| P/Sales | 1.36 | 1.56 | 0.23 | 0.27 |
| P/Cash Flow | 4.93 | 5.64 | 11.16 | 8.80 |
| P/Book Value | 1.02 | 1.17 | 1.44 | 1.63 |

## Appendix 2 – Peer Companies Multiples

| Industry Peer Firms (31/12/2012) | Market Cap ($m) | Enterprise Value ($m) | Net Debt ($m) | Net Debt/EV (%) | P/E | EV/EBITDA |
|---|---|---|---|---|---|---|
| BHP Billiton | 170,750.81 | 202,455.50 | 30,451.99 | 15.04% | 9.7x | 6.0x |
| Rio Tinto | 90,993.69 | 121,193.09 | 19,046.95 | 15.72% | 9.1x | 5.9x |
| Anglo American | 31,240.78 | 45,823.15 | 8,454.31 | 18.45% | 12.0x | 4.8x |

* Source: Thomson Reuters and JPM estimates

## Appendix 3 – Precedent Transactions Multiples

| Year Announced | 2001 | 2006 | 2010 | 2010 | 2011 | 2011 |
|---|---|---|---|---|---|---|
| Status | Completed | Completed | Completed | Withdrawn | Completed | Completed |
| Acquirer | BHP | Vale | Newcrest Mining | BHP Billiton | BHP Billiton | First Quantum Minerals |
| Target | Billiton | Inco | Lihir Gold | Potash Corp. of Saskatchewan | Petrohawk Energy Corp. | Inmet Mining Corp. |
| Deal Value ($m) | 11,510.99 | 17,150.30 | 9,018.25 | 39,761.24 | 11,776.25 | 5,057.55 |
| Attitude | Friendly | Hostile | Friendly | Hostile | Friendly | Hostile |
| Technique | Scheme of Arrangement | Tender Offer | Scheme of Arrangement | Tender Offer | Tender Offer | Scheme of Arrangement |
| Consideration | Stock Only | Cash Only | Cash and Stock | Cash Only | Cash Only | Cash and Stock |
| Premium (%) | 21.56 | 31.54 | 34.5 | 41.24 | 61.93 | 42.72 |
| Deal EV/EBITDA | 11.52x | 6.69x | 12.70x | 65.20x | 15.36x | 8.48x |
| Deal Equity/NI | 12.12x | 7.71x | 19.40x | 86.14x | 28.87x | 11.89x |
| Notes | – | – | Revised | – | – | Revised |

# Appendix 4 – Discounted Cash Flow Analysis

| JPM Research Estimates | Forecast Period | | | Cost of Capital | |
|---|---|---|---|---|---|
| *(USD $m)* | **2013** | **2014** | **2015** | Assumptions: | |
| **EBIT** | **8,085** | **12,051** | **14,751** | **Capital Structure** | |
| Depreciation & amortization | 5,635 | 6,168 | 6,701 | Gearing ratio | 38% |
| Change in working capital | −2,187 | −3,026 | −714 | | |
| Taxes paid | −1,232 | −2,320 | −3,442 | **Cost of Equity** | |
| | | | | Risk-free rate | 5.50% |
| **Cash flow from operations** | **10,301** | **12,873** | **17,296** | Equity risk premium | 5.50% |
| Capex Disposal proceeds | −7,161 | −5,915 | −4,963 | Levered beta | 1.50 |
| | − | − | − | | |
| **Un-levered Free Cash Flow** | **3,140** | **6,958** | **12,333** | **Cost of Debt** | |
| Net interest paid | −1,550 | −1,611 | −1,447 | Cost of debt | 7% |
| | | | | Tax rate | 23% |
| **Levered Free Cash Flow** | **1,590** | **5,347** | **10,886** | | |
| Debt raised/re-paid | − | − | − | − | − |
| Equity raised/re-paid | | | | | |
| Other investing/financing CFs | − | − | − | − | |
| **Free Cash Flow to Equity** | **1,590** | **5,347** | **10,886** | | |

# References

Betton, S., Eckbo, B.E. and Thorburn, K.S.. Chapter 15 – Corporate takeovers, in Eckbo, B.E., edited by, *Handbook of Empirical Corporate Finance, Volume 2*, 1st edition, Amsterdam: North-Holland, 2008.

Bruner R., *Applied M&A*, John Wiley & Sons, 2004.

Bruner, R., *Deals From Hell – M&A Lessons That Rise Above the Ashes,* Hoboken, NJ: Wiley, 2005. Damodaran A., *Applied Corporate Finance: A User's Manual*, John Wiley & Sons, 1999.

Damodaran A., *The dark side of valuation*, Prentice Hall, 2001.

Daniel Ammann, *The Secret Lives of Marc Rich: The King of Oil*, St. Martin's Griffin, 2009.Eckbo, B.E., Introduction to corporate takeovers: Modern empirical developments, Tuck School of Business Working Paper, 2011-92, 2010. http://ssrn.com/abstract=1767989 (last accessed on 27 August 2013).

Javier Blas and Sylvia Pfeifer, Dinner that put Glencore-Xstrata on the menu, *Financial Times*, 3 February 2012.

Jetley, G. and Ji, X., The shrinking merger arbitrage spread: Reasons and implications, *Financial Analyst Journal*, 66(2): 54–68, 2010.

O'Kane, D., Jamieson, F., Bell, R., Defay, B., Bateman, J. and Abate, A., Glencore Xstrata plc, *J.P. Morgan Cazenove Europe Equity Research*, 2 May 2013.PwC, Down, but not out, *Global Mining Deals*, March 2013.

Sanderse, M., Gabriel, A., Zaunscherb, E., Haissl, A. A. and Oguntade, A. O., Glencore-Xstrata: All to play for, *Morgan Stanley Research*, 7 May 2013.

Weston F., Mitchell M. L. and Mulherin J. H, *Takeovers, Restructuring and Corporate Governancev*, Prentice Hall, 2004.

# ADDITIONAL CASES

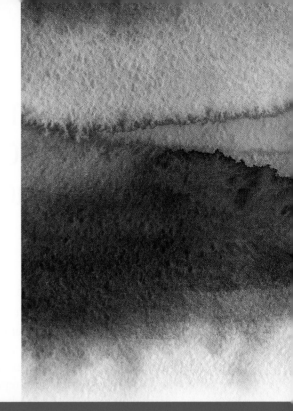

## PART IV

# CASE

# Enforcing financial reporting standards: The case of White Pharmaceuticals AG

## Abstract

As a consequence of accounting scandals, Germany – like many other countries – set up a supervisory body to control the compliance of capital market oriented companies with accounting regulations. The Financial Reporting Enforcement Panel (FREP) assumed their duty in July 2005 and has forced a number of companies to restate their financial statements. This case study adapts one of the real cases of the FREP and invites students to reflect on the enforcement of financial reporting standards: White Pharmaceuticals AG enters a strategic alliance to profit from the research and development of their partner. The company charges all payments that it conducts in the course of the alliance to their expense accounts. The FREP, however, finds that the final lump-sum payment should have been capitalized by White. The case reviews the accounting for research and development expenditure and also discusses the convergence of financial reporting standards in the US and Europe.

**Keywords:** Financial Reporting Enforcement, Research and Development, IFRS Standards

## The Case

### INTRODUCTION

Peter Schmidt, head of the accounting department of Germany-based White Pharmaceuticals AG,[1] had been waiting for the letter for quite a while now. When it finally came, his hands started shaking as he read "Financial Reporting Enforcement Panel" on the envelope. Opening the letter he recalled the painfully long days in his office during which he tried to answer countless questions to the panel's satisfaction. As he read through the letter, his face grew paler. This was exactly what he had warned the CFO of White Pharmaceuticals AG of and exactly what he had described as a worst case scenario. In the letter, dated November 18th 2009, the Financial Reporting Enforcement Panel (FREP) requested a restatement of White's financial statements for the year 2006. Income as well as intangible assets had been understated by 55 million Euros as White Pharmaceuticals AG

The sole responsibility for the content of the HHL Working Paper lies with the authors, Henning Zülch and Dominic Detzen. We encourage the use of the material for teaching or research purposes with reference to the source. The reproduction, copying and distribution of the paper for non-commercial purposes is permitted on condition that the source is clearly indicated. Any commercial use of the document or parts of its content requires the written consent of the author/s.

For further HHL publications see www.hhl.de/publications.

[1]All names, dates, and locations have been changed, as have the "characters" involved in the case.

had expensed a payment made to acquire research results. With the letter in his hand, Peter slowly walked to the office of Alexander Muller, White's Chief Financial Officer, and reflected on the events that had led to the examination by the FREP.

White Pharmaceuticals AG was founded in 1956 by Paul White and his brother Roland. Since its inception, the company had been headquartered in a small town near Frankfurt, Germany, and had specialized in various fields of pharmaceutical research. In recent years, White Pharmaceuticals AG had benefited from major breakthroughs with drugs for neurological diseases and subsequently experienced a remarkable growth with revenues that soon exceeded 1 billion Euros. In 2000, the current CEO and son of Paul White, Richard, decided to use the momentum to have his company listed on the German stock exchange. The initial public offering (IPO) was a huge success for Richard White who also took the opportunity to reward his employees for their contribution to White's recent success. At the same time, he made his intention quite clear that he did not want to rest but that he wanted to challenge the big pharmaceutical companies.

## THE COOPERATION AGREEMENT

In a meeting subsequent to the IPO, Mr. White asked his managerial staff for options to grow further and to expand into additional markets. His CFO, Alex Muller, proposed to sustain the recent growth by entering strategic alliances with other research companies. Richard White agreed with his CFO as he saw a huge potential for his company to both profit from joint research results and from entering new markets. His considerations also based on the fact that, following the IPO, White Pharmaceuticals AG had enough money to make strategic alliances attractive to potential partners. Thus, Mr. White encouraged his staff to follow this idea and find research companies that fit into their portfolio.

Soon, a US-based company called Neurocentral, Inc. was identified and offered a partnership which the company gratefully accepted as they had been facing serious funding problems recently. Neurocentral, Inc. was a medium-sized pharmaceutical company that also specialized in the development of neurological drugs. According to the terms of the partnership, White Pharmaceuticals AG received access to Neurocentral's research results by obtaining the sole rights to sell the jointly developed drugs worldwide. White would therefore be able to expand into additional markets while profiting from Neurocentral's good ties to the US Food and Drug Administration (FDA). For Neurocentral, Inc., on the other hand, the alliance meant that their funding problems were solved. Simultaneously, they could increase their competitiveness which had also suffered lately. Both companies were delighted with the alliance and signed the contract in 2001 feeling like they were getting the most out of the deal.

Thus, the companies jointly agreed on the development of a transdermal patch that treats a common form of epilepsy. Neurocentral, Inc. had made a lot of progress in the research and expected to start clinical studies in the near future. To fund this R&D project, White Pharmaceuticals AG was to provide its US counterpart with three forms of compensation that corresponded to the typical steps in a drug development process[2]: After signing the contract, Neurocentral, Inc. was to receive a non-refundable upfront payment of five million Euros that was directly linked to the development of the transdermal patch. Using this money, the American company could increase their research efforts and complete the research and the pre-clinical phase in the year 2001, a little earlier than expected. In addition, White Pharmaceuticals AG would make two milestone payments of ten million Euros each as soon as Neurocentral, Inc. reached pre-defined targets in the development of the patch. The payments would become due when Neurocentral completed Phase I and II of the clinical studies which would be when preliminary testing of the new drug provided first results on central characteristics like dosage range, efficacy and side effects. Provided that no complications arose, Neurocentral, Inc. estimated to finalize Phase I in 2002 and Phase II in 2004. The final component of the compensation package would include a lump-sum payment of 55 million Euros that White would transfer when Neurocentral, Inc. completed the final clinical studies (Phase III) successfully. Early estimations by Neurocentral's researchers showed that they expected the

---

[2]See Appendix for a depiction of the drug development process and the payment structure.

drug ready for approval in 2006. In exchange for their payments, White Pharmaceuticals AG received worldwide commercialization rights for the transdermal patch. Consequently, White would use their own resources to file for approval of the patch with both FDA and European Medicines Agency (EMA). The post-approval studies (Phase IV) would also be undertaken by White who would then continue to market the new drug.

## ACCOUNTING FOR THE AGREEMENT

Soon after the contract was signed and the corresponding upfront payment was made, Peter Schmidt was confronted with analyzing the partnership from an accounting perspective. For him, the key issue concerning the payments was quite clear. The subject revolved around the question whether to recognize an intangible asset or whether to expense the costs as the payments were made. He knew that IAS 38 sets the rules for the treatment of intangible assets and research and development expenditures. Here, he read that he needed to distinguish between separately acquired and internally generated intangible assets. The former are usually capitalized as the definition and recognition criteria of IAS 38 are fulfilled. Concerning internally generated intangibles, however, IAS 38 differentiates between a research and a development phase. While costs for research are to be expensed, costs that are incurred in the development phase are recognized as intangible assets if an additional set of criteria is fulfilled.

With these abstract explanations in mind, Peter sought to assess the upfront payment concerning a possible capitalization. He remembered that when he first started his job, Alex Muller told him that "we expense almost all of our R&D costs. That's what everyone does in the pharmaceutical industry. Besides, we never know if we will receive approval by EMA or FDA. Only if we have the authorization do we recognize the costs for the development of the approved drug. And we only capitalize those costs that we incur after the approval." Still unsure about what to do Peter called his colleague at Neurocentral, Inc. and asked him to assess the situation. Jeff Hudson, head of accounting at Neurocentral, Inc., was about to go to a meeting when his phone rang. Jeff was surprised by the question but did not have too much time to get involved with the issue. Thus, he simply said: "Look, Peter, I am kind of busy at the moment. But I can tell you that, here, in the US, we don't recognize costs that we incur when doing research for new drugs. SFAS No. 2 doesn't allow a capitalization. However, if we acquire R&D, that's a different story. In that case, we follow SFAS No. 141 and SFAS No. 142 and capitalize the acquired in-process R&D. But I'm not really sure what I would do in your situation. Besides, you're an IFRS Standards guy and, as far as I know, R&D accounting still differs on our continents." Peter didn't feel like his American counterpart had fully understood his problem but was still thankful for Jeff's quick assessment of the situation.

Feeling that he had to solve the issue himself, Peter considered the nature of the upfront compensation. White Pharmaceuticals AG conducted the payment to profit from the research carried out by Neurocentral, Inc. While White Pharmaceuticals AG received all rights to the research performed, Peter did not perceive the five million Euros as an acquisition of an intangible asset. Instead, he felt that White only provided Neurocentral with the funding for research activities that the company performed. Following this reasoning, the payment had to be regarded as if White's researchers were conducting the research. And, considering the status the research was in at that time, no one could tell if the project would eventually yield a product that White would be able to sell. Therefore, the up-front payment would fall under the definition of research expenditure which IAS 38 prohibits from capitalizing. Although being skeptical of his argumentation, he charged the five million Euros to White's R&D expenses.

Thereafter, the project proceeded as expected and Neurocentral, Inc. started the clinical studies in 2002. In the same year, they were able to complete the first phase of the studies which provided them with a safety profile of the transdermal patch. Acting upon their role in the collaboration agreement, White transferred the first milestone payment of ten million Euros as soon as they received the latest research report from their partner.

As a consequence of the payment, Peter was again confronted with the accounting for the alliance. Considering that the project had progressed to the development phase which, according to IAS 38, meant that incurred costs should be recognized, he wanted to discuss a possible capitalization of the payment with his CFO. In their meeting, Peter outlined his train of thought and explained that a capitalization may be necessary. He argued that White received all rights to the research performed and to the development carried out thus far. Therefore, the ten million Euros could be considered part of the intangible asset that White acquired in the course of the collaboration. Besides, Peter told Mr. Muller that IAS 38 required enterprises to recognize expenses that they incur in the development phase. Alex Muller listened carefully to what Peter Schmidt told him. However, he made clear that he assessed the payment differently: "I understand your reasoning, Peter, but I don't share your opinion. I believe that assessing the agreement is a two-step-process. First, we have to judge whether or not the transaction is an acquisition of R&D. I don't consider the agreement as an acquisition, but as an outsourcing of our R&D because we just fund the research and development conducted by Neurocentral. Thus, the second and central question that we have to ask is: Would we capitalize our expenses if we conducted the R&D in-house? And the answer is: No, we would not. At this point in the development process, we do not know if we will ever get a marketable product. And, if you read IAS 38, the standard tells you that an enterprise should only capitalize R&D if it can demonstrate that the intangible asset will yield future economic benefits. But as we don't have approval by either FDA or EMA yet, we cannot reasonably expect future economic benefits from the product. All this leads me to the conclusion that we don't have to capitalize the milestone payment."

Although Peter felt that he had made a valid point, Alex Muller's argumentation also sounded convincing. In the end, he decided to follow his CFO's reasoning as Mr. Muller had been in the business longer than Peter and could therefore reasonably be expected to know the relevant accounting practices in the industry. Thus, he recorded the milestone payment as part of White's expenses.

While Peter had struggled with the accounting treatment of the ten million Euros, Neurocentral, Inc. had begun with the second phase of the development. In the years 2003 and 2004, the transdermal patch was tested with 250 patients who were closely monitored to observe possible side effects of the drug. At the same time, these tests provided Neurocentral with first indications of the actual efficacy of the patch. Researchers at the American company and their counterparts in Europe were both delighted with the progress with which the project advanced. In 2004, Neurocentral, Inc. proudly notified White Pharmaceuticals AG that the second phase was completed successfully. In return, White transferred another ten million Euros expecting to soon receive a fully developed product. For Peter who still had his CFO's reasoning in mind, the milestone payment seemed of a similar nature as the one made in 2002. Concluding that no intangible asset was received in return for the ten million Euros, he again expensed the milestone payment as he had done with the previous one.

Subsequently, Neurocentral, Inc. conducted Phase III of the development process which typically is of much larger scale. As the company had not observed any severe side effects from the patch so far, they were able to limit the final clinical study to 1,000 patients. Over the course of two years, Neurocentral again tested the transdermal patch and observed a great effectiveness of the drug. What's more, no complications or additional side effects arose. Accordingly, the development process was completed in 2006 which was celebrated at both companies. After receiving all documents associated with the transdermal patch, White Pharmaceuticals AG went on to make the final lump-sum payment of 55 million Euros to Neurocentral, Inc. In addition, they used the documents received to compile the application for FDA and EMA approval.

Thus, the project had been completed and Peter faced the last payment resulting from the agreement. He realized that Mr. Muller's argumentation was still valid – White had filed for approval but not received an authorization for the drug yet. As a consequence, he again charged the 55 million Euros to White's expense accounts. Nevertheless, the official termination of the agreement made him reconsider the accounting treatment and he decided to openly discuss the issue with White's auditors.

## THE DISCUSSION WITH WHITE'S AUDITORS

At year's end, Peter sat down with the auditors and was asked if any extraordinary transactions had occurred. He described the circumstances of the alliance with Neurocentral, Inc. and asked the auditors for their opinion on the lump-sum payment. A few days later, after the auditors had analyzed the issue, they discussed whether White had acquired an intangible asset or whether the payment was part of White's R&D expense. The auditors, however, suggested that the issue may be open to interpretation. On the one hand, they shared Alex Muller's assessment and acknowledged that the lack of an official approval indeed made a capitalization questionable. On the other hand, they shared Peter's doubts and indicated that the approval only seemed to remain a legal formality. The clinical studies had been completed without any complications and White could present the necessary paperwork for an approval by FDA or EMA. This would lead to the conclusion that all criteria in IAS 38 were fulfilled and the costs incurred in the last stage of the development phase, i.e., 55 million Euros, should be recognized. In addition, the auditors declared that the transaction could also be interpreted as an acquisition of an intangible asset. Consequently, the price White had paid for the R&D could be seen to reflect White's expectations concerning an inflow of economic benefits. According to IAS 38, such a separate acquisition always resulted in an intangible asset that had to be recognized by the acquirer.

Regardless of these discussions, Alex Muller who joined Peter and the auditors at the meeting insisted on the fact that White only compensated Neurocentral, Inc. for the research and did not acquire an asset. He claimed that he had researched similar transactions and found that engaging another entity to conduct research did not constitute an acquisition of an asset. Thus, he asserted that the arrangement with Neurocentral, Inc. had to be evaluated as an outsourcing of research and development. Following this argumentation, he demanded to apply the same criteria as would be the case if the R&D was conducted in-house, i.e., by White's own research department. And, in that situation, they had to evaluate if all criteria of development costs were fulfilled. He, again, negated that White could already expect future economic benefits as White still did not have an approval by either FDA or EMA. Therefore, he pushed for an expense charge of the lump-sum payment. As the auditors could not provide an unequivocal interpretation that asserted the contrary and as they had specifically asked for managerial judgment, they eventually decided to follow Mr. Muller's reasoning and approved the expense charges.

## THE EXAMINATION

Although the transdermal patch turned out to be a huge success and the executive teams of both White Pharmaceuticals AG and Neurocentral, Inc. were eager to extend the alliance, they could not agree on a follow-up project and the collaboration was terminated. Consequently, Peter slowly forgot about his struggle of how to treat the payments to Neurocentral, Inc. Thus, in the summer of 2008, Peter was not in the least worried when White Pharmaceuticals AG received a letter by the Financial Reporting Enforcement Panel. In their letter, the FREP told White Pharmaceuticals AG that the company was chosen at random to be inspected by the new supervising authority. They would like to examine White's financial statements for the year 2006. Mr. Muller did not really know what was coming at them but he put Peter in charge of the FREP investigation as "this is an accounting thing and it's clearly your job to handle this."

As a first task, Peter was to provide the FREP with White's annual as well as quarterly financial statements including auditor's report and their summary of unadjusted audit differences. When two months passed without an additional notification by FREP, Peter started wondering what the examination would bring about. A little while later, White received another letter from the enforcement institution that indicated areas that the FREP would put an emphasis on in their examination. At the same time, they requested a number of documents to be sent back to the FREP within the next two weeks. The short time frame surprised Peter and he was glad that he could rely on his team to help him provide all documents necessary and answer all questions. Still, they struggled with several of the panel's queries and, in the end, barely made the deadline to send the material back. Relieved from this stress, he turned back to his routine business at White which had suffered in the prior weeks.

While having hoped that the examination was over, he was proved wrong by another notification that came about two months later. The institution requested more material and asked even more questions than before. Holding the letter in his hands, he started to realize that this would be a tough year for him. Over a period of ten months, Peter repeatedly received notifications and letters that he was to respond to in a very short period of time. Again and again, his usual habit of working eight to nine hours a day turned into a frenzy of long nights that often lasted until midnight. As soon as he had finished the latest request by FREP, he needed to take care of his usual work and started worrying when the next letter was coming.

On a regular basis, he met with Mr. Muller to talk about the status of the examination and to discuss how they should handle the panel's investigation. How should they communicate with the capital market? Should they openly inform investors of what was going on or should they wait until they received the results of the investigation? After long debates, Mr. Muller decided to wait and assured Peter that "everything will work out eventually" and that "investors don't need to know everything."

While pondering this issue, Peter realized that the FREP's questions soon circled around White Pharmaceuticals' payments to Neurocentral, Inc. and he recalled his insecurity concerning the treatment of the compensation. Looking at White's financial statements for the year 2006, he saw that the company expensed a total amount of 240 million Euros for research and development. This amount included 55 million Euros which represented the final lump-sum payment to Neurocentral, Inc. Suddenly it dawned on Peter that they might have made a mistake.

With FREP's concluding letter in his hand, Peter Schmidt was walking towards Mr. Muller's office. He prepared to tell his boss what had gone wrong. The FREP stated that White Pharmaceuticals AG had incorrectly expensed 55 million Euros in 2006. This amount should have been recognized because it represented the costs of a separately acquired intangible asset. In exchange for their payment, White had received a fully developed product which could reasonably be expected to result in an inflow of economic benefits. Therefore, White's income and assets had been understated by 55 million Euros. In addition, the FREP indicated that they had serious doubts about the treatment of the milestone payments. However, these doubts did not result in an additional finding.

The letter further read that if White Pharmaceuticals AG accepted the statement, the error would be released in the electronic German Federal Gazette. If White wanted to object, they had to address this issue with the Financial Supervisory Authority (*Bundesanstalt für Finanzdienstleistungsaufsicht,* BaFin) who would then carry out their own investigation. Knocking on the CFO's door, Peter wondered how investors would react upon learning that the examination had been concealed from them.

## Requirements

### RESEARCH AND DEVELOPMENT COSTS

1  The central issue of the case is the treatment of White Pharmaceuticals' payments to Neurocentral, Inc.

    1  How are research and development costs treated (a) according to IFRS Standards and (b) according to US-GAAP?

    2  How are separately acquired intangible assets treated (a) according to IFRS Standards and (b) according to US-GAAP?

    3  Assess the payments made by White according to the criteria set out in IAS 38. Which payment would you have recognized in Peter's place?

2  Costs for research and development are a major part of a pharmaceutical company's spending.

    1  Why does capitalizing R&D seem to be an area of managerial discretion, although there are explicit rules of how to treat R&D?

    2  Are there advantages (disadvantages) of capitalizing R&D?

    3  White's CFO tells Peter Schmidt that the pharmaceutical industry charges most of their R&D costs to expenses. Table 1 shows the ratio of capitalized R&D to total R&D expenditures in different industries. Can you imagine why industries differ in their treatment of R&D?

    4  The IFRS Standards Framework constitutes qualitative characteristics that financial statements are to fulfill. Do you think that the accounting for research and development costs corresponds to the qualitative characteristics of relevance and reliability?

**TABLE 1**  Capitalizing Development Costs in Germany

| Industry | ATL | BCU | CPH | FBI | IND | MTST | RCF |
|---|---|---|---|---|---|---|---|
| Capitalized R&D/ Total Costs for R&D (%) | 29.73 | 36.66 | 1.66 | 31.01 | 13.60 | 45.54 | 15.99 |

Note: (ATL=Automobile, Transportation, Logistics; BCU=Basic Resources, Construction, Utilities; CPH=Chemicals, Pharmaceuticals, Healthcare; FBI=Financial Services, Banks, Insurance; IND=Industrial; MTST=Media, Technology, Software, Telecommunication; RCF=Retail, Consumer, Food & Beverages; Hagerand Hitz 2007).

## GLOBAL ACCOUNTING STANDARDS: IFRS STANDARDS AND US-GAAP

The case study reviewed the different treatment of R&D costs according to IFRS Standards and US-GAAP. As the IASB and the FASB want to create uniform global accounting standards, many financial reporting standards will change and many companies face a complex process to adapt their accounting systems (see, for example, Gornik-Tomaszewski and Jermakowicz, 2010).

1  Can you think of advantages (disadvantages) of global accounting standards?
2  What is the impact on reporting entities that have to adapt their accounting?
3  The IASB and the FASB also plan to converge the rules for R&D expenditures. However, the project has been set on hold in 2009. Outline the boards' approach concerning the convergence. Can you imagine possible hindrances to the convergence of R&D accounting?

## ENFORCEMENT OF FINANCIAL REPORTING STANDARDS

1  In Germany, an institution that enforces financial reporting standards was only established in recent years.

   1  What is the reasoning behind an institution that enforces financial reporting standards?
   2  How are companies that are to be inspected selected? What does the German enforcement process look like?

2  At the end of our case, Peter receives a final letter by the FREP that presents an error finding to him. He is wondering what the consequences of this finding are.

   1  What are White's possible responses to the finding? Which way would you pursue? Why?
   2  How do you think investors will react to the error finding? How should White Pharmaceuticals AG have best reacted to the examination by the FREP?
   3  Who is to take responsibility for the restatements? Which role do you attribute to White's auditors?
   4  Imagine that Alex Muller asked Peter to appeal FREP's finding. What would be his motivations to do so? In your answer, outline arguments that Peter could use to successfully appeal the decision.
   5  Now, imagine that White's CFO decided to accept the finding. How would Peter go about restating White's financial statements?[3] In your answer, refer to IAS 8 and examine what decisions Peter has to make. Also, consider how White best let investors know about the restatement. What role do tax authorities play?

# References

S. Gornik-Tomaszewski and E.K. Jermakowicz, "Adopting IFRS Standards – Guidance for U.S. Entities Under IFRS Standards 1," *CPA Journal* 80(3) (2010): 12–18.

S. Hager and J.-M. Hitz, "Immaterielle Vermögenswerte in der Bilanzierung und Berichterstattung – eine empirische Bestandsaufnahme für die Geschaftsberichte deutscher IFRS Standards-Bilanzierer 2005" (Accounting for and Reporting of Intangible Assets – An Empirical Survey of German IFRS Standards Accounts in 2005). *Zeitschrift für internationale und kapitalmarktorientierte Rechnungslegung* (2007)(4): 205–218.

---

[3]Assume that White's financial year ends December 31st. Also, assume that White only presents one prior period in their annual report.

# Appendix

**FIGURE 1**  Drug Development Process and Payment Structure (Own depiction based on information from FDA)

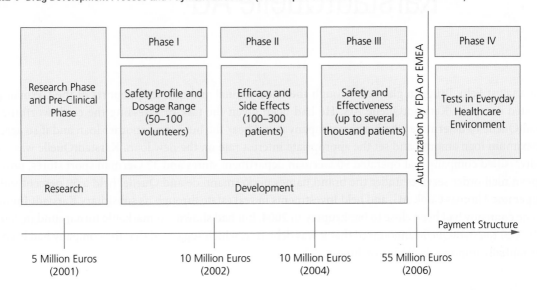

# CASE
# KarstadtQuelle AG

Credit analyst Felix Brüggen glanced through the latest annual and quarterly reports of the German publicly listed company KarstadtQuelle AG. He had been given the task of assessing the creditworthiness of KarstadtQuelle to determine whether the company could bear the burden of another loan and if so agree on the maximum loan amount and set the appropriate interest rate on the new loan. KarstadtQuelle was a German diversified company that operated 90 German department stores and 32 German sport stores, provided European mail order services under the brand names neckermann.de and Quelle, held a 50 percent stake in tour operator Thomas Cook AG, and held investments in real estate through its subsidiary Karstadt Immobilien.[1] The company had been close to bankruptcy in 2004, but had shown a remarkable turnaround in 2005. In March 2006 KarstadtQuelle announced that it was debt-free, which suggested that the company had been able to substantially improve its creditworthiness.

## KarstadtQuelle in 2004[2]

In the second half of 2004, KarstadtQuelle was on the verge of bankruptcy. The company did not reach its financial targets for that year and struggled under the debt load it had built up over the years, while lacking access to new long-term financing. The main reasons for the company's problems, which KarstadtQuelle's (new) management outlined in the company's 2005 Annual Report, were mismanagement and difficult market circumstances. The poor financial situation required drastic measures. In 2004 KarstadtQuelle's management board changed composition – by replacing the managing and finance directors – and the company reorganized the management boards of many of its subsidiaries. In addition, the company negotiated a new three-year credit facility of €1.75 billion with a syndicate of 16 banks, agreed with its current shareholders to issue new shares for an amount of approximately €500 million, and issued €140 million in convertible bonds. These capital increases were supported by the announcement of a new restructuring plan that was to be carried out in fiscal 2005. During 2004 KarstadtQuelle's share price decreased, however, by 61 percent, from €19.70 to €7.60.

## KarstadtQuelle in 2005

Fiscal year 2005 was labelled by management "the year of restructuring." KarstadtQuelle's restructuring program had the following components:

- *Divestments in retail.* The company would strengthen its 88 larger department stores – with sales space above 8,000 square metres and total revenues of €4.5 billion – and divest its 77 smaller department stores – with sales space below 8,000 square metres and total revenues of €0.7 billion. It also planned to

Professor Erik Peek prepared this case. The case is intended solely as the basis for class discussion and is not intended to serve as an endorsement, source of primary data, or illustration of effective or ineffective management.

[1]Thomas Cook AG has been proportionally consolidated in KarstadtQuelle's financial statements.
[2]This and the following sections are based primarily on material from KarstadtQuelle's 2005 Annual Report, its Interim Reports of March 2006 and June 2006, and its press releases issued during 2004, 2005, and 2006.

divest its specialty store chains, such as sports stores RunnersPoint and GolfHouse. These divestments should help KarstadtQuelle to expand its high-margin products in the department store business.

- *Focus within mail order.* In the mail order business, KarstadtQuelle would focus its efforts on growth in the specialty mail order segment and in the e-commerce segment.[3] The company would further strategically reorient its traditionally strong universal mail order business in Germany.
- *Cost savings.* KarstadtQuelle expected to be able to achieve €210 million in cost savings in its department store business and €150 million in cost savings in its universal mail order business by the year 2006.
- *Real estate.* The company considered segregating its real estate business from its department store (retail) business.
- *Reorientation of the group.* KarstadtQuelle would streamline its portfolio, abandon marginal operations, and outsource some of its processes in the retail business.

Although the financial and operational state of the company's mail order business appeared worse than anticipated, KarstadtQuelle's management were able to make some important changes to the segment in 2005. Mail order companies Quelle and neckermann.de were converted into limited liability companies and started to operate separately under their own management to improve these subsidiaries' decision processes. In the mail order segment the company also positioned Quelle and neckermann.de in the market as two sharply distinct brands and combined several separately operating service units into one to reduce costs.

KarstadtQuelle also sold several specialty stores as well as its small department stores. The divestiture program also resulted in the sale of Karstadt Hypothekenbank AG to the company's pension fund. After the sale Karstadt Hypothekenbank AG took over, from KarstadtQuelle's finance companies, financing of the company's hire purchase business in its mail order segment, thereby helping KarstadtQuelle to derecognize its discounted installment receivables (in accordance with IAS 39). The sale of Karstadt Hypothekenbank reduced KarstadtQuelle's net non-current liabilities by approximately €1 billion. The sale of the company's marginal operations and smaller department stores yielded close to €1.1 million. In addition, KarstadtQuelle sold and leased back its mail order logistics real estate at a cost of over €400 million. As a result of the restructuring, KarstadtQuelle was able to reduce its workforce by roughly one-fifth, or 25,000 employees.

In KarstadtQuelle's 2005 Annual Report, management reported that although performance in the mail order segment was still below plan, the company had reached its targets. In 2005 sales had declined from €17.2 billion to €15.8 billion, but the company had been able to cut its net loss from €1.6 billion to €316 million. During the fiscal year 2005, KarstadtQuelle's share price increased by 68 percent, from €7.60 to €12.74, to imply a market value of €2.69 billion.

## KarstadtQuelle in the first half of 2006

After the financial restructuring of the company in 2005, KarstadtQuelle's management considered the company's equity position too vulnerable. To reduce leverage further, the company sold its real estate portfolio – consisting of department stores, car parks, sport stores, and office buildings – for an amount of €4.5 billion. The real estate was sold to and leased back from an entity that was jointly owned by a subsidiary of Goldman Sachs – the Whitehall Fund – and KarstadtQuelle. KarstadtQuelle had a participation of 49 percent in the joint entity but, as it reported, carried no other risks than those arising from its equity contribution of €120 million. The operational management of the joint entity was in the hands of the Whitehall Fund. The first payment under the real estate transaction – €2.7 billion – was received on July 3, 2006. The second payment – the remaining €1.8 billion – would be received later in year 2006.

---

[3]Specialty mail order companies focus on selling one product type, such as baby products or fashion products, whereas universal mail order companies offer a broad assortment of product categories.

According to KarstadtQuelle, the real estate transaction had several positive effects. First, it yielded a high short-term cash inflow that helped the company to quickly reduce its financial liabilities. Second, it improved important balance sheet ratios such as the equity-to-assets ratio. Third, it resulted in a high non-recurring income component for fiscal 2006. Fourth and finally, it led to a lasting improvement in pre-tax profits to the order of €100 million.

The company continued to restructure its business. It repositioned its department stores by distinguishing "Premium" stores that sold high-margin products at prime locations from "Boulevard" stores that focused on selling brands in the middle to higher price segment. Further, KarstadtQuelle increased its purchase volume in Asia and set up local design centers in Europe and Asia to develop fashionable and timely products. To facilitate procurement in Asia, the company signed an agreement to cooperate with the Chinese export company Li & Fung. These actions aimed to reduce purchase expenses and increase inventory turnover, thereby reducing working capital by an estimated €500 million. The proceeds from the real estate transaction further helped KarstadtQuelle to invest another €200 million in restructuring its universal mail order business.

In the first half of 2006 KarstadtQuelle managed to report a net profit of €558.1 million. During this half year KarstadtQuelle's share price increased by 62 percent, from €12.74 to €20.59, to reach a market value of €4.34 billion.

## QUESTIONS

1 When preparing a report that summarizes the main factors affecting KarstadtQuelle's creditworthiness, which factors should the credit analyst focus on? How do these factors affect KarstadtQuelle's creditworthiness?

2 Assess whether KarstadtQuelle could bear the burden of another €500 million loan. If so, what would be the appropriate interest rate on this new loan?

**EXHIBIT 1**  KarstadtQuelle's consolidated financial statements

## INCOME STATEMENTS (€ thousands)

|  | Half year ending June 30, 2006 | Year ending December 31, 2005 | Half year ending June 30, 2005 | Year ending December 31, 2004 |
|---|---|---|---|---|
| Sales | 6,474,551 | 15,845,032 | 7,166,102 | 17,199,007 |
| Cost of sales and expenses for tourism services | (3,614,132) | (8,911,823) | (3,911,755) | (9,631,912) |
| **Gross income** | **2,860,419** | **6,933,209** | **3,254,347** | **7,567,095** |
| Other capitalized own costs | 13,987 | 50,691 | 22,242 | 53,519 |
| Operating income | 1,315,470 | 1,102,555 | 388,286 | 819,669 |
| Staff costs | (1,180,843) | (2,630,323) | (1,382,563) | (3,109,417) |
| Operating expenses | (2,321,642) | (5,152,129) | (2,245,903) | (5,575,730) |
| Other taxes | (10,702) | (29,344) | (13,644) | (30,262) |
| **Earnings before interest, tax, and depreciation and amortization (EBITDA)** | **676,689** | **274,659** | **22,765** | **(275,126)** |
| Depreciation and amortization (not including amortization of goodwill) | (145,297) | (343,329) | (171,828) | (425,115) |
| Impairment loss | (507) | (48,193) | (57,550) | (101,641) |
| **Earnings before interest, tax, and amortization of goodwill (EBITA)** | **530,885** | **(116,863)** | **(206,613)** | **(801,882)** |
| Amortization of goodwill | 0 | (8,399) | 205 | (152,446) |
| **Earnings before interest and tax (EBIT)** | **530,885** | **(125,262)** | **(206,408)** | **(954,328)** |
| Income from investments | 2,740 | (9,454) | 2,259 | 1,314 |
| Income from investments in associates | 4,259 | 16,681 | 8,535 | 12,481 |
| Net interest income | (192,055) | (292,953) | (153,537) | (326,863) |
| Other financial results | 19,634 | 15,783 | (12,911) | (165,371) |
| **Earnings before tax (EBT)** | **365,463** | **(395,205)** | **(362,062)** | **(1,432,767)** |
| Taxes on income | 194,500 | 81,180 | 117,053 | 178,008 |
| **Earnings from continuing operations** | **559,963** | **(314,025)** | **(245,009)** | **(1,254,759)** |
| Result from discontinued operations | 0 | (258) | (25,352) | (370,531) |
| **Net profit/loss before minority interests** | **559,963** | **(314,283)** | **(270,361)** | **(1,625,290)** |
| Profit/loss due to minority interests | (1,847) | (2,199) | (1,515) | (24) |
| **Net loss after minority interests** | **558,116** | **(316,482)** | **(271,876)** | **(1,625,314)** |

*(continued)*

**EXHIBIT 1** KarstadtQuelle's consolidated financial statements (Continued)

| | Half year ending June 30, 2006 | Year ending December 31, 2005 | Half year ending June 30, 2005 | Year ending December 31, 2004 |
|---|---|---|---|---|
| **BALANCE SHEETS (€ thousands)** | | | | |
| Intangible assets | 1,087,878 | 1,104,831 | 1,117,732 | 1,100,986 |
| Tangible assets | 1,061,660 | 2,452,839 | 2,659,840 | 2,786,185 |
| Shares in associates | 86,343 | 98,398 | 110,226 | 105,877 |
| Other financial assets | 624,494 | 535,220 | 1,032,739 | 1,405,772 |
| Other non-current assets | 96,764 | 94,167 | 129,746 | 116,313 |
| Deferred taxes | 220,891 | 228,249 | 283,529 | 164,914 |
| **Non-current assets** | **3,178,030** | **4,513,704** | **5,333,812** | **5,680,047** |
| Inventories | 1,547,838 | 1,621,095 | 1,700,643 | 1,823,904 |
| Trade receivables | 795,267 | 844,385 | 1,400,712 | 1,295,494 |
| Tax receivables | 127,316 | 50,430 | 89,381 | 61,800 |
| Other receivables and other assets | 1,011,858 | 1,139,128 | 1,046,039 | 911,201 |
| Purchase price receivable from real estate transaction | 2,690,203 | 0 | 0 | 0 |
| Cash and cash equivalents and securities | 770,550 | 707,163 | 657,504 | 661,156 |
| **Current assets** | **6,943,032** | **4,362,201** | **4,894,279** | **4,753,555** |
| Assets classified as held for sale | 481,506 | 262,658 | 1,942,263 | 1,209,587 |
| **Balance sheet total** | **10,602,568** | **9,138,563** | **12,170,354** | **11,643,189** |
| Subscribed share capital | 514,544 | 510,398 | 510,398 | 510,398 |
| Reserves | 790,711 | (237,068) | (196,053) | 58,663 |
| Minority interests | 12,192 | 16,745 | 31,595 | 26,783 |
| **Equity** | **1,317,447** | **290,075** | **345,940** | **595,844** |
| Long-term capital of minority interests | 0 | 0 | 53,203 | 58,983 |
| Non-current financial liabilities | 1,007,146 | 3,012,793 | 3,361,517 | 3,372,376 |
| Other non-current liabilities | 485,925 | 566,606 | 596,024 | 549,694 |
| Pension provisions | 886,923 | 906,756 | 859,101 | 891,911 |
| Other non-current provisions | 368,220 | 383,784 | 350,802 | 365,483 |
| Deferred taxes | 18,880 | 11,673 | 8,483 | 12,533 |
| **Non-current liabilities** | **2,767,094** | **4,881,612** | **5,229,130** | **5,250,980** |
| Current financial liabilities | 3,062,043 | 724,776 | 2,164,105 | 2,062,517 |
| Trade payables | 1,331,760 | 1,600,870 | 1,424,662 | 1,554,497 |
| Current tax liabilities | 180,695 | 201,746 | 151,775 | 229,840 |
| Other current liabilities | 1,405,913 | 768,855 | 1,286,692 | 799,186 |
| Current provisions | 506,277 | 609,677 | 564,313 | 626,136 |
| **Current liabilities** | **6,486,688** | **3,905,924** | **5,591,547** | **5,272,176** |
| Liabilities from assets classified as held for sale | 31,339 | 60,952 | 1,003,737 | 524,189 |
| **Balance sheet total** | **10,602,568** | **9,138,563** | **12,170,354** | **11,643,189** |

(*continued*)

**EXHIBIT 1**  KarstadtQuelle's consolidated financial statements (Continued)

| | Half year ending June 30, 2006 | Year ending December 31, 2005 | Half year ending June 30, 2005 | Year ending December 31, 2004 |
|---|---|---|---|---|
| **CASH FLOW STATEMENTS (€ thousands)** | | | | |
| EBITDA | 676,689 | 274,659 | 22,765 | (275,126) |
| Profit/loss from the disposal of fixed assets | (906,419) | (155,154) | (24,278) | (1,304) |
| Profit/loss from foreign currency | (4,457) | (1,907) | 3,038 | 4,919 |
| Decrease of non-current provisions (not including pension and tax provisions) | (2,178) | (95,099) | (18,760) | (59,880) |
| Addition to (Utilization of) restructuring provision | (130,367) | 255,853 | (84,830) | 583,809 |
| Other expenses/income not affecting cash flow | 146,904 | 168,307 | 98,454 | 146,161 |
| **Gross cash flow** | **(219,828)** | **446,659** | **(3,611)** | **398,579** |
| Changes in working capital | (68,114) | 1,006,822 | (173,859) | 93,576 |
| Changes in other current assets and liabilities | 317,002 | (231,280) | 114,760 | 165,831 |
| Dividends received | 1,165 | 13,278 | 2,803 | 24,958 |
| Payments/refunds of taxes on income | (46,068) | (8,253) | (37,395) | (46,452) |
| **Cash flow from operating activities** | **(15,843)** | **1,227,226** | **(97,302)** | **636,492** |
| Cash flow from acquisitions/divestments of subsidiaries less cash and cash equivalents disposed of | 79,572 | 250,388 | 10,080 | (3,060) |
| Purchase of tangible and intangible assets | (81,127) | (258,785) | (84,686) | (331,475) |
| Purchase of investments in non-current financial Assets | (140,295) | (7,953) | (69,020) | (83,283) |
| Cash receipts from sale of tangible and intangible Assets | 62,133 | 703,648 | 133,560 | 119,356 |
| Cash receipts from sale of non-current financial Assets | 8,522 | 43,723 | 40,665 | 32,835 |
| **Cash flow from investing activities** | **(71,195)** | **731,021** | **30,599** | **(265,627)** |
| Interest received | 72,957 | 134,202 | 62,773 | 131,533 |
| Interest paid | (185,698) | (377,162) | (190,584) | (331,834) |
| Pension payments | (54,135) | (62,272) | (90,365) | (95,867) |
| Cash receipts/payments under mortgage bond program and for (financial) loans | 334,309 | (1,546,621) | 297,971 | (192,959) |
| Payment of liabilities due under finance lease | (9,729) | (47,264) | (16,208) | (39,489) |
| Cash payments/cash receipts for dividends and capital increase | 3,979 | (1,520) | (571) | 473,006 |
| **Cash flow from financing activities** | **161,683** | **(1,900,637)** | **63,016** | **(55,610)** |
| **Changes in cash and cash equivalents affecting cash flow** | **74,645** | **57,610** | **(3,687)** | **315,255** |
| Changes in cash and cash equivalents due to changes in exchange rates or other changes caused by the consolidated companies | (11,258) | (14,856) | (1,020) | (14,367) |
| Cash and cash equivalents at the beginning of the Period | 707,163 | 653,162 | 662,211 | 352,274 |
| **Cash and cash equivalents at the end of the period** | **770,550** | **695,916** | **657,504** | **653,162** |

**EXHIBIT 2** Excerpts from the notes to the consolidated financial statements KarstadtQuelle's Annual Report 2005

## Consolidation

In the year under review the shares in Karstadt Hypothekenbank AG were exchanged for shares held by the II.KarstadtQuelle Pension Trust e.V. In Quelle Neckermann Versand Finanz GmbH & Co., KG and Karstadt Hypothekenbank AG deconsolidated. During the year the company was treated as a disposal group and its assets and liabilities recognized under Assets qualified as held for sale and Liabilities in connection with assets classified as held for sale. Impairment of €51,440 thousand resulting within the year from estimated sales proceeds from company assets proved to be no longer necessary in connection with this exchange.

## Sale of receivables

Individual group companies are selling trade receivables to Karstadt Hypothekenbank AG, which was transferred to the II.KarstadtQuelle Pension Trust e.V. under the CTA program. At the end of the fiscal year Karstadt Hypothekenbank AG took over from the finance companies the purchase of receivables being sold by these companies under the ABS programs. In this connection, the sale of receivables was classified as an actual derecognition under IAS 39. International companies in mail order are continuing to sell under asset-backed securitization (ABS) transactions their receivables to a finance company, which refinances the purchases on the capital market. Under the ABS program the purchasers of these receivables withhold part of the purchase price as security until receipt of the payments. If there is sufficient likelihood of realization, the anticipated payment is shown as a separate financial asset.

The vendors must assume responsibility for collecting the debts. At the balance sheet date adequate provisions are set aside for these commitments. For the assumption of the risks and interim financing, the vendors pay a program fee, which, depending on the classification of the sales, is shown as a true sale or a sale that does not qualify for derecognition under other operating expenses or interest.

## Operating income

| Amounts shown in € thousands | 2005 | 2004 |
|---|---|---|
| Income from the disposal of assets classified as held for sale | 167,613 | 12,949 |
| Income from advertising cost subsidies | 154,738 | 169,702 |
| Earnings from rental income and commissions | 131,155 | 103,239 |
| Income from charged-on goods and services | 57,800 | 55,283 |
| Income from the disposal of non-current assets | 52,080 | 11,885 |
| Income from the reversal of other liabilities | 37,514 | 27,883 |
| Income from exchange rate differences | 28,157 | 44,121 |
| Income from the reversal of other provisions | 27,697 | 19,851 |
| Income from deconsolidation | 20,471 | 10,659 |
| Income from other services | 18,779 | 21,569 |
| Income from the reversal of allowances | 9,783 | 8,310 |
| Other income | 396,768 | 334,218 |
| | 1,102,555 | 819,669 |

## Operating expenses

| Amounts shown in € thousands | 2005 | 2004 |
|---|---|---|
| Logistics costs | 1,431,003 | 1,459,007 |
| Catalogue costs | 893,853 | 861,938 |
| Operating and office/workshop costs | 693,058 | 777,016 |
| Advertising | 615,761 | 648,103 |
| Administrative costs | 559,386 | 479,393 |
| Restructuring costs | 269,342 | 651,455 |
| Allowances on and derecognition of trade receivables | 223,506 | 256,577 |
| Losses from the disposal of assets classified as held for sale | 60,050 | 1,894 |
| Outside staff | 32,435 | 23,632 |
| Expenses due to currency differences and losses | 26,250 | 49,040 |
| Losses from the disposal of fixed assets | 4,491 | 21,636 |
| Other expenses | 342,994 | 346,039 |
| | 5,152,129 | 5,575,730 |

## Net interest income

| Amounts shown in € thousands | 2005 | 2004 |
|---|---|---|
| Interest costs from pension expense | (133,384) | (137,104) |
| Other interest and similar income | 254,790 | 217,699 |
| Other interest and similar expenses | (414,359) | (407,458) |
| | (292,953) | (326,863) |

The previous year's value included non-recurring charges of €51.9 million from restructuring.

Through application of the new IAS 39, the Group's receivables sales were classified as non-disposal of receivables. Accordingly, the corresponding expenses from prefinancing of receivables (so-called program fees) are recognized under interest expenses. These amount to €55,641 thousand (previous year: €41,165 thousand) for the 2005 financial year. The previous year's amounts were adjusted accordingly for better comparability.

# Leases

Finance lease agreements have a firmly agreed-upon, basic leasing period of between 20 and 25 years and include a purchase option for the lessee after expiry of the basic leasing period. Assets under finance lease agreements have a carrying amount of €237,783 thousand (previous year: €262,686 thousand) at the balance sheet date. These assets relate to buildings, aircraft, and reserve engines where the carrying value of the future minimum lease payments covers the material purchase costs. For aircraft financing normally a purchase option for the residual value, plus an amount equal to 25 percent of the amount by which the fair value exceeds the residual value, exists after the expiry of the lease period. If the purchase option is not exercised, the aircraft is sold by the lessor. If the proceeds from the sale are lower than the residual value, the lessee must pay the difference to the lessor. The lessee is entitled to up to 75 percent of the amount by which the sales proceeds exceed the residual value.

The operating lease agreements comprise mainly building leases without purchase option or aircraft leases where the assessment of the criteria of IAS 17 resulted in classification as operating lease.

| Amounts shown in € thousands | Up to 1 year | | 1 to 5 years | | Over 5 years | |
|---|---|---|---|---|---|---|
| | 2005 | 2004 | 2005 | 2004 | 2005 | 2004 |
| **Finance lease agreements:** | | | | | | |
| Lease payments due in future | 38,328 | 65,875 | 320,653 | 185,498 | 138,313 | 131,161 |
| Discount | (759) | (36,209) | (35,783) | (48,924) | (31,598) | (14,162) |
| Present value | 37,569 | 29,666 | 284,870 | 136,574 | 106,715 | 116,999 |
| Lease payments under subleases | 1,152 | 0 | 4,606 | 0 | 5,758 | 0 |
| **Operating lease agreements:** | | | | | | |
| Lease payments due in future | 343,359 | 311,629 | 919,291 | 863,627 | 1,221,619 | 842,697 |
| Discount | (11,072) | (16,953) | (124,498) | (131,195) | (600,007) | (364,210) |
| Present value | 332,287 | 294,676 | 794,793 | 732,432 | 621,612 | 478,487 |
| Lease payments under subleases | 23,847 | 22,694 | 63,318 | 43,098 | 75,363 | 15,940 |

# Trade receivables

**Breakdown of trade receivables by business segment**

| (Amounts shown in € thousands) | 2005 | 2004 |
|---|---|---|
| Karstadt | 82,441 | 41,324 |
| Mail order | 602,074 | 1,093,715 |
| Thomas Cook | 82,113 | 73,508 |
| Services | 76,626 | 79,287 |
| Other | 1,131 | 7,660 |
| | 844,385 | 1,295,494 |

In connection with the application of IAS 39, sales of receivables under ABS programs were not subject to any further disposals at the beginning of the 2005 financial year. Accordingly, the previous year's figures of €622 million have been adjusted to suit the change in recognition. The reorganization of the receivables sale program at home with the sale of receivables amounting to €613 million to Karstadt Hypothekenbank AG at the end of the financial year, however, resulted in an actual disposal and thus to a marked reduction in trade receivables.

To secure claims under a global agreement for the sale of receivables, security was provided to Karstadt Hypothekenbank AG on existing and future trade receivables.

Under the syndicated loan agreement and the second lien, financing amounts totalling €243,414 thousand owed by customers to various Group companies were assigned as security for debtors' liabilities.

## Financial liabilities

| | Up to 1 year | | 1 to 5 years | | Over 5 years | |
|---|---|---|---|---|---|---|
| Amounts shown in € thousands | 2005 | 2004 | 2005 | 2004 | 2005 | 2004 |
| Bank loans and overdrafts | 231,438 | 734,047 | 797,776 | 694,086 | 326,934 | 469,513 |
| Liabilities under leasing agreements | 18,800 | 33,249 | 244,719 | 145,809 | 68,013 | 163,177 |
| Other financial liabilities | 474,538 | 1,295,221 | 200,511 | 677,130 | 1,374,840 | 1,222,661 |
| Total | 724,776 | 2,062,517 | 1,243,006 | 1,517,025 | 1,769,787 | 1,855,351 |

Interest-bearing bank loans and overdraft loans are recognized at the amount paid out less directly assignable issue costs. Financing costs, including premiums payable as repayments or redemption, are allocated with effect for income. Liabilities under lease agreements are shown at present value.

The terms and conditions of the facility were adjusted in December 2005 mainly with regard to the conclusion of the secondary loan facility explained below with regard to adherence to financial ratios. Note that €275 million of the loan facility had been utilized at the balance sheet date. The financial ratios to be adhered to relate to adjusted EBITDA, interest coverage, debt coverage, and the level of equity. For the mail order segment there is a further financial ratio relating to adjusted EBITDA.

To secure the Group's finances for the long term, in December of the financial year the KarstadtQuelle Group also agreed to a further secondary loan facility amounting to nominally €309 million, which had been fully utilized by the balance sheet date. The security provided for the liabilities was for the most part identical with the security underlying the syndicated loan facility, although ranking below the syndicated facility.

The loans secured by mortgage bear interest rates between 2.75 percent p.a. and 7.24 percent p.a. at the balance sheet date. The syndicated loan facility taken up the previous year and the recently concluded second-ranking loan facility bear interest on the basis of EURIBOR (or LIBOR, if drawing in currencies other than euros) plus margin and regulatory costs. In the case of the syndicated loan facility, the bullet facility is initially subject to a margin of 3.5 percent p.a., which will rise to 4.5 percent p.a. in 2006 and to 5.5 percent p.a. in 2007. For the seasonal facility and the revolving loan facility, initially a margin of 3.75 percent p.a. has been agreed from December 10, 2005, for the period of one year. Thereafter under certain circumstances it will rise to 4.75 percent p.a. The second-ranking loan facility bears interest with a margin of 12 percent.

Financial liabilities also include liabilities to customers of the KarstadtQuelle Bank from savings deposits, night money, balances on card accounts, promissory notes, and savings certificates amounting to €77,642 thousand.

Of first-ranking financial liabilities, €484,675 thousand (previous year: €742,172 thousand) are secured by mortgages and €350,372 thousand by other rights. In addition, there is first-ranking mortgage security amounting to €1,249,465 thousand (previous year: €1,419,737 thousand) under the Karstadt Hypothekenbank AG's (Essen) mortgage bond program. Liabilities of €91,238 thousand proportionate (previous year €74,060 thousand) arising from real estate financing at Thomas Cook are likewise supported by mortgage or similar security.

KarstadtQuelle AG has undertaken a guarantee to the Karstadt Hypothekenbank AG, Essen, for loans of Karstadt Finance B.V., Hulst, Netherlands, amounting to €1.8 billion, which translates to €1.3 billion at the balance sheet date.

Under the agreed-upon syndicated loan facility, a partial land charge assignment declaration agreement was reached with real estate management companies, and the creation of overall land charges and in some cases binding security pledges in respect of land charges was agreed upon. Additionally, shares in Thomas Cook AG and various fully consolidated Group companies and amounts due from customers of the various Group companies were assigned. Furthermore, unrecognized brands held by KarstadtQuelle AG, Karstadt Warenhaus GmbH, Quelle GmbH, and neckermann.de GmbH were assigned as security for liabilities of KarstadtQuelle AG.

Liabilities of €350,273 thousand (previous year: €391,850 thousand) arising from aircraft financing are secured by aircraft mortgages or are subject to availability limitations resulting from the financing structure.

Leasing liabilities carried as liabilities are effectively secured by the lessor's rights to buildings or aircraft specified in the finance lease.

# Pension provisions

The recognized amount from pension obligations results as follows:

| Amounts shown in € thousands | Commitments financed from funds | Commitments financed from provisions | 2005 | 2004 |
|---|---|---|---|---|
| Present value of future pension commitments (DBO) | 1,564,743 | 1,019,941 | 2,584,684 | 2,602,586 |
| Unrecognized actuarial gains/losses | (71,678) | (117,610) | (189,288) | (72,217) |
| Unrecognized past service costs | (119) | (336) | (455) | (634) |
| Fair value of plan assets | (1,485,424) | 0 | (1,485,424) | (1,504,939) |
| | 7,522 | 901,995 | 909,517 | 1,024,796 |
| Pension provisions in connection with disposal groups | 0 | (2,761) | (2,761) | (132,885) |
| | 7,522 | 899,234 | 906,756 | 891,911 |

Pension costs are as follows:

| Amounts shown in € thousands | Commitments financed from funds | Commitments financed from provisions | 2005 | 2004 |
|---|---|---|---|---|
| Service costs | 3,856 | 8,378 | 12,234 | 15,126 |
| Interest costs | 70,151 | 39,009 | 109,160 | 141,735 |
| Expected return on plan assets | (84,723) | 0 | (84,723) | (83,865) |
| Actuarial gains/losses with effect on income | 32 | 305 | 337 | 113,424 |
| Past service costs | 1,255 | 2,386 | 3,641 | 99 |
| Income from changes in plans/expenses from deconsolidation | 4,987 | 3,201 | 8,188 | 351 |
| | (4,442) | 53,279 | 48,837 | 186,168 |

Whereas the cost of pension claims acquired during the financial year is shown under staff costs, the interest and the expected return on plan assets and the actuarial losses affecting plan assets are recorded with effect for income and shown under financial results.

The composition of plan assets is calculated from the following table:

| Amounts shown in € thousands | 2005 | 2004 |
|---|---|---|
| Real estate, incl. dormant holdings | 987,966 | 1,091,060 |
| Corporate investments | 351,000 | 348,674 |
| Financial resources | 146,458 | 65,205 |
| | 1,485,424 | 1,504,939 |

The Group utilizes parts of the real estate assets for itself. The lease payments are made on the basis of usual market estimates. Furthermore, under their articles of incorporation, the pension trusts may lend up to 10 percent of their assets back to the Group in the form of cash and cash equivalents. An amount of €72,982 thousand (previous year: €26,971 thousand) results here at the balance sheet date.

## Other non-current provisions

| Amounts shown in € thousands | Staff | Guarantees/ warranties | Contingent losses resulting from pending transactions | Restructuring effects | Other |
|---|---|---|---|---|---|
| As at 01.01.2005 | 31,866 | 958 | 298 | 235,295 | 34,659 |
| Changes in consolidated companies | (123) | 0 | 0 | (626) | (128) |
| Currency differences | (8) | (2) | 0 | 8 | 0 |
| Recourse | (705) | (642) | 276 | (43,444) | (1,804) |
| Reversal | (13,283) | (23) | (248) | (6,704) | (678) |
| Appropriation | 965 | 647 | 0 | 72,227 | 11,660 |
| Reclassification acc. to IFRS Standards 5 | (285) | (1) | 0 | 8,694 | (701) |
| As at 31.12.2005 | 18,427 | 937 | 326 | 265,450 | 43,008 |

Staff provisions include provisions for severance. Other provisions relate mainly to litigation risks and payments and jubilee payments and death benefits. restoration liabilities.

# CASE

# Tesco: From Troubles to Turnaround[1]

**IVEY** | Publishing

"We set out to start rebuilding profitability whilst reinvesting in the customer offer, and we have done this,"[2] exclaimed Dave Lewis, chief executive officer (CEO) of Tesco PLC, while declaring the company's annual results on April 13, 2016. Tesco, a U.K.-based retailer with a market capitalization of £14.73 billion,[3] was Britain's biggest grocer both by market share and revenue.[4] The company had posted a £162 million pre-tax profit for fiscal year (FY) 2015/16, up from a loss of £6.38 billion in FY 2014/15.

In Tesco's 2016 annual report, Lewis stated, "This has been a significant year for Tesco. We have delivered unprecedented change over the past 12 months as we have begun to transform our business."[5] However, while the company had been able to churn out profitability, the net sales had consistently dropped since FY 2012/13. Similarly, the share price of the company had fallen by more than 20 per cent from January 2015 to January 2016, and by around 50 per cent from January 2014 to May 2016 (see **Exhibit 1**). What course of action would enable Lewis to improve Tesco's value for shareholders? What area(s) should he focus on in order to bolster Tesco's financial performance? What should Lewis do to improve Tesco's market share in the United Kingdom?

Anupam Mehta, Utkarsh Goyal, and Sanchit Taneja wrote this case solely to provide material for class discussion. The authors do not intend to illustrate either effective or ineffective handling of a managerial situation. The authors may have disguised certain names and other identifying information to protect confidentiality.

---

[1]This case has been written on the basis of published sources only. Consequently, the interpretation and perspectives presented in this case are not necessarily those of Tesco PLC or any of its employees.

[2]Tesco PLC, "Preliminary Results 2015/16," 1, accessed April 22, 2016, www.tescoplc.com/media/1866/prelim_2015-2016_results_statement.pdf.

[3]£ = GBP = Great Britain pounds; all currency amounts are in £ unless otherwise specified; TSCO share price = £1.81 on February 27, 2016; Outstanding shares = 8,140,701,516 on February 27, 2016; and Tesco PLC, "Share Price," accessed May 17, 2016, www.tescoplc.com/investors/share-price-information/share-price.

[4]Jane Denton, "Sales Boom Sees Aldi Overtake Upmarket Rival Waitrose to Become UK's Sixth-Biggest Supermarket," This is Money, April 8, 2015, accessed April 26, 2016, www.thisismoney.co.uk/money/markets/article-3030079/British-shoppers-quids-prices-fall-fastest-rate-records-began-Aldi-UK-s-sixth-biggest-supermarket.html; and "Top 10 UK Retailers by Sales in 2015," Retail Economics, accessed April 26, 2016, www.retaileconomics.co.uk/top10-retailers.asp.

[5]Tesco PLC, *Annual Report and Financial Statements 2016*, 4, accessed May 22, 2016, www.tescoplc.com/media/264194/annual-report-2016.pdf.

# The company

Tesco was established as a grocery and general merchandise retailer in 1919.[6] However, since 1990, the company had started to diversify by offering books, clothing, electronics, furniture, toys, petrol, software, financial services, and telecommunications/Internet services—all while expanding its reach geographically. Tesco offered both value range products (branded as "Tesco Value") and premium range products (branded as "Tesco Finest"). As of 2016, the company had 3,460 stores in the United Kingdom (see Exhibit 2), 6,902 stores around the world, and 476,000+ employees (see Exhibit 3).[7]

Tesco ranked as the world's fifth largest retailer in terms of revenue as of 2015.[8] Tesco's rank dropped from second in 2012 to fifth in 2013, attributed to the declining sales of the company.[9] Tesco had been listed on the London Stock Exchange since 1947,[10] and was a constituent of the Financial Times Stock Exchange 100 Index.[11] The firm had a market capitalization of approximately £18.1 billion as of April 22, 2015—the 28th-largest of any company with a primary listing on the London Stock Exchange.[12]

## BUSINESS MODEL

According to Tesco's 2015 annual report, the company's business model focused on four key areas: customers, products, reinvestment, and channels. The company had a simple mission: "To be the champion for customers, helping them to enjoy a better quality of life and an easier way of living."[13]

## GROWTH STRATEGY

Tesco had refocused its business under three operational headlines: (1) listening to, understanding, and reaching out to customers to create the best possible offer; (2) working with growers and suppliers to make great products, and helping to deliver the best value to customers; and (3) working across different channels to get those products to customers in the most convenient way possible. The company had a special blend of capability, skills, and reach, complemented by a rich heritage in retail, which management hoped would help to earn customer loyalty and subsequently create value for shareholders.[14]

## PAST PERFORMANCE

With close to 100 years of corporate history, Tesco had pioneered smaller convenience stores and provided products under its own brand.[15] The number of Tesco stores in the United Kingdom increased from 2,715 stores in FY 2010/11 to 2,979 stores in FY 2011/12.[16] This rapid expansion helped the company emerge as one of the biggest retail chains in the world. Tesco's financial performance was on an upward trend until FY 2011/12. The company's revenue increased from £60.46 billion in FY 2010/11 to £64.54 billion in FY 2011/12

[6]"History," Tesco PLC, accessed April 22, 2016, www.tescoplc.com/about-us/history.

[7]"Key Facts," Tesco PLC, accessed April 22, 2016, www.tescoplc.com/about-us/key-facts.

[8]J. William Carpenter, "The World's Top 10 Retailers (WMT, COST)," Investopedia, December 24, 2015, accessed May 5, 2016, www.investopedia.com/articles/markets/122415/worlds-top-10-retailers-wmt-cost.asp.

[9]Deloitte, "Top 10 Global Retailers Show Modest Growth in 2014," press release, September 25, 2014, accessed May 5, 2016, www2.deloitte.com/an/en/pages/about-deloitte/articles/consumerbusiness.html.

[10]Steve Hawkes, "Tesco Vows Shake-Up as Shares Crash by £5 Billion," Sun, January 13, 2012, accessed April 22, 2016, www.thesun.co.uk/sol/homepage/news/money/4057898/Tesco-vows-shake-up-as-shares-crash-by-5billion.html.

[11]"TESCO Share Price (TSCO)," London Stock Exchange, accessed April 22, 2016, www.londonstockexchange.com/exchange/prices-and-markets/stocks/summary/company-summary/GB0008847096GBGBXSET0.html.

[12]AJ Bell Media, "Markets: Indices," Telegraph, accessed April 30, 2016, http://shares.telegraph.co.uk/indices/?index=UKX.

[13]"Core Purpose and Values," Tesco PLC, accessed April 22, 2016, www.tescoplc.com/about-us/core-purpose-and-values.

[14]Tesco PLC, "Our Business Model," in Annual Report and Financial Statements 2015, 8, accessed April 22, 2016, www.tescoplc.com/media/1908/tescoar15_br_businessmodel.pdf.

[15]Richard Anderson, "Tesco Turns Stale as Competitors Freshen up Ideas," BBC News, April 22, 2015, accessed October 2, 2016, www.bbc.com/news/business-29310445.

[16]Tesco PLC, Annual Report and Financial Statements 2011, 2, 2011, accessed April 22, 2016, www.tescoplc.com/files/pdf/reports/tesco_annual_report_2011.pdf.

(an increase of 6.76 per cent), while the gross profit increased from £5.13 billion in FY 2010/11 to £5.26 billion in FY 2011/12 (an increase of 2.65 per cent) (see Exhibit 4).

However, Tesco's revenue then fell from £64.83 billion in FY 2012/13 to £63.5 billion in FY 2013/14 (see **Exhibit 4**). Tesco's then CEO, Philip Andrew Clarke, tried to revive the business with a plan to inject £1 billion to refurbish 430 stores and hire 8,000 new store workers to enhance the shopping experience for customers.[17] The idea was to turn Tesco into a multichannel retailer in an effort to revitalize its business and grow with customers' needs. Despite these efforts, profits and share prices continued to decrease. As a result, Clarke was fired.

## THE NEW CEO: DAVE LEWIS

Lewis became group chief executive of Tesco on September 1, 2014. He brought with him 28 years of experience at Unilever in a variety of roles, which took him across Greater Europe, Asia, and the Americas. His last three roles included chairman of Unilever in the United Kingdom and Ireland, president of the company's divisions in the Americas, and global president of the personal care division. During his career, Lewis had been responsible for a number of business turnarounds within these roles and areas.[18]

Upon Lewis's move to Tesco, former Tesco board director Andy Higginson said, "I think Dave Lewis is a great hire for Tesco. . . . He's very seasoned and a successful manager. He's got great values and will be very strong on sorting the strategy out."[19] Market analysts agreed that Lewis's appointment brought hope for Tesco, with one analyst noting that the appointment, coupled with the recent hiring of Alan Stewart from Marks & Spencer as Tesco's finance director, meant that "shareholders now have the change they have been pushing for."[20]

Lewis joined Tesco at a time when the company was undergoing a severe financial crisis. From the company's cash position to its decreasing sales, Tesco's new CEO had numerous issues to address. Soon after hiring Lewis in September 2014, Tesco experienced another massive setback in the form of an accounting scandal. Tesco's previous chairman Sir Richard Broadbent explained:

> The issues that have come to light over recent weeks are a matter of profound regret. We have acted quickly to clarify the financial performance of the company. A new management team is in place to address the root causes of the misstatement, and to develop and implement the actions that will build the company's future.[21]

The fraud was publicly exposed when the company's predicted profits for the first half of 2014 were cut back from £1.1 billion to £263 million. Accounting issues further affected Tesco's performance.

# The retail industry

Although the U.K. retail industry had grown steadily until 2013, the trend started to dip after this point. This decrease was attributed to the United Kingdom's slow economy at the time. The growth rate decreased from 2.3 per cent in 2014 to 2 per cent in 2015. With the country's gross domestic product growth hovering around 2

[17]Zoe Wood, "Tesco Profits Fall for First Time in Almost 20 years," *Guardian,* October 3, 2012, accessed April 31, 2016, www.theguardian.com/business/2012/oct/03/tesco-profits-fall-uk-supermarkets.

[18]"Tesco's Board and Executive Committee," Tesco PLC, accessed April 31, 2016, www.tescoplc.com/about-us/board-and-executive-committee/board/.

[19]Rupert Neate, "We Know Dave Lewis Can Sell Soap. Can He Really Run Tesco?" *Guardian,* July 27, 2014, accessed October 2, 2016, www.theguardian.com/business/2014/jul/27/dave-lewis-tesco-manage-dove.

[20]Paras Anand, Head of European Equities, Fidelity International, as quoted by Ben Marlow and Katherine Rushton, "Shareholders Split on Phil Clarke's Resignation from Tesco," *Telegraph,* July 21, 2014, accessed October 2, 2016, www.telegraph.co.uk/finance/newsbysector/epic/tsco/10980835/Shareholders-split-on-Phil-Clarkes-resignation-from-Tesco.html.

[21]"Tesco Shares Slump after Raised Profit Error," BBC News, October 23, 2014, accessed April 31, 2016, www.bbc.com/news/business-29735685.

per cent (which was less than the long-term economic growth rate), retail spending was projected to decrease by around 0.2 per cent every year until 2020.[22]

Several reports and trends exhibited a move toward technology and online retail in the U.K. retail industry. Moreover, the industry began to experience a dramatic shift toward discount retail stores, which were very simple in design. Due to the volatile economy, consumers started to prefer discount stores over all other offerings. The average 12-week market share of German discount stores such as Aldi and Lidl saw a rise of over 1 per cent from 2014 to 2016, while other competitors in the U.K. market saw negative market share growth during the same period (see Exhibit 5).[23]

## Tesco's financial results for FY 2014/15 and 2015/16

During FY 2014/15, there had been renewed focus on corporate governance. The company's board spent a significant proportion of its time examining and strengthening Tesco's processes throughout the group. Low-performing stores were shut down, and many staff members were laid off to reduce costs. Tesco closed 43 stores that were not yielding any profits and stalled the opening of 49 new stores. Moreover, the company regained ownership of 21 superstores to reduce rent exposure. In an attempt to focus on its core customers, Tesco also sold off all major non-core business. The company's Korean business, Homeplus, was sold for £4.2 billion as a measure to strengthen Tesco's balance sheet.[24]

In FY 2015/16, Lewis's primary focus was to turn Tesco back into a customer-centric business. Therefore, Lewis implemented many strategic changes with three focal points to help Tesco recover from the accounting scandal of 2014: (1) regaining competitiveness in core U.K. business; (2) protecting and strengthening the balance sheet and profits; and (3) rebuilding trust and transparency.[25]

Competition in the market was driving companies to lower their margins and offer deep discounts. Tesco's top competitors—Asda, Morrisons, and Sainsbury's—had a solid hold in the market, and new players— Aldi and Lidl—were competing fiercely for market share. Under these circumstances, Tesco focused on delivering the best competitive price for its customers. Tesco's 2015 strategic report stated, "In October 2015, we became the first—and still only—retailer in the [United Kingdom] to offer customers an immediate price match at the till with Brand Guarantee."[26] To ensure lower prices, Tesco invested all excess profits in the prices of products. In 2015, the company launched a range of products with an emphasis on lower prices. Capital expenditure was also cut from £2.88 billion in FY 2013/14 to £2.32 billion in FY 2014/15, and was further reduced to £1.04 billion in FY 2015/16 (see Exhibit 6).

When Tesco's results for FY 2015/16 were announced, everyone was surprised with the turnaround that Lewis had achieved since his arrival: the company that had faced huge losses in FY 2014/15 had now registered a net profit of £138 million in FY 2015/16 (see Exhibit 4). According to the company's 2016 strategic report, one of the most important changes was the establishment of a new purpose for Tesco: "Serving shoppers a little better every day."[27] This purpose began to guide all of Tesco's decisions and shape every action the company took.

Although Tesco's revenue decreased (from £62.28 billion in FY 2014/15 to £54.43 billion in FY 2015/16), international sales contributed a great deal toward overall sales, constituting 19.1 per cent of total revenue.

[22]"The Retail Forecast for 2013-2016," Centre for Retail Research, January 5, 2016, accessed April 31, 2016, www.retailresearch.org/retailforecast.php.

[23]"Great Britain - Grocery Market Share (12 weeks ending)," Kantar WorldPanel, 2016, accessed May 5, 2016, www.kantarworldpanel.com/en/grocery-market-share/great-britain.

[24]Ashley Armstrong, "Tesco Sells South Korean Homeplus Business for £4Bn," Telegraph, September 7, 2015, accessed April 24, 2016, www.telegraph.co.uk/finance/11848185/Tesco-sells-South-Korean-business-for-4bn.html.

[25]Tesco PLC, Strategic Report 2015, 3, accessed April 28, 2016, www.tescoplc.com/media/1189/tesco_cr15_strategicreport.pdf.

[26]Ibid, 4.

[27]Ibid.

[28]Tesco PLC, Annual Report and Financial Statements 2016, op. cit., 87.

Tesco focused on cost management, leading to reductions in the cost of sold goods and operating costs, which enabled the company to achieve an operating profit of £1.05 billion in FY 2015/16 (see Exhibit 4).[28]

## Challenges ahead

Mike Dennis, an analyst at Cantor Fitzgerald, predicted that Tesco would be fined roughly 1 per cent of U.K. grocery sales (approximately £350 million) attributed to the accounting scandal of 2014.[29] In addition, the Serious Fraud Office (SFO) could levy other fines, which, together, could amount to around £500 million. Tesco also had to repay or refinance £1.1 billion in bonds due in September 2016, and £330 million due in January 2017 (see Exhibit 7).[30] Additionally, the company had a pension deficit.[31] According to the analyst:

> [T]he possible fines and legal redress could be classified as exceptional costs but would also drain Tesco of needed cash resources [and] ability to repay debt, and potentially limit any margin recovery. . . . We believe, the implications of a stronger regulator, Groceries Code Adjudicator (GCA), a compliant grocery industry, and potential restrictions from the SFO could place significant limitations on Tesco's ability to recover margin and repay/refinance [bonds]. . . . The whole industry is currently trying to manage cost pressures, ranging from the living wage to higher rent and rates, as well as falling sales in supermarkets and hypermarkets. So, for Tesco specifically, and the industry, this might severely limit any future price reinvestment against the discounters and margin recovery.[32]

The results for FY 2015/16 were encouraging, but in April 2016,[33] Lewis acknowledged that Tesco's recovery would not be smooth, and that the company was still facing major challenges. Share prices fell as investors became cautious of the company's profit warning. Lewis also hinted at a likely fall in sales over the next year. Despite these statements, Lewis appeared optimistic in Tesco's 2016 annual report and financial statements, saying, "Of course there is still more to do—but we are on the road to recovery and momentum is building across the business."[34].

Given all of these efforts, would Tesco's new CEO be able to bring the company out of its downward spiral? Could he convince shareholders that Tesco was a worthy investment?

---

[29]Graham Ruddick, "Tesco to be Censured by Supermarket Watchdog Over Conduct with Suppliers," *Guardian,* January 25, 2016, accessed April 21, 2016, www.theguardian.com/business/2016/jan/25/tesco-censured-supermarket-watchdog-suppliers-groceries-code-adjudicator.
[30]Lynsey Barber, "Tesco Share Price Falls as Serious Fraud Office's Investigation is Set to Conclude," City A.M., January 25, 2016, accessed April 27, 2016, www.cityam.com/233040/the-serious-fraud-offices-tesco-investigation-is-set-to-conclude.
[31]Ruddick, op. cit.
[32]Barber, op. cit.
[33]Saabira Chaudhuri, "Tesco Shares Fall as Company Warns on Profit," *Wall Street Journal,* April 13, 2016, accessed April 22, 2016, www.wsj.com/articles/tesco-swings-to-full-year-profit-1460528432.
[34]Tesco PLC, *Annual Report and Financial Statements 2016,* op. cit., 6

**EXHIBIT 1**  TESCO's share prices, 2012 to 2016

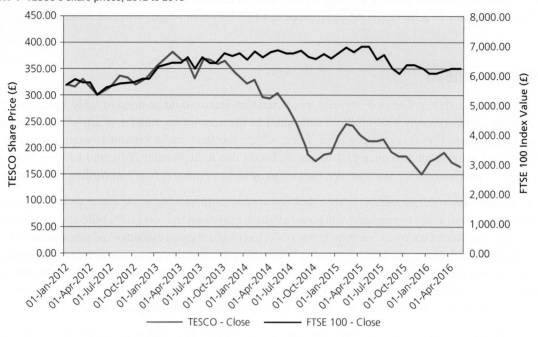

Source: "Tesco Share Price," Thomson Reuters, accessed April 22, 2016.

**EXHIBIT 2** TESCO store types in the united kingdom, with count and features

| Format | Year | Number of stores | Total area of stores (in square feet) | Mean area of each store (in square feet) | (%) of total space owned by Tesco |
|---|---|---|---|---|---|
| Tesco Extra | 2016 | 252 | 17,846,000 | 70,817 | 42.99 |
| | 2015 | 250 | 17,763,000 | 71,052 | 42.01 |
| | 2014 | 247 | 17,610,000 | 71,296 | 42.12 |
| | 2013 | 238 | 17,051,000 | 71,643 | 42.11 |
| Homeplus | 2016 | 0 | 0 | - | 0.00 |
| | 2015 | 11 | 488,000 | 44,364 | 1.15 |
| | 2014 | 12 | 523,000 | 43,583 | 1.25 |
| | 2013 | 12 | 523,000 | 43,583 | 1.29 |
| Tesco Superstores | 2016 | 478 | 14,002,000 | 29,293 | 33.73 |
| | 2015 | 487 | 14,254,000 | 29,269 | 33.71 |
| | 2014 | 482 | 14,110,000 | 29,274 | 33.75 |
| | 2013 | 481 | 14,053,000 | 29,216 | 34.70 |
| Tesco Metro | 2016 | 177 | 2,005,000 | 11,328 | 4.83 |
| | 2015 | 191 | 2,150,000 | 11,257 | 5.08 |
| | 2014 | 195 | 2,191,000 | 11,236 | 5.24 |
| | 2013 | 192 | 2,145,000 | 11,172 | 5.30 |
| Tesco Express | 2016 | 1,732 | 4,031,000 | 2,327 | 9.71 |
| | 2015 | 1,735 | 4,030,000 | 2,323 | 9.53 |
| | 2014 | 1,672 | 3,883,000 | 2,322 | 9.29 |
| | 2013 | 1,547 | 3,588,000 | 2,319 | 8.86 |
| One Stop | 2016 | 779 | 1,256,000 | 1,612 | 3.03 |
| | 2015 | 770 | 1,235,000 | 1,604 | 2.92 |
| | 2014 | 722 | 1,142,000 | 1,582 | 2.73 |
| | 2013 | 639 | 991,000 | 1,551 | 2.45 |
| Dobbies | 2016 | 36 | 1,652,000 | 45,889 | 3.98 |
| | 2015 | 35 | 1,648,000 | 47,086 | 3.90 |
| | 2014 | 34 | 1,638,000 | 48,176 | 3.92 |
| | 2013 | 32 | 1,540,000 | 48,125 | 3.80 |
| Tesco Dotcom | 2016 | 6 | 716,000 | 119,333 | 1.72 |
| | 2015 | 6 | 716,000 | 119,333 | 1.69 |
| | 2014 | 6 | 716,000 | 119,333 | 1.71 |
| | 2013 | 5 | 604,000 | 120,800 | 1.49 |

Source: Compiled by the case authors, based on Tesco PLC, *Annual Report and Financial Statements 2016,* 163–164, accessed May 22, 2016, www.tescoplc.com/media/264194/annual-report-2016.pdf; and Tesco PLC, *Annual Report and Financial Statements 2015,* 151–152, accessed April 22, 2016, www.tescoplc.com/files/pdf/reports/ar15/download_annual_report.pdf.

**EXHIBIT 3**  TESCO: Five-year record

|  | 2015/16 | 2014/15 | 2013/14 | 2012/13 | 2011/12 |
|---|---|---|---|---|---|
| Revenue (in £ millions) | 54,433 | 56,925 | 63,557 | 63,406 | 63,916 |
| Revenue growth (%) | −4.28 | −10.43 | 0.24 | −0.80 | − |
| Profit/(Loss) (in £ millions) | 129 | (5,766) | 970 | 24 | 2,814 |
| Profit/(Loss) growth (%) | | | | | |
| Number of stores | 6,902 | 6,849 | 7,305 | 6,653 | 6,049 |
| Average number of employees | 482,152 | 480,607 | 510,444 | 506,856 | 514,615 |

Source: Compiled by the case authors, based on Tesco PLC, *Annual Report and Financial Statements 2016*, 85, 163, accessed May 22, 2016, www.tescoplc.com/media/264194/annual-report-2016.pdf; Tesco PLC, *Annual Report and Financial Statements 2015*, 83, 151, 168, accessed April 22, 2016, www.tescoplc.com/files/pdf/reports/ar15/download_annual_report.pdf; Tesco PLC, *Annual Report and Financial Statements 2014*, 69, 138, 144, accessed April 22, 2016, www.tescoplc.com/files/pdf/reports/ar14/download_annual_report.pdf; Tesco PLC, *Annual Report and Financial Statements 2013*, 72, 136, accessed April 22, 2016, www.tescoplc.com/media/1456/tesco_annual_report_2013.pdf; and Tesco PLC, *Annual Report and Financial Statements 2012*, 90, accessed April 22, 2016, www.tescoplc.com/media/1455/tesco_annual_report_2012.pdf.

**EXHIBIT 4**  TESCO and subsidiaries, consolidated statement of operations and comprehensive loss

**INCOME STATEMENT**

| Fiscal year ends in February (in £ millions, except per share data) | 2015/16 | 2014/15 | 2013/14 | 2012/13 | 2011/12 | 2010/11 |
|---|---|---|---|---|---|---|
| Revenue | 54,433 | 62,284 | 63,557 | 64,826 | 64,539 | 60,455 |
| Cost of revenue | 51,579 | 64,396 | 59,547 | 60,737 | 59,278 | 55,330 |
| Gross profit | 2,854 | (2,112) | 4,010 | 4,089 | 5,261 | 5,125 |
| Operating expenses | 1,852 | 2,695 | 1,657 | 1,901 | 2,486 | 2,290 |
| Sales, general, and administrative Other operating expenses | (44) | 985 | (278) | | | |
| Total operating expenses | 1,808 | 3,680 | 1,379 | 1,901 | 2,486 | 2,290 |
| Operating income | 1,046 | (5,792) | 2,631 | 2,188 | 2,775 | 2,835 |
| Interest expense | 498 | 499 | 447 | 445 | 417 | 465 |
| Other income (expense) | (386) | (85) | 75 | 217 | 1,477 | 1,271 |
| Income before income taxes | 162 | (6,376) | 2,259 | 1,960 | 3,835 | 3,641 |
| Provision for income taxes | (54) | (657) | 347 | 574 | 879 | 864 |
| Minority interest | (9) | (25) | (4) | (4) | 8 | 16 |
| Other income | (9) | (25) | (4) | (4) | 8 | 16 |
| Net income from continuing operations | 216 | (5,719) | 1,912 | 1,386 | 2,956 | 2,777 |
| Net income from discontinuing operations | (87) | (47) | (942) | (1,266) | (142) | (106) |
| Other | 9 | 25 | 4 | 4 | (8) | (16) |
| Net income | 138 | (5,741) | 974 | 124 | 2,806 | 2,655 |
| Net income available to common shareholders | 138 | (5,741) | 974 | 124 | 2,806 | 2,655 |

Source: Compiled by the case authors, based on Tesco PLC, *Annual Report and Financial Statements 2016*, 85, accessed May 22, 2016, www.tescoplc.com/media/264194/annual-report-2016.pdf; Tesco PLC, *Annual Report and Financial Statements 2015*, 83, accessed April 22, 2016, www.tescoplc.com/files/pdf/reports/ar15/download_annual_report.pdf; Tesco PLC, *Annual Report and Financial Statements 2014*, 69, accessed April 22, 2016, www.tescoplc.com/files/pdf/reports/ar14/download_annual_report.pdf; Tesco PLC, *Annual Report and Financial Statements 2013*, 72, accessed April 22, 2016, www.tescoplc.com/media/1456/tesco_annual_report_2013.pdf; Tesco PLC, *Annual Report and Financial Statements 2012*, 90, accessed April 22, 2016, www.tescoplc.com/media/1455/tesco_annual_report_2012.pdf; and Tesco PLC, *Annual Report and Financial Statements 2011*, 94, accessed April 22, 2016, www.tescoplc.com/files/pdf/reports/tesco_annual_report_2011.pdf.

**EXHIBIT 5** Average market share growth (12 weeks ending) 2014–2016

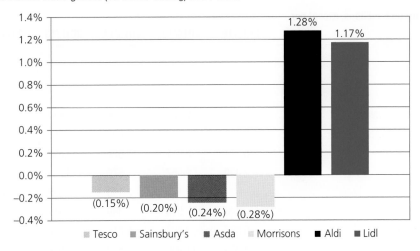

Source: Compiled by the case authors, based on Kantar WorldPanel, "Great Britain—Grocery Market Share (12 weeks ending)," Kantar WorldPanel, 2016, accessed May 5, 2016, www.kantarworldpanel.com/en/grocery-market-share/great-"www.kantarworldpanel.com/en/grocery-market-share/great-britain.

**EXHIBIT 6** TESCO and subsidiaries: Cash flow statement

| Fiscal year ends in February (in £ millions, except per share data) | 2015/16 | 2014/15 | 2013/14 | 2012/13 | 2011/12 | 2010/11 |
|---|---|---|---|---|---|---|
| Net cash provided by operating activities | 2,126 | 484 | 3,185 | 2,837 | 4,408 | 4,267 |
| Net cash used for investing activities | (615) | (2,015) | (2,854) | (278) | (3,183) | (1,859) |
| Net cash provided by (used for) financing activities | (604) | 814 | 56 | (2,365) | (1,366) | (3,036) |
| Effect of exchange rate changes | 1 | 78 | (105) | 26 | 24 | (46) |
| Net change in cash | 908 | (639) | 282 | 220 | (117) | (674) |
| Cash at beginning of period | 2,174 | 2,813 | 2,531 | 2,311 | (6,790) | (7,929) |
| Cash at end of period | 3,082 | 2,174 | 2,813 | 2,531 | (6,907) | (8,603) |
| Operating cash flow | 2,126 | 484 | 3,185 | 2,837 | 4,408 | 4,267 |
| Capital expenditure | (1,038) | (2,318) | (2,881) | (2,987) | (3,708) | (3,551) |
| Free cash flow | 1,088 | (1,834) | 304 | (150) | 700 | 716 |

Source: Compiled by the case authors, based on Tesco PLC, *Annual Report and Financial Statements 2016*, 89, accessed May 22, 2016, www.tescoplc.com/media/264194/annual-report-2016.pdf; Tesco PLC, *Annual Report and Financial Statements 2015*, 87, accessed April 22, 2016, www.tescoplc.com/files/pdf/reports/ar15/download_annual_report.pdf; Tesco PLC, *Annual Report and Financial Statements 2014*, 73, accessed April 22, 2016, www.tescoplc.com/files/pdf/reports/ar14/download_annual_report.pdf; Tesco PLC, *Annual Report and Financial Statements 2013*, 76, accessed April 22, 2016, www.tescoplc.com/media/1456/tesco_annual_report_2013.pdf; Tesco PLC, *Annual Report and Financial Statements 2012*, 94, accessed April 22, 2016, www.tescoplc.com/media/1455/tesco_annual_report_2012.pdf; and Tesco PLC, *Annual Report and Financial Statements 2011*, 98, accessed April 22, 2016, www.tescoplc.com/files/pdf/reports/tesco_annual_report_2011.pdf.

**EXHIBIT 7** TESCO and subsidiaries: Consolidated balance sheet

| FY ends in February (in £ millions, except per share data) | 2015/16 | 2014/15 | 2013/14 | 2012/13 | 2011/12 | 2010/11 |
|---|---|---|---|---|---|---|
| **Assets** | | | | | | |
| Current assets | | | | | | |
| Cash | | | | | | |
| Cash and cash equivalents | 3,082 | 2,165 | 2,506 | 2,512 | 2,305 | 2,428 |
| Short-term investments | 3,639 | 746 | 1,096 | 580 | 1,284 | 1,170 |
| Total cash | 6,721 | 2,911 | 3,602 | 3,092 | 3,589 | 3,598 |
| Inventories | 2,430 | 2,957 | 3,576 | 3,744 | 3,598 | 3,162 |
| Receivables | | 2,121 | 2,190 | 2,525 | 2,657 | 2,330 |
| Prepaid expenses | 440 | 516 | 388 | 417 | 420 | 387 |
| Other current assets | 5,237 | 3,453 | 5,816 | 3,318 | 2,599 | 2,562 |
| Total current assets | 14,828 | 11,958 | 15,572 | 13,096 | 12,863 | 12,039 |
| Non-current assets | | | | | | |
| Property, plant, and equipment | | | | | | |
| Land | 22,557 | 25,298 | 25,734 | 24,817 | | |
| Fixtures and equipment | | | | | 9,967 | 8,895 |
| Other properties | 10,468 | 11,493 | 10,851 | 10,826 | 27,058 | 25,767 |
| Property and equipment, at cost | 33,025 | 36,791 | 36,585 | 35,643 | 37,025 | 34,662 |
| Accumulated depreciation | (15,125) | (16,351) | (12,095) | (10,773) | (9,324) | (8,401) |
| Property, plant, and equipment, net | 17,900 | 20,440 | 24,490 | 24,870 | 27,701 | 26,261 |
| Goodwill | 2,517 | 2,288 | 2,286 | 2,954 | | |
| Intangible assets | 357 | 1,483 | 1,509 | 1,408 | 4,618 | 4,338 |
| Deferred income taxes | 49 | 514 | 73 | 58 | 23 | 48 |
| Other long-term assets | 8,253 | 7,531 | 6,234 | 7,743 | 5,576 | 4,520 |
| Total non-current assets | 29,076 | 32,256 | 34,592 | 37,033 | 37,918 | 35,167 |
| Total assets | 43,904 | 44,214 | 50,164 | 50,129 | 50,781 | 47,206 |
| **Liabilities and stockholders' equity** | | | | | | |
| Liabilities | | | | | | |
| Current liabilities | | | | | | |
| Short-term debt | 2,815 | 1,998 | 1,904 | 760 | 1,838 | 1,386 |
| Capital leases | 11 | 10 | 6 | 6 | | |
| Accounts payable | 4,545 | 5,076 | 5,831 | 6,036 | 5,971 | 5,782 |
| Taxes payable | 807 | 461 | 893 | 959 | 416 | 432 |
| Other current liabilities | 11,536 | 12,265 | 12,765 | 11,224 | 11,024 | 10,131 |
| Total current liabilities | 19,714 | 19,810 | 21,399 | 18,985 | 19,249 | 17,731 |
| Non-current liabilities | | | | | | |
| Long-term debt | 10,623 | 10,520 | 9,188 | 529 | 9,911 | 9,689 |
| Capital leases | 88 | 131 | 115 | 9,539 | | |
| Deferred taxes liabilities | 135 | 199 | 594 | 1,006 | 1,160 | 1,094 |
| Pensions and other benefits | 3,175 | 4,842 | 3,193 | 2,378 | | |
| Minority interest | (10) | | 7 | 18 | 26 | 88 |

| FY ends in February (in £ millions, except per share data) | 2015/16 | 2014/15 | 2013/14 | 2012/13 | 2011/12 | 2010/11 |
|---|---|---|---|---|---|---|
| Other long-term liabilities | 1,553 | 1,641 | 953 | 1,031 | 2,660 | 2,069 |
| Total non-current liabilities | 15,564 | 17,333 | 14,050 | 14,501 | 13,757 | 12,940 |
| Total liabilities | 35,278 | 37,143 | 35,449 | 33,486 | 33,006 | 30,671 |
| Stockholders' equity | | | | | | |
| Additional paid-in capital | 5,095 | 5,094 | 5,080 | 5,020 | 4,964 | 4,896 |
| Retained earnings | 3,265 | 1,985 | 9,728 | 10,535 | 12,369 | 11,197 |
| Accumulated other comprehensive income | 266 | (8) | (93) | 1,088 | 442 | 442 |
| Total stockholders' equity | 8,626 | 7,071 | 14,715 | 16,643 | 17,775 | 16,535 |
| Total liabilities and stockholders' equity | 43,904 | 44,214 | 50,164 | 50,129 | 50,781 | 47,206 |

Source: Compiled by the case authors, based on Tesco PLC, *Annual Report and Financial Statements 2016,* 87, accessed May 22, 2016, www.tescoplc.com/media/264194/annual-report-2016.pdf; Tesco PLC, *Annual Report and Financial Statements 2015,* 85, accessed April 22, 2016, www.tescoplc.com/files/pdf/reports/ar15/download_annual_report.pdf; Tesco PLC, *Annual Report and Financial Statements 2014,* 71, accessed April 22, 2016, www.tescoplc.com/files/pdf/reports/ar14/download_annual_report.pdf; Tesco PLC, *Annual Report and Financial Statements 2013,* 74, accessed April 22, 2016, www.tescoplc.com/media/1456/tesco_annual_report_2013.pdf; Tesco PLC, *Annual Report and Financial Statements 2012,* 92, accessed April 22, 2016, www.tescoplc.com/media/1455/tesco_annual_report_2012.pdf; and Tesco PLC, *Annual Report and Financial Statements 2011,* 96, accessed April 22, 2016, www.tescoplc.com/files/pdf/reports/tesco_annual_report_2011.pdf.

# CASE

## Valuing Europe's fastest growing company: HelloFresh in 2017

In May 2017 the *Financial Times* published its 2017 FT1000 ranking of Europe's fastest growing companies. Leading the financial newspaper's ranking was Berlin-based meal-box delivery company HelloFresh, the company that managed to grow its revenue from €2.3 million in 2012 to €305 million in 2015, a stunning growth rate of more than 400 percent per year. HelloFresh was founded in 2011 by Dominik Richter, Thomas Griesel, and Jessica Nilsson with a small investment that was soon complemented by a capital infusion of close to €2.5 million, made by start-up incubator Rocket Internet. Rocket Internet obtained a 60 percent stake in HelloFresh, valuing the start-up at around €4 million. Several funding rounds followed this first capital infusion, the most noteworthy capital event being an investment of €75 million made by Edinburgh-based investment manager Baillie Gifford in September 2015, in exchange for an equity stake of slightly less than 3 percent. This investment, which was made in anticipation of an initial public offering (IPO), valued the company at no less than €2.6 billion only four years after its inception. Soon after Baillie Gifford made its investment, Rocket Internet called off the IPO; other investors seemed unwilling to buy into the €2.6 billion valuation of HelloFresh. It took another one and a half years before Rocket Internet dared to make a second attempt at bringing HelloFresh to the Frankfurt Stock Exchange, this time at slightly more than half of its 2015 valuation.

## HelloFresh

HelloFresh's primary business model was to sell and deliver to customers' doors meal boxes that contained all the fresh ingredients needed to prepare a fixed number of healthy, self-cooked dinners, according to carefully crafted recipes. This business model was built strongly on customers' increasing preference for online shopping, convenience, healthy and sustainable food, and food waste reduction. The company started operations in 2012 in Germany and gradually expanded into nine other countries, including the United States, one of HelloFresh's fastest growing markets. HelloFresh kept most operational processes in-house, from recipe creation to sourcing, to production and packaging to delivery. The company's critical success factors were the efficiency of its supply chain and inventory management, the effectiveness of customer attraction and retention, and the development of data technology solutions that (a) supported cost-efficient recipe creation and sourcing and (b) facilitated targeted marketing and market penetration. By working closely with (mostly local) food suppliers HelloFresh managed to order ingredients on a just-in-time basis and keep inventories to a minimum.

In 2017 the online food market was in rapid development, which meant that making an investment in HelloFresh came with risks. One important market factor was that competition from online food retailers and delivery services was growing. Amazon's takeover of US-based food retailer Whole Foods had shaken up the food retail industry and motivated traditional food retailers to speed up their investments in online platforms.

Professor Erik Peek prepared this case. The case is intended solely as the basis for class discussion and is not intended to serve as an endorsement, source of primary data, or illustration of effective or ineffective management.

Furthermore, there were some examples of large competitors making steps to enter the meal delivery market. For example, consumer goods manufacturer Unilever entered into partnerships with delivery companies in the Netherlands and the United Kingdom, whereas food retailers Albertson and Lidl acquired HelloFresh's competitors Plated and Kochzauber.

Another important market factor was that customer acquisition was expensive, and according to some analysts customer attrition rates were high. HelloFresh reported that customer acquisition costs (CAC), consisting of all marketing costs other than customer care and overhead costs, amounted to an average of €82 per newly acquired customer. To put this number in perspective, the average revenue per customer in 2016 and the first half of 2017 was €181 per quarter. Given an average contribution margin, defined as revenue minus cost of sales and fulfilment expenses, of 18.3 percent of revenue, HelloFresh earned an average quarterly contribution margin of €33 per customer (€181 × 0.183). Consequently, ignoring discounting, it took HelloFresh an average of 2.7 quarters, or roughly eight months, to earn back the investment in acquiring one customer.

**Exhibit 1** shows the net present value of a €82 thousand investment to acquire 1,000 customers with different rates of customer attrition. To simplify calculations, it is assumed that customers who remain subscribed until month 13 will continue to do so for another two years. Under such a simplifying assumption, an €82 investment in the acquisition of one customer turns out to be a negative NPV investment if the monthly customer attrition rate equals 20 percent. Customer attrition rates of 15 percent or lower would yield positive NPVs. These calculations present a simplified version of reality; for example, in practice, customer attrition rates tend to decline the longer a customer cohort has been subscribed to a service. However, the calculations do illustrate the valuation relevance of HelloFresh's customer retention success as well as how low attrition rates must be to make the customer acquisition investments pay off. Some industry observers claimed that attrition rates of 20 percent or higher were far from inconceivable.

**Exhibit 2** shows the standardized income statements, balance sheets, and cash flow statements (all adjusted for operating leases) of HelloFresh for the fiscal years 2014 through 2016 and the half year ending on June 30, 2017. During its first years of operation, HelloFresh did not earn any profits or positive free cash flows, presumably because of the large investments in growth and customer acquisition that the company made. To help investors get a better view of the company's long-term profit potential, HelloFresh also disclosed non-GAAP performance measures for the fiscal quarters ending on or after December 2015. The non-GAAP performance measures that HelloFresh highlighted were its contribution margin, defined as revenue minus cost of sales and fulfilment expenses (excluding share-based payments); and adjusted EBITDA, defined as earnings before interest, taxes, depreciation, amortization, special items, and share-based payments. **Exhibit 3** shows the calculation of HelloFresh's non-GAAP performance. Further, **Exhibit 4** provides some non-financial indicators that are informative about HelloFresh's customer base, growth, orders, and revenues during 2015–2017.

## Valuing HelloFresh

Between December 2011 and June 2017, HelloFresh went through several funding rounds, each of which bears some information about how the company's current investors valued their holdings. **Exhibit 5** provides an overview of estimated amounts raised during this period and their implications for the company's value. All estimates are based on HelloFresh's Statements of Changes in Equity, which the company disclosed in its IPO prospectus. While Rocket Internet's initial capital infusion of €2.5 million valued HelloFresh at around €4 million, in fiscal 2012 HelloFresh raised another €4 million, granting a 30.7 percent stake in its equity. This funding transaction suggests that the company's investors valued HelloFresh at an amount of around €13.1 million (4.0/0.307) in 2012. After 2012 investors' valuation rapidly increased, from €47 million in 2013 to €131 million in 2014, before levelling off at €2.6 billion – making HelloFresh a "unicorn" company – in 2015 and 2016.

Prior to the initial public offering of October 2017, HelloFresh had 132,436,643 shares outstanding, of which 94 percent were held by five shareholders. The offering consisted of 31.05 million newly listed shares, of which

4.05 million were offered under an overallotment option, such that after the IPO 163,486,643 shares were traded on the Frankfurt Stock Exchange. HelloFresh's IPO was priced at the middle of the indicated price range, at €10.25 per share. At this price, HelloFresh's equity was valued at €1,357.5 million (163,486,643 × 10.25).

The company's book equity amounted to €56.4 million, or €0.43 per share, on June 30, 2017, the most recent fiscal quarter end prior to the IPO date. Given the proceeds of the public offering of €318.3 million (31.05 million × 10.25) and the underwriting and placement costs of €11.0 million, the post-IPO book value of HelloFresh's equity amounted to €364.7 million (56.4 + 318.3 − 11.0). HelloFresh's IPO price of €10.25 thus corresponded with a price-to-book multiple of 3.7 (1,357.5/364.7).

As indicated, the net proceeds from HelloFresh's initial public offering were €307.3 million. HelloFresh planned to invest an amount of €60 million in automation equipment, use around €28 million to pay off a loan from its main shareholder Rocket Internet, and invest €50 to €100 million in further growth. The company announced that it would hold the remainder of the proceeds, an estimated amount of €119 to €169 million, to improve its responsiveness to new business or acquisition opportunities.

## Blue Apron

One of HelloFresh's most comparable peers was US-based Blue Apron, Inc. Blue Apron had adopted a very similar business model, was founded in 2012, and also went public in 2017. In the years 2014 to 2016, Blue Apron's revenue grew from $77.8 million to $795.4 million. The meal box delivery company disclosed in its IPO prospectus that its customer acquisition costs amounted to an average of $94 per customer. Average quarterly revenue per customer amounted to $247; however, quarterly revenues per customer had decreased from $267 per customer in the first quarter of 2016 to $235 per customer in the first quarter of 2017. **Exhibit 6** shows some accounting and non-financial performance measures for Blue Apron for the fiscal quarters ending between March 31, 2015, and March 31, 2017.

In June 2017 Blue Apron listed 30 million of its Class A common stock for trading on the New York Stock Exchange at an IPO price of $10, significantly below the indicated price range of $15 to $17. The net proceeds of the public offering were $278 million, increasing Blue Apron's post-IPO book value of equity to $289 million and its invested capital to $441 million. The IPO price of $10 corresponded with an equity valuation of around $1.87 billion, a price-to-book multiple of 6.5 (1.87/0.289), and an enterprise value-to-invested capital ratio of 4.5 (2.02/0.441). By the time HelloFresh went public in October, Blue Apron's share price had halved, to a value just above $5.

## Required

Evaluate the IPO price of HelloFresh. What assumptions seem to be implicit in the company's initial valuation? Can these assumptions be justified?

**EXHIBIT 1**  The effect of customer attrition on the net present value of customer acquisition

| Month(s) | Customers | Contribution margin | Present value | Customers | Contribution margin | Present value | Customers | Contribution margin | Present value |
|---|---|---|---|---|---|---|---|---|---|
| 1 | 1,000 | 11,000 | 10,945 | 1,000 | 11,000 | 10,945 | 1,000 | 11,000 | 10,945 |
| 2 | 800 | 8,800 | 8,713 | 850 | 9,350 | 9,257 | 900 | 9,900 | 9,802 |
| 3 | 640 | 7,040 | 6,935 | 722 | 7,942 | 7,824 | 810 | 8,910 | 8,778 |
| 4 | 512 | 5,632 | 5,521 | 613 | 6,743 | 6,610 | 729 | 8,019 | 7,861 |
| 5 | 409 | 4,499 | 4,388 | 521 | 5,731 | 5,590 | 656 | 7,216 | 7,038 |
| 6 | 327 | 3,597 | 3,491 | 442 | 4,862 | 4,719 | 590 | 6,490 | 6,299 |
| 7 | 261 | 2,871 | 2,772 | 375 | 4,125 | 3,983 | 531 | 5,841 | 5,641 |
| 8 | 208 | 2,288 | 2,199 | 318 | 3,498 | 3,361 | 477 | 5,247 | 5,042 |
| 9 | 166 | 1,826 | 1,746 | 270 | 2,970 | 2,840 | 429 | 4,719 | 4,512 |
| 10 | 132 | 1,452 | 1,381 | 229 | 2,519 | 2,396 | 386 | 4,246 | 4,039 |
| 11 | 105 | 1,155 | 1,093 | 194 | 2,134 | 2,020 | 347 | 3,817 | 3,613 |
| 12 | 84 | 924 | 870 | 164 | 1,804 | 1,699 | 312 | 3,432 | 3,233 |
| 13–36 | 67 | 17,688 | 15,663 | 139 | 36,696 | 32,494 | 280 | 73,920 | 65,456 |
| | | | 65,718 | | | 93,739 | | | 142,258 |

**Assumptions**

| | | | | | | | | | |
|---|---|---|---|---|---|---|---|---|---|
| Contribution margin per customer (€) | | 11.00 | | | 11.00 | | | 11.00 | |
| Monthly attrition rate (%) | | 20% | | | 15% | | | 10 | |

**Net present value**

| | | | | | | | | | |
|---|---|---|---|---|---|---|---|---|---|
| PV of contribution margin per initial customer acquired (€) | | 65.72 | | | 93.74 | | | 142.26 | |
| Marketing outflow (€) | | 82.00 | | | 82.00 | | | 82.00 | |
| Net present value per initial customer (€) | | (16.28) | | | 11.74 | | | 60.26 | |

**EXHIBIT 2**  Income statements, balance sheets, and cash flow statements of HelloFresh SE on June 30, 2017 (standardized and adjusted for operating leases)

| Condensed income statements (€ mln) | 1st half of 2017 | 2016 | 2015 | 2014 |
|---|---|---|---|---|
| **Revenue** | **435.4** | **597.0** | **305.0** | **69.6** |
| Cost of sales | (180.5) | (257.3) | (146.1) | (31.1) |
| SG&A expense | (304.1) | (425.6) | (273.0) | (53.0) |
| Net other operating income | (1.4) | (3.6) | (1.4) | (1.2) |
| **Operating profit** | **(50.6)** | **(89.5)** | **(115.5)** | **(15.7)** |
| Interest income | 0.6 | 1.5 | 0.1 | 0.0 |
| Interest expense | (7.2) | (6.1) | (1.4) | 0.0 |
| **Profit before taxes** | **(57.2)** | **(94.1)** | **(116.8)** | **(15.7)** |
| Tax expense | 0.4 | 0.3 | 0.0 | 0.4 |
| **Profit after taxes** | **(56.8)** | **(93.8)** | **(116.8)** | **(15.3)** |
| Profit or loss to non-controlling interest | (0.1) | (0.1) | (3.0) | (0.8) |
| **Profit or loss to ordinary shareholders** | **(56.9)** | **(93.9)** | **(119.8)** | **(16.1)** |

| Condensed balance sheets (€ mln) | 1st half of 2017 | 2016 | 2015 | 2014 |
|---|---|---|---|---|
| Operating cash | 21.8 | 29.9 | 15.3 | 3.5 |
| + Trade receivables | 8.8 | 9.3 | 11.5 | 2.7 |
| + Inventories | 9.4 | 10.1 | 5.6 | 1.4 |
| + Other current assets | 10.2 | 12.6 | 9.4 | 2.0 |
| − Trade payables | (54.5) | (43.1) | (45.5) | (11.2) |
| − Other current liabilities | (21.8) | (19.4) | (12.5) | (1.6) |
| **Net working capital** | **(26.1)** | **(0.6)** | **(16.3)** | **(3.2)** |
| Non-current tangible assets | 148.9 | 150.9 | 47.9 | 1.5 |
| + Non-current intangible assets | 7.5 | 6.2 | 4.7 | 0.0 |
| − Deferred tax liabilities (net of assets) | 1.1 | 0.7 | 0.4 | 0.4 |
| − Other non-current liabilities | (11.4) | (15.5) | (10.2) | (0.3) |
| **Net non-current operating assets** | **146.1** | **142.3** | **42.8** | **1.6** |
| Excess cash | 93.5 | 29.5 | 95.7 | 17.4 |
| + Other non-operating investments | 13.4 | 13.9 | 9.2 | 0.0 |
| **Non-operating investments** | **106.9** | **43.4** | **104.9** | **17.4** |
| Current debt | 6.1 | 6.7 | 2.7 | 0.3 |
| + Non-current debt | 164.5 | 157.7 | 41.1 | 0.8 |
| **Debt** | **170.6** | **164.4** | **43.8** | **1.1** |
| **Ordinary shareholders' equity** | **56.4** | **20.6** | **87.6** | **15.7** |
| **Non-controlling interest in equity** | **(0.1)** | **0.0** | **0.0** | **(1.0)** |
| **Invested capital** | **226.9** | **185.0** | **131.4** | **15.8** |

| Condensed cash flow statements (€ mln) | 1st half of 2017 | 2016 | 2015 | 2014 |
|---|---|---|---|---|
| Profit before interest and tax | (50.5) | (89.6) | (115.5) | (15.8) |
| Taxes paid | 0.0 | (0.1) | 0.0 | 0.0 |
| Non-operating losses (gains) | 0.0 | 0.1 | 0.0 | 0.0 |
| Non-current operating accruals | 24.8 | 21.6 | 20.2 | 1.0 |
| Net (investments in) or liquidation of operating working capital | 14.0 | (7.8) | 11.2 | 3.2 |
| **Operating cash flow** | **(11.7)** | **(75.8)** | **(84.1)** | **(11.6)** |
| Interest Received | 0.0 | 0.1 | 0.1 | 0.0 |
| Net investments in non-current assets | (20.8) | (118.9) | (58.0) | (1.5) |
| **Free cash flow available to debt and equity** | **(32.5)** | **(194.6)** | **(142.0)** | **(13.1)** |
| Interest Paid | (4.6) | (1.5) | (0.0) | 0.0 |
| Net Debt issuance | 7.7 | 116.7 | 42.8 | 1.0 |
| **Free cash flow available to equity** | **(29.4)** | **(79.4)** | **(99.2)** | **(12.1)** |
| Net share issuance | 86.2 | 28.4 | 189.9 | 28.0 |
| **Net increase (decrease) in cash balance** | **56.8** | **(51.0)** | **90.7** | **15.9** |

Source: Prospectus for the public offering of HelloFresh on October 23, 2017, and author's calculations

**EXHIBIT 3**  Non-GAAP performance between the fourth quarter of 2015 (ending on December 31, 2015) and the second quarter of 2017 (ending on June 30, 2017)

| | Q4 2015 | Q1 2016 | Q2 2016 | Q3 2016 | Q4 2016 | Q1 2017 | Q2 2017 |
|---|---|---|---|---|---|---|---|
| **Revenue** | **106.9** | **141.4** | **150.1** | **146.8** | **158.7** | **205.3** | **230.1** |
| Cost of sales | (51.3) | (63.3) | (63.7) | (62.6) | (67.7) | (87.1) | (93.4) |
| Fulfilment expenses | (47.9) | (57.6) | (60.0) | (59.1) | (61.8) | (76.9) | (85.9) |
| Adding back: Share-based compensation expense included in cost of sales and fulfilment expenses | 1.0 | (0.3) | 0.3 | 0.5 | (0.3) | 0.3 | 0.0 |
| **Contribution margin** | **8.8** | **20.2** | **26.7** | **25.6** | **28.9** | **41.6** | **50.8** |
| Adding back: Fixed and overhead expenses included in cost of sales and fulfilment expenses | 5.0 | 8.6 | 9.7 | 10.3 | 11.7 | 14.9 | 15.9 |
| **Contribution margin excluding fixed and overhead expenses** | **13.8** | **28.7** | **36.5** | **35.9** | **40.6** | **56.6** | **66.7** |
| **Contribution margin** | **8.8** | **20.2** | **26.7** | **25.6** | **28.9** | **41.6** | **50.8** |
| Marketing expenses | (48.7) | (41.6) | (38.9) | (39.9) | (37.0) | (64.6) | (58.5) |
| General and administrative expenses | (12.0) | (7.5) | (7.3) | (8.2) | (7.7) | (9.3) | (11.2) |
| Other operating income and expenses | 0.4 | (1.4) | (1.2) | (0.2) | (0.9) | (0.1) | (1.3) |
| Adding back: Depreciation and amortization | 0.3 | 0.7 | 1.1 | 1.1 | 1.5 | 1.9 | 1.9 |
| Adding back: Share-based compensation included in marketing and G&A expenses | 15.0 | 1.8 | 0.8 | 0.9 | (1.7) | 0.8 | 0.7 |
| Adding back: Other special items | 1.8 | 0.5 | 0.3 | 0.2 | 0.6 | 0.1 | 0.7 |
| **Adjusted EBITDA** | **(34.3)** | **(27.3)** | **(18.4)** | **(20.5)** | **(16.3)** | **(29.6)** | **(16.9)** |

Source: Prospectus for the public offering of HelloFresh on October 23, 2017

**EXHIBIT 4**  Non-financial indicators between the first quarter of 2015 (ending on March 31, 2015) and the second quarter of 2017 (ending on June 30, 2017)

| | Q1 2015 | Q2 2015 | Q3 2015 | Q4 2015 | Q1 2016 | Q2 2016 | Q3 2016 | Q4 2016 | Q1 2017 | Q2 2017 |
|---|---|---|---|---|---|---|---|---|---|---|
| **Group** | | | | | | | | | | |
| Revenue (€ mln) | 45.4 | 67.1 | 85.5 | 106.9 | 141.4 | 150.1 | 146.8 | 158.7 | 205.3 | 230.1 |
| Active customers (th. persons) | 289 | 408 | 542 | 621 | 786 | 812 | 844 | 857 | 1,160 | 1,251 |
| Orders (mln) | 1.1 | 1.5 | 1.9 | 2.3 | 3.0 | 3.1 | 3.0 | 3.2 | 4.2 | 4.7 |
| Orders per customer | 3.68 | 3.67 | 3.50 | 3.75 | 3.85 | 3.83 | 3.58 | 3.77 | 3.62 | 3.74 |
| Meals (mln) | 7.7 | 10.9 | 13.7 | 17.0 | 22.0 | 22.7 | 22.2 | 23.9 | 30.6 | 33.7 |
| Average order value (€) | 42.73 | 44.75 | 45.01 | 45.92 | 46.80 | 48.25 | 48.53 | 49.12 | 48.85 | 49.17 |
| **USA** | | | | | | | | | | |
| Revenue (€ mln) | 13.0 | 22.8 | 31.8 | 36.1 | 61.5 | 71.5 | 74.3 | 79.5 | 120.1 | 143.3 |
| Active customers (th. persons) | 92 | 143 | 198 | 218 | 328 | 382 | 413 | 432 | 714 | 796 |
| Orders (mln) | 0.3 | 0.4 | 0.6 | 0.7 | 1.1 | 1.3 | 1.3 | 1.4 | 2.2 | 2.7 |
| Orders per customer | 2.81 | 2.99 | 3.00 | 3.02 | 3.34 | 3.36 | 3.21 | 3.22 | 3.14 | 3.40 |
| Meals (mln) | 1.7 | 2.8 | 3.9 | 4.3 | 7.5 | 8.9 | 9.2 | 9.7 | 15.4 | 18.3 |
| Average order value (€) | 50.61 | 53.46 | 53.46 | 54.81 | 56.08 | 55.74 | 56.04 | 57.10 | 53.54 | 53.03 |
| **International** | | | | | | | | | | |
| Revenue (€ mln) | 32.4 | 44.2 | 53.7 | 70.8 | 79.9 | 78.6 | 72.4 | 79.2 | 85.2 | 86.8 |
| Active customers (th. persons) | 197 | 265 | 344 | 403 | 458 | 430 | 431 | 425 | 446 | 455 |
| Orders (mln) | 0.8 | 1.1 | 1.3 | 1.7 | 1.9 | 1.8 | 1.7 | 1.8 | 2.0 | 2.0 |
| Orders per customer | 4.09 | 4.04 | 3.79 | 4.15 | 4.21 | 4.25 | 3.94 | 4.33 | 4.39 | 4.34 |
| Meals (mln) | 6.0 | 8.1 | 9.7 | 12.7 | 14.5 | 13.9 | 12.9 | 14.2 | 15.2 | 15.4 |
| Average order value (€) | 40.20 | 41.28 | 41.16 | 42.42 | 41.51 | 43.00 | 42.67 | 43.12 | 43.48 | 43.93 |

Source: Prospectus for the public offering of HelloFresh on October 23, 2017

**EXHIBIT 5** Investors and funding prior to the IPO of HelloFresh

**Part A: Funding and valuation throughout the years**

| Period end date | Ending share capital | Share capital issued | Equity stake issued | Proceeds (estimate) | Equity value estimate | Investors (if known) |
|---|---|---|---|---|---|---|
| December 31, 2011 | 32,457 | - | 59.5% | 2,500 | 4.2 | Rocket Internet |
| December 31, 2012 | 46,820 | 14,363 | 30.7% | 4,004 | 13.1 | Vorwerk Ventures and others |
| December 31, 2013 | 56,184 | 9,364 | 16.7% | 7,743 | 46.5 | - |
| December 31, 2014 | 69,415 | 13,231 | 19.1% | 24,998 | 131.1 | Insight Ventures, Phenomen Ventures and others |
| September 30, 2015 | 84,276 | 14,861 | 17.6% | 110,002 | 623.8 | Rocket Internet |
| December 31, 2015 | 125,005,120 | 3,600,576 | 2.9% | 75,001 | 2,603.9 | Baillie Gifford |
| December 31, 2016 | 126,983,480 | 1,035,672 | 0.8% | 21,573 | 2,645.1 | - |
| June 30, 2017 | 132,436,643 | 5,453,163 | 4.1% | 85,700 | 2,081.3 | Qatar Investment Authority and others |

Source: Prospectus for the public offering of HelloFresh on October 23, 2017, and author's calculations

**Part B: HelloFresh's shareholder structure immediately prior and after the IPO**

| Shareholder | Holdings prior to the IPO | Holdings after the IPO |
|---|---|---|
| Rocket Internet SE | 58.59% | 47.51% |
| Jeff Horing/Insight Ventures | 18.66% | 15.13% |
| Phenomen Ventures LP | 8.84% | 7.17% |
| Vorwerk & Co. KG | 4.43% | 3.59% |
| Qatar Investment Authority | 3.34% | 2.71% |
| Other shareholders | 5.62% | 4.56% |
| Treasury shares | 0.52% | 0.42% |
| Public float | 0.00% | 18.91% |
| | 100.00% | 100.00% |
| Number of shares issued | 133,128,752 | |
| Treasury shares | (692,109) | |
| Number of shares outstanding | 132,436,643 | |

Source: Prospectus for the public offering of HelloFresh on October 23, 2017

**EXHIBIT 6**  Accounting and non-financial data of Blue Apron, Inc

| | Q1 2015 | Q2 2015 | Q3 2015 | Q4 2015 | Q1 2016 | Q2 2016 | Q3 2016 | Q4 2016 | Q1 2017 |
|---|---|---|---|---|---|---|---|---|---|
| Revenue ($ mln) | 48.6 | 73.3 | 102.3 | 116.7 | 172.1 | 201.9 | 205.5 | 215.9 | 244.8 |
| Cost of sales (excl. depreciation and amortization) ($ mln) | (37.6) | (55.0) | (83.7) | (87.0) | (112.5) | (127.3) | (145.6) | (147.2) | (168.5) |
| Marketing expenses | (8.4) | (12.8) | (16.0) | (14.2) | (25.4) | (32.0) | (49.6) | (37.1) | (60.6) |
| Total operating expenses | (55.9) | (82.6) | (121.6) | (127.7) | (169.1) | (196.4) | (242.8) | (241.8) | (296.5) |
| Profit or loss | (7.3) | (9.3) | (19.4) | (11.0) | 3.0 | 5.5 | (37.4) | (26.1) | (52.2) |
| Adjusted EBITDA ($ mln) | (6.7) | (8.5) | (18.3) | (9.4) | 5.0 | 8.0 | (34.6) | (22.0) | (46.3) |
| Active customers (th. persons) | 213 | 242 | 247 | 272 | 649 | 766 | 907 | 879 | 1,036 |
| Orders (mln) | 0.8 | 1.2 | 1.8 | 2.0 | 2.9 | 3.4 | 3.6 | 3.7 | 4.3 |
| Orders per customer | 3.9 | 4.1 | 4.3 | 4.6 | 4.5 | 4.4 | 4.0 | 4.2 | 4.1 |
| Average order value ($) | 57.77 | 58.74 | 58.01 | 59.21 | 59.28 | 59.40 | 57.12 | 58.78 | 57.23 |

Source: Prospectus for the public offering of Blue Apron on June 19, 2017

# CASE

# Spotify's direct-listing IPO[1]

**IVEY** | Publishing

On the morning of April 3, 2018, Jennifer Wang, a portfolio manager with the hedge fund Super Tech, which focused on growing technology companies, was contemplating an investment in music streaming service Spotify Technology SA (Spotify). The company had planned an unusual direct listing that day on the New York Stock Exchange (NYSE). Unlike typical initial public offerings (IPOs), which used investment banks as underwriters to help firms sell shares in their transition to becoming public companies, Spotify's direct listing would instead have simply made the company's shares eligible for pubic trading on an exchange, but no capital would be raised. Wang wondered whether her fund should invest in Spotify and if so, what maximum price and investment horizon it should accept. She needed to do her own analysis to establish what she felt was a fair value for Spotify's stock, and her task was complicated by recent equity market turmoil.

## Music streaming

The music industry included songwriters, performance artists, talent managers, record labels, music broadcast entities (e.g., terrestrial radio, Internet radio, and television), and the live performance segment. The product—recorded songs developed and recorded by artists—was sourced and curated primarily by three major record labels: Sony BMG, Universal Music Group, and Warner Music Group. Together, these three labels controlled 80 per cent of the market for popular music.[2] These labels signed artists and coordinated the process that produced, manufactured, distributed, and marketed artists' performed songs. Songs were marketed—introduced to the public—when they were featured on broadcast media. Artists were paid royalties for their songs based on a statutory rate in the United States. Recording artist mechanical royalties[3] were set at US$0.08[4] for each song of five minutes or less in length and $0.0155 per minute for each song that was more than five minutes long. Record labels generally negotiated artist contracts that paid a percentage of this statutory rate

---

[1]This case has been written on the basis of published sources only. Consequently, the interpretation and perspectives presented in this case are not necessarily those of Spotify or any of its employees.
[2]Heather McDonald, "The Big Three Record Labels," The Balance, November 13, 2017, accessed February 27, 2018, https://www.thebalance.com/big-three-record-labels-2460743.
[3]A mechanical royalty arises when music is sold or streamed. In contrast, performance royalties arise when music is performed publicly. Streaming services like Spotify pay both mechanical and performance royalties.
[4]All currency amounts are in US$ unless specified otherwise.

(e.g., 75 per cent). After various promotional and touring costs, artists could receive a net 10 per cent royalty on physical record sales and 5–8 per cent on sales from Internet downloads.[5]

Music streaming was a way for users to consume audio content without having to download the files to their devices. Typically, music streaming required users to have a streaming application (app) and wireless access to the Internet. Prior to music streaming, users had to download audio files in various formats such as MP3, WMA, or AAC. Unlike downloaded music, music streamed was not saved to a user's hard drive. Instead, the audio files were delivered in small packets, buffered, and played almost simultaneously (see **Exhibit 1**).[6]

The major players in the music streaming industry included Spotify, Apple Inc. (Apple), Google LLC (Google); and Amazon.com, Inc. (Amazon) (see **Exhibit 2**). As of February 2018, Spotify had 140 million active users of its free service and an additional 70 million paid subscribers in 61 countries.

Apple had dominated the digital download industry following the launch of its iTunes Store in 2003. In 2015, it launched Apple Music, which offered streaming services to consumers at a price of $9.99 a month for individuals and $14.99 a month for families of up to six users.[7] It had a catalogue of 45 million songs and was available in 115 countries. As of February 2018, Apple Music had 30 million subscribers in the United States and 36 million globally. It was growing 5 per cent per month in the United States (faster than Spotify's 2 per cent per month)[8] and was expected to surpass Spotify in the U.S. market by the summer of 2018.[9]

Google Play Music was Google's music streaming service. It allowed users to listen to customized Internet radio station streams for free and had a paid service with a 40 million-song library.[10] Google Play Music had about 7 million subscribers in total in July 2017. Google also operated another video and song streaming service: YouTube Red. Both Google Play Music and YouTube Red cost users $10 per month.[11]

Amazon had two music streaming services—Prime Music and Amazon Music Unlimited—with a combined 16 million paid subscribers. Prime Music, available to Amazon's Prime members, allowed users to stream over two million songs without ads. Amazon Music Unlimited had tens of millions of songs in its library and was available to Prime members for $7.99 a month and to other customers at $9.99 a month.[12]

## Spotify's background

Daniel Ek and Martin Lorentzon founded Spotify on April 23, 2006, in Stockholm, Sweden. They launched the public beta version of the Spotify music streaming site in the spring of 2007,[13] and the company was officially launched on October 7, 2008. Ek was the firm's founder and chief executive officer (CEO), and Lorentzon was its co-founder and chair of the board. Other key executives included Barry McCarthy, the chief financial

[5]Lee Ann Orbringer, "How Music Royalties Work," HowStuffWorks, May 24. 2003, accessed February 27, 2018, https://entertainment.howstuff-works.com/music-royalties6.htm.

[6]Mark Harris, "What Is Streaming Music?," Lifewire, February 8, 2018, accessed February 27, 2018, https://www.lifewire.com/what-is-stream-ing-music-2438445.

[7]Caitlin McGarry, "Apple Music Turns iTunes into a Streaming Service," MacWorld, June 8, 2015, accessed February 27, 2018, https://www.macworld.com/article/2932738/apple-music-turns-itunes-into-a-streaming-service.html.

[8]Anne Steele, "Apple Music on Track to Overtake Spotify in U.S. Subscribers," *Wall Street Journal*, February 5, 2018, accessed February 27, 2018, https://www.wsj.com/articles/apple-music-on-track-to-overtake-spotify-in-u-s-subscribers-1517745720.

[9]Andrew Liptak, "Apple Music Is Set to Surpass Spotify in Paid US Subscribers This Summer," The Verge, February 4, 2018, accessed Febuary 27, 2018, https://www.theverge.com/2018/2/4/16971436/apple-music-surpass-spotify-us-subscribers.

[10]Ara Wagoner, "Google Play Music: Everything You Need to Know!," Android Central, January 11, 2018, accessed February 27, 2018, https://www.androidcentral.com/google-play-music.

[11]Jonathan Vanian, "Google Play Music and YouTube Red May Merge," *Fortune*, July 27, 2017, accessed February 27, 2018, http://fortune.com/2017/07/27/google-play-music-youtube-red/.

[12]Hugh McIntyre, "Report: Amazon Is the Third-Largest Company in On-Demand Streaming Music," *Forbes/Media & Entertainment* (blog), October 27, 2017, accessed February 27, 2018, https://www.forbes.com/sites/hughmcintyre/2017/10/27/report-amazons-prime-music-is-the-third-biggest-on-demand-streaming-music-platform/#ec7efbb46ba3; and "Amazon Music Unlimited," Amazon, accessed February 27, 2018, https://www.amazon.com/gp/dmusic/promotions/AmazonMusicUnlimited.

[13]Rasmus Fleischer, "Writing the Early History of Spotify," Copyriot, June 14, 2017, accessed March 28, 2018, https://copyriot.se/2017/06/14/writing-the-early-history-of-spotify-excerpt-from-a-forhcoming-book/.

officer; Chris Maples, the managing director of U.K. operations; and Kate Vale, the managing director and sales director for Australia and New Zealand.[14] In August 2009, when Spotify was valued at $250 million and had 75 employees, its owners included Bolag Andel Rosello (Lorentzon), which held 28.6 per cent; Instructus (Ek) at 23.3 per cent; Northzone Ventures at 11.9 per cent; Enzymix Systems (F. Hagnö) at 5.8 per cent; Sony BMG at 5.8 per cent; Universal Music at 4.8 per cent; Warner Music a 3.8 per cent; Wellington IV Tech at 3.8 per cent; Creandum II LP at 3.5 per cent; Swiftic (Strigéus) at 2.6 per cent; Creandum II KB at 2.4 per cent; EMI at 1.9 per cent; Merlin at 1.0 per cent; and SBH Capital (B. Hagnö) at 0.8 per cent.[15]

On February 22, 2018, Spofity revealed that the shareholders of its ordinary shares included Ek (25.7 per cent); Lorentzon (13.2 per cent); Sony Music Entertainment Ltd. (5.7 per cent); entities affiliated with Technology Crossover Ventures (5.4 per cent); Tiger Global Management LLC (6.9 per cent); and Tencent Holdings Limited (7.5 per cent).[16]

Spotify's "freemium" business model offered two services to customers. The first was a basic, free-to-use music streaming service with limited functionality (i.e., a limited number of song skips was allowed, the sound quality was average, and listeners could not access songs offline) and advertising content interspersed between songs. The premium service was priced at $9.99 a month ($5.00 for students), had higher functionality, and did not contain advertising. This premium service also allowed users to listen to songs offline (i.e., to save the songs to their devices) and had enhanced sound quality, with song bitrates increased to 320 kilobits per second.[17] Within the premium service was a family option for up to five members of the same household, priced at $14.99 a month.[18]

Spotify paid out 70 per cent of its revenues to copyright holders; principally, the big record labels. Its focus on negotiating and establishing a system for royalty payments set it apart from its major competitors, such as Grooveshark, and allowed it to avoid infringement lawsuits. However, paying out the majority of its revenues in royalties meant that the firm had t continually seek capital as it grew (see Exhibit 3) and that it had never posted a profit. By September 2016, Spotify had paid out a cumulative total of $5 billion in royalties to rights holders, an in June 2017, it announced plans to pay more than $2 billion in guaranteed royalties over the next two years.[19]

## ACQUISITIONS, FUNDING, AND FINANCIAL PERFORMANCE

In March 2014, Spotify purchased The Echo Nest Corporation, a music intelligence firm, for €49.7 million.[20] Echo Nest's capabilities included understanding how users accessed music: it had developed software tools to curate and drive music discovery for users. Other firms Spotify acquired between 2013 and 2017 included Soundtrap AB, Niland API, Mediachain, MightyTV, Sonalytic, CrowdAlbum, Seed Scientific, Tunigo, Preact, and Cord Project Inc., each for an undisclosed sum.[21] These acquired firms focused mainly on technology that identified songs and their creators (or rights holders), blockchain data solutions that connected apps to media,[22] and software that created better-quality personalized song recommendations.

[14]"Company Overview of Spotify Limited," Bloomberg, accessed February 28, 2018, https://www.bloomberg.com/research/stocks/private/people.asp?privcapld=49444968.

[15]Michael Arrington, "This Is Quite Possibly the Spotify Cap Table," Tech Crunch, August 7, 2009, accessed February 27, 2018, https://techcrunch.com/2009/08/07/this-is-quite-possibly-the-spotify-cap-table/.

[16]Spotify Technology SA, *Form F-1 Registration Statement as Filed with the United States Securities and Exchange Commission on February 28, 2018*, 147, accessed March 29, 2018, https://www.sec.gov/Archives/edgar/data/1639920/000119312518063434/d494294df1.htm#494294_20.

[17]Ulyssestone, "Spotify's Latest Statement on Sound Quality and Bitrate," Spotify Classical Playlists (blog), September 23 2011, accessed February 27, 2018, www.spotifyclassical.com/2011/09/spotifys-latest-statement-on-sound.html.

[18]"Premium for Family," Spotify, accessed February 27, 2018, https://support.spotify.com/us/account_payment_help/premium_for_family/premium-for-family/.

[19]Peter Kafka, "Spotify Has Guaranteed to Pay Big Music Labels Billions over the Next Two Years," Recode, June 15, 2017, accessed February 27, 2018, https://www.recode.net/2017/6/15/15807382/spotify-revenue-2016-financials-guarantee-payment-universal-merlin.

[20]€ = EUR = euro; €1.00 = US$1.22 as of April 2018.

[21]"Acquisitions: Spotify," Crunchbase, accessed February 27, 2018, https://www.crunchbase.com/search/acquistions/field/organizations/num_acquisitions/spotify.

[22]"Building a More Connected World for Creators and Audiences," Mediachain, accessed February 27, 2018, www.mediachain.io/.

On March 29, 2016, Spotify announced it was raising $1 billion in convertible debt from a group of investors including the private equity firm TPG, the hedge fund Dragoneer Investment Group LLC, and clients of the Goldman Sachs Group Inc. The annual interest payment on the debt would be 5 per cent per year and would increase by one percentage point every six months until Spotify went public or the rate reached 10 per cent, whichever came first. In addition, the debt was convertible into equity at a 20 per cent discount to Spotify's share price if an IPO were held within a year of the closing of the deal. The discount would continue to increase by 2.5 percentage points every six months after that initial year.[23] Spotify added the $1 billion to its $600 million in cash on hand. Prior to raising this current round of convertible debt, Spotify had raised $1 billion from investors such as Founders Fund; Accel Partners; Technology Crossover Ventures; and Kleiner, Perkins, Caufield and Byers.[24]

In December 2017, private trades in Spotify stock valued the firm at above $19 billion.[25] This was an increase from the $16 billion valuation accorded to Spotify in the fall of 2017. Further, in early December 2017, Tencent Music Entertainment, a subsidiary of the Chinese tech giant Tencent, purchased stock in the firm, valuing Spotify at $20 billion. Some of the Spotify shares in the transaction came from Spotify's convertible debt placement: TPG and Dragoneer were allowed to convert their debt into equity at a $10 billion valuation and then sell it to Tencent at a $20 billion valuation. The amount of debt converted was not made public.[26]

According to Spotify's annual income statements, balance sheets, cash flow statements, and segment information (see Exhibits 4–7), the company generated revenues of €4,090 million in 2017 and had a net loss of €1,233 million. Its revenues had grown 52.2 per cent, from €1,940 in 2015 to €2,952 in 2016, and another 38.6 per cent from 2016 to 2017. Its net loss had grown 134.3 per cent, from €230 million in 2015 to €539 million in 2016, and another 129.1 per cent from 2016 to 2017.

## DISPUTES AND CRITICS

In October 2014, Taylor Swift's album 1989 was missing from Spotify's playlist, and Swift publicly removed the rest of her song catalogue in November 2014. She stated,

> [A]ll I can say is that music is changing so quickly, and the landscape of the music industry itself is changing so quickly, that everything new, like Spotify, all feels to me a bit like a grand experiment. And I'm not willing to contribute my life's work to an experiment that I don't feel fairly compensates the writers, producers, artists, and creators of this music. And I just don't agree with perpetuating the perception that music has no value and should be free.[27]

Spotify playfully responded with a promoted playlist entitled "What to Play While Taylor's Away."[28] By June 2017, Swift, seemingly interested in earning some of the royalties being paid to music streaming artists, put her full playlist back on Spotify.[29] A member of another band, Radiohead, had announced in 2013 that "I feel like as musicians we need to fight the Spotify thing," and the band kept its music off of the site.[30] But Radiohead relented, and its music was on Spotify by mid-2016.[31]

[23]Douglas MacMillan, "Spotify Raises $1 Billion in Debt Financing," *Wall Street Journal*, March 29, 2016, accessed February 27, 2018, https://www.wsj.com/articles/spotify-raises-1-billion-in-debt-financing-1459284467.

[24]Ibid.

[25]Reuters, "Spotify Price Tag Rises ahead of Filing for NYSE Listing, Value Sits around US$19 Billion: Sources," *Financial Post*, December 14, 2017, accessed March 29, 2018, http://business.financialpost.com/technology/spotify-price-tag-rises-ahead-of-filing-for-nyse-listing-value-sits-around-us19-billion-sources.

[26]Theodore Schleifer and Peter Kafka, "How Spotify Solved a $1 Billion Debt Problem that Will Help It IPO," Recode, January 3, 2018, accessed February 27, 2018, https://www.recode.net/2018/1/3/16847786/spotify-tag-tencent-debt-dragoneer-ipo-music-streaming.

[27]Kaitlyn Tiffany, "A History of Taylor Swift's Odd, Conflicting Stances on Streaming Services," The Verge, June 9, 2017, accessed February 27, 2018, https://www.theverge.com/2017/6/9/15767986/taylor-swift-apple-music-spotify-statements-timeline.

[28]Ibid.

[29]Hilary Weaver, "Taylor Swift Gives In, a Little, to Spotify," *Vanity Fair, Vanities* (blog), November 7, 2017, accessed February 27, 2018, https://www.vanityfair.com/style/2017/11/taylor-swift-gives-in-to-streaming-services.

[30]Stuart Dredge, "Thom Yorke Calls Spotify 'The Last Desperate Fart of a Dying Corpse,'" *Guardian*, October 7, 2013, accessed February 27, 2018, https://www.theguardian.com/technology/2013/oct/07/spotify-thom-yorke-dying-corpse.

[31]Amy X. Wang, "Radiohead Surrendered to Spotify—But May Have Won the War," Quartz, June 17, 2016, accessed February 27, 2018, https://qz.com/704210/one-of-the-biggest-opponents-of-spotify-is-ready-to-surrender-but-it-may-have-won-the-war/.

In late December 2017, Spotify was sued by Wixen Music Publishing Inc. (Wixen). Wixen was alleging that Spotify was using thousands of songs without a license and without compensating the music publisher and was seeking $1.6 billion in damages—or $150,000 per song. According to Wixen, while Spotify had signed deals with the music labels to acquire rights to sound recordings of songs, it had failed to acquire the rights for the song compositions. The Wixen lawsuit would be the fourth outstanding lawsuit against Spotify, and the biggest. Others, by songwriter Bob Gaudio and Bluewater Music Services Corporation, collectively represented a few thousand song compositions and, potentially, hundreds of millions of dollars in damages if the maximum of $150,000 for statutory damages were awarded.[32]

Spotify had already settled one lawsuit alleging song composition infringement. In May 2017, Spotify paid $43 million to settle a class-action lawsuit initiated by a group of songwriters who had accused the streaming service of using their songs without their permission and failing to pay royalties on the music.[33]

There were potentially tens of millions of copyrighted song compositions. In statements it made to the United States Copyright Office, Spotify indicated that it was attempting to locate and identify the owners of these songs. In reaching deals with the major publishers, Spotify relied on Harry Fox Agency to advise it on its compliance on the issue of song licenses.[34]

## PREPARATIONS FOR DIRECT LISTING

In July 2017, Spotify executives met with the U.S. Securities and Exchange Commission to explore the process of going public via an IPO (see **Exhibit 8**). By this time it had raised $1 billion in a convertible note and had hired three investment banks to assist with the IPO process: Goldman Sachs Group Inc., Morgan Stanley, and Allen & Company LLC.[35] The private discussions progressed, but no IPO was held in 2017.

On February 28, 2018, Spotify fielded a prospectus to sell share on the NYSE. Rather than going public via a traditional IPO process, Spotify was planning a direct listing after regulatory filings were approved. There would be no investor road show (i.e., presentations by management to analysts and potential investors) before the IPO date, and there would be no quiet period during which analysts, issuers, company insiders, and other parties would be restricted from discussing or promoting the stock. There would also be no stock sales to selected clients coordinated by investment banks. Pundits believed that the major reason Spotify was seeking to list its shares was because of the convertible debt terms.

On March 15, the company live-streamed an unusual investor day event that included a playlist of music such as "I'm Waiting for the Man," by The Velvet Underground, which announced the appearance of CEO Ek, and ending with "Closing Time," by Semisonic. Senior executives presented a vision for the company, and the chief financial officer discussed some of the company's financial aspects.[36] Spotify prioritized growth—particularly in mobile, podcasts, and cars—over profits in the short term. Spotify positioned itself in the "discovery" business, as opposed to the "access" business of its competitors. In order to reach as wide an audience as possible, Spotify said its free, ad-supported tier would remain. According to the head of research and development, this offered "Something for nothing. It's the greatest value proposition in the history of the world." CEO Ek defended the direct listing by claiming, "I think the traditional model for taking a company public isn't a good fit for us."[37] It was also revealed that the shares would start trading on April 3.

[32]Eriq Gardner, "Spotify Hit with Two Lawsuits Claiming 'Staggering' Copyright Infringement," Hollywood Reporter, July 18, 2017, accessed February 27, 2018, https://www.hollywoodreporter.com/thr-esq-spotify-hit-two-lawsuits-claiming-staggering-copyright-infringement-1021771.

[33]Sherisse Pham, "Spotify Sued for $1.6 Billion over Tom Petty, Doors Songs," CNN Tech, January 3, 2018, accessed February 27, 2018, http://money.cnn.com/2018/01/03/technology/spotify-lawsuit-wixen-songs/index.html.

[34]Gardner, op. cit.

[35]Lucas Shaw, "SEC Is Studying Spotify's Plan to Bypass IPO in NYSE Listing," Bloomberg, August 21, 2017, accessed February 27, 2018, https://www.bloomberg.com/news/articles/2017-08-21/sec-is-said-to-study-spotify-plan-to-bypass-ipo-in-nyse-listing.

[36]Maureen Farrell and Austen Hufford, "Spotify Sets April 3 as First Trading Day," *Wall Street Journal*, March 15, 2018, accessed March 29, 2018, https://www.wsj.com/articles/spotify-sets-april-3-as-first-trading-day-1521154370); and "Live Analysis: Spotify's IPO Investor Day," *Wall Street Journal*, March 152018, accessed March 29, 2018, htttps://www.wsj.com/livecoverage/spotify-ipo?mod=djemalertNEWS.

[37]Maureen Farrell, op. cit.

Spotify's listing was already being called a non-IPO, since the company would start trading directly and would not be raising any cash or selling shares in the event. It would pay equity capital market fees of $30 million in total to Goldman Sachs Group Inc., Morgan Stanley, and Allen & Company LLC. These three banks would assist Spotify with the listing.[38] The banks could engage in price stabilization following the listing, but they would not have a so-called *greenshoe* option, which would have allowed them as underwriters to buy an additional 15 per cent of shares, to facilitate stabilization. The direct listing would also not include a lock-up period for insider; this meant that selling volume in the early days of secondary trading would be very unpredictable and could be large.

## SPOTIFY'S VALUATION

Two common approaches to valuing companies included the discounted cash flow (DCF) analysis and the use of market multiples from comparable firms and recent transactions, such as the ratio of enterprise value to earnings before interest, taxes, depreciation, and amortization (EBITDA). Wang needed a list of peers and key data to estimate Spotify's value using multiples analysis from comparable firms (see Exhibit 9). She initially selected firms with a range of sizes and implied values but wondered whether she should narrow the set. DCF analysis started with an estimate of a firm's free cash flows over a set number of years; then, those cash flows were discounted by the firm's cost of capital to arrive at an estimate of the overall firm value. Interest-bearing debt was subtracted to arrive at an estimate of the equity value.

On March 26, Spotify released guidance that indicated it expected revenue to rise by 22–27 per cent annually in the first quarter of 2018, to between €1.1 billion and €1.15 billion ($1.37 billion to $1.43 billion), and by 20–30 per cent over the full year of 2018, to between €4.9 billion and €5.3 billion ($6.1 billion to $6.6 billion). Commentators noted that sales growth was forecast to decelerate relative to 2017 growth.[39]

In estimating Spotify's equity value using DCF analysis, Wang carefully reviewed the popular blog and analysis of well-known New York University professor and valuation expert Aswath Damodaran.[40] She used some of his DCF model assumptions, modified with her own assessment, to estimate free cash flows for the next 10 years. She used the 2017 revenue base of €4,090 million and assumed annual growth of 25 per cent for 2018–2022, followed by growth of 20 per cent in 2023, 15 per cent in 2024, 11 per cent in 2025, 8 per cent in 2026, and 5 per cent in 2027. She estimated that Spotify's annual "steady-state" growth rate beyond the next 10 years would be 3 per cent, but she wanted to test a growth rate of 5 per cent as part of her sensitivity analysis.

To determine a discount rate for her analysis, Wang assumed a market risk premium of 5 per cent. Because Spotify was no yet being publicly traded, she compiled data on peer firms to determine an appropriate beta (see Exhibit 9). She noted that Spotify did not have any outstanding interest-bearing debt. Given tax-loss carryforwards, she assumed Spotify would not pay any taxes through 2022 and would then face a 25 per cent tax rate. She assumed there were 178.11 million shares outstanding. Among other assumptions (see Exhibit 10), for simplicity, she assumed a valuation date of December 31, 2017 for discounting purposes.

## ECONOMIC AND MARKET CONDITIONS

The U.S. economy recorded real gross domestic product growth of 2.6 per cent in the fourth quarter of 2017, down from the third-quarter 2017 growth of 3.2 per cent.[41] The Economic Intelligence Unit forecast growth for the U.S. economy in 2018 and 2019 of 2.3 per cent a year. In January 2018, the Federal Reserve kept its target

---

[38]Greg Roumeliotis and Liana Baker, "Spotify Makes Confidential Filing for U.S. IPO: Source," Reuters, January 3, 2018, accessed February 27, 2018, https://www.reuters.com/article/us-spotify-ipo/spotify-makes-confidential-filing-for-u-s-ipo-source-idUSKBN1ES1IP.

[39]Eric Jhonsa, "As Spotify Nears Its IPO Tuesday, There's Some Good News and Some Bad News," TheStreet, April 2, 2018, accessed April 2, 2018, htttps://www.thestreet.com/story/14534795/1/spotify-new-guidance-is-a-very-mixed-bag.html.

[40]Aswath Damodaran, "Stream On: An IPO Valuation of Spotify," Musings on Markets (blog), March 16, 2018, accessed March 19, 2018, http://aswathdamodaran.blogspot.ca/2018/03/stream-on-ipo-valuation-of-spotify.html.

[41]"U.S. Economy at a Glance," Bureau of Economic Analysis, accessed February 27, 2018, https://www.bea.gov/newsreleases/glance.htm.

federal funds rate unchanged at 1.25–1.50 per cent.[42] This move had been expected by the market; pundits expected the Federal Reserve to continue increasing the federal funds rate as inflation rose.[43] In late March 2018, a 10-year U.S. government treasury bond was yielding 2.85 per cent. For comparison, the yields for the other Treasury bonds were as follows: 1.71 per cent for one month; 1.79 per cent for three months; 1.94 per cent for six months; 2.06 per cent for one year; 2.33 per cent for two years; and 2.64 per cent for five years.[44] In 2017, the Dow Jones Industrial Average had its best-performing year since 2013, advancing by 25 per cent. The Standard and Poor's (S&P) 500 index gained 19 per cent, and the Nasdaq Stock Market (NASDAQ) gained 28 per cent.[45] A pull-back in stocks in early February 2018 saw the Dow Jones briefly fall by more than 10 per cent from its high. In late March 2018, the Dow Jones had a price-to-earnings (P/E) ratio of 25.2 versus 21.1 a year earlier. It had a dividend yield of 2.24 per cent versus 2.36 a year earlier. The S&P 500 had a P/E ratio of 24.9 versus 24.5 a year earlier and a dividend yield of 1.93 versus 1.97 a year earlier.[46] The Chicago Board Options Exchange (CBOE) Volatility Index (VIX), a measure of anticipated market volatility, spiked from a muted level of below 10 at the beginning of 2018 to over 37 on February 5, before receding to just below 20 in late March.[47]

In 2017, there had been a global rebound in IPO activity, and 374 IPOs had raised $141.4 billion, up from 268 IPOs and $106.3 billion in 2016. IPO activity had yet to reach the highs of 2014, when $238.4 billion was raised from 413 issues.[48] However, on March 23, 2018, file-sharing service Dropbox Inc. went public and saw its first-day share price increase by 36 per cent on the same day that the S&P 500 dropped 2 per cent and both Facebook and Amazon fell by over 3 per cent.[49] In 2017, Snap Inc., which owned the popular social media app Snapchat, surged 44 per cent above its $17 listing price in the first day of trading, but it had struggled since July of that year to trade above the listing price.

## The investment decision

The direct-listing date had arrived, and it was decision time for Wang. She was still uncertain about whether her fund should invest in Spotify, particularly given the recent market turmoil. She needed to be comfortable that she would be buying in at a fair price, and she also wondered what the investment horizon should be.

Wang wondered whether Spotify's direct listing was simply a unique occurrence or whether this IPO might also disrupt the traditional underwriting process, just as Spotify had disrupted the music industry. More immediately, she also wondered what would happen in the short term. Stephen Gandel, writing for Bloomberg, captured investors' uncertainty about how Spotify's shares might trade on its first day when he said, "The shares could plunge, soar, or soar and then plunge, or plunge and soar, or not trade at all because of a mismatch between buyers and sellers."[50]

Early on April 3, 2018, the designated market maker on the NYSE, Citadel Securities LLC, set the "reference price" for Spotify's direct listing at $132. In a traditional IPO, the reference price was the offering price, but in the case of a direct listing, Citadel selected a reference price based on recent private market transactions and

[42]"United States Fed Funds Rate," Trading Economics, accessed February 27, 2018, https://tradingeconomics.com/united-states/interest-rate.
[43]Ibid.
[44]"Treasury Yield Curve," U.S. Department of the Treasury, accessed March 27, 2018, https://www.treasury.gov/resource-center/data-chart-center/interest-rates/Pages/Historic-Yield-Data-Visualization.aspx.
[45]Matt Egan and Danielle Winer-Bronner, "It Was an Epic Year for Stocks," CNN Money, December 29, 2017, accessed February 27, 2018, http://money.cnn.com/2017/12/29/investing/stocks-2017-wall-street/index.html.
[46]"P/Es & Yields on Major Indexes," *Wall Street Journal* Market Data Center, accessed March 29, 2018, http://www.wsj.com/mdc/public/page/2_3021-peyield.html.
[47]"CBOE Volatility Index," MarketWatch, accessed March 29, 2018, https://www.marketwatch.com/investing/index/vix/charts.
[48]Ryan Vlastelica, "IPO Activity Surged in 2017, Thanks to Pickup among Tech Stocks," MarketWatch, December 18, 2017, accessed February 27, 2018, https://www.marketwatch.com/story/ipo-activity-surged-in-2017-thanks-to-pick-up-in-tech-stocks-2017-12-15.
[49]Peter Cohan, "After 36% Pop, Don't Rush into Dropbox Stock," *Forbes/Investing* (blog), March 26, 2018, accessed March 29, 2018, https://www.forbes.com/sites/petercohan/2018/03/26/after-36-pop-dont-rush-into-dropbox-stock/#1918c84370c0.
[50]Stephen Gandel, "IPO of the Year Could Be Spotify's Non-IPO," Bloomberg Gadfly, January 8, 2018, accessed February 27, 2018, https://www.bloomberg.com/gadfly/articles/2018-01-08/spotify-set-to-blaze-ipo-trail-and-make-bankers-shudder.

independent valuations (see Exhibit 9). Wang settled down in front of her computer at 9:30 a.m., contemplating whether to place an order. Market clearing usually happened fairly quickly, so she knew she only had a bit of time to move ahead if she hoped to get in on the first clearing trade of the day. Given the size of the company and the novelty of the listing process, she suspected market clearing might take longer than expected. By 10:30 a.m., trading had not opened but Citadel Securities had posted an initial bid-ask range of $145–$155. A little after 11:00 a.m., the range moved up to $150–$160, suggesting that demand was strong. Now Wang wondered whether she should jump in or stay on the sidelines.

**EXHIBIT 1**  The evoluton of music streaming

The music streaming industry emerged around 2000 when a streaming format was created using Adobe's Flash application. The universal adoption of Flash meant that users did not need to download proprietary streaming formats based on Windows (Media Player) or Apple (QuickTime) in order to listen to or view streams of content. The first major company to commercialize music streaming was Pandora Internet Radio, an Internet-based radio station and music recommendation service. Later renamed Pandora Media, the company continued to focus on its business model of providing customized but non-interactive Internet radio stations to listeners, earning the majority of its revenues from advertising.

One of the earliest firms focused on the current interpretation of music streaming—defined as a service that allowed users to select customized playlists of songs and have the audio files played on their devices in real-time—was Grooveshark, which was launched in March 2006. Grooveshark allowed users to sell their MP3 files to each other via a proprietary peer-to-peer network. By April 2008, Grooveshark allowed users to select and play audio files without downloading an application.

One of the biggest issues that Grooveshark and other firms in the nascent industry faced was how to manage copyright infringement issues for music being played. The large record labels such as Universal Music Group, Sony Music Entertainment, and Warner Music Group alleged that Grooveshark allowed its users to upload and share music without paying royalties to copyright holders. Grooveshark was faced with a $17 billion lawsuit in 2011 and was shut down on May 1, 2015.

Total industry revenues from recorded music were $4.0 billion for the first half of 2017, up from $3.4 billion in the first half of 2016. Total revenues from streaming music services accounted for 62 per cent of the market in 2017, or $2.5 billion. This was up 48 per cent from the first half of 2016.

There were over 30.4 million consumers paying for streaming in the United States, resulting in $1.7 billion in paid streaming subscription revenues for the first half of 2017. This was up from $1.067 billion in the first half of 2016. In the same two periods, digital and customized radio revenues were $493 million and $407 million respectively, and ad-supported, on-demand music streaming revenues were $273 million and $199 million respectively.

The standard business model in music streaming was a "freemium" model that saw one group of users receive a free service with limited features and advertising, while other users paid for a premium service that had more features (e.g., users could fast forward or skip songs) and was ad-free. Spotify offered a $10 a month unlimited subscription service. Spotify paid about 70 per cent of total revenues to the record labels and other music rights holders. This equated to about $0.006 and $0.0084 every time a song was streamed.

---

Note: All currency amounts are in US$.

Sources: Created by the case authors using data from Mark Harris, "What Is Streaming Music?," Lifewire, February 8, 2018, accessed February 27, 2018, https://www.lifewire.com/what-is-streaming-music-2438445; Sam Parr, "How Pandora's Founder Convinced 50 Early Employees to Work 2 Years Without Pay," The Hustle, May 27, 2016, accessed February 27, 2018, https://thehustle.co/pandora-speech; Chris Morrison, "Grooveshark Offers P2P Music Downloads — But Is It Legal?," Venturebeat, December 5, 2007 accessed February 27, 2018, https://venturebeat.com/2007/12/05/grooveshark-offers-p2p-music-downloads-but-is-it-legal/; Brittany Spanos, "Grooveshark Shuts Down after Eight Years," Rolling Stone, May 1, 2015, accessed February 27, 2018, https://www.rollingstone.com/music/news/grooveshark-shuts-down-after-eight-years-20150501; Joshua P. Frielander, "News and Notes on 2017: Mid-Year RIAA Revenue Statistics," Recording Industry Association of America, accessed February 27, 2018, www.riaa.com/wp-content/uploads/2017/09/RIAA-Mid-Year-2017-News-and-Notes2.pdf, "How Is Spotify Contributing to the Music Business?," Spotify, November 3, 2014, accessed February 27, 2018, https://wayback.archive-it.org/all/20141103193456/http://www.spotifyartists.com/spotify-explained/.

**EXHIBIT 2**  Recording industry association of america statistics

### United States Estimated Retail Dollar Value
### (In US$ millions, net after returns)

| DIGITAL SUBSCRIPTION & STREAMING | 2016 | 2017 | % CHANGE 2016–2017 |
|---|---|---|---|
| Paid Subscription—Units, Millions | 20.2 | 30.4 | 50.60% |
| Paid Subscription—Dollar Value | $994.9 | $1,487.7 | 49.50% |
| Limited Tier Paid Subscription | %71.7 | $224.7 | 213.40% |
| On-Demand Streaming (Ad-Supported) | $199.3 | $273.2 | 37.10% |
| SoundExchange Distributions | $403.4 | $339.5 | −15.80% |
| Other Ad-Supported Streaming | $3.7 | $153.1 | 4021.20% |
| **Total Streaming Revenues** | **$1,673.0** | **$2,478.1** | **48.10%** |
| | | | |
| **DIGITAL PERMANENT DOWNLOAD** | | | |
| Download Single—Units, Millions | 412.5 | 316.2 | −23.4% |
| Download Single—Dollar Value | $496.6 | $384.6 | −22.6% |
| Download Album | $464.6 | $344.1 | −25.9% |
| Ringtones & Ringbacks | $21.4 | $16.7 | 22.0% |
| Other Digital | $10.9 | $11.7 | 7.3% |
| **Total Digital Download Revenues** | **$993.5** | **$757.0** | **−23.8%** |
| | | | |
| **TOTAL DIGITAL VALUE** | **$2,666.50** | **$3,235.10** | **21.3%** |
| Synchronization Royalties | $100.40 | $118.70 | 18.20% |
| | | | |
| **PHYSICAL** | | | |
| CD—Units Shipped, Millions | 38.6 | 35.2 | −8.6% |
| CD—Dollar Value | $443.5 | $430.6 | −2.9% |
| LP/EP | $176.1 | $181.7 | −3.2% |
| Music Video | $16.4 | $14.5 | −11.3% |
| Other Physical | $4.9 | $5.3 | 10.0% |
| **Total Physical Units** | **$46.8** | **$43.5** | **−7.2%** |
| **Total Physical Value** | **$640.8** | **$632.2** | **−1.3%** |
| | | | |
| **TOTAL DIGITAL AND PHYSICAL** | | | |
| Total Units | 515.1 | 402.2 | −21.9% |
| Total Value | $3,407.7 | $3,986.0 | 17.0% |

| % of Shipments | 2016 | 2017 |
|---|---|---|
| Physical | 19.0% | 16.0% |
| Digital | 81.0% | 84.0% |

Note: CD = compact disc; LP = long playing album; EP = extended playing album

Source: Created by the case authors using data from Joshua P. Friedlander, *2017 Mid-Year RIAA Shipment and Revenue Statistics,* 4, Recording Industry Association of America, 2017, accessed February 27, 2018, https://www.riaa.com/reports/2017-mid-year-riaa-shipment-revenue-statistics-riaa/.

**EXHIBIT 3**  Spotify funding round (in US$)

| Announced Date | Transaction Name | Number of Investors | Money Raised | Lead Investors |
|---|---|---|---|---|
| June 30, 2017 | Secondary Market—Spotify | 1 | | |
| July 28, 2016 | Secondary Market—Spotify | 3 | | |
| March 30, 2016 | Debt Financing—Spotify | 2 | $1 billion | |
| January 27, 2016 | Convertible Note—Spotify | 1 | $500 million | |
| January 21, 2016 | Secondary Market—Spotify | | | |
| November 1, 2015 | Secondary Market—Spotify | 1 | $150 million | |
| August 30, 2015 | Secondary Market—Spotify | 2 | | |
| June 10, 2015 | Series G—Spotify | 16 | $526 million | |
| November 25, 2014 | Secondary Market—Spotify | 2 | | |
| September 1, 2014 | Secondary Market—Spotify | 1 | | |
| January 1, 2014 | Secondary Market—Spotify | 1 | | |
| November 21, 2013 | Series F—Spotify | 1 | $250 million | TCV |
| November 15, 2012 | Series E—Spotify | 6 | $100 million | Goldman Sachs |
| January 1, 2012 | Secondary Market—Spotify | 1 | | |
| June 17, 2011 | Series D—Spotify | 5 | $100 million | Accel Partners |
| February 1, 2010 | Series C—Spotify | 1 | €11.6 million | Founders Fund |
| August 4, 2009 | Series B—Spotify | 3 | $50 million | Horizons Ventures |
| October 1, 2008 | Series A—Spotify | 5 | $21.6 million | |

Source: Adapted from "Spotify > Funding Rounds," Crunchbase, accessed February 27, 2018, https://www.crunchbase.com/organization/spotify/funding_rounds/funding_rounds_list.

**EXHIBIT 4**  Spotify consolidated statement of operations

**For the year ended December 31**

**(in € millions, except share and per share data)**

|  | 2015 | 2016 | 2017 |
|---|---|---|---|
| Revenue | 1,940 | 2,952 | 4,090 |
| Cost of revenue | 1,714 | 2,551 | 3,241 |
| **Gross profit** | **226** | **401** | **849** |
| Research and development | 136 | 207 | 396 |
| Sales and marketing | 219 | 368 | 567 |
| General and administrative | 106 | 175 | 264 |
|  | **461** | **750** | **1,227** |
| **Operating loss** | **−235** | **−349** | **−378** |
| Finance income | 36 | 152 | 118 |
| Finance costs | −26 | −336 | −974 |
| Share in earnings of associates and joint ventures | — | −2 | 1 |
| **Finance income/(costs) — net** | **10** | **−186** | **−855** |
| **Loss before tax** | **−225** | **−535** | **−1,233** |
| Income tax expense | 5 | 4 | 2 |
| **Net loss attributable to owners of the parent** | **−230** | **−539** | **−1,235** |
| **Net loss per share attributable to owners of the parent** | | | |
| Basic and diluted | −1.62 | −3.63 | −8.14 |
| **Weighted-average ordinary shares outstanding** | | | |
| Basic and diluted | **141,946,600** | **148,368,720** | **151,668,769** |

Source: Created by the case authors using data from Spotify Technology SA, Form F-1 Registration Statement as filed with the United States Securities and Exchange Commission on February 28, 2018, F-3, accessed March 29, 2018, https://www.sec.gov/Archives/edgar/data/1639920/000119312518063434/d494294df1.htm#rom494294_20.

**EXHIBIT 5** Spotify balance sheets

**As at December 31**
**(in € millions)**

| | 2015 | 2016 | 2017 |
|---|---|---|---|
| **Assets** | | | |
| **Non-current assets** | | | |
| Property and equipment | 81 | 85 | 73 |
| Intangible assets including goodwill | 73 | 80 | 162 |
| Investment in associates and joint ventures | 1 | 0 | 1 |
| Long-term investment | 0 | 0 | 910 |
| Restricted cash and other non-current assets | 21 | 23 | 54 |
| Deferred tax assets | 4 | 3 | 9 |
| | 180 | 191 | 1,209 |
| | | | |
| **Current assets** | | | |
| Trade and other receivables | 244 | 300 | 360 |
| Income tax receivable | 3 | 6 | 0 |
| Short-term investments | 0 | 830 | 1,032 |
| Cash and cash equivalents | 597 | 755 | 477 |
| Other current assets | 27 | 18 | 29 |
| | 871 | 1,909 | 1,898 |
| **Total assets** | 1,051 | 2,100 | 3,107 |
| | | | |
| Equity/(Deficit) and liabilities | | | |
| Equity/(Deficit) | | | |
| Share capital | 0 | 0 | 0 |
| Other paid in capital | 797 | 830 | 2,488 |
| Other reserves | 85 | 122 | 177 |
| Accumulated deficit | −653 | −1,192 | −2,427 |
| **Equity/(Deficit) attributable to owners of the parent** | 229 | −240 | 238 |
| | | | |
| **Non-current liabilities** | | | |
| Convertible notes | 0 | 1,106 | 944 |
| Accrued expenses and other liabilities | 16 | 10 | 56 |
| Provisions | 8 | 4 | 6 |
| Deferred tax liabilities | 0 | 0 | 3 |
| | 24 | 1,120 | 1,009 |

**EXHIBIT 5**  Spotify balance sheets (Continued)

### Current liabilities

| | | | |
|---|---:|---:|---:|
| Trade and other payables | 119 | 201 | 341 |
| Income tax payable | 5 | 6 | 9 |
| Deferred revenue | 92 | 149 | 216 |
| Accrued expenses and other liabilities | 485 | 673 | 881 |
| Provisions | 15 | 57 | 59 |
| Derivative liabilities | 82 | 134 | 354 |
| | **798** | **1,220** | **1,860** |
| **Total liabilities** | **822** | **2,340** | **2,869** |
| **Total equity/(deficit) and liabilities** | **1,051** | **2,100** | **3,107** |

Source: Created by the case authors using data from Spotify Technology SA, *Form F-1 Registration Statement as filed with the United States Securities and Exchange Commission on February* 28, 2018, F-5, accessed March 29, 2018, https://www.sec.gov/Archives/edgar/data/1639920/000119312518063434/d494294df1.htm#rom494294_20.

**EXHIBIT 6** Spotify cash flow statements

### For the year ended December 31
### (in € millions)

|  | 2015 | 2016 | 2017 |
|---|---|---|---|
| **Operating activities** | | | |
| Net loss | −230 | −539 | −1235 |
| Adjustments to reconcile net loss to net cash flows | | | |
| Depreciation of property and equipment | 26 | 32 | 46 |
| Amortization of intangible assets | 4 | 6 | 8 |
| Share-based payments expense | 28 | 53 | 65 |
| Impairment loss on trade receivables | 0 | 15 | 0 |
| Finance income | −36 | −152 | −118 |
| Finance costs | 26 | 336 | 974 |
| Income tax expense | 5 | 4 | 2 |
| Share in earnings of associates and joint ventures | 0 | 2 | −1 |
| Net foreign exchange (gains)/losses | −33 | 42 | −3 |
| Changes in working capital: | | | |
| Increase in trade receivables and other assets | −121 | −60 | −112 |
| Increase in trade and other liabilities | 251 | 245 | 447 |
| Increase in deferred revenue | 25 | 77 | 77 |
| Increase in provisions | 20 | 38 | 8 |
| Interest received | 2 | 5 | 19 |
| Interest paid | −1 | 0 | 0 |
| Income tax paid | −4 | −4 | 2 |
| **Net cash flows (used in)/from operating activities** | **−38** | **100** | **179** |
| **Investing activities** | | | |
| Business combinations, net of cash acquired | −7 | −7 | −49 |
| Investment in associates and joint ventures | −1 | −1 | 0 |
| Purchase of equipment | −44 | −27 | −36 |
| Purchase of intangibles | −5 | −3 | −10 |
| Purchase of short-term investments | 0 | −1,397 | −1,386 |
| Sales and maturities of short-term investments | 0 | 609 | 1,080 |
| Change in restricted cash | −10 | −1 | −34 |
| **Net cash flows used in investing activities** | **−67** | **−827** | **−435** |

**EXHIBIT 6**  Spotify cash flow statements (Continued)

### Financing activities

| | | | |
|---|---|---|---|
| Finance lease payments | −4 | −5 | −4 |
| Proceeds from issuance of convertible notes, net of costs | 0 | 861 | 0 |
| Proceeds from issuance of new shares, net of costs | 474 | 0 | 0 |
| Proceeds from issuance of warrants | 0 | 27 | 9 |
| Proceeds from exercise of share options | 6 | 33 | 29 |
| **Net cash flow from financing activities** | **476** | **916** | **34** |
| **Net increase in cash and cash equivalents** | **371** | **190** | **−222** |
| Cash and cash equivalents at January 1 | 206 | 597 | 755 |
| Net foreign exchange gains/(losses) on cash and cash equivalents | 20 | −32 | −56 |
| **Cash and cash equivalents at December 31** | **597** | **755** | **477** |

Source: Created by the case authors using data from Spotify Technology SA, *Form F-1 Registration Statement as filed with the United States Securities and Exchange Commission on February* 28, 2018, F-7, accessed March 29, 2018, https://www.sec.gov/Archives/edgar/data/1639920/000119312518063434/d494294df1.htm#rom494294_20.

**EXHIBIT 7**  Spotify segment information (in € millions)

| | 2015 | 2016 | 2017 |
|---|---|---|---|
| **Premium** | | | |
| Revenue | 1,744 | 2,657 | 3,674 |
| Cost of revenue | 1,492 | 2,228 | 2,868 |
| **Gross profit** | **252** | **429** | **806** |
| **Ad Supported** | | | |
| Revenue | 196 | 295 | 416 |
| Cost of revenue | 227 | 330 | 373 |
| **Gross loss** | **−31** | **−35** | **43** |
| **Consolidated** | | | |
| Revenue | 1,940 | 2,952 | 4,090 |
| Cost of revenue | 1,714 | 2,551 | 3,241 |
| **Gross profit** | **226** | **401** | **849** |

*Reconciliation of gross profit*

General expenditures, finance income, finance costs, taxes, and share in earnings of associates and joint ventures are not allocated to individual segments as these are managed on an overall group basis. The reconciliation between reportable segment gross profit and loss to consolidated loss before tax is as follows:

| | 2015 | 2016 | 2017 |
|---|---|---|---|
| **Segment gross profit** | **226** | **401** | **849** |
| Research and development | −136 | −207 | −396 |
| Sales and marketing | −219 | −368 | −567 |
| General and administrative | −106 | −175 | −264 |
| Finance income | 36 | 152 | 118 |
| Finance costs | −26 | −336 | −974 |
| Share in earnings of associates and joint ventures | — | −2 | 1 |
| **Loss before tax** | **−225** | **−535** | **−1,233** |

| | 2015 | 2016 | 2017 |
|---|---|---|---|
| *Revenue by country* | | | |
| United States | 741 | 1,173 | 1,577 |
| United Kingdom | 268 | 342 | 444 |
| Luxembourg | 1 | 1 | 3 |
| Other countries | 930 | 1,436 | 2,066 |
| | **1,940** | **2,952** | **4,090** |

**EXHIBIT 8**  NYSE listing standards and trading following ipos and direct listings

To list shares for trading on the New York Stock Exchange (NYSE) through a traditional firm-commitment initial public offering (IPO), which involved satisfying requirements of the *Securities Act* of 1933 and the *Securities Exchange Act* of 1934, a company had to demonstrate an aggregate market value of publicly held shares of at least US$40 million. That valuation determined as the offering price in the IPO multiplied by the number of shares to be outstanding after completion of the IPO. The offering price also had to exceed US$4.

A firm not previously completing an SEC registered public share offering might also list on the NYSE without contemporaneously selling securities and meeting all related legal requirements; this allowed public trading of shares previously created through private placements. For such "direct listings," the NYSE required a higher minimum number for the aggregate market value of publicly traded shares. The firm had to provide a valuation developed by an independent valuation agent. If the company's unregistered securities actively traded in a trading system for unregistered securities operated by a national securities exchange or registered broker dealer (e.g., a "private placement market" such as SharesPost), the NYSE required that the minimum of the independent agent valuation and the valuation implied from recent transactions in a private placement market be at least US$100 million. Under a NYSE rule change approved February 8, 2018, by the SEC, a firm could list on the NYSE without having recent trading in a private placement market if the independent agent valuation of the firm exceeded US$250 million.

The processes through which trading commenced on the NYSE for IPOs and direct listings were similar. Each firm selected a designated market maker (DMM), who was required to set the clearing price for the first trade on the exchange. That clearing price was based on orders to buy and sell received by the DMM. If the DMM anticipated that the clearing price would change by 5 per cent or more from a "reference price," it had to first publish a pre-opening indication of the clearing price to market participants. For traditional IPOs, the reference price was the IPO offering price; for direct offerings, the reference price was the recent price in a private placement market, if one existed, or the number implied by the independent valuation. The DMM might also publish order imbalance information. After publishing the pre-opening indication of the clearing price, it had to wait at least three minutes for the market to react before finalizing the opening price and commencing trading. The DMM could revise the pre-opening indication of a clearing price, in which case the waiting period could be extended. Once the DMM was satisfied that an opening price that would allow orderly clearing of trades had been identified and the requisite waiting period had passed, format trading could commence.

Although market clearing on the first day of trading for IPOs and direct listings looked similar, there were important differences in terms of how the firms got to that first trading day. In an IPO, the issuer retained investment banks to first conduct due diligence and prepare filing documents (S-1s for domestic issuers and F-1s for foreign issuers). Under the *Securities Exchange Act* of 193, domestic firms pursing a direct listing were required to file Form 10 with the SEC. Foreign firms were required to file Form 20-F(R). Firms could also register under the *Securities Act* of 1933 using Form S-1 or F-1. The issuer could use an investment bank to help prepare those documents and navigate the SEC approval process, but that was not required. While regulatory filings were being reviewed by the SEC, issuing firm executives, underwriters, and potential investors met at roadshows. The underwriters solicited indications of interest from investors and gained insights regarding an appropriate price. For a direct offering, there was no roadshow, so a potentially important first step in price discovery was missing.

There were two other important differences between IPOs and direct listings that could potentially have an effect on secondary market trading. First, IPOs generally included lockups that precluded certain insiders from trading for some period. Direct IPOs had no lockups, so the number of insiders trading was not limited. The resulting supply and demand imbalances in the early aftermarket could be large and unpredictable. A second important difference related to underwriter stabilization. In an IPO, underwriters were permitted to post stabilizing bids in order to prevent early price declines. Such stabilizing activities were possible for a direct IPO, should the filing firm retain an underwriter; however, the costs savings relative to an IPO could be significantly diminished, given the costs of stabilization and resulting legal liability. Stabilization would be more challenging in a direct offering compared to a traditional IPO, given features of share issuance. To facilitate stabilization in an IPO, the underwriter was permitted to oversell the offering using an overallotment (or *greenshoe*) option, Stabilizing bids could then be covered by the oversold shares. Since direct offerings involved no share sales, it was more costly (and risker) for the underwriter to post stabilizing bids.

---

Note: For an advisor to be considered independent, it could not control more than 5 per cent of the shares of the issuer. The advisor was also required to have not provided any investment banking services to the issuer within the past 12 months.

Sources: Created by the case authors using data from United States Securities and Exchange Commission, Release No. 34-820627: Self-Regulatory Organizations; New York Stock Exchange LLC; Notice of Filing of Amendment No. 3 and Order Granting Accelerated Approval of Proposed Rule Change, as Modified by Amendment No. 3, to Amend Section 102.01B of the NYSE Listed Company Manual to Provide for the Listing of Companies that List Without a Prior Exchange Act Registration and that Are Not Listing in Connection with an Underwritten Initial Public Offering and Related Changes to Rules 15, 104, and 123D, February 2, 2018, accessed February 27, 2018, https://www.sec.gov/rules/sro/nyse/2018/34-82627.pdf; Bob Bryan and Hollis Johnson, "Snap Just Went Public—Here's a Behind-the-Scenes Look at What a Typical IPO Is Like," Business Insider, March 2, 2017, accessed February 27, 2018, www.businessinsider.com/what-happens-during-an-ipo-on-nyse-snap-ipo-2017-3#and-then-comes-the-waiting-17 (for a description of the opening process for the E.L.F. IPO in 2016, in which the article indicated the average waiting time to market opening was approximately 11 minutes); Alan Jones, "Demystifying Direct Listing," PwC's Deals (blog), June 9 2017, accessed February 27, 2018, http://usblogs.pwc.com/deals/demystifying-direct-listings/; John C. Coffee Jr., "The Spotify Listing: Can an 'Underwriter-less' IPO Attract Other Unicorns?," CLS Blue Sky Blog, January 16, 2018, accessed February 27, 2018, http://clsbluesky.law.columbia.edu/2018/01/16/the-spotify-listing-can-an-underwriter-less-ipo-attract-other-unicorns/#_ednref1 (for a discussion of the differences between IPOs and direct listings and their relative pros and cons).

**EXHIBIT 9**  Key data from comparable firms (N US$)

| Company Name | Close Price (3/28/18) | Shares Outstanding | Market Capitalization | LTM[1] Net Debt | Total Enterprise Value | LTM Tangible Book Value[2]/ Share | LTM Total Revenue | LTM EBITDA | LTM1 Year Total Revenues Growth % |
|---|---|---|---|---|---|---|---|---|---|
| Alibaba Group Holding Limited | 178.91 | 2,569.5 | 459,705.2 | −15,074.3 | 456,971.0 | 9.38 | 36,081.5 | 14,222.7 | 57.71% |
| Amazon.com, Inc. | 1,431.42 | 484.1 | 692,960.7 | 13,161.0 | 706,121.7 | 22.70 | 177,866.0 | 15,039.0 | 30.80% |
| Apple Inc. | 166.48 | 5,074.0 | 844,721.7 | 45,247.0 | 889,968.7 | 26.01 | 239,176.0 | 74,174.0 | 9.65% |
| Baidu, Inc. | 223.10 | 348.2 | 77,675.0 | −11,997.8 | 68,388.2 | 42.96 | 13,485.5 | 4,361.8 | 20.21% |
| Comcast Corporation | 33.28 | 4,644.5 | 154,569.2 | 61,119.0 | 217,888.2 | −9.97 | 84,526.0 | 27,812.0 | 5.13% |
| eBay Inc. | 40.11 | 1,012.1 | 40,594.5 | 4,152.0 | 44,746.5 | 3.13 | 9,567.0 | 2,941.0 | 6.55% |
| Facebook, Inc. | 153.03 | 2,905.0 | 444,552.3 | −41,711.0 | 402,841.3 | 18.67 | 40,653.0 | 23,228.0 | 47.09% |
| Netflix, Inc. | 285.77 | 433.9 | 124,009.5 | 3,676.6 | 127,686.1 | −15.67 | 11,692.7 | 910.6 | 32.41% |
| Pandora Media, Inc. | 4.96 | 254.9 | 1,264.2 | −227.8 | 1,527.2 | 0.04 | 1,466.8 | −289.0 | 5.92% |
| The Walt. Disney Company | 98.54 | 1,503.7 | 148,172.2 | 21,414.0 | 174,522.2 | 3.29 | 55,704.0 | 16,912.0 | 0.96% |
| Time Warner Inc. | 94.20 | 779.9 | 73,462.0 | 21,123.0 | 94,621.0 | −8.49 | 31,271.0 | 9,081.0 | 6.66% |
| Twenty-First Century Fox, Inc. | 35.88 | 1,852.5 | 66,165.3 | 13,985.0 | 82,104.3 | −2.15 | 29,351.0 | 6,540.0 | 4.59% |
| Twitter, Inc. | 28.45 | 748.1 | 21,284.5 | −2,609.4 | 18,675.1 | 5.12 | 2,443.3 | 344.8 | −3.41% |
| Wayfair Inc. | 65.14 | 88.5 | 5,765.1 | −204.5 | 5,560.6 | −0.58 | 4,720.9 | −174.2 | 39.66% |

(continued)

**EXHIBIT 9** Key data from comparable firms (N US$) (Continued)

| Company Name | LTM EBIT Margin% | NTM Revenue[3] | NTM EBITDA[3] | 5 Year Beta | TEV/Total Revenues LTM - Latest | TEV/EBITDA LTM - Latest | P/TangBV LTM - Latest | NTM TEV/Forward Total Revenue (Capital IQ) | NTM TEV/Forward EBITDA (Capital IQ) |
|---|---|---|---|---|---|---|---|---|---|
| Alibaba Group Holding Limited | 31.30% | 50,077.4 | 21,196.8 | 2.58 | 13.10 | 44.20 | 19.70 | 9.13 | 21.56 |
| Amazon.com, Inc. | 2.30% | 233,498.4 | 26,976.2 | 1.55 | 4.00 | 47.00 | 63.10 | 3.02 | 26.18 |
| Apple Inc. | 26.90% | 263,346.4 | 80,278.7 | 1.18 | 3.70 | 12.00 | 6.40 | 3.38 | 11.09 |
| Baidu, Inc. | 18.50% | 15,953.0 | 4,214.0 | 1.77 | 5.20 | 16.30 | 5.40 | 4.29 | 16.23 |
| Comcast Corporation | 20.80% | 89,550.3 | 29,456.6 | 1.16 | 2.60 | 7.80 | NM[4] | 2.43 | 7.40 |
| eBay Inc. | 23.70% | 1,962.0 | 3,721.6 | 1.06 | 4.70 | 15.20 | 12.80 | 4.08 | 12.02 |
| Facebook, Inc. | 49.70% | 55,284.6 | 33,601.3 | 0.66 | 9.90 | 17.30 | 8.20 | 7.29 | 11.99 |
| Netflix, Inc. | 7.20% | 15,862.5 | 1,923.0 | 0.96 | 10.90 | 140.20 | NM | 8.05 | 66.40 |
| Pandora Media, Inc. | −23.00% | 1,505.8 | −98.2 | −0.40 | 1.00 | 0.00 | 111.40 | 1.01 | NM |
| The Walt. Disney Company | 25.30% | 58,771.3 | 17,847.8 | 1.31 | 3.10 | 10.20 | 30.00 | 2.97 | 9.78 |
| Time Warner Inc. | 26.90% | 32,566.3 | 9,448.4 | 0.92 | 3.00 | 10.60 | NM | 2.91 | 10.01 |
| Twenty-First Century Fox, Inc. | 20.40% | 31,296.1 | 7,492.9 | 1.26 | 2.80 | 12.60 | NM | 2.62 | 10.96 |
| Twitter, Inc. | 1.90% | 2,704.5 | 964.7 | 0.80 | 7.60 | 54.20 | 5.60 | 6.91 | 19.36 |
| Wayfair Inc. | −4.80% | 6,242.3 | −99.1 | 1.27 | 1.20 | 0.00 | NM | 0.89 | NM |

Notes: [1] LTM = last 12 months; EBITDA = earnings before interest, taxes, depreciation, and amortization; [2] Tangible book value = assets, net of goodwill and other intangibles, less liabilities; [3] NTM = next 12 months; NTM financials were consensus (average) analyst forecasts as compiled by Standard & Poor's Capital IQ; [4] NM = not measurable.
Source: Created by the case authors using data from "Spotify—Quick Comparable Analysis," Standard & Poor's Capital IQ, accessed March 29, 2018.

**EXHIBIT 10** Additional discounted cash flow assumptions

| Year | EBIT Margin* | Capital Expenditures Less Depreciation Less Increases in Working Capital** |
|------|------|------|
| 2018 | −2.08% | 255.63 |
| 2019 | −0.41% | 319.53 |
| 2020 | 1.26% | 399.41 |
| 2021 | 2.94% | 499.27 |
| 2022 | 4.61% | 624.08 |
| 2023 | 6.28% | 624.08 |
| 2024 | 7.95% | 561.68 |
| 2025 | 9.63% | 473.68 |
| 2026 | 11.30% | 382.39 |
| 2027 | 12.97% | 258.11 |

Notes: EBIT = earnings before interest and taxes; * EBIT as a percentage of revenue, as assumed in Damodaran's model; negative margins in 2018 and 2019; ** in € millions; as indicated in Damodaran's model as "reinvestment" in order to preserve the sales-to-capital ratio at 4.0.

Source: Case writer estimates and Aswath Damodaran, "Stream On: An IPO Valuation of Spotify," published in Musings on Markets (blog), March 16, 2018, accessed March 29, 2018, http://aswathdamodaran.blogspot.ca/2018/03/stream-on-ipo-valuation-of-spotify.html.

# The Air France–KLM merger

*We have always been convinced of the necessity of consolidation in the airline industry. Today, we announce a combination with KLM that will create the first European airline group, which is a milestone in our industry. This will bring significant benefits to customers, shareholders and employees. Capitalizing on the two brands and on the complementary strengths of both companies, we should, within SkyTeam, be able to capture enhanced growth opportunities.*

— Jean-Cyril Spinetta, Chairman and CEO of Air France

*KLM has been pointing out the need for consolidation in light of the challenges facing our industry, and we have not made it a secret we were looking for a strong European partner. Through this innovative partnership with Air France and our subsequent expected participation in the SkyTeam alliance, we are confident that we have secured a sustainable future for our company. Our valuable Schiphol hub will be an integral part of the dual hub strategy of the new airline group, allowing us to build on what KLM and its staff have achieved over nearly 85 years.*

— Leo van Wijk, President and CEO of KLM

On September 30, 2003, Air France and KLM Royal Dutch Airlines – two European airlines that provided international passenger and cargo airline services – issued a press release that announced their planned merger. The merger envisaged the creation of the leading European airline Air France– KLM. In 2003 both airlines were the primary national ("flag carrying") airlines in their home countries, France and the Netherlands. However, poor industry conditions put pressure on the airlines' growth and operating margins. In the fiscal year ending on March 31, 2003, Air France, the larger of the two airlines, reported an increase in total sales of slightly more than one percent to €12,687 million and a net profit of €120 million (€0.55 per share). KLM performed worse than Air France. In the same fiscal year, KLM reported a decrease in total sales of slightly less than one percent to €6,485 million and a loss (before extraordinary items) of €186 million (€3.97 per share).

For a number of years, KLM had been searching for a strategic partner, which seemed to be of essential importance given the deteriorating industry conditions. Initially, KLM attempted to form an alliance with the Italian flag carrier, Alitalia. However, this alliance soon appeared to be unsuccessful because of the poor functioning of Milan Malpensa Airport, an unexpected delay in the privatization of Alitalia, and cultural incompatibilities between the Italians and the Dutch.[1] After breaking with Alitalia, KLM continued to search for another partner. In early 2000 talks about joining forces with British Airways remained unfruitful, as KLM and its main shareholder, the Dutch state, were unwilling to hand over control to the British flag carrier.[2] In the second half of 2003, Air France came to the rescue.

Professor Erik Peek prepared this case. The case is intended solely as the basis for class discussion and is not intended to serve as an endorsement, source of primary data, or illustration of effective or ineffective management.

[1] "KLM Ends Venture with Alitalia, Imperiling US Airline Alliance," *Wall Street Journal*, May 1, 2000; "Alitalia Is Seeking Damages for Breakup with KLM," *Wall Street Journal*, August 2, 2000.
[2] "Europe's Flag Airlines: Going Nowhere," *Businessweek*, February 26, 2001.

# KLM Royal Dutch Airlines[3]

KLM Royal Dutch Airlines was founded in 1919, which, at the time of the merger, made it the oldest continuously operating airline in the world. Landmarks in the company's history were its very first scheduled flight to London in 1920, its first intercontinental flight to Jakarta (formerly Batavia) in 1924, and its operating scheduled flights to New York from 1946.

Over the years the core activities of KLM remained very much the same. The airline provided worldwide passenger and cargo transport, engineering and maintenance, and, in a later stage, charter and low-cost scheduled flights. KLM operated its charter and low-cost flights primarily through its subsidiaries Buzz and Transavia. In 1994 KLM served 153 cities in 81 countries on six continents and ranked eighth among the largest international airlines based upon ton-kilometre traffic on international flights. Nine years later KLM served 350 cities in 73 countries on six continents and ranked fifth among the largest international airlines.

In its prospectus from 1994, which accompanied the issuance of 18.5 million additional ordinary shares, the airline summarized its most important operating risks. First, the airline operated in an industry that was cyclical and highly competitive. The cyclical nature could have a strong adverse effect on KLM's profitability because, as every other airline, it had a high degree of operating leverage (high fixed-to-variable cost ratio). Second, the airline's profitability depended strongly on exchange rate fluctuations as well as on fluctuations in aircraft fuel prices. Third, because in many parts of the world airlines and international air traffic were highly regulated, KLM's operations could be affected by foreign governments' actions of protectionism.

Within this uncertain economic environment, KLM's corporate objective was "… to position itself as an airline operating worldwide from a European base that provides quality service for passengers and cargo shippers at competitive cost levels." The strategy that KLM used to attain this objective was to:

- *Increase customer preference.* KLM focused on achieving a high level of customer satisfaction, for example, by closely monitoring customer demand and by expanding its "Flying Dutchman" frequent flyer program.
- *Strengthen its market presence around the world.* KLM strengthened its market presence in the world's major air transportation markets by expanding its hub-and-spoke operations at Schiphol Airport and by creating alliances with other European, American, and Asian airlines. For example, in 1989 KLM had acquired a 20 percent stake in Northwest Airlines, a North American airline having its operations hubs in Boston, Detroit, and Minneapolis. This acquisition helped KLM to gain better access to American destinations. The alliance between KLM and Northwest implied that both airlines operated as a joint venture on transatlantic flights, while KLM did all their marketing in Europe and Northwest in the United States.
- *Reduce its costs to at least an internationally competitive level.* During the early 1990s KLM launched a restructuring programme that aimed to reduce its costs and increase its productivity. The programme included spinning off noncore business units, network optimization, eliminating the first class section on intercontinental flights, redesigning business processes, and acquiring more efficient aircraft. KLM launched a second restructuring program, Focus 2000, in 1996, and a third one, Baseline, in 2000.

In 2003 KLM's shares were listed on the Amsterdam Euronext Exchange and on the New York Stock Exchange. Since early in KLM's history, the Dutch state had been KLM's primary shareholder. The state's ownership interest in KLM gradually decreased over the years, from 38 percent of the votes in 1994 to 14 percent in 2003. Nonetheless, the state remained able to effectively influence the airline's major (non-operating) decisions through various mechanisms. First, up to the date of the merger, the state had the option to obtain a 50.1 percent voting interest to prevent any undesirable accumulation of share ownership in the hands of others. This option was especially important to prevent a country imposing restrictions on KLM exercising international traffic rights. Because such traffic rights were the result of bilateral treaties between governments and tied to domestically owned airlines, countries could deny these rights to KLM if in their view the airline was no longer in Dutch

---

[3]Material in this section is drawn from KLM's 1994 prospectus, its 2002/2003 Annual Report, and its corporate website.

hands. Second, the articles of association offered the state the right to appoint a majority of the Supervisory Board. Third, the state held the majority of KLM's priority shares, through which it had a veto over important decisions such as the issuance of shares, payments of stock dividends, and changes in the articles of association.

## The merger agreement[4]

During 2002, while renewed negotiations between British Airways and KLM reached deadlock, KLM representatives also started to meet with Air France representatives to talk about the possibilities of cooperation. Parallel to these meetings, Air France's North American alliance partners, Continental Airlines and Delta Airlines, discussed possible cooperation with KLM's North American alliance partner, Northwest Airlines. In August 2002 the three North American airlines signed a ten-year agreement to improve schedule connections between the airlines and to share codes, frequent flyer programs, and airport lounges. After the signing of the agreement, the three airlines encouraged Air France and KLM to start similar cooperation in Europe. However, because the French state was planning to privatize Air France (i.e., reduce its shareholdings to a level below 20 percent), Air France and KLM envisaged a closer form of cooperation. Initially, both parties discussed the option of creating a dual listed company structure. Air France and KLM would keep their separate listings but cross-hold 50 percent of the shares of each other's operating subsidiaries. Because Air France had a substantially greater market value than KLM, Air France would also become the direct owner of 52 percent of KLM's shares and certain of its assets would be excluded from the transaction. However, the idea of creating a dual listed company structure appeared too complex, and both airlines soon opted for a simpler alternative, which they presented to their shareholders on September 30, 2003.

The alternative proposal implied that the former shareholders of KLM and Air France became shareholders of the publicly listed holding company Air France–KLM, which would hold 100 percent of the shares of two private operating companies, Air France and KLM. Former Air France shareholders would receive one Air France–KLM share for every Air France share that they held. In exchange for ten KLM shares, former KLM shareholders would receive 11 Air France–KLM shares plus ten Air France–KLM warrants. The warrants had a strike price of €20.00, were exercisable after 18 months and had an exercise period of three-and-a-half years. Three warrants gave the warrant holder the right to purchase two Air France–KLM shares.

Based on Air France's closing price on September 29, 2003, the estimated value of one warrant was equal to €1.68 (according to the Air France–KLM merger announcement). This warrant value was based on the following assumptions:

- The September 29 Air France–KLM share price was €13.69.
- The risk-free rate equaled 2.89 percent.
- The estimated future volatility of the Air France–KLM share price was 40 percent.
- Estimated dividends per share were €0.096, €0.144, and €0.188 during the exercise period (based on I/B/E/S estimates).

Based on the Air France–KLM share price of €13.69 and a warrant value of €1.68, the total value of the offer for KLM shareholders equaled €16.74 per share (11/10 × €13.69 + €1.68), which implied a premium of 40 percent over KLM's closing share price on September 29, 2003. After the share exchange, former KLM shareholders would own 19 percent of the ordinary shares (and voting rights) of Air France–KLM. The share exchange offer would commence only after approval from the EU and US competition authorities, and if no third party announced a public offer for either KLM's shares or Air France's shares.

The transaction between Air France and KLM was not a full-blown merger. The two private operating companies, Air France and KLM, remained separate entities, in particular because it was important to preserve

---

[4]Material in this section is drawn from the Air France–KLM merger prospectus (April 5, 2004).

the two established brand names. Further, the Dutch state retained the option to acquire a 50.1 percent voting interest in KLM (the operating company) if necessary to preserve KLM's landing rights.

## Motivation for the merger

Airline industry analysts tend to distinguish two phases of evolution in a deregulated airline industry – that is, the expansion phase and the consolidation phase. To illustrate, in the 1970s the US government deregulated the US airline industry, which led to a serious expansion of supply from 1978 to 1990. In this expansion phase, US airlines responded by cutting their costs, but their operating margins experienced a secular decline. In the early stages of consolidation, from 1986 onwards, mergers resulted in the elimination of several brands, but did not restrict or reallocate capacity. Since the mergers initially raised costs, profit margins remained under pressure. In the later stages of the consolidation phase, US airlines reallocated their capacity from unprofitable (geographical) areas to profitable (geographical) areas. This significantly improved US airlines' profit margins. In the mid-1990s the European airline industry was in a different stage of development than the US airline industry. At that time, European airlines had just entered into the earlier stages of consolidation by creating alliances. However, alliances made it difficult to reallocate capacity and improve profitability. Furthermore, government interference hindered efficient allocation of capacity.[5]

During the late 1990s and the early 2000s, the profit potential of the European airline industry changed substantially. At the end of the 1990s, Europe had an increasing number of large and small airlines, many airports close together, and most governments supporting loss-making national airlines. Government support resulted in very few unprofitable companies leaving the market. At the same time, many airlines started downgrading their product by offering low levels of service on short-haul flights to compete on costs. All major airports had capacity constraints, which (in combination with their slot trading system that favoured current slot-owners) made access to established airports difficult for new entrants. However, new entrants, such as Ryanair and easyJet were moving to smaller, local airports to avoid the capacity constraints of the major airports. These new entrants further intensified the competition (on costs) in the European airline industry. Finally, the use of web booking systems made the market more transparent. Customers were able to easily compare prices, which substantially reduced switching costs.

After 2000 the profit potential of the European airline industry improved slightly. The European Commission had allowed governments to cover insurance risks and costs faced by airlines after the September 11, 2001, terrorist attacks; however, other forms of government support were no longer allowed. Further, after September 2001, many airlines significantly reduced (fixed) capacity, which reduced competition. Finally, more and more countries signed bilateral "open skies" agreements with the United States, implying that European airlines could fly to any place in the United States, at any fare, at any time (but only from their home countries). In early 2004 a European agreement with the United States was being negotiated, implying that, for example, the German national airline Lufthansa would be allowed to fly from Milan to New York. Nonetheless, KLM's return on equity during the fiscal years ending in 2001, 2002, and 2003 was 3.7, −7.8, and −24.1 percent, respectively.

**Exhibit 1** reports KLM and Air France's motivation for entering into the merger agreement, as it was set out at the merger presentation on September 30, 2003.

---

[5]See "Global Airlines: Survival of the Fittest," *Goldman Sachs Global Research,* September 22, 1997.

## Response of the Dutch Investor Association

In early 2004 the Dutch Investor Association (VEB; Vereniging voor Effectenbezitters) began to oppose the merger proposal. The VEB was of the opinion that during the months following the merger, KLM's value had increased substantially due to changed circumstances, which would justify a higher takeover price. KLM shareholders had to decide before May 5, 2004 (just before KLM's publication of its 2003/2004 financial statements) whether they wanted to offer their shares to Air France. The VEB claimed that KLM shareholders should be able to take the latest financial results into account when making their decision. Air France and KLM, supported by a Dutch court decision on April 29, 2004, refused this claim. **Exhibit 2** sets out the VEB's objections in detail.

On May 6, 2004, KLM announced that net profit, operating profit, and revenues for the fiscal year 2003/2004 were €24 million, €120 million, and €5,870 million, respectively.

## QUESTIONS

1 Evaluate the motivating factors behind the Air France–KLM merger. Does the merger effectively address the strategic challenges faced by KLM and Air France?
2 Calculate the present value of the synergies. To what extent is the actual market response to the merger announcement consistent with the estimated value of the expected performance improvements?
3 To what extent can the premium be justified by the expected performance improvements (as presented in **Exhibit 1**)?
4 Critically analyze each of the VEB's objections to the proposed takeover price (as presented in **Exhibit 2**). Do you have any evidence that Air France shareholders agree with the VEB?
5 If you were a shareholder of KLM, would you support this merger proposal?

**EXHIBIT 1** Appendix to the offer document

# Strategic rationale of the transaction

The airline industry is fragmented and its current competitive structure, with national carriers for each individual country, is an inheritance from a former era. This has contributed to low profitability and lack of value creation for shareholders. The need for structural changes and consolidation in Europe is widely accepted, but has not yet commenced as a consequence of regulatory and political constraints.

The single European market and its current enlargement to some 455 million inhabitants reinforce the need for consolidation.

The evolution of the European regulatory framework highlighted by (i) the November 2002 European Court of Justice ruling and (ii) the mandate given in June 2003 to the European Commission to negotiate the open sky agreement with the US, now creates an attractive environment for a value creating combination.

If commercial alliances have contributed over the past years to initiate the first steps towards consolidation, deeper cooperation is now needed to generate significant and sustainable synergies.

The proposed transaction between Air France and KLM is the first significant move in this context and will create a leading airline group in Europe with aggregated revenues of EUR 19.2 billion (2002/03 fiscal year).

The combination with KLM is a major step in Air France's strategy. In parallel, KLM's strategy over the years has consistently been built on two pillars: the strengthening of its own organization, as well as the participation in a global alliance, for which it seeks a strong European partner. The combination with Air France is the achievement of this strategy.

The transaction will benefit from the complementarities of the two airlines' operations:

- Two reputable and strong brands that will be further strengthened.
- Two operational hubs (Paris CDG and Amsterdam Schiphol) which are among the most efficient in Europe and provide significant development potential.
- Two complementary networks both in medium and long haul. In medium haul Air France has a strong position in Southern Europe and KLM has developed a strong position in Northern and North Eastern Europe, and both will be able to expand their positions in Central and Eastern Europe. The long haul networks currently consist of 101 destinations of which only 31 are common (essentially the world's largest cities with high traffic volumes).
- A combined network of 226 destinations with 93 new destinations for KLM passengers and 48 new destinations for Air France passengers.
- A strong presence in cargo where Air France and KLM are the fourth and eleventh largest in the world respectively but with complementary capabilities and expertise.

- A strong combination in the field of aircraft maintenance, creating one of the largest MRO providers worldwide.
- SkyTeam will eventually become the second largest global airline alliance with its partners being able to offer passengers a more truly worldwide network.

## Synergies

Potential synergies arising from the proposed transaction have been thoroughly assessed and quantified by a joint working group of Air France and KLM who have reviewed the feasibility and quantum of the synergies and their build-up over time.

### SALES AND DISTRIBUTION

By coordinating the two sales organizations, the new group will have an improved presence around the world and will be able to offer a wider range of products to passengers. Cost savings could be achieved by coordinating the sales structures of the two companies. A joint negotiation position with catering and ground-handling partners could also lead to additional benefits.

### NETWORK/REVENUE MANAGEMENT AND FLEET

By full code sharing, harmonizing the flight schedules, and optimizing common management revenue policy, the two airlines will be able to offer more destinations, a larger number and more convenient connections for passengers, and improved sales performance.

### CARGO

The offering of an improved product through a more extensive network in combination with coordinated freighter planning, should lead to an increase of revenues. Cost savings should also be possible by more efficient hub handling.

### ENGINEERING AND MAINTENANCE

The two airlines will be able to integrate purchasing of stock, to create centres of excellence in engineering and optimize the use of existing E&M [engineering and maintenance] platforms.

### IT

Converging the IT applications used by both airlines should generate considerable cost savings in the medium term.

### OTHER

Optimizing and harmonizing other activities such as simulator utilization and joint purchasing of goods should deliver further cost savings.

The identified potential synergies are expected to result in an annual improvement of the combined operating income (earnings before interest and tax) of between EUR 385 million and EUR 495 million, following a gradual implementation over a period of five years, with further upward potential thereafter.

Approximately 60 percent of potential synergies are expected to be derived from cost savings.

This does not include additional expected synergies from marketing cooperation with respective partners. Furthermore, any improvement from the common fleet policy and lower capital expenditure requirements have not yet been determined and have not been taken into account in these estimates.

## KLM RESTRUCTURING PLAN

The KLM restructuring plan, which was announced in April 2003, with targeted annual operating income improvement of EUR 650 million by April 1, 2005, are additional to the synergies mentioned above. The KLM management remains fully committed to achieving this objective.

## Estimated value of the synergies

### Synergies by activity (Euro amounts in mn)

| Activity | Main actions | Year 3 (2006/2007) | Year 5 (2008/2009) |
|---|---|---|---|
| Sales/Distribution | Coordination of sales structures; Sales cost improvements; Handling and catering. | €40 | €100 |
| Network, revenue management, fleet | Network/scheduling management; Revenue management harmonization; optimization of fleet utilization; Coordinated management. | €95–130 | €30–195 |
| Cargo | Network optimization; Commercial alignments; support services. | €35 | €35 |
| Maintenance | Procurement; Insourcing; pooling (stocks etc.). | €25 | €60–€65 |
| IT systems | Progressive convergence of IT systems | €20 | €50–€70 |
| Other | Procurement synergies | €5–€10 | €10–€30 |
| Total cost savings | | €220–€260 | €385–€495 |

### Total expected synergies per year (Euro amounts in millions)

| | 2004/2005 | 2005/2006 | 2006/2007 | 2007/2008 | 2008/2009 | Long-term |
|---|---|---|---|---|---|---|
| Total savings | 65–75 | 110–135 | 220–260 | 295–370 | 385–495 | >600 |

**EXHIBIT 2**  Press release of the Dutch Investor Association (VEB): "Air France shareholders get it on the cheap," April 19, 2004[a]

After two postponements on 22 March and 31 March, KLM and Air France announced they intend to pursue their merger plans unchanged. This means that Air France will make an offer worth €784 million, whereby each KLM share will be worth 1.1 Air France shares plus a warrant. Far too low an offer.

Half a year has gone by since the merger was announced on 30 September 2003. In the intervening six months a number of circumstances have emerged that would justify a higher bid. The prospectus and the bid offer show that KLM is worth considerably more than was apparent until now. There are other questions that remain unanswered that would provide a clearer view of KLM's value. Here are ten reasons why the Air France bid is far too low.

### NET EQUITY PER SHARE IS €34

KLM net worth (assets after debt) is €1,501 million, or €34.14 per share. At an Air France share price of €15 the offer amounts to €17.80 per KLM share. The bid is thus equivalent to just over its net equity value. Air France shareholders will obtain half KLM for free.

A further point is that KLM owns significant intangible assets that are not valued on the balance sheet. This includes the KLM brand name and the landing rights owned by KLM which have a definite economic value. Since these important intangibles are not valued at all in the balance sheet, a price in excess of net equity value stands to reason.

### THE BID IS WORTH A MERE SEVEN TIMES EARNINGS (2004) AND FIVE TIMES EARNINGS (2005)

Analysts forecast a substantial increase of profit for fiscal 2004/2005 and the following fiscal. They predict earnings in the €100–€110 million range in 2004. In the following year they could reach the €150–€170 million range. This equates to €2.50 and €3.60 per share. The bid is thus seven times expected earnings for 2004 and five times expected earnings for 2005. Compared with other listed companies, whose average p/e ratio is 14, this is a very low valuation. Prices paid for other airline companies score are 17 times 2004 earnings and 11 times 2005.

### REAL ESTATE ASSETS INCLUDE A SURPLUS VALUE OF AT LEAST €248 MILLION, OR €5.60 PER SHARE

The bid documentation (p. F-158) prepared by Air France and KLM reveals significant hidden reserves in KLM's stock of real estate. These are valued in KLM's balance sheet at €331 million. Price at purchase was €728 million, 55 percent of which has been written off. According to KLM these assets are now worth €248 million more. Put against 44.2 million shares on the market this corresponds to a surplus value

of €5.60 per share. Specialists say the surplus value is closer to the €450–€650 million bracket!

### UNLIKE AIR FRANCE, KLM HAS ACCUMULATED A PENSION FUND SURPLUS OF €2.4 BILLION

According to French GAAP (Generally Accepted Accounting Principles) KLM equity is worth about €3 billion, roughly double the equity according to Dutch GAAP and four times the value of the bid. Some significant modifications have been made to arrive at these figures. On the one hand the pension fund reserve has been added to shareholder equity. This is worth €2.4 billion. Against that a negative adjustment has to be made for contingent tax liabilities falling upon KLM of €811 million. French GAAP values equity per share at €69.

### THE EXCHANGE RATIO IS PARTLY THE RESULT OF OPERATING RESULTS IN 2002/2003 AND 2003/2004: THESE WERE SERIOUSLY DEPRESSED BY THE SARS HEALTH SCARE AND THE CRISIS IN IRAQ

KLM has been looking for a partner for years. There were several previous rounds of negotiation with British Airways. In 2001 a merger attempt with Alitalia failed. Processing the consequences of this failure was unpleasant. KLM was obliged to pay Alitalia €275 million, which was equivalent to €6 per KLM share. The media reported that KLM had refused an out of court settlement worth €50 million. The Alitalia costs appear as a charge in the 2002/2003 accounts. Last year operating results came under pressure as a result of the SARS health scare which significantly reduced passenger traffic to and from Asia. The first quarter of calendar 2003 put heavy pressure on both sales and profit as a result of the coming war in Iraq and the danger of terrorist attacks directed at aircraft. It is obvious that these factors depressed the price negotiations which clearly took account of current operational results. KLM would have been far better served by sitting it out until it could enter into negotiations from a more comfortable and more profitable situation.

### THE LAST TWO QUARTERS SHOW RESULTS SIGNIFICANTLY ABOVE THE ESTIMATES OF ANALYSTS

The merger and the price were announced on 30 September. In the intervening period KLM published its quarterly results, first on 23 October 2003 (Q2) and then on 22 January 2004 (Q3). KLM's results exceeded – even significantly – expectations. This has led to KLM anticipating a slightly positive result for 2003/2004 – despite SARS, Iraq, the low dollar and a poor economy. These improvements alone would have justified an adjustment of the price.

[a] Reprinted with permission from the Vereniging van Effectenbezitters.

The earnings trend on the French side is less attractive. In the last nine months Air France net profit has fallen from €143 million to €80 million.

## AIR FRANCE GETS CONTROL OF KLM WITHOUT PAYING A PREMIUM

Air France will be the masters in the newly merged company. Previous Air France shareholders will hold onto an 81 percent share in the company. The CEO will be a Frenchman, Jean-Cyrille Spinetta. In both the Executive and the Supervisory Boards the Dutch will be in a minority. Of the eight Executive Board Directors four will be Dutch and four will be French. Although both companies pay lip-service to the mantra of a merger, it is in reality a takeover. Air France pitches a bid priced in its own shares for KLM and gains control. It might be that the changing of the guard will take place in stages to allow landing rights to be preserved, but after three years this formal structure will be dissolved as well. In cases of takeover, a control premium payable in addition to the standard economic valuation is the norm. Air France is not paying it.

## KLM HAS STARTED A COST SAVINGS PROGRAMME WORTH €650 MILLION, BUT KLM SHAREHOLDERS WILL GET ONLY 19 PERCENT OF THE BENEFIT

On 8 May 2003 KLM announced a cost cutting programme designed to yield €650 million in savings. The major share of these cost reductions has still to be carried out. On 22 January KLM announced that €125 millions worth of savings had been achieved. Clearly, successful execution of the programme will lead to better profitability at KLM. If the cost reduction programme is implemented in full and half of the benefits are given back to the customer in the form of reduced fares, operational results will go up by €325 million. Stripping out 35 percent corporation tax, this leads to a contribution of €211 million to the bottom line. If the transaction goes through, KLM shareholders will own 19 percent of the joint company, as a result of which only 19 percent of these benefits will flow to KLM shareholders. But every single percentage point of the improvement will have come from the business they used to own.

## KEY FACTORS SHOW THAT KLM SHOULD OBTAIN OVER 30 PERCENT OF THE MERGED AIRLINE

On a total passengers carried basis KLM is the world's tenth largest airline and Air France is number three. Taken by sales, Air France with revenues worth €12.7 billion is about twice the size of KLM (revenues of €6.5 billion). A revenue criterion thus leads to a 66:34 ratio: KLM shareholders deserve a one-third share in the merged airline. Other measures of size lead to the same ratio. Based on four criteria – sales, number of aircraft, shareholder equity, and headcount – an average ratio comes out at 69:31. The figure means that the KLM figure should be 63 percent higher than the agreed 19 percent. If there are no signs of structural differences in profitability between Air France and KLM – and nothing has emerged to show this – these yardsticks can be used to make a reliable estimate of what the share swap ratio should be.

## BENEFITS OF SYNERGY

The bid prospectus (p. 50) lists significant benefits of synergy the two companies expect to achieve if the merger goes through. Year One factors for €75 million in synergy benefits, rising to €450 million in Year Five. Clearly KLM shareholders should be compensated for these synergies in the form of a proper price offer, or share swap. It is scarcely an adequate response to claim that, because Air France has brought out an offer priced in shares, KLM shareholders will thereby participate in the benefits. For whatever reasons that they may consider relevant – let us say, for issues of control – KLM shareholders may decide to decline the offer to become Air France shareholders. If they accept the merger and do decide to become Air France shareholders they will share in the benefits of synergy to the tune of a mere 19 percent.

## KEY DATES

Above are ten reasons why the offer for KLM is far too low. In terms of procedure there are two important dates. On Monday 19 April an Extraordinary General Meeting of Shareholders will be held. Information about the offer will be given, questions will be answered, and a proposal to change the Articles of Association – which will permit the merger – will be put to the vote. At 11 am on 3 May the offer will close. Prior to that KLM shareholders will have to decide whether they want to accept or reject the bid. If less than 70 percent of the shares are tendered the transaction will be a dead letter. If less than 95 percent of shares are tendered, KLM's share listing will be maintained.

We have tried to shed light on the true worth of KLM. It is significantly higher than the current bid offer. This will not dispense KLM shareholders from taking their own decision. That can be based on other decisions such as enthusiasm over the prospects of Air France, a need for cash or whatever.

Peter Paul de Vries
Chairman of Vereniging van Effectenbezitters (Dutch Investor Association)

**EXHIBIT 3** Abridged merger prospectus

# Unaudited condensed pro forma consolidated financial information

The following unaudited condensed pro forma consolidated financial information is being provided to give you a better understanding of what the results of operations and financial position of Air France–KLM might have looked like had the offer of Air France for KLM common shares occurred on an earlier date. The unaudited condensed pro forma financial information is based on the estimates and assumptions set forth in the notes to such information. The unaudited condensed pro forma consolidated financial information is preliminary and is being furnished solely for illustrative purposes and, therefore, is not necessarily indicative of the combined results of operations or financial position of Air France–KLM that might have been achieved for the dates or periods indicated, nor is it necessarily indicative of the results of operations or financial position of Air France–KLM that may, or may be expected to, occur in the future. No account has been taken within the unaudited condensed pro forma consolidated financial statements of any synergy or efficiency that may, or may be expected to, occur following the offer.

For accounting purposes, the combination will be accounted for as Air France's acquisition of KLM using the purchase method of accounting under both French and US GAAP. Under French GAAP, this determination has been based on the assessment of effective control of KLM by Air France, primarily through the ability of Air France to control the significant decisions of KLM as a result of its deciding vote on the strategic management committee. Under US GAAP, Air France believes that its ability to cast the deciding vote for majority matters of the strategic management committee, combined with its ownership of 49 percent of the voting share capital of KLM, and its ownership of all of the outstanding depositary receipts related to the administered shareholdings which will exist following the completion of the exchange offer, will provide Air France with a controlling financial interest in KLM, and that consolidation of KLM provides the most meaningful presentation of the combined financial position and results of operations of Air France–KLM. We have also concluded that Air France should initially measure all assets, liabilities, and non-controlling interests of KLM at their fair values at the date of completion of the exchange offer.

As a result of the above considerations under French GAAP and US GAAP, the accompanying unaudited pro forma financial information includes adjustments to reflect the fair values of KLM's net assets as further described in the accompanying footnotes. The final combination will be accounted for based on the final determination of the transaction value and the fair values of KLM's identifiable assets and liabilities at the date of exchange of control. Therefore, the actual goodwill amount, as well as other balance sheet items, could differ from

the preliminary unaudited condensed pro forma consolidated financial information presented herein, and in turn affect items in the preliminary unaudited condensed pro forma consolidated income statements and balance sheet, such as amortization of intangible assets, income of equity affiliates, long-term assets, negative goodwill, prepaid pension assets, and related income taxes.

The following unaudited pro forma consolidated financial information gives pro forma effect to the offer, after giving effect to the pro forma adjustments described in the notes to the unaudited pro forma consolidated financial information. The unaudited condensed pro forma consolidated income statements for the financial year ended March 31, 2003 and for the six months ended September 30, 2003 give effect to the offer and the business combination as if they had occurred on April 1, 2002. The unaudited condensed pro forma consolidated balance sheet as of September 30, 2003 gives effect to the offer and the business combination as if they had occurred on September 30, 2003. The unaudited condensed pro forma consolidated financial information of Air France–KLM is based on the historical consolidated financial statements of Air France, which are included elsewhere in this prospectus, and on the historical consolidated financial statements of KLM, which are included in KLM's Annual Report on Form 20-F for the year ended March 31, 2003, as amended, and in the unaudited interim condensed consolidated financial statements for the six months ended September 30, 2003 filed by KLM on Form 6-K dated December 30, 2003, incorporated by reference in this prospectus. The historical financial statements of Air France and KLM are prepared in accordance with French GAAP and Dutch GAAP, respectively. Dutch GAAP differs in some respects from French GAAP. Accordingly, the historical financial statements of KLM have been adjusted to French GAAP for all periods presented in this unaudited condensed pro forma consolidated financial information.

Air France has presented the unaudited condensed pro forma consolidated financial information in accordance with both French GAAP and US GAAP for the year ended March 31, 2003 and as of September 30, 2003 and for the six-month period then ended in order to fulfill regulatory requirements in the United States. The combined entity will continue to prepare its consolidated financial statements in accordance with French GAAP until application of IFRS Standards becomes mandatory within the European Union for financial years beginning on or after January 1, 2005. Air France will also provide additional information in accordance with US GAAP in order to fulfill regulatory requirements in the United States.

These unaudited condensed pro forma consolidated financial statements are only a summary and should be read in conjunction with the historical consolidated financial statements and related notes of Air France and KLM.

## UNAUDITED CONDENSED PRO FORMA COMBINED INCOME STATEMENT
## FOR THE SIX-MONTH PERIOD ENDED SEPTEMBER 30, 2003

|  | French GAAP | | |
|---|---|---|---|
| (euro amounts in mn) | **Air France** | **KLM** | **pro forma combined** |
| Net sales | €6,193 | €3,036 | €9,229 |
| Salaries and related costs | (2,025) | (922) | (2,947) |
| Depreciation and amortization | (618) | (218) | (806) |
| Aircraft fuel | (657) | (396) | (1,053) |
| Landing fees and other rents | (654) | (268) | (922) |
| Aircraft maintenance materials and outside repairs | (186) | (263) | (449) |
| Aircraft rent | (239) | (133) | (372) |
| Selling expenses and passenger commissions | (533) | (191) | (724) |
| Contracted services and passenger revenues | (533) | (286) | (819) |
| Other operating expenses | (660) | (264) | (924) |
| Income (loss) from operations | 88 | 95 | 213 |
| Restructuring costs | (11) | (75) | (86) |
| Interest expense | (71) | (53) | (124) |
| Interest income and other financial income, net | 65 | 26 | 91 |
| Other income (expense), net | 0 | 7 | 7 |
| Gain on sale of stock subsidiaries | 0 | 12 | 12 |
| Income of equity affiliates | 22 | 7 | 32 |
| Income (loss) before taxes and minority interests and goodwill amortization | 93 | 19 | 145 |
| Income tax | (32) | 4 | (38) |
| Minority interest | (1) | 0 | (1) |
| Goodwill amortization and impairment | (8) | (2) | 115 |
| Income (loss) from continuing operations | €52 | €21 | €221 |

The accompanying notes are an integral part of the unaudited condensed pro forma consolidated financial statements.

**UNAUDITED CONDENSED PRO FORMA COMBINED INCOME STATEMENT FOR THE YEAR ENDED MARCH 30, 2003**

| (euro amounts in mn) | French GAAP | | |
| --- | --- | --- | --- |
| | Air France | KLM | pro forma combined |
| Net sales | €12,687 | €6,367 | €19,054 |
| Salaries and related costs | (3,856) | (1,714) | (5,570) |
| Depreciation and amortization | (1,310) | (528) | (1,776) |
| Aircraft fuel | (1,369) | (866) | (2,235) |
| Landing fees and other rents | (1,362) | (525) | (1,887) |
| Aircraft maintenance materials and outside repairs | (477) | (642) | (1,119) |
| Aircraft rent | (521) | (256) | (777) |
| Selling expenses and passenger commissions | (1,157) | (486) | (1,643) |
| Contracted services and passenger revenues | (1,086) | (594) | (1,680) |
| Other operating expenses | (1,357) | (663) | (2,020) |
| Income (loss) from operations | 192 | 93 | 347 |
| Restructuring costs | (13) | 0 | (13) |
| Interest expense | (161) | (140) | (301) |
| Interest income and other financial income, net | 76 | (4) | 72 |
| Other income (expense), net | 0 | (42) | (42) |
| Gain on sale of stock subsidiaries | 4 | 6 | 10 |
| Income of equity affiliates | 29 | (4) | 31 |
| Income (loss) before taxes and minority interests and goodwill amortization | 127 | (91) | 104 |
| Income tax | 13 | 30 | 22 |
| Minority interest | (4) | 0 | (4) |
| Goodwill amortization and impairment | (16) | (4) | 230 |
| Income (loss) from continuing operations | €120 | € (65) | €352 |

The accompanying notes are an integral part of the unaudited condensed pro forma consolidated financial statements.

## UNAUDITED CONDENSED PRO FORMA COMBINED BALANCE SHEET, SEPTEMBER 30, 2003

| (euro amounts in mn) | French GAAP | | |
| --- | --- | --- | --- |
| | Air France | KLM | pro forma combined |
| Current assets: | | | |
| Cash and cash equivalents | €1,202 | €55 | €1,257 |
| Short-term investments and restricted cash | 169 | 475 | 644 |
| Accounts receivables | 1,574 | 728 | 2,302 |
| Inventories | 209 | 145 | 354 |
| Prepaid expenses and other | 559 | 2,511 | 1,981 |
| Total current assets | 3,713 | 3,914 | 6,538 |
| Flight and ground equipment, net | 6,353 | 2,350 | 8,674 |
| Flight and ground equipment under capital lease, net | 1,515 | 2,592 | 3,708 |
| Investment in equity affiliates | 312 | 216 | 484 |
| Investment in securities | 103 | 0 | 66 |
| Deferred income taxes | 76 | 53 | 657 |
| Other non-current assets | 154 | 10 | 164 |
| Intangible assets | 159 | 48 | 207 |
| Goodwill | 103 | 12 | 103 |
| Total assets | €12,488 | €9,195 | €20,705 |
| Current liabilities: | | | |
| Current maturities of long-term debt | €223 | €16 | €239 |
| Short-term obligation (other) | 297 | 148 | 445 |
| Current obligation under capital leases | 113 | 151 | 265 |
| Trade payables | 1,204 | 546 | 1,750 |
| Deferred revenue on ticket sales | 807 | 471 | 1,278 |
| Taxes payable | 4 | 11 | 15 |
| Accrued salaries, related benefits and employee-related liabilities | 559 | 236 | 795 |
| Other current liability | 626 | 329 | 955 |
| Total current liabilities | 3,833 | 1,908 | 5,741 |
| Long-term debt | 2,349 | 591 | 2,940 |
| Non-current obligation under capital leases | 1,204 | 2,453 | 3,657 |
| Pension liability | 601 | 4 | 641 |
| Provisions | 450 | 223 | 1,906 |
| Other non-current liability | 0 | 212 | 212 |
| Deferred tax liability, non-current | 0 | 747 | 747 |
| Minority interest | 29 | 0 | 29 |
| Total stockholders' equity | 4,022 | 3,058 | 4,833 |
| Total liabilities and stockholders' equity | €12,488 | €9,195 | €20,705 |

The accompanying notes are an integral part of the unaudited condensed pro forma consolidated financial statements.

# Excerpts from the notes to the pro forma financial statements – significant differences between Dutch GAAP and French GAAP (euro amounts in millions, except per share data)

KLM prepares its consolidated financial statements in accordance with Dutch GAAP, which differ in certain material respects from French GAAP. For purposes of preparing the unaudited condensed pro forma consolidated financial information, KLM's historical consolidated financial statements have been adjusted to conform to French GAAP as applied by Air France for each period presented. These adjustments have been made based on estimates of the management of Air France and KLM. These adjustments are unaudited, and may not fully reflect the application of French GAAP for the periods presented as if KLM had prepared its financial statements using French GAAP. Upon completion of the exchange offer, Air France and KLM will perform a detailed review of their accounting policies and financial statement classifications, and additional adjustments may be required to conform the KLM financial statements to Air France–KLM's financial statements as presented under French GAAP.

Although Air France and KLM do not expect that this detailed review will result in material changes to accounting policies or classifications other than noted below, no such assurance can be given at this time. The table below summarizes the net effect of French GAAP adjustments on KLM's stockholders' equity as of September 30, 2003:

| Note | Differences | Stockholders' equity at September 30, 2003 |
|---|---|---|
| 1 | Pension benefits | €2,355 |
| 2 | Derivative instruments | 11 |
| 4 | Accounting for treasury stock | 23 |
| 7 | Frequent flyer program | (16) |
| 5 | Deferred income taxes | (811) |
| | Stockholders' equity without tax | €1,562 |

## NOTE 1 PENSION BENEFITS

Under Dutch GAAP, pension costs for KLM's defined benefit pension plans are generally expensed on the basis of the actuarially determined contributions that KLM is required to pay under various worldwide pension schemes. Air France accounts for the costs and obligations of its pension plans in accordance with French GAAP, which does not significantly differ from IAS 19.

This French GAAP adjustment provides for the costs and obligations related to KLM's pension plans as if these amounts had been determined using IAS 19 as applied on a historical basis of accounting. This adjustment, reflected in the "French GAAP adjustment" third column of the condensed pro forma income statements resulted in a decrease in Salaries and related costs by €45 million and €170

million for the six months ended September 30, 2003 and for the year ended March 31, 2003, respectively. The KLM balance sheet at September 30, 2003 was adjusted as follows in this respect: an increase in the "Prepaid expenses and other" caption of €2,336 million and a decrease in Provisions by €19 million resulting in an increase in stockholders' equity before tax by €2,355 million.

## NOTE 2 DERIVATIVE INSTRUMENTS

Under Dutch GAAP, derivatives are recorded separately on the balance sheet and are accounted for at fair value. Changes in the fair value of derivatives which meet certain criteria for cash flow hedge accounting may be deferred and recognized in other comprehensive income until such time as the hedged transaction is recognized. Ineffective portions of hedges are recognized immediately in earnings. Under French GAAP qualifying hedge instruments are presented on the balance sheet net of the hedged item. For cash flow hedges, changes in values of derivative instruments are deferred, as no separate presentation of other comprehensive income is included under French GAAP.

Certain derivatives do not meet the criteria for hedge accounting under Dutch GAAP, but do meet criteria for hedge accounting under French GAAP. As a result, changes in fair values of certain derivatives have been included in income under Dutch GAAP but would have been deferred under French GAAP. The French GAAP adjustment gives effect to reclassifications to reflect net presentation of qualifying hedges, and reverses the effects of changes in fair values of cash flow hedges that had been included in other comprehensive income under Dutch GAAP. In addition, the impacts on income of some non-qualifying derivatives under Dutch GAAP which meet French GAAP criteria have been reversed. The September 30, 2003 balance sheet impacts are described in the following table (in € millions):

| | |
|---|---|
| Flight equipment | €(110) |
| Other non-current assets | (409) |
| Long-term debt | (291) |
| Capital lease obligation | (239) |
| Stockholders' equity before tax | 11 |

Before tax, the income (loss) statement adjustment amounts to €(13) million and €(11) million for the six months ended September 30, 2003 and the year ended March 31, 2003, respectively.

## NOTE 3 RECOGNITION OF RESTRUCTURING COSTS

Under Dutch GAAP, €75 million (with a €26 million tax effect) arising from decisions made by KLM's Board of Managing Directors have been classified as extraordinary items in the unaudited condensed pro forma consolidated financial information. Under French GAAP, the expense of €49 million relating to the restructuring provision would have been recognized as the actual costs were incurred. The provision balance at March 31, 2003 is reversed in the balance sheet as a Dutch GAAP to French GAAP adjustment. During the six months ended September 30, 2003, the restructuring costs did qualify for French GAAP purposes and consequently were recorded in the Dutch GAAP to French GAAP reconciliation, with an impact of €75 million on restructuring costs with a related tax impact of €26 million.

## NOTE 4 ACCOUNTING FOR TREASURY STOCK

Under French GAAP, treasury shares held by Air France to fulfill commitments under employee stock option plans are accounted for as an asset. Provisions are recorded in order to record the shares at the lower of cost or market value, with related gains and losses recognized in the income statement. Under Dutch GAAP, the purchase price of these shares is deducted from stockholders' equity. The French GAAP adjustment reclassifies €23 million of KLM's acquired treasury shares to short-term investments and recognizes a realized income on the sale of those shares for an amount of €13 million for the six month period ended September 30, 2003 and a loss of €(16) million in the income statement for the year ended March 31, 2003.

## NOTE 5 DEFERRED INCOME TAXES

These adjustments reflect the deferred tax impacts of the French GAAP adjustments listed above, except for treasury stock adjustments which are tax exempted in the Netherlands. Income tax effect has been calculated using the KLM current tax rate of 34.5 percent. The net tax effect of French GAAP adjustments is a decrease in stockholders' equity of KLM of €811 million (an increase by €747 million of the deferred tax liabilities and a decrease by €64 million of the deferred tax assets).

For the year ended March 31, 2003, the deferred income taxes caption also reflects the French GAAP reclassification, from operating income and income tax to extraordinary items, net of tax, of the outcome of the dispute between KLM and Alitalia.

## NOTE 6 LEASE DEPOSITS

Under Dutch GAAP, lease deposits are either classified as investments in debt securities or other noncurrent assets, or deducted from financial debt, while under French GAAP lease deposits are offset with financial debt (obligation under capital leases). This reclassification leads to the decrease of financial debt and lease deposits by €475 million.

## NOTE 7 FREQUENT FLYER PROGRAM

Under Dutch GAAP, the liability recorded for the accrued costs related to flight awards earned by members of the frequent flyer program is classified as a long-term liability. Under French GAAP, amounts accrued related to the Fréquence Plus frequent flyer program are included in advance ticket liability in the consolidated balance sheet of Air France and classified as a current liability for purposes of the pro forma financial information. The French GAAP adjustment reclassifies €42 million

provision recorded by KLM under Dutch GAAP to unearned revenue in accordance with French GAAP as applied by Air France. This reclassification impacts provision for €26 million, stockholders' equity for €10 million and deferred tax assets for €6 million.

## NOTE 8 INVENTORY

Under Dutch GAAP, certain rotable and exchangeable parts have been classified in inventories. Under French GAAP, these items are classified as flight equipment. The net book value of these rotable parts and exchangeable components is €66 million at September 30, 2003.

## NOTE 9 OTHER

Under French GAAP, unrealized foreign exchange gain or loss on working capital elements is classified in financial income or expense. This reclassification amounts to €17 million and €22 million for the six months ended September 30, 2003 and the year ended March 31, 2003, respectively. In addition, as required under French GAAP, the Goodwill amortization or impairment caption has been reclassified to a separate line item below operating income. This reclassification amounts to €2 million and €4 million for the six months ended September 30, 2003 and the year ended March 31, 2003, respectively.

## NOTE 10 DISCONTINUED OPERATION AND EXTRAORDINARY ITEMS

Under French GAAP, KLM would have presented the disposal of its business "Buzz" as a discontinued operation in the income statement. This disposal was consummated during the six months ended September 30, 2003.

In addition, the outcome of the dispute between KLM and Alitalia would have been presented as an extraordinary item net of tax under French GAAP. This results in a reclassification of €(276) million and €95 million from operating income and income tax to extraordinary items, respectively, in the KLM pro forma French GAAP income statement for the year ended March 31, 2003. Discontinued operation net of tax, extraordinary items net of tax and cumulative effect of change in accounting principles are captions below income (loss) from continuing operations and are not presented in the pro forma condensed income statements.

# Excerpts from the notes to the pro forma financial statements – pro forma adjustments (euro amounts in millions, except per share data)

Under French GAAP, Air France is the acquirer of KLM and will account for its acquisition of KLM using the purchase method of accounting. Under the purchase method, Air France will allocate the total purchase price of KLM to the acquired assets and liabilities (including previously unrecognized items) based on their relative fair values as determined on the date of the transaction. This unaudited condensed pro forma consolidated financial information has been prepared and presented assuming that Air France will acquire a 100 percent controlling economic interest in KLM following the completion of the combination and the conditional acquisition of the Cumulative Preference Shares A. Under French GAAP, the estimated aggregate purchase price has been calculated as follows (in € millions, except number of shares and per share data):

| | |
|---|---:|
| KLM common shares outstanding | 46,810,000 |
| Exchange ratio into Air France's shares | 1.10 |
| Equivalent number of Air France's shares | 51,491,000 |
| Air France's share price | 13.34 |
| Estimated fair value of Air France shares issued | 686.9 |
| Estimated fair value of Air France warrants issued | 73.5 |
| Estimated fair value of preferred and priority shares | 35.5 |
| Estimated transaction-related expenses | 15.1 |
| Total estimated purchase price consideration | 811.0 |

The preliminary allocation of its purchase price reflected herein presents preliminary estimates of fair values as determined at September 30, 2003. Such estimates are based on an independent appraisal. The actual allocation of the purchase price will be based on the fair values determined at the date of the transaction, which may differ, in some respects, from those presented below. The estimated excess of purchase price consideration over the approximate value of KLM's net assets, the estimated fair value adjustments and the estimated negative goodwill are as follows (in € millions):

| | |
|---|---:|
| Total estimated purchase price consideration | 811 |
| Less: KLM's net assets under French GAAP | (3,058) |
| Consideration of fair values of acquired assets and liabilities: | |
| Reduction in fair value of aircraft | (675) |
| Reduction in reported value of intangible assets | (12) |
| Incremental fair value of buildings and lands | 248 |
| Reduction in fair value of equity investment | (44) |
| Reduction in fair value in pension and post-retirement plans and increase in pension provision | (1,125) |
| Deferred tax adjustments | 528 |
| Other items, net | 66 |
| Excess of the fair value of net assets acquired over purchase consideration | (1,233) |

Preliminary estimates of fair values and the final purchase price allocation may materially differ from preliminary amounts and allocations provided in this section. This analysis presents a preliminary

allocation of purchase price to the assets and liabilities of KLM, based on independent appraisals conducted at September 30, 2003. The final allocation of purchase price will be completed at the latest at the end of the fiscal year following the acquisition fiscal period, and will be based on valuations and appraisals conducted as of the date of the exchange offer closing date, as specified under French GAAP. We have identified aircraft and pension plans valuations as the most significant areas for potential material discrepancies between pro forma and final purchase price allocation.

Aircraft market value references are principally US dollar-based and therefore, the euro-denominated fair value of the KLM fleet may fluctuate significantly based on €/$ exchange rate fluctuations. The exchange rate retained for the purpose of the pro forma purchase price allocation was $1.13 per €1.00. Should this exchange rate fluctuate to $1.18 for €1.00 or $1.24 for €1.00, the downward fair value adjustment to the KLM fleet would increase by €140 million or €270 million, respectively. Should the exchange rate fluctuate oppositely to $1.07 for €.00, the downward fair value adjustment to the KLM fleet would decrease by €155 million.

The purchase price allocation may also differ significantly from our preliminary estimates, based on market conditions and assumptions prevailing to the pension plans valuation, mainly based on long term discount rates, anticipated inflation, stock market current valuation, overall economic prospects, and changes in agreements applicable to pensions in the Netherlands and to KLM employees. As further discussed below, the purchase price allocation may also need to be revised in case the overfunded pension plan assets recognition would be limited by the asset ceiling rules introduced by IAS 19.

Under French GAAP, in accordance with the accounting rules governing the purchase method of accounting, Air France is not allowed to recognize intangible assets, such as KLM's trademark or certain take-off and landing slots, when a negative residual goodwill amount results from the purchase price allocation.

KLM sponsors a number of pension benefit plans across the various locations where it operates. As of September 30, 2003, total obligations in respect of these plans amount to €7,055 million, and available pension funds assets have been fair valued at €8,260 million. Benefit plans for employees outside the Netherlands account for less than 5 percent of total obligations. In the Netherlands, pension benefits consist of final or average career salary plans which are funded through separate legal entities to which employees also contribute. Other post-employment benefits consist of sponsored medical coverage for some retirees, resulting in an estimated obligation ("PBO") for these plans of €67 million with no related assets. The adjustment to the carrying value of the KLM pension plans is based on this preliminary assessment of PBO and current values of plan assets. As of September 30, 2003, some plans have assets in excess of the PBO estimated by external actuaries. Under French GAAP, the amount of net asset which can be recognized is limited by the asset ceiling rules introduced by IAS 19.

These rules limit the amount of net asset which can be recognized on the employer's balance sheet to the present value of any economic benefits available in the form of refunds from the plans or reductions in future contributions to the plans. Following the proposed transaction, the asset ceiling limitation will also consider amounts of cumulative unrecognized actuarial losses and past service costs in determining the maximum asset to be recorded by the combined companies. As of September 30, 2003, the amount of net asset recognized is €1,247 million.

Following the completion of the transaction, Air France will perform a full valuation of the acquired KLM plans, in order to determine the actual amount of pension assets to be included in the allocation of purchase price to the acquired plans of KLM. This valuation will occur as of the closing date for the proposed transaction. It is not possible to predict at this time what the final value of the pension asset will be or whether the amount of such asset to be recorded by Air France will need to be reduced by a provision as a result of the asset ceiling restrictions. As a result, the final value to be allocated to the acquired plans could be subject to significant change. Furthermore, the amount of net pension asset recorded would be subject to reconsideration of the asset ceiling test, which could result in significant increases or decreases of the provision/non-cash impacts to Air France's results of operations.

For purposes of the presentation of the pro forma condensed consolidated income statements, the adjustments listed above have been presented as if the transaction had occurred on the first day of the first period presented. The impacts of the pro forma allocation of purchase consideration affect the results of operations for the six-month period ended September 30, 2003 and the year ended March 31, 2003 as follows:

- Note 11 Tangible assets. Reflects adjustments to the reported depreciation of KLM based on the reduction in the fair value of the fixed assets.
- Note 12 Investments in equity affiliates. Reflects adjustments to the carrying value of KLM's investments in affiliates, primarily KLM's 50 percent investment in Martinair. For purposes of the pro forma income statements, the decrease in the carrying value of Martinair has been attributed to the fleet assets having an estimated remaining useful life of seven years. The amortization of these adjustments results in an increase to the reported income from this equity investee of €3 million and €6 million for the six months ended September 30, 2003 and the year ended March 31, 2003, respectively.
- Note 13 Goodwill. This adjustment reflects the elimination of the amounts of historical goodwill and goodwill amortization of €2 million for the six-month period ended September 30, 2003 and €4 million for the year ended March 31, 2003.
- Note 14 Negative goodwill. For French GAAP purposes, the excess of the purchase consideration over the fair value of the

individual assets and liabilities recognized above results in residual negative goodwill of €1,233 million. Under French GAAP, the residual negative goodwill is allocated to the income statement on a straight line method over a period that reflects assumptions made and management plans as of the acquisition date. On a preliminary basis, Air France's management has estimated that a five-year period would satisfy these criteria. Therefore, for pro forma purposes, the negative goodwill amount has been amortized over a five-year period which results in a positive adjustment to net income of €246 million per year ended March 31, 2003 and €123 million for the six months ended September 30, 2003.

The above list is not exhaustive, and there may be other assets and liabilities which may have to be adjusted to fair value when both final valuations and allocations are made following the completion of the exchange offer.

Air France will complete the determination of fair values and the allocation of the purchase price after the completion of the exchange offer. French GAAP allows Air France to complete the purchase price allocation no later than the end of the fiscal year subsequent to the fiscal year in which the exchange offer was completed. The determination of fair values will be based on an independent appraisal.

The exchange ratio agreed between Air France and KLM implicitly valued KLM at less than KLM's net asset value. KLM performs an impairment test whenever there is an indication that the carrying amounts of its assets may not be recoverable. KLM has performed impairment tests on its owned and financially leased aircraft in a manner consistent with Statement of Financial Accounting Standards No. 144 (SFAS 144) under US GAAP as well as in accordance with the Guideline of the Council for Annual Reporting No. 121 (RJ 121) under Netherlands GAAP. SFAS 144 requires the recognition of an impairment loss if the carrying amount of a long-lived asset or group of assets is not recoverable and exceeds its fair value. The carrying amount of an asset or group of assets is generally not recoverable if it exceeds the sum of the undiscounted, pre-tax, future cash flows expected to result from the use and eventual disposition of the asset or group of assets. Assets must be grouped at the lowest level for which identifiable cash flows are largely independent of the cash flows of other assets. Under Netherlands GAAP, KLM compared the carrying amount of each asset group (cash generating unit) to its recoverable amount, which is defined as the higher of the net selling price and its value in use.

In conducting its impairment tests, KLM grouped its fleet assets into four groups:

- KLM's wide body fleet,
- KLM's 737 fleet,
- KLM's regional fleet, and
- Transavia's fleet.

KLM's wide body fleet, which is used for long-haul destinations, consists of a total of five different kinds of aircraft. Impairment tests for KLM's wide body fleet were conducted for each of these kinds of aircraft, because KLM monitors and optimizes its employment of, and revenues from, each of these kinds of aircraft separately. Therefore, KLM considers this the lowest level for which identifiable cash flows are largely independent of the cash flows of other assets. Impairment tests for KLM's 737 fleet, KLM's regional fleet, and Transavia's fleet were conducted at the fleet level instead of by aircraft type or subtype level because in KLM's operations the aircraft composing those fleets are generally interchangeable and therefore cash flows of types or subtypes are not meaningfully identifiable. In its impairment tests KLM:

- calculated total cash flows during the estimated economic life of each type of asset by multiplying the estimated annual cash flows from that asset type by the remaining average economic life of that asset type;
- estimated future cash flows based on historical cash flows and KLM's business plan for 2004–2005;
- estimated the residual asset value at the end of each aircraft's estimated economic life by reference to KLM's depreciation calculations, the Aircraft Value Reference Guide (published by the Aircraft Value Reference Company), and KLM's historical sales experience;
- considered the estimated residual asset value as a cash inflow at the end of the asset's economic life;
- assumed that KLM would replace each of its aircraft at the end of its economic life, and did not take into account expected changes in yields.

Based on undiscounted cash flows, the asset groups described above passed the recoverability test under SFAS 144 and RJ 121. Although KLM assumed that its aircraft would be replaced at the end of their economic life, KLM also considered the potential scenario involving a gradual decline in operations, under which KLM would be unable to invest in replacement aircraft, and concluded that such a scenario would take decades to transpire and is remote within the time-frame covered by KLM's estimated future cash flows.

KLM's management and supervisory boards agreed to accept Air France's offer at a significant discount to KLM's net asset value after they reviewed all of the strategic options available to KLM, including remaining an independent company, and concluded that at that time there was no superior strategic alternative to the combination. In assessing the offer in light of the fact that the consideration offered by Air France was below KLM's net asset value, the KLM management and supervisory boards considered certain factors, including the benefits that KLM believed may arise from combining certain complementary features of Air France's and KLM's businesses, KLM's expectation that cost savings and revenue-increasing synergies could be realized following completion of the offer, and the benefits associated with KLM's expected admission into the SkyTeam alliance (subject to KLM's fulfilling the admission criteria) following completion of the offer. The factors that the KLM management and supervisory boards considered in arriving at their decisions to approve and recommend the offer to holders of KLM's common shares are described in KLM's Solicitation/ Recommendation Statement on Schedule 14D-9, which has been filed with the Securities and Exchange Commission and which is being mailed to KLM's shareholders together with this prospectus.

**EXHIBIT 4**  KLM–Air France merger announcement, September 30, 2003

**A:** KLM share price from June 30, 2003 to May 5, 2004

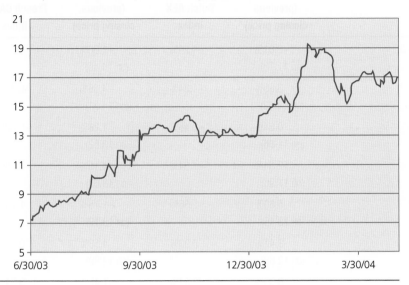

Source: Thomson Datastream.

**B:** Air France share price from June 30, 2003 to May 5, 2004

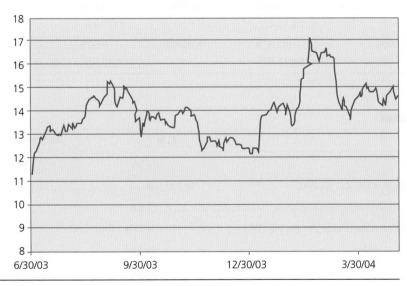

Source: Thomson Datastream.

## C: Stock returns (and prior day's closing share prices) surrounding the merger announcement

| | KLM return (previous closing price) | Dutch AEX Index | Air France return (previous closing price) | French CAC40 Index |
|---|---|---|---|---|
| 3 days before announcement (day −3) | −2.81% (on 11.75) | −1.24% | −1.66% (on 14.45) | −1.02% |
| 2 days before announcement (day −2) | 3.85% (on 11.42) | −1.34% | −4.86% (on 14.21) | −0.43% |
| 1 day before announcement (day −1) | 0.84% (on 11.86) | −0.46% | 1.26% (on 13.52) | −0.87% |
| Day of the announcement (day 0) | 12.54% (on 11.96) | −1.84% | −4.16% (on 13.69) | −1.68% |
| 1 day after announcement (day +1) | −5.69% (on 13.46) | 1.56% | −1.75% (on 13.12) | 1.79% |
| 2 days after announcement (day +2) | 3.47% (on 12.68) | 0.93% | 4.58% (on 12.89) | 0.06% |
| 3 days after announcement (day +3) | −0.30% (on 13.12) | 2.87% | −1.48% (on 13.48) | 3.24% |
| From day −10 to day +10 | 14.78% (on 11.91) | −1.54% | −4.62% (on 14.50) | 0.18% |
| From day −5 to day 5 | 16.06% (on 11.27) | −2.68% | −5.67% (on 14.64) | −0.35% |
| From September 30, 2003, to May 5, 2004 | 45.90% (on 11.96) | 10.60% | 6.50% (on 13.69) | 16.96% > |

Source: Thomson Datastream.

## D: Valuation data and other information

| | KLM | Air France |
|---|---|---|
| Closing price on September 30, 2003 | 11.96 | 13.69 |
| Number of ordinary shares outstanding on September 30, 2003 | 46,809,699 | 219,780,887 |
| Beta | 1.63 | 1.36 |
| Yield on government bonds with ten years' maturity on September 30, 2003 | 4.14% | 4.13% |
| Statutory tax rate in 2003 | 34.5% | 35.43% |
| Effective tax rate in 2003 | 32.0% | 13.27% |

# CASE

# Measuring impairment at Dofasco

**IVEY** | Publishing

It was December 15, 2008, when Joanne Bell received an e-mail with the most recent earnings projections for ArcelorMittal Dofasco. Bell had just joined the ArcelorMittal Dofasco financial accounting team after a few years of audit experience at a large Chartered Accountancy (CA) firm. She was perplexed by the challenge before her and knew she had a long night ahead.

ArcelorMittal Dofasco had undergone significant ownership changes in the past few years. When the firm had first been acquired, the market had placed a premium share value on the Dofasco subsidiary. However, in light of the recent economic downturn, the financial accounting group at Dofasco was required to reassess the values assigned to the subsidiary's net assets and determine whether a change in asset fair values existed as a result of the revised economic outlook.

Bell's supervisor, Sean Collins, the director of financial accounting at Dofasco had called a group meeting for the next day to discuss the implications of the economic situation on the value of the intangible assets recognized at Dofasco's acquisition.

## The steel industry in Canada

The steel industry was one of Canada's largest manufacturing industries with sales of $14 billion and production of 14.9 million tons. In 2008 the steel industry provided 30,000 direct jobs to the Canadian economy. Although steel manufacturing companies were located across Canada, the majority of the companies were located in Ontario. See **Exhibit 1** for geographic dispersion of steel manufacturers.

Modern steelmaking in Canada consisted of two different methods: the integrated process and the electric arc furnace process. The integrated process was the traditional steelmaking process, which combined iron ore, coke, limestone, and scrap metal in a blast furnace to produce molten iron. The molten iron was then refined in a basic oxygen furnace to produce liquid steel, which was cast into slabs at the customer's request. Integrated steelmakers were highly capital-intensive and produced two million to four million tons of steel annually.[1]

[1]Industry Canada, "An Overview of Steel Products and Processes," www.ic.gc.ca/eic/site/pm-mp.nsf/eng/mm01289.html, accessed August 12, 2009.

The electric arc furnace process relied primarily on recycled scrap steel, which was reheated to produce liquid steel. These steel manufacturers were known as mini-mill steelmakers. Mini-mill steelmakers were typically less capital-intensive than integrated steel makers and had the capacity to produce 250,000 to one million tons of steel annually.[2]

As a result of the capital-intensive nature of the business, the steel industry was challenged by high fixed costs and, as a result, preferred large batch sizes for production. To secure volume contracts, a steel company relied heavily on strong customer relationships and its ability to effectively match product technology with evolving customer needs. Successful steel companies generated sufficient cash flow to satisfy their financial debt, reinvest in technologies and foster growth and innovation with their customers.

The Canadian steel industry had undergone dynamic changes in recent years as a result of changes in the global industry. During the 1990s, the global steel industry was hugely fragmented, largely state-owned and crippled with debt. Profits were scarce as industry players struggled to manage high fixed costs, labour-intensive operations and stagnant growth. Shortly after the turn of the millennium, the industry experienced a renaissance in terms of profitability and rate of growth. This renaissance was a result of consolidation in the industry, which allowed for greater efficiencies in production and the ability to better access and serve global markets. Furthermore, the trend toward fully integrated business models reduced steelmakers' risk from input price volatilities by spurring greater self-sufficiency in sourcing their raw material supplies. Developing economies such as Brazil, Russia, India, and China experienced consistently above-average gross domestic product (GDP) growth, leading to vast business opportunities, especially for those companies already present in global markets. **Exhibit 2** highlights the financial improvements resulting from the steel industry trend toward greater efficiency.

## Dofasco Inc.

Clifton and Frank Sherman founded the Dominion Steel Casting Company in 1912 to manufacture castings for Canadian railways. In 1917, the company merged with its subsidiary, the Hamilton Steel Wheel Company. In 1980, the company, located in Hamilton, Ontario, Canada, adopted the name Dofasco Inc.

Dofasco's product lines include hot-rolled, cold-rolled, galvanized, Extragal™, Galvalume™, and tinplate flat-rolled steels, in addition to tubular products, laser-welded blanks, and Zyplex™, a proprietary laminate.[3] Although Dofasco's single largest market was the automotive industry, the company also targeted customers in the construction, energy, manufacturing, pipe and tube, appliance, packaging, and steel distribution industries.

Dofasco had been a pioneer of innovative steelmaking throughout its history. For example, Dofasco introduced the first universal steel plate mill in Canada and was the first company in North America to adopt basic oxygen furnace technology. In 1996, Dofasco led North America in adopting an electric arc furnace and slab caster. By diverging from its traditional integrated steelmaking process and operating a mini-mill, Dofasco moved into a leading position as a North American steel solutions provider.

In addition, since the company's founding, Dofasco had maintained a reputation for commitment to both its employees and the Hamilton community, reflected in its corporate philosophy: "Our product is steel. Our strength is people. Our home is Hamilton."[4] Dofasco was the first Canadian manufacturer to introduce employee profit-sharing, and it maintained a history of positive labor relations. The Dofasco profit-sharing plan had been acknowledged as the core element and reason behind Dofasco's non-unionized workforce at

[2]*Ibid.*
[3]"Dofasco Inc. 2004 Annual Report," www.sedar.com, accessed July 31, 2009.
[4]Meredith Macleod and Naomi Powell, "Unions Not the Dofasco Way," *Hamilton Spectator,* March 20, 2008, www.thespec.com/News/Business/article/342323, accessed August 12, 2009.

the Hamilton plant. In 1997, Dofasco became the first Canadian company to sign a voluntary Environment Management Agreement with the federal and provincial governments, and the company played a leadership role in the Hamilton Industrial Environmental Association. Dofasco donated millions of dollars to regional charitable campaigns, hospitals and educational institutions and was regarded as an outstanding corporate citizen.

## A hostile takeover

On November 23, 2005, Arcelor SA (Arcelor), the world's second-largest steelmaker, put forth an unsolicited proposal to Dofasco shareholders, offering $55 per share in an attempt to gain control of Dofasco. Arcelor, which was based in Luxembourg, had grown through consolidation focusing on acquisitions in developing economies. In alignment with its corporate strategy, Arcelor management hoped to use Dofasco as a springboard into the North American steel market.

Although Arcelor offered a 27.3 percent premium over Dofasco's previous day's stock closing price, the bid was not supported by Dofasco management, and Dofasco's board of directors urged shareholders not to tender the offer. During the same day, Dofasco shares increased 34.2 percent, which suggested that investors would wait for another bid.[5] Analysts believed that through the purchase of Dofasco, a supplier to the Ford Motor Company, Arcelor's share of the North American automotive steel market would increase from 1 percent to 12 percent. In Europe, Arcelor supplied the steel in one out of every two cars.[6]

On November 25, 2005, a white knight entered the bidding when German-based steelmaker Thyssen-Krupp AG (ThyssenKrupp), the world's ninth largest steelmaker, announced a friendly offer of $61.50 per common share for control of Dofasco.[7] Dofasco's board of directors unanimously recommended accepting the offer because, unlike Arcelor, ThyssenKrupp would allow Dofasco both to continue operations under its own name and management and to continue some form of the profit-sharing system. ThyssenKrupp planned for the Dofasco plant to become ThyssenKrupp's new North American headquarters.[8]

A bidding war for control of Dofasco continued between Arcelor and ThyssenKrupp into January of 2006. Analysts were not surprised, citing Dofasco's location and several internally generated intangible assets – including raw materials contracts, intellectual capacity through product and operational innovations, and strong customer relations (see **Exhibit 3**) – as attractive and valuable qualities of the company.[9]

Finally, on January 24, 2006, Arcelor outbid ThyssenKrupp by offering $71 per common share or $4.939 billion for control of Dofasco. ThyssenKrupp announced that it would not increase its offer because doing so would downgrade its own credit ratings and go beyond the point of creating economic value. Dofasco's white knight had stepped aside, and Dofasco's board of directors publicly announced their support for the Arcelor offer and agreed to a closing date of March 1, 2006.

**Exhibit 4** provides the details of the external valuation at the March 1, 2006 closing date for the acquisition, which was completed by DeJong Evaluation at the request of Dofasco's board of directors. **Exhibits 5 and 6** provide excerpts from Dofasco's balance sheet just prior to the acquisition and the estimated fair values of Dofasco's net assets at the date of acquisition.

[5]"Arcelor Launches $4B Bid for Dofasco," November 24, 2005, www.redorbit.com/news/science/313090/arcelor_launches_4b_bid_for_dofasco/index.html, accessed August 12, 2009.

[6]"Arcelor Raises Offer for Dofasco," *New York Times,* December 23, 2005, www.nytimes.com/2005/12/23/business/world business/23iht-arcelor.html, accessed August 11, 2009.

[7]"ThyssenKrupp Tops Arcelor SA's Bid for Dofasco," November 28, 2005, www.streetinsider.com/Mergers+and+Acquisitions/ThyssenKrupp+Tops+Arcelor+SAs+Bid+for+Dofasco/406983.html.

[8]"Dofasco and ThyssenKrupp Announce a Friendly All-Cash Deal," press release, November 28, 2005, www.dofasco.ca/bins/content_page.asp?cid=2347-2349-100900, accessed August 11, 2009.

[9]"Arcelor Raises Offer for Dofasco," *New York Times,* December 23, 2005, www.nytimes.com/2005/12/23/business/world business/23iht-arcelor.html, accessed August 11, 2009.

# A steel giant is born

Days after the Dofasco board of directors announced support for Arcelor's bid for Dofasco, India-based Mittal Steel Company NV (Mittal) announced an unsolicited US$22.8 billion offer for Arcelor. Mittal's bid for Arcelor was an attempt to form a global powerhouse and establish itself as the only steelmaker capable of producing more than 100 million tons of steel annually. An Arcelor–Mittal merger represented a milestone in the global steel industry. As a combined entity, the company would be capable of tripling the capacity of Mittal's nearest rival, Japan's Nippon Steel, and would hold 10 percent of the global market share.[10]

Mittal Steel was the world's largest steel manufacturer with shipments of 49.2 million tons and revenues of more than US$28.1 billion in 2005. The company had 16 steelmaking operations in four continents, customers in more than 150 countries and 224,000 employees. The company was headed by Lakshmi Mittal, one of the world's richest men, who had an estimated fortune of more than £15 billion.[11]

Operating both integrated and mini-mill facilities, Mittal Steel had set the pace for consolidation and globalization in the steel industry (see **Exhibit 7** for a list of recent acquisitions). Furthermore, the company produced most of its iron ore and coking coal manufacturing inputs through ownership of mines. Lakshmi Mittal believed that US$1.6 billion in annual savings synergies could be reached before 2008 through the amalgamation of Arcelor's operations with those of Mittal.[12]

Despite attempts by Arcelor's board and management to circumvent the acquisition using both a white knight strategy[13] and a poison pill strategy[14], in June 2006, Arcelor agreed to a US$33.1 billion takeover by Mittal. The takeover price represented more than a 50 percent increase in the Arcelor share price prior to the initial takeover talks in January.[15] Furthermore, Mittal and Arcelor reached an agreement to combine the two companies in a merger of equals, as ArcelorMittal, headquartered in Luxembourg.

# ArcelorMittal

Following the merger, ArcelorMittal continued to pursue its growth strategy, by undertaking 35 transactions in 2007 (see **Exhibit 8** for the geographic range of these transactions). The company became known as having proven expertise in acquiring companies and turning around under-performing assets. As a result of several successful acquisitions in 2007, the company boasted earnings before interest taxes, depreciation, and amortization (EBITDA) of US$19.2 billion, making 2007 a record year for the company.[16]

# The sudden global recession

ArcelorMittal started out 2008, believing it would be another promising year as a result of rapidly increasing commodity prices and full-capacity utilization fueled by China's rapid growth. However, by mid-2008, the subprime mortgage crisis in the United States had contributed to a banking crisis that led to the demise of

---

[10]James Kanter et al., "Arcelor Agrees to Mittal Takeover," *New York Times,* www.nytimes.com/2006/06/25/business/world business/25iht-steel. html?pagewanted=1&_r=1, accessed August 11, 2009.

[11]"Mittal Steel Unveils Arcelor Bid," *BBC News,* news.bbc.co.uk/2/hi/business/4653516.stm, accessed August 17, 2009.

[12]"Mittal Shareholders Approve ArcelorMittal Merger," *Reuters,* August 28, 2007, http://in.reuters.com/article/businessNews/idIN India-29195120070828, accessed August 17, 2009.

[13]A "white knight strategy" refers to a situation where a potential acquirer is sought out by a target company's management to take over the company to avoid a hostile takeover.

[14]A "poison pill strategy" is a strategy designed to fend off a hostile takeover attempt.

[15]James Kanter et al., "Arcelor Agrees to Mittal Takeover," *New York Times,* www.nytimes.com/2006/06/25/business/world business/25iht-steel. html?pagewanted=1&_r=1, accessed August 16, 2009.

[16]Lakshmi N. Mittal, "Steel Sans Frontiers: Why Global Is a Good Business Model," speech to the Federation of Industrialists (Luxembourg) (FEDIL), January 22, 2008, www.fedil.lu/Uploads/Publications/Documents/71_1_SpeechLakshmiNMittal.pdf, accessed December 3, 2008.

massive financial institutions and tremendous credit market constraints. A Depression-era plunge in world equity markets wiped out trillions of dollars of wealth and collapsed consumer confidence. The economy rapidly deteriorated, forcing a sudden halt to capital goods projects and durable goods spending, which greatly affected steel operations across the globe. Companies and governments were less inclined to invest in infrastructure improvements. Decreased confidence among consumers limited the purchase of automobiles, and rising unemployment put a strain on the construction market. All markets had limited opportunities to obtain financing, which further decreased incentives for companies, governments and consumers to demand steel products.

Consequently, the market prices for steel plummeted in the fourth quarter of 2008, from record highs experienced in August 2008, thus forcing steel companies to sharply cut back production (see **Exhibit 9**). By the end of 2008, most steel entities were operating at a very low production level of 40 percent.[17]

At Dofasco, production levels averaged 60 percent, as a result of the North American automotive market significantly scaling back projection levels and compounded by the risk that a few of the major North American car manufacturers would be forced into bankruptcy protection. Sales and margins suffered in the last quarter of 2008. As a result of the significantly changed market conditions, the favourable outlook at the time of the Dofasco acquisition in 2006 had changed dramatically, and a much more negative outlook was anticipated until at least the end of 2010 (see **Exhibit 10** for 2008 enterprise value estimates).

## Bell's task

Bell pulled out the memo prepared by Collins, the director of financial accounting at Dofasco (see **Exhibit 10**), which summarized his thoughts on the potential future cash flows for Dofasco and the resulting valuation of the division. Bell knew that the dismal forecasted earnings for the operations implied a potential impairment of the operation's assets under International Financial Reporting Standards but she was unsure of what the actual impairment loss might be. She knew that she would also have to review the March 1, 2006, fair value estimates and determine how the original $4.939 billion purchase price had been allocated to the various tangible and intangible assets and liabilities. Her understanding was that despite the large premium paid for the Dofasco shares, no portion of the purchase price discrepancy was allocated to goodwill, though she was unclear as to why this would have been the case. She wondered what the impact of the economic downturn might have been on any goodwill, had it been recorded. Bell also pulled out the DeJong fair value assessments for the various intangibles that were part of the purchase on March 1, 2006 (see **Exhibits 11, 12, 13,** and **14**). She understood that the evaluators had relied on an income approach, by using the projected EBITDA derived from each intangible to determine its value. She wondered how the revised EBITDA projections would change the recoverable value of Dofasco's intangible assets.

Bell knew she had a long night in front of her trying to understand both the original acquisition and the current values of the assets. She didn't want to disappoint her new supervisor by appearing unprepared for the meeting! She pulled out her summary of the impairment rules included in the International Financial Reporting Standards (see **Exhibit 15**), took a sip of her chai latte, put her pen to paper, and got to work.

---

[17]Interview with ArcelorMittal Dofasco Management, August 17, 2009.

**EXHIBIT 1**  Number of iron and steel mills in Canada by region

Source: Adapted from Statistics Canada, "Number of Establishments in Canada by Type and Region: December 2008 – Iron and Steel Mills and Ferro-Alloy Manufacturing (NAICS 3311)," Canadian Business Patterns Database, December 2008, www.ic.gc.ca/cis-sic/cis-sic.nsf/ILF-/cis3311etbe.html#est1, accessed August 12, 2009.

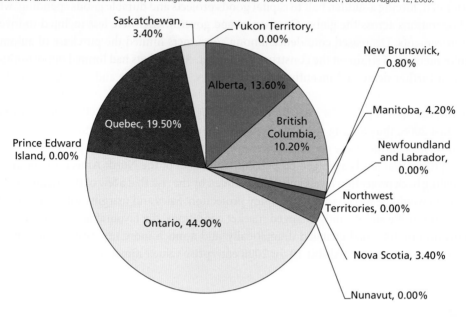

**EXHIBIT 2**  Steel manufacturing revenues per employee

Source: Statistics Canada, "Manufacturing Revenues per Employee: 1998–2007 – All Employees vs. Production Employees: Iron and Steel Mills and Ferro-Alloy Manufacturing (NAICS 3311)," special tabulation, unpublished data, Annual Survey of Manufactures, 1998–2003; Annual Survey of Manufactures and Logging, 2004 to 2007, www.ic.gc.ca/cis-sic/cis-sic.nsf/IDE/cis3311-pere.html, accessed August 12, 2009.

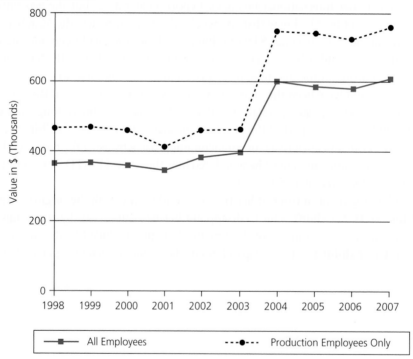

**EXHIBIT 3** Dofasco Inc. – internally generated intangible assets, January 2006

## Environmental permits and licenses

Environmental permits and licenses exist in the form of Certificates of Approvals, which are acquired from the Ministry of Environment (MOE). Dofasco requires permits for emitting substances into the air (i.e., air emission, noise), water (i.e., water usage and discharge) and land (i.e., waste generating sites). Without these certificates, Dofasco could not legally run its steel operations.

## Customer lists

A significant customer relationship requires the existence of some customer identifying records and some obligation or advantage on the part of the business or customer to continue the relationship. Dofasco is believed to have an identifiable customer base as it has the following qualities with regard to its customer relationship:

1 Offers exclusive products or services to such customers
2 Not dependent on brand for customer attraction
3 Little need for advertising and promotional activities
4 Not contingent on Dofasco's manufacturing location
5 Sells goods and services for which a significant cost is associated with substitution.

## Supply contracts

Dofasco's natural gas supply contracts are expected to provide the company economic benefits.

## Internal research and development

New Product Development (NPD) initiatives were identified during the valuation process and characterized as one of the following:

1 Advanced High Strength Steels – Lightweight, high-strength steel for automotive sector.
2 Other Steel Products – Other grades of hot-rolled and cold-rolled steel products for use in the automotive markets.
3 Coating – New coating applications for use in exposed steel products. Limited use in automotive market.

Source: ArcelorMittal Dofasco Financial Accounting Group.

**EXHIBIT** 4 Dofasco Inc. company valuation

# DEJONG EVALUATION
## MEMO

| | |
|---|---|
| **To:** | Sean Collins, Director of Financial Accounting at Dofasco |
| **From:** | DeJong Evaluation |
| **Date:** | 01-Mar-06 |
| **Re:** | Fair Value Assessment – Enterprise Value |

### DOFASCO'S STEEL OPERATIONS
### ENTERPRISE VALUE-AS OF MARCH 1, 2006

| CAD $ mn | 2006 | 2007 | 2008 | 2009 | 2010 | 2011 -> (Residual) |
|---|---|---|---|---|---|---|
| EBITDA | $400 | $550 | $600 | $650 | $700 | $700 |
| Synergies from acquisition | 50 | 100 | 100 | 150 | 150 | 150 |
| Total | 450 | 650 | 700 | 800 | 850 | 850 |
| Income tax rate of 34.12% | 154 | 222 | 239 | 273 | 290 | 290 |
| After-tax earnings | 296 | 428 | 461 | 527 | 560 | 560 |
| Cash flow adjustments | | | | | | |
| Capital expenditures | −100 | −100 | −100 | −100 | −100 | −100 |
| Change in working capital | 30 | 90 | 50 | 50 | – | – |
| Net cash flow | 226 | 418 | 411 | 477 | 460 | 460 |
| Terminal value | | | | | | 5,500 |
| Discount factor (9%) | 0.917 | 0.842 | 0.772 | 0.708 | 0.650 | 0.596 |
| **Present value of net cash flow** | **$208** | **$352** | **$317** | **$338** | **$299** | **$3,279** |
| **Total Enterprise value** | **$4,794** | | | | | |

Source: ArcelorMittal Dofasco Financial Accounting Group.

**EXHIBIT 5** Dofasco Inc. – excerpt from consolidated balance sheet[1] February 28, 2006 (in CDN$ mn)

### Current Assets

| | |
|---|---|
| Cash and cash equivalents | $ 50.00 |
| Short-term investments | – |
| Accounts receivable | 655.44 |
| Inventories | 1,421.67 |
| Future income taxes | 74.70 |
| Other current assets | 26.56 |

### Fixed and other assets

| | |
|---|---|
| Fixed assets | 2,258.71 |
| Future income tax assets | 47.02 |
| Accrued pension benefit | 90.07 |
| Investments and other assets | 30.43 |
| **Total Assets** | **$4,654.61** |

### Current Liabilities

| | |
|---|---|
| Short-term borrowings | $ 225.03 |
| Accounts payable and accrued liabilities | 607.50 |
| Income and other taxes payable | 46.00 |
| Dividends payable | 25.95 |
| Current requirements on long-term debt | 49.97 |

### Long-term liabilities

| | |
|---|---|
| Long-term debt | 695.29 |
| Future income tax liabilities | 84.78 |
| Employee future benefits | 735.33 |
| Other long-term liabilities | 57.30 |
| Minority Interest | 43.46 |
| Total Liabilities | $2,570.61 |
| **Net Carrying Value** | **$2,084.00** |

[1] Prepared in accordance with Canadian Generally Accepted Accounting Principles(GAAP).
Source: ArcelorMittal Dofasco Financial Accounting Group.

**EXHIBIT 6**  Dofasco Inc. – estimated fair values at acquisition[1] March 1, 2006 (in CDN$ mn)[2]

| | |
|---|---:|
| **Current Assets** | |
| Cash and cash equivalents | $ 50.00 |
| Short-term investments | |
| Accounts receivable | 605.00 |
| Inventories | 1,600.00 |
| Future income taxes | 74.70 |
| Other current assets | 49.89 |
| **Fixed and other assets** | |
| Fixed assets | |
| Land | 120.00 |
| Building | 964.00 |
| Machinery and equipment | 3,960.00 |
| Construction in progress | 110.00 |
| Future income tax assets | 47.02 |
| Accrued pension benefit | – |
| Investments and other assets | 31.43 |
| **Total Assets** | $7,612.04 |
| **Current Liabilities** | |
| Short-term borrowings | $ 225.03 |
| Accounts payable and accrued liabilities | 651.00 |
| Income and other taxes payable | 46.00 |
| Dividends payable | 25.95 |
| Current requirements on long-term debt | 49.97 |
| **Long-term liabilities** | |
| Long-term debt | 595.29 |
| Future income tax liabilities | 84.78 |
| Employee future benefits | 1,055.33 |
| Other long-term liabilities | 57.30 |
| Minority Interest | 43.46 |
| Total Liabilities | $2,834.11 |
| **Net Fair Value** | $4,777.93 |

[1] Fair values provided by DeJong Evaluation.

[2] DeJong Evaluation expected any purchase price discrepancy to be allocated mostly to definite life intangibles rather than to goodwill.

Source: ArcelorMittal Dofasco Financial Accounting Group.

**EXHIBIT 7**  Recent Mittal Steel Company NV acquisitions

| YEAR | COMPANY | COUNTRY |
|------|---------|---------|
| 1997 | Thyssen Duisberg | Germany |
| 1998 | Inland Steel | USA |
| 1999 | Unimetal | France |
| 2001 | Sidex | Romania |
| 2001 | Annaba | Algeria |
| 2003 | Nova Hut | Czech Republic |
| 2004 | BH Steel | Bosnia |
| 2004 | Balkan Steel | Macedonia |
| 2004 | PHS | Poland |
| 2004 | Iscor | South Africa |
| 2005 | ISG | USA |
| 2005 | Hunan Valin | China |
| 2005 | Kryvorizhstal | Ukraine |

Source: ArcelorMittal, "History," www.arcelormitta.com/index.php?lang=en&page=15, accessed August 18, 2009.

**EXHIBIT 8**  ArcelorMittal 2007 takeover transactions by country

| | |
|---|---|
| Argentina | Poland |
| Austria | Russia |
| Brazil | Slovakia |
| Canada | South Africa |
| China | Turkey |
| Estonia | United Kingdom |
| France | United States |
| Germany | Uruguay |
| Italy | Venezuela |
| Mexico | |

Source: ArcelorMittal, "History," www.arcelormittaL.com/mdex.php?lang=en&page=15, accessed August 18, 2009.

**EXHIBIT 9**  Historical steel prices

Source: ArcelorMittal Dofasco Marketing Group.

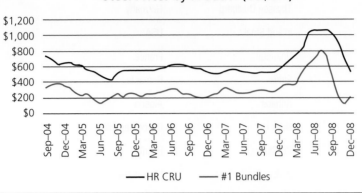

Note: NT = Net Tons (2000 lbs); HR CRU = Price of hot roll steel monitored by CRU Steel Price Index; #1 Bundles = Price of scrap bundles in the Chicago area.

**EXHIBIT 10**  Dofasco enterprise value December 15, 2008

## DOFASCO
## ENTERPRISE VALUE
## DECEMBER 15, 2008

File   Edit   View   Favorites   Tools   Help

# DOFASCO™                                    ArcelorMittal

| | |
|---|---|
| To: | Dofasco Financial Accounting Group |
| From: | Sean Collins, Director of Financial Accounting at Dofasco |
| Date: | 15-Dec-08   6:46 PM |
| Re: | Dofasco Enterprise Value -Year End 2008 |

Hello Team,

Below you will find the earnings projections for ArcelorMittal Dofasco. You will notice a substantial change from the projections made and enterprise value at Arcelor's acquisition on March 1, 2006. These projections will guide our discussions regarding the impairment of intangible assets tomorrow.

Note that the 9 percent Arcelor Historical Discount Rate was applied for the enterprise valuation by DeJong Evaluation on March 1, 2006. A 13 percent ArcelorMittal Corporate Discount Rate is applied broadly across other ArcelorMittal subsidiaries.

Company sales managers are predicting a 20 percent–30 percent decline in revenues as a result of the current economic situation. As a team I expect us to determine the implication of this decline on the valuation of ArcelorMittal Dofasco's identified intangible assets.

I am looking forward to a productive meeting tomorrow morning.

S.C.

## DOFASCO'S STEEL OPERATIONS
## ENTERPRISE VALUE – AS OF DECEMBER 31, 2008

| CAD $ mn | 2009 | 2010 | 2011 | 2012 | 2013 | 2014 |
|---|---|---|---|---|---|---|
| EBITDA | $250 | $400 | $500 | $500 | $500 | $500 |
| Less: Tax | 85 | 136 | 171 | 171 | 171 | 171 |
| After-Tax Earnings | 165 | 264 | 329 | 329 | 329 | 329 |
| Cash flow adjustments | | | | | | |
| Capital expenditures | −80 | −90 | −90 | −90 | −90 | −90 |
| Change in working capital | 90 | 90 | 50 | 50 | – | – |
| Net operating free cash flow | $260 | $400 | $460 | $460 | $410 | $410 |
| Terminal cash value | | | | | | $3,000 |
| **Valuation Using Arcelor Historical Discount Rate** | | | | | | |
| Discount Factor (9%) | 0.917 | 0.842 | 0.772 | 0.708 | 0.650 | 0.596 |
| Present Value of Cash Flow | $238.5 | $336.7 | $355.2 | $325.9 | $266.5 | $1,788.8 |
| Enterprise Value | $3,311.6 | | | | | |
| **Valuation Using ArcelorMittal Corporate Discount Rate** | | | | | | |
| Discount Factor (13%) | 0.885 | 0.783 | 0.693 | 0.613 | 0.543 | 0.480 |
| Present Value of Cash Flow | $230.1 | $313.3 | $318.8 | $282.1 | $222.5 | $1,441.0 |
| Enterprise Value | $2,807.8 | | | | | |

Source: ArcelorMittal Dofasco Financial Accounting Group.

**EXHIBIT 11**  DeJong evaluation – environmental permit valuation estimates

## DEJONG EVALUATION
### MEMO

| | |
|---|---|
| **To:** | Sean Collins, Director of Financial Accounting at Dofasco |
| **From:** | DeJong Evaluation |
| **Date:** | 01-Mar-06 |
| **Re:** | Fair Value Assessment – Dofasco Permits and Licenses |

As the employment of environmental permits is vital to Dofasco's operations, the fair value of these permits is determined by the earnings foregone in the absence of the permits on hand. DeJong Evaluation has provided both high and low estimates for the earnings foregone in the absence of environmental permits. The estimated cost to acquire the necessary environmental permits would be approximately $1.4M, which includes the consulting and application fees along with the necessary site reviews conducted by the Ministry of Environment. This cost is factored into the foregone earnings provided below. The permits expire at the end of 2011.

Net working capital and fixed assets are key supportive assets to this intangible asset. In order to accurately determine the fair value of the permits, a required return on assets directly related to the permit use must be deducted from the after-tax earnings applied in the valuation. Furthermore, a 11 percent discount rate has been adopted as the appropriate rate of return specific to intangible assets. Intangible assets are considered to be the highest risk asset component of an overall business enterprise as may have little, if any, liquidity, and poor versatility for redeployment elsewhere in the business enterprise.

**FAIR VALUE DATA**

| CAD $ mn | 2006 | 2007 | 2008 | 2009 | 2010 | 2011 |
|---|---|---|---|---|---|---|
| **Total Earnings Foregone** | | | | | | |
| High *end value* | $350 | $375 | $400 | $425 | $440 | $450 |
| Low *end value* | $345 | $365 | $395 | $415 | $425 | $435 |
| **Income Tax Rate** | 34.12% | | **Discount Rate** | 11% | | |
| **After-tax returns on contributory assets** | | | | | | |
| | $235 | $245 | $260 | $270 | $270 | $270 |
| **Discount Factor (11%)** | 0.901 | 0.812 | 0.731 | 0.659 | 0.593 | 0.535 |
| *High Value* | −$3.98 | $1.66 | $2.57 | $6.58 | $11.79 | $14.15 |
| Present Value | $32.78 | | | | | |
| *Low Value* | −$6.95 | −$3.68 | $0.17 | $2.24 | $5.93 | $8.86 |
| Present Value | $6.57 | | | | | |

**EXHIBIT 12**  DeJong evaluation – customer lists valuation estimates

## DEJONG EVALUATION
### MEMO

**To:**        Sean Collins, Director of Financial Accounting at Dofasco
**From:**      DeJong Evaluation
**Date:**      01-Mar-06
**Re:**        Fair Value Assessment – Dofasco Customer Lists

Dofasco's ability to meet customer needs has prompted much of its steel-making and product innovations. Furthermore, Dofasco's specialized product offering has developed long-term relationships in many of its markets. Arcelor citied Dofasco's strong customer relations as value driver for the purchase of Dofasco. Value derived from customer lists is expected to expire after eight years.

The income approach, using an excess earnings method to value the acquired customer relationships has been applied. The excess earnings method estimates the fair value of an asset based on expected future economic benefits discounted to present value. DeJong evaluators have provided both high and low EBITDA margin estimates. Margin estimates are based on a High and Low range of production costs such as market price fluctuations for raw material inputs.

Net working capital, fixed assets, technology and Dofasco's assembled workforce are key supportive assets to this intangible asset. In order to accurately determine the fair value of the Dofasco's customer relationships, a required return on assets directly related to the customer lists use must be deducted from the after-tax earnings applied in the valuation. Furthermore, a 11 percent discount rate has been adopted as the appropriate rate of return specific to intangible assets. Intangible assets are considered to be the highest risk asset component of an overall business enterprise as may have little, if any, liquidity, and poor versatility for redeployment elsewhere in the business enterprise.

### FAIR VALUE DATA

| CAD $ mn | 2006 | 2007 | 2008 | 2009 | 2010 | 2011 | 2012 | 2013 | 2014 | 2015 |
|---|---|---|---|---|---|---|---|---|---|---|
| Revenue | | | | | | | | | | |
| Automotive | $976 | $1,065 | $978 | $882 | $813 | $630 | $450 | $270 | $90 | $– |
| Construction | 490 | 538 | 491 | 456 | 425 | 349 | 271 | 194 | 116 | 38 |
| Distribution | 386 | 362 | 284 | 223 | 189 | 114 | 38 | – | – | – |
| Consumer | 296 | 308 | 270 | 237 | 213 | 169 | 21 | 73 | 24 | – |
| Total | $2,148 | $2,273 | $2,023 | $1,798 | $1,640 | $1,262 | $880 | $537 | $230 | $38 |
| **EBITDA Margin – High** | 10.8% | 18.2% | 22.8% | 24.6% | 24.6% | 24.6% | 24.5% | 24.6% | 24.8% | 23.7% |
| **EBITDA – High** | $232.0 | $413.0 | $461.0 | $442.0 | $403.0 | $310.0 | $216.0 | $132.0 | $57.0 | $9.0 |
| **EBITDA Margin – Low** | 9.9% | 16.4% | 21.2% | 23.4% | 23.3% | 23.3% | 23.3% | 23.4% | 23.5% | 22.5% |
| **EBITDA – Low** | $213.4 | $371.7 | $428.7 | $419.9 | $382.9 | $294.5 | $205.2 | $125.4 | $54.2 | $8.6 |
| **Earnings After Tax** | *Tax Rate* | 34.12% | | | | | | | | |
| **EBITDA – High** | $152.8 | $272.1 | $303.7 | $291.2 | $265.5 | $204.2 | $142.3 | $87.0 | $37.6 | $5.9 |
| **EBITDA – Low** | $140.6 | $244.9 | $282.4 | $276.6 | $252.2 | $194.0 | $135.2 | $82.6 | $35.7 | $5.6 |
| **After-Tax Return on Contributory Assets** | | | | | | | | | | |
| Net working capital | $17.3 | $17.7 | $15.6 | $13.7 | $12.6 | $9.7 | $6.7 | $4.1 | $1.8 | $0.3 |
| Fixed assets | 167.0 | 222.4 | 203.6 | 183.3 | 170.9 | 131.2 | 91.5 | 55.3 | 24.0 | 4.0 |
| Technology | 15.5 | 19.8 | 16.6 | 16.4 | 15.2 | 11.7 | 8.1 | 5.0 | 2.1 | 0.4 |
| Assembled workforce | 9.0 | 11.9 | 11.1 | 9.0 | 9.1 | 7.0 | 4.9 | – | 1.0 | 0.2 |
| Total | $208.8 | $271.8 | $246.9 | $222.4 | $207.8 | $159.6 | $111.2 | $64.4 | $28.9 | $4.9 |
| **Net Return on Customer Relationship** | | | | | | | | | | |
| High | −$56.0 | $0.3 | $56.8 | $68.8 | $57.7 | $44.6 | $31.1 | $22.6 | $8.7 | $1.0 |
| Low | −$68.2 | −$26.9 | $35.5 | $54.2 | $44.4 | $34.4 | $24.0 | $18.2 | $6.8 | $0.7 |
| **Present Value of Net Return on Customer Relationship** | | | **Discount Rate** | | | | 11% | | | |
| Discount Factor | 0.901 | 0.812 | 0.731 | 0.659 | 0.593 | 0.535 | 0.482 | 0.434 | 0.391 | 0.352 |
| Future Returns – High | −$50.4 | $0.2 | $41.5 | $45.3 | $34.2 | $23.9 | $15.0 | $9.8 | $3.4 | $0.4 |
| Present Value – High | $123.3 | | | | | | | | | |
| Future Returns – Low | −$61.4 | −$21.9 | $26.0 | $35.7 | $26.4 | $18.4 | $11.6 | $7.9 | $2.6 | $0.3 |
| Present Value – Low | $45.6 | | | | | | | | | |

**EXHIBIT 13**  DeJong evaluation – Dofasco supply contracts

## DEJONG EVALUATION
**MEMO**

| | |
|---|---|
| **To:** | Sean Collins, Director of Financial Accounting at Dofasco |
| **From:** | DeJong Evaluation |
| **Date:** | 01-Mar-06 |
| **Re:** | Fair Value Assessment – Dofasco Supply Contracts |

After a review of Dofasco's significant supply contracts, it appears that Dofasco's natural gas contract is its sole contract which holds significant value relative to current market terms. DeJong has determined the present value of this contract to be approximately $10 million CAD. These natural gas contracts will be useful over the next two years.

A 11 percent discount rate has been adopted as the appropriate rate of return specific to intangible assets. Intangible assets are considered to be the highest risk asset component of an overall business enterprise as may have little, if any, liquidity, and poor versatility for redeployment elsewhere in the business enterprise.

### FAIR VALUE DATA

| CAD $ mn | 2006 | 2007 |
|---|---|---|
| Supply Contract Benefit | **$6.5** | **$5.1** |
| Discount Factor (11%) | 0.901 | 0.812 |
| Future Benefit | **$5.9** | **$4.1** |
| Present Value | **$10.0** | |

Source: ArcelorMittal Dofasco Financial Accounting Group.

**EXHIBIT 14**  DeJong evaluation – internal development valuation estimates

# DEJONG EVALUATION
## MEMO

**To:**        Sean Collins, Director of Financial Accounting at Dofasco

**From:**      DeJong Evaluation

**Date:**      01-Mar-06

**Re:**        Fair Value Assessment – New Product Development

Only those new product development (NPD) initiatives, where research and development activities have been substantially completed and near the commercialization stage will be considered for the 'internal research and development' intangible asset valuation. The estimated fair value of these significant NPD initiatives will be determined based on several factors, which include the projected after-tax earnings on the sales of the new products in the market, less costs to develop. Similar to the valuation of other intangibles, this process is known as the earnings approach to asset valuation. Given Dofasco's capacity restraints, after-tax earnings foregone on existing product that would have otherwise been produced (ie., opportunity cost) should also be considered.

The useful life of this intangible asset will range from 10 to 15 years; this assumes these NPDs will be replaced by new NPDs following that period. A discount rate of 15 percent was determined to be the minimal expected return on the NPDs.

In order to assess the reasonability of the earnings approach, the research and development costs incurred to date such as salaries and benefits of those employees involved in the projects, cost of materials, testing, overhead and upfront licensing fees have been determined. These costs are known as the 'costs to replicate.' The costs to replicate must be exceeded by an estimated future economic benefit of the initiative to confirm that the NPD projects have future inherit value. The current after tax cost to replicate is $7.5 million CAD. Currently value exists beyond the 'costs to replicate.'

### FAIR VALUE DATA

| CAD $ mn | 2006 | 2007 | 2008 | 2009 | 2010 | 2011 | 2012 | 2013 | 2014 | 2015 |
|---|---|---|---|---|---|---|---|---|---|---|
| **EBITDA from NPD – High Estimates** | | | | | | | | | | |
| Advanced High Strength Steels | $1 | $2 | $4 | $5 | $5 | $5 | $5 | $5 | $5 | $5 |
| Other Steel Products | 5 | 8 | 9 | 10 | 10 | 10 | 10 | 10 | 10 | 10 |
| Coating | 1 | 2 | 4 | 4 | 4 | 4 | 4 | 4 | 4 | 4 |
| Total | $7 | $12 | $17 | $19 | $19 | $19 | $19 | $19 | $19 | $19 |
| **EBITDA from NPD – Low Estimates** | | | | | | | | | | |
| Advanced High Strength Steels | $1 | $1 | $2 | $2 | $2 | $2 | $2 | $2 | $2 | $2 |
| Other Steel Products | 4 | 6 | 8 | 8 | 8 | 8 | 8 | 8 | 8 | 8 |
| Coating | 1 | 1 | 2 | 2 | 2 | 2 | 2 | 2 | 2 | 2 |
| Total | $6 | $8 | $12 | $12 | $12 | $12 | $12 | $12 | $12 | $12 |
| Costs to complete NPD | $5 | $4 | $3 | $– | $– | $– | $– | $– | $– | $– |
| Foregone operating margin on products no longer produced | $3 | $3 | $3 | $3 | $3 | $3 | $3 | $3 | $3 | $3 |
| **Discount Rate** 15.00%    **Tax Rate**    34.12% | | | | | | | | | | |
| Discount Factor | 0.870 | 0.756 | 0.658 | 0.572 | 0.497 | 0.432 | 0.376 | 0.327 | 0.284 | 0.247 |
| Value of NPD – High Estimates | –$0.6 | $2.5 | $4.8 | $6.0 | $5.2 | $4.6 | $4.0 | $3.4 | $3.0 | $2.6 |
| **Present Value – High Estimates** | $35.5 | | | | | | | | | |
| Value of NDP – Low Estimates | –$1.1 | $0.5 | $2.6 | $3.4 | $2.9 | $2.6 | $2.2 | $1.9 | $1.7 | $1.5 |
| **Present Value – Low Estimates** | $18.2 | | | | | | | | | |

Source: ArcelorMittal Dofasco Financial Accounting Group.

**EXHIBIT 15** Summary of IAS 36 – impairment of assets

## Cash-generating units

Under international accounting standards (IAS 36), intangible assets that do not generate independent cash flows on their own are grouped into cash-generating units (CGU). A CGU is the smallest group of assets that generates cash inflows, which are largely independent of the cash flows from other assets or groups of assets.

Goodwill is assigned to a CGU or to a group of CGUs, which are expected to benefit from the synergies of the combination.

## Lifespan of intangible assets

Intangible assets are classified as having either indefinite or definite lives. In general, when no legal, regulatory, contractual, competitive, economic, or other factors limit the useful life of an intangible to the enterprise, the useful life of an intangible asset is considered to be **indefinite**. Conversely, **definite** life intangibles have a foreseeable limit to the period which the asset is expected to benefit the entity. Definite life intangible assets are amortized over their useful life or pattern of expected future benefits.

## Impairment testing under IAS 36 – assets other than goodwill

| | Definite Life Assets | Indefinite Life Assets |
|---|---|---|
| *Impairment Assessment Timing* | Assessed for circumstances of impairment at each reporting date. Determine the recoverable amount if impairment seems possible. | Assessed for impairment any time during an annual period, provided it is performed at the same time every year. Determine the recoverable amount for the asset or CGU. |
| *Impairment Test* | Compare the carrying amount of the asset to the recoverable amount. When the recoverable amount is less than the carrying amount, an impairment loss exists. The recoverable amount is the higher of: <br> a) the *fair value less costs to sell,* which is the amount that could be obtained from a sale of the asset in an arm's-length transaction less the costs directly attributable to the sale; or <br> b) the *value in use,* which is the present value of future cash flows expected to be derived from the asset or cash-generating unit. | Compare the carrying amount of the asset to the recoverable amount. When the recoverable amount is less than the carrying amount, an impairment loss exists. The recoverable amount is the higher of: <br> a) the *fair value less costs to sell,* which is the amount that could be obtained from a sale of the asset in an arm's-length transaction less the costs directly attributable to the sale; or <br> b) the *value in use,* which is the present value of future cash flows expected to be derived from the asset or cash-generating unit. |
| *Impairment Loss* | The impairment loss is equal to the carrying amount of the asset or CGU less the recoverable amount. | The impairment loss is equal to the carrying amount of the asset or CGU less the recoverable amount. |

An impairment loss recognized in prior periods for an asset other than goodwill can be reversed if there has been a change in the estimates used to determine the asset's recoverable amount since the last impairment loss was recognized. Under such circumstances, the carrying amount of the asset is increased to its recoverable amount; however, the increased carrying amount cannot exceed the original carrying amount (net of any accumulated amortization).

*(continued)*

**EXHIBIT 15**  Summary of IAS 36 – impairment of assets (Continued)

# Impairment testing under IAS 36 – goodwill

A CGU to which goodwill has been allocated must be tested for impairment at least annually, at the same time every year or whenever there is an indication that the unit may be impaired (see examples above). The impairment test involves comparing the carrying amount of the CGU, including the goodwill, with the recoverable amount of the CGU. If the carrying amount of the CGU exceeds the recoverable amount of the CGU, the entity must recognize an impairment loss.

An impairment loss from goodwill should be allocated to reduce the carrying amount of the CGU in the following order:

1  Reduce the carrying amount of any goodwill allocated to the CGU; and then
2  Reduce the carrying amount of each asset in the CGU on a pro rata basis.[1]

Impairment losses for goodwill cannot be reversed as subsequent increases in value of goodwill are believed to be internally generated rather than a reversal of the previous impairment.

---

[1]However, a carrying amount of an asset cannot be reduced below the highest of its fair value less costs to sell (if determinable), its value in use (if determinable) and zero.

# CASE

# The initial public offering of PartyGaming Plc

On June 30, 2005, PartyGaming Plc offered 781,629,050 of its ordinary shares for public trading on the London Stock Exchange. The offer price of the shares was 116 pence per ordinary share. The number of shares offered for public trading represented approximately 19.5 percent of PartyGaming's 4 billion shares outstanding.

An investment in PartyGaming's shares was not without risks. In its prospectus, PartyGaming warned its prospective investors that they:

> … should be aware that an investment in PartyGaming Plc involves a high degree of risk and that, if certain of the risks described in Part 3 occur, they may lose all or a very substantial part of their investment. Accordingly, an investment in the Shares is only suitable for investors who are particularly knowledgeable in investment matters and who are able to bear the complete loss of their investment.

## PartyGaming and its industry[1]

PartyGaming was founded in 1997. Between 1997 and 2005 the company had become one of the largest online gaming suppliers in the world. In 2005 the company generated the largest proportion of its revenues from accommodating online poker games, partly by means of its own website PartyPoker.com – the world's leading online poker site. Specifically, online poker produced 92 percent of the company's revenues; the remaining 8 percent came from online casino and bingo games. The company had achieved its leading position in online poker through a timely entry into the online poker market, supported by effective online and offline sales and marketing, a reliable technology, and high-level customer support.

In 1997 Ruth Parasol started PartyGaming with the launch of the Starluck casino site, which was operated and managed from the Caribbean. Three years later Anurag Dikshit and Vikrant Bhargava – who would later become the company's Operations and Marketing Directors – became investors in PartyGaming and started to develop the company's poker business. The poker site PartyPoker.com was launched in 2001 from Canada. With the help of famous poker player Mike Sexton, PartyGaming was able to attract a lot of publicity for its new website by organizing the "PartyPoker.com Million" tournament, for which the qualification rounds took place online. In 2002 and 2003 PartyGaming launched PartyBingo.com and moved its operations to Hyderabad (India) and its headquarters to Gibraltar.

The online gaming market had experienced rapid growth in the years just prior to 2005. Primary drivers of this growth were the increasing worldwide popularity of the internet as well as the increasing customer

Professor Erik Peek prepared this case. The case is intended solely as the basis for class discussion and is not intended to serve as an endorsement, source of primary data, or illustration of effective or ineffective management.

[1]The material in this and the following sections largely draws from PartyGaming's IPO prospectus (June 14, 2005).

awareness of the sector's existence. Increasing customer awareness had resulted from greater television exposure and intensified marketing activities by the major industry players. In addition, online gaming companies had invested in their growth by developing new products and improving payment processing, transaction services, and customer support. Industry analysts did not expect this growth to stop in the near term. The online sector's share of the global gaming market was expected to increase from 3 to 8 percent between 2004 and 2009.

Industry analysts estimated the size of the global online and offline gaming market to be $243 billion (in revenues) in 2004 and $282 billion in 2009. The online gaming market was estimated to generate revenue of approximately $8.2 billion in 2004 and $22.7 billion in 2009. In 2004 online casino and bingo games accounted for 29 percent of the online gaming revenues, whereas online poker games accounted for 13 percent. Respectively, 50 percent, 27 percent, and 15 percent of the global online gaming revenues had been generated from the United States, Europe, and Asia. Industry analysts expected the US share of the global online gaming market to decline to 40 percent in 2009 as a result of the above-average market growth in Europe and Asia. The key drivers of such growth would be the increasing number of internet users, the increasing popularity of gaming, the increasing marketing investments made by the industry players, and the development of new distribution channels, such as mobile phones.

Poker had become more popular over the years mostly because of the increased television coverage of poker tournaments and the exposure of the game on popular television shows. Because many of the poker players around the world were still playing offline, the online poker market could potentially grow from the migration of offline players to online play. Analysts estimated that this migration, in combination with the attraction of new poker players, could make the online poker market's revenues grow from slightly more than $1 billion in 2004 to close to $6.4 billion in 2009 – representing 28 percent of the global online gaming market. In comparison, analysts estimated that the online casino market would grow from $2,157 million (in revenues) in 2004 to $5,587 million in 2009. According to PartyGaming's management, there were a number of barriers to entry to the online poker market, creating a competitive advantage for the company:

- *Player liquidity.* To be able to organize games with a wide range of stakes at all times of players' choosing, online poker providers needed to have a large customer base.
- *Software control.* The leading online poker providers had invested significant amounts in software. Having control over their own software helped them to make the software improvements that were necessary for attracting and retaining customers.
- *Payment processing expertise.* To attract and maintain customers, online poker providers must be able to provide a wide range of payment methods (credit cards, e-checks, online wallets) and must have built a reputation for quick, efficient, and error-free payment processing.
- *Customer support.* Online poker providers must make significant investments in customer service operations.
- *Marketing and global reach.* Online poker providers needed to have significant market resources to penetrate new geographic markets and increase advertising expenditures as competition increased.

Having the mission to be the world's largest gaming company, with the most trusted brands, innovative technology, and high-level customer service, PartyGaming focused its strategy on the following areas: (1) sustain brand value and maintain leadership in its current markets; (2) expand to markets outside the United States, first in Europe, later in Asia; (3) continue to provide innovative technology and high-level customer support; (4) stretch the "Party" brand to other games, either acquired or self-developed; and (5) make use of alternative delivery channels, such as mobile phones and interactive television.

In 2004 PartyGaming was the undisputed market leader in the online poker segment. Based on the average ring game rake – the amount of money the provider takes from the pot – the company had a market share of 54 percent. The five next-largest providers of online poker gaming all had market shares between 5 and 8 percent.

# The risks

As pointed out, an investment in PartyGaming's ordinary shares involved substantial risks. The following risks were especially high:

- *Regulatory risks.* One apparent risk affecting the online gaming market in 2005 was that in many countries national gaming laws had been developed to govern offline gaming activities and were not particularly suited to govern online gaming activities. Consequently, in some of PartyGaming's geographical segments there was much uncertainty about whether the supply of online gaming was legal or not. In some countries foreign suppliers of online gaming were not able to obtain a license, and it was uncertain whether and how local regulators would bring actions against foreign suppliers who had no license but were not physically present. PartyGaming ran the risk that regulators would change their laws and take actions that would inhibit the company's ability to process payments and advertise in a particular country. The advantage of these regulatory risks was, however, that they prevented many other companies from entering PartyGaming's industry, thereby reducing competition.
- *Taxation risks.* PartyGaming and most of its group companies had their domicile in Gibraltar, where they were exempt from paying taxes because they offered no services to Gibraltarians or Gibraltar residents. However, in early 2005 the European Commission and the governments of Gibraltar and the United Kingdom had agreed to abolish the Gibraltar exempt company tax regime by the end of 2010. PartyGaming would even lose its tax exempt status – and become subject to a 35 percent tax rate – on December 31, 2007, if it had a change in ownership before June 30, 2006, and immediately lose its tax exempt status if it had a change in ownership after June 30, 2006. At the time of the IPO, it was still unclear what regulators would consider a "change in ownership." PartyGaming expected that the IPO would not be treated as a change in ownership. The company's principal shareholders had agreed not to dispose of their shares within two years of the IPO. Further, the decision to abolish the exempt company tax regime had been appealed to the European Court. Finally, the government of Gibraltar was seeking alternative ways to provide companies with an attractive tax regime.
- *Technology risks.* PartyGaming ran the risk that hackers would attempt to gain access to its systems and disrupt its services. Further, the growing demand for the company's online gaming services could lead to a situation in which its technological architecture as well as the technological architecture of its third-party providers was not developed enough to ensure the absence of errors, failures, interruptions, or delays in the provision of its services. Finally, PartyGaming needed to make investments in technology that facilitated the delivery of its online gaming services to customers who were not using personal computers but other devices such as mobile phones or television set-top devices.
- *Competitive risks.* Other companies in PartyGaming's industry offered formidable competition. At the time of the IPO there were more than 2,000 online gaming sites and more than 200 online poker sites competing for the same customers. An increasing proportion of PartyGaming's revenues came from "third-party skins" – third-party brands that used PartyGaming's platform and shared their revenues. Third-party skins were competition to the company's own operations and brought significant risks of disputes and litigation.
- *Intellectual property rights.* A substantial part of PartyGaming's technology and know-how was proprietary and any misappropriated or unauthorized disclosure of its technology and know-how could harm the company's competitive advantage. Similarly, the use of "Party" domain names or the "Party" brand by third parties without approval could harm the value of the company's brand. In some countries where PartyGaming operated, national laws did not sufficiently protect the company's intellectual property rights, or actions to enforce its intellectual property rights were costly. PartyGaming also ran the risk that other technology companies would claim that their intellectual property rights were infringed by PartyGaming, which could result in litigation.

- *Risks of international expansion.* Because of the legal uncertainties in the United States, PartyGaming planned to expand internationally. Competition outside the United States was, however, stronger than within the United States. Further, international expansion would bring a number of additional risks, such as legal, political, cultural, and currency risks. Operating on an international scale could also increase the company's transaction costs.

- *Short operating history.* PartyGaming's short operating history made it difficult to assess the company's prospects. In its prospectus, the company reported that it did not expect that its rapid historic growth would persist in the future. In order to grow, PartyGaming should innovate new products and services, countering the declining growth of the online poker market. The company also expected that when growth declined, the cyclicality and seasonality (lower yields per active player day in the second quarter, higher yields in the first and fourth quarters) of its operations would become more pronounced.

- *Principal shareholders.* After the IPO, the principal shareholders of PartyGaming would hold close to 73 percent of the company's ordinary shares. Consequently, they could have a decisive influence on the company's financial and operating decisions as well as the success of any takeover offer.

Although PartyGaming had no physical presence in the United States, it did not block US customers from signing up to the company's websites. The company generated almost 87 percent of its revenues from the United States, where the regulatory risks were significant. It advertised its gaming sites in the United States and made use of the services of US payment processors to collect from and pay out funds to its US customers. At the time of the IPO the US Department of Justice considered the US operations of PartyGaming illegal. Further, at least seven US states had laws that explicitly prohibited online gaming, while many other states prohibited all forms of unlicensed gaming. US federal laws were, however, inconclusive about whether online gaming was indeed illegal, and the status of state laws in the matter was unclear. The company had not received an official notification from any US authority that it sought to bring action against the company for its US operations. Any future action by US authorities to issue an injunction, impose fines or imprisonment, or seize gaming proceeds could, however, impose considerable (legal) costs upon the company and reduce the company's revenues and profits.

US law enforcement officials targeted their enforcement activities at US-based companies that provided services such as IT, payment processing, and advertising to PartyGaming. In particular, they alleged the violation of US laws to discourage US banks from processing online gaming transactions and US media from advertising online gaming sites. As a consequence, several banks, such as Citibank; financial service companies, such as PayPal; and media companies, such as Discovery had decided not to provide any services to PartyGaming. Another threat to PartyGaming's US operations was posed by the proposals of the US Congress to prohibit online gaming or the provision of payment processing services to online gaming companies. Over the past years, several proposals were made but did not receive sufficient support to be passed. In 2005 the US Congress would consider the "Kyl Bill," which sought to prohibit the processing of online gaming transactions. At the time of the IPO, this proposal seemed to lack sufficient support from the US Congress.

## PartyGaming's governance

In early 2005 PartyGaming's Board of Directors comprised four executive directors and four nonexecutive directors. All nonexecutive directors were denoted as independent. The company's board had established an audit committee, a remuneration committee, a nominations committee, and an ethics committee. The company's CEO was Richard Lawrence Segal, who had joined the company in August 2004, after having been the CEO of cinema operator Odeon Limited for seven years.

Two executive directors were also principal shareholders of PartyGaming. After the IPO, Anurag Dikshit, Operations Director, would own 31.6 percent of the company's shares; and Vikrant Bhargava, Marketing Director, would own 16.3 percent. Two other principal shareholders were co-founder Ruth Parasol – owning 16.3

percent – and her husband, Russell DeLeon – owning 9.0 percent. Each of the principal shareholders had agreed not to sell any shares during the 12 months following the IPO. Principal shareholders owning more than 15 percent of the company's shares had the right to nominate one nonexecutive director. However, they also agreed that at any time at least half of the company's board would comprise independent directors.

# PartyGaming's performance

At the time of the IPO, PartyGaming's management considered the company's key strengths to be its high-margin business model, its strong marketing programme and brand name, its large active player base, its high-quality and innovative technology, its offering of a wide variety of pay-in and withdrawal methods, its high-level 24/7 customer support, its well-developed systems of risk management and fraud detection, and its strong management team.

To sustain brand value and attract active players, PartyGaming made significant investments in marketing. The company made use of a variety of marketing strategies, such as television and radio advertising, affiliate marketing (sharing revenues with other sites that market PartyGaming sites), direct mail, sign-up bonuses, and sponsorships. In addition, PartyGaming invested in the retention of customers by organizing the PartyPoker.com Million Tournaments, for which the qualification rounds were held online, introducing player loyalty programmes (award schemes), and awarding bonuses to existing players who pay in new funds.

Evidence of PartyGaming's marketing success is shown by the large increase in the company's registered poker and casino players prior to 2005. **Exhibit 1** shows the number of registered and active poker and casino players by period, as well as the average yield per player day. The number of active players, the average daily active players, active player days (average daily active players times the number of days in a period), and yield per active player day were PartyGaming's key performance indicators. The yield per active player day followed a seasonal pattern. In 2003 (2004) the yield per active poker player day was $21.0 ($19.8), $18.1 ($18.7), $18.8 ($18.9), and $20.0 ($19.1) in the first, second, third, and fourth quarter, respectively. Although PartyGaming had a large player base, the company was reliant on a relatively small number of customers. For example, close to 10 percent of the active poker players contributed 70 percent of the company's revenues from poker games. Similarly, 5 percent of the active casino players contributed 82 percent of the company's revenues from casino games.

**Exhibit 2** shows PartyGaming's financial statements for the fiscal years 2003 and 2004, as well as for three fiscal quarters. These figures illustrate PartyGaming's growth in revenues and profits. One apparent development was the strong decline in equity between 2003 and 2004. The reason for this decline was the acquisition of PartyGaming Holdings Limited by PartyGaming Plc in 2004. PartyGaming acquired its interest in PartyGaming Holdings Limited in a transaction under common control. An acquisition under common control occurs when the acquirer and the target firm are both controlled by the same party. As a result of this transaction, PartyGaming Plc became the group's ultimate parent company. International Accounting Standards did not require acquisitions under common control to be accounted for using the purchase method. Consequently, PartyGaming used the pooling method to account for the acquisition, and the deficit in equity reflected the group's cumulative profits as if the new group structure had always been in place.

## QUESTIONS

1 The initial offer price of PartyGaming's ordinary shares was 116 pence per share. Which sales growth and net operating profit margin assumptions are consistent with an offer price of 116 pence?

2 Using your own assumptions, estimate the value of PartyGaming's ordinary shares at the time of the IPO. How do the risks that PartyGaming faced affect your value estimate?

**EXHIBIT 1** Information about PartyGaming's registered and active players

| | Fiscal year ending December 31, 2002 | Fiscal year ending December 31, 2003 | Fiscal year ending December 31, 2004 | Three months ending March 31, 2005 |
|---|---|---|---|---|
| Total registered poker players | 105,000 | 1,283,000 | 5,225,000 | 6,603,000 |
| Total registered casino players | 535,000 | 903,000 | 1,296,000 | 1,376,000 |
| Registered real-money poker players | 20,000 | 210,000 | 806,000 | 1,020,000 |
| Of which active players (in the last month of the period) | 6,000 | 125,000 | 324,000 | 411,000 |
| Registered real-money casino and bingo players | 282,000 | 320,000 | 374,000 | 388,000 |
| Of which active players (in the last month of the period) | 4,000 | 9,000 | 13,000 | 14,000 |
| Average daily active poker players | 1,297 | 17,043 | 77,094 | 121,570 |
| Average yield per active poker player day ($) | 20.8 | 19.5 | 19.1 | 18.6 |
| Average daily active casino and bingo players | 580 | 832 | 1,797 | 1,875 |
| Average yield per active casino and bingo player day ($) | 90.7 | 96.9 | 73.9 | 73.1 |

Source: PartyGaming's IPO prospectus (June 14, 2005). The item "total registered players" includes "play money" players who participate in games for free.

**EXHIBIT 2** PartyGaming's consolidated income statements, balance sheets, cash flow statements, and pro forma income
statement and segment information for two fiscal years and three fiscal quarters

**CONSOLIDATED INCOME STATEMENTS ($ mn)**

|  | Three months ending March 31, 2005 | Three months ending December 31, 2004 | Three months ending March 31, 2004 | Fiscal year ending December 31, 2004 | Fiscal year ending December 31, 2003 |
|---|---|---|---|---|---|
| Revenue – net gaming revenue | 222.6 | 194.0 | 115.4 | 601.6 | 153.1 |
| Other operating revenue/(expenses) | −0.3 | 0.4 | 0.0 | 0.1 | 0.4 |
| Administrative expenses |  |  |  |  |  |
| – other administrative expenses | −23.3 | −21.6 | −15.8 | −73.1 | −29.4 |
| – share-based payments | −4.6 | −2.3 | 0.0 | −3.2 | 0.0 |
| – strategic review costs | −1.5 | 0.0 | 0.0 | 0.0 | 0.0 |
| Distribution expenses | −64.6 | −48.8 | −28.7 | −142.2 | −34.9 |
| **Profit from operating activities** | 128.3 | 121.7 | 70.9 | 383.2 | 89.2 |
| Finance income | 0.6 | 0.8 | 0.2 | 1.4 | 0.0 |
| Finance costs | −3.0 | −4.4 | −0.1 | −12.9 | 0.0 |
| Share of losses of associate | −0.3 | 0.0 | 0.0 | 0.0 | 0.0 |
| **Profit before tax** | 125.6 | 118.1 | 71.0 | 371.7 | 89.2 |
| Tax | −8.2 | −7.4 | −3.9 | −21.6 | −5.6 |
| **Profit after tax** | 117.4 | 110.7 | 67.1 | 350.1 | 83.6 |
| Minority interest | 0.0 | 0.0 | −1.6 | −1.6 | −6.6 |
| **Profit from ordinary activities attributable to equity holders of the parent** | 117.4 | 110.7 | 65.5 | 348.5 | 77.0 |
| Net earnings per share ($ cents) | 3.11 | 2.93 | 1.73 | 9.23 | 2.04 |
| Net earnings per share ($ cents) – diluted | 3.09 | 2.91 | 1.72 | 9.16 | 2.02 |
| Weighted average shares outstanding | 3,776 | 3,776 | 3,776 | 3,776 | 3,776 |
| Weighted average shares outstanding, diluted | 3,803 | 3,803 | 3,803 | 3,803 | 3,803 |

**EXHIBIT 2** PartyGaming's consolidated income statements, balance sheets, cash flow statements, and pro forma income statement and segment information for two fiscal years and three fiscal quarters (Continued)

### *PRO FORMA* INCOME STATEMENT AND SEGMENT INFORMATION ($ mn)

| | Three months ending March 31, 2005 | Three months ending December 31, 2004 | Three months ending March 31, 2004 | Fiscal year Ending December 31, 2004 | Fiscal year ending December 31, 2003 |
|---|---|---|---|---|---|
| **Revenues** | | | | | |
| – Poker | 210.3 | 183.5 | 102.9 | 553.0 | 123.7 |
| – Casino/Bingo | 12.3 | 10.5 | 12.5 | 48.6 | 29.4 |
| – Other | 0.0 | 0.0 | 0.0 | 0.0 | 0.0 |
| **Administrative expenses** | | | | | |
| – Transaction fees | −10.1 | −8.9 | −6.2 | −29.3 | −9.8 |
| – Staff costs | −10.5 | −8.0 | −4.3 | −21.8 | −8.3 |
| – Depreciation and amortization | −1.7 | −1.4 | −0.8 | −4.6 | −1.1 |
| – Other overheads | −7.1 | −5.6 | −4.5 | −20.6 | −10.2 |
| **Distribution expenses** | | | | | |
| – Affiliate fees | −23.6 | −18.8 | — | −53.7 | −13.3 |
| – Customer acquisition and retention (primarily advertising) | −24.1 | −14.5 | — | −37.6 | −10.6 |
| – Chargebacks (amounts unrecoverable from customers) | −11.6 | −10.2 | — | −36.7 | −8.2 |
| – Customer bonuses | −3.7 | −4.1 | — | −10.0 | −1.6 |
| – Web-hosting | −1.6 | −1.2 | — | −4.2 | −1.2 |
| **Profit before tax** | | | | | |
| – Poker | 128.0 | 118.0 | 64.5 | 360.1 | 81.2 |
| – Casino/Bingo | 6.2 | 6.0 | 6.7 | 28.4 | 8.2 |
| – Other | −8.6 | −5.9 | −0.2 | −16.8 | −0.2 |
| **Impairment losses – trade receivables** | −11.7 | −10.1 | −10.3 | 42.2 | −9.9 |
| **Impairment losses – other** | 0.0 | 0.0 | 0.0 | 0.0 | −0.4 |

**EXHIBIT 2**  PartyGaming's consolidated income statements, balance sheets, cash flow statements, and pro forma income
statement and segment information for two fiscal years and three fiscal quarters (Continued)

## CONSOLIDATED BALANCE SHEETS ($ mn)

| | Three months ending March 31, 2005 | Three months ending December 31, 2004 | Three months ending March 31, 2004 | Fiscal year ending December 31, 2004 | Fiscal year ending December 31, 2003 |
|---|---|---|---|---|---|
| Intangible assets | 7.7 | 7.7 | 8.0 | 7.7 | 0.0 |
| Property, plant, and equipment | 25.4 | 13.3 | 9.1 | 13.3 | 5.7 |
| Investment in associates | 1.5 | 0.0 | 0.0 | 0.0 | 0.0 |
| **Total non-current assets** | 34.6 | 21.0 | 17.1 | 21.0 | 5.7 |
| Trade and other receivables | 132.9 | 107.8 | 76.5 | 107.8 | 53.2 |
| Cash and cash equivalents | 78.3 | 133.9 | 131.7 | 133.9 | 74.6 |
| Short-term investments | 3.5 | 0.0 | 0.0 | 0.0 | 0.0 |
| **Total current assets** | 214.7 | 241.7 | 208.2 | 241.7 | 127.8 |
| **Total assets** | 249.3 | 262.7 | 225.3 | 262.7 | 133.5 |
| Bank overdraft | 2.9 | 1.8 | 2.3 | 1.8 | 0.0 |
| Trade and other payables | 46.4 | 39.5 | 18.7 | 39.5 | 14.4 |
| Shareholder loans | 229.3 | 223.9 | 0.0 | 223.9 | 0.0 |
| Income taxes | 36.2 | 28.0 | 10.7 | 28.0 | 6.7 |
| Client liabilities and progressive prize pools | 124.1 | 104.6 | 49.1 | 104.6 | 35.4 |
| Provisions | 7.9 | 4.7 | 3.0 | 4.7 | 1.9 |
| **Total current liabilities** | 446.8 | 402.5 | 83.8 | 402.5 | 58.4 |
| Trade and other payables | 5.0 | 6.1 | 7.5 | 6.1 | 0.0 |
| Shareholder loans | 80.2 | 258.9 | 0.0 | 258.9 | 0.0 |
| **Total non-current liabilities** | 85.2 | 265.0 | 7.5 | 265.0 | 0.0 |
| Share capital | 0.1 | 0.0 | 0.0 | 0.0 | 0.0 |
| Share premium account | 0.4 | 0.4 | 0.4 | 0.4 | 0.4 |
| Retained earnings | 534.4 | 417.0 | 134.0 | 417.0 | 68.6 |
| Other reserve | −825.4 | −825.4 | −0.4 | −825.4 | −0.4 |
| Share option reserve | 7.8 | 3.2 | 0.0 | 3.2 | 0.0 |
| **Equity attributable to equity holders of the parent** | −282.7 | −404.8 | 134.0 | −404.8 | 68.6 |
| **Minority interest** | 0.0 | 0.0 | 0.0 | 0.0 | 6.5 |
| **Total liabilities and shareholders' equity** | 249.3 | 262.7 | 225.3 | 262.7 | 133.5 |

**EXHIBIT 2** PartyGaming's consolidated income statements, balance sheets, cash flow statements, and pro forma income
statement and segment information for two fiscal years and three fiscal quarters (Continued)

**CONSOLIDATED CASH FLOW STATEMENTS ($ mn)**

| | Three months ending March 31, 2005 | Three months ending December 31, 2004 | Three months ending March 31, 2004 | Fiscal year ending December 31, 2004 | Fiscal year ending December 31, 2003 |
|---|---|---|---|---|---|
| Profit before tax | 125.6 | 118.1 | 71.0 | 371.7 | 89.2 |
| Adjustment for: | | | | | |
| Amortization of intangibles | 0.0 | 0.1 | 0.0 | 0.3 | 0.2 |
| Interest expense | 3.0 | 4.4 | 0.1 | 12.9 | 0.0 |
| Interest income | −0.6 | −0.8 | −0.2 | −1.4 | 0.0 |
| Depreciation of property, plant, and equipment | 1.7 | 1.3 | 0.8 | 4.3 | 0.9 |
| Gains on sale of property, plant, and equipment | 0.0 | 0.0 | 0.0 | 0.0 | 0.1 |
| Increase in share-based payments reserve | 4.6 | 2.3 | 0.0 | 3.2 | 0.0 |
| Loss on investment in associate | 0.3 | 0.0 | 0.0 | 0.0 | 0.0 |
| **Operating cash flows before movements in working capital and provisions** | 134.6 | 125.4 | 71.7 | 391.0 | 90.4 |
| Increase in trade and other receivables | −24.6 | −15.3 | −23.3 | −54.6 | −48.1 |
| Increase in trade and other payables | 26.5 | 31.3 | 15.2 | 89.9 | 43.4 |
| Increase in provisions | 3.2 | Å|3.5 | 1.1 | 2.8 | 0.4 |
| Income taxes paid | −0.8 | 0.0 | 0.0 | 0.0 | 0.0 |
| **Cash generated/(used) by working capital** | 4.3 | 12.5 | −7.0 | 38.1 | −4.3 |
| **Net cash from operating activities** | 138.9 | 137.9 | 64.7 | 429.1 | 86.1 |
| Purchases of property, plant, and equipment | −13.8 | −4.0 | −4.1 | −11.9 | −5.9 |
| Purchases of intangible assets | 0.0 | 0.0 | 0.0 | 0.0 | −0.2 |
| Retained earnings | 534.4 | 417.0 | 134.0 | 417.0 | 68.6 |
| Purchase of minority interest in subsidiary | 0.0 | 0.0 | −5.8 | −5.8 | 0.0 |
| Interest received | 0.6 | 0.5 | 0.2 | 1.4 | 0.0 |
| Purchase and cancelation of own shares | 0.0 | 0.0 | −0.1 | −2.0 | −3.1 |
| Investment in associated undertaking | −1.8 | 0.0 | 0.0 | 0.0 | 0.0 |
| Increase in short-term investments | −3.5 | 0.0 | 0.0 | 0.0 | 0.0 |
| **Net cash used in investing activities** | −18.5 | −3.5 | −9.8 | −18.3 | −9.2 |
| Issue of shares | 0.0 | 0.0 | 0.0 | 0.9 | 0.0 |
| Interest paid | −3.8 | −4.6 | −0.1 | −11.0 | 0.0 |
| Equity dividends paid | 0.0 | 0.0 | 0.0 | 0.0 | −8.1 |
| Payments to shareholders | −173.3 | −113.5 | 0.0 | −343.2 | 0.0 |
| **Net cash used in financing activities** | −177.1 | −118.1 | −0.1 | −353.3 | −8.1 |

Source: PartyGaming's IPO Prospectus (June 14, 2005). Note that at the time of the IPO, the total number of shares outstanding was 4,000,000,000.

# CASE
## Two European hotel groups (A): Equity analysis*

## Accor[1]

In 2017 France-based Accor was Europe's second largest and the world's sixth largest hotel group (based on the number of rooms). The company employed more than 250 thousand people and operated restaurants, (online) travel agencies, and 4,300 hotels with 616,181 rooms in 99 countries. Major brand names owned by Accor included Raffles, Sofitel, Novotel, Mercure, Ibis, and HotelF1. Fifty-two percent of the company's hotel rooms were located in Europe and 27 percent in the Asia-Pacific region. Accor did not own all of its hotels. In 2017 about 26 percent of its rooms were owned or leased, 41 percent were operated under management contracts, and 33 percent were franchised. Accor's hotel business generated close €1.7 billion in revenues, while its other businesses generated €277 million in revenues.

In its hotel business, Accor served several segments, ranging from the upscale segment with Sofitel or Raffles to the economy segment with Ibis Budget or HotelF1. The company's preferred operating structure depended on the type of segment. For example, Accor preferred to operate its hotels under management contracts in the upscale segment and franchised in the budget segment. Under a management contract structure, Accor typically signed a 30- to 50-year agreement to manage one or more hotels, some of which were partly or fully owned by AccorInvest. AccorInvest was a property company that started off as one of Accor's operating segments but became a separate legal entity during 2017. In early 2018 Accor partly divested AccorInvest by selling a majority stake to a group of institutional investors, while planning to retain a substantial minority stake for strategic reasons.

Accor denoted 2016 as a "transformative year" and 2017 as a "turning point," not only because the company started to prepare a spin-off of AccorInvest but also because it continued to invest in new brands, including BHG in Brazil and Mantra in Australia. During 2017 Accor also continued to diversify its activities into new businesses. These businesses included (a) the rental of luxury private homes, presumably motivated by the success of Airbnb; (b) AccorLocal, providing local services to residents living nearby the company's hotels; and (c) new providers of online booking services, such as Gekko. Accor's management anticipated that 2018 would be a year of strong growth. The hotel group planned to open another 45,000 new hotel rooms per year in 2018 and the following years, primarily in the midscale and economy segment. Management also announced that it would continue to acquire and integrate businesses focused on innovative travel services, as it did in 2017, thereby slowly lowering its emphasis on traditional hotel services.

**Exhibit 1** provides some of Accor's key performance indicators during the fiscal year ending December 31, 2017. **Exhibit 2** shows Accor's financial statements for the fiscal years ending December 31, 2016, and 2017. In 2017 Accor's total revenues grew by 17.7 percent, of which 9.8 percent came from the company's expansion of its capacity and 7.9 percent represented growth on a like-for-like basis (e.g., because of increases in occupancy rates or average room rates).

Professor Erik Peek prepared this case. The case is intended solely as the basis for class discussion and is not intended to serve as an endorsement, source of primary data, or illustration of effective or ineffective management.

[1]Most of the material in this section comes from Accor's 2017 Annual Report.

# NH Hotel Group[2]

Spain-based NH Hotel Group competed with Accor primarily in the midscale (NH) and upscale (NH Collection, nhow, and Hesperia) segments of the European hotel market. In 2017 NH Hotel Group ranked sixth among Europe's largest hotel groups, after Accor and companies such as UK-based InterContinental Hotels and Whitbread. The total number of rooms that NH Hotel Group operated was 58,916 at the end of 2017. About 56 percent of these rooms were leased, 21 percent were owned, and 22 percent were managed. In 2017 the company's hotel business generated close to €1.2 billion in revenues; its catering activities generated close to €0.3 billion in revenues.

NH Hotel Group's largest shareholder was Chinese conglomerate HNA, which owned 29 percent of NH's equity but lost its representation on the company's board after a battle with the British hedge fund Oceanwood. At the end of 2017 the Spanish hotel group Barcelo indicated an interest in acquiring NH Hotel Group at a price of around €2.2 billion. The acquisition would create a hotel group owning 600 hotels and generating annual revenues of close to €3.7 billion, while giving family-owned Barcelo control in the combined group. Although shareholder HNA was seeking to find buyers for its shares in NH Hotel Group, NH's board turned down Barcelo's offer in January 2018 based on strategic considerations. The board, nonetheless, indicated being open to other offers.

**Exhibit 3** shows NH Hotel Group's financial statements for the fiscal years ending December 31, 2016, and 2017. In 2017 the company's total revenues grew by close to 7 percent. NH Hotel Group was profitable in 2016 and 2017, following a series of losses in prior years.

## QUESTIONS

1  Are the financial statements of Accor and NH Hotel Group comparable? Which adjustments to the financial statements would you consider necessary before comparing the companies' financial performance? Make use of the information from **Exhibit 3** where necessary.

2  Discuss which valuation multiples are potentially useful in valuing Accor and NH Hotel Group and compare these multiples for the two companies at the end of fiscal year 2017. What may explain the observed difference in valuation multiples between Accor and NH Hotel Group?

[2]Most of the material in this section comes from NH Hotel Group's 2017 Annual Report.

**EXHIBIT 1** Key performance indicators for Accor and NH Hotel Group in fiscal 2017: Revenue per available room (RevPAR) and rooms available at fiscal year end

| | Segment | Occupancy rate | | Average room rate | | RevPAR | | Number of rooms end 2017 | Leased or owned | Managed | Franchised |
|---|---|---|---|---|---|---|---|---|---|---|---|
| | | fiscal 2017 (%) | Change from last year (%p) | fiscal 2017 (€) | Change from last year (%) | fiscal 2017 (€) | Change from last year (%) | 2017 | | | |
| **Accor by geographic segment** | France and Switzerland | 67.8 | 3.3 | 82.0 | (0.9) | 56.0 | 4.2 | 151,537 | 32.2% | 11.7% | 56.1% |
| | Rest of Europe | 73.6 | 1.9 | 80.0 | 3.8 | 59.0 | 6.5 | 168,865 | 49.4% | 12.9% | 37.7% |
| | Middle East & Africa | 61.6 | 2.9 | 118.0 | (3.9) | 72.0 | 0.8 | 47,951 | 6.5% | 85.5% | 8.0% |
| | Asia-Pacific | 70.0 | 3.1 | 82.0 | 1.2 | 57.0 | 5.8 | 168,375 | 3.7% | 74.8% | 21.5% |
| | North and Central America | 74.6 | 0.8 | 212.0 | 4.4 | 158.0 | 5.7 | 27,702 | 7.1% | 83.3% | 9.6% |
| | South America | 54.5 | 0.3 | 62.0 | (3.8) | 34.0 | (3.4) | 51,751 | 36.9% | 39.8% | 23.2% |
| | **Total** | **68.8** | **2.5** | **89.0** | **0.9** | **61.0** | **4.7** | **616,181** | **26.4%** | **40.6%** | **33.0%** |
| **Accor by operating segment** | Luxury and upscale | 68.0 | 3.0 | 155.0 | 0.7 | 106.0 | 5.4 | 142,500 | 9.7% | 75.4% | 14.9% |
| | Midscale | 69.4 | 3.0 | 87.0 | 0.4 | 60.0 | 4.8 | 203,802 | 27.3% | 38.8% | 33.9% |
| | Economy | 68.7 | 1.9 | 57.0 | 1.0 | 39.0 | 3.9 | 264,229 | 35.3% | 22.5% | 42.2% |
| | Multi-brand | | | | | | | 5,650 | 0.9% | 72.0% | 27.1% |
| | **Total** | **68.8** | **2.5** | **89.0** | **0.9** | **61.0** | **4.7** | **616,181** | **26.4%** | **40.6%** | **33.0%** |
| **NH Hotel Group by geographic segment** | Spain | 73.1 | 4.2 | 92.2 | 9.7 | 67.5 | 14.4 | 16,641 | 65.7% | 30.7% | 3.6% |
| | Italy | 69.0 | 2.1 | 115.5 | 6.8 | 79.8 | 9.0 | 7,904 | 92.0% | 8.0% | 0.0% |
| | Germany | 71.8 | 2.6 | 84.7 | (0.6) | 60.9 | 2.0 | 10,261 | 100.0% | 0.0% | 0.0% |
| | Benelux | 70.4 | 6.7 | 105.2 | 7.4 | 74.1 | 14.7 | 8,460 | 94.5% | 5.5% | 0.0% |
| | Rest of Europe | 80.0 | 5.5 | 93.8 | 1.0 | 75.0 | 6.5 | 3,967 | 67.1% | 27.5% | 5.4% |
| | Latin America | 62.7 | 0.2 | 79.7 | 1.7 | 50.0 | 2.0 | 11,407 | 49.7% | 50.3% | 0.0% |
| | Other regions | | | | | | | 276 | 99.6% | 0.4% | 0.0% |
| | **Total** | **70.8** | **2.4** | **95.2** | **5.1** | **67.4** | **8.7** | **58,916** | **76.4%** | **22.3%** | **1.4%** |

Source: 2017 financial statements of Accor SA and NH Hotel Group SA and author's calculations

**EXHIBIT 2** Accor's and NH Hotel Group's standardized consolidated income statements, balance sheets, and cash flow statements for the fiscal years ending December 31, 2016 and 2017

| | Accor | | NH Hotel Group | |
|---|---|---|---|---|
| Income statements (€ mln) | 2017 | 2016 | 2017 | 2016 |
| Revenue | 1,937.0 | 1,646.0 | 1,546.1 | 1,447.9 |
| Operating expenses | (1,445.0) | (1,249.0) | (1,429.8) | (1,380.2) |
| **Operating profit** | **492.0** | **397.0** | **116.2** | **67.7** |
| Investment and interest income | 55.0 | 31.0 | 2.6 | 3.4 |
| Net non-recurring income or expense | (91.0) | (146.0) | 4.4 | 42.4 |
| Interest expense | (96.0) | (92.0) | (76.7) | (72.3) |
| **Profit before taxes** | **360.0** | **190.0** | **46.5** | **41.2** |
| Tax expense | 51.0 | 2.0 | (33.5) | (7.9) |
| **Profit after taxes** | **411.0** | **192.0** | **13.0** | **33.2** |
| Profit or loss to non-controlling interest | (40.0) | (33.0) | (3.7) | (3.4) |
| **Profit or loss to ordinary shareholders (of continued operations)** | **371.0** | **159.0** | **9.3** | **29.8** |
| Profit or loss of discontinued operations | 71.0 | 106.0 | (0.3) | (2.3) |
| Cost of goods sold/procurement | (67.0) | (64.0) | (75.7) | (66.9) |
| Personnel expenses | (810.0) | (723.0) | (427.1) | (415.9) |
| Depreciation and amortization | (134.0) | (109.0) | (123.1) | (114.2) |
| Net other operating income/expense | (434.0) | (353.0) | (803.9) | (783.3) |
| Statutory tax rate (%) | 34.4 | 34.4 | 25.0 | 25.0 |
| Effective tax rate (%) | (14.2) | (1.1) | 72.1 | 19.3 |
| Weighted average shares outstanding (thousands) | 287,488 | 259,054 | 340,805 | 341,042 |
| Weighted average shares outstanding, diluted (thousands) | 288,291 | 259,925 | 391,628 | 391,865 |
| End-of-year share price (€) | 43.00 | 35.43 | 5.91 | 3.75 |

**EXHIBIT 2** Accor's and NH Hotel Group's standardized consolidated income statements, balance sheets, and cash flow statements for the fiscal years ending December 31, 2016 and 2017 (Continued)

| Condensed balance sheets (€ mln) | Accor | | NH Hotel Group | |
|---|---|---|---|---|
| | 2017 | 2016 | 2017 | 2016 |
| Operating cash (5% of revenue) | 96.9 | 82.3 | 77.3 | 72.4 |
| + Trade receivables | 403.0 | 374.0 | 132.6 | 146.2 |
| + Inventories | 8.0 | 8.0 | 9.8 | 9.9 |
| + Other current assets | 294.0 | 252.0 | 54.2 | 67.2 |
| − Trade payables | 398.0 | 384.0 | 223.0 | 229.8 |
| − Other current liabilities | 690.0 | 587.0 | 87.6 | 101.2 |
| **Operating working capital** | **(286.2)** | **(254.7)** | **(36.7)** | **(35.3)** |
| | | | | |
| Non-current tangible assets | 662.0 | 562.0 | 1,583.2 | 1,701.4 |
| + Non-current intangible assets | 3,802.0 | 3,897.0 | 262.8 | 244.2 |
| − Deferred tax liabilities (net of assets) | 292.0 | 366.0 | 29.4 | 22.6 |
| − Other non-current liabilities (non-interest-bearing) | 0.0 | 0.0 | 39.0 | 34.0 |
| **Net non-current operating assets** | **4,172.0** | **4,093.0** | **1,777.5** | **1,889.0** |
| | | | | |
| Excess cash | 1,019.2 | 1,143.7 | 2.9 | 66.3 |
| + Minority equity investments | 672.0 | 596.0 | 9.4 | 10.6 |
| + Other non-operating investments | 169.0 | 257.0 | 92.3 | 110.0 |
| **Non-operating investments** | **1,860.2** | **1,996.7** | **104.7** | **186.9** |
| | | | | |
| Current debt | 343.0 | 884.0 | 278.5 | 38.0 |
| + Non-current debt | 2,870.0 | 2,308.0 | 521.9 | 890.7 |
| **Debt** | **3,213.0** | **3,192.0** | **800.4** | **928.7** |
| | | | | |
| Ordinary shareholders' equity | 5,484.0 | 5,656.0 | 1,108.5 | 1,111.9 |
| + Non-controlling interest in equity | 341.0 | 267.0 | 43.5 | 44.0 |
| − Net assets held for sale | 3,292.0 | 3,280.0 | 106.8 | 44.0 |
| **Group equity** | **2,533.0** | **2,643.0** | **1,045.2** | **1,111.9** |
| | | | | |
| **Invested capital** | **5,746.0** | **5,835.0** | **1,845.6** | **2,040.5** |

**EXHIBIT 2**  Accor's and NH Hotel Group's standardized consolidated income statements, balance sheets, and cash flow statements for the fiscal years ending December 31, 2016 and 2017 (Continued)

| Cash flow statements (€ mln) | Accor | | NH Hotel Group | |
| --- | --- | --- | --- | --- |
| | 2017 | 2016 | 2017 | 2016 |
| Profit before interest and tax | 492.0 | 397.0 | 146.8 | 112.9 |
| Taxes paid | (98.4) | (114.4) | (55.8) | (40.3) |
| Non-operating losses (gains) | (155.0) | (216.0) | (30.5) | (45.3) |
| Non-current operating accruals | 188.0 | 140.0 | 128.9 | 129.7 |
| Net (investments in) or liquidation of operating working capital | 37.0 | (4.0) | 13.3 | (5.8) |
| **Operating cash flow** | **463.6** | **202.6** | **202.6** | **151.2** |
| | | | | |
| Interest received | 0.0 | 0.0 | 1.3 | 2.0 |
| Dividends received | 23.0 | 13.0 | 0.0 | 0.0 |
| Net (investments in) or liquidation of non-current assets | (371.0) | (3,027.0) | (43.4) | 270.4 |
| **Free cash flow available to debt and equity** | **115.6** | **(2,811.4)** | **160.6** | **423.6** |
| | | | | |
| Interest paid | (46.6) | (46.6) | (101.7) | (80.9) |
| Debt (repayment) or issuance | 127.0 | 137.0 | (164.6) | (329.7) |
| **Free cash flow available to equity** | **196.0** | **(2,721.0)** | **(105.8)** | **13.0** |
| | | | | |
| Dividend payments | (200.0) | (215.0) | (18.6) | (1.1) |
| Net share (repurchase) or issuance | 26.0 | 1,733.0 | 0.0 | (2.4) |
| **Net increase (decrease) in cash balance** | **22.0** | **(1,203.0)** | **(124.3)** | **9.5** |

Source: 2017 financial statements of Accor SA and NH Hotel Group SA and author's calculations

**EXHIBIT 3** Excerpts from the notes to Accor's and NH Hotel Group's financial statements for the fiscal year ending on December 31, 2017

## A. Accor

### NOTE 3 SPIN-OFF AND CONTEMPLATED DISPOSAL OF ACCORINVEST

[. . .] In 2013, AccorHotels launched a plan to reorganize its business model around two strategic businesses, HotelServices (hotel management and franchising business) and HotelInvest (hotel owner-operator business).

On July 12, 2016, after three years of transformation to create a more efficient business model, the Group announced a project to turn HotelInvest into a subsidiary and open up its share capital to external investors. The aim of the project is to strengthen AccorHotels' financial resources in order to maximize the Group's overall value by stepping up the pace of business growth and seizing new development opportunities.

In early December 2016, AccorHotels initiated negotiations with potential investors with a view to selling a significant stake in the new group, while maintaining business relationships. AccorHotels would continue to be the preferred manager of the hotels operated by the new group and would also continue to own the brands, which would be licensed to the hotels under management contracts. [. . .]

The AccorInvest assets and liabilities were classified as assets held for sale at December 31, 2016, in accordance with IFRS Standards 5. AccorHotels considers that the planned divestment will lead to the loss of control of AccorInvest under IFRS Standards 10. On completion of the transaction, the rights held by the Group (voting rights at Shareholders' Meetings and contractual rights resulting from the agreements governing future relations between the parties, the shareholders' agreement and hotel management contracts) will not give it the power to unilaterally direct its relevant activities, i.e. operation of the hotels and strategic management of the hotel portfolio. Consequently, on completion date, the assets and liabilities of AccorInvest will be derecognized and the Group's stake in the company net assets will be recognized under "Investments in associates", to the extent of the retained residual interest. The classification as assets held for sale was maintained at December 31, 2017.

### NOTE 9.2 TANGIBLE ASSETS

Property, plant and equipment are depreciated on a straight-line basis over their estimated useful lives, determined by the components method, from the date when they are put in service, as follows:

|  | Economy hotels | Luxury Upscale and Midscale hotels |
|---|---|---|
| Buildings and related costs | 35 years | 50 years |
| Building improvements, fixtures and fittings | 7 to 25 years | 7 to 25 years |
| Equipment | 5 to 10 years | 5 to 10 years |

[. . .] Property, plant and equipment break down as follows:

| (€ millions) | December 2016 Net book value | December 2017 | | |
|---|---|---|---|---|
| | | Gross value | Amortization and depreciation | Net book value |
| Land | 33 | 59 | (5) | 54 |
| Buildings | 329 | 782 | (417) | 365 |
| Fixtures | 85 | 279 | (162) | 117 |
| Equipment and furniture | 94 | 253 | (160) | 93 |
| Construction in progress | 21 | 36 | (2) | 33 |
| **PP&E** | **562** | **1,408** | **(746)** | **662** |

## NOTE 12 INCOME TAX EXPENSE

In 2017, the Group has a €51 million income tax benefit, favourably driven by the following one-off items:

- tax relief of €37 million (including interests) received following the Steria ruling confirming the right to a 5% expense deduction on European-source dividends for the period 2009 to 2013;
- accrual for a €26 million income tax receivable for retroactive cancelation of the 3% dividend tax paid over 2015 to 2017, as a result of the French Constitutional Council decision;
- deferred tax benefits recognized on differences between the tax basis and the net book value of intangible assets acquired to AccorInvest in Germany and Netherlands for €73 million as part of the spin-off of the company; and
- favorable adjustment on deferred taxes for €59 million resulting from the change in US Federal tax rate from 35% to 21% enacted as part of the US Tax Cuts and Jobs Act.

## NOTE 13.2 MINORITY INTERESTS

The Group holds 52.69% of the capital and voting rights of Orbis SA, the Orbis Group's parent company which is listed on the Warsaw Stock Exchange. The following table presents selected financial information for Orbis:

| (€ millions) | 2016 | 2017 |
|---|---|---|
| Revenue | 315 | 342 |
| Net profit | 50 | 53 |
| Non-current assets | 479 | 560 |
| Current assets | 147 | 147 |
| Current liabilities | 59 | 68 |
| Non-current liabilities | 566 | 639 |

## NOTE 14.1 OFF-BALANCE SHEET COMMITMENTS

Off-balance sheet commitments (which are not discounted) given at December 31, 2017 break down as follows:

| (€ millions) | Less than 1 year | 1 to 5 years | Beyond 5 years |
|---|---|---|---|
| Commitments related to development | 1,032 | 1 | |
| Commitments increasing net debt | 69 | 183 | 196 |
| Commitments given in the normal course of business | 25 | 51 | 11 |
| Security interests given on assets | | 81 | |
| Contingent liabilities | | 1 | |

Commitments of development projects are mainly a commitment linked to the acquisition of Mantra Group for €908 million (see Note 14.3), Gekko acquisition for €85 million and €35 million for a commitment to acquire a stake in Orient-Express and additional stake in Mama Shelter. Commitments that increase debt mainly include rent guarantees for the headquarters buildings in the amount of €240 million (€172 million discounted at 7%) and rent guarantees for hotels related to continued activities (Orbis, etc.) in the amount of €129 million (€86 million discounted at 7%).

## B. NH Hotel Group

### NOTE 4.1 PROPERTY PLANT AND EQUIPMENT

Property, plant and equipment are valued at their original cost. They are subsequently valued at their reduced cost resulting from cumulative depreciation and, as appropriate, from any impairment losses they may have suffered. [. . .]

The Group depreciates its property, plant and equipment following the straight line method, distributing the cost of the assets over their estimated useful lives, in accordance with the following table:

| | Estimated years of useful life |
|---|---|
| Buildings | 33 – 50 |
| Plant and machinery | 10 – 30 |
| Other plant, fixtures and furniture | 5 – 10 |
| Other fixed assets | 4 – 5 |

### NOTE 8 PROPERTY PLANT AND EQUIPMENT

The breakdown and movements under this heading during 2017 and 2016 were as follows (in thousands of euros):

| Cost | Balance at 31/12/2016 | [...] | Balance at 31/12/2017 |
|---|---|---|---|
| Land and building | 1,695,856 | | 1,601,557 |
| Plant and machinery | 795,269 | | 791,302 |
| Other plant, fixtures and furniture | 457,987 | | 440,680 |
| Other fixed assets | 794 | | (529) |
| Property, plant and equipment in progress | 25,713 | | 27,452 |
| | **2,975,619** | | **2,860,462** |
| **Accumulated depreciation** | | | |
| Buildings | (326,752) | | (342,842) |
| Plant and machinery | (532,735) | | (545,332) |
| Other plant, fixtures and furniture | (350,744) | | (342,127) |
| Other fixed assets | (434) | | 10 |
| | **(1,210,665)** | | **(1,230,291)** |
| Impairment | (63,526) | | (47,007) |
| **Net book value** | **1,701,428** | **[...]** | **1,583,164** |

## NOTE 18 TAX NOTE

[. . .] The reconciliation between the consolidated comprehensive profit or loss statements, the corporation tax base, current and deferred tax for the year, is as follows:

| (€ thousands) | 2017 | 2016 |
|---|---|---|
| Profit (loss) for the financial year - continuing | 76,436 | 44,358 |
| Profit (loss) for the year from discontinued operations | (3,718) | (2,274) |
| **Consolidated statements of comprehensive profit and loss before taxes** | **72,718** | **42,084** |
| Accounting consolidation adjustments | 5,022 | 7,584 |
| Due to permanent differences | 54,307 | (11,888) |
| Due to temporary differences | (5,408) | 24,043 |
| **Tax base (taxable profit or loss)** | **126,642** | **61,821** |
| Current taxes to be refunded (to pay) | 157 | 4,756 |
| Total current tax income (expense) | (33,148) | (16,907) |
| Total deferred tax income (expense) | 1,610 | 12,835 |
| Total other tax income (expense) | (1,973) | (3,866) |
| Total Corporation Tax income / (expense) | (33,511) | (7,938) |

## NOTE 24.5 OPERATING LEASES

At 31 December 2017 and 2016, the Group had made undertakings concerning future minimal rental payments by virtue of non-cancelable operating lease agreements, which expire as set out in the table below.

The current value of the rental payments has been calculated by applying a post-tax discount rate in keeping with the cost of capital of each of the countries and includes the commitments which the Group estimates will have to be met in the future to guarantee a fixed income or minimum return from hotels operated under a management agreement.

| **Present value** (€ thousands) | 2017 | 2016 |
|---|---|---|
| Less than one year | 261,801 | 259,112 |
| Between two and five years | 876,540 | 867,428 |
| More than five years | 1,211,109 | 1,151,056 |
| Total | 2,349,450 | 2,277,596 |

# Two European hotel groups (B): Debt analysis

## CASE

At the end of fiscal year 2017, European hotel group Accor had a substantial amount of publicly traded nonconvertible bonds outstanding. The company had issued several tranches of bonds between 2013 and 2017, with maturities ranging from one to eight years and coupon rates ranging from 0.05 percent (for the one-year bond) to 2.76 percent (for Polish zloty-denominated long-term bonds). On December 31, 2017, the carrying value of Accor's bonds was €2,748 million. The company had bank debt in the amount of €30 million, €209 million of current and non-current provisions, and €202 million of finance lease liabilities. At the end of fiscal 2017, one of the world's largest rating agencies, Standard and Poor's, had rated Accor and its public debt at BBB−.

Accor's competitor NH Hotel Group had €400 million of public debt outstanding at the end of fiscal year 2017. During 2016 the company had issued secured senior bonds for an amount of €285 million. These bonds had a coupon rate of 3.75 percent. One year later NH Hotel Group issued another tranche of secured senior bonds, for an amount of €115 million at 3.17 percent, to help the company retire and refinance a €250 million tranche of senior secured bonds that it had issued in 2013 at a coupon rate of 6.875 percent. In addition to the public secured senior bonds, at the end of fiscal 2017 NH Hotel Group had a mortgage loan of around €40 million, subordinated loans of €40 million, and current and non-current provisions of close to €60 million.

On October 31, 2013, NH Hotel Group had placed a tranche of 2,500 convertible bonds with institutional investors, maturing on October 31, 2018. The bonds had an issue price of €100,000 and an annual interest rate of 4 percent. One bond was exchangeable for 20,329 NH shares at an exchange price of €4.919 per share. If bondholders would not exchange their bonds for shares, NH Hotel Group would fully redeem the bonds on October 31, 2018.

### QUESTION

1 Determine a credit rating for NH Hotel Group's debt. Compare the rating to Accor's rating. If NH Hotel Group's credit rating differs from Accor's rating, what explains the difference?

Professor Erik Peek prepared this case. The case is intended solely as the basis for class discussion and is not intended to serve as an endorsement, source of primary data, or illustration of effective or ineffective management.

**EXHIBIT 1**  Selected historical financial information

| (in €mln) | | 2017 | 2016 | 2015 | 2014 | 2013 |
|---|---|---|---|---|---|---|
| Profit or loss | Accor | 411.0 | 192.0 | 246.0 | 227.0 | 125.0 |
| | NH Hotels | 13.0 | 33.2 | (2.8) | (41.9) | (33.4) |
| After-tax interest expense | Accor | (63.0) | (60.4) | (46.6) | (38.0) | (54.4) |
| | NH Hotels | (57.5) | (54.2) | (55.3) | (51.6) | (52.8) |
| Revenue | Accor | 1,937.0 | 1,646.0 | 5,581.0 | 5,454.0 | 5,425.0 |
| | NH Hotels | 1,546.1 | 1,447.9 | 1,376.6 | 1,247.0 | 1,232.2 |
| Debt | Accor | 3,213.0 | 3,192.0 | 3,170.0 | 3,171.0 | 2,601.0 |
| | NH Hotels | 800.4 | 928.7 | 944.6 | 883.0 | 976.4 |
| Equity | Accor | 5,484.0 | 5,656.0 | 3,762.0 | 3,657.0 | 2,538.0 |
| | NH Hotels | 1,108.5 | 1,111.9 | 1,088.1 | 1,112.5 | 1,000.5 |
| Non-controlling interest in equity | Accor | 341.0 | 267.0 | 225.0 | 213.0 | 214.0 |
| | NH Hotels | 43.5 | 44.0 | 38.0 | 24.2 | 153.0 |
| Operating cash flow | Accor | 970.0 | 865.0 | 886.0 | 875.0 | 848.0 |
| | NH Hotels | 229.6 | 176.6 | 90.3 | 32.1 | 40.3 |
| Investment cash flow | Accor | (1,248.0) | (3,738.0) | (280.0) | (1,447.0) | (120.0) |
| | NH Hotels | (42.3) | (23.7) | (216.8) | (38.3) | 96.2 |
| Financing cash flow | Accor | 54.0 | 1,677.0 | (230.0) | 1,505.0 | (305.0) |
| | NH Hotels | (243.8) | (94.4) | (6.8) | (103.9) | (41.7) |
| Market capitalization | Accor | 12,417.8 | 10,086.9 | 9,413.5 | 8,594.1 | 7,802.6 |
| | NH Hotels | 2,101.6 | 1,346.8 | 1,765.4 | 1,392.3 | 1,320.9 |

Source: 2013–2017 financial statements of Accor SA and NH Hotel Group SA

**EXHIBIT 2**  Excerpts from Accor's and NH Hotel Group's annual reports for the fiscal year ending on December 31, 2017

# A. Accor

## NOTE 3 SPIN-OFF AND CONTEMPLATED DISPOSAL OF ACCORINVEST

[…] The AccorInvest assets and liabilities were classified as assets held for sale at December 31, 2016, in accordance with IFRS Standards 5. AccorHotels considers that the planned divestment will lead to the loss of control of AccorInvest under IFRS Standards 10. On completion of the transaction, the rights held by the Group (voting rights at Shareholders' Meetings and contractual rights resulting from the agreements governing future relations between the parties, the shareholders' agreement and hotel management contracts) will not give it the power to unilaterally direct its relevant activities, i.e. operation of the hotels and strategic management of the hotel portfolio. Consequently, on completion date, the assets and liabilities of AccorInvest will be derecognized and the Group's stake in the company net assets will be recognized under "Investments in associates", to the extent of the retained residual interest. […]

The contribution of AccorInvest to the consolidated balance sheet is as follows:

| (€ millions) | Dec. 2016 | Dec. 2017 |
|---|---|---|
| Goodwill and other intangible assets | 352 | 345 |
| Tangible assets | 3,119 | 3,683 |
| Other non-current assets | 167 | 168 |
| Non-current assets | 3,639 | 4,196 |
| Receivables and other current assets | 476 | 442 |
| Cash and cash equivalents | 292 | 128 |
| Assets held for sale | 28 | 3 |
| **ASSETS** | **4,435** | **4,769** |
| Financial debts | 133 | 234 |
| Other non-current liabilities | 148 | 202 |
| Non-current liabilities | 281 | 436 |
| Trade payables | 368 | 363 |
| Other current liabilities | 519 | 726 |
| **LIABILITIES** | **1,168** | **1,526** |

## NOTE 11.3.2 ANALYSIS OF GROSS FINANCIAL DEBT

The maturity profile of bonds and bank borrowings is one of the indicators used to assess the Group's liquidity position. At December 31, 2017, maturities of long and short-term debt were as follows:

| 2018 | 2019 | 2020 | 2021 | 2022 | Beyond |
|---|---|---|---|---|---|
| 138 | 336 | 72 | 952 | 188 | 1,093 |

In 2017, financial costs amount to €71 million. Future financial costs are estimated at €163 million for the period from January 2018 to December 2020 and €70 million thereafter. […] These estimates are based on the average cost of debt at the end of the period, after hedging, assuming that no facilities will be rolled over at maturity.

At December 31, 2017, 86% of long and short-term debt was fixed rate, with an average rate of 2.04%, and 14% was variable rate, with an average rate of 2.12%. At December 31, 2017, fixed rate debt was denominated primarily in EUR (88%), while variable rate debt was denominated mainly in euro (76%), in polish zloty (21%) and in Mauritian rupee (3%).

Bonds at December 31, 2017 break down as follows:

| Nominal amount | Local currency | Date of issuance | Maturity | Initial interest rate (%) | Dec. 2016 | Dec. 2017 |
|---|---|---|---|---|---|---|
| 700 | M EUR | June 2012 | June 2017 | 2.88 | 367 | 0 |
| 250 | M EUR | August 2009 | November 2017 | 6.04 | 250 | 0 |
| 138 | M EUR | December 2017 | December 2018 | 0.05 | 0 | 138 |
| 600 | M EUR | March 2013 | March 2019 | 2.50 | 334 | 335 |
| 300 | M PLN | June 2015 | June 2020 | 2.76 | 68 | 72 |
| 900 | M EUR | February 2014 | February 2021 | 2.63 | 906 | 904 |
| 200 | M PLN | July 2016 | July 2021 | 2.69 | 45 | 48 |
| 60 | M EUR | December 2014 | February 2022 | 1.68 | 60 | 60 |
| 150 | M CHF | June 2014 | June 2022 | 1.75 | 139 | 128 |
| 500 | M EUR | September 2015 | September 2023 | 2.38 | 466 | 471 |
| 600 | M EUR | January 2017 | January 2024 | 1.25 | 0 | 593 |
| **Bonds** | | | | | **2,635** | **2,748** |

On January 18, 2017, AccorHotels successfully set the terms of a 7-year bond issue for an amount of €600 million with an annual coupon of 1.25%. With this issue, AccorHotels took advantage of the favorable conditions on the credit market to optimize its average cost of debt and extend the average maturity. On December 20, 2017, the Group issued a one year bond for €138 million with an annual coupon of 0.05%. During the year, the Group reimbursed two bonds at maturity. [...]

At December 31, 2017, AccorHotels had two unused confirmed lines of credit representing a total of €2,150 million, one for €350 million expiring in June 2018 and the other for €1,800 million expiring in June 2019.

## NOTE 13.1.4 PERPETUAL SUBORDINATED NOTES

On June 30, 2014, AccorHotels issued €900 million worth of perpetual subordinated notes. The notes have no fixed maturity; their first call date is June 30, 2020. The interest rate on the notes is set at 4.125% up until June 30, 2020 and will be reset every five years thereafter, with a 25-bps step-up in June 2020 and a 275-bps step-up in June 2040. Interest is payable on the notes only in those periods for which a dividend is paid to shareholders. Due to their characteristics and in accordance with IAS 32, the notes have been recorded in equity for €887 million net of transaction costs. Interest on the notes is also recorded in equity. In 2017, interest payments on perpetual subordinated notes amounted to €37 million.

## B. NH Hotel Group

## NOTE 15 DEBT IN RESPECT OF BOND ISSUES AND BANK BORROWINGS

The balances of the "Bonds and other negotiable securities" and "Debts with credit institutions" items at 31 December 2017 and 2016 were as follows:

| (€ thousands) | 2017 Long-term | 2017 Short-term | 2016 Long-term | 2016 Short-term |
|---|---|---|---|---|
| Convertible bonds | – | 244,606 | 238,724 | – |
| Guaranteed senior bonds maturing in 2019 | – | – | 250,000 | – |
| Guaranteed senior bonds maturing in 2023 | 400,000 | – | 285,000 | – |
| Borrowing costs | – | 5,125 | – | 6,248 |
| Arrangement expenses | −12,285 | −3,536 | −10,087 | −4,015 |
| **Debt instruments and other marketable securities** | **387,715** | **246,195** | **763,637** | **2,233** |
| Mortgages | 32,945 | 7,496 | 33,078 | 4,325 |
| Unsecured loans | 867 | 2,238 | 2,158 | 9,072 |
| Subordinated loans | 40,000 | – | 40,000 | – |
| Credit lines | – | 2,008 | – | 9,944 |
| Arrangement expenses | −2,566 | −917 | −2,516 | −1,015 |
| Borrowing costs | – | 899 | – | 900 |
| **Debts with credit institutions** | **71,246** | **11,724** | **72,720** | **23,226** |
| **Total** | **458,961** | **257,919** | **836,357** | **25,459** |

[…] On 30 October 2013 the Parent Company placed guaranteed senior bonds, which mature in 2019, at the nominal value of 250,000 thousand euros. The nominal yearly interest rate for said issuance of notes is 6.875%. At 31 December 2017, these bonds are fully canceled through early amortisation or refinancing. […]

On 23 September 2016 the Parent Company placed guaranteed senior bonds, which mature in 2023, at the nominal value of 285,000 thousand euros. The nominal yearly interest rate for said issuance of notes is 3.75%. On 4 April 2017, the parent company issued an extension of guaranteed senior bonds maturing in 2023 for a nominal amount of 115,000 thousand euros with an implicit cost until maturity of 3.17%. The outstanding nominal amount at 31 December 2017 is 400,000 thousand euros. […]

[…] at the beginning of the year the Group owed 250,000 thousand of bonds to their holders which have been fully refinanced or amortised in full throughout 2017.

In this regard, in April 2017, the parent company issued an extension of guaranteed senior notes maturing in 2023 for a nominal amount of 115,000 thousand euros with an implicit cost until maturity of 3.17%. This extension led to the conversion of 121,505 thousand euros in guaranteed senior notes maturing in 2019 with an annual nominal interest of 6.875%. […]

[…] The detail, by maturity, of the items included under "Non-Current and Current Payables" is as follows (in thousands of euros):

| Instrument | Total | 2018 | 2019 | 2020 | 2021 | 2022 | Remainder |
|---|---|---|---|---|---|---|---|
| Mortgage loans | 40,441 | 7,496 | 2,756 | 2,605 | 2,554 | 2,141 | 22,889 |
| Subordinated loans | 40,000 | – | – | – | – | – | 40,000 |
| Convertible bonds | 250,000 | 250,000 | – | – | – | – | – |
| Guaranteed senior notes mat. in 2023 | 400,000 | – | – | – | – | – | 400,000 |
| Unsecured loans | 3,105 | 2,238 | 600 | 267 | – | – | – |
| Credit lines | 2,008 | 2,008 | – | – | – | – | – |
| **SUBTOTAL** | **735,554** | **261,742** | **3,356** | **2,872** | **2,554** | **2,141** | **462,889** |
| Arrangement expenses | −19,304 | −4,453 | −3,064 | −3,243 | −3,197 | −2,765 | −2,582 |
| **Borrowing at 31/12/2017** | **716,880** | **257,919** | **292** | **−371** | **−643** | **−624** | **460,307** |

# CASE

# Fiat Group's first-time adoption of IFRS Standards

In June 2002 the Council of the European Union adopted new regulations that required companies listed in the EU to prepare their consolidated financial statements in accordance with the International Financial Reporting Standards (IFRS Standards). According to the new rules, companies must apply IFRS Standards no later than in the fiscal year starting in 2005. Member states of the EU could, however, allow companies that were listed outside the EU and that prepared their statements in accordance with US Generally Accepted Accounting Principles (US GAAP) to apply IFRS Standards in either 2006 or 2007.

The decision of the European Council also affected Italy-based car manufacturer Fiat, which had its shares traded on the Italian Stock Exchange and reported its financial statements in accordance with Italian accounting standards (henceforth Italian GAAP). The Fiat Group decided not to apply IFRS Standards earlier than required and reported its first IFRS Standards-based annual report in fiscal year 2005.

## Business description and financial performance

In 2005 the Italy-based Fiat Group generated its revenues primarily from the production and sales of passenger vehicles, tractors, agricultural equipment, and light commercial vehicles. Its portfolio of passenger car brands included large-volume brands such as Fiat, Alfa Romeo, and Lancia (generating €19.5 billion in revenues), as well as luxury, high-margin brands such as Maserati and Ferrari (generating €1.8 billion in revenues). In addition to these activities, the Fiat Group produced components and production systems, provided administrative and financial services to its group companies, published a daily newspaper (*La Stampa*), and sold advertising space for multimedia customers. Total revenues amounted to €46.5 billion in 2005. The company's pre-tax profit was €1 billion.

The Fiat Group had its ordinary shares traded on the Italian Stock Exchange and had American Depository Receipts (ADRs) traded on the New York Stock Exchange. About one quarter of the group's ordinary shares were widely held, 45 percent were in the hands of banks and other institutional investors, and 30 percent were held by Fiat's primary shareholder, IFIL Investments, which was controlled by the Agnelli family. Through IFIL Investments and several other investment vehicles, the Agnelli family, who were the founders of Fiat, held a substantial voting block in the group. Fiat Group's board of directors consisted of three executive directors and 12 nonexecutive directors, of which eight were considered "independent" from the company and its major shareholder. The company's chairman of the board of directors was Luca Cordero di Montezemolo, former protégé of Fiat's longtime boss, Gianni Agnelli, chief executive officer (CEO) of Fiat's subsidiary Ferrari and chairman of Italy's employers' association Confindustria. The vice-chairman was John Elkann, who was a member of the Agnelli family, and the CEO was Sergio Marchionne.

Professor Erik Peek prepared this case. The case is intended solely as the basis for class discussion and is not intended to serve as an endorsement, source of primary data, or illustration of effective or ineffective management.

This section is based primarily on the Fiat Group's 2005 Annual Report and Report on Corporate Governance.

The first half of the 2000s was not a successful period for the Fiat Group. Italian GAAP-based revenues declined from €57.5 billion in 2000 to €46.7 billion by 2004. Possible causes for the group's underperformance were the economic slowdown in Europe, the group's continued diversification into unrelated industries, and its lack of innovation and development of new car models. In fiscal year 2005, however, the company reported a slight increase in (IFRS Standards-based) revenues of 2 percent and its first net profit since 2000, inducing management to designate the year 2005 as a "turning point" for Fiat. In spring 2006 analysts expected the Fiat Group's revenues to grow from €46.5 billion in 2005 to approximately €50.5 billion in 2006 and €52.2 billion in 2007. They also expected the Fiat Group to remain profitable in the next two years. Estimated pre-tax profits for 2006 and 2007 were €1.2 billion and €1.7 billion, respectively.[1] **Exhibit 1** shows the Fiat Group's stock price and accounting performance during the first half of the 2000s as well as its debt ratings in January 2006. In the first half of 2006 the Fiat Group made two Eurobond issues, each for €1 billion.

# First-time adoption of IFRS Standards

### THE GENERAL RULE

In June 2003, the International Accounting Standards Board (IASB) issued IFRS Standards 1 on firms' first-time adoption of IFRS Standards. The objective of this new standard was to ensure that all firms preparing their financial statements for the first time in accordance with the IFRS Standards (1) execute the transition to new reporting principles in a consistent manner and (2) provide sufficient additional disclosures to help the users of their statements understand the effects of the transition. IFRS Standards 1 requires that a first-time adopter applies *retrospectively* the IFRS Standards that are *effective at the reporting date* of its first IFRS Standards-based statements. Retrospective application of current IFRS Standards means that the firm recognizes all its assets and liabilities not only as though it has always applied IFRS Standards but also as though the current IFRS Standards version has always been effective and prior IFRS Standards versions have never existed.[2] This illustrates that IFRS Standards 1 aimed especially to improve comparability across first-time adopters, as opposed to improving comparability between first-time adopters and current users of IFRS Standards, whose assets and liabilities are often affected by prior IFRS Standards versions.

As well as the *reporting date* of the first IFRS Standards statements, the *transition date* is important for the application of IFRS Standards 1. The transition date is the beginning of the earliest fiscal year for which the first-time adopter prepares full IFRS Standards-based comparative statements. All first-time adopters are required to prepare an opening balance sheet at the transition date, although they are not required to publicly disclose this opening balance sheet. The accounting policies that a first-time adopter must use to prepare its opening balance sheet are the same policies that it uses to prepare its first IFRS Standards-based financial statements (including the comparative statements).

Retrospective application of the IFRS Standards does not imply that on the transition date the first-time adopter can revise the estimates that it made for the same date under previous reporting standards. For example, if a first-time adopter receives information after the transition date that suggests that the economic life of one of its assets is three years instead of the previously assumed two years, the IFRS Standards-based opening balance sheet on the transition date must reflect the "old" economic life assumption of two years. Hence IFRS Standards 1 explicitly forbids the first-time adopter to modify its prior financial statements with hindsight.

### EXEMPTIONS

Retrospective application of current IFRS Standards may carry costs that exceed the benefits of the information that it produces. The IASB acknowledged the importance of a cost-benefit trade-off and included several exemptions from full retrospective application:

---

[1]Source: Reuters consensus estimates.
[2]IFRS Standards 1 allows first-time adopters to apply new IFRS Standards that will become effective on a date after the reporting date but that permit earlier application.

- The international standard on business combinations (IFRS Standards 3) requires firms to recognize their acquisitions of other firms using purchase accounting. Under purchase accounting, a firm separately discloses on its balance sheet the fair value of the acquired assets as well as the excess of the purchase price over this amount (labelled goodwill). Under a few other accounting regimes, such as in the United Kingdom, firms can — or could — record some of their acquisitions using pooling accounting, whereby the acquirer recorded only the historical cost of the acquired assets on its balance sheet. Retrospective application would require a firm to restate all past business combinations that it recorded using the pooling method. IFRS Standards 1 allows first-time adopters not to restate business combinations that occurred prior to the transition date. If a firm nevertheless chooses to restate a business combination that occurred on a date prior to the transition date, it must also restate all other business combinations that occurred after this particular date.
- When a firm records its property, plant and equipment, intangible assets, and investment property at their (depreciated) historical cost, IFRS Standards 1 allows it to assume that these assets' fair values at the transition date are the assets' historical cost. IFRS Standards 1 refers to this assumed value as the assets' "deemed cost." Alternatively, if the firm has revalued any of these assets prior to the adoption of IFRS Standards and the revalued amount is broadly comparable to fair value under IFRS Standards, it can use the revalued amount as deemed cost.
- A first-time adopter may choose to immediately recognize (into equity) the cumulative actuarial gains and losses on all its pension plans. By doing so the first-time adopter avoids splitting the cumulative gains and losses that have arisen since the inception of the plans into a recognized and an unrecognized portion, which may be a difficult exercise when the firm uses the "corridor approach" for recognizing actuarial gains and losses.[3]
- A firm that consolidates the translated values of subsidiaries' foreign currency-denominated assets on its balance sheet recognizes the cumulative translation difference, which arises because exchange rates fluctuate over the years, as a separate component in equity. Because separately reporting restated cumulative translation differences generates little additional information, a first-time adopter can choose to add the cumulative translation differences to equity and reset the line item to zero upon adoption.
- International accounting rules require a firm to separate the debt from the equity component of convertible debentures — or similar compound financial instruments — and account for these separately. Consequently, the equity component of compound financial instruments may remain on the firm's balance sheet after the debt component is no longer outstanding. IFRS Standards 1 allows a first-time adopter not to separate the debt and equity components of compound financial instruments if the debt component is no longer outstanding on the transition date.
- A subsidiary that becomes a first-time adopter later than its parent can choose between reporting its assets and liabilities in accordance with IFRS Standards 1 — using its own transition date — or reporting its assets and liabilities in accordance with the reporting principles used by its parent — using its parent's transition date. A parent that becomes a first-time adopter later than its subsidiary must report its subsidiary's assets and liabilities in its consolidated financial statements as they are reported in the subsidiary's financial statements.
- International rules require firms to report stock options using the fair value method, under which they record an expense for stock option compensation when the options are issued. The value of the options issued is estimated using a recognized option valuation model and is then expensed over the vesting period. A first-time adopter is, however, not required to use this method for options that it issued prior to November 7, 2002, or that vested before the later of the following two dates: (1) the transition date and (2) January 1, 2005.

---

[3] Unrecognized actuarial losses arise, for example, when a change in a firm's actuarial assumptions increases its pension obligation, but the resulting change in the obligation is not recognized as a pension expense. Under the "corridor approach," the firm annually compares the cumulative unrecognized actuarial gains and losses to the greater of 10 percent of the pension obligation or 10 percent of the fair value of the pension plan assets. When the cumulative unrecognized actuarial gains and losses exceed their benchmark, the firm amortizes the difference over the remaining working lives of the active employees.

This list of optional exemptions is nonexhaustive because every time the IASB issues a new reporting standard, it may decide to exempt a first-time adopter from retrospective application of the new standard. In addition to these optional exemptions, IFRS Standards 1 includes a few mandatory exemptions. For example, a first-time adopter cannot rerecognize assets and liabilities that it derecognized prior to January 1, 2004, under its previous accounting principles.

### REQUIRED DISCLOSURES

According to IFRS Standards 1, a first-time adopter needs to disclose at least the following information in its first-time IFRS Standards-based financial statements:

- At least one year of comparative information under IFRS Standards. The comparative information of firms that adopted IFRS Standards before January 1, 2006, such as the Fiat Group and most other listed firms in the EU, need not comply with the international standards on financial instruments (IAS 32 and IAS 39) and on insurance contracts (IFRS Standards 4). However, these firms must disclose the nature of the adjustments that would make the comparative information comply with these three reporting standards.
- A reconciliation of equity under IFRS Standards and equity under previous reporting standards at the transition date and at the end of the latest fiscal year prior to the first-time adoption of IFRS Standards.
- A reconciliation of the profit or loss under IFRS Standards and under previous reporting standards in the latest fiscal year prior to the first-time adoption of IFRS Standards.
- The additional disclosures required by the international standard on the impairment of assets (IAS 36) if the firm recognized or reversed an impairment loss in its opening IFRS Standards balance sheet.[4]
- An explanation of the material adjustments made to the cash flow statement.
- The aggregate adjustments that the firm made to the carrying amounts of the assets for which it uses the fair values as deemed cost.

## The Fiat Group's first-time adoption of IFRS Standards

For the Fiat Group the reporting date of its first IFRS Standards statements was December 31, 2005. The company's transition date was January 1, 2004. Despite not being required to do so, the Fiat Group publicized its opening balance sheet for January 1, 2004, on May 11, 2005, in an appendix to the company's interim report for the first quarter of 2005. In addition to the 2004 opening balance sheet, the first-quarter report included an IFRS Standards-based 2004 closing balance sheet, an IFRS Standards-based 2004 income statement, and a reconciliation of IFRS Standards-based and Italian GAAP-based opening and closing equity for fiscal year 2004.

**Exhibit 4** reports excerpts from Appendix 1 to the 2005 financial statements of the Fiat Group. In this appendix, the group outlined the effects of the transition to IFRS Standards on its balance sheet and income statement.

### QUESTIONS

1  What are Fiat's key accounting policies? Which of Fiat's key accounting policies are affected by the adoption of IFRS Standards?
2  Summarize the differences between Fiat's key accounting methods under Italian GAAP and those under IFRS Standards. What characterizes the differences between the two sets of methods? From the perspective of a minority investor in the company's shares, which methods provide better information about the economic performance of Fiat?
3  Summarize the main factors that affect management's reporting incentives and strategy in fiscal year 2005. Which factors might reduce management's incentive to fully comply with the IFRS Standards?

[4]These disclosures are, for example, the amount of impairment, with an indication of the income statement item under which the impairment was categorized; the events that gave rise to the impairment (reversal); the nature of the impaired asset or cash generating unit; and the discount rate used to determine the value in use or the basis for determining the net selling price.

**EXHIBIT 1**  Market performance and accounting performance for the Fiat Group

### Fiat's stock price and the MSCI World Automobiles Price Index from January 2000 to December 2005

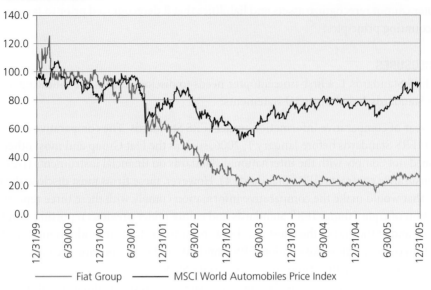

—— Fiat Group    —— MSCI World Automobiles Price Index

Source: Thomson Datastream.

### Fiat's Accounting Performance from 2000 to 2005

| (in € millions) | 2005 (IFRS Standards) | 2004 (Italian GAAP) | 2003 (Italian GAAP) | 2002 (Italian GAAP) | 2001 (Italian GAAP) | 2000 (Italian GAAP) |
|---|---|---|---|---|---|---|
| Consolidated revenues | 46,544 | 46,703 | 47,271 | 55,649 | 58,006 | 57,555 |
| Operating result | 2,215 | −833 | −510 | −762 | 318 | 855 |
| Group interest in net result | 1,331 | −1,586 | −1,900 | −3,948 | −455 | 644 |
| Group interest in stockholders' equity | 8,681 | 5,099 | 6,793 | 7,641 | 12,170 | 13,320 |
| Return on equity (in %) | 15.3 | −26.7 | −26.3 | −39.9 | −3.5 | 5.1 |
| Cash flow from operations | 3,716 | −358 | −1,947 | 1,053 | 2,435 | N.A. |

Source: Annual reports of the Fiat Group.

### Fiat's Debt Ratings in January 2006

| Rating agency | Rating (long-term senior unsecured) | Date of rating | Rating (short-term senior unsecured) | Date of rating |
|---|---|---|---|---|
| Standard and Poor's | BB− | 8/1/2005 | B | 8/2/2005 |
| Fitch | BB− | 1/20/2006 | B | 1/20/2006 |
| Moody's | Ba3 | 1/31/2006 | | |

Source: Reuters.

**EXHIBIT 2**  Fiat Group's shareholders and directors

On December 31, 2005, the Fiat Group had 1,092,246,316 ordinary shares, 103,292,310 preference shares and 79,912,800 savings shares outstanding and trading on public exchanges. All shares had a par value of €5. Holders of ordinary shares had voting rights but holders of preference shares and savings shares had limited or no voting rights. The ordinary shares were held by the following investors or investor groups:

| Investor (group) | Percentage (%) |
|---|---|
| IFIL Investments S.p.A. (controlled by IFI S.p.A., in turn controlled by Giovanni Agnelli & C. S.a.p.a.) | 30.46 |
| Banca Intesa | 6.08 |
| Unicredito | 5.58 |
| Capitalia | 3.80 |
| BNL | 2.73 |
| Generali | 2.38 |
| Libyan Arab Foreign Inv. Co. | 2.28 |
| International Institutional Investors | approx. 12.5 |
| Italian Institutional Investors | approx. 10 |
| Other stockholders | approx. 24 |

Source: Annual reports of the Fiat Group.

| Director | Age | Position | Background |
|---|---|---|---|
| Luca Cordero di Montezemolo | 59 | Chairman of the Board[3] | Chairman and CEO of Ferrari S.p.A. since 1991; Director of La Stampa, Pinault-Printemps-Redoute S.A., Tod's, Indesit Company; Chairman of Bologna Fiere; President of Confindustria (the Federation of Italian Industries). |
| Andrea Agnelli | 31 | Director | Past positions at Iveco, Piaggio S.p.A., Auchan S.A., Juventus F.C. S.p.A., Ferrari S.p.A. and Philip Morris International Inc. |
| Roland Berger | 68 | Director[3] | Chairman of the Supervisory Board of Roland Berger Strategy Consultants, Munich. |
| Tiberto Brandolini d'Adda | 58 | Director | Chairman and CEO of Sequana Capital (formerly Worms & Cie); General Partner of Giovanni Agnelli & C.; Vice Chairman and Member of the Executive Committee of IFIL S.p.A. |
| John Philip Elkann | 30 | Vice Chairman of the Board[1,3] | Chairman of Itedi S.p.A., IFIL S.p.A., and Giovanni Agnelli & C. S.a.p.a.z.; Member of the Boards of Exor Group SA, IFI S.p.A., and RCS Media Group. |
| Luca Garavoglia | 31 | Director[1] | Chairman of Davide Campari-Milano S.p.A., parent company of the Campari Group. |
| Gian Maria Gros-Pietro | 64 | Director[1] | President of Federtrasporto (Italian association of transportation companies); Member of the Directive Committee and General Council of Assonime (Italian listed companies association), the Board of the Union of Industrialists of Rome, Confindustria's General Council, the Board of Edison S.p.A., the Board of SEAT Pagine Gialle S.p.A., the Executive Committee and the General Council of the Aspen Institute Italia, the International Business Council of the World Economic Forum, and the Supervisory Board of Sofipa Equity Fund; Chairman of Autostrade S.p.A.; Vice President of I.G.I. (Istituto Grandi Infrastrutture); Senior Advisor for Italy of Société Générale Corporate & Investment Banking. |

| Director | Age | Position | Background |
|----------|-----|----------|------------|
| Hermann-Josef Lamberti | 50 | Director[2] | Chief Operating Officer and Member of the Board of Management at Deutsche Bank AG; Chairman of the Supervisory Board of Deutsche Bank Privat und Geschaftskunden AG; Member of the Supervisory Board of Carl Zeiss AG and Deutsche Börse AG; Non-executive Director of Euroclear plc and Euroclear Bank SA. |
| Sergio Marchionne | 54 | CEO[3] | CEO of Fiat S.p.A., Fiat Auto Holding B.V. and Fiat Auto S.p.A.; Chairman of the Board of Directors of Lonza Group Ltd.; Director of Serono Ltd.; Member of the Supervisory Board of Hochtief; Chairman of Société Générale de Surveillance Holding SA, Banca Unione di Credito, CNH (Case New Holland) and ACEA (European Automobile Manufacturers Association); Member of the General Councils of Confindustria and Assonime (the Association of listed Italian companies); Permanent member of the Fondazione Giovanni Agnelli. |
| Virgilio Marrone | 60 | Director | General Manager and CEO of IFI S.p.A.; Member of the boards of SanPaolo IMI S.p.A. and the Exor Group. |
| Vittorio Mincato | 70 | Director[2] | Past CEO of Eni S.p.A; Chairman of Poste Italiane S.p.A.; Member of CNEL (the Italian National Committee for Economy and Labor); Chairman of Assonime, the Executive Board of Confindustria and the Boards of Directors of Parmalat S.p.A., the Teatro alla Scala Foundation, the Accademia Nazionale di Santa Cecilia, and the Accademia Olimpica; Vice President of the Union of Industrialists of Rome. |
| Pasquale Pistorio | 70 | Director[3] | Past President and CEO and Current Honory Chairman of SGS-THOMSON Microelectronics (STMicroelectronics); Member of numerous organizations, including the Internal Advisory Council of the Government of Singapore, the ICT Task Force of the United Nations, the International Business Council of the World Economic Forum, and the Boards of Telecom Italia S.p.A. and Chartered Semiconductor Manufacturing; Chairman of ENIAC, the technological platform for nanoelectronics of the EU; Vice President of Confindustria for innovation and research. |
| Carlo Sant'Albano | 42 | Director | Managing Director and General Manager of IFIL S.p.A; Member of the Boards of Sequana Capital, Juventus F.C. and Alpitour. |
| Ratan Tata | 68 | Director | Chairman of Tata Sons Limited, the holding company of the Tata Group; Chairman of the major Tata companies including Tata Steel, Tata Motors, Tata Power, Tata Consultancy Services, Tata Tea, Tata Chemicals, Indian Hotels and Tata Teleservices Limited; Associated with a number of important business and philanthropic organizations in India and abroad. |
| Mario Zibetti | 67 | Director[2] | Past senior partner at Arthur Andersen S.p.A.; Member of the Board of Directors of Ersel Finanziaria S.p.A., Comital- Cofresco S.p.A. and Fabio Perini S.p.A. |

[1] Member of the Nominating and Compensation Committee
[2] Member of the Internal Control Committee
[3] Member of the Strategic Committee
Source: Form 20-F 2005 of the Fiat Group.

**EXHIBIT 3**  Letter from the chairman and the chief executive officer, December 2005

2005 marked a turning point for Fiat. We delivered on our commitments, we met all of our targets and we even exceeded a number of them. We had promised that 2004 would be Fiat's final year of net losses — and we achieved net income of over 1.4 billion euros in 2005. We had committed to a drastic cut in net industrial debt — and it was reduced by two-thirds. We had decided to focus on the relaunch of our Automobile activities, and in the last quarter of 2005 Fiat Auto posted a trading profit of 21 million euros after 17 consecutive quarters of losses. This has contributed to restoring Fiat's credibility, not only in Italy, but internationally, as evidenced by the improvement in our debt ratings and our ability to attract a large number of institutional investors in our debt raising activities. Our reputation has also benefited from the launch of new models across all brands that have been received extremely well by the public for their creativity, style, technology, and innovation, qualities that have distinguished the best Fiat cars since the firm was founded.

These breakthroughs, as well as all the other operational and financial improvements highlighted in this annual report, could not have been achieved without the strenuous efforts of the entire Fiat community, each and every one of whose members contributed to the relaunch of the Group with dedication and discipline. To do so, the Fiat people had to endorse fundamental changes in attitude, to assume greater responsibility and accountability, and to show their determination to deliver. We would like to express our sincere thanks to all of them.

During 2005, we also built a strong base for more effective and profitable operations in the future. First of all, we successfully resolved all pending strategic and financial issues: we settled our outstanding matters with General Motors and received a 1.56 billion euro cash payment; the Italenergia Bis transaction led to a 1.8 billion euro reduction in net industrial debt; and finally, conversion of the Mandatory Convertible Facility resulted in a 3 billion euro debt reduction and a sharp improvement in Group equity.

Fiat's business governance structure, especially in Automobiles, was right-sized to match realistic demand and market conditions. In Autos we have put in place a fully market-oriented organization, unbundling the brands: Fiat, Lancia, and Alfa Romeo now face the customer on their own, while sharing key functions such as manufacturing, quality and safety.

Everything is driven by the brands and for the brands. Similarly, in Agricultural and Construction Equipment, Case New Holland was reorganized along four brands rather than regions. And we have begun to aggressively streamline processes throughout the organization. The Company will reap the benefits of these structural improvements in 2006 and beyond.

Last year, we made other important decisions that will shape the Group's future, in the form of targeted industrial alliances with major international partners. Seven such agreements were struck in the Automobile Sector — with Pars Industrial Development Foundation (PIDF), PSA-Tofas, Zastava, Suzuki, Ford, Severstal Auto, and Tata Motors — while another partnership was established in commercial vehicles and industrial engines, between Iveco and SAIC.

Though much was done in 2005 to set the Company on course towards a real, lasting rebirth of our Group, the process is far from over and much remains to be done. Nonetheless, today's Fiat is a much different company from what it was just a year ago. The Group improved all key financial indicators. Our cash position — about 7 billion euros at 2005 year end — is strong. The financial markets are showing increased confidence in our prospects, as demonstrated by the steady appreciation of the Fiat share price. We have nearly completed the process of making our Internal Control System fully Sarbanes Oxley compliant, a move that will further enhance confidence in the Group at the international level. The Fiat we are talking about is a Group with a reinvigorated managerial structure, a leaner organization, a solid financial structure, and stronger market positions thanks to new products. This new Fiat can achieve new, challenging targets in 2006.

At Group level, we aim to deliver positive cash flow from operations, a trading profit between 1.6 and 1.8 billion euros, and net income of about 700 million euros. While we do not expect market conditions for our operating Sectors to change materially this year, we have set high trading margin targets (trading profit as a percentage of revenues) for all of them: 7 percent to 7.5 percent at CNH, 5.5 percent to 6 percent at Iveco, and 3.5 percent to 4 percent in Components and Production Systems. The Automobile Sector should also turn in a positive performance, with a trading margin of 0.5 percent to 1 percent. This result will be supported by the full-year contribution of new models already rolled out. These will be joined in coming months by other new models, as we implement our aggressive product renewal plan calling for the launch of 20 new cars and the restyling of 23 current models between 2005 and 2008.

We made a clean break with the past, while respecting all commitments made to stakeholders. We are clearly within reach of recovering our position as a competitive automotive Group. This is why we are keeping up the pressure that has enabled us to get this far, demanding much from ourselves and from all the men and women of the Fiat community. We have no intention of lessening the momentum that has allowed Fiat to generate a series of steady improvements, quarter after quarter, throughout 2005. We will remain focused on reducing costs in non-essential areas, while continuing to invest in innovation. We will complement our advanced technological resources with better commercial organization and more efficient services. Finally, we will continue to seek new international opportunities, implementing our strategy of targeted alliances with key partners who will help us reduce capital commitments, and share investments and risks. It is for all these reasons that we feel confident about our future.

Turin, February 28, 2006

Luca Cordero di Montezemolo — Chairman

Sergio Marchionne — Chief Executive Officer

**EXHIBIT 4**  Excerpts from Appendix 1 of Fiat's 2005 financial statements: Transition to International Financial Reporting Standards

Following the coming into force of European Regulation No. 1606 dated July 19, 2002, starting from January 1, 2005, the Fiat Group adopted International Financial Reporting Standards (IFRS Standards) issued by the International Accounting Standards Board (IASB). This Appendix provides the IFRS Standards reconciliations of balance sheet data as of January 1 and December 31, 2004, and of income statement data for the year ended December 31, 2004, as required by IFRS Standards 1 — First-time Adoption of IFRS Standards, together with the related explanatory notes. This information has been prepared as part of the Group's conversion to IFRS Standards and in connection with the preparation of its 2005 consolidated financial statements in accordance with IFRS Standards, as adopted by the European Union.

## Reconciliations required by IFRS Standards 1

As required by IFRS Standards 1, this note describes the policies adopted in preparing the IFRS Standards opening consolidated balance sheet at January 1, 2004, the main differences in relation to Italian GAAP used to prepare the consolidated financial statements until December 31, 2004, as well as the consequent reconciliations between the figures already published, prepared in accordance with Italian GAAP, and the corresponding figures remeasured in accordance with IFRS Standards. The 2004 restated IFRS Standards consolidated balance sheet and income statement have been prepared in accordance with IFRS Standards 1 — First-time Adoption of IFRS Standards. In particular, the IFRS Standards applicable from January 1, 2005, as published as of December 31, 2004, have been adopted, including the following:

- IAS 39 — Financial Instruments: Recognition and Measurement, in its entirety. In particular, the Group adopted derecognition requirements retrospectively from the date on which financial assets and financial liabilities had been derecognized under Italian GAAP.
- IFRS Standards 2 — Share-based Payment, which was published by the IASB on February 19, 2004 and adopted by the European Commission on February 7, 2005.

## Description of main differences between Italian GAAP and IFRS Standards

The following paragraphs provide a description of the main differences between Italian GAAP and IFRS Standards that have had effects on Fiat's consolidated balance sheet and income statement. Amounts are shown pre-tax and the related tax effects are separately summarized in the item R. Accounting for deferred income taxes.

### A. DEVELOPMENT COSTS

Under Italian GAAP applied research and development costs may alternatively be capitalized or charged to operations when incurred.

Fiat Group has mainly expensed R&D costs when incurred. IAS 38 — Intangible Assets requires that research costs be expensed, whereas development costs that meet the criteria for capitalization must be capitalized and then amortized from the start of production over the economic life of the related products.

Under IFRS Standards, the Group has capitalized development costs in the Fiat Auto, Ferrari-Maserati, Agricultural and Construction Equipment, Commercial Vehicle and Components Sectors, using the retrospective approach in compliance with IFRS Standards 1.

The positive impact of 1,876 million euros on the opening IFRS Standards stockholders' equity at January 1, 2004, corresponds to the cumulative amount of qualifying development expenditures incurred in prior years by the Group, net of accumulated amortization. Consistently, intangible assets show an increase of 2,090 million euros and of 2,499 million euros at January 1, 2004, and at December 31, 2004, respectively.

The 2004 net result was positively impacted by 436 million euros in the year, reflecting the combined effect of the capitalization of development costs incurred in the period that had been expensed under Italian GAAP, and the amortization of the amount that had been capitalized in the opening IFRS Standards balance sheet at January 1, 2004. This positive impact has been accounted for in Research and Development costs.

In accordance with IAS 36 — Impairment of Assets, development costs capitalized as intangible assets shall be tested for impairment and an impairment loss shall be recognized if the recoverable amount of an asset is less than its carrying amount, as further described in paragraph I. Impairment of Assets.

### B. EMPLOYEE BENEFITS

The Group sponsors funded and unfunded defined benefit pension plans, as well as other long term [sic] benefits to employees.

Under Italian GAAP, these benefits, with the exception of the Reserve for Employee Severance Indemnities ("TFR") that is accounted for in compliance with a specific Italian law, are mainly recorded in accordance with IAS 19 — Employee Benefits, applying the corridor approach, which consists of amortizing over the remaining service lives of active employees only the portion of net cumulative actuarial gains and losses that exceeds the greater of 10 percent of either the defined benefit obligation or the fair value of the plan assets, while the portion included in the 10 percent remains unrecognized.

With the adoption of IFRS Standards, TFR is considered a defined benefit obligation to be accounted for in accordance with IAS 19 and consequently has been recalculated applying the Projected Unit Credit Method. Furthermore, as mentioned in the paragraph "Optional exemptions," the Group elected to recognize all cumulative actuarial gains and losses that existed at January 1, 2004, with a negative impact on opening stockholders' equity at that date of 1,247 million euros.

Consequently pension and other post-employment benefit costs recorded in the 2004 IFRS Standards income statement do not include any amortization of unrecognized actuarial gains and losses deferred in previous years in the IFRS Standards financial statements under the corridor approach, and recognized in the 2004 income statement under Italian GAAP, resulting in a benefit of 94 million euros.

The Group has elected to use the corridor approach for actuarial gains and losses arising after January 1, 2004.

Furthermore, the Group elected to state the expense related to the reversal of discounting on defined benefit plans without plan assets separately as Financial expenses, with a corresponding increase in Financial expenses of 127 million euros in 2004.

## C. BUSINESS COMBINATIONS

As mentioned above, the Group elected not to apply IFRS Standards 3 — Business Combinations retrospectively to business combinations that occurred before the date of transition to IFRS Standards.

As prescribed in IFRS Standards 3, starting from January 1, 2004, the IFRS Standards income statement no longer includes goodwill amortization charges, resulting in a positive impact on Other operating income and expense of 162 million euros in 2004.

## D. REVENUE RECOGNITION — SALES WITH A BUY-BACK COMMITMENT

Under Italian GAAP, the Group recognized revenues from sales of products at the time title passed to the customer, which was generally at the time of shipment. For contracts for vehicle sales with a buy-back commitment at a specified price, a specific reserve for future risks and charges was set aside based on the difference between the guaranteed residual value and the estimated realizable value of vehicles, taking into account the probability that such option would be exercised. This reserve was set up at the time of the initial sale and adjusted periodically over the period of the contract. The costs of refurbishing the vehicles, to be incurred when the buy-back option is exercised, were reasonably estimated and accrued at the time of the initial sale.

Under IAS 18 — Revenue, new vehicle sales with a buy-back commitment do not meet criteria for revenue recognition, because the significant risks and rewards of ownership of the goods are not necessarily transferred to the buyer. Consequently, this kind of contract is treated in a manner similar to an operating lease transaction. More specifically, vehicles sold with a buy-back commitment are accounted for as Inventory if they regard the Fiat Auto business (agreements with normally a short-term buy-back commitment) and as Property, plant and equipment if they regard the Commercial Vehicles business (agreements with normally a long-term buy-back commitment). The difference between the carrying value (corresponding to the manufacturing cost) and the estimated resale value (net of refurbishing costs) at the end of the buy-back period is depreciated on a straight-line basis over the duration of the contract. The initial sale price received is accounted for as a liability. The difference between the initial sale price and the buy-back price is recognized as rental revenue on a straight-line basis over the duration of the contract.

Opening IFRS Standards stockholders' equity at January 1, 2004 includes a negative impact of 180 million euros mainly representing the portion of the margin accounted for under Italian GAAP on vehicles sold with a buy-back commitment prior to January 1, 2004, that will be recognized under IFRS Standards over the remaining buy-back period, net of the effects due to the adjustments to the provisions for vehicle sales with a buy-back commitment recognized under Italian GAAP.

This accounting treatment results in increases in the tangible assets reported in the balance sheet (1,001 million euros at January 1, 2004 and 1,106 million euros at December 31, 2004), in inventory (608 million euros at January 1, 2004 and 695 million euros at December 31, 2004), in advances from customers (equal to the operating lease rentals prepaid at the date of initial sale and recognized in the item Other payables), as well as in Trade payables, for the amount of the buy-back price, payable to the customer when the vehicle is bought back. In the income statement, a significant impact is generated on revenues (reduced by 1,103 million euros in 2004) and on cost of sales (reduced by 1,090 million euros in 2004), while no significant impact is generated on the net operating result; furthermore, the amount of these impacts in future years will depend on the changes in the volume and characteristics of these contracts year-over-year. Notwithstanding this, these changes are not expected to have a particularly significant impact on Group reported earnings in the coming years.

## E. REVENUE RECOGNITION — OTHER

Under Italian GAAP the recognition of disposals is based primarily on legal and contractual form (transfer of legal title).

Under IFRS Standards, when risks and rewards are not substantially transferred to the buyer and the seller maintains a continuous involvement in the operations or assets being sold, the transaction is not recognized as a sale.

Consequently, certain disposal transactions, such as the disposal of the 14 percent interest in Italenergia Bis and certain minor real estate transactions, have been reversed retrospectively: the related asset has been recognized in the IFRS Standards balance sheet, the initial gain recorded under Italian GAAP has been reversed and the cash received at the moment of the sale has been accounted for as a financial liability.

In particular, in 2001 the Group acquired a 38.6 percent shareholding in Italenergia S.p.A., now Italenergia Bis S.p.A. ("Italenergia"), a company formed between Fiat, Electricity de France ("EDF") and certain financial investors for the purpose of acquiring control of the Montedison–Edison ("Edison") group through tender offers. Italenergia assumed effective control of Edison at the end of the third quarter of that year and consolidated Edison from October 1, 2001. In 2002 the shareholders of Italenergia entered into agreements which resulted, among other things, in the transfer of a 14 percent interest in Italenergia from Fiat to other shareholders (with a put option that would require Fiat to repurchase the shares transferred in certain circumstances) and the assignment to Fiat of a put option to sell its shares in Italenergia to EDF in 2005, based on market values at that date, but subject to a contractually agreed minimum price in excess of book value.

Under Italian GAAP, Fiat accounted for its investments in Italenergia under the equity method, based on a 38.6 percent shareholding through September 30, 2002 and a 24.6 percent shareholding from October 1, 2002; in addition it recorded a gain of 189 million euros before taxes on the sale of its 14 percent interest in the investee to other shareholders effective September 30, 2002.

Under IFRS Standards, the transfer of the 14 percent interest in Italenergia to the other shareholders was not considered to meet the requirements for revenue recognition set out in IAS 18, mainly due to the existence of the put options granted to the transferees and de facto constraints on the transferees' ability to pledge or exchange the transferred assets in the period from the sale through 2005. Accordingly, the gain recorded in 2002 for the sale was reversed, and the results of applying the equity method of accounting to the investment in Italenergia was recomputed to reflect a 38.6 percent interest in the net results and stockholders' equity of the investee, as adjusted for the differences between Italian GAAP and IFRS Standards applicable to Italenergia.

This adjustment decreased the stockholders' equity at January 1, 2004 and at December 31, 2004 by an amount of 153 million euros and 237 million euros, respectively. Furthermore this adjustment increased the investment for an amount of 291 million euros at January 1, 2004 and of 341 million euros at December 31, 2004 and financial debt for amounts of 572 million euros at January 1, 2004 and of 593 million euros at December 31, 2004, as a consequence of the non-recognition of the transfer of the 14 percent interest in Italenergia.

## F. SCOPE OF CONSOLIDATION

Under Italian GAAP, the subsidiary B.U.C. — Banca Unione di Credito — as required by law, was excluded from the scope of consolidation as it had dissimilar activities, and was accounted for using the equity method.

IFRS Standards does not permit this kind of exclusion: consequently, B.U.C. is included in the IFRS Standards scope of consolidation. Furthermore, under Italian GAAP investments that are not controlled on a legal basis or a de facto basis determined considering voting rights were excluded from the scope of consolidation.

Under IFRS Standards, in accordance with SIC 12 — Consolidation — Special Purpose Entities, a Special Purpose Entity ("SPE") shall be consolidated when the substance of the relationship between an entity and the SPE indicates that the SPE is controlled by that entity.

This standard has been applied to all receivables securitization transactions entered into by the Group (see paragraph Q. Sales of receivables below), to a real estate securitization transaction entered into in 1998 and to the sale of the Fiat Auto Spare Parts business to "Societá di Commercializzazione e Distribuzione Ricambi S.p.A." ("SCDR") in 2001.

In particular, in 1998 the Group entered in a real estate securitization and, under Italian GAAP, the related revenue was recognized at the date of the legal transfer of the assets involved. In the IFRS Standards balance sheet at January 1, 2004, these assets have been written back at their historical cost, net of revaluations accounted before the sale, if any. Cash received at the time of the transaction has been accounted for in financial debt for an amount of 188 million euros at January 1, 2004.

The IFRS Standards stockholders' equity at January 1, 2004 was negatively impacted for 105 million euros by the cumulative effect of the reversal of the capital gain on the initial disposal and of the revaluation previously recognized under Italian GAAP, net of the related effect of asset depreciation, as well as the recognition of financial charges on related debt, net of the reversal of rental fees paid, if any. The impact on the 2004 net result is not material.

Furthermore, in 2001 the Group participated with a specialist logistics operator and other financial investors in the formation of "Societá di Commercializzazione e Distribuzione Ricambi S.p.A." ("SCDR"), a company whose principal activity is the purchase of spare parts from Fiat Auto for resale to end customers. At that date Fiat Auto and its subsidiaries sold their spare parts inventory to SCDR recording a gain of 300 million euros. The Group's investment in SCDR represents 19 percent of SCDR's stock capital and was accounted for under the equity method for Italian GAAP.

Under IFRS Standards, SCDR qualifies as a Special Purpose Entity (SPE) as defined by SIC 12 due to the continuing involvement of Fiat Auto in SCDR operations. Consequently, SCDR has been consolidated on a line by line basis in the IFRS Standards consolidated financial statements, with a consequent increase in financial debt of 237 million euros and of 471 million euros at January 1, 2004 and at December 31, 2004, respectively. Opening stockholders' equity at January 1, 2004 was reduced by 266 million euros by the amount corresponding to the unrealized intercompany profit in inventory held by SCDR on that date; this amount did not change significantly at the end of 2004.

## G. PROPERTY, PLANT AND EQUIPMENT

Under Italian GAAP and IFRS Standards, assets included in Property, Plant and Equipment were generally recorded at cost, corresponding to the purchase price plus the direct attributable cost of bringing the assets to their working condition.

Under Italian GAAP, Fiat revalued certain Property, Plant and Equipment to amounts in excess of historical cost, as permitted or required by specific laws of the countries in which the assets were located. These revaluations were credited to stockholders' equity and the revalued assets were depreciated over their remaining useful lives.

Furthermore, under Italian GAAP, the land directly related to buildings included in Property, Plant and Equipment was depreciated together with the related building depreciation.

The revaluations and land depreciation are not permitted under IFRS Standards. Therefore IFRS Standards stockholders' equity at January 1, 2004 reflects a negative impact of 164 million euros, related to the effect of the elimination of the asset revaluation recognized in the balance sheet, partially offset by the reversal of the land depreciation charged to prior period income statements.

In the 2004 IFRS Standards income statement, the above-mentioned adjustments had a positive impact of 14 million euros in 2004 due to the reversal of the depreciation of revalued assets, net of adjustments on gains and losses, if any, on disposal of the related assets, and to the reversal of land depreciation.

## H. WRITE-OFF OF DEFERRED COSTS

Under Italian GAAP, the Group deferred and amortized certain costs (mainly start-up and related charges). IFRS Standards require these to be expensed when incurred.

In addition, costs incurred in connection with share capital increases, which are also deferred and amortized under Italian GAAP, are deducted directly from the proceeds of the increase and debited to stockholders' equity under IFRS Standards.

## I. IMPAIRMENT OF ASSETS

Under Italian GAAP, the Group tested its intangible assets with indefinite useful lives (mainly goodwill) for impairment annually by comparing their carrying amount with their recoverable amount in terms of the value in use of the asset itself (or group of assets). In determining the value in use the Group estimated the future cash inflows and outflows of the asset (or group of assets) to be derived from the continuing use of the asset and from its ultimate disposal, and discounted those future cash flows. If the recoverable amount was lower than the carrying value, an impairment loss was recognized for the difference.

With reference to tangible fixed assets, under Italian GAAP the Group accounted for specific write-offs when the asset was no longer to be used. Furthermore, in the presence of impairment indicators, the Group tested tangible fixed assets for impairment using the undiscounted cash flow method in determining the recoverable amount of homogeneous group of assets. If the recoverable amount thus determined was lower than the carrying value, an impairment loss was recognized for the difference. Under IFRS Standards, intangible assets with indefinite useful lives are tested for impairment annually by a methodology substantially similar to the one required by Italian GAAP. Furthermore, development costs, capitalized under IFRS Standards and expensed under Italian

GAAP, are attributed to the related cash generating unit and tested for impairment together with the related tangible assets, applying the discounted cash flow method in determining their recoverable amount.

Consequently, the reconciliation between Italian GAAP and IFRS Standards reflects adjustments due to both impairment losses on development costs previously capitalized for IFRS Standards purposes, and the effect of discounting on the determination of the recoverable amount of tangible fixed assets.

## L. RESERVES FOR RISKS AND CHARGES

Differences between Italian GAAP and IFRS Standards refer mainly to the following items:

- Restructuring reserve: the Group provided restructuring reserves based upon management's best estimate of the costs to be incurred in connection with each of its restructuring programs at the time such programs were formally decided. Under IFRS Standards the requirements to recognize a constructive obligation in the financial statements are more restrictive, and some restructuring reserves recorded under Italian GAAP have been eliminated.
- Reserve for vehicle sales incentives: under Italian GAAP Fiat Auto accounted for certain incentives at the time at which a legal obligation to pay the incentives arose, which may have been in periods subsequent to that in which the initial sale to the dealer network was made. Under IAS 37 companies are required to make provision not only for legal, but also for constructive, obligations based on an established pattern of past practice. In the context of the IFRS Standards restatement exercise, Fiat has reviewed its practice in the area of vehicle sales incentives and has determined that for certain forms of incentives a constructive obligation exists which should be provided under IFRS Standards at the date of sale.

## M. RECOGNITION AND MEASUREMENT OF DERIVATIVES

Beginning in 2001 the Fiat Group adopted — to the extent that it is consistent and not in contrast with general principles set forth in the Italian law governing financial statements — IAS 39 Financial Instruments: Recognition and Measurement. In particular, taking into account the restrictions under Italian law, the Group maintained that IAS 39 was applicable only in part and only in reference to the designation of derivative financial instruments as "hedging" or "non-hedging instruments" and with respect to the symmetrical accounting of the result of the valuation of the hedging instruments and the result attributable to the hedged items ("hedge accounting"). The transactions which, according to the Group's policy for risk management, were able to meet the conditions stated by the accounting principle for hedge accounting treatment, were designated as hedging transactions; the others, although set up for the purpose of managing risk exposure (inasmuch as the Group's policy does not permit speculative transactions), were designated as "trading." The main differences between Italian GAAP and IFRS Standards may be summarized as follows:

- Instruments designated as "hedging instruments" — under Italian GAAP, the instrument was valued symmetrically with the underlying hedged item. Therefore, where the hedged item was not adjusted to fair value in the financial statements, the hedging instrument was also not adjusted. Similarly, where the hedged item had not yet been recorded in the financial statements (hedging of future flows), the valuation of the hedging instrument at fair value was deferred. Under IFRS Standards:
- In the case of a fair value hedge, the gains or losses from remeasuring the hedging instrument at fair value shall be recognized in the income statement and the gains or losses on the hedged item attributable to the hedge risk shall adjust the carrying amount of the hedged item and be recognized in the income statement. Consequently, no impact arises on net income (except for the ineffective portion of the hedge, if any) and on net equity, while adjustments impact the carrying values of hedging instruments and hedged items.
- In the case of a cash flow hedge (hedging of future flows), the portion of gains or losses on the hedging instrument that is determined to be an effective hedge shall be recognized directly in equity through the statement of changes in equity; the ineffective portion of the gains or losses shall be recognized in the income statement. Consequently, with reference to the effective portion, only a difference in net equity arises between Italian GAAP and IFRS Standards.
- Instruments designated as "non-hedging instruments" (except for foreign currency derivative instruments) — under Italian GAAP, these instruments were valued at market value and the differential, if negative compared to the contractual value, was recorded in the income statement, in accordance with the concept of prudence. Under IAS 39 the positive differential should also be recorded. With reference to foreign currency derivative instruments, instead, the accounting treatment adopted under Italian GAAP was in compliance with IAS 39.

In this context, as mentioned in the consolidated financial statements as of December 31, 2003, Fiat was party to a Total Return Equity Swap contract on General Motors shares, in order to hedge the risk implicit in the Exchangeable Bond on General Motors shares. Although this equity swap was entered into for hedging purposes it does not qualify for hedge accounting and accordingly it was defined as a non-hedging instrument. Consequently, the positive fair value of the instrument as of December 31, 2003, amounting to 450 million euros, had not been recorded under Italian GAAP. During 2004 Fiat terminated the contract, realizing a gain of 300 million euros.

In the IFRS Standards restatement, the above mentioned positive fair value at December 31, 2003 has been recognized in opening equity, while, following the unwinding of the swap, a negative adjustment of the same amount has been recorded in the 2004 income statement.

## N. TREASURY STOCK

In accordance with Italian GAAP, the Group accounted for treasury stock as an asset and recorded related valuation adjustments and gains or losses on disposal in the income statement.

Under IFRS Standards, treasury stock is deducted from stockholders' equity and all movements in treasury stock are recognized in stockholders' equity rather than in the income statement.

## O. STOCK OPTIONS

Under Italian GAAP, with reference to share-based payment transactions, no obligations or compensation expenses were recognized.

In accordance with IFRS Standards 2 — Share-based Payment, the full amount [of the] fair value of stock options on the date of grant must be expensed. Changes in fair value after the grant date have no impact on the initial measurement. The compensation expense corresponding to the option's fair value is recognized in payroll costs on a straight-line basis over the period from the grant date to the vesting date, with the offsetting credit recognized directly in equity.

The Group applied the transitional provision provided by IFRS Standards 2 and therefore applied this standard to all stock options granted after November 7, 2002 and not yet vested at the effective date of IFRS Standards 2 (January 1, 2005). No compensation expense is required to be recognized for stock options granted prior to November 7, 2002, in accordance with transitional provision of IFRS Standards 2.

## P. ADJUSTMENTS TO THE VALUATION OF INVESTMENTS IN ASSOCIATES

These items represent the effect of the IFRS Standards adjustments on the Group portion of the net equity of associates accounted for using the equity method.

## Q. SALES OF RECEIVABLES

The Fiat Group sells a significant part of its finance, trade and tax receivables through either securitization programs or factoring transactions.

A securitization transaction entails the sale without recourse of a portfolio of receivables to a securitization vehicle (special purpose entity). This special purpose entity finances the purchase of the receivables by issuing asset-backed securities (i.e., securities whose repayment and interest flow depend upon the cash flow generated by the portfolio). Asset-backed securities are divided into classes according to their degree of seniority and rating: the most senior classes are placed with investors on the market; the junior class, whose repayment is subordinated to the senior classes, is normally subscribed for by the seller. The residual interest in the receivables retained by the seller is therefore limited to the junior securities it has subscribed for.

Factoring transactions may be with or without recourse on the seller; certain factoring agreements without recourse include deferred purchase price clauses (i.e., the payment of a minority portion of the purchase price is conditional upon the full collection of the receivables), require a first loss guarantee of the seller up to a limited amount or imply a continuing significant exposure to the receivables cash flow.

Under Italian GAAP, all receivables sold through either securitization or factoring transactions (both with and without recourse) had been derecognized. Furthermore, with specific reference to the securitization of retail loans and leases originated by the financial services companies, the net present value of the interest flow implicit in the instalments, net of related costs, had been recognized in the income statement.

Under IFRS Standards:

- As mentioned above, SIC 12 — Consolidation — Special Purpose Entities states that an SPE shall be consolidated when the substance of the relationship between the entity and the SPE indicates that the SPE is controlled by that entity; therefore all securitization transactions have been reversed.

- IAS 39 allows for the derecognition of a financial asset when, and only when, the risks and rewards of the ownership of the assets are substantially transferred: consequently, all portfolios sold with recourse, and the majority of those sold without recourse, have been reinstated in the IFRS Standards balance sheet.

The impact of such adjustments on stockholders' equity and on net income is not material. In particular, it refers mainly to the reversal of the gains arising from the related securitization transactions on the retail portfolio of receivables of financial service companies, realized under Italian GAAP and not yet realized under IFRS Standards.

With regards to financial structure, the reinstatement in the balance sheet of the receivables and payables involved in these sales transactions causes a significant increase in trade and financial receivables and in financial debt balances, and a worsening in net debt. In particular, in consequence of these reinstatements, trade receivables increase by 3,563 million euros and 2,134 euros at January 1, 2004 and at December 31, 2004, respectively; at the same dates, financial receivables increase by 6,127 million euros and 6,997 euros, and financial debt increased by 10,581 million euros and 10,174 million euros, respectively.

## R. ACCOUNTING FOR DEFERRED INCOME TAXES
This item includes the combined effect of the net deferred tax effects, after allowance, on the above mentioned IFRS Standards adjustments, as well as other minor differences between Italian GAAP and IFRS Standards on the recognition of tax assets and liabilities.

**Effects of transition to IFRS Standards on the consolidated balance sheet at January 1, 2004**

| (in € millions) | Italian GAAP | Reclassifications | Adjustments | IAS/IFRS Standards | |
|---|---|---|---|---|---|
| Intangible assets, of which: | 3,724 | | 1,774 | 5,498 | Intangible assets, of which: |
| Goodwill | 2,402 | | | 2,402 | Goodwill |
| Other intangible fixed assets | 1,322 | | 1,774 | 3,096 | Other intangible fixed assets |
| Property, plant and equipment, of which: | 9,675 | (945) | 817 | 9,547 | Property, plant and equipment |
| Property, plant and equipment | 8,761 | (31) | | | |
| Operating leases | 914 | (914) | | | |
| | | 31 | | 31 | Investment property |
| Financial fixed assets | 3,950 | 70 | (121) | 3,899 | Investment and other financial assets |
| Financial receivables held as fixed assets | 29 | (29) | | | |
| | | 914 | (50) | 864 | Leased assets |
| Deferred tax assets | 1,879 | | 266 | 2,145 | Deferred tax assets |
| **Total Non-Current assets** | **19,257** | **41** | **2,686** | **21,984** | **Non-current assets** |

| (in € millions) | Italian GAAP | Reclassifications | Adjustments | IAS/IFRS Standards | |
|---|---|---|---|---|---|
| Net inventories | 6,484 | | 1,113 | 7,597 | Inventories |
| Trade receivables | 4,553 | (682) | 2,678 | 6,549 | Trade receivables |
| | | 12,890 | 7,937 | 20,827 | Receivables from financing activities |
| Other receivables | 3,081 | (148) | 541 | 3,474 | Other receivables |
| | | 407 | 10 | 417 | Accrued income and prepaid expenses |
| | | | | 2,129 | Current financial assets, of which: |
| | | 32 | | 32 | Current equity investments |
| | | 515 | 260 | 775 | Current securities |
| | | 430 | 892 | 1,322 | Other financial assets |
| Financial assets not held as fixed assets | 120 | (120) | | | |
| Financial lease contracts receivable | 1,797 | (1,797) | | | |
| Financial receivables | 10,750 | (10,750) | | | |
| Securities | 3,789 | (3,789) | | | |
| Cash | 3,211 | 3,214 | 420 | 6,845 | Cash and cash equivalents |
| **Total Current assets** | **33,785** | **202** | **13,851** | **47,838** | **Current assets** |
| Trade accruals and deferrals | 407 | (407) | | | |
| Financial accruals and deferrals | 386 | (386) | | | |
| | | | 21 | 21 | Assets held for sale |
| **TOTAL ASSETS** | **53,835** | **(550)** | **16,558** | **69,843** | **TOTAL ASSETS** |
| **Stockholders' equity** | **7,494** | **(934)** | | **6,560** | **Stockholders' equity** |
| | | | | 7,455 | Provisions, of which: |
| Reserves for employee severance indemnities | 1,313 | 1,503 | 1,224 | 4,040 | Employee benefits |
| Reserves for risks and charges | 5,168 | (1,550) | (203) | 3,415 | Other provisions |
| Deferred income tax reserves | 211 | (211) | | | |
| Long-term financial payables | 15,418 | 6,501 | 14,790 | 36,709 | Debt, of which: |
| | | | | 10,581 | Asset-backed financing |
| | | | | 26,128 | Other debt |
| **Total Non-current liabilities** | **22,110** | **6,243** | | | |

## Effects of transition to IFRS Standards on the consolidated balance sheet at January 1, 2004 (Continued)

| (in € millions) | Italian GAAP | Reclassifications | Adjustments | IAS/IFRS Standards | |
|---|---|---|---|---|---|
| | | 568 | (223) | 345 | Other financial liabilities |
| Trade payables | 12,588 | | (297) | 12,291 | Trade payables |
| Others payables | 2,742 | | 1,948 | 4,690 | Other payables |
| Short-term financial payables | 6,616 | (6,616) | | | |
| **Total Current liabilities** | **21,946** | **(6,048)** | | | |
| | | 211 | 274 | 485 | Deferred tax liabilities |
| Trade accruals and deferrals | 1,329 | | (21) | 1,308 | Accrued expenses and deferred income |
| Financial accruals and deferrals | 956 | (956) | | | |
| | | | | | Liabilities held for sale |
| **TOTAL LIABILITIES AND STOCKHOLDERS' EQUITY** | **53,835** | **(550)** | **(934)** | **69,843** | **TOTAL STOCKHOLDERS' EQUITY AND LIABILITIES** |

## Effects of transition to IFRS Standards on the income statement for the year ended December 31, 2004

| (in € millions) | Italian GAAP | Reclassifications | Adjustments | IAS/IFRS Standards | |
|---|---|---|---|---|---|
| Net revenues | 46,703 | | (1,066) | 45,637 | Net revenues |
| Cost of sales | 39,623 | 675 | (1,177) | 39,121 | Cost of sales |
| **Gross operating result** | **7,080** | | | | |
| Overhead | 4,629 | 51 | 21 | 4,701 | Selling, general and administrative costs |
| Research and development | 1,810 | 1 | (461) | 1,350 | Research and development costs |
| Other operating income (expenses) | (619) | 346 | (142) | (415) | Other income (expenses) |
| **Operating result** | **22** | **(381)** | **409** | **50** | **Trading profit** |
| | | 154 | (4) | 150 | Gains (losses) on the disposal of equity investments |
| | | 496 | 46 | 542 | Restructuring costs |
| | | (243) | | (243) | Other unusual income (expenses) |
| | | **(966)** | **359** | **(585)** | **Operating result** |
| | | (641) | (538) | (1,179) | Financial income |

| (in € millions) | Italian GAAP | Reclassifications | Adjustments | IAS/IFRS Standards | |
|---|---|---|---|---|---|
| Result from equity investments | 8 | | 127 | 135 | Result from equity investments |
| Non-operating income (expenses) | (863) | 863 | | | |
| EBIT | (833) | | | | |
| Financial income (expenses) | (744) | 744 | | | |
| Income (loss) before taxes | (1,577) | | (52) | (1,629) | Result before taxes |
| Income taxes | (29) | | (21) | (50) | Income taxes |
| Net result of normal operations | (1,548) | | (31) | (1,579) | Net result of normal operations |
| Result from discontinued operations | | | | | Result from discontinued operations |
| Net result before minority interest | (1,548) | | (31) | (1,579) | Net result before minority interest |

# Index